V-RAY 5 FOR 3DS MAX 2020

V-RAY 5 FOR 3DS MAX 2020

3D RENDERING WORKFLOWS

VOLUME 1

JAMIE
CARDOSO

CRC Press
Taylor & Francis Group
Boca Raton London New York

CRC Press is an imprint of the
Taylor & Francis Group, an **informa** business

First edition published 2021
by CRC Press
2 Park Square, Milton Park, Abingdon, Oxon, OX14 4RN

and by CRC Press
6000 Broken Sound Parkway NW, Suite 300, Boca Raton, FL 33487-2742

First edition published by CRC 2016

CRC Press is an imprint of Informa UK Limited

British Library Cataloguing-in-Publication Data
A catalogue record for this book is available from the British Library

ISBN: 978-0-367-72429-0 (hbk)
ISBN: 978-0-367-62550-4 (pbk)
ISBN: 978-1-003-15476-1 (ebk)

Typeset in Minion Pro
by Deanta Global Publishing Services, Chennai, India

Access the Support Material: https://www.routledge.com/9780367724290

Contents

Preface

V-Ray rendering engine was created by Chaos Group in 1997. It was originally available as a rendering plug-in for 3ds max only but later integrated into other platforms such as cinema 4D, Maya, Sketchup, etc.

At the start, it was competing with other rendering engines, such as Final Render, Brazil, and Mental Ray. However, it quickly outranked its competitors to become the most popular rendering engine today.

Its current popularity is such that even Oscar-winning film studios, such as ILM (Industry of Light & Magic), have incorporated it into their rendering pipeline.

Recent reports suggest that ninety percent of companies/industries using rendering applications have at least one copy of V-Ray in their rendering pipeline.

V-Ray's meteoric rise is mostly attributed to its ease of use, support group, constant updates/improvements, and rendering speed.

Acknowledgments

I would like to take this opportunity to personally thank Sean Connelly and Taylor & Francis for this amazing opportunity, and for being ever so patient with me throughout the process.

In addition, I would like to thank my family and friends, who have been my greatest supporters.

I would like to also thank everyone who contributed directly and indirectly to the production and completion of this book.

Special thanks to Shawn Lochman, Elitsa Dimitrova, Graham Macfarlane, James Goodman, Chaos Group, Teodora Mircheva, Ana Savova, Martin Minev, Nadeem Bhatti, George P, Maher Zebian, Geoff Chilvers, Giacomo Arteconi, Andrew Gibbon, Jacob Adamiec, Mateusz Wawrzyniak, and Mark Simpkin.

Finally, I would like to express my eternal gratitude for the continuous support from friends, family, esteemed colleagues, my book readers, my LinkedIn connections, followers, and my blog viewers: You rock!

Author

Jamie Cardoso is a renowned author, reviewer, computer artist, and technologist, with years of experience in creating state-of-the-art 3d photomontages, verified views, VR, AR, XR, MR, Stereos, and photorealistic interior and exterior visualizations for architects and designers.

In collaboration with well-established marketing/design agencies and visualization companies, he has helped create iconic buildings and spaces such as the Gherkin, the Shard, the Welsh Assembly, 107 Cheapside, Heron Tower, Jaguar headquarters, Asos, Virgin Cruises, One Hyde Park, Google, Battersea Power Station Development, and many more.

Much of Jamie's work and contributions have been featured in such books and magazines as *Area Autodesk, 3D World, CG Society, TutsPlus, CG Architect, Evermotion, Chaos Group, and Udemy*, to name but a few. Jamie also co-authored two successful books entitled *Realistic Architectural Visualization with 3ds max and Mental Ray* (Focal Press, 1st edition 2007, 2nd edition 2009). And most recently, a new book with Taylor & Francis, entitled *3D Photorealistic Rendering: Interiors and Exteriors with V-Ray & 3Ds Max* (A K Peters/CRC Press, 2016). In his spare time (whenever that is), he shares some of his knowledge with users, by posting free step-by-step-tutorials on his blog, YouTube channel, Instagram, LinkedIn, Facebook, and Twitter.

To connect with him, simply Google: Jamie Cardoso.

1

Clients, Projects, Pre-Production, Production, and Post-Production Overview

1 Clients, Projects, and Production

Approaching Clients

Emails

"Cold emails" are one of the best ways to fish for clients, when executed properly.

There's a higher chance of your emails being opened and read when you do the following:

- Ensure the subject of your email starts with "RE:"

Email recipients are more likely to open such types of emails because the "RE" implies it's a reply to an existing conversation.

- As a sender, never use generic email addresses such as info@, contact@, etc.

Email recipients are more inclined to open personalized email addresses such as jamiec@ and jamie.cardoso@, because such email accounts don't come across as spams or as "mass emails."

Also, servers are less likely to automatically send your emails to the "junk" box.

- Prior to sending an email, ensure to send it to someone's personal email address, as opposed to general/public email addresses such as info@ and contact@

General/public email addresses tend to be ignored as they come across as unsolicited.

However, it's worth noting that very small companies (one to five employees) tend to open unsolicited emails.

Otherwise, it's always best to address emails to specific individuals at companies, especially those involved in marketing and communications (e.g., mary.eugene@ arcthitects.com).

- Always start an email with "Dear" (e.g., Dear Jane), followed by a "Hi" emoji ().

This will also increase the chances of your email being opened, especially on a mobile phone.

- Start by wishing the recipient well and in good health.
- Quickly introduce yourself and your firm's speciality.
- Embed compelling images similar to the spaces/products the client creates (maximum of four) into your email and a link to your website and/or portfolio.

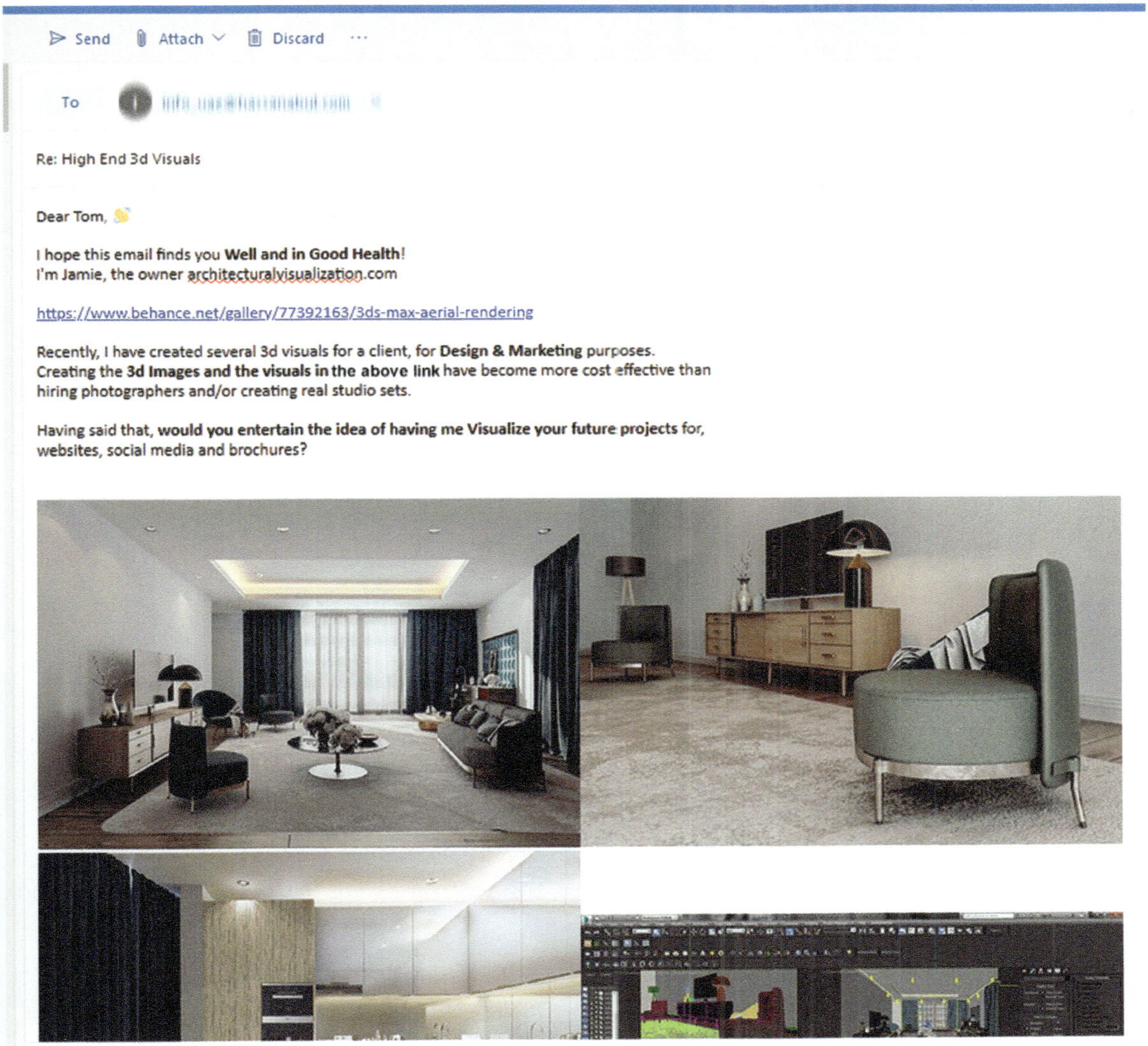

Composing emails.

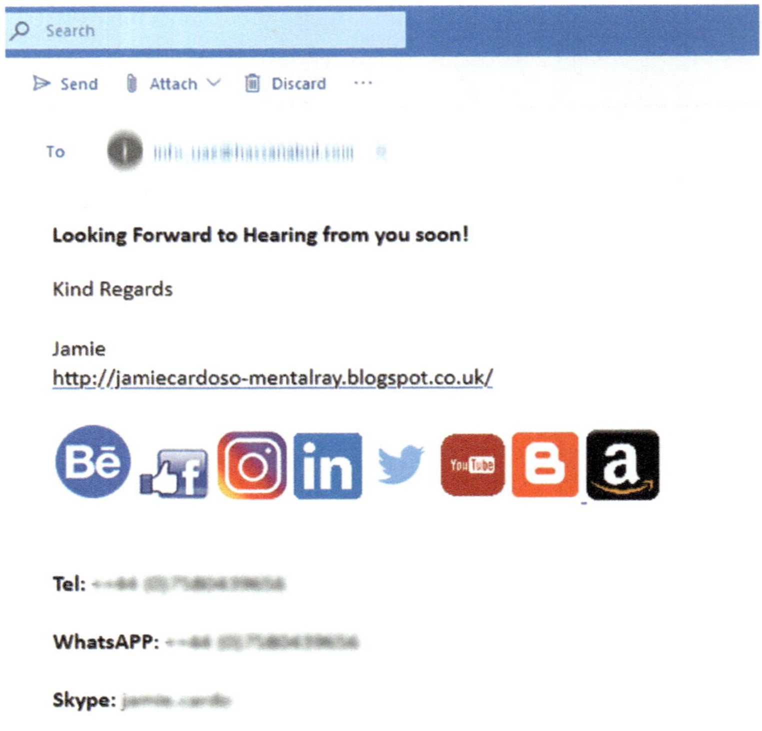

Email signature

To find key email addresses at companies, first visit their website.

It's often under:

https://architect.com/people/

https://architect.com/aboutus/people

https://architect.com/studio/people

If perchance you can't find any relevant email addresses from their website, simply use the website https://hunter.io/

This service allows users to find personal email addresses of employees of a company, by simply copying and pasting a website's URL into its search box (e.g., https://architect.com).

It also allows users to work out an individual's email address (if not publicly available) by seeing how a company's emails are formatted (e.g., jcardoso@architects.co.uk).

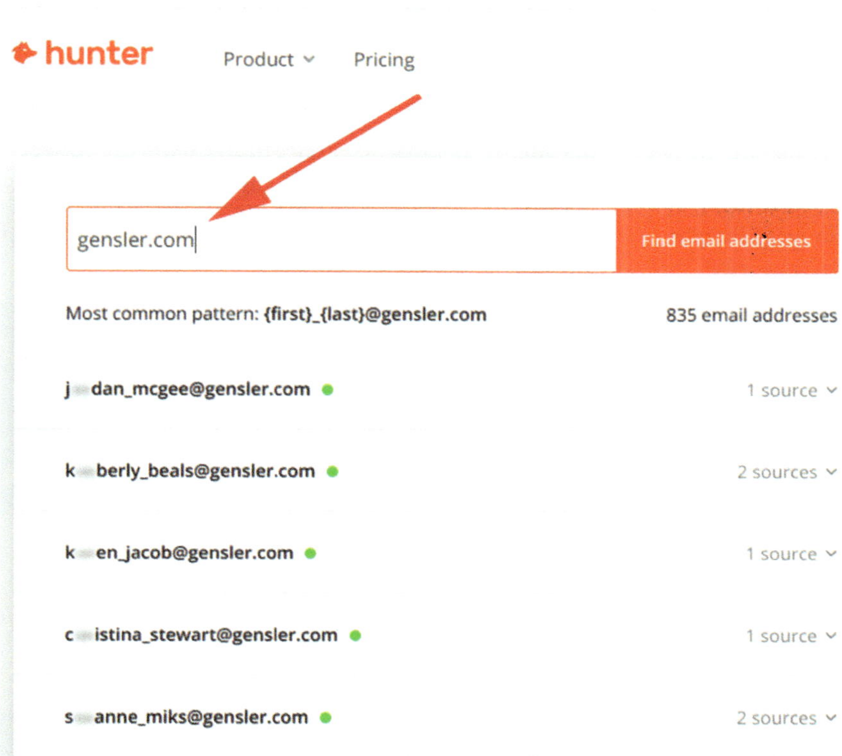

Email hunter

Calls

It's often best to communicate via email/messaging to keep a record of everything.

However, some clients also like to engage via phone calls using WhatsApp, Skype, Zoom, or messenger.

Such clients find it quicker and easier to layout their ideas using the above-mentioned mediums of communication.

Having said that, always keep a note of key instructions/requests during conversations.

Taking notes

Meeting the Client

There are times when you might be invited to meet a client at their office, or vice versa.

Depending on what you intend to showcase (e.g., images, animations, etc.), tablets are one of the most useful devices for meetings.

Google Chromecast devices can also be used in conjunction with your phone or tablet to cast content on a TV screen.

Tablets

Chromecast

If it's VR content (virtual reality), then you need at least two headsets and a laptop to launch the content from.

In terms of dress codes, dressing casually smart works perfectly for most office environments.

Smart casual is a dress code that comprises well-fitting, neat, and appropriate pieces that are slightly less formal than a business casual or business professional dress code. However, smart casual is much more elevated and put together than dressing for off-hours and avoids items that are too casual or loose-fitting.

VR headsets

For more information about how to dress casually smart, simply Google: smart casual

- First-time meetings are often set to evaluate personalities and to reassure expertise
- When visiting a client, always turn up at least 10 minutes before the agreed time.
- Punctuality conveys respect toward the client and your organizational skills.
- Always start by introducing yourself with a smile and a handshake (if you're not social distancing).
- If offered a drink, always accept it by saying, "Yes please; thank you." People often offer you a drink to be cordial and to make you feel comfortable in their premises.
- It's also a good opportunity to smile and engage in a quick conversation.
- Instead of delving into a work-related conversation immediately, start by saying something humorous about the weather or something humorous about your journey to their office. Or, simply mention something complementary about your client's office.
- Most clients tend to remember/appreciate people who are respectfully humorous about themselves and complementary toward the client.
- While discussing the project and receiving instructions from a client, always take notes throughout.
- Taking notes is a great way of showing you are listening and acknowledging them.
- While engaging in discussions, make humble suggestions when appropriate, to showcase your expertise and problem-solving skills.
- Furthermore, once the project discussions are over, try to leave the office in a similar way you have started; by saying something humorous (e.g., about the weather or your journey), followed by a handshake and stating how great it was to meet them.
- Finally, once you have repeated the above steps a few times (through trial and errors), you will gradually become better and better at it.

Emails/Newsletter

It's good practice to send your clients newsletter emails periodically (once a month), about projects you have recently finished, and new Video/Blog posts.

Clients are easily persuaded and distracted by new competitors and recommendations by colleagues.

Your monthly emails will help remind your clients of your relationship with them, and your expertise in the field.

LOGO

No. 0031
May 2020

From the Studio:
A round up of news from Jamie Cardoso

Project News:
What we've been working on

We've created another gorgeous 360° kitchen configurator for Blossom Avenue kitchens. This online configurator has a choice of two kitchen interiors with millions of possible cabinet, handle and worktop combinations.

Second Nature Kitchens (New CG Images)
Back in November we shared a collection of images for Second Nature – the leading independent kitchen brand in the UK. Once again they've commissioned us to expand their brochure with a magnificent collection of new kitchen CGI's which we've added to our portfolio page.

Newsletter

Social Media and Forums

Having a strong social media presence will help remind your clients of your relevance, and expose your work to potential new clients.

When it comes to social media, users and clients often have a very short attention span.

To stay on their radar, try to post relevant content as often as you possibly can (once a week or every two weeks if possible).

Some of the best social media platforms to showcase your work are as follows:

LinkedIn

Instagram

https://archinect.com/forum

https://www.skyscrapercity.com/forums/architecture.4/

https://www.behance.net/

YouTube

When posting content, always use popular titles such as:

3d, 3d rendering, 3d visualization, 3d visualizer, 3ds max, architectural rendering, interior design rendering, 3d architectural visualization, etc.

And hashtags such as:

#3dvisualization #3drendering #3d #architecturalvisualization #render #archviz #digitalart #illustration #rendering #illustrator #3dartist #3drender #renders #archdaily #architecturedesign #architecture #photoshop #architect #renderings #autodesk #autocad #rendered #design #scene #modelling #rendering3d #realestate

To have a better insight into words, your clients often search to find your type of services, use sophisticated tools such as the Google ads keyword plan.

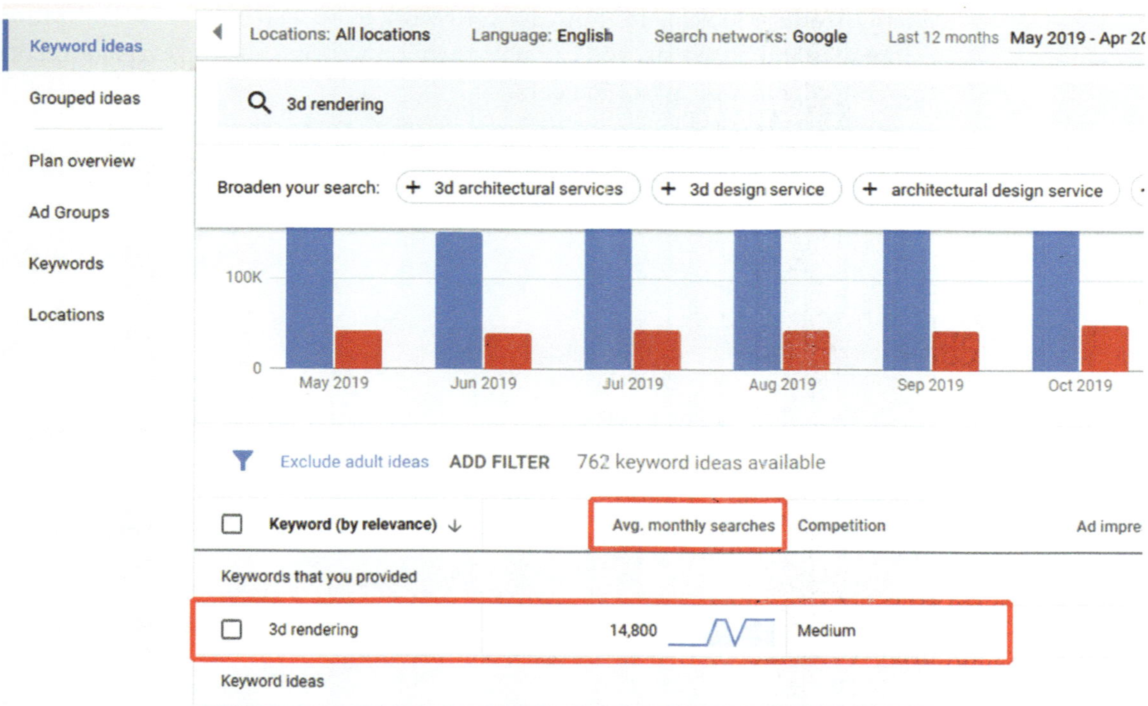
Keyword ideas
Grouped ideas
Plan overview
Ad Groups
Keywords
Locations
Locations: All locations
Language: English
Search networks: Google
Last 12 months May 2019 - Apr 20
3d rendering
Broaden your search:
3d architectural services
3d design service
architectural design service
100K
0
May 2019
Jun 2019
Jul 2019
Aug 2019
Sep 2019
Oct 2019
Exclude adult ideas
ADD FILTER
762 keyword ideas available
Keyword (by relevance)
Avg. monthly searches
Competition
Ad impre
Keywords that you provided
3d rendering
14,800
Medium
Keyword ideas

Google ads keyword plan

Finally, if you're looking to showcase your work to be seen by other visualization companies and 3d artists, you can post them on websites such as evermotion.org, cgarchitect.com, and artstation.com.

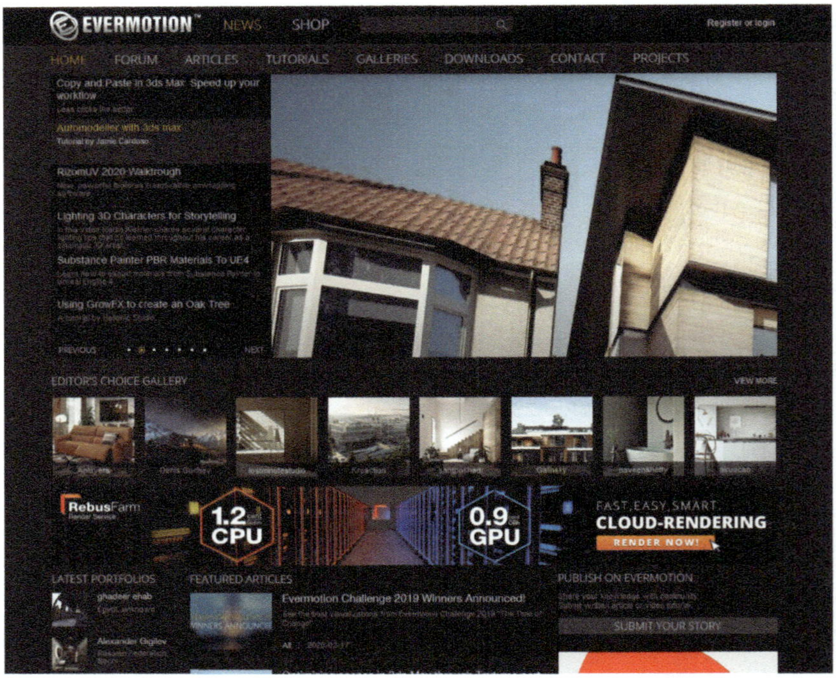

Evermotion website

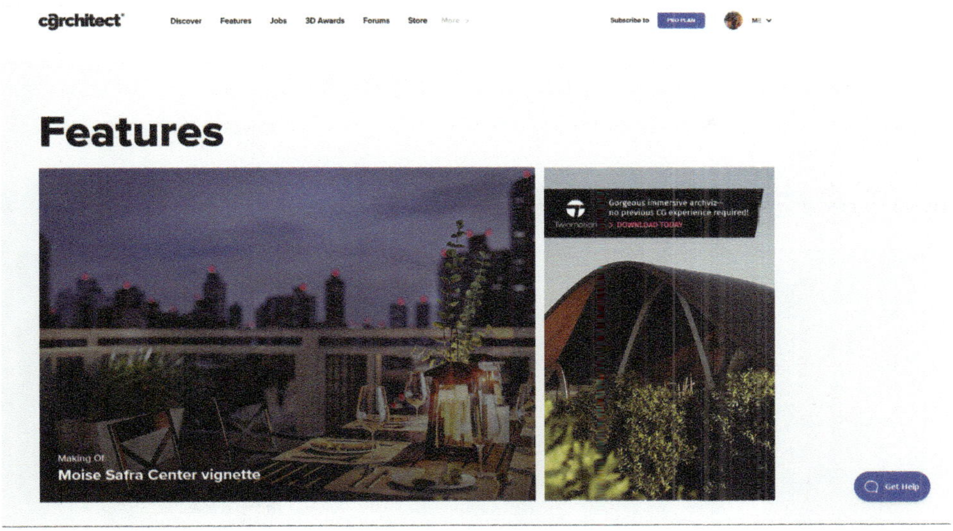

CG Architect *website*

Artstation website

Projects

Most potential projects will start with a client sending you an email with the overall brief, drawings, mood boards, deliverables, and deadlines.

In this first-case scenario, you are expected to quickly go through the entire information pack provided, ask questions, and come up with the final quotation.

There are also times when all you have are drawings/PDFs.

In such cases, you'll be left with the task of creating mood boards/art direction, ask questions, etc.

1 Clients, Projects, and Production

Before providing the final quotation, you should do the following:

- Check the drawings and/or the 3d models thoroughly, prior to committing to the final budget and deadline.

Check thoroughly for key information such as the dwg drawings

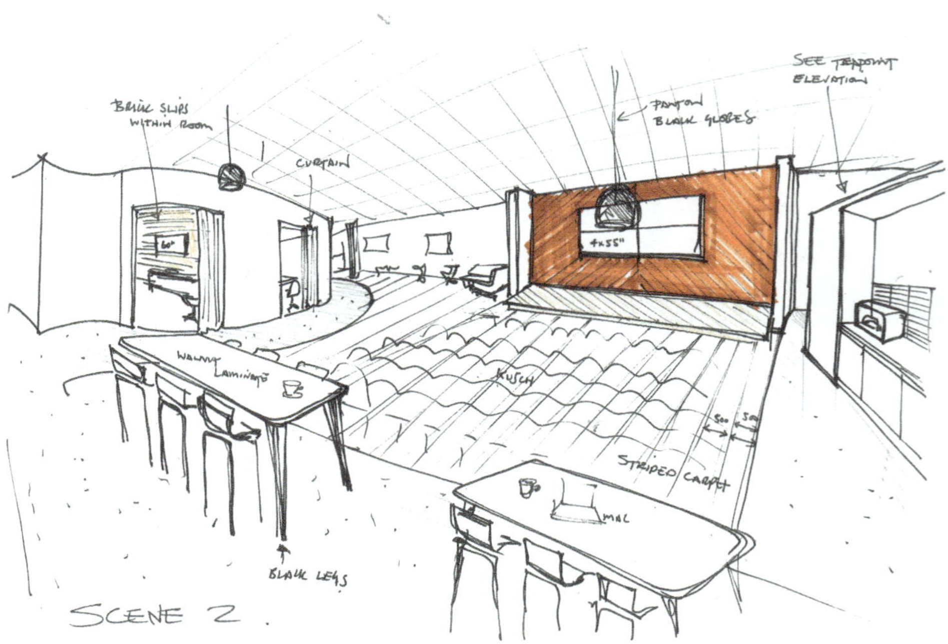

And sketches

Upon receiving the drawings/model from a client, it's utterly important to ensure assets are not riddled with artifacts or incomplete (e.g., missing textures, drawings, etc.).

Failing to do so may inevitably affect the original budget and the final deadline.

- With the client's help, mark-up one or more camera positions that will help capture some of the most complementary parts of the space/design.

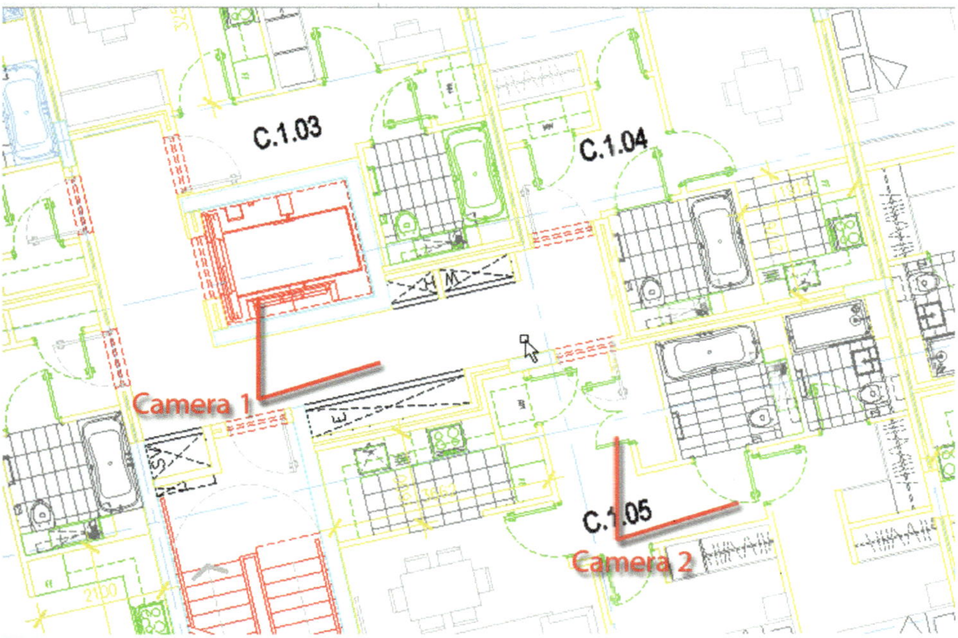

Marked-up drawings and/or sketches

During the process of marking up camera positions with the client, gather as much information as possible about furniture, mood boards, etc.

This will help you previsualize camera compositions, lighting, colors, 3d assets, etc.

Camera positions will help you forecast the amount of time involved in creating the space and its content.

- Once the above steps have been ironed out, the budget and the project deadline can be set.

The best way to manage clients' expectations is for artists/companies to be honest with themselves on matters of expertise, speed, and available resources.

1 Clients, Projects, and Production

Nowadays, clients expect quicker turnarounds, higher quality, and lower prices.

The less the time you spend on a project, the bigger the profit margins.

To help achieve this, only model the essentials such as drawings and bespoke furniture unavailable for download.

Otherwise, it's common practice to download ready-to-render 3d models/assets with shaders and textures from manufacturers' websites, evermotion, 3sky, 3dbee, etc.

Some of these ready-to-render 3d assets are free, and most of them may cost as little as $6 each.

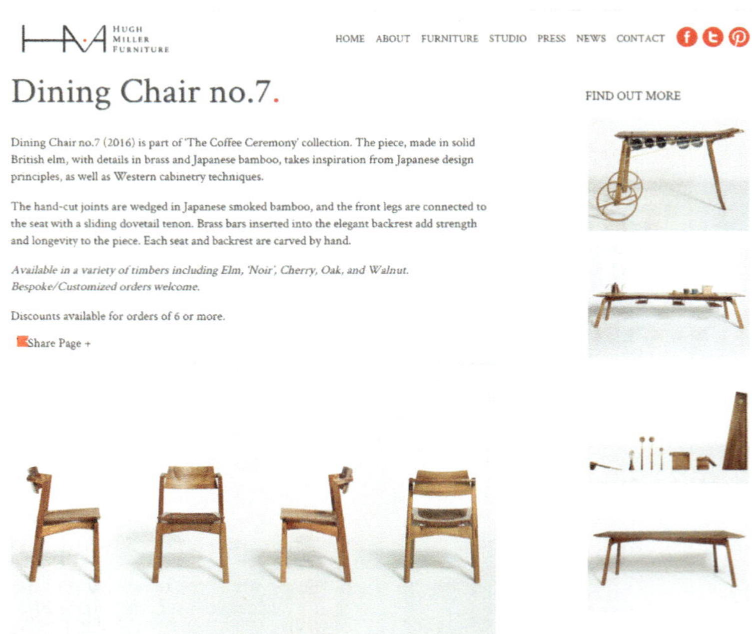

Bespoke furniture

Manufacturers' website to download

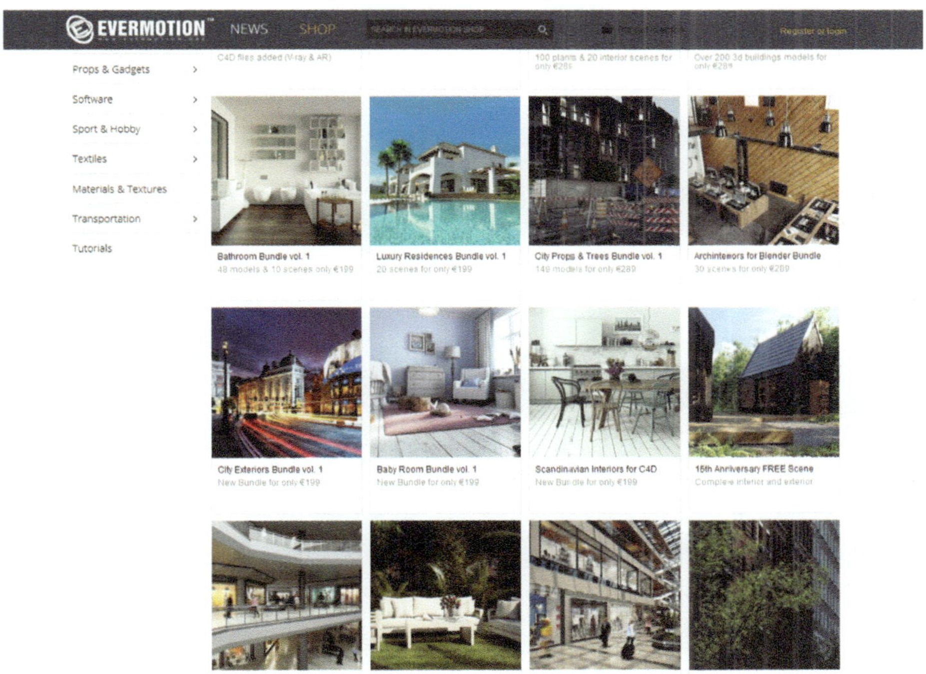

Evermotion website

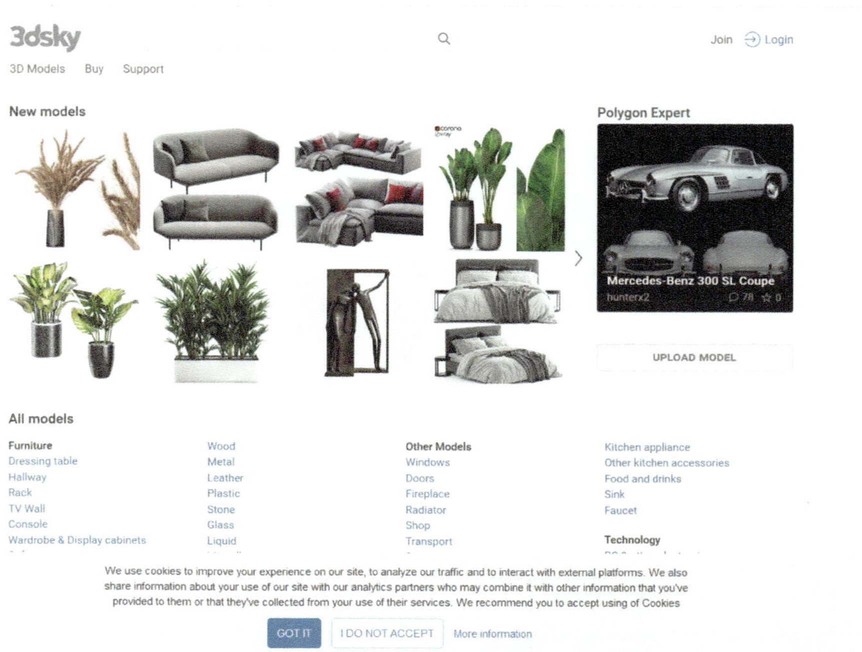
3dsky
Join Login
3D Models Buy Support
New models
Polygon Expert
Mercedes-Benz 300 SL Coupe
UPLOAD MODEL
All models
Furniture
Dressing table
Hallway
Rack
TV Wall
Console
Wardrobe & Display cabinets
Wood
Metal
Leather
Plastic
Stone
Glass
Liquid
Other Models
Windows
Doors
Fireplace
Radiator
Shop
Transport
Kitchen appliance
Other kitchen accessories
Food and drinks
Sink
Faucet
Technology
We use cookies to improve your experience on our site, to analyze our traffic and to interact with external platforms. We also share information about your use of our site with our analytics partners who may combine it with other information that you've provided to them or that they've collected from your use of their services. We recommend you to accept using of Cookies
GOT IT
I DO NOT ACCEPT
More information

3dsky website

60% OFF » Save on 3D Assets in June
3D Bee.IT
high quality,
photorealistic &
production ready
3D models & 3D scans

3dbee.it website

Pricing Projects

The pricing of a project is always based on one-person hours, or days required to finish a project (hence the term man-days/hours).

Daily rates often start from as little as $150 to $700 (8 hours per day).

To avoid pricing yourself out of the market, simply visit a useful website called Salary Expert:

https://www.salaryexpert.com/salary/browse/countries/3d-artist.

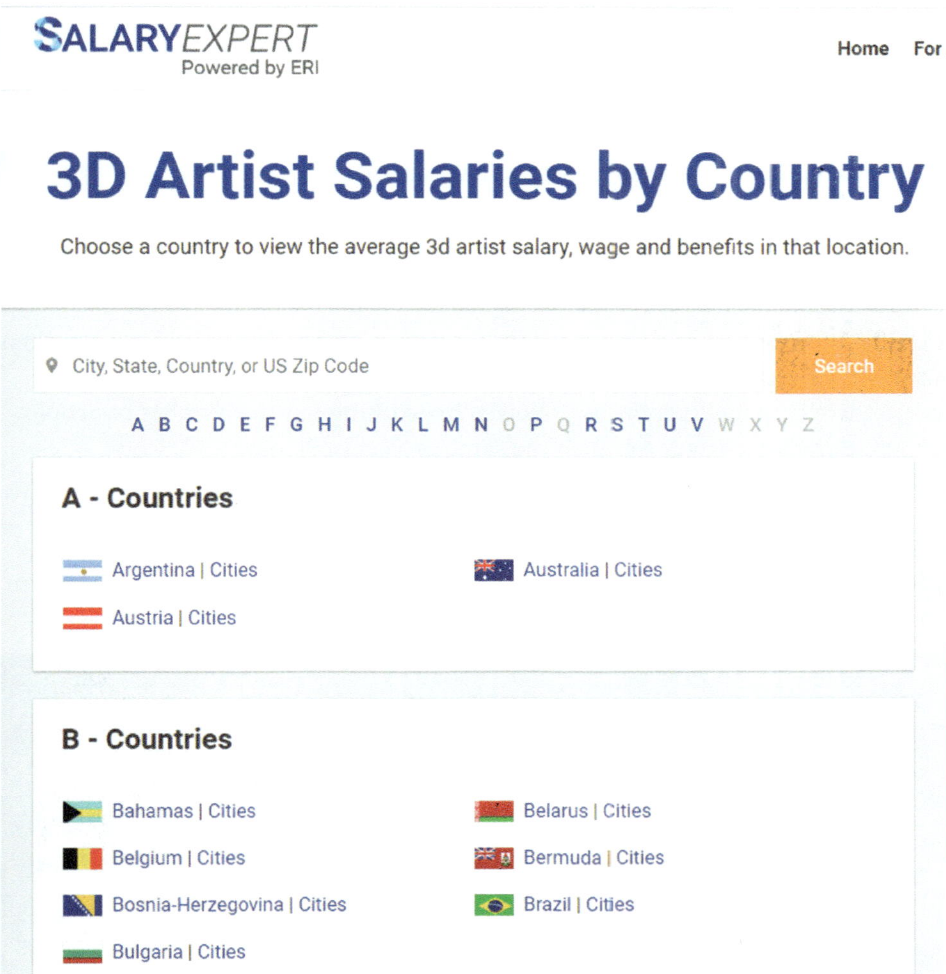

salaryexpert.com

To quickly work out the day rate of an experienced freelancer, simply divide a 3d artist's annual salary by 52 (number of weeks in one year), and the result by 5 (number of days in one week).

I.E: UK £50.000 ÷ 52 = £961.00 ÷ 5 = £192.00

So the average day rate for experienced freelancers in the UK should be around £192. There are always exceptions where some freelancers may charge slightly more (£250–700/day).

If it's an ongoing contract with a company (longer than five days), some freelancers tend to reduce their prices down to £150 per day to make it feasible for clients to keep them for months at time.

If you are approaching clients as a solid company with an office and overheads, then you need to always multiply your day rate by 2, at least.

Alternatively, as a company, to make it feasible to clients, set the project with a fixed price (e.g., normal day rate multiplied by 2 or more) based on the following guidelines:

For instance, if it takes six months for one person to finish a project but the client wants it delivered within 30 days, one would normally price it as if it were one person working for six months, followed by working out the number of people and resources necessary to finish the same project in 30 days.

To work out the final budget, companies/artists also factor in the cost of hiring freelancers (if necessary), usage of render farms, and 3d assets.

garagefarm.net is currently the best, most reliable, and the cheapest render farm in the market.

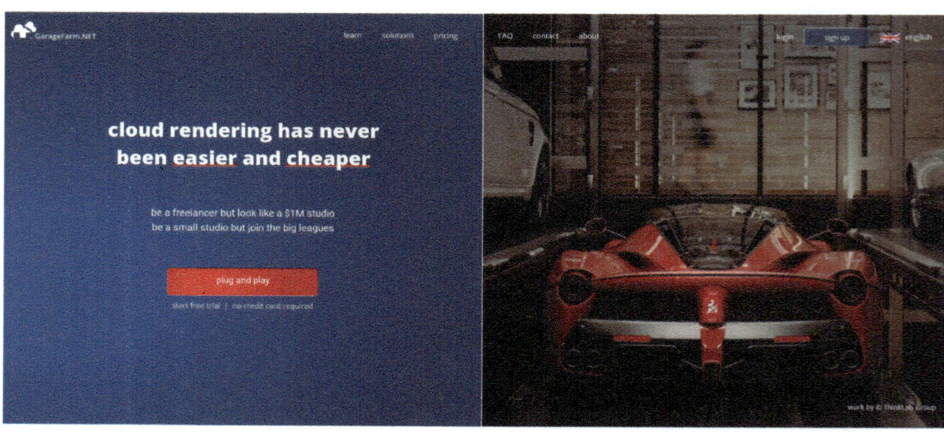

Garagefarm website

Since clients often insist on negotiating prices down, always start with a higher price in order to be able to negotiate down to something more reasonable and sustainable for both parties.

Furthermore, the final deadline and budget should also reflect potential revisions throughout the project.

It's standard practice to accept two different sets of revisions per camera view, for as long as it doesn't deviate from the original brief. Otherwise, it is subject to additional costs (this should also be highlighted in the contract).

Finally, the user should always try to persuade the client (politely) to be more prompt and decisive with general comments and feedback in order to help meet the deadline, and stay on budget.

There are instances when clients expect artists/companies to aid them with their design concepts and color decisions (mostly interior designers). In such exceptional cases, one should *not* try to have a fixed budget and deadline (if possible), as costs may rise exponentially!

Instead, try to work out a day rate.

Contracts

Contracts should always include the following terms and conditions:

1. Project description
2. Deliverables
3. Deadline
4. Comments
5. Fees
6. Acceptance
7. Application
8. Obligations
9. Definitions
10. Cost and expenses
11. Cancellations, weather, postponements
12. Intellectual property rights and release
13. Payment stages
14. Confidential information
15. Liabilities
16. General

The resource files should include an example of what a standard contract should look like.

Standard contract cover

QUOTE

Estimate Description — To create a high quality animation film capturing the essence and excitement surround construction and design.

Description	Quantity	Rate		Line Total
Animation Days	60	350		21000
Render Farm	1	3000		3000
Assets/Music/Software	1	1000		1000

Discount	
Excl VAT	25000
20% VAT	5000
TOTAL	**30000.00**

Deliverables — A 2-2.5 minute animation rendered in HD, delivered in MP4 via Dropbox, Vimeo or ReviewStudio. With the following licensing to be conveyed to your comapany ,
Publicity, and Collateral for 1 film, in perpetuity.

Deadline — Film will be delivered by 31st May 2018 (4 weeks turnaround).

Comments — The entire project will be divided into three separate phases:

Phase 1: Create an animatic (a very draft screen preview) of the entire film, as described in your word document named " Storyboard ".
The sole purpose of the full animatic is to depict the pace of, 3d cameras/characters; storyline; and the full content/composition of the animation.
We will also provide you with up to 10 fully rendered frames (of your choice) along the animation path, to illustrate the final quality

Company Logo

Standard contract quote

QUOTE cont.

Comments Continued	of the whole video (e.g. high resolution 1920 x 1080). This is also an opportunity for you to comment on the animation and its entire content/composition. **Phase 2:** Render the full animation with all comments incorporated. **Phase 3:** Finetune tweaks/comments (if any); followed by re-rendering and doing the post-production. All comments/changes should not deviate from the original brief or could be subject to additional fees. There will be 2 animation styles: For the construction phases, a diagrammatical animation style will be employed. For the revealing end "hero" animation a photorealistic style will be employed. We have budgeted for no more than 1 minute of photo realistic style animation. This price assumes all 3D construction data is provided to **Company** at the start of the project. **Payment Stages** We require £7,500 payment as cleared funds by 17th May 2018, £7,500 payment as cleared funds by 31st May 2018, and the remainder within 30 days of invoice. All animations will be watermarked until client signoff.

Standard contract quote continuation

Invoices

Invoices should include details such as:

1. Project description
2. Days/rates
3. Total fee
4. Invoice number and date
5. Your company and the client's name
6. Your company and the client's address
7. Your company and the client's VAT number
8. Your company's bank or PayPal details

The resource files should include an example of what a standard invoice should look like.

To be in good graces of the client, as a sign of good gesture, try to provide extra/complementary visuals (if possible), and be flexible with late payments.

Having said that, as mentioned in the contract, always have a watermark on your 3d visuals until the final payment is cleared.

The resource files should include an example of what a standard invoice should look like.

DESCRIPTION	DAYS	RATE
	10	$xxxx
Create three Interior 3d Visualisations for, **ArchViz ltd**		
		Total $5250.00

INVOICE 2020 No: 0001 Date: 25-May-2020

Company ltd

Company number: xxxxxxx
Vat number: xxxxxxx

Paypal: xxxxxx@hotmail.com

BANK: Name
Account No: xxxxxxxx

Sort Code: xxxxxx

IBAN: xxxxxxxxXXXXXX

BIC : xxxxxxxx

BANK address: xxxxxxxx

Bill to:

Client's Name
Address
Website
Vat number

Standard invoice

Pre-Production

The pre-production phase is often used as a stepping-stone to all the subsequent steps, such as production and post-production.

Photo reference relevant to the 3d composition

Once all of the abovementioned options have been taken into consideration, and there's a mutual agreement on the time and budget, the user can begin discussing matters regarding the art direction, if not previously addressed.

During this process, the user and/or the client should begin creating digital mood-boards depicting suggestions about the color of the artificial lights, natural light color, time of the day, light effects, camera angles, camera effects, overall color/feel, etc.

The images/photos should resemble the 3d rendering one is trying to create. These similarities should be in the composition, time of the day, and colors.

Also, the proposed photo references should be striking enough to convince the client or/and the art director.

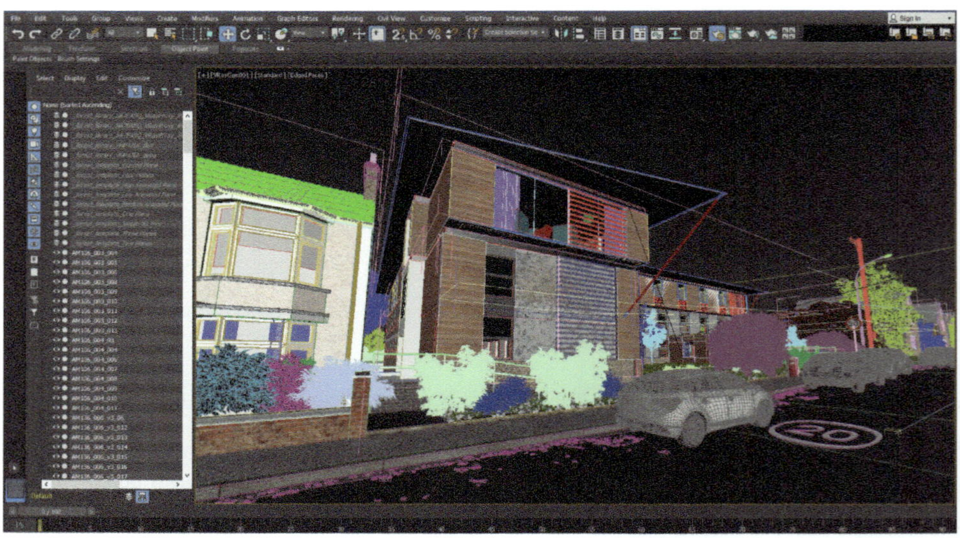

The 3d composition

The final result

Some good resources for online photo references are the websites:

https://www.behance.net/search?search=architecture

http://www.barratthomes.co.uk/new-homes/greater-london/h634701-great-minster-house/gallery-set/gallery-pages/

https://thecoolhunter.net/category/architecture/

It's also common for clients to have their own set of photos as guide and/or source of inspiration.

As mentioned earlier, this process usually takes a few hours, or days, depending on the client, budget, or the project in question.

It's worth noting that, most of the abovementioned steps are usually adopted by companies/users commissioned to produce compelling "Hero shots" for marketing/campaign purposes.

However, if one is working in a fast-paced environment—whereby users are expected to model 3d scenes from scratch—and create multiple camera renders on a daily basis, then some of the pre-production steps such as the art direction might be impossible due to time constraints.

However, in such instances, users can still guide themselves through their own selection of private photo references/images whilst using their own artistic license and trained eyes to produce the expected images and "manage" clients' expectations.

NOTE

Most of the topics in this section and the next will be discussed in greater detail in later chapters.

Production Overview

The production process is typically the stage where the user begins modeling/assembling the agreed 3d shots, followed by shading, texturing, and rendering the views.

The process consists of the following steps:

1. Create the 3d model from the drawings supplied by the client.

As mentioned earlier, focus the modeling solely on areas visible to the camera previously signed off.

It's common practice to create and place cameras halfway through the modeling process. Cameras are typically raised to 1.65 meters (average eye level).

Alternatively, you can create cameras after modeling relevant areas of the scene.

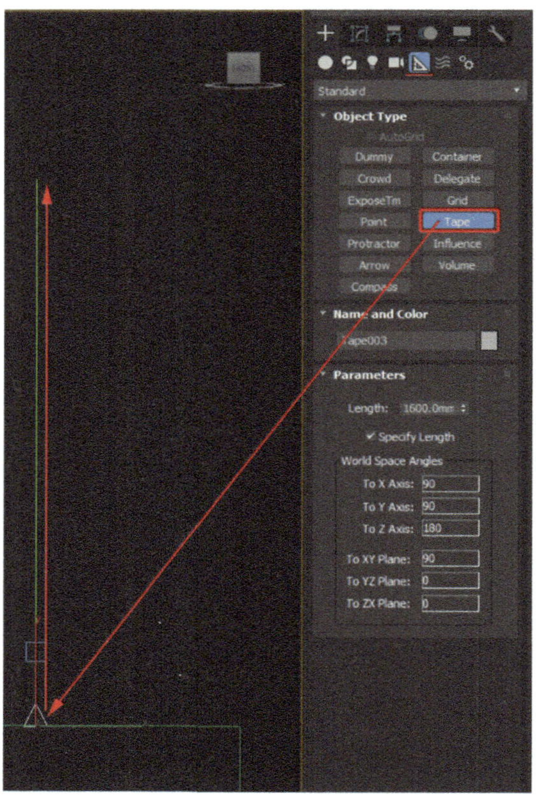

Create a camera at an average eye level

2. Following that, one can adjust the camera and the composition to make the overall image more appealing.

As mentioned earlier, good photo references are useful guides to make the final renders more interesting.

Next, create/place artificial lights and/or sunlight in the scene to help sign off the camera composition and most of the 3d model.

During this stage, users can produce an appealing chalk render to help "sell/sign off" the chosen view.

Chalk renders consist of a basic white material/texture applied as an override render material.

A simple chalk render

To produce appealing chalk renders, users often insure that materials such as glass, water, transparent objects, window frames, picture frames, objects with glow, and bump/displacements are not part of the chalk override material/render.

Also, the final chalk renders should look interesting in modeling details—well-lit and with a good image sampler (antialiasing).

Lighting a scene realistically is one of the most important and crucial parts of the production.

When lighting, the prime focus should be in ensuring there's a clear definition between dark and bright areas in the scene (i.e., depth and contrast).

Most scenes consist of sunlight, ambient/diffused light, and interior artificial lights.

The ambient/diffused lights should always be present in most lit scenes.

The sunlight can be recreated with a sunlight object.

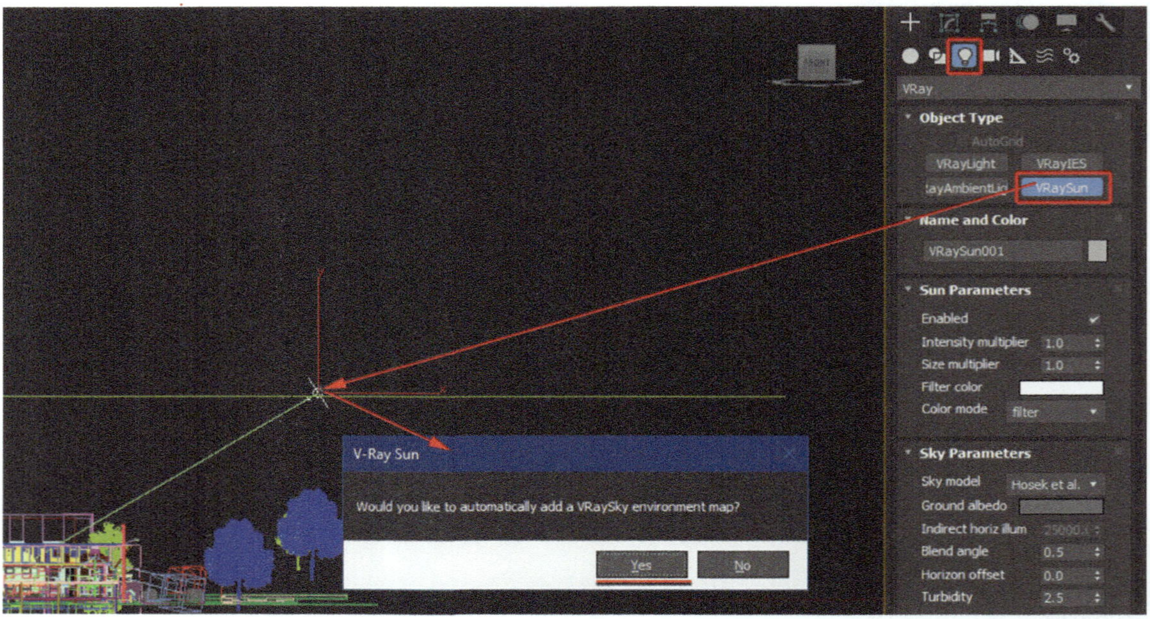

Sunlight object

The ambient light is usually reproduced with a dome light and plane lights (for glass windows/openings).

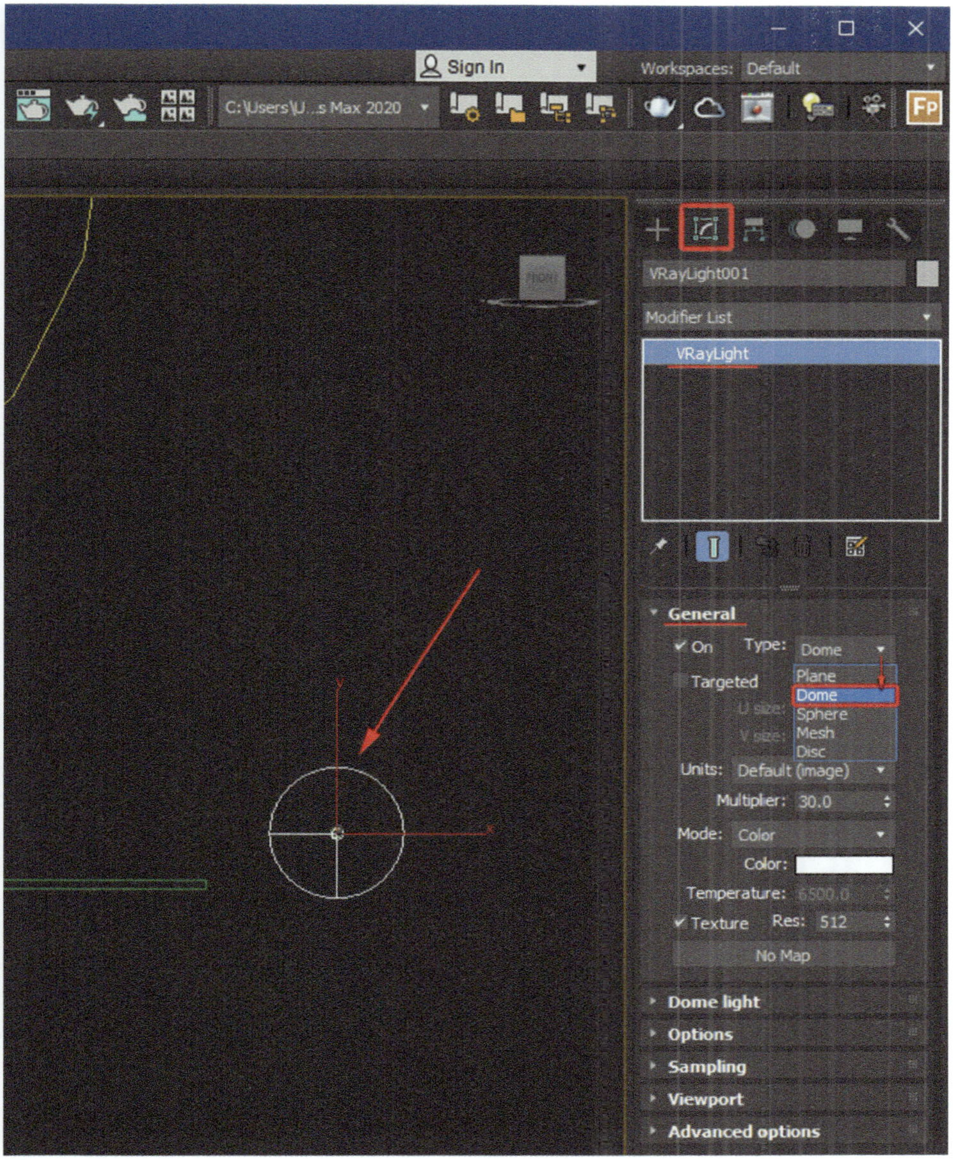

VRay dome light

Some users choose to simply apply an HDRI to the dome texture toggle, to create both direct and indirect light.

However, it will be challenging to later control these two separate elements in post-production and/or with the LightMix in the Frame Buffer.

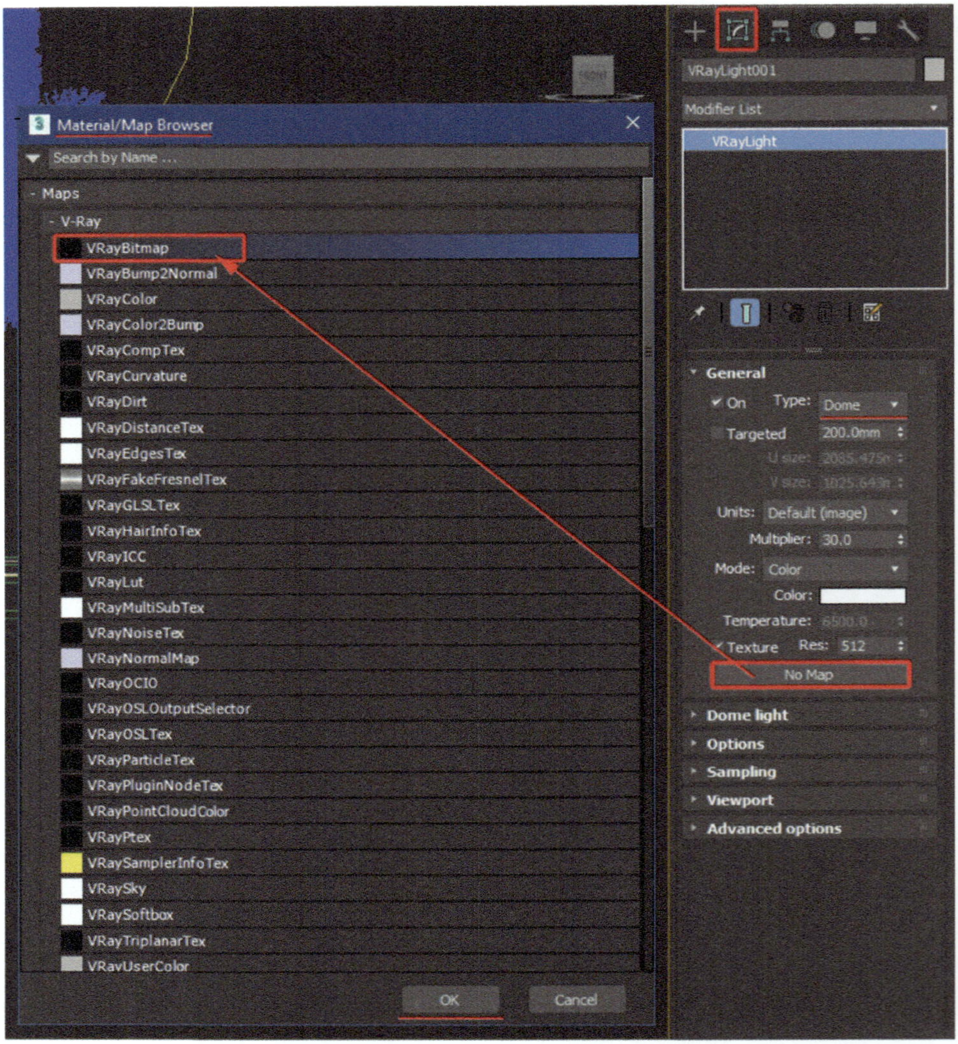
Material/Map Browser
Search by Name ...
- Maps
- V-Ray
VRayBitmap
VRayBump2Normal
VRayColor
VRayColor2Bump
VRayCompTex
VRayCurvature
VRayDirt
VRayDistanceTex
VRayEdgesTex
VRayFakeFresnelTex
VRayGLSLTex
VRayHairInfoTex
VRayICC
VRayLut
VRayMultiSubTex
VRayNoiseTex
VRayNormalMap
VRayOCIO
VRayOSLOutputSelector
VRayOSLTex
VRayParticleTex
VRayPluginNodeTex
VRayPointCloudColor
VRayPtex
VRaySamplerInfoTex
VRaySky
VRaySoftbox
VRayTriplanarTex
VRayUserColor
OK
Cancel
VRayLight001
Modifier List
VRayLight
General
On
Type:
Dome
Targeted
200.0mm
Units:
Default (image)
Multiplier:
30.0
Mode:
Color
Color:
Temperature:
Texture
Res:
512
No Map
Dome light
Options
Sampling
Viewport
Advanced options

Add VRayBitmap to the Texture toggle

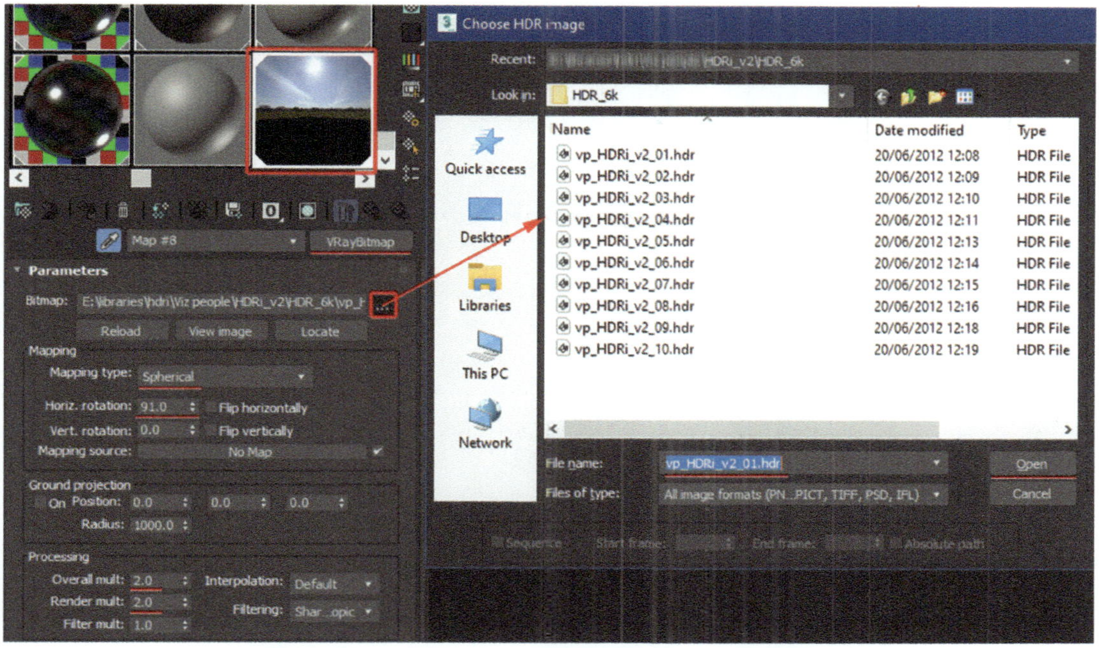
Choose HDR image
Recent:
Look in:
HDR_6k
Quick access
Desktop
Libraries
This PC
Network
Name
Date modified
Type
vp_HDRi_v2_01.hdr 20/06/2012 12:08 HDR File
vp_HDRi_v2_02.hdr 20/06/2012 12:09 HDR File
vp_HDRi_v2_03.hdr 20/06/2012 12:10 HDR File
vp_HDRi_v2_04.hdr 20/06/2012 12:11 HDR File
vp_HDRi_v2_05.hdr 20/06/2012 12:13 HDR File
vp_HDRi_v2_06.hdr 20/06/2012 12:14 HDR File
vp_HDRi_v2_07.hdr 20/06/2012 12:15 HDR File
vp_HDRi_v2_08.hdr 20/06/2012 12:16 HDR File
vp_HDRi_v2_09.hdr 20/06/2012 12:18 HDR File
vp_HDRi_v2_10.hdr 20/06/2012 12:19 HDR File
File name: vp_HDRi_v2_01.hdr
Files of type: All image formats (PN...PICT, TIFF, PSD, IFL)
Open
Cancel
Map #8
VRayBitmap
Parameters
Bitmap: E:\libraries\hdri\Viz people\HDRi_v2\HDR_6k\vp_
Reload
View image
Locate
Mapping
Mapping type: Spherical
Horiz. rotation: 91.0
Flip horizontally
Vert. rotation: 0.0
Flip vertically
Mapping source: No Map
Ground projection
On Position: 0.0 0.0 0.0
Radius: 1000.0
Processing
Overall mult: 2.0
Interpolation: Default
Render mult: 2.0
Filtering: Shar...opic
Filter mult: 1.0

Add HDRI to the VRayBitmap

The artificial lights can be recreated with IES photometric lights.

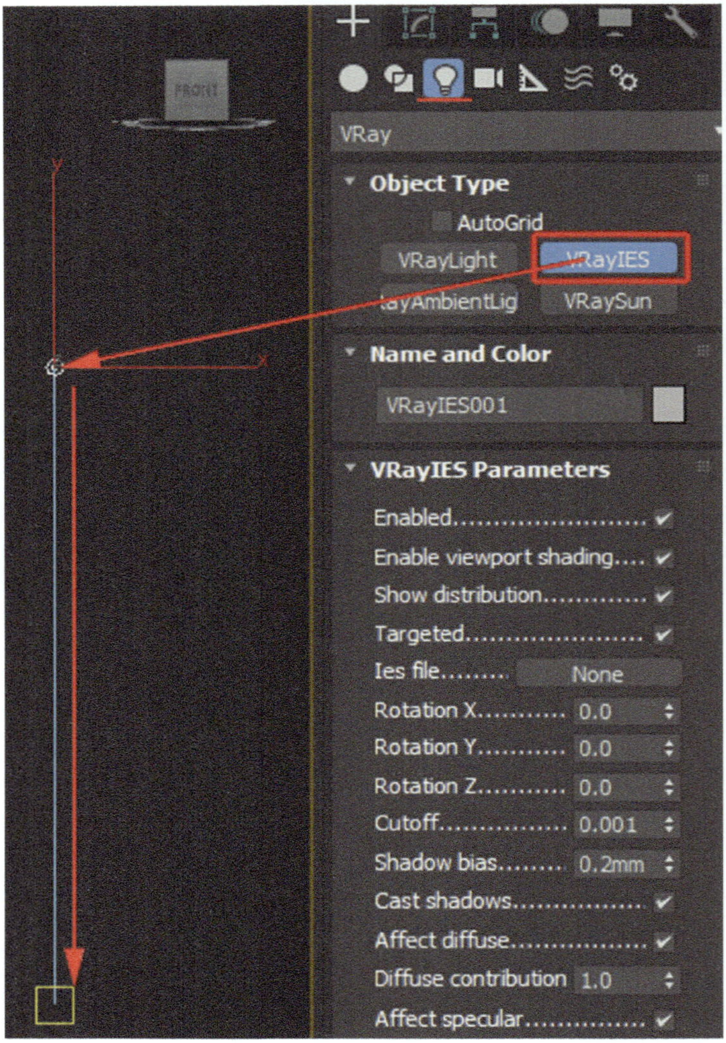

VRay IES lights

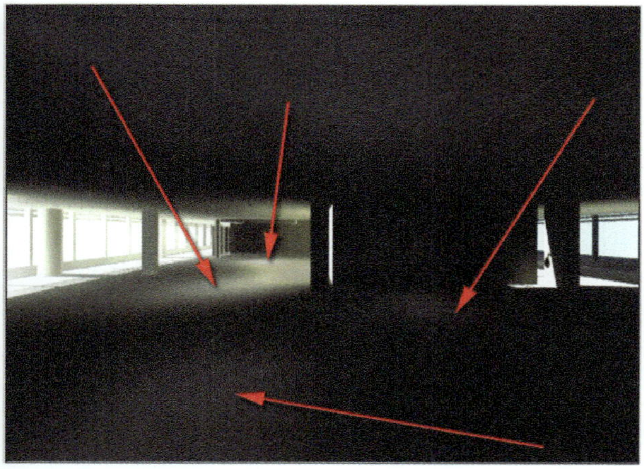

Chalk render highlighting depth and pools of light

Always choose IES web files that cast pools of light, whenever possible.

The 14.IES is widely used to generate such effects; it can be found in this book's resource files.

These pools of light will help create details, contrast, and depth in the entire scene. In addition, ensure these pools of light don't overlap with each other. To prevent overexposed hot spots generated by the pools of light, simply space each light adequately, followed by test rendering periodically regions of the scene.

To add further light details in the scene, users usually position these lights close to the walls, so their web patterns can be cast onto the walls.

To create more realistic patterns of light, position/rotate some of the lights so that the pools of light are projected in an oblique direction.

The light colors also play an important role in making a scene look more appealing. Blue and yellow tones are often seen in most striking images/photos.

Yellow light colors usually represent the artificial lights; blue colors represent the ambient/diffused light.

The sunlight color is usually white, unless it's sunset.

Before illuminating a scene, one should always determine where the main light source should be coming from.

This is often determined by the chosen camera view, and the number of glass windows/openings close to the camera and/or visible in the shot.

The rule of thumb is to always choose the sunlight as the main light source in interior and exterior daylight scenes. In exterior daylight scenes, this choice is always a given.

In interior daylight scenes, one should choose the sunlight as the main light source, only when there are glass windows/openings visible and/or close to the camera view. In such cases, users should have a strong direct/angled sunlight cast onto surfaces, with hints of blue on areas indirectly lit by the ambient/diffused light.

Artificial lights caught in sun-lit areas should be dimmed or switched off, in order for the sunlight to have more prominence.

The indirectly lit areas can have the artificial lights switched on, with the ambient light in the mix.

Sun as the main source of light for an interior daylight scene

Sun as the main source of light for an exterior daylight scene

In all other interior daylight scenarios, users frequently choose artificial lights and the ambient/diffused light as the main light sources.

When such happens, the sunlight should ideally be casting a direct light, in the distance; so the ambient and artificial lights can have more dominance in the scene.

Artificial lights as the main source of light for an interior daylight scene

In exterior night scenes, the main light sources should be the dome/ambient/diffused light and the artificial lights.

Dome and artificial lights as the main source of light for an exterior night scene

3. Once the chalk render is signed off by the client, one can begin creating shaders and details in areas closer to the camera. These extra modeling details will help make the render appear more realistic.

For instance, details such as shadow gaps, general table contents, carpet, fur, chamfered edges, realistic plants/trees/grass, slightly uneven surfaces/tiles, creases, and subtle asymmetry and clutter always make a 3d scene look more appealing and realistic.

Detailed modeling

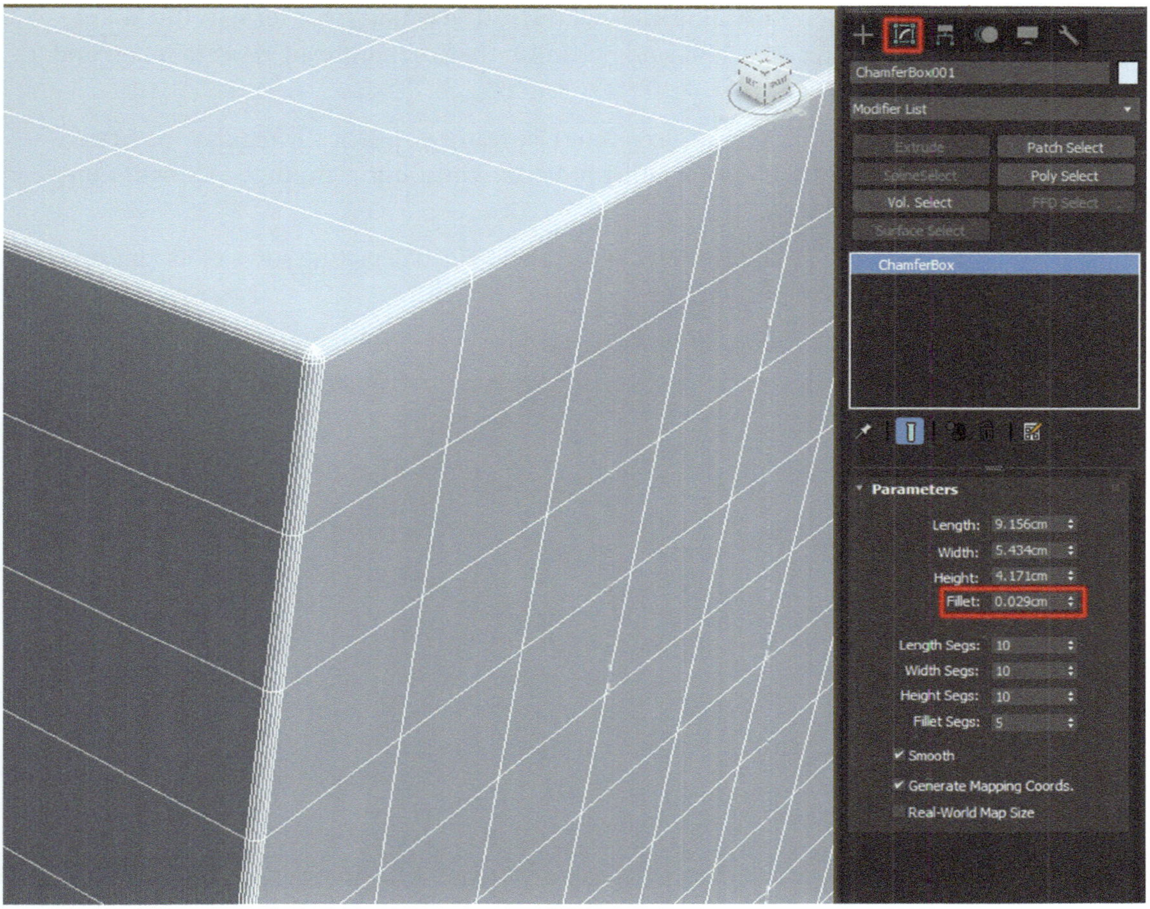

Chamfered edges

Having a vast library of pre-modeled assets from previous projects will help speed up the modeling process.

To really expedite the process of building your 3d scene with assets and materials in less than one day, simply use an amazing plug-in called "Project Manager."

In Project Manager, models, materials, textures, and other assets are neatly divided into five different tabs.

The "Models Tab" allows users to merge 3d files using a variety of options such as replace, export, and render existing models.

This amazing plug-in also supports substance textures—interactive rendering previews for IES files and materials.

Furthermore, it's compatible with all 3d Max image file formats (including PSD, Vrimg, etc.), and automatically attaches thumbnail views to image and file libraries.

Its amazing drag-and-drop interface features drastically reduces the time/effort involved in completing projects, whilst using groundbreaking intuitive workflows.

The book resources comes with a short video depicting some of its amazing functionalities: at

https://3d-kstudio.com/product/project-manager/

Project Manager plug-in

To quickly create trees, plants, ground, rocks, grass, gravel, hedges, ceiling details/services, etc., simply use ITоо tools such as Forest Pack and Rail Clone.

With a click of a button, users can create and customize landscapes and environments with great ease.

ITоо products can truly condense days/weeks of work into a few hours.

For more information about ITоо products, please visit https://www.itoosoft.com/forestpack

ITоо Forest Pack

Below are some of many guidelines one should keep an eye out for while shading and texturing the scene:

A. Ensure there's a photorealistic texture applied to most objects in the scene (even when the material is white).

Realistic white wall

Having a realistic texture applied to a white wall often makes a surface appear more realistic than otherwise. In real life, even pristine surfaces come with subtle details that we usually take for granted.

When these subtle details are removed, our eyes may subsequently perceive the surface or the overall image to be unrealistic/CG.

These illusive details are generally captured in a photo of a texture.

Websites such as cgtextures.com have a range of realistic textures for walls and most surfaces. You may not find specific colors for all surfaces. However, one can use Photoshop to modify surface colors.

Alternatively, you may create your own textures by photographing them yourself.

B. Bump/displacement maps usually add more realism to a surface/texture.

To emulate and reinforce the appearance of a convincing bump/displacement surface, users frequently create and plug a grayscale version of the diffuse texture into the bump toggle.

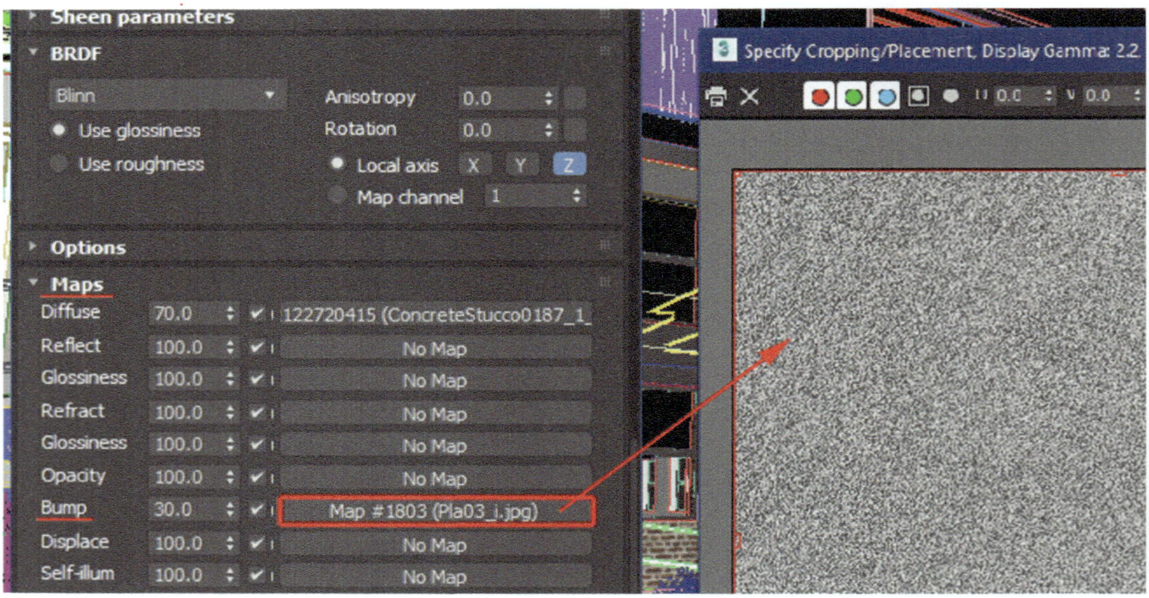

Bump toggle

Bump rendering results

To create a grayscale version of the diffused map, simply open the texture in Photoshop first.

Next, desaturate and tweak with its contrast, followed by saving it as a separate file name.

The more the contrast between the black and white colors, the sharper the bump/displacement.

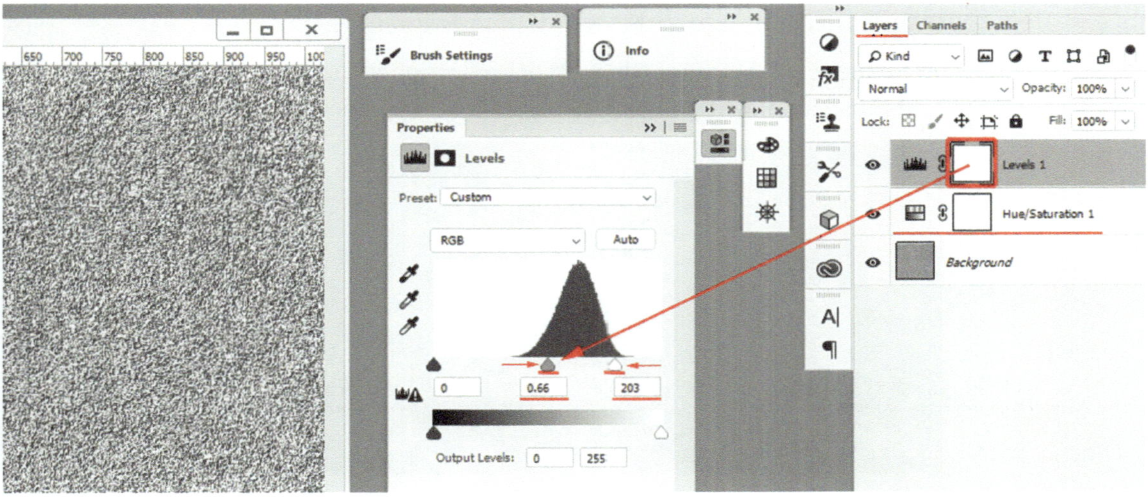

Creating a grayscale bump texture in Photoshop

While the bump effect adds more realism to a surface, the displacement will certainly increase its photorealism dramatically.

Displacing a 3d surface only adds value to a rendered image when the object in question is closer to the camera. Otherwise, the displacement details will go unnoticed on distant objects.

Displacement effects close to the camera

C. Add reflective/glossy surfaces whenever possible: these surfaces generally make a scene more interesting and realistic.

HDRIs (high dynamic range image) can also help add extra reflection/glossy details. If the HDRI is being used for reflection purposes only, ensure it is plugged to the environment reflection/refraction override toggle only. Otherwise, it will also contribute to the overall illumination.

Also, there will be times when HDRI reflection values such as position, rotation, and intensity may require changing drastically in order to be visible in the scene.

HDRI reflections on surfaces

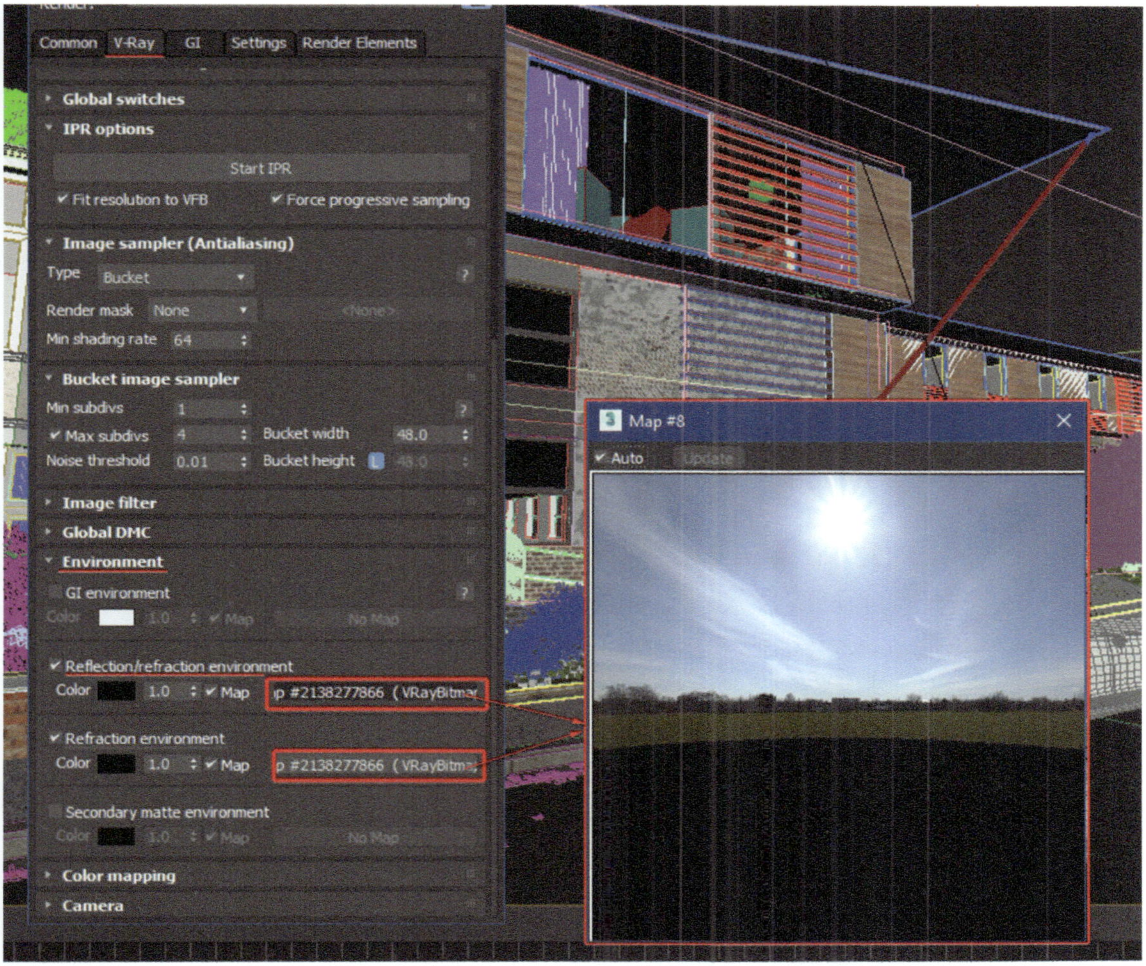

HDRI map

D. Uneven reflectivity: most surfaces in real life reflect light unevenly. To emulate this effect, simply plug a grayscale version of the diffuse map texture onto the reflectivity toggle.

As mentioned earlier, the grayscaling process can be achieved in Photoshop. The higher the grayscale contrast, the sharper the reflections.

E. Highlighted glossiness: adding glossy highlights on surfaces frequently helps to make a scene more interesting and realistic.

Reflective surfaces with highlights and glossiness

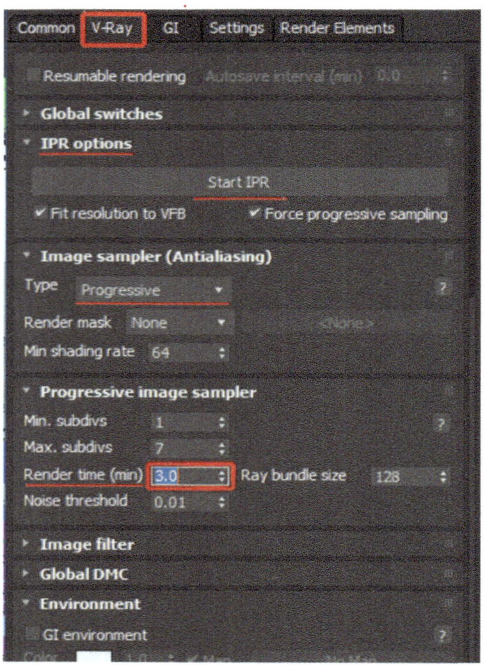

IPR and Progressive rendering parameters

Rendering

A variety of different test renders are carried out during the production stage. It is common practice to start with draft renders while setting up the lights and the chalk renders.

Users have an array of choices such as IPR, Progressive, or Bucket rendering

IPR (interactive production rendering) works in conjunction with progressive rendering settings to generate quick and draft renders while tweaking in real time.

Users simply need to click on the Start IPR button.

Progressive renderings are quick renders that occur immediately after you update material settings, render settings, lighting, etc.

Unlike the IPR, it doesn't allow users to make changes while the renders are taking place.

If you happen to have a simple scene, it's a quick workflow.

Otherwise, it may hinder the progression of your work by automatically rendering your scene every time you make a slight change.

IPR is probably a better choice to continue the work whilst rendering.

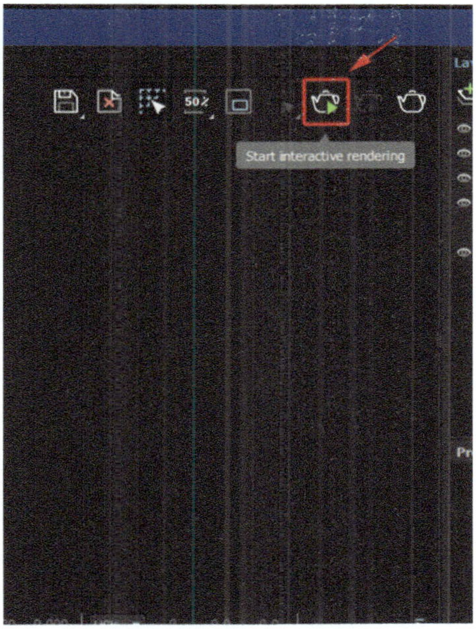

Start interactive rendering

Last rendered VFB

Alternatively, simply use the Bucket rendering type with lower/draft settings.

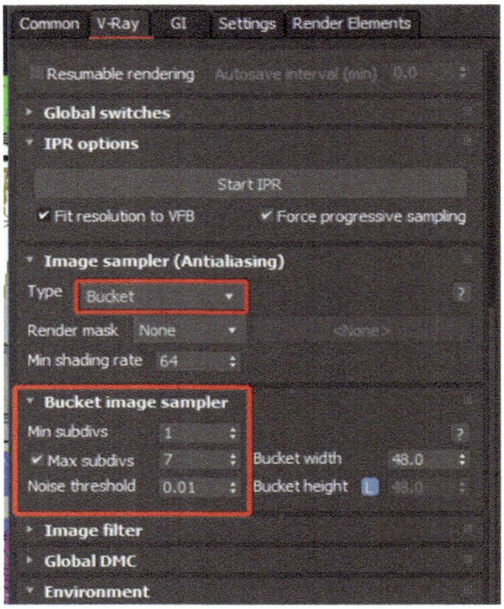

Bucket rendering with draft settings

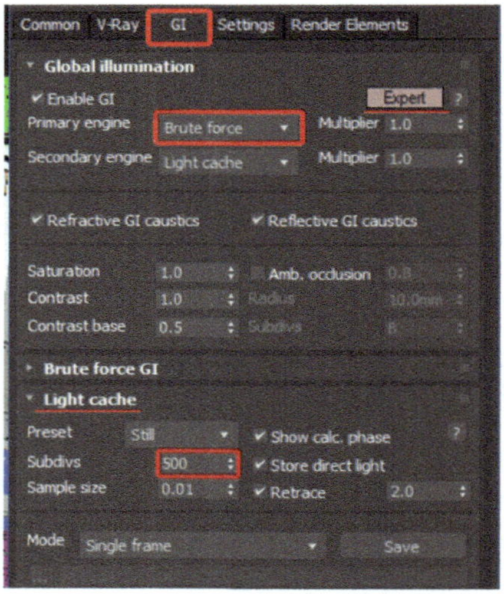

GI draft settings

Once satisfied with the overall lighting and the scene, one can increase the light and render settings for the final high-resolution render (i.e., 3000 pixels).

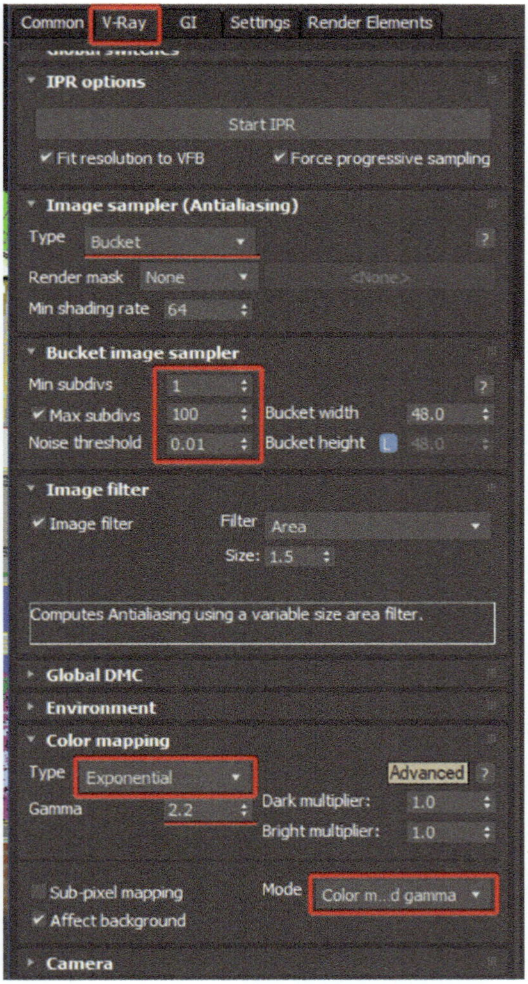

Common
V-Ray
GI
Settings
Render Elements
IPR options
Start IPR
Fit resolution to VFB
Force progressive sampling
Image sampler (Antialiasing)
Type
Bucket
Render mask
None
<None>
Min shading rate
64
Bucket image sampler
Min subdivs
1
Max subdivs
100
Bucket width
48.0
Noise threshold
0.01
Bucket height
L
48.0
Image filter
Image filter
Filter
Area
Size:
1.5
Computes Antialiasing using a variable size area filter.
Global DMC
Environment
Color mapping
Type
Exponential
Advanced
Gamma
2.2
Dark multiplier:
1.0
Bright multiplier:
1.0
Sub-pixel mapping
Mode
Color m...d gamma
Affect background
Camera

High image sampler settings

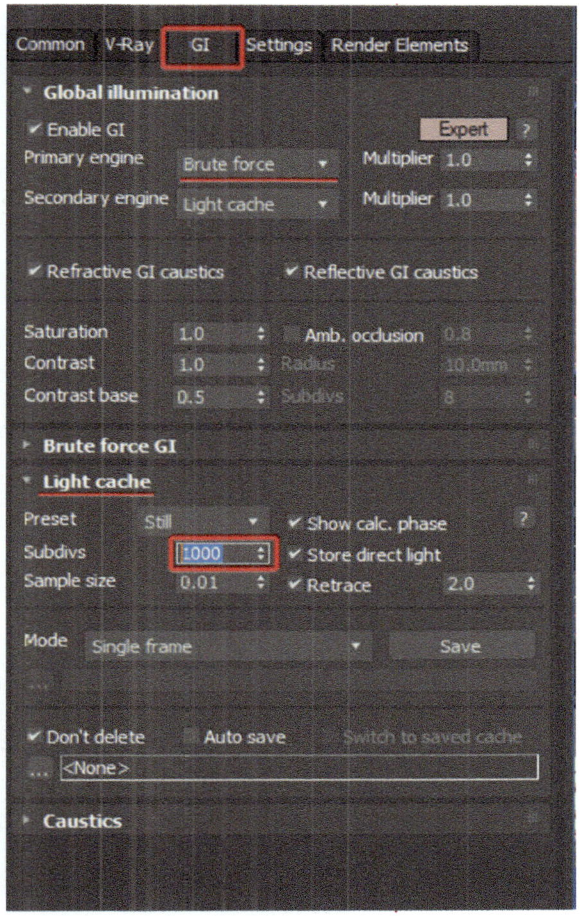

Common
V-Ray
GI
Settings
Render Elements
Global illumination
Enable GI
Expert
Primary engine
Brute force
Multiplier
1.0
Secondary engine
Light cache
Multiplier
1.0
Refractive GI caustics
Reflective GI caustics
Saturation
1.0
Amb. occlusion
0.8
Contrast
1.0
Radius
10.0mm
Contrast base
0.5
Subdivs
8
Brute force GI
Light cache
Preset
Still
Show calc. phase
Subdivs
1000
Store direct light
Sample size
0.01
Retrace
2.0
Mode
Single frame
Save
Don't delete
Auto save
Switch to saved cache
<None>
Caustics

GI high settings

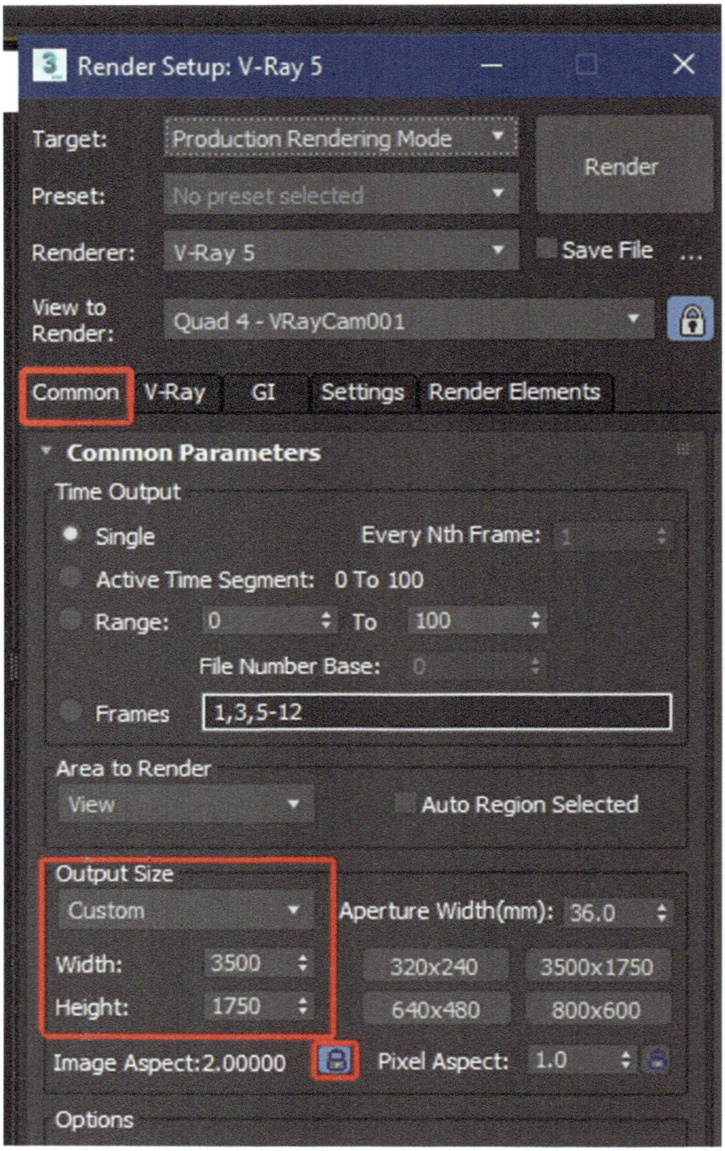
Render Setup: V-Ray 5
Target: Production Rendering Mode
Preset: No preset selected
Render
Renderer: V-Ray 5
Save File
View to Render: Quad 4 - VRayCam001
Common
V-Ray
GI
Settings
Render Elements
Common Parameters
Time Output
Single
Every Nth Frame: 1
Active Time Segment: 0 To 100
Range: 0 To 100
File Number Base: 0
Frames 1,3,5-12
Area to Render
View
Auto Region Selected
Output Size
Custom
Aperture Width(mm): 36.0
Width: 3500
Height: 1750
320x240
3500x1750
640x480
800x600
Image Aspect: 2.00000
Pixel Aspect: 1.0
Options

Higher resolution output size

Before sending the final render, it's common practice to do region renders, to ensure shaders/textures and the image quality are at the highest level.

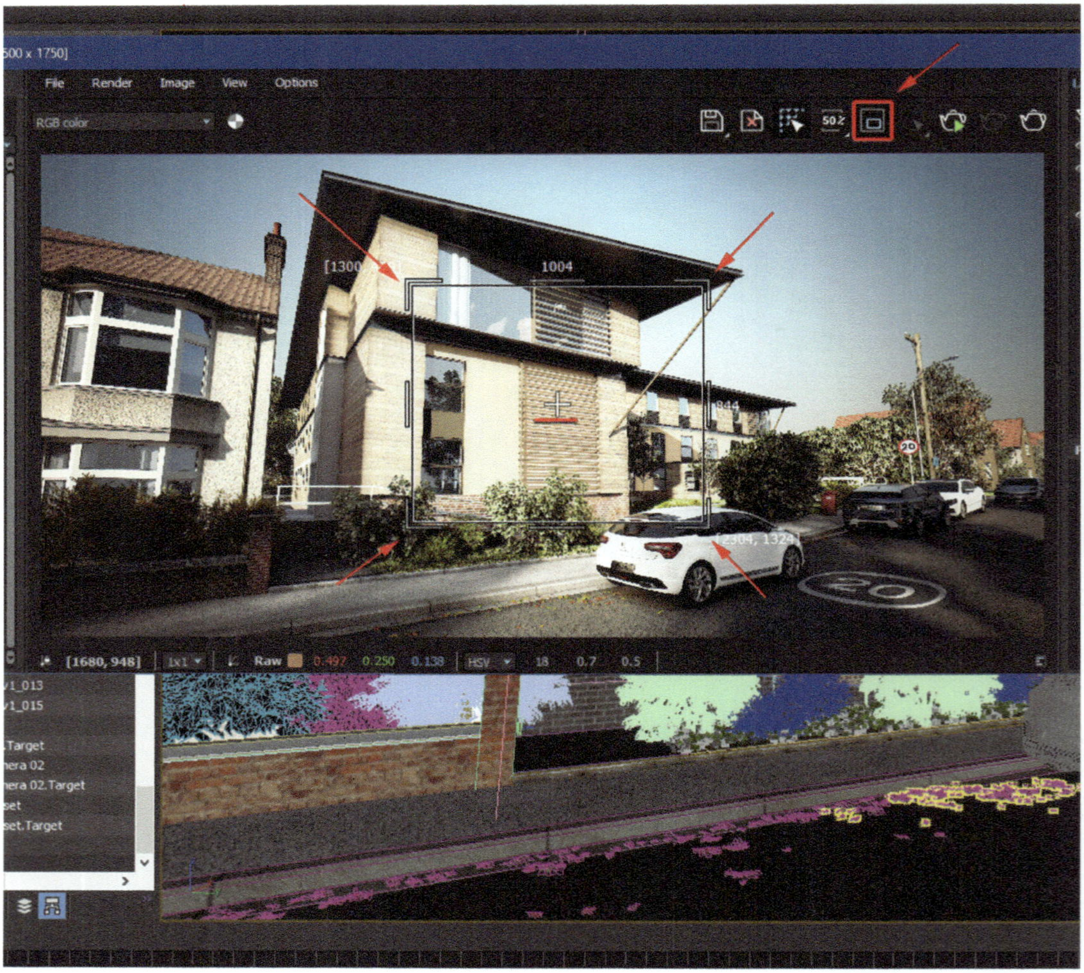

Region renders

With the lighting, shaders, and textures fine-tuned, one can begin adding the render elements and test rendering them (without saving).

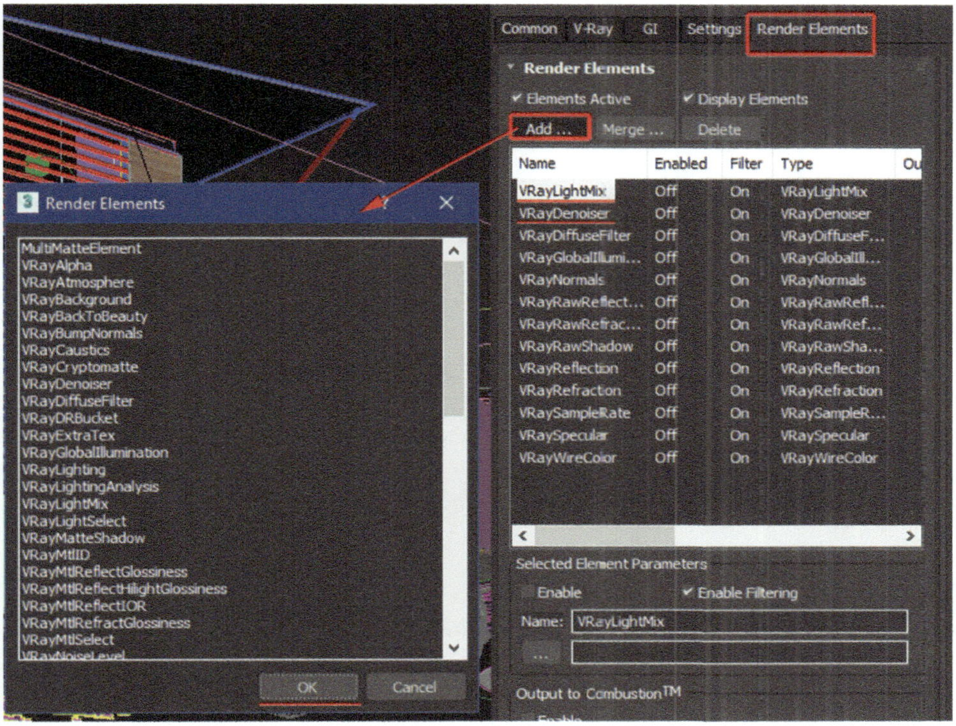

Adding render elements

The subsequent step is to name the final output file and render it.

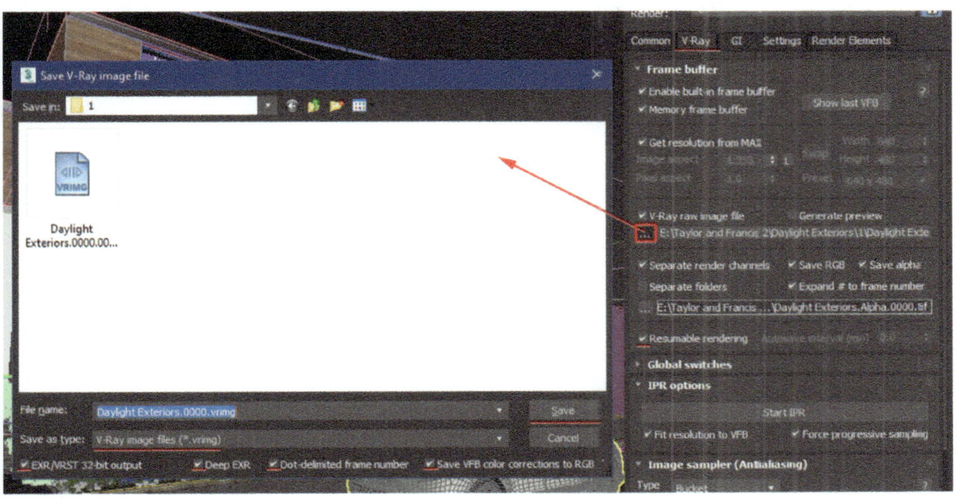

Name and save to VRay image file

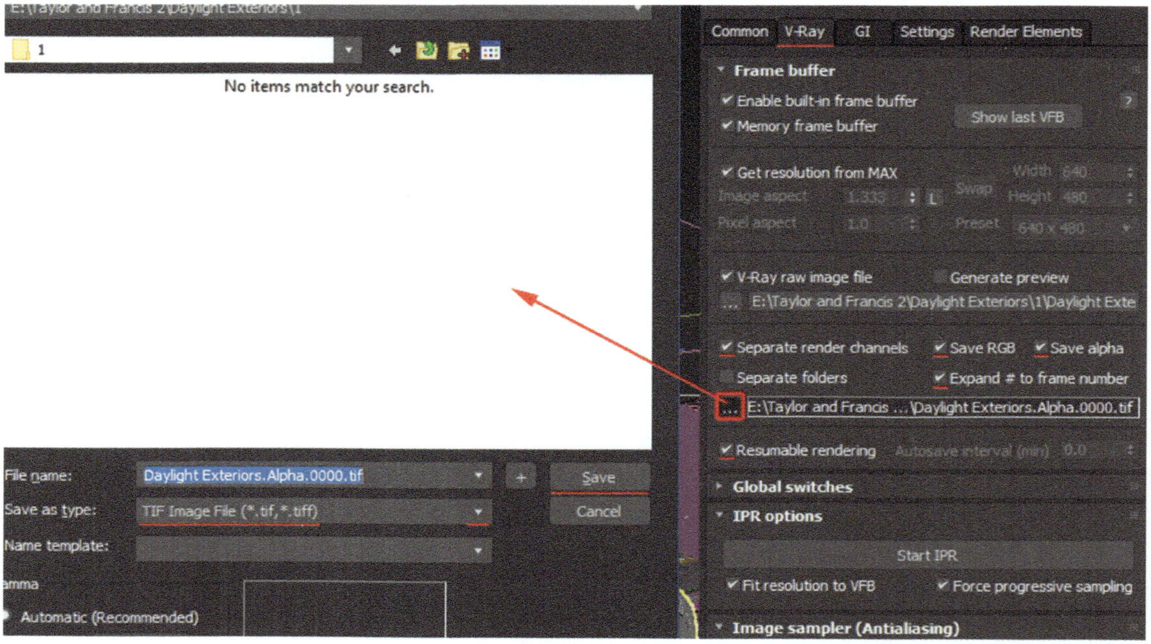

Name and save to tiff image file

Post-Production Overview

Post-production is often used to tweak specific materials, replace backgrounds, and fine-tune the overall image.

While most users are recommended to get the raw renders looking as good as possible from 3ds max, post-production work will always be necessary to take the final image to the next level.

More often than not, even in cases when the raw renders are already very good, adjusting render elements and the overall image in post-production work will turn a good image into an excellent one.

To enhance materials in post, multiple render passes are frequently mixed with key Photoshop blending modes and adjustment layers.

Some of the most popular render passes for post-production are specular, reflection, lightselect, reflection filter, diffuse material, MultiMattElement, Refraction, etc.

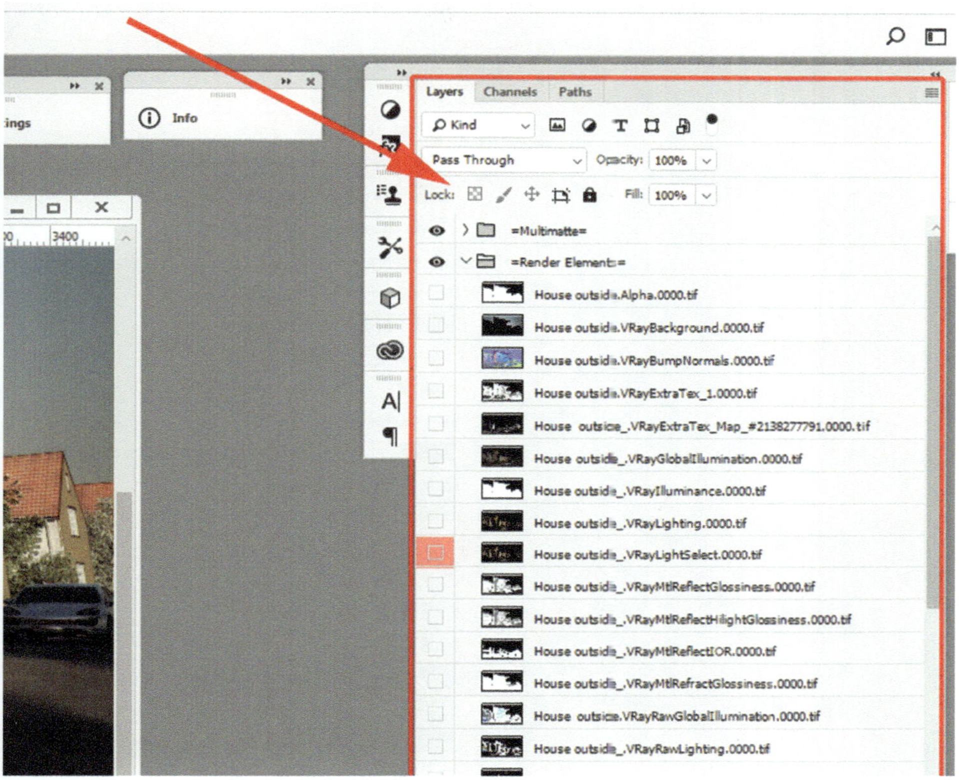

Render elements in a Photoshop stack

For better control of each material in post, some render passes are copied and moved into one specific group folder, with a mask attached to it.

To blend multiple render passes within each material group folder, users choose blending modes such as screen, multiply, overlay, etc.

As mentioned earlier, adjustment layers are also used within the group folders to control the material contrast and its colors.

Some of the widely used adjustment layers are levels, curves, photo filter, exposure, color balance, hue/saturation, and brightness/contrast.

These adjustment layers can also be used to grade and fine-tune the overall image.

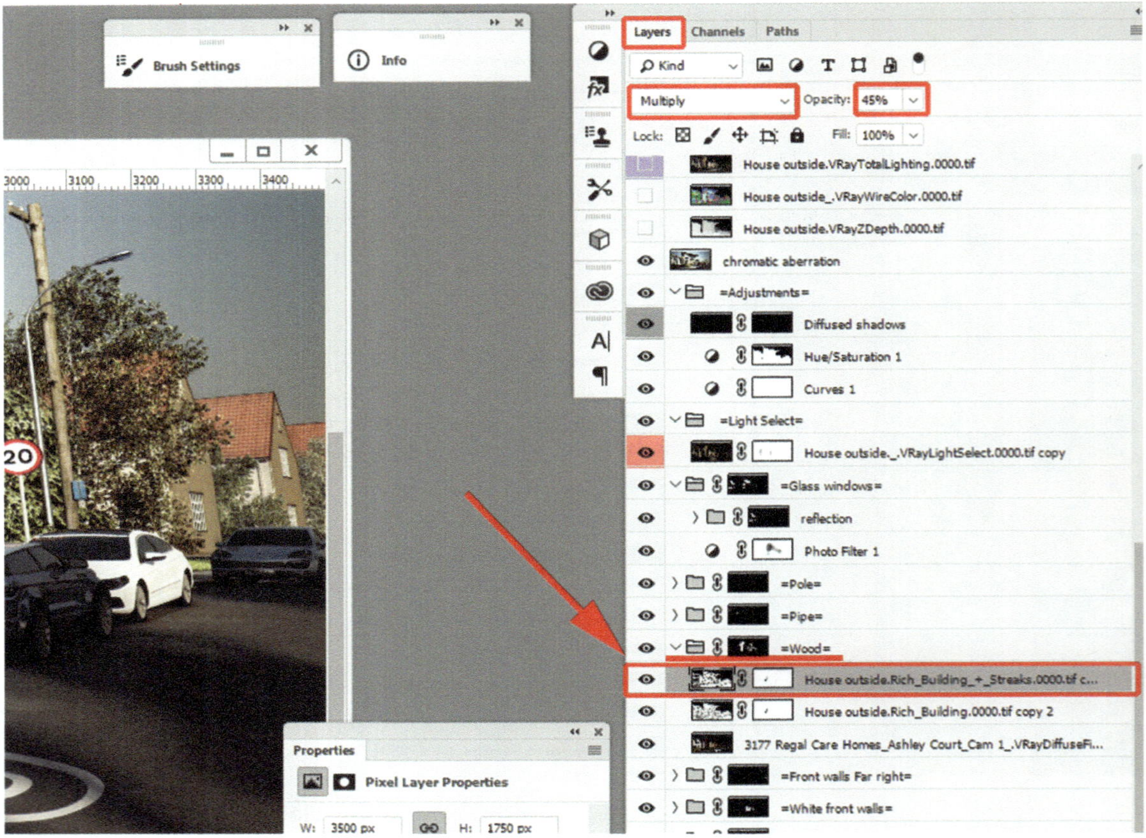
Brush Settings
Info
Layers
Channels
Paths
Kind
Multiply
Opacity: 45%
Lock:
Fill: 100%
House outside.VRayTotalLighting.0000.tif
House outside_.VRayWireColor.0000.tif
House outside.VRayZDepth.0000.tif
chromatic aberration
=Adjustments=
Diffused shadows
Hue/Saturation 1
Curves 1
=Light Select=
House outside._.VRayLightSelect.0000.tif copy
=Glass windows=
reflection
Photo Filter 1
=Pole=
=Pipe=
=Wood=
House outside.Rich_Building_+_Streaks.0000.tif c...
House outside.Rich_Building.0000.tif copy 2
3177 Regal Care Homes_Ashley Court_Cam 1_.VRayDiffuseFi...
=Front walls Far right=
=White front walls=
Properties
Pixel Layer Properties
W: 3500 px
H: 1750 px
3000
3100
3200
3300
3400
20

Tweaking specific materials in Photoshop

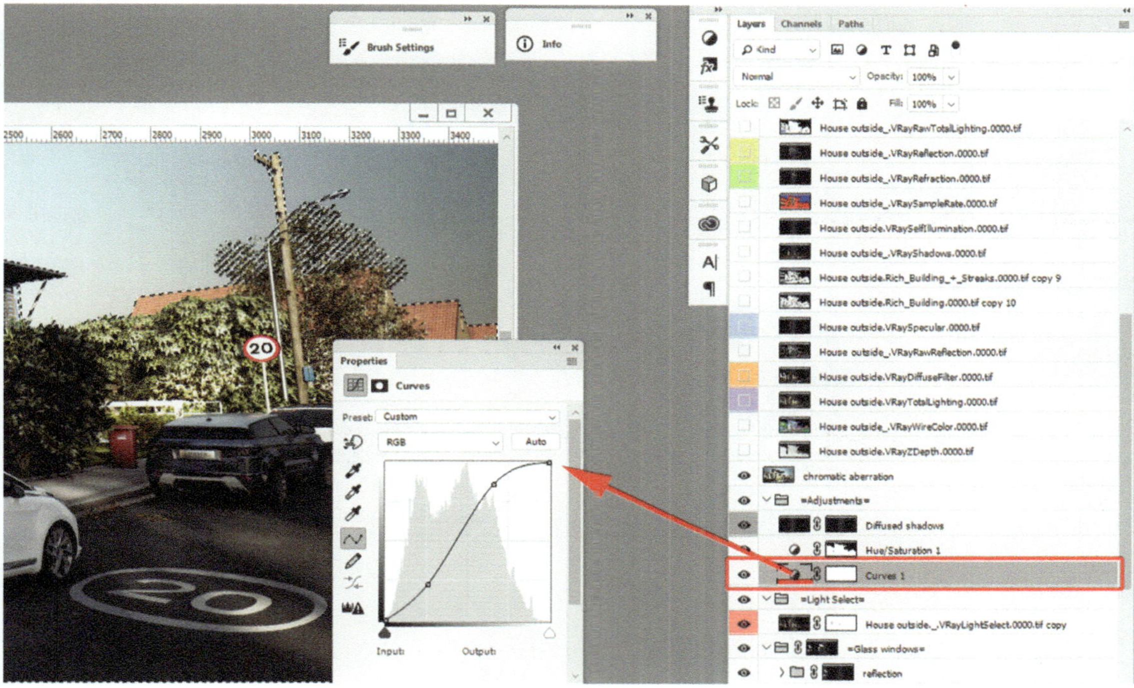

Different adjustment layers being used

Alternatively, users and companies often use reputable companies such as epictor.com to help expedite the post-production process in a few hours.

Epictor offers amazing services such as full post-production work from raw renders, integrating people in visualizations, and much more.

For more information about them, please visit http:'/www.epictor.com/

Finally, vishopper.com offers some of the best and cheapest cut out people library to be added in post-production.

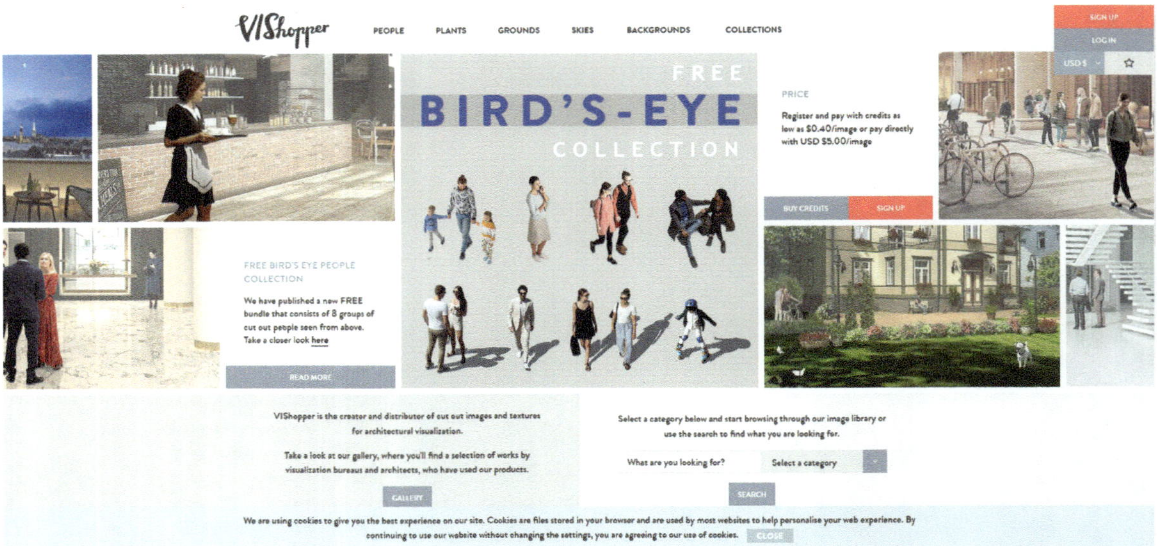
VIShopper
PEOPLE
PLANTS
GROUNDS
SKIES
BACKGROUNDS
COLLECTIONS
SIGN UP
LOG IN
USD $
FREE
BIRD'S-EYE
COLLECTION
PRICE
Register and pay with credits as low as $0.40/image or pay directly with USD $5.00/image
BUY CREDITS
SIGN UP
FREE BIRD'S EYE PEOPLE COLLECTION
We have published a new FREE bundle that consists of 8 groups of cut out people seen from above. Take a closer look here
READ MORE
VIShopper is the creator and distributor of cut out images and textures for architectural visualization.
Take a look at our gallery, where you'll find a selection of works by visualization bureaus and architects, who have used our products.
GALLERY
Select a category below and start browsing through our image library or use the search to find what you are looking for.
What are you looking for?
Select a category
SEARCH
We are using cookies to give you the best experience on our site. Cookies are files stored in your browser and are used by most websites to help personalise your web experience. By continuing to use our website without changing the settings, you are agreeing to our use of cookies.
CLOSE

vishopper.com website

2

Creating Materials and Shaders in V-Ray 5

2 Creating Materials and Shaders

V-Ray 5 is fully integrated with 3ds max, and comes equipped with a list of robust and powerful procedural maps and shaders to help achieve complex and striking results.

By default, most V-Ray 5 material presets are ready to render.

In the discussions that will follow, we will focus primarily on the VRayMtl parameters/presets and some of its most popular procedural maps.

In order to access the VRayMtl parameters, V-Ray 5 needs to be installed and loaded first.

To load VRay, press F10 to open the Render Setup dialog. Alternatively, simply click on its main toolbar button.

In the Render Setup dialog, go to the Common tab.

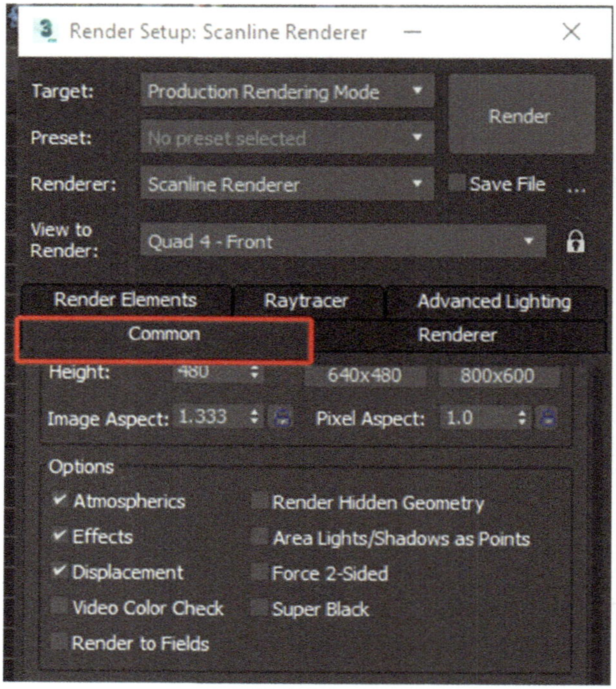

Go to the common tab

Scroll down and open the Assign Renderer rollout parameters. Click on its Production toggle.

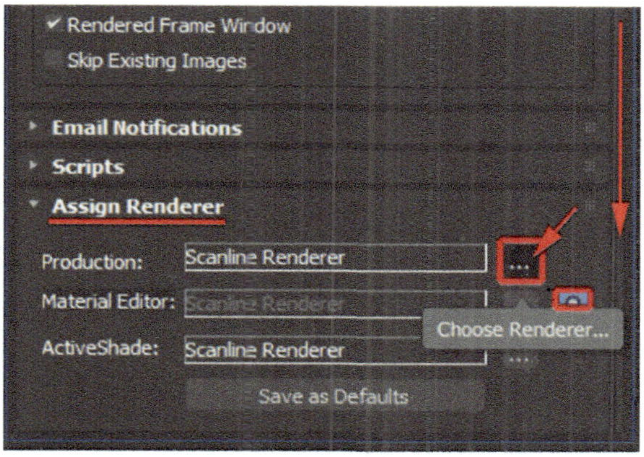

Assign Renderer rollout parameters

Pick the V-Ray 5 render in the Choose Renderer dialog. The VRay renderer should load automatically.

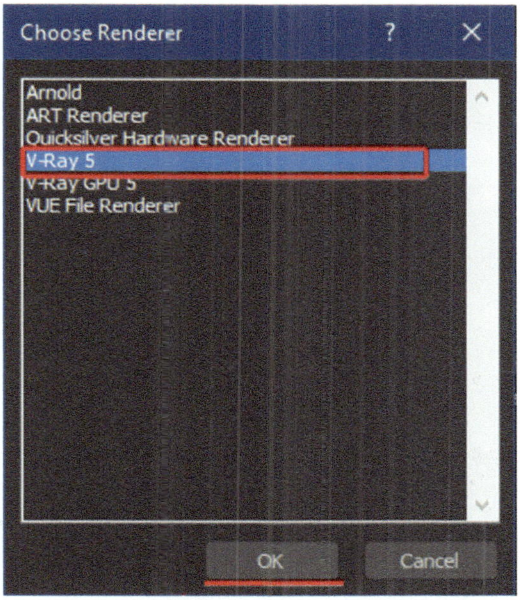

Choose the VRay renderer to load in the scene

To begin using the VRayMtl, simply open the Material Editor (M).

For the purpose of this discussion, we will be using the Compact Material Editor version, as opposed to Slate (node base).

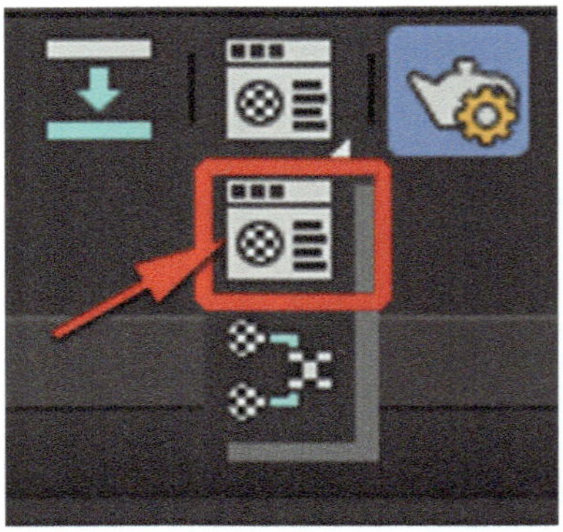

Choose the Compact Material Editor version

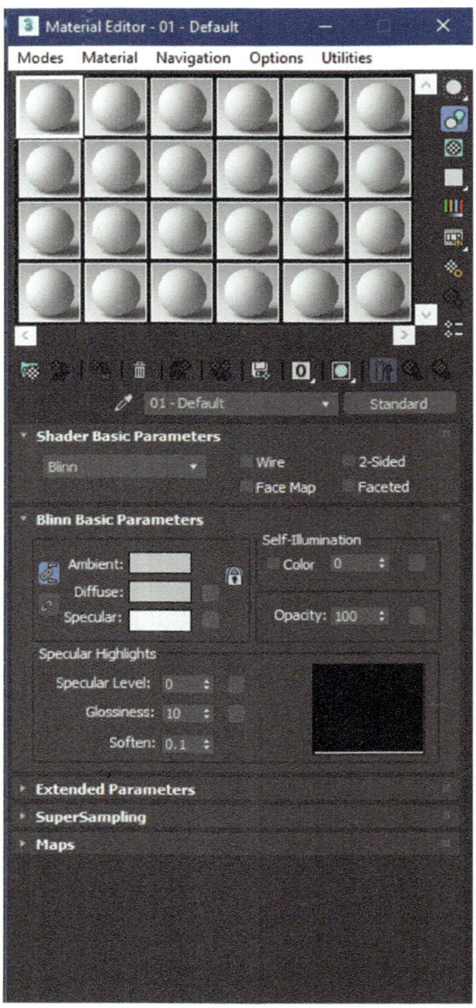

Material Editor open

This chapter assumes the standard material was automatically loaded in the Material Editor dialog.

Otherwise, you should probably see the Physical Material instead.

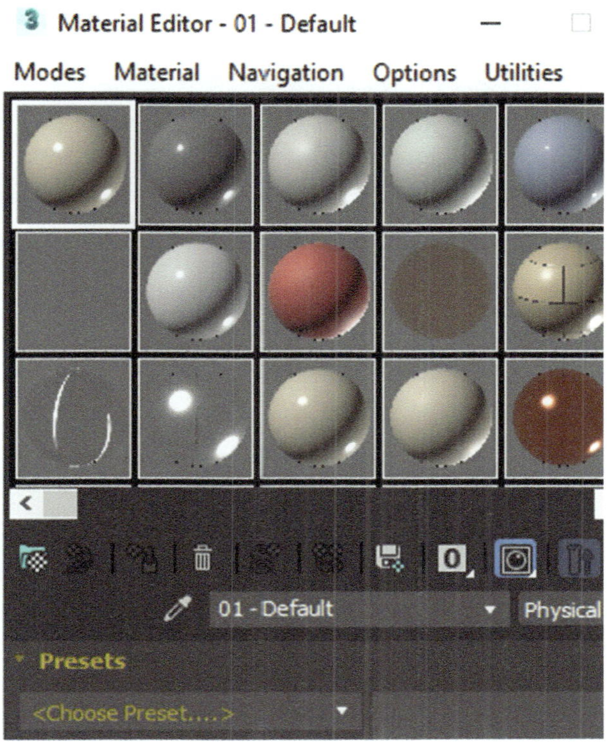

Physical Material loaded

By default, 3ds max has the Custom UI and Defaults Switcher set to DesignVIZ. ART, which automatically loads the Physical Materials.

To change this, simply go to the Customize toolbar and choose the Custom UI and Defaults Switcher option.

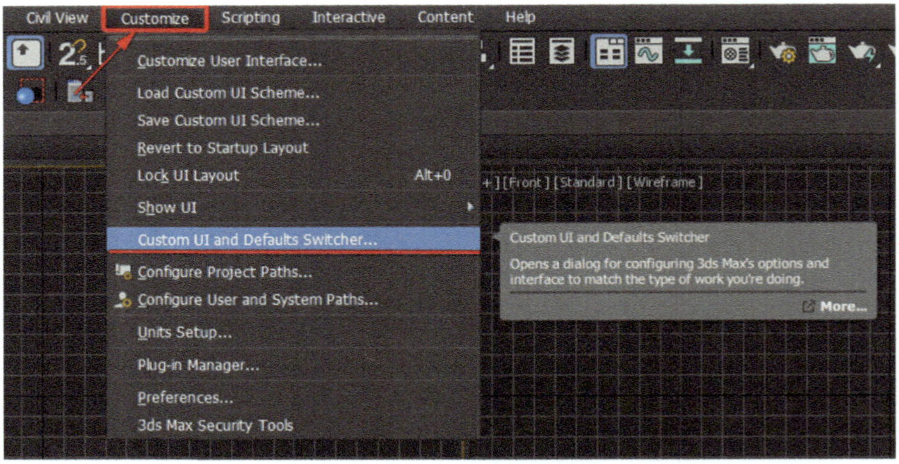

Custom UI and Defaults Switcher

Currently, you may have the DesignVIZ.ART loaded.

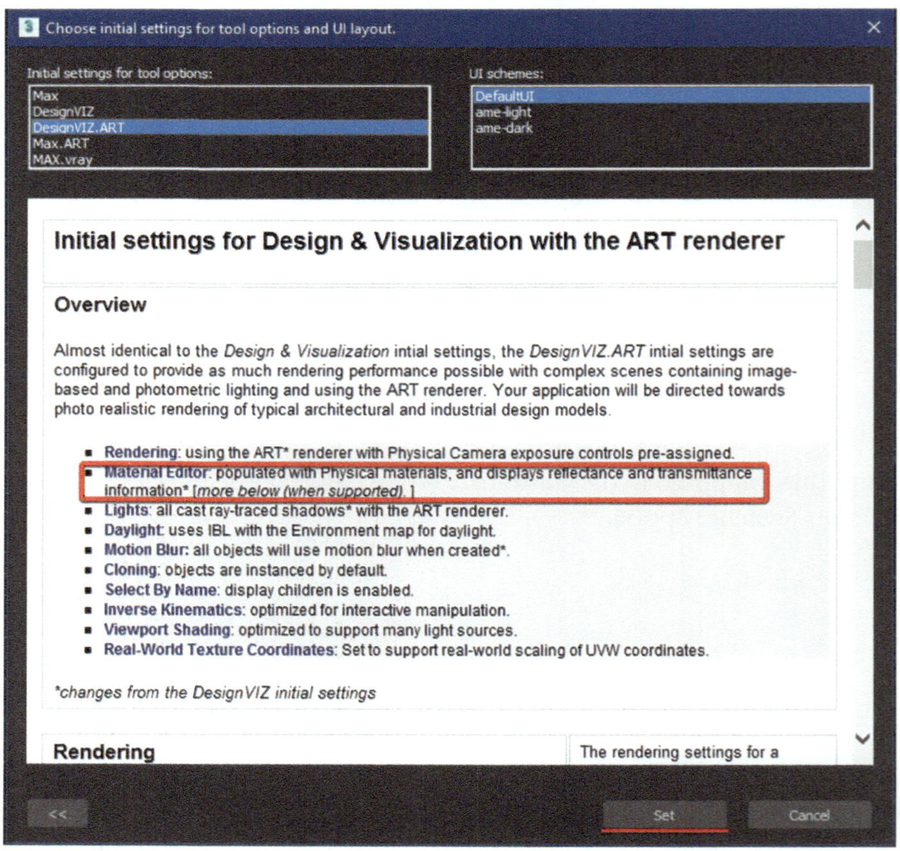

DesignVIZ.ART loaded

To change it, simply select the Max.vray DefaultUI cption, and click to Set.

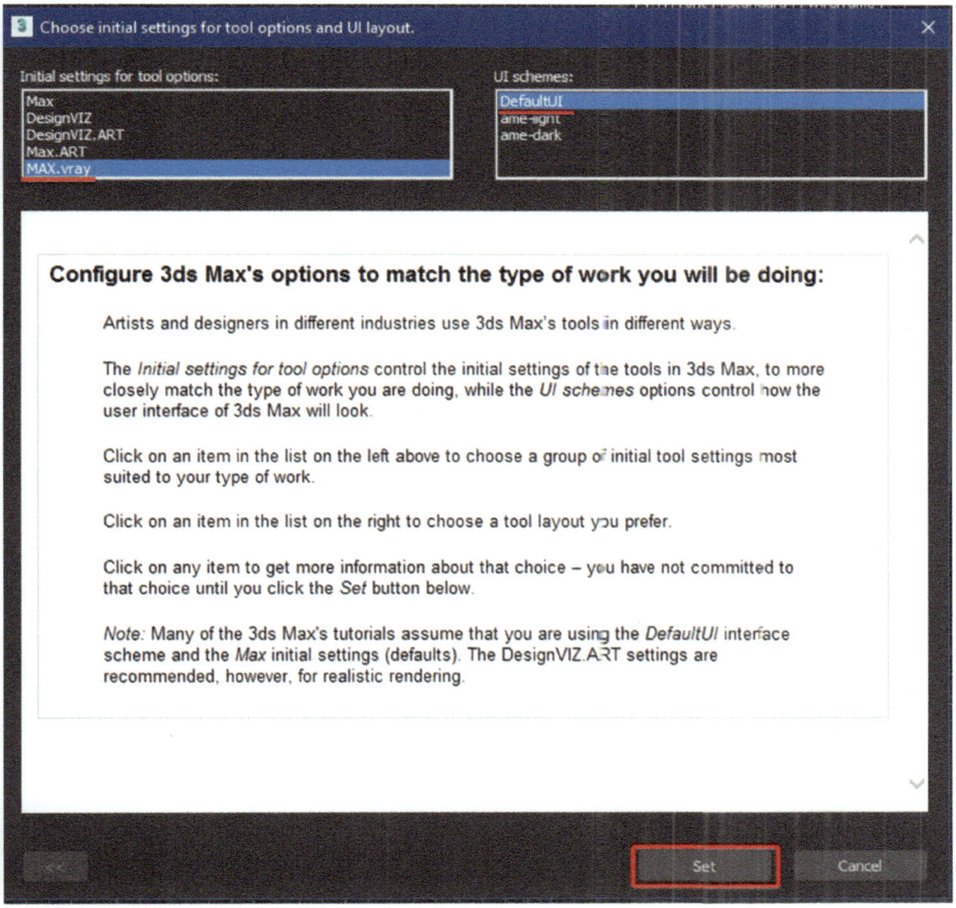

Max.vray DefaultUI option

However, this action might remove the new VRay toolbar, along with the new Asset Browser.

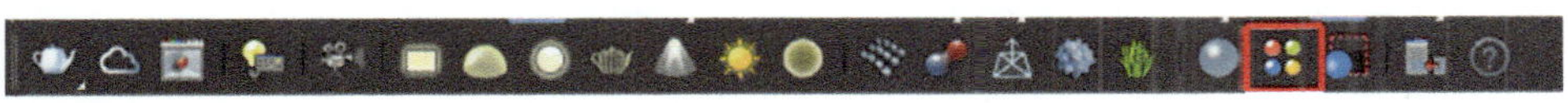

New VRay toolbar with Asset Browser

Currently, there's no way to pull back the new VRay Asset Browser from the Customize User Interface.

For this reason alone, users will be required to close 3ds max and uninstall V-Ray 5 first.

NOTE

Next time you open a brand new 3ds max scene, the Material Editor should automatically load with VRay materials by default.

Next, open 3ds max and set the Custom UI and Defaults Switcher to be Max.ray.

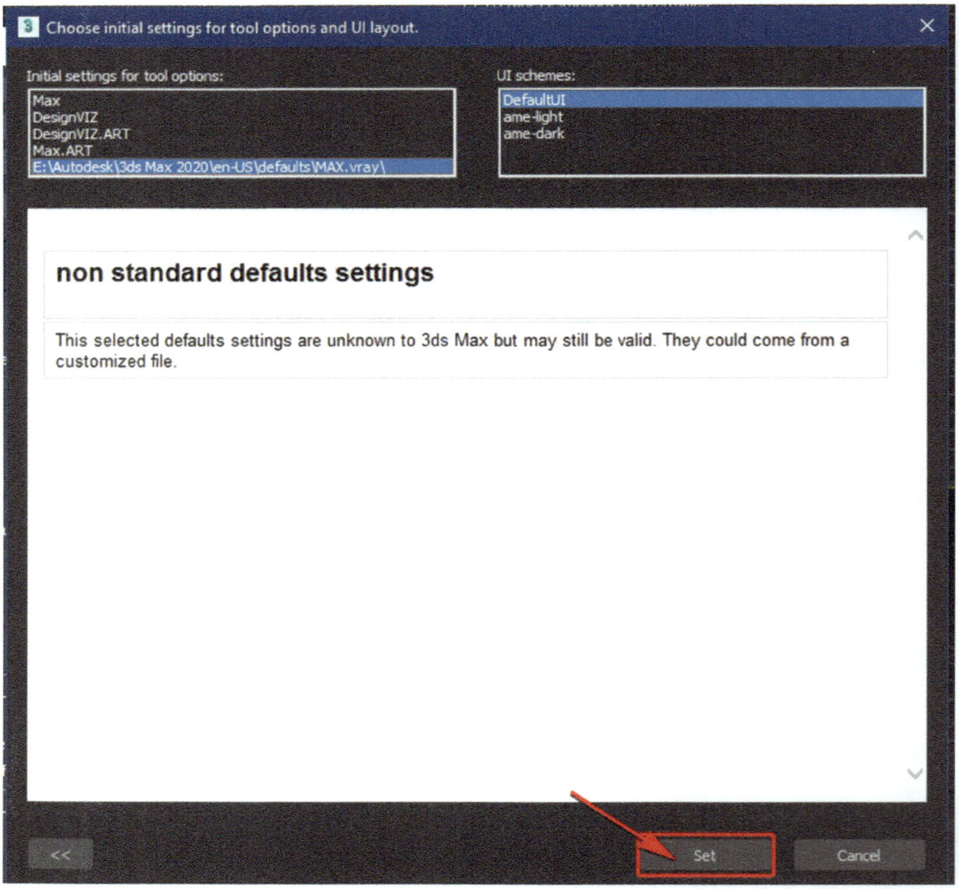

Max.vray DefaultUI option

Close 3ds max and reinstall V-Ray 5.

Next time you open 3ds max, the new VRay toolbar should appear automatically, along with the VRay materials loaded in the Material Editor dialog.

To continue, let's assume most readers didn't reinstall V-Ray 5, and have the Standard Materials automatically loaded in the Material Editor.

To load the VRayMtl, simply click on the Standard toggle, and choose the VRayMtl from the Material/Map Browser list.

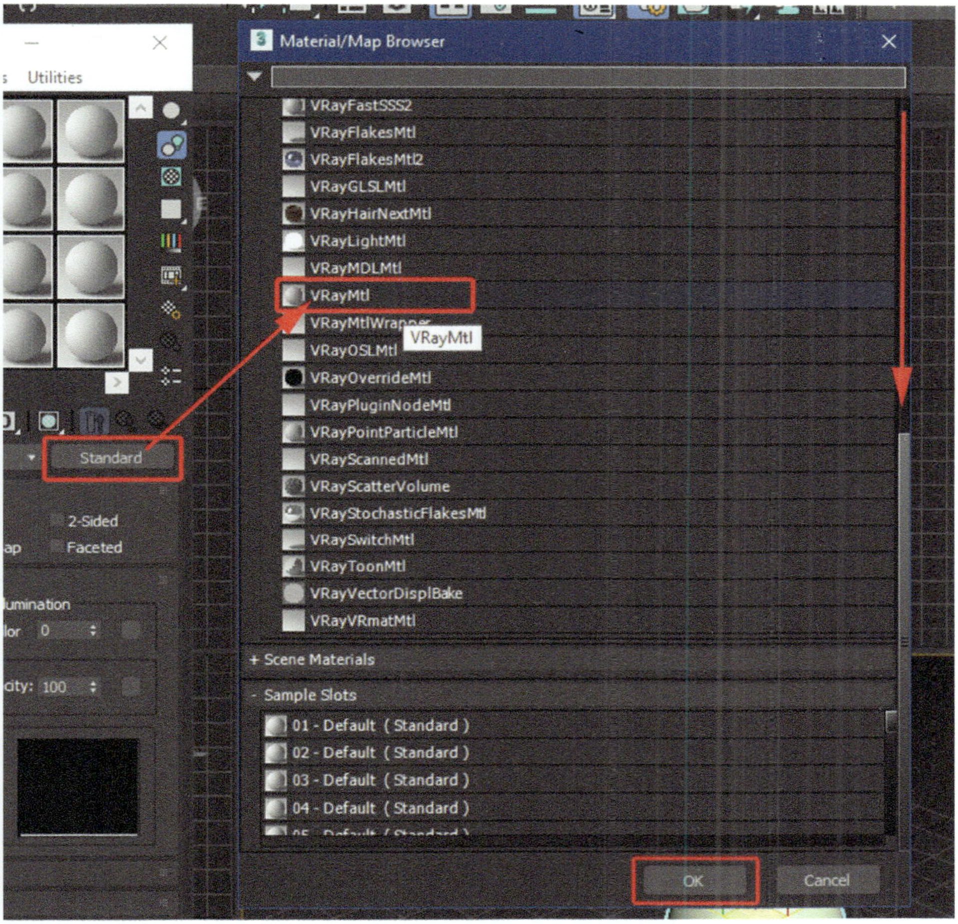

Load VRayMtl

If you happen to have the Physical Material loaded, simply click on toggle to load the VRayMtl.

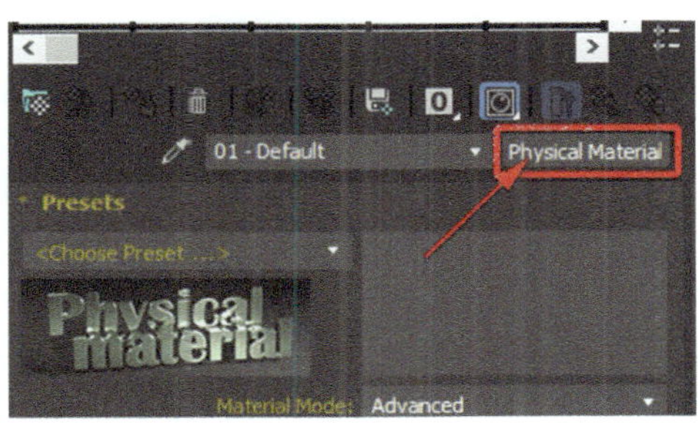

Click on the Physical Material toggle

Because V-Ray 5 displays the shaders and lighting more accurately in the material slots, the shader preview may take slightly longer to update.

To avoid this, simply go to the Settings tab.

Under the System rollout parameters, enable the native 3ds max material swatches.

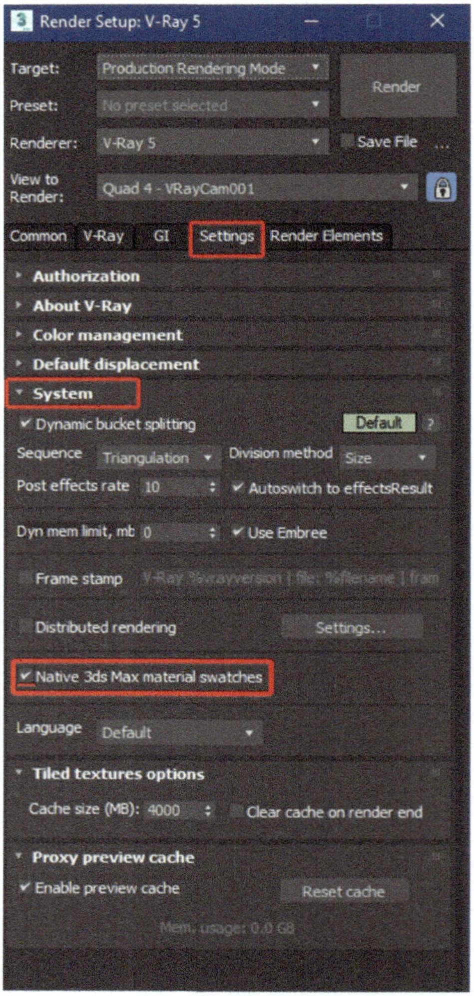

Native 3ds max material swatches

For realistic material previews, users can still use the VRay Asset Browser toolbar.

This new VRay material library can also be found in *C:\Users\User\Documents\V-Ray Material Library*

Alternatively, simply visit the Chaos Group website to download it from there:

https://docs.chaosgroup.com/display/VMAX/V-Ray+Asset+Browser

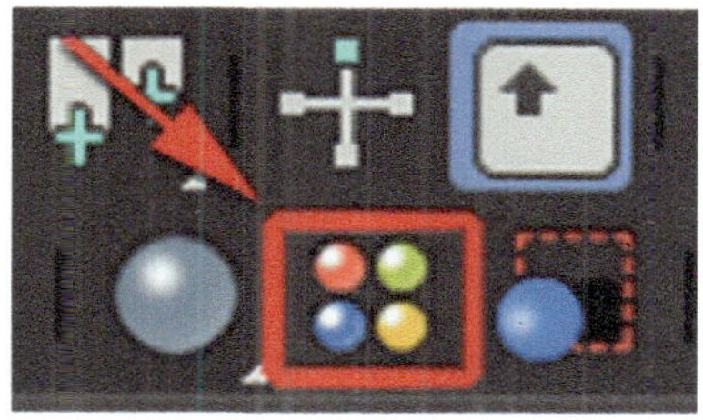

VRay Asset Browser toolbar

VRay Asset Browser dialog comes with a huge range of ready-to-render Material Library presets that are fast to display, and provides a full preview of its physical properties.

Most of its physical properties derive from the VRayMtl parameters we will be discussing in this chapter.

The Material Library presets are a massive help to speed up users' workflow.

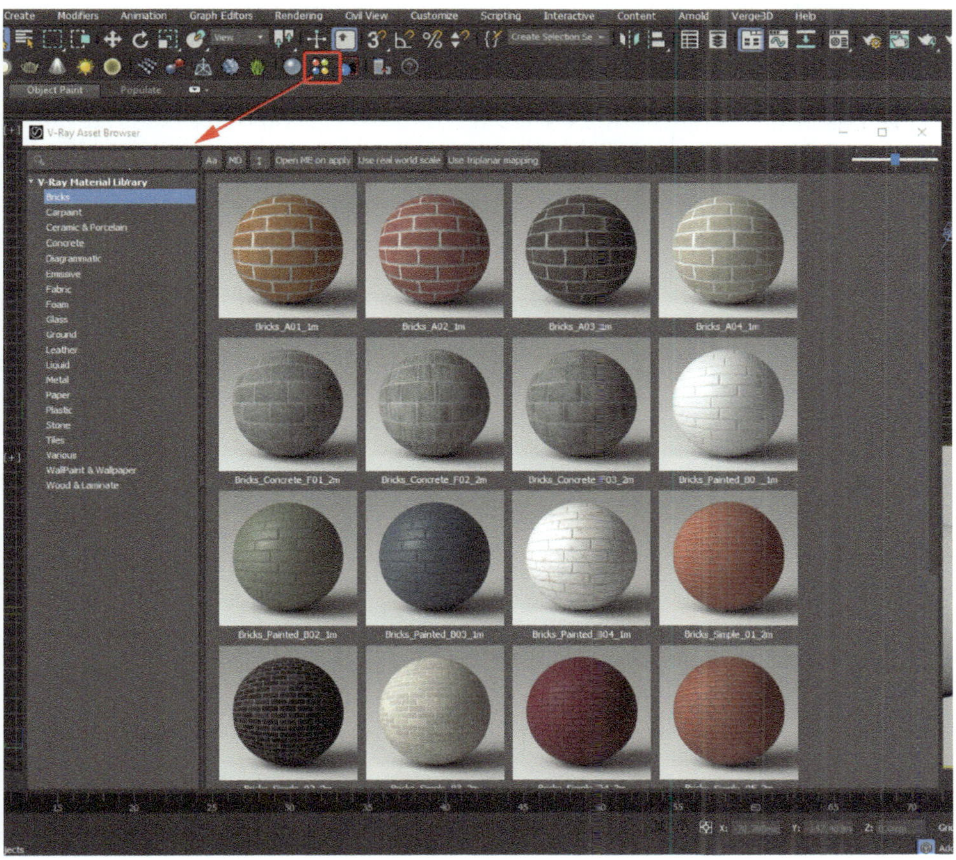

VRay Asset Browser dialog

VRay Asset Browser comes with the following functionalities:

Filter case sensitive: When enabled (it turns blue), this button takes into consideration the upper and lower cases of text typed in the search bar.

This text field is often used to quickly search for specific materials.

Filter by metadata: When enabled, it filters the searches by metadata.

Sort by name: When enabled, it sorts the materials displayed in the dialog alphabetically.

Open ME on apply: When enabled, the Material Editor dialog(M) opens automatically when materials are applied to objects.

Users need to right click on a specific material slot and choose to Apply to selected objects.

NOTE

This function can be found inside the coordinates rollout of textures applied. It may *not* work, sometimes (bug), and users will be required to enable it manually.

Use real-world scale: When enabled, it automatically enables the real-world scale function of selected VRayBitmaps, when applied via the VRay Asset Browser dialog.

This function applies to the tiling and other material values.

Always enable this button prior to applying materials to selected objects or adding materials to scene/material slot.

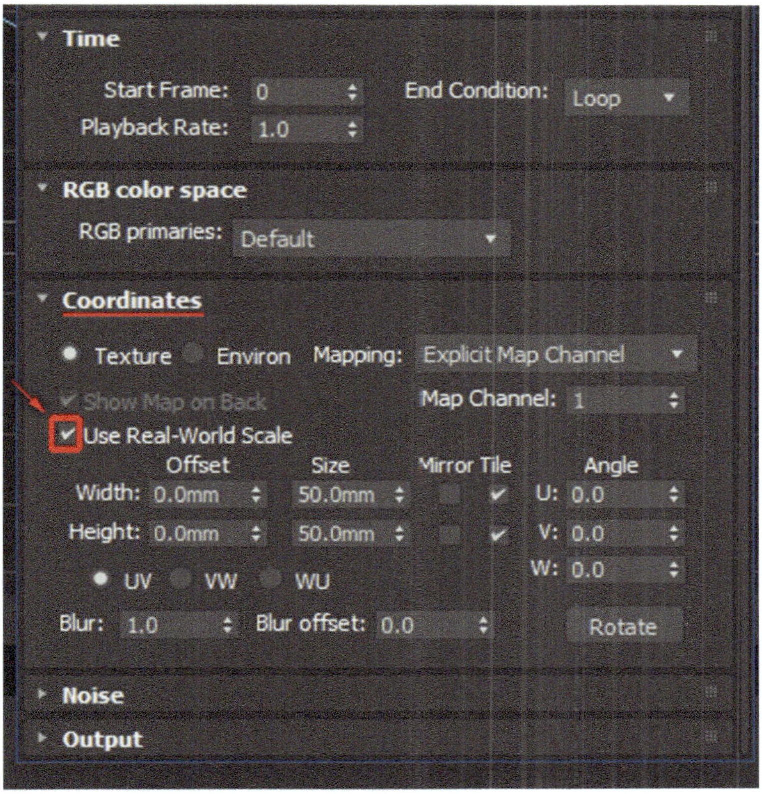

Use Real-world scale

Use triplanar mapping: When enabled, it adds the VrayTriplanarTex procedural map.

It serves as a substitute for UVW maps on objects. It's useful to apply it on objects without UVWs (merged 3d assets, etc.).

Always enable this button prior to applying materials to selected objects. Or prior to adding materials to scene/material slot.

As mentioned earlier, users can apply materials from the VRay Material Browser dialog, by simply right clicking on a specific material slot and choosing to Apply to Selected object(s).

Users can also choose to Preview the material, Add to scene, and Add to favorites.

The option to Add to scene loads the selected material in the material slot.

Some of the VRay preset materials come with a VRayBitmap procedural map applied to its diffuse toggle and a TX file assigned to it.

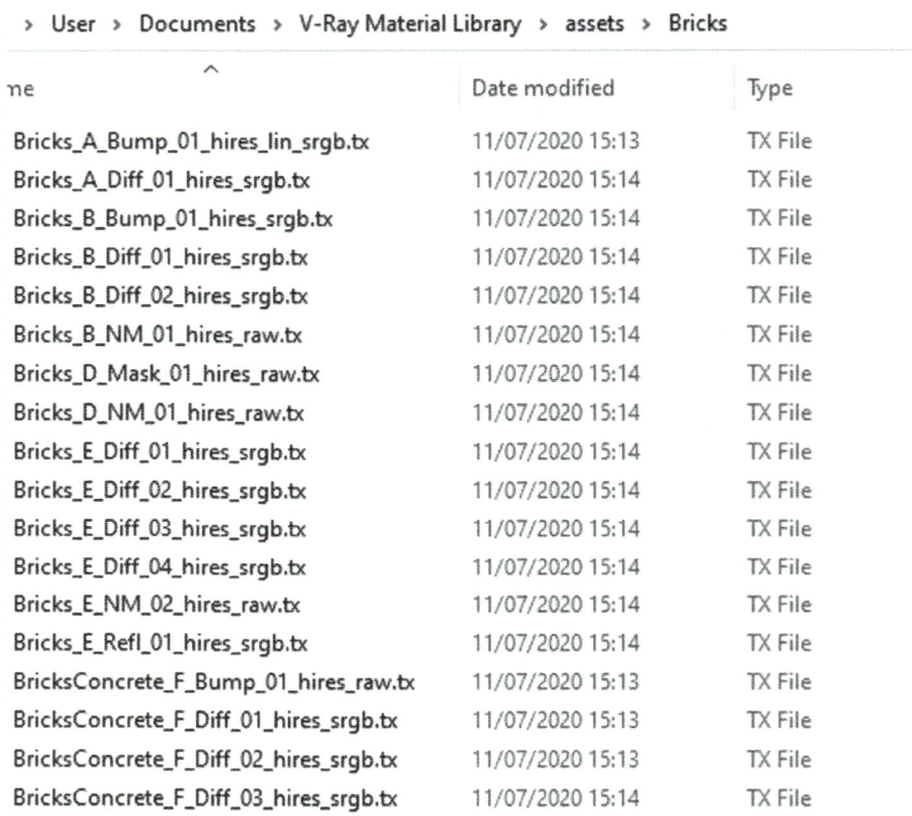

ne	Date modified	Type
Bricks_A_Bump_01_hires_lin_srgb.tx	11/07/2020 15:13	TX File
Bricks_A_Diff_01_hires_srgb.tx	11/07/2020 15:14	TX File
Bricks_B_Bump_01_hires_srgb.tx	11/07/2020 15:14	TX File
Bricks_B_Diff_01_hires_srgb.tx	11/07/2020 15:14	TX File
Bricks_B_Diff_02_hires_srgb.tx	11/07/2020 15:14	TX File
Bricks_B_NM_01_hires_raw.tx	11/07/2020 15:14	TX File
Bricks_D_Mask_01_hires_raw.tx	11/07/2020 15:14	TX File
Bricks_D_NM_01_hires_raw.tx	11/07/2020 15:14	TX File
Bricks_E_Diff_01_hires_srgb.tx	11/07/2020 15:14	TX File
Bricks_E_Diff_02_hires_srgb.tx	11/07/2020 15:14	TX File
Bricks_E_Diff_03_hires_srgb.tx	11/07/2020 15:14	TX File
Bricks_E_Diff_04_hires_srgb.tx	11/07/2020 15:14	TX File
Bricks_E_NM_02_hires_raw.tx	11/07/2020 15:14	TX File
Bricks_E_Refl_01_hires_srgb.tx	11/07/2020 15:14	TX File
BricksConcrete_F_Bump_01_hires_raw.tx	11/07/2020 15:13	TX File
BricksConcrete_F_Diff_01_hires_srgb.tx	11/07/2020 15:13	TX File
BricksConcrete_F_Diff_02_hires_srgb.tx	11/07/2020 15:13	TX File
BricksConcrete_F_Diff_03_hires_srgb.tx	11/07/2020 15:14	TX File

TX file extensions in the folder

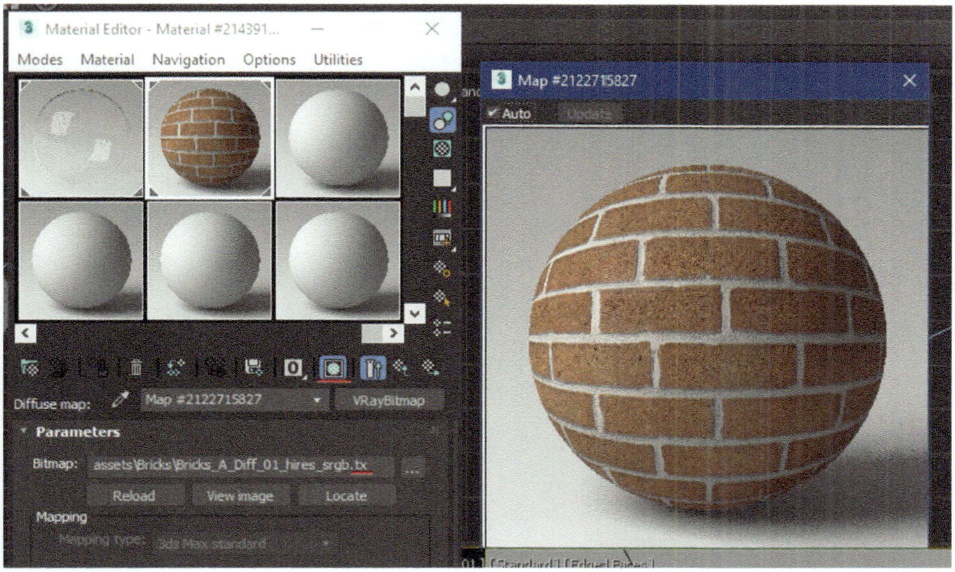

TX file assigned

TX file formats are extremely useful for memory cache efficiency, when rendering textures and reducing aliasing artifacts.

These file formats contain prefiltered levels of details of a texture (from low to high resolution).

Each level of detail is loaded according to its proximity to the camera/view.

The high-resolution version is automatically loaded for close-ups—and the low resolution when further away.

When the VrayTriplanarTex is applied, it automatically goes into the Mapping source toggle.

VRayTriplanarTex will be later discussed in more detail.

Right click to assign materials and apply VrayTriplanarTex

To apply each VRay material from the Material Editor, users need to select a material slot and objects in the scene, followed by clicking on the Assign Material to Selection button.

Assign a VRayMtl to objects in the scene

Basic Parameters

This chapter is an overview of VRay materials and parameters, not step-by-step tutorials, as depicted from Chapter 6 and onwards.

However, to test some of the parameters described here, please open the 3ds max file under the name VRay Materials.max

This 3ds max scene comes with a VRay Frame Buffer file format (vfbl) and a LUT file loaded in its VRay Frame Buffer dialog.

The LUT file associated with this chapter is under the name 3DCollective_sRGB _Agfa_Futura_03Hard.cube

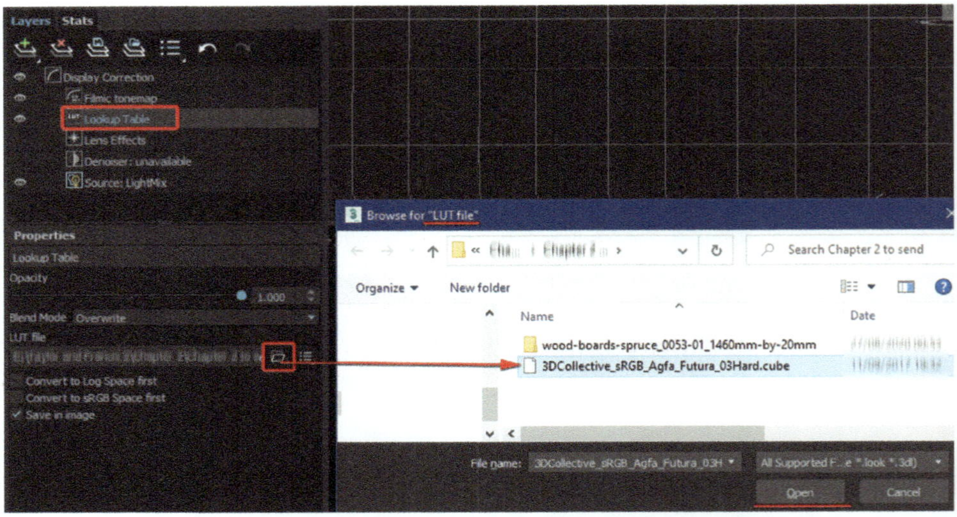

Load LUT file

The VRay Frame Buffer file format associated with this chapter is under the name VRay Materials.vfbl

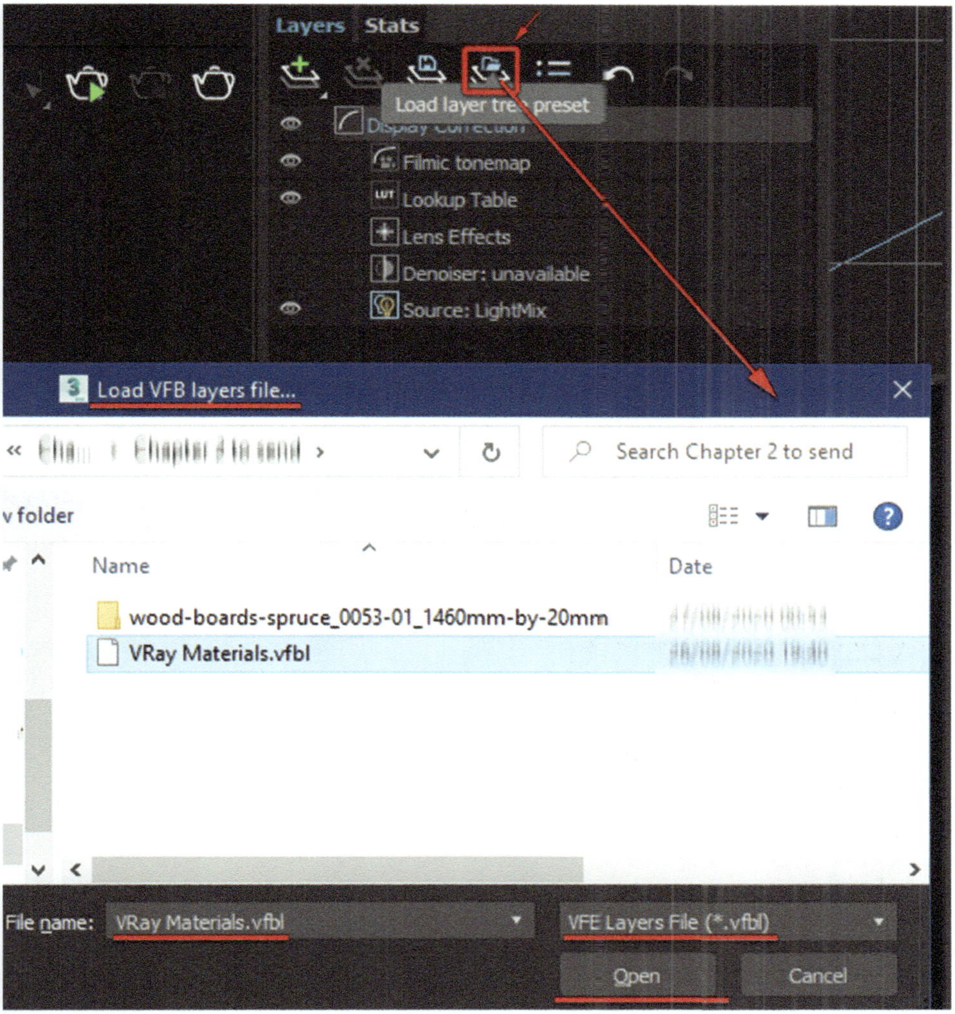

Load VRay Frame Buffer file

Diffuse

Diffuse color: This color swatch enables users to pick and choose a diffuse color by using the Color Selector dialog.

To access the Color Selector dialog, simply left click on its color swatch and hold down. Once the Color Selector dialog appears, pick a color in the Hue section. Or type in a specific value and adjust its Whiteness slider.

Alternatively, one can sample colors by selecting the Sample Screen Color picker and picking a color inside or outside 3ds max.

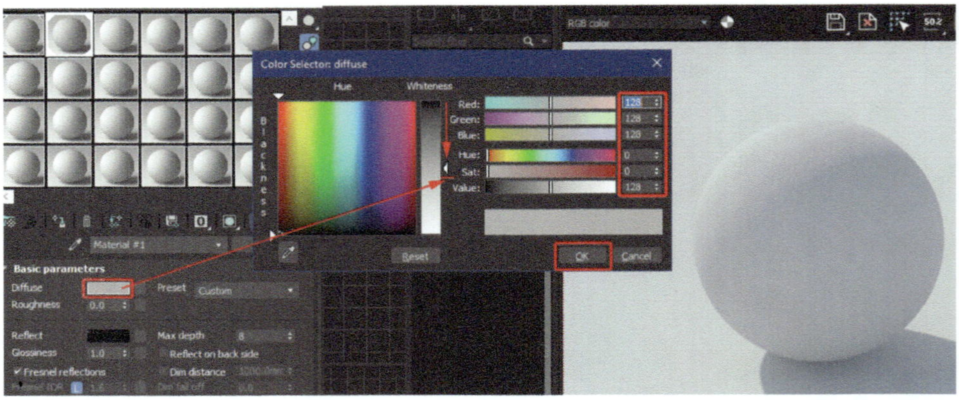

Use the Diffuse color swatch

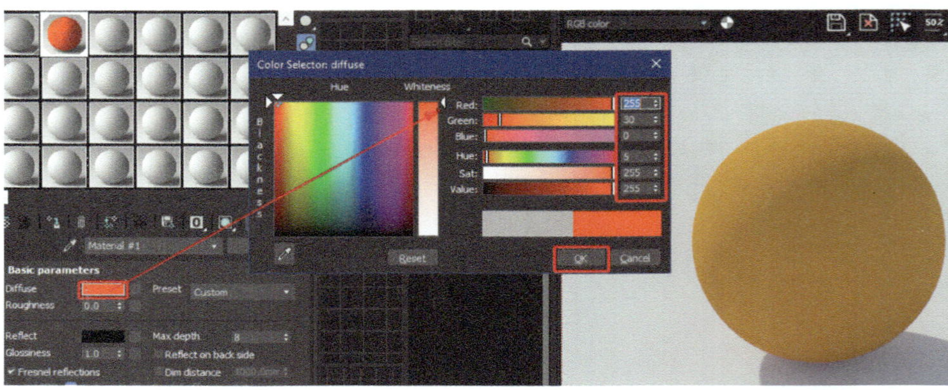

Set different colors

Sample colors with Sample Screen Color picker

Diffuse toggle: The diffuse toggle allows users to plug a host of standard and VRay procedural maps listed in the Material/Map Browser.

The VRayBitmap procedural map is often used to apply textures to its Bitmap toggle, as previously shown. It's worth noting that reflective surfaces will affect the original diffuse color and/or its texture.

Users often increase the Metalness function value to darken materials, when materials lose too much of their original color because of reflectivity.

Some of the chapters ahead will show other ways to fix this problem.

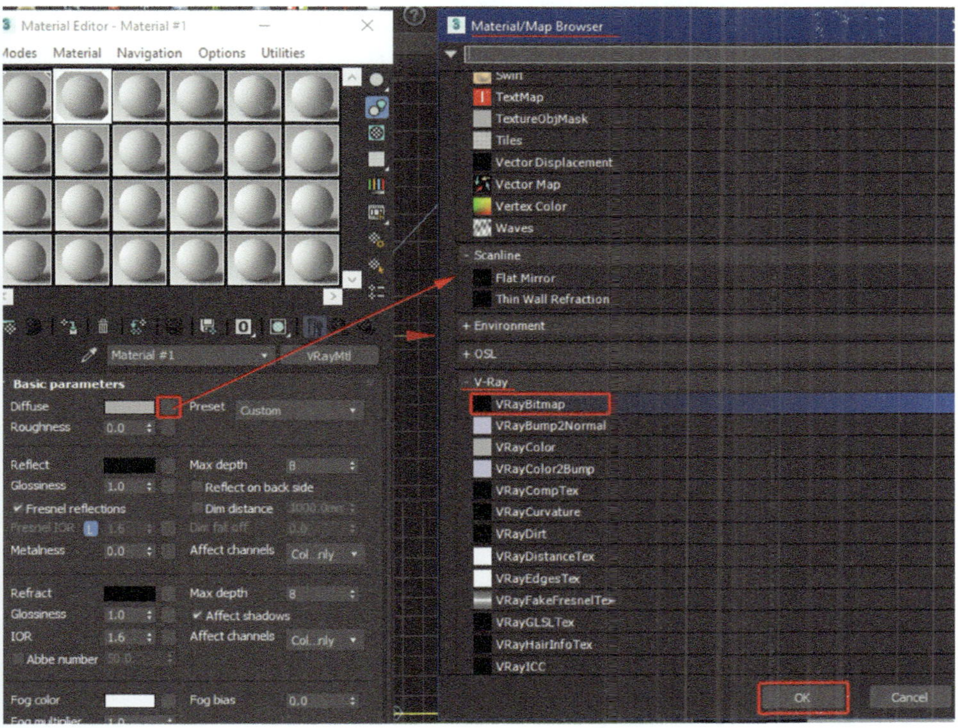

List of procedural maps

Roughness toggle: The toggle enables users to plug textures and other procedural maps from the Material/Map Browser list.

This toggle works best with black and white and grayscale textures/procedural maps. Once a texture is applied, it automatically overrides the numerical values.

Roughness value: This function determines how coarse a surface appears.

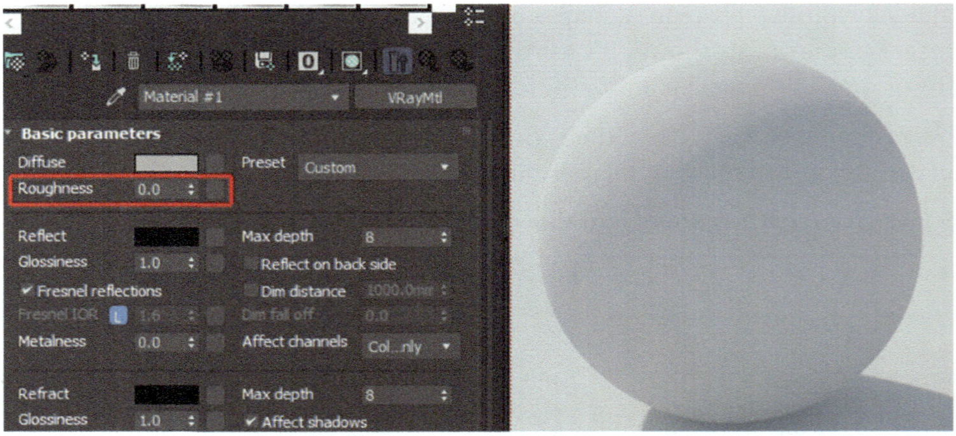

Roughness value set to 0.0

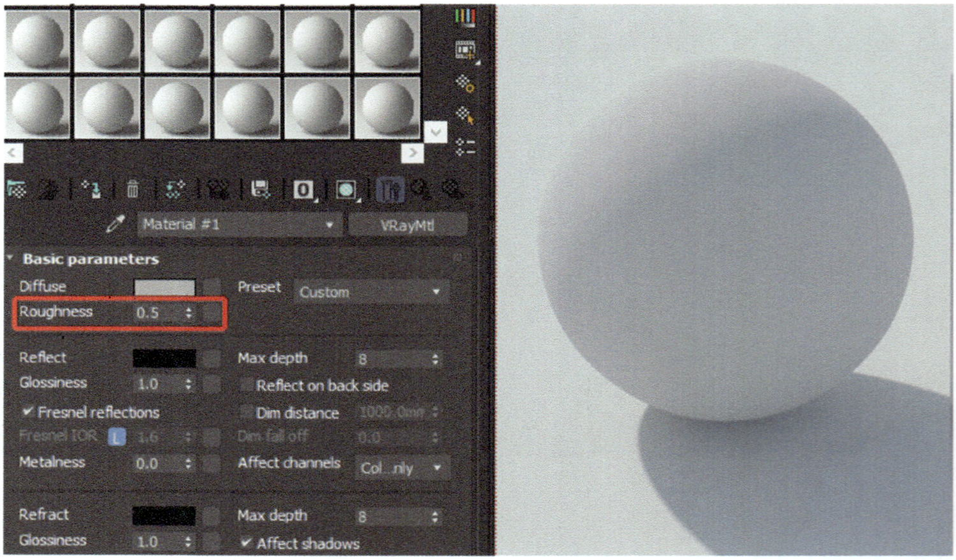

Roughness value set to 0.5

Preset rollout: This is a downsized version of the VRay Asset Browser dialog.

Unlike the VRay Asset Browser dialog, the Preset rollout allows users to choose a smaller number of material presets available from the dropdown list.

The preview for each material preset is available from the material slot.

VRay material presets

To maximize the material slot, simply double click on it.

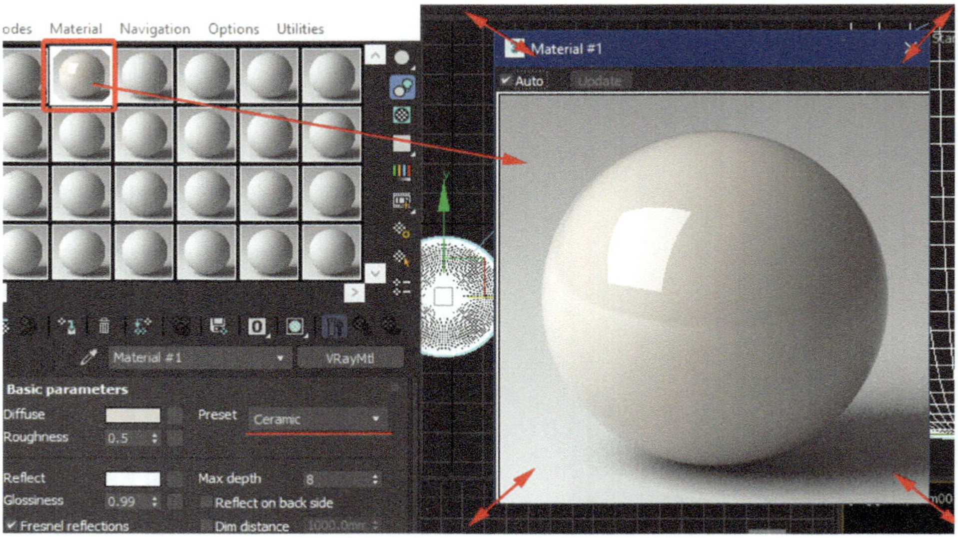

Material slot maximized

Reflect

Reflect Color: This color swatch allows users to pick and choose the Reflect intensity/color by using the Color Selector dialog.

The default color is black, which is equivalent to no reflections.

Darker colors yield less reflections, and lighter colors (e.g., white) yield the opposite effect.

It's also common for users to set specific colors (e.g., orange/brass color) when creating metallic surfaces such as brass.

Reflect toggle: This toggle enables users to set the reflectivity of the surface by plugging textures and other procedural maps from the Material/Map Browser list.

It works best with black and white and grayscale textures. Artists often plug a gray texture to this toggle to realistically emulate a surface reflecting light unevenly.

Once a texture/procedural map is applied to the toggle, it automatically overrides the color swatch values.

Fresnel reflections: When enabled, the reflections and highlights are calculated automatically by the camera/viewing angle of the surface. This function is turned on by default.

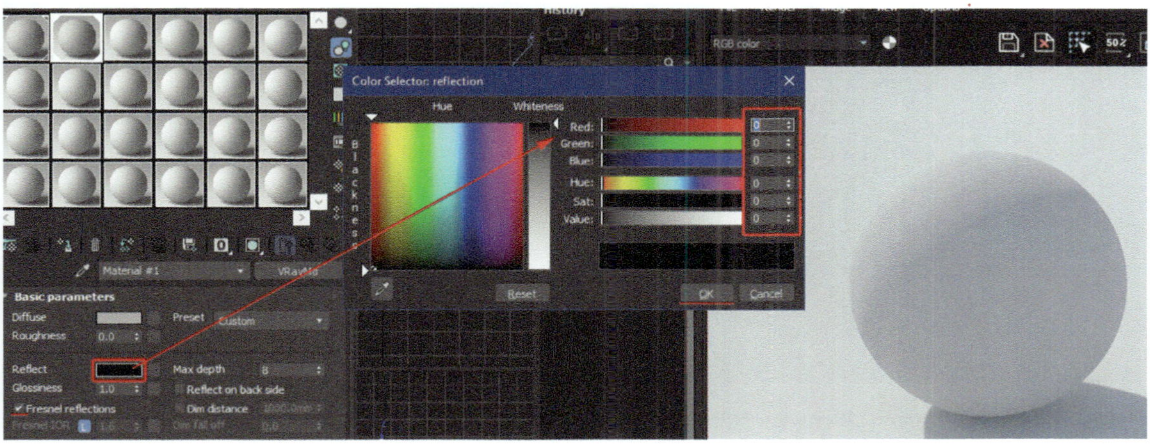

Reflect Color Selector set to 0.0, with the Fresnel reflections enabled

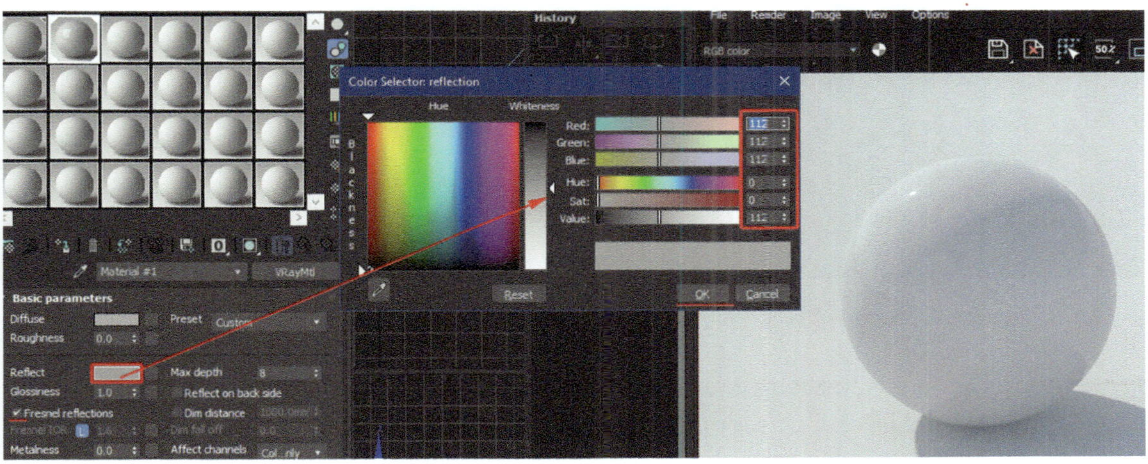

Reflect Color Selector set to 112, with the Fresnel reflections enabled

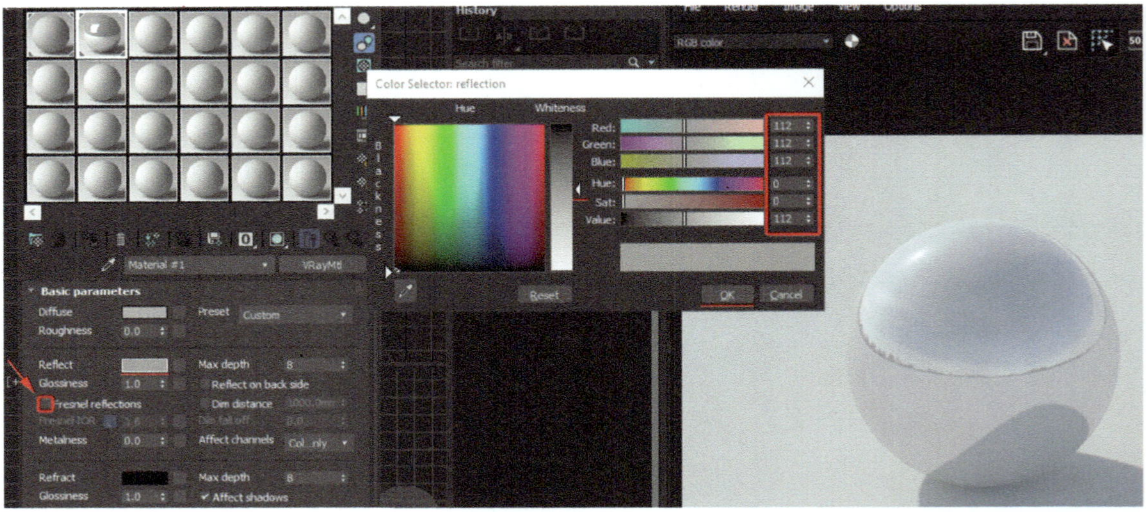

Reflect Color Selector set to 112, with the Fresnel reflections disabled

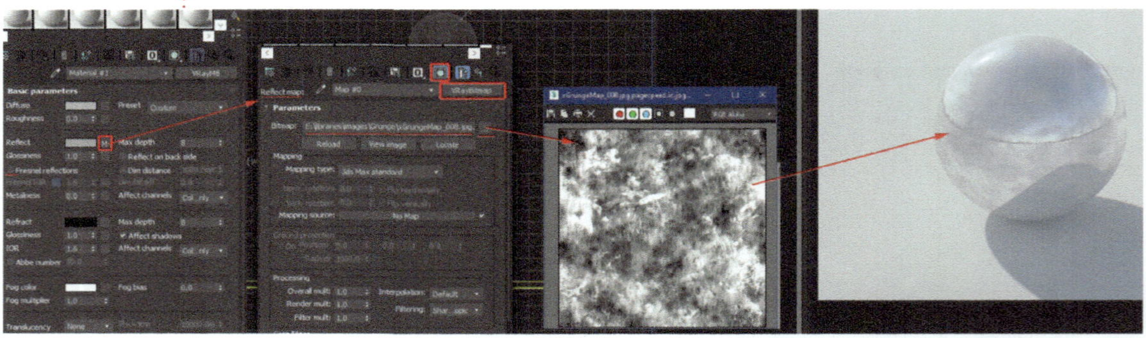

Reflect toggle, with gray texture applied

At times, having the Reflect toggle with a grayscale texture, in conjunction with the Fresnel reflections enabled, can yield appealing results. It's just a matter of trying what works best (e.g., with or without Fresnel turned on).

The more contrast the grayscale texture, the sharper the reflections/glossiness.

To achieve the opposite effect (e.g., more diffused results), the grayscale texture needs to have less contrast (e.g., more gray than black areas).

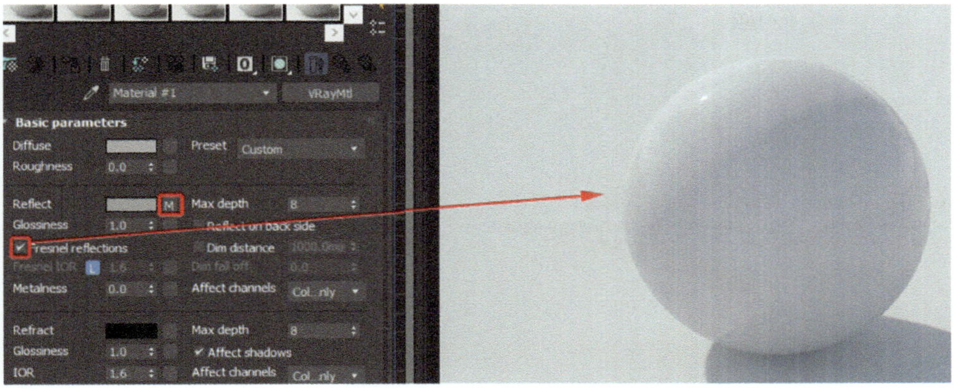

Reflect toggle, with gray texture and Fresnel reflections enabled

There are also instances when users might be required to invert the grayscale texture inside the Reflect toggle in order to achieve specific results.

To do so, simply go inside the Reflect map coordinates, and scroll down to the Output rollout.

In the Output rollout parameters, enable the Invert function. It works in exact same way as the Invert tool in Photoshop (Ctrl+i)

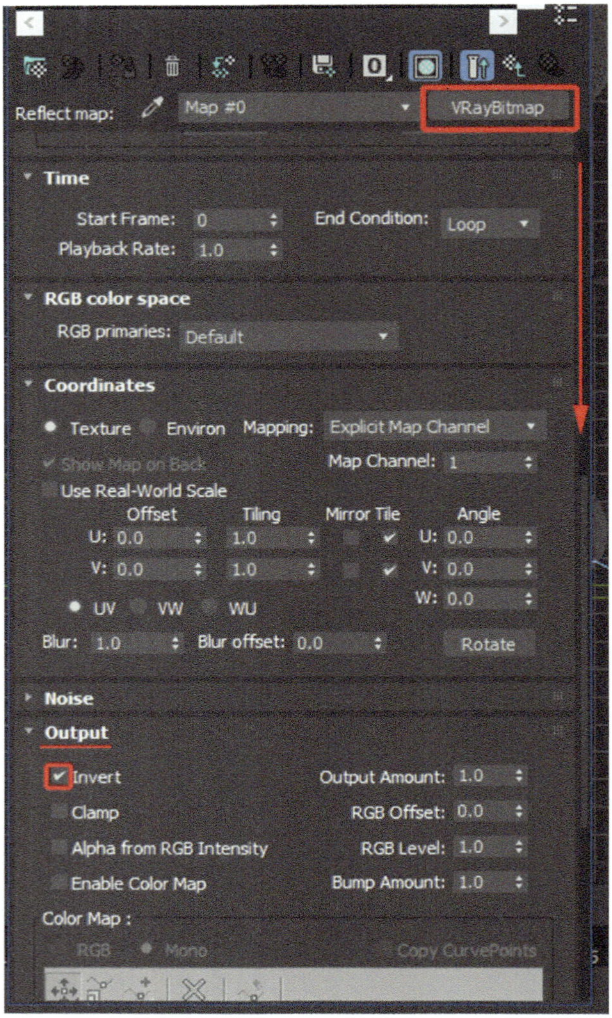

Reflect map grayscale texture inverted

The Reflect toggle texture can also be mixed/blended with its color swatch to produce specific results. To do so, simply scroll down to the Maps rollout and reduce the Reflect toggle's numerical values.

NOTE

This amazing technique can also be used with any function with a toggle.

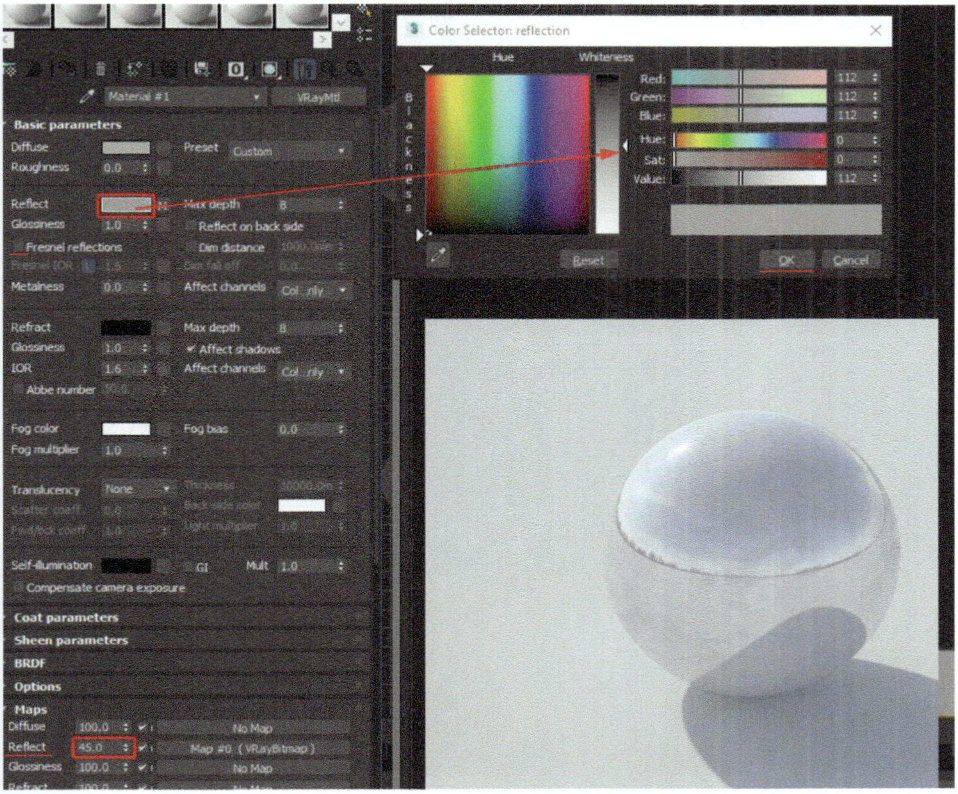

Reflect toggle mixed with the Reflect color swatch

It is also common practice for users to apply the Falloff procedural map to help control the Fresnel effects manually.

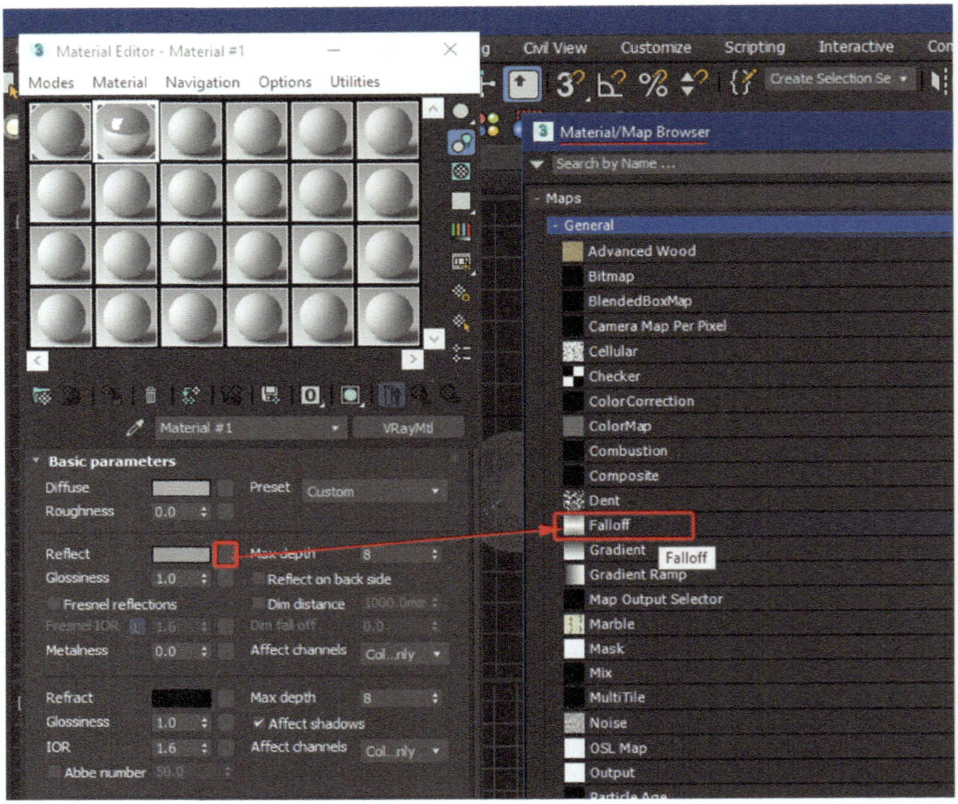

Apply Falloff procedural map to the Reflect toggle

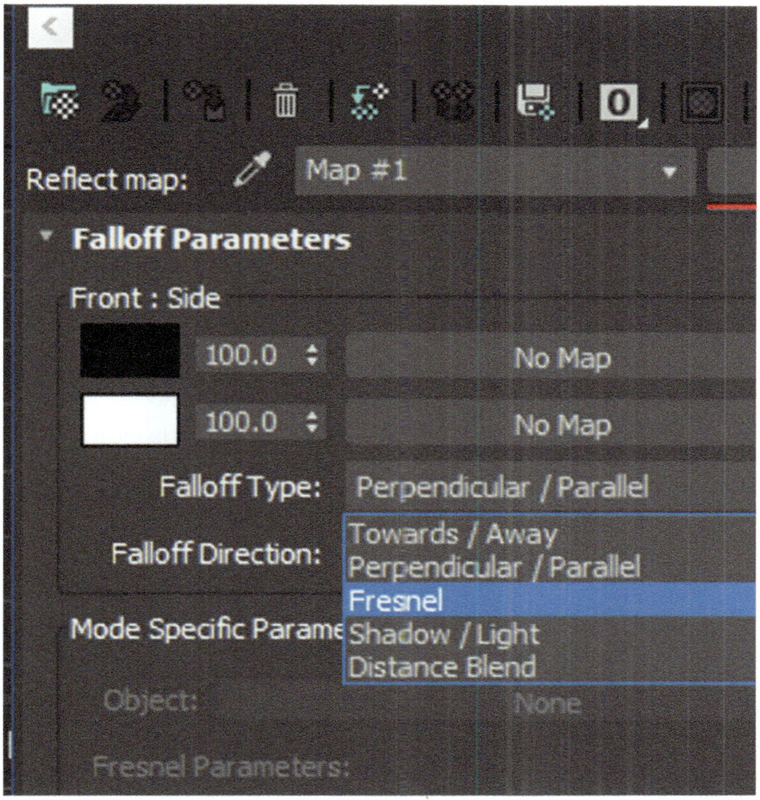

Choose the Fresnel Falloff Type

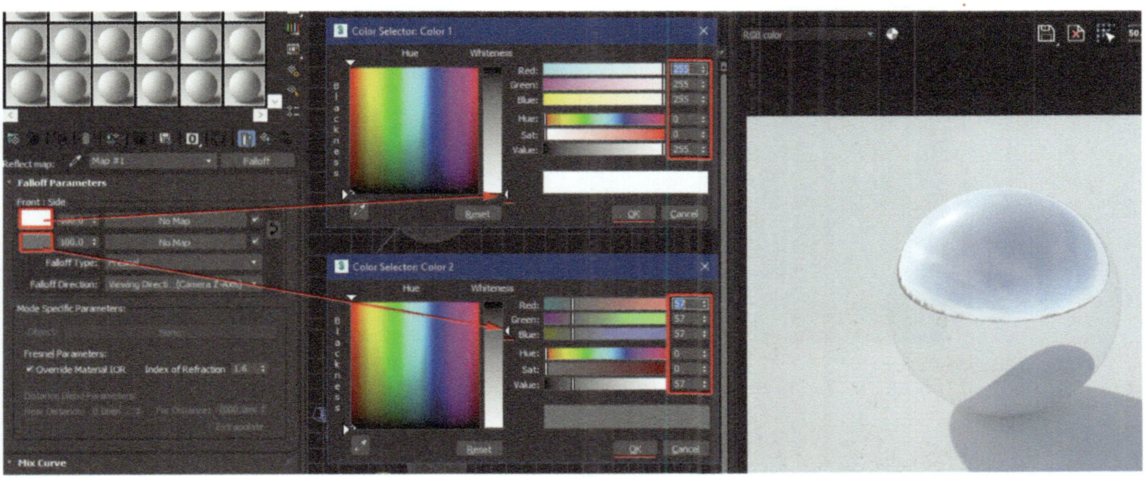

Adjust the Front: Side color values to achieve different reflection results

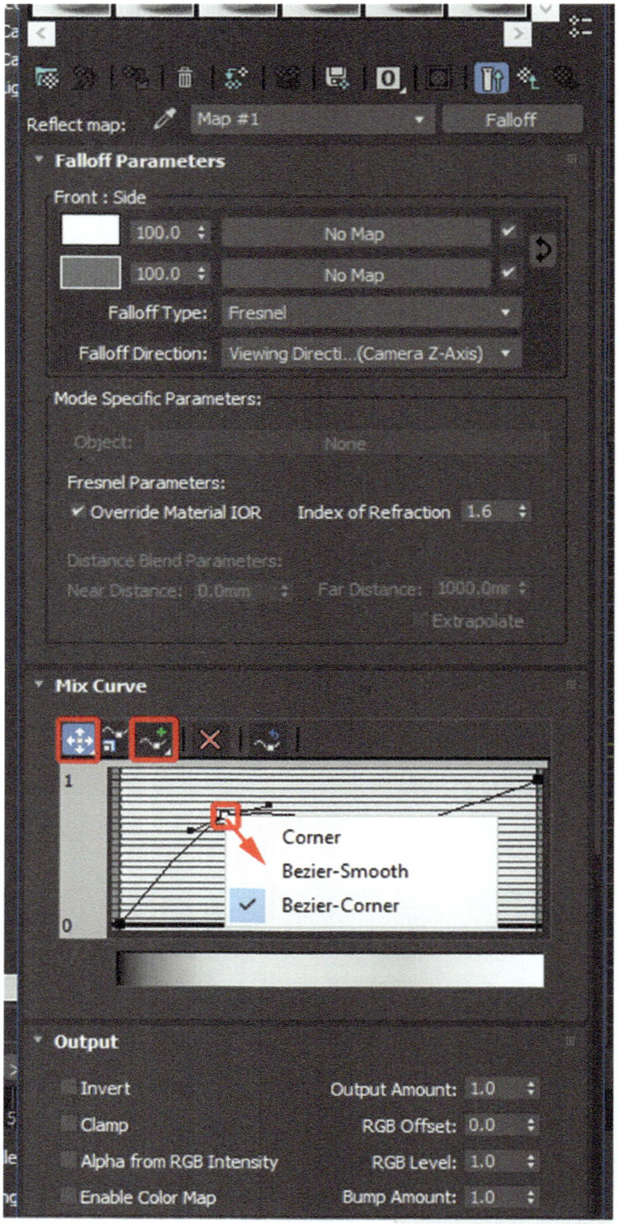

Tweak the Mix Curve points to help control the reflections

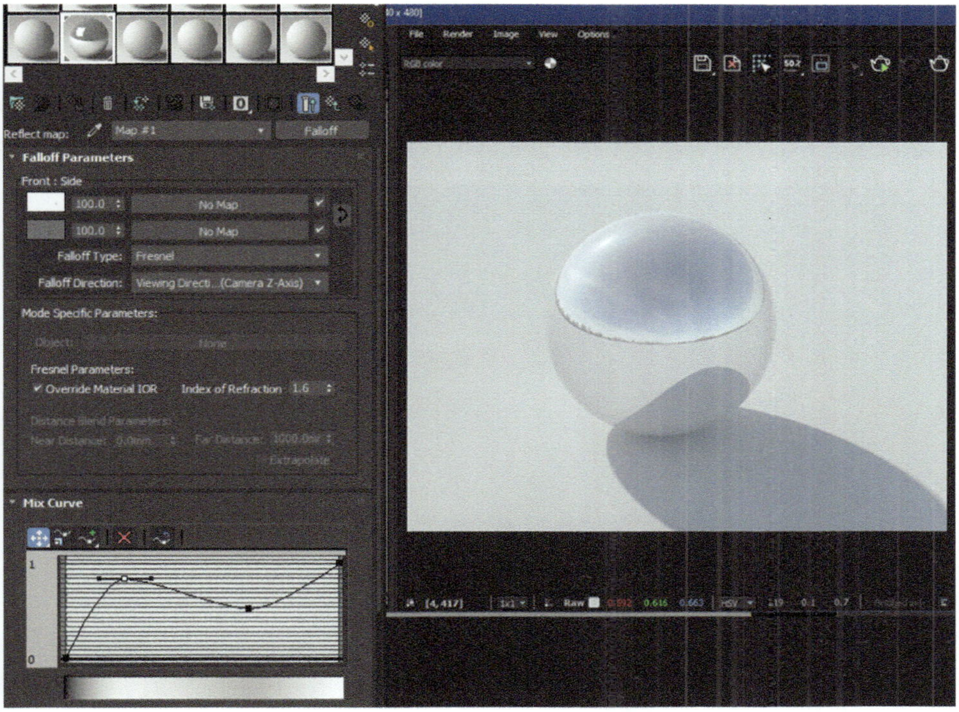

Final results

Fresnel reflections: This function is padlocked with Fresnel IOR, and it's set 1.6 by default. To manually change this, simply click on the L (padlock) button.

Its adjacent toggle allows users to plug bitmaps and/or procedural maps to it.

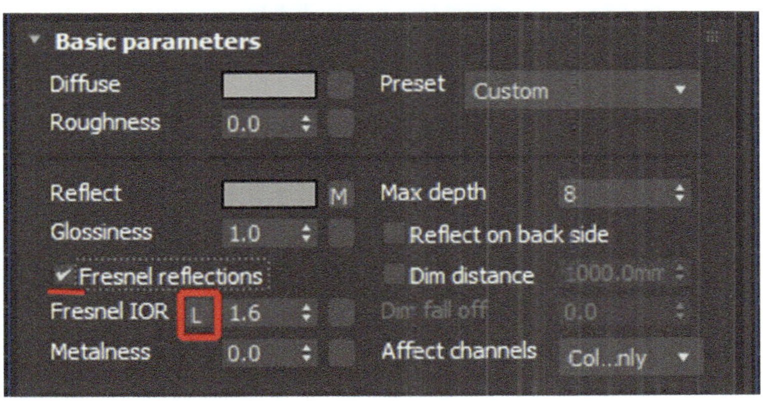

Fresnel IOR with the padlock(L) unlocked

Glossiness: This function determines the appearance of glossy highlights and the type of reflections on surfaces. Its value is set to 1.0 by default.

The value of 1.0 yields a sharp/linear highlight with sharp/linear reflections.

The appearance of highlights is only noticeable when there is reflectivity on the surface. Otherwise, the glossiness values will be redundant.

Lower values yield blurrier reflections and wider highlights.

For perfect highlight results, users should *not* reduce the Glossiness values below 0.5.

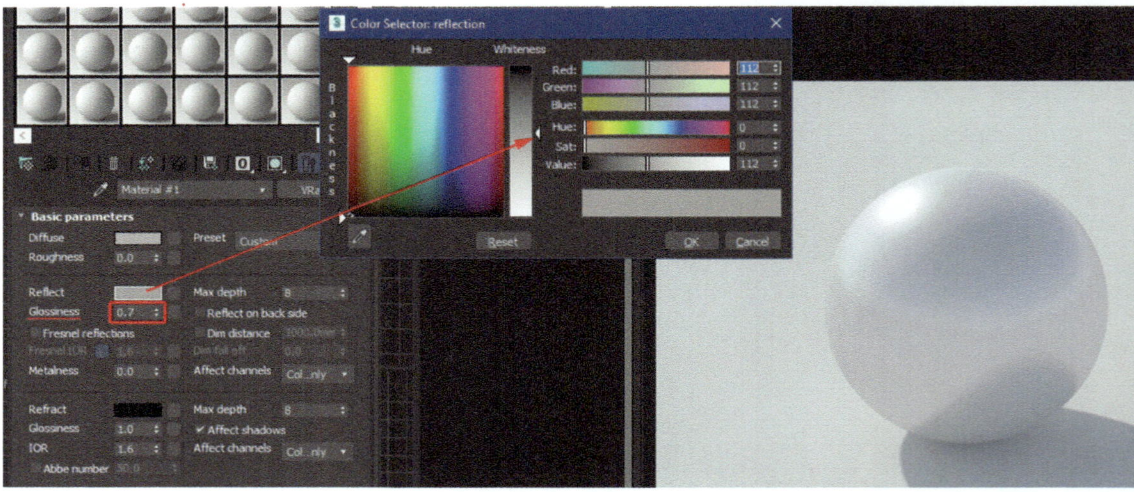

Glossiness value set to 0.7, with the Fresnel reflections turned off

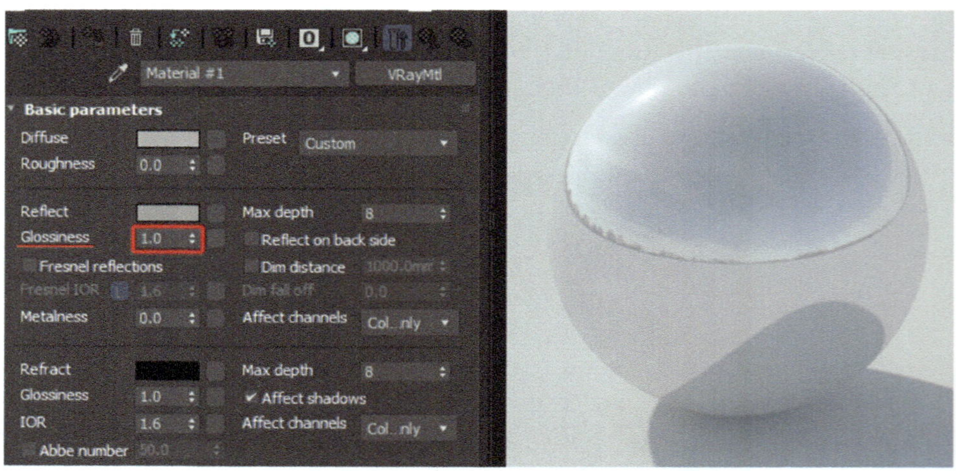

Roughness value set to 1.0, with the Fresnel reflections turned off

Glossiness toggle: This toggle allows users to plug a grayscale texture or/and a procedural map to it. Once applied, it automatically overrides its numerical values.

Once a texture/procedural map is applied to the toggle, it automatically overrides the Glossiness values.

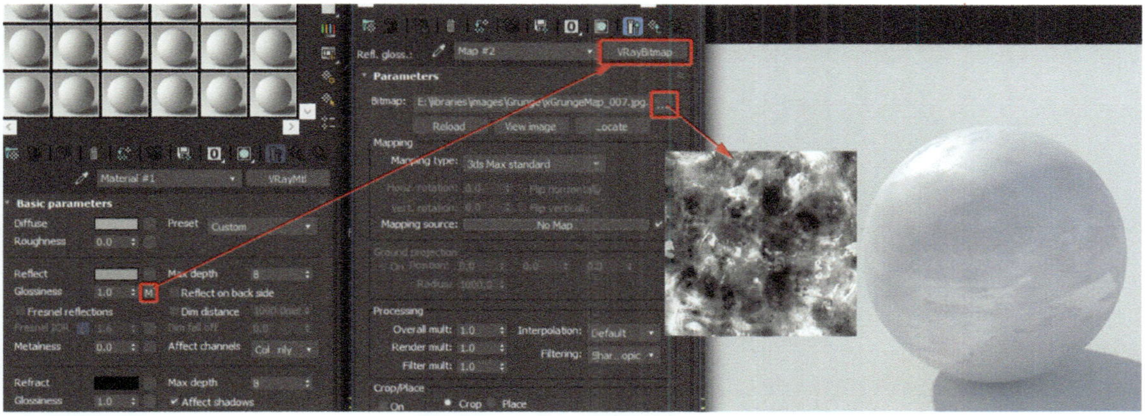

VRayMtl with grayscale texture applied to the Glossiness toggle

Metalness: This function yields a metallic look to surfaces. Values range from 0.0 to 1.0.

The value of 1.0 darkens the surface and yields a more metallic look.

Users should only enter values 0.0 or 1.0, respectively. Values in-between yield physically inaccurate results.

The Metalness function works best when the Reflect color swatch is set to full white (255).

To match PBR setups from external applications, users often plug the roughness texture to the Glossiness toggle, and enable the Use roughness function under the BRDF rollout parameters.

Metalness toggle: The toggle enables users to plug a grayscale texture or/and a procedural map to it. Once applied, it automatically overrides its numerical values.

NOTE

When enabled, the Use roughness function will automatically switch the Glossiness function to Roughness.

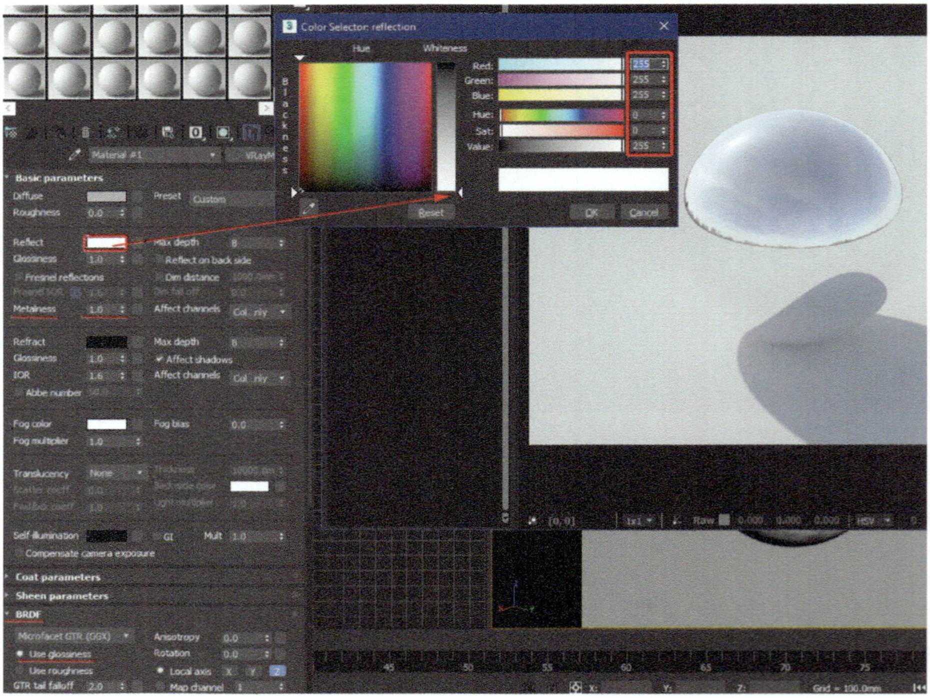

Metalness value set 1.0 with Use glossiness function enabled

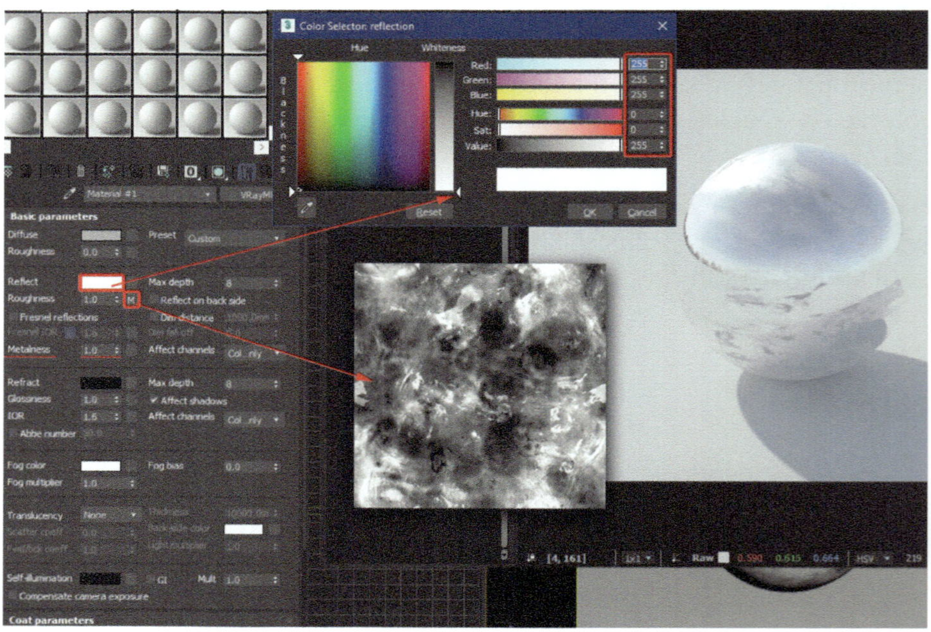

Metalness with Use roughness enabled and texture applied

Max depth- This function sets the number of times a ray can be reflected, before it stops, and begins using the Exit color.

This function is quite useful for scenes with numerous reflections/refractions bouncing off each other. Increasing the Max depth value will eradicate any potential black areas (exit color) in the reflections/refractions.

However, it may increase the rendering time.

Max depth value is set to 5 by default.

Reflect on backside: This function works best on glass thickness.

The Refract color determines the opacity of a surface. A full white Refract color (255) makes a surface fully transparent.

To create a typical glass material, simply set its Diffuse color to Black 0, Reflect color 193, Refract color 255 (white), and the Fog color 109,57,220 (greenish tint).

Alternatively, simply load a Glass preset from VRay Asset Browser dialog.

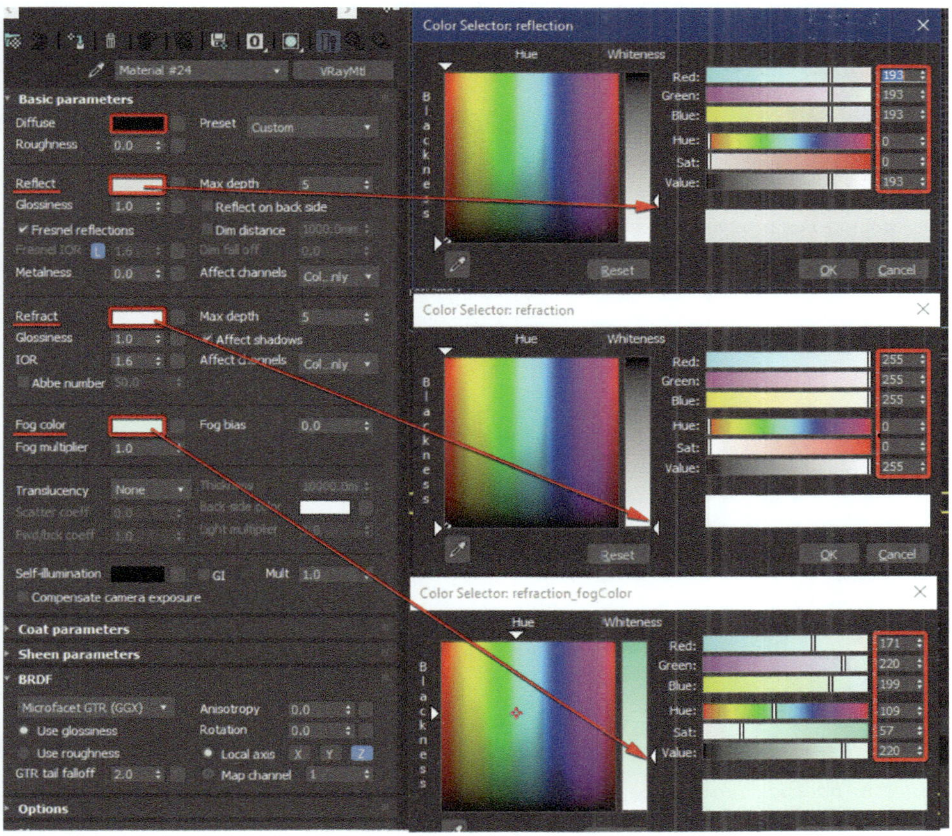

Glass material created

When the Reflect on backside function is turned on, VRay takes into consideration internal and back face reflections of an object, which will subsequently increase the rendering times (inevitably).

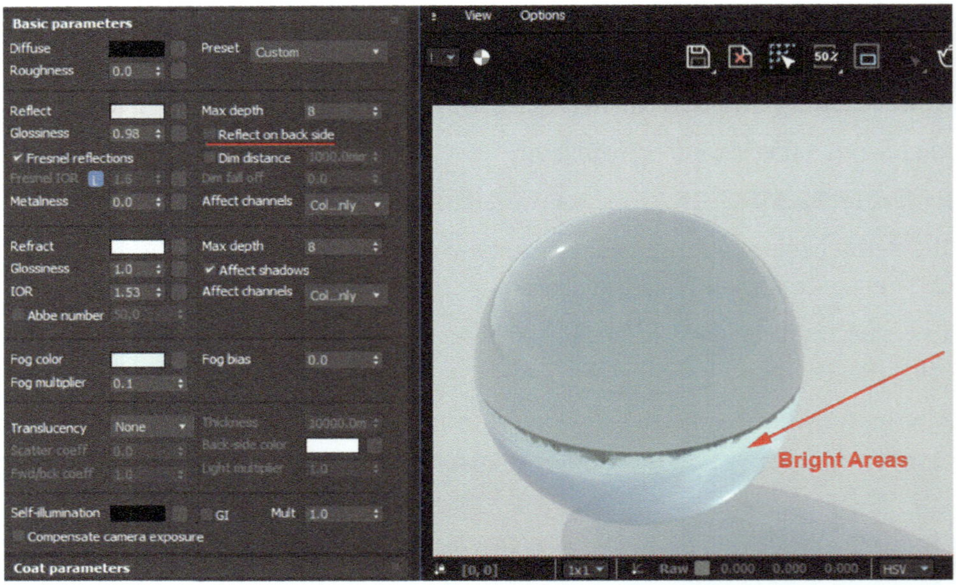

Reflect on backside turned off

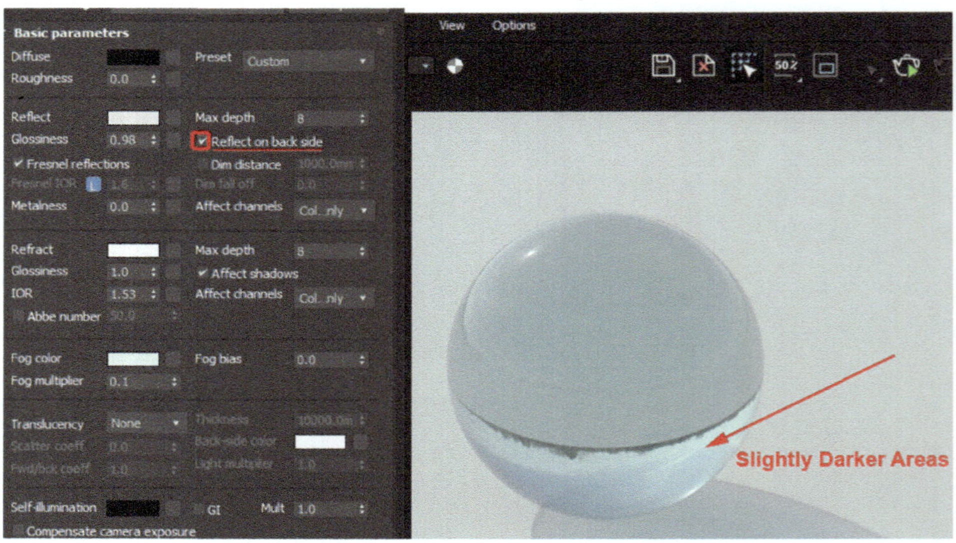

Reflect on backside turned on

Dim distance: When enabled, it restricts the distance of traced rays by entering the numerical radius. Disabled by default.

Dim fall off: When enabled, it sets the falloff radius of Dim distance. It is automatically enabled when the Dim distance is turned on.

It's grayed out by default.

Affect channels: This function controls how the render channels are being affected by the Reflection. It's set to Color only by default.

Refract

Refract: The color swatch of this function controls the opacity of a surface—black (e.g., 0.0) being completely opaque, and white(e.g., 255) being fully transparent.

Default color value is 0.0 (fully opaque). When the Refract color value is 0.0 (black), VRayMtl immediately uses the Diffuse base color instead.

Refract toggle: The refract toggle allows users to plug textures and/or procedural maps to it. Grayscale and/or black/white textures work best.

NOTE

The main opacity of an object should always be controlled via refraction, as opposed to object properties (right click>object properties>Opacity).

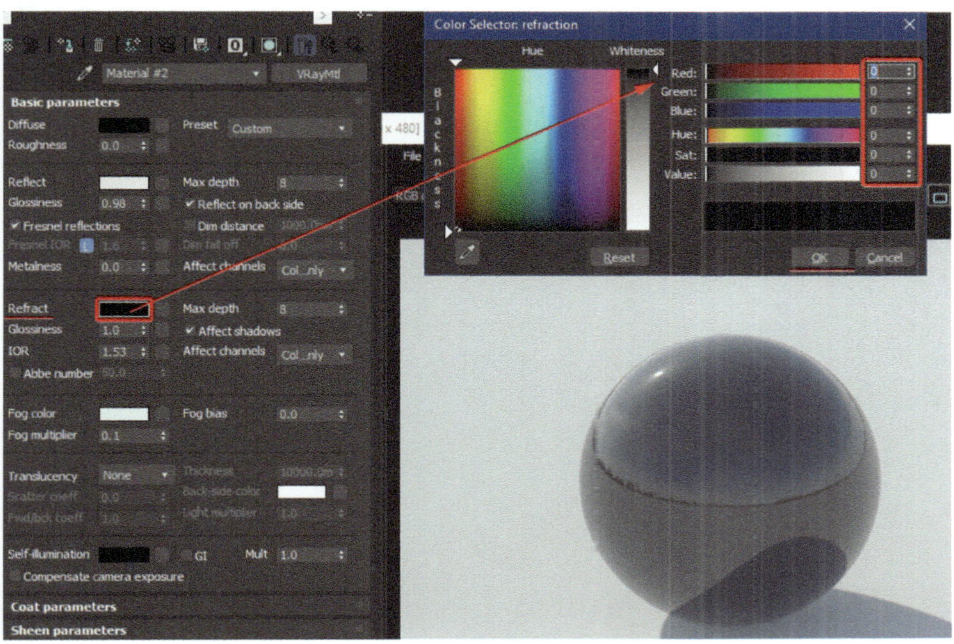

Refract color value set to 0.0 (black)

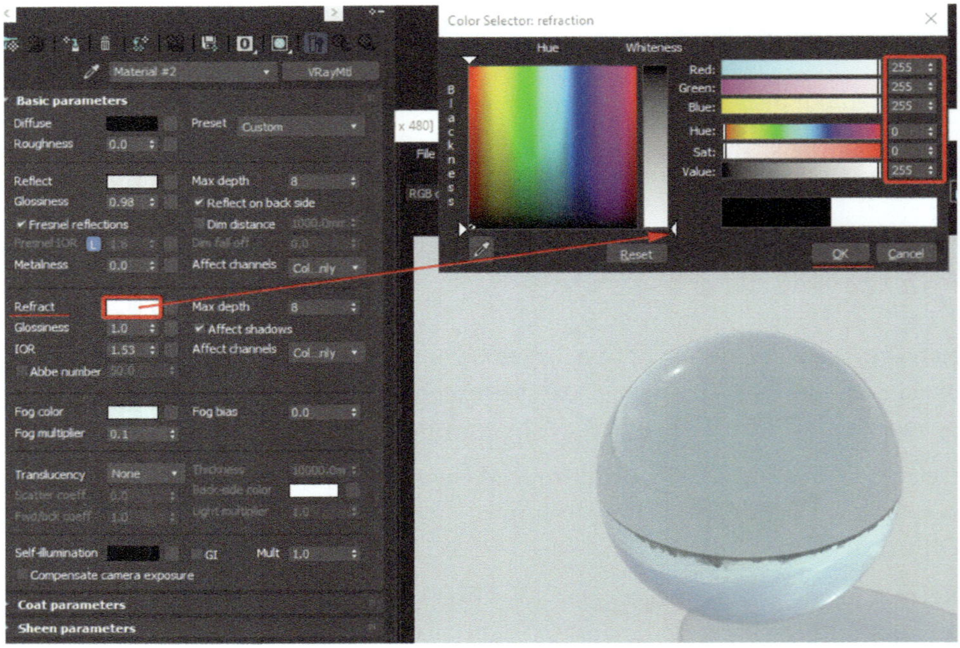

Refract color value set to 255 (white)

Glossiness: This function controls the sharpness of refractions. The value of 1.0 equals to sharp refractions.

The value of 0.0 is equivalent to completely diffused refractions. Users often reduce these values to emulate translucent surfaces.

It's worth noting that decreasing these values will subsequently increase the rendering times of this surface.

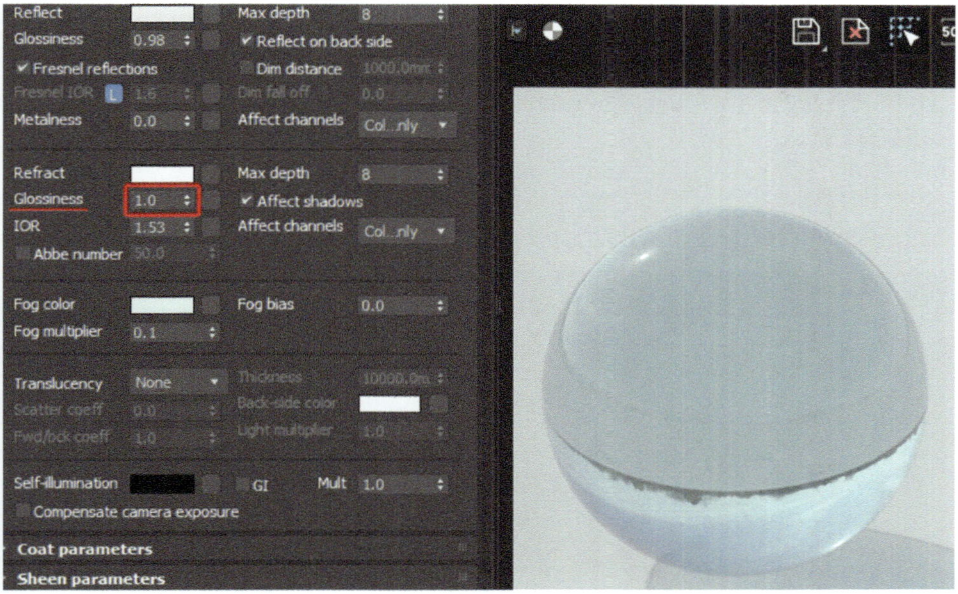

Glossiness value of 1.0

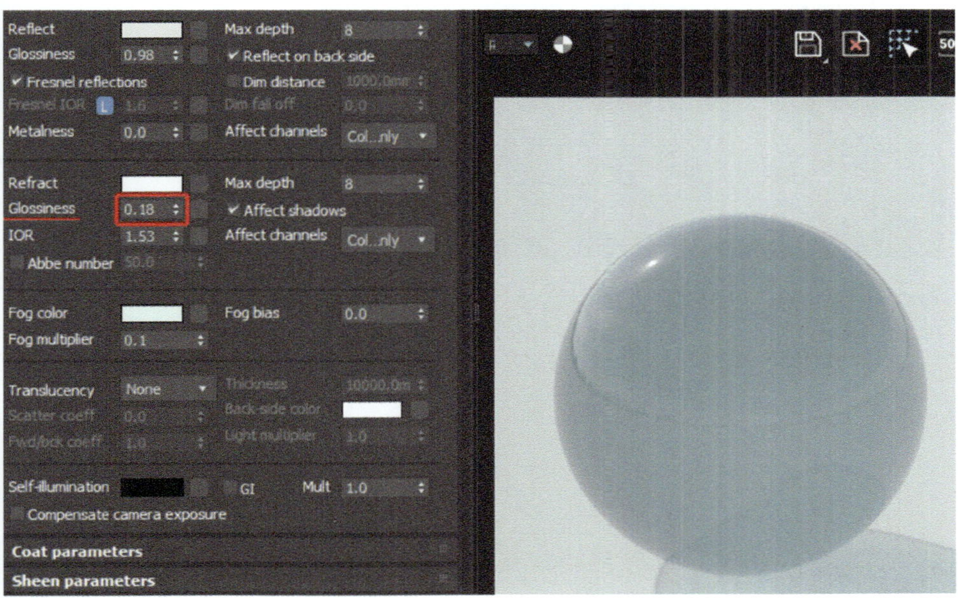

Glossiness value of 0.18

IOR: The Index of Refraction determines how a light interacts/bends through a transparent surface.

IOR effects are not visible on completely solid surfaces. Surfaces need to be partially or fully transparent.

An IOR value of 1.0 is equal to no refraction on a transparent surface. The default value is 1.6.

For a more detailed list of refractive indices, please visit the following website:

https://en.wikipedia.org/wiki/List_of_refractive_indices

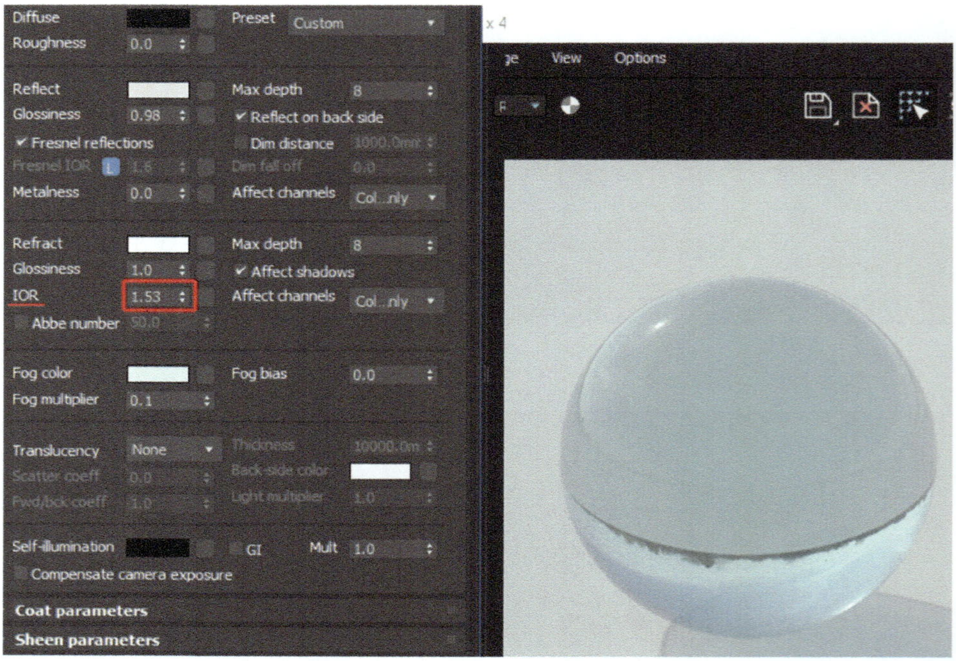

Refraction IOR value of 1.53

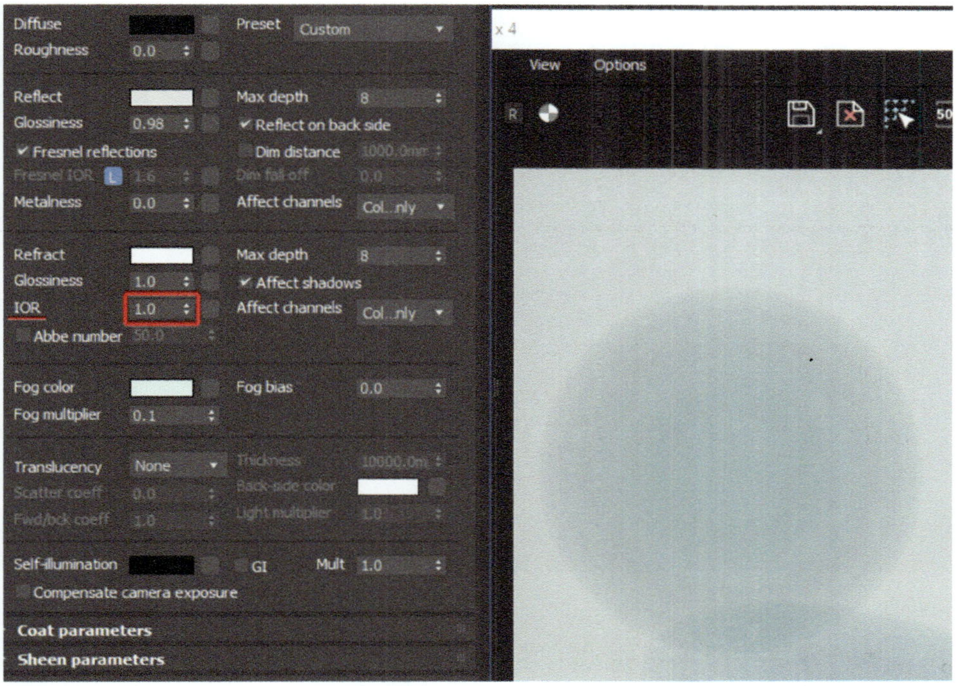

Refraction IOR value of 1.0

Abbe number: When enabled, it computes the light wavelength dispersion more accurately and photo realistically. However, the rendering times may skyrocket drastically.

The results are more noticeable when its value is set to a minimum of 10.

Also, Abbe values help reinvigorate a spectrum of true light colors, which become apparent on the rim of objects and on caustic effects (if enabled).

This function is more visible when there are physical lights interacting with an object—as opposed to HDRI being used as a light source.

Disabled by default.

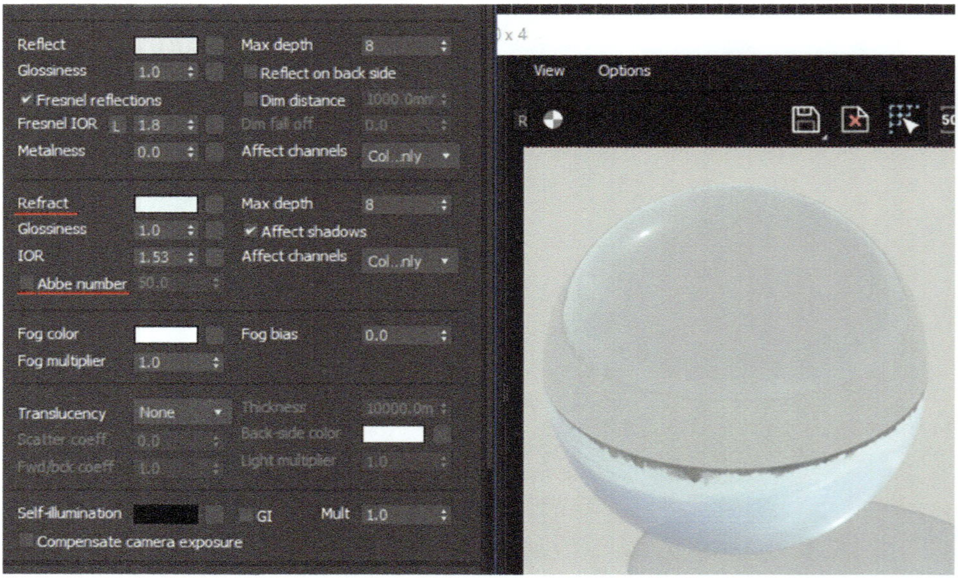

Abbe number disabled

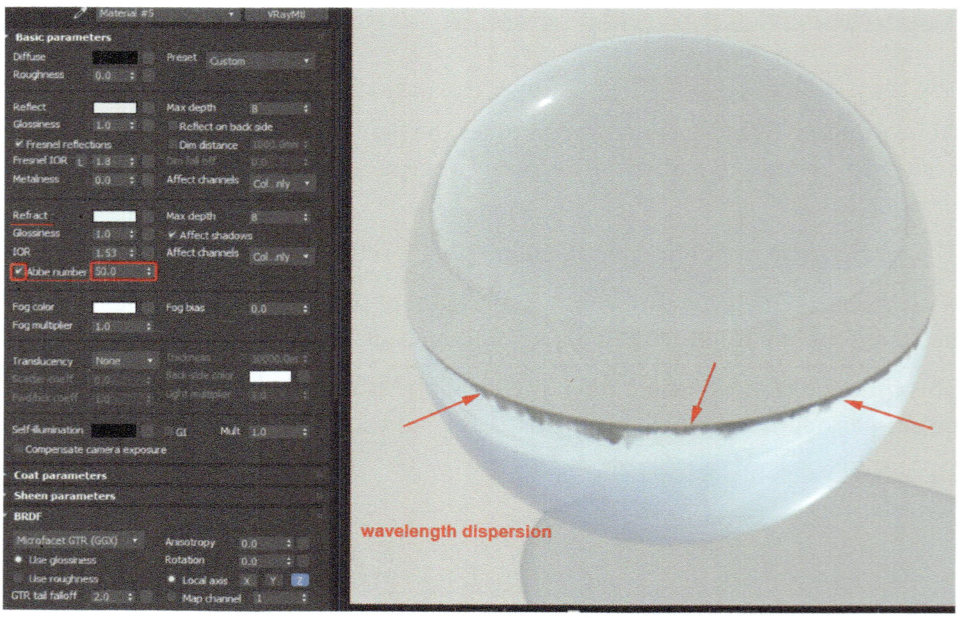

Abbe number enabled with value set to 50.0

Max depth: This function determines the number of times a ray can be refracted, before it stops, and begins using the Exit color.

Max depth value is set to 8 by default. Increasing it will subsequently increase the rendering times of this surface.

Affect shadows: This function allows the light to pass through transparent surfaces (e.g., refractive objects) and cast its transparent shadows. The shadow colors may vary, depending on the surface.

This function is only noticeable on objects that are transparent (refract color *not* completely black).

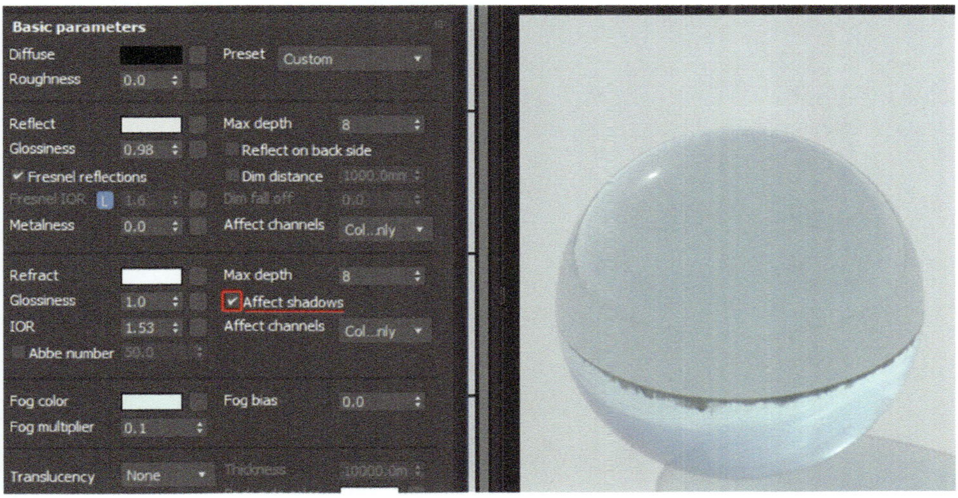

Affect shadows enabled

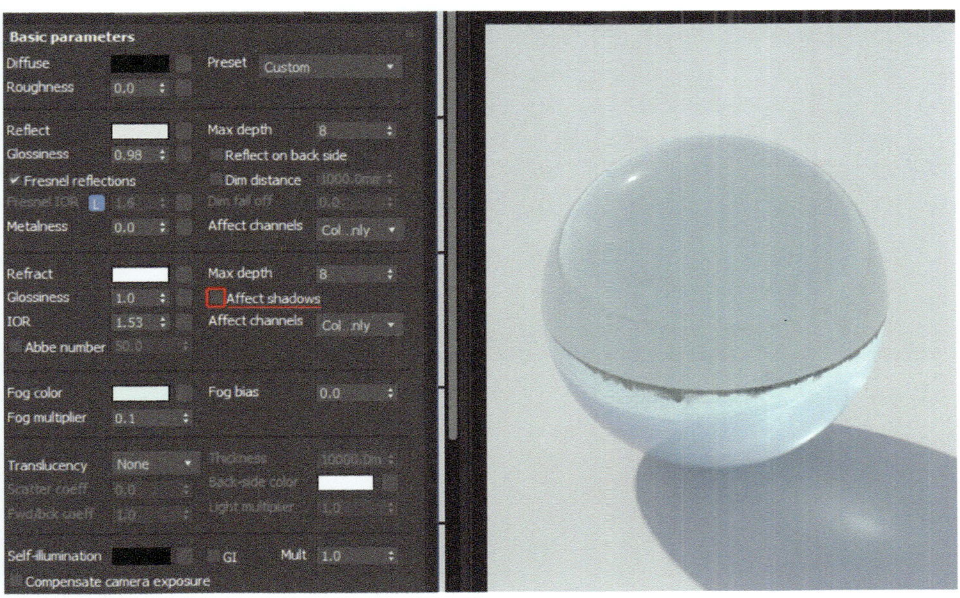

Affect shadows disabled

Refract Affect channels: When the surface is transparent, this specific function allows users to choose the channels to be affected by refraction, in the rendering channels (e.g., Alpha MultimatteElement).

Professionals often choose the All channels option, as it helps to insert the background and other elements behind a refractive/transparent surface.

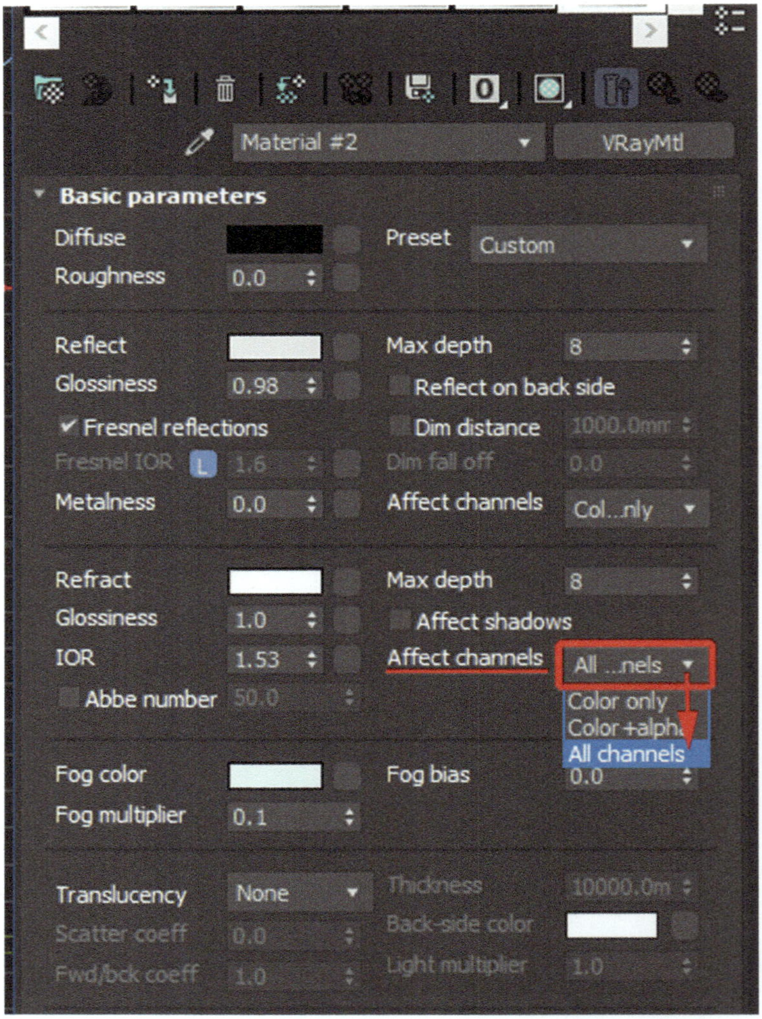

Affect channels set to All channels

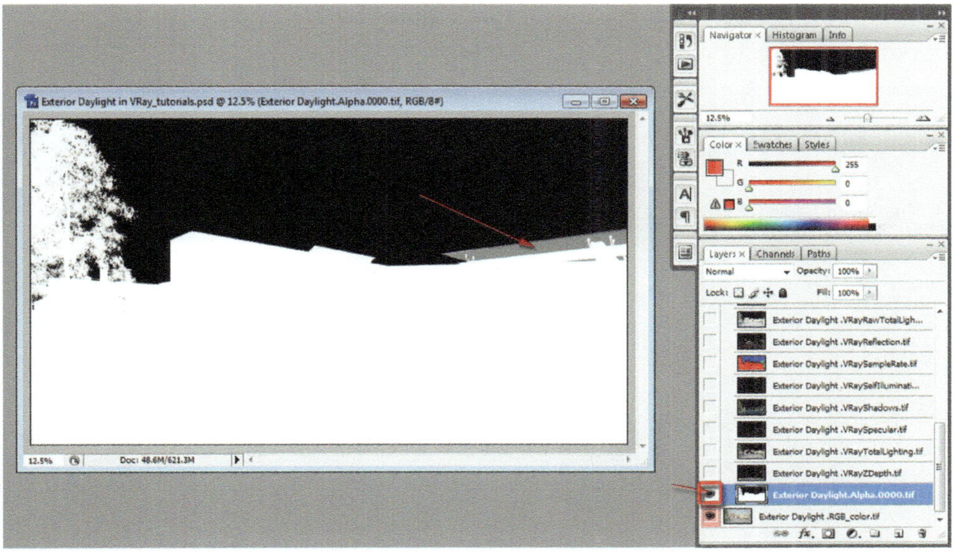

Affect channels result in the Alpha channel

Background Sky inserted behind the glass

Fog

Fog color: This function enables users to change the color of refractive objects and/or emulate the effect of a more opaque object, depending on its size.

Darker colors make refractive objects look more opaque, and lighter colors yield the opposite effect.

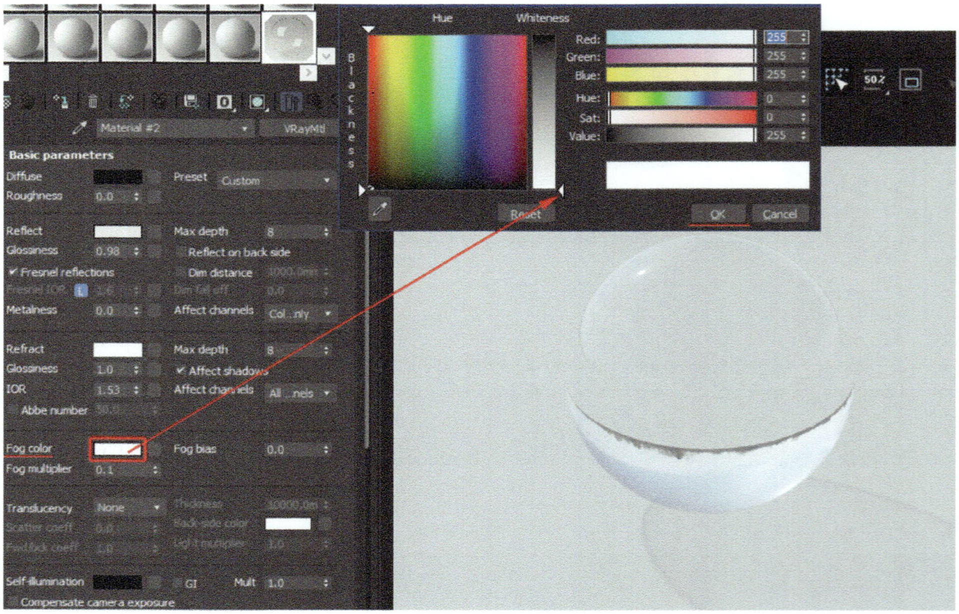

Fog color set to white

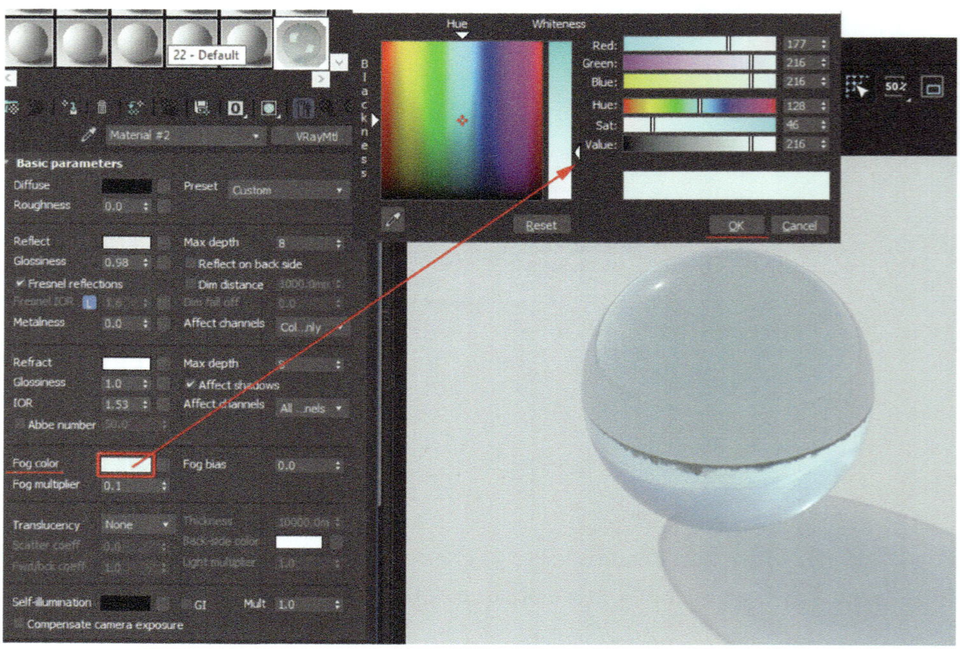

Fog color set to light green

Fog multiplier: This function determines the density/influence of the fog. Default value 0.1.

Fog bias: The function allows users to control the density of objects (refractive surfaces mainly).

Default value is 0.0.

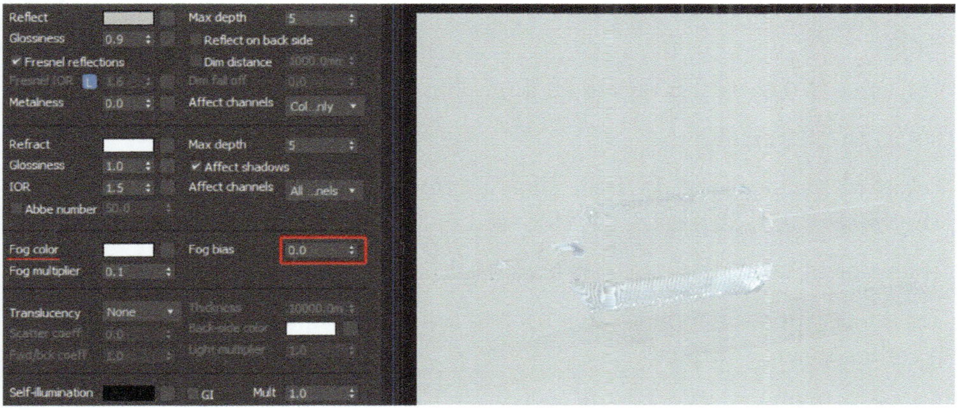

Fog bias set to 0.0

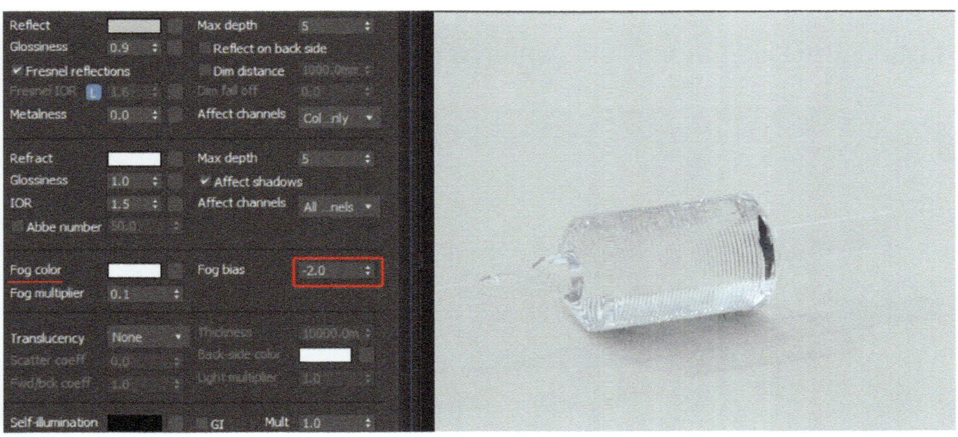

Fog bias set to 2.0

Translucency

Translucency: This function works in conjunction with refractions to calculate the amount of subsurface scattering on a surface. It's set to None by default.

There are three types of translucent models: Hard wax model, Soft (water) model, and Hybrid model.

VRay Asset Browser comes with robust presets to emulate hard surfaces such as marble (Hard wax model), water, and Hybrid models such as real translucent plastics, skin, milk, and fruit juice.

Scatter coefficient: This function determines the amount of scattering inside a surface.

The value of 0.0 scatters rays in all directions. The value of 1.0 does the opposite.

It's set to 0.0 by default.

Forward/backward coefficient: This function controls the scattering direction. The value of 0.0 scatters the rays forward.

The value of 1.0 scatters the rays backward.

Thickness: This function is often used to limit the propagation of the rays traveling inside a surface.

It's set to 10.000 mm by default.

Backside color: This function determines the color of the subsurface scattering effect. It's set to white (255) by default.

Light multiplier: This function controls the strength of translucency.

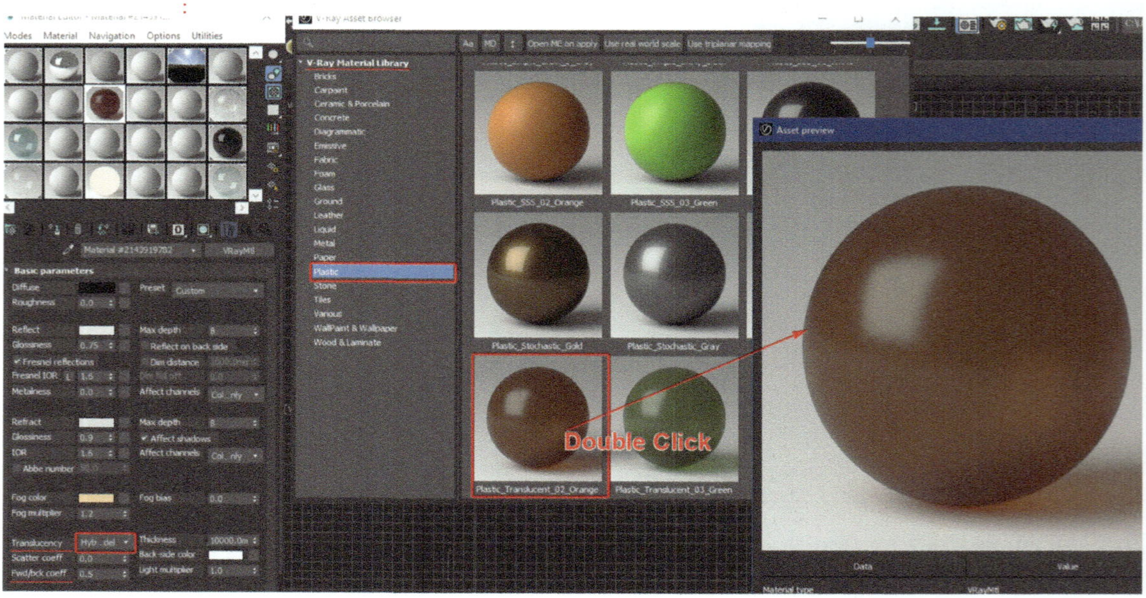

Plastic with translucency set as Hybrid model

Self-illumination

This function allows users to choose the Self-illumination color from its color swatch, or plug a texture or/and a procedural map to its toggle.

To test this material, there's a scene named Self-illumination.max

Self-illumination color: The self-illumination color swatch is set to black by default.

Compensate camera exposure: When enabled, this function automatically adjusts the self-illumination intensity to compensate for the exposure of the scene.

GI: This function uses the Global Illumination settings to light up a scene. Otherwise, it will simply illuminate itself without contributing to the GI. Disabled by default.

Multiplier: This function controls the intensity of the self-illumination. Default value is set to 1.0.

The self-illumination effect is more apparent in dark/dim scenes.

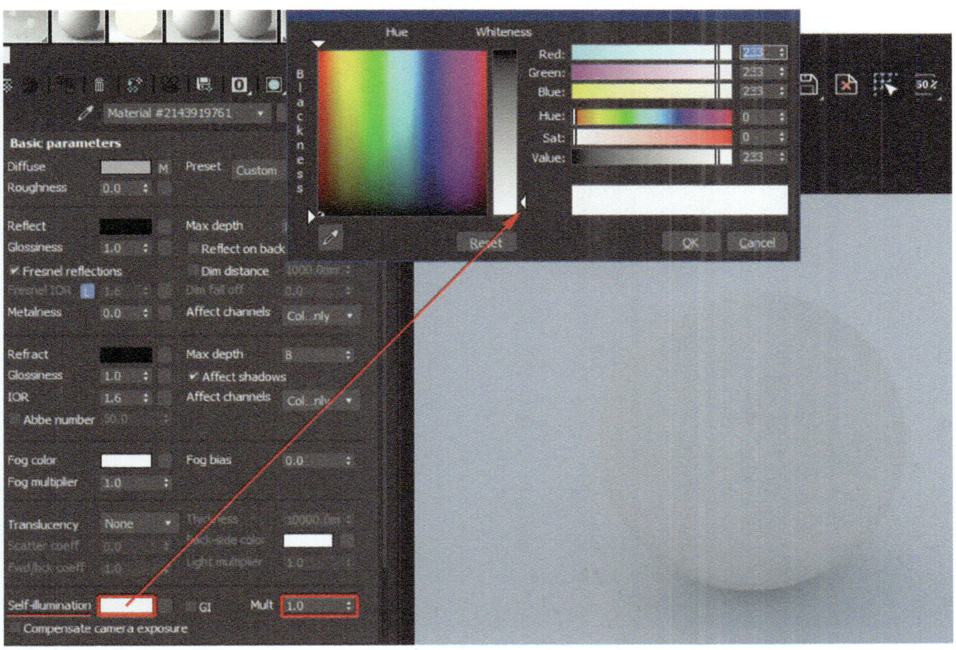

Self-illumination color set to white with Mult set to 1.0

NOTE

When using a bitmap/texture in the Self-illumination toggle, ensure its color swatch is black; otherwise, the texture will not be visible in the viewport.

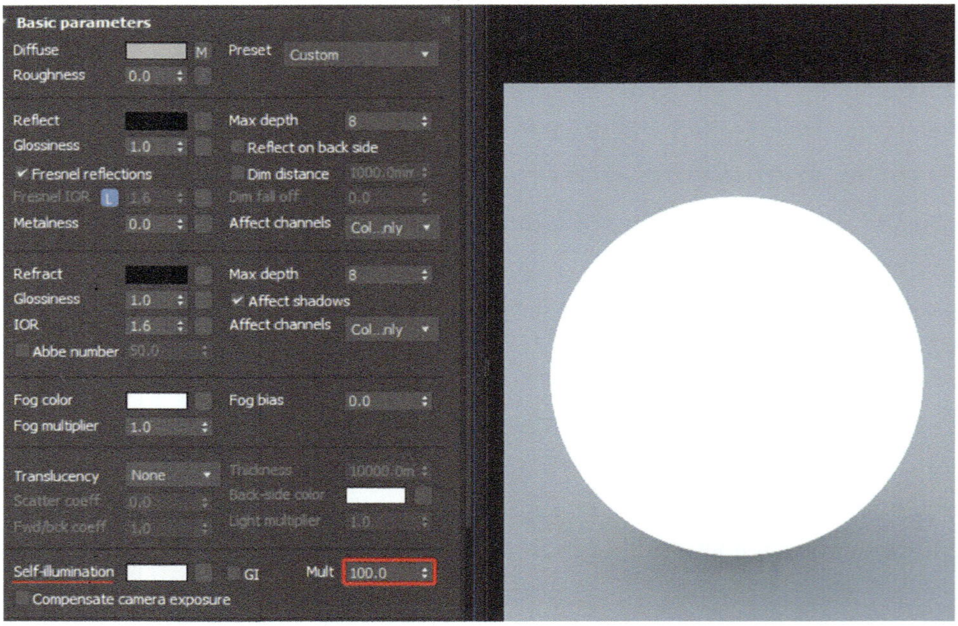

Self-illumination color set to white with Mult set to 100.0

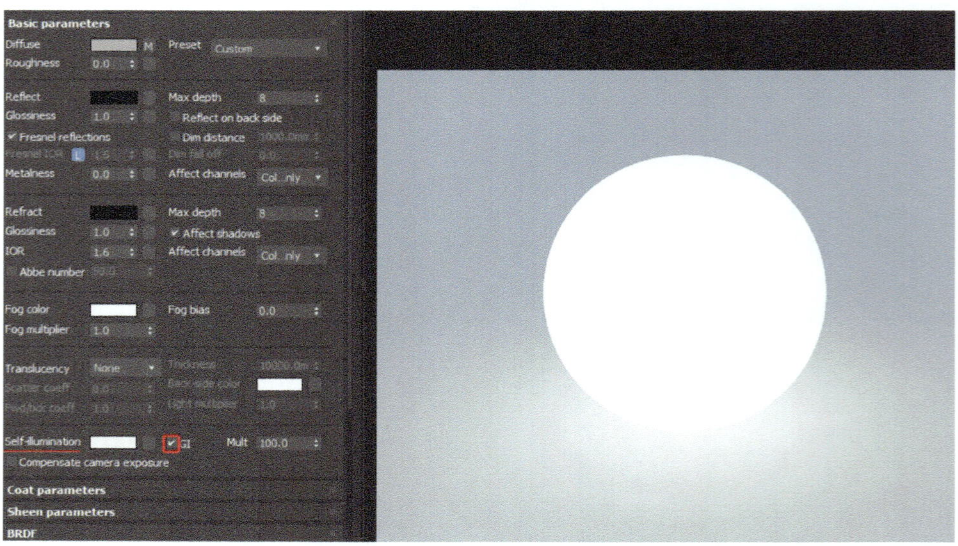

Self-illumination with GI enabled

Self-illumination with compensate camera exposure enabled

Coat Parameters

To test this material parameters, there is a scene under the name VRay Materials .max

Coat amount: This function controls the blending amount (visibility) of the Coat color, Coat glossiness, Coat IOR, etc.

The value of 0.0 makes the Coat color or its map/layer in the toggle completely invisible.

The value of 1.0 makes the Coat color or its map/layer in the toggle completely visible and blending with the diffuse color or map/layer in the toggle.

Users can also use its adjacent toggle to plug materials or/and procedural maps.

The Coat amount is set to 0.0 by default.

Coat glossiness: This function sets the amount of glossiness and reflectivity of the coat.

Its toggle can be used to plug materials or/and procedural maps.

The default glossiness value is set to 1.0.

Coat IOR: This function sets the index of refraction of the Coat.

Users can plug materials or/and procedural maps to its adjacent toggle.

Its default IOR value is set to 1.6.

Coat color: This function controls the color of the coat.

Its adjacent toggle can be used to plug materials or/and procedural maps.

The default Coat color is set to white.

Lock coat bump to base bump: When enabled, it reinvigorates the base bump map over the coat bump map (if any).

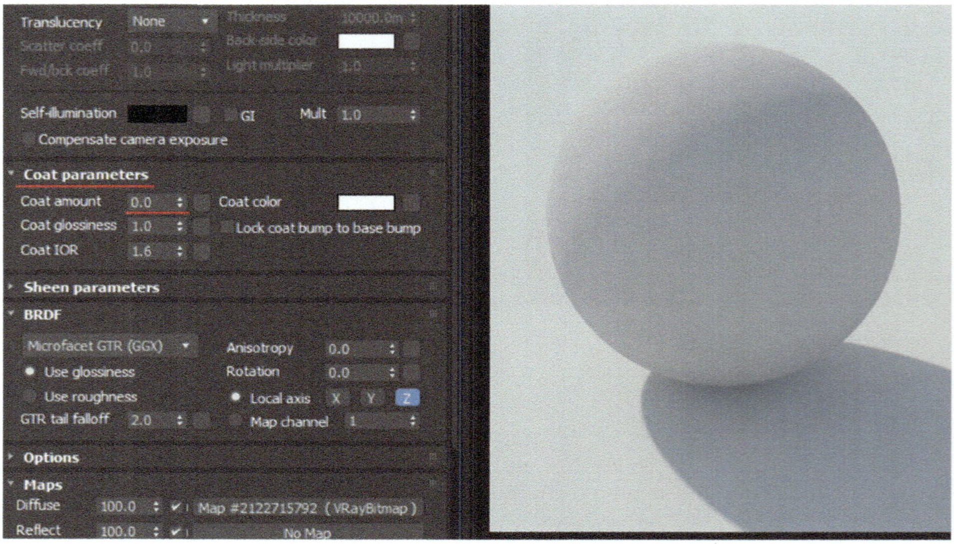

Coat amount set to 0.0

Coat amount set to 1.0

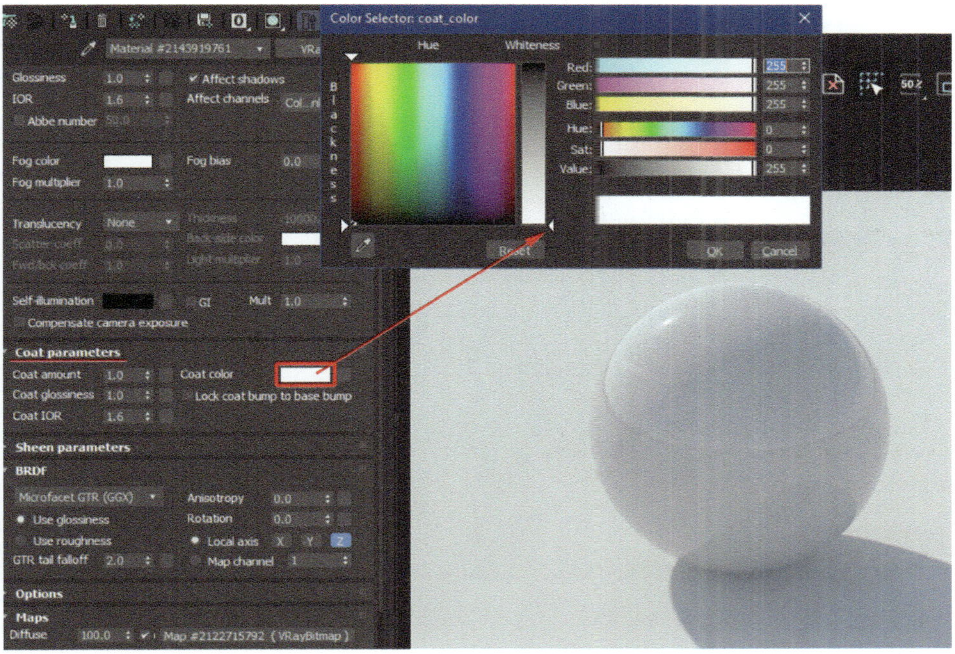
Color Selector: coat_color
Hue
Whiteness
Blackness
Red:
Green:
Blue:
Hue:
Sat:
Value:
255
255
255
0
0
255
Reset
OK
Cancel
Material #2143919761
Glossiness
IOR
Abbe number
Affect shadows
Affect channels
Fog color
Fog multiplier
Fog bias
Translucency
None
Scatter coeff
Fwd/bck coeff
Thickness
Back-side color
Light multiplier
Self-illumination
GI
Mult
Compensate camera exposure
Coat parameters
Coat amount
Coat glossiness
Coat IOR
Coat color
Lock coat bump to base bump
Sheen parameters
BRDF
Microfacet GTR (GGX)
Use glossiness
Use roughness
GTR tail falloff
Anisotropy
Rotation
Local axis
Map channel
Options
Maps
Diffuse
Map #2122715792 (VRayBitmap)

Coat color set to white

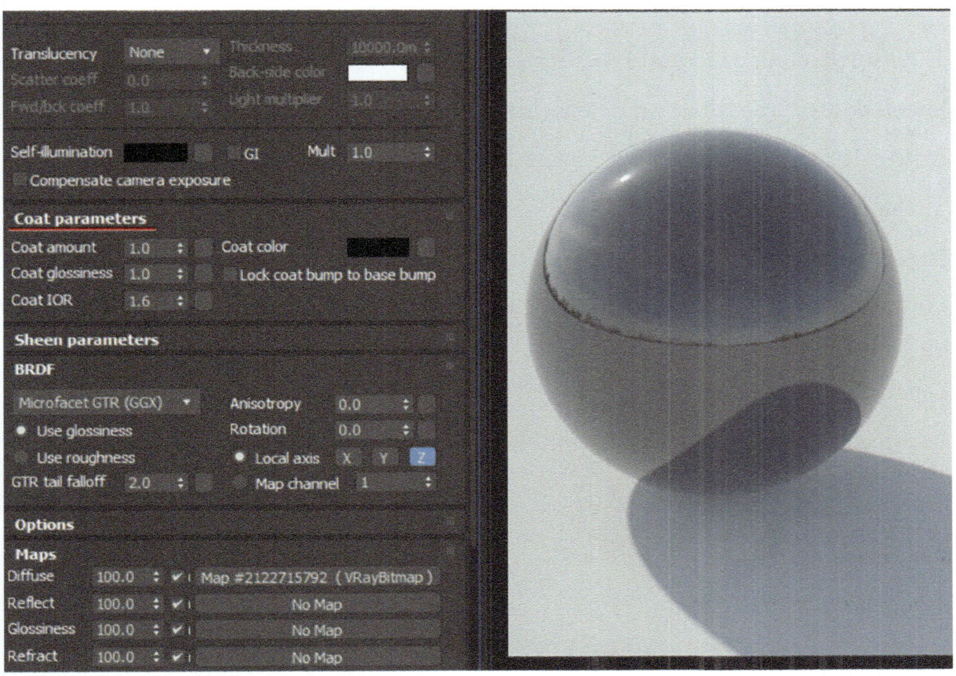
Translucency
None
Thickness
10000.0m
Scatter coeff
Back-side color
Fwd/bck coeff
Light multiplier
Self-illumination
GI
Mult
1.0
Compensate camera exposure
Coat parameters
Coat amount
1.0
Coat color
Coat glossiness
1.0
Lock coat bump to base bump
Coat IOR
1.6
Sheen parameters
BRDF
Microfacet GTR (GGX)
Anisotropy
0.0
Use glossiness
Rotation
0.0
Use roughness
Local axis
X
Y
Z
GTR tail falloff
2.0
Map channel
1
Options
Maps
Diffuse
100.0
Map #2122715792 (VRayBitmap)
Reflect
100.0
No Map
Glossiness
100.0
No Map
Refract
100.0
No Map

Coat color set to black

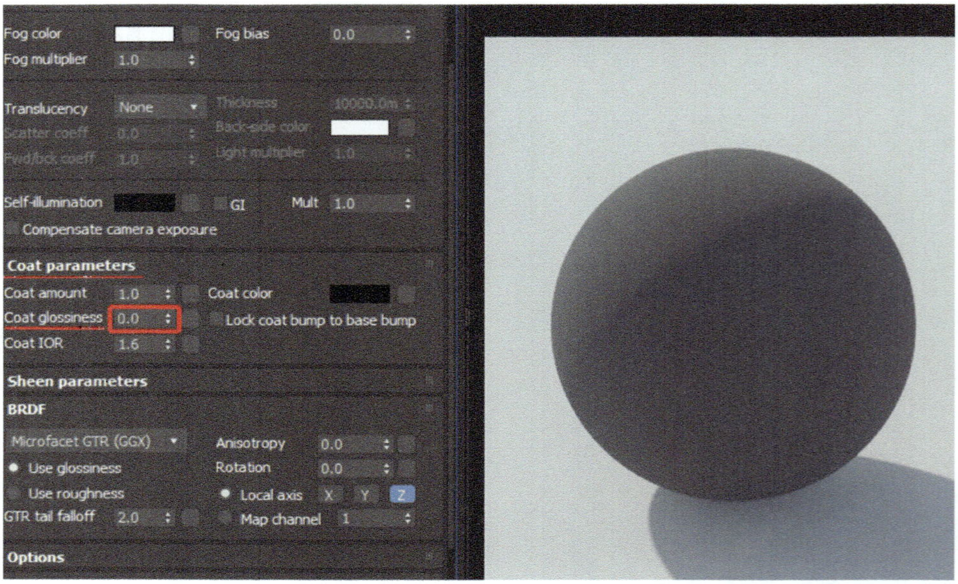

Coat glossiness/reflectivity set to 0.0

Sheen Parameters

This function helps to emulate surfaces such as velvet and satin.

Sheen color: This function determines the color of the sheen.

Its toggle can be used to plug materials or/and procedural maps.

The default color is black.

Sheen glossiness: This function controls the sharpness of the shine.

Lower values yield a more diffused shine (velvet look), and higher values have the opposite effect.

Default value is set to 0.8.

Its adjacent toggle can be used to plug materials or/and procedural maps.

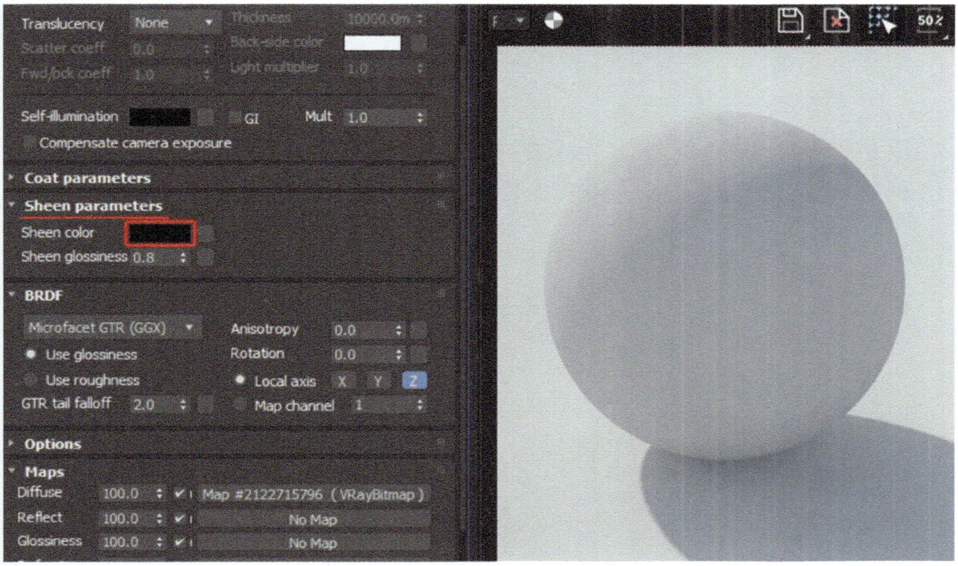

Sheen color set to black

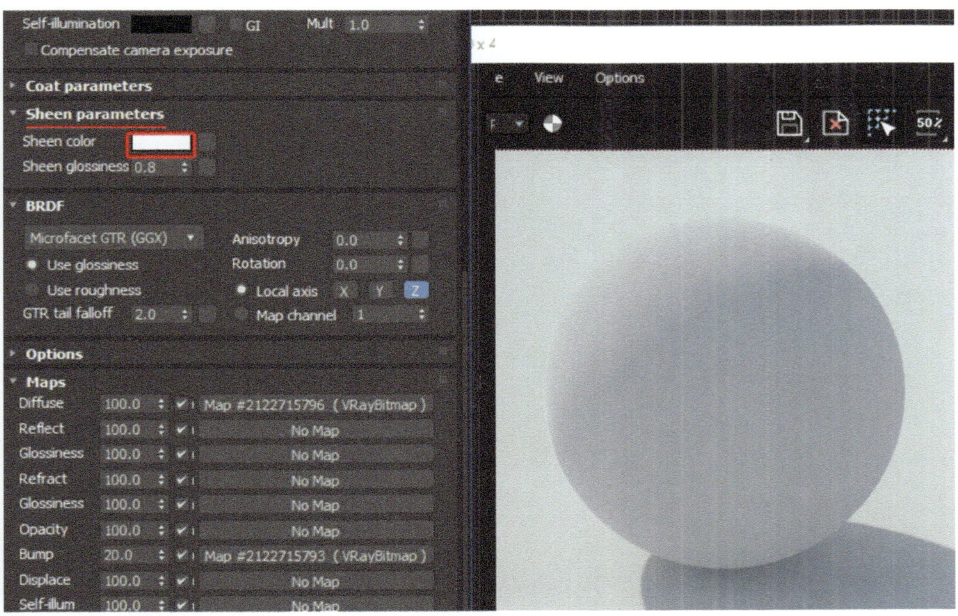

Sheen color set to white

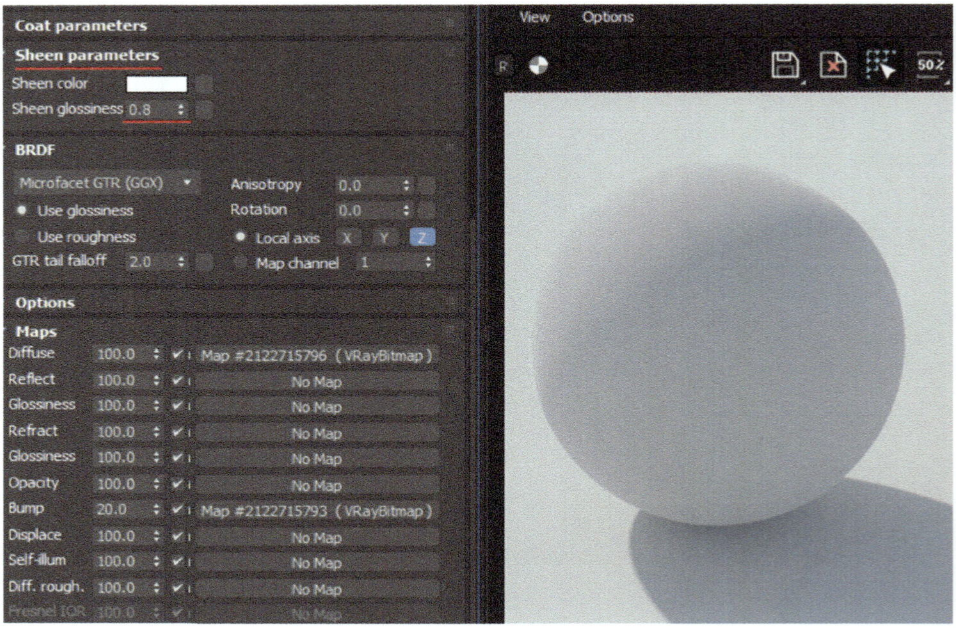

Sheen glossiness set to 0.8

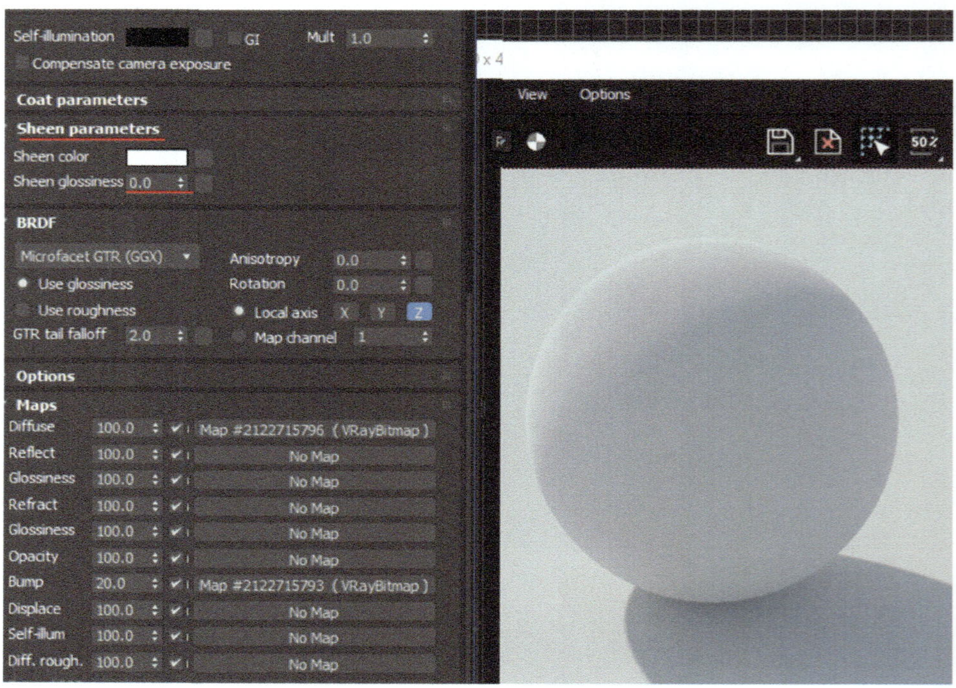

Sheen glossiness set to 0.0 (full velvet)

BRDF Rollout

For the purpose of illustrating this group parameters, the Aluminium_Anodized_Bronze material was used.

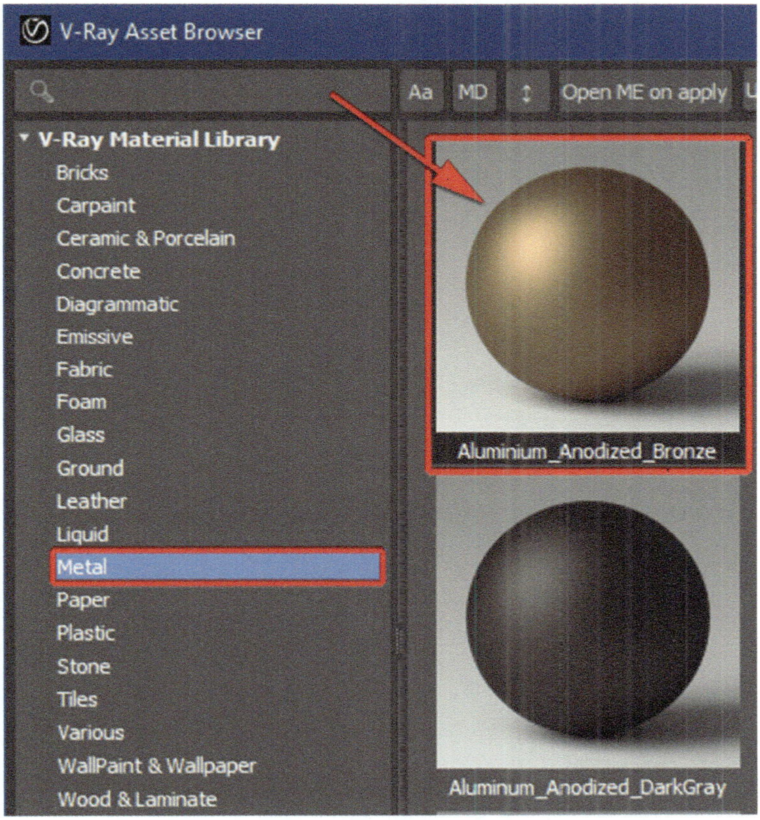

Aluminium_Anodized_Bronze material

Bidirectional reflectance distribution function (BRDF) parameters control the appearance of the glossy highlights and the reflections on a surface.

There are currently four types of BRDF:

1. **Microfacet GTR (GGX):** GGX is the most recent and flexible BRDF type and yields better representation of most materials due to its ability to control the shape of the specular lobe.
2. **Phong:** This type of BRDF yields a small/sharp glossy highlight.
3. **Blinn:** The glossy highlights of this type of BRDF are wider and less sharp.
4. **Ward:** This BRDF produces even wider and more metallic glossy highlights.

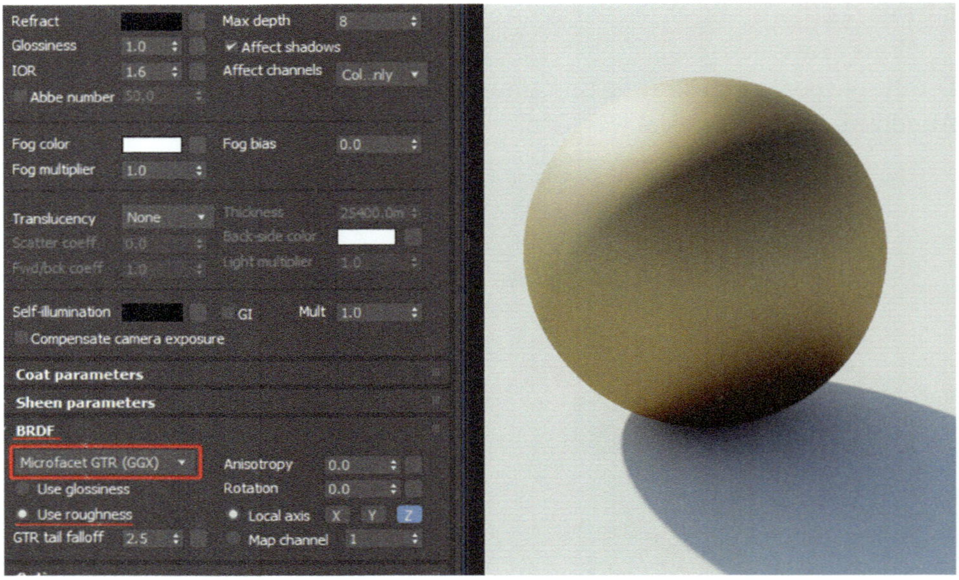

BRDF Microfacet GTR (GGX) type with Use roughness

BRDF Microfacet GTR (GGX) type with Use glossiness

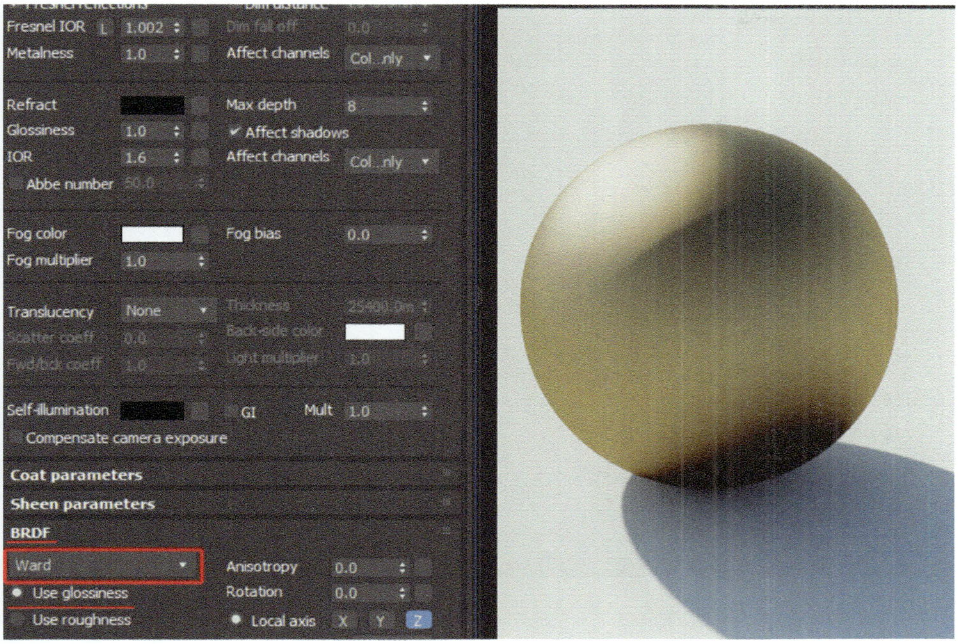

BRDF Ward type with glossiness

Use glossiness: This function is enabled by default, and it uses the Reflect Glossiness parameters (in the Basic parameters) to yield the glossy highlights on a surface.

Use roughness: When enabled, this function automatically switches the Reflect Glossiness function to Roughness type (in the Basic parameters) to emulate a more satin/matte glossy surface.

Anisotropy: This function dictates the direction of the glossy highlights. Users can also plug grayscale texture or/and a procedural map to its toggle. Default value is 0.0.

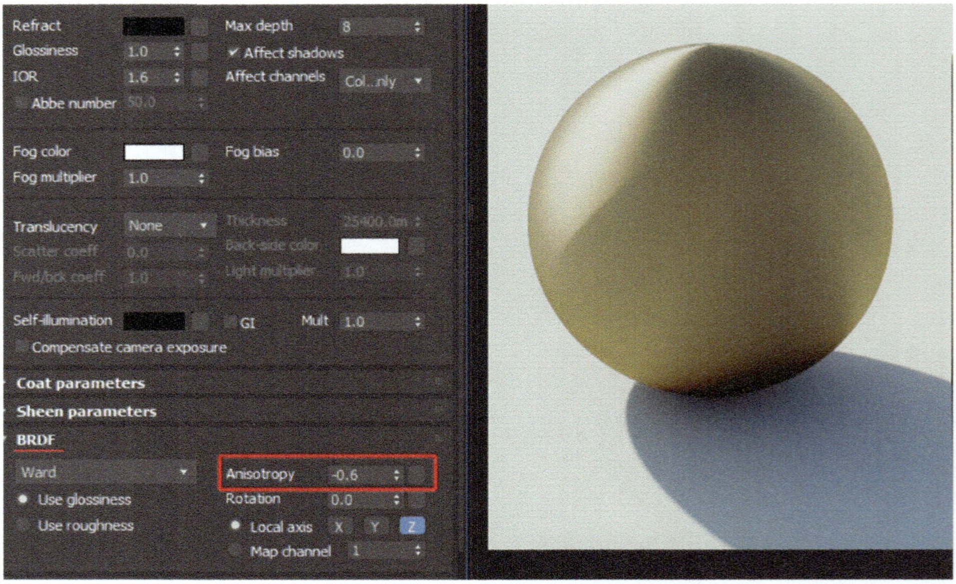

Anisotropy value set to 0.6

Rotation: It allows users to manually set the direction (in degrees) of the reflections and highlights.

Users can apply a grayscale texture or/and a procedural map in its toggle. Default value is 0.0.

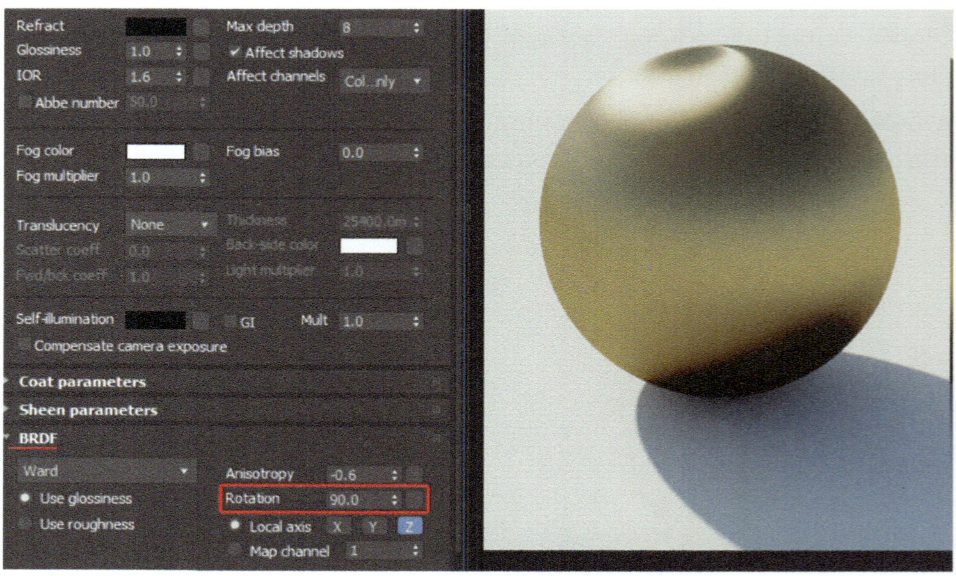

Rotation value set to 90.0

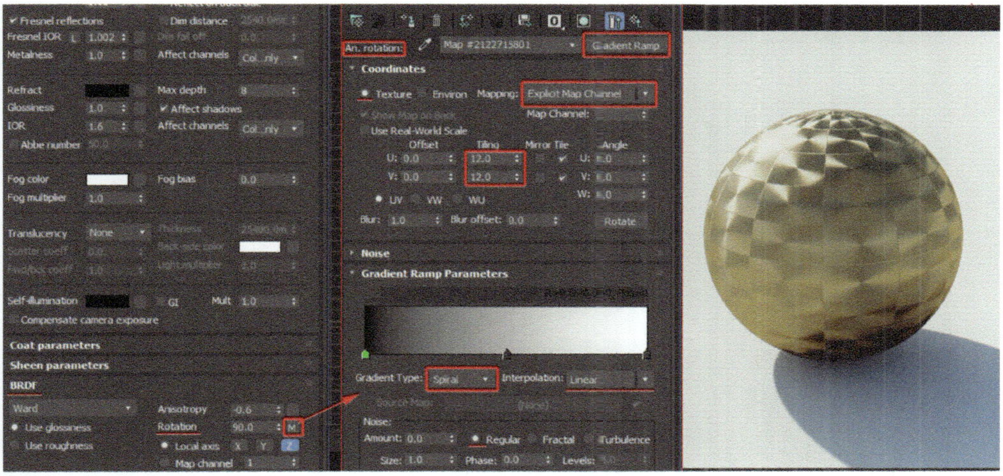

Gradient Ramp procedural map, applied to Rotation toggle

Options Rollout

Trace reflections: This function enables reflections to be traced, when a surface is reflective. If reflections are not contributing much to a surface, this function can be disabled, to speed the rendering times.

Enabled by default.

Trace refractions: It allows refractions to be traced, when a surface is reflective/ refractive. Also, if refractions are not contributing much to a surface, this function can be disabled, to speed the rendering times of the surface.

Enabled by default.

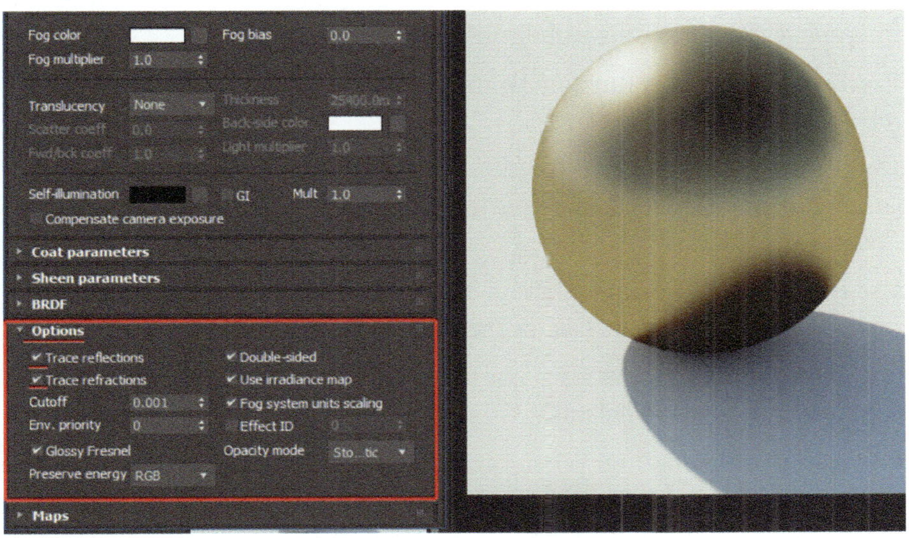

Trace reflections and refractions enabled

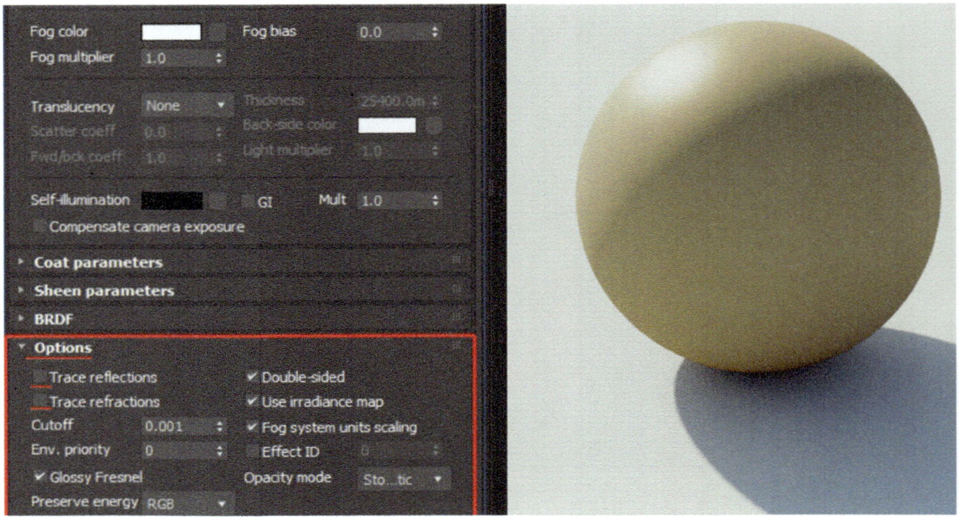

Trace reflections and refractions disabled (faster rendering), but the shine remains

Cutoff: This function sets the trace limit of reflections and refractions. High values reduce the tracing time (with a risk of artifacts), and low values increase the rendering times drastically (with more accuracy).

Default value is 0.01.

Env.priority: This function prioritizes the environment being used for reflections and refractions.

Default value is 0.

Gloss Fresnel: When turned on, it takes into consideration the glossy Fresnel to interpolate the reflections and refractions.

Preserve energy: This function controls how the diffuse, reflections, and refractions affect each other.

Double-sided: This function is quite useful to correct surfaces with one side, or surfaces with one of its faces requiring flipping the normals (e.g., black/dark). Enabled by default.

Use Irradiance map: This function uses the irradiance map computation to calculate its surface, if enabled in the Global Illumination render settings.

Otherwise, it will automatically use the brute force (more accurate), if the GI is turned on. Enabled by default.

Fog system units scaling: When turned on, this function makes the fog color dependent on the system units (it often darkens glass/transparent surfaces).

Effect ID: When turned on, this function allows the reflections/refractions to affect specific material ID numbers (which need to be specified/entered).

Default value is 0.

Opacity mode: This function determines how the opacity is sampled.

Maps Rollout

For the purpose of illustrating the functionalities of the rollout parameters, the Bricks_A01_m material was used.

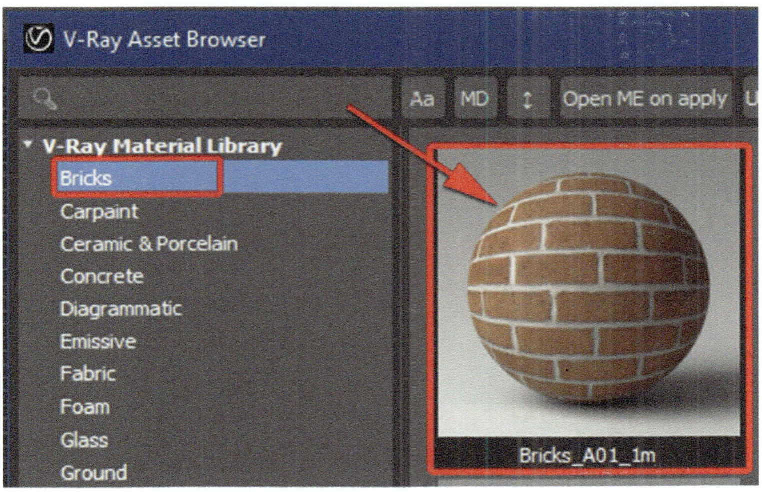

Bricks_A01_m material

Most Map toggles displayed under this rollout are directly connected to the textures/procedural maps being used in the VRay basic parameters.

When a texture/procedural map is being used in a toggle, it automatically overrides the colors and/or values displayed.

NOTE

The Use real-world scale function was not applied.

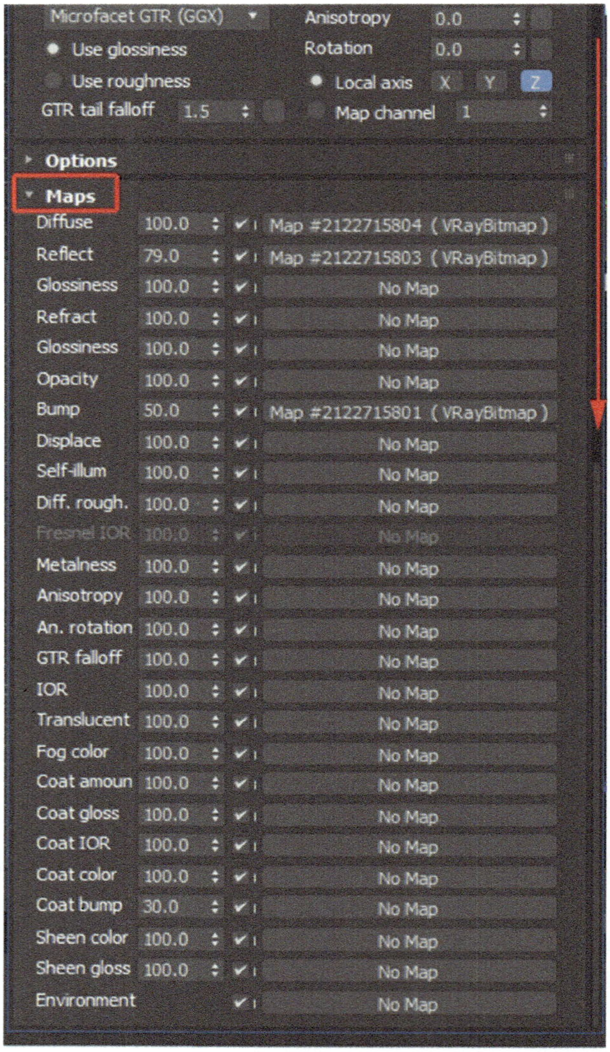

Maps rollout

The toggles being used have a capital letter M in them, and the toggles not being used are empty (e.g., none).

Users can increase or decrease the contribution of each toggle being used (in percentages) by typing in a value, or use its adjacent spinner.

The default value of each toggle is 100%.

In addition, users can completely disable any toggle being used, by simply disabling its adjacent tick box. When such happens, the toggle with the capital M will automatically become lowercase (e.g., m)

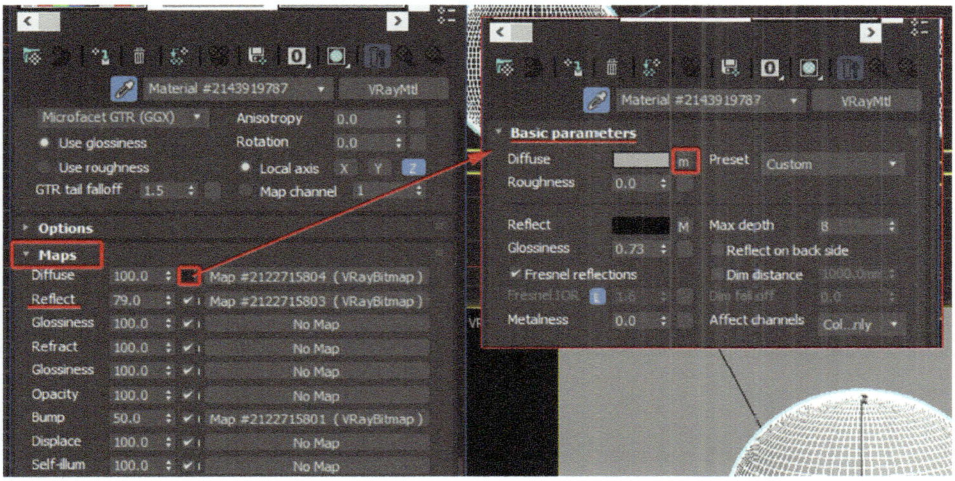

Diffuse Toggle disabled and Reflect percentage reduced to 79.0

Bump: It allows users to plug a texture and/or a procedural map to its toggle. It works best with grayscale and/or black and white bitmaps.

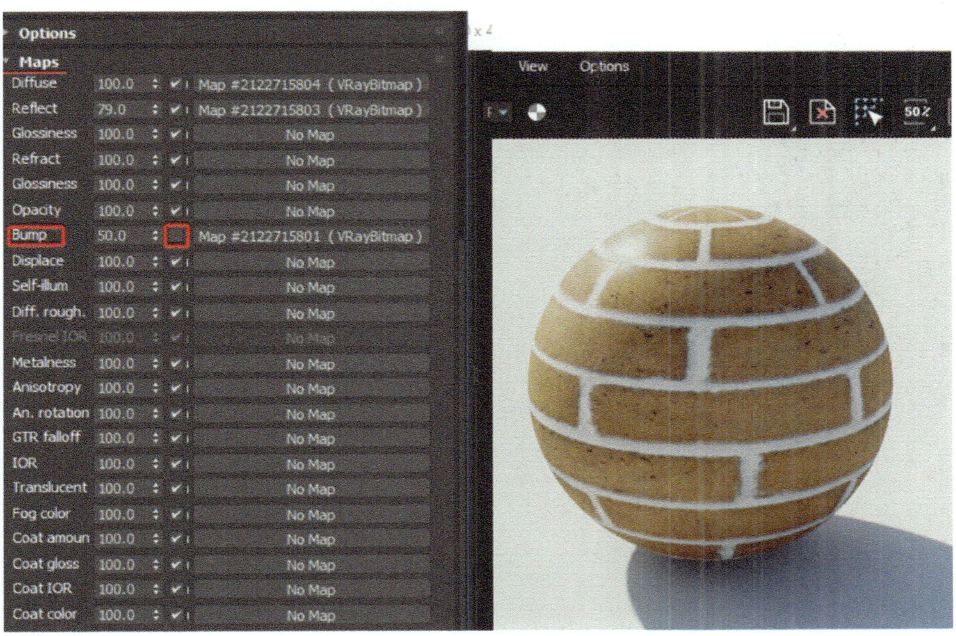

Bump map disabled

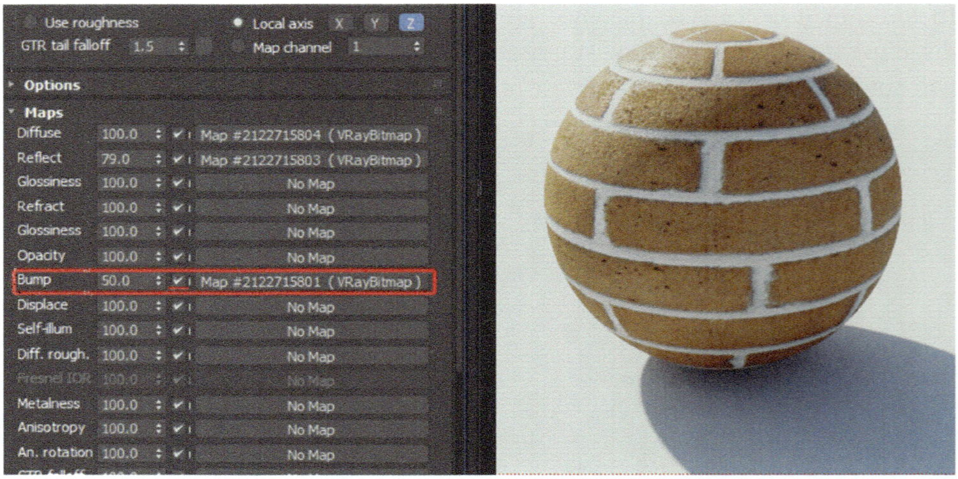

Bump map enabled

For the purpose of illustrating the Displace functionalities, a standard VRayMtl was loaded, as previously shown.

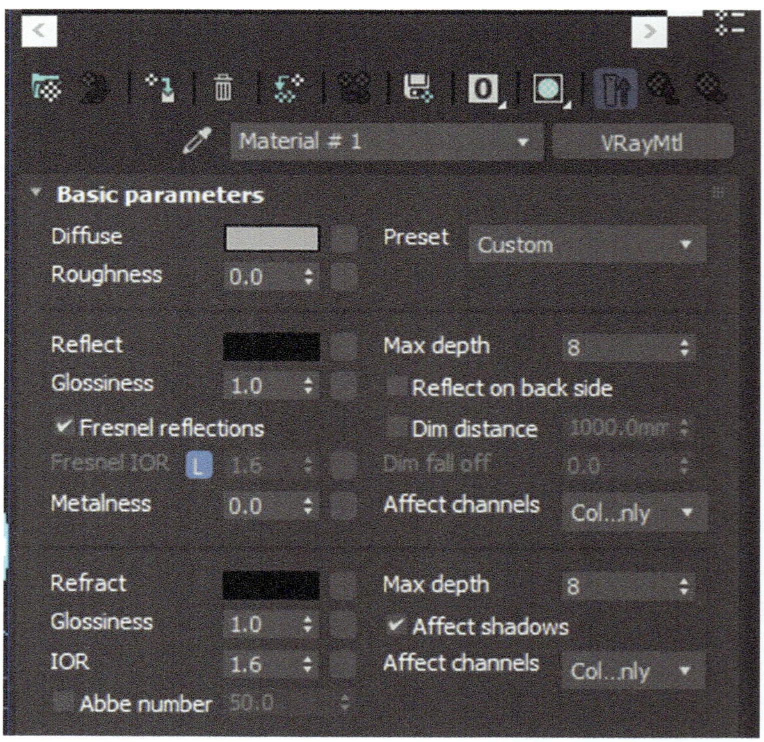

Standard VRayMtl was loaded

Displace: This function physically modifies a geometry according to its mapping coordinates. For accurate results, users are recommended to have a detailed geometry (many segments).

Users can plug a texture and/or a procedural map to its toggle. Also, it works best with grayscale and/or black and white bitmaps.

It's worth noting that this type of displacement is very time-consuming to render.

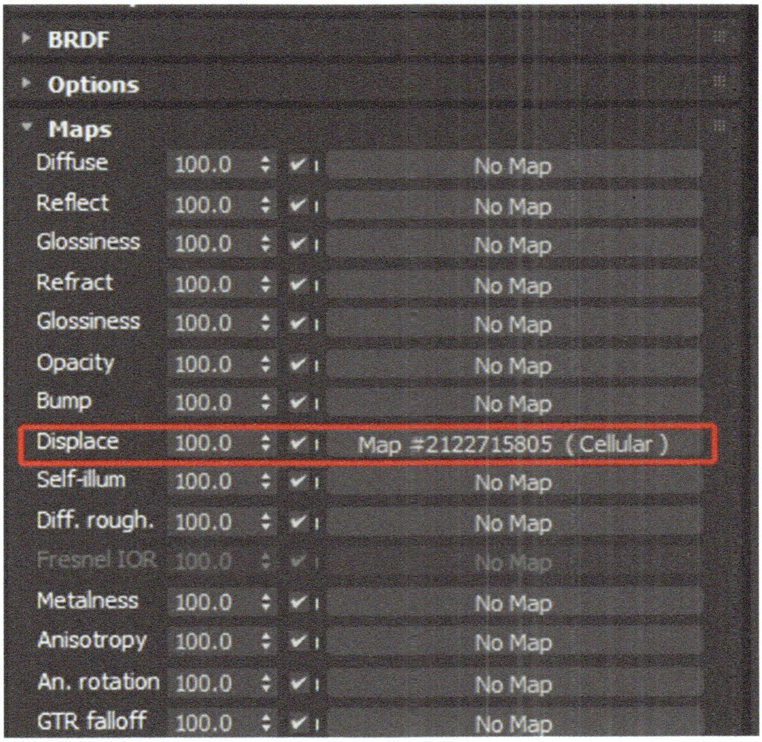

Displace function with a procedural map

For relatively fast and accurate results, professionals tend to use the VRayDisplacementMod instead. When using this modifier, the Displace toggle needs to be disabled.

This VRay modifier can be accessed from the Modify list.

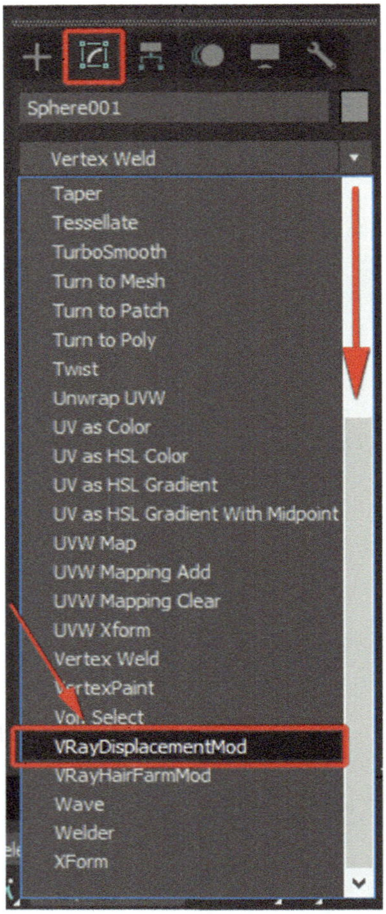

VRayDisplacementMod from the Modify list

NOTE

The VRayDisplacementMod works best when the UWM Map modifier is applied first. Otherwise, the procedural map/texture applied will not tile accordingly.

Also, the 2D mapping (landscape) option is the fastest to render from the three types.

To apply a grayscale texture or/and a procedural map, simply use the Texmap toggle.

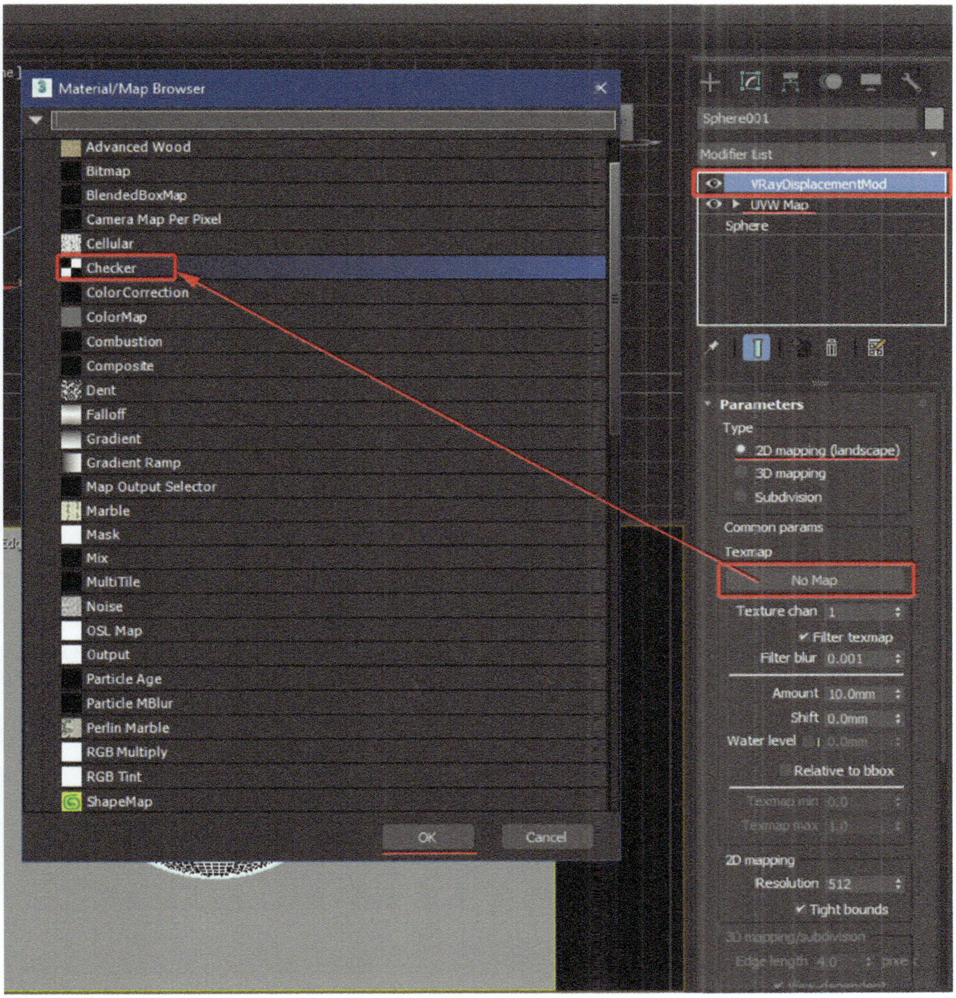

Use the Texmap toggle to access the Material/Map Browser

To edit the texture or/and the procedural map, simply drag/drop it into a toggle, and choose to instance it.

Also, ensure the toggle is disabled, to prevent doubling it up. Following that, enable the Show shaded Material in Viewport button.

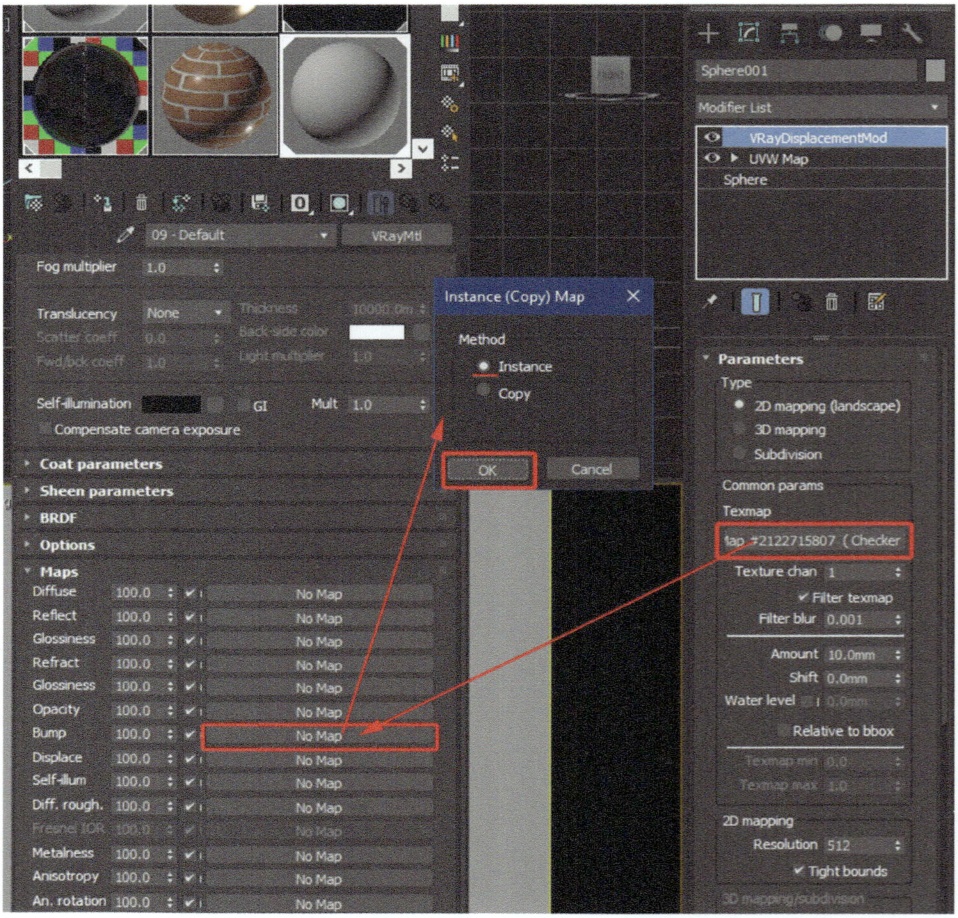
Sphere001
Modifier List
VRayDisplacementMod
UVW Map
Sphere
09 - Default
VRayMtl
Fog multiplier 1.0
Translucency None
Thickness
Scatter coeff 0.0
Back-side color
Fwd/bck coeff 1.0
Light multiplier 1.0
Self-illumination
GI
Mult 1.0
Compensate camera exposure
Instance (Copy) Map
Method
Instance
Copy
OK
Cancel
Coat parameters
Sheen parameters
BRDF
Options
Maps
Diffuse 100.0 No Map
Reflect 100.0 No Map
Glossiness 100.0 No Map
Refract 100.0 No Map
Glossiness 100.0 No Map
Opacity 100.0 No Map
Bump 100.0 No Map
Displace 100.0 No Map
Self-illum 100.0 No Map
Diff. rough. 100.0 No Map
Fresnel IOR 100.0 No Map
Metalness 100.0 No Map
Anisotropy 100.0 No Map
An. rotation 100.0 No Map
Parameters
Type
2D mapping (landscape)
3D mapping
Subdivision
Common params
Texmap
lap #2122715807 (Checker
Texture chan 1
Filter texmap
Filter blur 0.001
Amount 10.0mm
Shift 0.0mm
Water level
Relative to bbox
Texmap min 0.0
Texmap max 1.0
2D mapping
Resolution 512
Tight bounds
3D mapping/subdivision

Drag and drop the Texmap content

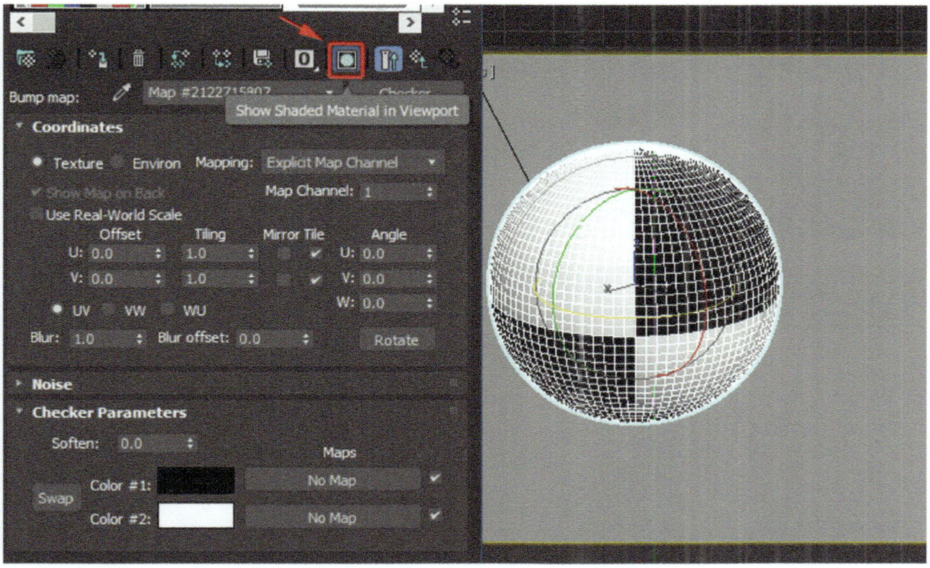

Enable Show shaded Material in Viewport

Furthermore, when using the VRayDisplacementMod modifier, the texture/procedural map parameters should always be kept at 1.0 in the Material Editor.

All texture/procedural map changes such as tiling should occur at the Modify level only (e.g., with UVW Mapping, MapScaler).

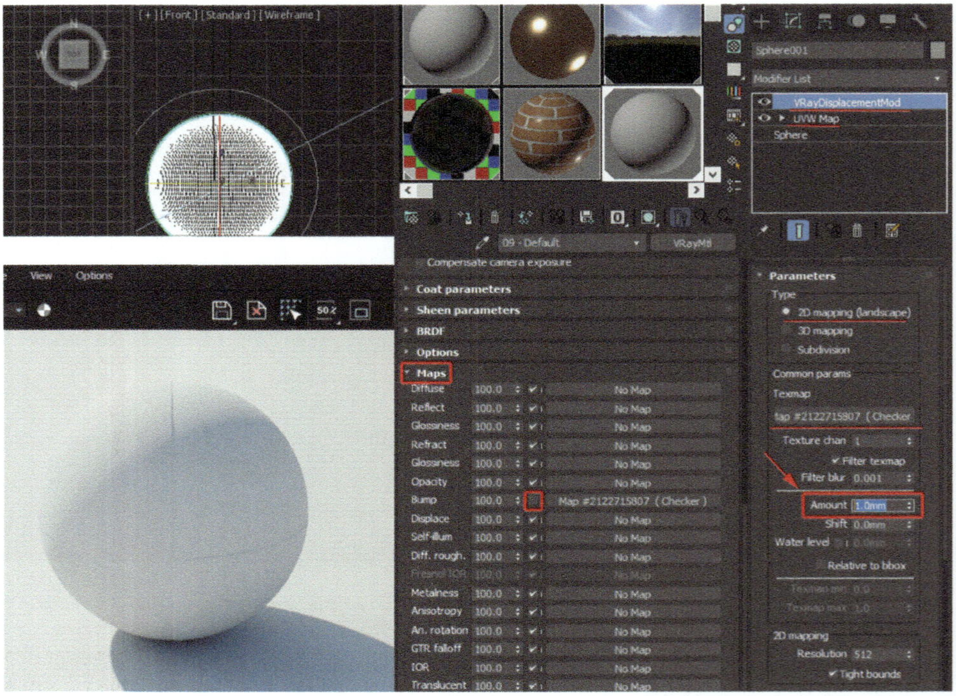

VRayDisplacementMod Amount set to 1.0 mm

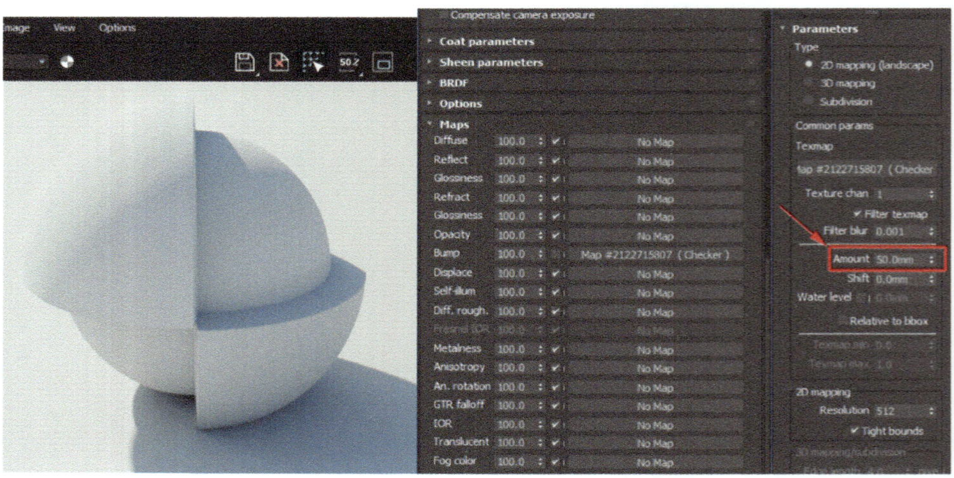

VRayDisplacementMod Amount set to 50.0 mm

Opacity: This function only works when textures and/or procedural maps are plugged to its toggle.

For best results, use grayscale and/or black and white textures/procedural maps.

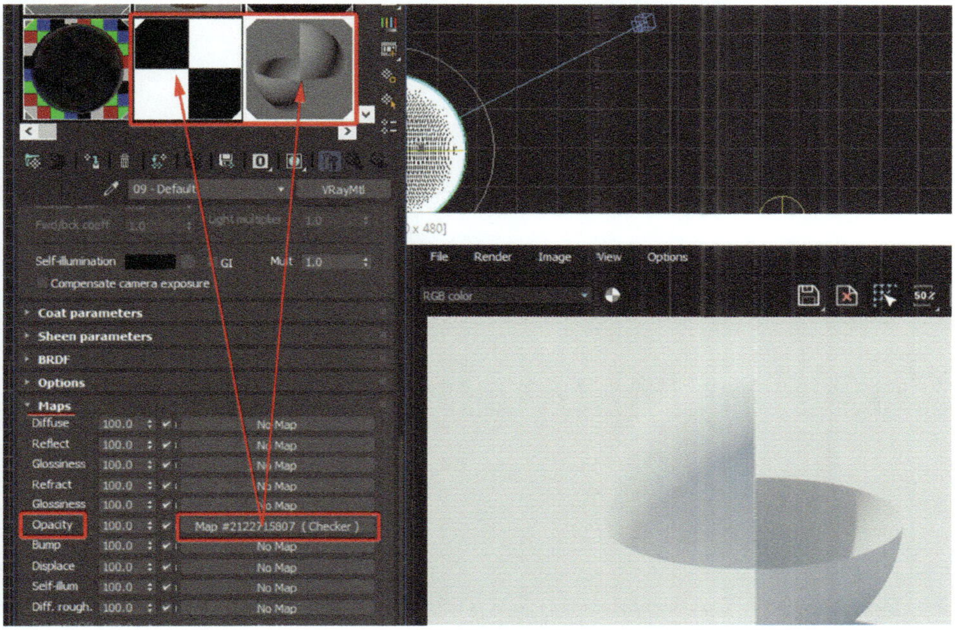

Checker procedural map applied to Opacity toggle

More VRay Shaders and Procedural Maps

While VRay has a host of shaders and procedural maps, the following discussion will focus mainly on the most used ones, by artists and industry professionals.

VRayBitmap

This procedural map is often used as the basis to plug Bitmaps and other procedural maps.

Its Bitmap toggle is often used to plug textures and file formats such as JPG, PNG, HDR, EXR, TIFF, and TX.

Its Mapping source toggle allows users to plug amazing procedural maps such as VRayUVWRandomizer, VRayTriplanarTex, and VRayMultiSubTex.

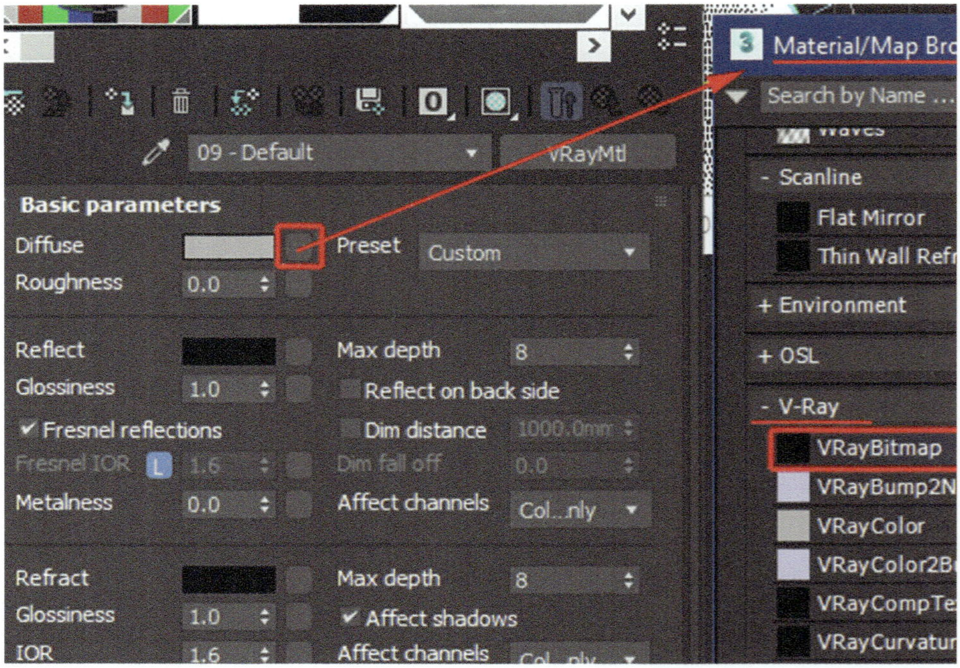
Material/Map Bro
Search by Name ...
09 - Default
VRayMtl
Basic parameters
Diffuse
Preset
Custom
Roughness
0.0
Reflect
Max depth
8
Glossiness
1.0
Reflect on back side
Fresnel reflections
Dim distance
1000.0mm
Fresnel IOR
1.6
Dim fall off
0.0
Metalness
0.0
Affect channels
Col...nly
Refract
Max depth
8
Glossiness
1.0
Affect shadows
IOR
1.6
Affect channels
- Scanline
Flat Mirror
Thin Wall Refr
+ Environment
+ OSL
- V-Ray
VRayBitmap
VRayBump2N
VRayColor
VRayColor2B
VRayCompTe
VRayCurvatur

VRayBitmap in the Material Browser

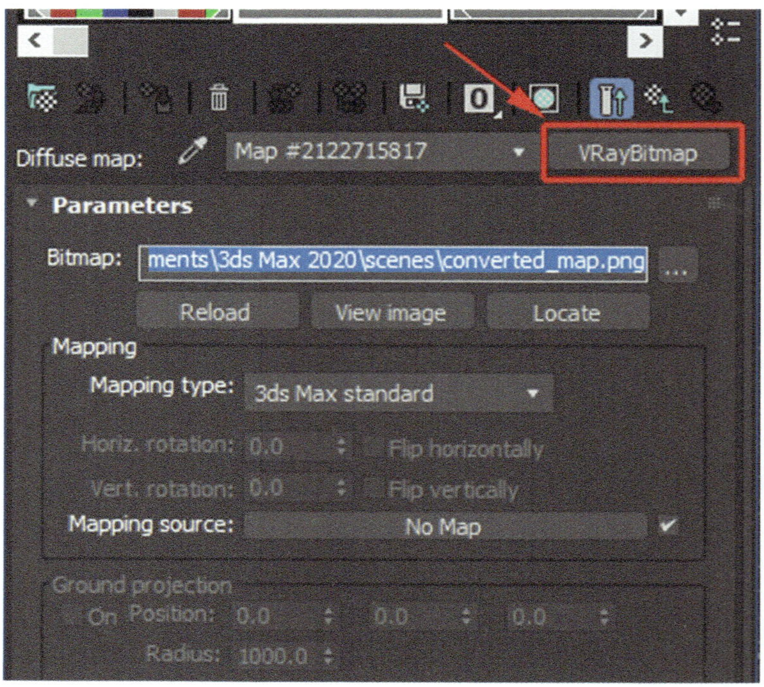
Diffuse map:
Map #2122715817
VRayBitmap
Parameters
Bitmap:
ments\3ds Max 2020\scenes\converted_map.png
Reload
View image
Locate
Mapping
Mapping type:
3ds Max standard
Horiz. rotation:
0.0
Flip horizontally
Vert. rotation:
0.0
Flip vertically
Mapping source:
No Map
Ground projection
On
Position:
0.0
0.0
0.0
Radius:
1000.0

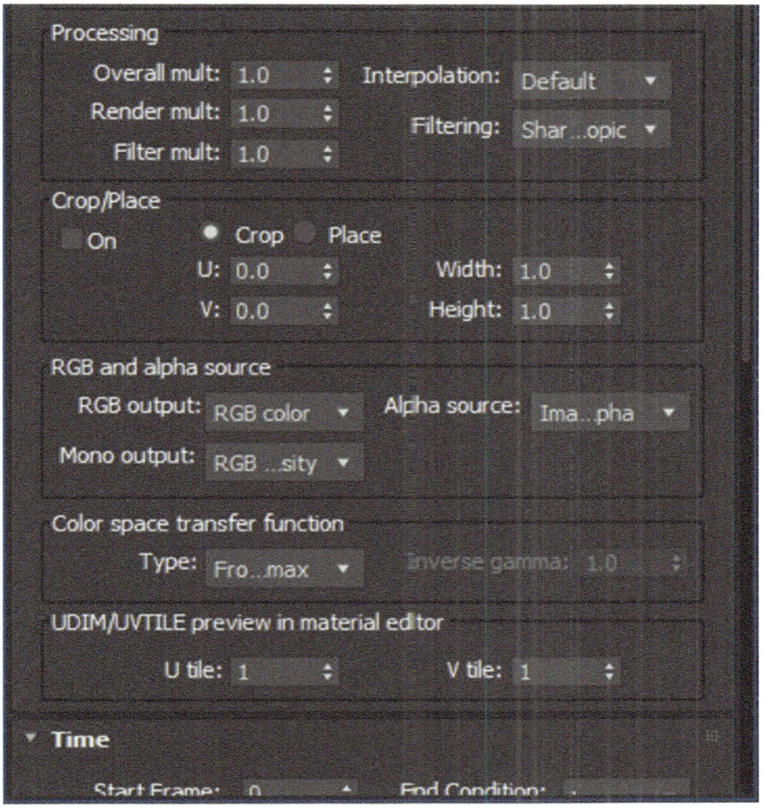

VRayBitmap loaded

Bitmap: This toggle allows users to locate and load file formats such as JPG, PNG, HDR, EXR, TIFF, and TX.

Reload: When clicked, this button reloads the bitmap currently loaded.

View image: When clicked, this button opens the loaded bitmap inside 3ds max.

Locate: When clicked, it locates the loaded bitmap, by opening it in a separate folder.

Mapping type: This function determines how the bitmaps are displayed.

The most commonly used mapping types are 3ds max standard and Spherical.

3ds max standard type uses the standard tiling style often applied on surfaces.

When enabled, it automatically uses the Coordinates group to tile the loaded bitmap.

Spherical type is often used for HDR maps plugged in the Environment toggle.

NOTE

This button doesn't work with file formats such as TX.

NOTE

This button doesn't work with file formats such as TX.

Horizontal rotation: This function controls the horizontal rotation of a bitmap.

This function is only available when the mapping type is *not* set to 3ds max standard.

Vertical rotation: This function controls the vertical rotation of a bitmap.

This function is only available when the mapping type is *not* set to 3ds max standard.

Mapping source: This function allows users to plug useful procedural maps such as VRayUVWRandomizer, VRayTriplanarTex, and VRayMultiSubTex.

Ground projection: This function only works when applied to the environments map toggle.

When enabled, it helps to ground the lower section of the environment map onto an imaginary plane that will receive shadows.

This function is particularly useful for 3d scenes with environment maps and floating objects without a physical ground (geometry) to cast shadows onto.

Position: This function controls the position coordinates of the projected environment map.

Overall mult: This function determines the overall intensity/brightness of the loaded material in the material editor preview and while rendering.

Render mult: This function determines the overall intensity/brightness of the loaded material, only while rendering.

Filter mult: This function controls the blurriness of the loaded image. Higher values yield blurrier results and faster rendering of the blurred image.

Interpolation: This function controls the rendering interpolation of textures (Bilinear, Bicubic, Biquadratic).

Filtering: This function controls the filtering method (isotropic, elliptical, sharp isotropic)

Crop/place: When enabled, this function allows users to Crop or Place the loaded texture.

U and V: These two functions allow users to control the U/V tiling of the loaded material.

Width and height: These two functions allow users to control the width/height of the loaded material.

The remaining parameters are self-explanatory, and can be found at: http://docs.chaosgroup.com/

VRayUVWRandomizer

This exquisite procedural map allows users to randomize the position, rotation, and scale of bitmaps.

It can only be plugged from the Mapping source toggle of the VRayBitmap and VRayTriplanarTex texture nodes.

Once VRayUVWRandomizer is loaded, the bitmap tiling is overridden/controlled by its Coordinate parameters.

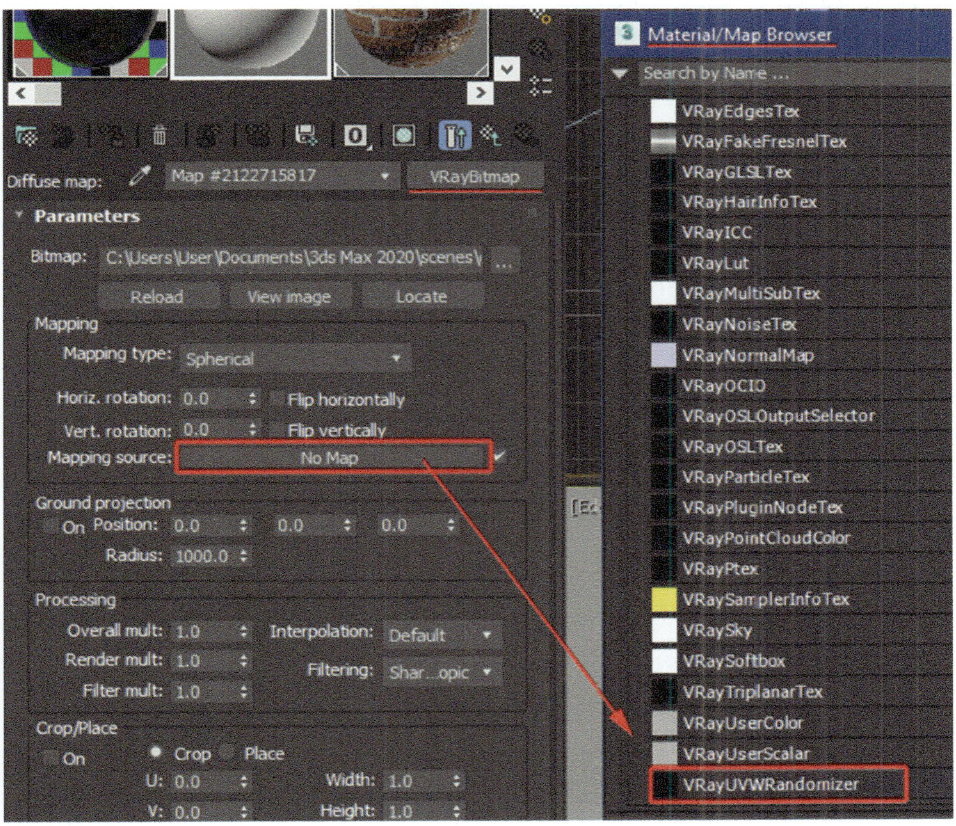

VRayUVWRandomizer in the Material Browser

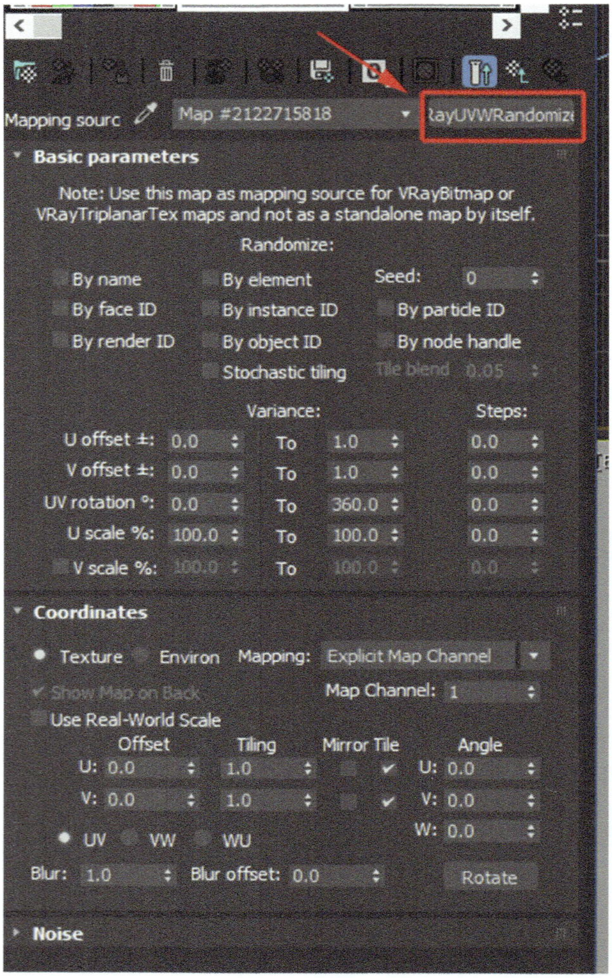

VRayUVWRandomizer loaded

To test the functionalities of this procedural map, please open the file under the name VRayUVWRandomizer.max

By name: When enabled, this function randomizes (color index) bitmaps by its name.

By face ID: When enabled, this function randomizes (color index) bitmaps by the face IDs of an object.

By render ID: When enabled, this function randomizes bitmaps (color index) of object's face ID.

By element: When enabled, this function randomizes bitmaps (color index) by the element IDs of an object.

By instance ID: When enabled, this function randomizes bitmaps (color index) by the face IDs of an object.

By object ID: When enabled, this function randomizes bitmaps (color index) by the face IDs of an object.

Stochastic tiling: When enabled, this function automatically changes the UV mapping tile.

Seed: This function allows users to change the pattern randomization by entering different values.

By particle ID: When enabled, this function randomizes bitmaps (color index) by the face IDs of particles.

By node handle: When enabled, this function randomizes bitmaps (color index) by the face IDs of an object.

Variance: This group controls the offset, rotation, and scale variations.

U offset (horizontal)**:** This function controls the horizontal position of your bitmap. Always enter values that are different from the V offset (vertical) values.

V offset (vertical)**:** This function controls the vertical position of your bitmap. Always enter values that are different from the U offset (horizontal) values.

UV rotation: This function controls the rotation of your bitmap in U or V axis.

U scale % (horizontal)**:** This function controls the horizontal scale of your bitmap.

V scale % (vertical)**:** This function controls the vertical scale of your bitmap in percentages.

Steps: This function controls the variation intervals. Entering values higher than 1 can really make a difference on the overall look of a bitmap.

Always enter different step values in U and V directions.

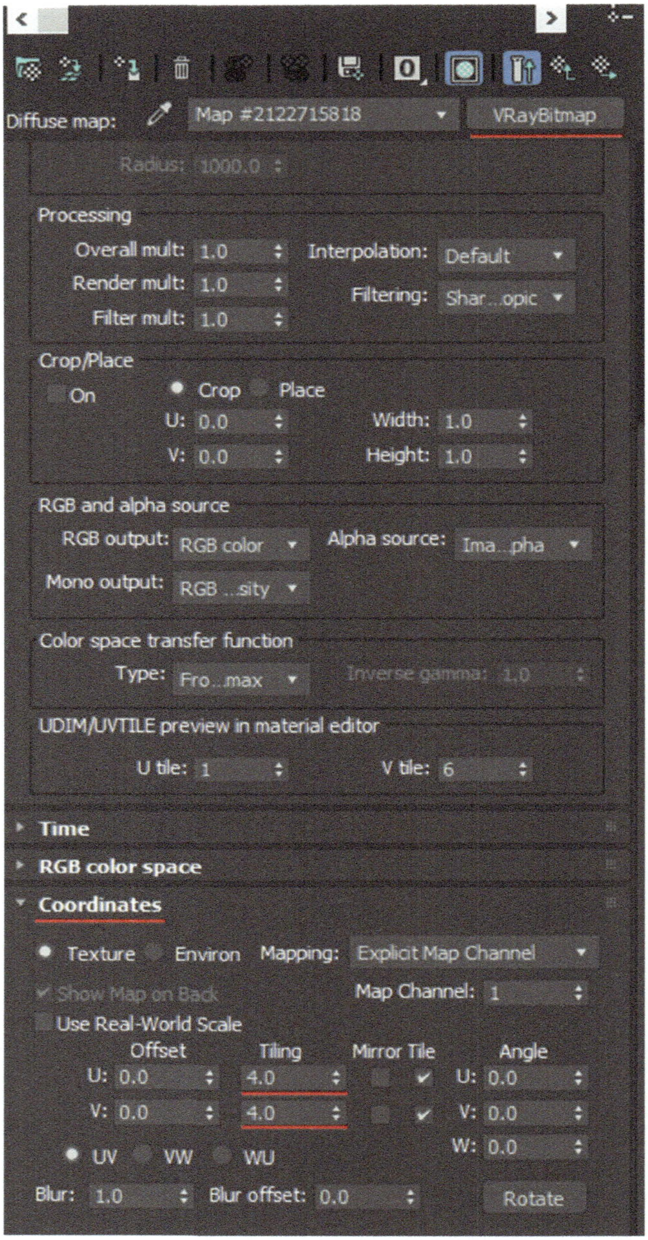
Diffuse map:
Map #2122715818
VRayBitmap
Radius: 1000.0
Processing
Overall mult: 1.0
Interpolation: Default
Render mult: 1.0
Filtering: Shar...opic
Filter mult: 1.0
Crop/Place
On
Crop
Place
U: 0.0
Width: 1.0
V: 0.0
Height: 1.0
RGB and alpha source
RGB output: RGB color
Alpha source: Ima...pha
Mono output: RGB ...sity
Color space transfer function
Type: Fro...max
Inverse gamma: 1.0
UDIM/UVTILE preview in material editor
U tile: 1
V tile: 6
Time
RGB color space
Coordinates
Texture
Environ
Mapping: Explicit Map Channel
Show Map on Back
Map Channel: 1
Use Real-World Scale
Offset
Tiling
Mirror Tile
Angle
U: 0.0
4.0
U: 0.0
V: 0.0
4.0
V: 0.0
UV
VW
WU
W: 0.0
Blur: 1.0
Blur offset: 0.0
Rotate

x 480]

Brick material without VrayUVWRandomizer

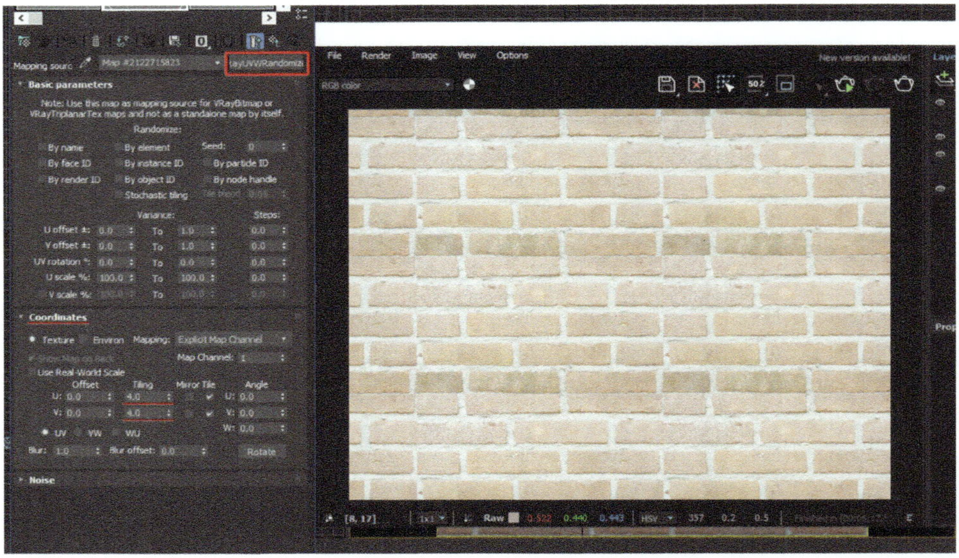
Basic parameters
Coordinates
Noise
File
Render
Image
View
Options

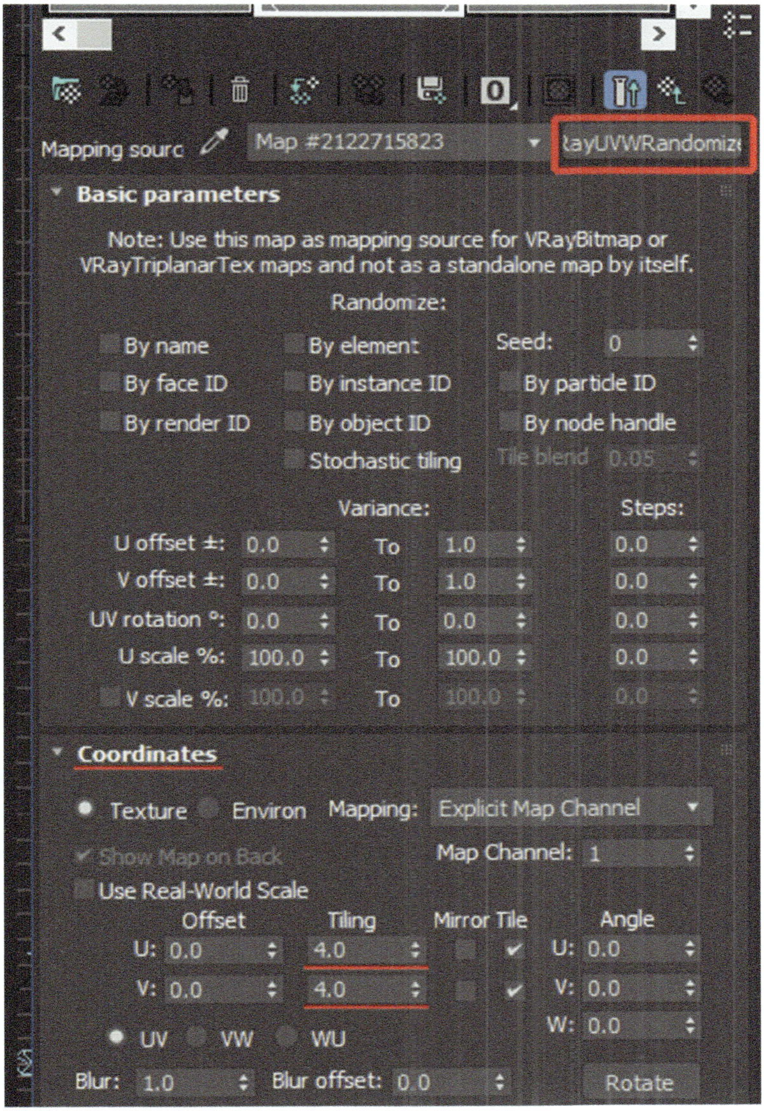
Mapping sourc
Map #2122715823
RayUVWRandomize
Basic parameters
Note: Use this map as mapping source for VRayBitmap or VRayTriplanarTex maps and not as a standalone map by itself.
Randomize:
By name
By element
Seed: 0
By face ID
By instance ID
By particle ID
By render ID
By object ID
By node handle
Stochastic tiling
Tile blend 0.05
Variance:
Steps:
U offset ±: 0.0 To 1.0 0.0
V offset ±: 0.0 To 1.0 0.0
UV rotation °: 0.0 To 0.0 0.0
U scale %: 100.0 To 100.0 0.0
V scale %: 100.0 To 100.0 0.0
Coordinates
Texture
Environ
Mapping: Explicit Map Channel
Show Map on Back
Map Channel: 1
Use Real-World Scale
Offset
Tiling
Mirror Tile
Angle
U: 0.0 4.0 U: 0.0
V: 0.0 4.0 V: 0.0
W: 0.0
UV VW WU
Blur: 1.0
Blur offset: 0.0
Rotate

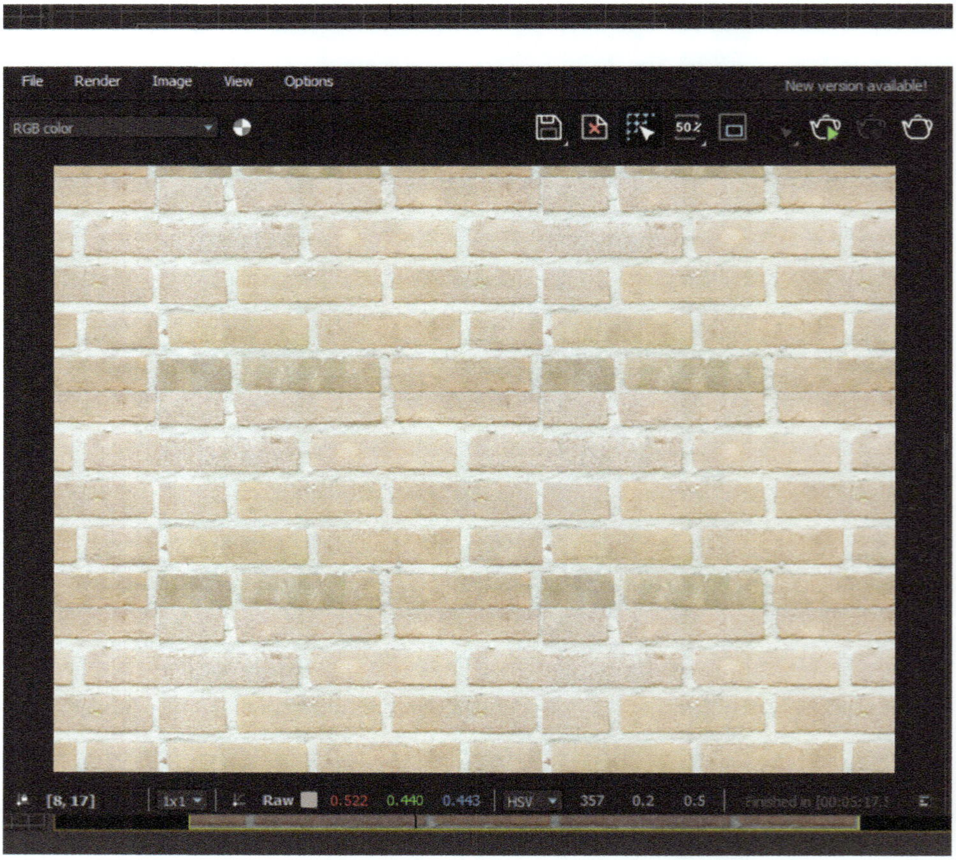
File
Render
Image
View
Options
New version available!
RGB color
[8, 17]
1x1
Raw
0.522
0.440
0.443
HSV
357
0.2
0.5

Brick material with VrayUVWRandomizer

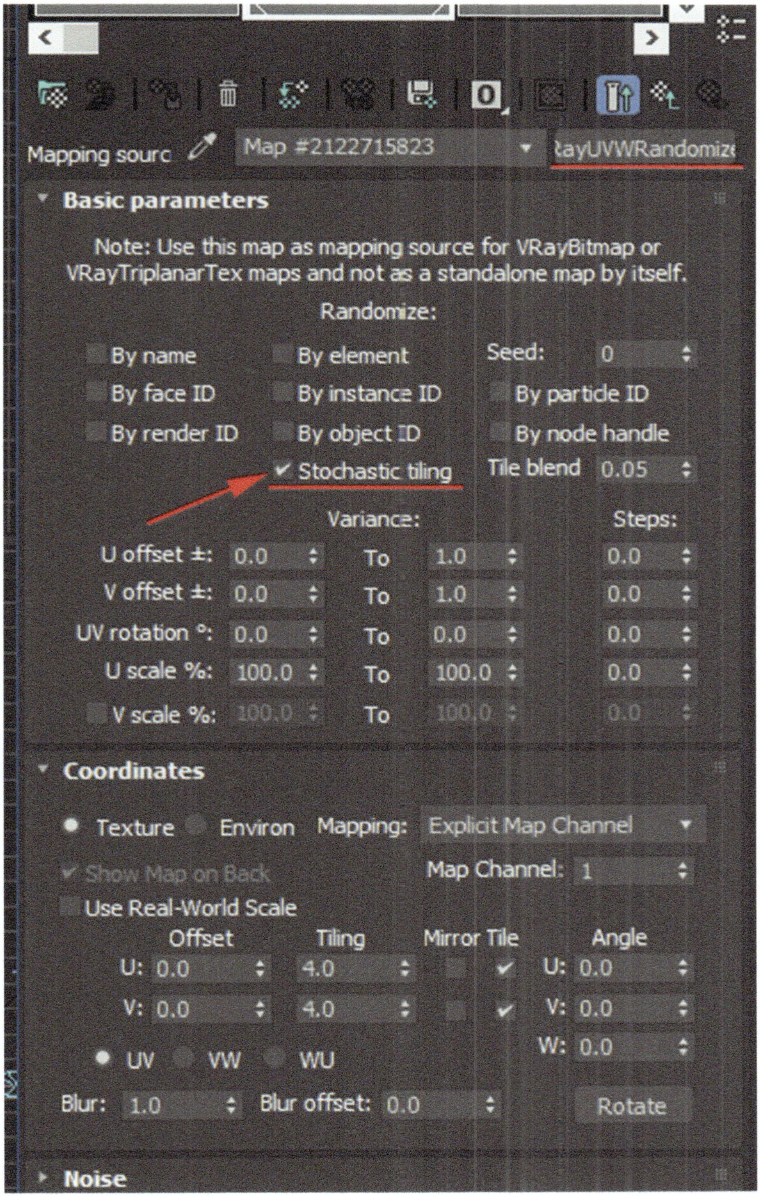
Mapping sourc
Map #2122715823
RayUVWRandomize
Basic parameters
Note: Use this map as mapping source for VRayBitmap or VRayTriplanarTex maps and not as a standalone map by itself.
Randomize:
By name
By element
Seed:
By face ID
By instance ID
By particle ID
By render ID
By object ID
By node handle
Stochastic tiling
Tile blend
Variance:
Steps:
U offset ±:
V offset ±:
UV rotation °:
U scale %:
V scale %:
To
Coordinates
Texture
Environ
Mapping:
Explicit Map Channel
Show Map on Back
Map Channel:
Use Real-World Scale
Offset
Tiling
Mirror Tile
Angle
UV
VW
WU
Blur:
Blur offset:
Rotate
Noise

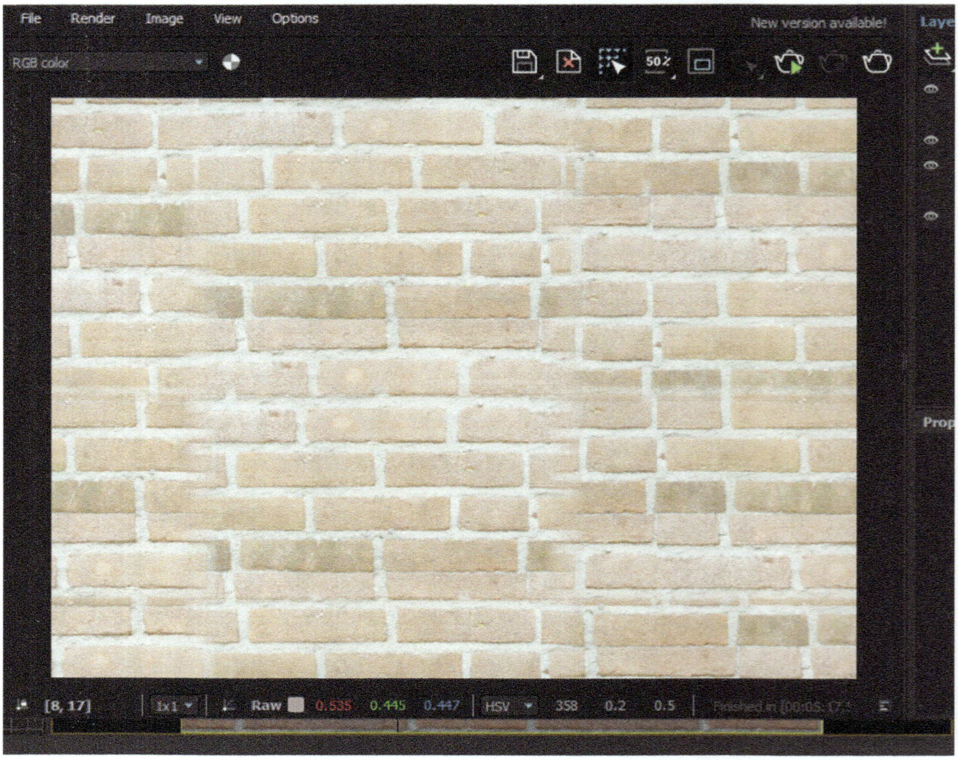

VrayUVWRandomizer with Stochastic tiling enabled

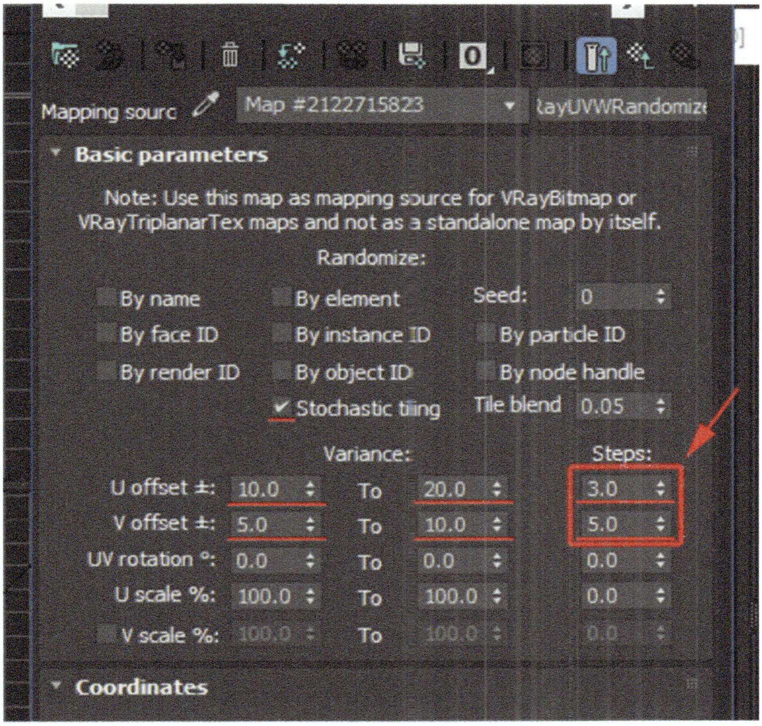
Mapping sourc
Map #2122715823
RayUVWRandomize
Basic parameters
Note: Use this map as mapping source for VRayBitmap or VRayTriplanarTex maps and not as a standalone map by itself.
Randomize:
By name
By element
Seed:
0
By face ID
By instance ID
By particle ID
By render ID
By object ID
By node handle
Stochastic tiling
Tile blend
0.05
Variance:
Steps:
U offset ±:
10.0
To
20.0
3.0
V offset ±:
5.0
To
10.0
5.0
UV rotation °:
0.0
To
0.0
0.0
U scale %:
100.0
To
100.0
0.0
V scale %:
100.0
To
100.0
0.0
Coordinates

VrayUVWRandomizer with Stochastic and U, V offset

VRayMultiSubTex

NOTE

VRayMultiSubTex colors are *not* visible in the viewport (only in the render).

This unique procedural map allows users to randomize bitmaps and colors, based on material IDs, faces, elements, etc.

VRayMultiSubTex is best used with multiple bitmaps to emulate randomized materials across one surface.

To apply it, simply click on the diffuse toggle and choose the VRayMultiSubTex from the Material/Map Browser dialog, under VRay rollout.

20 Total IDs are loaded by default. However, for the purpose of this exercise, it was set for a Total of 15 IDs instead.

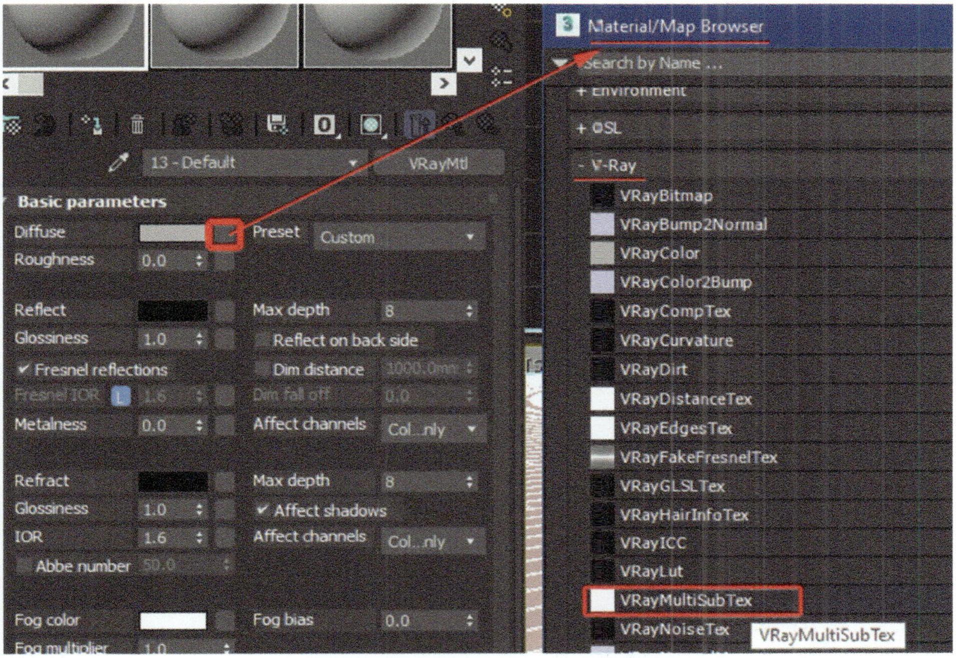
Material/Map Browser
Search by Name ...
+ Environment
+ OSL
- V-Ray
VRayBitmap
VRayBump2Normal
VRayColor
VRayColor2Bump
VRayCompTex
VRayCurvature
VRayDirt
VRayDistanceTex
VRayEdgesTex
VRayFakeFresnelTex
VRayGLSLTex
VRayHairInfoTex
VRayICC
VRayLut
VRayMultiSubTex
VRayNoiseTex
VRayMultiSubTex
13 - Default
VRayMtl
Basic parameters
Diffuse
Preset
Custom
Roughness
0.0
Reflect
Max depth
8
Glossiness
1.0
Reflect on back side
Fresnel reflections
Dim distance
Metalness
0.0
Affect channels
Col..nly
Refract
Max depth
8
Glossiness
1.0
Affect shadows
IOR
1.6
Affect channels
Col..nly
Abbe number
Fog color
Fog bias
0.0

Load VRayMultiSubTex procedural map

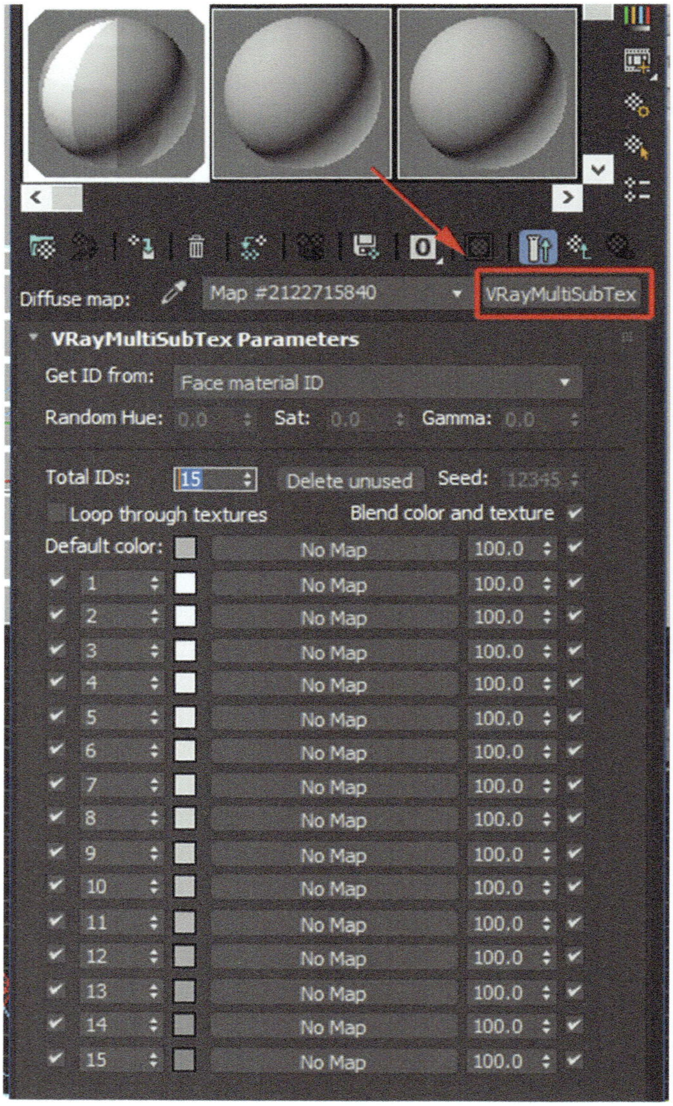

VRayMultiSubTex loaded

To test the functionalities of this procedural map, please open the file under the name VRayMultiSubTex.max

Get ID from: This function determines the type of ID to get from.

It is set to Face material ID by default.

Random by Face material ID is also quite popular to randomly distribute Bitmaps and/or colors across a surface.

To set Face material IDs, simply select a specific object with multiple faces, and add the Editable Poly modifier to it.

Under its Selection rollout, enable the Element type and select one element in the viewport.

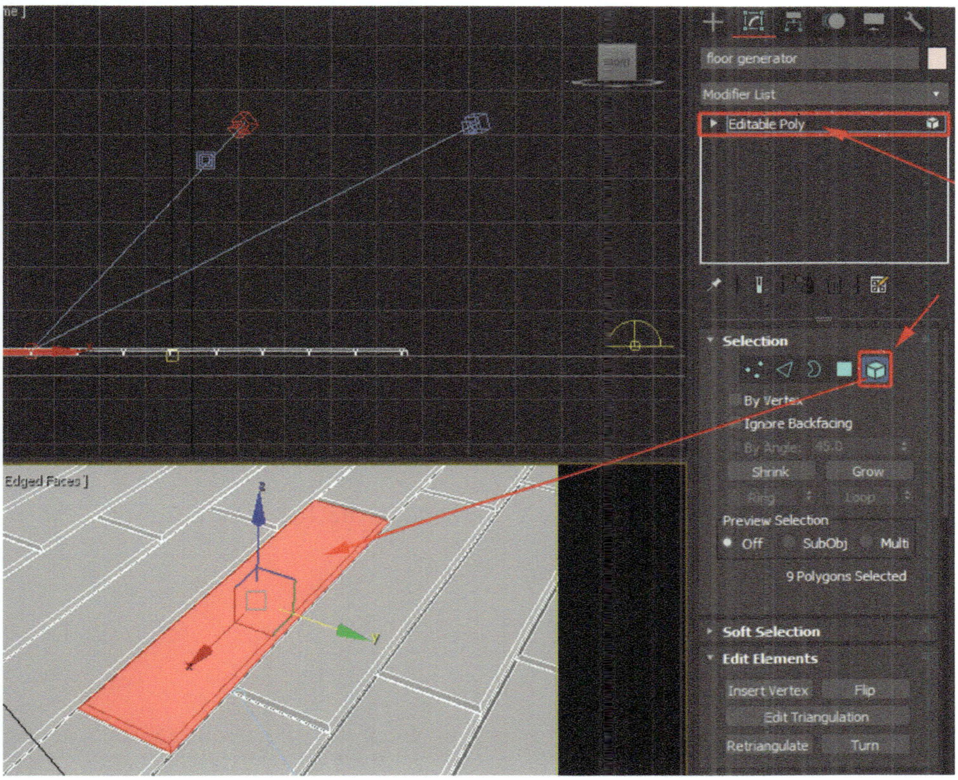

Editable Poly by Element

Users can choose to manually enter a specific material ID number for each selected element, by scrolling down to its Polygon:Material IDs rollout parameters, and typing in any number in the Set ID name field.

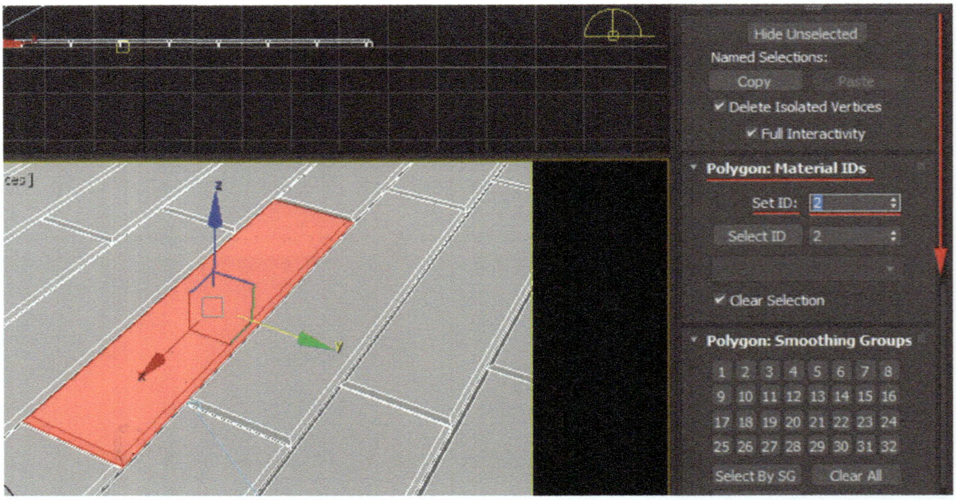

Set element ID numbers manually

Alternatively, simply add the MaterialByElement modifier to automatically add ID numbers to each separate element randomly.

Users can also set the total count of ID numbers on the entire surface by entering a number in the ID Count.

This ID count number should always match with the Total IDs number in the VRayMultiSubTex.

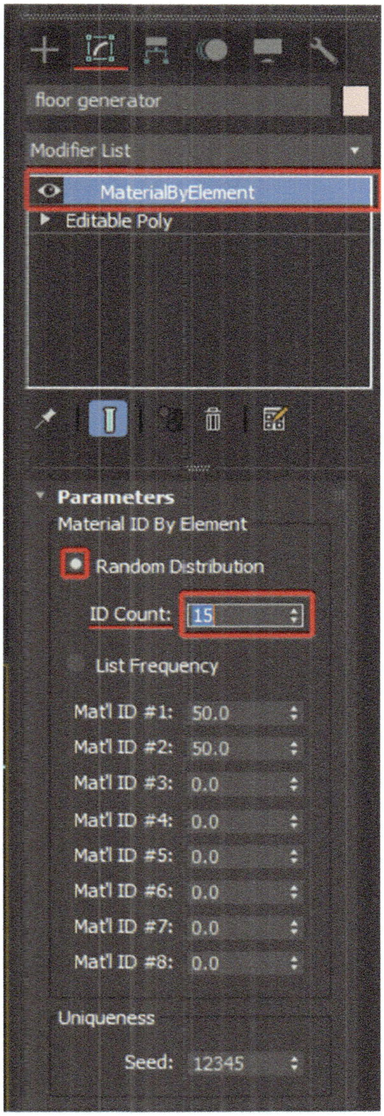

Add MaterialByElement modifier

To check which ID numbers were randomly assigned to each element, simply add another Editable Poly modifier on top of the MaterialByElement, and select each element to see the ID numbers randomly assigned (between 1 and 15).

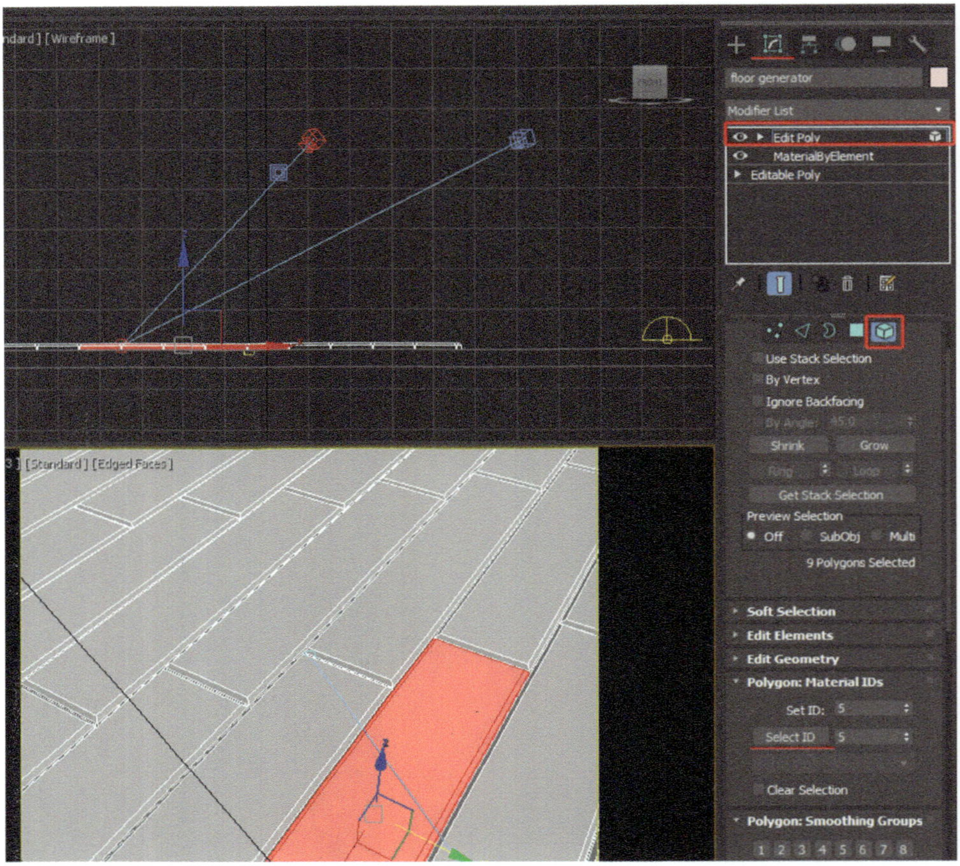

Editable Poly added on top of MaterialByElement

These ID numbers work in conjunction with the ID numbers displayed in the VRayMultiSubTex.

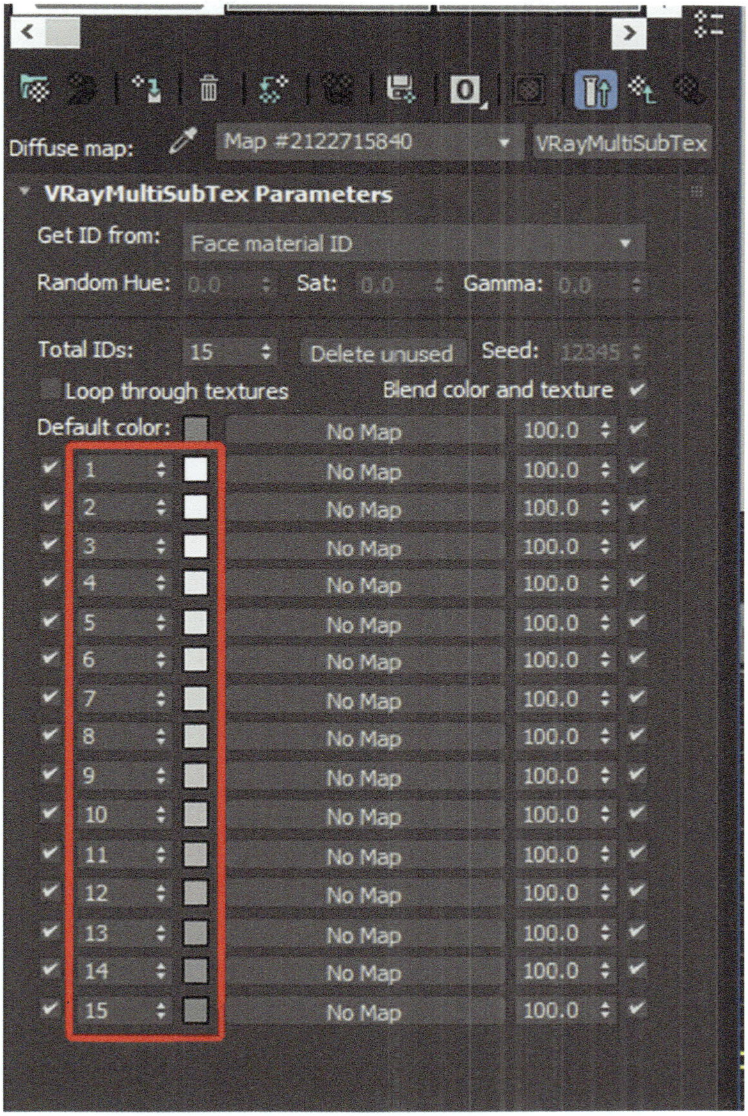

Material ID numbers from colors

Or the bitmap/procedural map ID number being used in the toggle (if any).

To choose a material ID number, simply click and hold.

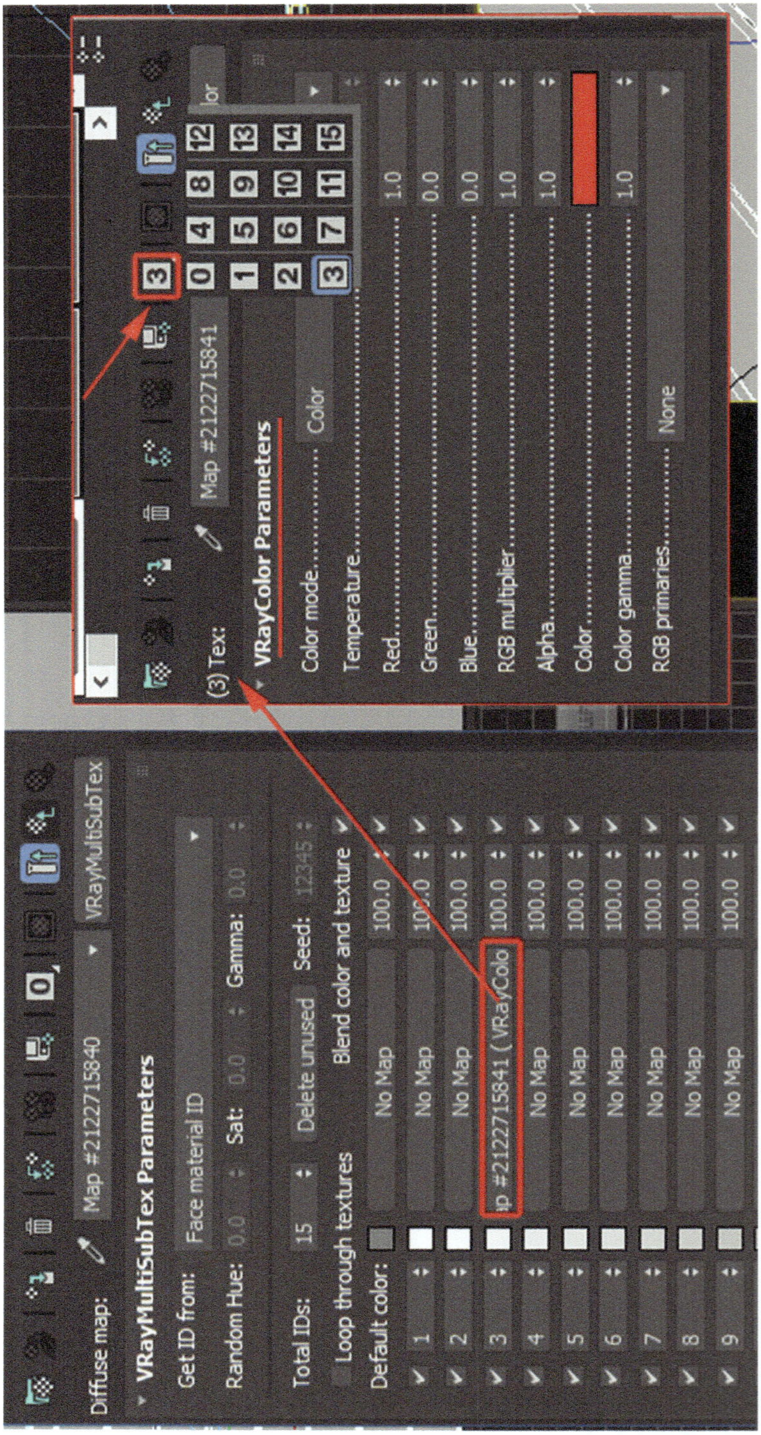
Diffuse map:
Map #2122715840
VRayMultiSubTex
VRayMultiSubTex Parameters
Get ID from:
Face material ID
Random Hue:
Sat:
Gamma:
Total IDs:
15
Delete unused
Seed:
Loop through textures
Blend color and texture
Default color:
No Map
ap #2122715841 (VRayColo
(3) Tex:
Map #2122715841
VRayColor Parameters
Color mode
Color
Temperature
Red
Green
Blue
RGB multiplier
Alpha
Color gamma
RGB primaries
None

Material ID numbers from Procedural Maps

To assign object IDs, simply select an object in the scene and right click on it. Choose the Object Properties option in the quad menu.

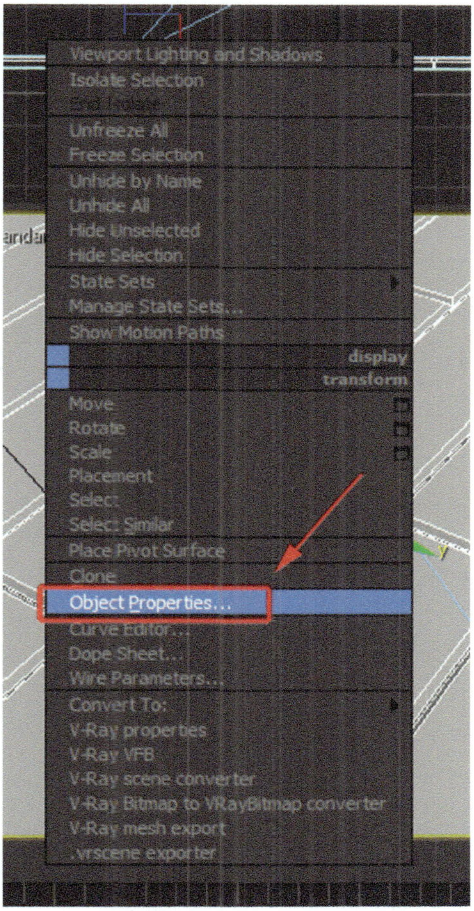

Object Properties in Quad menu

In the General tab, under G-Buffer group, type in a specific number that matches one of the MaterialByElement object ID numbers (if the Object ID option is being used).

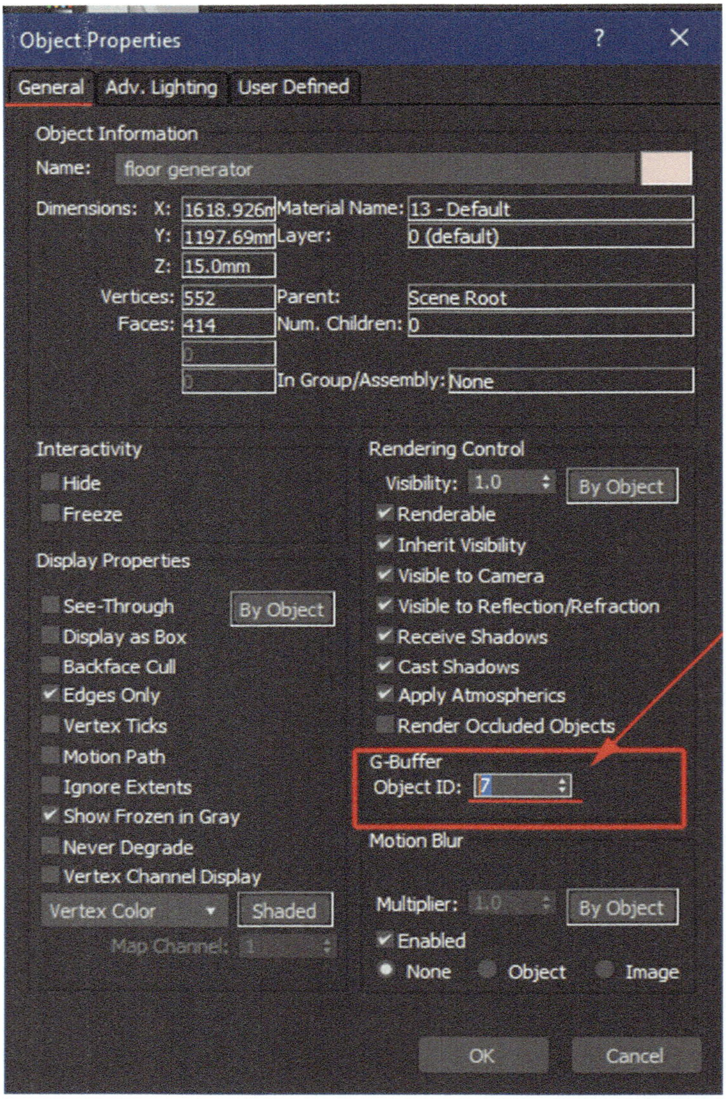

G-Buffer Object ID number

Random Hue: This function only becomes available if any of the Radom ID modes are chosen from the list (Random by Node Handle, Random by Face material ID, Random by Object ID, etc.).

It randomizes the hue colors, procedural maps, and bitmaps being used under Default color list.

Default value is 0.0.

Sat: Only available if any of the Radom ID modes are chosen from the list (Random by Node Handle, Random by Face material ID, Random by Object ID, etc.).

It randomizes the saturation colors, procedural maps, and bitmaps being used under Default color list.

Default value is 0.0.

Gamma: It becomes available if any of the Radom ID modes are chosen from the list (Random by Node Handle, Random by Face material ID, Random by Object ID, etc.).

It randomizes the gamma colors, procedural maps, and bitmaps being used under Default color list.

Default value is 0.0.

Total IDs: This function sets the total number of IDs being used/displayed under the Default color list.

Default value is 20.

Delete unused: When clicked, it deletes disabled slots under the Default color list.

Seed: This function randomizes patterns, if the Random by name option is chosen from the list.

Entering different numbers will yield different pattern results.

Loop through textures: This function is useful when the number of Face material IDs or Object IDs in the scene exceeds the Total IDs number specified in the list.

It automatically applies one of the listed colors or/and textures specified in the list.

Blend color and texture: When enabled, this function automatically blends the current color displayed in the swatch with loaded bitmap/procedural map plugged in the toggle.

The default value of 100 uses 100% of the loaded bitmap/procedural map plugged in the toggle (if any is being used).

Otherwise, no blending will occur with default color swatch only.

The value of 50 uses 50% the loaded bitmap/procedural map plugged in the toggle, and 50% of the color swatch.

NOTE

Different wood board textures from the folder, wood-boards-spruce_0053-01_1460mm-by-20mm, were used in each of the 15 toggles to achieve the final result.

Default color: This is the default base color or/and procedural map whose IDS are not matched. It works mainly with Object ID and Face material ID options.

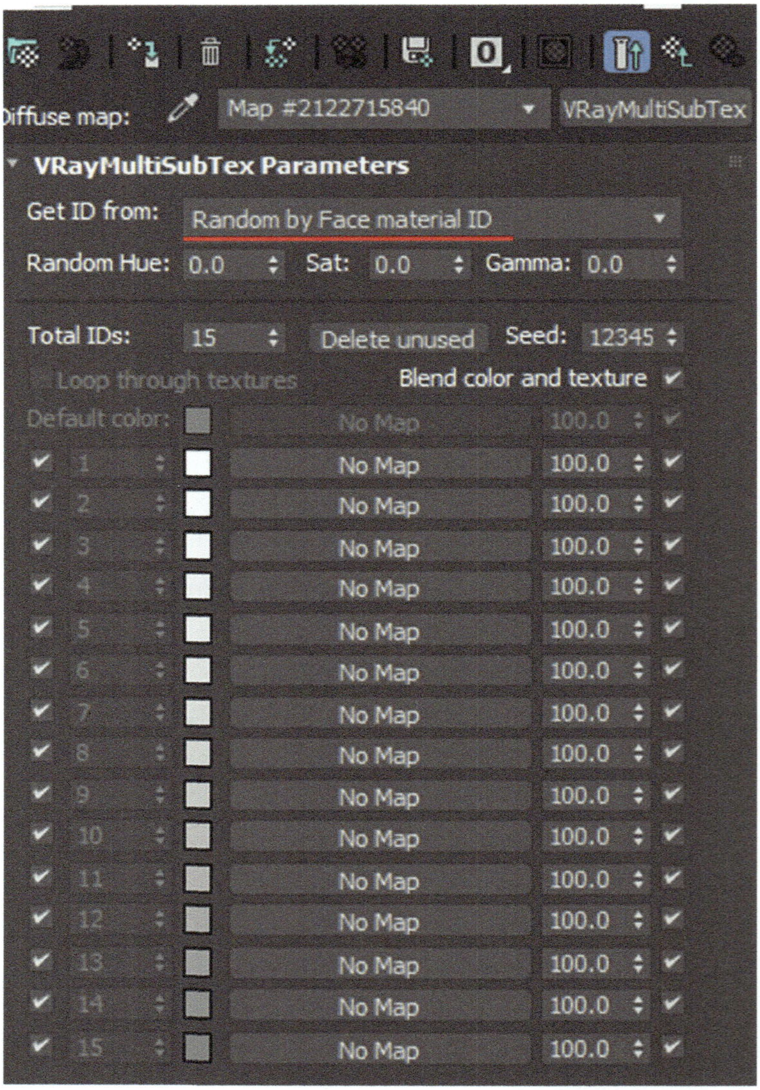

File
Render
Image
View
Options
New version available!
RGB color
[481, 64]
1x1
Raw
0.717
0.745
0.796
HSV
218
0.1
0.8

Random by Face material ID colors only

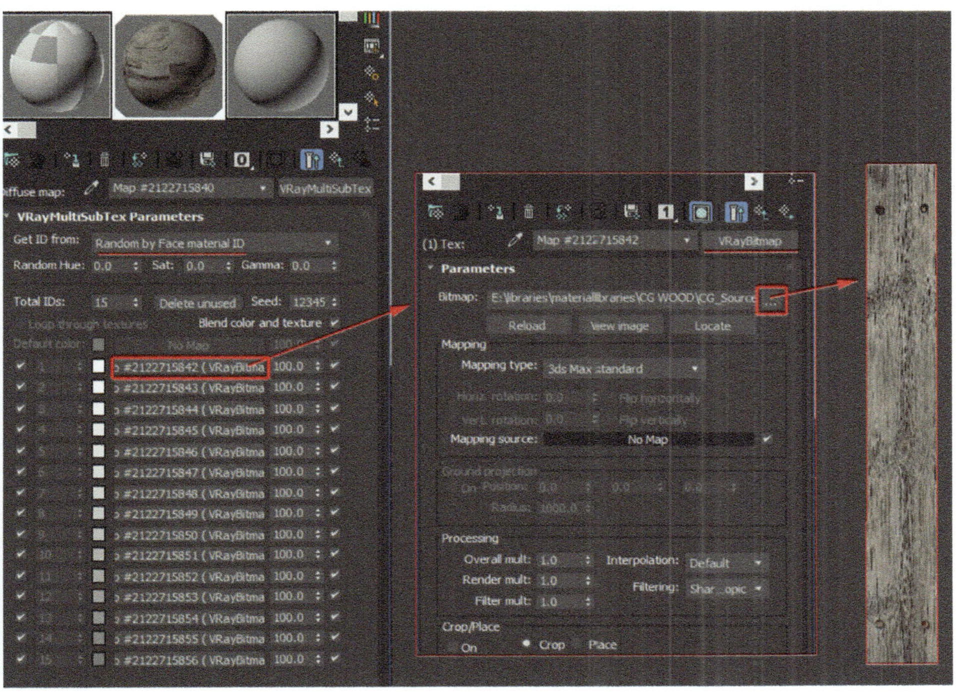
Diffuse map:
Map #2122715840
VRayMultiSubTex
VRayMultiSubTex Parameters
Get ID from:
Random by Face material ID
Random Hue:
Sat:
Gamma:
Total IDs:
Delete unused
Seed:
12345
Blend color and texture
#2122715842 (VRayBitma
(1) Tex:
Map #2122715842
VRayBitmap
Parameters
Bitmap:
Reload
View image
Locate
Mapping
Mapping type:
3ds Max standard
Mapping source:
No Map
Processing
Overall mult:
Interpolation:
Default
Render mult:
Filtering:
Filter mult:
Crop/Place
Crop
Place

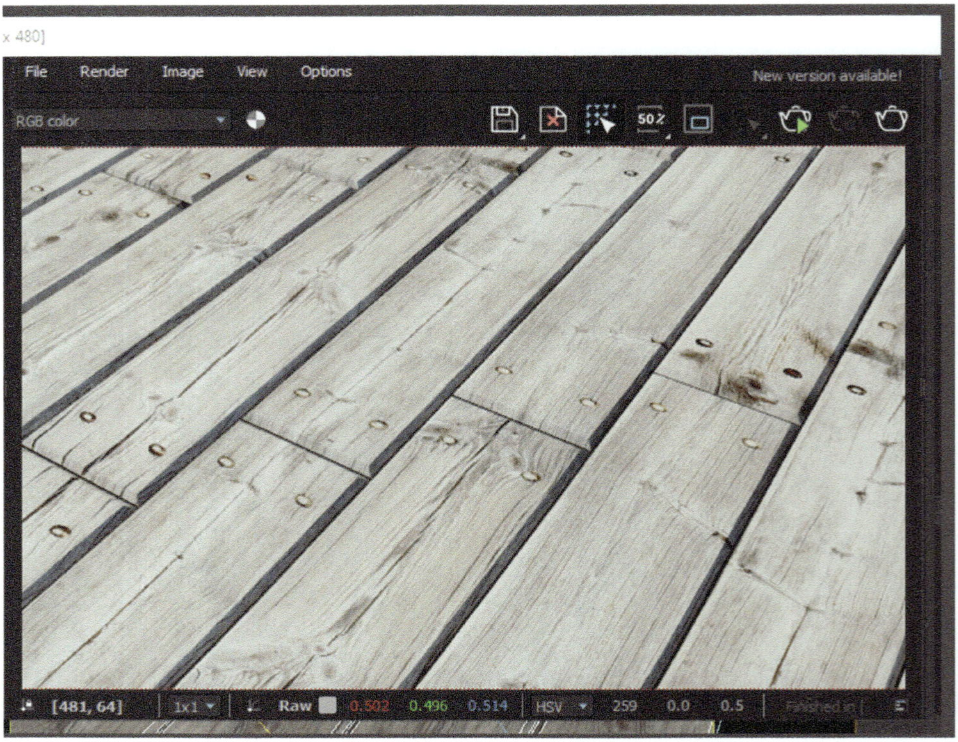
x 480]
File
Render
Image
View
Options
New version available!
RGB color
50%
[481, 64]
1x1
Raw
0.502
0.496
0.514
HSV
259
0.0
0.5

Random by Face material ID Bitmaps

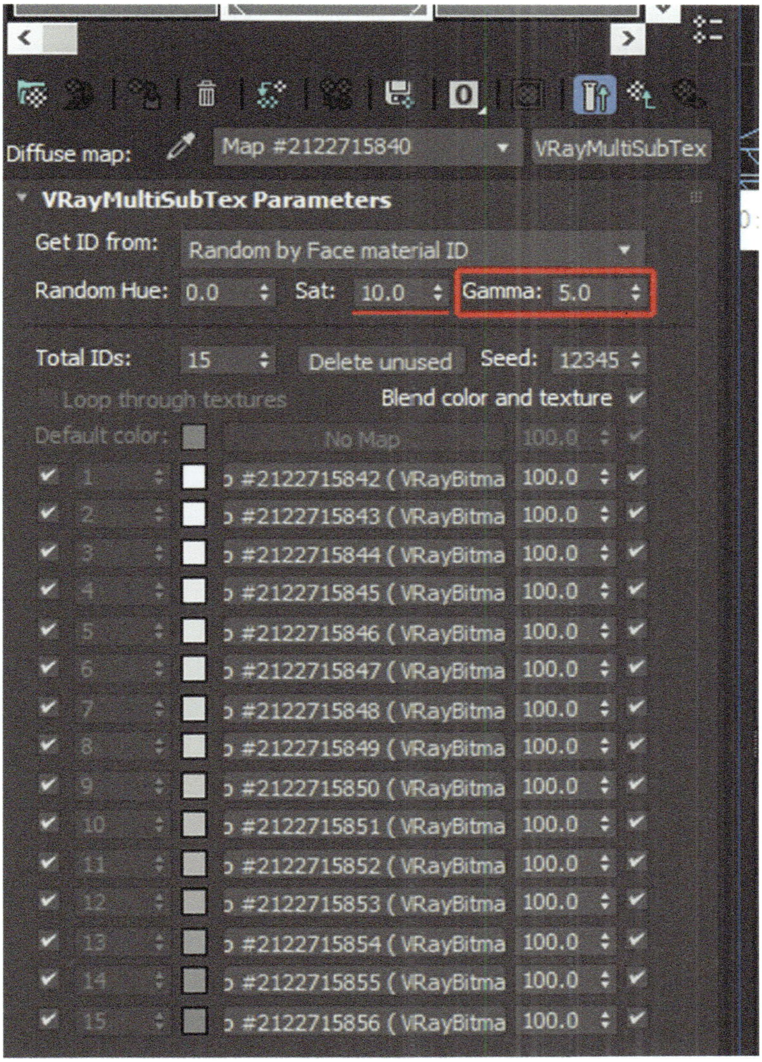
Diffuse map:
Map #2122715840
VRayMultiSubTex
VRayMultiSubTex Parameters
Get ID from:
Random by Face material ID
Random Hue: 0.0
Sat: 10.0
Gamma: 5.0
Total IDs: 15
Delete unused
Seed: 12345
Loop through textures
Blend color and texture
Default color:
No Map
100.0
1
#2122715842 (VRayBitma
100.0
2
#2122715843 (VRayBitma
100.0
3
#2122715844 (VRayBitma
100.0
4
#2122715845 (VRayBitma
100.0
5
#2122715846 (VRayBitma
100.0
6
#2122715847 (VRayBitma
100.0
7
#2122715848 (VRayBitma
100.0
8
#2122715849 (VRayBitma
100.0
9
#2122715850 (VRayBitma
100.0
10
#2122715851 (VRayBitma
100.0
11
#2122715852 (VRayBitma
100.0
12
#2122715853 (VRayBitma
100.0
13
#2122715854 (VRayBitma
100.0
14
#2122715855 (VRayBitma
100.0
15
#2122715856 (VRayBitma
100.0

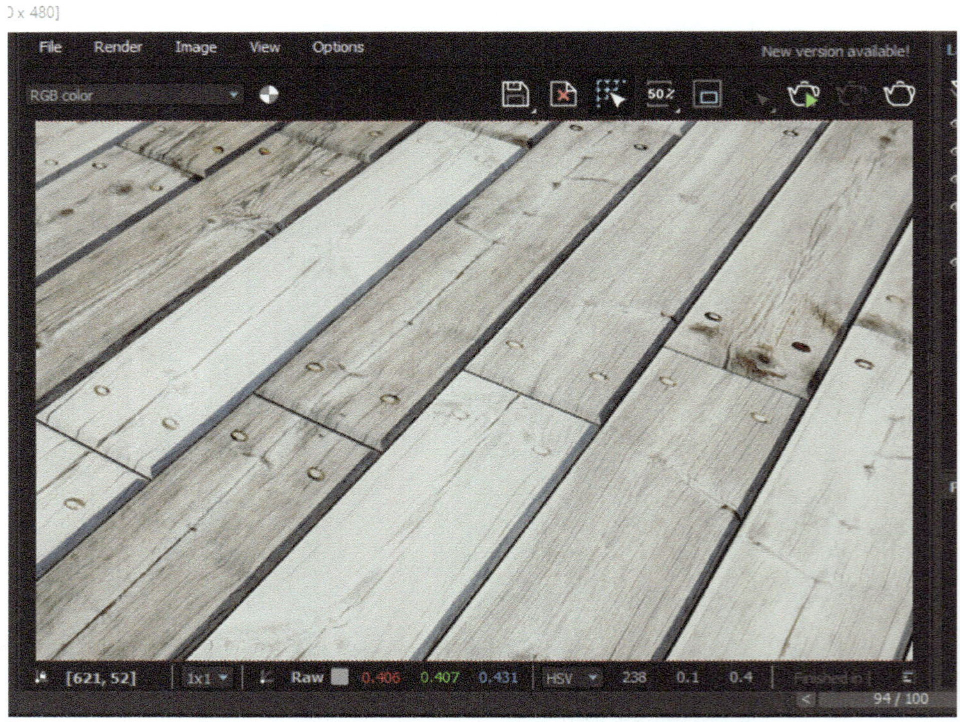

Random Gamma set to 5.0 and Saturation set to 10.0

VRayTriplanarTex

VRayTriplanarTex procedural map is extremely useful to apply on objects without the appropriate UVW map.

It works by projecting one or more bitmaps along the axis of a surface.

To apply it, simply click on an existing VRayBitmap already being used.

In the material/Map Browser, choose the VRayTriplanarTex procedural map from the list.

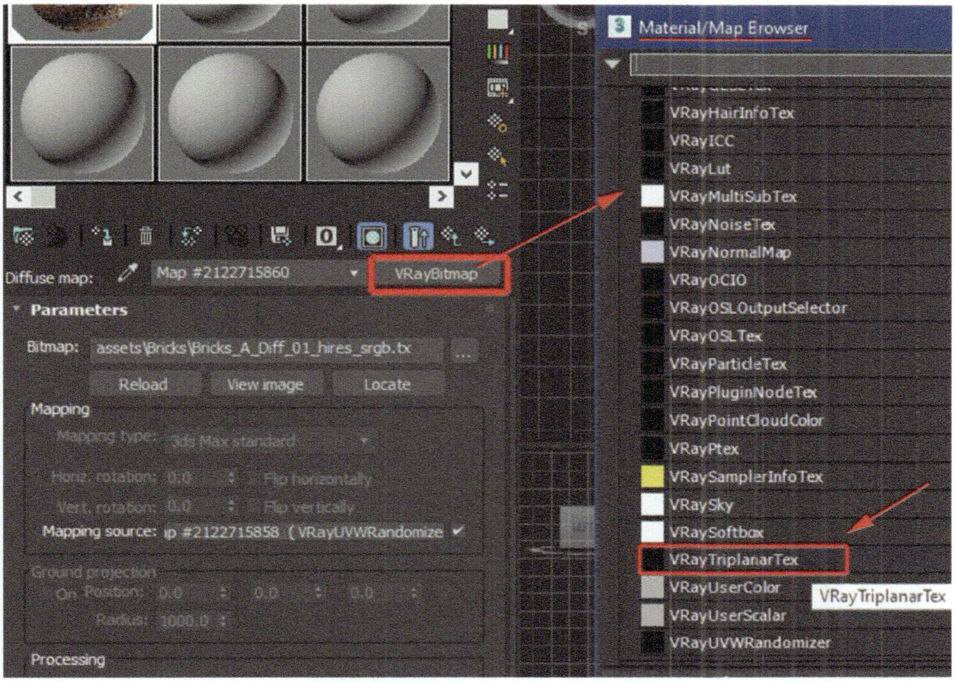

Choose the VRayTriplanarTex

Keep old map as sub-map

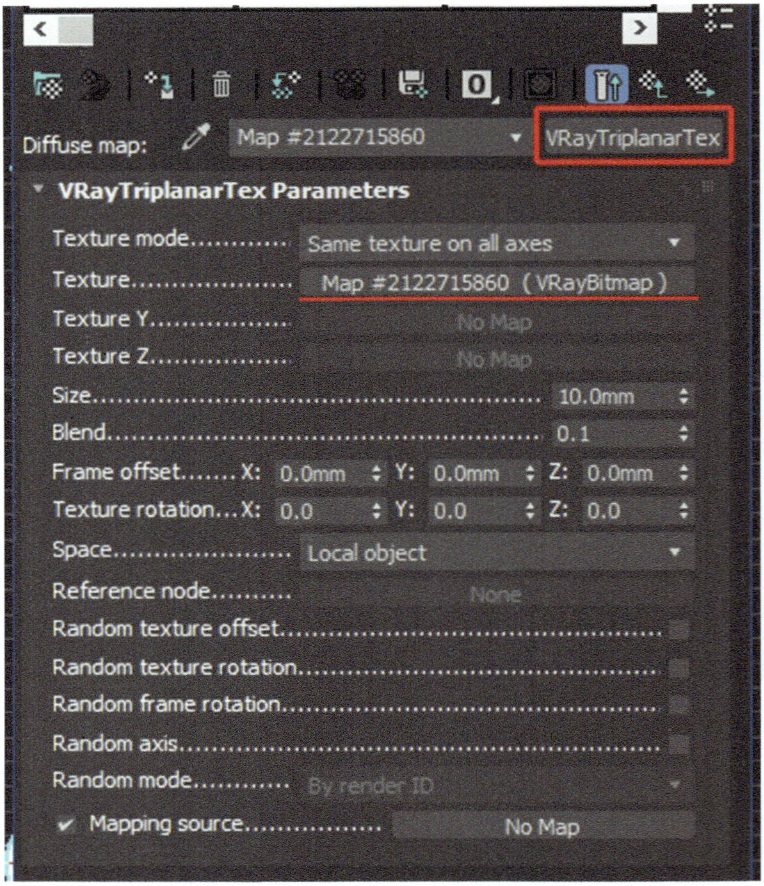

VRayTriplanarTex loaded

However, if other toggles are also being used (for reflections, bump, etc.), this procedural map needs to be applied to them also (with the same parameter values).

NOTE

Currently, VRayTriplanarTex procedural map is being used in the diffuse toggle.

Texture mode: This function controls how the textures will be projected.

The option to use, Same texture on all axis, projects one texture (bitmap) on all axis of a surface.

The option to use, different texture on each axis, projects different textures on each axis.

Texture: This toggle allows users to load textures and/or procedural maps.

Texture Y: This toggle only becomes available if the Texture mode is set to Different texture on each axis.

It allows users to load textures and/or procedural maps on Y-axis.

Texture Z: This toggle only becomes available if the Texture mode is set to Different texture on each axis.

It allows users to load textures and/or procedural maps on Z-axis.

Size: This function controls the size of the texture. Higher values tile the texture further.

Blend: This function is only useful when the Texture mode is set to Different texture on each axis.

It allows users to set the amount of blend/blur between texture borders.

Frame offset: This function allows users to move the texture in X-, Y-, and Z-axes.

Texture rotation: The function controls the rotation of textures.

Space: This function determines the projection space of the texture.

It's set to local object by default.

Users can also set the space type to Reference to another node, and select a specific object in the scene. The selected object is often moved and/or rotated to see major changes the Material editor dialog.

The world space is used by default.

Frame offset values are more apparent in the render.

Random: texture offset, rotation, frame rotation, axis, mode.

When enabled, this function randomly applies values to the parameters discussed earlier.

Mapping source: This function's toggle allows users to plug the VRayUVWRandomizer to it.

NOTE

These values are more noticeable when separate objects in the scene have the same VRayTriplanarTex applied (e.g., group of objects or different objects attached).

NOTE

These values are more noticeable when separate objects in the scene have the same VRayTriplanarTex applied (e.g., group of objects or different objects attached).

NOTE

When the Texture mode is set to Different texture on each axis, the Size values need to be increased considerably in order for textures to be visible in the render.

NOTE

These values are more noticeable when separate objects in the scene have the same VRayTriplanarTex applied (e.g., group of objects or different objects attached).

NOTE

This function is more noticeable when separate objects have the same VRayTriplanarTex applied (e.g., group of objects or different objects attached).

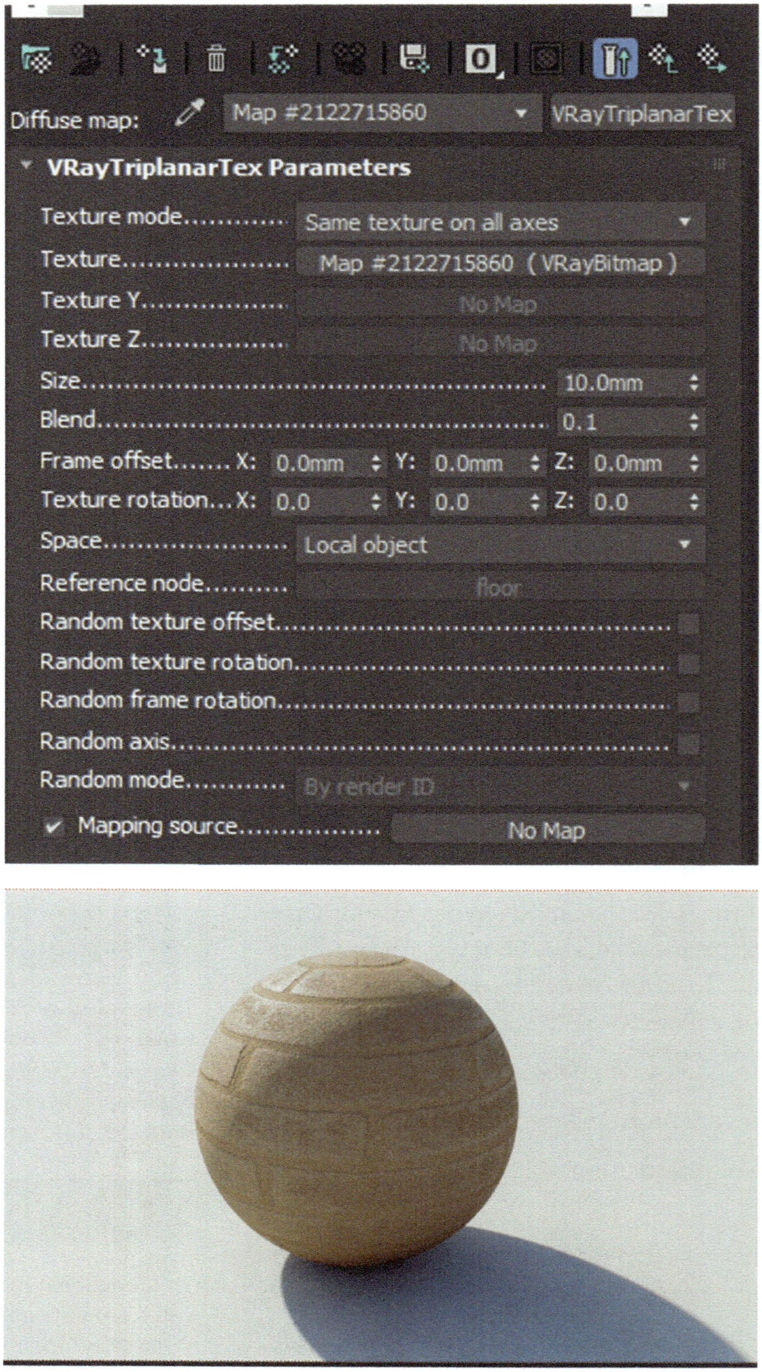

Size set to 10 mm

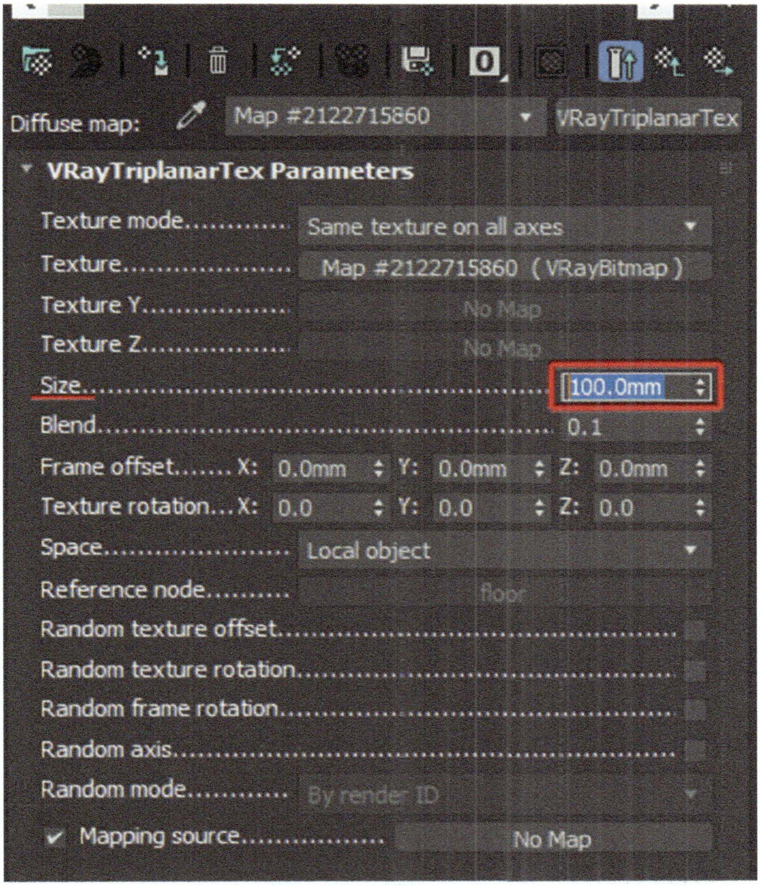

Size set to 100 mm

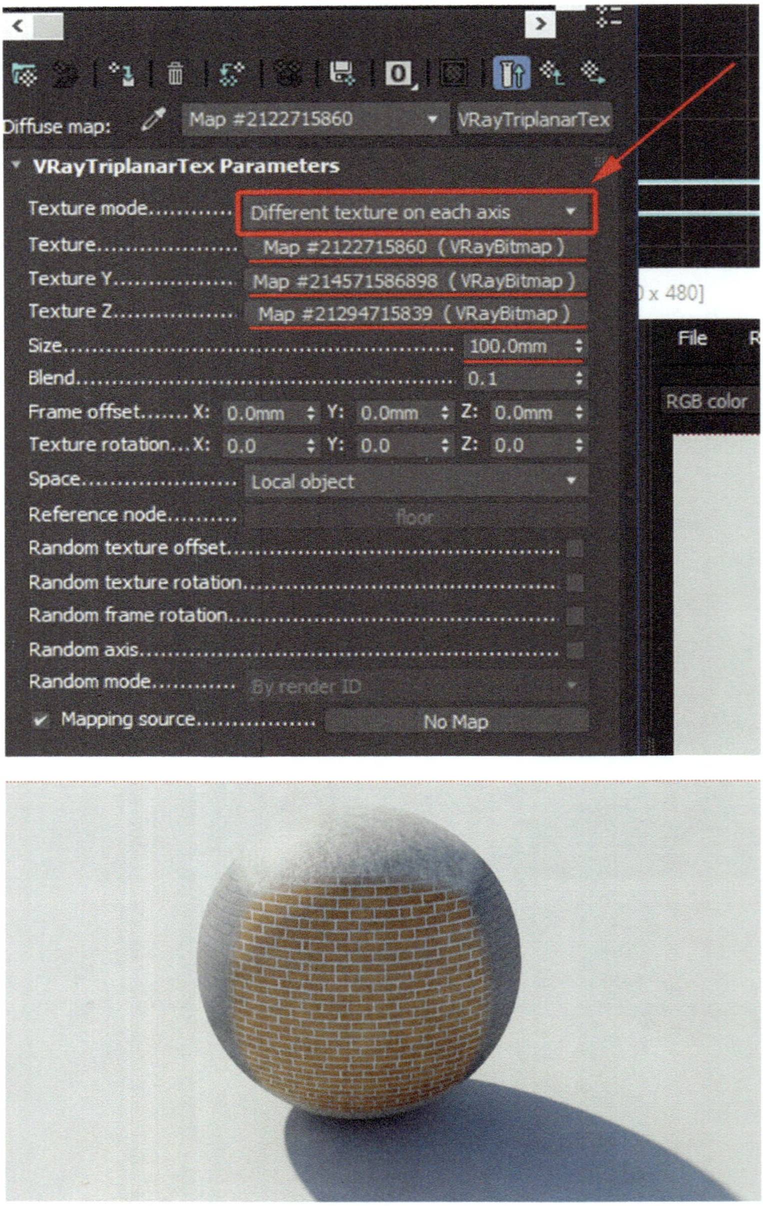

Different texture on each axis

To achieve similar results, simply use multiple materials/textures of your choice.

NOTE

A variety of different materials from VRay Asset Browser were used to achieve this result.

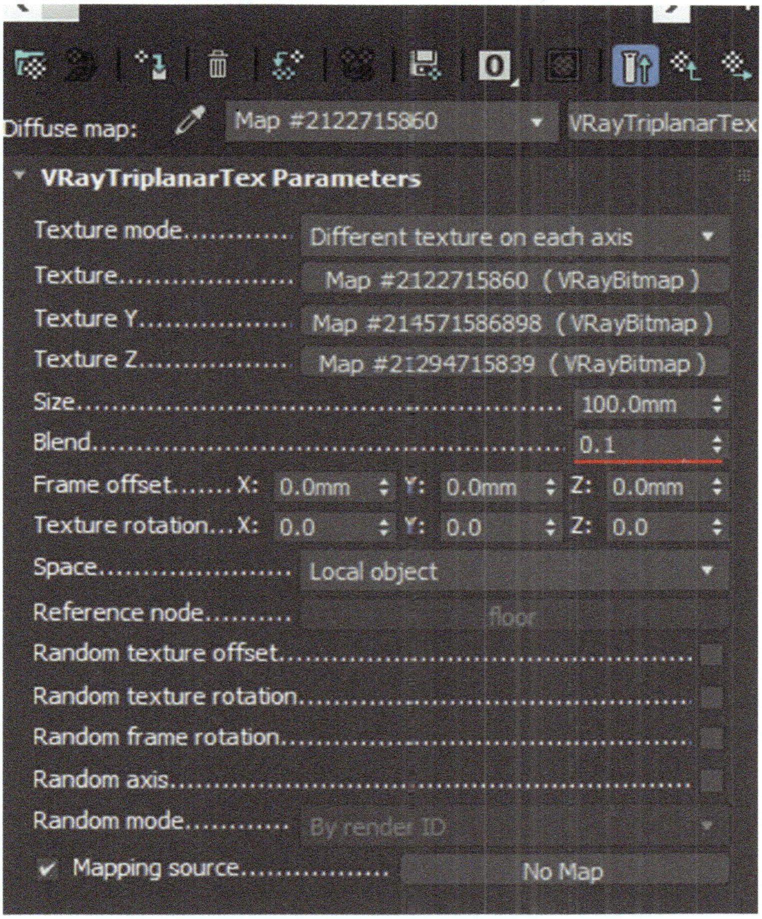

Blend value set to 0.1

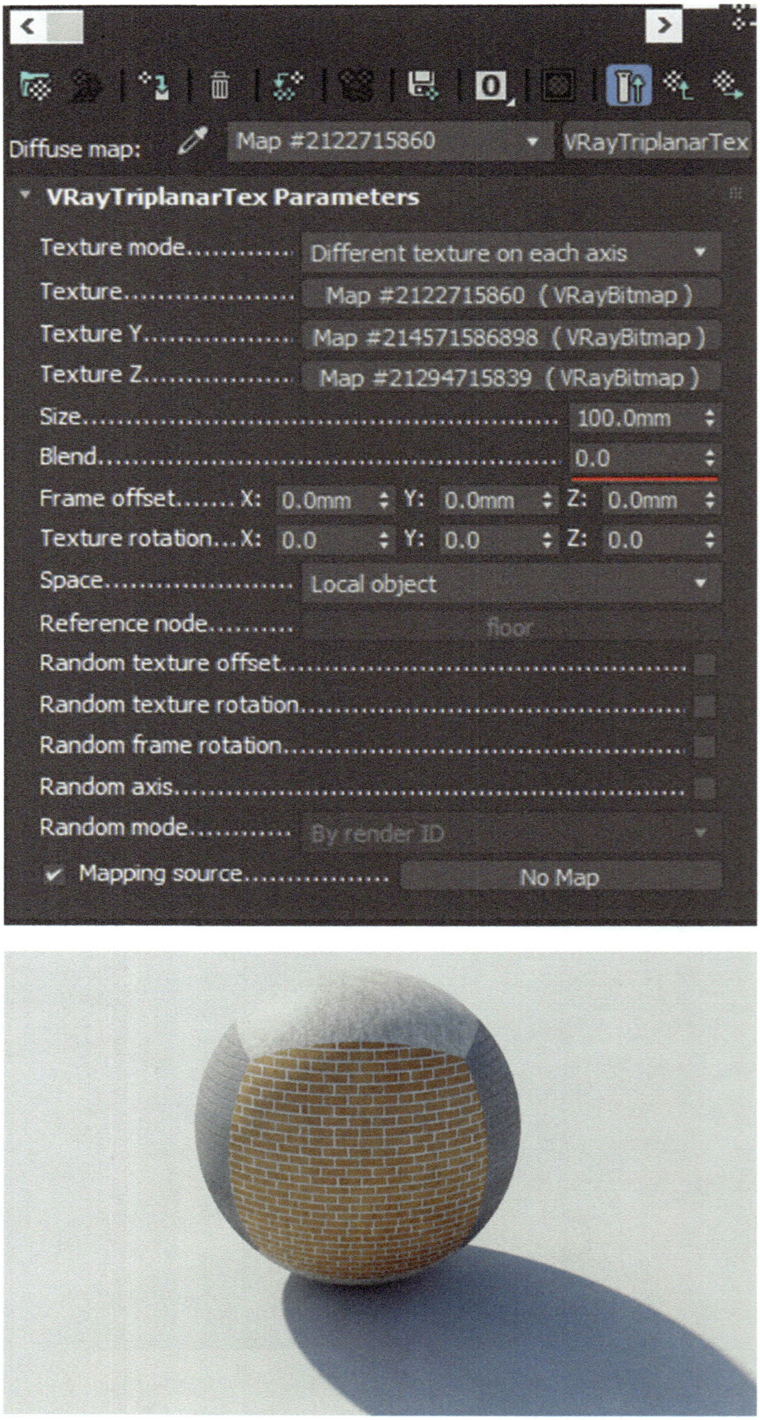

Blend value set to 0.0

In the best-case scenario, only one of the angled faces will display a different material.

To correct this problem (bug), go to the Editable Poly or Mesh modifier, and specify the Face ID numbers.

Use some of the steps shown previously.

Hold down the Ctrl key to select multiple faces, if required.

Do not use the MaterialByElement modifier.

Back in the Material Editor dialog (M), click on the Diffuse toggle and choose the VRayMultiSubTex procedural map.

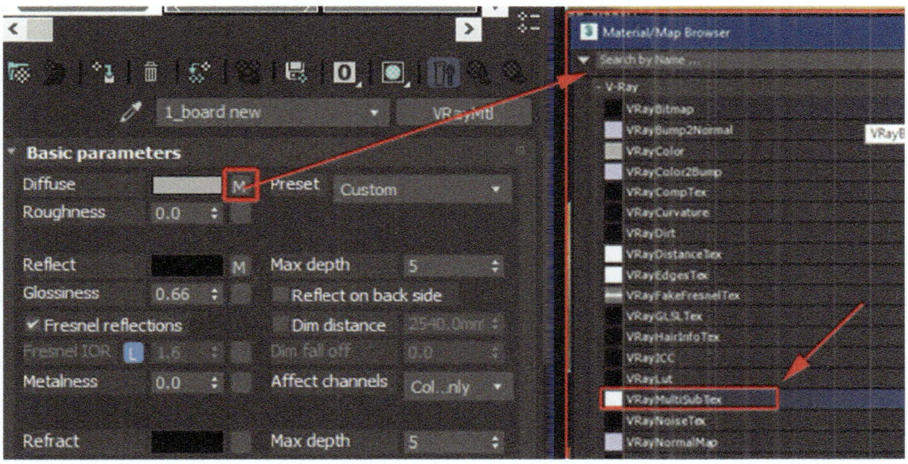

Apply the VRayMultiSubTex

In the VRayMultiSubTex parameters, set the Get ID from Face material ID. This will recognize the ID faces previously numbered accordingly.

Under Total IDs, set the total number of IDs you want.

In the Default color toggle, apply the VRayColor2Bump to add detail to the surface.

Set its material ID number to coincide with the face number previously set. And add the VRayTriplanarTex procedural map, as previously shown.

Under VRayTriplanar Parameters, set the Texture mode as Different texture on each axis.

Copy the same texture or a different one into X, Y, and Z toggles.

Set its size. And set the space as Local object.

Also, set its Material ID number to coincide with the face number previously set.

NOTE

Objects with angled faces will yield undesirable results.

Repeat the same steps for the remaining Total IDS listed in the VRayMultiSubTex Parameters. Use different ID numbers, and set the Frame offset in X with deferent values.

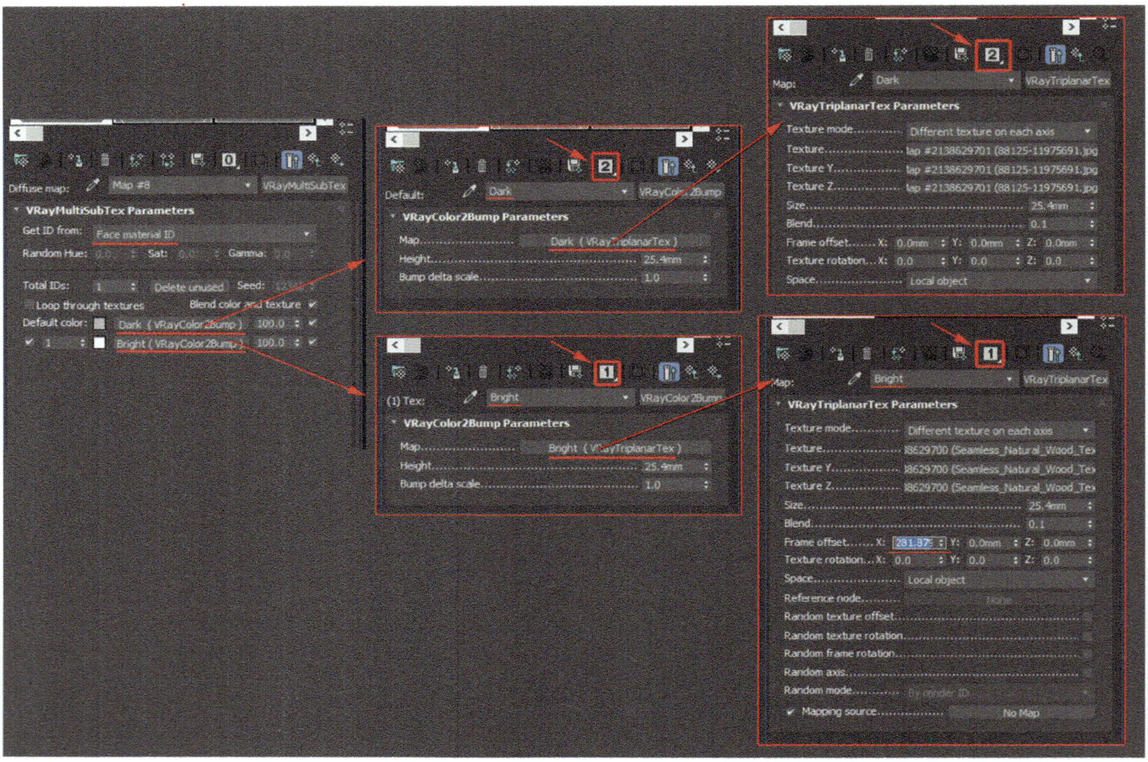

Apply the VRayTriplanarTex

VRayPointCloudColor

NOTE

This procedural map is only available via the Diffuse toggle.

VRayPointCloudColor procedural map allows users to accurately render point cloud objects in 3ds max without the renders having to look self-illuminated.

To use a specific bitmap, apply the VRayBitmap procedural map first, and load the VRayPointCloudColor via the Mapping source toggle.

VRayPointCloudColor doesn't have any parameters.

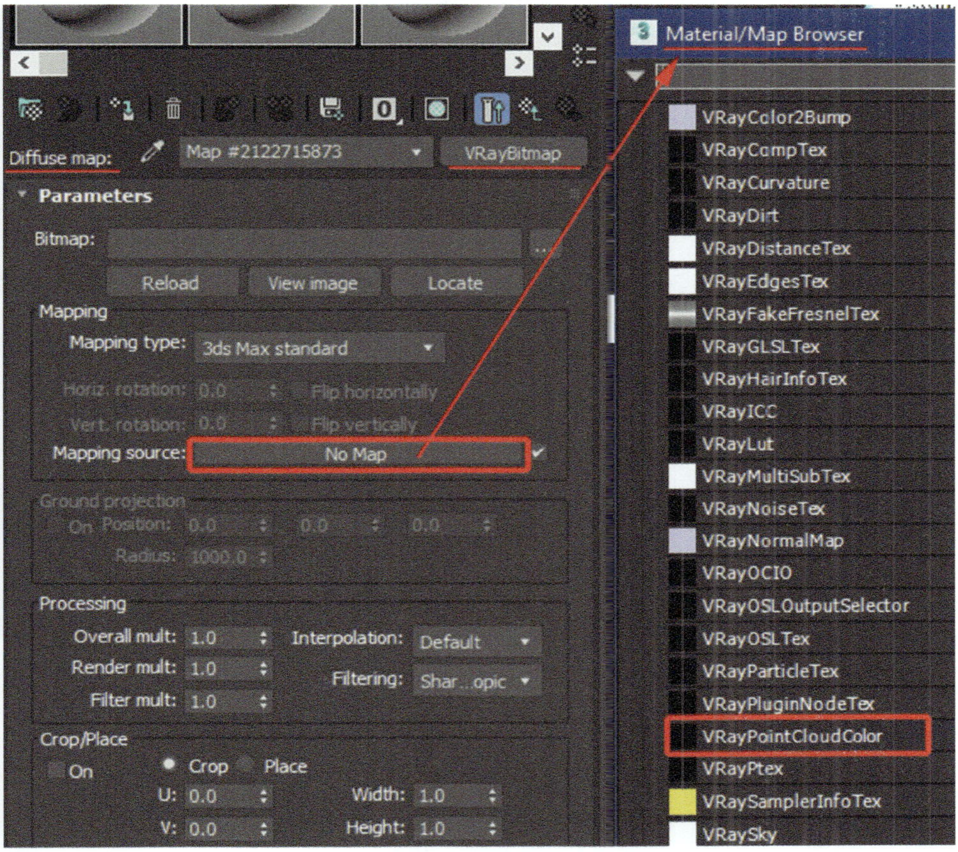

Load VRayPointCloudColor via Mapping source

VRayDirt

This amazing procedural map allows users to emulate dirt or ambient occlusion effects around the crevices of objects.

Users can apply VRayDirt directly to the Diffuse toggle of a material.

Or Via the Render Elements (VRayExtraTex>VRayDirt).

Either way, VRayDirt increases the rendering times slightly.

To apply it via the Diffuse toggle of a material, simply click on the existing VRayBitamp or Bitmap, and choose VRayDirt from the Material Map/Browser dialog.

NOTE

VRayDirt is less apparent on spherical surfaces.

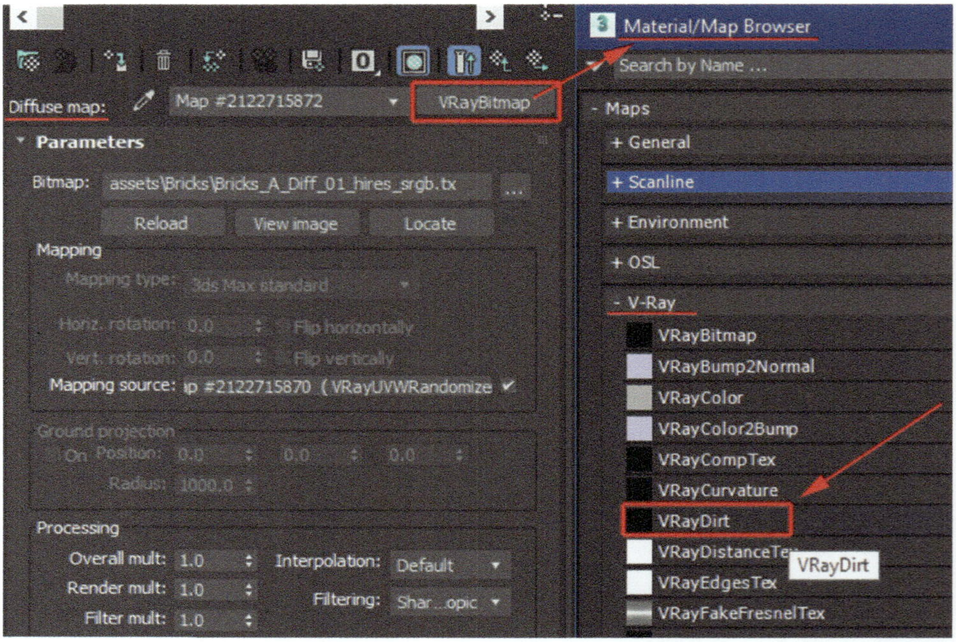
Material/Map Browser
Search by Name ...
Diffuse map:
Map #2122715872
VRayBitmap
Parameters
Bitmap: assets\Bricks\Bricks_A_Diff_01_hires_srgb.tx
Reload
View image
Locate
Mapping
Mapping type: 3ds Max standard
Horiz. rotation: 0.0
Flip horizontally
Vert. rotation: 0.0
Flip vertically
Mapping source: ap #2122715870 (VRayUVWRandomize
Ground projection
On Position: 0.0 0.0 0.0
Radius: 1000.0
Processing
Overall mult: 1.0
Render mult: 1.0
Filter mult: 1.0
Interpolation: Default
Filtering: Shar...opic
- Maps
+ General
+ Scanline
+ Environment
+ OSL
- V-Ray
VRayBitmap
VRayBump2Normal
VRayColor
VRayColor2Bump
VRayCompTex
VRayCurvature
VRayDirt
VRayEdgesTex
VRayFakeFresnelTex

Load VRayDirt

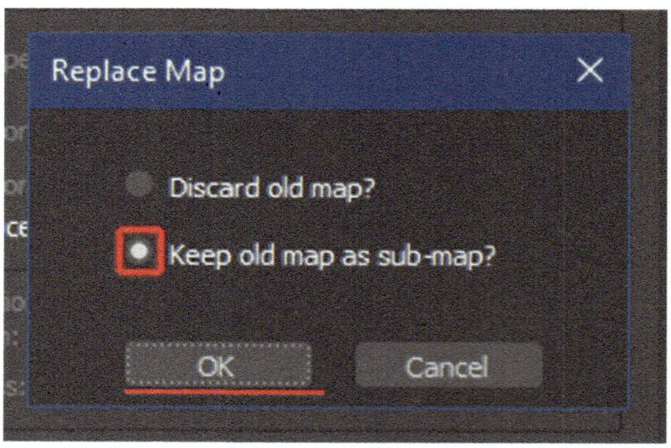
Replace Map
Discard old map?
Keep old map as sub-map?
OK
Cancel

Keep old map as sub-map

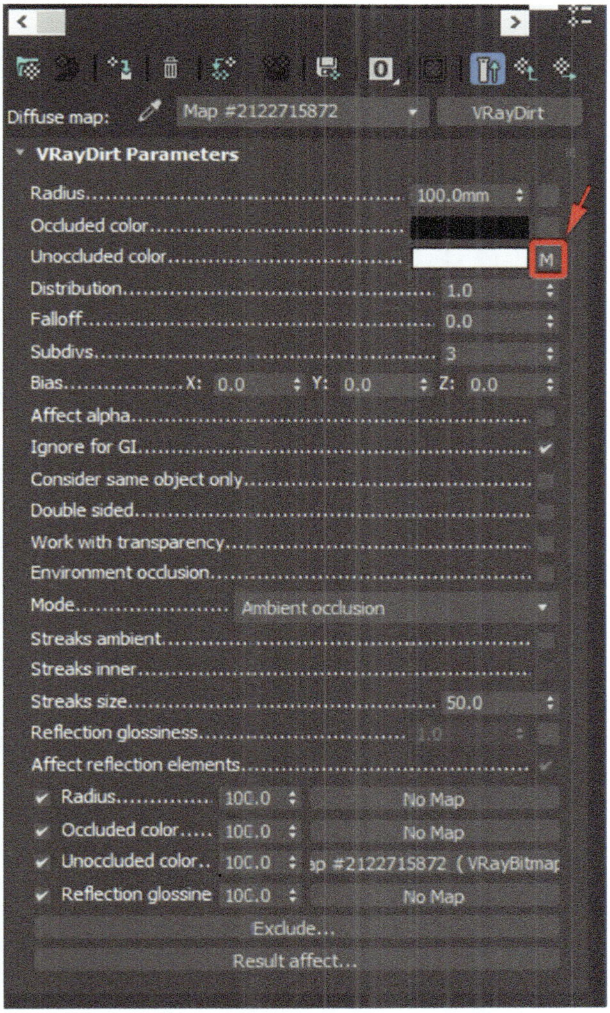

VRayDirt loaded

To apply VRayDirt via render element, simply go to the Render Setup dialog, and open the Render Element Tab.

Under Render Elements group, click to Add, and choose the VRayExtraTex procedural map from its dialog.

Once loaded, click on its Texture toggle and load the VRayDirt from the Material/Map Browser dialog.

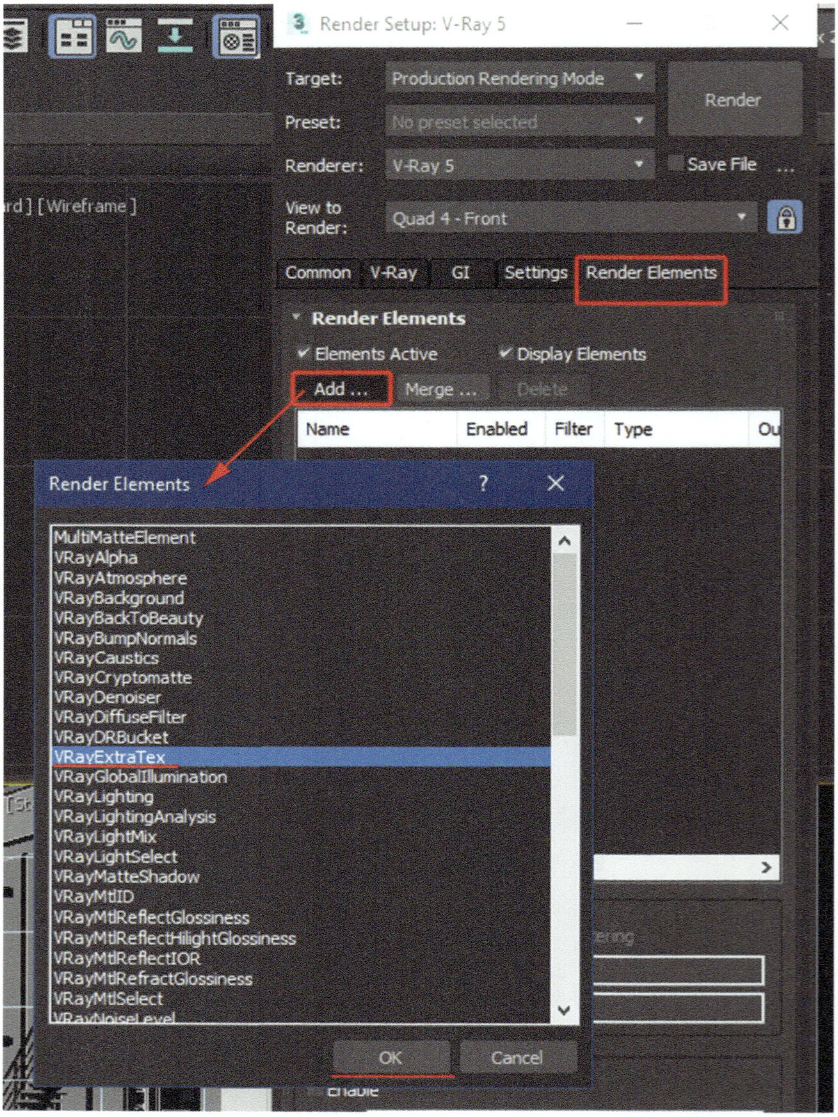

Add VRayExtraTex Render Element

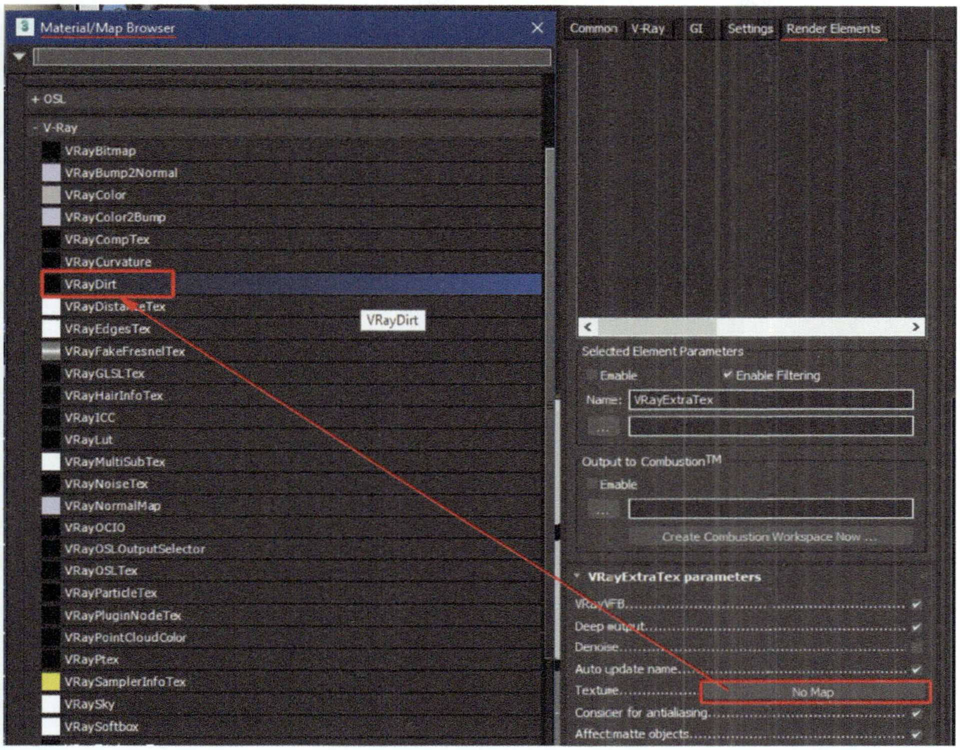

Add VRayDirt

To edit its parameters, drag the VRayDirt from VrayExtraTex toggle onto an empty material slot.

Choose the Instance Method.

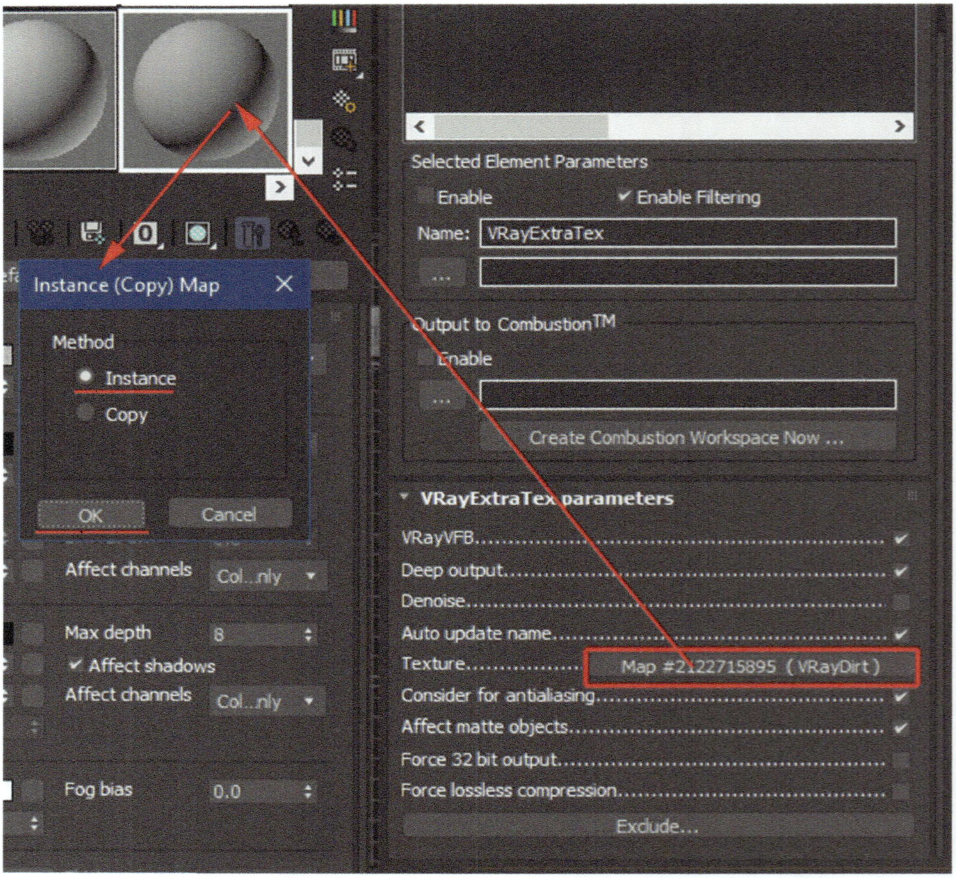
Selected Element Parameters
Enable
Enable Filtering
Name:
VRayExtraTex
Output to CombustionTM
Enable
Create Combustion Workspace Now ...
Instance (Copy) Map
Method
Instance
Copy
OK
Cancel
Affect channels
Col...nly
Max depth
8
Affect shadows
Affect channels
Col...nly
Fog bias
0.0
VRayExtraTex parameters
VRayVFB
Deep output
Denoise
Auto update name
Texture
Map #2122715895 (VRayDirt)
Consider for antialiasing
Affect matte objects
Force 32 bit output
Force lossless compression
Exclude...

Drag and drop the VRayDirt onto material slot

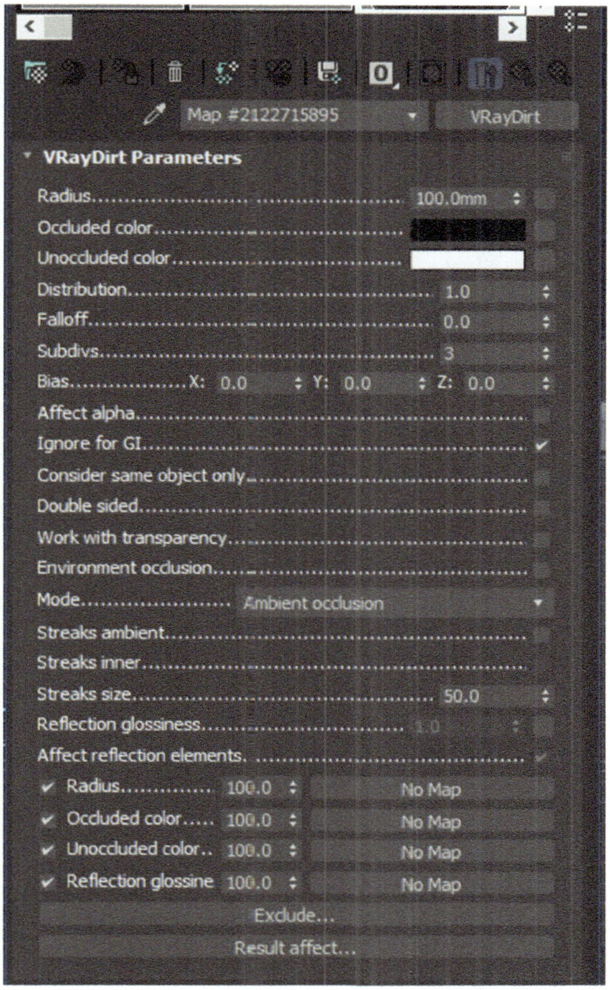

VRayDirt loaded

It's quicker to preview and adjust the VRayDirt parameters as a material override (under VRay global switches) tab.

Once satisfied with the results, you can copy/paste the final parameters onto the diffuse toggle, and disable the override.

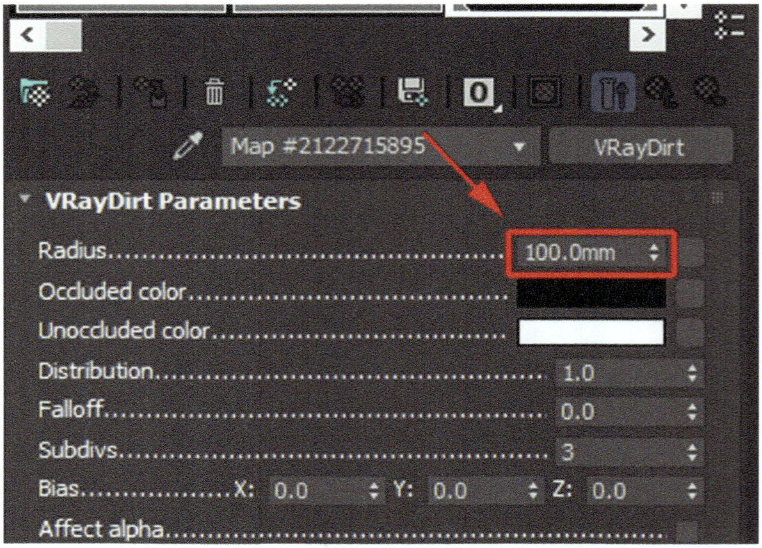

VRayDirt Radius set to 100 mm

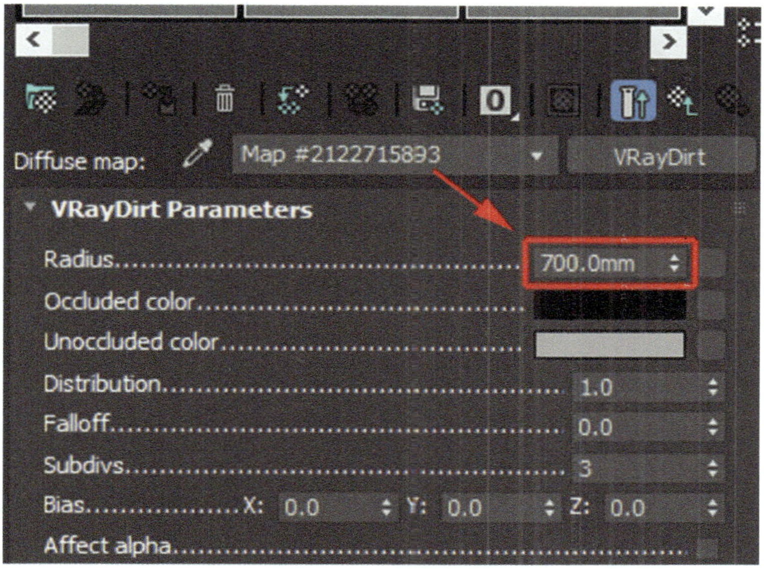

VRayDirt Radius set to 700 mm

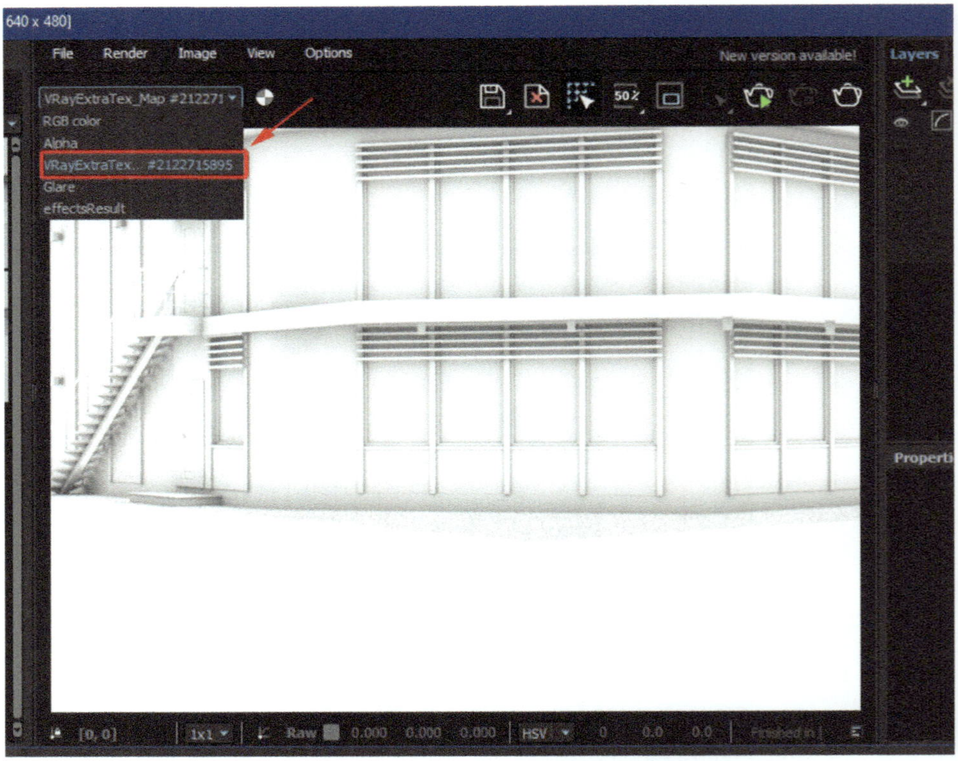

VRayDirt Radius set to 700 mm in Render Elements

It's common practice for users to focus mainly on the Z-axis to create streaks in a vertical direction.

NOTE

Enabling the Streaks ambient function will *not* yield streaks. One of the Bias axes needs to have a value applied (e.g., 30).

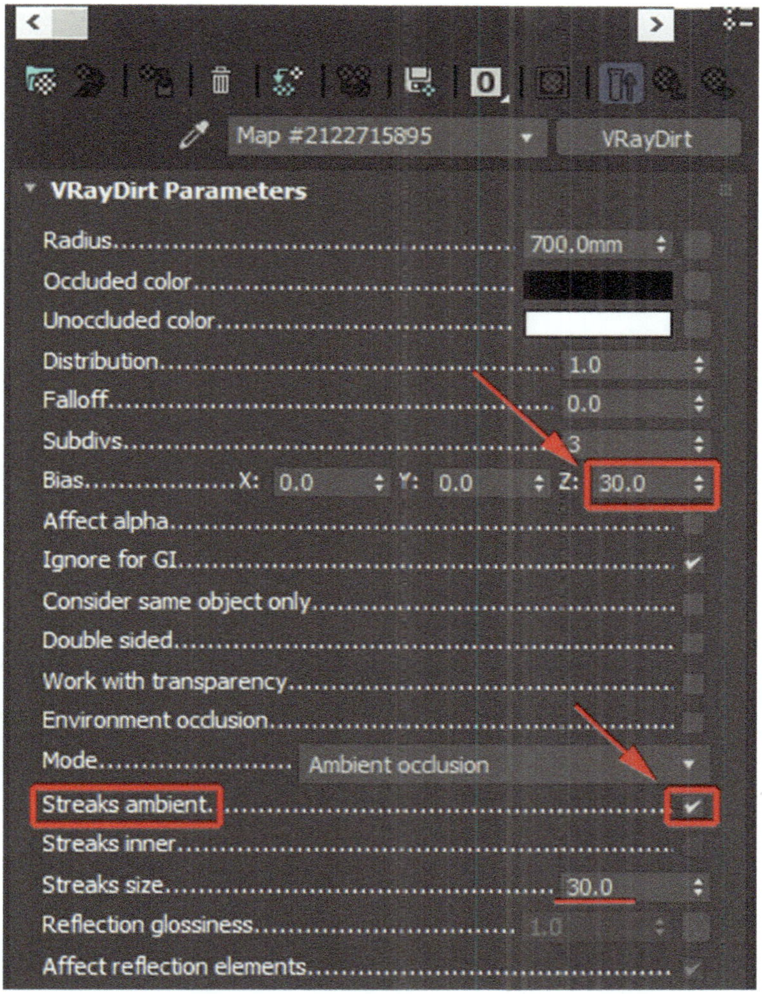
Map #2122715895
VRayDirt
VRayDirt Parameters
Radius
700.0mm
Occluded color
Unoccluded color
Distribution
1.0
Falloff
0.0
Subdivs
3
Bias
X: 0.0
Y: 0.0
Z: 30.0
Affect alpha
Ignore for GI
Consider same object only
Double sided
Work with transparency
Environment occlusion
Mode
Ambient occlusion
Streaks ambient
Streaks inner
Streaks size
30.0
Reflection glossiness
1.0
Affect reflection elements

VRayDirt Streaks ambient with Z bias set to 30

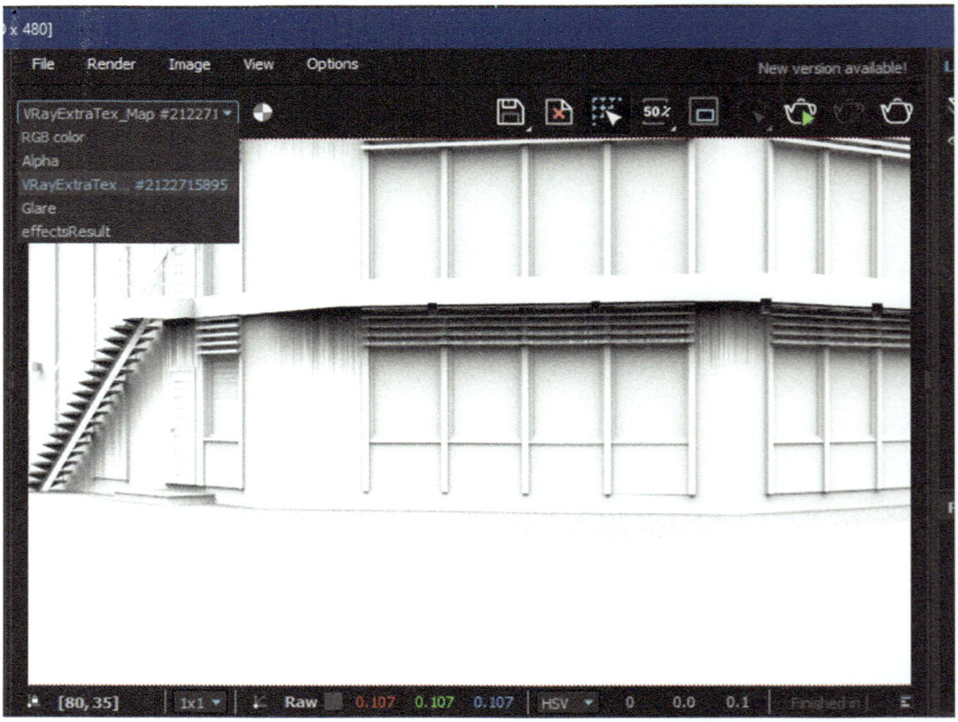

VRayDirt Streaks in Render Elements

Radius: This function sets the radius of the VRayDirt.

Default value is 100 mm.

Occluded color: This function controls the color of the VRayDirt.

Default color is black (0).

Unoccluded color: This function controls the main color/shade of objects.

When VRayDirt is used in the Diffuse toggle, users often have procedural maps plugged to this toggle (e.g., VRayMtl, VRayBitmap).

Distribution: This function narrows the spread of the VRayDirt.

The smaller the value, the wider the VRayDirt.

Default value is 1.0.

Falloff: This function controls the amount of gradient on the VRayDirt.

High values reduce the spread of the gradient. Keep the default value (0.0) to have a wide gradient.

Default value is 0.0.

Subdivs: This function controls the quality of the VRayDirt. High values yield smother results (less grainy) at a cost of longer rendering times.

The default value is often OK.

Default value is 3.

Bias: This function sets the direction of the VRayDirt. Z-axis sets the direction of the VRayDirt vertically.

The default value of 0.0 (in X, Y, and Z axes) sets the ambient occlusion in all directions.

Affect alpha: When turned on, the alpha values of the Occluded and Unoccluded colors/toggles are applied.

Enabling this function doubles the rendering times.

Disabled by default.

Ignore for GI: When enabled (by default), this function omits the VRayDirt preview during the precalculation process of the render.

By default, VRayDirt is only visible during the rendering time. No precalculation.

Enabled by default.

Consider same object only: By default (disabled), VRayDirt is spread to nearby objects.

When this function is enabled, the ambient occlusion will no longer affect adjacent objects.

Disabled by default.

Double-sided: When turned on, this function affects crevices and edges of objects.

It often creates undesirable results.

Disabled by default.

Work with transparency: When turned on, this function takes into consideration transparent objects in the scene, including mapped opacity.

Disabled by default.

Environment occlusion: This function takes into consideration the Environment contribution on unoccluded areas.

Disabled by default.

Mode: This function controls how the VRayDirt will be used (Ambient Occlusion, Reflection occlusion, Inner occlusion, ambient + inner occlusion).

Set to Ambient Occlusion mode by default.

Streaks ambient: When enabled, this function adds streaks to the ambient occlusion.

Streaks are only visible when the bias value is set in one direction (positive values) or the other (negative values).

VRayDirt will be projected in both directions without streaks, if the Bias values are set to 0.0 (in X, Y, Z).

It's common practice for users to focus mainly on Z-axis to create streaks in one direction.

The value of 30 seems to work well in most scenes.

Disabled by default.

Streaks inner: This function only becomes available when the Inner occlusion mode is set.

When enabled, it adds streaks to crevices.

Disabled by default.

Streak size: This function controls the width of each streak. The bigger the value, the more the streaks overlap horizontally.

Default value is 50.0.

This will reduce the rendering times substantially.

Instead, create a separate scene with a basic VRayMtl as an override material, and use multiple passes of VRayDirt as render elements (e.g., with streaks, without streaks).

These VRaydirt render passes/elements can be later used in post-production by overlaying them (Multiply blending mode) against the main render, in Photoshop, AfterEffects, Nuke, etc.

NOTE

When sending the final high-resolution renders, it's best Not to use VRayDirt as render element in your main scene.

Reflection glossiness: This function becomes available if the Mode is set to Reflection occlusion (Phong, Blinn, Ward).

It controls the direction of the rays traced for Reflection Occlusion.

Affect reflection elements: This function becomes available if the Mode is set to Reflection occlusion (Phong, Blinn, Ward).

When turned on, the ambient reflection affects the reflection in the render element.

Exclude: This toggle allows users to choose objects to exclude from VRayDirt.

VRayAerialPerspective

This truly amazing procedural map works in conjunction with the VRySun and VRaySky to emulate perspective atmospheric effects such as fog or haze.

Unlike the VRayEnvironmentFog, it's much faster to render and does not cast volumetric shadows.

To apply it, simply open the environment dialog by pressing 8 on your keyboard, or by going to the Rendering toolbar and choosing the Environment option from the list.

Next, in the Environment and Effects dialog, under Atmosphere group, click the Add toggle and choose the VRayAerialPerspective.

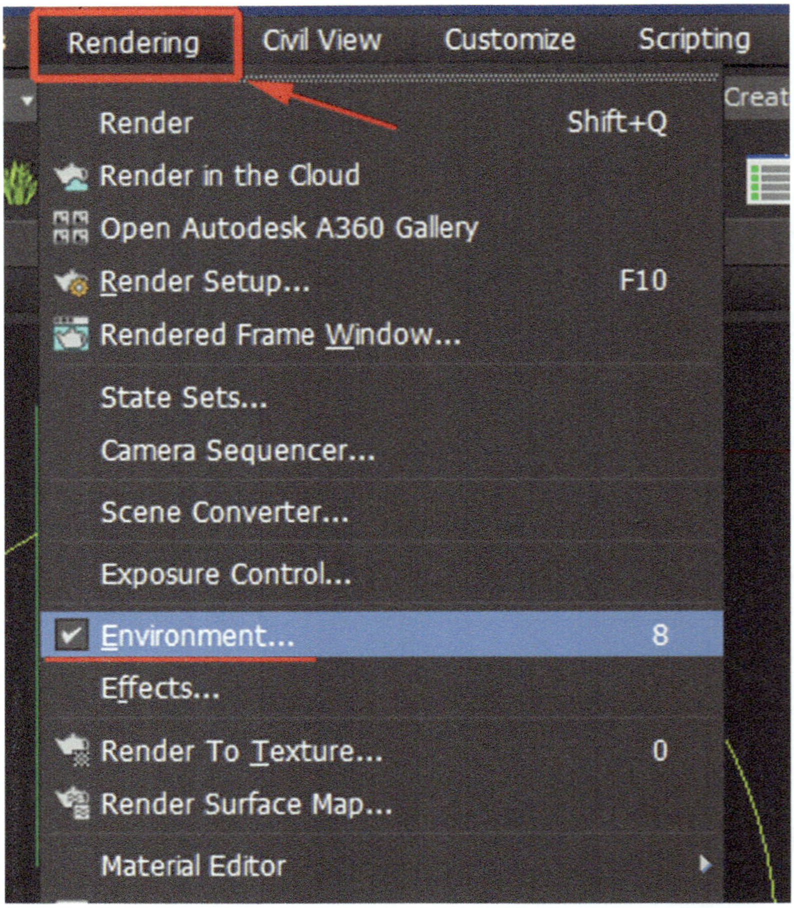
Rendering
Civil View
Customize
Scripting
Render
Shift+Q
Render in the Cloud
Open Autodesk A360 Gallery
Render Setup...
F10
Rendered Frame Window...
State Sets...
Camera Sequencer...
Scene Converter...
Exposure Control...
Environment...
8
Effects...
Render To Texture...
0
Render Surface Map...
Material Editor

Open the Environment dialog

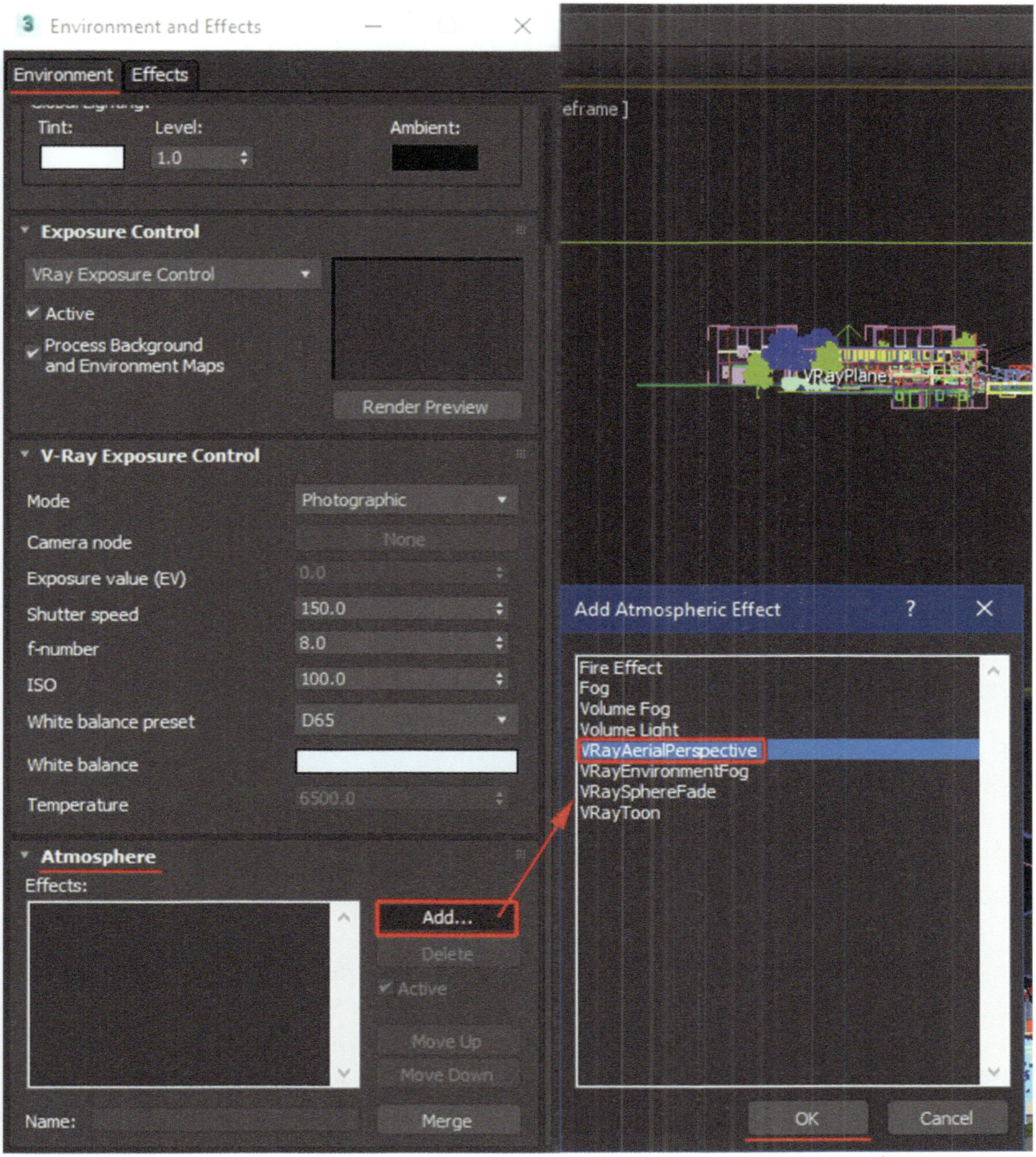
Environment and Effects
Environment
Effects
Tint:
Level:
1.0
Ambient:
Exposure Control
VRay Exposure Control
Active
Process Background and Environment Maps
Render Preview
V-Ray Exposure Control
Mode
Photographic
Camera node
None
Exposure value (EV)
0.0
Shutter speed
150.0
f-number
8.0
ISO
100.0
White balance preset
D65
White balance
Temperature
6500.0
Atmosphere
Effects:
Add...
Delete
Active
Move Up
Move Down
Name:
Merge
VRayPlane
Add Atmospheric Effect
Fire Effect
Fog
Volume Fog
Volume Light
VRayAerialPerspective
VRayEnvironmentFog
VRaySphereFade
VRayToon
OK
Cancel

Add VRayAerialPerspective

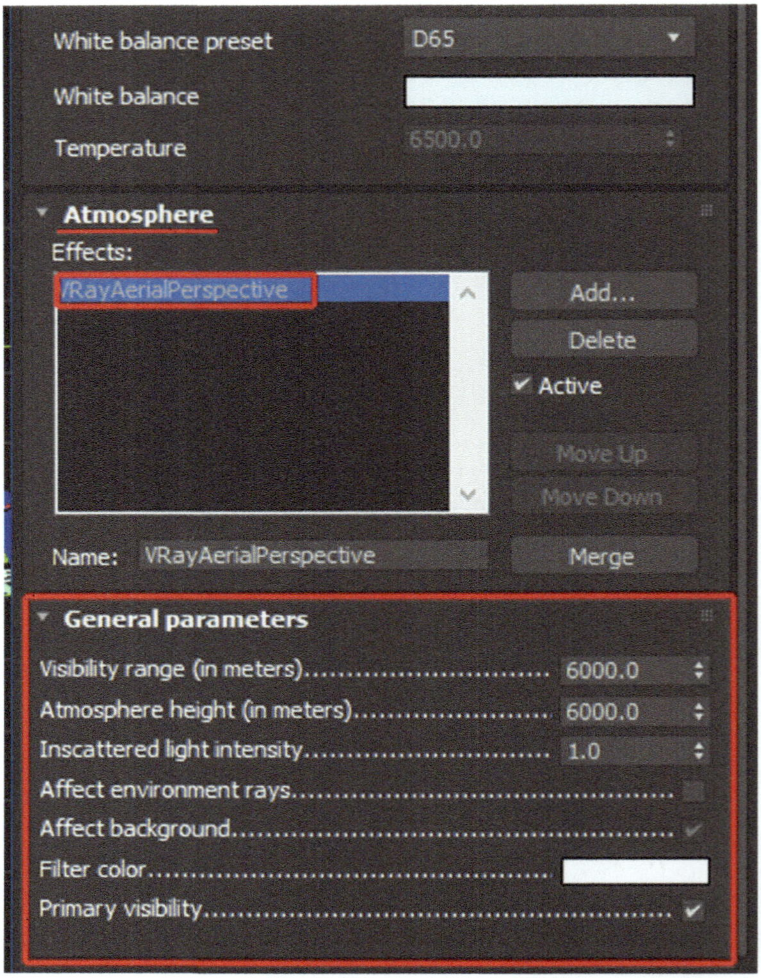

VRayAerialPerspective Loaded

Visibility range (in meters): This function controls the fog/haze proximity to the camera.

Low values bring the fog/haze closer to the camera. And high values do the opposite.

Default value is 6000.0 (far away).

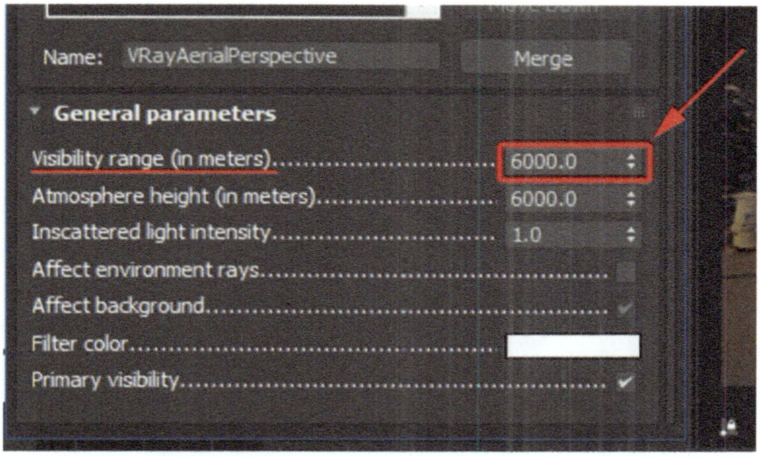

Visibility range 6000.0

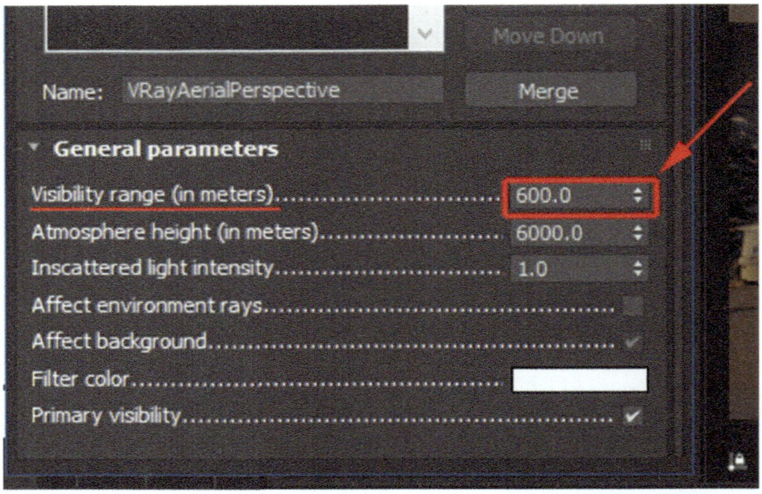

Visibility range 600.0

Atmosphere height (in meters) : This function controls the height of the fog/haze.

Low values reduce the height of the fog/haze. And high values do the opposite.

Default value is 6000.0.

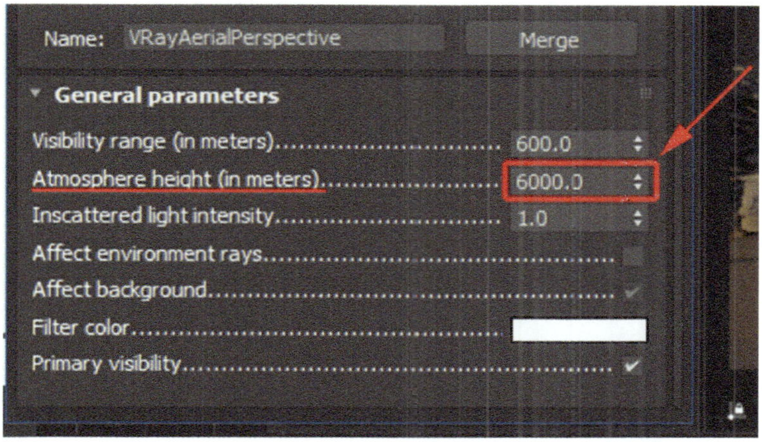

Atmosphere height 6000.0

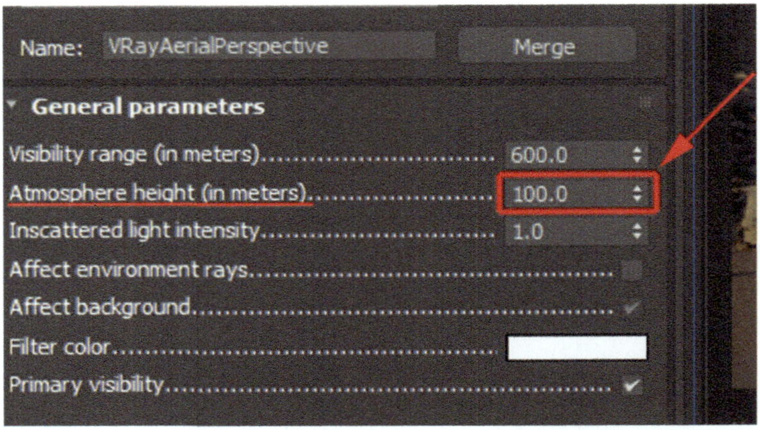

Atmosphere height 100.0

Inscattered light intensity: This function controls how much light passes through the fog/haze.

Values lower than 1.0 reduce the brightness/shadows in the scene. Values higher than 1.0 yield the opposite effect.

Default value is 1.0.

Affect Environment rays: When enabled, this function blends the fog/haze with the horizon (sky).

Disabled by default.

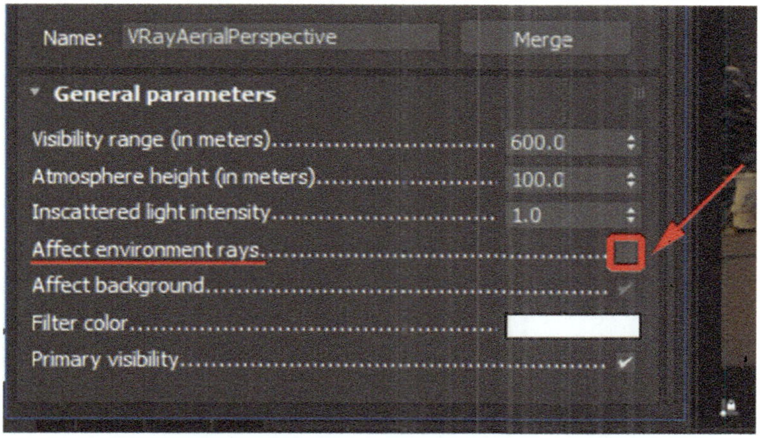

Affect Environment rays disabled

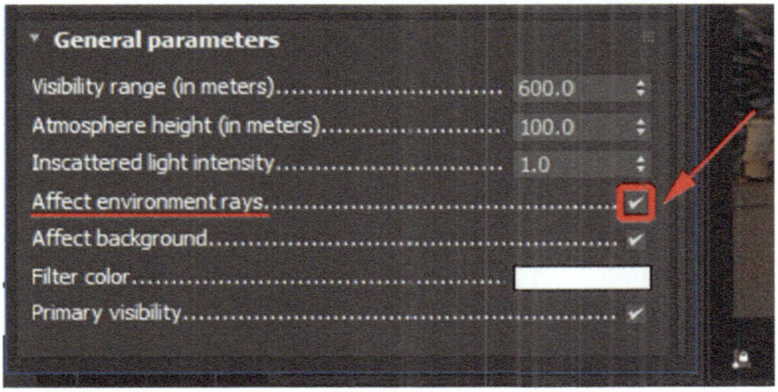

Affect Environment rays enabled

Affect background: This function adds the fog/haze to the background. When disabled, the background is darker (assuming the Filter color is white). Enabled by default.

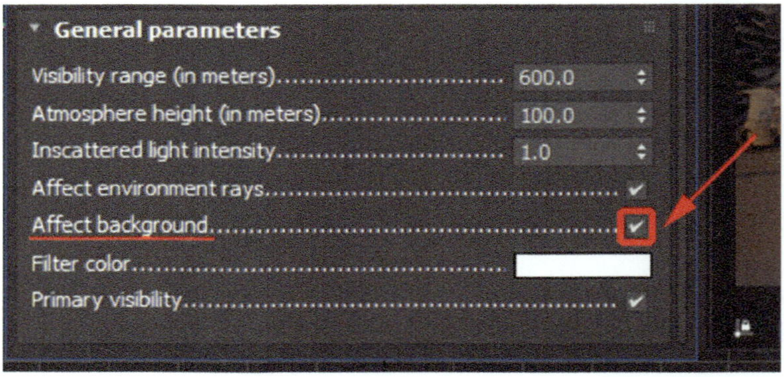

Affect background enabled

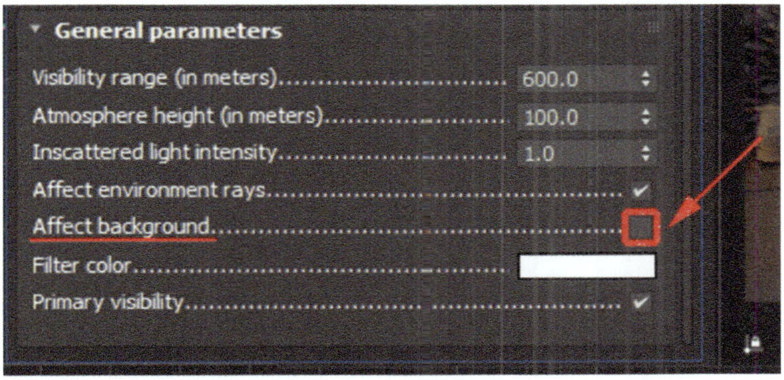

Affect background disabled

Filter color: This function controls the color of the fog/haze.

Default color is white.

Primary visibility: This function enables the visibility of the fog/haze.

Enabled by default.

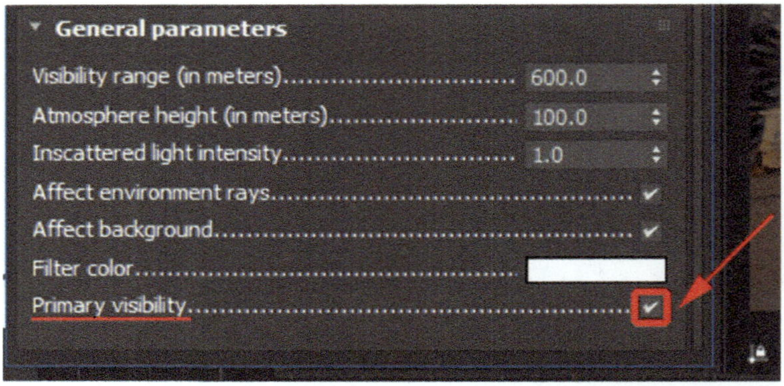

Primary visibility enabled

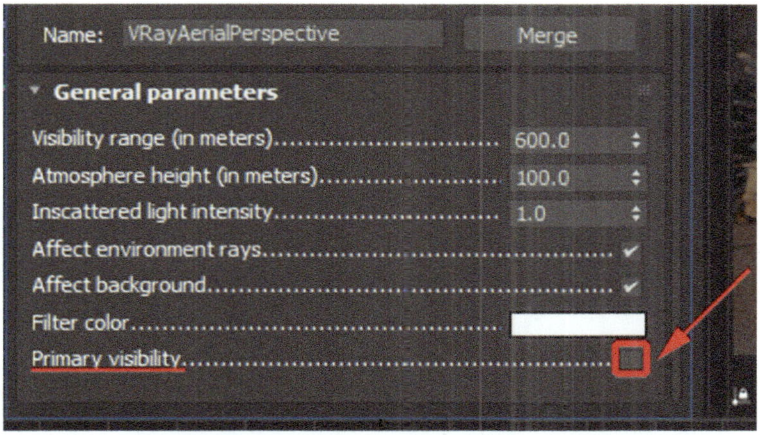

Primary visibility disabled

VRayLightMtl

This shader is primarily used to add self-illumination to objects. And it can easily be accessed through the Material/Map Browser dialog, under the VRay rollout list.

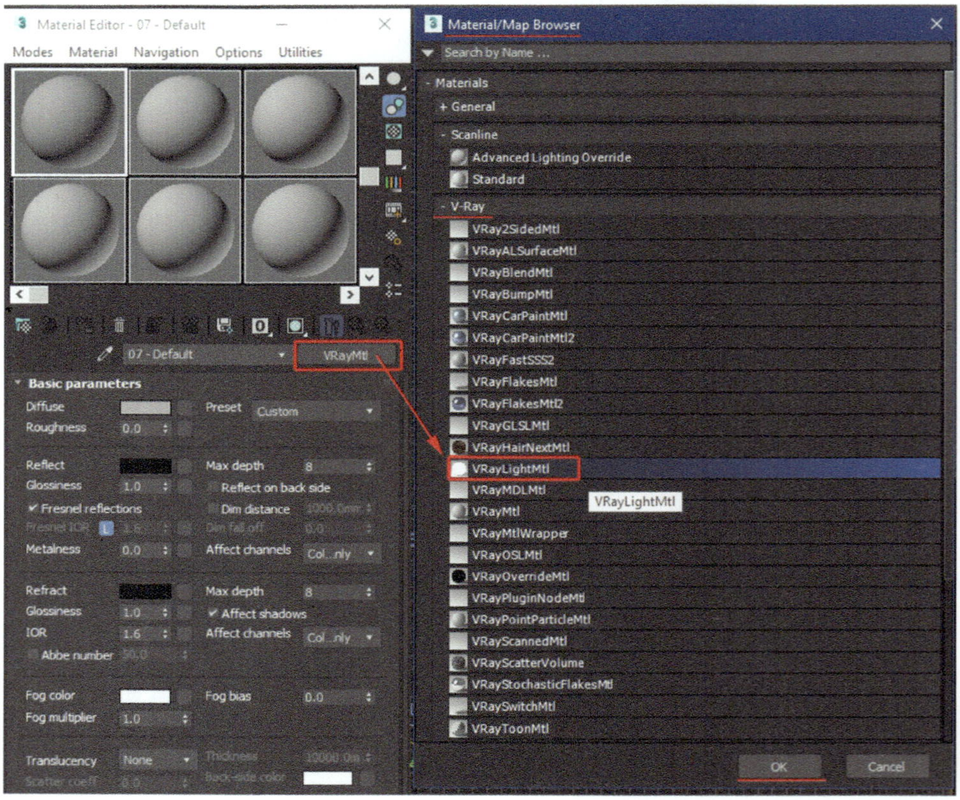

VRayLightMtl in the Material/Map Browser

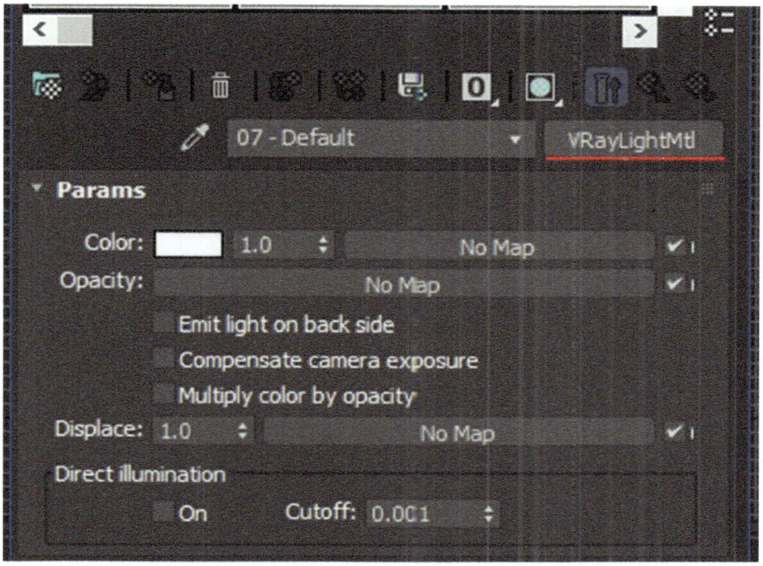

VRayLightMtl parameters

VRayLightMtl works in exact same way as the VRay Self-Illumination function. In addition, it comes with the following features:

Opacity: This function allows users to plug textures and/or procedural maps to its toggle.

As with most opacity toggles, it works best when a grayscale and/or black and white texture/procedural map is used.

Emit light on back side: This function allows the light to be emitted from a side of an object that is not emitting light.

Disabled by default.

Compensate camera exposure: This function is quite useful for scenes where the exposure controls are causing the self-illumination to be slightly dimmed. Turning this function on will essentially make the self-illumination more visible, by compensating for the exposure.

Disabled by default.

Multiply color by opacity: When turned on, it increases the color of the light material, based on the texture/procedural map applied to the Opacity toggle.

Disabled by default.

Displace: This function is only available when the Direct illumination is disabled. Users can plug a texture/procedural map to it.

Displacement works best with grayscale and black and white materials.

Direct illumination: When turned on, it emits light in the same manner as a VRay Mesh light. As such, it can be time-consuming to render.

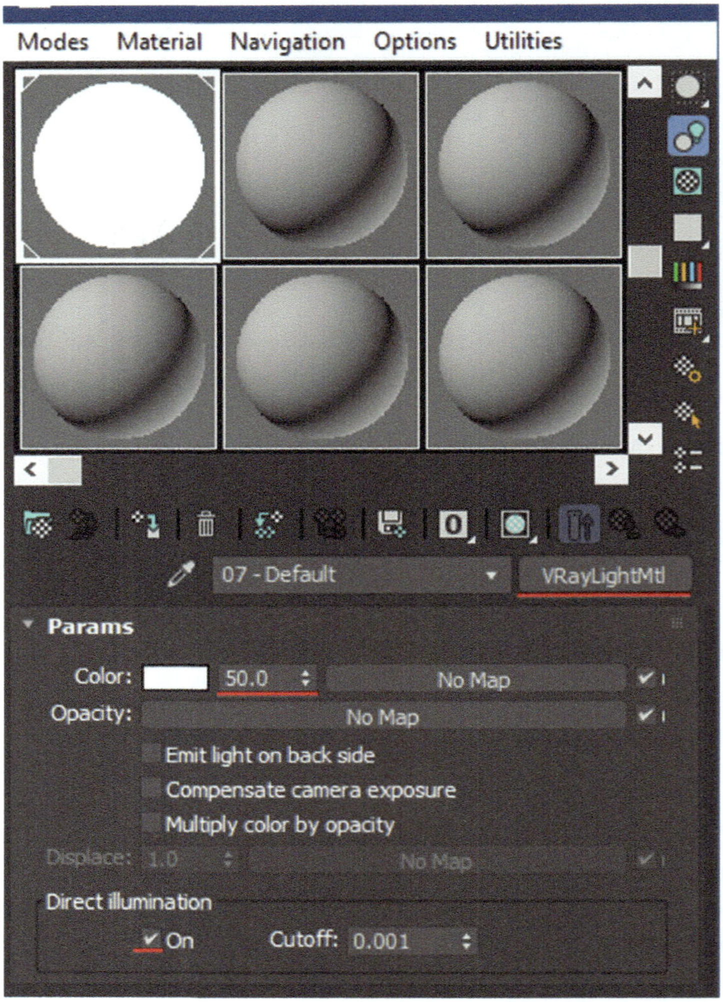

VRayLightMtl with the Direct Illumination enabled

VRayMtlWrapper

This shader only works if the Global Illumination (GI) and/or the Caustics are enabled in rendering parameters.

It's mainly used to allow certain materials to receive or generate GI and Caustics.

To access it, simply select an existing material slot and click on the main shader toggle, followed by choosing the VRMtlWrapper shader from the Material/Map Browser list.

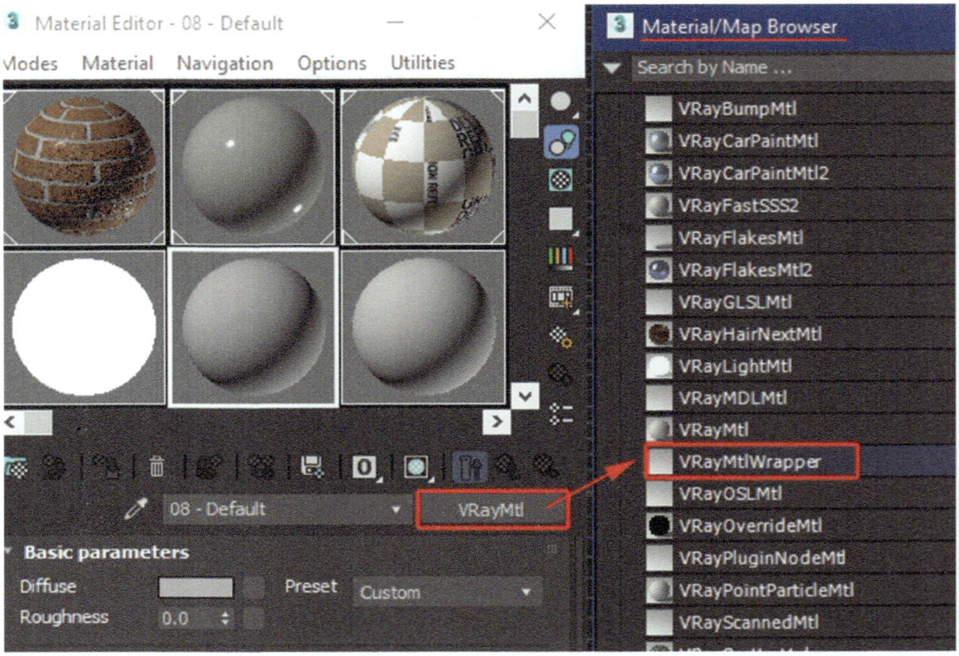

Choose the VRMtlWrapper shader from the Material/Map Browser

The Replace Material dialog should be prompted. Choose to Keep old material as sub-material.

Choose to Keep old material as sub-material

Its parameters should load up automatically.

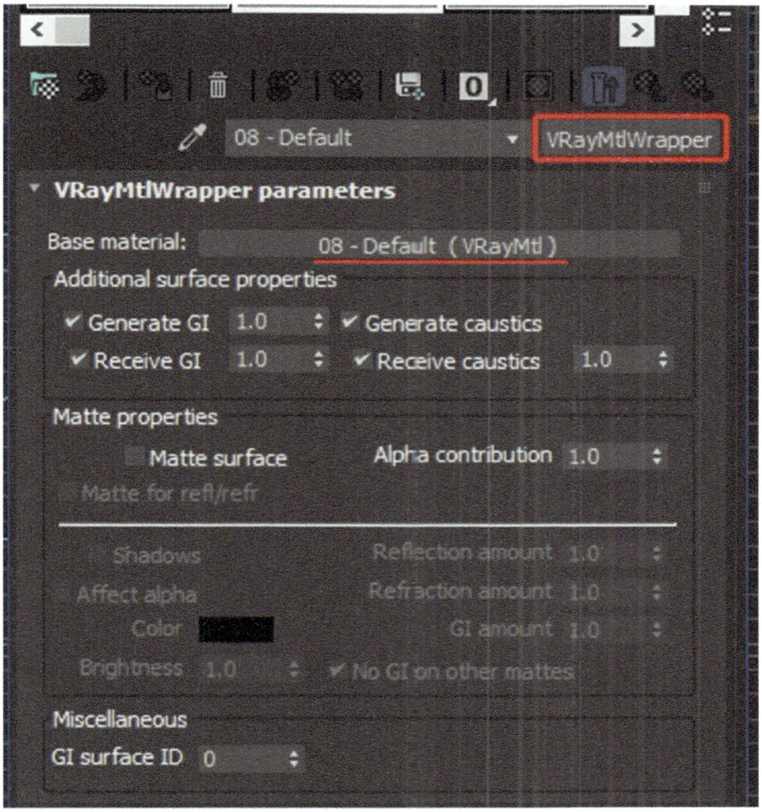

VRMtlVrapper parameters

Base material: The sub-material is kept in this toggle.

Generate GI: This function enables users to increase or decrease the quantity of GI being generated by the Base material.

Receive GI: The function allows users to increase or decrease the amount of GI being received by the Base material. Its value is set 1 0 by default.

This feature is widely used to make shadows/indirectly lit areas darker, or brighter.

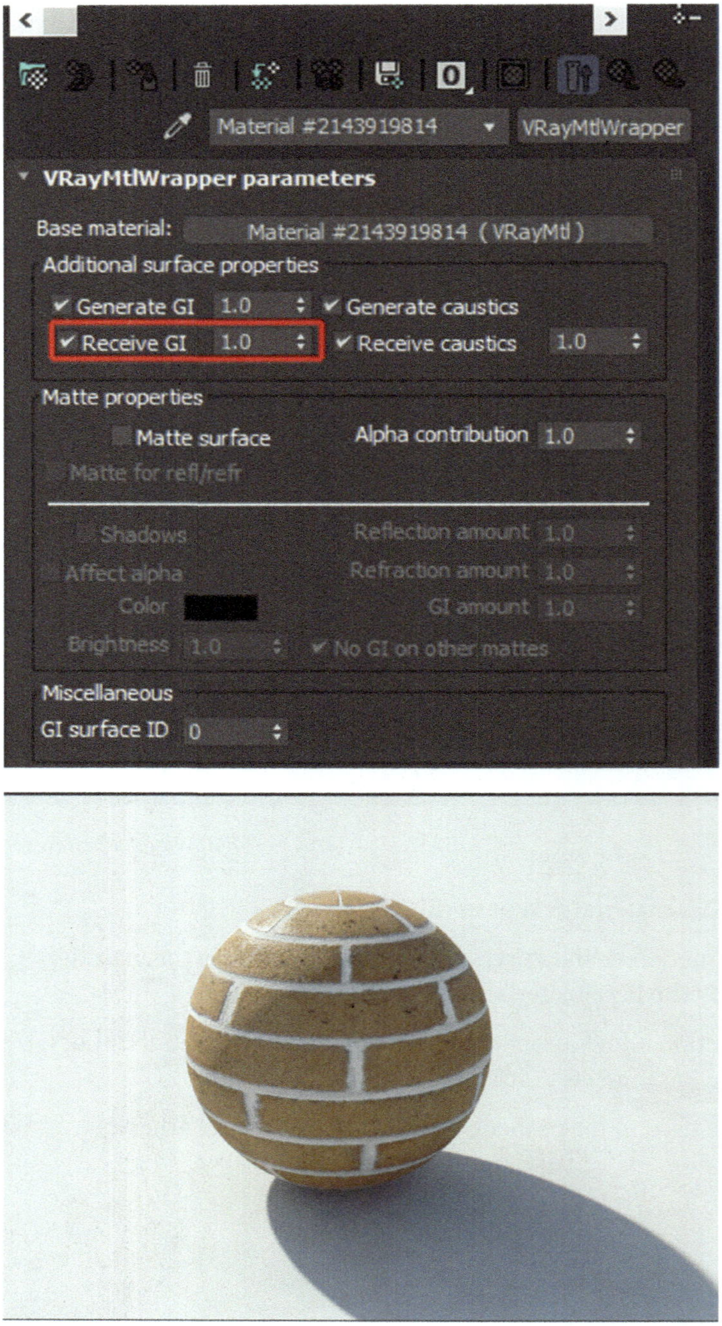

Receive GI set to 1.0

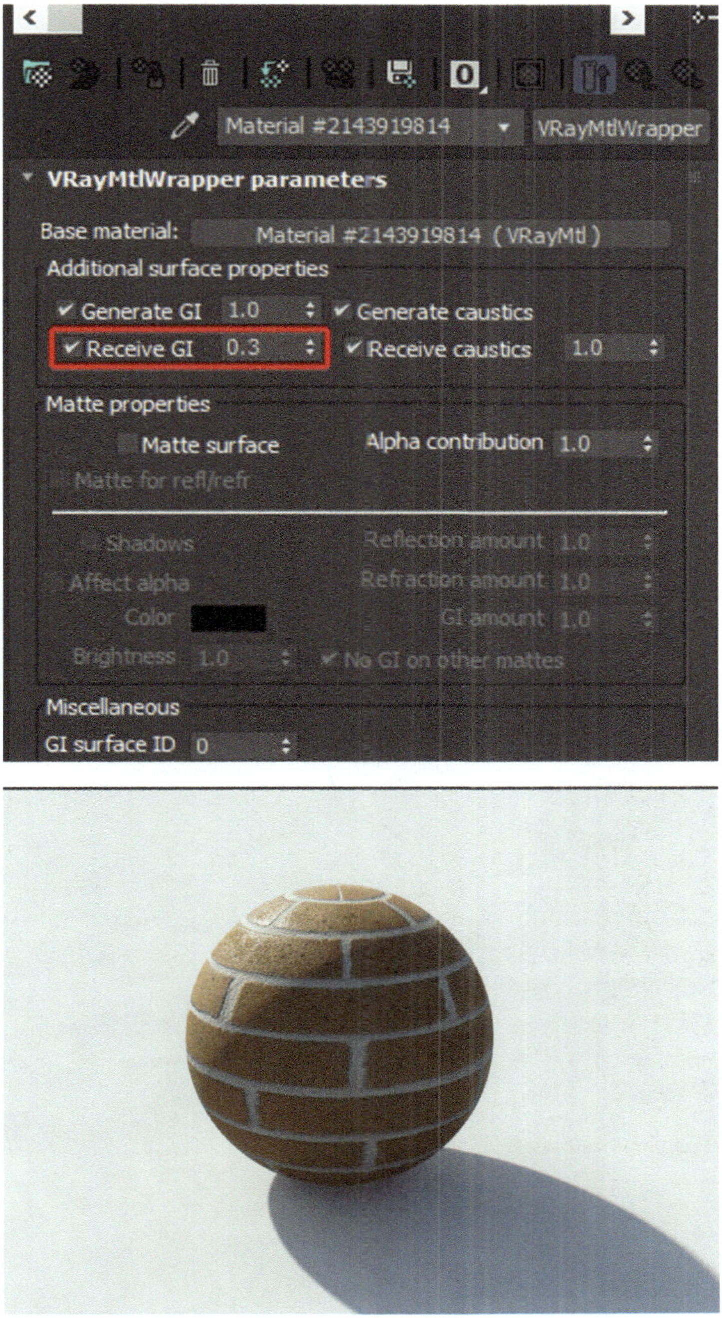

Receive GI set to 0.3

Generate caustics: When turned on, it allows caustics to be generated. Enabled by default.

Receive caustics: Users can increase or decrease the amount of caustics being received by the object. Its value is set 1.0 by default.

VRayOverrideMtl

This shader is mostly used as an override to correct GI "color bleeding" artifacts, reflections, refractions, and shadows.

It can easily be accessed by clicking on the main shader toggle, followed by choosing the VRayOverrideMtl from the Material/Map Browser dialog.

Following that, in the Replace Material dialog, choose to Keep old material as sub-material.

The VRayOverrideMtl should load up automatically thereafter.

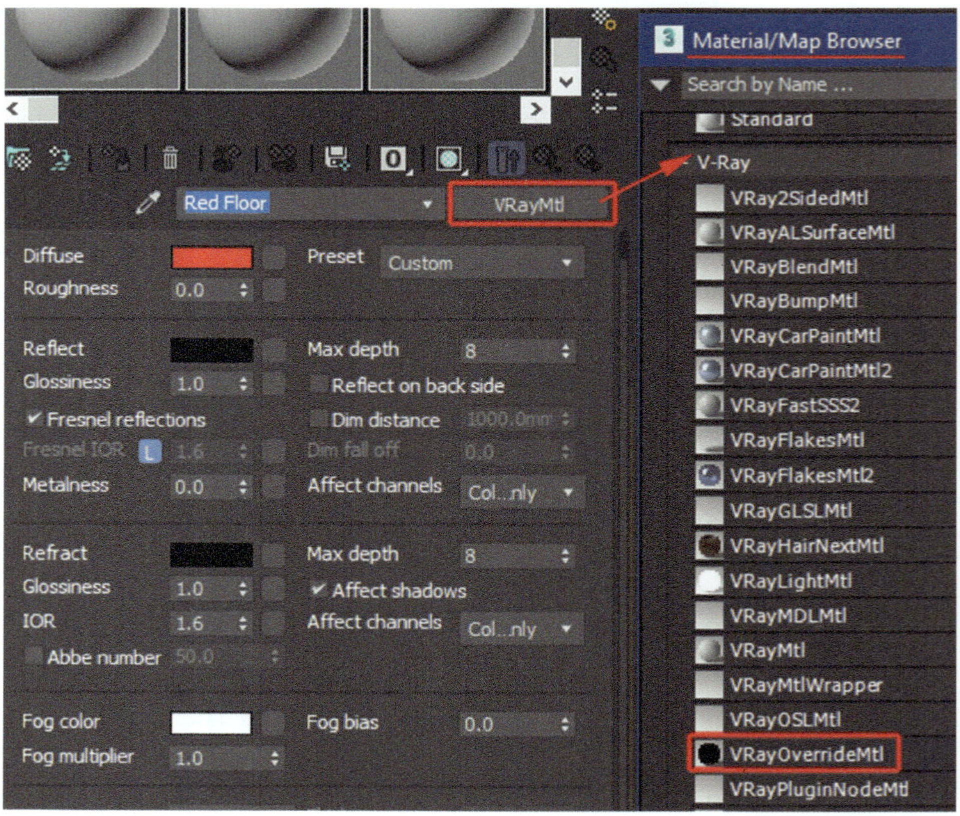

Choose the VRayOverrideMtl shader

Choose to Keep old material as sub-material

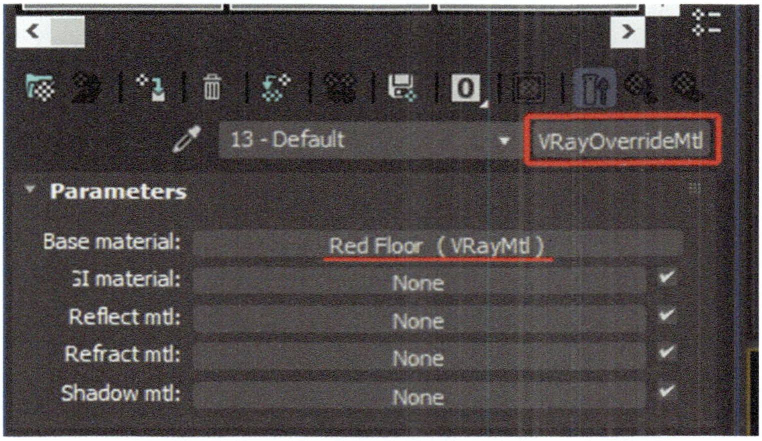

VRayOverrideMtl shader loaded

Base material: This is the toggle where the base *sub-material* is kept in.

GI: The toggle allows users to plug a material, to be used as a new source of GI reflectance. This toggle is very useful to override GI "color bleeding" effects on nearby objects.

Reflect mtl: This function can be used to override its material appearance, when "seen" on other reflective objects.

Refract mtl: This toggle works in a similar way to Reflect mtl. It can be used to change how the refractions are seen by other reflective surfaces.

Shadow myl: The toggle allows users to override the shadow appearance when cast onto its surface.

The examples below depict how the "color bleeding" and the reflection colors were easily changed/corrected, by simply plugging different shaders (white VRayMtl) in both GI and Reflect mtl toggles.

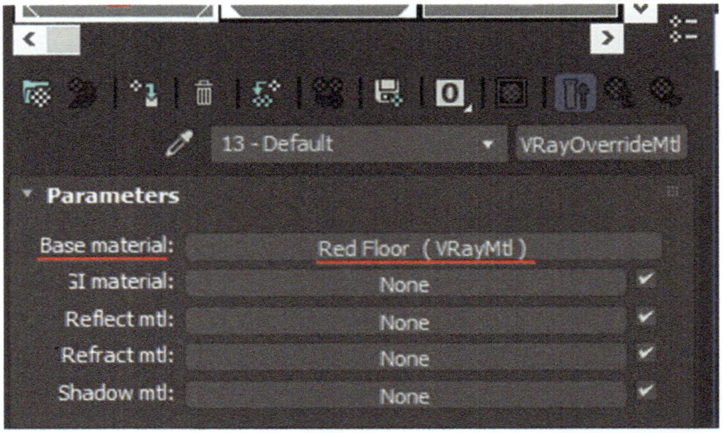
13 - Default
VRayOverrideMtl
Parameters
Base material:
Red Floor (VRayMtl)
GI material:
None
Reflect mtl:
None
Refract mtl:
None
Shadow mtl:
None

Color reflected and spilling from the Red floor

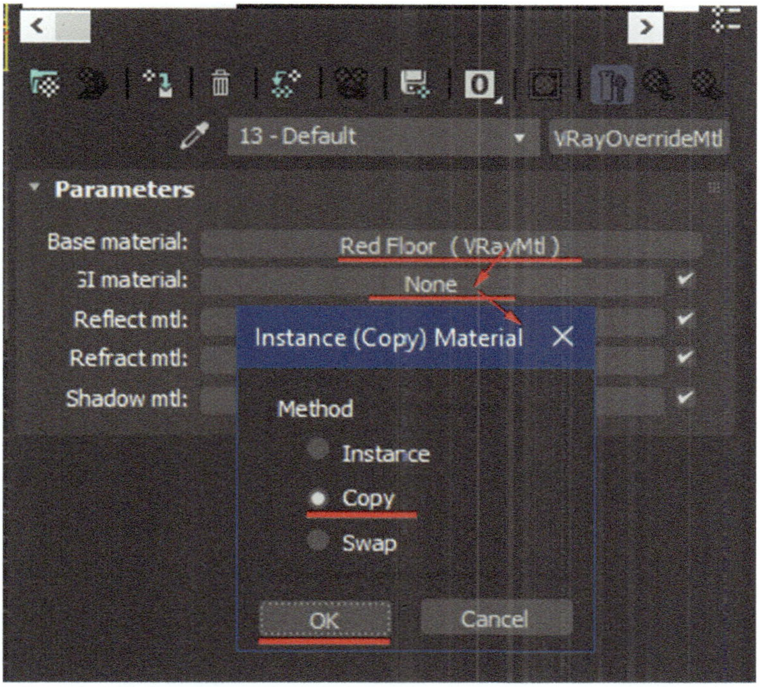

Copy Base material to GI material

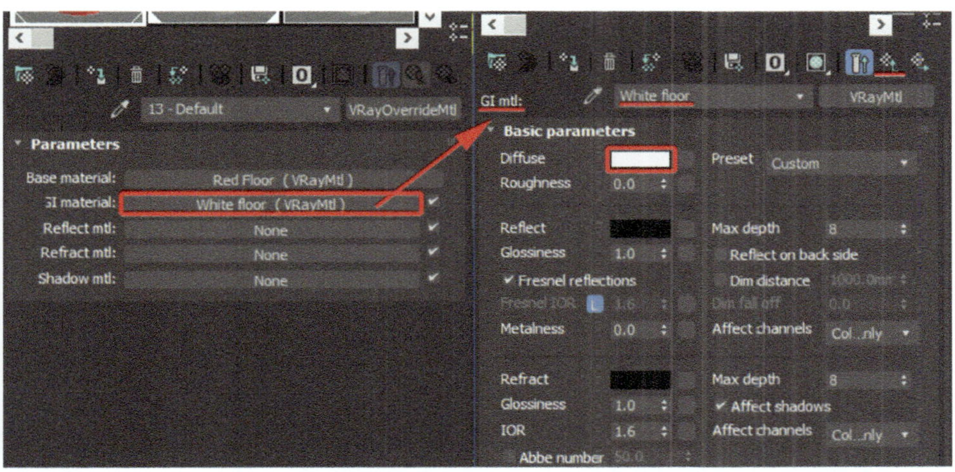

GI mtl color changed to white, and renamed

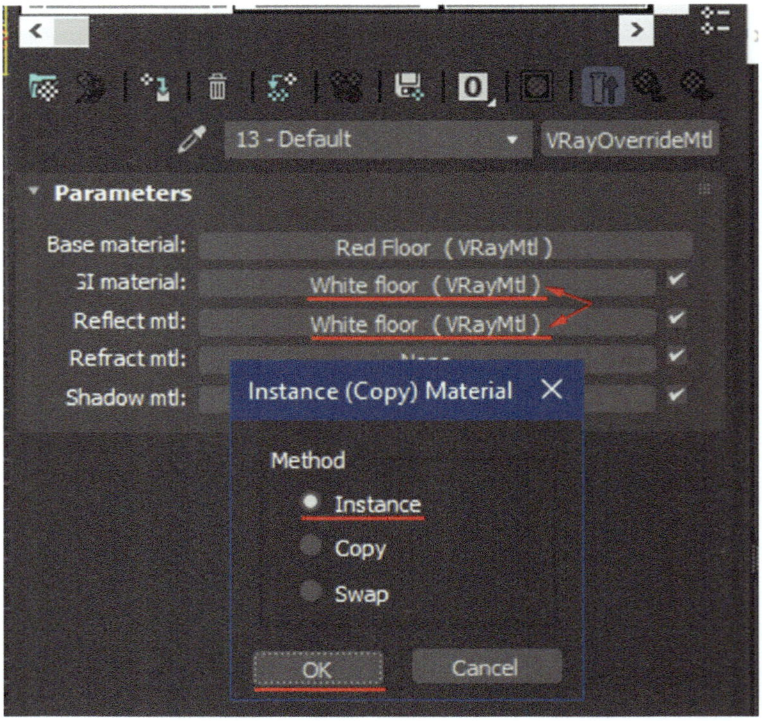

Copy instance the GI toggle

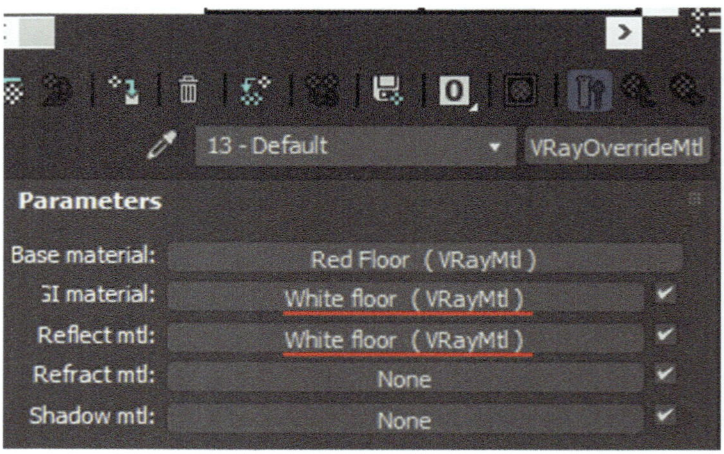

Final result, no color spills or red reflections

VRay2SidedMtl

This material is mostly used to emulate translucent objects. Its properties are more apparent when there's a strong light hitting its surface internally or/and externally (lamp shades or plant leaves).

To access this shader, simply click on the main VRayMtl toggle, and choose the VRay2SidedMtl shader from the Material/Map Browser list.

Following that, choose to keep old material as sub-material, in the Replace Material dialog.

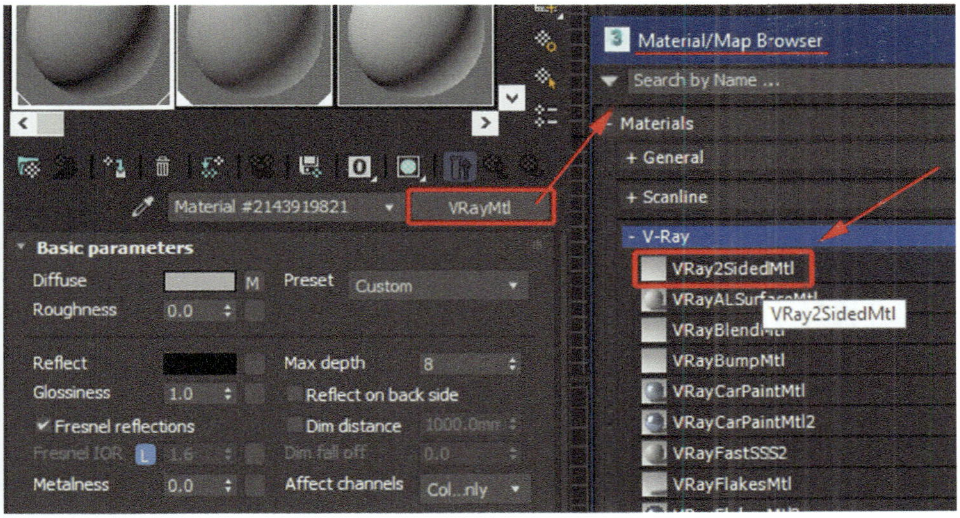

VRay2SidedMtl shader

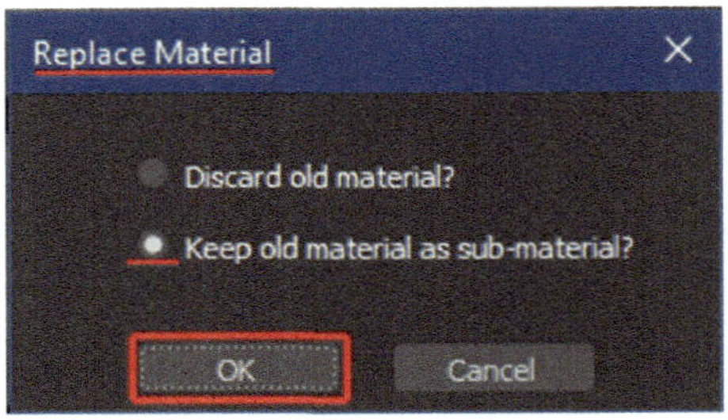

Choose to keep old material as sub-material option

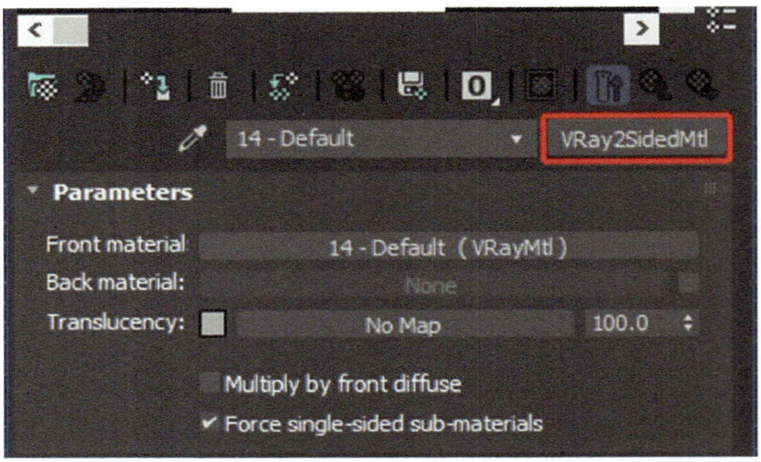

VRay2SidedMtl shader loaded

Front: This toggle allows users to set up the Front material surface. Often more opaque and with a slight difference in color (preferably).

Back material: The material for this toggle is frequently setup to be less opaque (e.g., more refractive/transparent) and with a slight difference in color (generally the light color-yellowish).

In addition, being a more refractive material, users normally enable its refraction to Affect shadows.

Translucency: This function allows users to control the transition between the two surfaces (Front and Back material) with the Color Selector, or a procedural map through its toggle.

If the toggle is being used, the numerical values allow users blend the toggle content, with the color selector values.

To create a translucent lamp shade, simply go inside the Front material toggle and make it more transparent in the Refract color swatch.

Also, rename it as White Material.

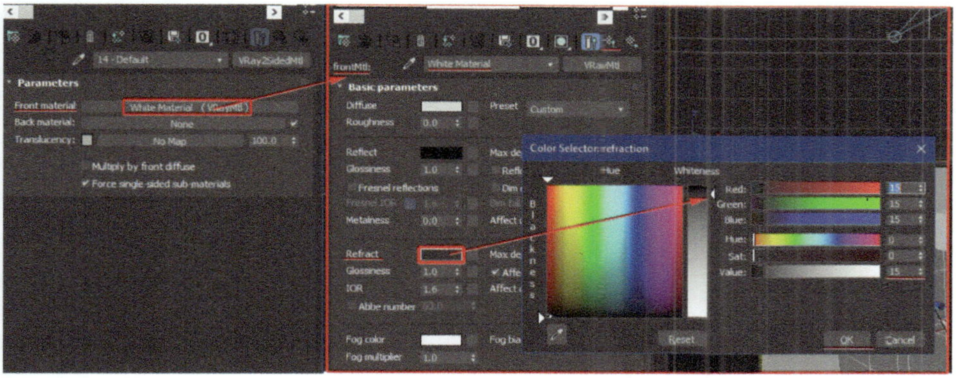

Change the Front material Refract color

Next, copy (drag and drop) the Front material toggle into the Back material toggle.

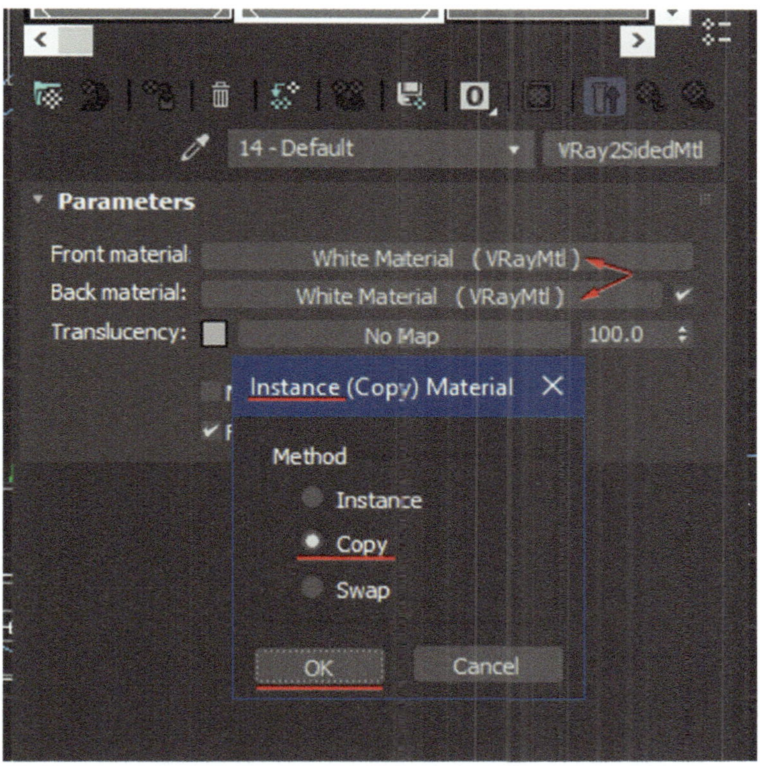

Copy the Front material toggle into the Back material

Rename the Back material as Yellow Material and change its diffuse color swatch.

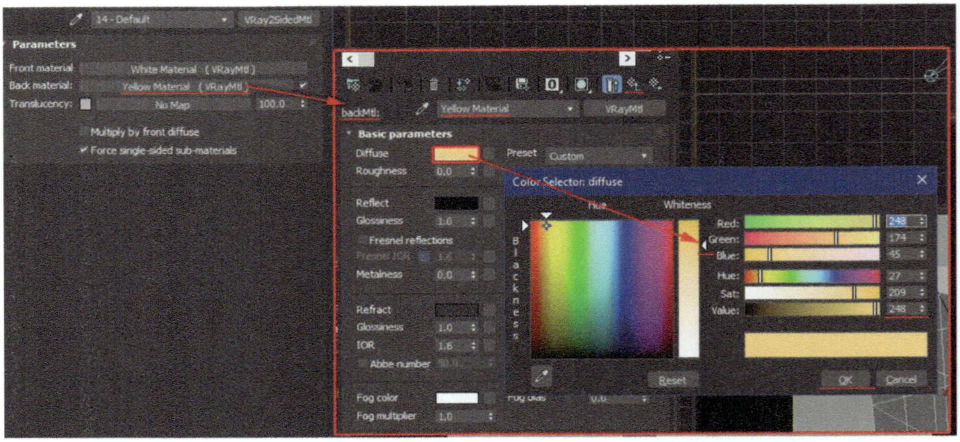

Rename the Back material and change its diffuse color

NOTE

In order to see the light through a translucent object, ensure its Multiplier is high enough, invisible to the camera, and set it to cast shadows.

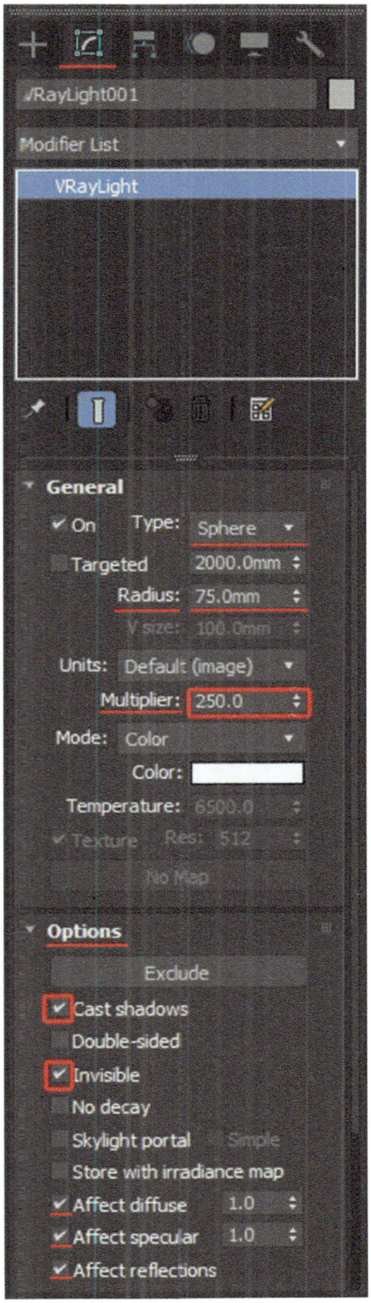
VRayLight001
Modifier List
VRayLight
General
On
Type:
Sphere
Targeted
2000.0mm
Radius:
75.0mm
Units:
Default (image)
Multiplier:
250.0
Mode:
Color
Color:
Temperature:
Options
Exclude
Cast shadows
Double-sided
Invisible
No decay
Skylight portal
Store with irradiance map
Affect diffuse
1.0
Affect specular
1.0
Affect reflections

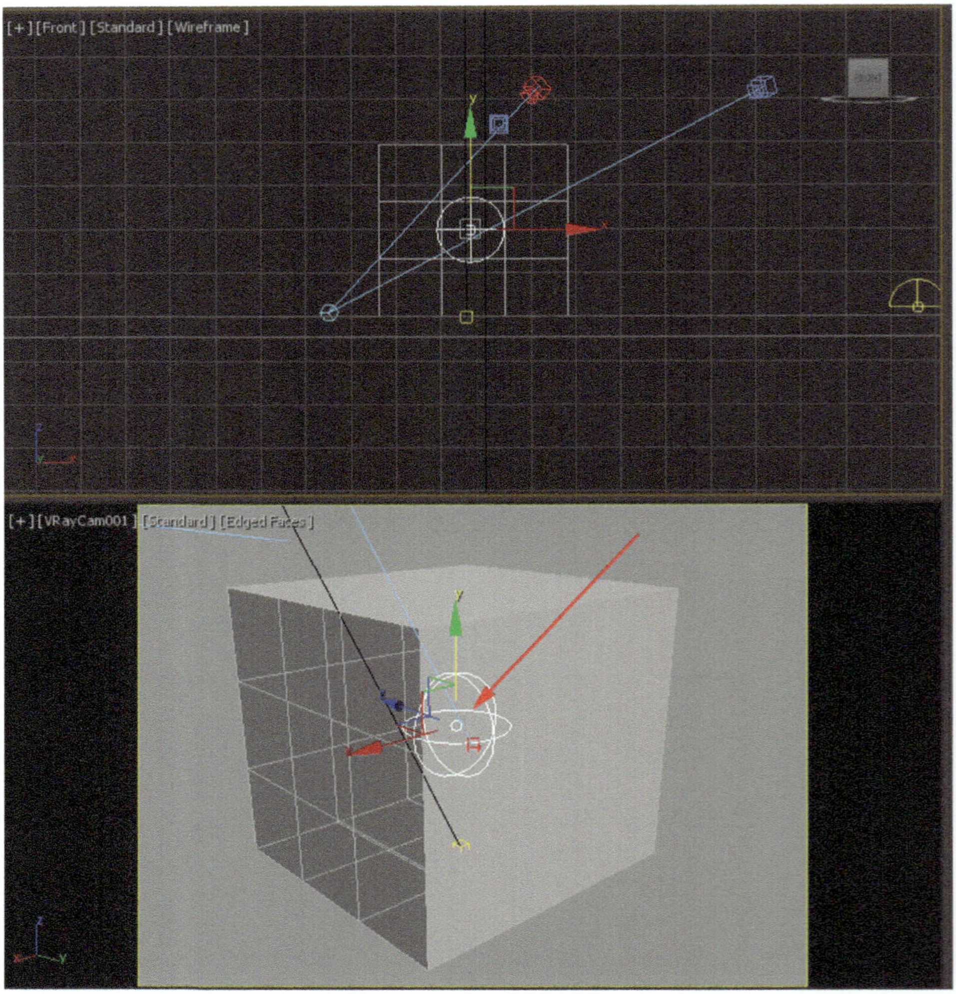
[+] [Front] [Standard] [Wireframe]
[+] [VRayCam001] [Standard] [Edged Faces]

Sphere Light parameters

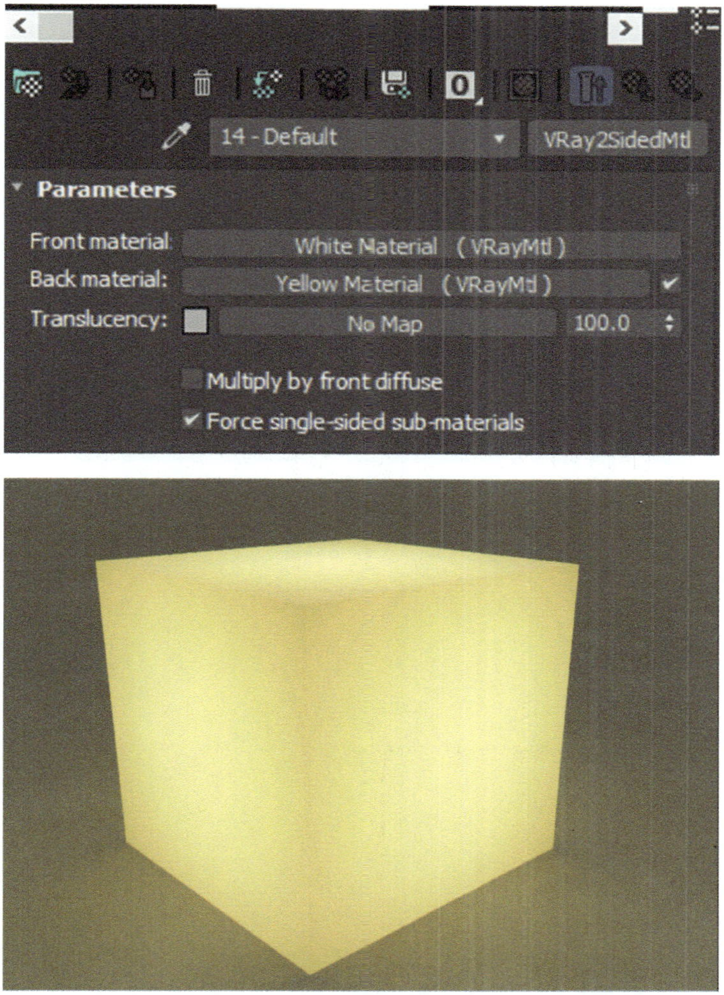

An object with a VRay2SidedMtl shader, and a physical light inside

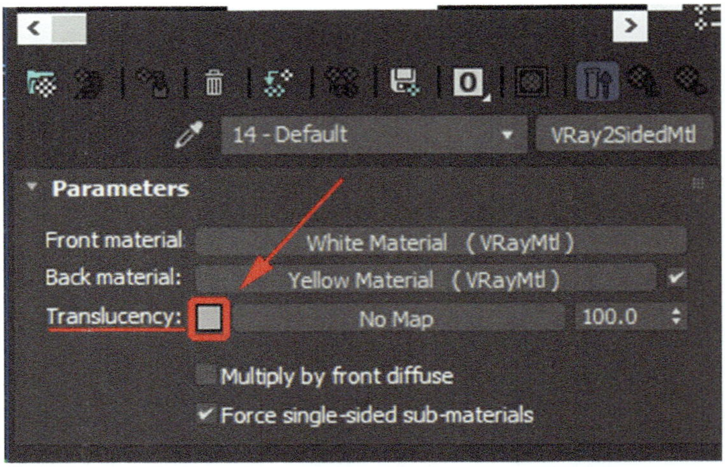

Translucency set to gray

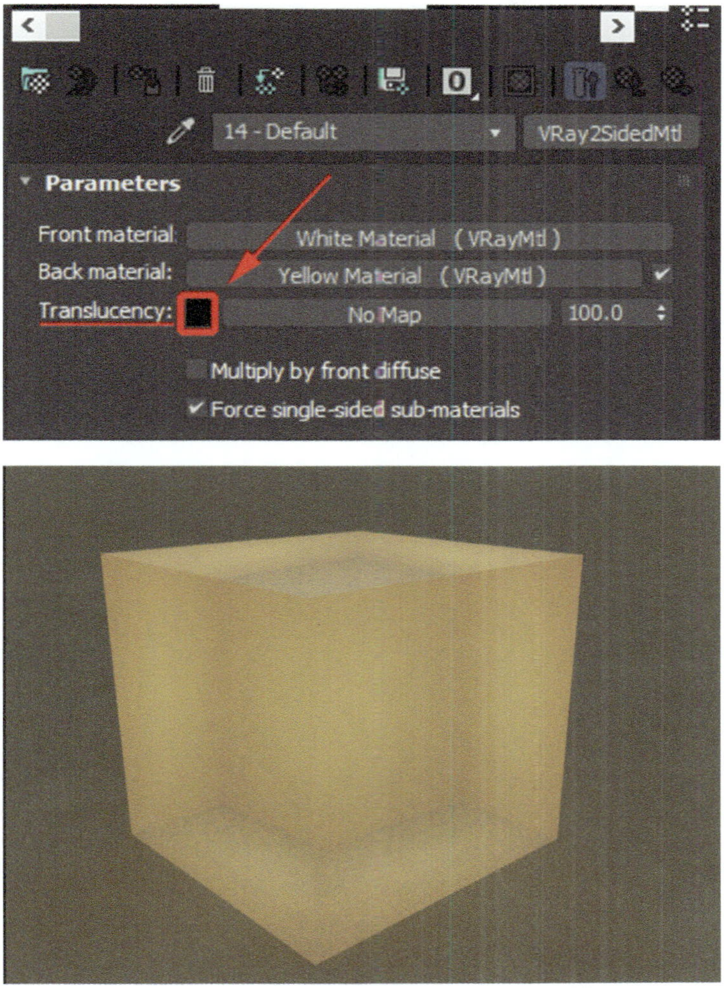

Translucency set to black

There are times when you may want the physical light to be visible in the camera. The results may not be desirable by default.

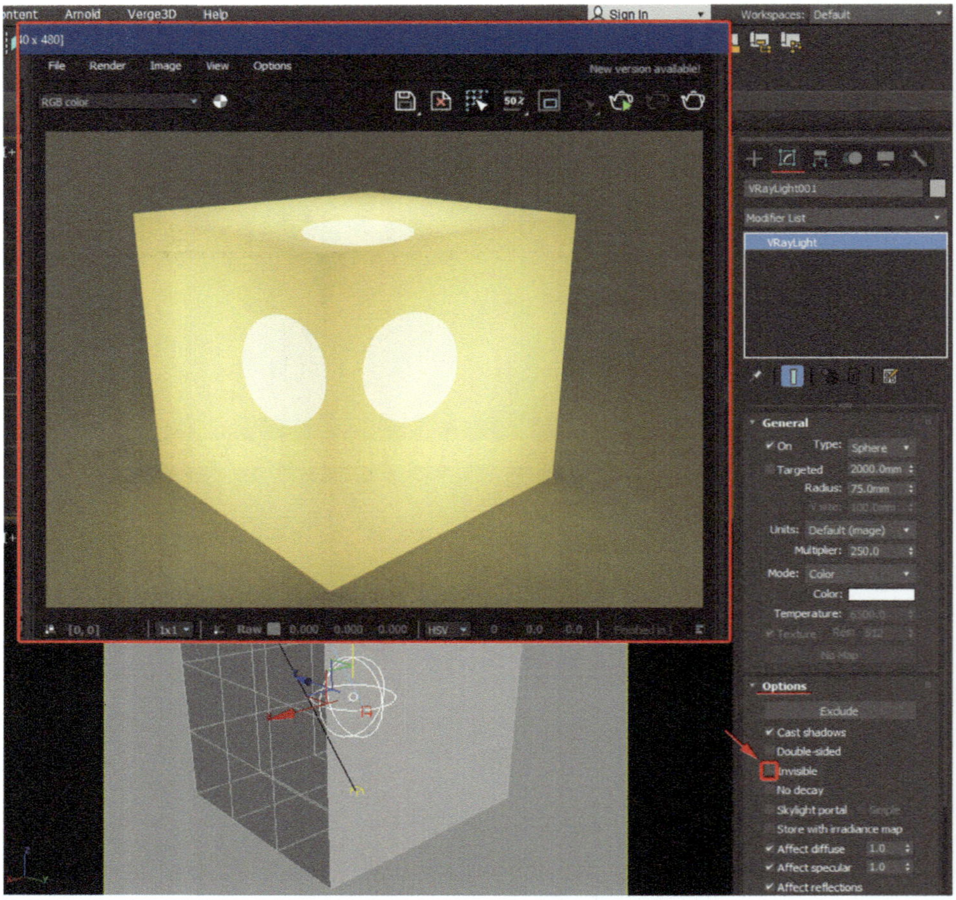

Light visible in the render

To correct this, always go to the Front material toggle, and change its Refract Glossiness value to 0.5.

These settings have already been discussed in detail.

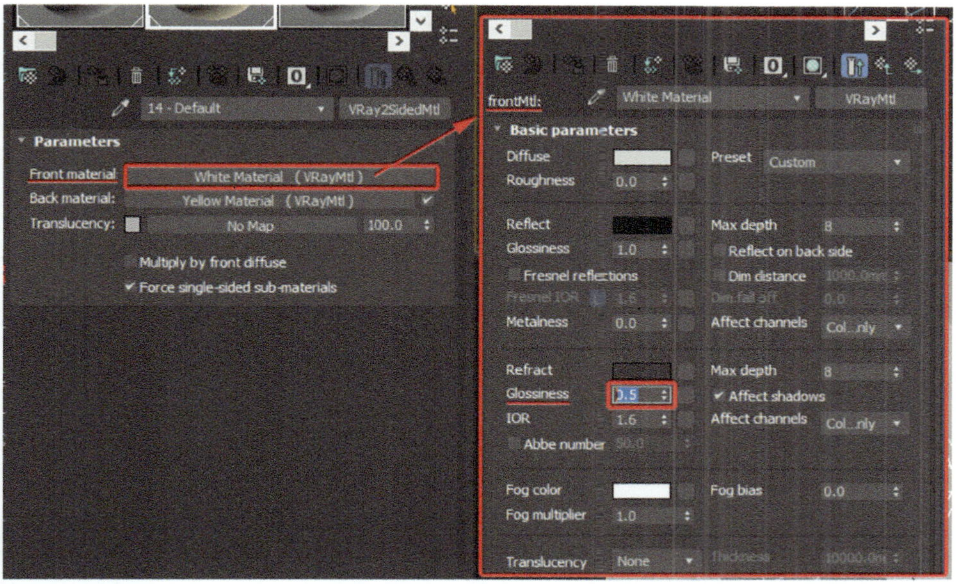

Change the Front material refraction Glossiness to 0.5

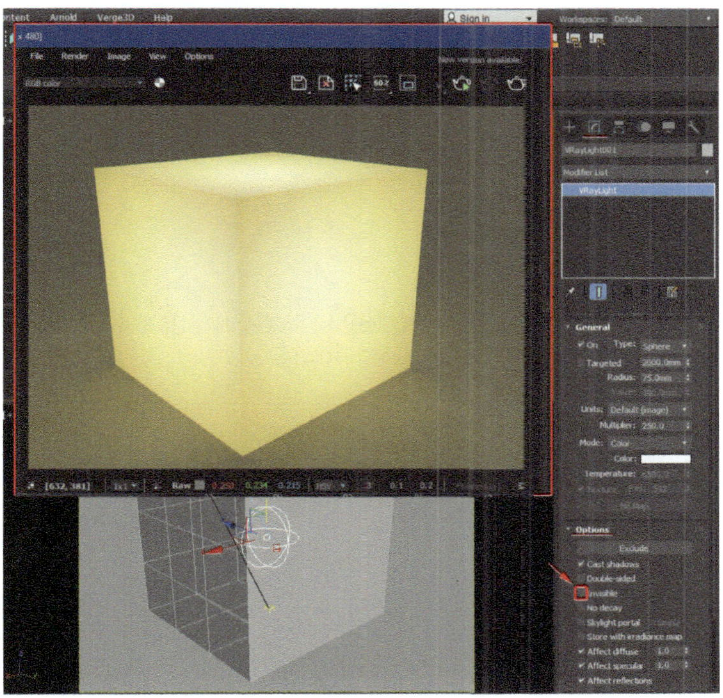

Final result with refraction Glossiness set to 0.5

VRayBlendMtl

To help highlight the functionalities of this shader, the Aluminium_Anodized_Bronze material was used as the base material.

This material was previously loaded from the VRay Asset Browser dialog.

VRayBlendMtl is very useful to create unique and exquisite materials, by blending multiple shaders together.

However, because of its complexity, it may take slightly longer to compute.

Materials can be blended through a toggle, or the color selector dialog.

To load it, simply click on the main shader toggle and pick the VRayBlendMtl from the Material/Map Browser dialog list. And choose to keep old material as sub-material in the Replace Material dialog.

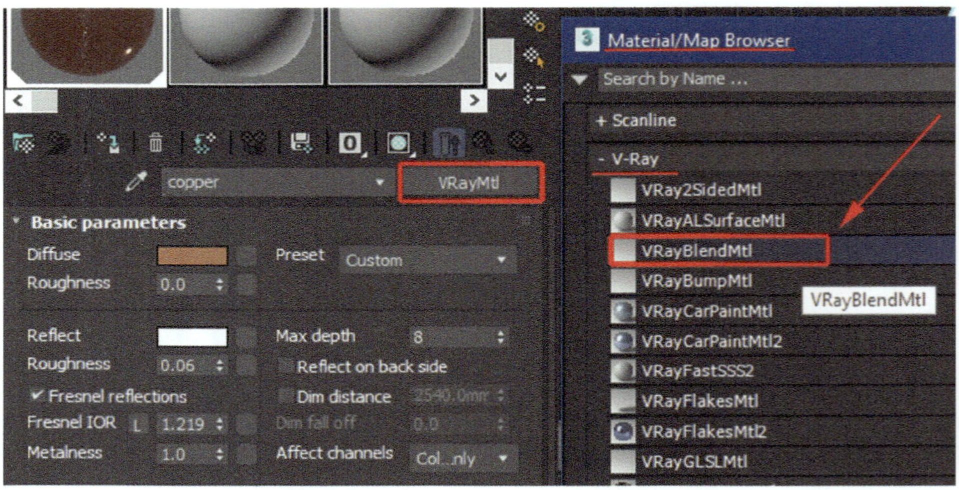

Select the VRayBlendMtl

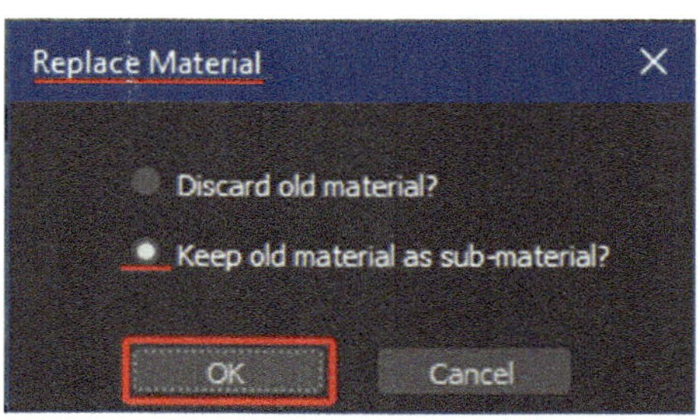

Choose to *keep old material as sub-material*

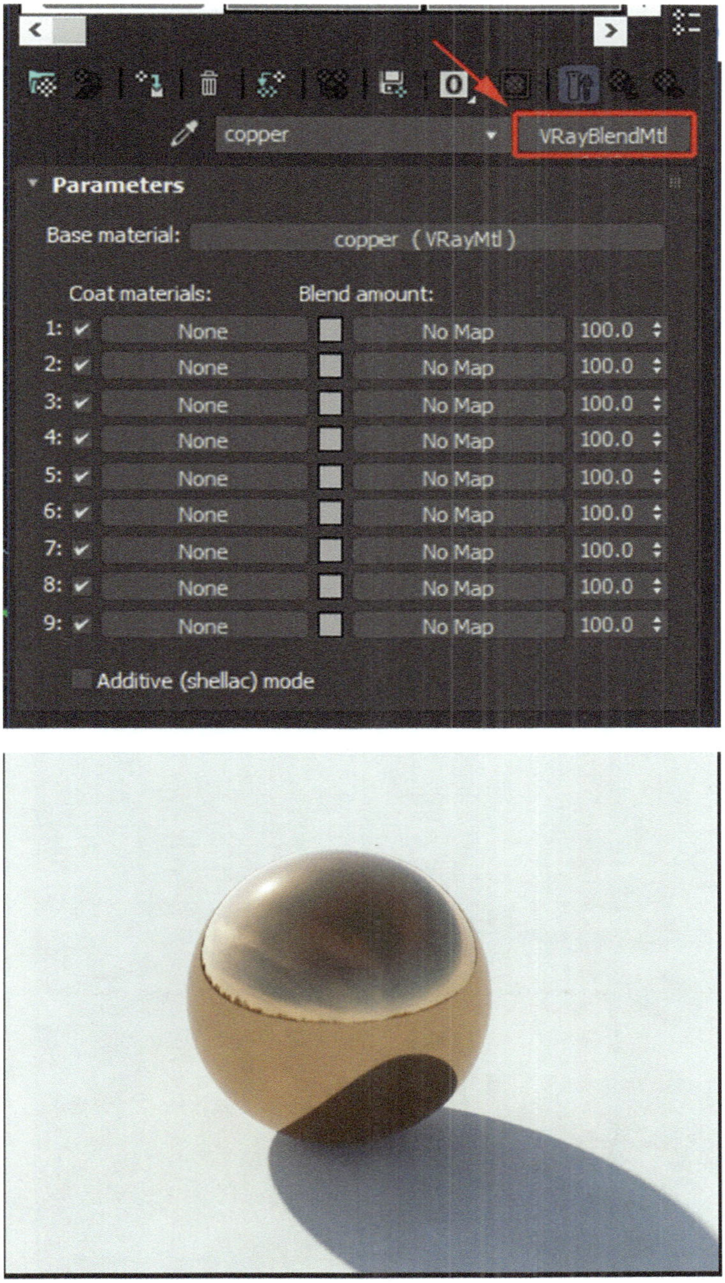

VRayBlendMtl loaded

Base material: This toggle is used as a the base sub-material.

Coat materials: This function has nine listed toggles that can be used to mix shaders with the Blend amount.

To demonstrate this functionality, the material Metal_Pattern_K_bmp_5cm was loaded from the VRay Asset Browser dialog.

When a VRayMaterial is loaded in its toggle, it automatically blends with the Base material.

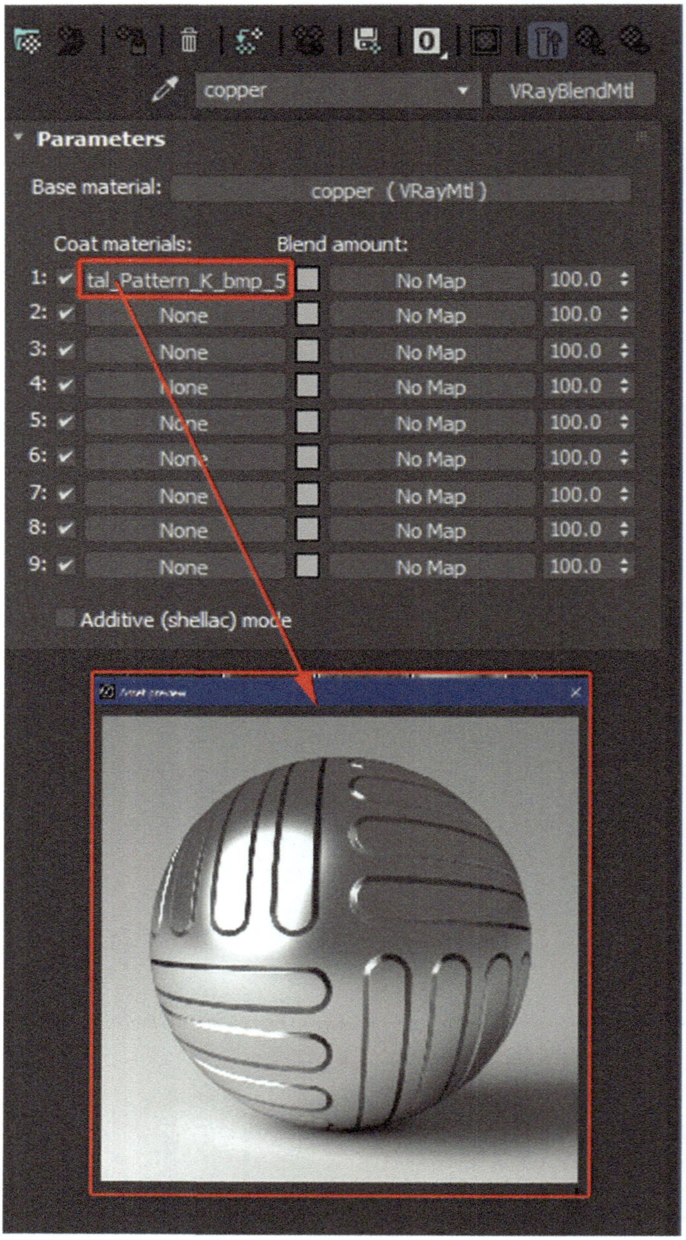

Coat materials with a toggle loaded

Blend amount: The function consists of nine listed toggles, with color swatches and numerical values to set the blend amount.

When a procedural map/bitmap is plugged into its toggle, it automatically overrides the color swatch.

Black and white or grayscale bitmaps work best.

The adjacent numerical values only work when there's a procedural map/bitmap inside the toggle.

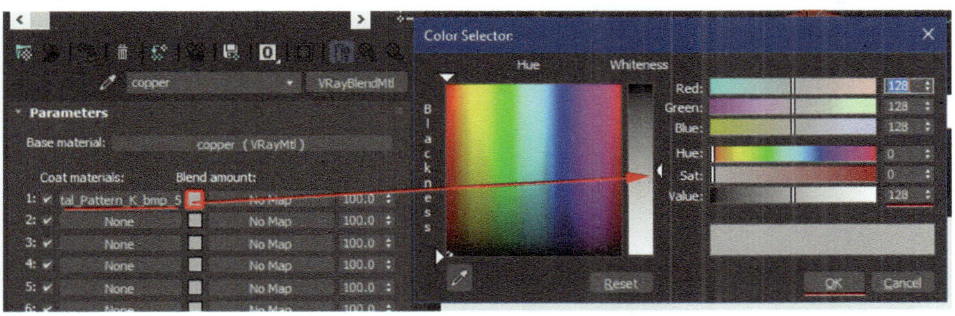

Blend amount set to 128

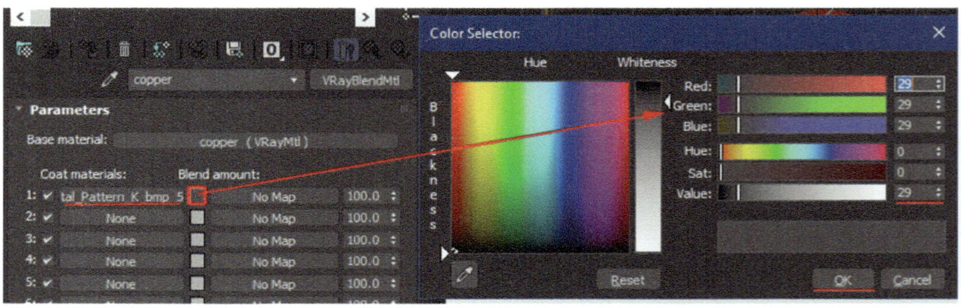

Blend amount set to 29

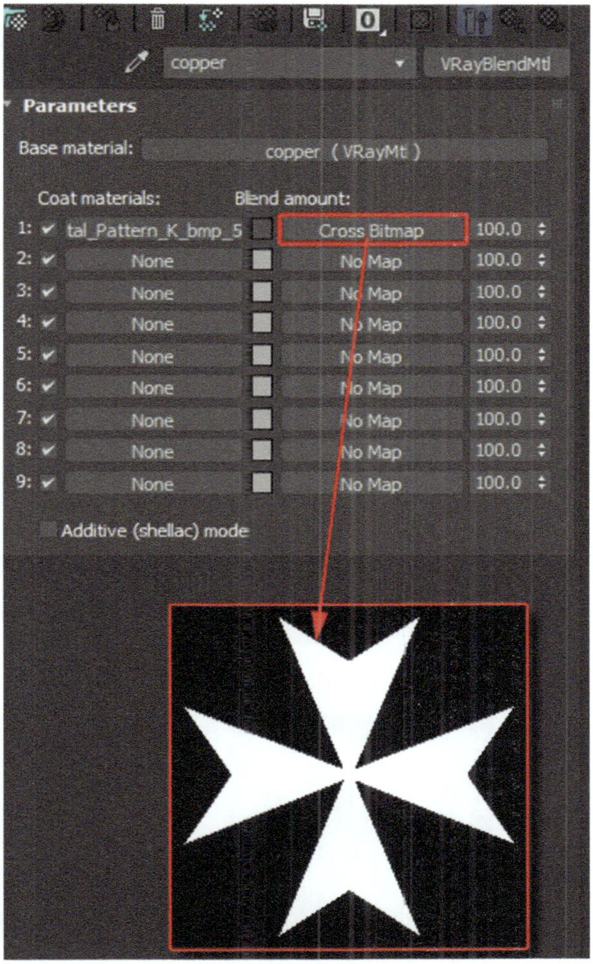
copper
VRayBlendMtl
Parameters
Base material:
copper (VRayMtl)
Coat materials:
Blend amount:
1: tal_Pattern_K_bmp_5
Cross Bitmap
100.0
2: None
No Map
100.0
3: None
No Map
100.0
4: None
No Map
100.0
5: None
No Map
100.0
6: None
No Map
100.0
7: None
No Map
100.0
8: None
No Map
100.0
9: None
No Map
100.0
Additive (shellac) mode

Bitmap applied to the Blend amount toggle

This bitmap is available in the resource files

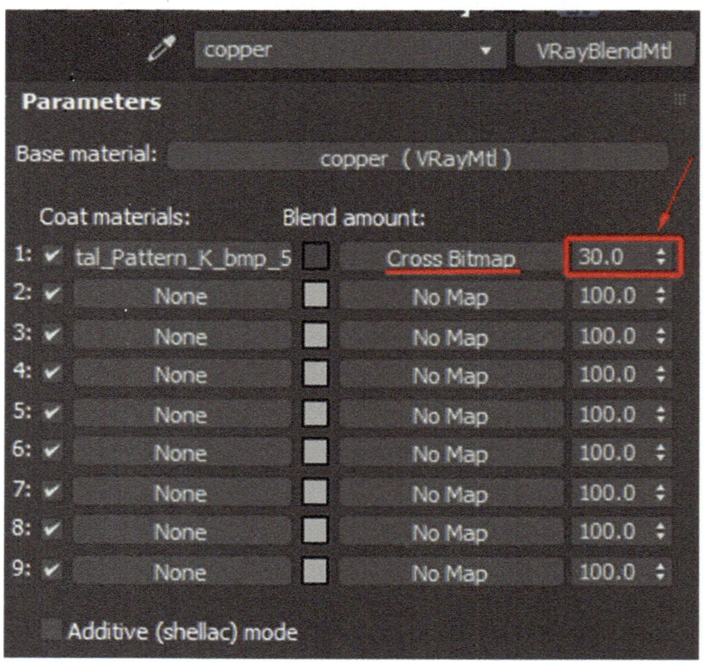

Blend amount Bitmap set to 30.0

VRayCarPaintMtl

As the name suggests, this shader emulates the physical properties of a metallic car pain finish.

Depending on System Unit Setup being used, a UVW Map modifier might be required in order for the flake layer to be visible.

To access it, simply click on the main shader toggle and choose the VRayCarPaintMtl from the Material/Map Browser dialog.

The shader should load up automatically.

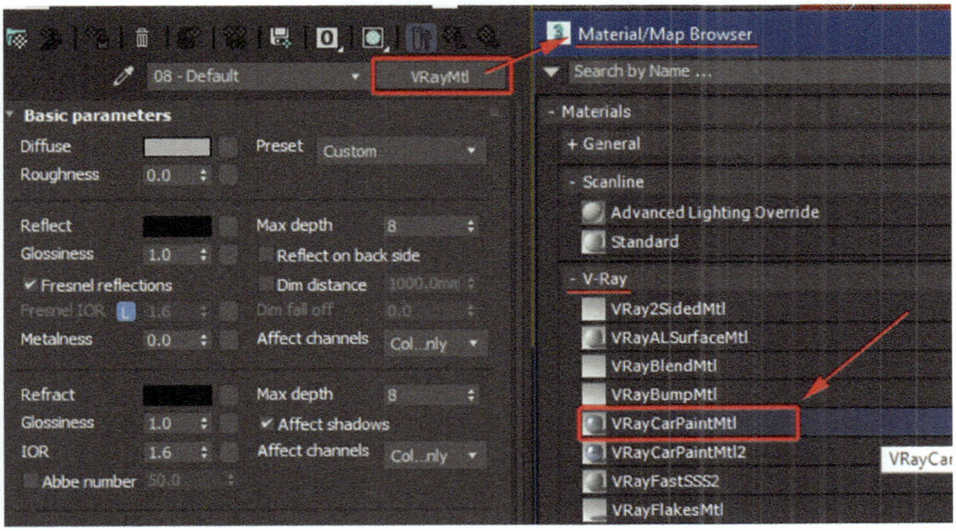

Choose the VRayCarPaintMtl shader

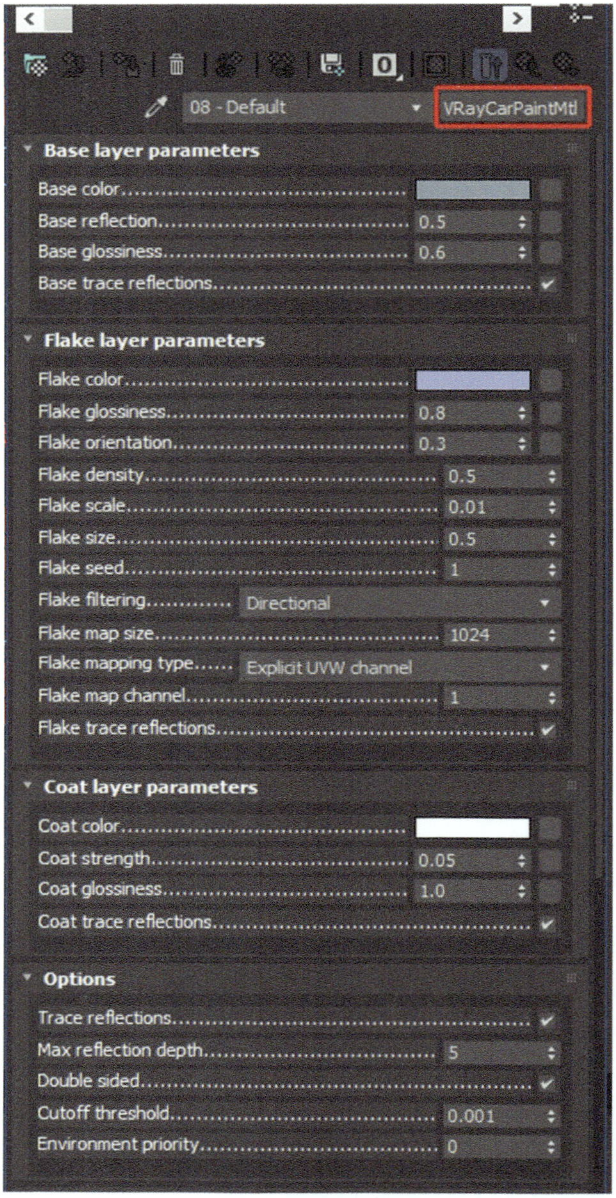

VRayCarPaintMtl shader loaded automatically

Base color: This function determines the main color of VRayCarPaintMtl.

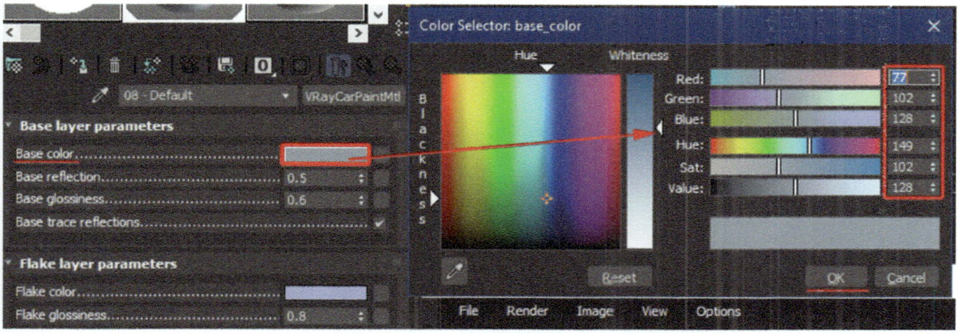
Color Selector: base_color
Hue
Whiteness
Blackness
Red:
Green:
Blue:
Hue:
Sat:
Value:
77
102
128
149
102
128
Reset
OK
Cancel
File
Render
Image
View
Options
08 - Default
VRayCarPaintMtl
Base layer parameters
Base color
Base reflection
0.5
Base glossiness
0.6
Base trace reflections
Flake layer parameters
Flake color
Flake glossiness
0.8

VRayCarPaintMtl base color: blue

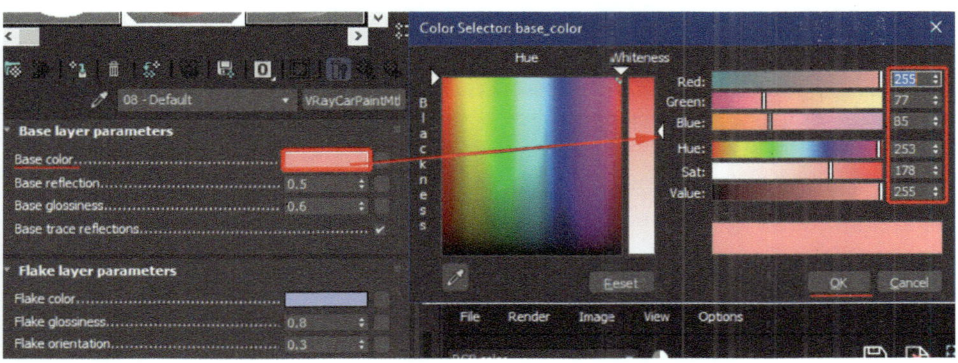
Color Selector: base_color
Hue
Whiteness
Blackness
Red:
Green:
Blue:
Hue:
Sat:
Value:
255
77
85
253
178
255
Reset
OK
Cancel
File
Render
Image
View
Options
08 - Default
VRayCarPaintMtl
Base layer parameters
Base color
Base reflection
0.5
Base glossiness
0.6
Base trace reflections
Flake layer parameters
Flake color
Flake glossiness
0.8
Flake orientation
0.3

VRayCarPaintMtl base color: red

Base reflection: This function controls the amount of reflectivity, with its numerical values. Default value is 0.5.

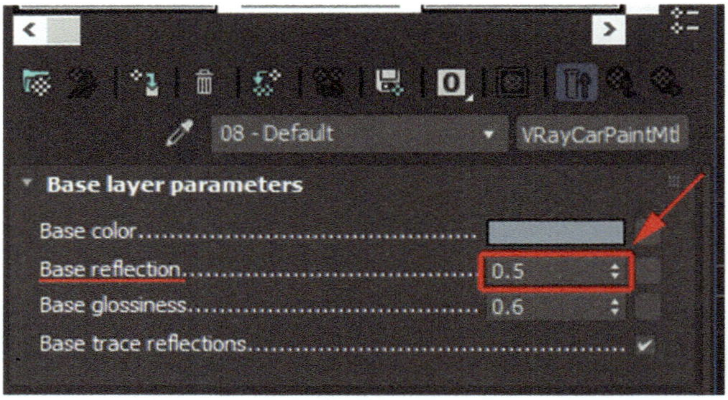

VRayCarPaintMtl base reflection: 0.5

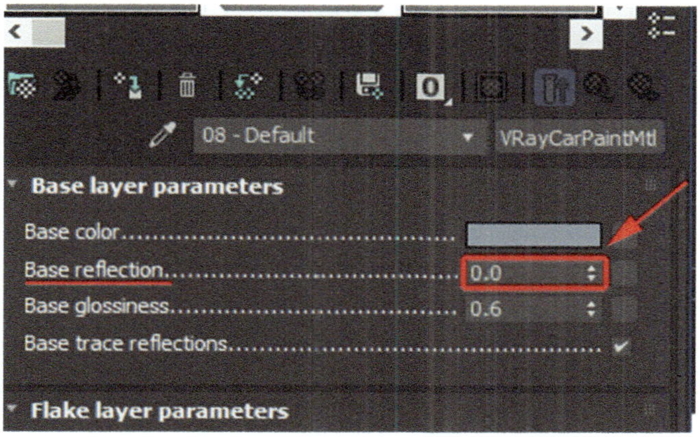

VRayCarPaintMtl base reflection: 0.0

Base glossiness: This function's numerical values determine the amount of glossiness on the surface. Default value is 0.6.

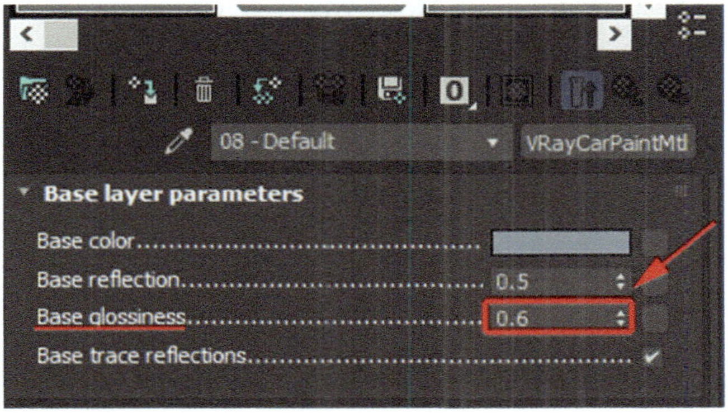

VRayCarPaintMtl base glossiness: 0.6

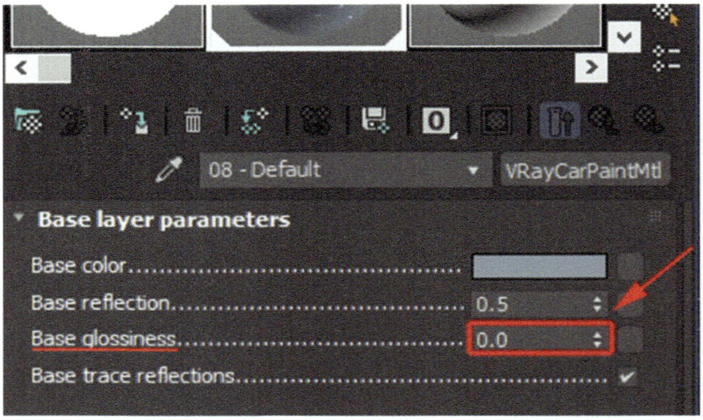

VRayCarPaintMtl base glossiness: 0.0

Base trace reflections: If enabled, this option allows the reflections to be traced. Enabled by default.

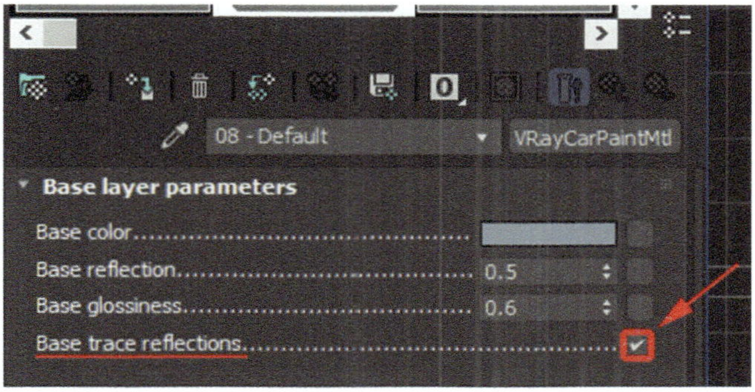

VRayCarPaintMtl base trace reflections: enabled

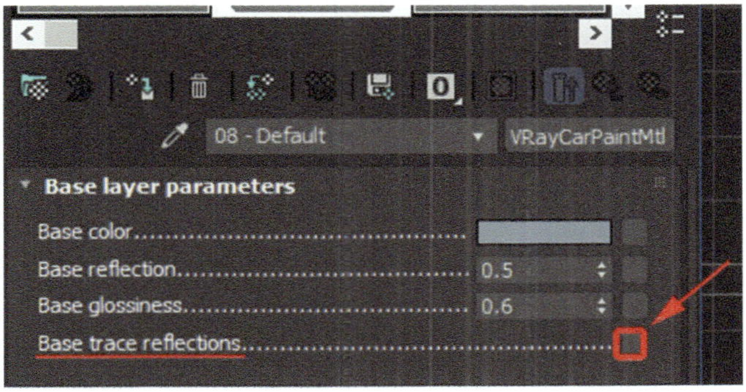

VRayCarPaintMtl base trace reflections: disabled

Flake color: This color swatch enables users to choose the flake color through the Color Selector dialog.

Default color is blue.

Flake glossiness: Its numerical values allow the users to control the amount of glossiness on the flake. Default value is 0.8.

Flake orientation: This function's numerical values control the orientation of the flake. This option is widely used to randomize the flake rotation.

Default value is 0.3.

Flake density: This function controls the density/number of flakes seen on the surface.

Default value is 0.5.

Flake scale: This option controls the structure of the flakes.

Default value is 0.01.

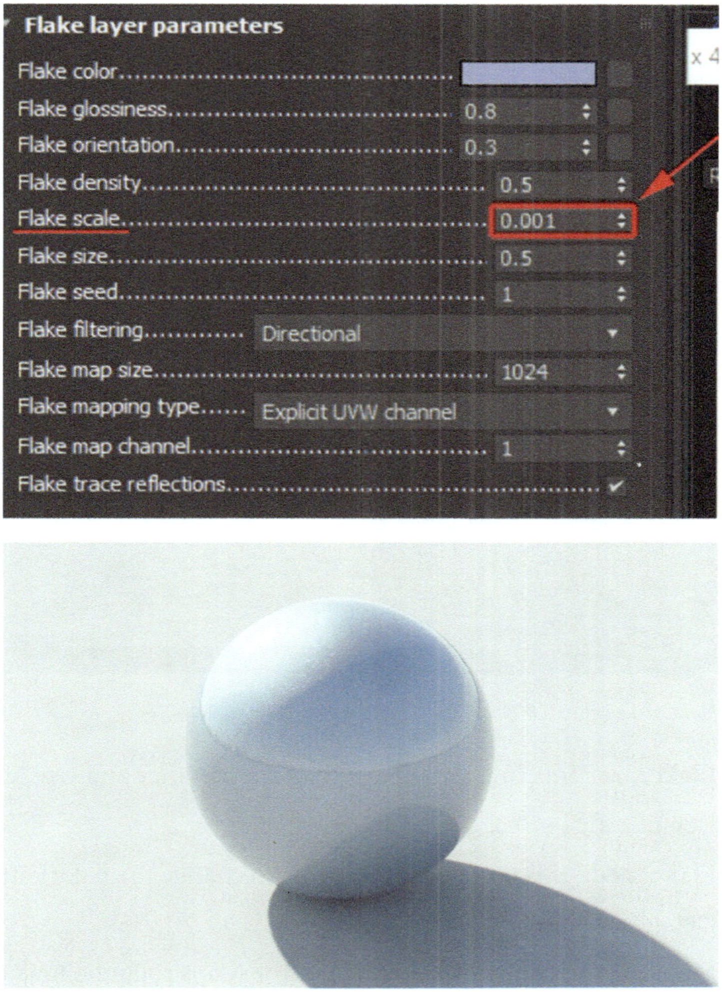

Flake scale set to 0.001

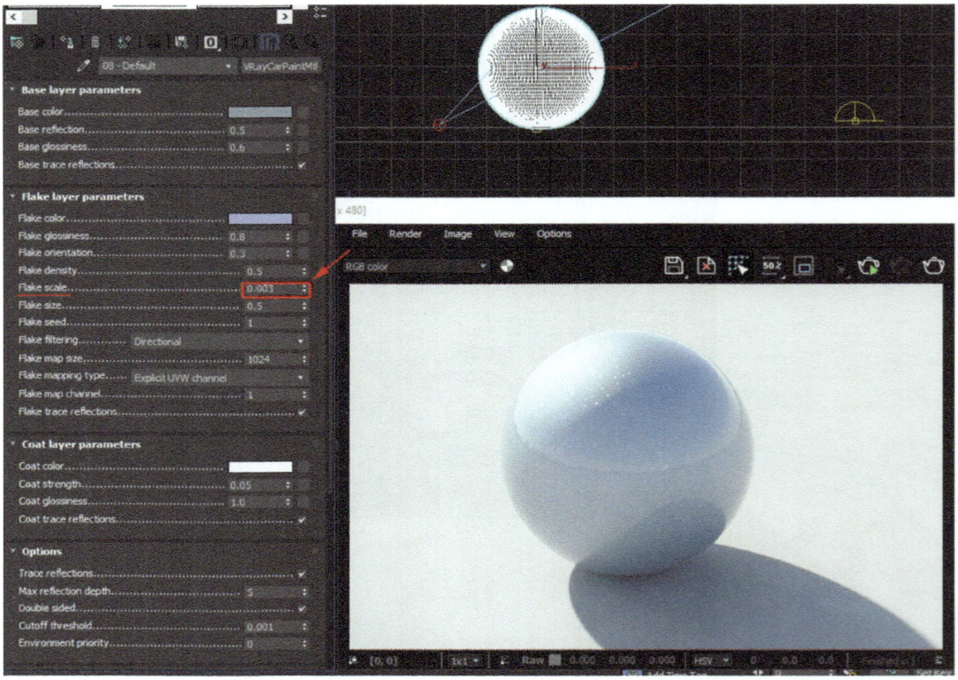

Flake scale set to 0.003

Flake size: This function determines the distance and size of the flakes.

Default value is 0.5.

Flake seed: This option enables users to change the flake pattern.

Default value is 1.

Maps: The list of toggles seen under the Maps rollout allows users to plug procedural maps in them. The procedural maps can be used at 100% value, or blended, by reducing the numerical values.

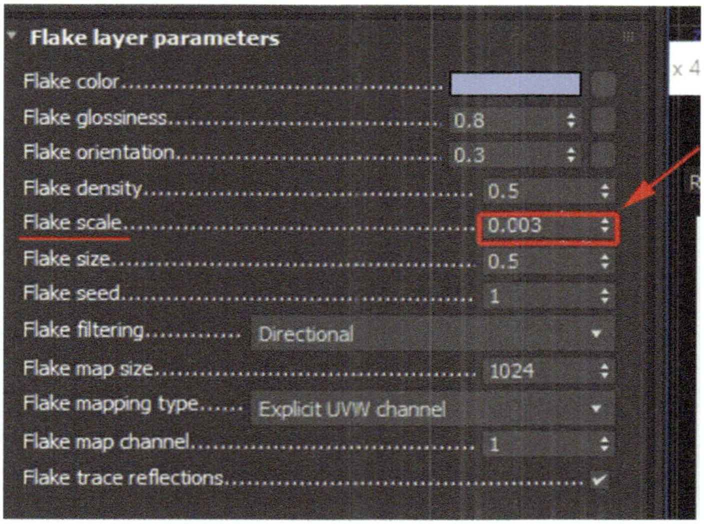

Coat color white

Coat color red

VRayEdgesTex

To test the functionality of this procedural map, please open the file under the name of VRayEdgesTex.max

This procedural map is widely used on top of a material or color to create edges/wirelines around the surface. It can be plugged through the diffuse toggle, or as a render element, to be composed in post.

It can also be used to emulate chamfered edges on corners/edges of surfaces through the Bump toggle.

The render below depicts a metal box prior to using the VRayEdgesTex in its Bump toggle.

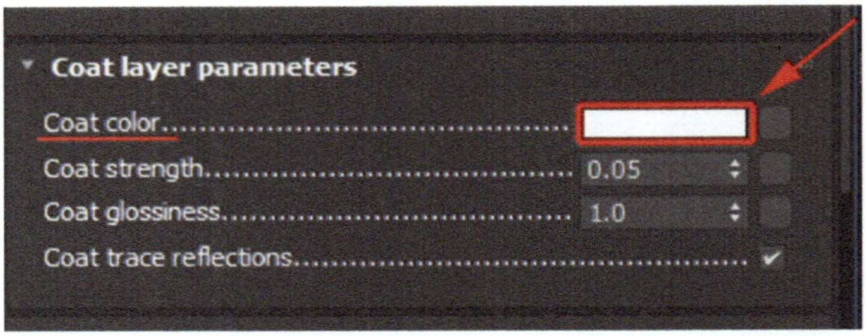

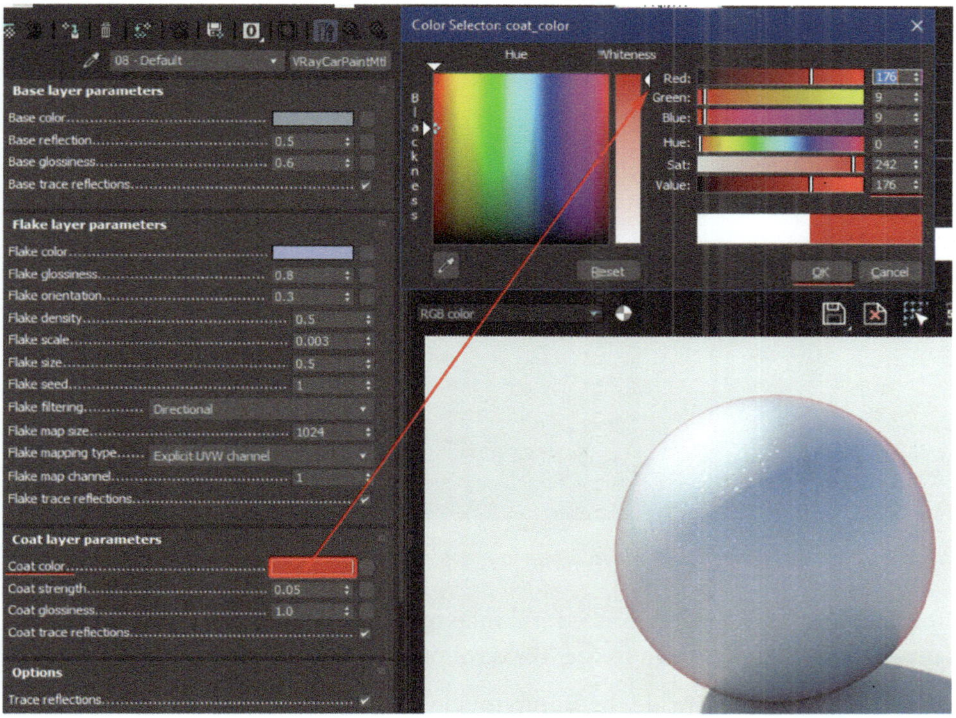
08 - Default
VRayCarPaintMtl
Base layer parameters
Base color
Base reflection 0.5
Base glossiness 0.6
Base trace reflections
Flake layer parameters
Flake color
Flake glossiness 0.8
Flake orientation 0.3
Flake density 0.5
Flake scale 0.003
Flake size 0.5
Flake seed 1
Flake filtering Directional
Flake map size 1024
Flake mapping type Explicit UVW channel
Flake map channel 1
Flake trace reflections
Coat layer parameters
Coat color
Coat strength 0.05
Coat glossiness 1.0
Coat trace reflections
Options
Trace reflections
Color Selector: coat_color
Hue
Whiteness
Blackness
Red: 176
Green: 9
Blue: 9
Hue: 0
Sat: 242
Value: 176
Reset
OK
Cancel
RGB color

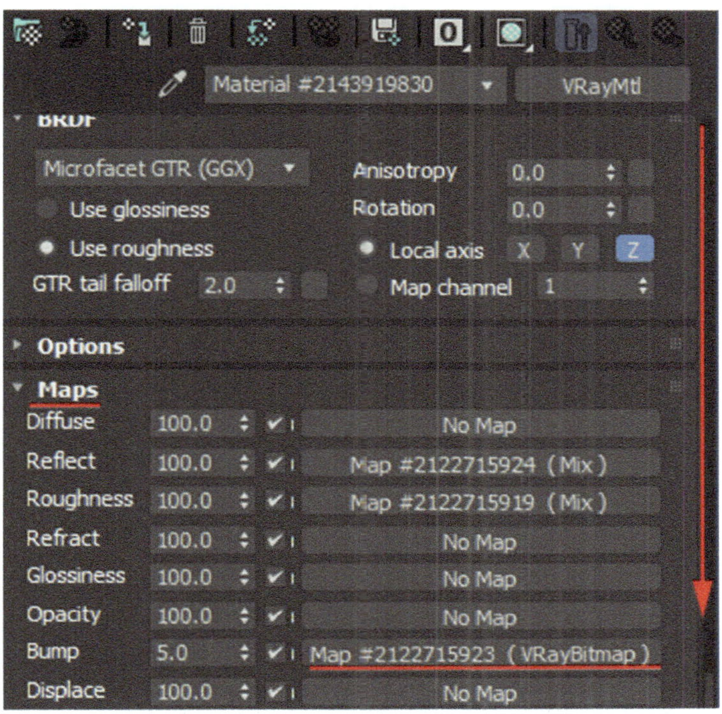
Material #2143919830
VRayMtl
BRDF
Microfacet GTR (GGX)
Anisotropy 0.0
Use glossiness
Rotation 0.0
Use roughness
Local axis X Y Z
GTR tail falloff 2.0
Map channel 1
Options
Maps
Diffuse 100.0 No Map
Reflect 100.0 Map #2122715924 (Mix)
Roughness 100.0 Map #2122715919 (Mix)
Refract 100.0 No Map
Glossiness 100.0 No Map
Opacity 100.0 No Map
Bump 5.0 Map #2122715923 (VRayBitmap)
Displace 100.0 No Map

Metal box without VRayEdgesTex in its Bump toggle

To add the VRayEdgesTex procedural map to the Bump toggle, simply scroll down to the Maps rollout and click on the Bump toggle.

Inside the Bump toggle, click on the VRayBitmap toggle to open the Material/Map Browser dialog.

In the Material/Map Browser dialog, under the VRay rollout, choose the Mix procedural map from its list.

NOTE

The following steps assume you already have an existing bitmap/procedural map plugged into the Bump toggle.

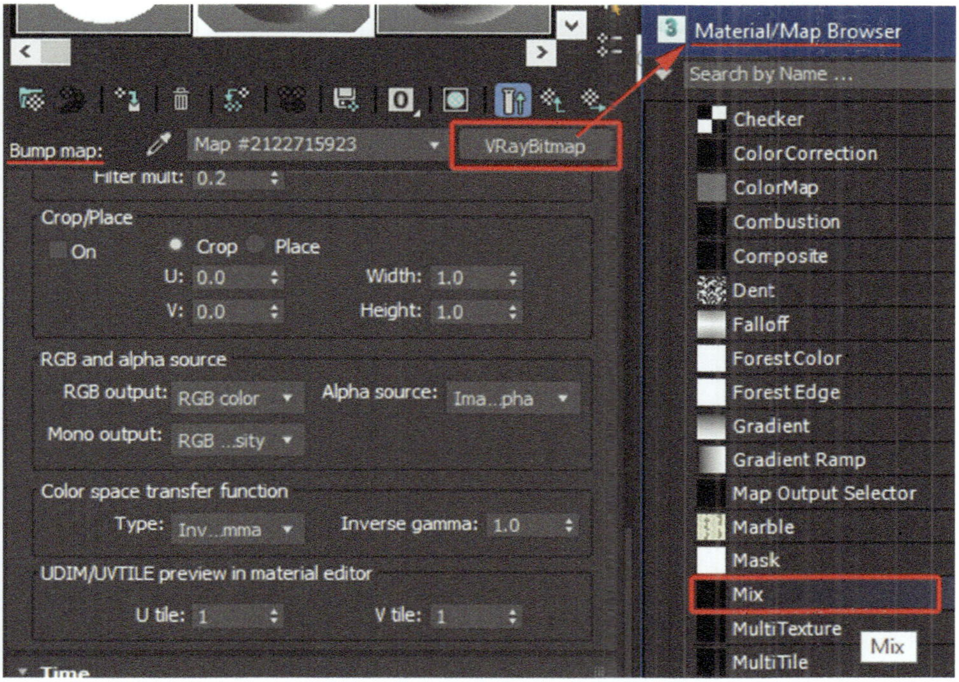

Choose the Mix procedural map

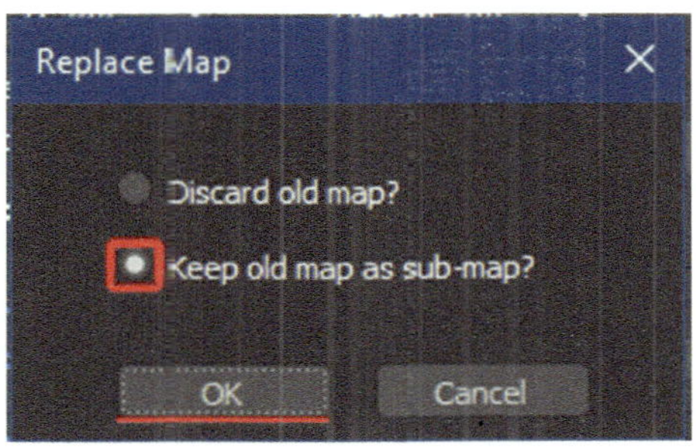

Keep old map as sub-map

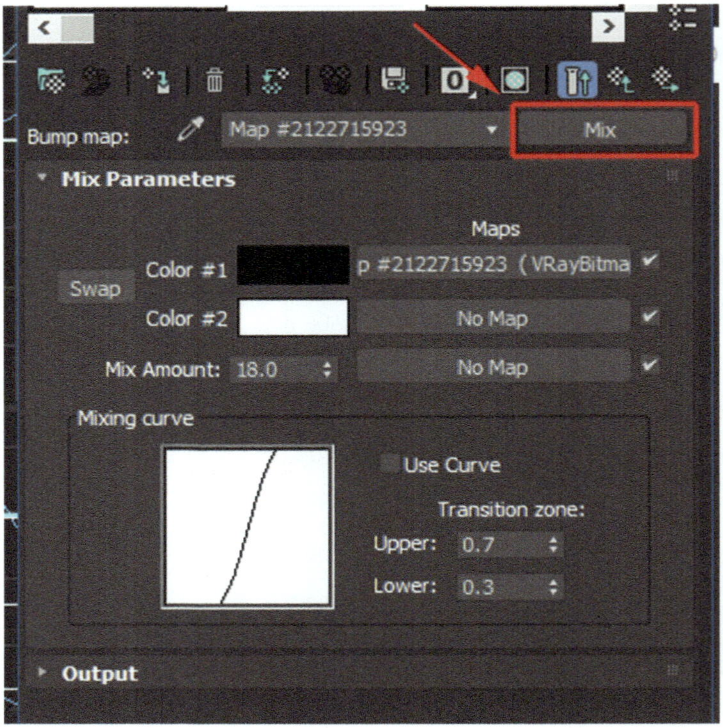

Mix procedural map loaded

The Mix procedural map will help keep the prominence of both VRayEdgesTex and the original bump bitmap (Color #1).

Color # and #2: These toggles allow users to plug procedural maps and/or Bitmaps to it.

Alternatively, users can simply use their color swatches.

Mix Amount: This function controls the amount of blend between Color #1 and Color #2.

With the default value set to 0.0, Color #1 will be 100% visible.

Users can also plug procedural maps and/or bitmaps to control the Mix Amount.

Grayscale and black and white bitmaps work best in the Mix Amount toggle.

Mixing curve: This group overrides the Mix amount values when the Use Curve function is enabled.

The upper and lower values control the transition zone/gradient.

To load the VRayEdgesTex, click on the Color #2 toggle, and choose the VRayEdgesTex procedural map from the Material/Map Browser dialog.

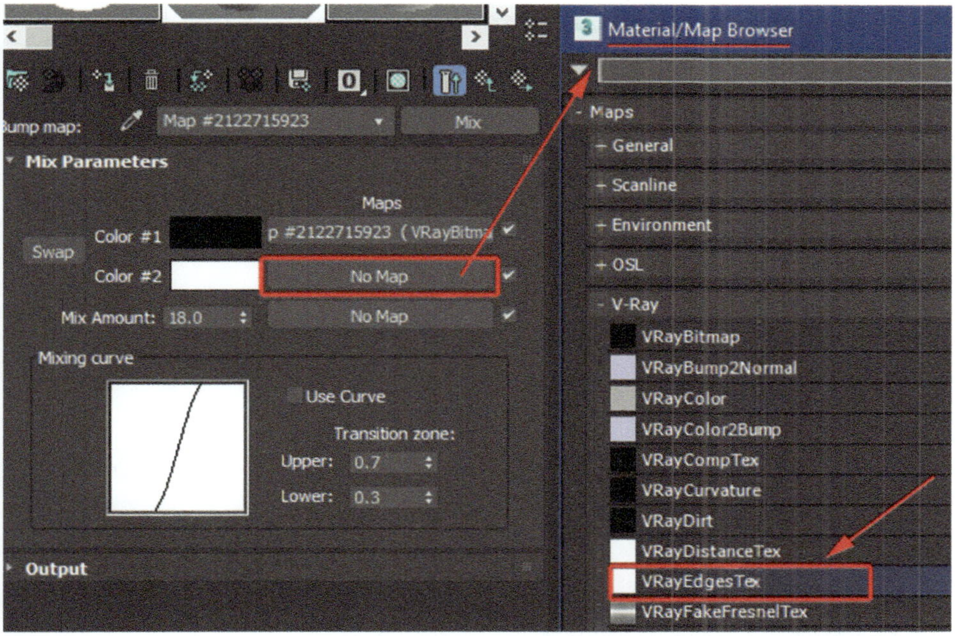

Load VRayEdgesTex

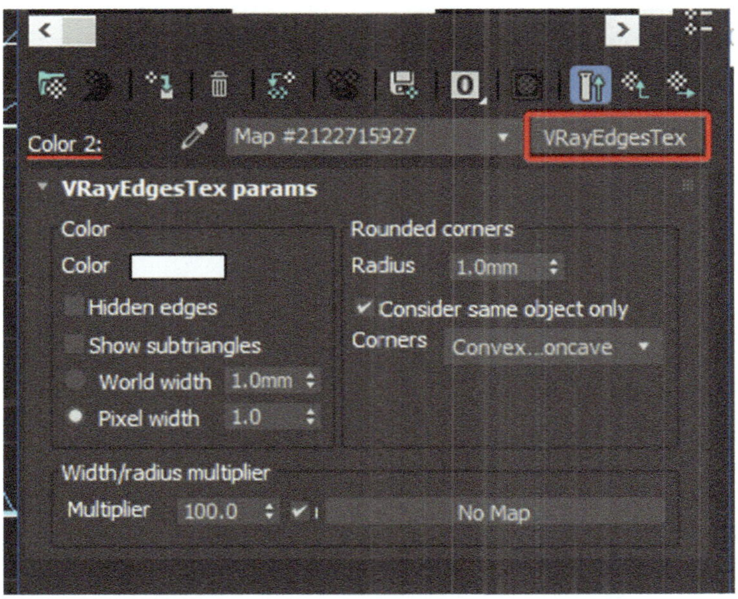

VRayEdgesTex procedural map loaded

Color: This color swatch sets the direction of the Bump, when used in the bump toggle.

White color produces an outward bump.

Black color produces an inward bump.

When applied in the diffuse toggle, it serves as the wireframe color (White) wrapped around the geometry.

Hidden edges: When enabled in the diffuse toggle, this function displays hidden wireframe edges of a geometry.

Disabled by default.

Show subtriangles: When enabled in the Diffuse toggle, this function displays the subtriangles of a geometry (in wireframe mode).

Disabled by default.

World width: When enabled in the Diffuse toggle, it displays the wireframe thickness based on your scene's system units.

Disabled by default.

Pixel width: When applied to the Diffuse toggle, this function controls the wireframe thickness, in pixel units.

Enabled and set to 1.0 by default.

Round corners: This group controls the bevel/chamfer size on objects, when applied to the Bump toggle.

Radius: This function controls the size of the bevel/chamfer.

Set to 1 mm by default.

Consider same object only: When enabled, this function will apply the bevel/chamfer effect on the objects applied only.

Enabled by default.

Corners: This function allows users to choose the type of corners to apply the Rounded corners to.

It is set to affect convex and concave by default.

Depending on the size of the object or the scenes' Unit Setup, one can set up appropriate Radius value.

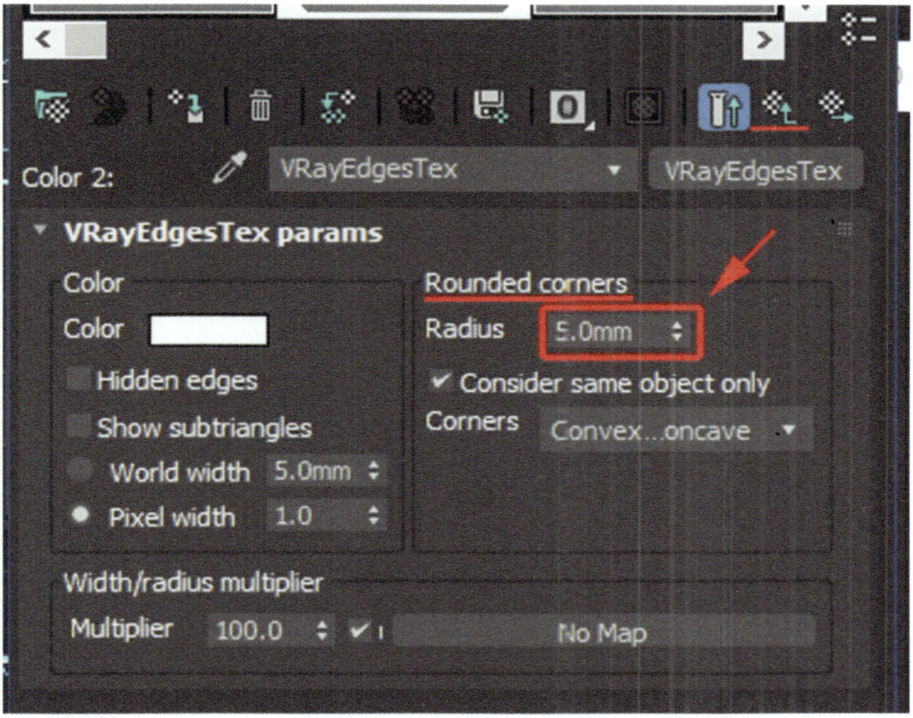

Radius value set to 5 mm.

Because we are currently using the VRayEdgesTex mixed with the main Bump bitmap, we need to increase the Mix amount value, in order for the Round corners to be visible in the render.

To do so, click on the Go to Parent button, to go back to the Mix main parameters.

Increase the Mix Amount value to about 18.0.

These values were achieved after few region renders to see what worked best.

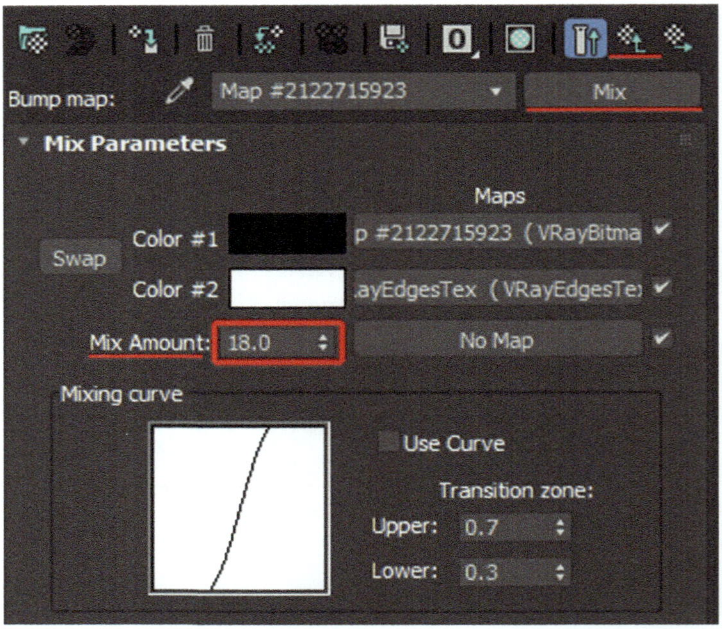
Bump map:
Map #2122715923
Mix
Mix Parameters
Maps
Color #1
p #2122715923 (VRayBitma
Swap
Color #2
.ayEdgesTex (VRayEdgesTe
Mix Amount:
18.0
No Map
Mixing curve
Use Curve
Transition zone:
Upper:
0.7
Lower:
0.3

Mix amount set to 18.0.

Conclusion

This chapter has introduced users to some of the most popular VRay shaders and procedural maps, followed by guiding users through the process of accessing and using them.

Some functionalities and parameters were discussed in more detail than others, by relevance.

Finally, new procedural maps will be introduced and discussed in more detail throughout this book.

For more information about other VRay shaders and procedural maps, please visit:

http://docs.chaosgroup.com/

3

Cameras and Lighting in VRay

3 Cameras and Lighting in VRay

Camera and lights are the building blocks of any 3d scene.

NOTE

As referred to earlier, the VRay renderer needs to be loaded in the scene first, prior to using some of the tools and techniques covered in this chapter.

As such, this chapter will focus on both VRay camera parameters and lights, to help highlight their invaluable role in the framing and mood of a scene.

To test some of the topics covered here, please open the 3ds max file, VRay Cameras.max

If you're ever prompted with the message, File Load: Units Mismatch dialog, simply choose to Adopt the File's Unit Scale. And OK to open it.

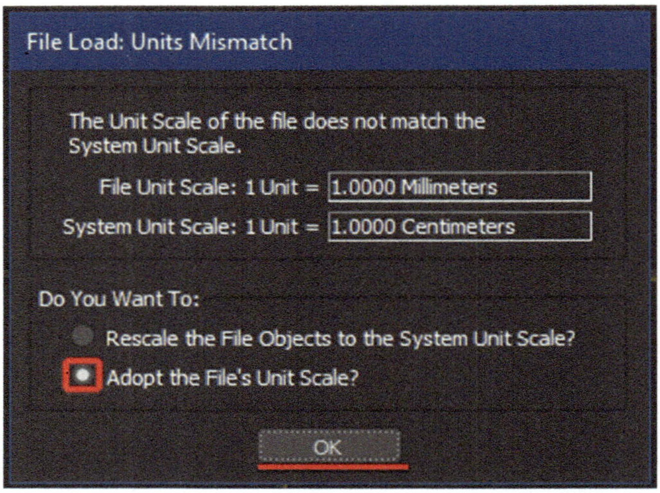

File Load: Units Mismatch dialog

Cameras: VRayPhysicalCamera

This type of camera is more popular of the two, and it emulates the physical properties of a real camera.

To create a VRayPhysicalCamera, go to the Create command panel and click on the Cameras button.

Under Cameras group, select the Standard menu and choose VRay from the list.

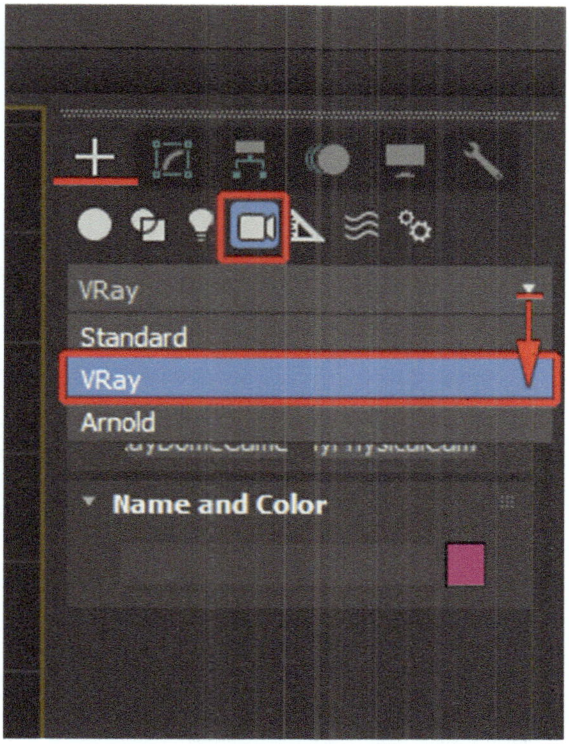

Choose the VRay menu from the Cameras group

In the VRay Object Type group, select the VRayPhysicalCamera button, followed by clicking its cursor in the top viewport and dragging it across the screen to create the camera target.

Right click after the camera creation to exit, and go to the Modify command panel thereafter.

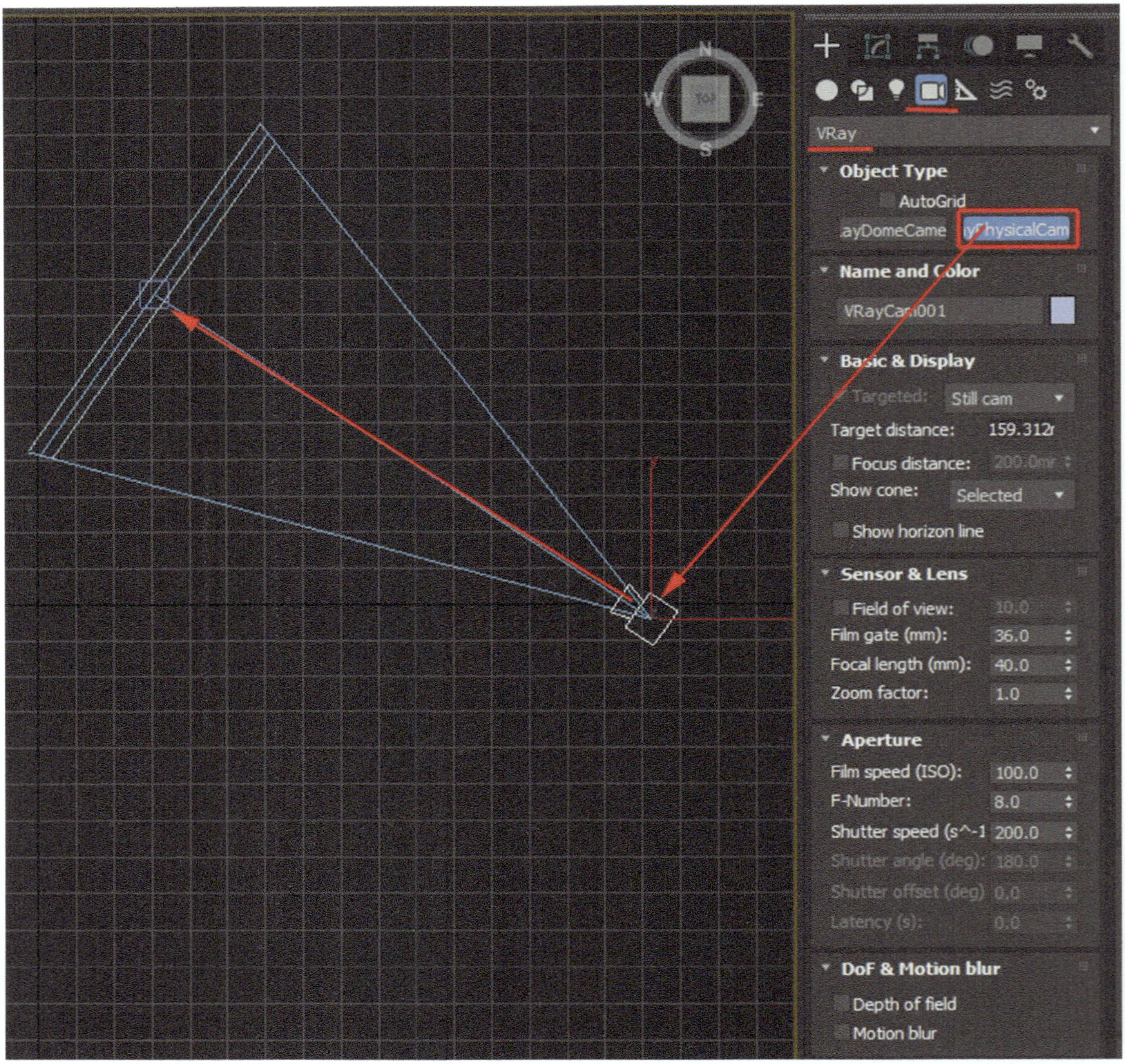

Create a VRayPhysicalCamera in the Top Viewport

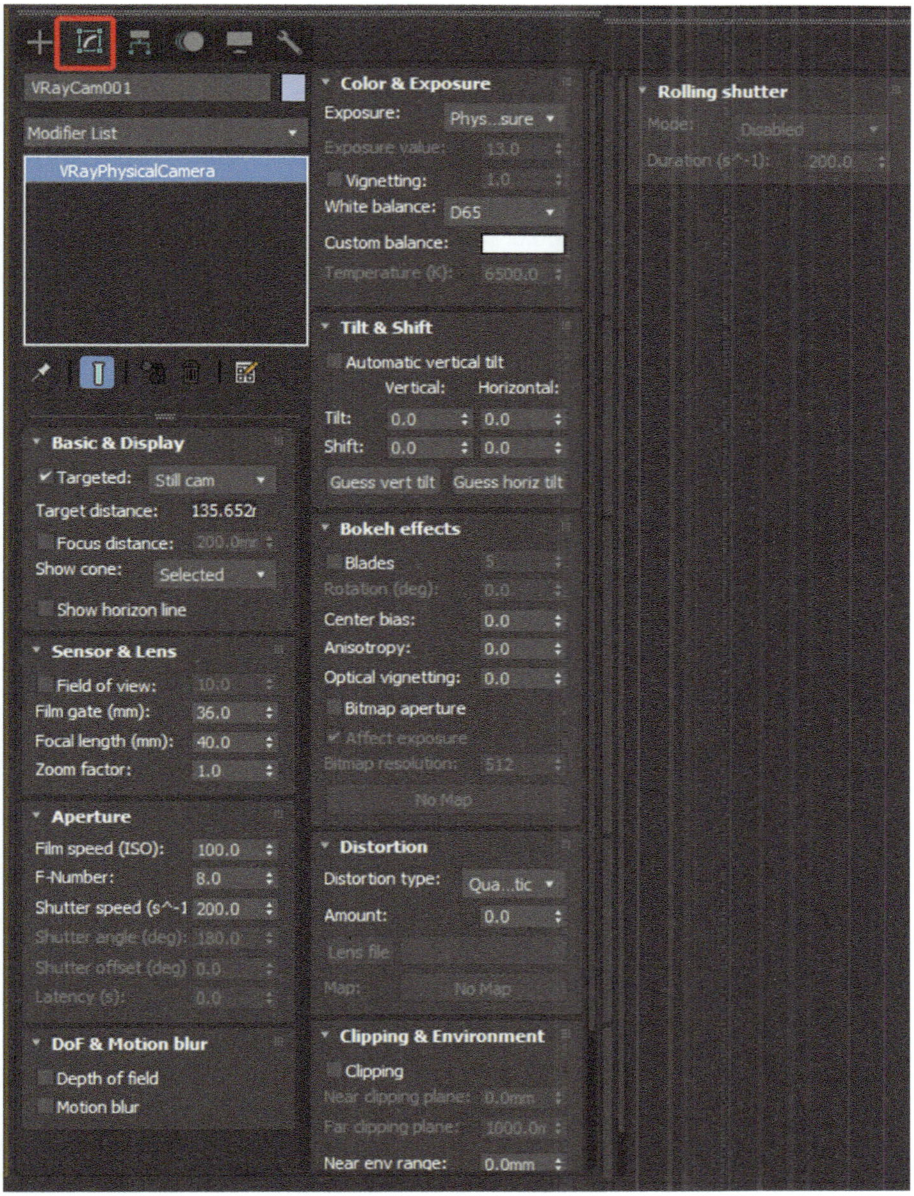

VRayPhysicalCamera parameters

Targeted: When enabled, this function adds a target to the physical camera. The target can be moved by the user to set the direction of the camera.

To move the camera itself, one has to either select both the camera and its target or simply disable the Target function.

Enabled by default.

Type: This camera function allows users to choose from three types of cameras available:

Still cam: This camera comes with a host of typical parameters to emulate a still camera.

Default shutter speed set to 200.0.

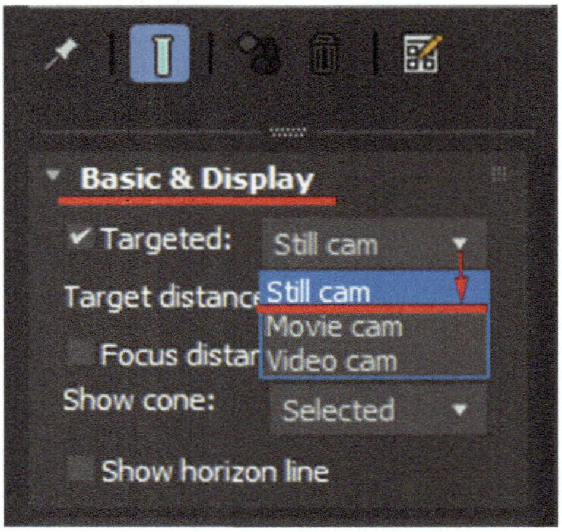

Physical camera options

Movie cam: This type of camera emulates a movie camera from motion pictures, using a standard shutter angle set to 180.

Video cam: This camera type emulates a standard video camera without shutter, and with CCD matrix.

Latency set to 0.0 by default.

Target distance: The function sets the distance of the target camera.

Focus distance: Its function value sets a new camera distance.

Disabled by default.

Horizon line: When turned on, it displays the exact position of horizon line in the camera viewport.

This tool is quite useful for matching camera views in photomontages or verified views.

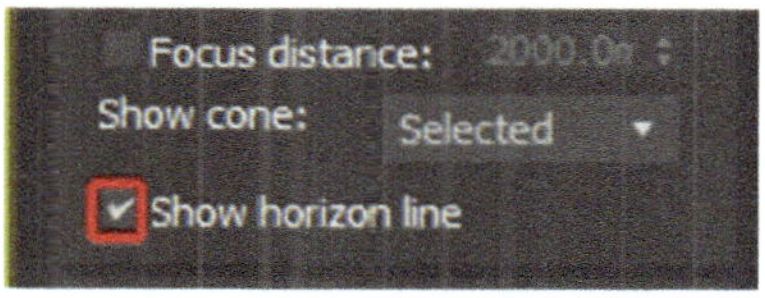

Show horizon line enabled

Horizon line visible in the camera viewport

Sensors & Lens

Field of view: When enabled, this function is an alternative to using the Film gate and Focal length functions.

High values have the effect of a camera zooming in.

Lower values have the opposite effect.

Disabled by default.

Film gate(mm): This function determines the horizontal size of the film gate, in millimeters. It's worth noting that the values displayed here are directly connected to the Units Setup dialog.

High values have the effect of a camera zooming in

Lower values have the opposite effect.

Default value is 36.0.

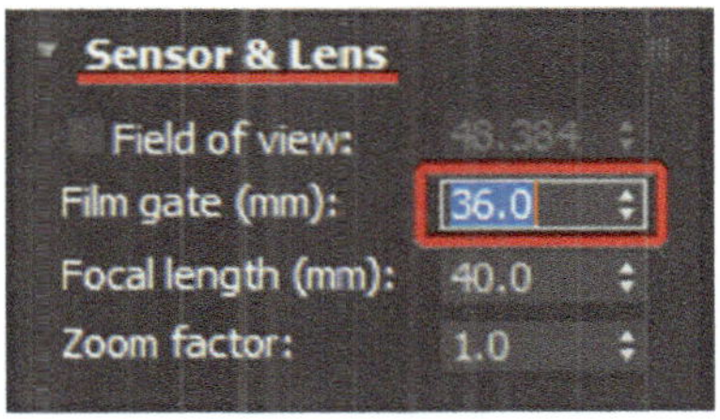

Film gate value set to 36.0

Film gate value set to 36.0 render

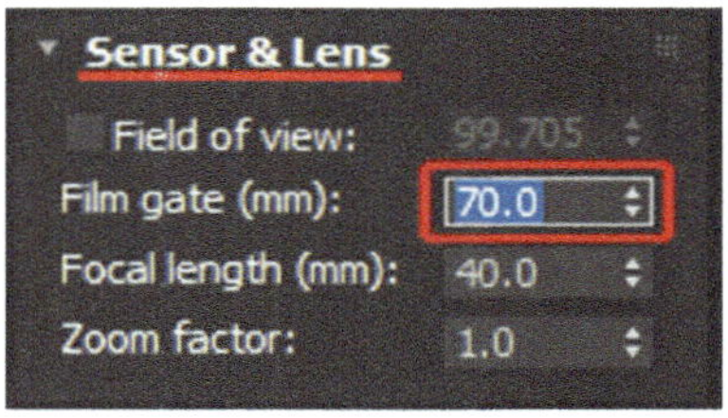

Film gate value set to 70.0

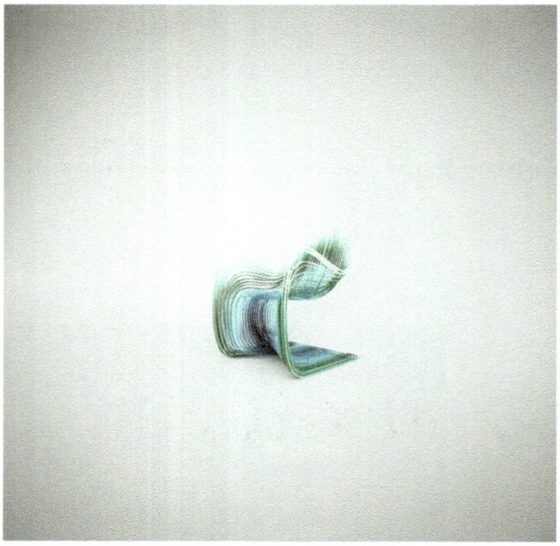

Film gate value set to 70.0 render

Focal length (mm): This function emulates the Focal length of a real camera lens.

High values have the effect of a camera zooming in.

Lower values have the opposite effect.

Default value is 40.0.

Zoom factor: This function allows the camera to zoom in and zoom out of the scene.

Default value is 1.0.

Aperture

Film speed (ISO): It controls the camera sensitivity. Lower values darken the render.

Higher values produce opposite results.

Default value is 200.0.

F-number: This function is often used to increase or decrease the render brightness, when the exposure function is turned on.

High values decrease the render brightness. Low values yield opposite results.

Default value is 8.0.

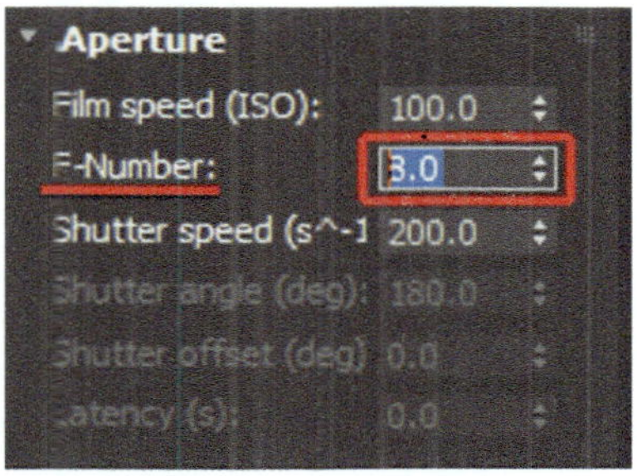

f-number value set to 8.0

f-number value set to 8.0 render

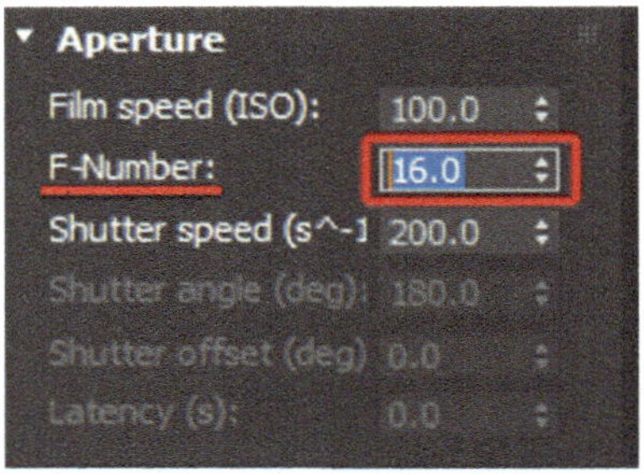

f-number value set to 16.0

f-number value set to 16.0 render

Shutter speed: This function controls the overall exposure time of the camera. Lower numerical values yield brighter results. Higher values have the opposite effect.

Default value is 200.00.

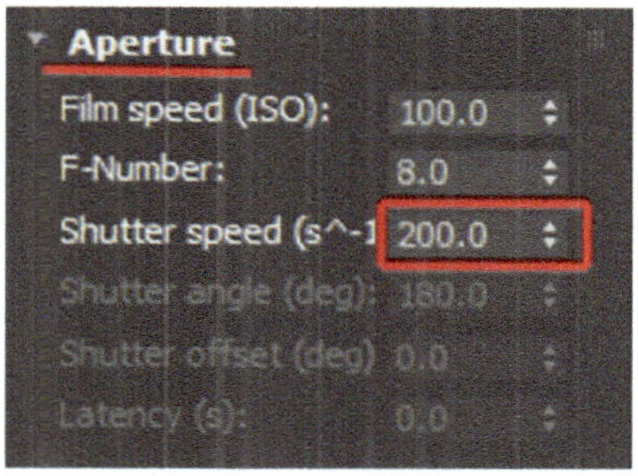

Shutter speed set to 200.0

Shutter speed set to 200.0 render

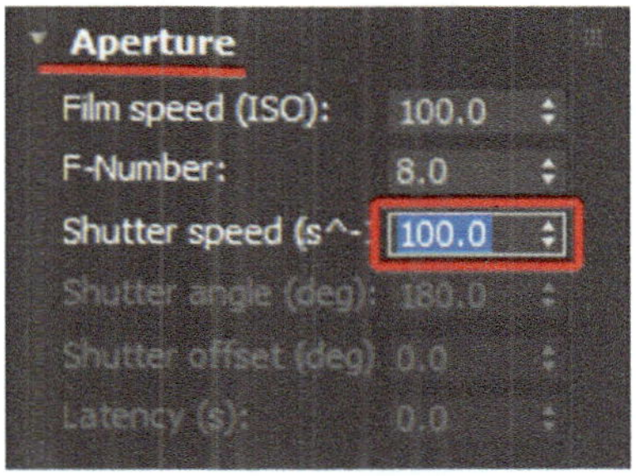

Shutter speed set to 100.0

Shutter speed set to 100.0 render

Shutter angle (deg): This option determines the shutter angle of the camera, in degrees.

Disabled by default.

It becomes live (180.0) when the camera type is set to a Movie cam.

Shutter offset (deg): It becomes live simultaneously with the shutter angle, when the camera type is set to a Movie cam.

Its numerical values determine the shutter offset of the Movie Cam type.

Latency (s): This function is only available when the Cam type is set to Video cam. It controls the Charge-Coupled-Device (CCD) latency of a Video cam.

Default value is 0.0.

DoF and Motion Blur

Depth of field: When enabled, it adds the Depth of Field effect to the camera.

For stronger results, it's imperative to enable the Focus distance function and decrease the F-Number value.

Low Focus distance values add the DoF effect in areas closer to the camera.

High Focus distance values add the DoF effect in areas further away from the camera.

We will cover this process in more detail in the chapters ahead.

Disabled by default.

NOTE

The DoF effect increases the rendering time drastically. It's often best to add the DoF effect in post-production, using the VRayZdepth render element.

Motion blur: When enabled, it adds the motion blur effect to a moving object.

For strong results, ensure the Shutter speed value is low (20.0) and the object is moving or/and rotating in the rendered frame (animated). The motion blur effect will never be visible at the beginning or end of a frame (only in the frames in-between).

Disabled by default.

> **NOTE**
>
> The motion blur effect increases the rendering time substantially.

Color and Exposure

Exposure parameters control the overall brightness of the render, in conjunction with other functions such as F-number, ISO, and shutter speed.

Enabled by default.

Physical exposure: This exposure type is controlled by the F-number and shutter speed values.

Exposure value (EV): When loaded, this type of exposure is controlled by the Exposure values entered, shutter speed, and F-number.

Disabled by default.

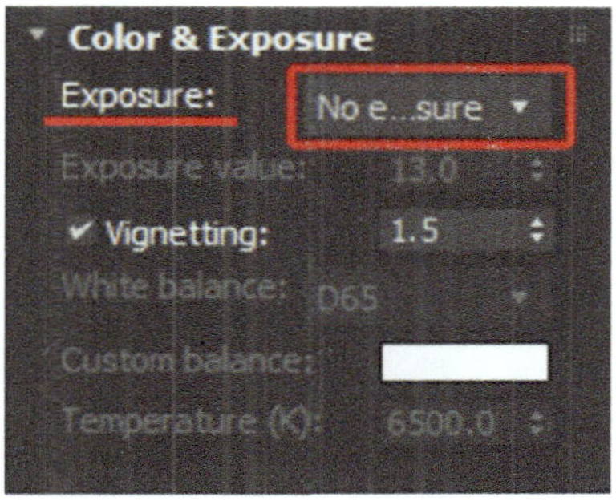

Exposure disabled

Exposure disabled render

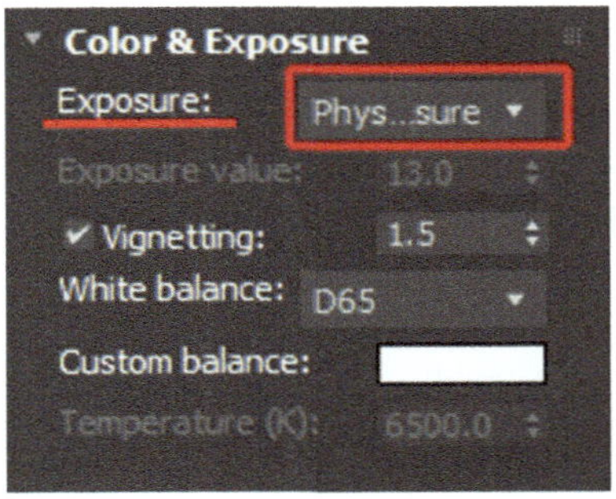

Exposure enabled

Exposure enabled render

Vignetting: When enabled, it creates a slightly more contrasting image by darkening the four corners of the render. This real camera effect is known as vignetting.

The higher the values, the more apparent and darker the vignetting effect.

Disabled by default.

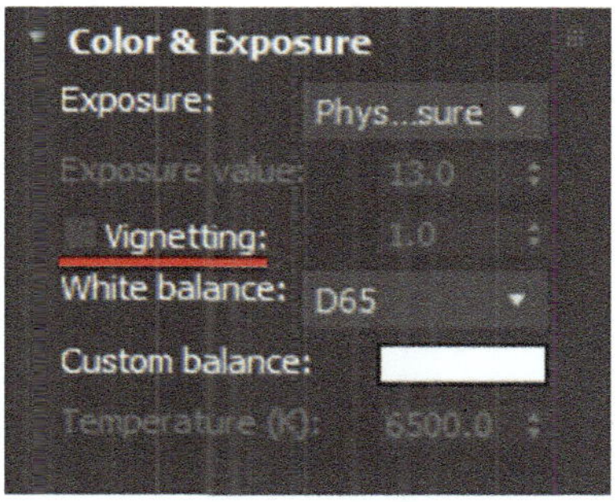

Vignetting disabled

Vignetting disabled render

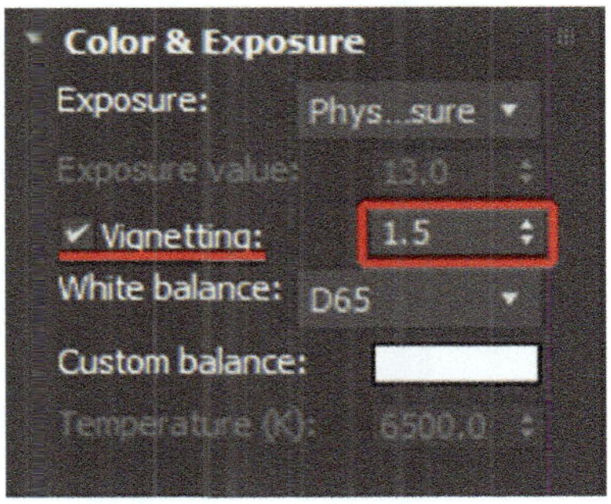

Vignetting enabled, value 1.5

Vignetting enabled, value 1.5 render

White balance: As the name suggests, its parameters control the colors that will appear white or whiter in the render.

It's widely used to balance out overpowering colors in the scene.

The pull-down menu comes with numerous presets such as Custom, Neutral, Daylight, D75, D65, D55, D50, and Temperature.

Default preset is D65.

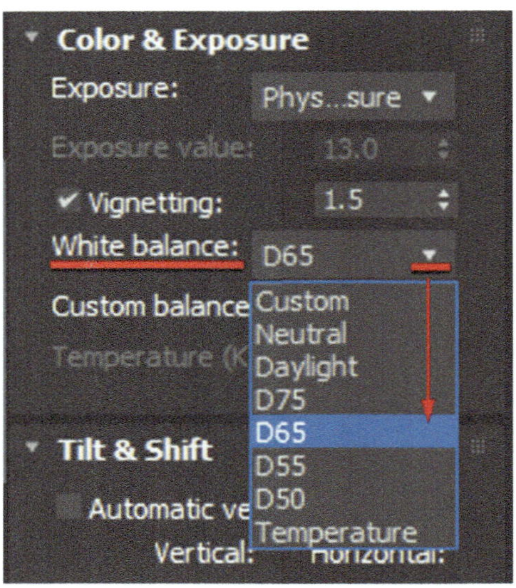

White balance pulled-down menu

Custom balance: This color swatch allows users to pick or sample a custom color from the Color Selector dialog. The color displayed here will look more toward white in the render.

Default color is white (255).

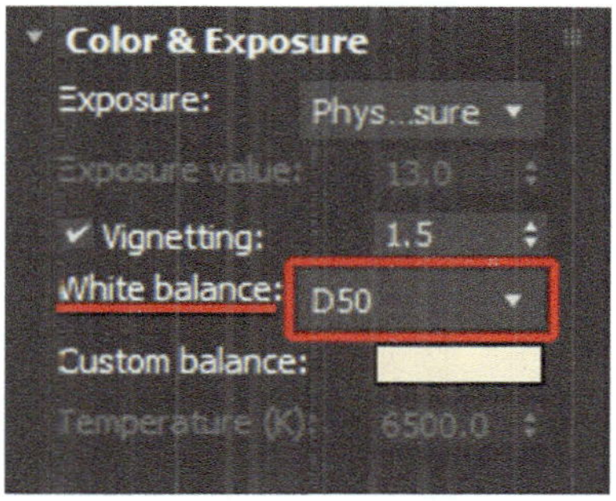

White balance set to D50

White balance set to D50 render

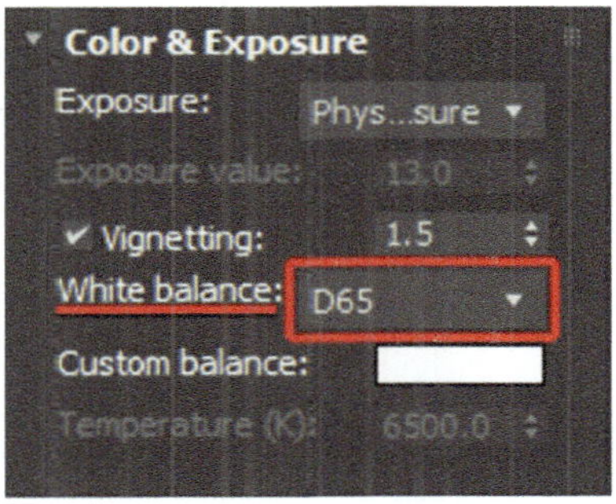

White balance set to D65

White balance set to D65 render

Temperature: This option becomes live when the Temperature preset is chosen from the default White Balance dropdown menu.

It allows users to type in a numerical color temperature value, if selected. For information about color temperature values, simply Google **kelvin color chart**.

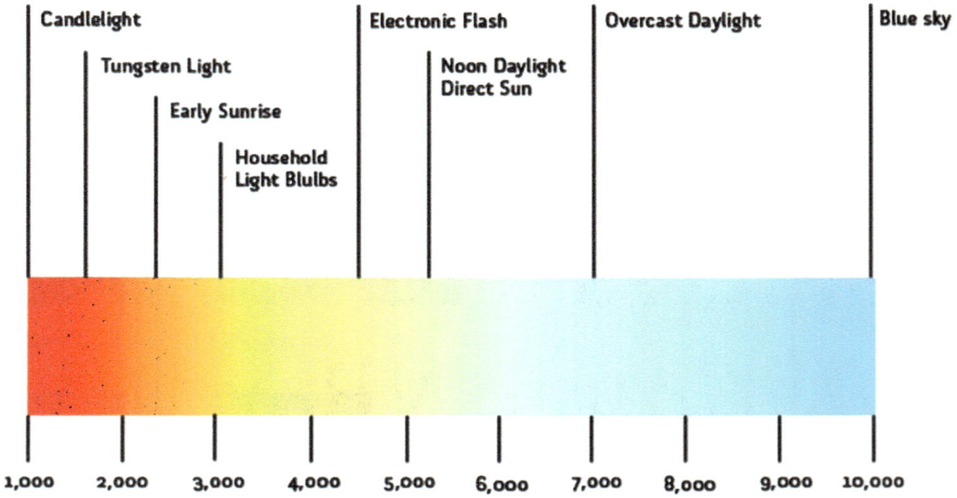

Kelvin color chart

Tilt and Shift

Automatic vertical tilt: When enabled, this function automatically corrects vertical tilt.

In addition, the Guess vert tilt and Tilt functions become automatically unavailable (grayed out).

Disabled by default.

Tilt

Vertical: This function is used to correct the verticals of distorted cameras, by entering a value.

Default value is 0.0.

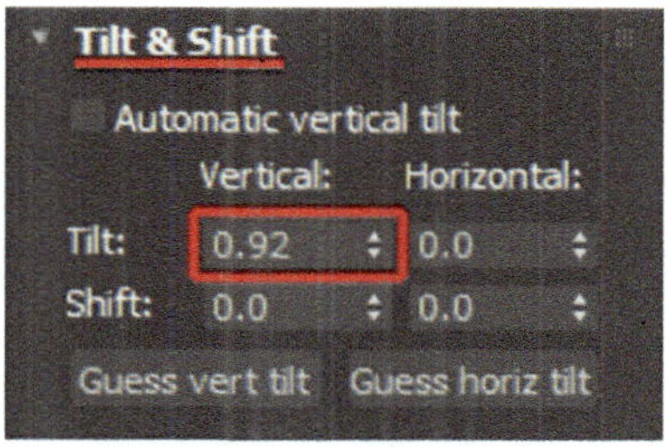

Vertical tilt value set to 0.92

Vertical tilt value set to 0.92 render

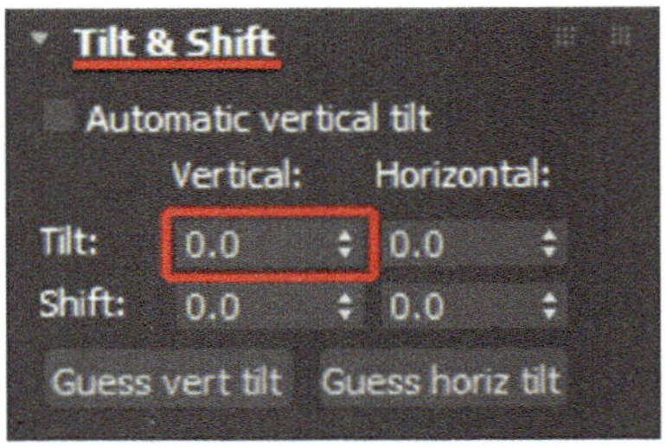

Vertical tilt value set to 0.0

Vertical tilt value set to 0.0 render

Horizontal: This function allows users to correct the camera distortion/tilt horizontally, by entering a value.

Default value is 0.0.

Shift

Vertical: This function enables users to offset/move (shift) the camera target vertically.

Positive values shift the camera up. Negative values shift the camera in the opposite direction.

Default value is 0.0.

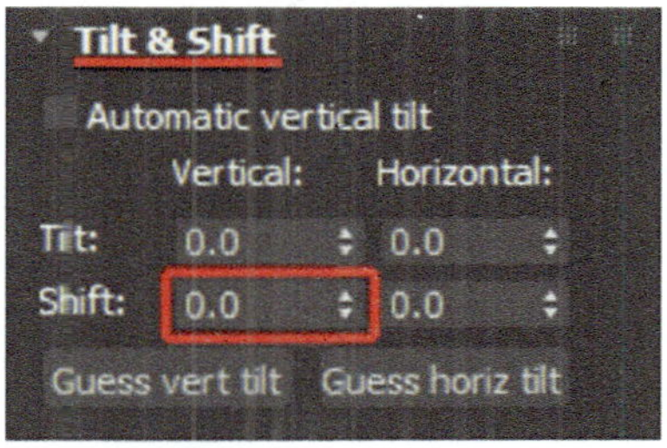

Vertical Shift value set to 0.0

Vertical Shift value set to 0.0 render

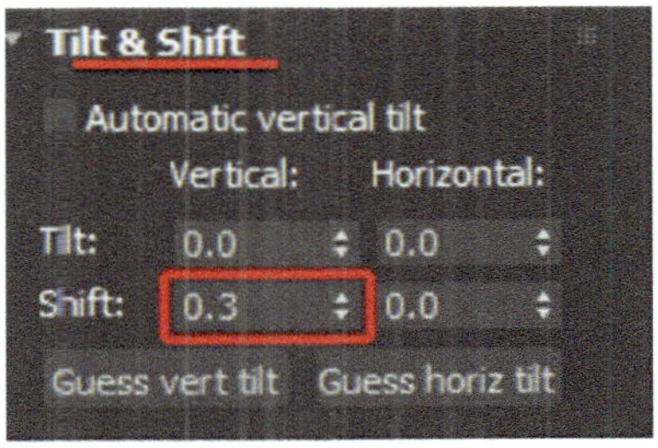

Vertical Shift value set to 0.3

Vertical Shift value set to 0.3 render

Horizontal: The function offsets/moves (shifts) the camera target horizontally. High values shift the camera to the right, and low values shift the camera in the opposite direction.

Default value is 0.0.

Guess vert tilt: When clicked, the button automatically guesses the vertical tilt values.

Guess horiz tilt: When clicked, the button automatically guesses the camera distortion tilt, horizontally.

Bokeh Effects

In a real production environment, the DOF, bokeh effects, etc., are often applied in post-production.

It is done so due to these effects being extremely time-consuming to fine-tune/render in 3ds max, especially when there's a need for quick turnarounds.

In the VRayPhysicalCamera, the bokeh effect is only visible if/when the Depth of field function is enabled.

The bokeh effect is mostly visible in overly bright areas of an image (overexposed).

Through the camera lenses, the bokeh effect is depicted in a circular or polygonal shape.

Disabled by default.

Blades: This function controls the shape of the bokeh effect. The higher the number of blades, the more circular the bokeh effect.

When disabled, the bokeh effect is totally circular.

Default value is 5.

Disabled by default.

Rotation (deg): This function controls the rotation of the blades (bokeh).

Default value is 0.0.

Disabled by default.

Center bias: This function controls the brightness of the bokeh. Negative values brighten the center of the bokeh effect.

Positive values brighten the outer edge of the bokeh effect.

Default value is 0.0.

Anisotropy: This function stretches the bokeh effect horizontally or vertically to emulate anamorphic lenses.

Default value is 0.0.

Optical vignetting: This function determines the strength of the optical vignetting.

Default value is 0.0.

Bitmap aperture: This function allows users to load a bitmap to control the shape (and scratches) of the bokeh effect.

Black and white bitmaps work best. White areas of a bitmap are interpreted as transparent.

Disabled by default.

Affect exposure: This function affects the overall exposure of the render.

Disabled by default.

Bitmap resolution: This function controls the sampled resolution of the loaded bitmap.

Disabled by default.

NOTE

This function is extremely slow to calculate and yields noise effects.

Distortion

Distortion type: This function controls the type of camera distortion (Quadratic, Cubic, Lens file, Texture).

Default distortion, Quadratic.

Popular camera tracking applications, such as Boujou, use the Cubic distortion camera type.

Amount: This function controls the amount of distortion.

Default value is 0.0.

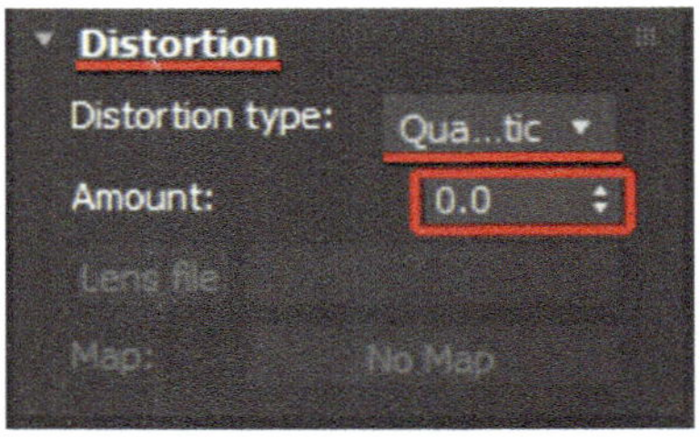

Quadratic distortion set to 0.0

Quadratic distortion set to 0.0 render

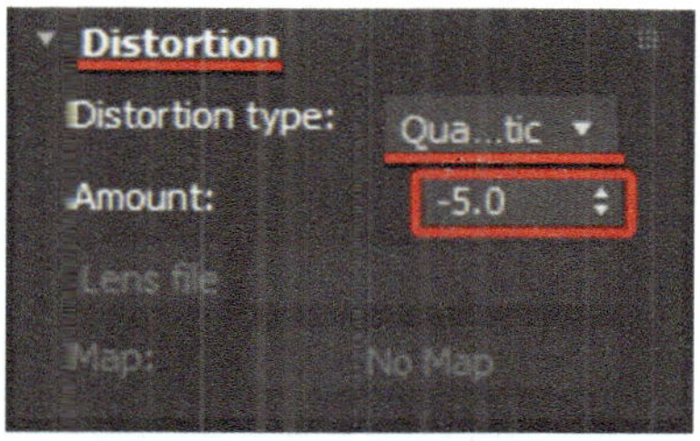

Quadratic distortion set to −5.0

Quadratic distortion set to −5.0 render

Lens file: This distortion type allows users to load a lens file type, often generated by the VRay Lens Analysis tool.

Texture: This distortion type allows users to load a Map from third-party applications such as Nuke, to set the camera distortion.

Clipping and Environment

Clipping: When enabled, it allows the selected camera to clip/slice objects within a specified distance, using the near clipping plane and the far clipping plane options.

The clipping option is widely used in tight/close shots, where objects such as doors and walls are obstructing the camera composition.

Near clipping plane: This function controls where the nearest clipping plane starts from.

Far clipping plane: This option determines where the far clipping plane starts from.

Clipping disabled

Clipping disabled render

Clipping enabled, with far clipping to 2178

Clipping enabled, with far clipping to 2178 render

Near env range: This function controls the near environment range of atmospheric effects in 3ds max.

Far env range: This function controls the far environment range of atmospheric effects in 3ds max.

Rolling shutter: This function controls/stabilizes the direction of the motion blur.

Disabled by default.

When enabled, it controls the amount of motion blur.

There are four types of rolling shutters to choose from: top to bottom, bottom to top, left to right, and right to left.

Duration (s^{-1}): This function controls the time the shutter passes an image in 1/seconds.

The Rolling shutter function only becomes live when the Motion blur function is enabled.

Lighting in VRay

In the discussion that will follow, we will begin by introducing some of the most popular VRay lights and take users through the process of using them to light a scene.

NOTE

To test some of the VRayLight parameters discussed here, simply open the 3ds max scene named VRay Lights.max.

It's worth noting that it is common practice to copy/instance lights whenever possible, as they are faster to compute.

VRayLight

To create a VRaylight, go to the Create command panel and click on the Lights button.

Under Lights group, select the Photometric menu and choose VRay from its dropdown list.

Choose the VRay menu from the Lights group

Under VRay Object Type group, select the VRayLight button, followed by clicking and dragging the cursor across the viewport to create it.

To exit creation, simply right click.

Next, go to the Modify command panel to see its parameters.

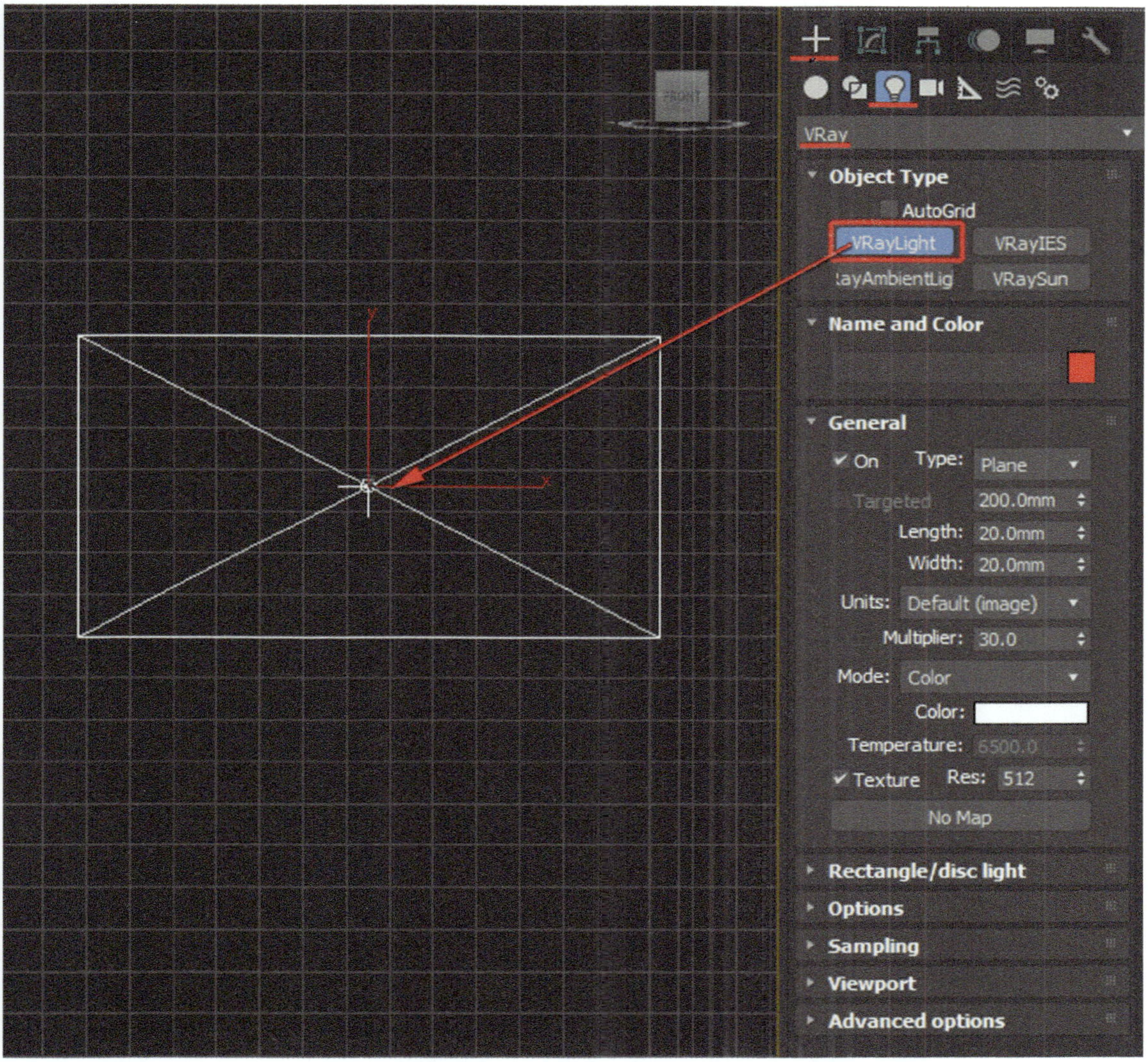
VRay
Object Type
AutoGrid
VRayLight
VRayIES
ayAmbientLig
VRaySun
Name and Color
General
On
Type:
Plane
Targeted
200.0mm
Length:
20.0mm
Width:
20.0mm
Units:
Default (image)
Multiplier:
30.0
Mode:
Color
Color:
Temperature:
6500.0
Texture
Res:
512
No Map
Rectangle/disc light
Options
Sampling
Viewport
Advanced options

Create VRayLight object in the viewport

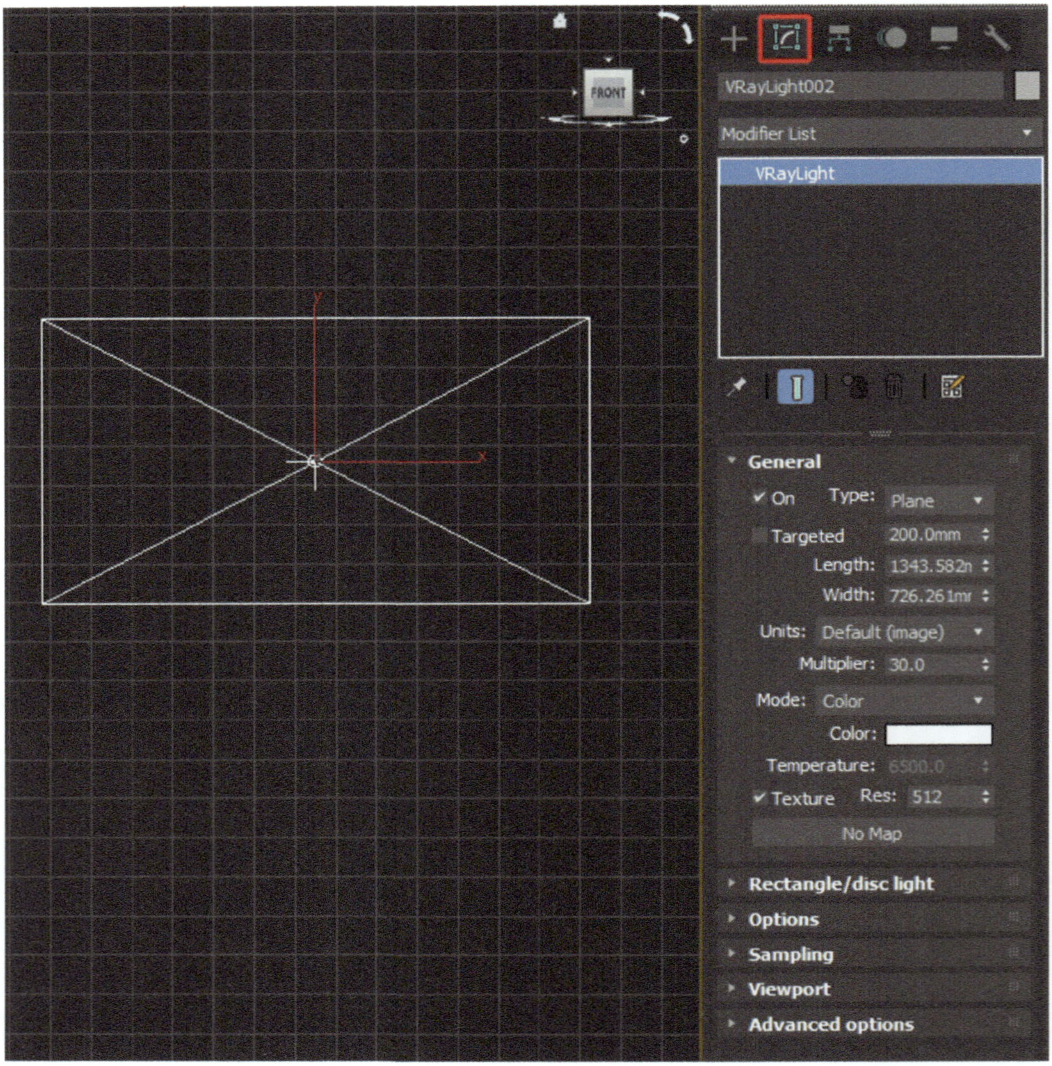

VRayLight parameters in the Modify panel

Plane Light

On: This function allows the light to be turned on and off.

Enabled by default.

Type: This function allows users to choose from a list of light types such as Plane, Dome, Sphere, Mesh, and Disc

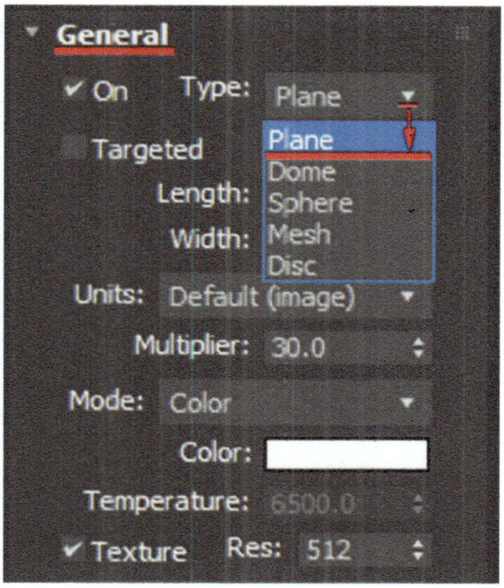

VRayLight types

Targeted: When enabled, it automatically creates a target direction of the light (only seen in the viewport).

The light target helps the user to see and change the direction of the light, if required.

Length: This value determines the length of the light object.

Width: This function controls the width of the light object.

The bigger the light size, the softer the shadows will be. This feature is coherent with most VRay lights.

It's worth noting that plane lights can be scaled independently with the Select and Uniform Scale toolbar, without affecting the size of other instanced lights in the scene.

As mentioned earlier, instanced lights are substantially quicker to render than copied lights.

Select and Uniform Scale toolbar

Units: This function allows users to choose from a list of well-known light units to light a scene.

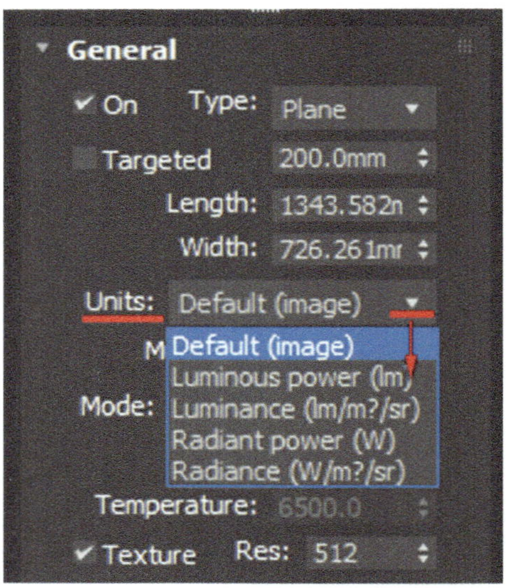

List of different light units

Default (image): This intensity unit is based on the Color Mode and the Multiplier value (30.0 by default). The overall intensity is also dependent on the physical scale/size of the light object.

Luminous power (Im): It determines the light power in lumens. This unit acts independently from the physical size of the light object.

Luminance (Im/m²/sr): This intensity is measured in lumens square meters per steradian.

Radiant power (W): This numerical intensity unit is measured in watts. Also, this unit acts independently from the physical size of the light object.

Radiance (W/m²/sr): This unit of intensity is measured in watts in square meter per steradian. The overall intensity of this unit is dependent on the physical scale/ size of the light object.

Multiplier: The default numerical value is based on the type of units chosen.

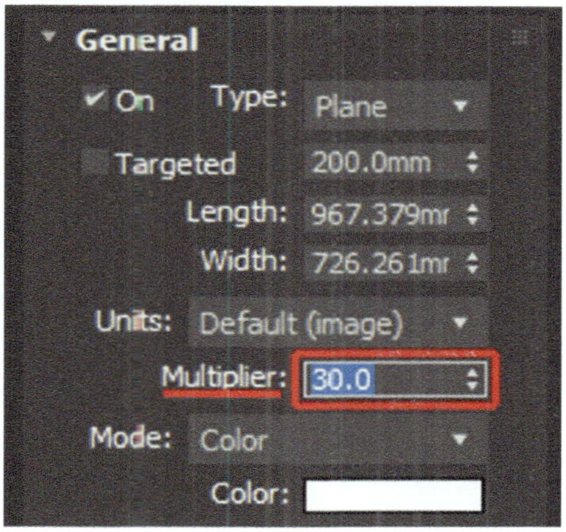

Multiplier value set to 30.0

Multiplier value set to 30.0 render

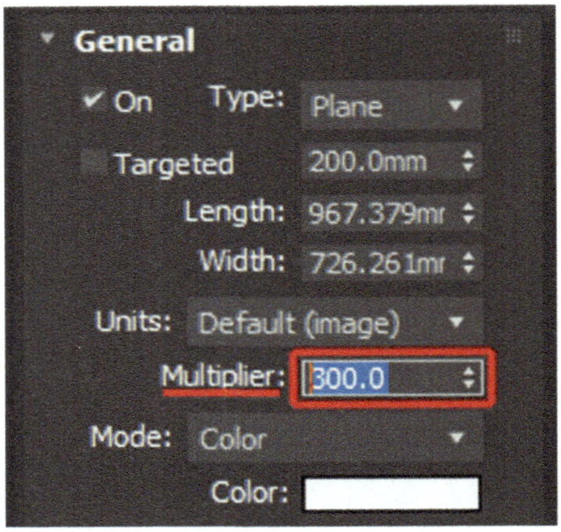

Multiplier value set to 300.0

Multiplier value set to 300.0 render

Mode: This function controls the color of the light source. Users have the option between Color and Temperature modes.

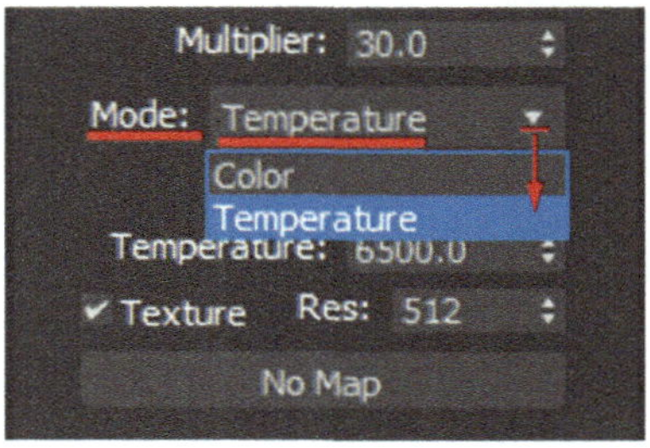

Color modes

Color: This mode allows users to click on the color swatch to choose/sample a color from the Color Selector dialog.

Temperature: If this mode is chosen, users are able to type in a color temperature value.

For more information about color temperature values, simply refer to the color chart depicted earlier or Google: **kelvin color chart**

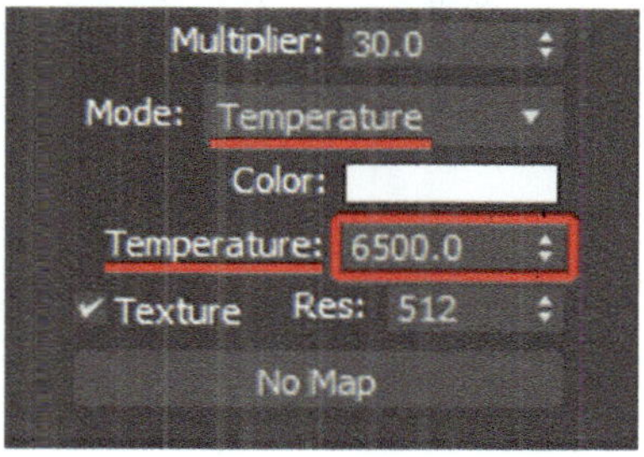

Color Temperature set to 6500.0

Color Temperature set to 6500.0 render

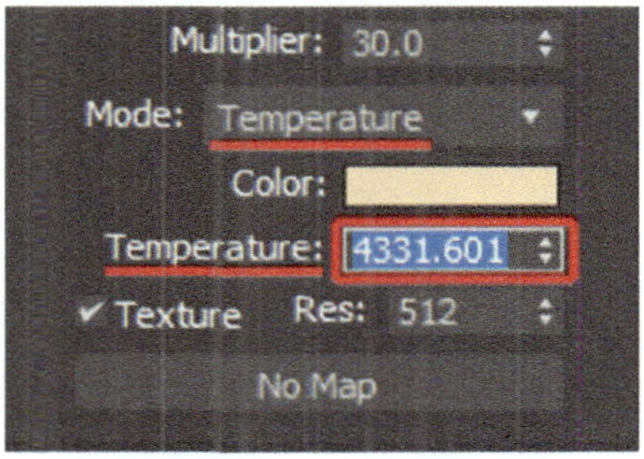

Color Temperature set to 4331.601

Color Temperature set to 4331.601 render

NOTE

HDRI works best in open spaces.

Texture: When enabled, this toggle allows users to plug a Bitmap or an HDRI via the VRayBitmap procedural map.

High Dynamic Range Images have greater dynamic range of luminosity than the normal images.

As such, they can be used to illuminate a scene accurately.

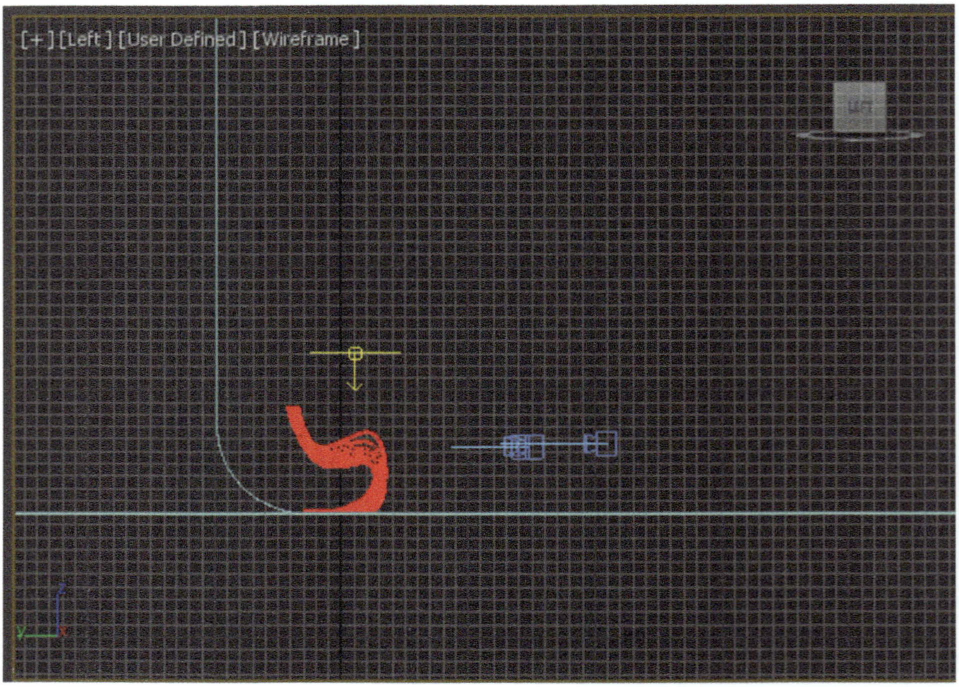

Open space studio without ceilings or surrounding walls

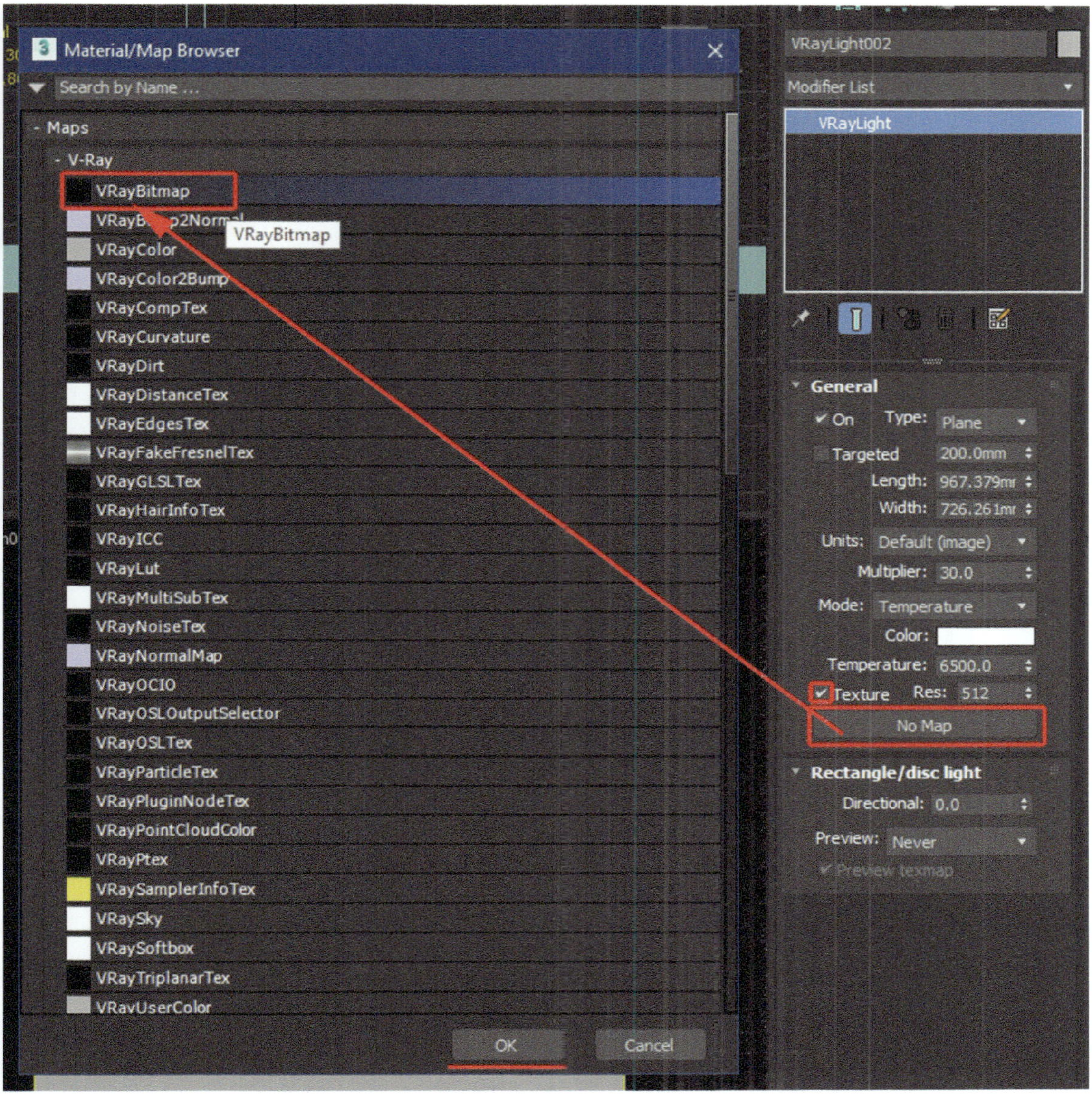

Pick the VRayBitmap procedural map

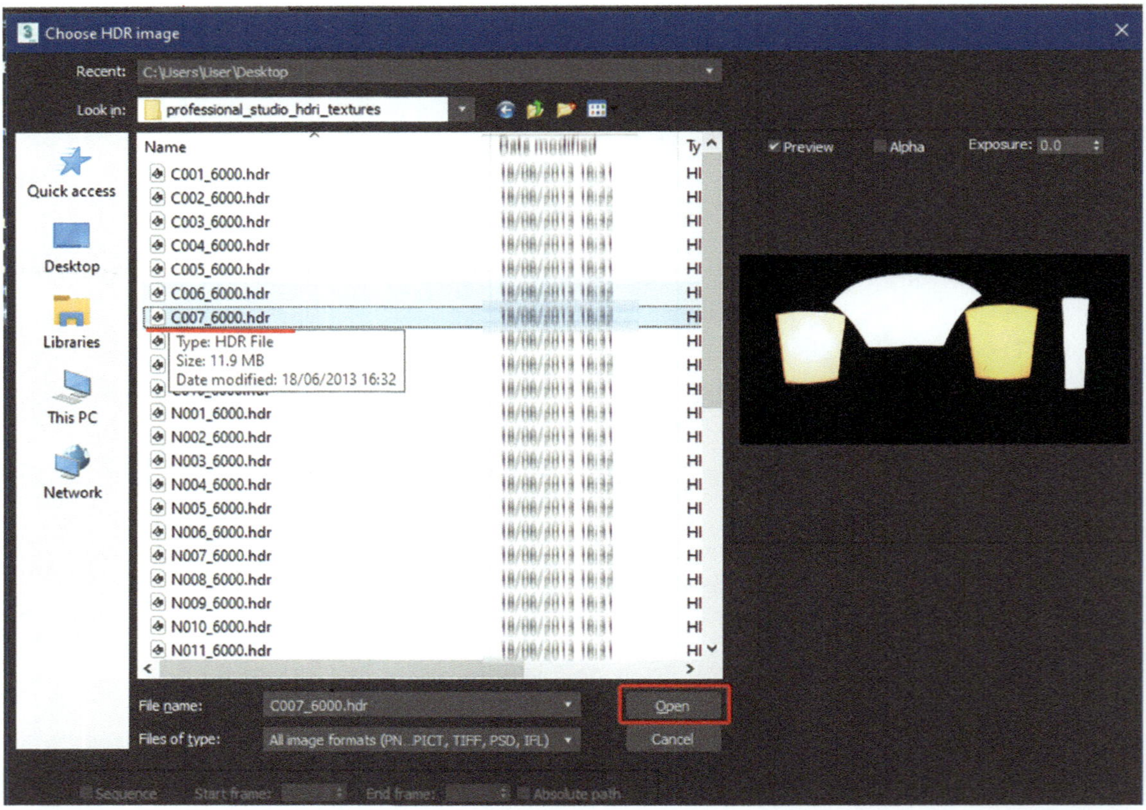

Pick the HDRI

Once applied, users can edit it, by simply dragging and dropping it into the Material Editor slot.

Choose the Instance option, from the Instance Copy Map dialog.

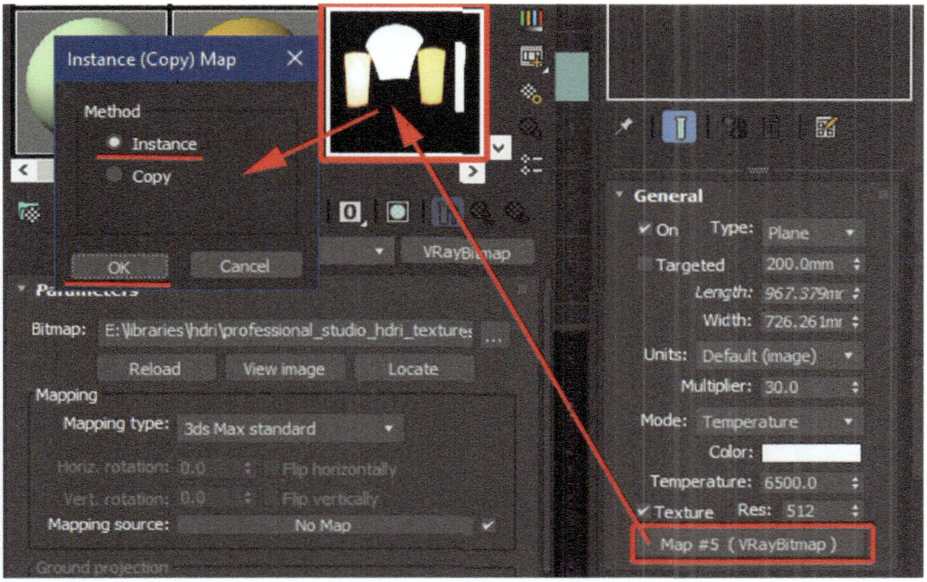

Drag and drop the VRayBitmap into a Material slot

In the VRayBitmap parameters, set the Mapping type to Spherical.

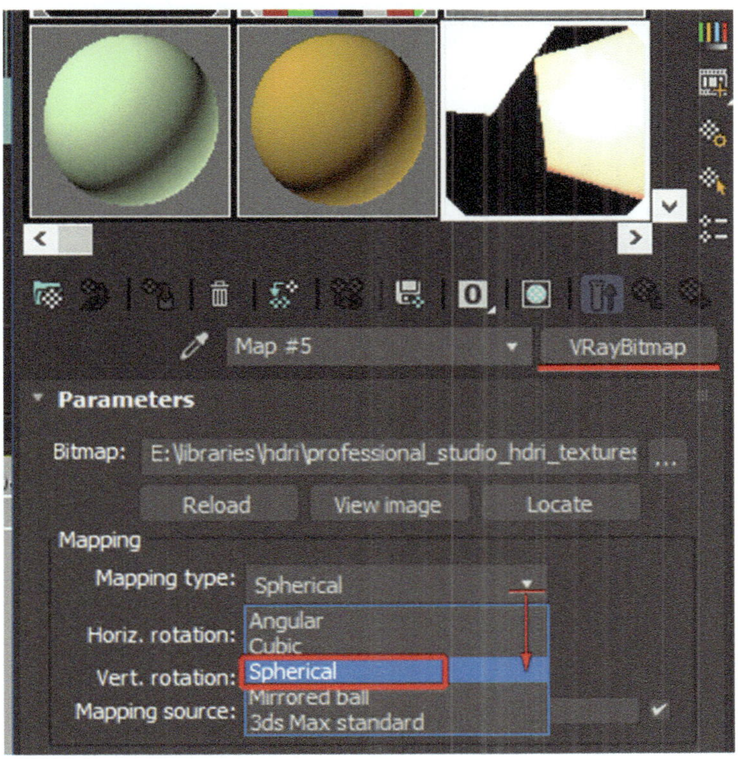

Spherical Mapping type

Use the Horiz.rotation, Vert.rotation, Flip and Crop/Place tools to move, rotate, and/or crop the HDRI to fit a specific area.

Plane lights can also be used to plug light procedural maps such as VRaySoftbox.

This light procedural map is often used to emulate a studio softbox light by creating gradients around the edges of the plane light.

This is also a good technique to remove hard edges from the plane lights.

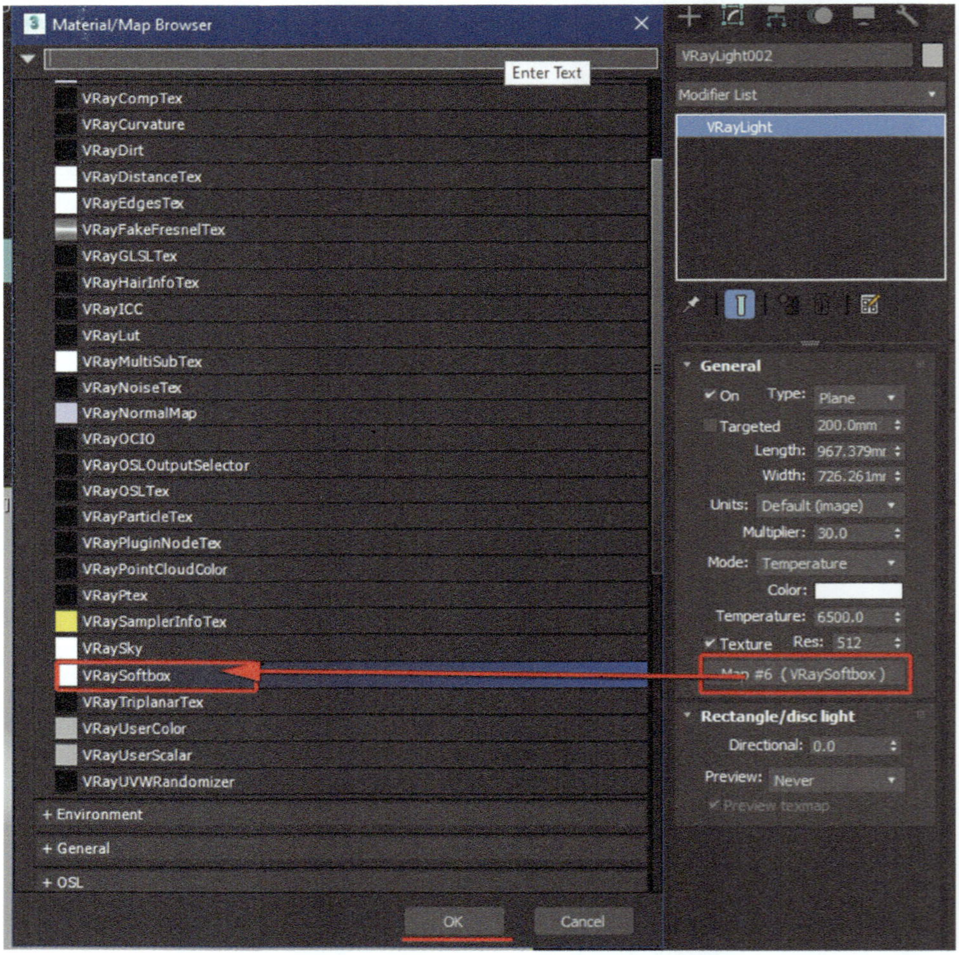

VRaySoftbox procedural map

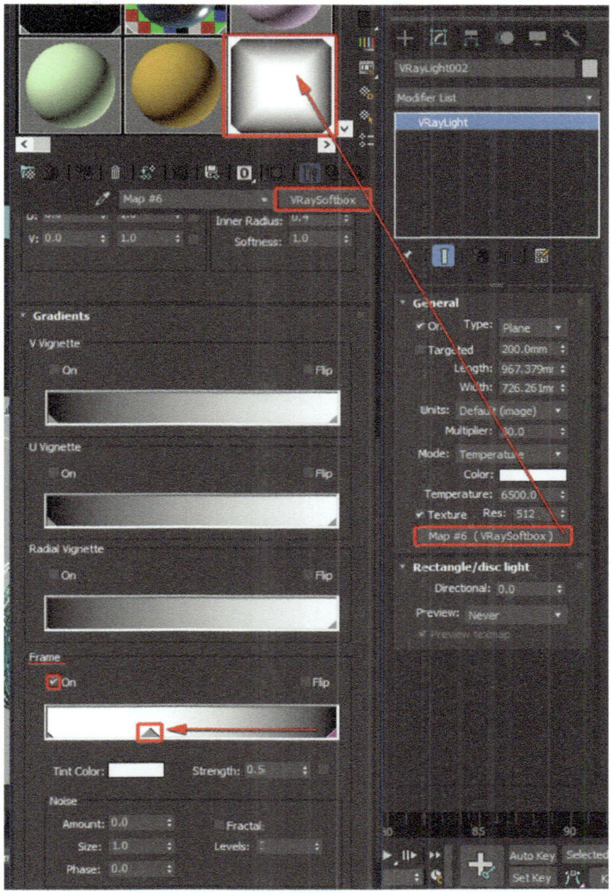

Frame function enabled and soft edges created

Also, users can apply black and white bitmaps on its Base parameters to emulate dust/scratches effects.

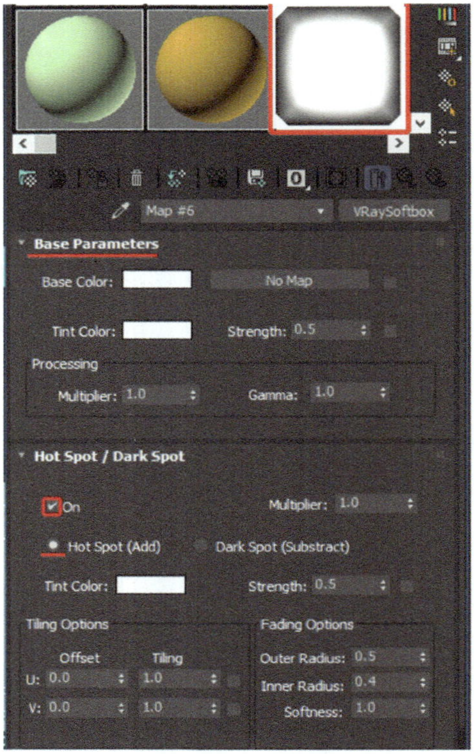
Map #6
VRaySoftbox
Base Parameters
Base Color:
No Map
Tint Color:
Strength: 0.5
Processing
Multiplier: 1.0
Gamma: 1.0
Hot Spot / Dark Spot
On
Multiplier: 1.0
Hot Spot (Add)
Dark Spot (Substract)
Tint Color:
Strength: 0.5
Tiling Options
Offset
Tiling
U: 0.0
1.0
V: 0.0
1.0
Fading Options
Outer Radius: 0.5
Inner Radius: 0.4
Softness: 1.0

Hot Spot enabled

Hot Spot enabled render

Rectangle/disc light

This option is only available when the light type is Plane or Disc.

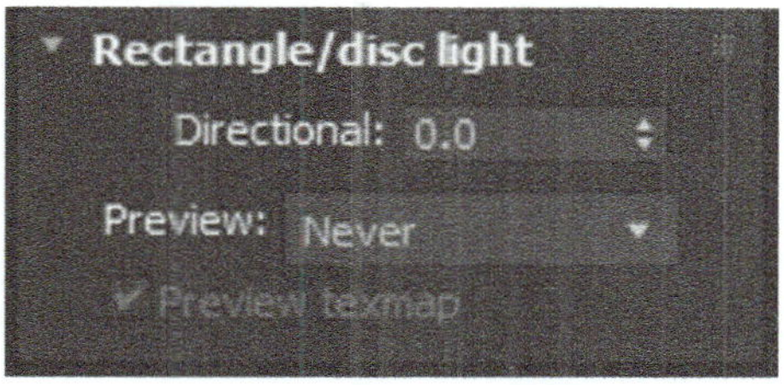

Rectangle/disc group

Directional: This function controls the direction of the light. With the default value set to 0.0, the light is spread.

When the directional value is increased toward the value 1.0, the light emission is less spread and more localized/directional.

Default value is 0.0

Preview: This function provides users with the option to preview the light in the viewport.

Never: This option will never preview the light in the viewport.

Always: This option will always preview the light in the viewport.

Selected: This option will only preview the selected light in the viewport.

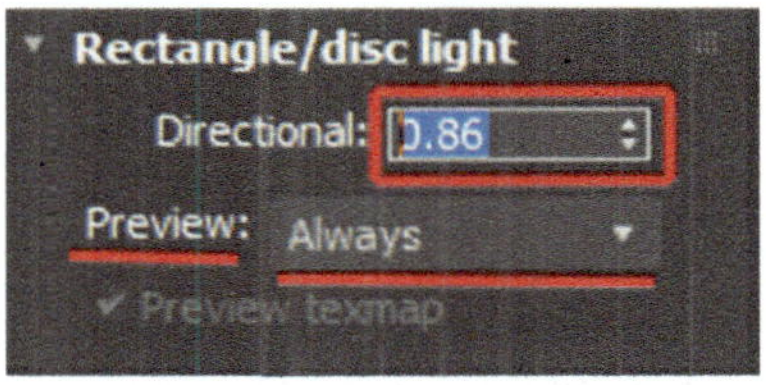

Directional value set to 0.86

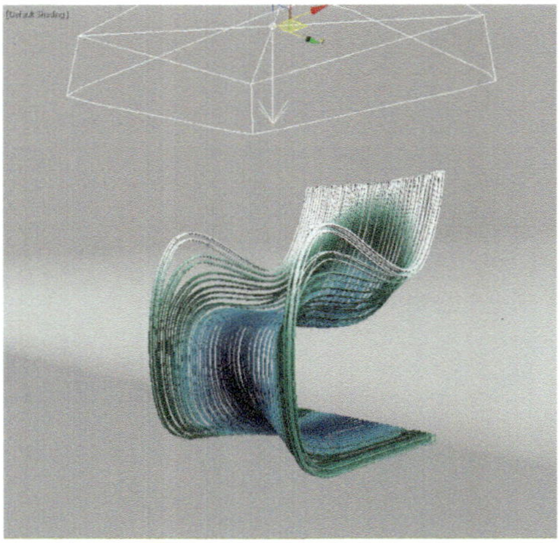

Directional value preview in the viewport

Directional value set to 0.86 render

Options

Exclude: This toggle allows users to pick and choose scene objects to be excluded from the effects of this light.

The left and right arrows in the middle allow users to add or remove listed scene objects.

To add objects, simply select them from Scene Objects list, and click on the button with an arrow point toward the right.

To remove objects, select them from the Include or Exclude list, followed by clicking on the button with an arrow pointing toward the left.

By default, the dialog is set to Exclude both, Illumination and Shadow Casting.

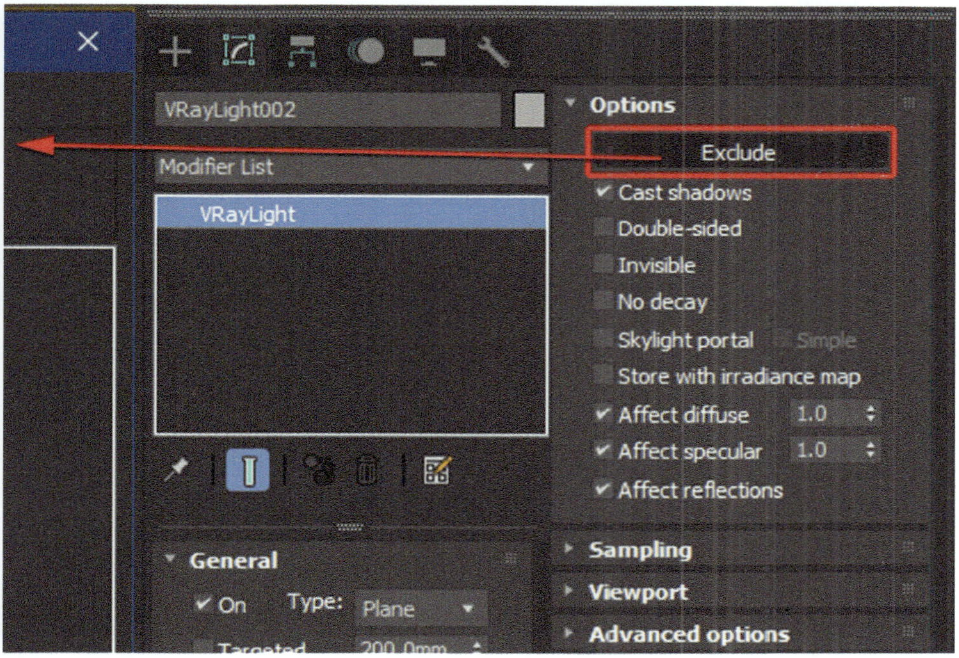

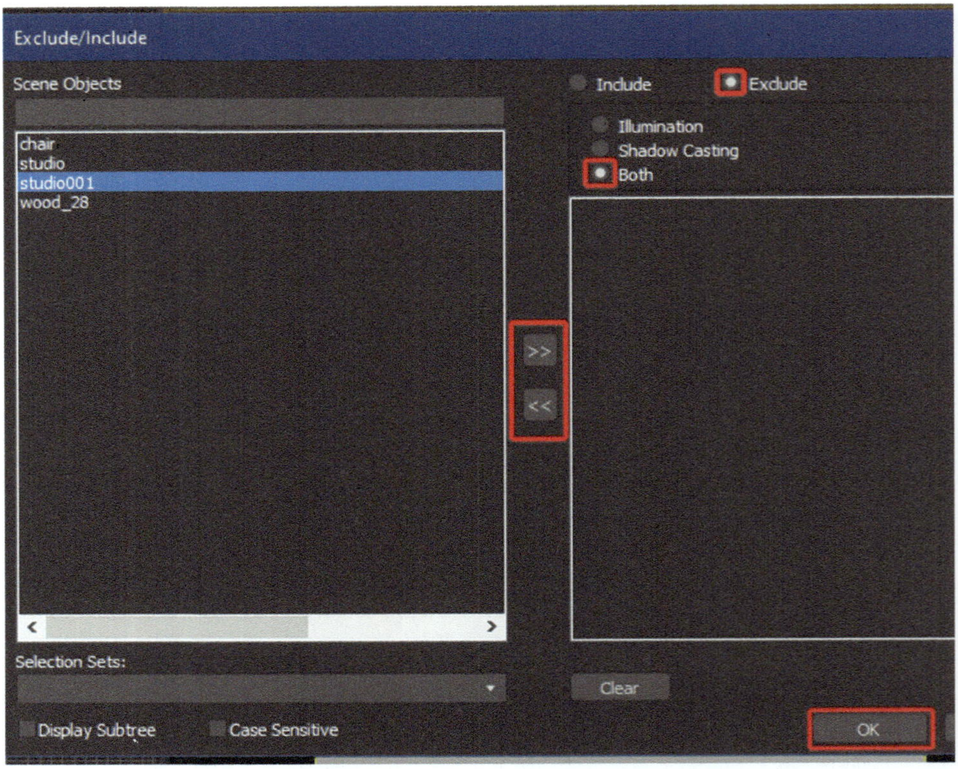

Exclude/Include **toggle**

Cast shadows: This function enables the light to cast shadows in the scene.

Enabled by default.

Double-sided: If enabled, it allows both sides of the plane light to cast light and shadows (if turned on).

Disabled by default.

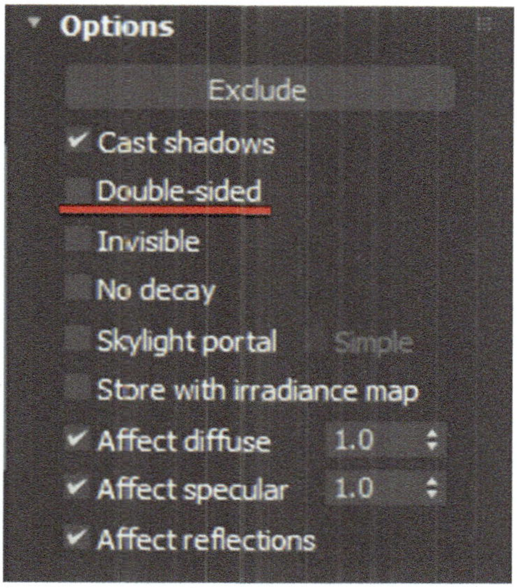

Double-sided option disabled

Double-sided option disabled render

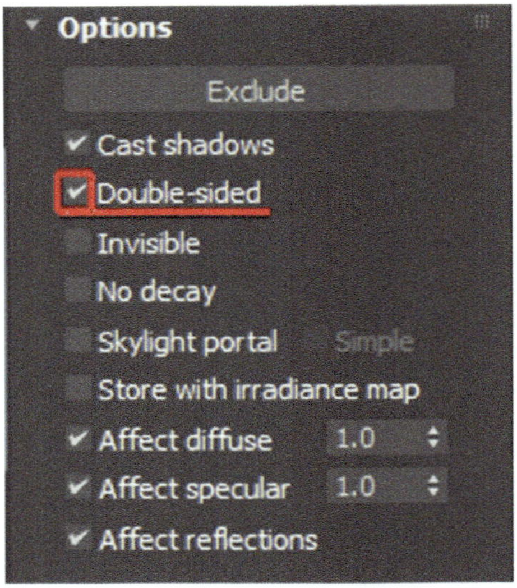

Double-sided option enabled

Double-sided option enabled render

Invisible: This function allows the light object to be invisible in the render. Disabled by default.

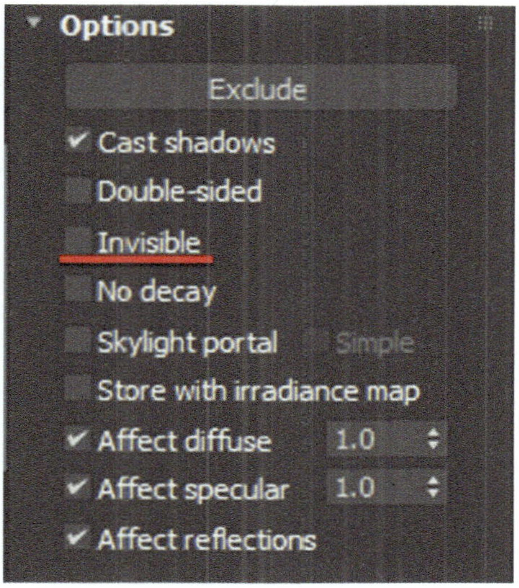

Invisible option disabled

Invisible option disabled render

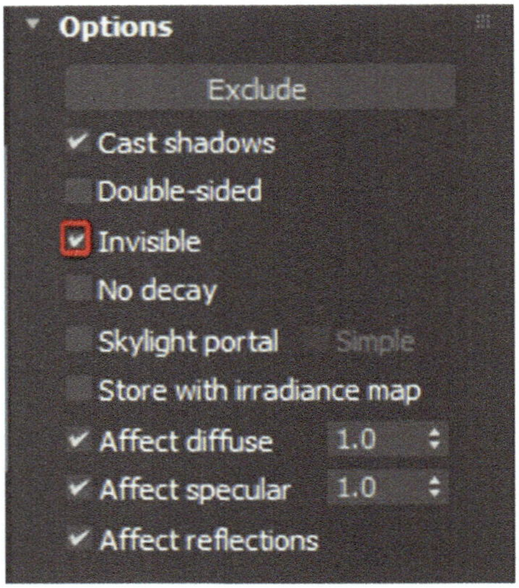

Invisible option enabled

Invisible option enabled render

No decay: When turned on, this function allows the light to travel infinitely without decaying/dimming, from its emitter/source.

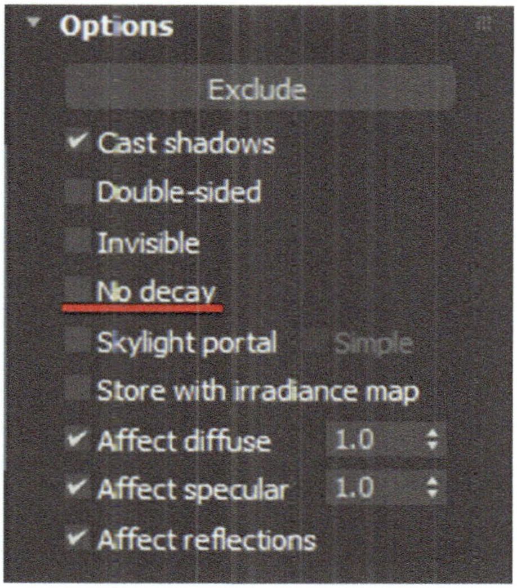

No decay option disabled

No decay option disabled render

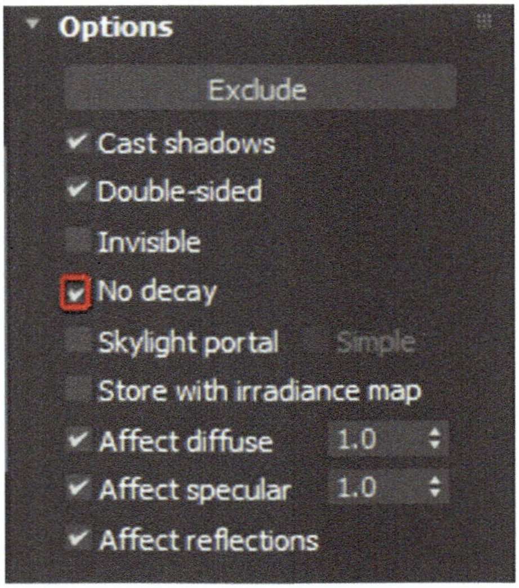

No decay option enabled

No decay option enabled render

Skylight portal: When on, this function uses the environment intensity to cast light and shadows.

Disabled by default.

Simple: It livens up when the Sky portal option is enabled. When on, it computes the sky portal lighting much quicker.

Store with irradiance map: When enabled, this function caches this light effect and stores them in the irradiance map (if enabled).

While this process saves the precalculation time, the shadows will be less accurate.

This option is widely used to correct light artifacts from Dome light or VRay mesh light (e.g., graininess and/or splotches).

Disabled by default.

Affect diffuse: This function allows this light source to affect the diffuse object. Enabled by default.

Affect specular: It enables this light source to affect the specular/glossiness of objects. Enabled by default.

Affect reflections: This option allows the light object/shape to be visible on reflections. Enabled by default.

Sampling

Shadow bias: This function controls the position of the shadows. Low values bring shadows close to the objects. High values do the opposite.

Default value is 0.02 mm.

Cutoff: This function controls the light distance/reach (and therefore its intensity). The lower the light distance, the quicker its render computation.

Default value is 0.001.

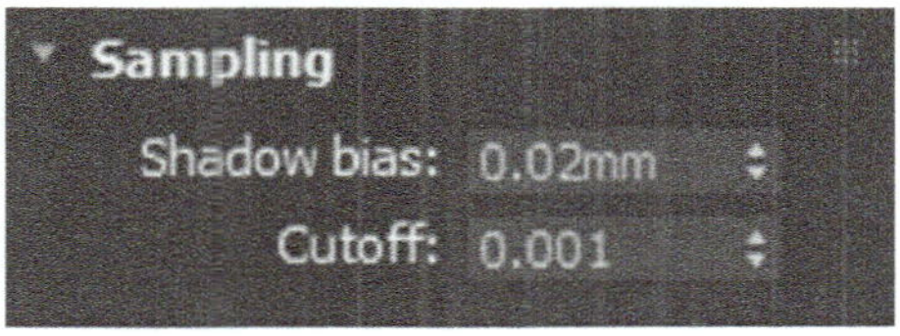

Sampling group

Viewport

Enable viewport shading: When turned on, the light effects will be seen in the shaded viewport (not wireframe).

Enabled by default.

Viewport wire color: If enabled, it allows users to choose a wire color for the light object.

To change the default color, simply click on its color swatch to bring up the Color Selector dialog.

Default color, yellow.

Disabled by default.

Icon text: This function enables the light name (text) in the viewport.

Disabled by default.

Viewport group

Advanced Options

Use MIS: This function (Multiple Importance Sampling) uses the direct and indirect lighting to compute its contribution.

Enabled by default.

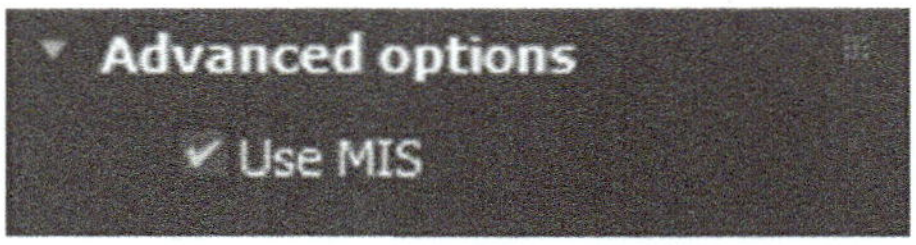

Advanced options group

Dome Light

When chosen, it automatically emulates the effect of diffused environment light and shadows. This effect is independent from the dome light location in the scene.

It's worth noting that VRaySky has a similar effect.

For this reason, when a Dome light is chosen, the environment light is doubled up, if the VRaySky is being used.

NOTE

Dome light works best in open spaces.

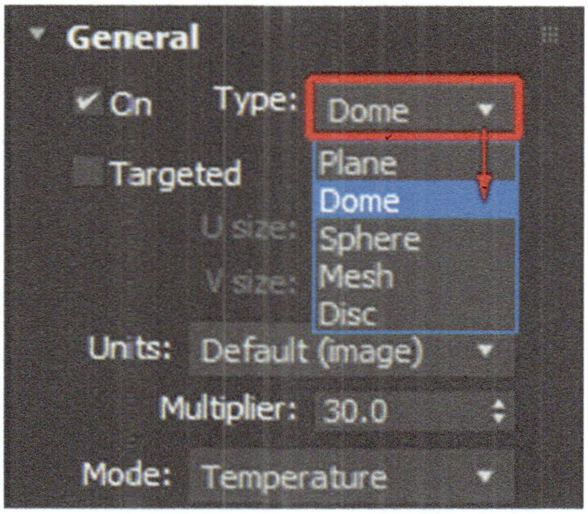

Dome light chosen

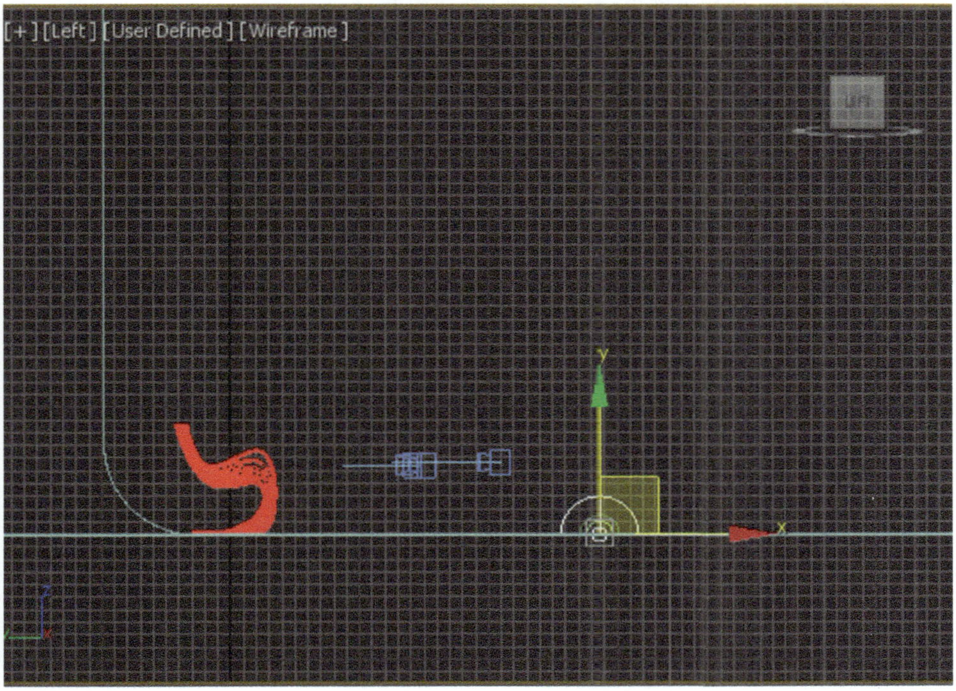

Dome light object in the viewport

Texture: This toggle is used to plug an HDRI via VRayBitmap, as previously shown.

Users often plug HDRI of a sky with sunlight to emulate both direct and indirect lighting.

HDRI only casts direct shadows if the image is sharp, as opposed to blurred.

Also, to cast direct shadows, the HDRI needs to have a very bright spot (sunlit exterior HDRI), else bright spots start emulating artificial lights.

NOTE

The Texture function needs to be enabled.

HDRI with sky and the sun

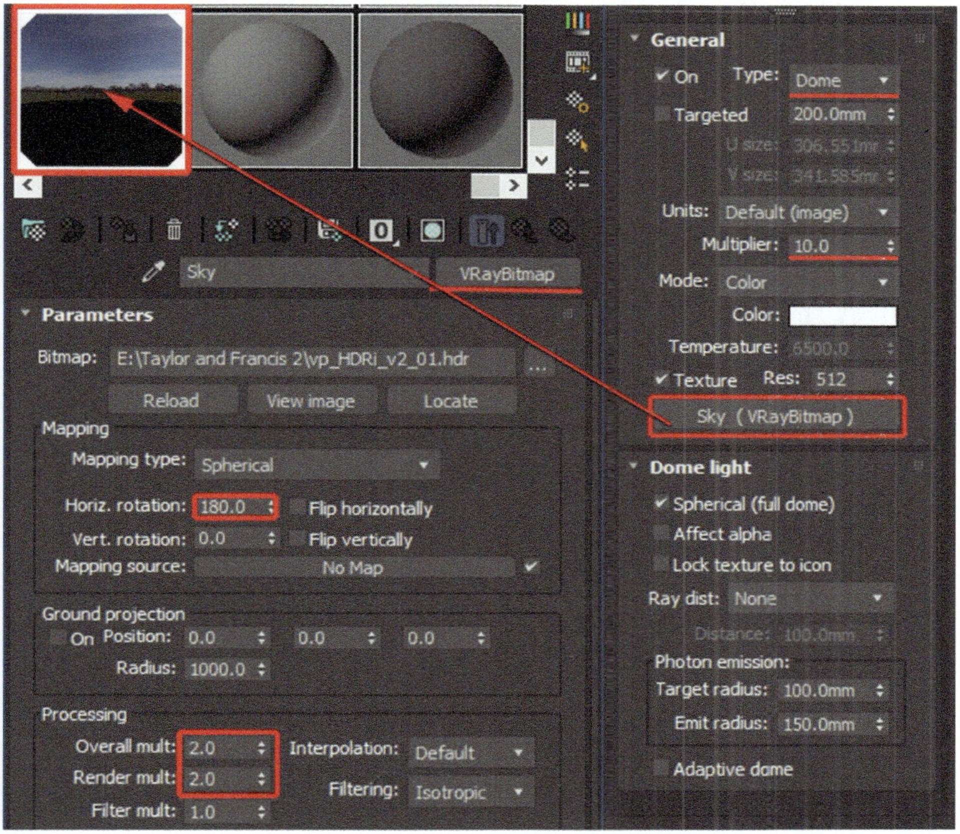

HDRI with sky and the sun applied

HDRI with sky and the sun render

Alternatively, users can plug HDRI of a cloudy sky to emulate diffused shadows and create a separate VRaySun object for the direct light.

This will provide users with the flexibility to control both light sources separately.

When lighting a scene with an HDRI, it's recommended that users disable the VRaySky in the Environment Map toggle (8).

VRaySky has a similar dynamic range to HDRI. In addition, the dome light Multiplier value shouldn't be set too high to prevent overexposing the scene.

Dome Light

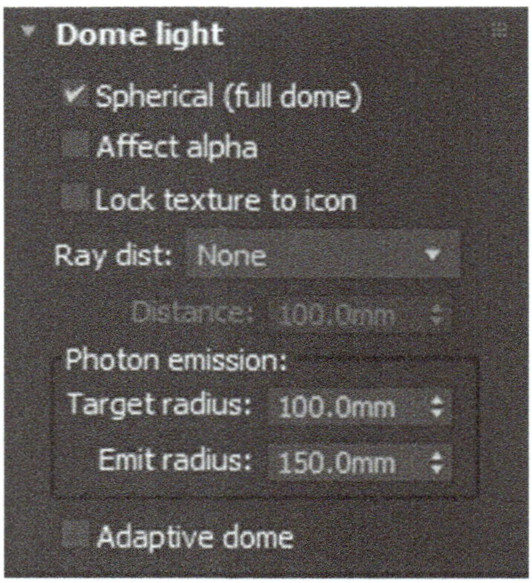

Dome light group

Spherical (full dome): This function applies the lighting spherically (full dome). Otherwise, hemispherical (if the spherical function is disabled).

Enabled by default.

Affect alpha: When enabled, the dome color or image (HDR) wrapped around the dome will be displayed as a solid render element (White), as opposed to alpha (Black).

Disabled by default.

Render elements such as alpha channels will be covered in more detail in the chapters ahead.

Lock texture to icon: When enabled, it locks/links the dome color/HDRI to the dome object in the scene.

So when the dome object is rotated in the scene, the color/HDRI will also be rotated automatically.

Disabled by default.

The Invisible function needs to be disabled in order for the Lock texture to work.

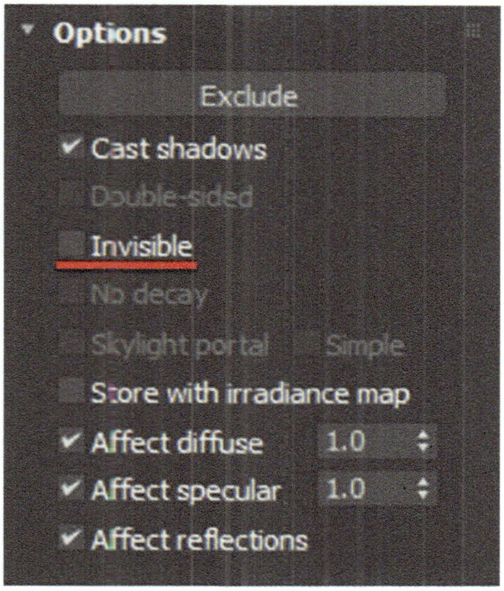

Invisible option disabled

Ray dist: It allows users to specify the maximum distance VRay will trace the shadows to.

None by default.

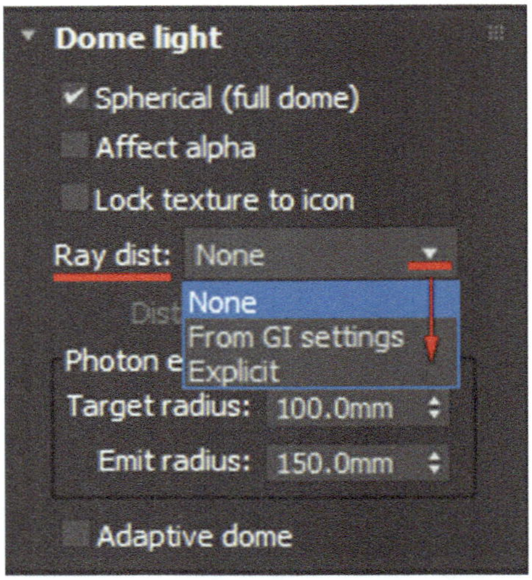

Ray distance options

From GI settings: This option uses the Global illumination parameters to trace the shadows.

Explicit: This option allows users to specify the distance.

Default value is 100 mm.

Target radius: This function controls the photon emission radius. This icon is displayed in the viewport.

Default value is 100 mm.

Emit radius: This function controls the photon emission radius. This icon is displayed in the viewport.

Default value is 150 mm.

Adapt dome: When enabled, this function helps to reduce/eliminate the noise/grain often generated by the dome light.

Disabled by default.

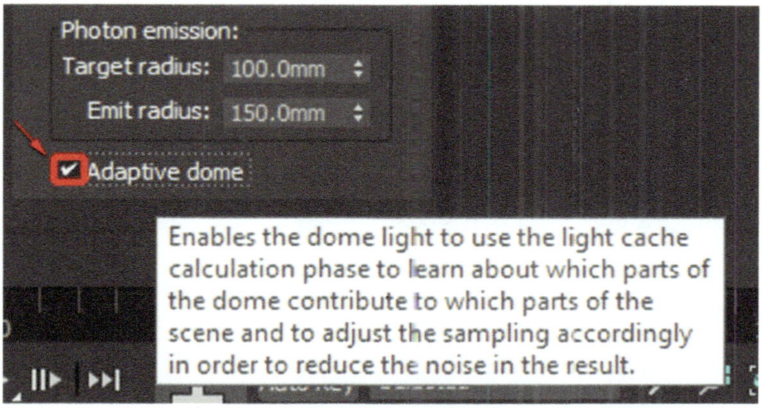

Adapt dome function

VRay Sphere Light

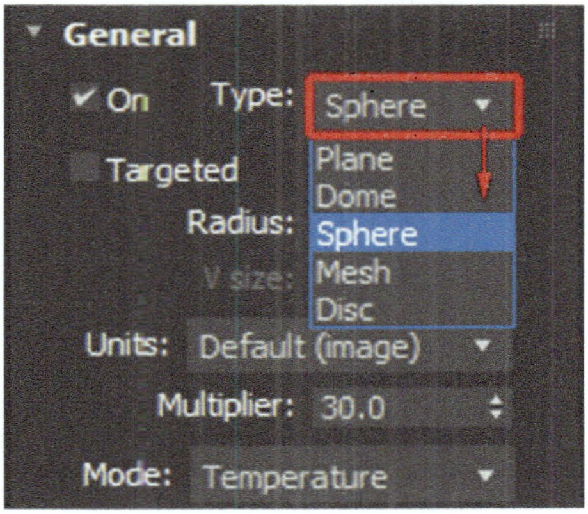

Sphere light chosen

This type of light becomes spherical, when chosen. The light is emitted from all sides (spherically).

The intensity is based on the size of sphere radius.

Bigger sphere radius result in softer shadows.

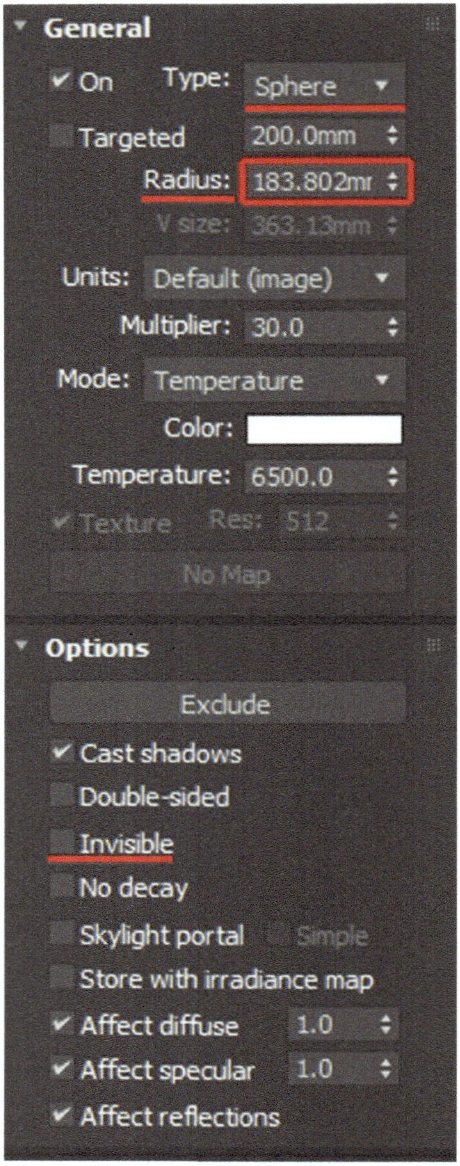
General
On
Type:
Sphere
Targeted
200.0mm
Radius:
183.802mr
V size:
363.13mm
Units:
Default (image)
Multiplier:
30.0
Mode:
Temperature
Color:
Temperature:
6500.0
Texture
Res:
512
No Map
Options
Exclude
Cast shadows
Double-sided
Invisible
No decay
Skylight portal
Simple
Store with irradiance map
Affect diffuse
1.0
Affect specular
1.0
Affect reflections

Sphere light options

Sphere light options render

VRay Mesh Light

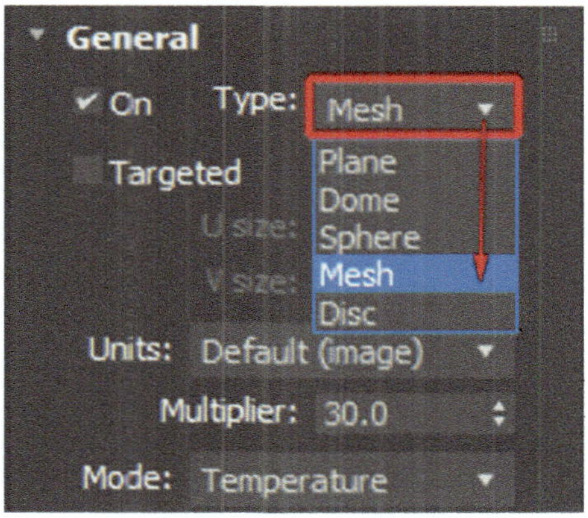

Mesh light chosen

When a Mesh light type is chosen, the mesh light options group becomes available.

The Pick mesh toggle allows users to pick any mesh/geometry in the scene, to be used as a light emitter.

NOTE

To pick a mesh, simply unhide the geometry named, Torus Knot001.

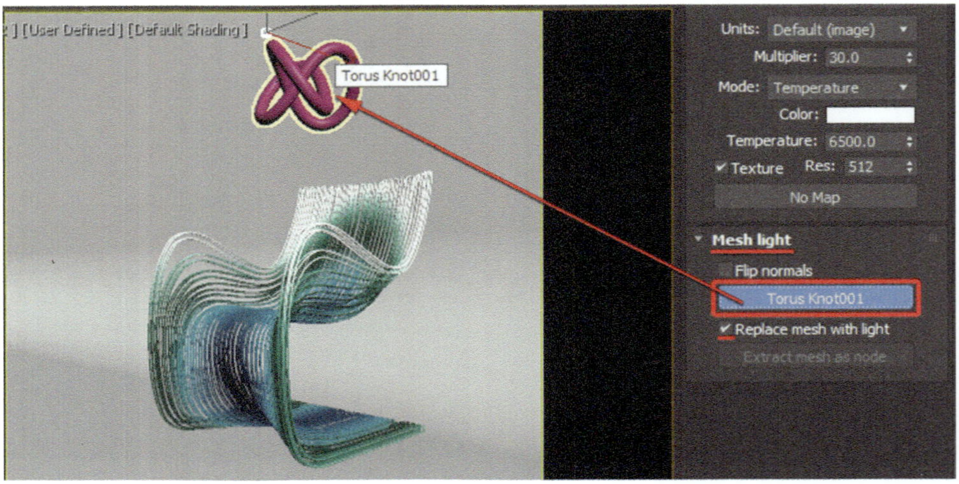

Pick a mesh/geometry in the scene

Once the mesh/geometry is picked, it is automatically transformed into a physical light source (if the Replace mesh with light option is enabled).

Also, the geometry/mesh is automatically added to the Modify stack.

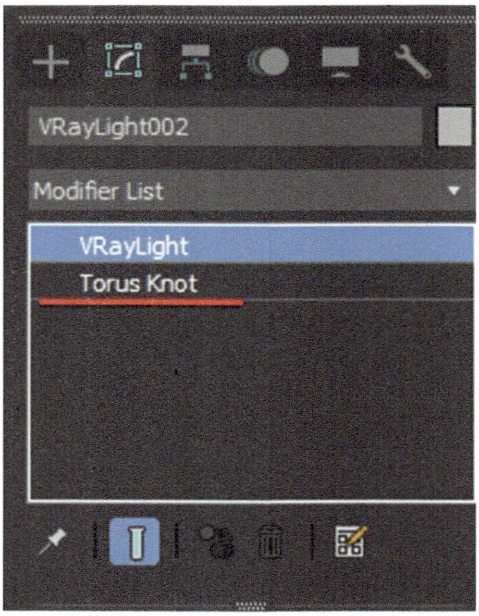

Geometry/mesh automatically added to the Modify stack

Scene lit with a Mesh light

Rendering a scene lit with a Mesh light can be time-consuming to render.

Also, it may yield grainy results, unless the Image Sampler Noise threshold value is low (0.07 or lower).

Extract mesh as node: This option allows users to extract the original mesh from mesh light by clicking on its button.

VRay Disc Light

When the Disc light type is chosen, the rectangle/disc light parameters group becomes available, along with the radius values.

The wider the radius, the softer the shadows.

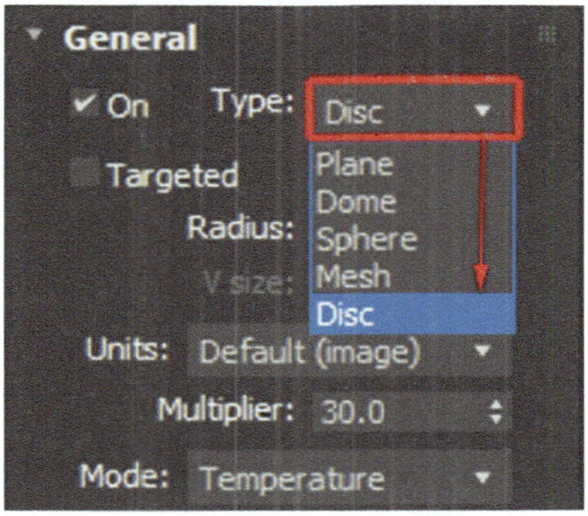

Disc light chosen

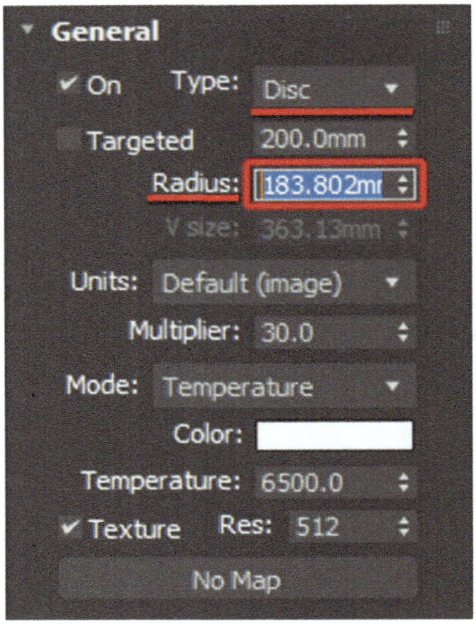

Disc light parameters

Disc light render

VRayIES

VRayIES lights are often used to recreate existing artificial light profile distributions for interior scenes.

Companies such as ERCO and Color Kinetics have a host of exiting IES light profiles ready for download:

https://www.erco.com/download/en/

https://www.colorkinetics.com/global/support/ies

To create a VRayIES light, use some of the steps described earlier, followed by selecting the VRayIES button, clicking the cursor in the Front/Left viewport, and dragging it down to create it.

Right click to exit light creation.

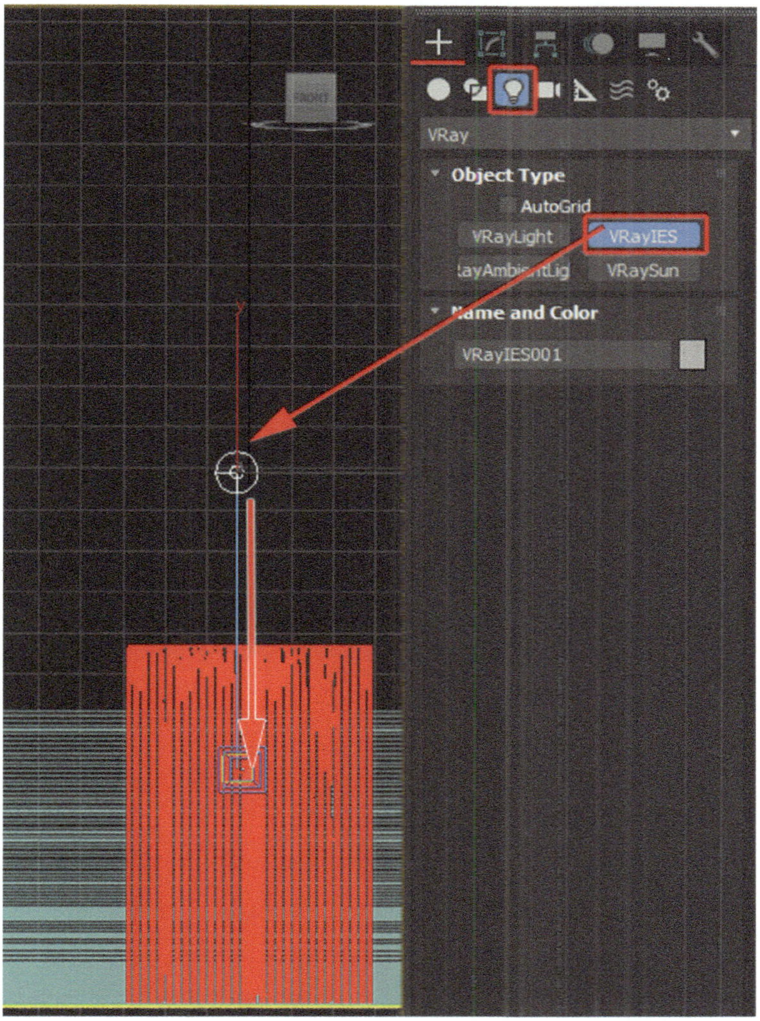

To create a VRayIES light

Once the VRayIES light has been created (with its target facing downward), users can disable the Targeted function to move the VRayIES light.

Most of the VRayIES parameters are self-explanatory. The following discussion will focus mainly on the most important ones.

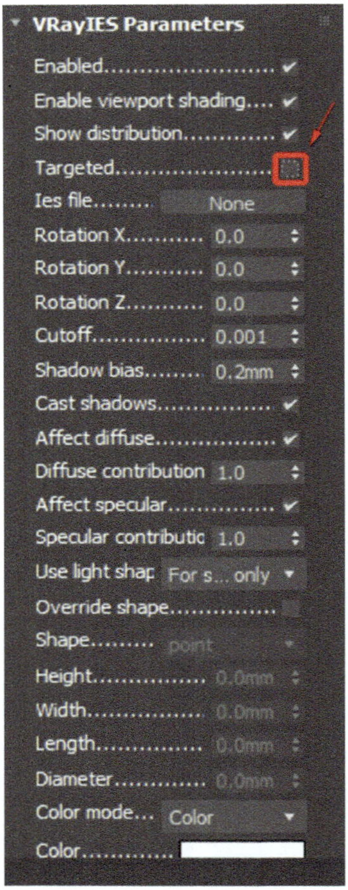

VRayIES light parameters

Enable: It enables the light to be turned on or off.

Show distribution: It shows the distribution of the IES light in the viewport.

IES file: This toggle allows users to locate and plug IES light profile.

IES web profiles are based on a real-world light distribution. IES 14 is one of the most popular light profiles used to create patterns of pools of light on the floor and walls.

NOTE

IES 14 is included in the book resources.

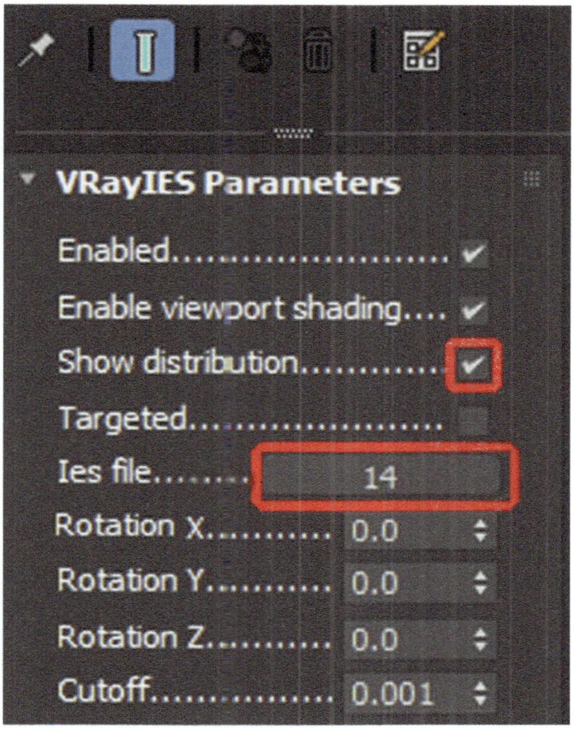
VRayIES Parameters
Enabled
Enable viewport shading
Show distribution
Targeted
Ies file 14
Rotation X 0.0
Rotation Y 0.0
Rotation Z 0.0
Cutoff 0.001

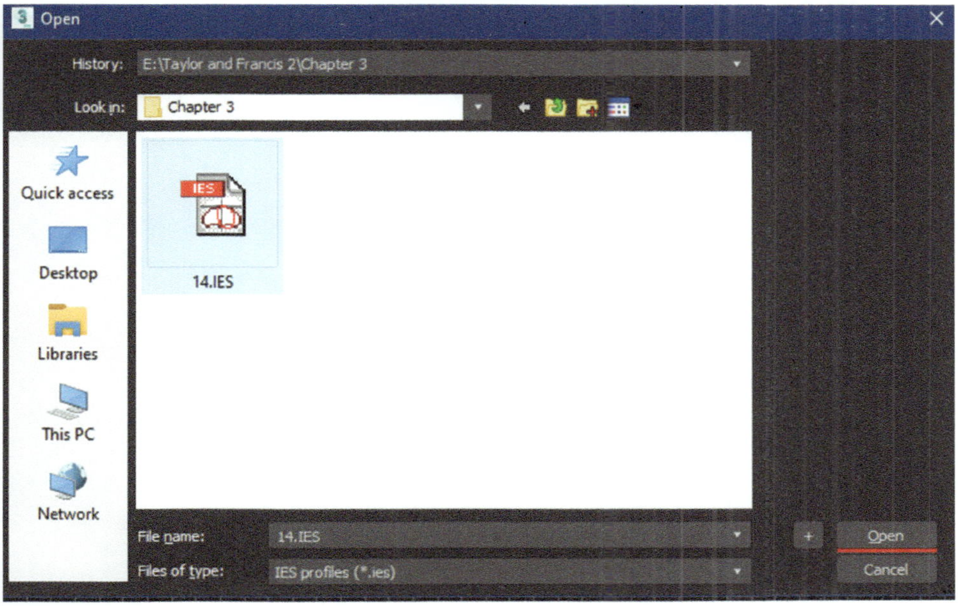
Open
History: E:\Taylor and Francis 2\Chapter 3
Look in: Chapter 3
Quick access
Desktop
Libraries
This PC
Network
14.IES
File name: 14.IES
Files of type: IES profiles (*.ies)
Open
Cancel

IES web file 14 loaded

To preview the IES distribution in the shaded viewport, simply click on the User Defined text and choose the Light and Shadows option followed by choosing to Illuminate with scene Lights.

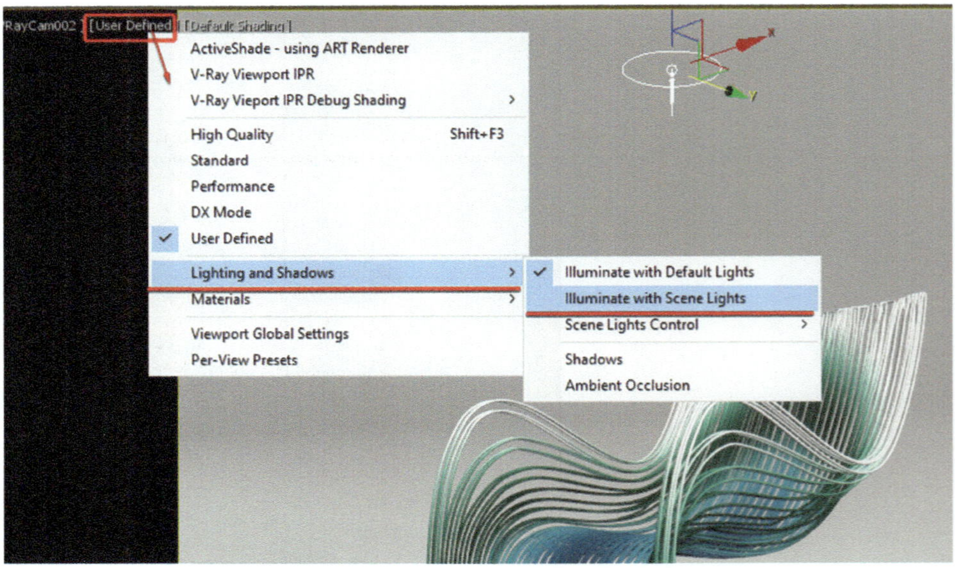

Illuminate with scene Lights

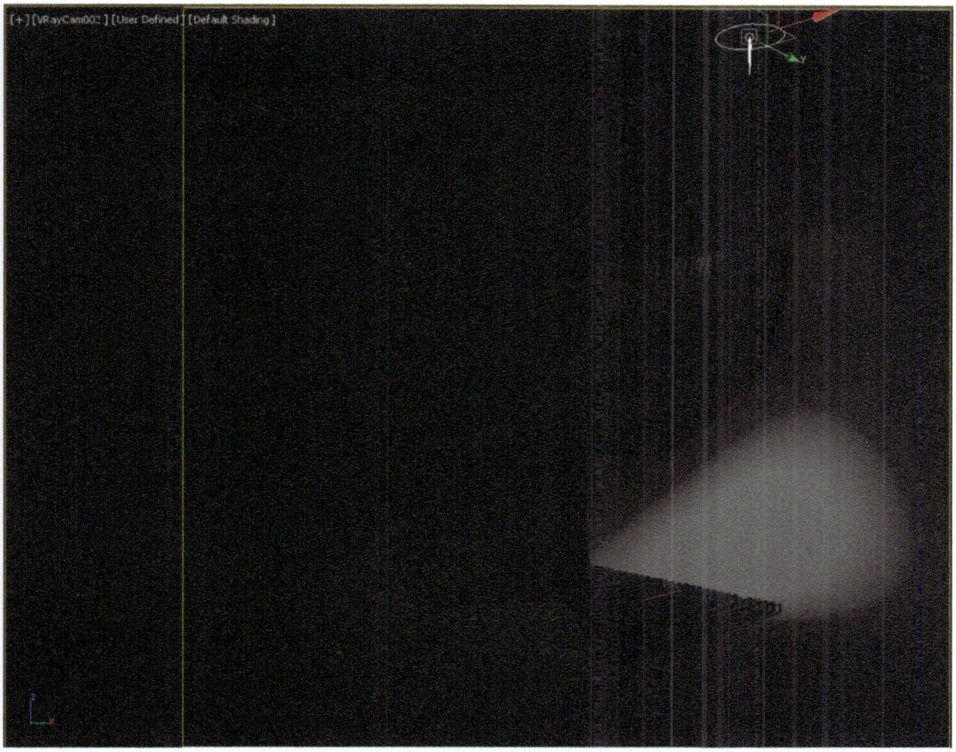

Illuminate with scene Lights in the viewport

If you happen to have a good graphics card, enable the VRay Viewport IPR (Interactive Production Rendering) to display a fast and accurate preview of the final render in the viewport.

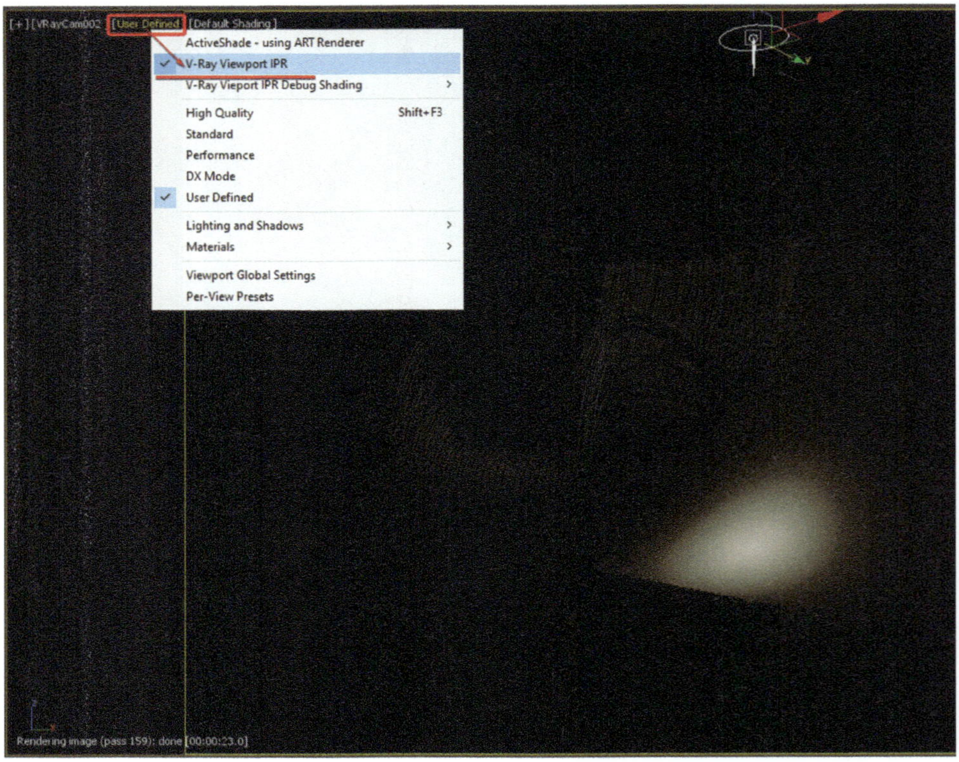

VRay Viewport IPR

Affect diffuse: This function determines whether the IES light will affect the diffuse color of objects or not.

Enabled by default.

Diffuse contribution: This function controls the intensity of the lights on the diffuse color of objects.

Default value is 1.0.

Affect specular: This function determines whether the IES light will affect the specular/glossiness of objects or not.

Enabled by default.

Specular contribution: This function controls how much the IES light will affect the specular/glossiness of objects.

Default value is 1.0.

Use light shape: This function controls how the shape of the light will be factored in to process the shadows and the illumination.

For shadows only is used by default.

Override shape: If chosen, it disables the IES profile shape, and enables functions such as Shape, Height, Width, Length, and Diameter.

Override Intensity: This function controls how the IES light intensity will be used.

Rescale: This function matches the light intensity defined by the user.

Replace: This function recalculates (multiplies) the intensity based on the IES distribution.

Intensity type: This function determines the units of the light intensity.

Intensity value: This function controls the intensity of the IES light.

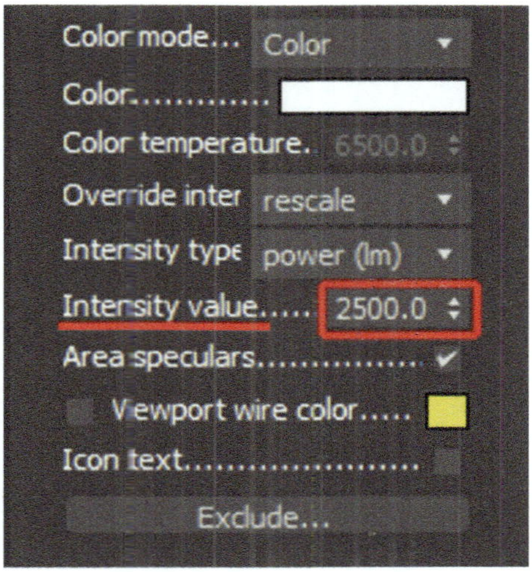

Intensity value set to 2500.0

Intensity value set to 2500.0 render

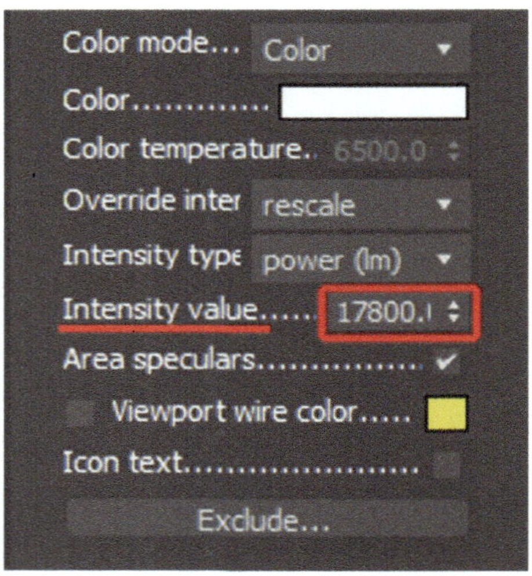

Intensity value IES power set to 17800.0

Intensity value set to 17800.0 render

VRaySun

The VRaySun emulates the physical properties of a real sunlight.

It's always best to have all four viewports in display (Top, Right, Left, Camera/ Perspective) before creating the VRaySun object.

This will help control its position and placement in the scene.

When the VRaySun is created, a dialog to automatically add a VRaySky in the environment map is prompted.

If there's already a Bitmap, you'll be asked to replace it, if desired.

The VRaySky works like an HDRI for diffused lighting and shadows.

The intensity of the VRaySky and VRaySun vary, depending on the sun position.

NOTE

To test some of the VRaySun parameters discussed here, simply open the 3ds max scene named VRay Sun.max.

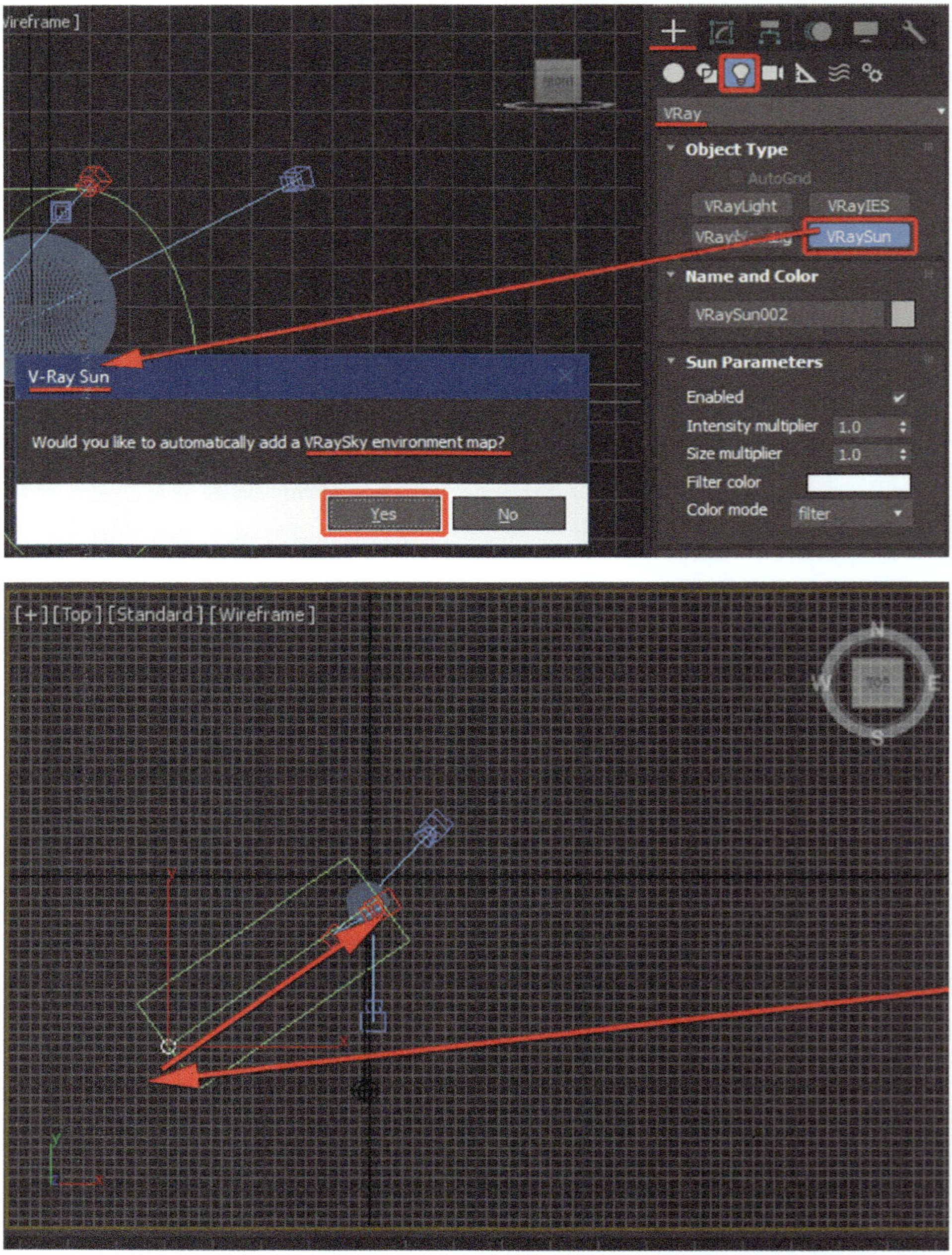

Creating the VRaySun

Move the VRaySun object up to a position where shadows are cast across the camera.

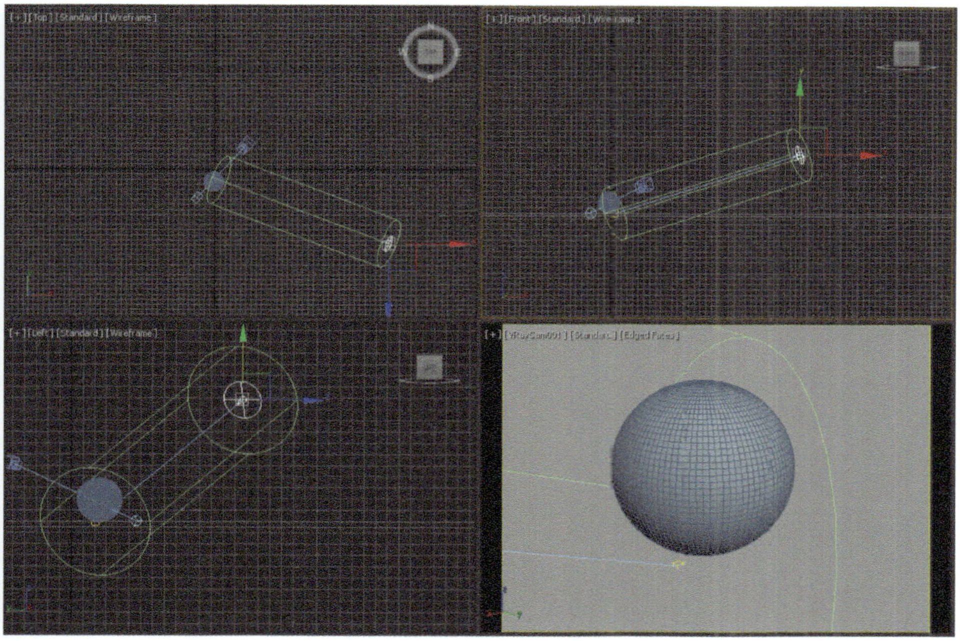

Position the VRaySun object

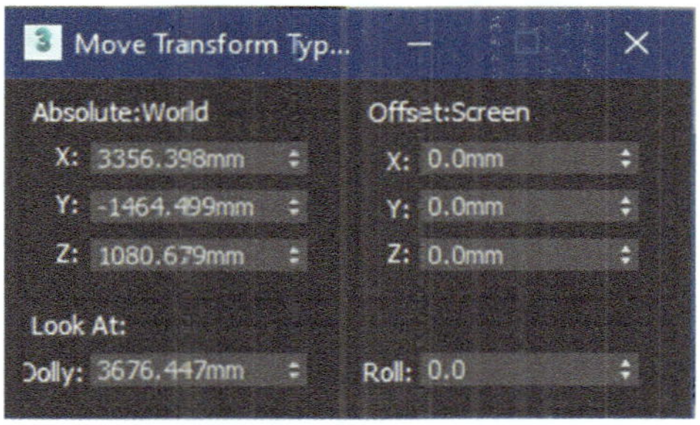
Move Transform Typ...
Absolute:World
X: 3356.398mm
Y: -1464.499mm
Z: 1080.679mm
Look At:
Dolly: 3676.447mm
Offset:Screen
X: 0.0mm
Y: 0.0mm
Z: 0.0mm
Roll: 0.0

VRaySun position

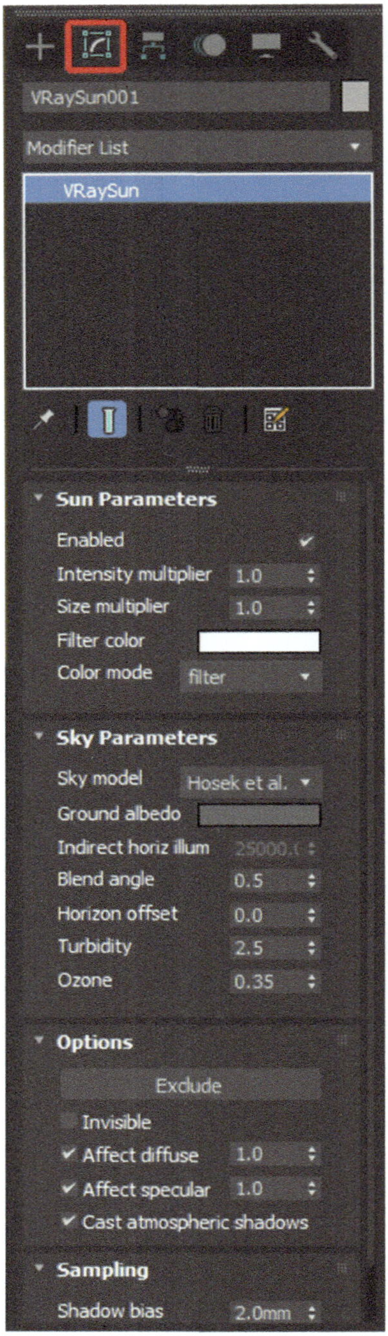
VRaySun001
Modifier List
VRaySun
Sun Parameters
Enabled
Intensity multiplier 1.0
Size multiplier 1.0
Filter color
Color mode filter
Sky Parameters
Sky model Hosek et al.
Ground albedo
Indirect horiz illum
Blend angle 0.5
Horizon offset 0.0
Turbidity 2.5
Ozone 0.35
Options
Exclude
Invisible
Affect diffuse 1.0
Affect specular 1.0
Cast atmospheric shadows
Sampling
Shadow bias 2.0mm

VRaySun Modify parameters

VRaySun rendered

Sun Parameters

Enabled: This function turns the VRaySun on or off.

Intensity multiplier: This function controls the intensity of the sun.

Default value is 1.0.

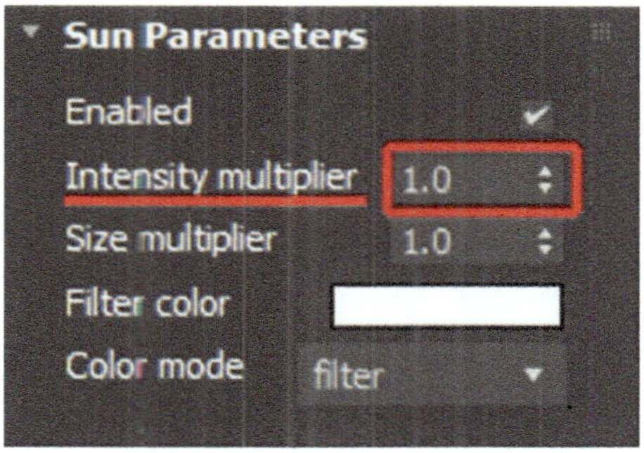

Intensity multiplier set to 1.0

Intensity multiplier set to 1.0 render

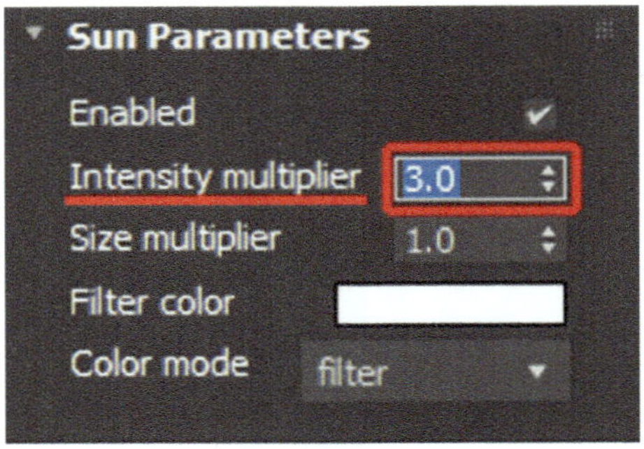

Intensity multiplier set to 3.0

Intensity multiplier set to 3.0 render

Size multiplier: This option controls the size of the sun in the VRaySky (it's visible on reflections).

The bigger the Size multiplier, the softer the shadows.

Filter color: This function controls the color of the VRaySun.

As the VRaySun object is moved downward, the default color changes automatically–white by default.

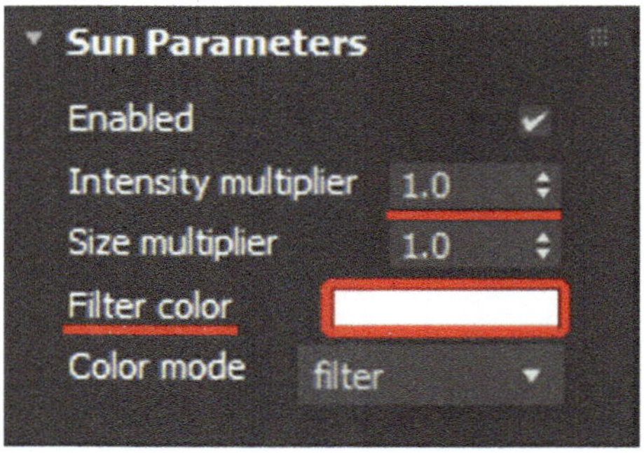

VRaySun default Filter color white

VRaySun default Filter color white render

Filter color automatically changed with sun moved down

Color mode: This function controls how the VRaySun is affected by Filter color.

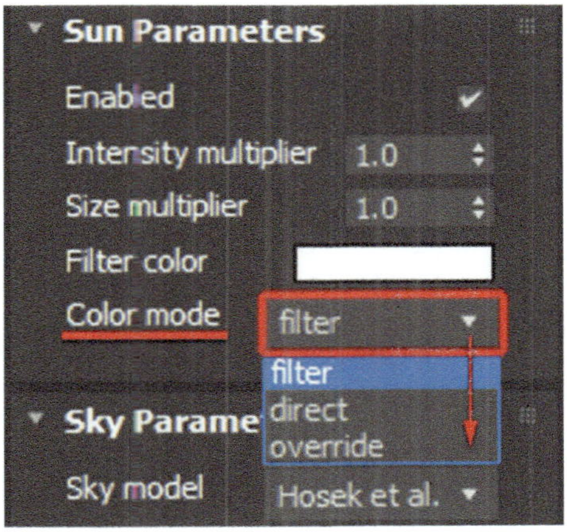

Color mode options

Filter: This option uses the color specified in the Filter color function.

Direct: This option uses the VRaySun color to coincide with the filter color. The intensity of the VRaySun is automatically controlled by the Intensity multiplier function.

Override: This option uses the VRaySun to coincide with the filter color. The intensity of the VRaySun is controlled by its position

Sky Parameters

NOTE

Always use the Improved Sky model type, as it uses a more photo-realistic and sophisticated Sky.

Sky model: This function allows users to choose a specific sky model from its dropdown menu. This sky model is directly connected to the VRaySky.

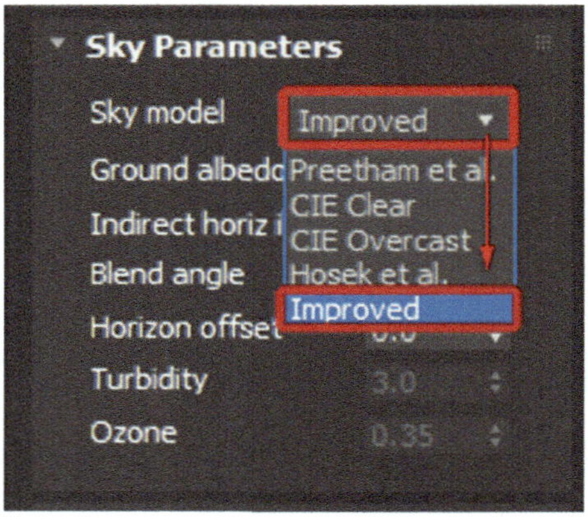

Sky model options

Ground albedo: This function controls the color of the ground (below the horizon line).

Indirect horiz illum: This function controls the indirect illumination on horizontal surfaces, generated by the sky VRaySky.

Blend angle: This function controls the size of the gradient seen in the VRaySky.

Horizon offset: This function allows users to offset the default horizon position.

Turbidity: It controls the color of the sky and the sun. Lower values yield bluer/clear skies, while higher values produce yellowish/orangish skies.

Ozone: This function controls mainly the color of the sunlight. Higher values yield bluer tones; and lower values produce more yellowish hues.

Options

Exclude: This toggle allows users to choose specific objects in the scene to exclude from the effects of the VRaySun.

Invisible: This option controls the visibility of the VRaySun in the sky.

Visible by default.

Affect diffuse: Allows the VRaySun to affect the diffuse color of objects in the scene.

Enabled by default.

Affect specular: It enables the VRaySun to affect the specular/glossiness of objects in the scene.

Enabled by default.

Cast atmospheric shadows: When enabled, atmospheric shadows will affect the scene.

Enabled by default.

Sampling

Shadow bias: This function controls the position of the shadows. Lower values bring the shadows closer to objects.

High values yield the opposite effect.

Default value is 2.0 mm.

Values higher than 5 mm may result in shadow artifacts.

Photon emit radius: It sets the radius/perimeter of the photon areas (seen in the viewport).

Users often increase it big enough to encapsulate the area seen by the camera.

VRay Light Lister

This amazing function (dialog) allows users to control the functionality of all VRay lights in the scene.

Some of these functionalities include the ability to rename lights, select lights, change light Multiplier, Color, Temperature, Type, Units, etc.

To open its dialog, simply click on the Tools toolbar and choose the VRay Light Lister from the dropdown menu.

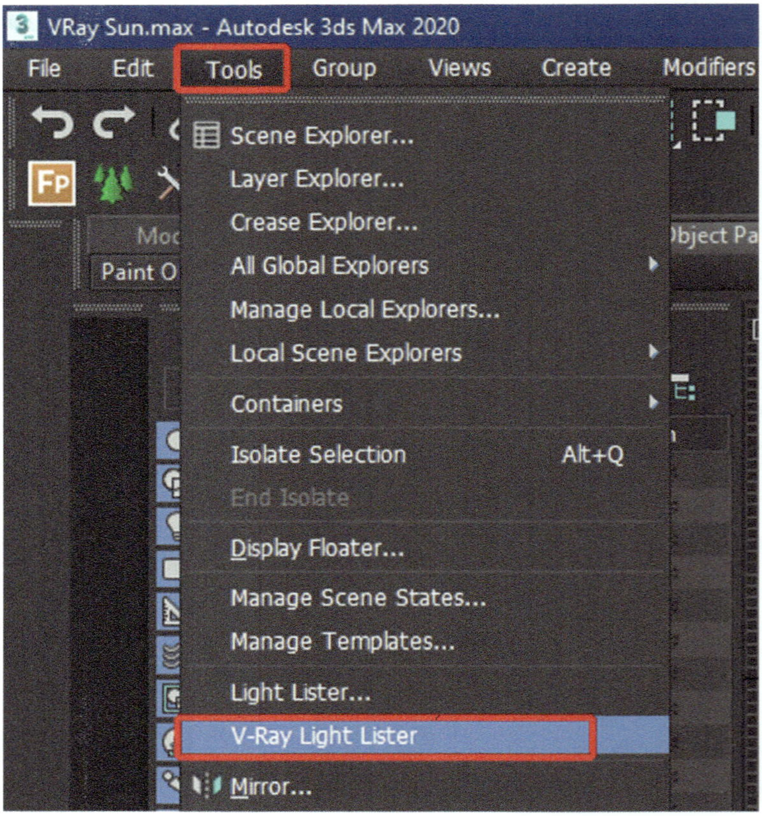

Choose VRay Light Lister

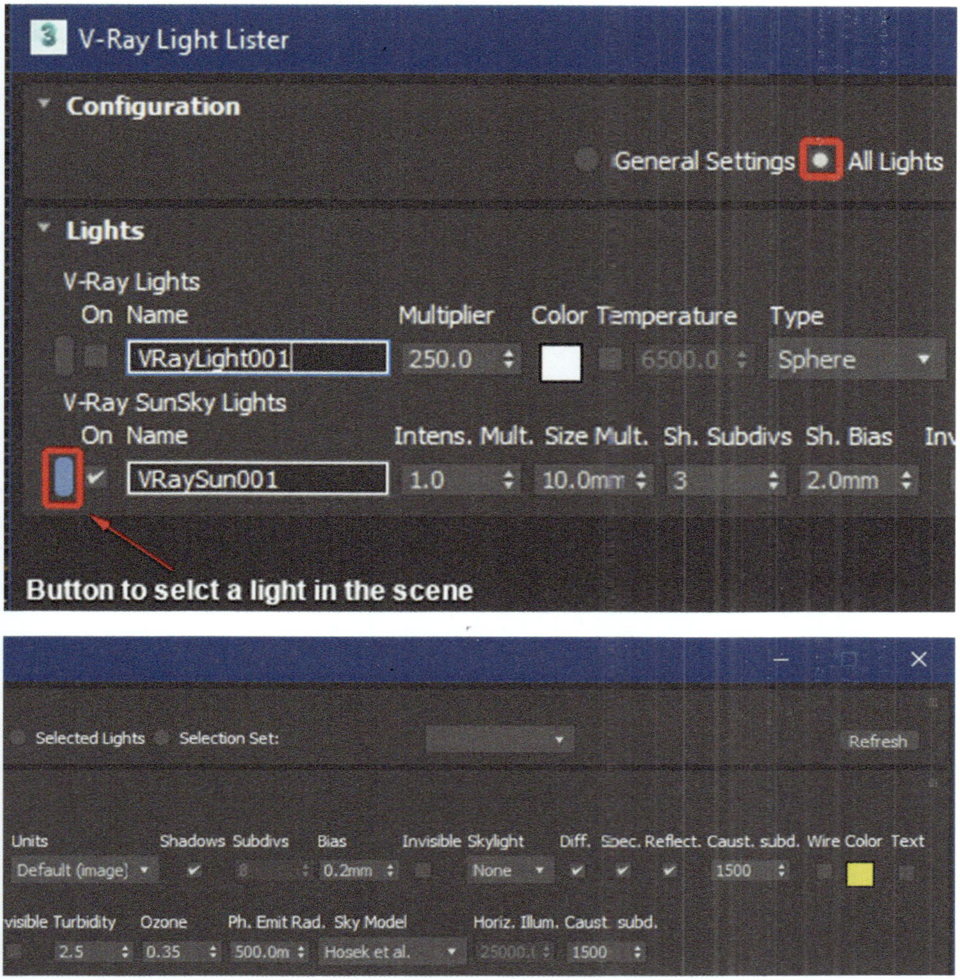
V-Ray Light Lister
Configuration
General Settings
All Lights
Lights
V-Ray Lights
On Name
Multiplier
Color Temperature
Type
VRayLight001
250.0
6500.0
Sphere
V-Ray SunSky Lights
On Name
Intens. Mult.
Size Mult.
Sh. Subdivs
Sh. Bias
VRaySun001
1.0
10.0mm
3
2.0mm
Button to selct a light in the scene
Selected Lights
Selection Set:
Refresh
Units
Shadows
Subdivs
Bias
Invisible
Skylight
Diff.
Spec.
Reflect.
Caust. subd.
Wire Color
Text
Default (image)
0.2mm
None
1500
visible
Turbidity
Ozone
Ph. Emit Rad.
Sky Model
Horiz. Illum.
Caust. subd.
2.5
0.35
500.0m
Hosek et al.
1500

VRay Light Lister dialog

NOTE

To test some of the VRaySun parameters discussed here, simply open the 3ds max scene named Daylight system.max.

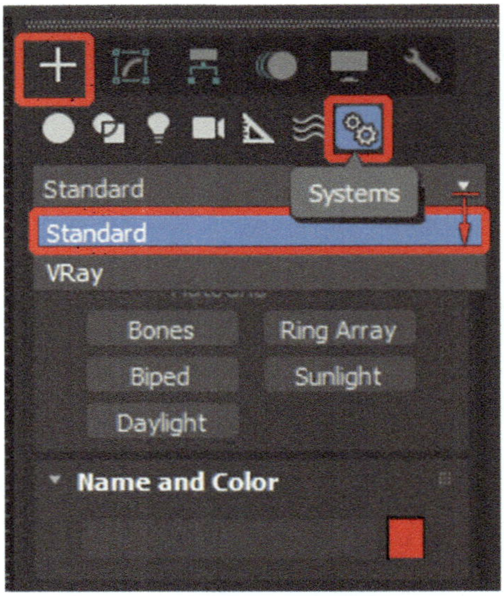

Choose the Standard System option

Daylight System

The daylight system object allows users to accurately pick and choose the geographical location, movement, and the angle of the sun around the earth.

To create it, ensure to have all four viewports in display.

Open the Create main toolbar and choose the Standard mode, followed by selecting the Systems button.

Under Systems Object type, select the Daylight button, followed by clicking and dragging its cursor in the Top viewport to create the compass and the sun object.

Release the left click and drag the mouse to begin setting the distance of the sun's head from the ground. Right click to exit creation.

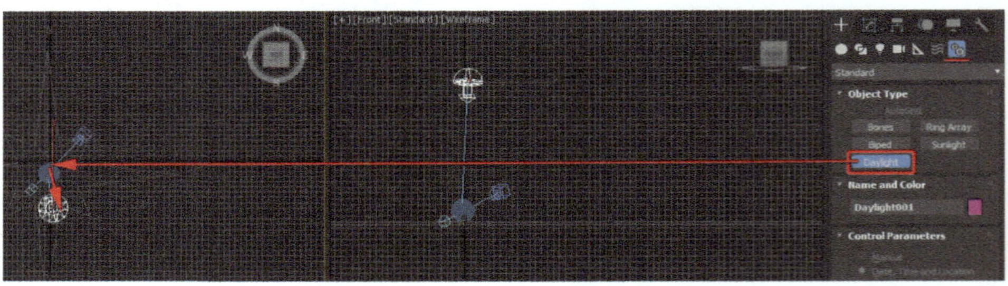

Creating the Daylight System object

To load the VRaySun, simply open the Modify command panel.

In the Sunlight option, pick the VRaySun from its dropdown menu.

A dialog should be prompted to automatically add a VRaySky in the Environment Map. Choose the Yes option.

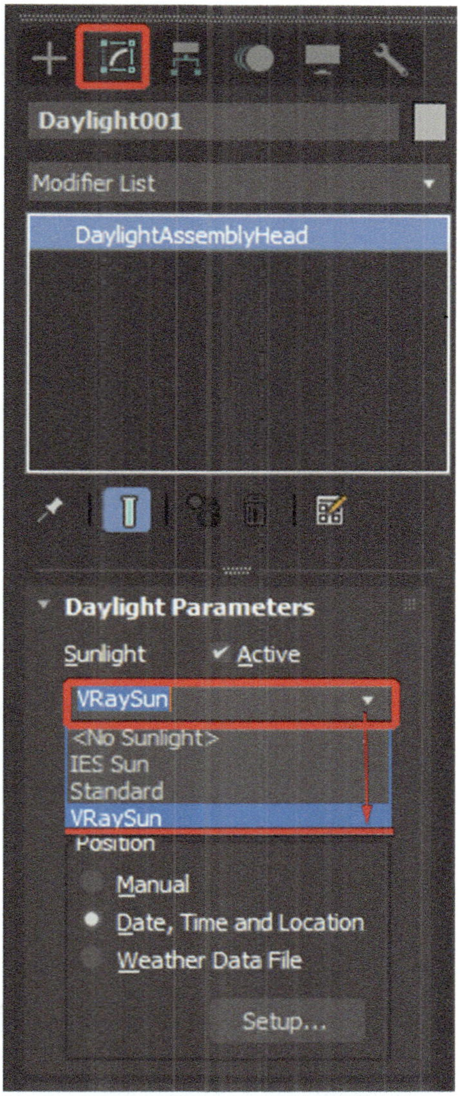

Choose the VRaySun option

Under Skylight, choose the No Skylight option.

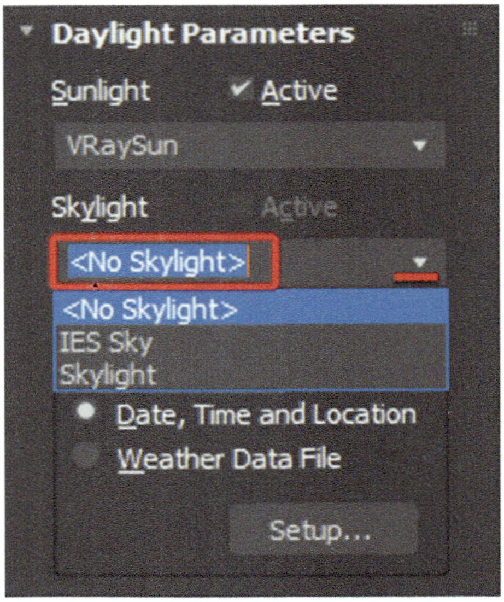

Choose the No Skylight option

VRaySun already has the Skylight parameters discussed earlier.

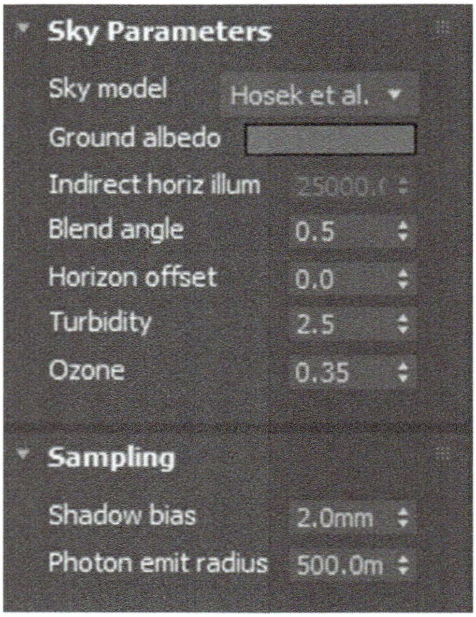

VRaySun Sky Parameters

To pick a location and setup the Time, simply click on the Setup button.

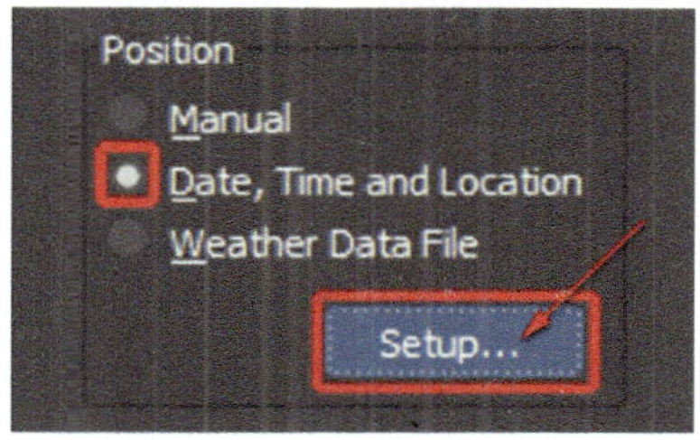

Position Setup button

The Motion command panel should open automatically.

The Control Parameters allow users to setup the Year, Month, Day, Hours, Mins, and Secs, by typing in the relevant numerical values.

To find a location, simply click on the Get Location toggle to bring up its dialog.

The Map area allows users to pick a location by clicking on it, or by selecting a continent from the Map dropdown menu, and choosing a City from its list.

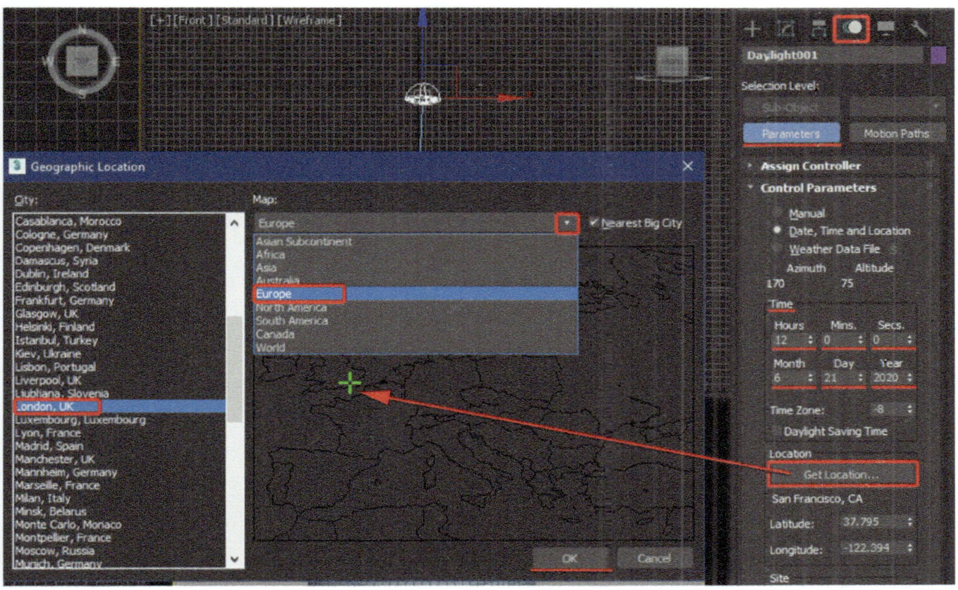

Choose a geographic location

The other parameters should *never* be tweaked/adjusted when using the Daylight System for accuracy.

Geographic Location render

Conclusion

This chapter has taken users through the process of accessing and using VRay camera parameters, along with some of the most popular VRay lights.

Users were also introduced to the Daylight System, and shown how to fine-tune some of its common parameters.

For more detailed information about VRay lights, Cameras, and other topics discussed here, please visit Chaos group official website:

http://docs.chaosgroup.com/

4

Rendering in VRay

4 Rendering in VRay

This chapter will take users through V-Ray 5s most useful rendering parameters, and show how to get the best out of them in a real production environment.

As previously stated, to access VRay tools and parameters, the VRay renderer needs to be loaded first.

To test some of the parameters being discussed in this chapter, please open the file under the name Rendering in VRay.max.

If there's a File Load Mismatch, choose Adopt the File's Unit Scale.

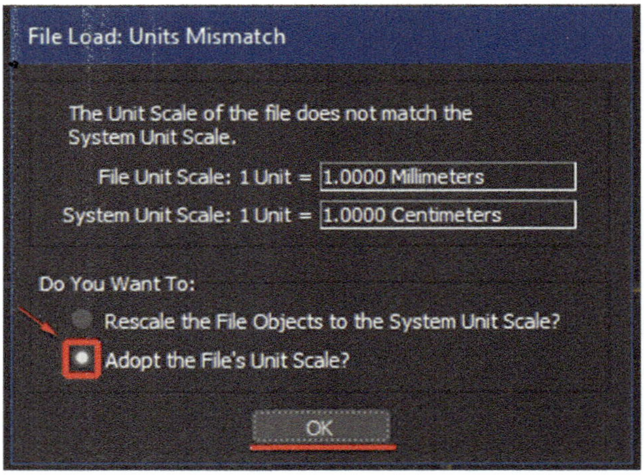

Choose Adopt the File's Unit Scale

Render Setup: VRay

To open the Render Setup dialog, simply press F10 or click on its icon from the main toolbar.

Render Setup button

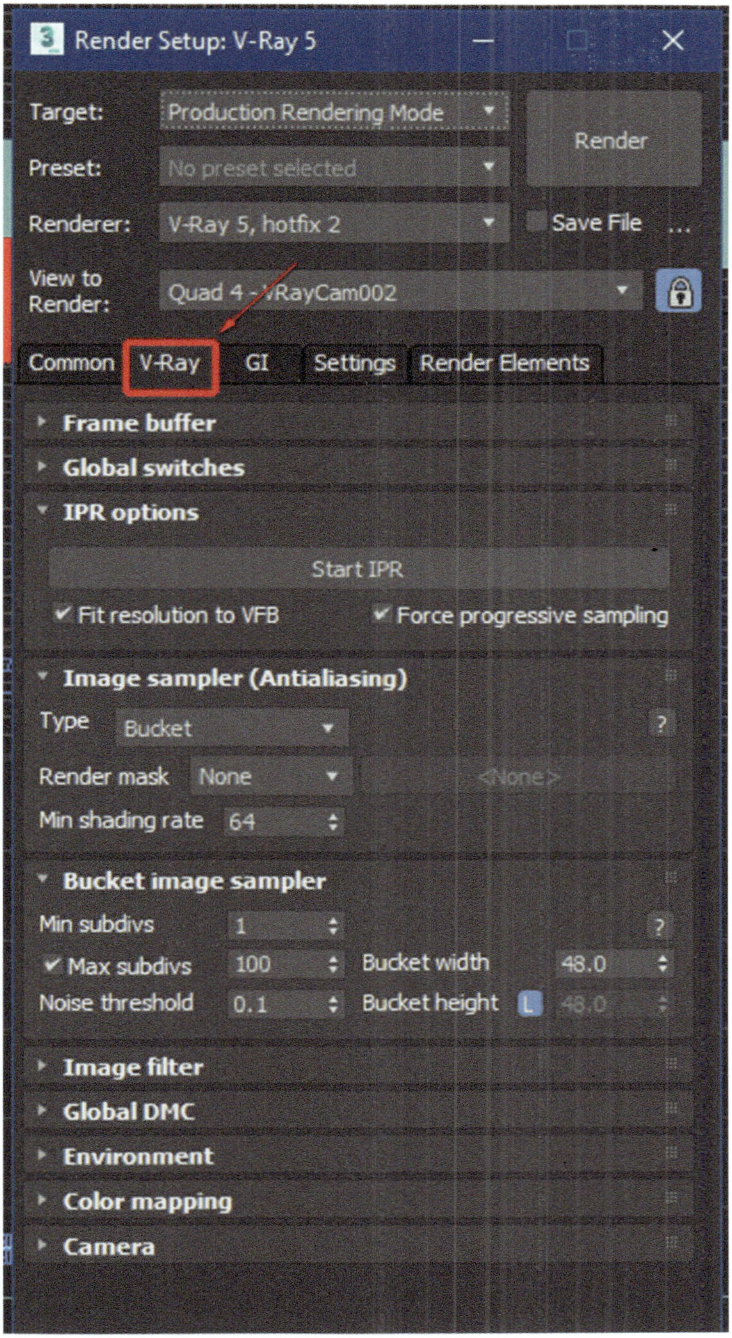
Render Setup: V-Ray 5
Target:
Production Rendering Mode
Render
Preset:
No preset selected
Renderer:
V-Ray 5, hotfix 2
Save File
View to Render:
Quad 4 - VRayCam002
Common
V-Ray
GI
Settings
Render Elements
Frame buffer
Global switches
IPR options
Start IPR
Fit resolution to VFB
Force progressive sampling
Image sampler (Antialiasing)
Type
Bucket
Render mask
None
<None>
Min shading rate
64
Bucket image sampler
Min subdivs
1
Max subdivs
100
Bucket width
48.0
Noise threshold
0.1
Bucket height
48.0
Image filter
Global DMC
Environment
Color mapping
Camera

Render Setup dialog

Under VRay tab, extend the Frame buffer rollout parameters.

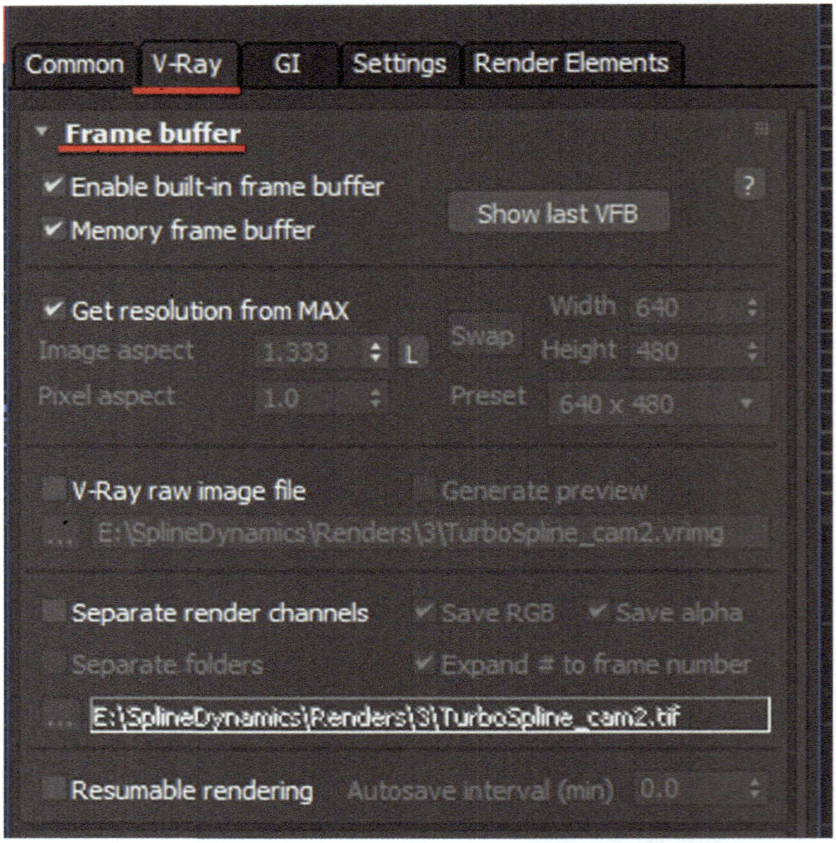

Frame buffer rollout parameters

Enable built-in frame buffer: This function uses the VRay frame buffer to render the scene. Enabled by default.

Memory frame buffer: When enabled, this option saves/displays all the rendering data into the memory of the Frame buffer. The rendering data is what's viewed in the VRF (e.g., RGB, Alpha, etc.), while the rendering is taking place and after the rendering is finished.

Enabled by default.

Show last VFB: This toggle opens up the VRay frame buffer by clicking on its button.

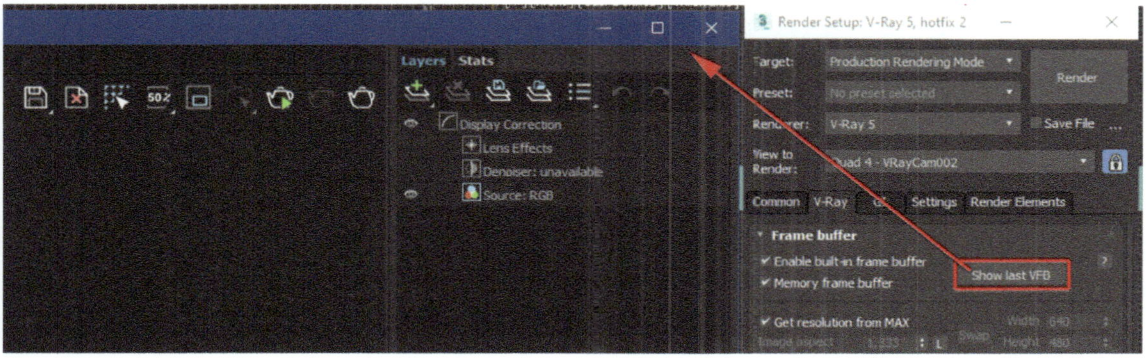

Show last VFB

The VRay frame buffer button can also be accessed from the main toolbar.

Show last VFB toolbar button

NOTE

For the purpose of this chapter, please load the VRay image file under the name Rendering in VRay. 0000.vrimg

VRay Frame Buffer Parameters

File—Load Image: This button allows users to locate and load files into the VFB. Users can choose load from any of the listed file types.

VRay image file (*.vrimg) is the most commonly used files.

VRay image file (*.vrimg) format is specific to VRay, and typically big in size. It's mainly because it contains key render data such as render passes and render logs.

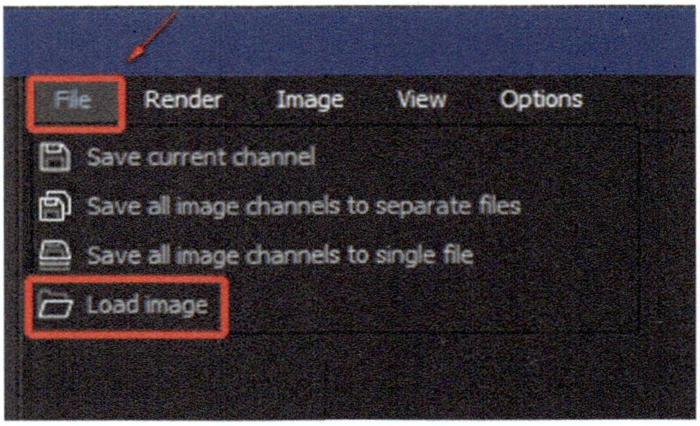

Load Image **dialog**

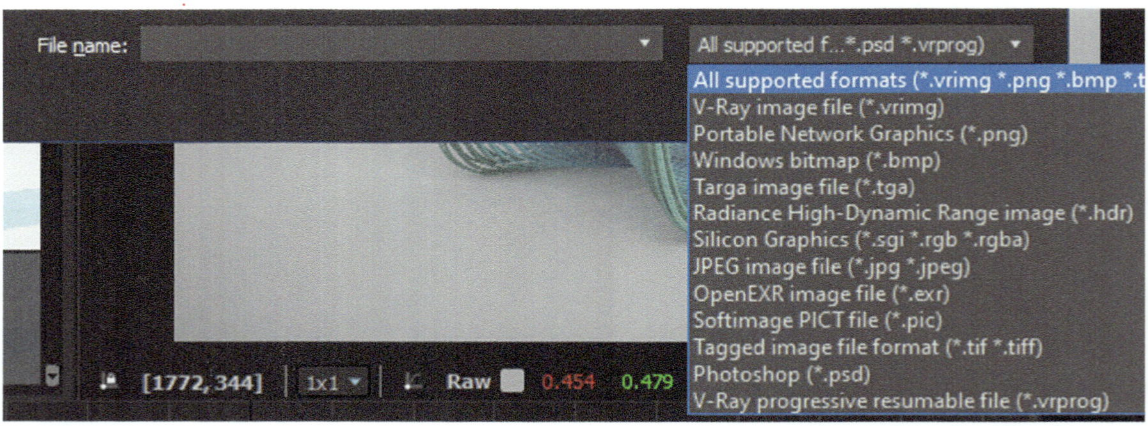

Supported file formats

Once the VRay image file (*.vrimg) is loaded in the frame buffer, it allows users to save them in a variety of file formats such as exe and tiff.

Users can also utilize the VRay image file (*.vrimg) to continue rendering previously crashed files, region renders, render selected objects in the scene, and use Frame Buffer functionalities such as Lens Effects, LUT files, VFB L, Layers, and much more.

To create/generate VRay image files (*.vrimg), simply open the Render Setup dialog (F10).

In VRay tab, under Frame buffer, enable and name the VRay raw image file function before rendering the final scene.

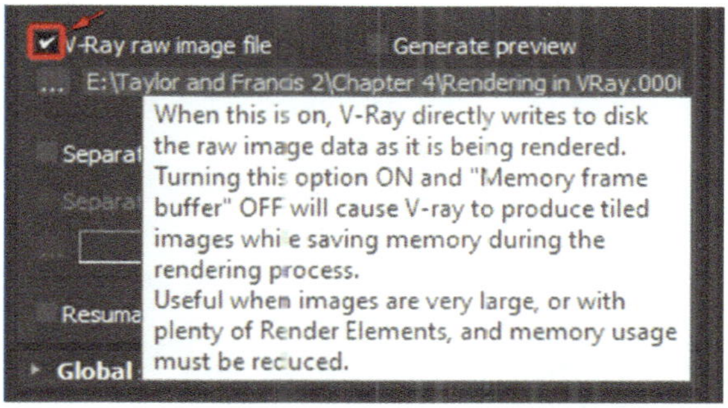

Enable and name VRay raw image file function

File—Save all image channels to single file: This function automatically saves all image channels/render elements listed in the frame buffer into a single file (OpenEXR image file).

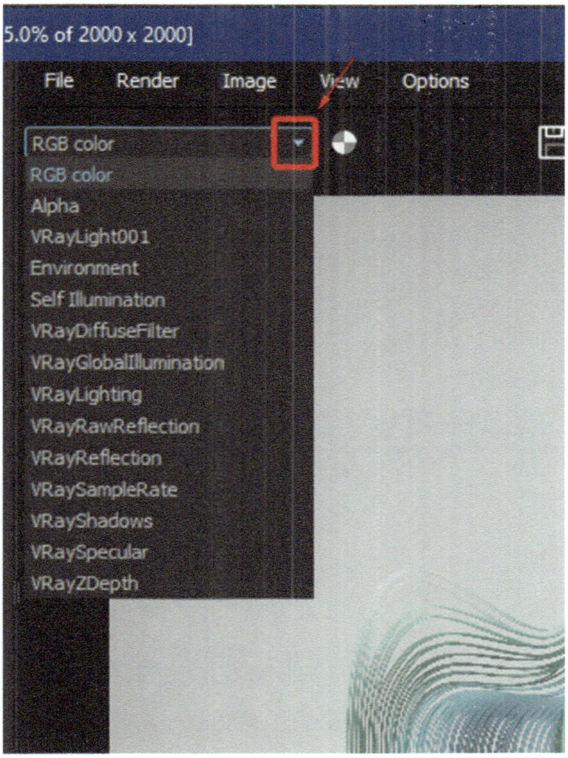

Listed rendered channels/elements

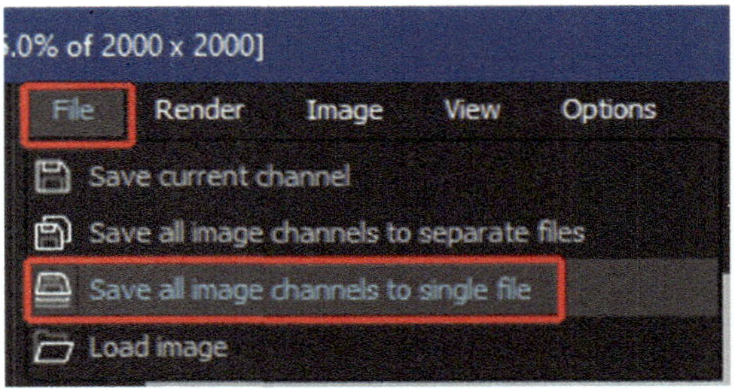

Save all image channels to single file

Clicking this function will prompt a dialog, for users to type in the file name, choose a location to save files into, and the file extension (OpenEXR image file).

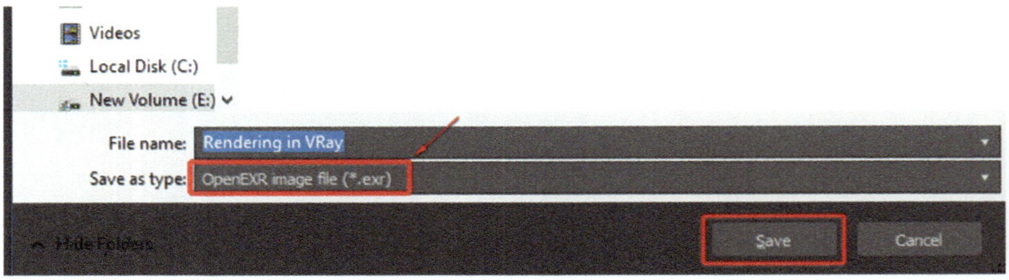

OpenEXR image in the Save dialog

Users can also Save all image channels to single file by clicking and holding down the button on the VRay Frame Buffer, followed by choosing it from the dropdown list.

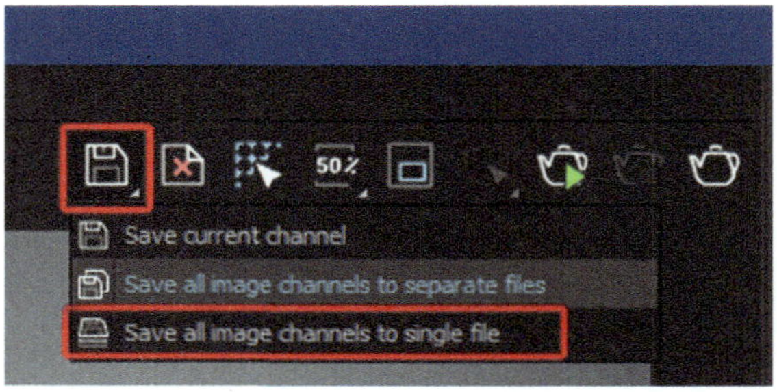

Save all image channels to single file button

File—Save all image channels to separate files: This function is the most used one.

It automatically saves all image channels/render elements listed in the frame buffer into separate individual render elements/channels, each named accordingly.

Clicking this function will prompt a dialog, for users to type in the file name, choose a location to save the files into and the file extension. Users often choose TIF Image File formats.

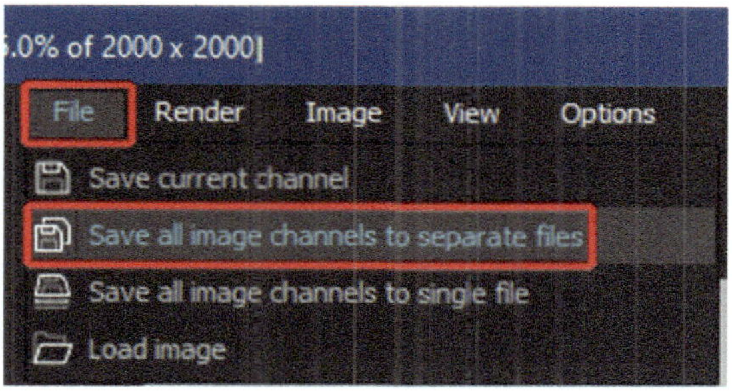

Save all image channels to separate files

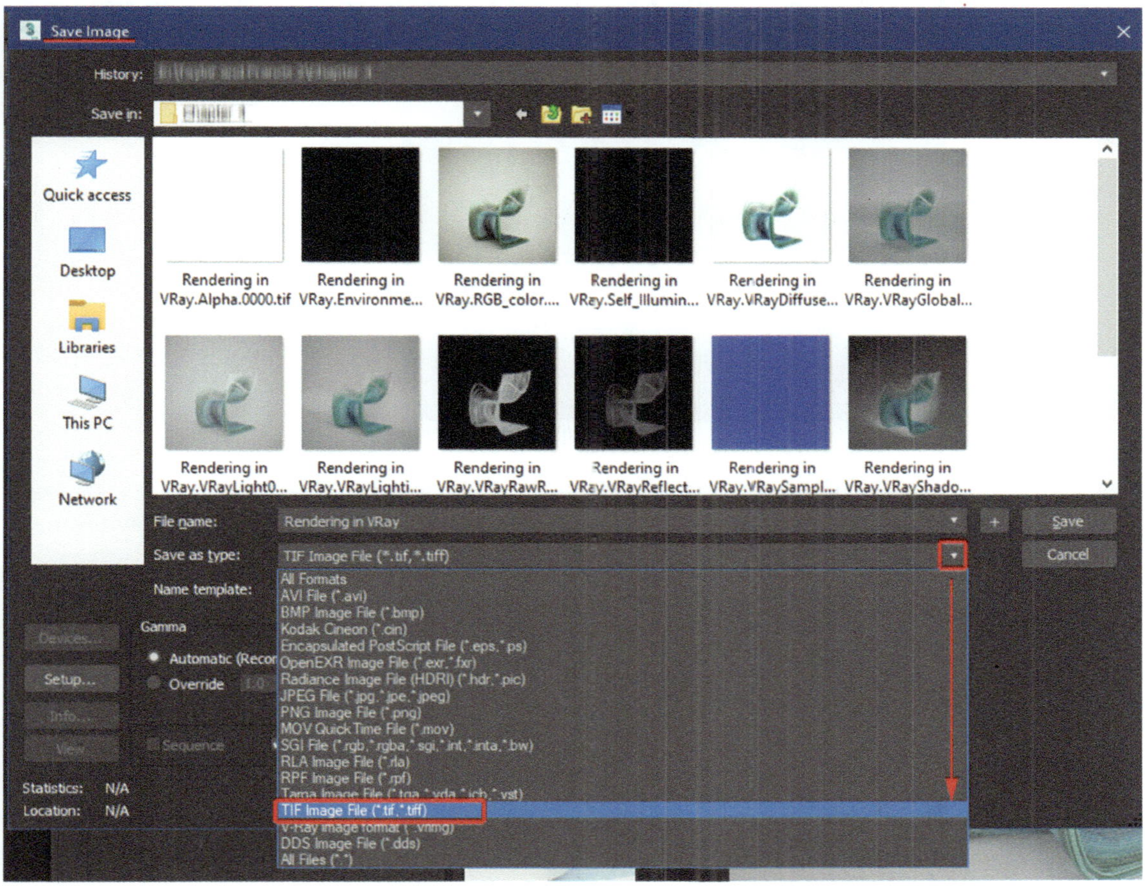

Saved separate files as TIF Image File

Users can also Save all image channels to separate files by clicking and holding down the button on the VRay Frame Buffer, followed by choosing it from the dropdown list.

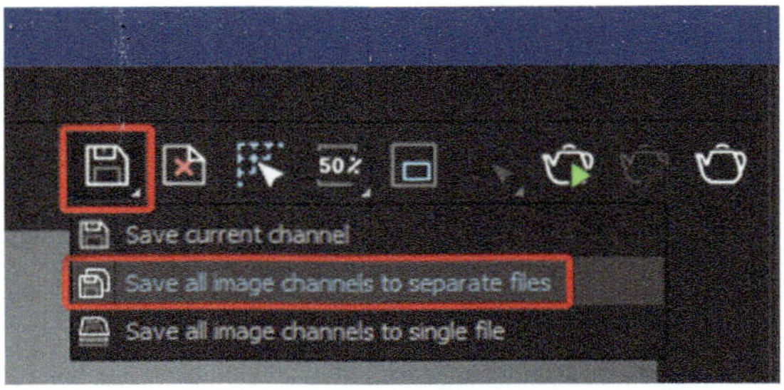

Save all image channels to separate files button

File—Save current channel: This button enables users to save the image currently being displayed in the frame buffer. Clicking this button will prompt the Save Image dialog, for users to choose a path location, the file extension type, and name the file.

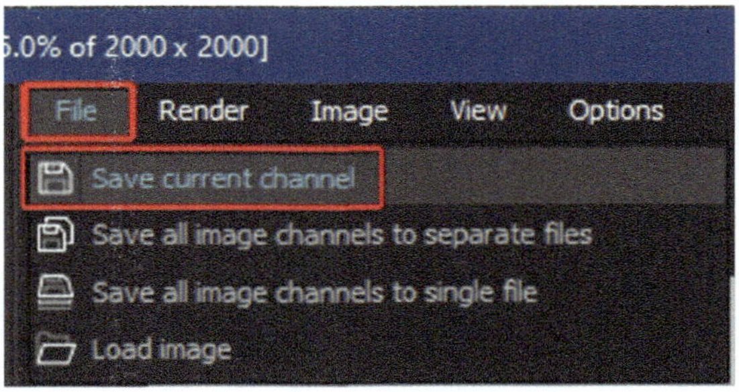

Save current channel

Users can also Save current channel by clicking its button on the VRay Frame Buffer.

Save current channel button

Render—Start interactive rendering: When enabled, this function starts the interactive rendering. Interactive rendering works in conjunction with the IPR (Interactive Production Rendering).

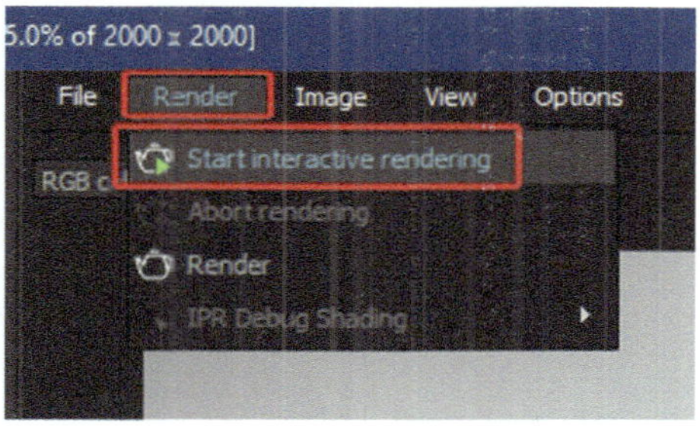

Start interactive rendering

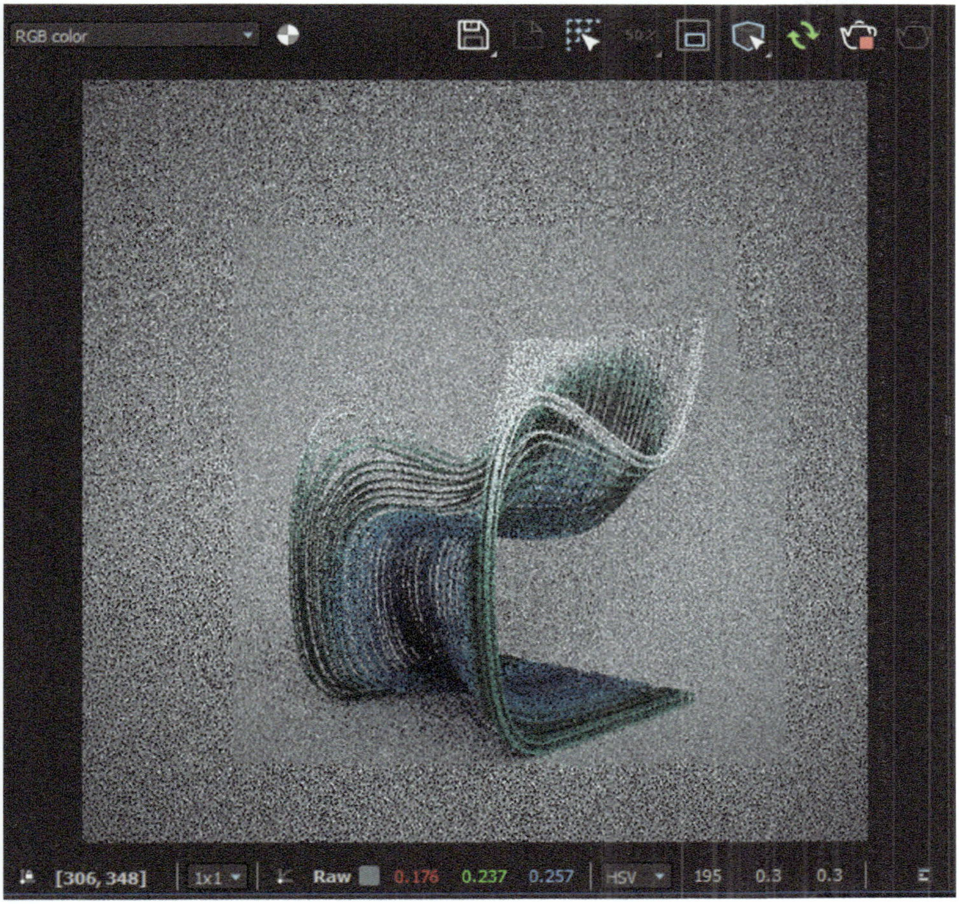

Interactive rendering process

Interactive rendering function automatically uses the Progressive Image sampler settings to quickly render the final results.

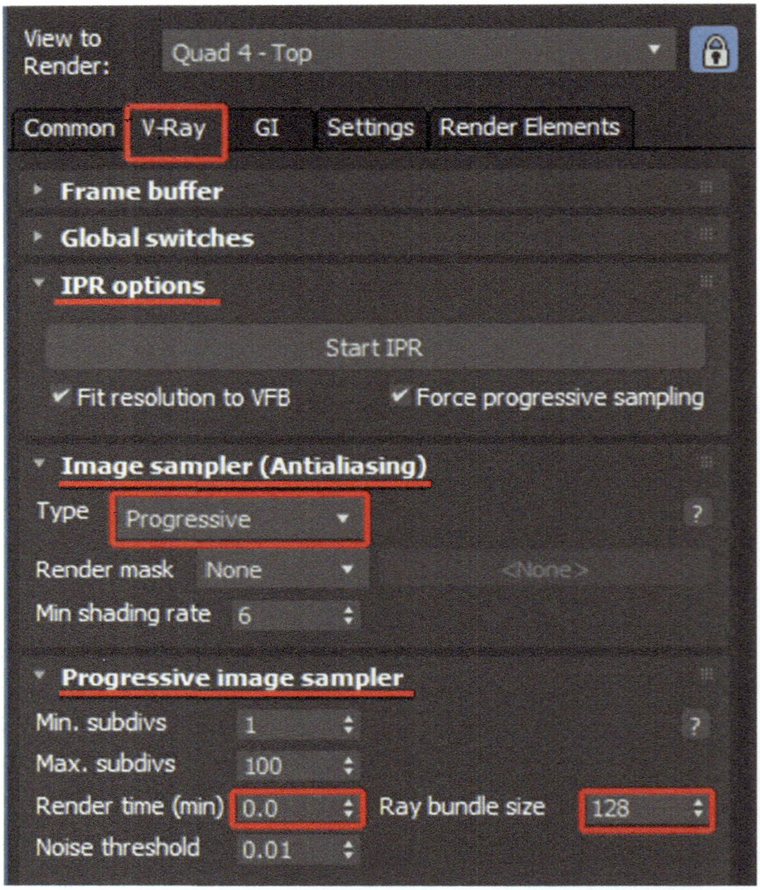

Progressive Image sampler

This function can also be used by clicking its button on VRay Frame Buffer

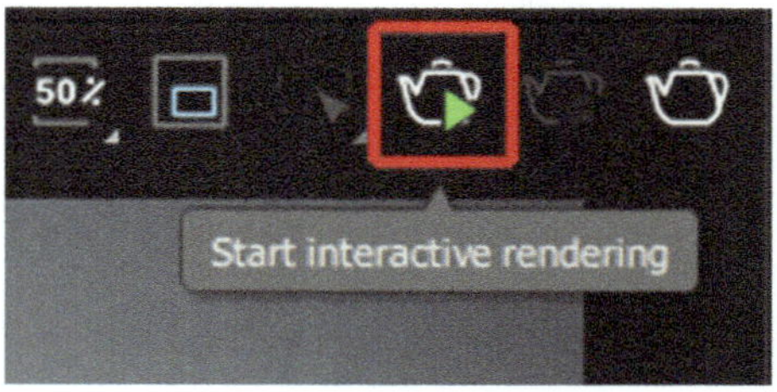

Start interactive rendering button

By clicking the button twice, it will automatically switch to Refresh interactive rendering.

This button will automatically render interactively every time a camera is moved and/or parameters are changed. Users can input new changes while the render is taking place, interactively.

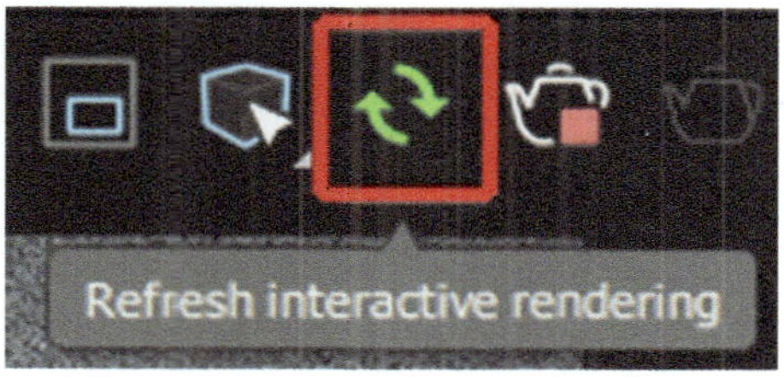

Refresh interactive rendering button

To stop interactive rendering, simply click the button to Abort rendering. This button only becomes available while interactive rendering is taking place.

Grayed out by default.

Abort rendering button

Users can also Abort rendering trough the Render tool dropdown list.

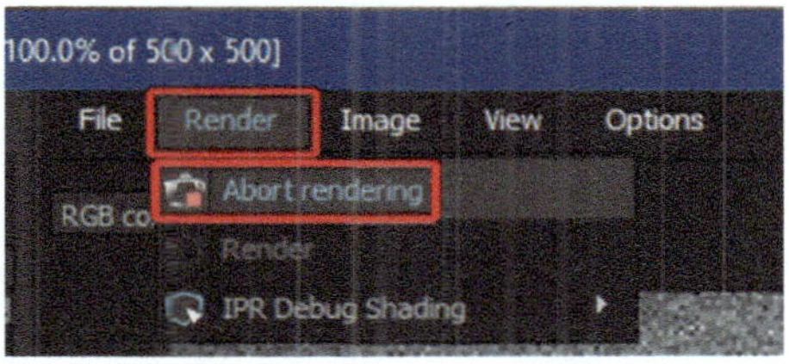

Abort rendering via Render dropdown list

Render: When clicked, it renders the current camera or viewport.

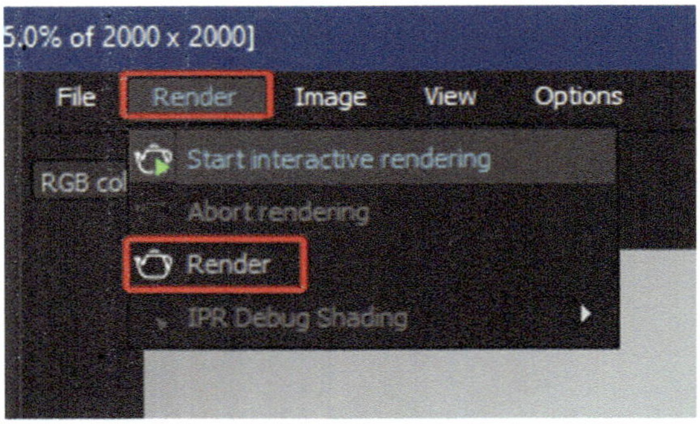

Render function

This function can also be enabled via its button on the VRay Frame Buffer.

Render button

Render—IPR Debug Shading: This function only becomes available when the Start interactive rendering is chosen, or the IPR button (Interactive Production Rendering) is clicked, under VRay IPR options. Also, the IPR button is available from the main toolbar (click and hold to choose from the list).

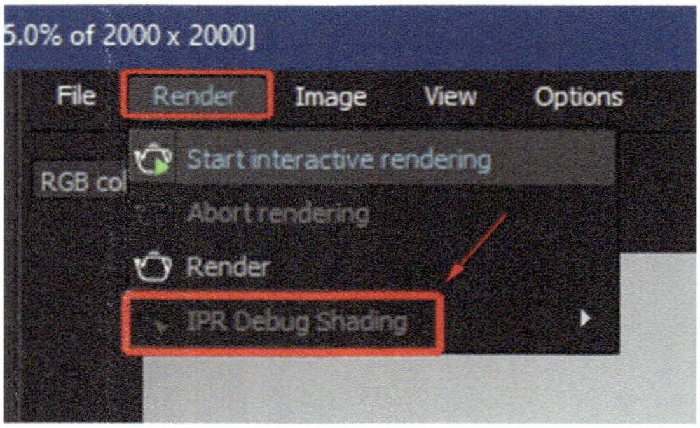

IPR Debug Shading

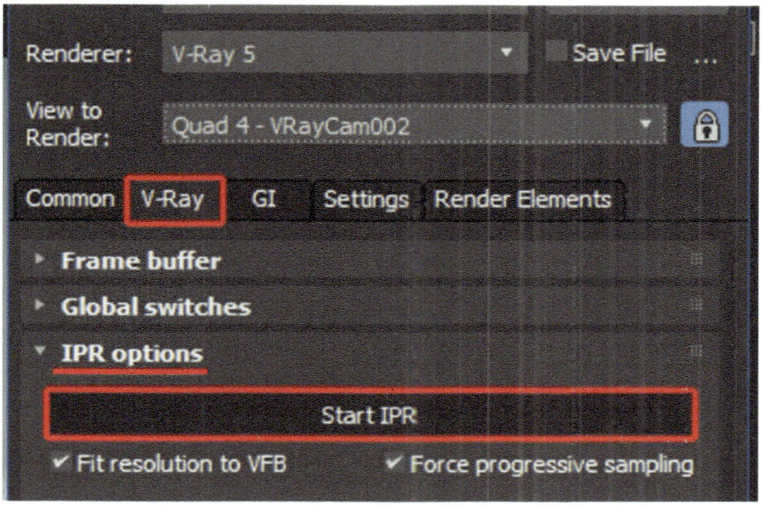

Start IPR options

IPR Mode button

Once enabled, the IPR Debug Shading becomes available with options Isolate Selected, Isolate locked selection, Lighting, Ambient Occlusion, Wireframe, Normals, and UVs.

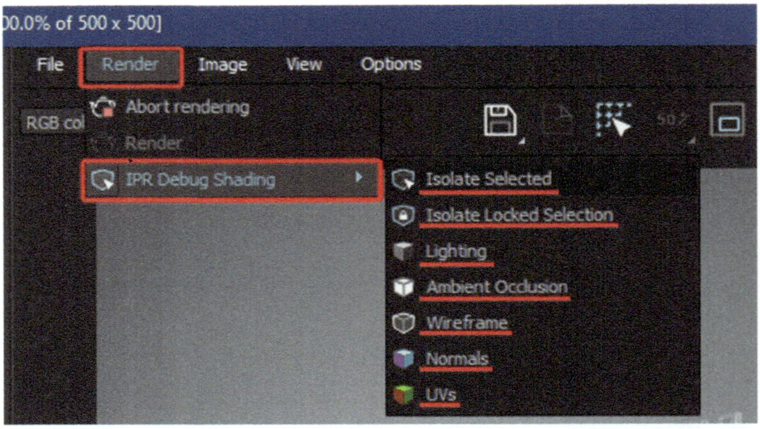

IPR Debug Shading available options

Once the IPR or Interactive rendering is enabled, the IPR options can also be accessed via the VRay Frame Buffer button.

Grayed out by default.

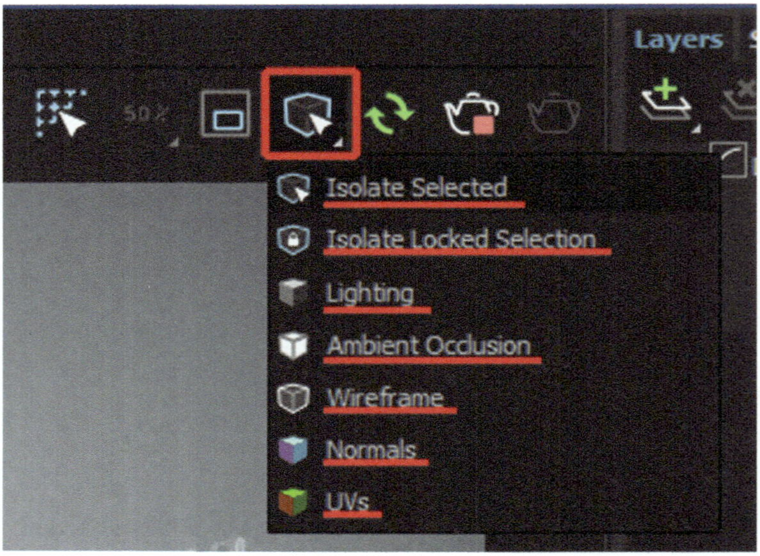

IPR Debug Shading available button

The IPR can also be activated via the viewport.

To do so, simply click on the User Defined text, and choose the VRay Viewport IPR option.

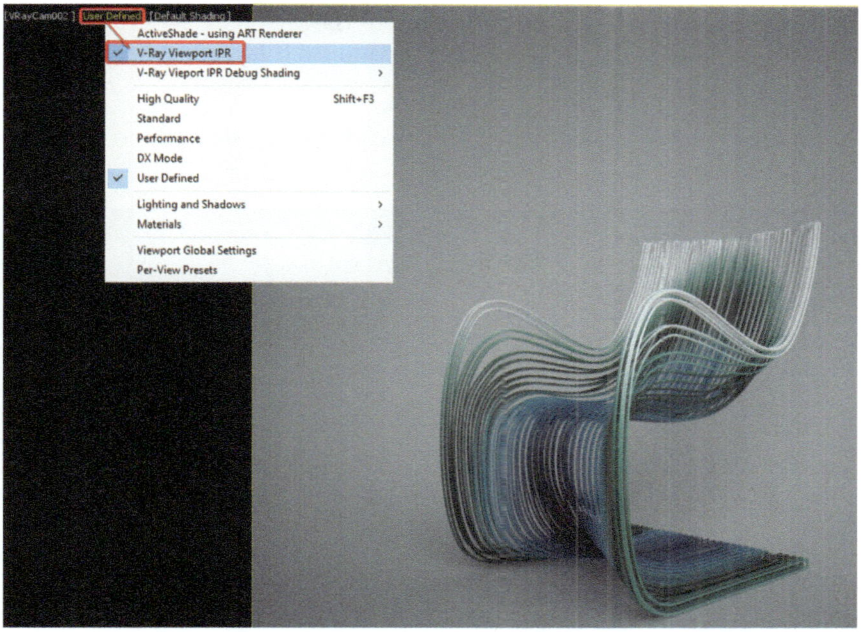

VRay Viewport IPR option and rendered

IPR can use the CPU (default) or the VRay GPU to carry out the Interactive Production Renderings.

To do so, simply go to Render Setup dialog, and load VRay GPU 5 from the Renderer dropdown list.

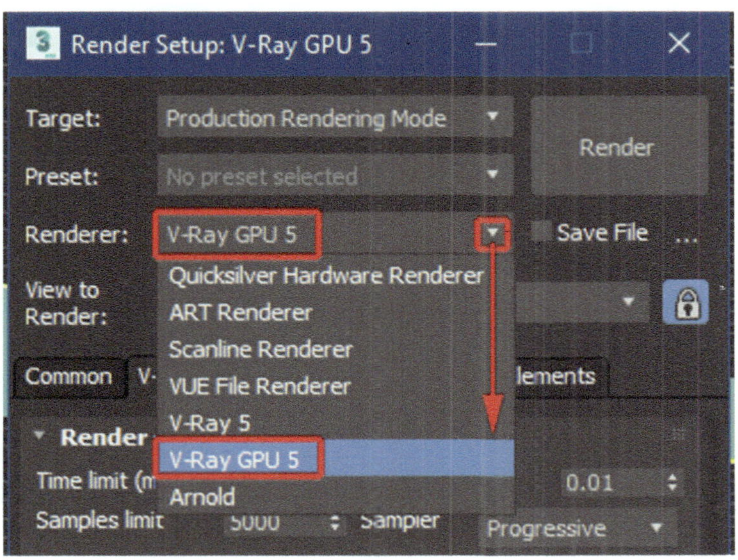

VRay GPU 5 loaded

Image—Follow mouse: If buckets are still rendering, when enabled, VRay automatically renders buckets where the mouse is hovering over in the VRay Frame Buffer.

If the area the mouse is hovering has already been rendered, no buckets will appear.

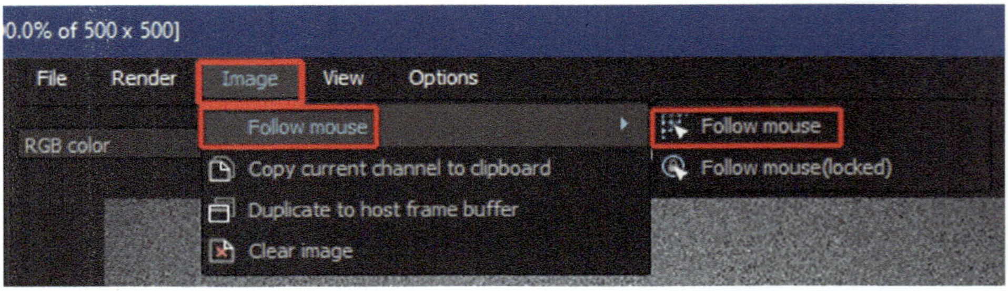

Follow mouse function

This function only works if the Image sampler type is set to Bucket.

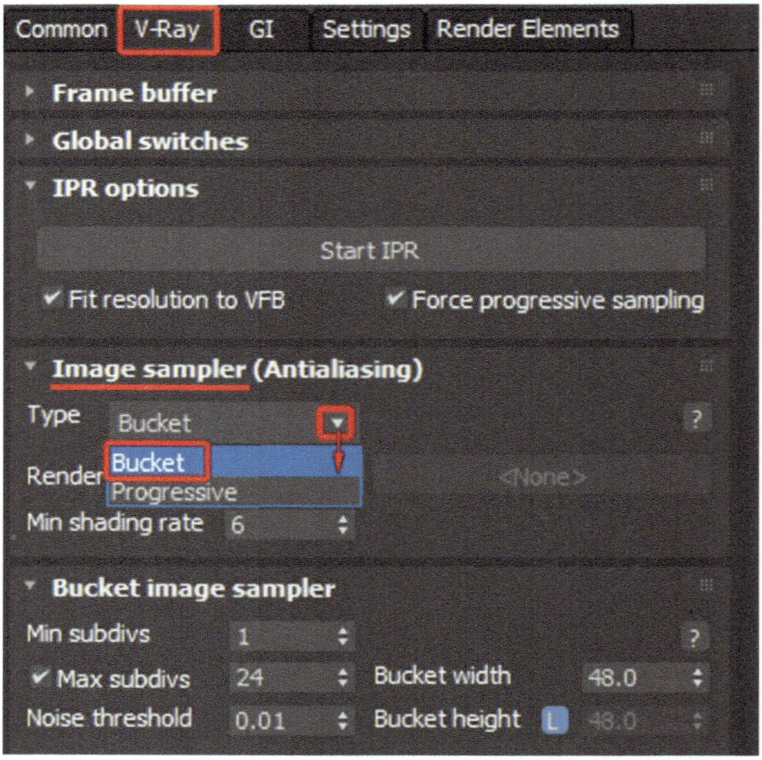

Bucket Image sampler

This function can also be enabled by clicking its button on the VRay Frame Buffer.

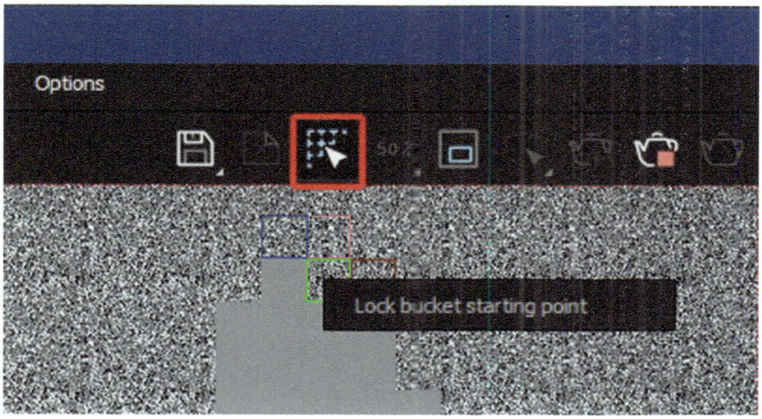

Follow mouse button

Image—Follow mouse/Lock bucket starting point: This function locks the bucket starting point on the VRay Frame Buffer, and no longer follows the mouse.

Users can enable it via the Image dropdown list, or by right clicking on the VRay Frame Buffer and clicking it.

Image—Copy current channel to clipboard: When selected, this function copies the image/channel to clipboard.

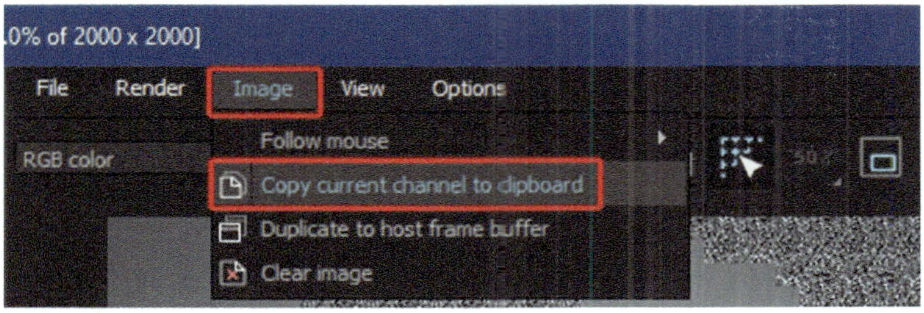

Copy current channel to clipboard function

Image—Duplicate to host frame buffer: When chosen, this function duplicates the image/render displayed in the frame buffer into a new dialog.

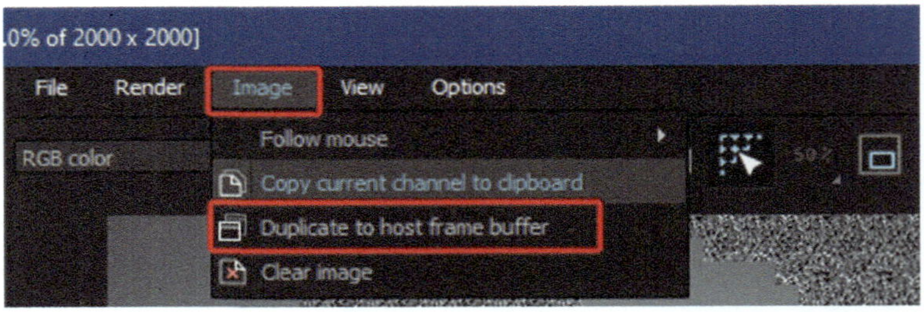

Duplicate to host frame buffer function

Image—Clear image: Clicking this button clears (removes) the channel/render being displayed in the VRay Frame Buffer.

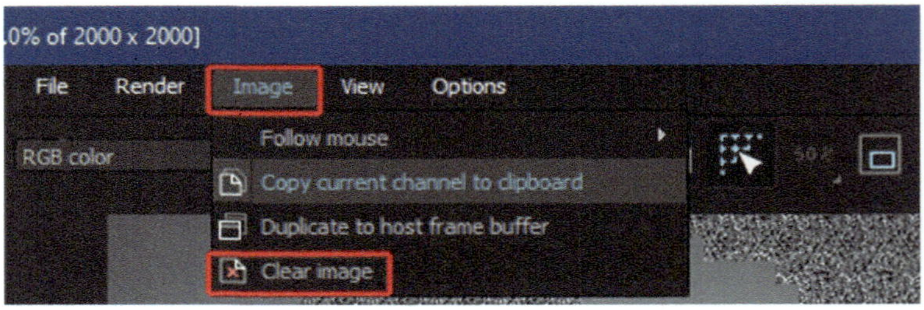

Clear image function

This function can also be accessed from the VRay Frame Buffer

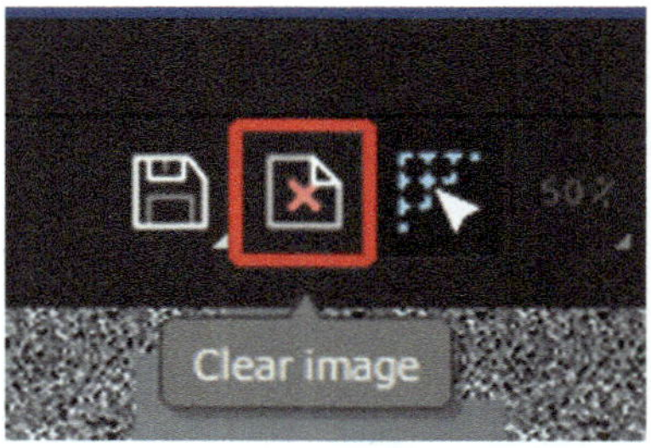

Clear image function button

View—Display color space: This function controls the color balance of your renders in the VRay Frame Buffer.

Users have the option to choose from color spaces such as sRGB, OCIO, ICC, Gamma 2.2, or None

Default color space, sRGB.

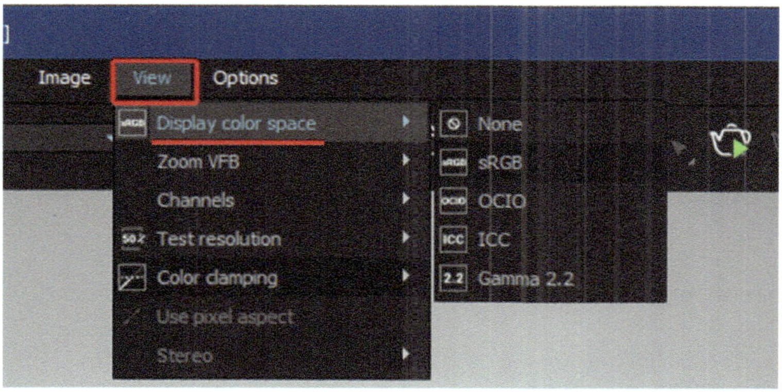

Display color space options

View—Zoom VFB: This function allows users to zoom in from a variety of zoom percentages (50%, 100%, and 150%).

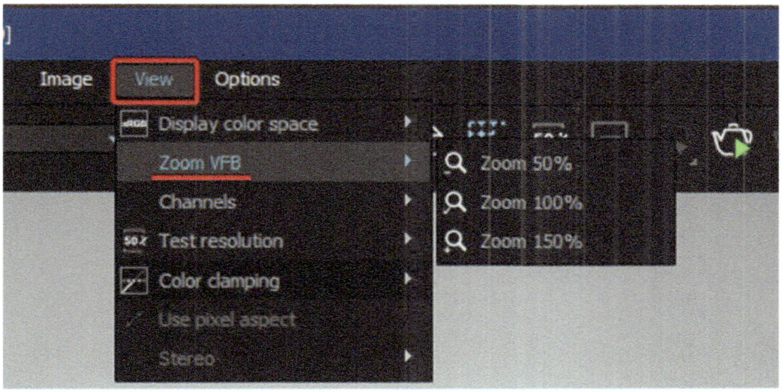

Zoom VFB options

View—Channels: This function allows users to view the render in a variety of different channels such as red, green, blue, alpha channels and Monochromatic.

NOTE

A dotted red line will always be present around the VFB, if the zoom exceeds 100% of the original image/render.

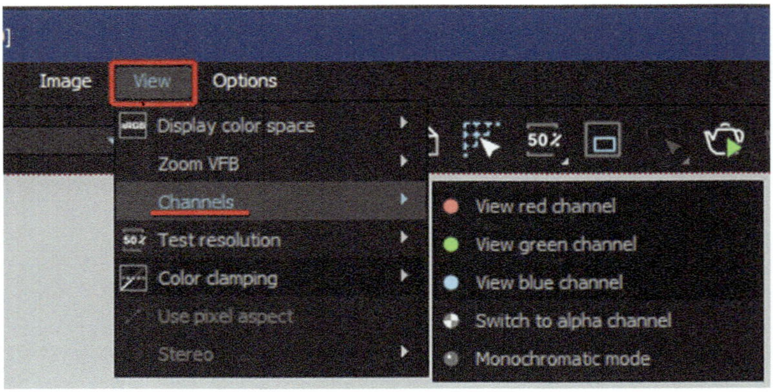

View channels options

View in Monochromatic mode

View—Test resolution: This function allows users to test the resolution in the VFB.

Default value is 50%.

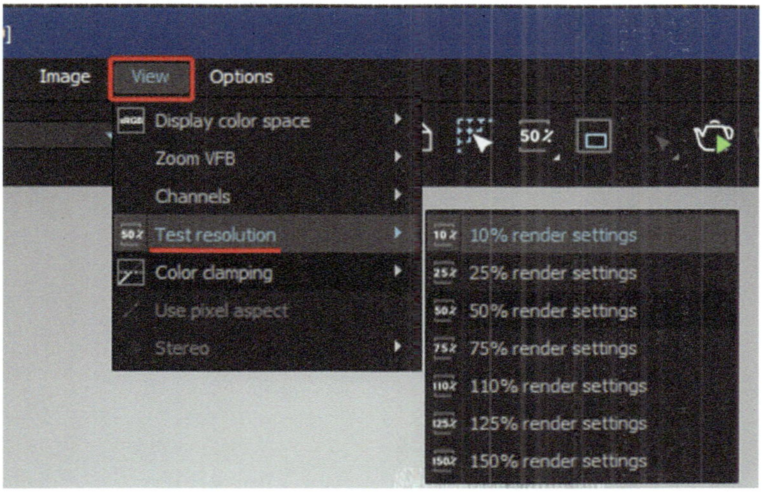

Test resolution options

This function can also be accessed via the VFB button.

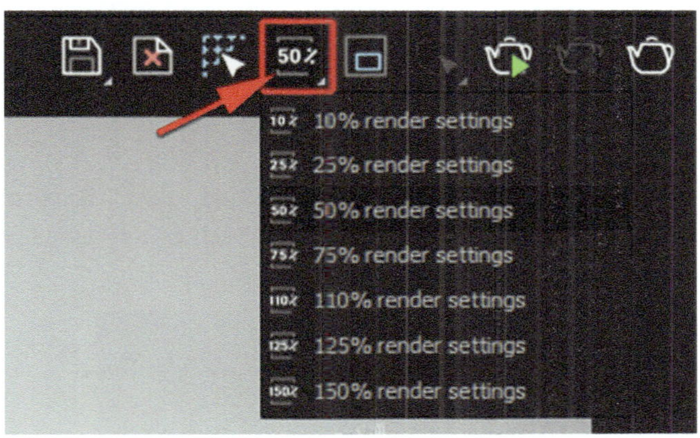

Test resolution options button

View—Color clamping: This function allows users to Force color clamping or View clamped colors in the VFB.

Force color clamping by default.

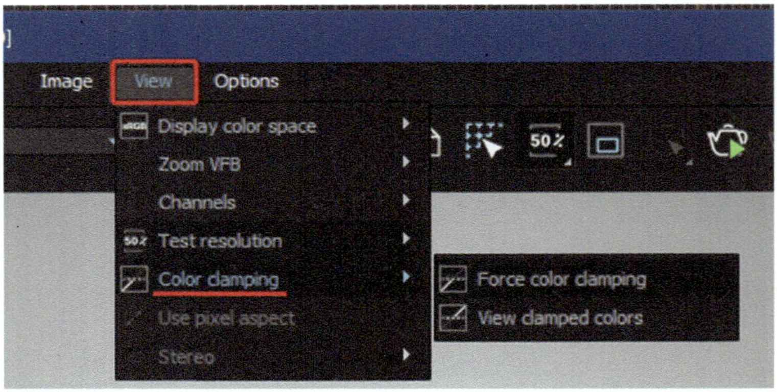

Color clamping options

View—Use pixel aspect: This function allows the visualization of the pixel aspect ratio.

Grayed out by default.

View—Stereo: This function previews the stereoscopic render in the VFB.

This function only becomes available if a stereoscopic render is being executed (split screens).

Grayed out by default.

Options—VFB settings: This function allows users to open the VFB Settings dialog and set up keep parameters such as Render view, Render Region controls, History, and Layers.

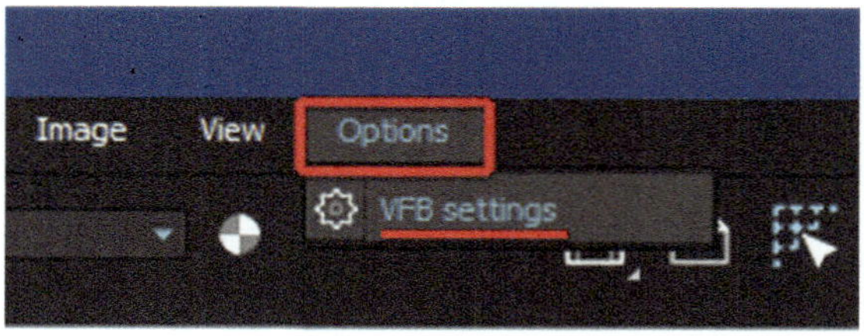

Options

Render View: This tab allows users to set the Zoom Multiplier values and the Bucket outlines colors (Different color by bucket, White, Black, and None).

The Show Advanced Settings (when enabled) provides users with additional and more complex functionalities.

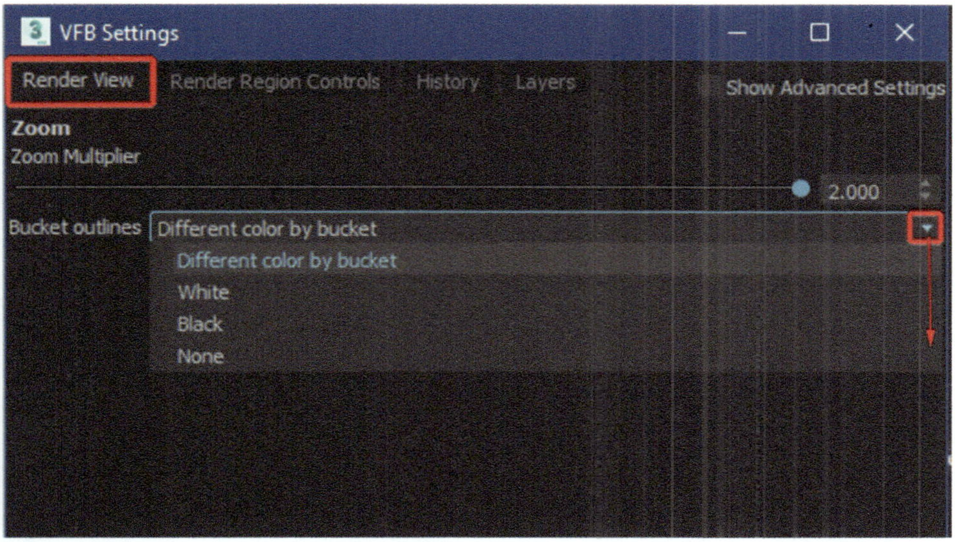

Render View tab

Render Region Controls: This tab controls the Region Render settings, with functionalities to Show controls on hover only and Show region sizes.

The Show Advanced Settings (when enabled) provides users with additional and more complex functionalities.

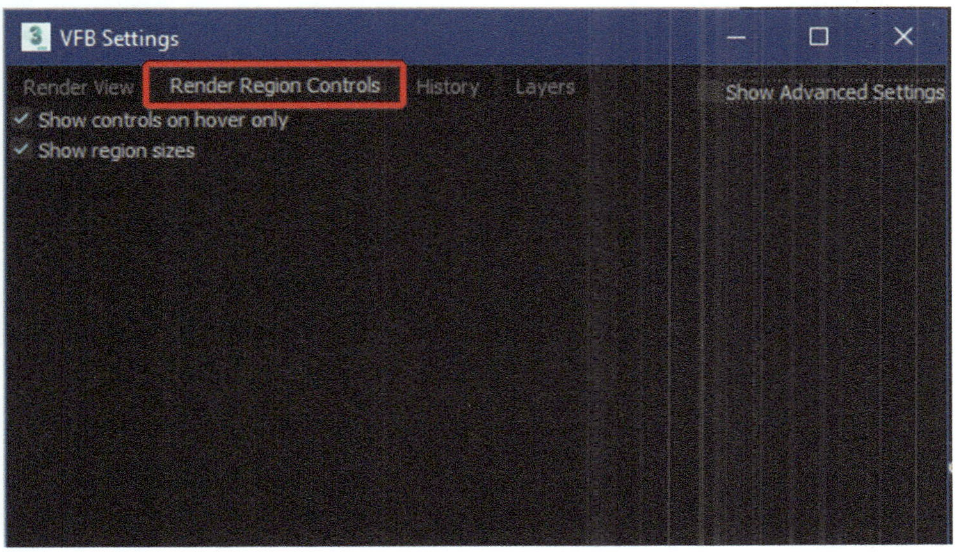

Render Region Controls tab

History: This unique tab allows users to Enable the History of rendered frames in the VFB History list.

If disabled and the Location is not set, no renders will appear in the VFB History section.

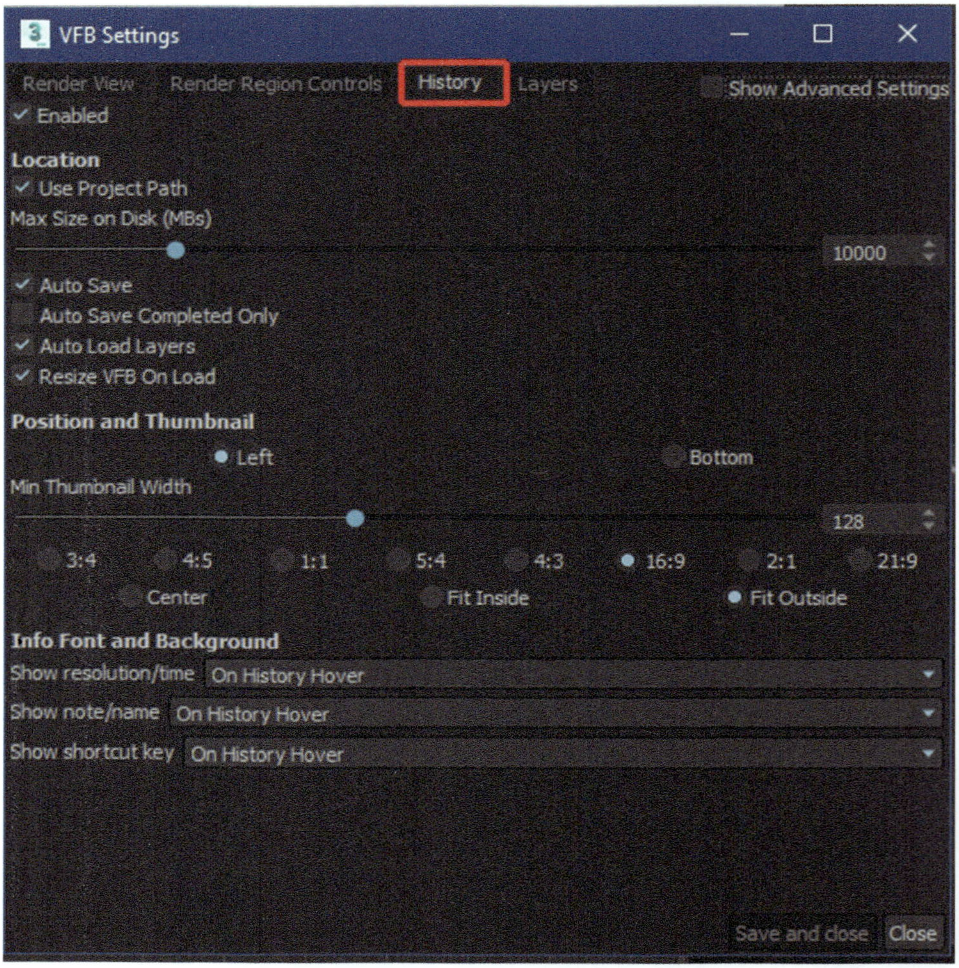

History functionalities tab

History in VFB disabled

When the History location is set, every time a frame is rendered, it will automatically appear in the History list.

Similarly, when you click on its thumbnail in the History list, it will immediately appear in the VFB.

History in VFB Set to a location

Save to history button: Clicking this button, automatically adds the current render in the VFB to the History list.

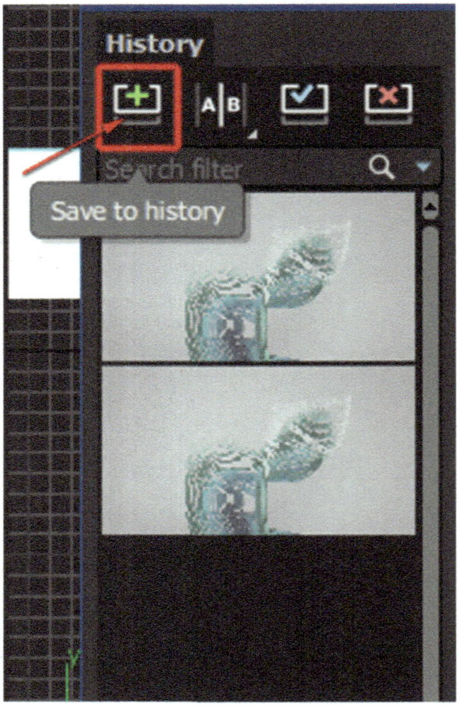

Save to history button

A/B horizontal: This button allows users to compare two or more renders in the VFB History horizontally (A/B), vertically (A/B), or (A/B/C/D). To enable this button, simply click on it.

When the option is A/B horizontal, a vertical white line should appear promptly in the middle of the VFB dividing two renders listed in the History list.

The vertical white line can be moved across horizontally.

To choose from one of the three options available, simply click and hold the button.

Once there is more than one render saved in the VFB History list, users can select and right click to choose Edit note, Set A, Set B, Load to VFB, Delete, Load layers, Load VRay settings, Open scene, or Reload history.

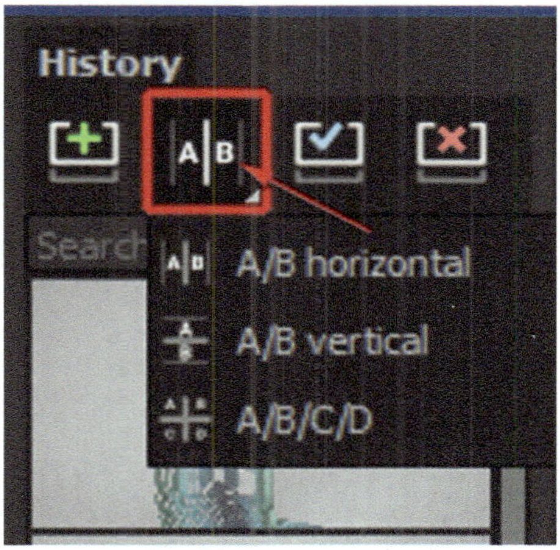

A/B button

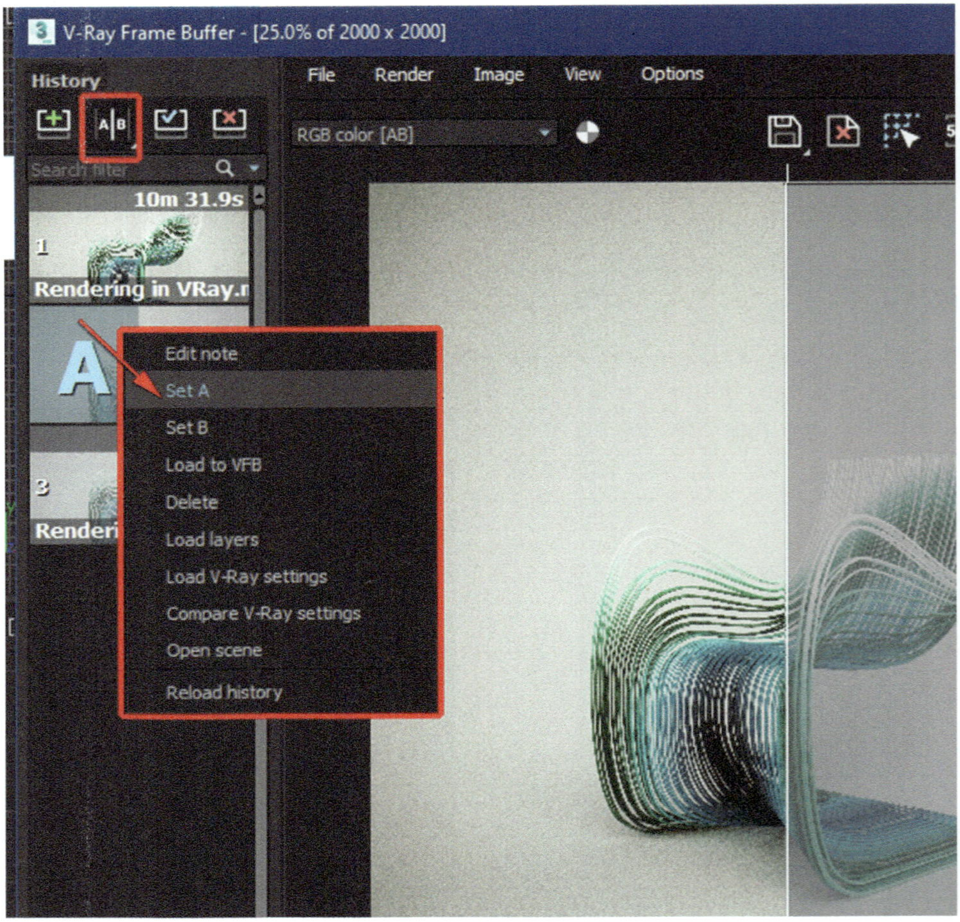

VFB history options

Load to VFB button: This button allows users to load to VFB.

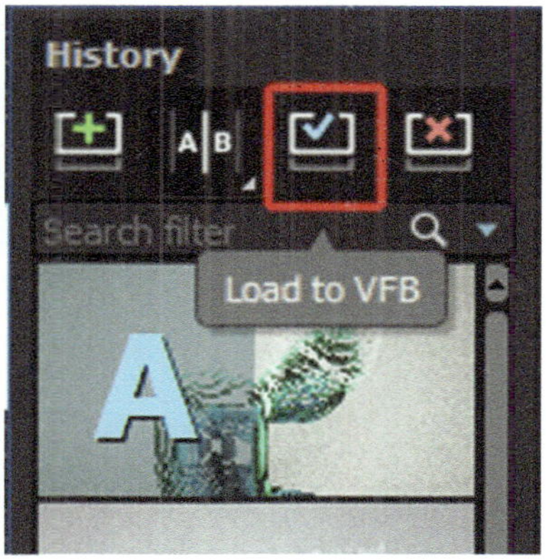

Load to VFB button

Delete button: This button allows users to delete any selected render in the VFB History list.

Delete button

Search filter: This text field allows users to type in and search for specific saved renders in the VFB History list.

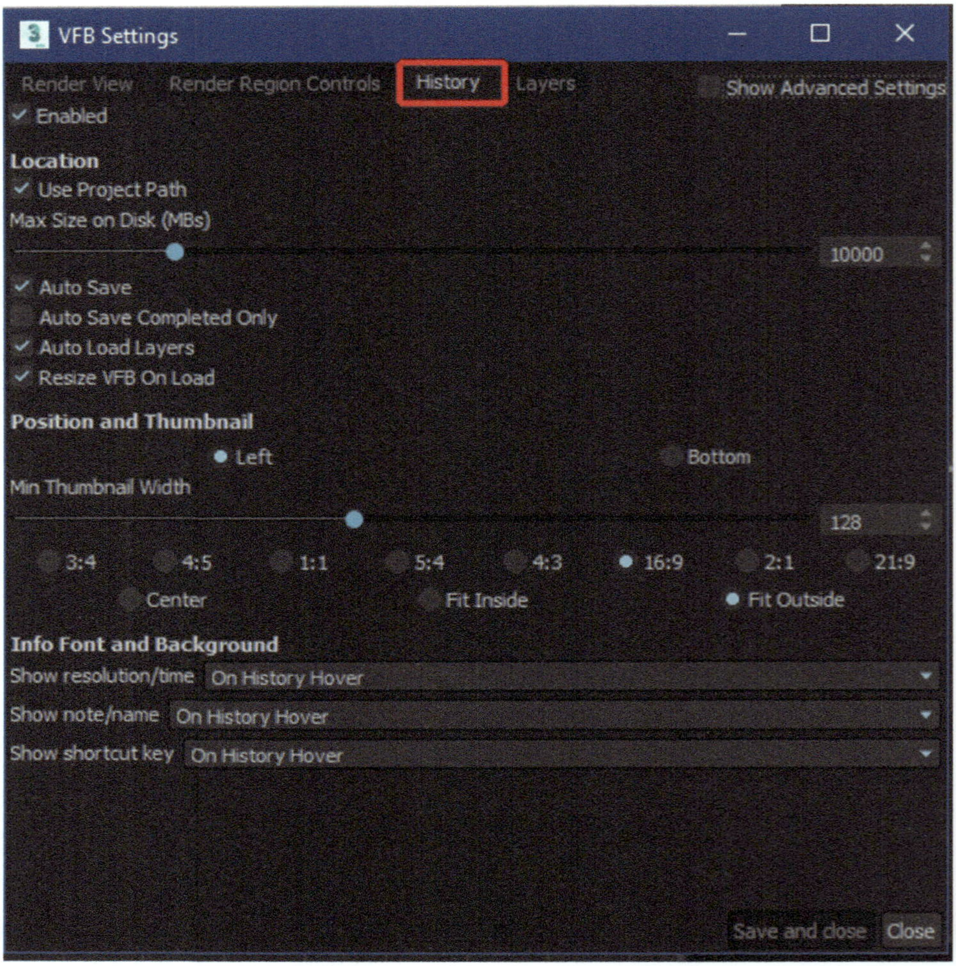

History functionalities tab

Location—Use Project Path: When enabled, it automatically uses the default location of where the current 3ds max file is saved.

This location is depicted when hovering over the saved render in the history section/list of the VFB.

Max Size on Disk (MBs): This function controls the maximum size of each of the renders saved in history list displayed in the VFB.

Users can utilize the slider or simply type in a specific value.

Auto Save: If enabled, it automatically saves the recent render into the VFB history list/location.

Auto Save Completed Only: When enabled, it only saves the completed renders into the VFB history list/location.

Auto load layers: When enabled, every time a thumbnail in the VFB history is clicked, it automatically appears in the main VFB with all its render elements/passes loaded (if any).

Resize VFB on Load: If enabled, every time a thumbnail in VFB history is clicked, it automatically resizes the VFB to fit the original render.

Position and Thumbnail: These parameters control the position and size of thumbnails displayed in the VFB history list.

Info Font and Background: These parameters control the font (text) and background information displayed on history thumbnails.

Users have the option to change functionalities such as Show resolution/time, Show note/name, and Show shortcut key.

Layers: This tab allows users to set, save, and load recent preset paths.

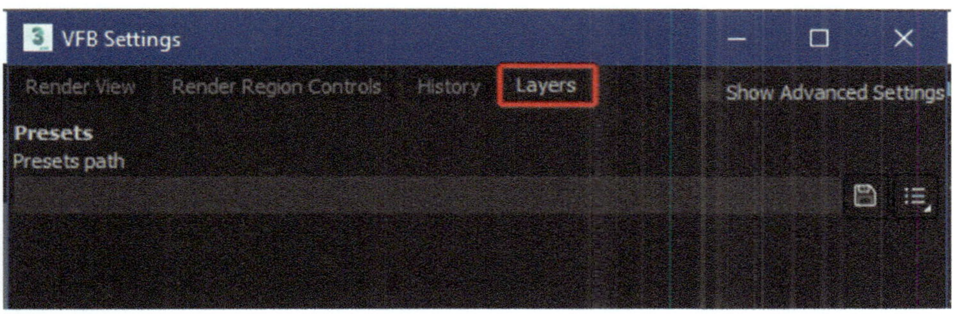

Layers tab

Save and close: When clicked, this button saves and closes the dialog.

Close: When clicked, this button closes the dialog.

Region render button: This button allows users to enable it (by clicking it), followed by clicking and dragging it in the VFB to draw a region to render.

Layers tab

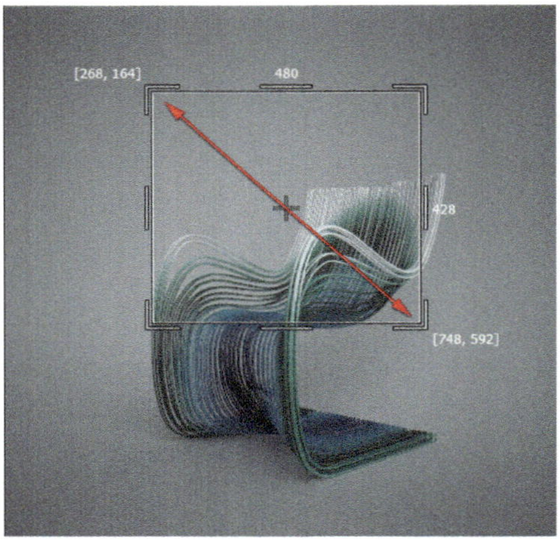

Click and drag in VFB to draw a region

The cross in the middle allows users to click and move the region anywhere in the VFB.

The eight handles around the drawn region allows users to click/select any of them individually, followed by stretching them in any direction (X- and Y-axes) to draw a specific region.

To disable the region render, simply deselect its button.

VFB layers: This tab allows users to view all available layers from its list by clicking on its button first, followed by choosing a specific adjustment layer to add to the list.

By default, there are two adjustment layers loaded and enabled: Display correction, and the Sources: RGB.

Lens Effects and the Denoiser are loaded but not enabled.

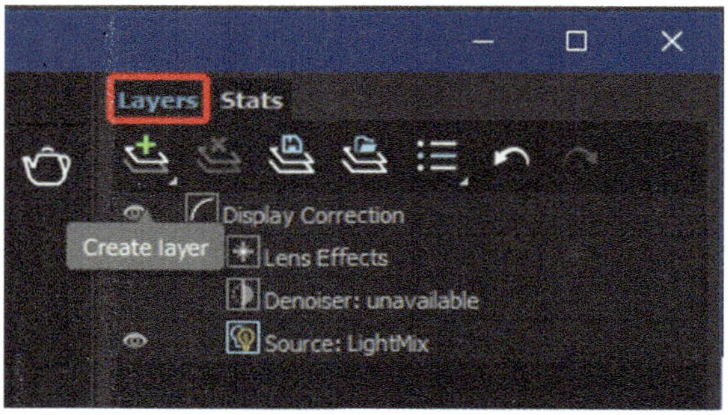

Default Adjustment layers

By selecting and right clicking any of the listed layers, users have the option to Reset, Save, Load Delete, New Layer, Duplicate, and Blend Modes.

The grayed out options are *not* available to the default layers.

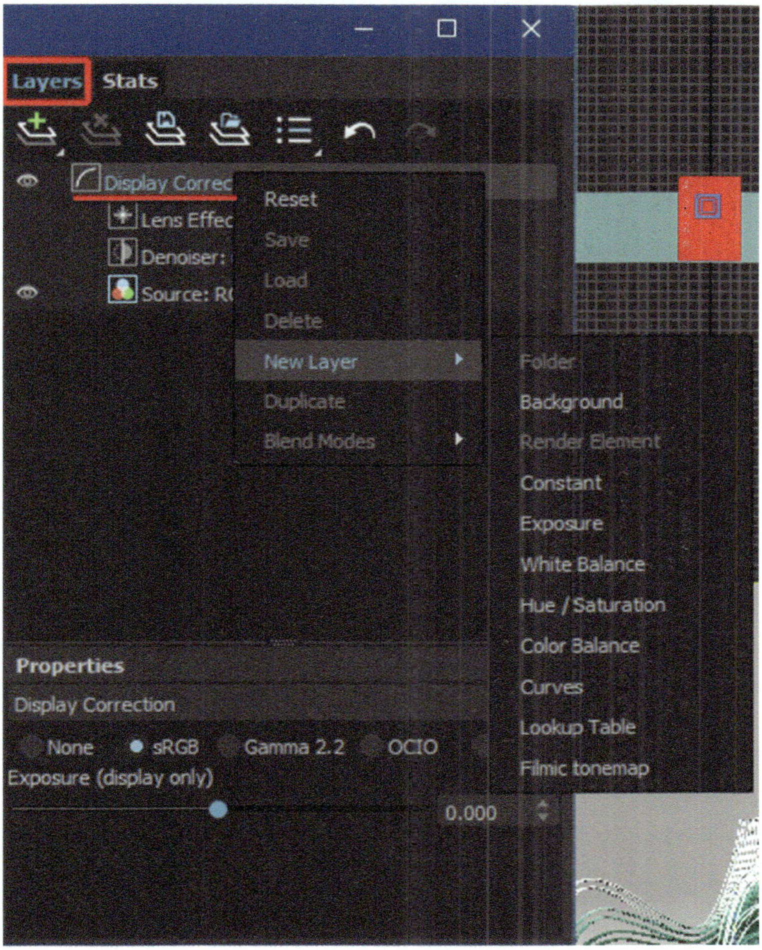

Right click options available

Each adjustment layer selected/chosen comes with its unique adjustable properties.

To make any layer visible (and saved in VFB), simply select on its layer first.

Next, enable its function under Properties and click on the empty section where the eye icon should be.

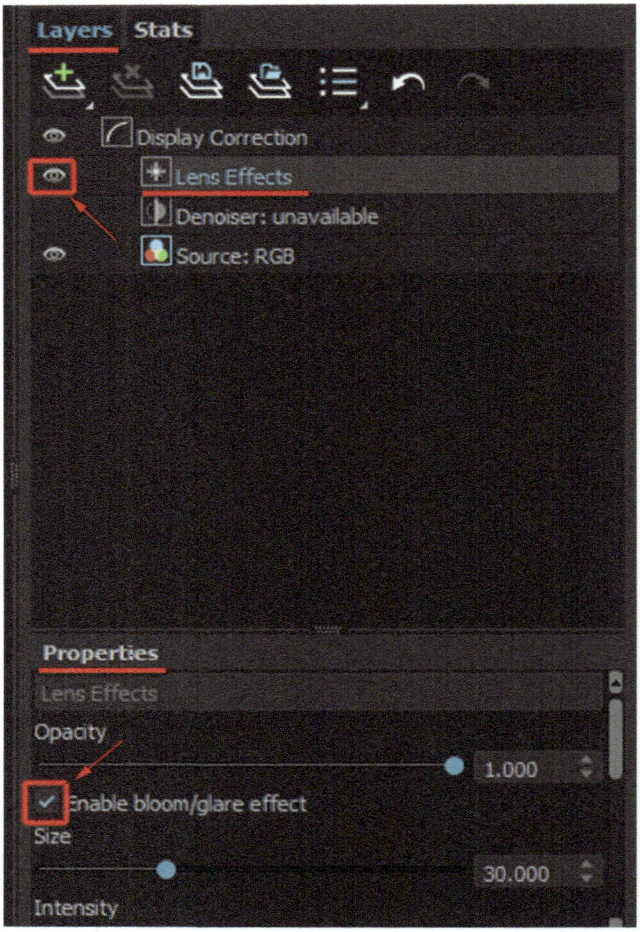

Enable Adjustment layers

The Denoiser and Light Mix only become available under Layers once added in the Render Elements and rendered.

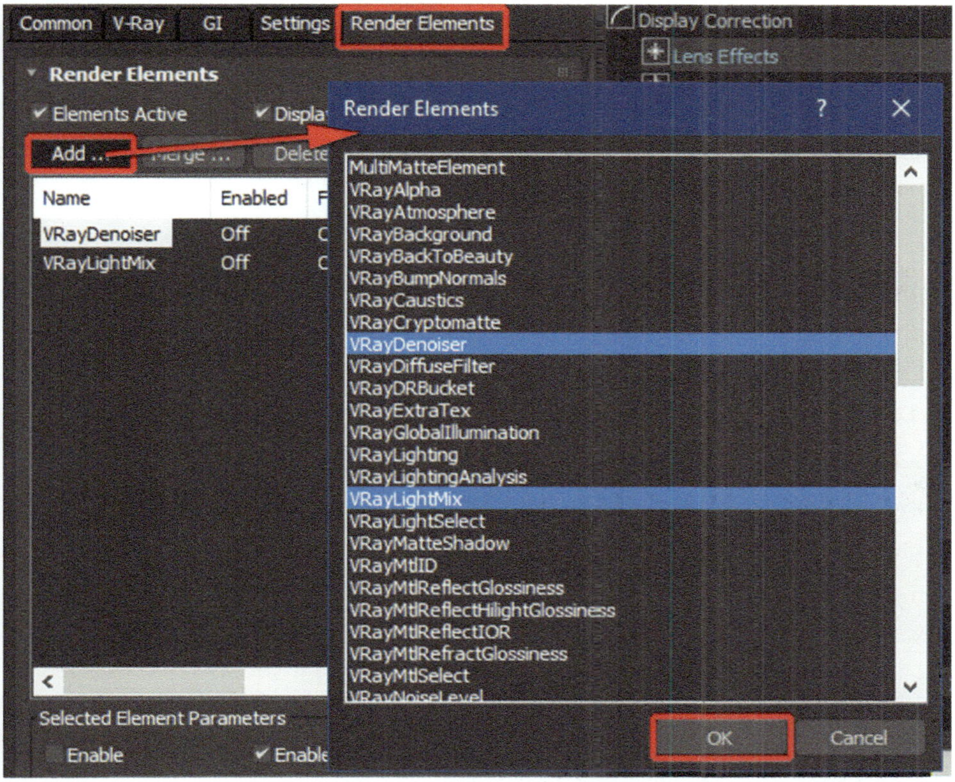

Enable Adjustment layers

Finally, before rendering, the GI Primary engine needs to be set to Brute force in order for LightMix to work.

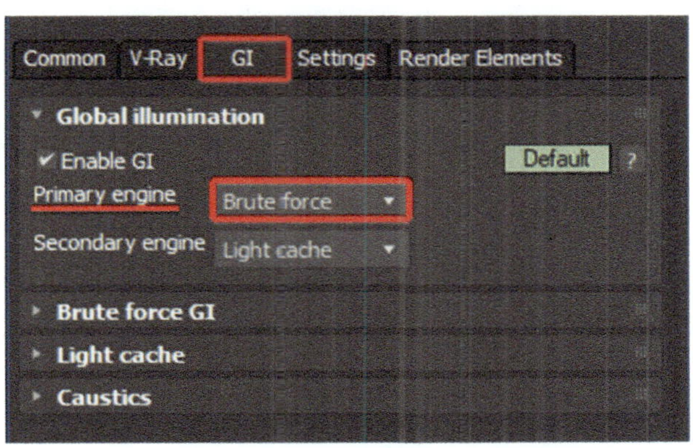

Primary engine set to Brute force

NOTE

Because Denoiser often "smears" shadows/parts of a render and adds additional rendering time, it's common practice for some users to disable/remove it, sometimes.

Once a render is carried out with the LightMix added, users are prompted with Properties such as All, VRaylight, Evironment, Self-Illumination, and Rest.

Each of the listed functions has a default value of 1.000, with white color swatch (255).

Every physical light in the scene is listed by its original name. Instanced lights are listed as one (same).

If you intend to control lights separately via LightMix, you need to copy them instead.

Reset/Refresh: This button resets any added changes.

Save: This button allows users to Save the current settings as LightMix file (*.lightmix).

Load: This toggle allows users to load any presaved LightMix file (*.lightmix).

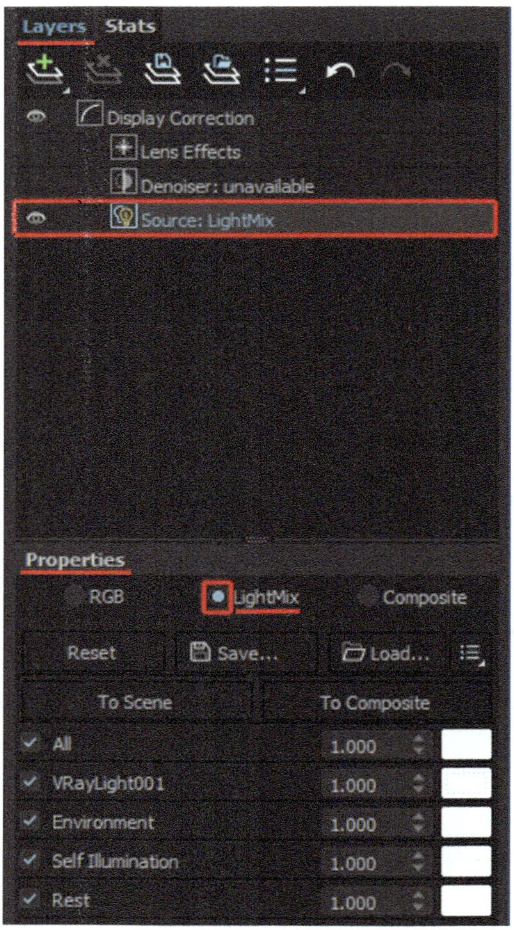

LightMix Properties

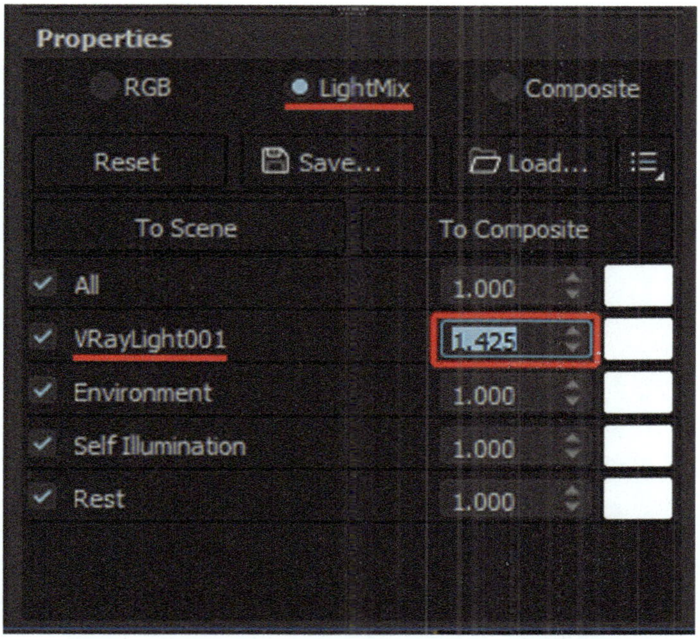

VRayLight set to 1.425

VRayLight set to 1.425 rendered

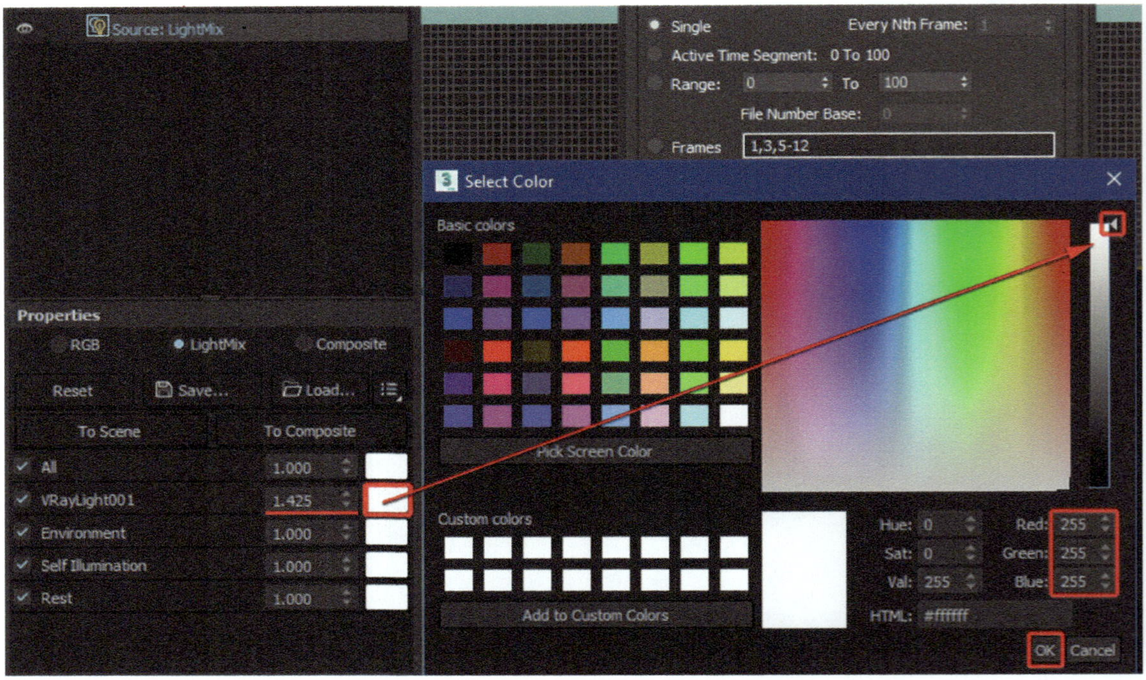

VRayLight color set to white (255)

VRayLight color set to white (255) rendered

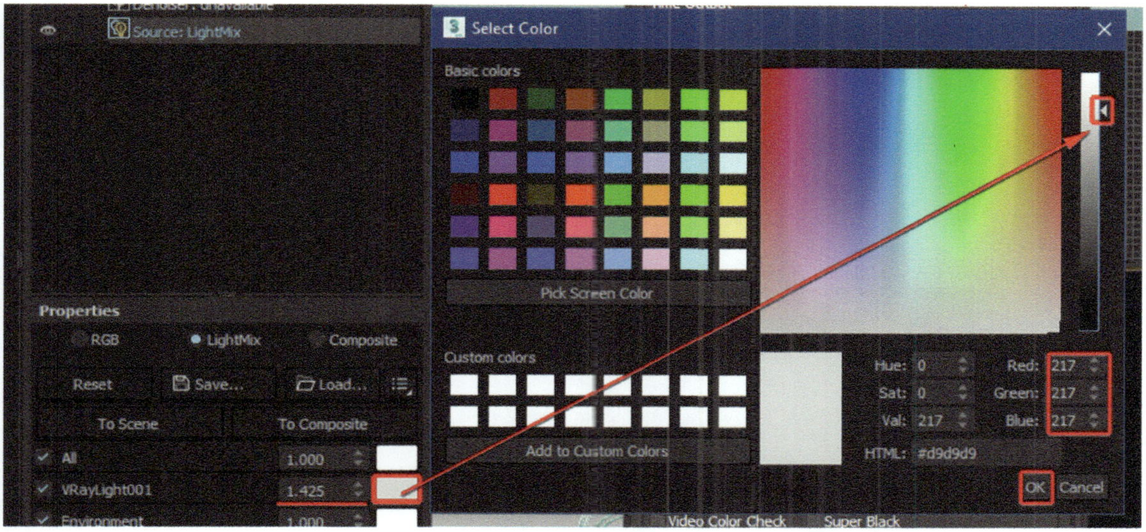

VRayLight color set to gray (217)

VRayLight color set to gray (217) rendered

Most adjustment layers listed are similar to those commonly used in Adobe Photoshop and other post-production applications such as Adobe After Effects and Nuke.

For the purpose of this exercise, we are going to focus on adjustment layers such as Filmic tonemap, Lookup Table, Hue/Saturation, and lens Effects

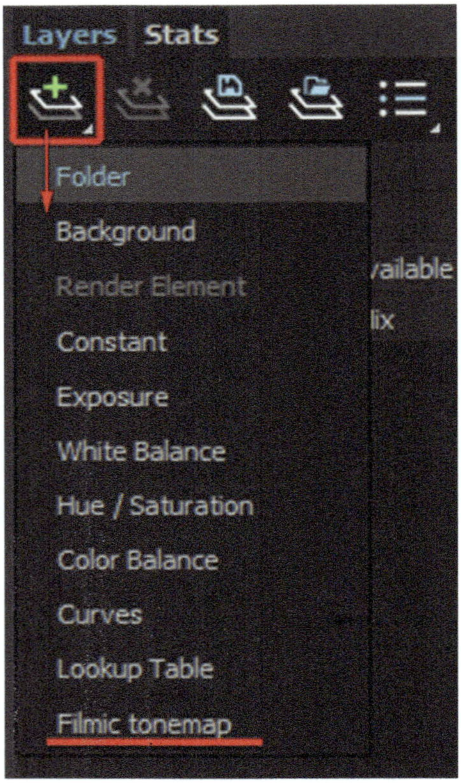

Layers tab and button

Filmic tonemap: This adjustment layer allows users to accurately control the overall contrast of a render by fine-tuning functions such as Blend Mode, Tone mapping space, Type, Log space, Shoulder strength, Linear strength, Linear angle, Toe strength, and White point.

For this scene, the functions that really made a difference were the Shoulder strength and Toe strength.

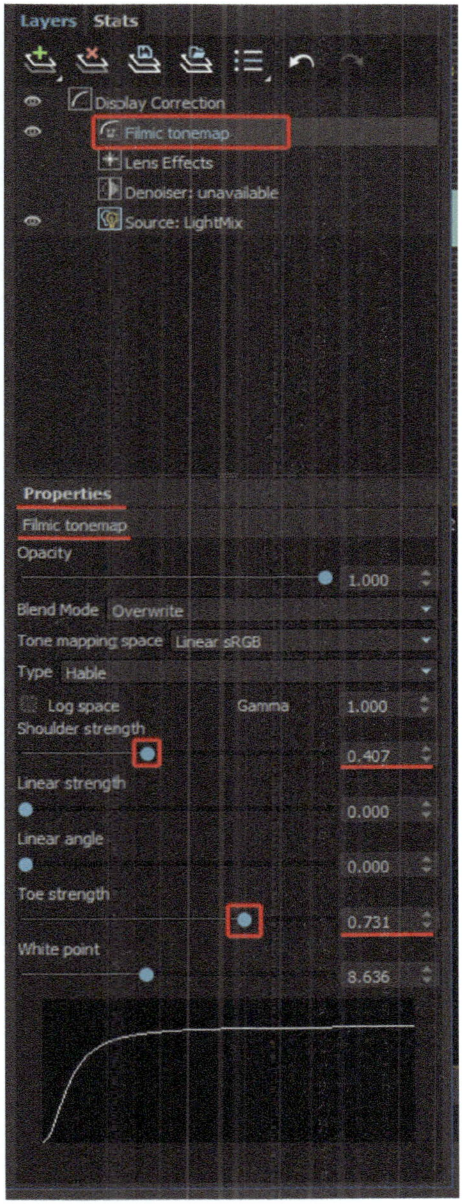

Filmic tonemap settings

Hue/Saturation: This adjustment layer is mostly used to saturate and/or desaturate renders.

For this scene, the function that really made a difference was the Saturation.

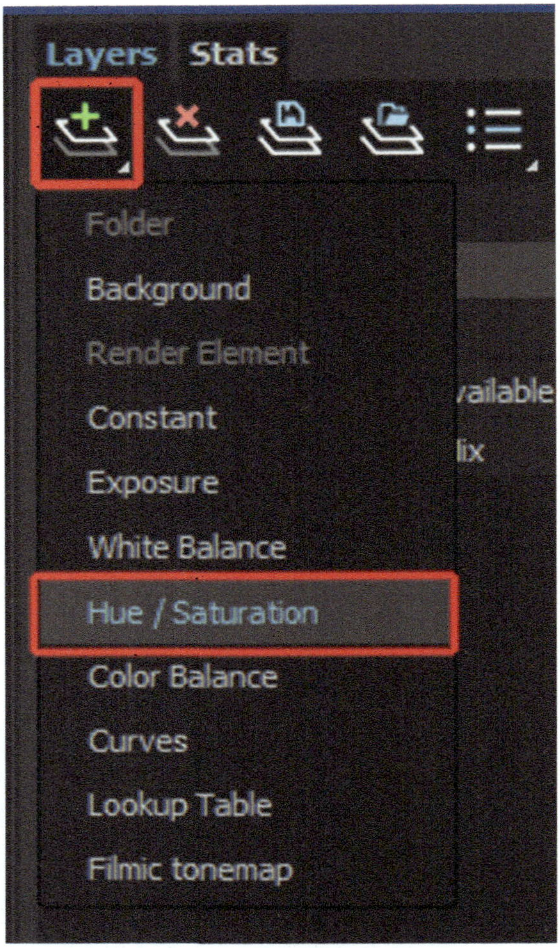
Layers
Stats
Folder
Background
Render Element
Constant
Exposure
White Balance
Hue / Saturation
Color Balance
Curves
Lookup Table
Filmic tonemap

Add Hue/Saturation layer

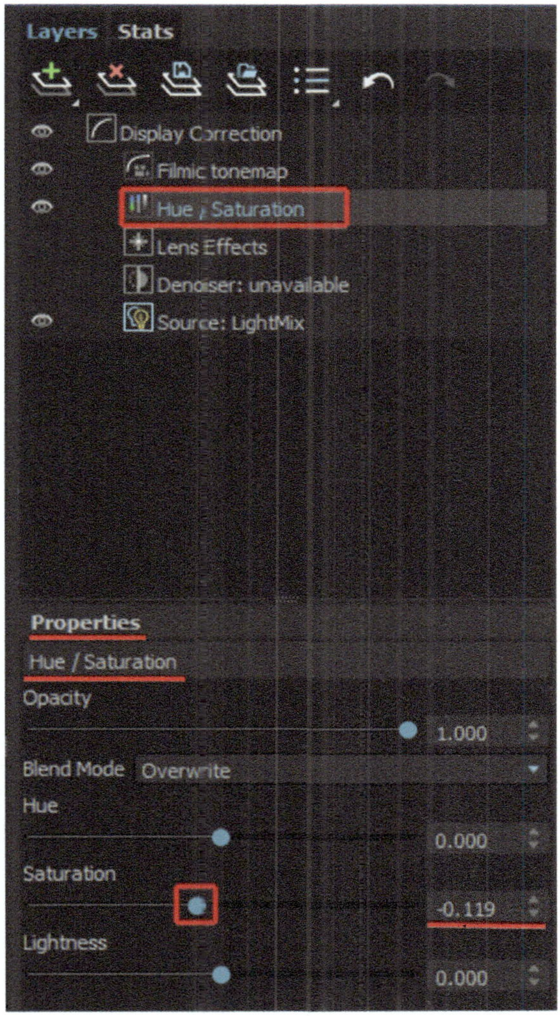

Hue/Saturation settings

Lookup Table: This adjustment layer allows users load pre-saved LUT files to color grade your final renders.

To bake/save the LUT file with the final render, simply enable the function to Save in image.

For this scene, I have used a LUT file under the name of 3DCollective_sRGB_Agfa_Futura_03Hard.cube

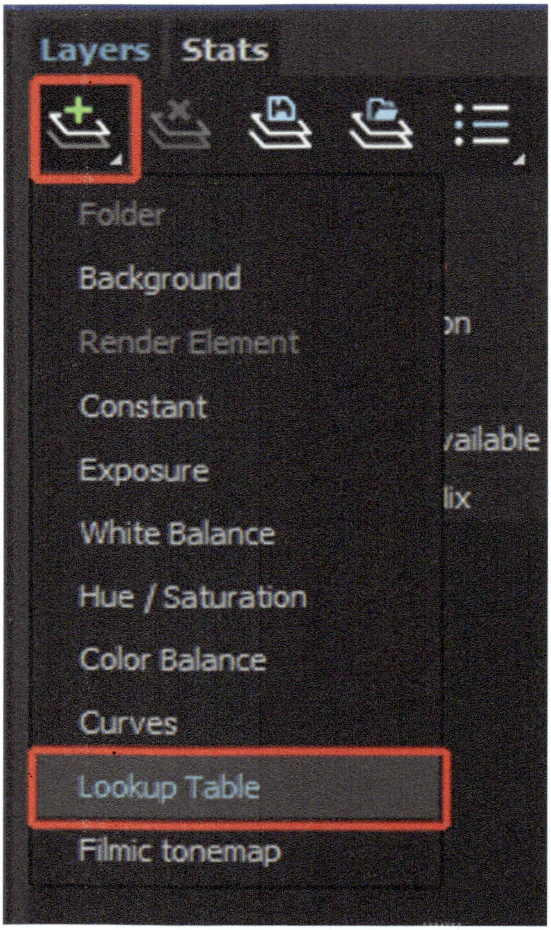
Layers
Stats
Folder
Background
Render Element
Constant
Exposure
White Balance
Hue / Saturation
Color Balance
Curves
Lookup Table
Filmic tonemap

Add Lookup Table layer

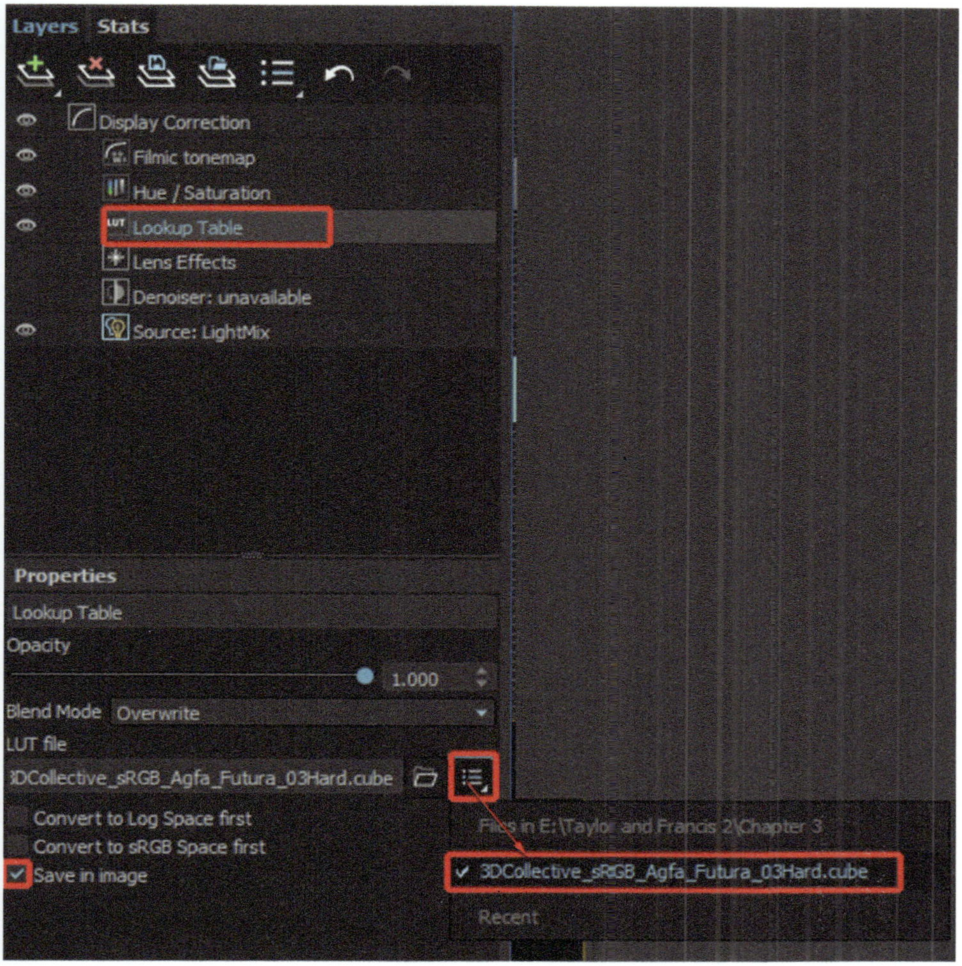

Lookup Table settings

Lookup Table final result

This LUT file was download from a website called 3dcollective.es.

However, LUT files can also be created in Photoshop.

To do so, simply add your own adjustment layers first.

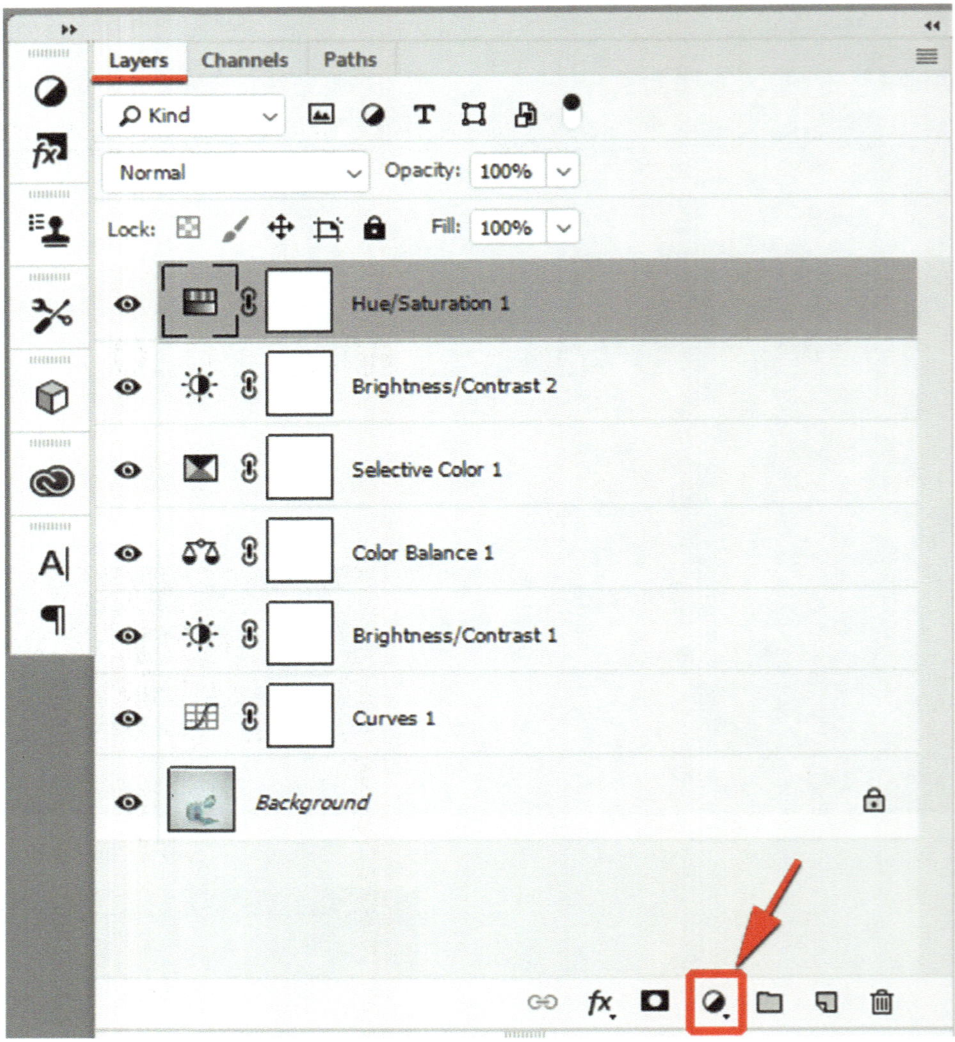

Add adjustment layers in Photoshop

Next, go to File, Export, and choose the Color Lookup Tables option.

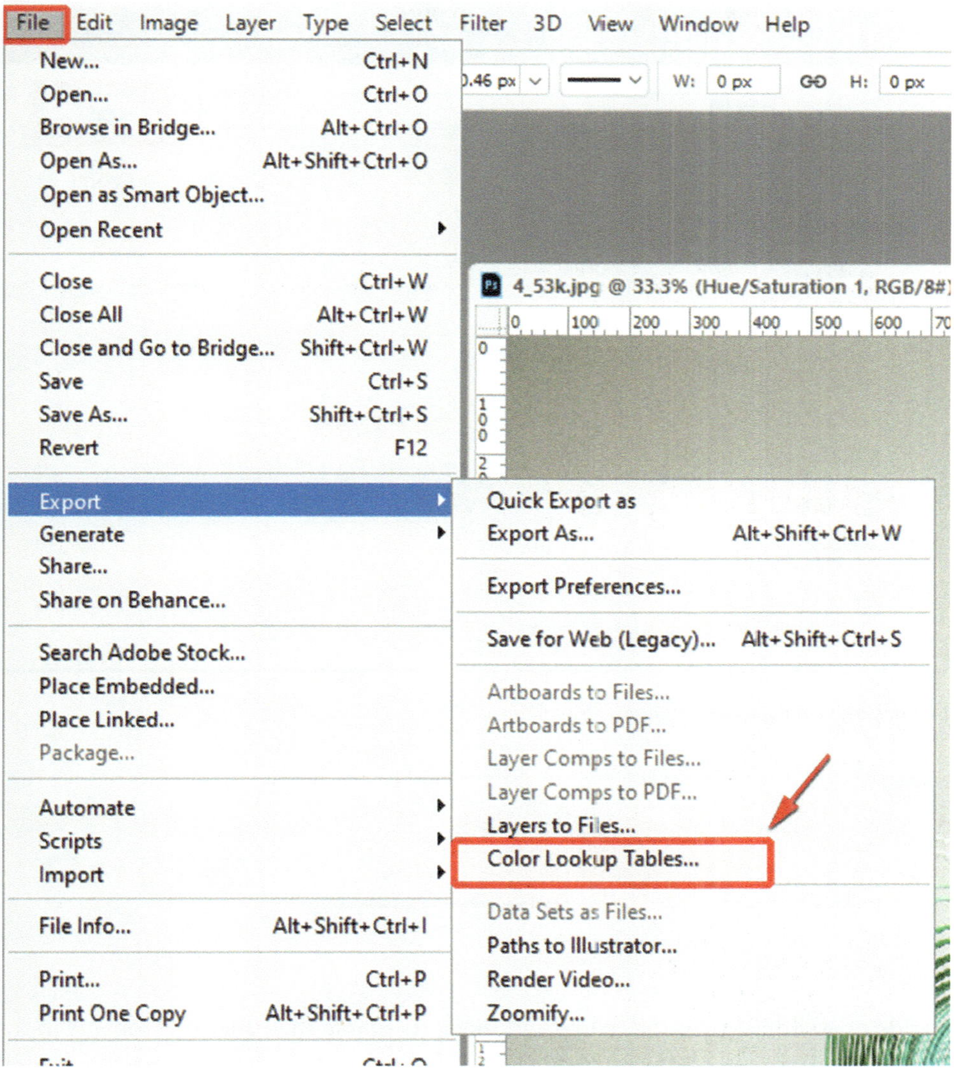

Add Color Lookup Tables option

Adjust and OK to close the dialog.

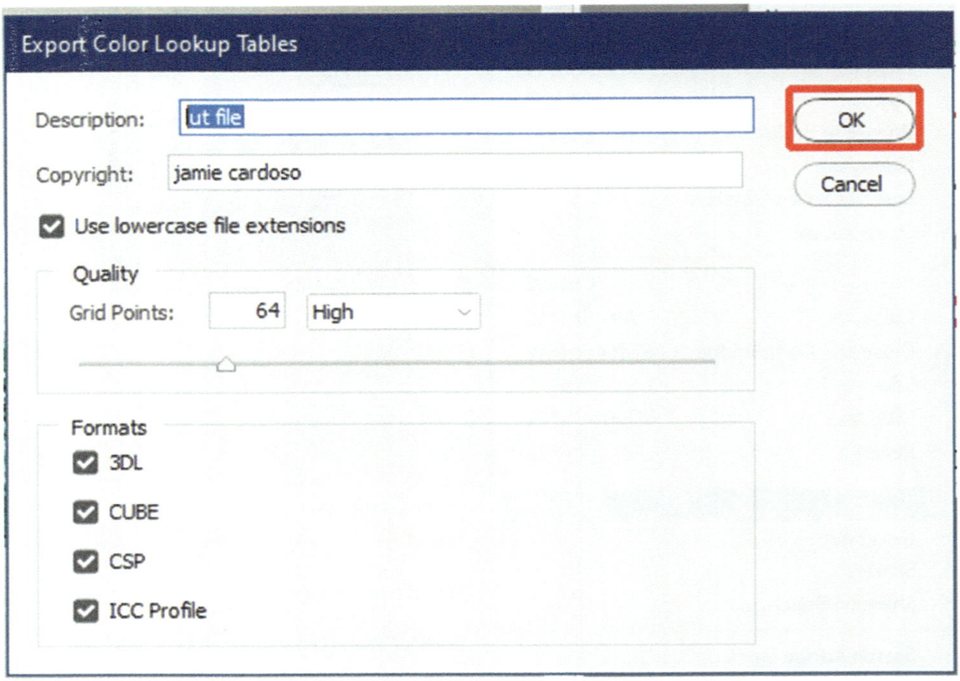

Export Color Lookup Tables dialog

Save the LUT file

In 3ds max, after loading it, you might need to enable the function Convert to Log Space first.

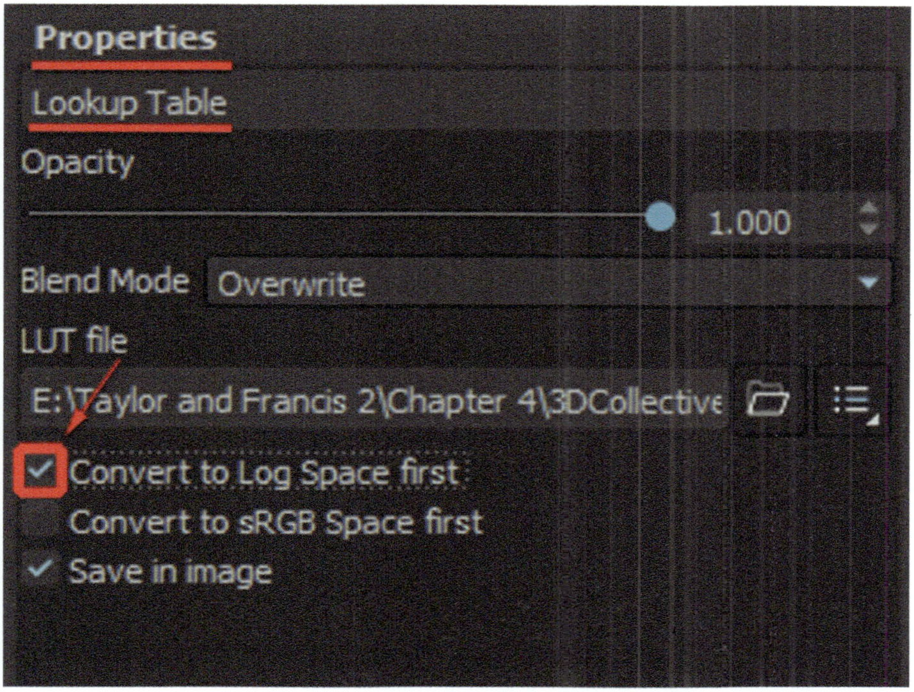

Convert to Log Space first

Lens Effects: To enable this default layer, users need to select it first, and then turn on the function Enabled bloom/glare effect.

This effect is only visible in finished rendered scenes with high contrast (bright and dark areas) and scenes with extreme highlight/bright spots, such as the sun and visible light sources. Users can set its Bloom Size, Intensity, Rotation, Threshold, Saturation, and Aperture.

NOTE

When you enable the Lens Effects in a fresh/new 3d scene, it will *not* show in VFB until the render is completed. Subsequent Lens Effects values can be adjusted while the render is taking place.

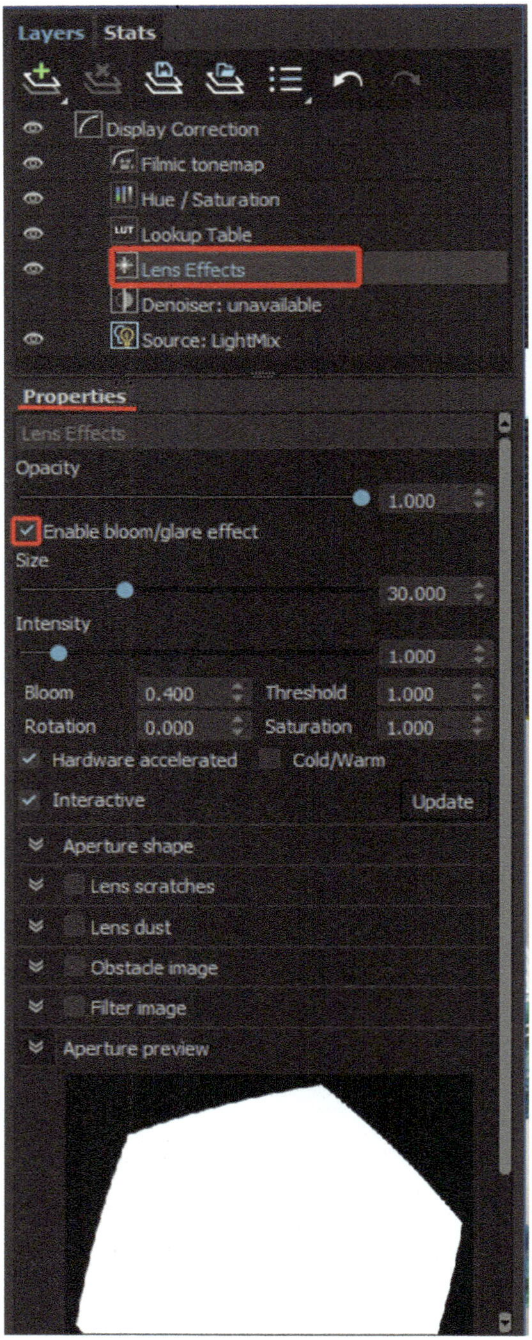

Lens Effects Properties

NOTE

There are times when you will need to right click and Reset the Lens Effects and increase values in order to appear in VFB. Also, click to Update.

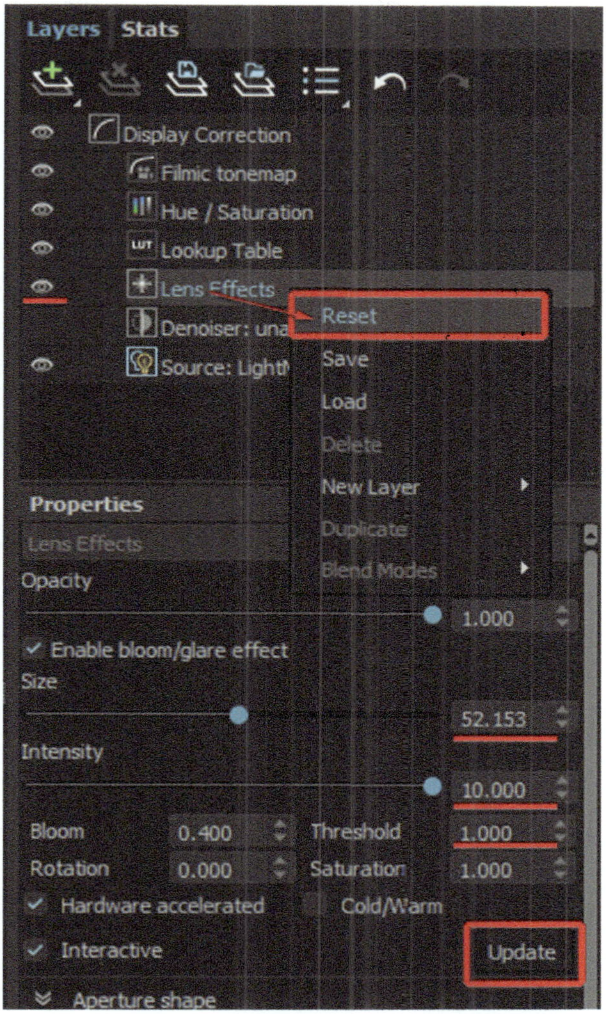

Lens Effects Reset and readjusted

The LightMix value might also need increasing at times.

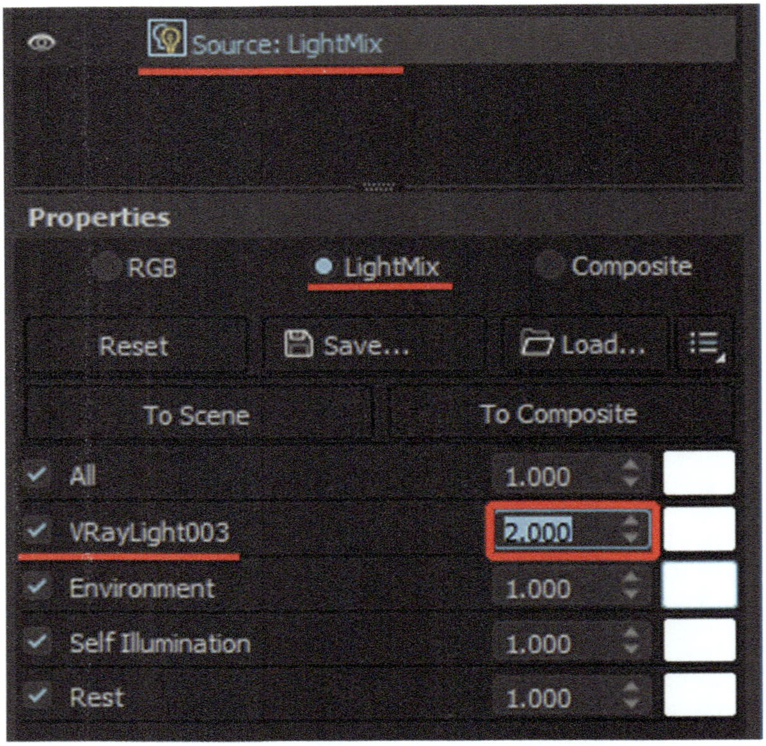

LightMix value increase to 2.000

Lens Effects final result in the VFB

NOTE

This button is grayed out (not available) when any of the default layers are selected (Display Correction, Lens Effects and Denoiser).

Delete selected layers button: This button allows users to delete a selected layer from this.

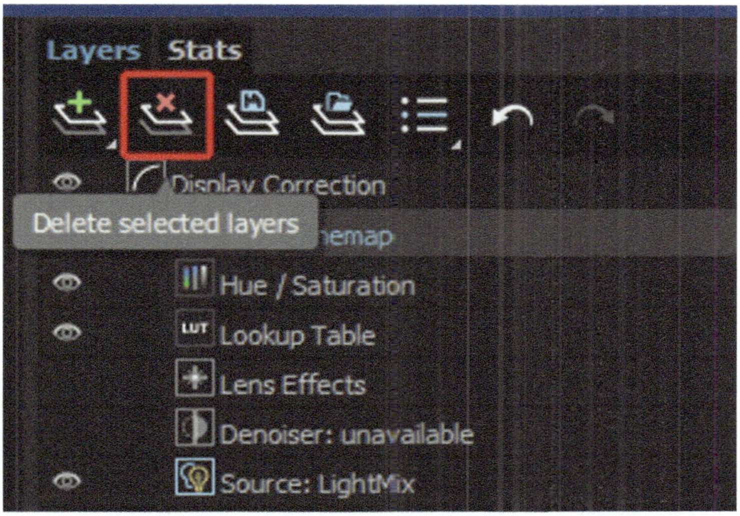

Delete selected layers button

Save layer tree preset button: This button allows users to save the list of layers added as a *. vfbl file format.

This file format can later be added in another 3ds max scene.

For the purpose of this exercise, a file under the name of Rendering in VRay.vfbl was saved. It can be loaded using the Load layer tree preset.

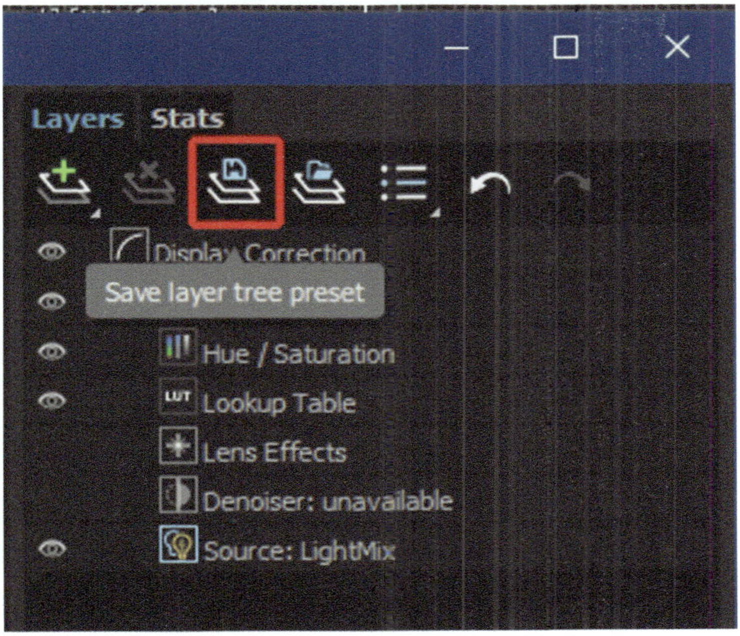

Save layer tree preset button

NOTE

The LightMix might not load with the original settings, if the VRayLight names and types differ (might require rerendering with scene lights).

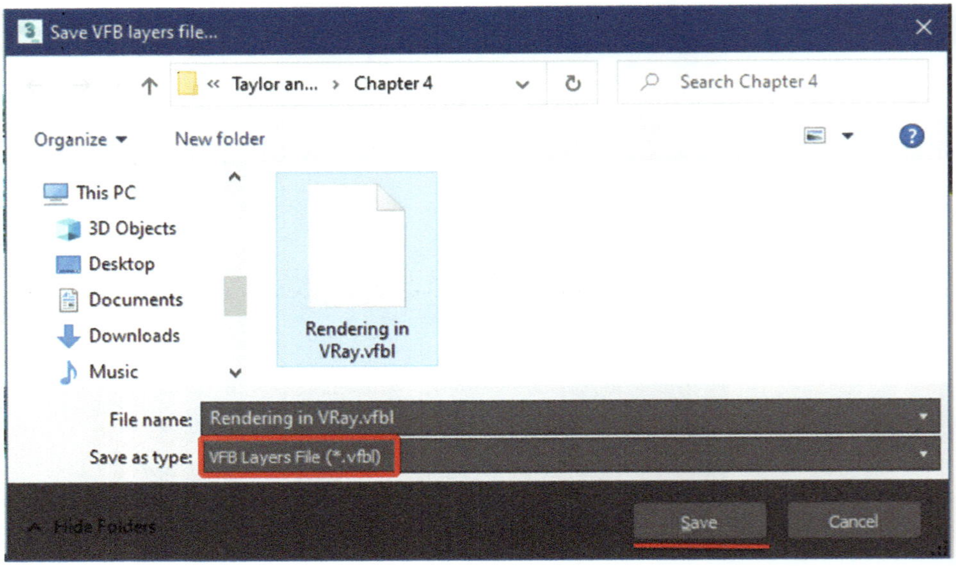

vfbl file saved

Load layer tree preset button: This button allows users to load and pre-saved vfbl file formats. For the purpose of this exercise, a file under the name of Rendering in VRay.vfbl was loaded.

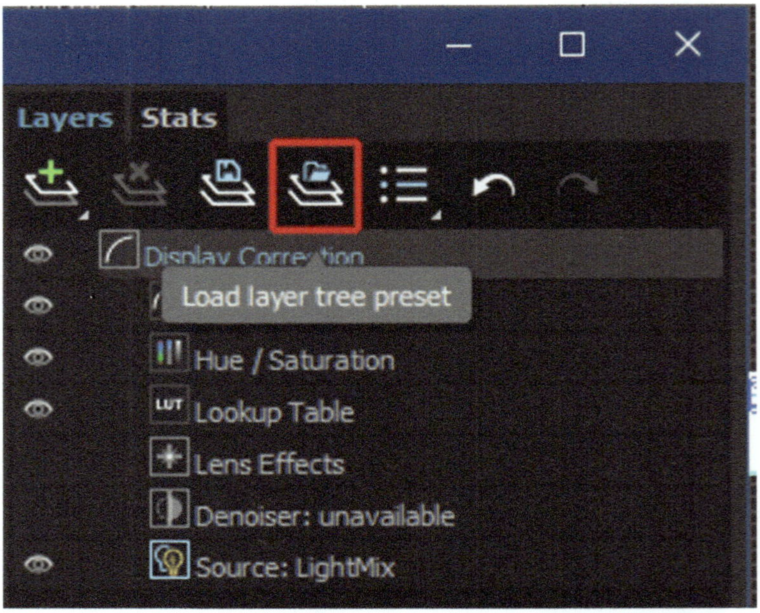

Load layer tree preset button

Undo/Redo Loading layers from file: These buttons allows users to undo or redo actions in the Layers tab.

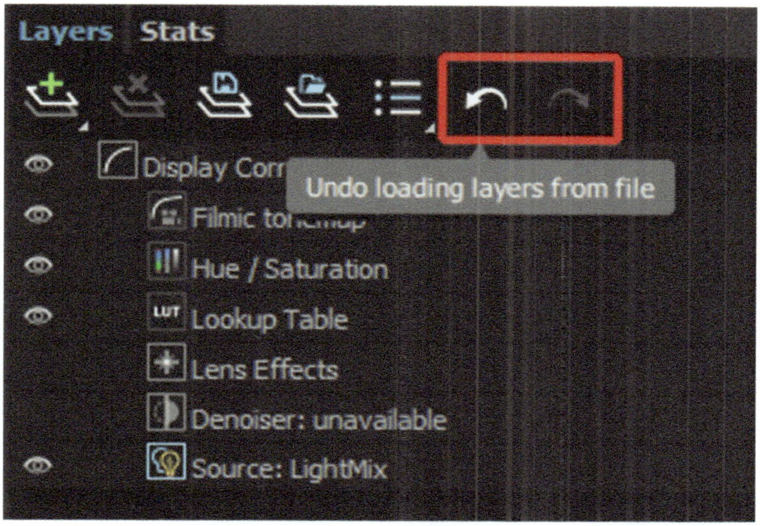

Undo/Redo Layers' actions

Show log button: Clicking this button unhides or hides the VRay messages dialog.

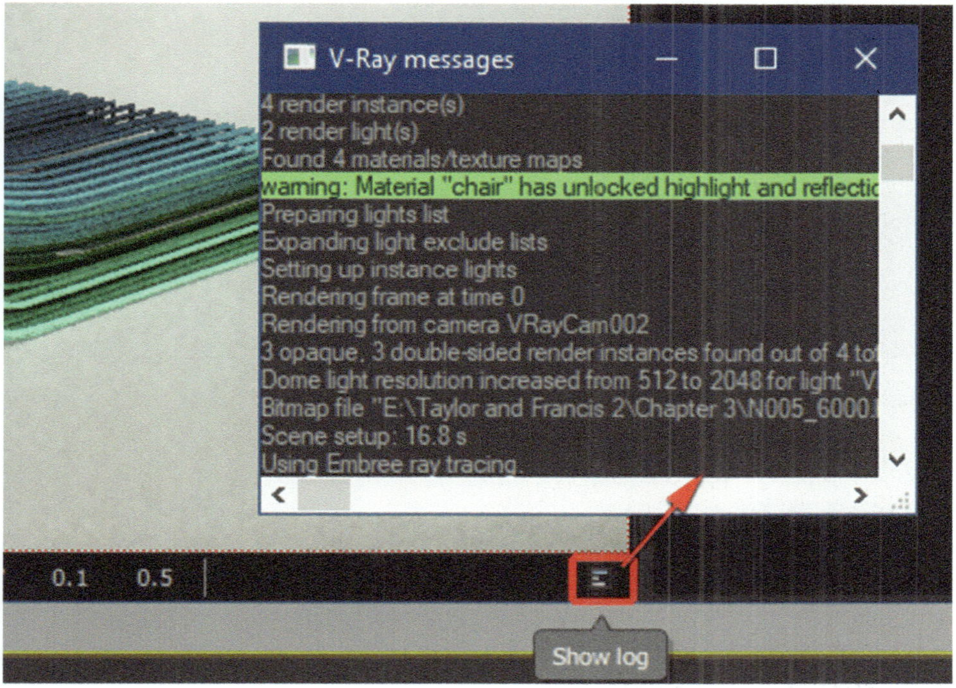

Show log button

HSV: Displays the colors in Hue, Saturation, and Value under where the current mouse is on VFB.

Web: Displays colors in HEX of the pixel under where the current mouse is on VFB.

8bit: It displays the colors in 8-bit palette under where the current mouse is on VFB.

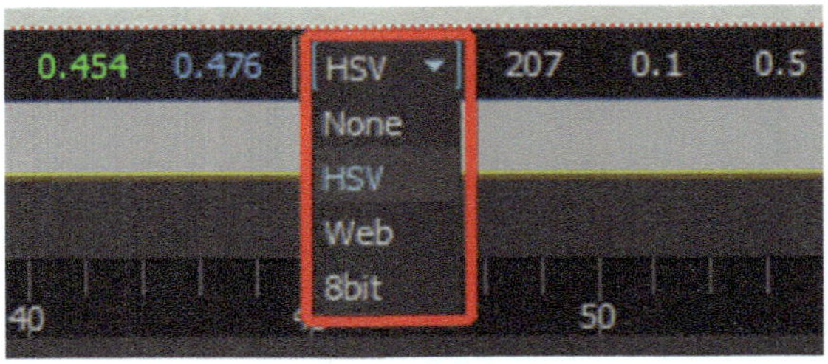

Color displays under the mouse

Show corrected colors button: It displays the corrected colors in the VFB. Enabled by default.

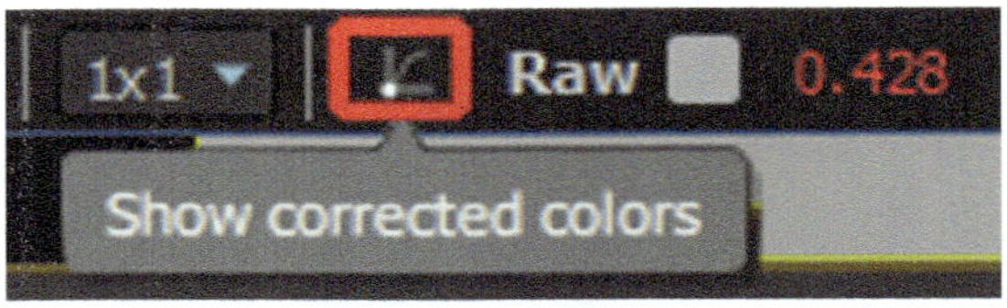

Show corrected colors button

Lock pixel info coordinates button: When enabled, it locks the mouse pointer coordinates and displays the pixel information. Unlocked by default.

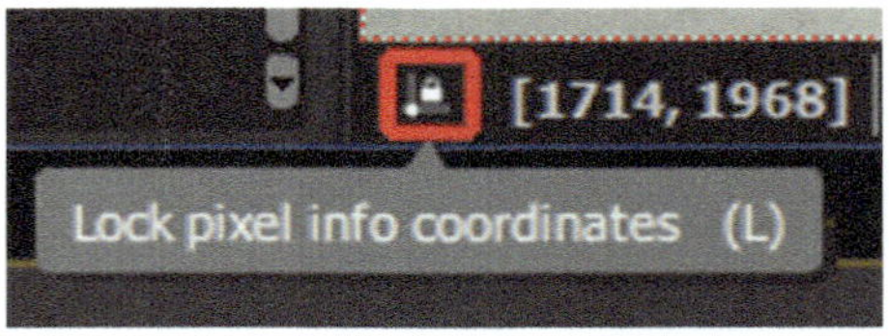

Lock pixel info coordinates button

VRay Raw Image File

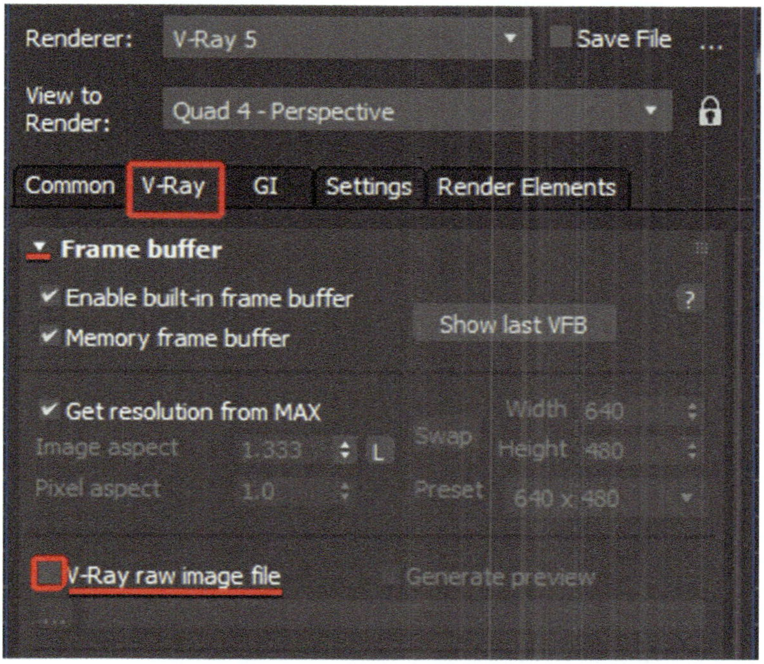

VRay raw image file

VRay raw image file: When enabled, it renders the raw image format directly into the disk (bucket by bucket as the render progresses). This feature is quite useful when rendering extremely high-resolution images that may cause the VFB to crash during the rendering process.

Disabling the Memory frame buffer function while using this option will still render your high-resolution images into the*. vrimg file.

The function to Generate preview allows users to have a small preview of the render in progress.

The toggle to Save VRay image file allows users to find a location to save the *.vrimg file. Users can also enable functions such as EXR and Deep EXR.

VRay image file formats are often massive in size because of key render data stored in them.

As mentioned earlier, the *. vrimg file can be loaded into the VFB and saved out in any specific file format.

NOTE

Only enable this function prior to sending the final renders.

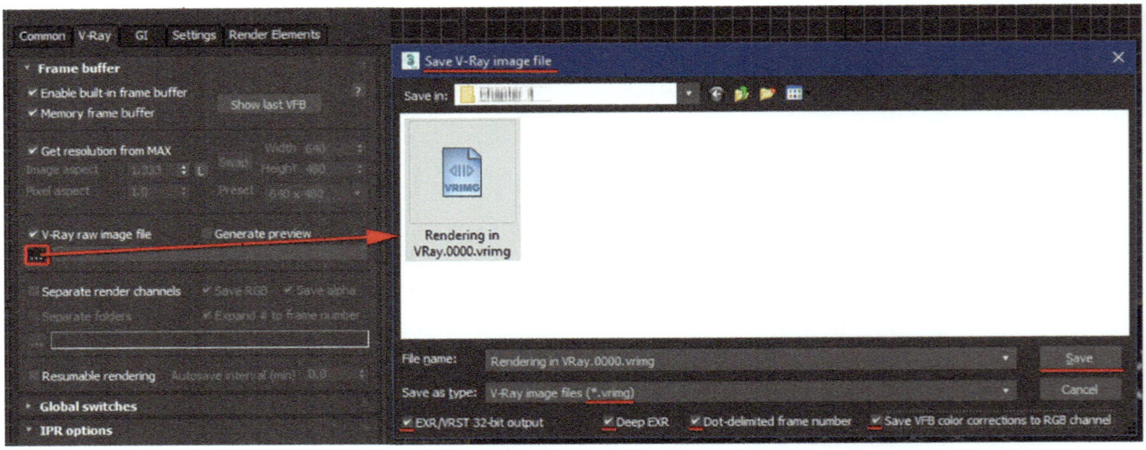

Save VRay image file toggle

Separate render channels: When enabled, it saves the render elements/channels (if added) into separate/individual files when rendered.

Also, when enabled, functions such as Save RGB, Save alpha, and Expand # to frame number are automatically enabled.

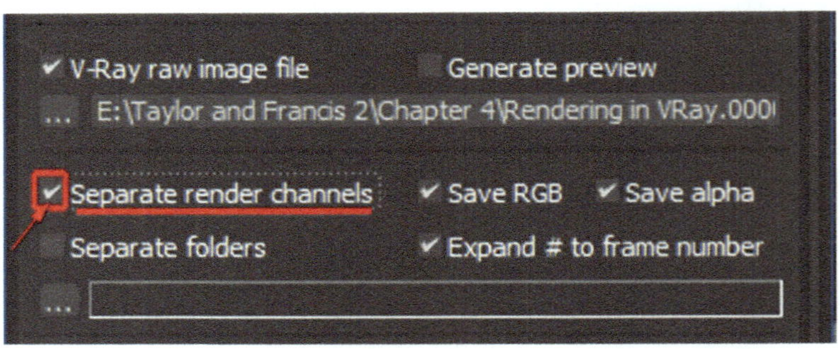

Separate render channels

Separate folders: When enabled, it renders each element/channel into a separate folder. Disabled by default.

NOTE

Only use this toggle prior to sending the final renders.

Browse toggle: This toggle allows users to name the file to be rendered and specify its folder destination and file format.

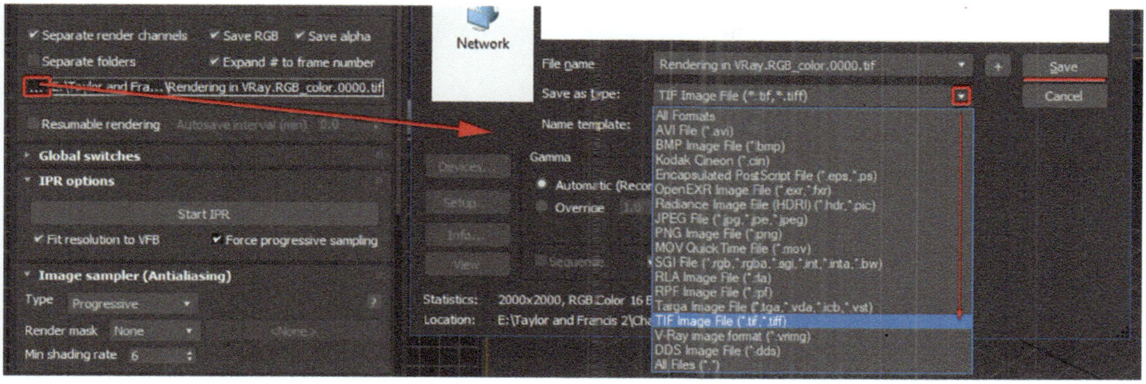

Browse toggle

Resumable rendering: When enabled, it only works in conjunction with VRay raw image file (*. vrimg) to save the rendering progress. If by chance the computer shuts down abruptly, users can continue the render from where the last bucket finished before crashing.

No precalculation will be computed as long as users don't change any of the original settings/parameters.

NOTE

Only use this function prior to sending the final renders. And remember to disable it after the render is completed. Otherwise, it might render black.

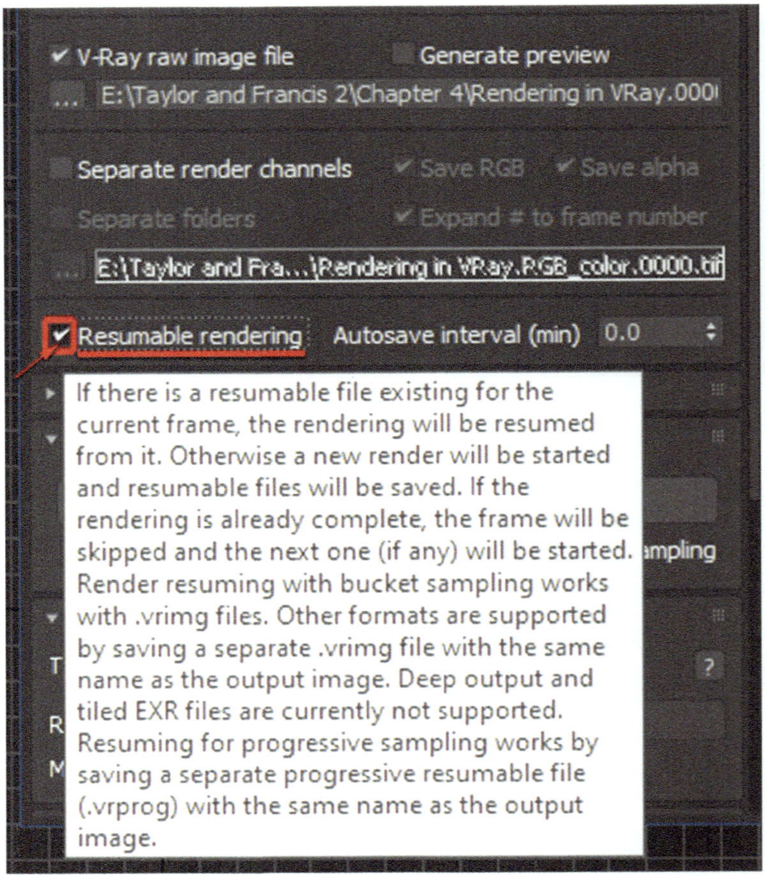

Resumable rendering function

Autosave interval (min): This function only works in conjunction with Resumable rendering and VRay raw image file. The value of 0.0 only saves when the render is completed.

Otherwise, it will save every minute specified/typed in.

Global Switches

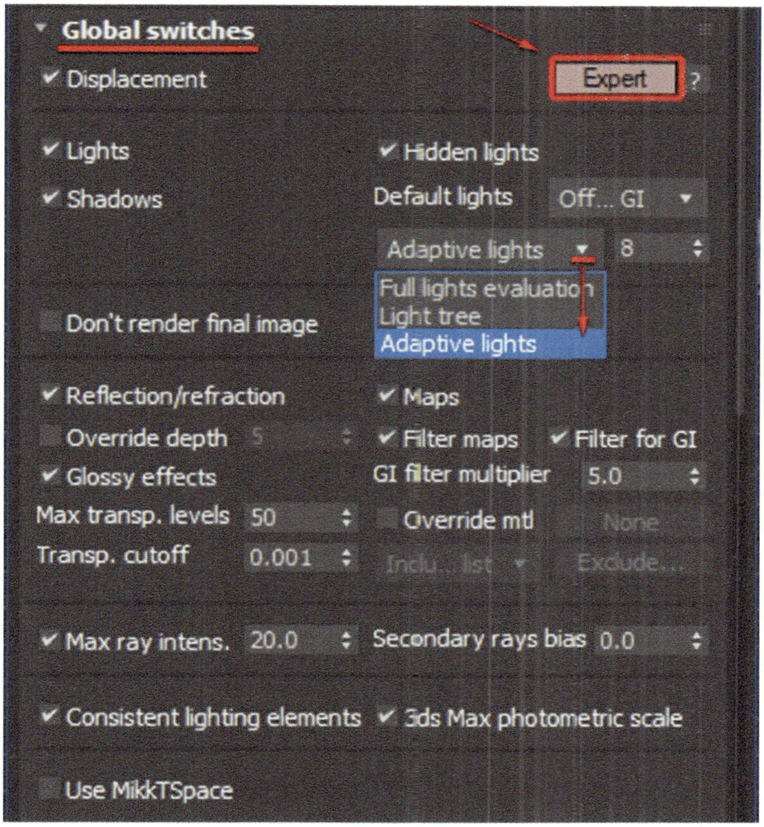

Global switches Expert options

To see more of Global switches functions, simply click on the Basic button twice to get to the Expert mode.

Displacement: When on, it renders the displacement effects applied on materials. Enabled by default.

Lights: When on, it renders the light effects in the scene. Enabled by default.

Shadows: If turned on, it renders the shadows. Enabled by default.

Hidden lights: When on, it renders the effects of hidden/isolated lights. Enabled by default.

Adaptive lights: Controls how many lights are sampled in the scene, based in the light cache points. It's best used in scenes with many lights.

Light tree: This mode is the fastest to compute, as it only calculates lights based on their proximity to the camera.

Full lights evaluation: This option calculates all lights in the scene (time-consuming).

Don't render final image: When enabled, it computes the pre-pass without rendering it. It's quite useful for saving the GI precalculation.

Disabled by default.

Reflection/refraction: It computes the refraction of objects in the scene, if enabled.

Enabled by default.

Override depth: If enabled, it overrides the depth value of all materials in the scene with a specified value entered.

This function is only used when there are merged objects/materials with extremely high depth values that are causing the renders to slow down.

Disabled by default.

Glossy effects: It calculates the glossy effects on reflections and refractions. Otherwise, glossy effects on reflections will be mirror-like (nondiffused). Enabled by default.

Override mtl: This toggle allows users to plug a material/shader to override all materials in the scene.

This function is quite useful for quick chalk renders or light studies, whereby the entire scene has one basic white/gray material, with lights turned on.

The Include/Exclude toggles allows users to pick and choose which objects in the scene to exclude from the override material.

IPR Options

IPR options

Interactive Production Render options allows users to execute quick and interactive renders using the Progressive image sampler parameters.

As mentioned earlier, this function can also be accessed via the main toolbar or the Viewport.

Start IPR: This button starts the IPR rendering in the VFB, when clicked.

Fit resolution to VFB: This function forces the original render size to fit the VFB size. Enabled by default.

Force progressive sampling: When enabled, this function uses the Progressive image sampler parameters to compute the renders. Enabled by default.

While the IPR is taking place in the VFB, users can right click and choose Real Zoom, View Navigation, Reinitialize, Select object (Ctrl+Click), Get object material (Shift+Click), and Set focus distance (Alt+Click).

Every time one of the functions is chosen, the IPR updates the render in the VFB.

VFB IPR options

NOTE

IPR works with both Bucket and Progressive image samplers

NOTE

This function is for display purposes in the VFB only.

Image Sampler (Antialiasing)

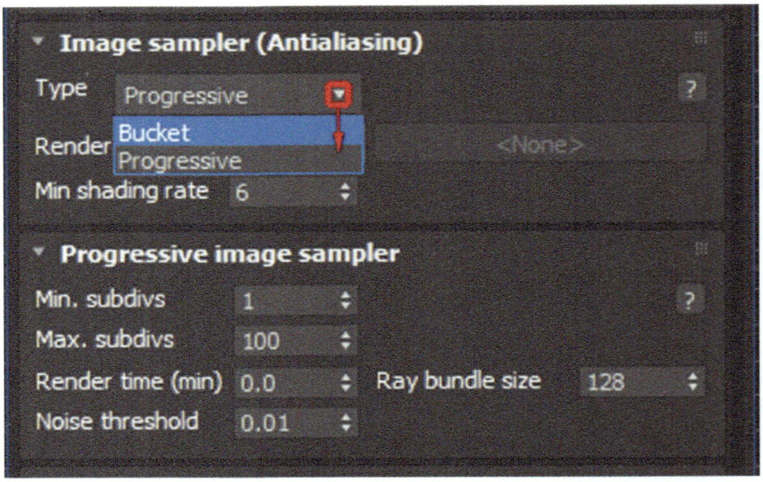

Image sampler types

This rollout controls the final quality of the renders.

Type: This function allows users to choose Progressive (default) or Bucket type from its dropdown list.

Render mask: This function doesn't work well with region renders. It allows users to choose from a list of different types of areas/masks to render such as Texture, Selected, Include/Exclude list, and Layers.

This tool is quite useful for final renders that require one or two object surfaces to be changed. Instead of having to rerender the entire scene, users can select the objects in question and rerender them.

Default, none.

NOTE

I often set it to 64 for final renders.

Min shading rate: This amazing function allows users to increase the render quality without affecting the rendering times. The higher the value, the better the shading quality.

Default value is 6.

Progressive Image Sampler

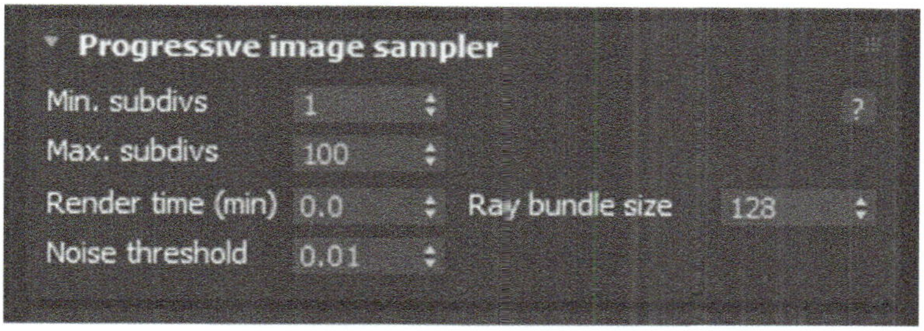

Progressive image sampler options

This image sampler type is often used for test renders while building the scene. It cannot be used for strip network renders, etc.

Min. subdivs: This function controls the minimum number of samples required to process the antialiasing. The higher the value, the slower the rendering times.

Default value is 1.

NOTE

For optimal results, this value should always be kept at 1.

Max. subdivs: The function controls maximum number of samples required to process the antialiasing.

Default value is 100.

NOTE

For optimal results, this value should always be kept at 100.

Render time (min): The values entered here specify the total number of minutes a render should take, regardless of its final quality. The default value of 0.0 sets the rendering time to progressively unlimited, until the final quality is achieved.

If the renders are set to Interactive (IPR), users can continue making changes to the scene and materials while rendering interactively in the viewport or VFB simultaneously.

Ray bundle size: This function controls the number rays calculated on each machine (if many) when the render is set to distributed.

Default value is 128.

Noise threshold: This function is the main parameter to control the overall quality of renders. The smaller the value, the better the quality.

However, rendering times will increase.

For draft renders, the value of 0.1 should be sufficient.

For high-resolution progressive renders, values between 0.007 to 0.01 often work perfectly.

Default value is 0.01.

Progressive Noise threshold set to 0.01

Progressive Noise threshold set to 0.007

Bucket Image Sampler

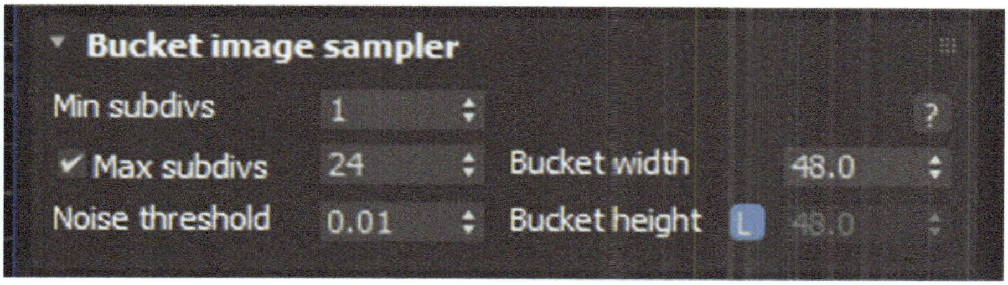

Bucket image sampler options

This image sampler type is often used for final renders and animations via network rendering using strips, etc.

Min subdivs: It controls the minimum number of samples necessary to compute each rendered pixel.

Default value is 1.

Max subdivs: It controls the maximum number of samples necessary to compute each rendered pixel.

Default value is 24.

Noise threshold: This function is the main parameter that controls the overall quality of a render. The smaller the value, the better the quality.

However, rendering times will increase.

For draft renders, the value of 0.1 should be sufficient.

For final high-resolution renders, values between 0.007 and 0.01 often work perfectly.

NOTE

For optimal results, this value should always be kept at 1.

NOTE

For optimal "universal workflow" settings, this value should be set to 100.

Bucket Noise threshold set to 0.1

Bucket Noise threshold set to 0.007

Bucket width and height: The default value of 48 pixels sets the size of each bucket rendered on VFB.

NOTE

Uncloaking the padlock allows user to set the bucket's width and height sizes individually.

Image Filter

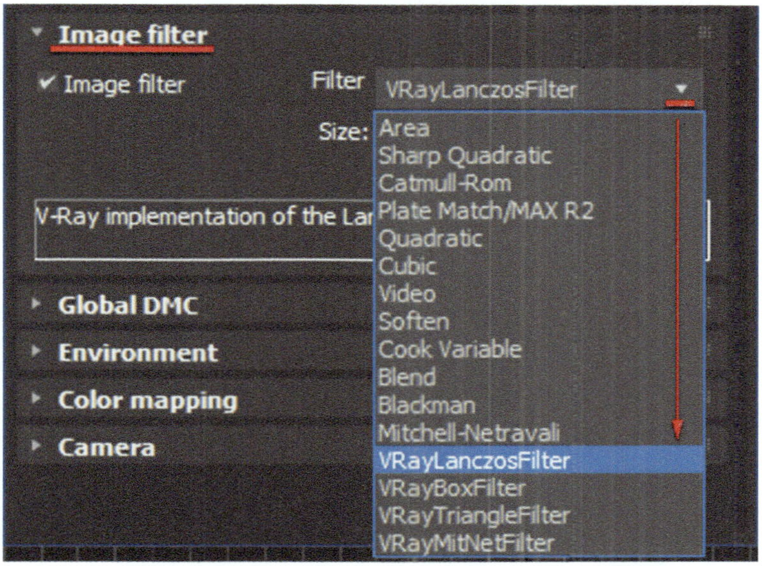

Image filter options

This section controls the filter applied to the renders.

Image filters such as Mitchell-Netravali yield sharp results and increase the rendering times slightly.

VRayLanczosFilter by default.

I often use the Area filter.

Global DMC

This section controls how the noise is processed.

Lock noise pattern: When enabled, it forces similar noise patterns to be locked.

It's mainly used for animations.

Disabled by default.

Blue noise sampling: When enabled, it optimizes the noise pattern uniformly across a render.

Enabled by default.

Global DMC group

Environment

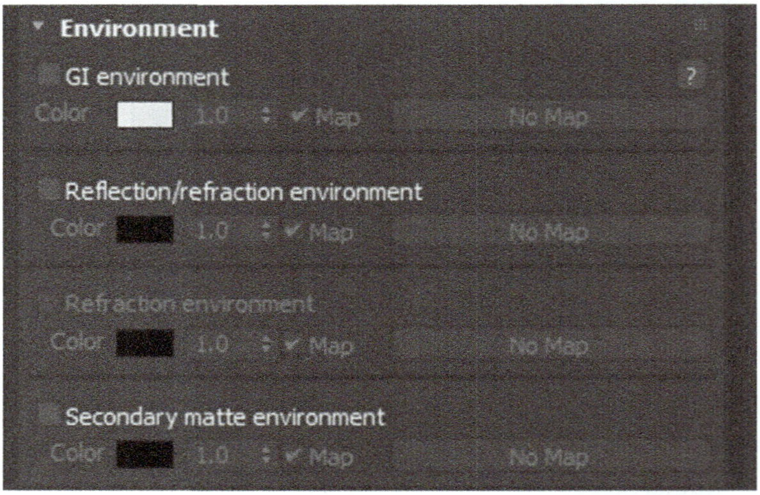

Environment rollout parameters

When used, the environment parameters will override the Environment map toggle.

GI environment: If turned on, it controls the environment/background Global Illumination parameters.

Color: This function allows users to pick a color from its color swatch dialog and control the intensity with its values.

Map: Users often plug a VRayBitmap with an HDRI in this toggle to produce accurate environment lighting.

Reflection/refraction environment: If turned on, i: controls the global reflection/refraction of the environment.

Map: VRayBitmap with an HDRI is often used in this toggle to produce the environment's reflection/refraction.

Color Mapping

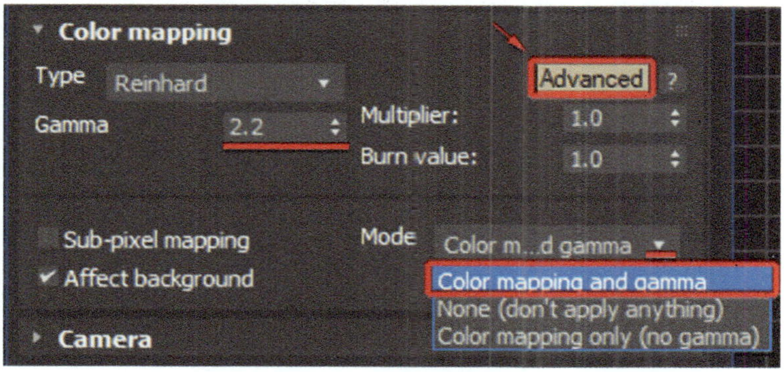

Color mapping rollout parameters

These parameters control how the overall render is processed and saved in your computer.

Type: This function allows users to choose the Color mapping type from its dropdown list. One of the most popular ones is the Linear multiply.

I personally prefer the Exponential type, because of its overall photographic look and the ability to balance overexposed renders.

Reinhard by default.

Gamma: This function controls the gamma value. The value of 2.2 is the most accurate one.

Users should also set the gamma from Preference Settings to 2.2.

NOTE

Ensure to click on the Default button to bring up the Advanced parameters.

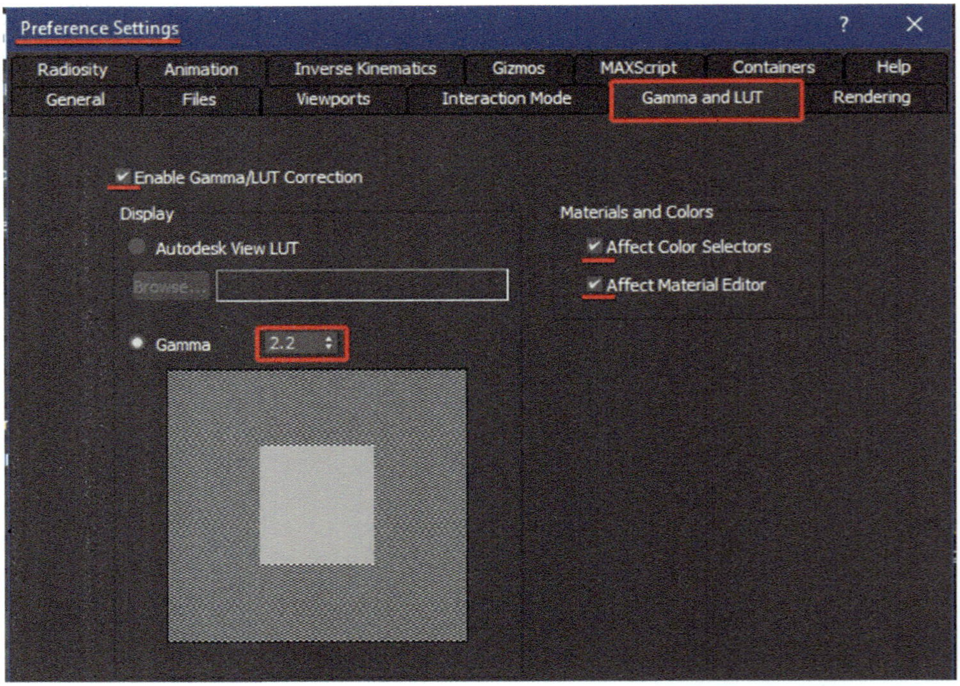

Gamma Preference Settings to 2.2

Multiplier: This function controls the intensity of the multiplier in the render. Default value is 1.0.

Burn value: This option controls the intensity of exposed/burnt areas in the render. Default value is 1.0.

This function is quite useful to help integrate Photomontages or Verified views. In addition, it can be used to help reduce overly bright areas.

Sub-pixel mapping: This function applies the color mapping to individual sub-pixel samples.

Also, it helps to remove artifacts such as bright pixel dots on a render. It often increases the rendering time slightly, when enabled.

Disabled by default.

Affect background: When on, the color mapping is applied to the environment map.

For photomontages, users often disable this option to avoid doubling the gamma. Enabled by default.

Mode: This option controls how the VFB renders are saved into your hard drive.

Scenes from earlier versions of 3ds max should be merged in a scene setup with Color mapping and gamma mode. Otherwise, saved images/renders may differ from what is seen in the VFB.

Default mode, Color mapping only (no gamma).

NOTE

Color mapping and gamma mode is the best, because it saves the renders exactly as seen in the VFB. Ensure to always setup your scene in this manner prior to beginning a project.

Global Illumination

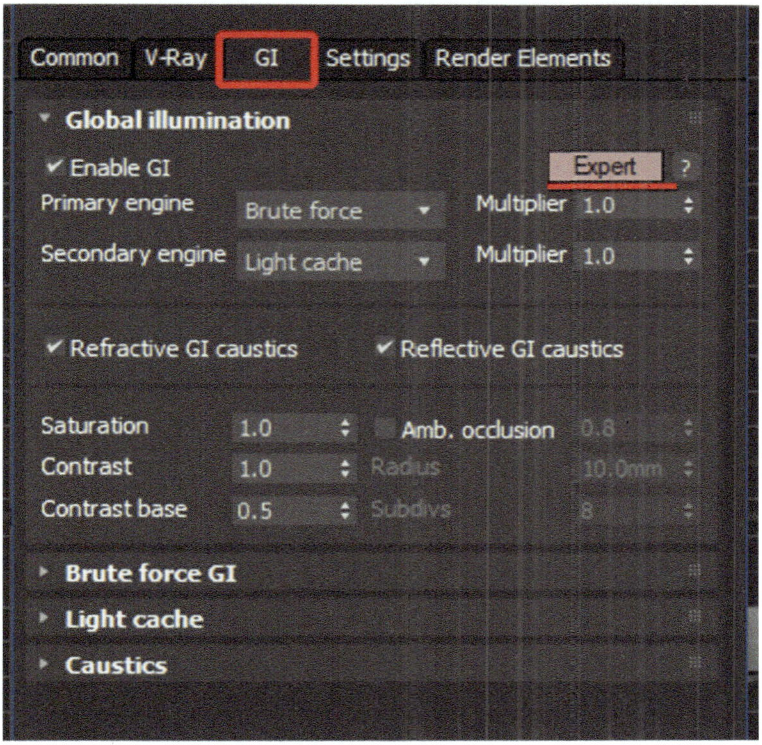

Global Illumination parameters

NOTE

Ensure to click on the Default button twice to bring up the Expert parameters.

Enable GI: This function activates the Global Illumination.

Enabled by default.

Primary engine: This option computes the GI primary bounces. Its dropdown menu allows users to choose other prime engines such as Irradiance or Light cache.

Furthermore, in V-Ray 5, lights, render elements, and most parameters only work with Brute force.

Brute force by default.

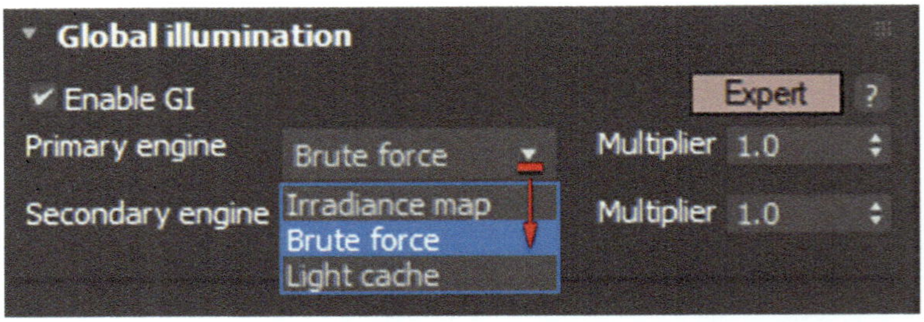

Brute force primary engine

NOTE

Brute force is the most accurate primary engine. Its parameters are grayed out because it's physically accurate (unbiased).

Secondary engine: This option computes the GI secondary bounces. Light cache is the default secondary engine.

Multiplier: For both, primary and secondary engines, this function helps to reinvigorate or diminish their influence in the GI calculation.

Default value is 1.0.

Refractive/Reflective GI caustics: When enabled, these functions allow the GI caustics to be computed on refractive and/or reflective (transparent) surfaces.

Enabled by default.

NOTE

They only work when the Caustics rollout parameters are enabled.

Caustics parameters are disabled by default.

Saturation: This option controls the color saturation of the GI effect. Higher values cause the GI to produce more saturated colors.

Default value is 1.0.

Contrast: This function determines the overall contrast of the GI. Higher values increase the GI contrast.

Default value is 1.0.

Contrast base: This option controls the base contrast values. Default value is 0.5.

Amb. occlusion: When on, it adds connecting shadows on indirectly lit areas globally. Disabled by default.

NOTE

Ambient occlusion works in a similar way to VRayDirt (previously covered).

Radius: This option controls the propagation of the connecting shadows from its starting point. Default value is 10 mm.

Subdivs: This option controls the smoothness of the connecting shadows. Higher values yield smoother results.

Default value is 8.

Light Cache

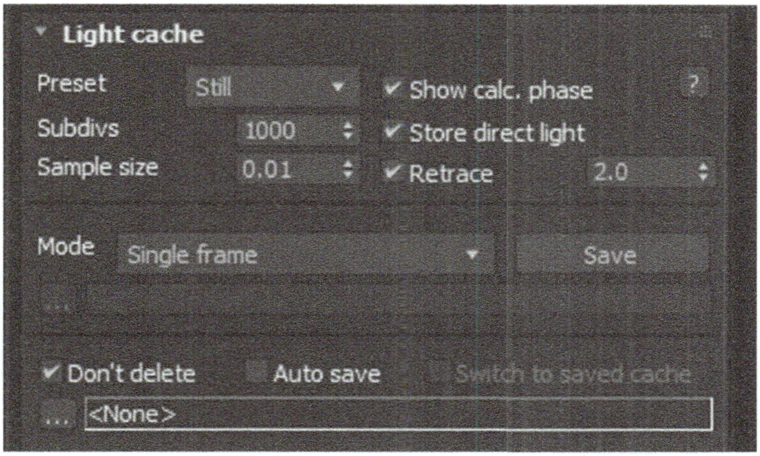

Light cache parameters

This secondary GI engine is an approximation (biased). It's ideal for most high resolution still renders and animations.

Preset: This function allows users to choose between Still and Animation presets.

The Still preset comes with the default Subdivs value set to 1000.

The Animation preset comes with the default Subdivs value set to 3000.

Subdivs: This function determines the accuracy of the light cache calculation. Extremely high values produce results closer to Brute force (unbiased).

Values between 1000 and 3000 work well for most scenes. Default value is 1000.

Sample size: This function controls the spatial detail of light cache. The default value of 0.01 works well for most scenes and animations.

Default value is 0.01.

Show calc. phase: This function displays the precalculation of the light cache in the VFB, prior to rendering.

Enabled by default.

Store direct light: This function caches the direct light (if any) in the light cache calculation.

Enabled by default.

NOTE

The value of 8.0 is ideal for animations.

Retrace: This function retraces the light in tight areas such as corners. Having this option turned on prevents light leaks and flickering.

Default value is 2.0. Higher values increase the light cache precalculation time.

Mode: This option allows users to choose between Single Frame or From file mode.

Default Mode is Single frame.

Save: This toggle allows users to name and save a Light cache file (*.vrlmap)

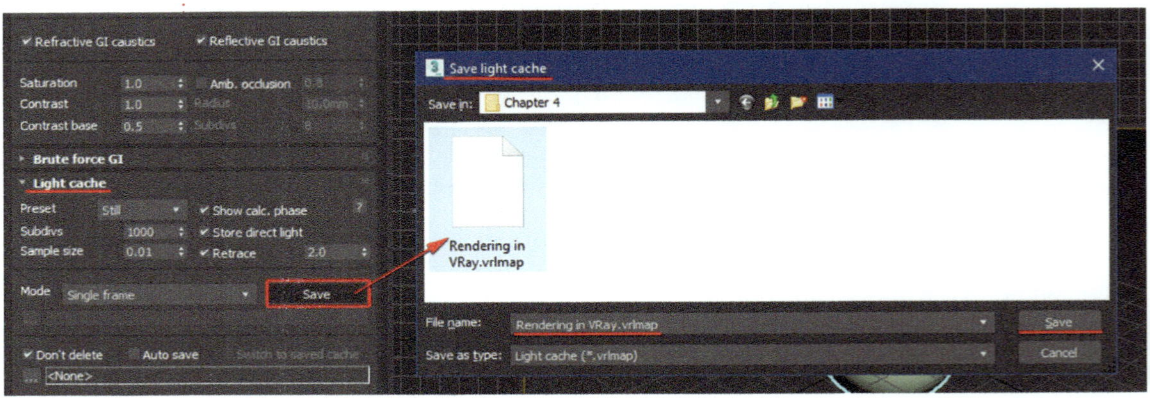

Save Light cache dialog

Don't delete: When turned on, it keeps the light cache in memory after rendering. It's faster for subsequent renders.

However, it uses up computer memory.

Enabled by default.

Auto save: When enabled, it automatically saves the light cache file entered in the toggle below (<None>).

Disabled by default.

Switch to saved cache: This function only becomes available if the Auto save option is enabled.

It automatically uploads the saved light cache file in the toggle below (<none>), after being saved previously.

Users tend to enable the Don't render final image option while saving the light cache file. Having this function enabled will allow users to save the light cache precalculation file without having to render the image.

Also, ensure to disable the Don't render final image option, prior to sending the final render.

Settings

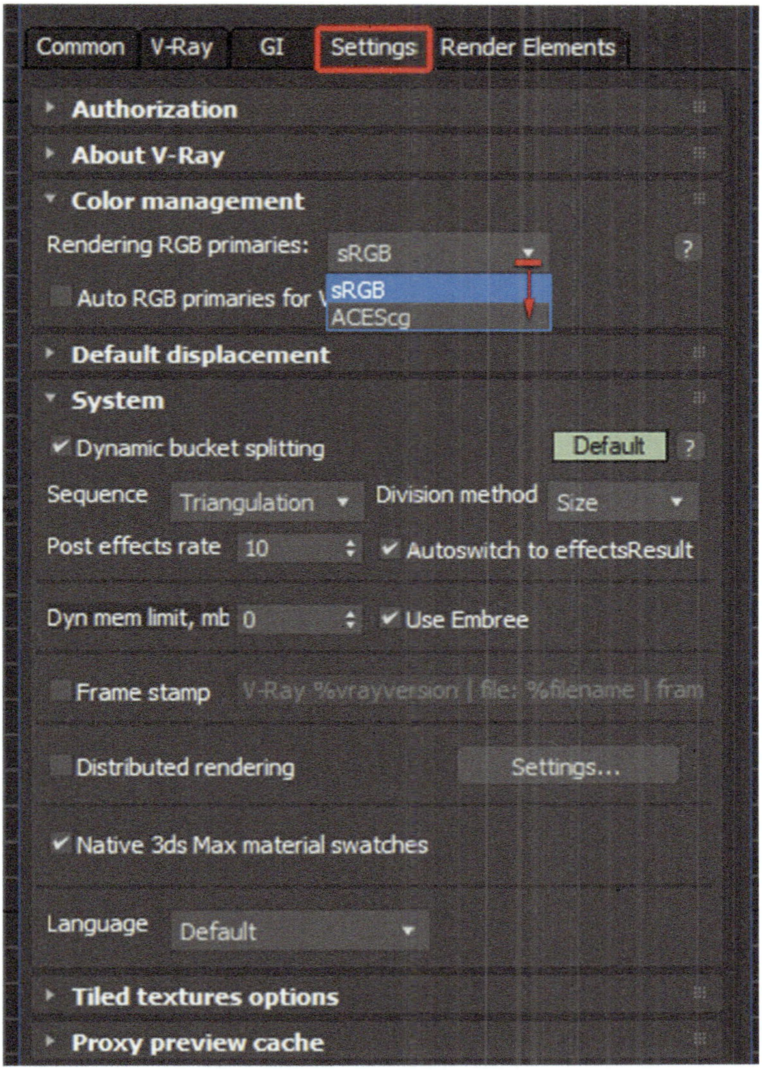

Settings parameters

Color Management

Rendering RGB primaries: This option allows users to choose between sRGB and ACEScg color display spaces.

sRGB is the default color space for most monitors.

Auto RGB primaries for VRayBitmap textures: When enabled, this function forces the RGB primaries for VRayBitmap textures.

Disabled by default.

Default Displacement

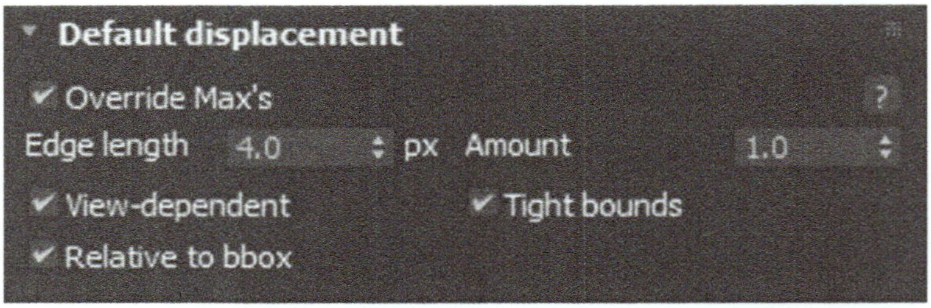

Default displacement parameters

Override Max's : When enabled, it uses VRay's micro-triangulation system to calculate displacement values. Enabled by default.

Edge length: This function controls the edge length of the displacement, in pixels (if view-dependent). Default value is 4.0.

Amount: This option controls the default scaling amount of the displacement. Default value is 1.0.

View-dependent: When enabled, the Edge length is in pixels; otherwise, world units. Enabled by default.

Relative to bbox: This function forces the displacement to be relative to the bounding box. Enabled by default.

Tight bounds: When enabled, it computes the displacement as closely as possible to the original mesh (preserves the integrity of the original mesh). Enabled by default.

System

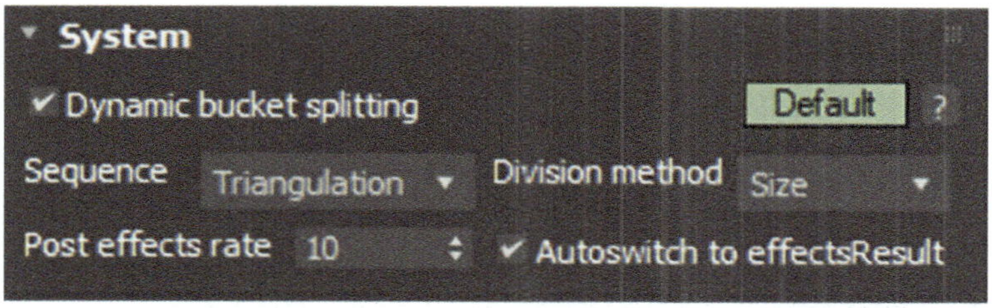

System parameters

Dynamic bucket splitting: It automatically splits the bucket rendering size according to the bucket width value. In addition, it automatically decides whether to reduce or increase the bucket size depending on the areas of the VFB being rendered.

Enabled by default.

Sequence: It determines the sequence/movement of the bucket rendering in the VFB. Default sequence is triangulation.

Post-effects rate: This function determines the frequency of progressive rendering updates on the VFB. The value of 0 disables render updates during progressive rendering.

High values updates progressive renders more frequently. The default value of 10 is often sufficient.

Division method: This function controls how the render is divided in buckets when rendering in VFB. Users can choose between Size and Count division methods.

Both methods use pixels to measure the buckets. The Image sampler type needs to be set to Bucket.

Autoswitch to effectsResult: This function uses the effectsResult channel/render element to display the final render result. It's mostly useful when effects are being used under the VFB Layers tab.

Enabled by default.

Dyn mem limit, mb: This option sets the memory limit to compute a render. This function is quite useful to increase or decrease the rendering power, depending on one's resources.

The default value of 0 uses as much memory as possible to compute the final render.

Use Embree: This function uses the Intel Embree raycaster. Enabled by default.

Dyn mem limit, mb parameters

Frame stamp: When enabled, the bottom part of the VRay Frame buffer will display key render information such as VRay Version (VRay %vrayversion) and File name (file: %filename).

Disabled by default.

Frame stamp parameters

Distributed rendering: When enabled, it uses the distributed rendering system to allocate assigned computers to the rendering calculation.

Computers are assigned/allocated through the Settings toggle.

The more the computers are assigned, the faster the renders will be. Distributed rendering only works in conjunction with VRay Spawner.

For more information about VRay Spawner, please visit http://docs.chaosgroup.com/

Distributed rendering is disabled by default.

Settings: This toggle allows users to add/allocated computers to the distributed rendering process.

VRay distributed rendering settings dialog has the following functionalities:

Add server: This function allows users to type in the machine/server name or IP address.

Edit server: It allows users to edit an existing machine/server name or IP address. To do so, simply select the listed Host name, followed by clicking on the Edit server function.

Remove server: It enables users to select and remove existing servers from the list.

Resolve servers: This function allows VRay to automatically resolve incorrect server names/IP addresses listed in the dialog.

NOTE

Always enable the functions to Restart servers on render end and Transfer missing assets. This will prevent numerous problems associated with remote servers.

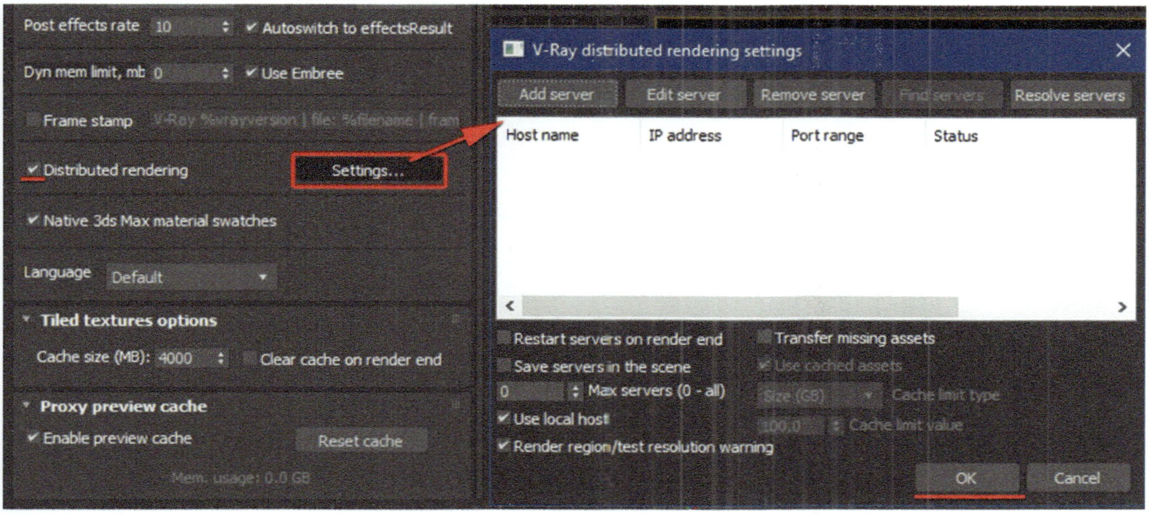

Settings dialog

Native 3ds max material swatches: This function allows users to enable the Native 3ds max material editor.

As mentioned earlier, this function should be enabled for quick previews of materials in the Material Editor slots. Otherwise, material previews will be more realistic, at a cost of slower performance.

Disabled by default.

Native 3ds max material swatches function

Language: This function allows users to choose a preferred language to translate the VRay tooltips.

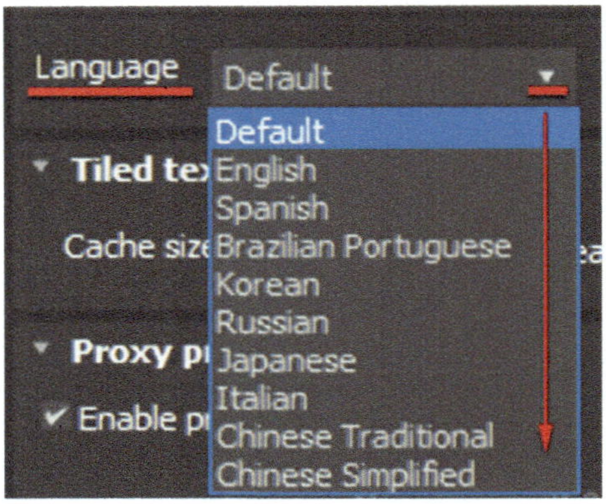

Language options

Tiled Textures Options

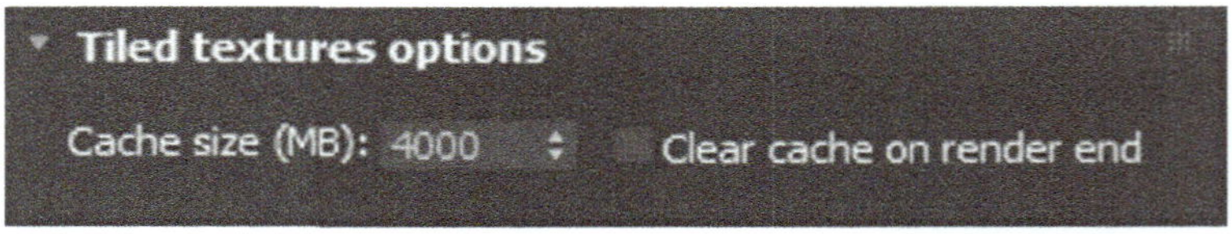

Tiled textures options

Cache size (MB): This function allows users to specify the maximum amount of memory (MB) to be used to cache tiled textures (OpenEXR and TIFF files). If set to 0, VRay will use as much memory as required.

Default value is 4000.

Clear cache on render end: When enabled, it clears the texture cached after a render is completed.

Proxy Preview Cache

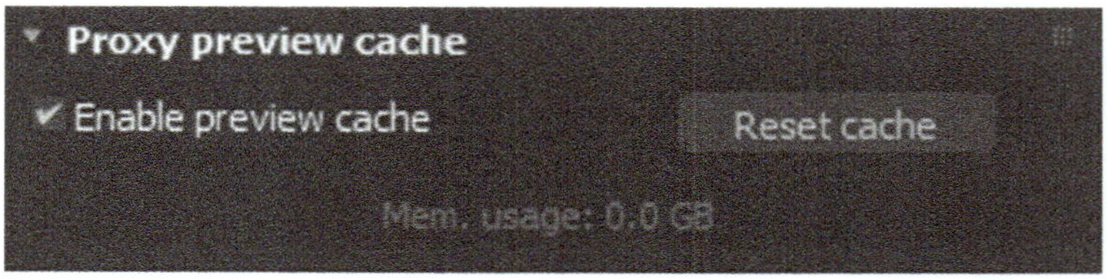

Proxy preview cache parameters

Enable preview cache: This function allows the viewport to preview all VRayProxy objects in the scene, which speeds up the viewport performance. Enabled by default.

Chapter 5 will showcase how to create VRayProxies.

Reset cache: Clicking this button clears up the cached information.

Render Elements

Render Elements are often used to help enhance the overall render, key physical properties of materials, and lights in post-production.

Most render elements can only be used if/when the function to Separate render channels is enabled (except for VRayLightMix and VRayDenoiser).

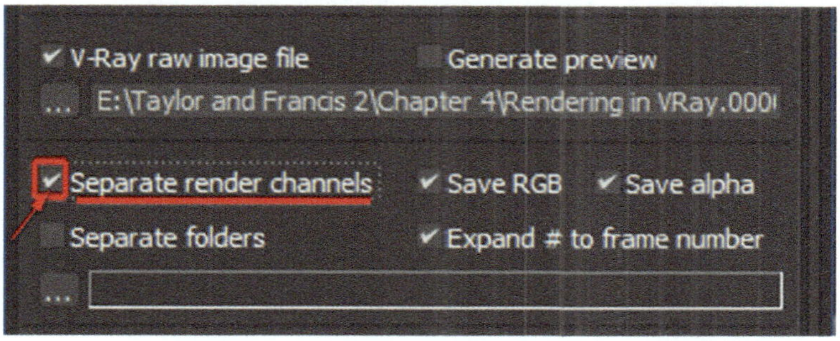

Separate render channels

To add a render element, go to the Render Elements tab first.

Under Render Elements, click on the Add button, followed by selecting one or more of the listed elements in the dialog. Then click OK.

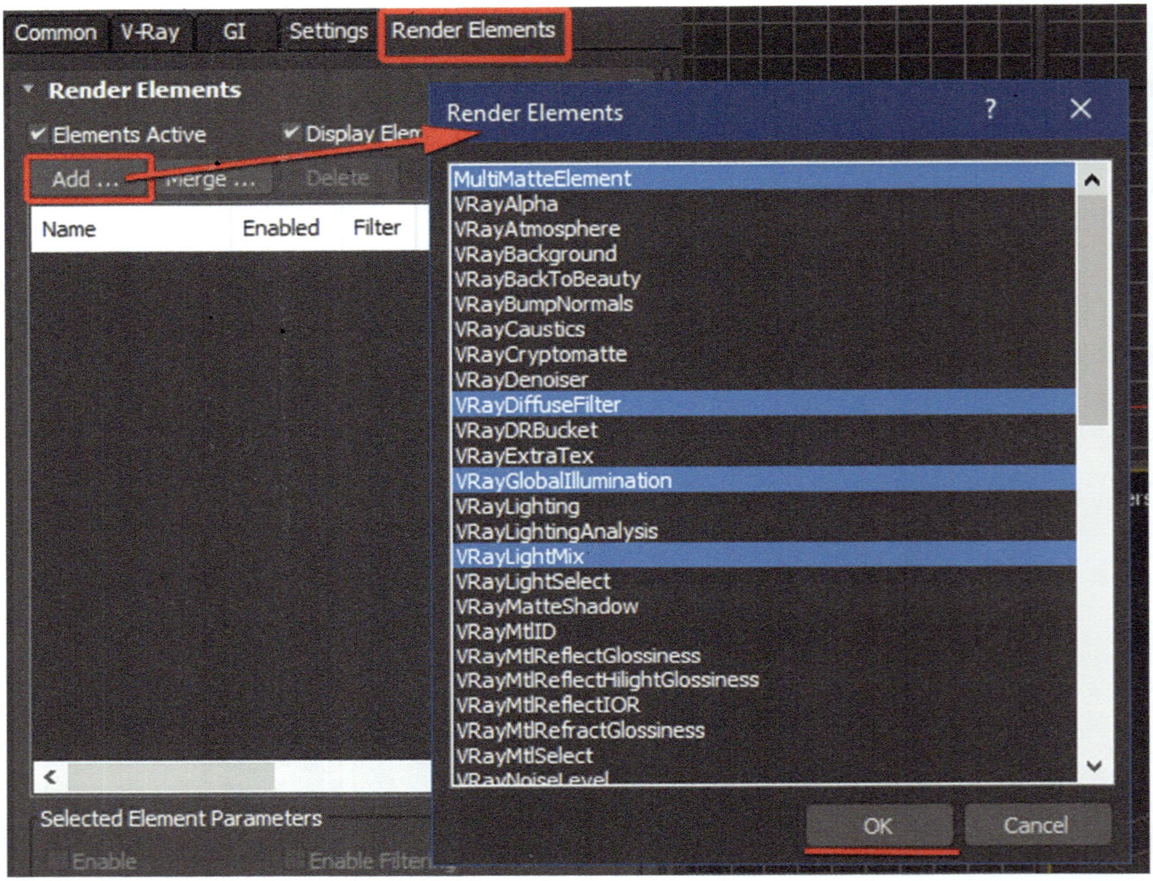

Add Render Elements

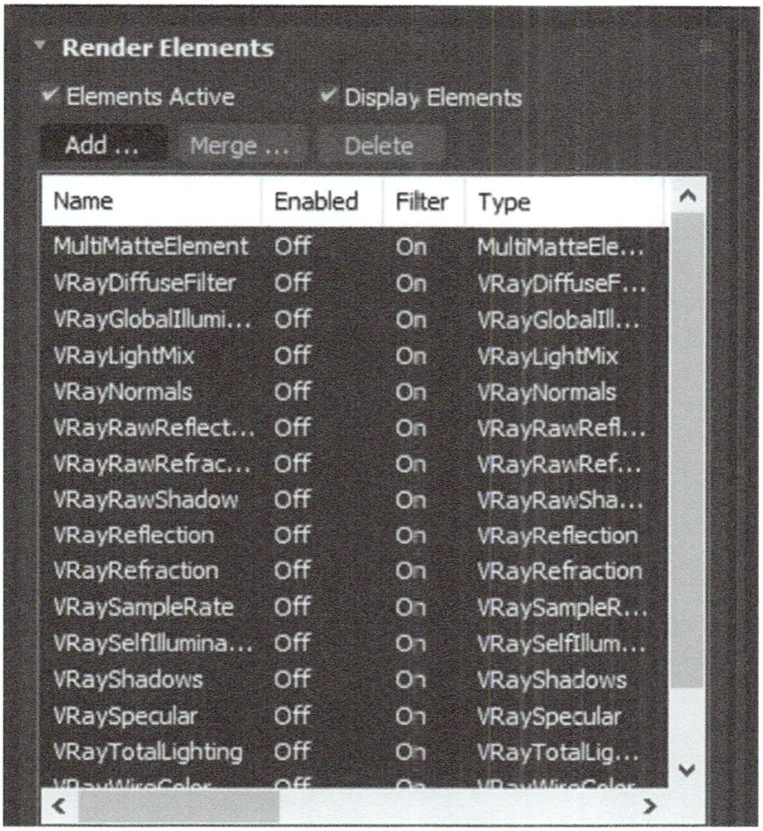

Add Render Elements added

When selected individually, each render element comes with its own set of parameters.

Some of the most useful render elements are as follows:

VRayLightMix

This render element allows users to control the intensity and color of all lights in the scene, via the VFB.

By default, it is set to Group by Instanced lights. This option displays all instanced lights in the scene as one Layer in the VFB.

If you want the flexibility to manipulate the instanced lights individually, simply choose the option to Group by Individual lights.

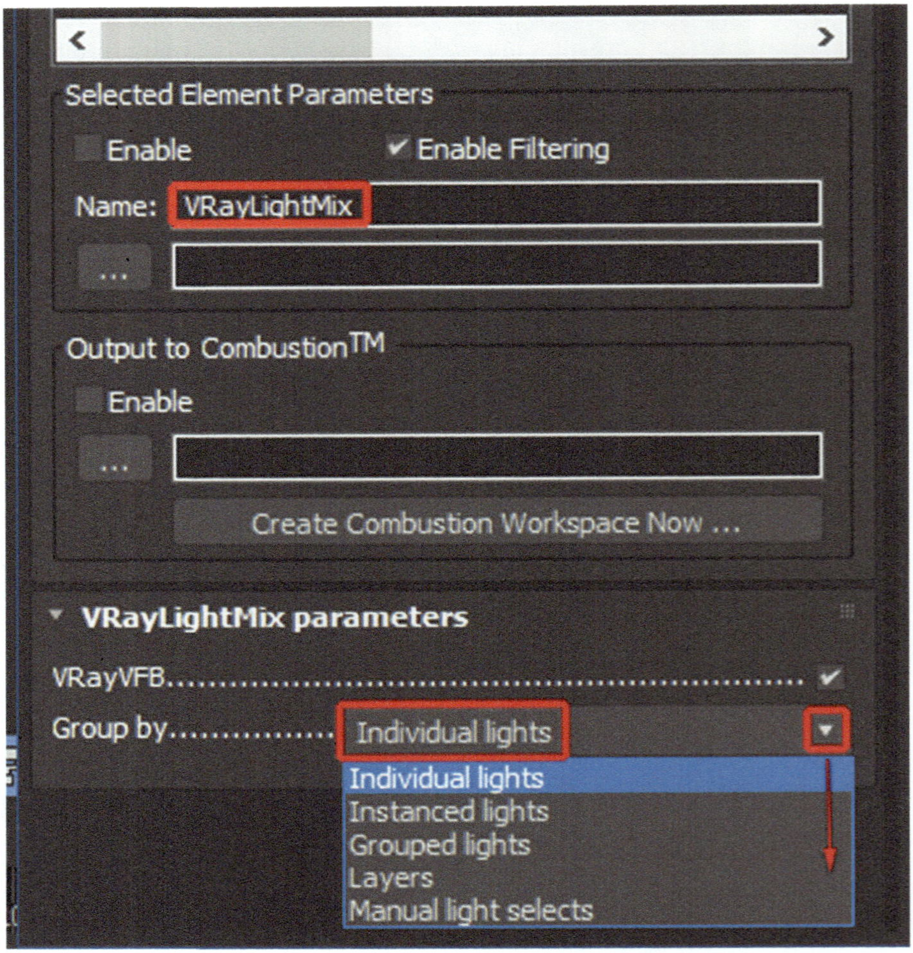
Selected Element Parameters
Enable
Enable Filtering
Name: VRayLightMix
...
Output to Combustion™
Enable
...
Create Combustion Workspace Now ...
VRayLightMix parameters
VRayVFB
Group by
Individual lights
Individual lights
Instanced lights
Grouped lights
Layers
Manual light selects

VRayLightMix parameters

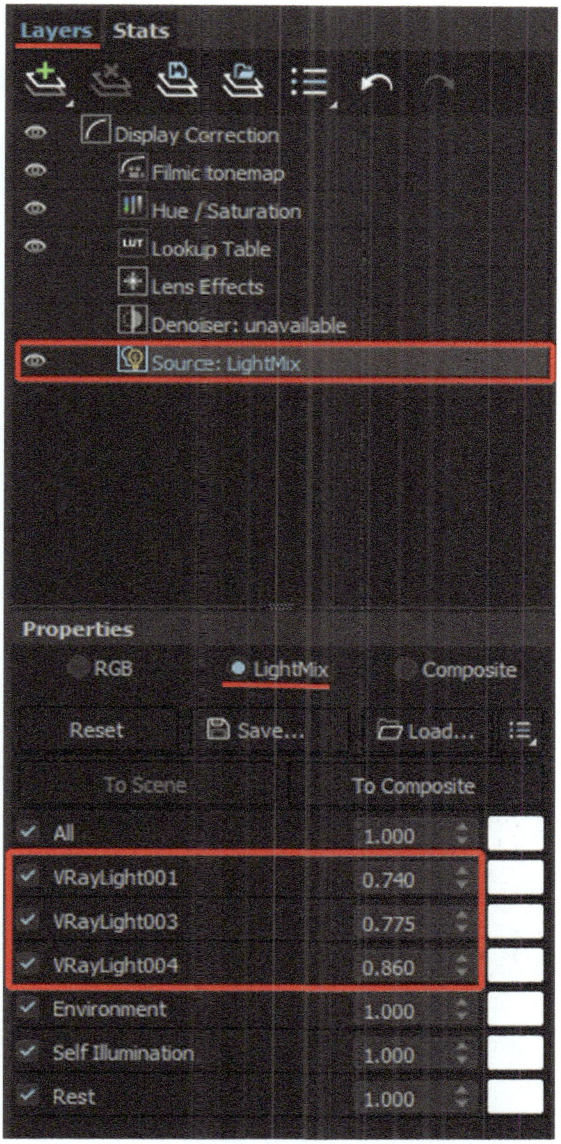

LightMix with instanced lights displayed individually

MultiMatteElement

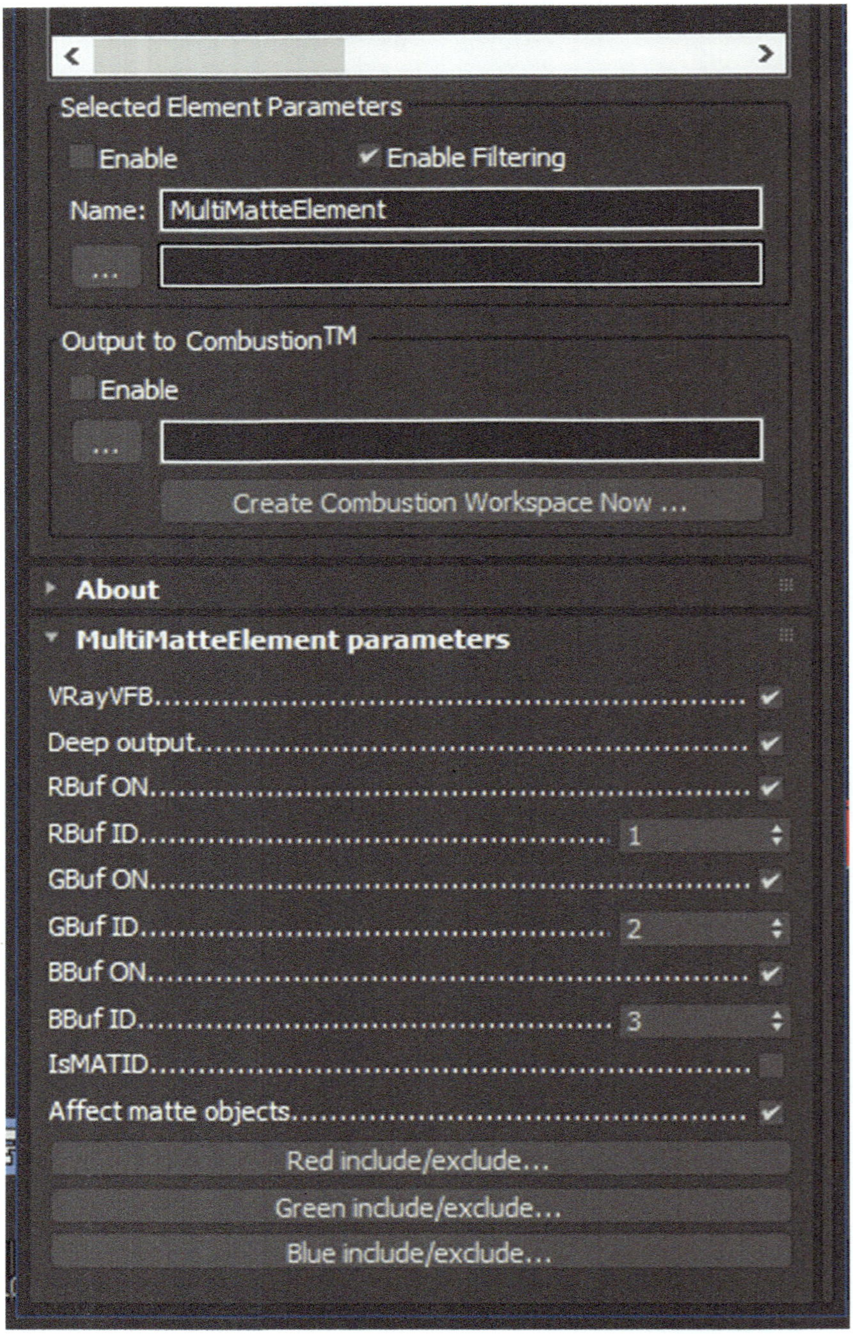
Selected Element Parameters
Enable
Enable Filtering
Name:
MultiMatteElement
...
Output to CombustionTM
Enable
...
Create Combustion Workspace Now ...
About
MultiMatteElement parameters
VRayVFB
Deep output
RBuf ON
RBuf ID
1
GBuf ON
GBuf ID
2
BBuf ON
BBuf ID
3
IsMATID
Affect matte objects
Red include/exclude...
Green include/exclude...
Blue include/exclude...

MultiMatteElement

This render element represents the true R (red), G (green), and B (blue) colors, which are extremely accurate to select in post-production (they don't yield jagged edges).

The RBuf, GBuf, and BBuf IDs allow users to specify numbers associated with each color. By default, the RBuf ID (red) is associated with id number 1.

The GBuf ID (green) is associated with id number 2, and the BBuf ID (blue) is associated with id number 3.

The IsMATID function determines whether the id numbers are related to materials or object ids.

If disabled (default), the numbers are related to object ids.

Each object id number needs to coincide with one of the numbers specified here.

To create object id numbers, simply select any object in the scene and right click to bring up the quad menu.

Choose the Object Properties option.

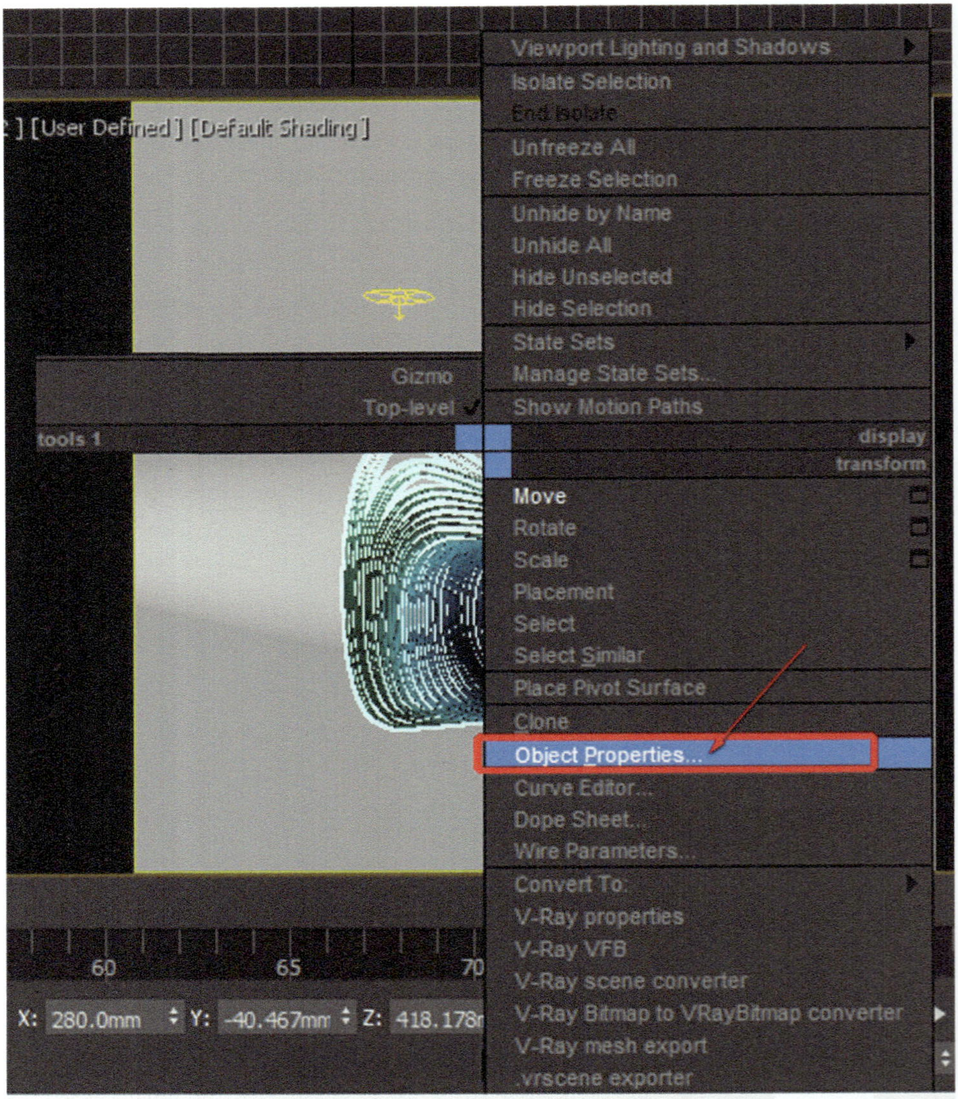

Choose the Object Properties option

In the Object Properties dialog, under G-Buffer Object ID, enter a number to coincide with any of the ID numbers listed in the MultimatteElement parameters.

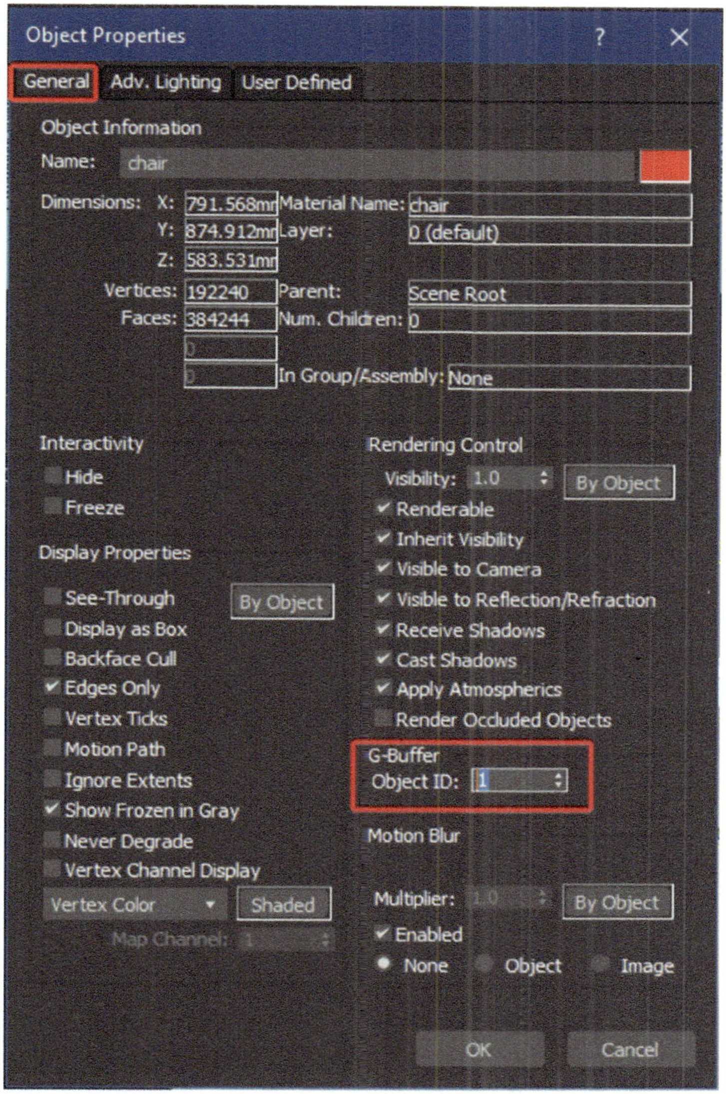

G-Buffer Object ID number

Repeat the same actions to other objects in the scene, entering ID numbers 2 and 3 to coincide with the MultimatteElement numbers.

The final result (when rendered) should look similar to the image below.

MultimatteElement with RGB colors rendered

If you have more objects in the scene you want to add different object ID numbers to, you need to add a second MultimatteElement to the list, and name it differently (MultimatteElement 2).

Also, the RGB ID numbers need to differ from the previous ones (4, 5, 6). The new objects in the scene need to have id numbers to coincide with the new MultimatteElement 2.

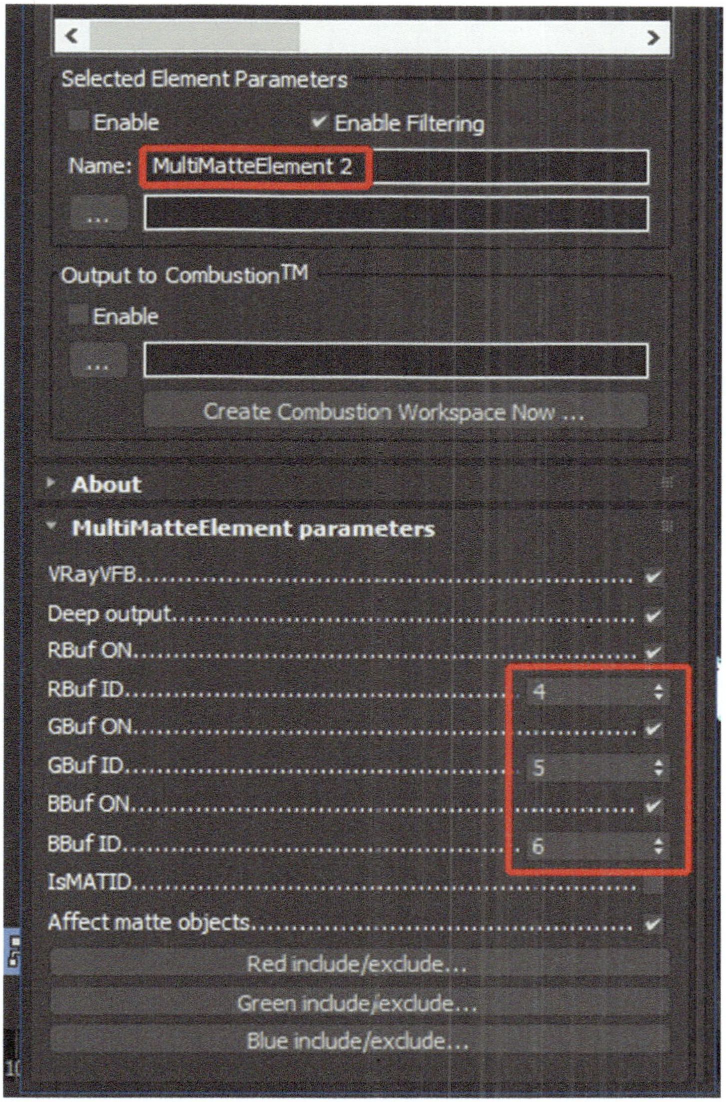

MultiMatteElement 2 with different ID numbers

Second MultimatteElement with RGB colors rendered

If you want to have a new MultimatteElement with IDs associated with materials instead, simply enable the IsMAID function.

Also, name the new render element differently (MultiMatteElement _sub 1).

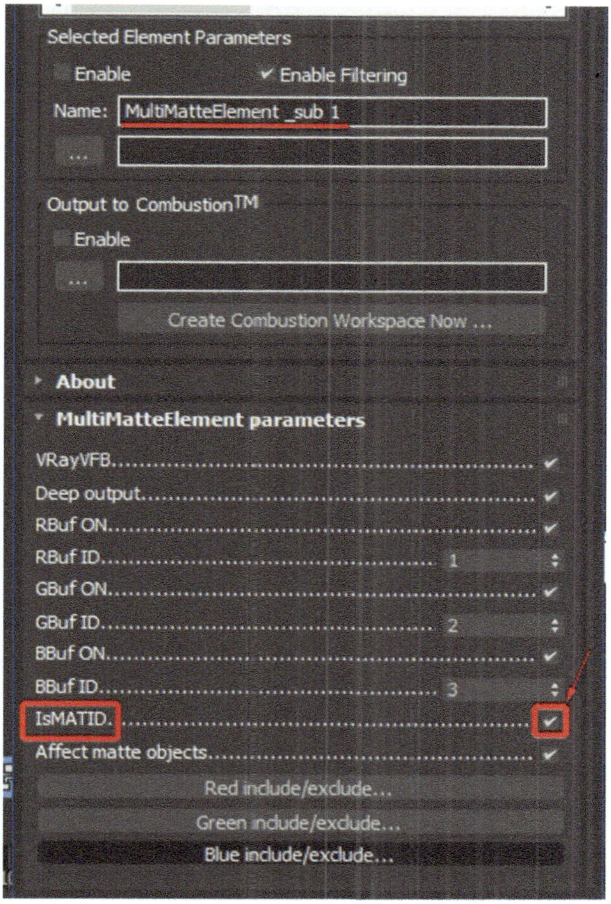

IsMAID function enabled

In the Material Editor, change the material number to coincide with one of the MultiMatteElement _sub 1 ids (select and hold).

Change the material ID number

Repeat the same action to other materials in the scene.

In the end, users often end up with a long list of different MultiMatteElements: some of the render elements affecting the object IDs, and others affecting the material IDs.

To select the colors in post, simply go to the Channels tab, hold down the Ctrl key, and select one of the three listed colors.

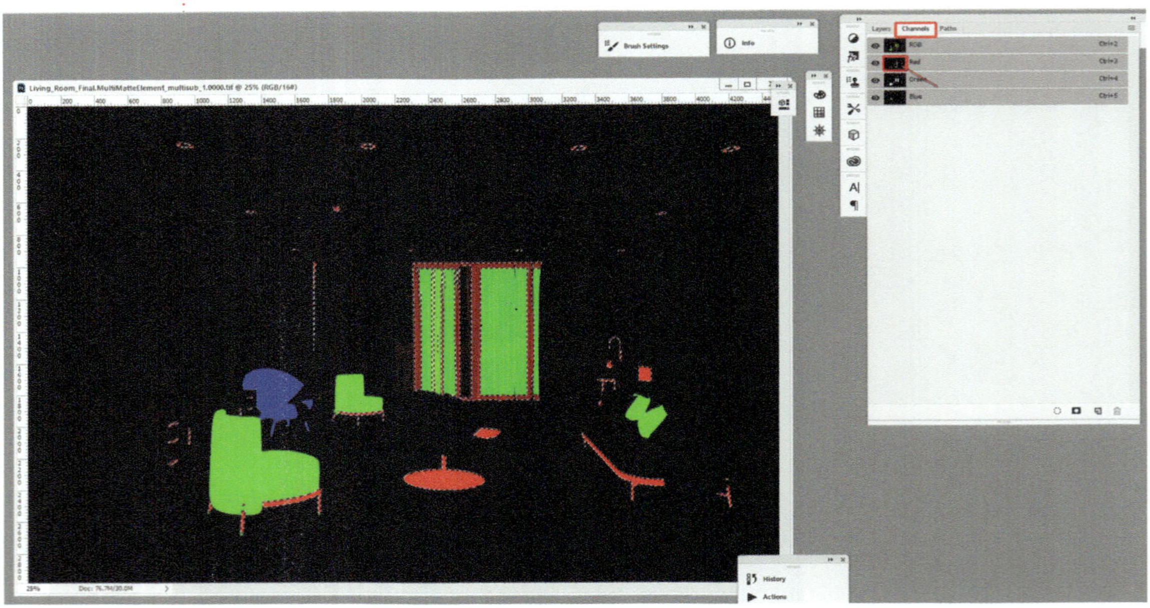

Select colors in post-production

Next, select the Layers tab and create a new group, clicking its button.

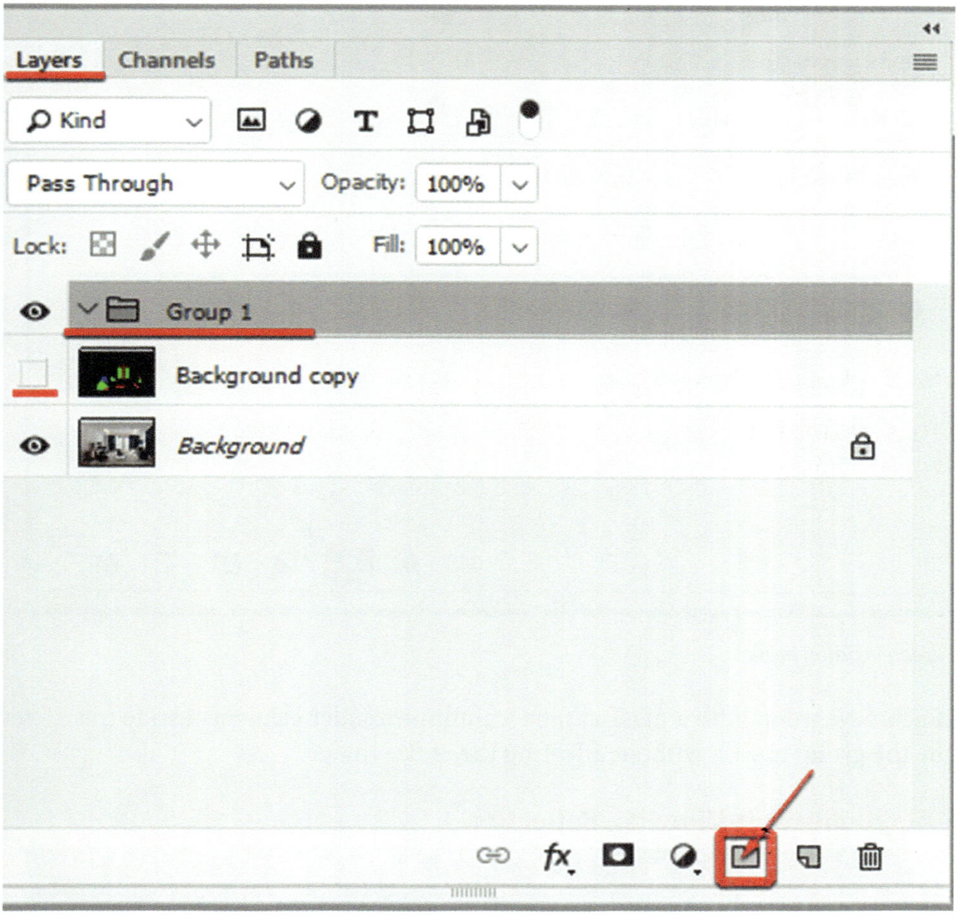

Create a new Group

While the selection is still on, click on the mask button to create a group mask.

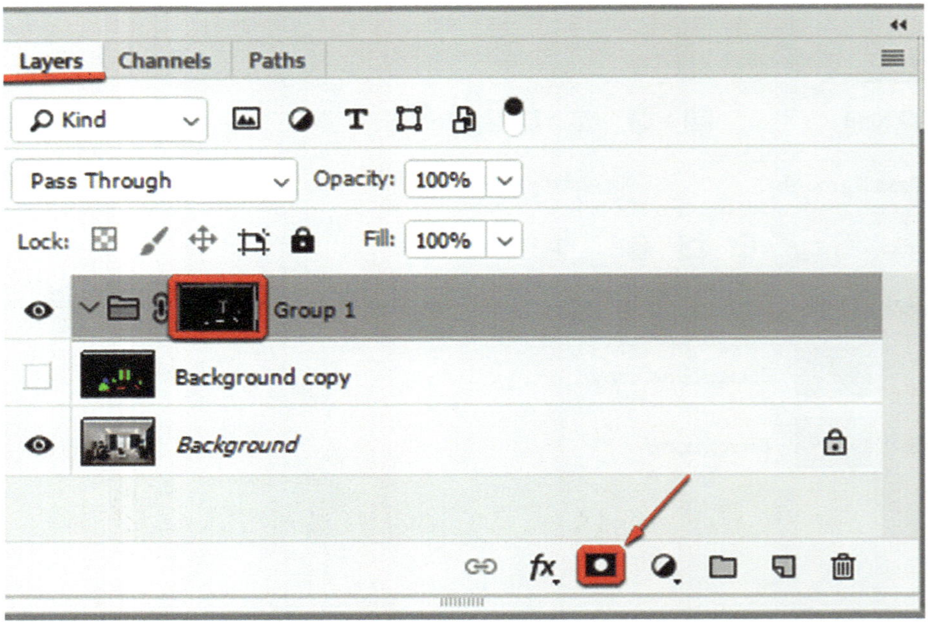

Create a group mask

Each new group with a mask can have multiple render elements inside (restricted by the group mask), without affecting the entire image.

VRayReflection/VRayRawReflection

VRayReflection render element

VRayRawReflection render element

These two render elements are quite useful to extra reflections from materials. If there are no reflections in the scene, these elements will render black.

In post-production, VRayReflection works best with Screen blending mode.

VRayRawReflection works best with Normal blending mode, and the opacity reduced accordingly.

VRaySampleRate

This render element is quite useful see areas of the scene that are problematic to render (green and red). Green areas are slightly problematic to render, but red areas are the most severe.

NOTE

In 3ds max, when enabling reflections on materials, it's best to always disable the Fresnel reflections function in order to see reflections in the render element.

VRaySampleRate render element

VRayBackToBeauty

This render element allows VRay to save the VRay Frame Buffer layers applied (beauty) and without it (raw render).

This render element also adds automatically the VRaySSS2 pass (only seen while rendering).

VRaySpecular

VRaySpecular render element

This render element is amazing to add/control specular/glossy highlights in post-production. If there are no specular/glossy highlights in the scene, this element will render black.

In post-production, VRaySpecular works best with Screen blending mode.

NOTE

In 3ds max, when enabling reflections/highlights on materi-als, it's best to always disable the Fresnel reflections function, in order to see specular/highlights in the render element.

VRayRefraction/VRayRawRefraction

VRayRefraction render element

VRayRawRefraction render element

These render elements help to control the refractions/transparency in post-production. If there is no refraction/transparency in the scene, these elements will render black.

In post-production, VRayRefraction works best with Screen blending mode.

VRayRawRefraction works best with Normal blending mode in post-production.

VRayDiffuseFilter

VRayDiffuseFilter render element

This element renders mainly colors, shades, and textures, without GI, lighting, or shadows. It's quite useful to help control the colors and textures of objects in post-production (reducing its layer opacity slightly).

In post-production, it works best with Normal blending mode.

VRayWireColor

VRayWireColor render element

This render element is an alternative to the MultiMatteElement. Unlike MultiMatteElement, it automatically creates colors based on objects' wire color in 3ds max.

Users often use the Magic wand tool to select VRayWireColors in post-production. This method of selection is not accurate and often leaves selection edges jagged.

VRayZDepth

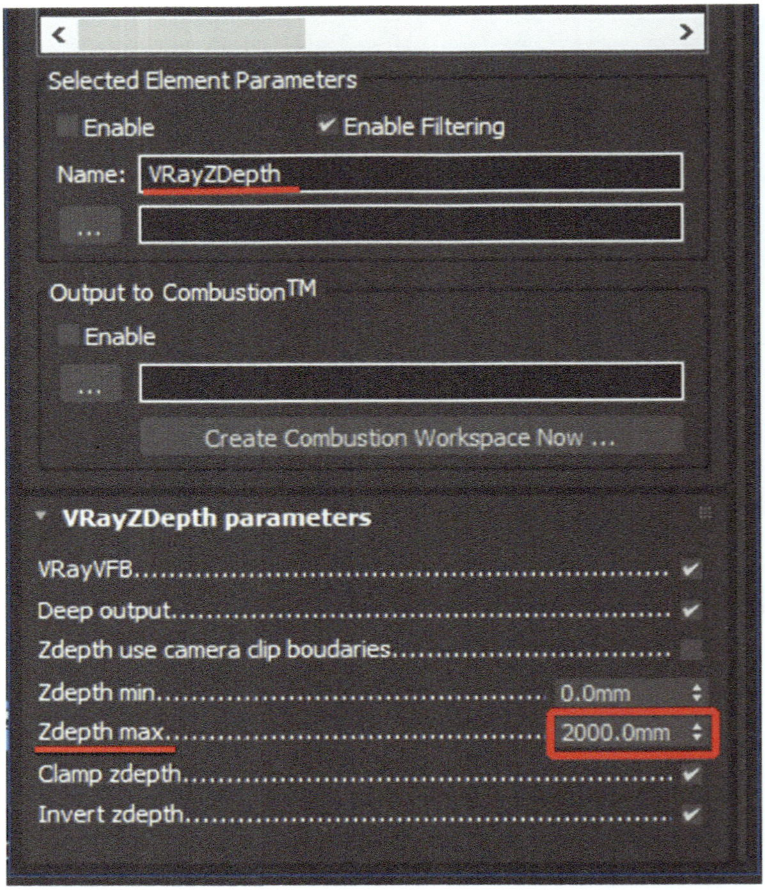

VRayZDepth render element

This render element is often used to create effects such as fog and depth of field in post-production.

To set the distance in 3ds max, simply enter a value in ZDepth max function.

Set the ZDepth max value

To create the depth of field effect in post-production, go to its Channels tab. Hold down the Ctrl key and select its RGB or Red channel.

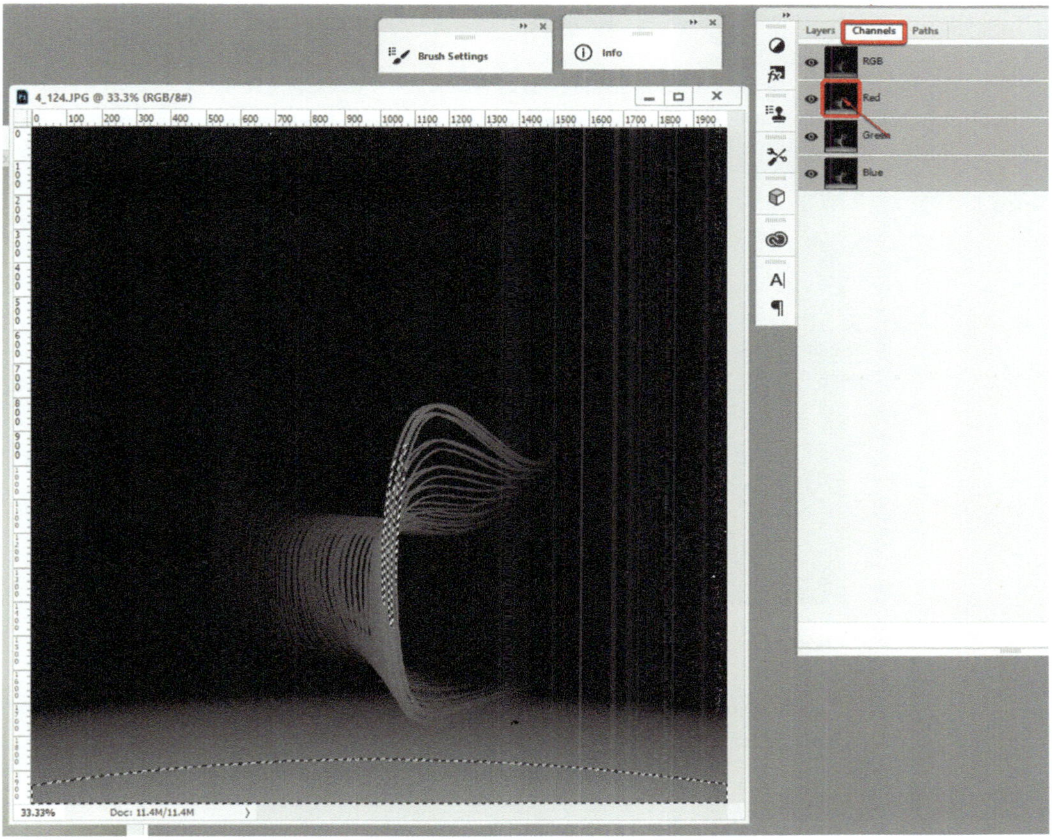

Red channel selected

While the selection is still on, click on the Select tool and choose Save selection.

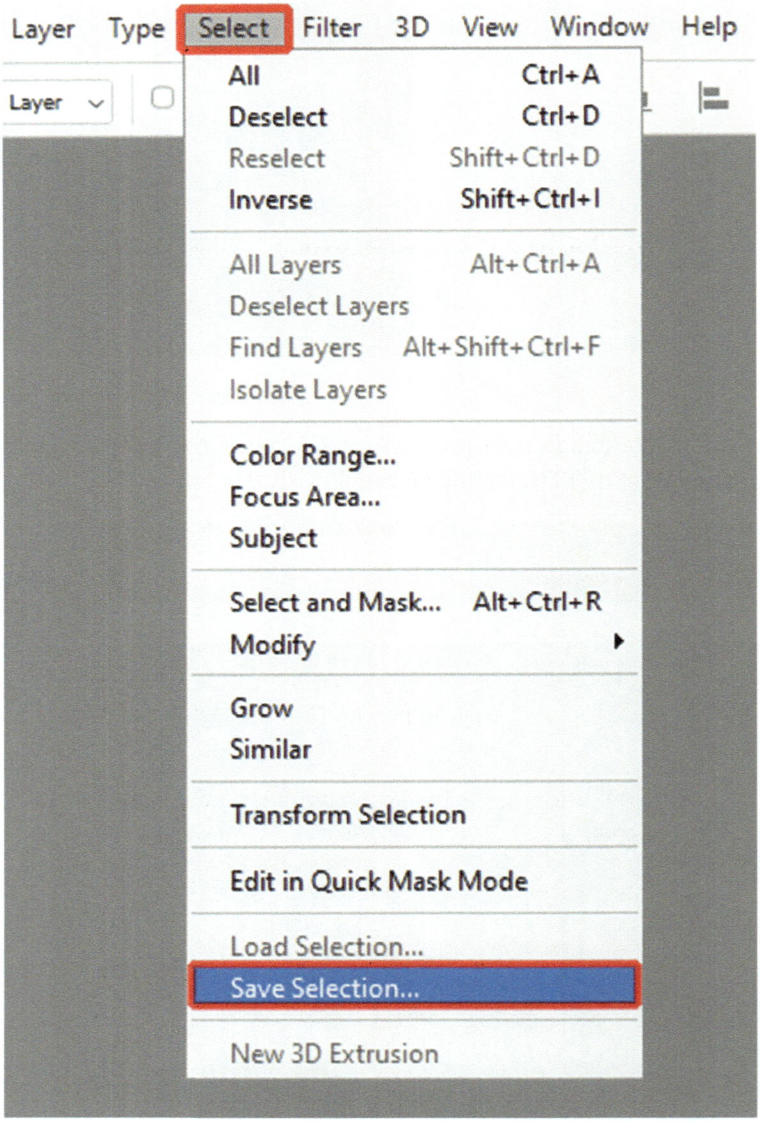

Choose Save selection

In Save Selection dialog, choose the Destination document (main render) and Name the new selection accordingly.

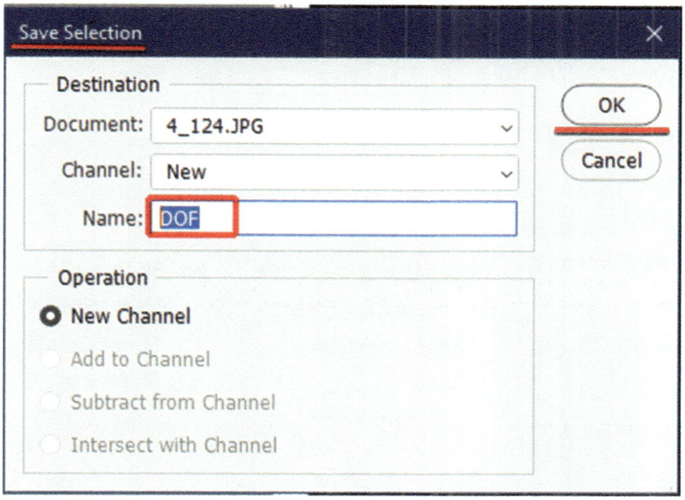

Name selection

Select the main render. Right click and choose Duplicate Layer.

It's always good practice to work on a Duplicated layer, not the original one.

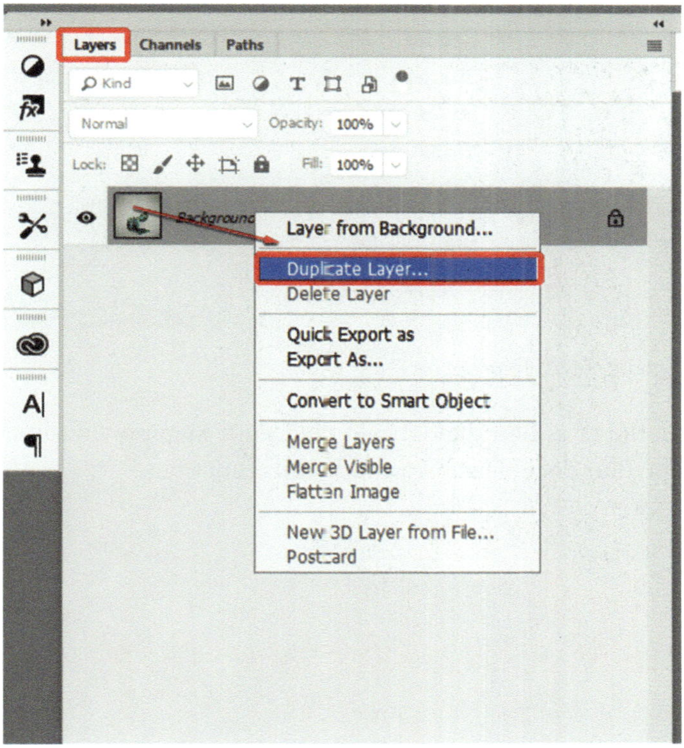

Duplicate layer

Next, go to the Filter tab. Under Blur, choose the Lens Blur option.

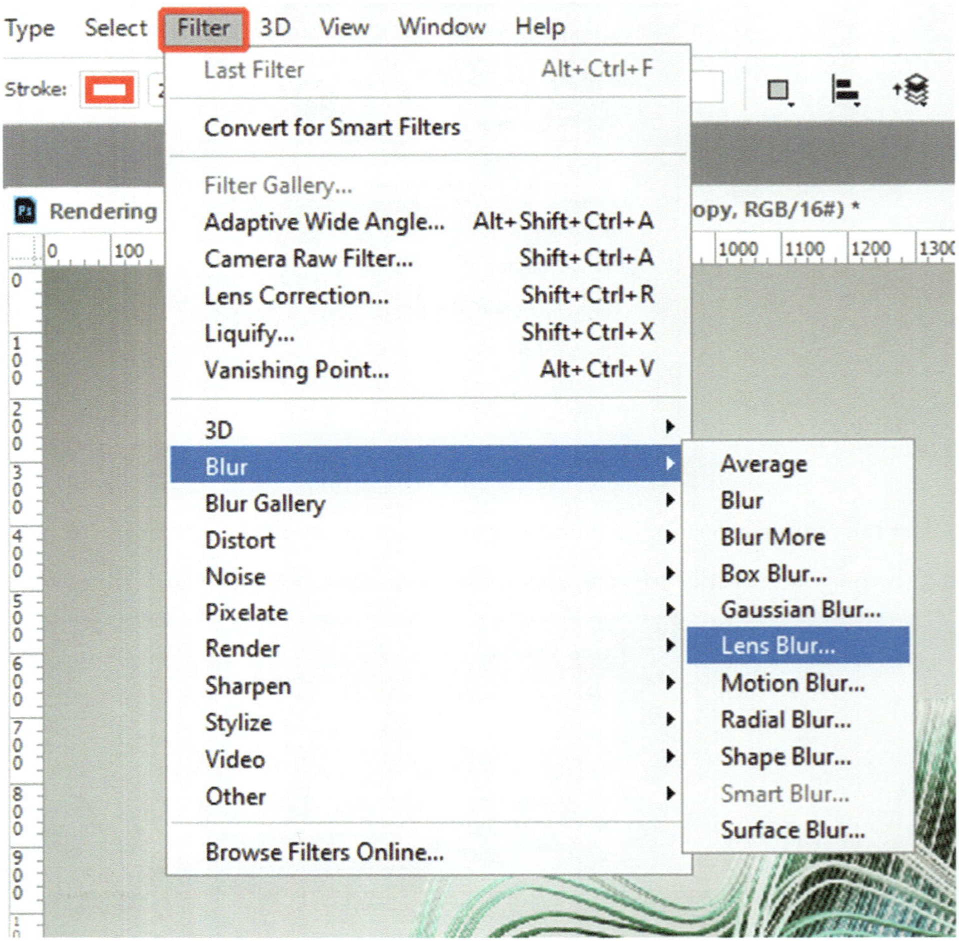

Choose the Lens Blur option

In the Lens Blur dialog, load the Depth Map previously saved (DOF) and adjust the Blur Focal Distance and Radius functions.

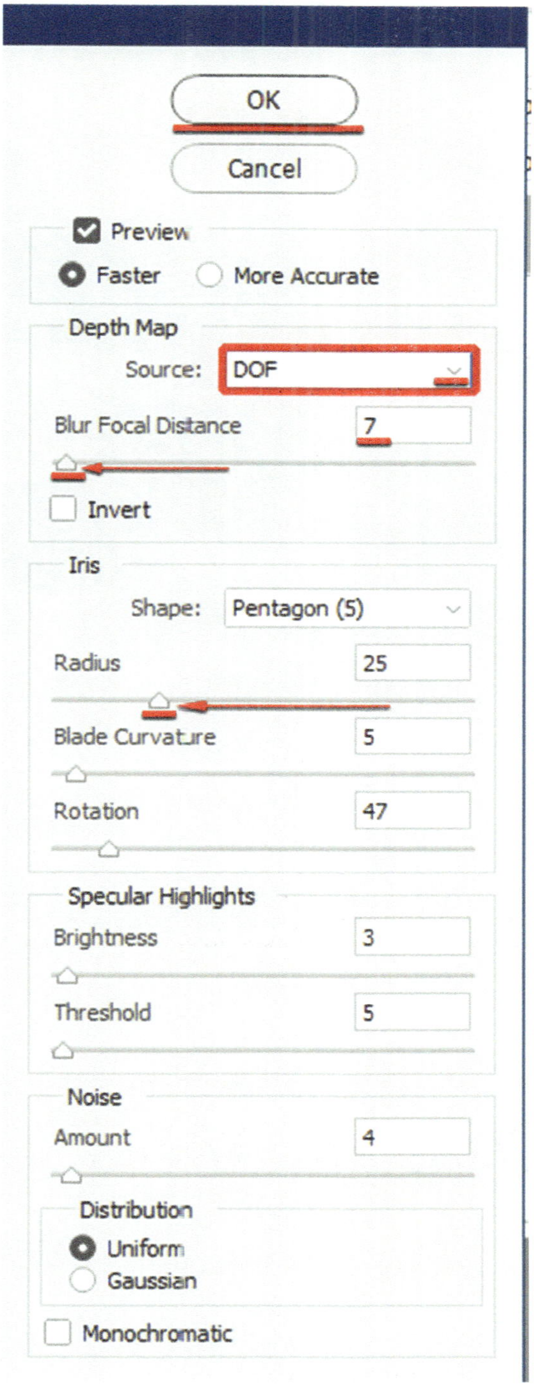
OK
Cancel
Preview
Faster
More Accurate
Depth Map
Source:
DOF
Blur Focal Distance
7
Invert
Iris
Shape:
Pentagon (5)
Radius
25
Blade Curvature
5
Rotation
47
Specular Highlights
Brightness
3
Threshold
5
Noise
Amount
4
Distribution
Uniform
Gaussian
Monochromatic

Choose and adjust the Lens Blur option

VRayNormals

VRayNormals render element

This amazing render element is often used as a final step to add extra highlights to the overall render.

To do so, place the VRayNormals render element on top of your final post-processed image. And add the Levels adjustment layer.

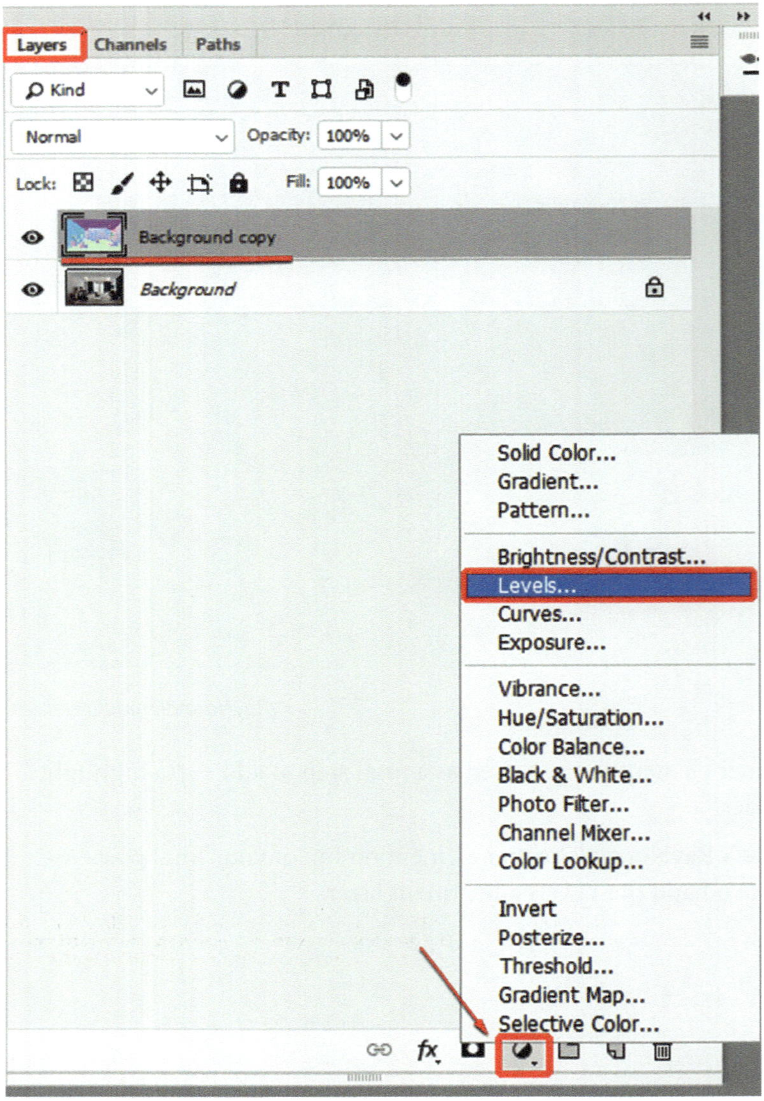

Add the Levels adjustment layer

To increase contrast between the colors displayed, move the Levels midpoint to the far right (0.09).

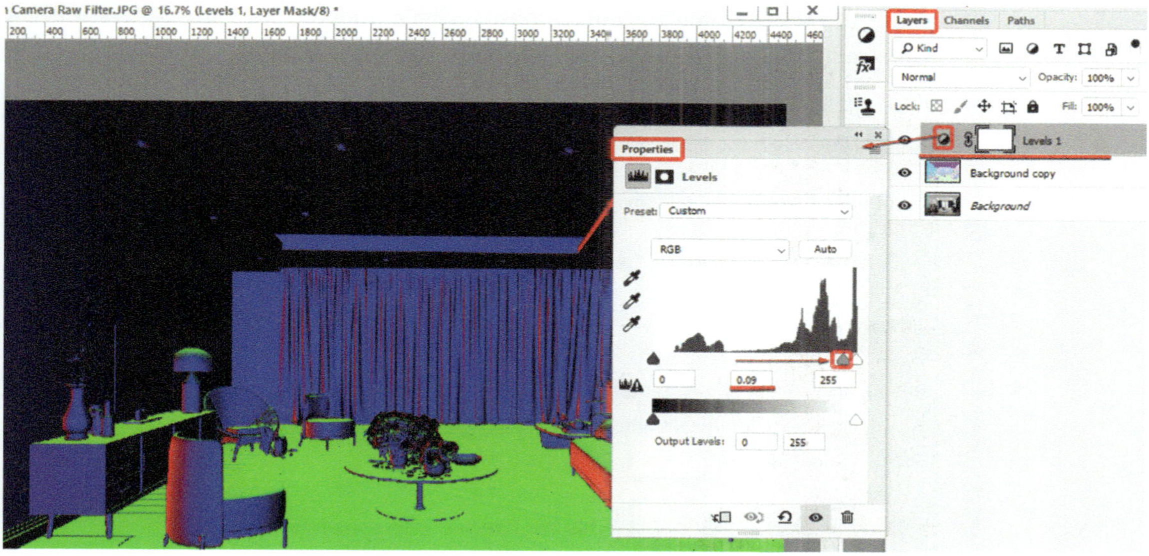

Increase Levels contrast

To restrict the Levels effects to the layer directly below it (VRayNormals), simply hold down the Alt key and hover over the Levels adjustment layer until you see the clipping mask sign.

While holding down the Alt key, click to clip it to the layer directly below it. The Levels adjustment layer is now only affecting the VRayNormals layer.

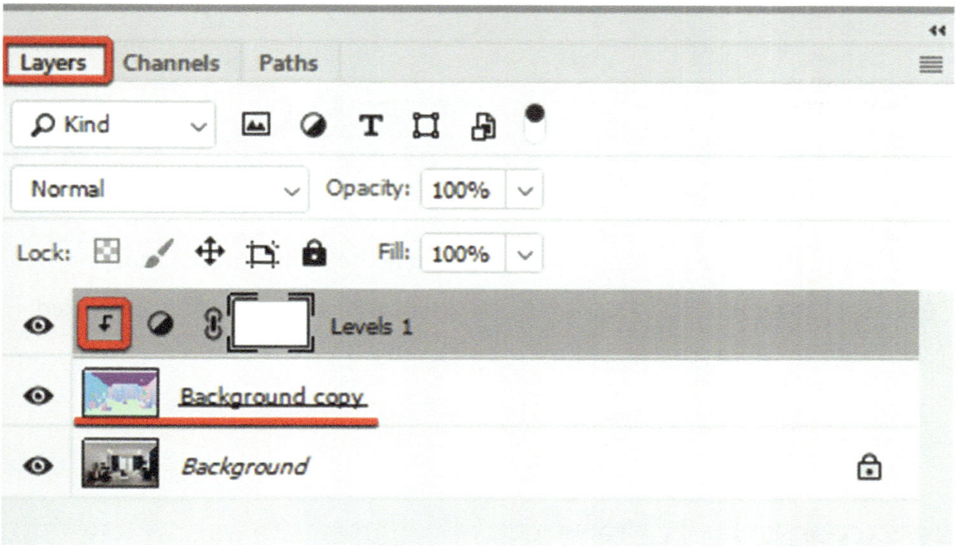

Levels clipped to the VRayNormals layers

Next, Add the Hue/Saturation, Channel Mixer, and another Hue/Saturation adjustment layer on top. Ensure to clip all to the layers below.

All Adjustment layers are now connected to the VRayNormals layer below.

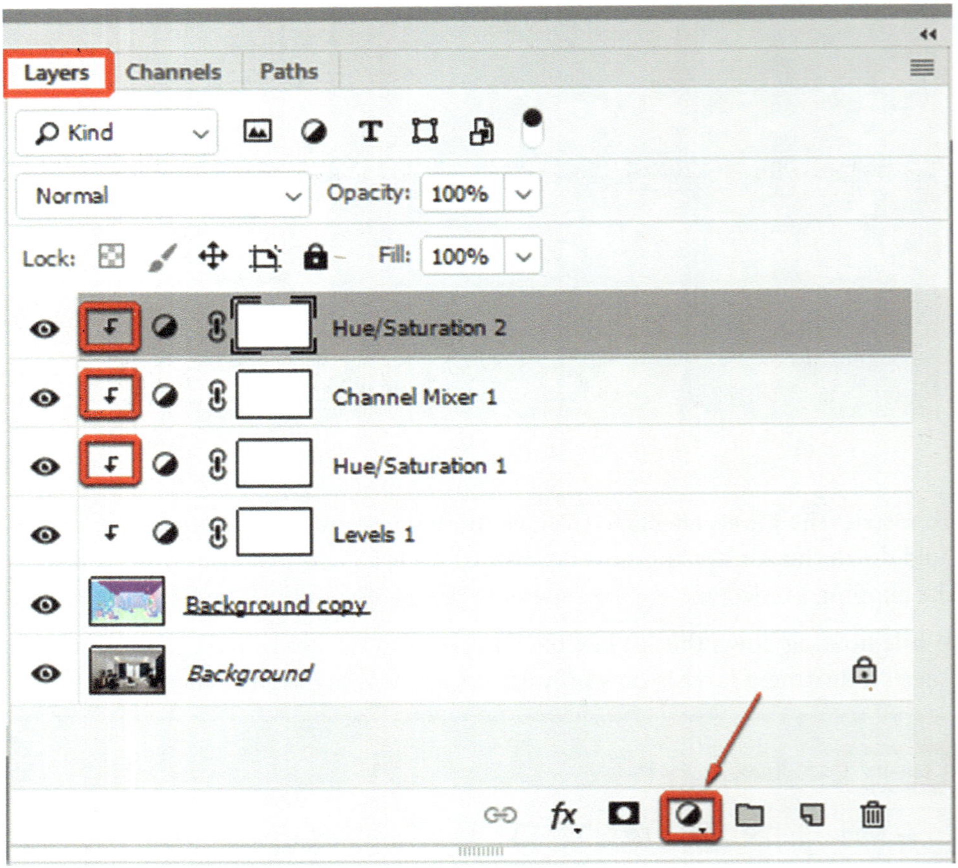

New Adjustment layers added

Next, select the Channel Mixer layer and enable the Monochrome function.

To adjust the highlighted areas of the image, begin moving the sliders for Red, Green, and Blue.

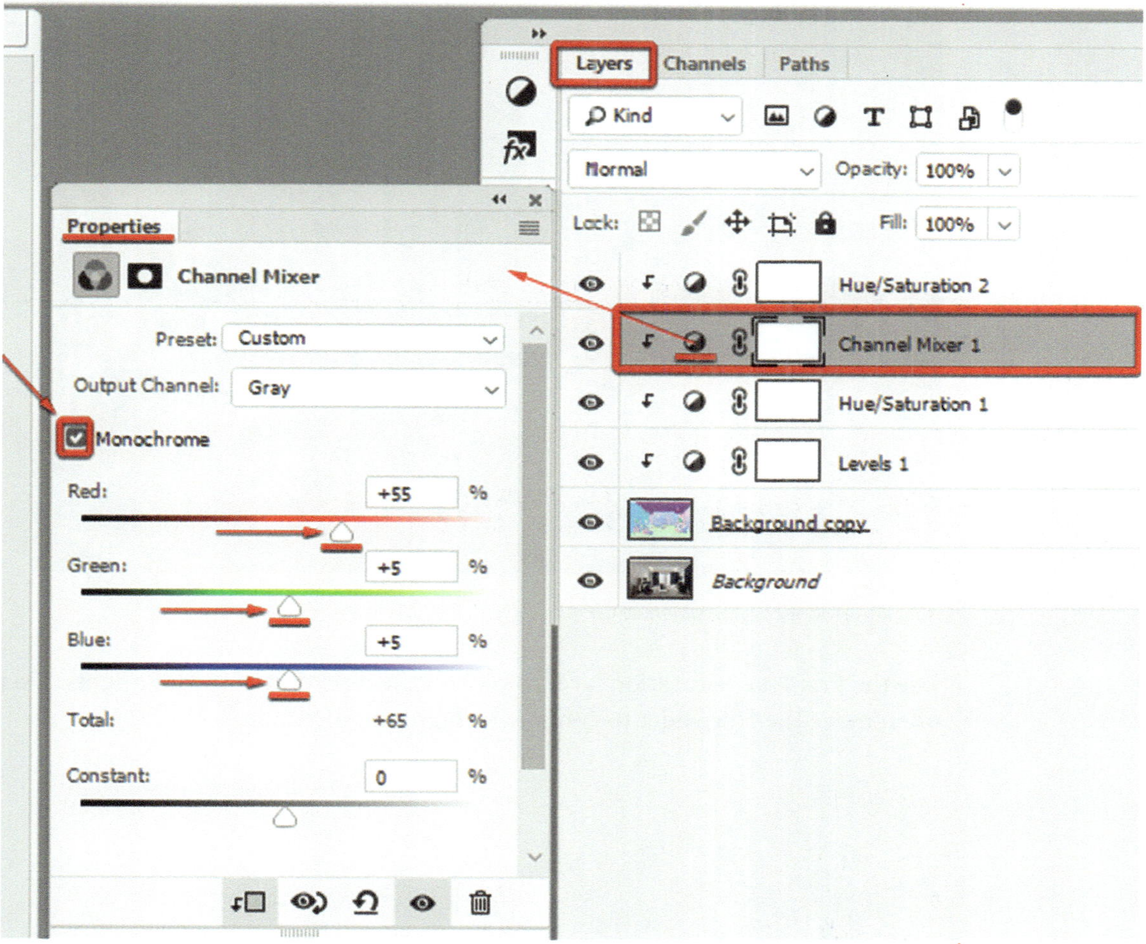
Layers
Channels
Paths
Kind
Normal
Opacity: 100%
Lock:
Fill: 100%
Hue/Saturation 2
Channel Mixer 1
Hue/Saturation 1
Levels 1
Background copy
Background
Properties
Channel Mixer
Preset: Custom
Output Channel: Gray
Monochrome
Red: +55 %
Green: +5 %
Blue: +5 %
Total: +65 %
Constant: 0 %

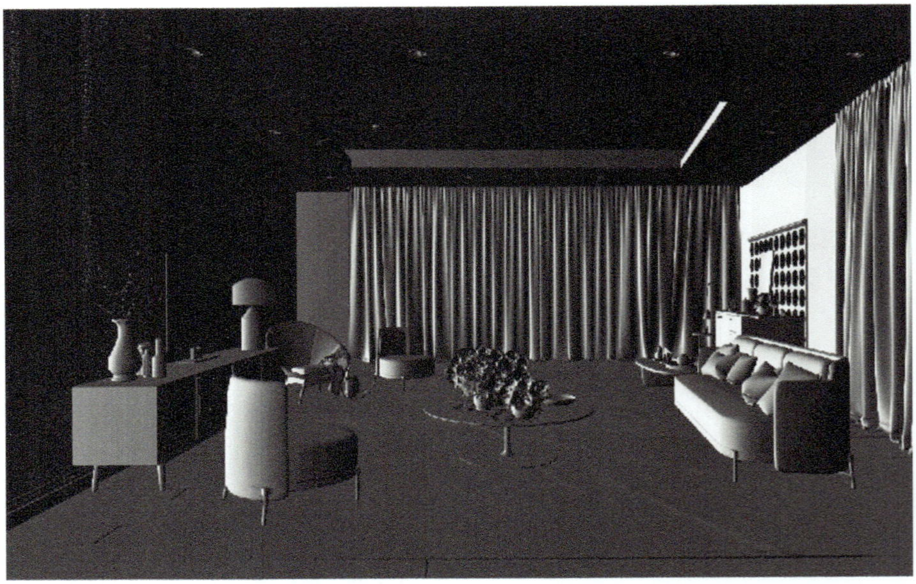

Adjust the Monochrome sliders of Channel Mixer

Use the first Hue/Saturation layer to control the direction of the highlights. Users often move the Hue slider to control the highlight direction.

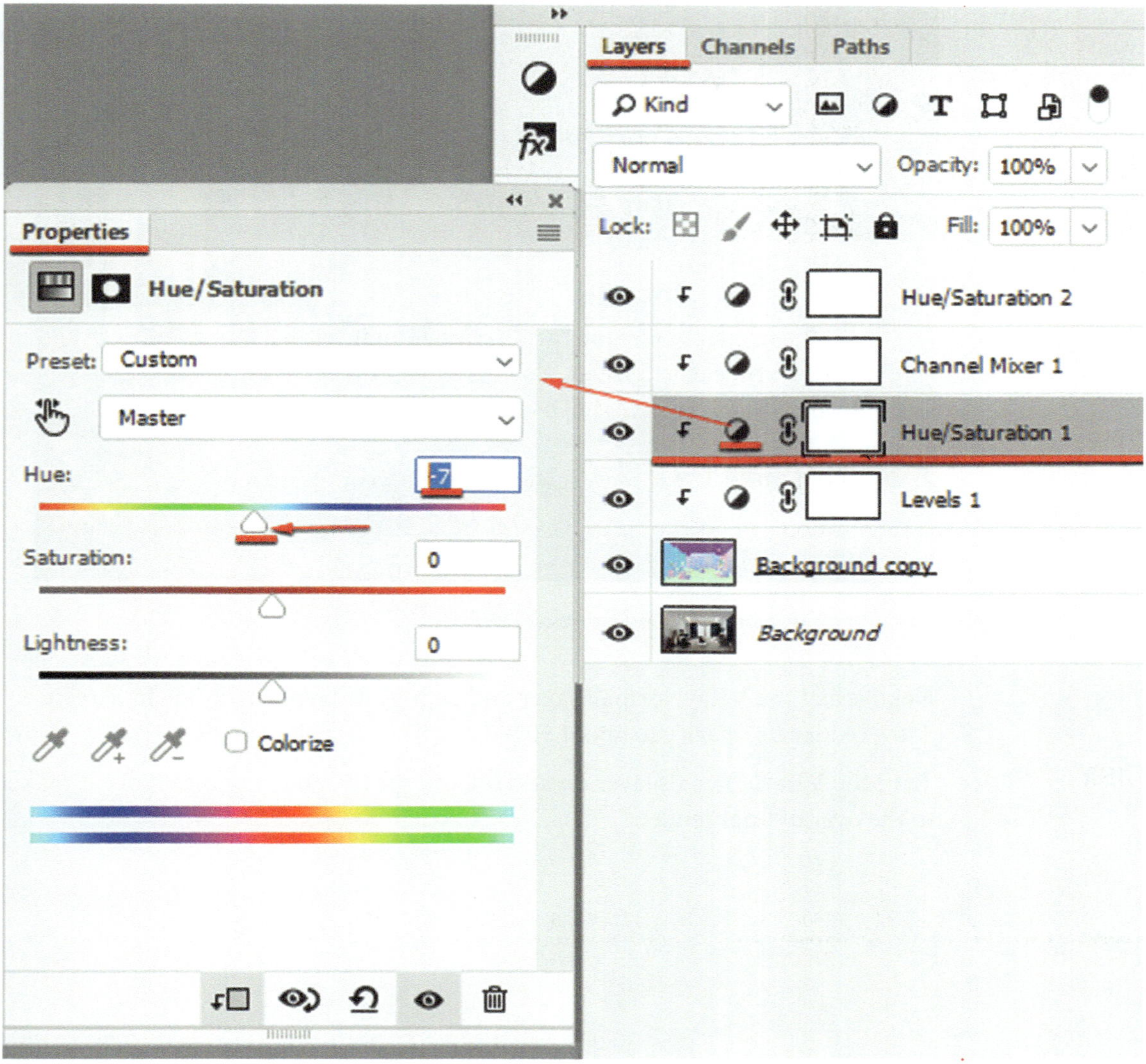
Layers
Channels
Paths
Kind
Normal
Opacity: 100%
Lock:
Fill: 100%
Hue/Saturation 2
Channel Mixer 1
Hue/Saturation 1
Levels 1
Background copy
Background
Properties
Hue/Saturation
Preset: Custom
Master
Hue:
-7
Saturation:
0
Lightness:
0
Colorize

Control the highlights with Hue/Saturation slider

Next, select the VRayNormals layer and change its blending mode to Screen. Also, reduce its opacity to about 50%.

Turn the VRayNormals layer on and off and see the amazing difference it makes to the overall final render.

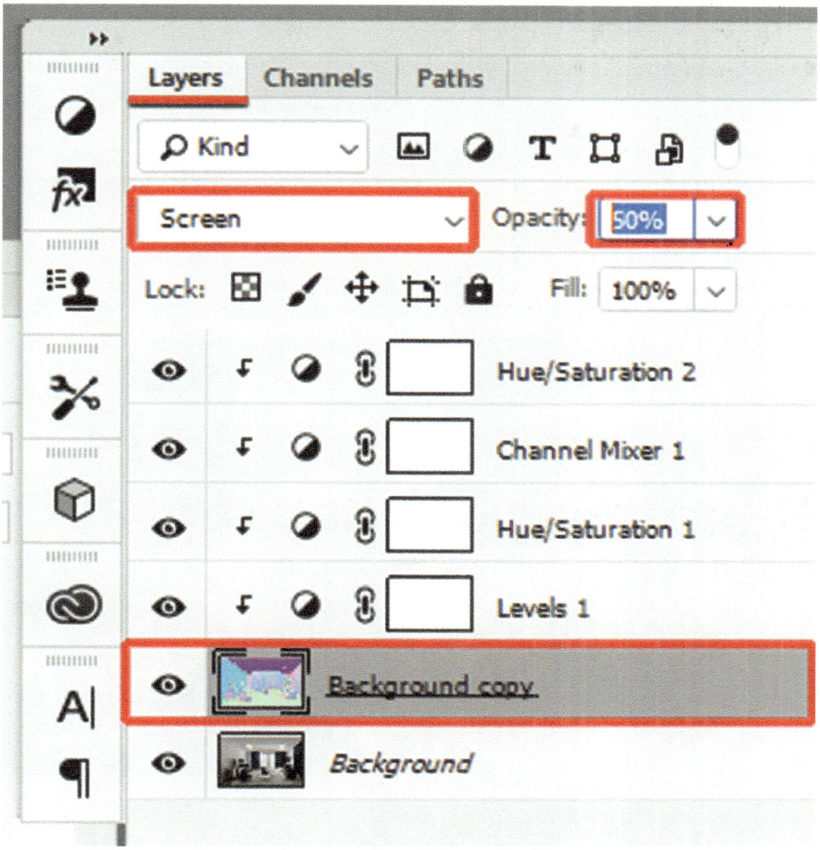
Layers
Channels
Paths
Kind
Screen
Opacity: 50%
Lock:
Fill: 100%
Hue/Saturation 2
Channel Mixer 1
Hue/Saturation 1
Levels 1
Background copy
Background

Change the VRayNormals layer blending mode to a Screen type

Furthermore, you can add a layer mask to the VRayNormals layer, and brush away highlights on unwanted areas.

To do so, while the VRayNormals layer is still selected, click on the layer mask button to add it to the selected layer.

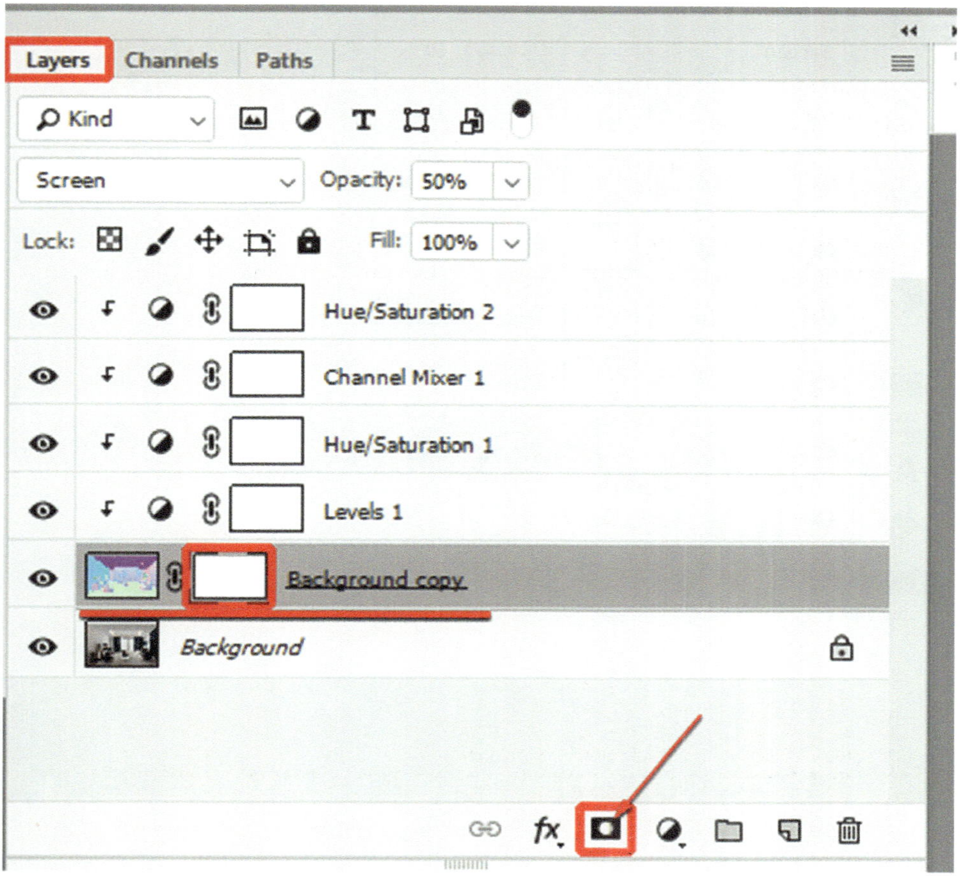

Added Layer mask

Layer masks work best with black and white colors in the background toolbar (X). With a brush tool enabled (B), black/dark colors take away pixels with each brush stroke.

White/brighter colors do the opposite.

Before you begin brushing away pixels (B), ensure the Layer mask is selected and the brush opacity is set. The lower the brush opacity value, the slower the pixels will be taken away.

A brush opacity set to 100% immediately takes away pixels.

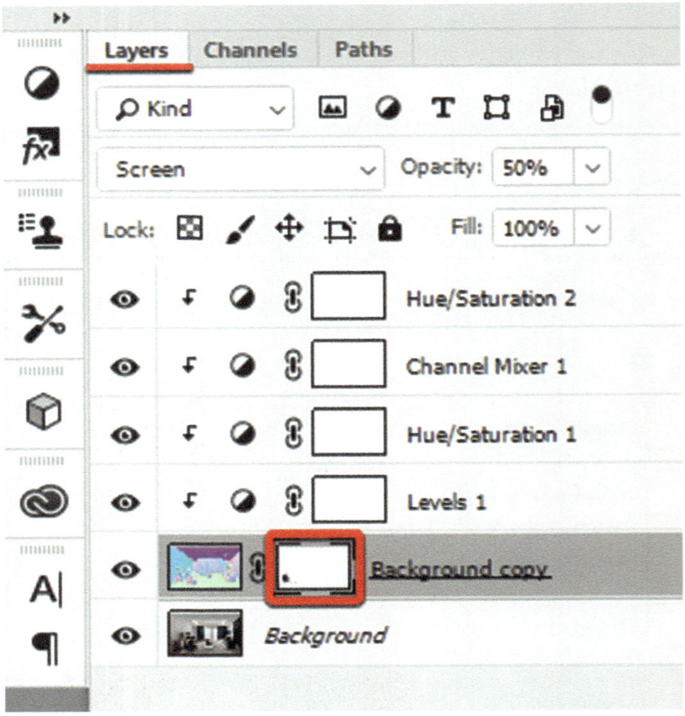

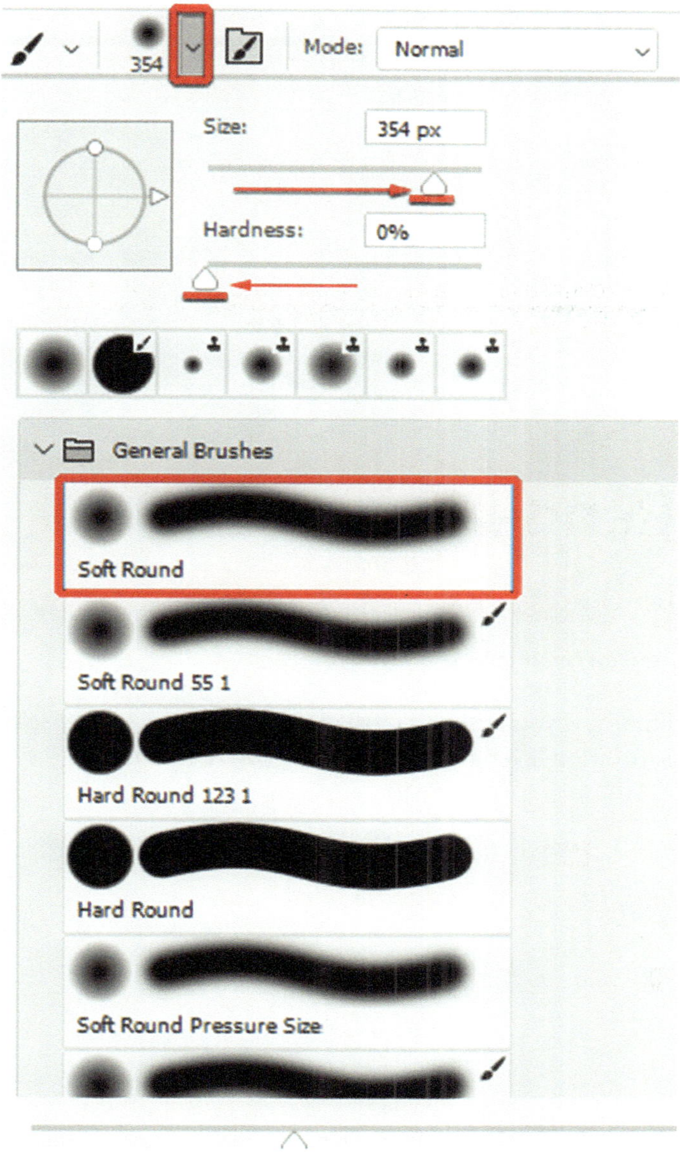
354
Mode:
Normal
Size:
354 px
Hardness:
0%
General Brushes
Soft Round
Soft Round 55 1
Hard Round 123 1
Hard Round
Soft Round Pressure Size

User Layer mask to brush away pixels

Finally, if you wish to colorize the highlights, simply select the top Hue/ Saturation layer and enable the Colorize function.

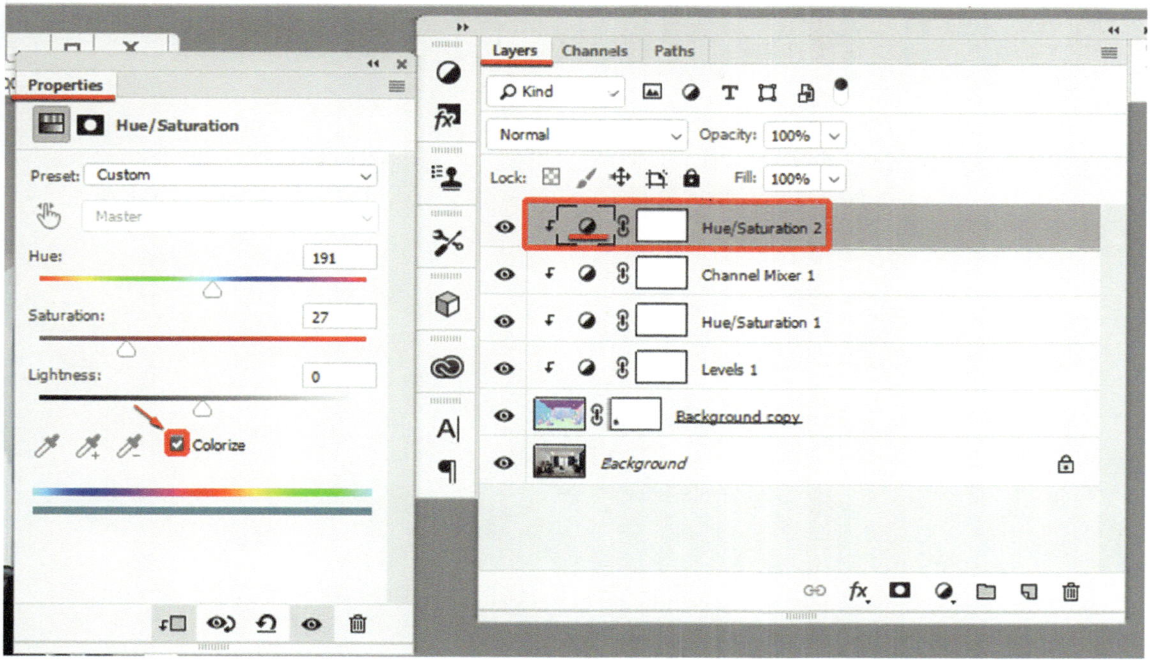

Colorize the highlights with Hue/Saturation

Chapters 8, 9, and 12 will take users through the process of using some of these render elements.

Conclusion

This chapter has introduced and navigated users through some of the key VRay rendering parameters and render elements.

For more detailed information about VRay rendering parameters, please visit the following VRay official website:

http://docs.chaosgroup.com/

5

Tips and Tricks

5 Tips and Tricks

Always "Adopt the File's Unit Scale" when opening a new file. This will prevent scenes from being rescaled and looking inaccurate.

However, there are only a "handful" of exceptions when one might be required to choose "Rescale the File Objects to the System Unit Scale" option.

It only happens when the incoming file is not accurate and requires rescaling.

One should also use the same approach for incoming gamma settings.

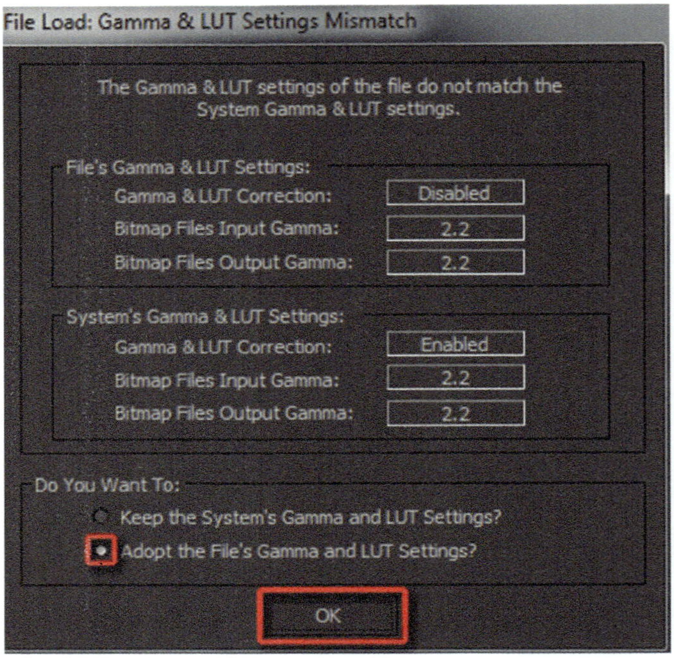

Rescale the File Objects to the System Unit Scale

Before importing 2D drawings (DWGs) into 3ds max, it's important to do the following:

- Ensure to have the original 2D drawing completely "cleaned/stripped" from AutoCAD or micro-station (e.g., omit unnecessary text and other layers). This action will reduce the incoming file size, when imported into max.
- Drawings are often created far away from the 0.0.0 point; therefore, 3ds max and most 3d applications will have difficulty in displaying/representing lines or objects accurately at such distances.

  Therefore, it's imperative to reposition the drawings as close to 0.0.0 point as possible, prior to importing them into 3ds max.

- One of the most popular techniques to reposition the drawings is to first create a dummy/point/line at 0.0.0 point.

  Select the drawing layers from the file, and move/snap them onto the previously created dummy/point/line (i.e., at 0.0.0 point).

- Once the drawings are close/or at the 0.0.0 point, it's important to save the file under a different name, to prevent overwriting the original file.

  Prior to importing the Cad file into max, ensure to bind all files in AutoCAD.

  To bind Xreferenced files, simply type in "Xref" to enable its dialog box.

  Next, in the dialog box, select the relevant files and right click to enable its pop-up list. The pop-up list should give the user the option to click on the "bind" function, or not.

  In some cases, one may be required to explode objects in AutoCAD in order to ensure that specific objects/lines are imported, and without artifacts.

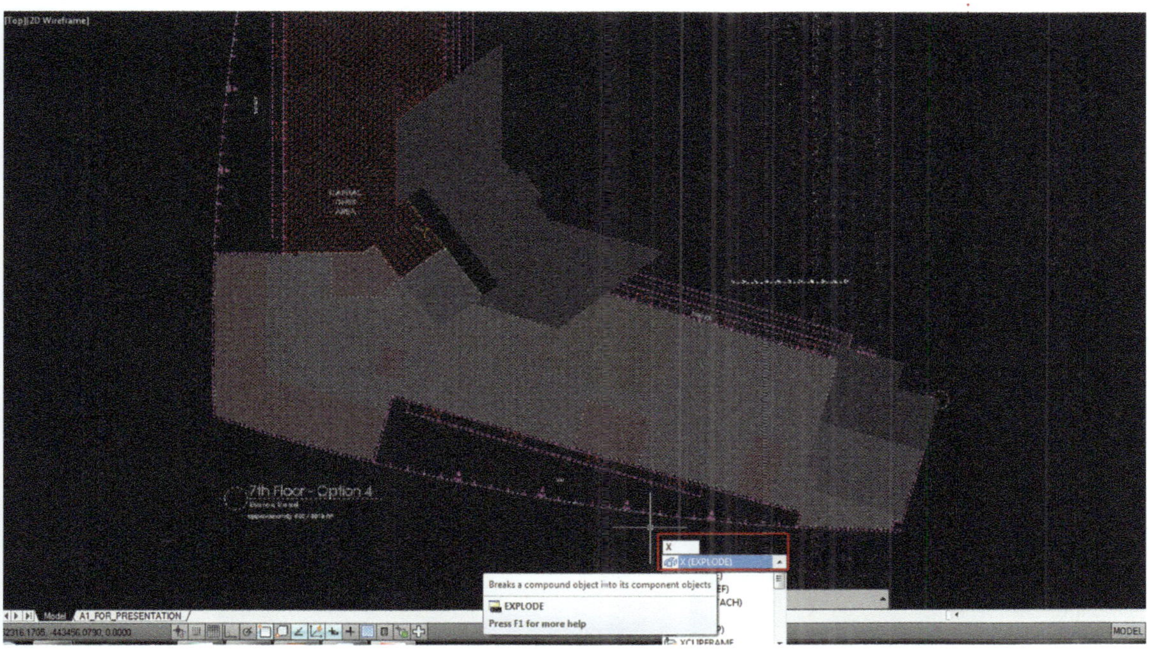

Explode objects in AutoCAD

There are occasions when drawings will come with multiple elevations and sections—therefore, unwise to be imported as a whole in 3ds max.

5 Tips and Tricks

The common approach is to first use the rectangular selection (click and drag to region select a specific area), followed by typing the "Ctrl+C" to copy the selection, creating a new document by typing the "Ctrl+N," and pasting the previously copied drawing to its original position in the new document by typing "Paste+O" + "Enter" button + double click the "middle mouse button" anywhere in the viewport.

- In MicroStation, professionals often select the "fence" tool, draw around the desired area, and type in the "FF=" to save the drawing under a different name.

Note that, by default MicroStation is set to automatically save the file every time a change is made to the drawing. For this reason, one is required to "fence save" first, prior to moving/snapping the drawings to the dummy line/point/object.

It's worth mentioning that the DGN (i.e., MicroStation) file has to be saved as DWG first, prior to being imported into 3ds max.

- It's also important to have the metric system setup (e.g., millimeters, meters), as opposed to keeping the default system to "Generic Units."

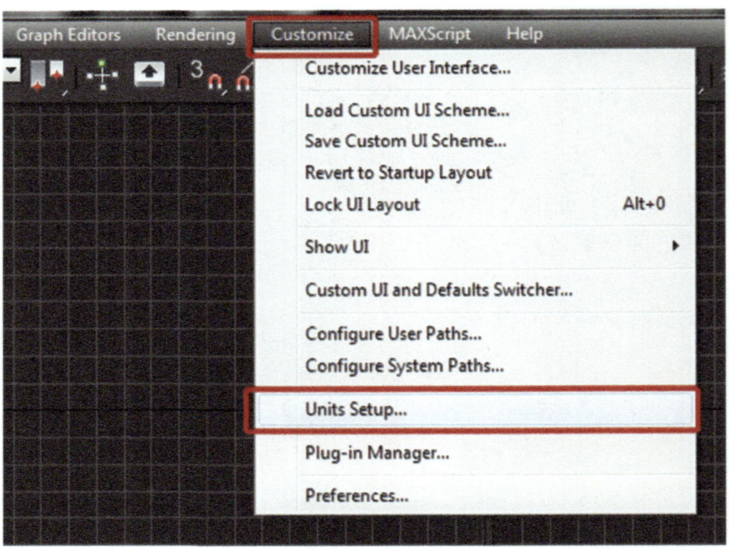

Open units setup

Choose the metric unit scale

Also one needs to set the system to "Respect System Units in Files." These two functions will prove vital in ensuring that incoming files are not disproportionate in size and/or automatically rescaled.

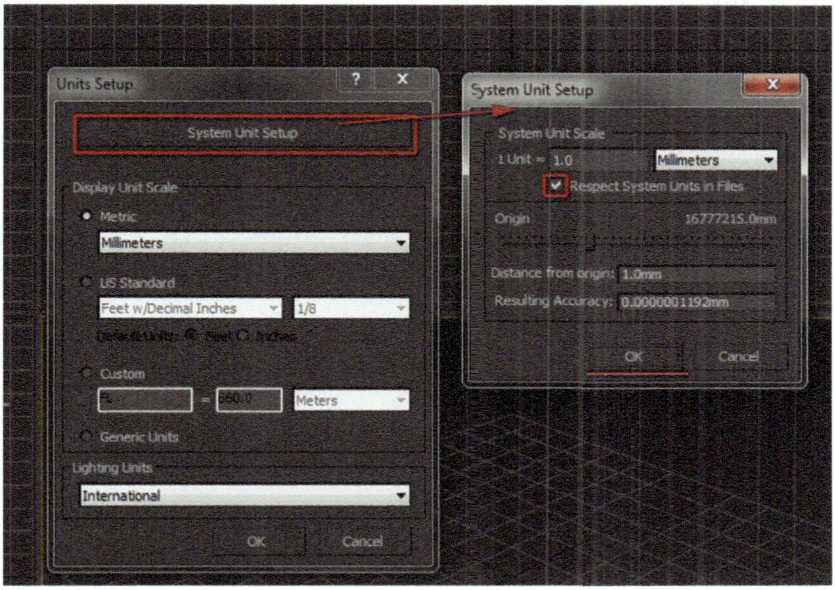

Choose Respect System Units in Files

Furthermore, one should pay extra attention to the "model scale" group in the "AutoCAD DWG/DFX Import Options" dialog box.

The "Incoming file units" function should be left untouched.

Simply enable or disable the "Rescale" function, depending on the total value of the "Resulting model size" function.

The rule of thumb is to always choose the smaller metric value displayed on the "Resulting model size" text field.

Also, the "Curve steps" values should be increased if the smooth curves of the incoming drawings are not accurate in the main 3d software. This function will essentially increase the number of vertices in such areas.

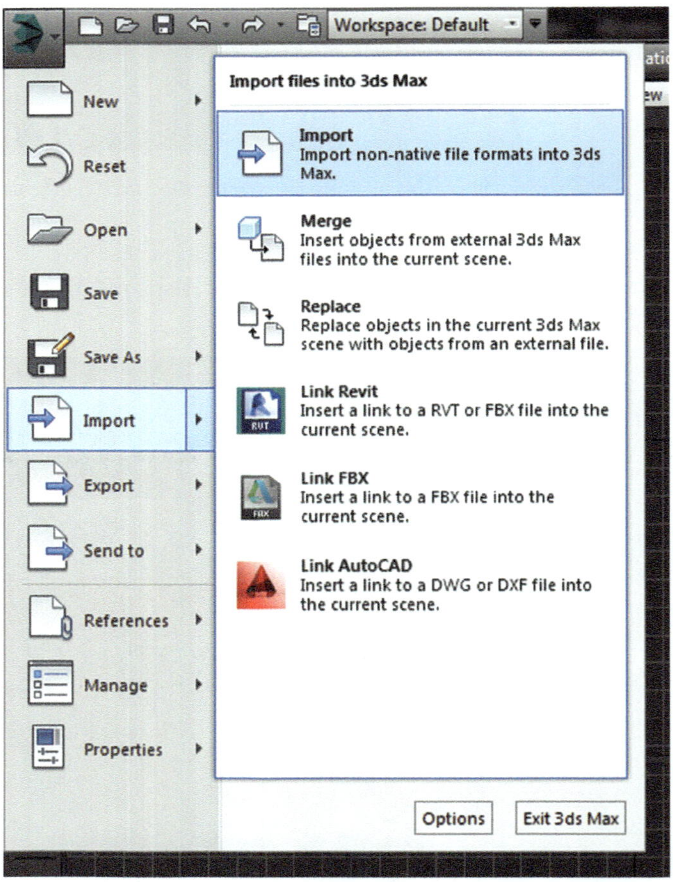

Import function

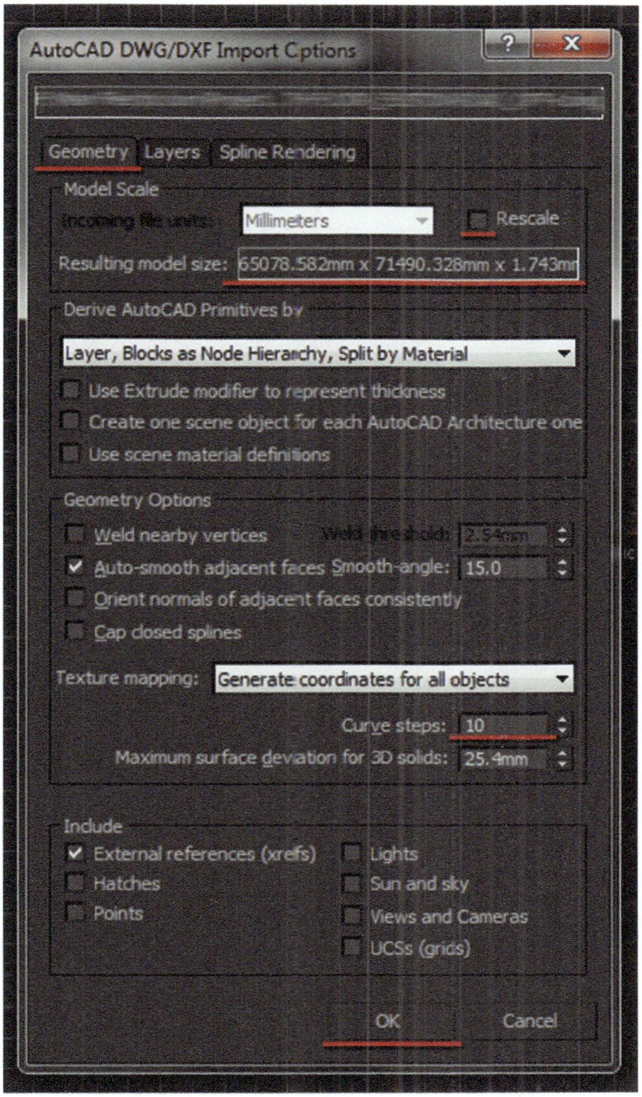

AutoCAD DWG/DXF Import Options

Once the drawing is imported into the scene, it's common practice to quickly check the dimensions of walls, stairs, chairs, etc., with the "Tape" helper. This precautionary measure is to ensure that the scale of the imported file is correct.

Doors are often 2.2 m in height; chairs 400/600 mm in width, etc. Some professionals find it easier to continuously switch the metric "Display Unit Scale" between meters, millimeters, centimeters, etc., depending on the amount of value required to input (e.g., small values = millimeters; large values = meters).

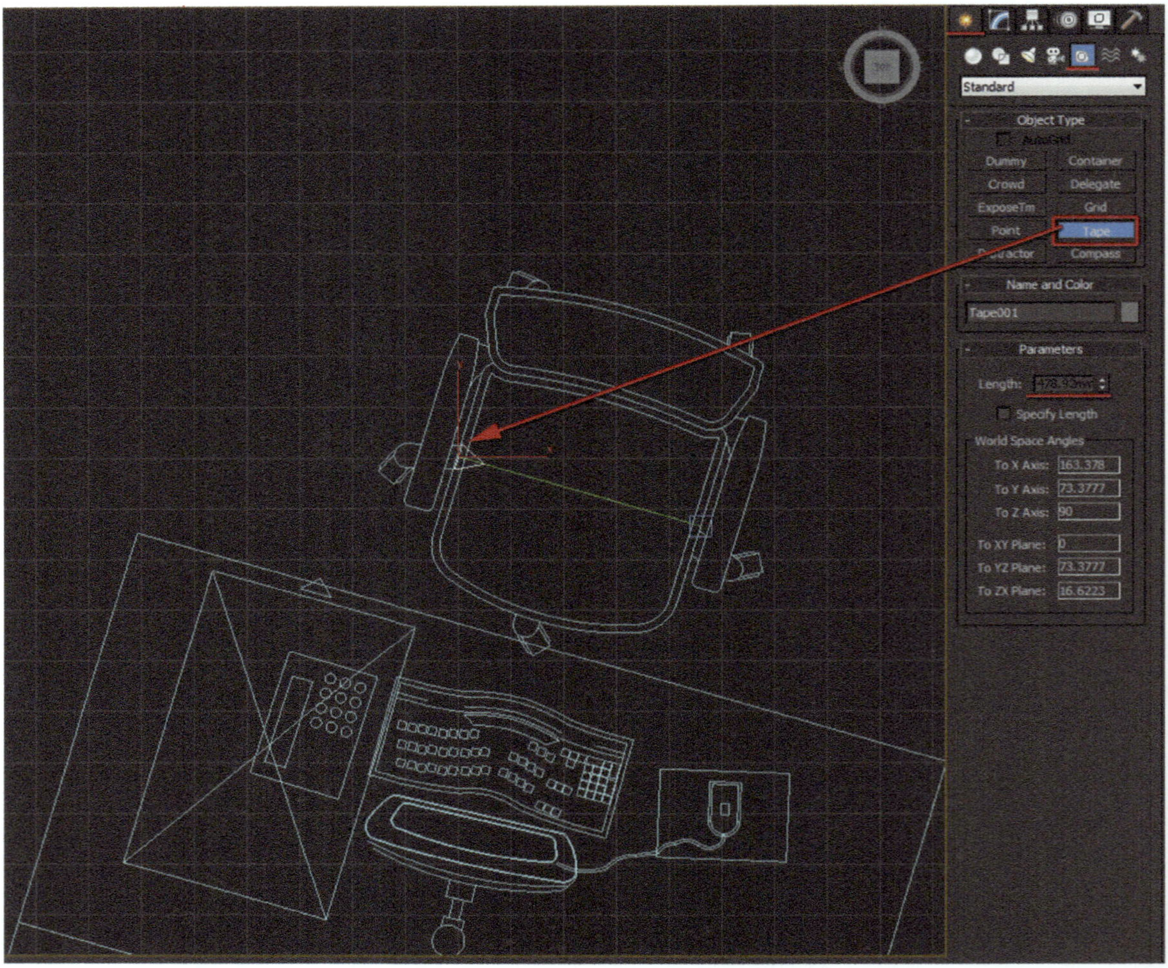

Use the Tape tool to measure scene elements

- Once the drawing is in the scene, select it in its entirety by first pressing the H to open the Select From Scene dialog, followed by clicking on the Select All button and OK to close the dialog.

With all objects in the scene selected, one can then group it.

It is common practice to name the group in accordance to its original name (e.g., 2D_DWG_Level 1).

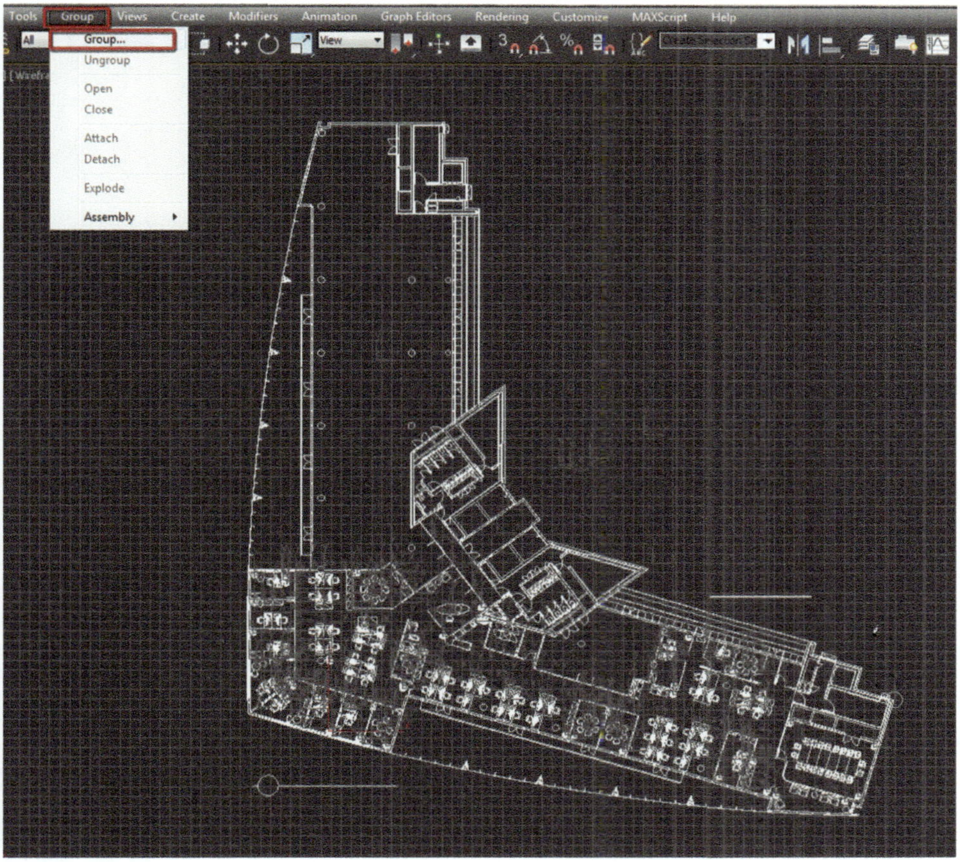

Group DWGs

Some users also choose to create a layer under a similar name. However, the only drawback is the fact that all the drawing content will be culminated into one single color.

To prevent this artifact, simply place the script under the name of color layer in the following folder:

C:\Program Files\Autodesk\3ds max 2014\scripts\Startup

To create new layer, simply select the relevant objects in the scene, followed by opening the layer dialog, clicking the Create New Layer button, and renaming it, if necessary.

When renaming the layers of objects, one should create names such as "#3D_DWG_Ceiling...".

This is to ensure layers of relevance always stay on top of the list, as it can easily be overlooked/lost among the other named layers.

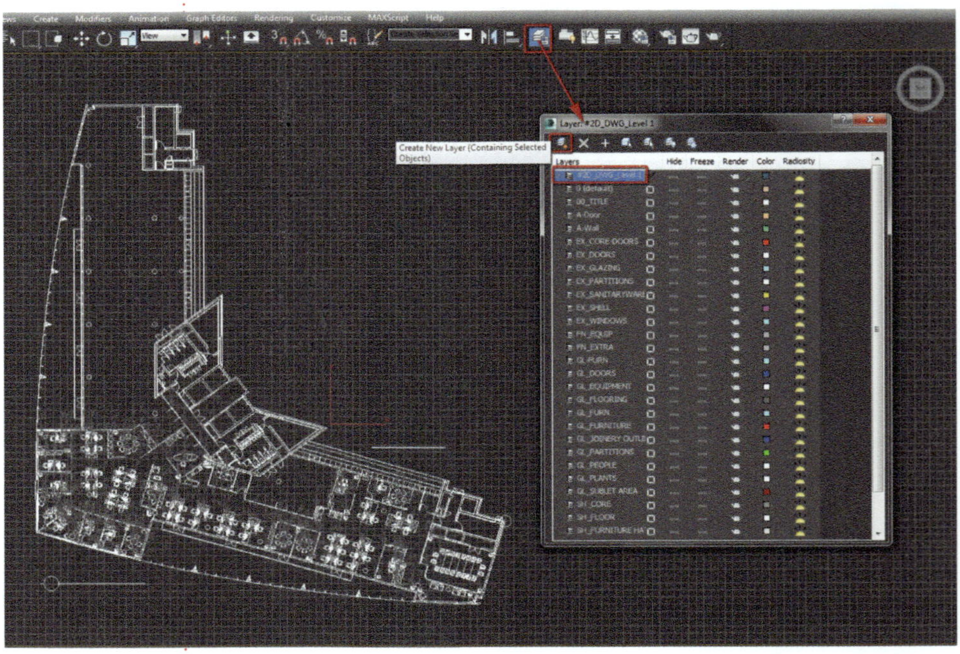

Create New Layer dialog

To edit, move, or delete layer/folder, one has to select it from the dialog list first (e.g., highlighted).

To rename a layer/folder from the list, one is required to double click it, followed by typing in the name.

Some studios find it easier to work with layers mainly, due to its ease of use and its flexibility to provide control over the contents in the scene.

While selecting an object in the scene and creating a new layer, the dialog box adds/moves the selected object of the list into to the newly created layer.

It works almost like a folder that one can select as a group, or to select individual objects from its content list, to turn on/off, to freeze, etc.

When a layer/folder is created and the objects are automatically moved into this newly created layer/folder, the main "layer" dialog box list will still retain the unused copies of the objects names in the list.

These unused names/layers can be found on the root of the dialog box, or inside another layer/folder.

It is also common practice to delete all unused layers/objects from the list in order to clean/tidy up the dialog box.

The layer under the name of "0(default)" is the default layer created automatically, and *cannot*/should *not* be deleted.

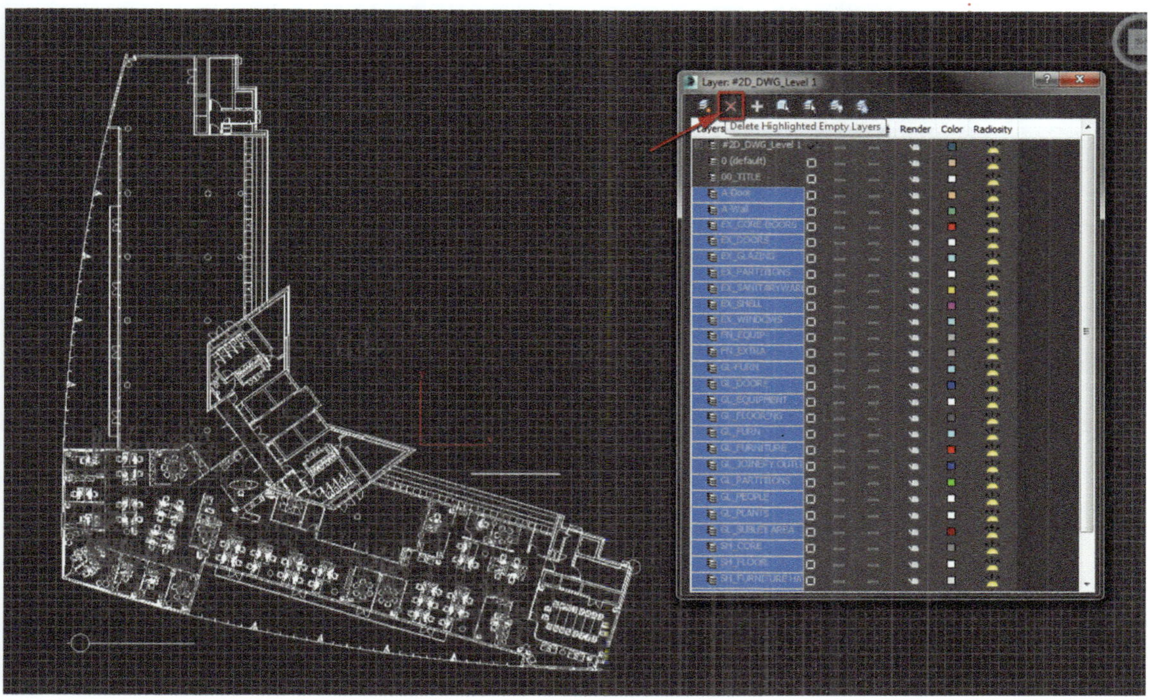

Delete unused layers

If the user doesn't manually create a new layer/folder, most objects created in the scene will be automatically added/moved into this default layer/folder.

Although one can select and move the contents of this default layer/folder, users are unable to delete it (e.g., "0(default)," even when empty.

As with all new layers/folders created by the user, one is able to select and move its content into a different layer/folder, and delete the empty layer/folder thereafter.

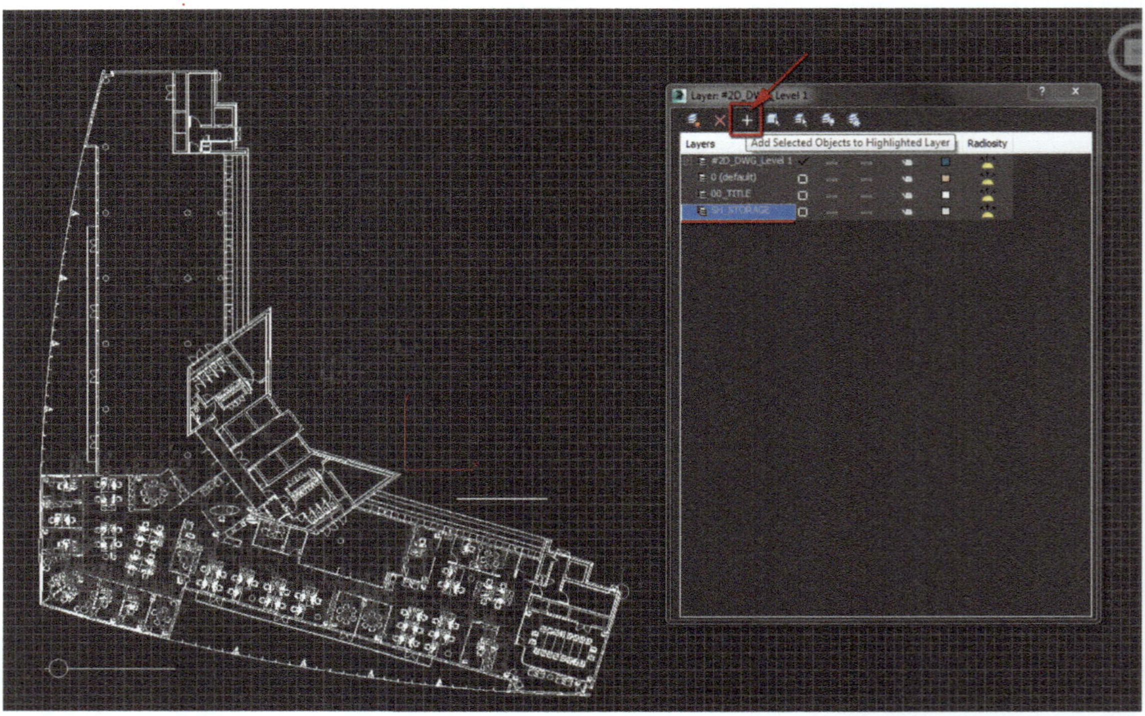

Adding selected objects in the scene into the highlighted layer

- Before beginning to trace the drawing to create 3d objects, it is imperative to do the following:
- Set up the snap tools parameters and the toggle to 2.5 (2d).

Since the drawings are in 2d (e.g., splines), professionals usually change the "snaps toggle" from the default "3" to "2.5," by simply left clicking and holding down on the tools' icon from the "main toolbar."

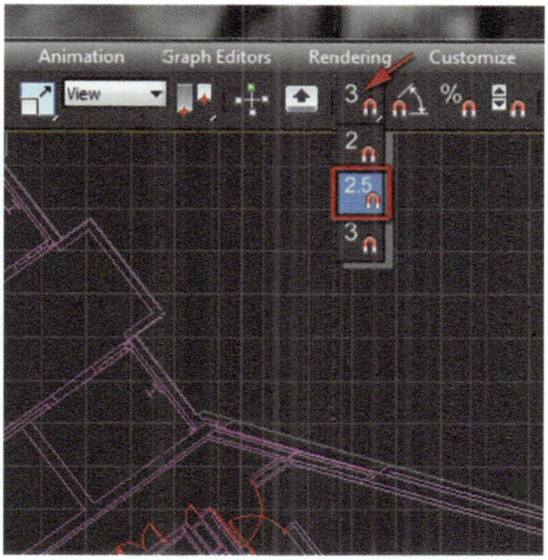

Choose the 2.5 toggle

To quickly snap the splines while tracing the drawing, one is required to change some key parameters:

Right click on the "snaps toggle" icon from the "main toolbar." Its dialog box should pop up.

Enable the "vertex" and "endpoint" functions.

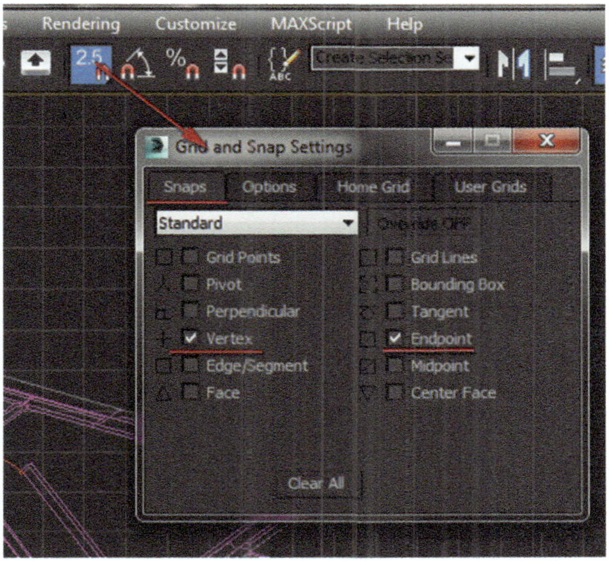

Right click to open its Grid and Snap Settings dialog

Also, in the "options" tab, enable the "snap to frozen objects" function. This will ensure that even frozen drawings/splines can be traced and snapped onto.

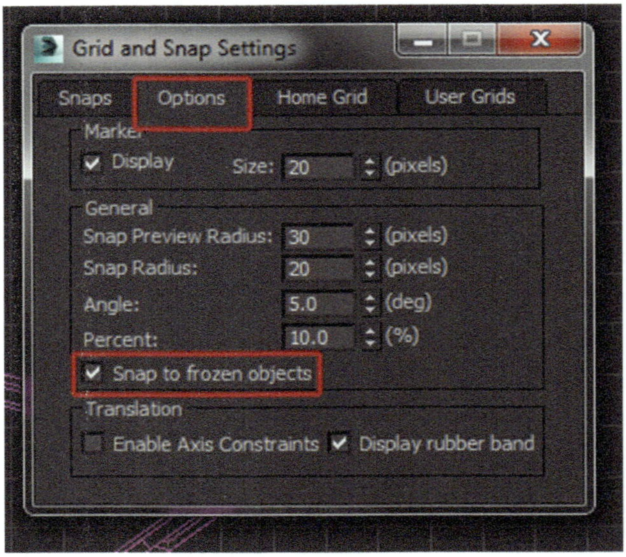

Enable the snap to frozen objects function

Some Users may be wondering why not simply extrude the 2d drawing lines in 3ds max?

Most drawings' vertices are not welded (e.g., opened), and often *not* drawn on the same plane/level, and therefore difficult to extrude as a whole. Even when welding vertices globally with a target distance value.

Welding the drawings manually often takes much longer than tracing them.

DWG plans are always more accurate than the elevations or sections.

To ensure the elevations and sections line up with the plan, one should trace/draw the simplest area of the drawing plan that is relevant to the section or elevation first. Extrude it thereafter.

Next, position the elevation or section to match this newly created object. One should use the same procedure to position the following elevations and sections.

There are times when it's difficult to trace and create objects from rotated DWG drawings.

To make this process easier, users are often required to create a grid helper from the rotated DWG drawing and use it as the basis to trace and create objects from a specific angle.

- The following step is to use the, Auto grid pivot point, script to automatically create and align a grid to any particular spline or object angle.

One should start by selecting the relevant spline in the viewport, followed by clicking on the MAXScript main toolbar and choosing the Run Script option.

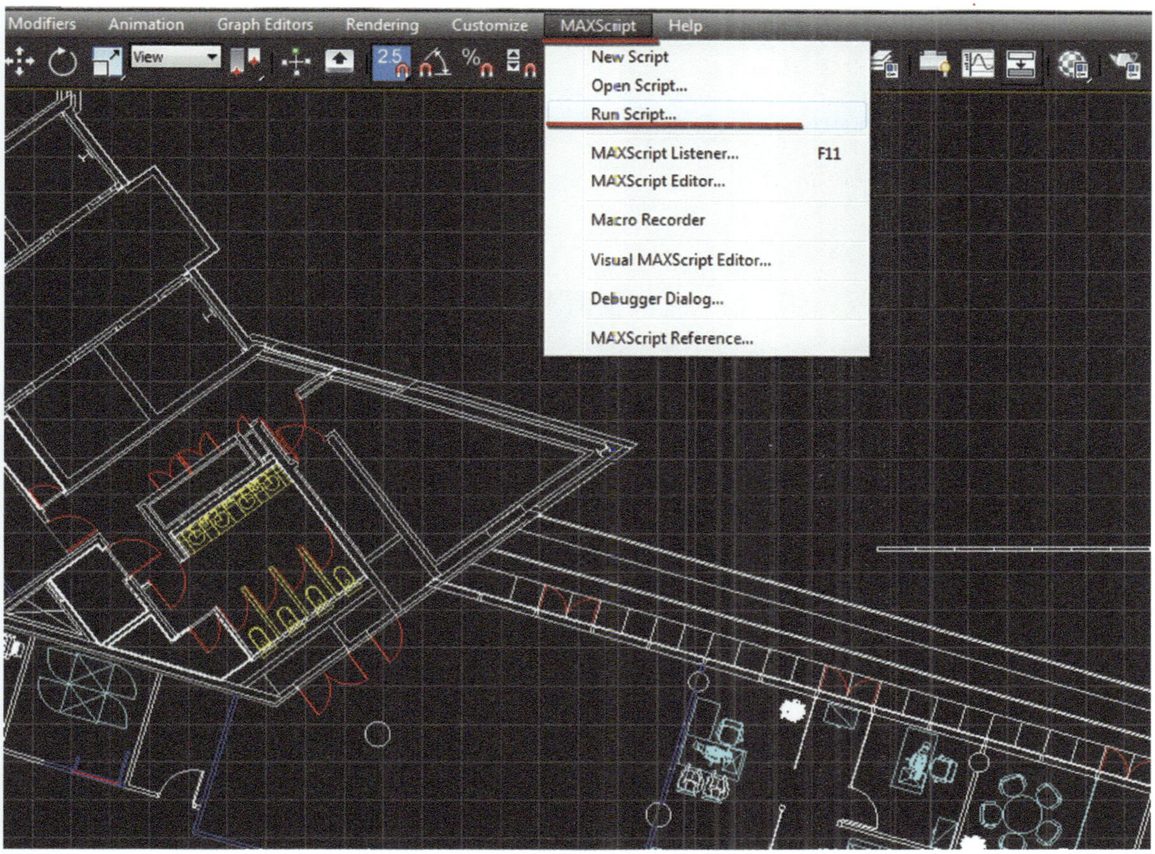

Choose the Run Script option

Next, locate and open the Auto grid pivot point, script.

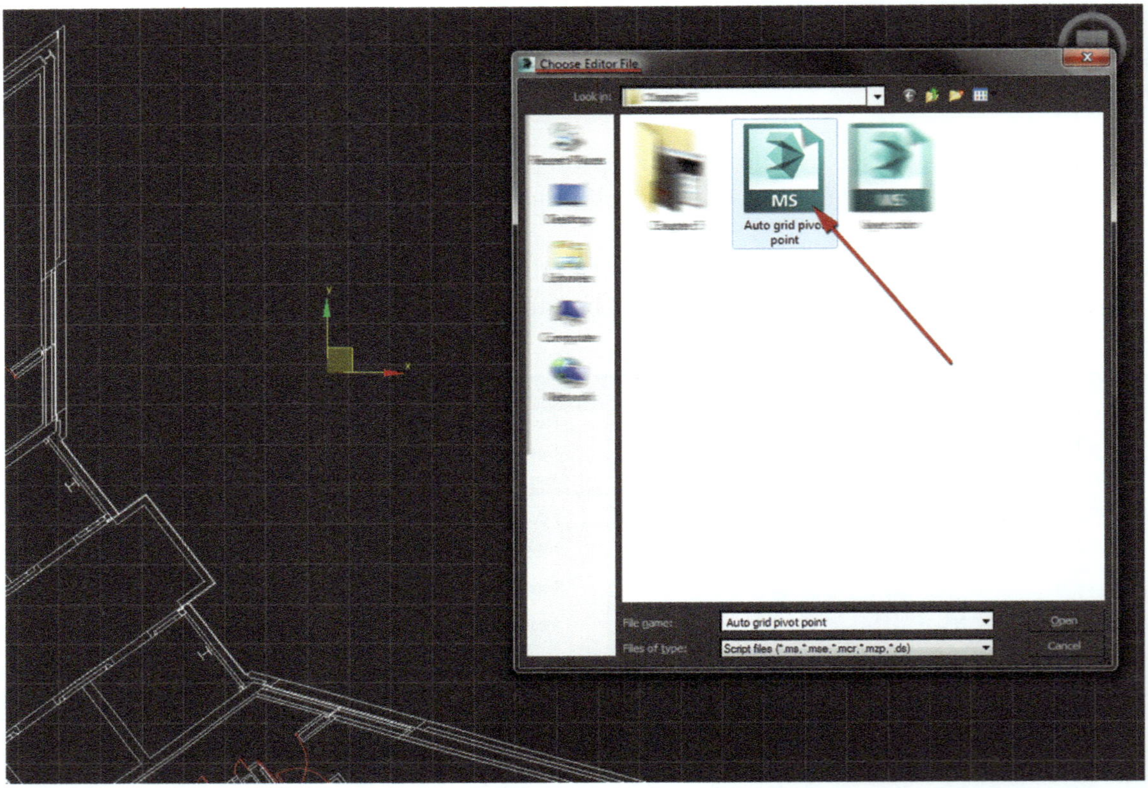

Open the Auto grid pivot point script

The grid should appear and activate itself automatically.

If the grid is too small, one can use its Modify parameters to increase it.

Layer:EX_SHELLGrid
Modifier List
Grid
Parameters
Grid Size
Length: 13446.72
Width: 8418.0mm
Spacing
Grid: 10.0mm

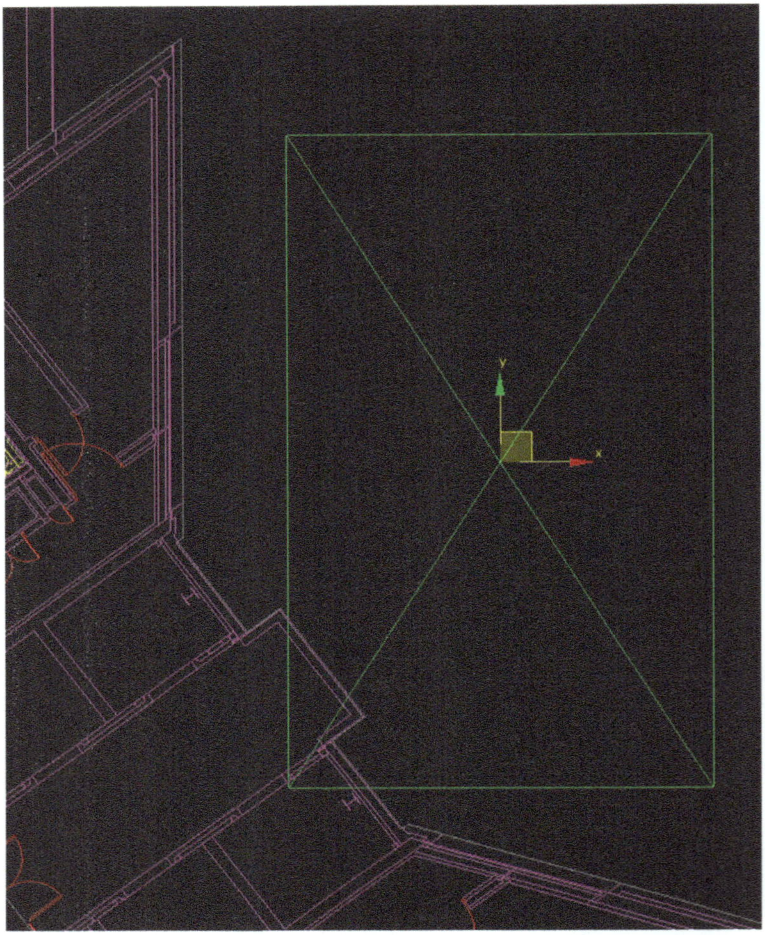

Modify the grid parameters, if necessary

From this point, one can begin tracing and creating shapes and geometry from the grid angle/position.

To view the rotated drawing plan in a straight angle, simply do the following:

Right click on the top viewport text and select the "Extended Viewports" function.

Next, choose the "Grid" option, followed by choosing the "top" view.

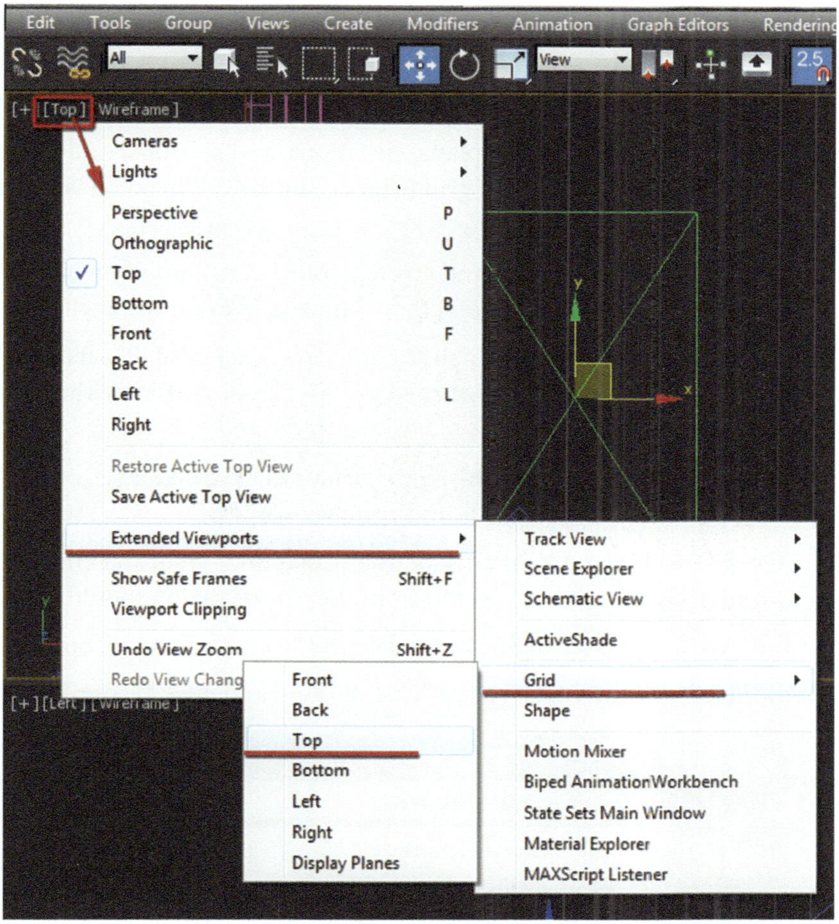

Change the viewport to grid top

The drawing should automatically rotate and position itself correctly. The grid tool is the ideal solution when working with rotated drawings.

This way one is *not* required to rotate the drawings individually.

The grid helper can also be very useful when setting max to automatically create objects at a certain height level (i.e., 2.5 m) without having to manually move the objects from the 0.0.0 point.

To do so, simply move the grid to the desired height level on the left or right viewport.

Before moving/rotating the grid, ensure to *deactivate* it, and set the view to normal viewport first (e.g., *not* grid view).

5 Tips and Tricks

Once finished moving and rotating the grid helper, simply activate it again.

If you desire to start tracing lines in the "front" viewport, simply create a grid in the front viewport.

As drawings are produced in plans, elevations, and sections, professionals often have to work with a variety of grid helpers, at different height levels, and in different viewports.

One good technique to trace and create a spline continuously without having to exit creation is occasionally press the "I" and "Z" key on the keyboard.

It is also important to set a key shortcut to freeze selected objects. This is to ensure that even objects from opened groups can be frozen, without the need to close the group first.

Professionals often resort to this key shortcut to have better selection control of objects, when working in dense and complex scenes.

To access this dialog simply click on the "Customize" tab, and choose the "customize User Interface" option from the list. Its dialog should open.

In the "Action" list, scroll down to select the "freeze selection" option.

In the "hotkey" function, type in "Ctrl+F" keys and click "assign" to apply it.

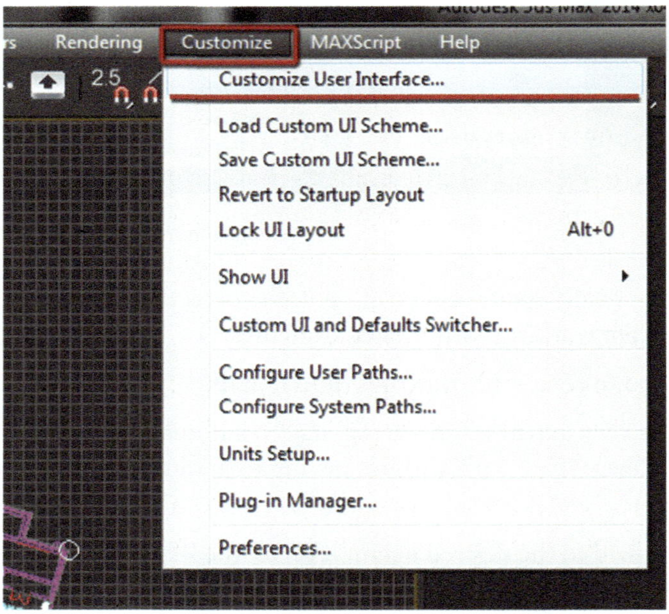

Choose the Customize User Interface option

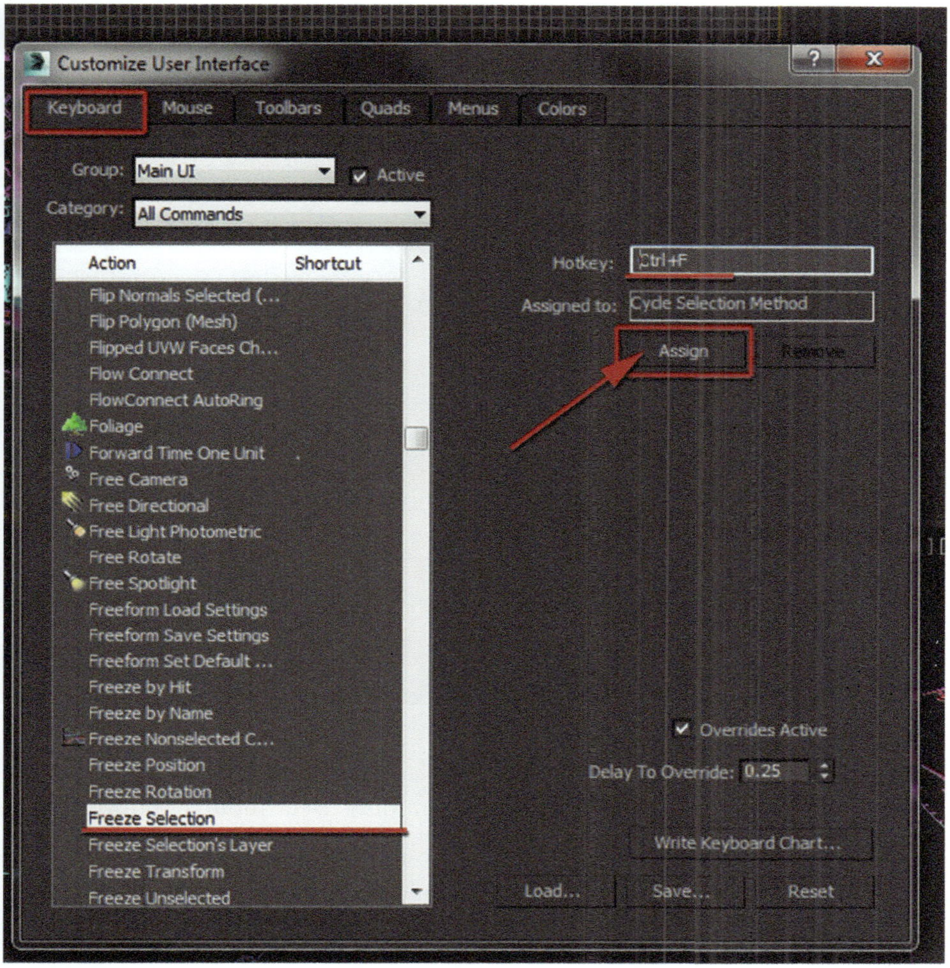

Assign a Hotkey

It's also important to set the viewport "orbit selected" tool to rotate around the selected object. This function enables users to rotate the viewport around the axis of the selected object.

Orbit Selected

Furthermore, set max to show the most commonly used “modify” buttons such as extrude and UVW map.

Doing this will save users time, by *not* having to constantly search and pick for commonly used modifiers from the dropdown list menu.

To customize and display the modifier buttons, simply click and hold the “configure modifier sets” button, and choose the same from the pop-up list.

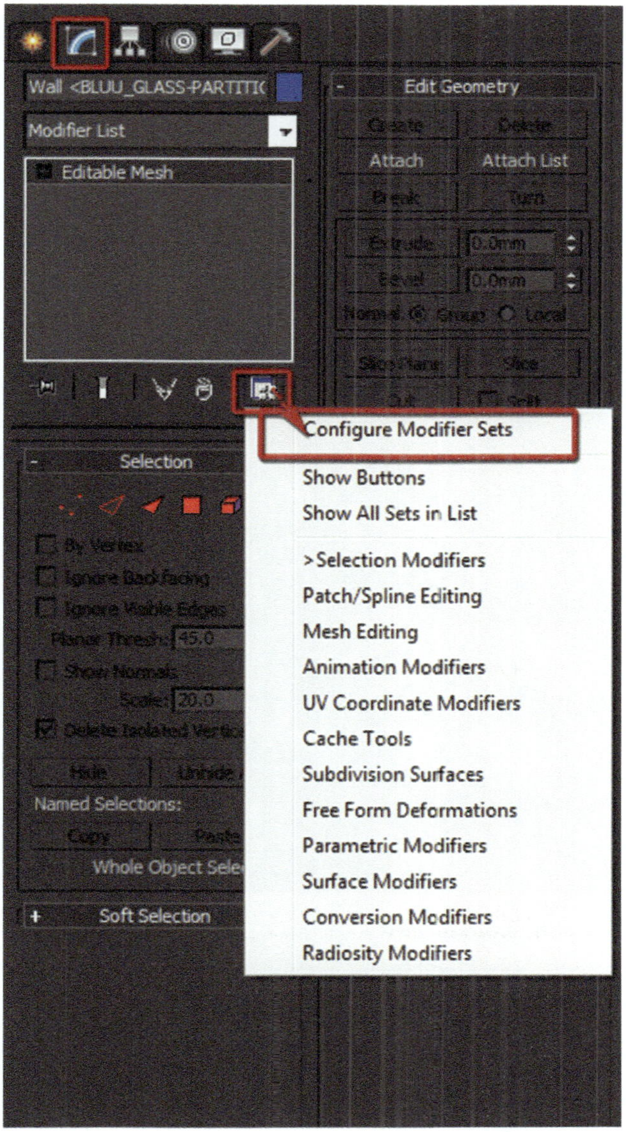

Choose configure Modifier Sets

In its dialog, drag and drop your commonly used modifiers from the list onto the "modifiers" group buttons (e.g., add and replace). Also, scroll down the list to pick other useful modifiers.

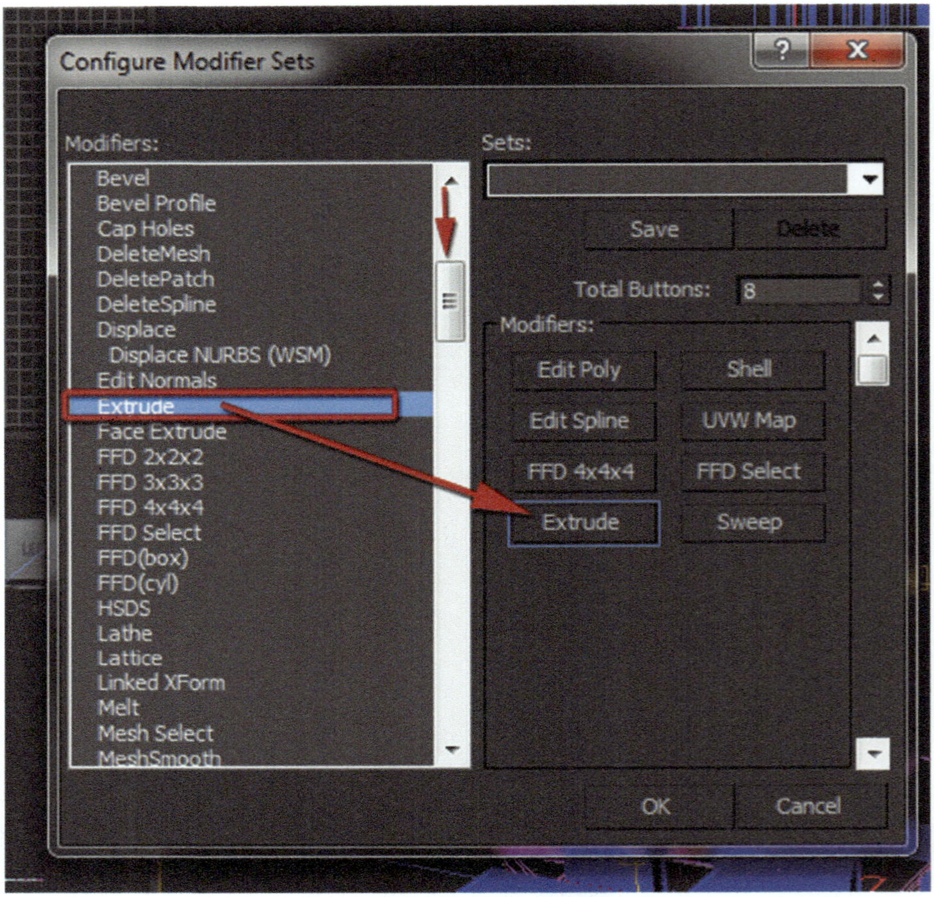

Drag and drop modifiers

Once finished, close the dialog and set the "configure modifier sets" to "show buttons."

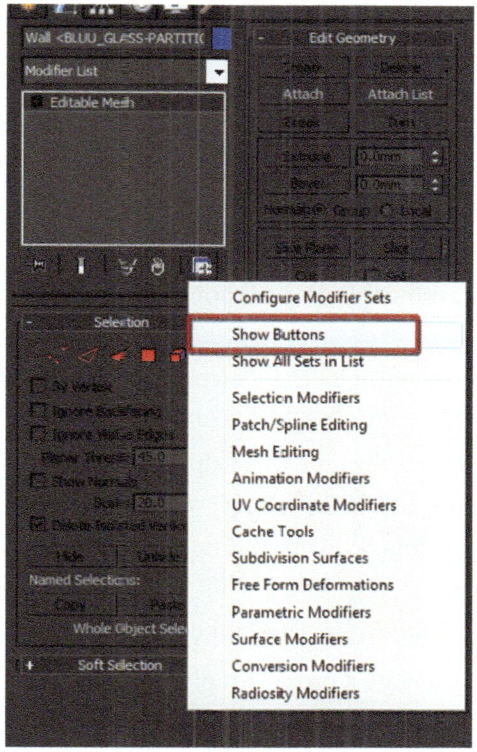

Choose Show Buttons

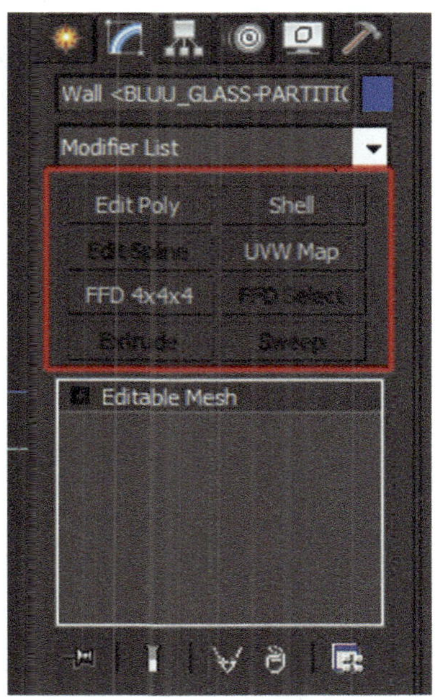

Buttons displayed

5 Tips and Tricks

While it's important to use photo references and drawings to help create convincing 3d models, one should concentrate mainly in detailing objects that are closer to the camera.

Objects in the distance often look acceptable with a realistic texture and a good shader applied.

Moreover, it is also crucial to pay extra attention to scale relationships between objects by using 2d drawings around you as photos reference points, as our eyes can inexplicably pinpoint scale discrepancies, when apparent!

Finally, when creating and detailing models, it is worth finding an efficient way of navigating in the viewport, by occasionally displaying the less relevant objects as boxes (i.e., box display mode) and/or hiding them when necessary.

This technique will help speed up the viewport performance while navigating and creating geometry of the 3d scene.

Although not always necessary, creating proxies is also a great technique of working and rendering efficiently.

VRay proxies can reduce the max file size and rendering times astronomically.

To create a proxy, simply select the object in question and right click to bring up the quad menu.

Choose the VRay mesh export option to open its dialog.

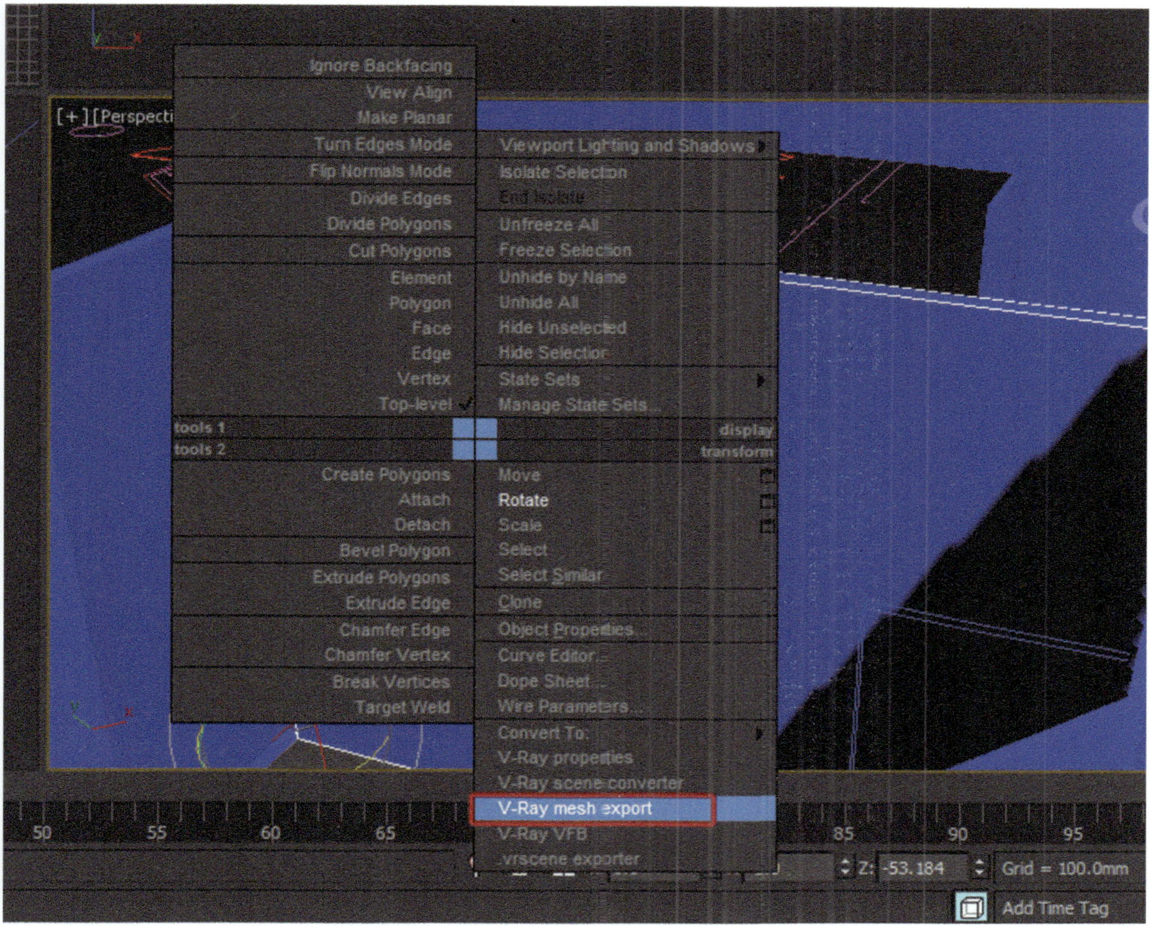

Choose the VRay mesh export option

The Folder toggle allows users choose the location where the proxy mesh will be saved into.

The File name field allows users to name/rename the vrmesh file.

The file name should be kept as simple as possible (e g., sphere.vrmesh).

To prevent unexpected proxy artifacts, always choose the option Export each selected object in a separate file.

Finally, always choose the Automatically create proxies option.

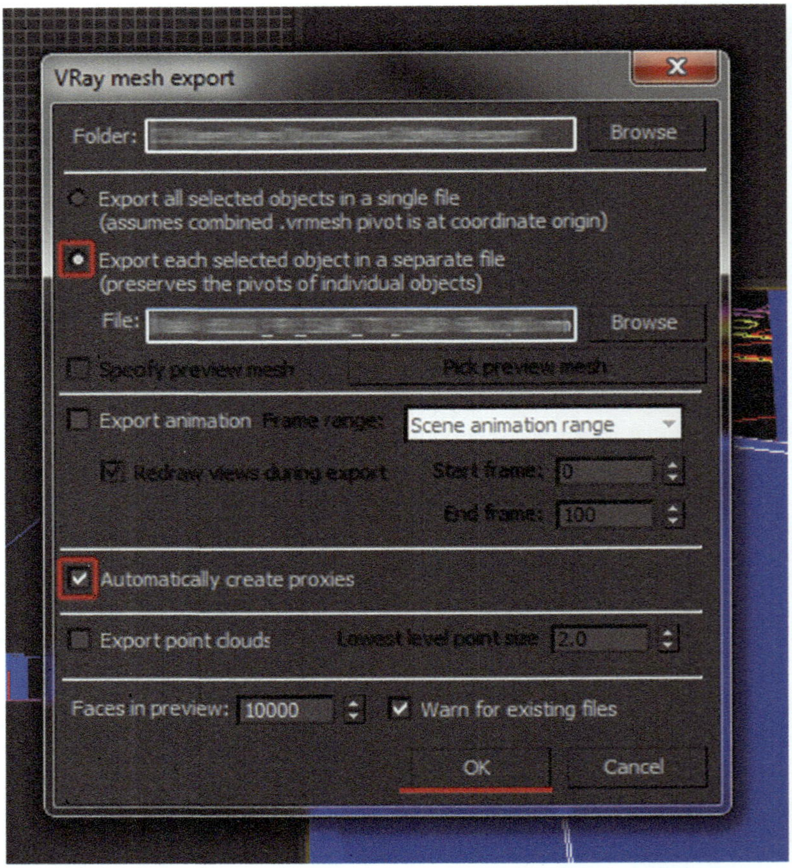

VRay mesh export dialog

To control the display and other aspects of the VRayProxy, simply open the Modify panel.

The Scale function allows users to control the size of the proxy in the scene. The value of 1.0 is often correspondent to the original size of the object.

The Display group controls the preview of the proxy object in the viewport. Users often choose the Bounding box display type for very dense objects such as trees, grass, and hair.

The Import as mesh function allows users to retrieve the original mesh. Complex geometry may take a considerable amount of time to retrieve. In some cases, it may even crash the system.

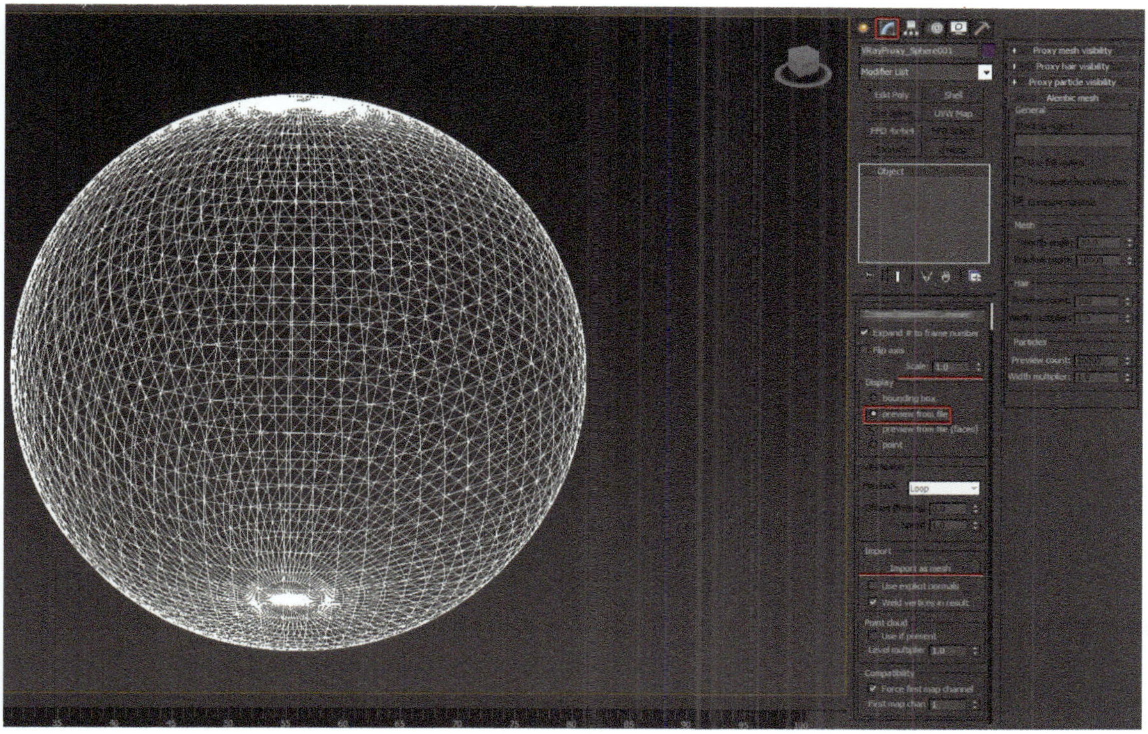

VRayProxy Modify parameters

Producing realistic textures is another important part of the production process.

When textures are applied in a competent manner, the ideal 3d scene should look convincing or close to it even before the lights and the indirect illumination have been implemented.

It's common mistake for users to take high-resolution photos of a smaller area of an object or a surface, as opposed to high-resolution photos of the entire object/surface.

The above-described approach often leads to users having to resort to Photoshop to build the entire texture of an object or a surface by tiling it.

This methodology will subsequently cause the final texture to look artificially tiled and with lack of important details that frequently make a texture look convincing and realistic.

A widely used technique to prevent such from occurring is to take high-resolution photo of the entire object/surface desired or take a high-resolution photo of an extensive area of the relevant object/surface.

This approach will capture all the important details of the entire surface (i.e., scratch, dust, AO, subtle discrepancies, etc.) without having to resort Photoshop to tile the surface.

Script for Verified Views

In architectural visualization, typing in individual survey point values in 3ds max can be very time-consuming, especially when working with multiple camera views for verified views.

Most verified views come with at least 10 individual survey points per camera.

Below is an example of a typical survey data spreadsheet provided by the surveyor.

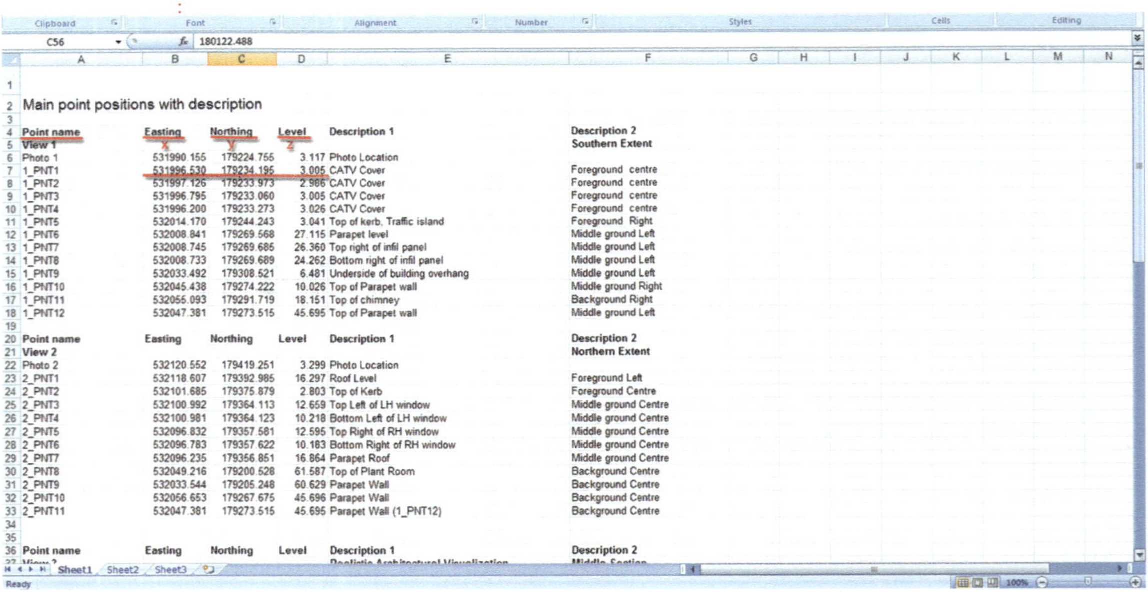

	A	B	C	D	E	F
1						
2	Main point positions with description					
3						
4	**Point name**	**Easting**	**Northing**	**Level**	**Description 1**	**Description 2**
5	**View 1**	X	Y	Z		**Southern Extent**
6	Photo 1	531990.155	179224.755	3.117	Photo Location	
7	1_PNT1	531996.530	179234.195	3.005	CATV Cover	Foreground centre
8	1_PNT2	531997.126	179233.973	2.986	CATV Cover	Foreground centre
9	1_PNT3	531996.795	179233.060	3.005	CATV Cover	Foreground centre
10	1_PNT4	531996.200	179233.273	3.026	CATV Cover	Foreground centre
11	1_PNT5	532014.170	179244.243	3.041	Top of kerb, Traffic island	Foreground Right
12	1_PNT6	532008.841	179269.568	27.115	Parapet level	Middle ground Left
13	1_PNT7	532008.745	179269.685	26.360	Top right of infil panel	Middle ground Left
14	1_PNT8	532008.733	179269.689	24.262	Bottom right of infil panel	Middle ground Left
15	1_PNT9	532033.492	179308.521	6.481	Underside of building overhang	Middle ground Left
16	1_PNT10	532045.438	179274.222	10.026	Top of Parapet wall	Middle ground Right
17	1_PNT11	532055.093	179291.719	18.151	Top of chimney	Background Right
18	1_PNT12	532047.381	179273.515	45.695	Top of Parapet wall	Middle ground Left
19						
20	**Point name**	**Easting**	**Northing**	**Level**	**Description 1**	**Description 2**
21	**View 2**					**Northern Extent**
22	Photo 2	532120.552	179419.251	3.299	Photo Location	
23	2_PNT1	532118.607	179392.985	16.297	Roof Level	Foreground Left
24	2_PNT2	532101.685	179375.879	2.803	Top of Kerb	Foreground Centre
25	2_PNT3	532100.992	179364.113	12.659	Top Left of LH window	Middle ground Centre
26	2_PNT4	532100.981	179364.123	10.218	Bottom Left of LH window	Middle ground Centre
27	2_PNT5	532096.832	179357.581	12.595	Top Right of RH window	Middle ground Centre
28	2_PNT6	532096.783	179357.622	10.183	Bottom Right of RH window	Middle ground Centre
29	2_PNT7	532096.235	179356.851	16.864	Parapet Roof	Middle ground Centre
30	2_PNT8	532049.216	179200.528	61.587	Top of Plant Room	Background Centre
31	2_PNT9	532033.544	179205.248	60.629	Parapet Wall	Background Centre
32	2_PNT10	532056.653	179267.675	45.696	Parapet Wall	Background Centre
33	2_PNT11	532047.381	179273.515	45.695	Parapet Wall (1_PNT12)	Background Centre
34						
35						
36	**Point name**	**Easting**	**Northing**	**Level**	**Description 1**	**Description 2**

Survey data spreadsheet

The View name or number is often referred to the camera.

The Easting value is the equivalent of the X position in 3ds max. The Northing value is the equivalent of Y position in max.

The Level value is the equivalent of the Z position in max.

The script, SurveyPointImporter, will help create and position each survey value automatically/accurately in 3ds max as instanced point helpers.

The great advantage of having survey points in 3ds max as instanced helper points is that their sizes in the camera viewport can be set to have a Constant Screen Size.

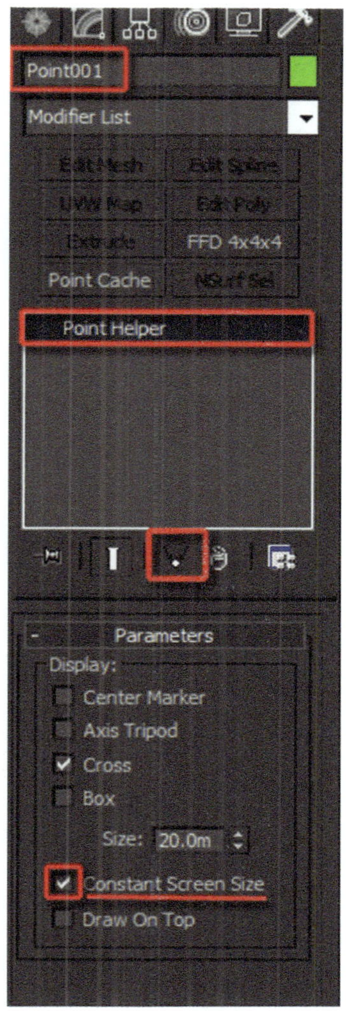

Instanced Point Helper

It's worth noting that the first line of code of this script is set to go to the root of C drive and extract/open a csv file type (spreadsheet) under the name of surveypoints.csv (e.g.,

f = openFile "c:/surveypoints.csv" mode:"rt"

Tip: It's imperative to have forward slash (e.g., /) specified in the file location. Not back slash.

This means that every time one runs this script, it will automatically look for a file under the above-mentioned name (e.g., surveypoints.csv), the file extension/type (e.g., csv), and the specified location, as described above (c:/).

However, you can change the location and the file name as you see fit (not the file extension: cvc).

Example: **f = openFile"F:/scene tests/Wembley Stadiumsurveypoints.csv" mode:"rt"**

Once satisfied, simply name and save the script as a maxscript file type.

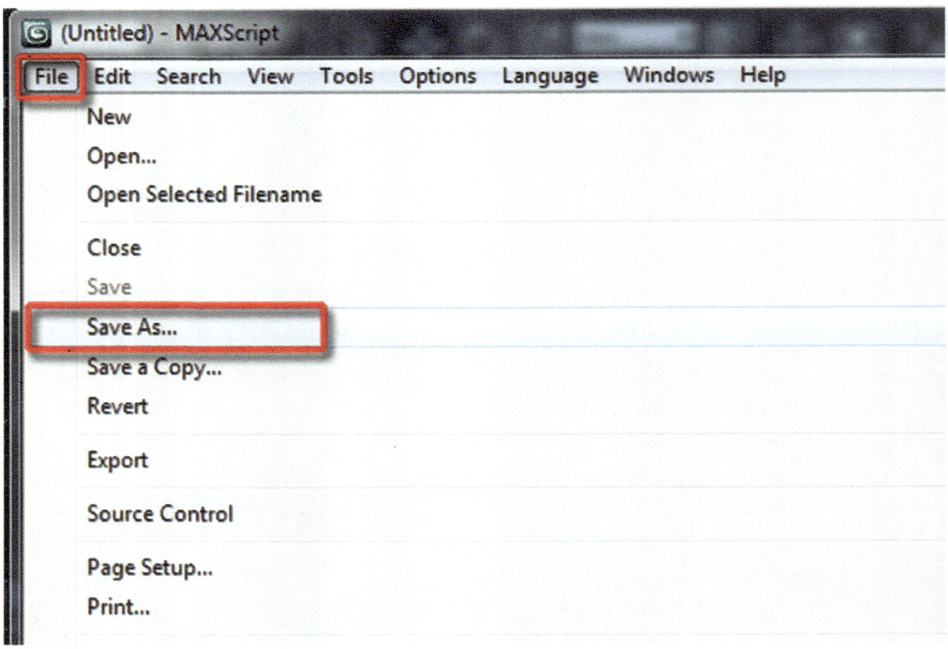

Choose Save the script

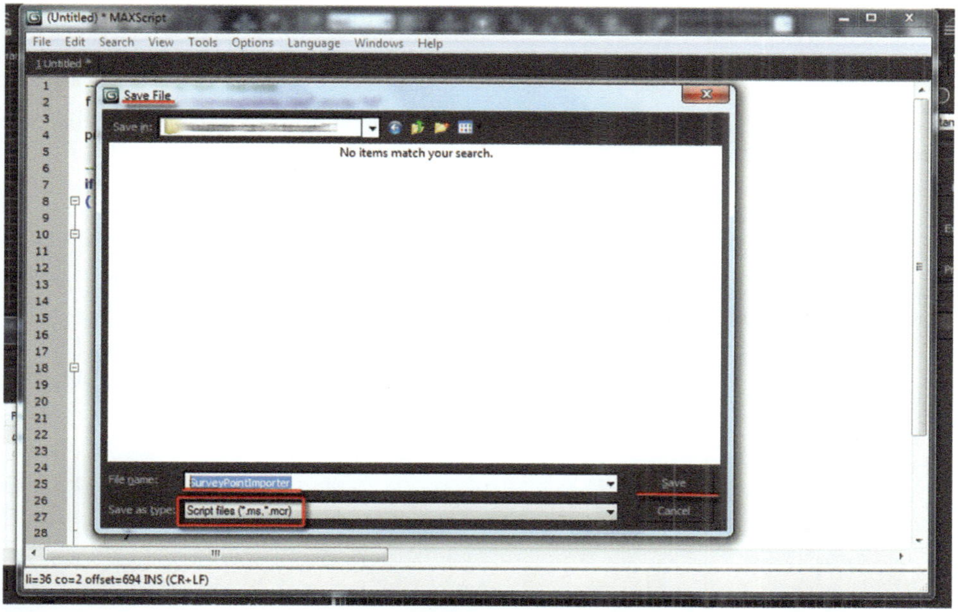

Rename and Save the script

Once saved, close the dialog box.

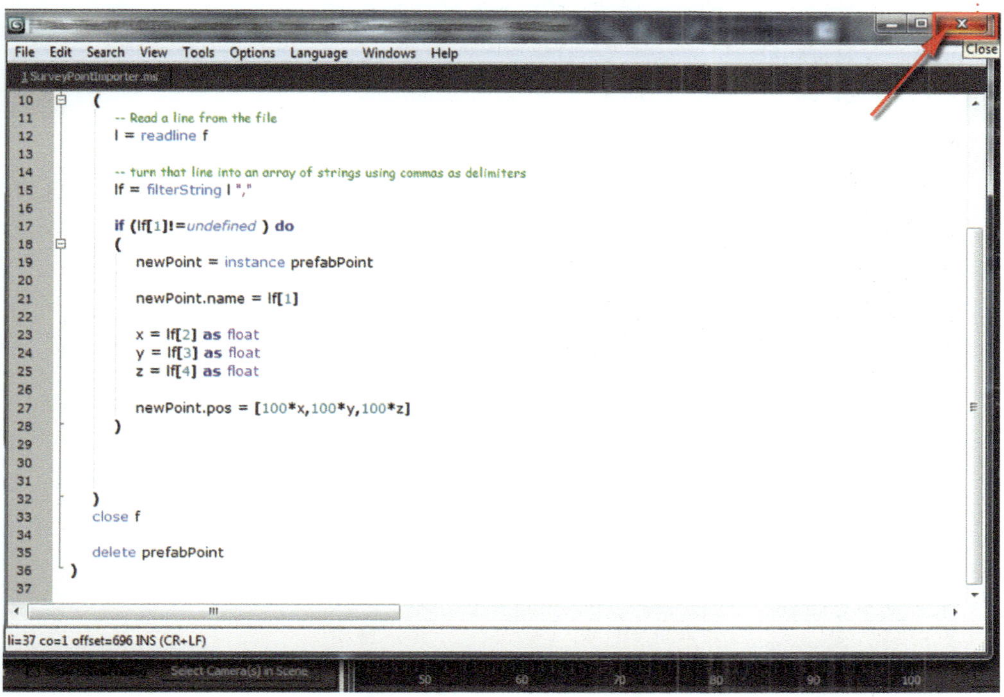

Close the dialog box

To run the script, simply click on the MAXScripttoolbar and choose Run Script.

All survey points should be created automatically.

Tip: At times it may seem there's only survey point in the scene due to its gigantic size in the viewport. If the survey points are too big, simply reduce its size manually.

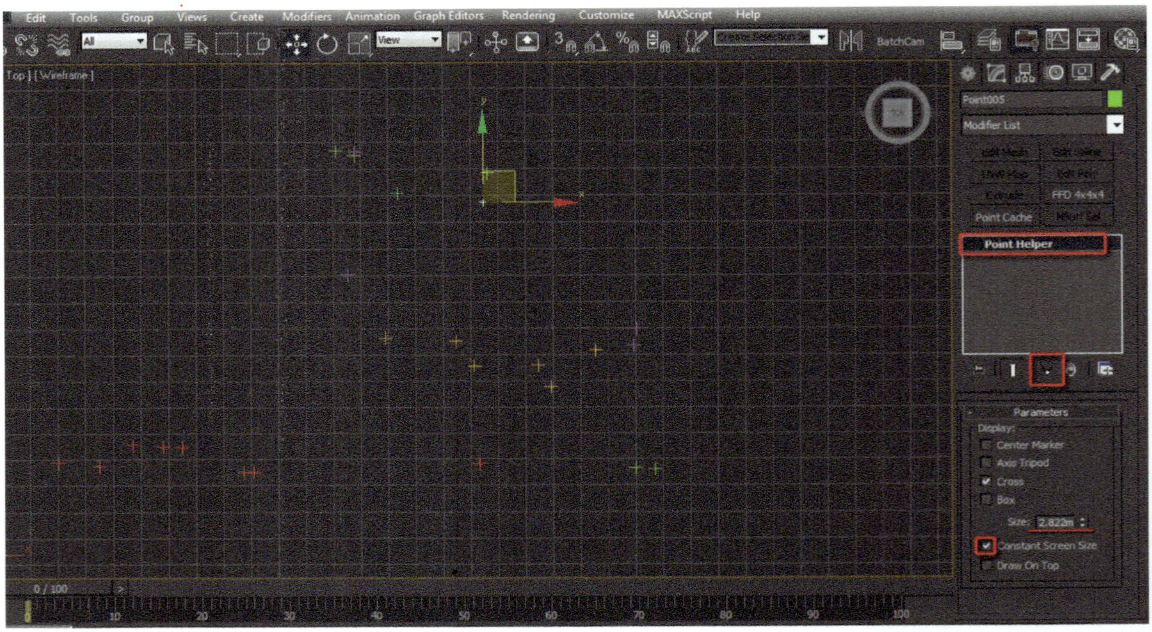

Survey points created automatically in 3ds max

It's worth noting that the last three or four digits of the survey values might be slightly off.

It is *not* a script error: 3ds max has difficulty with accuracy when working or displaying numbers/units that are too far away from 0.0.0.

If perchance there's a script error reading the spreadsheet file, simply open the spreadsheet file in a notepad application and resave it as a cvc file format.

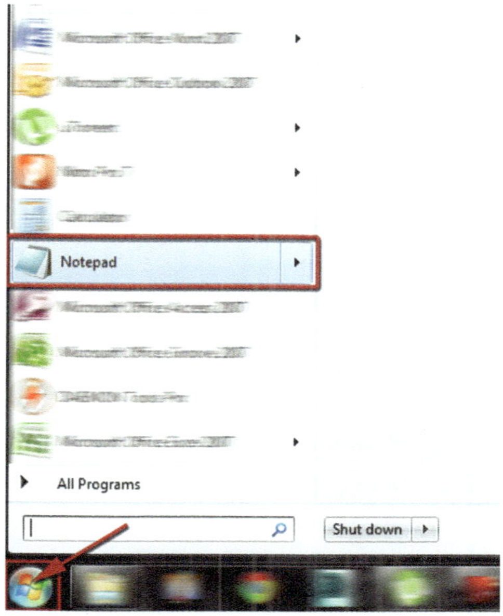

Use the Notepad application to open and resave the spreadsheet file

The subsequent step is to create and position the 3d cameras according to the values (X Y Z) depicted in cvc file.

In addition, one can also begin camera-matching each view according to the camera info and the photography provided.

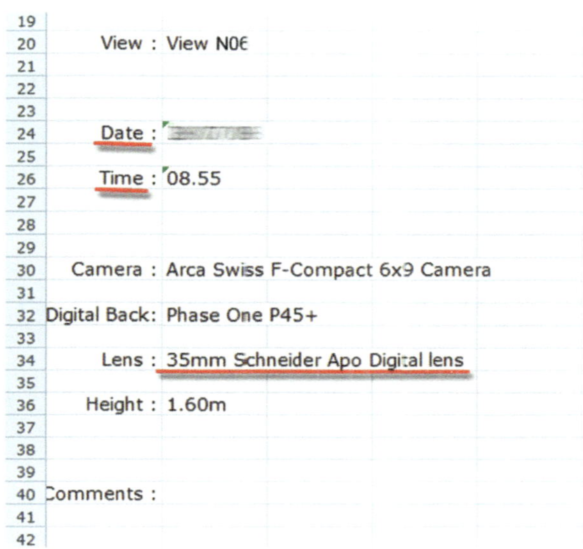

Camera data

5 Tips and Tricks

While camera matching, one can use tools such as 2D Pan Zoom Mode zoom in into an camera position, without affecting the camera itself.

To begin zooming in, simply right click on the plus sign on the top left corner of the camera viewport, and choose the 2D Pan Zoom Mode option.

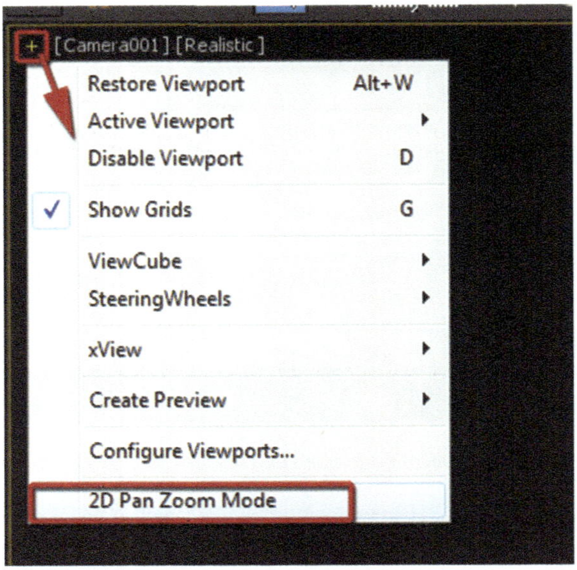

2D Pan Zoom Mode option

To return to the original camera position, simply right click on the 2D Pan Zoom text and choose Exit 2D Pan Zoom Mode option.

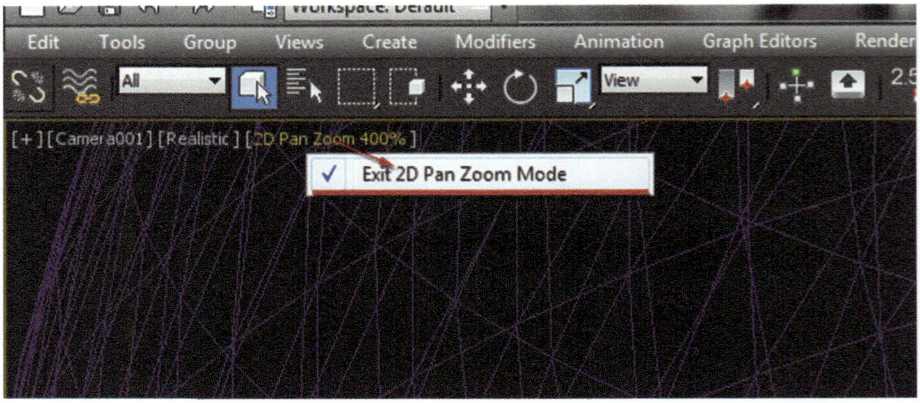

Exit *2D Pan Zoom Mode option*

Using the vanishing line to correct camera shifts for verified views

Users are often required to create vanishing lines in Photoshop, in order to correct camera shifts from photos taken for verified views or photomontages.

To create the vanishing lines, users simply go to the Tools sidebar and choose the Line Tool from the list.

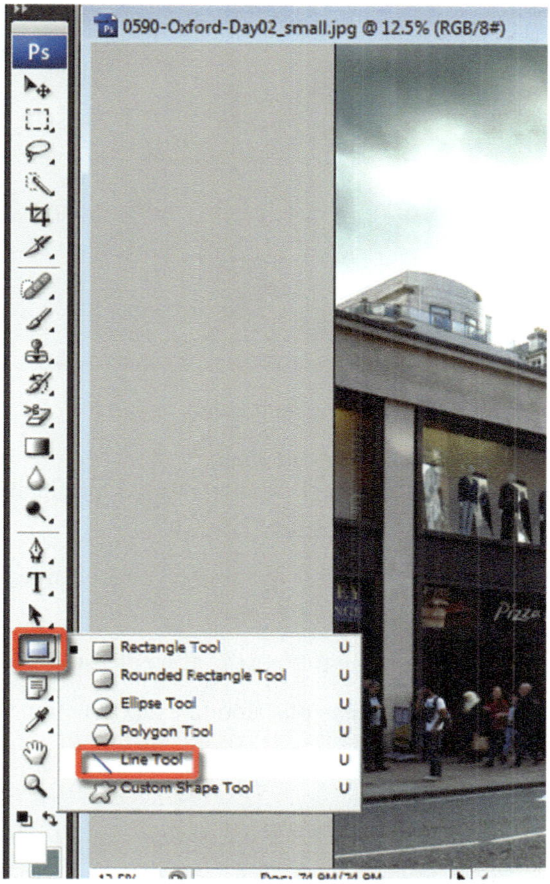

Use the Line Tool in Photoshop

To create the vanishing line, simply set the line weight to a visible size (i.e., 5 px) and begin creating it, by clicking and dragging it.

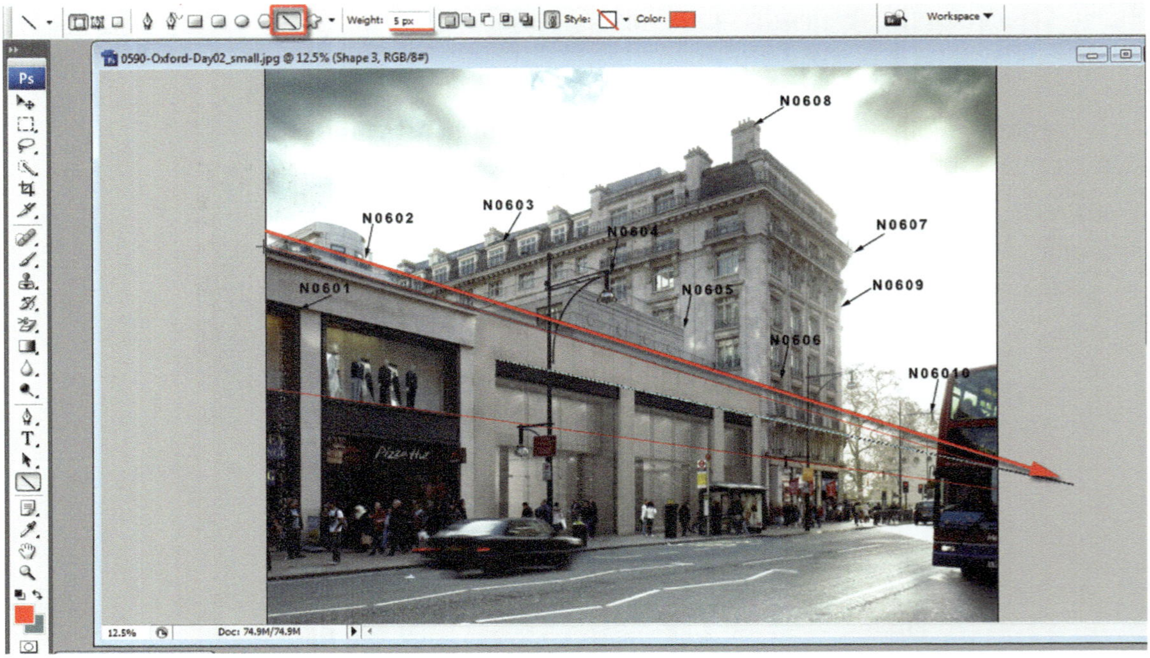

Create the first vanishing line with Line Tool in Photoshop

Once the vanishing lines are created, duplicate the background layer (Ctrl+J) and enable the canvas Ruler (Ctrl+R).

It's worth noting that it's imperative to duplicate layer prior to using the Crop tool in a nondestructive way.

Next, click on the top part of the ruler and drag it down to create a guide.

Ensure the guide is positioned exactly where the vanishing lines meet.

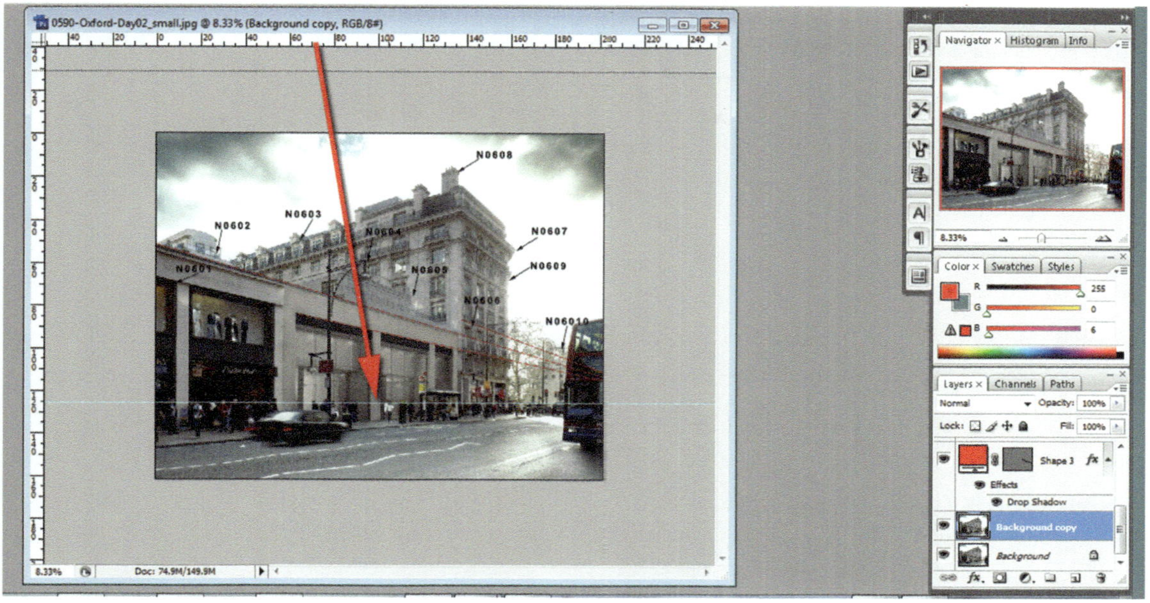

Create a Guide line in Photoshop

To correct the camera shift, the vanishing line (guide) needs to divide canvas into two equal sides. This exercise will require extending the canvas.

To Crop extend the Canvas in a nondestructive way, first zoom out of the canvas and enable the Crop tool (C).

Next, drag down the Crop tool until its midpoint is positioned at the center of the guide (vanishing line).

Before cropping, ensure that the "Hide" option is enabled, as opposed to "Delete." Once satisfied, simply press "Enter" to crop extend the document/canvas.

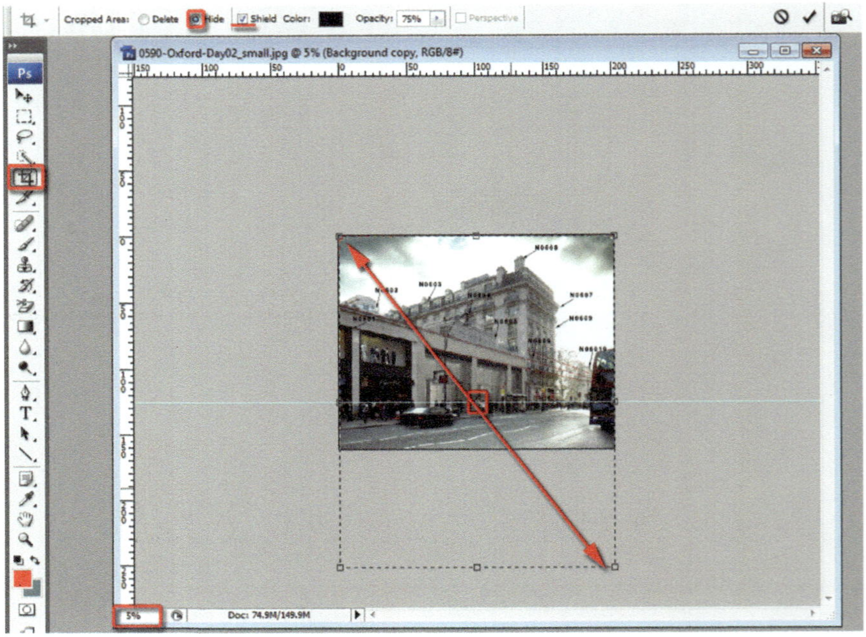

Drag down the Crop tool to the center of the Guideline

Extended Crop

Following that, create a rectangular selection around the extended area with the marquee tool. Create a new layer (Ctrl+Shift+Alt+N), fill the selection with a Paint Bucket tool (G), and save the document as a PSD file.

Also, save another version in a JPEG format.

Create and fill the selection with a Paint Bucket tool

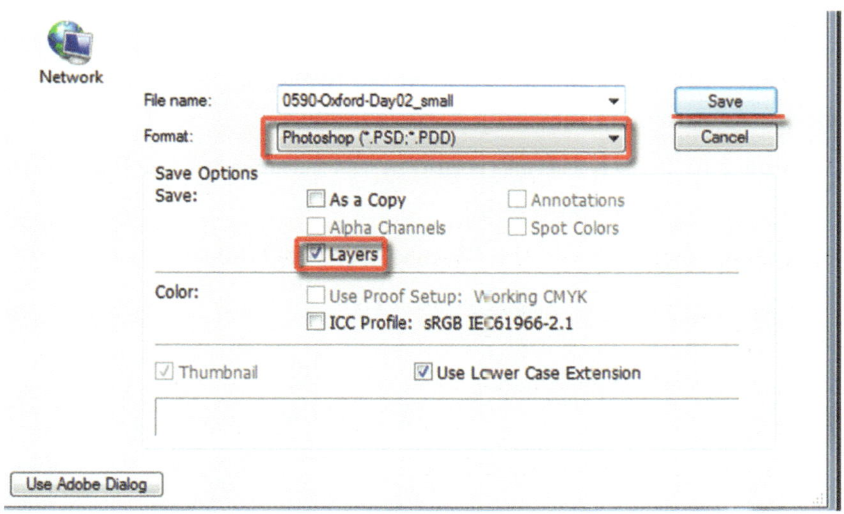

Save the document as a PSD file and as a JPEG

Once the document is saved as a PSD file, you'll be able to go backward and forward between the original and cropped versions at any point in future.

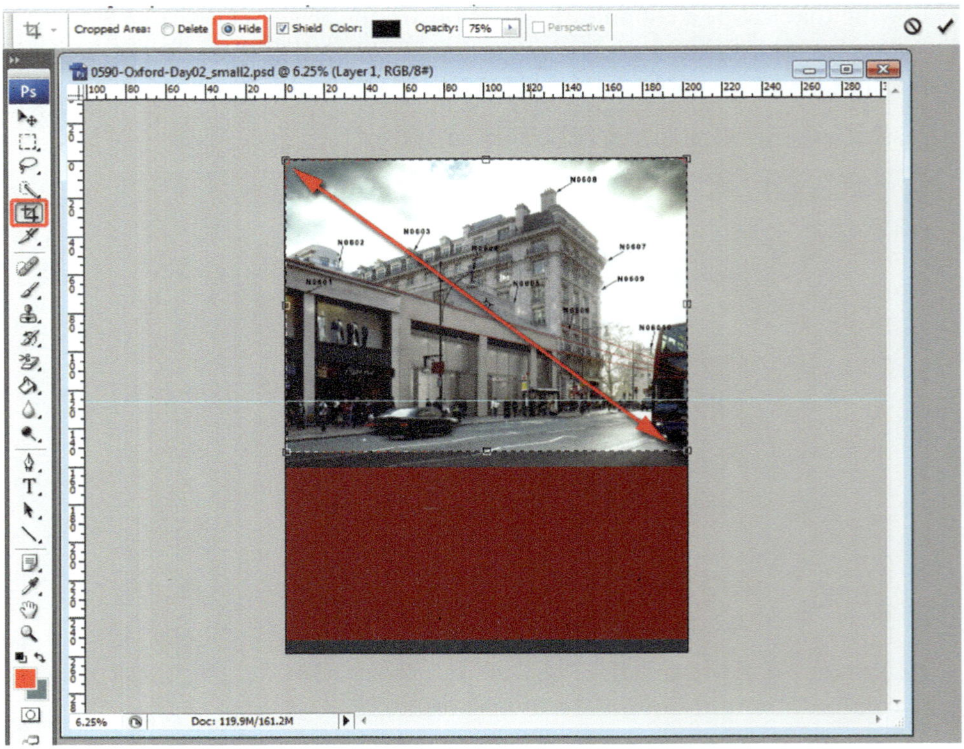

Edit the PSD document if/when desired

The JPEG format should be later used as a background image in the camera viewport, for camera matching purposes only.

The image to be used as background in 3ds max needs to be reduced in size for camera-matching purposes only.

Very large images used in the 3ds max viewport tend to slow down the graphics card.

0590-Oxford-Day02_small_test.psd @ 33.3% (Layer 1, RGB/8#)
Duplicate...
Image Size...
Canvas Size...
File Info...
Print...
33.33%

Right click and select the Image Size option

Image Size Dialog

In 3ds max, to insert the resized background image, first set and lock its width and height output size to match the resized incoming background image (e.g., 1500 x 1872).

Next, go to the camera viewport and right click on the viewport display type (e.g., wireframe, realistic, shaded, etc.).

On the dropdown quad menu, choose the Viewport Background, followed by selecting the Configure Viewport Background option (Alt+B).

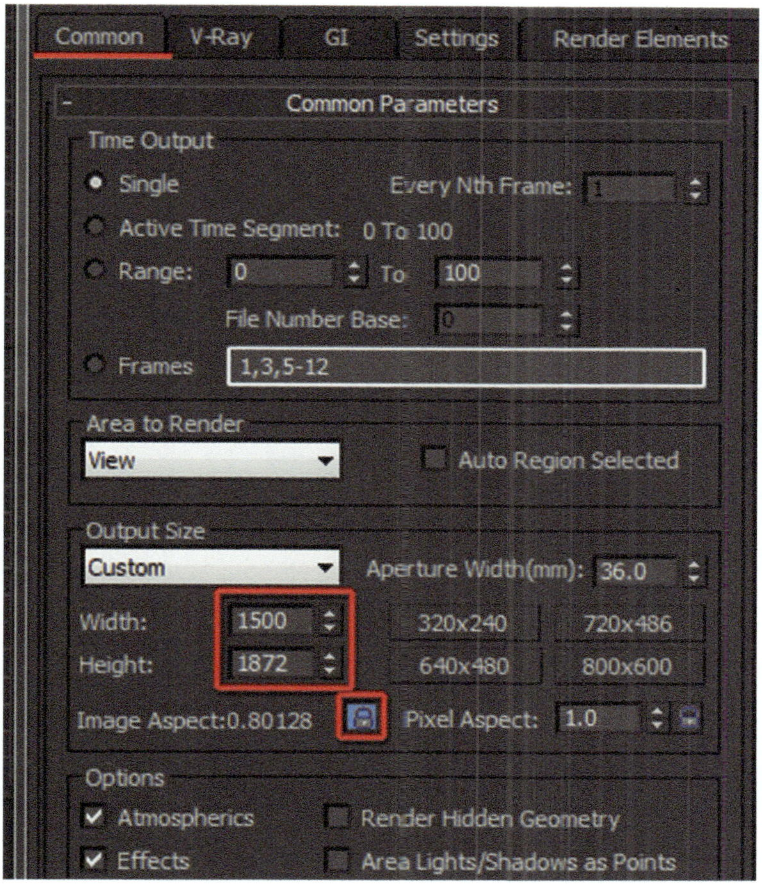
Common
V-Ray
GI
Settings
Render Elements
Common Parameters
Time Output
Single
Every Nth Frame:
Active Time Segment: 0 To 100
Range: 0 To 100
File Number Base: 0
Frames 1,3,5-12
Area to Render
View
Auto Region Selected
Output Size
Custom
Aperture Width(mm): 36.0
Width: 1500
Height: 1872
320x240
720x486
640x480
800x600
Image Aspect:0.80128
Pixel Aspect: 1.0
Options
Atmospherics
Render Hidden Geometry
Effects
Area Lights/Shadows as Points

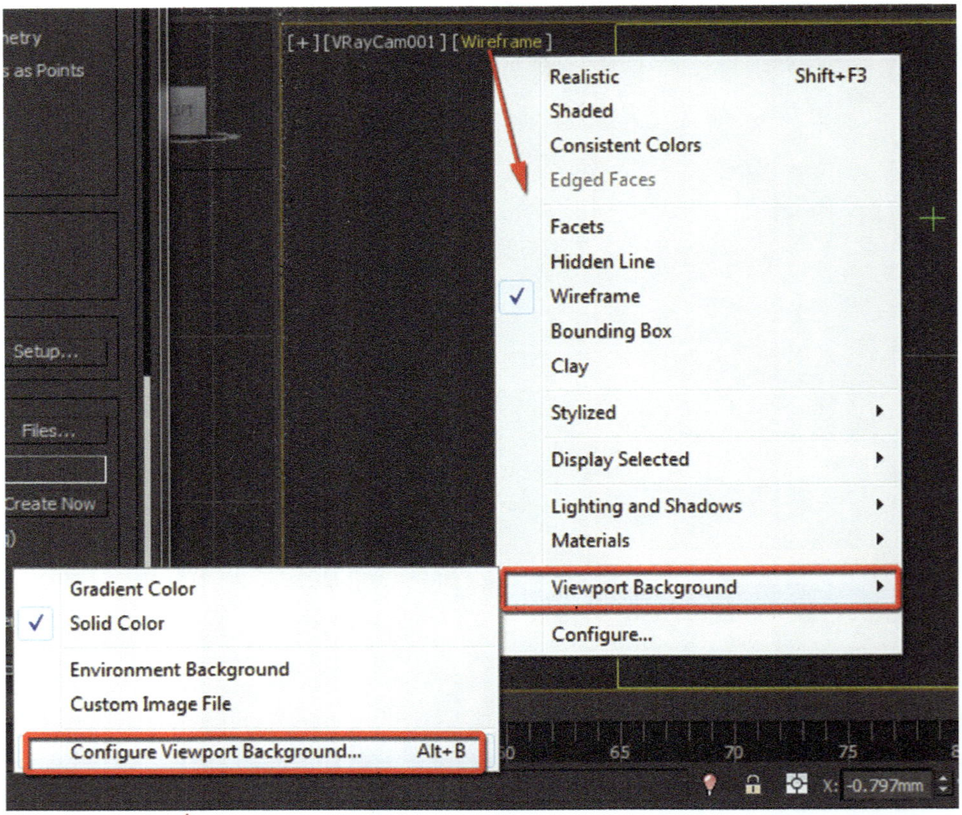

Select the Configure Viewport Background option

In the Configure Viewport Background dialog, open the Background tab and choose the Use Files option.

In the Setup dialog, choose the Match Rendering Output option, followed by clicking on the Files toggle to select and open the Background image.

Use the Shift+F to enable the Show Safe Frames option.

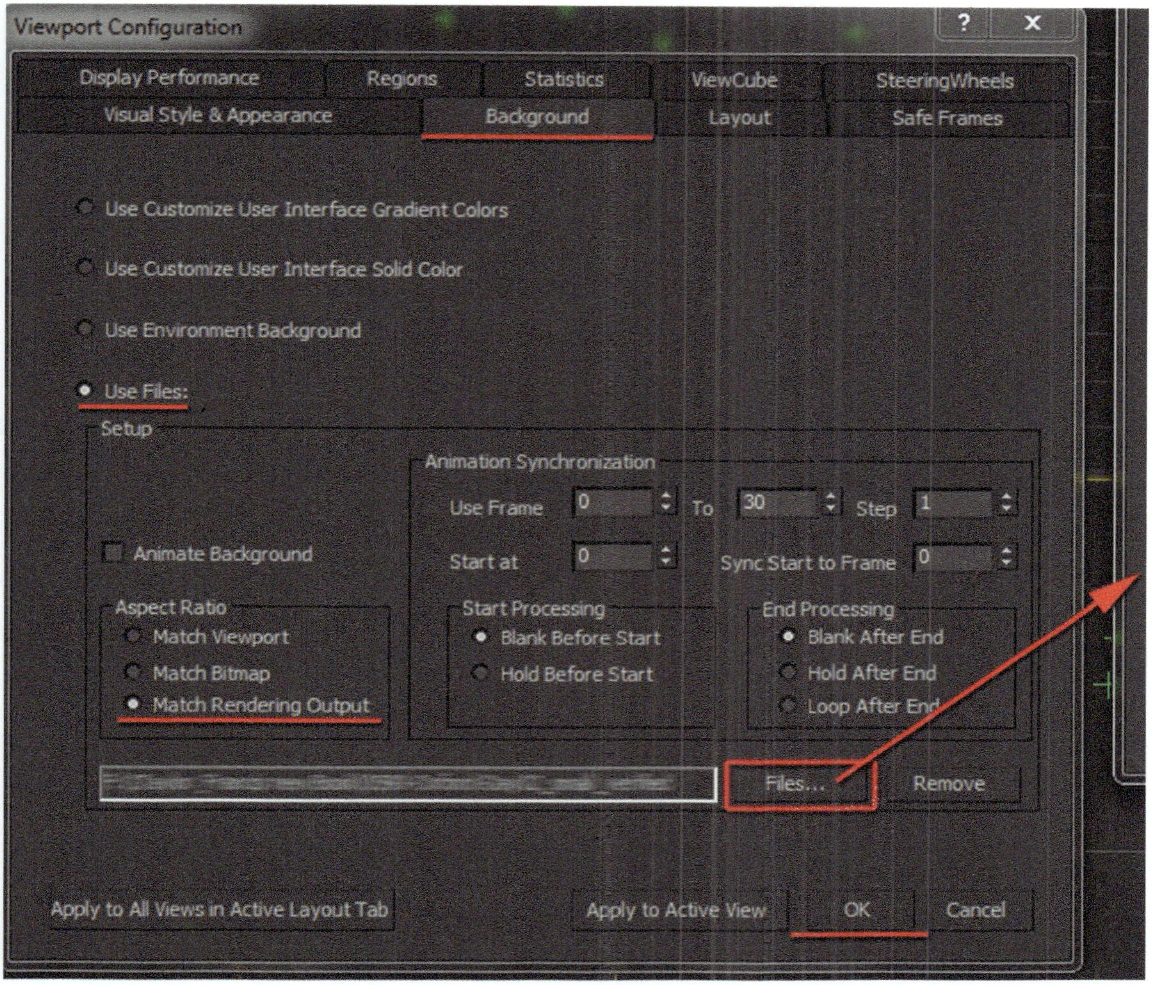
Viewport Configuration
Display Performance
Regions
Statistics
ViewCube
SteeringWheels
Visual Style & Appearance
Background
Layout
Safe Frames
Use Customize User Interface Gradient Colors
Use Customize User Interface Solid Color
Use Environment Background
Use Files:
Setup
Animation Synchronization
Use Frame
0
To
30
Step
1
Animate Background
Start at
0
Sync Start to Frame
0
Aspect Ratio
Match Viewport
Match Bitmap
Match Rendering Output
Start Processing
Blank Before Start
Hold Before Start
End Processing
Blank After End
Hold After End
Loop After End
Files...
Remove
Apply to All Views in Active Layout Tab
Apply to Active View
OK
Cancel

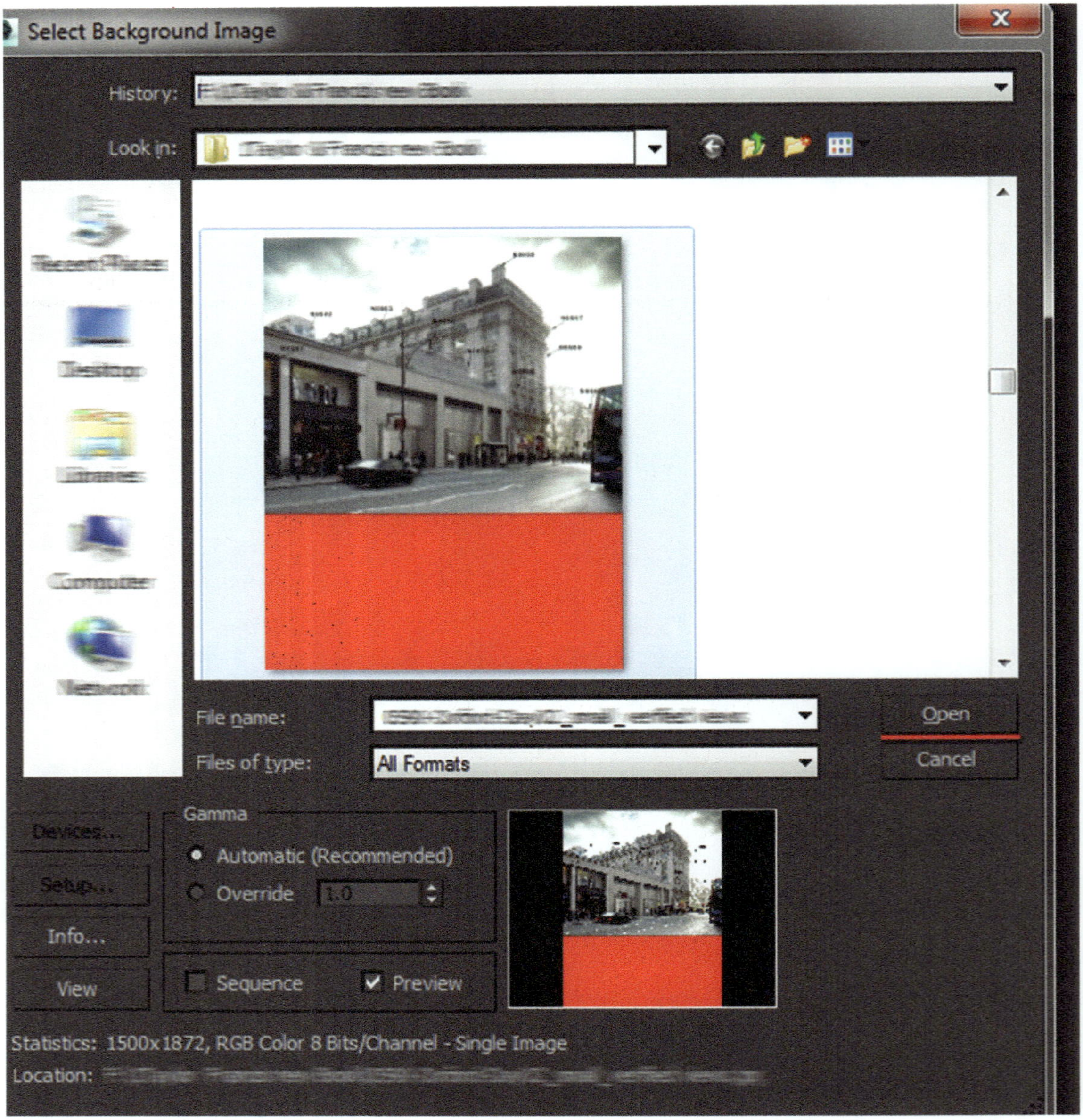
Select Background Image
History:
Look in:
File name:
Files of type:
All Formats
Open
Cancel
Gamma
Automatic (Recommended)
Override
1.0
Devices...
Setup...
Info...
View
Sequence
Preview
Statistics: 1500x1872, RGB Color 8 Bits/Channel - Single Image
Location:

Load up the Background image

Background image loaded

After camera-matching the view, one can then resize the final output size to high resolution (e.g., 6000 x 7488).

To transfer some of the camera data (e.g., ISO speed, F-stop, Exposure time, Day, time) into the VRayPhysicalCamera, simply select and right click on the raw photo, followed by selecting/opening the Properties option and opening its Details tab.

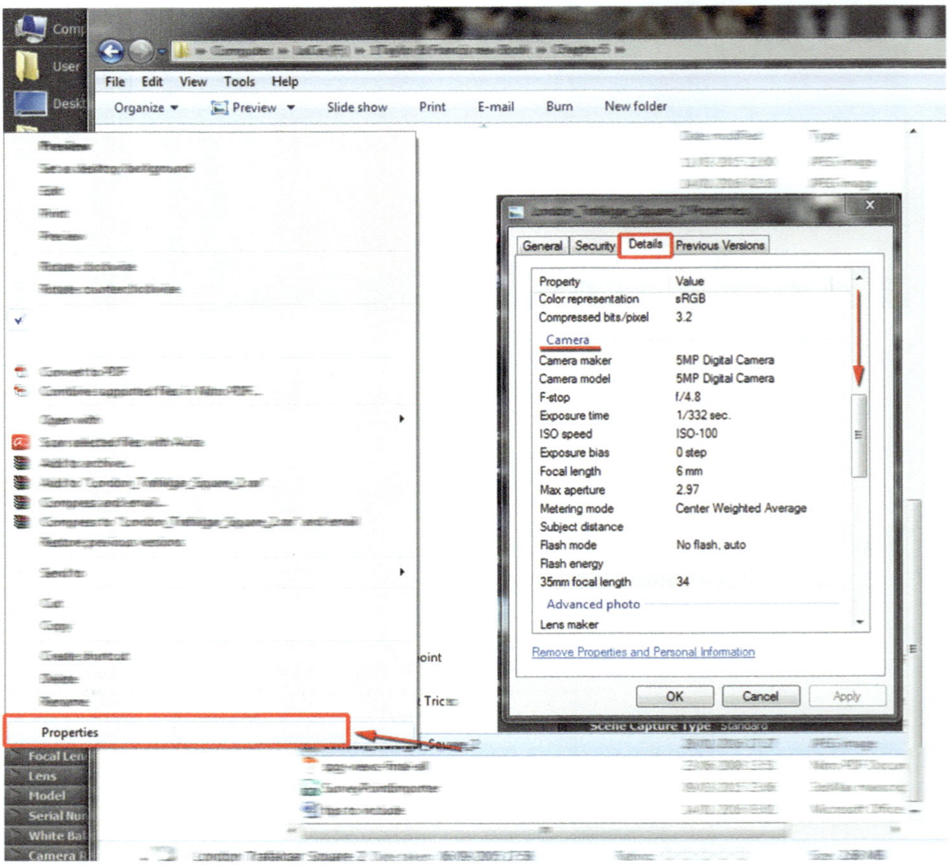

Camera Details tab

In architectural visualization/verified views, it's common for users to have an AutoCAD drawing with the survey reference.

Architectural companies often use this drawing (in conjunction with the cameras and point helpers) to help with the alignment against the existing context model.

To align the matched survey and cameras with the context model, one is required to first save the working scene containing the survey points, cameras, and the AutoCAD drawing (if available).

Next, open the main scene containing the context model, building, and lights.

Following that, open the XRef scene dialog and add the scene containing the matched survey data with cameras.

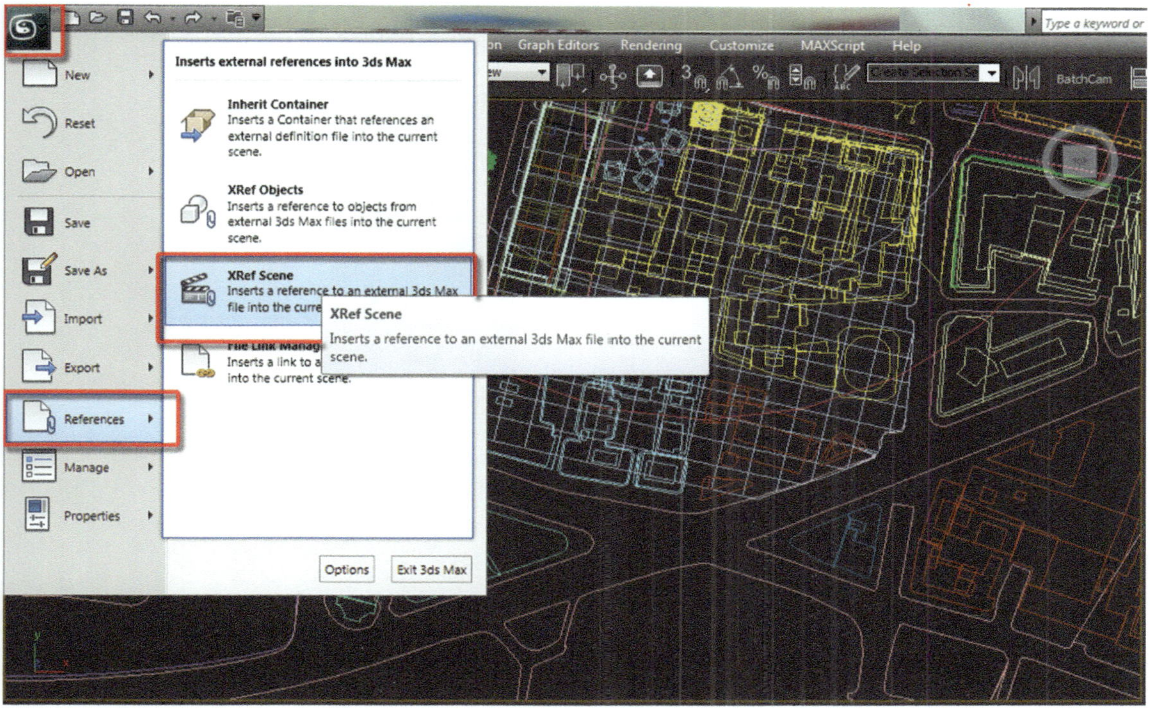

XRef Scene

[+] [Top] [Wireframe + Edged Faces]
XRef Scenes
XRef Files:
Add...
Open File
History:
Look in:
Thumbnail
Name
Date
Type
Size
Tags
verified ...
File name:
verified views
Files of type:
3ds Max (*.max)
Open
Cancel
XRef File:
Update File:
Display Options:
Ignore:
Parent:
Select:
All
None
Invert
Close
None Selected
Welcome to M
Click or click-and-drag to select objects

Add the scene

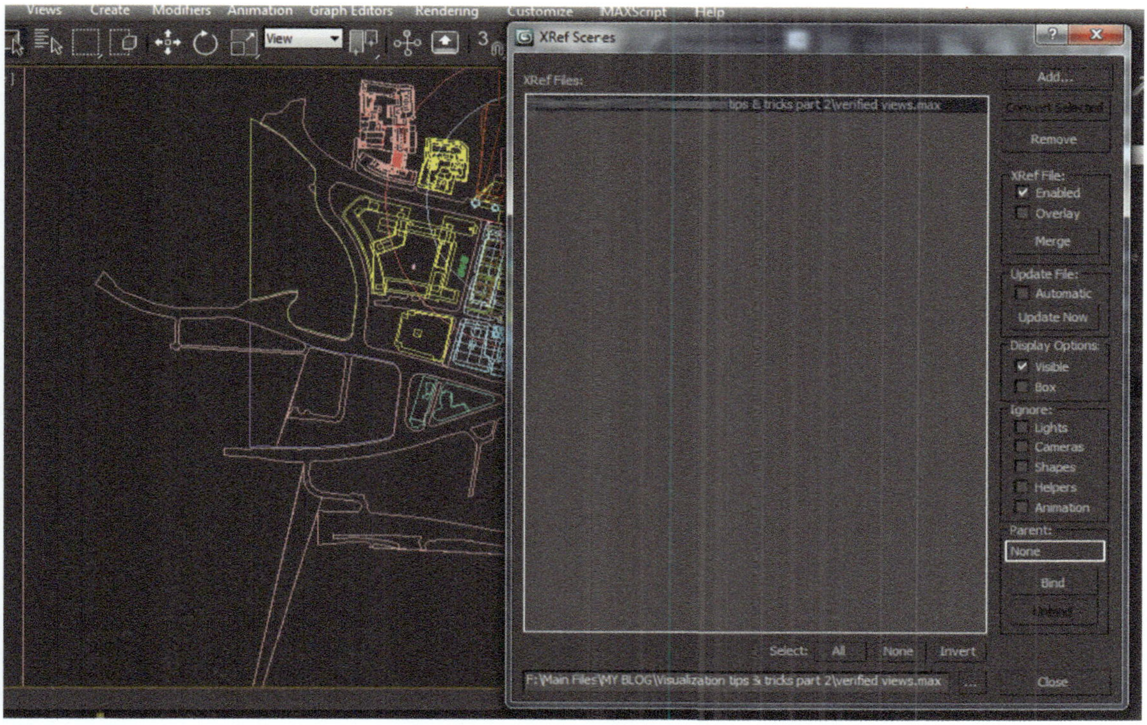

Loaded scene

It's common for the matched survey points and cameras to be miles away from the 0.0.0 point and the main scene.

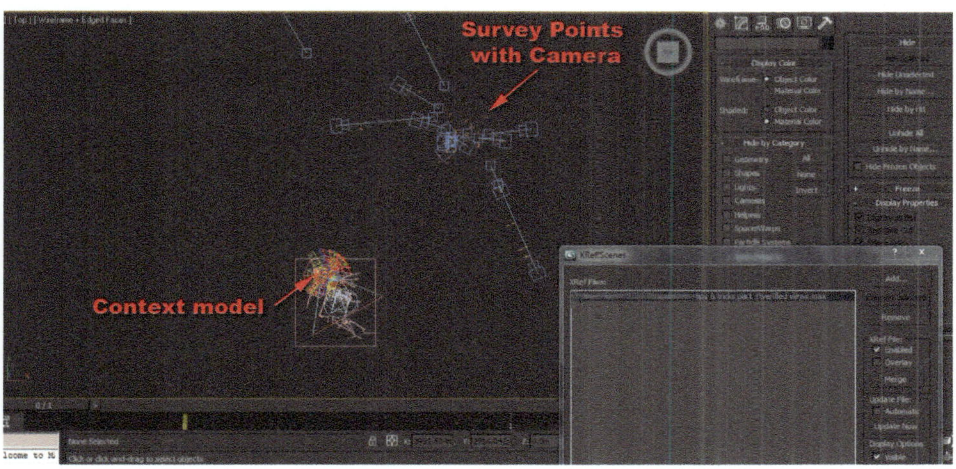

Context model and survey points away from each other

To line up the XRef survey points with the main scene, create a dummy object and bind it to the XRef scene.

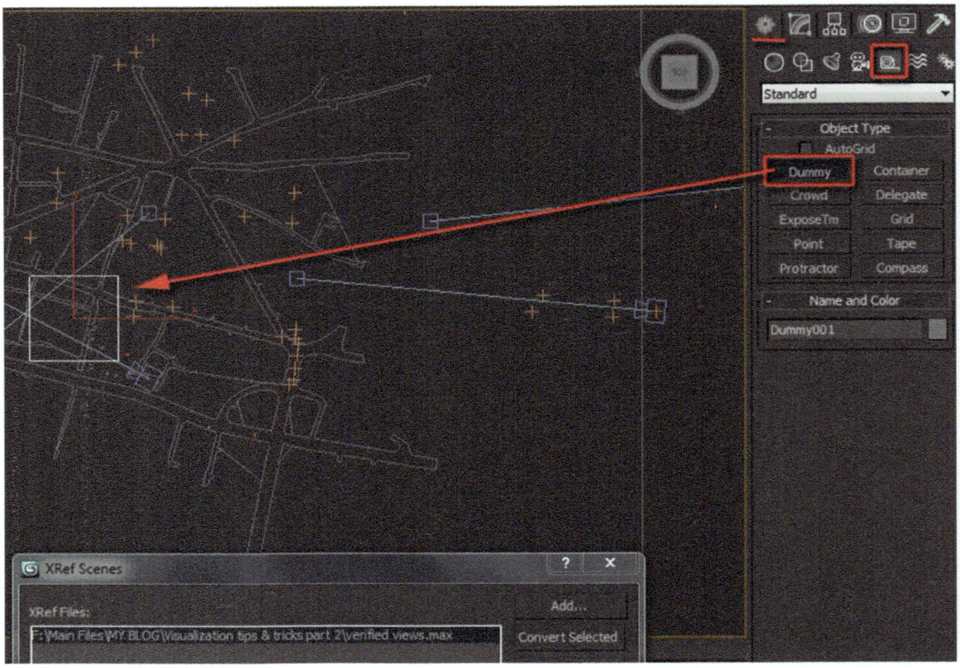

Create a Dummy object

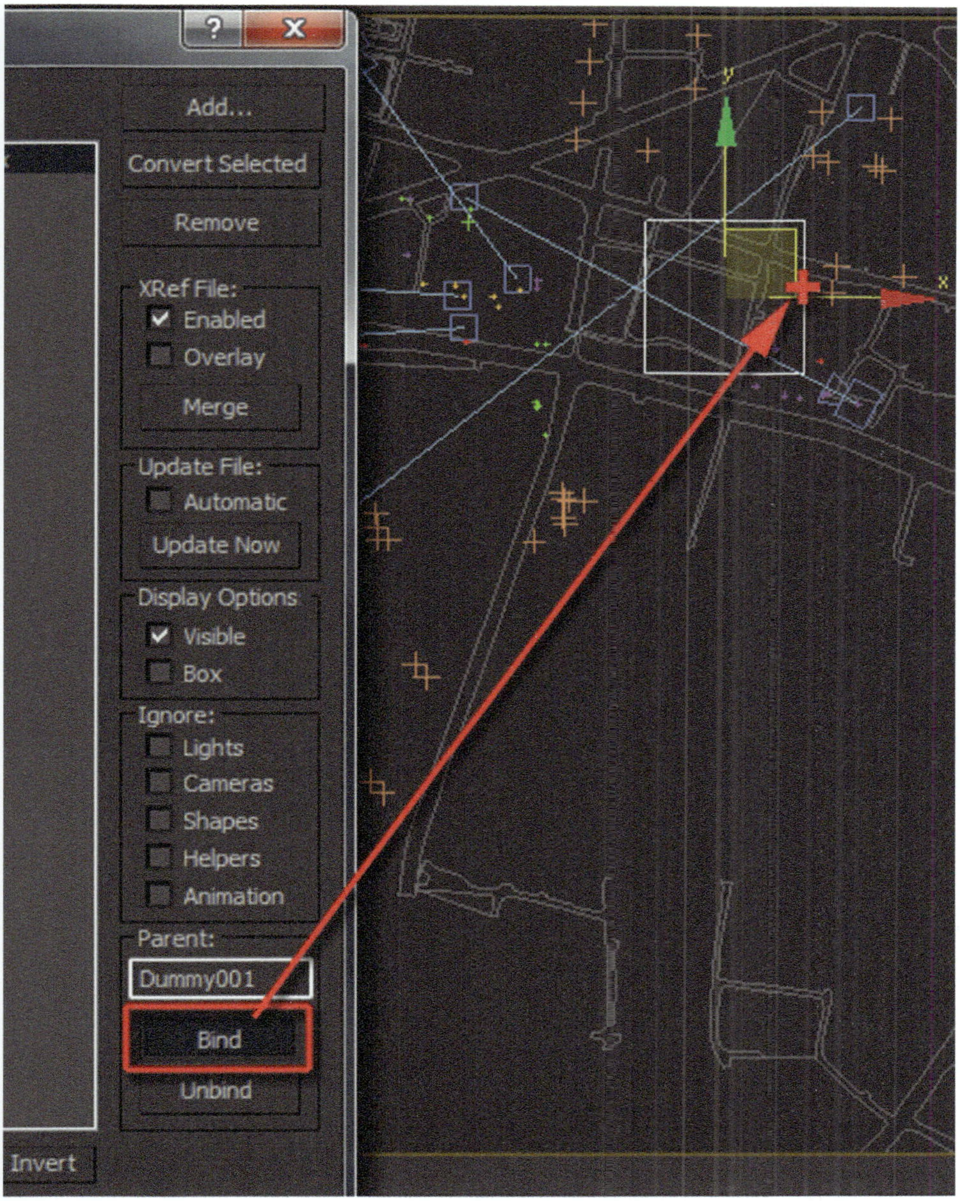

Bind the Dummy object

Following that, move and/or rotate the dummy in order to line up perfectly with the main scene.

Dummy object and scene aligned

An XRef and a dummy object were used to ensure the original survey point values remained intact from their original scene location.

Camera-Matching without a Survey Data

Before beginning the process of camera-matching a photo, it's imperative to be aware of the following:

1. Have an almost accurate dimension of a relevant object in the photo (e.g., at least one object in the photo).
2. Be aware that photos are usually taken at eye level (e.g., 1.65 meters), unless stated otherwise.
3. The average height of most people in photos is between 1.70 and 1.75 meters, unless there's an exception.
4. The average door height is around 2.2 meters, unless there's an exception.
5. The average height of a chair is about 0.4 meters, unless there's an exception.

Start by setting up the Output size to match the incoming background photo to be camera-matched.

Background photo Image Size

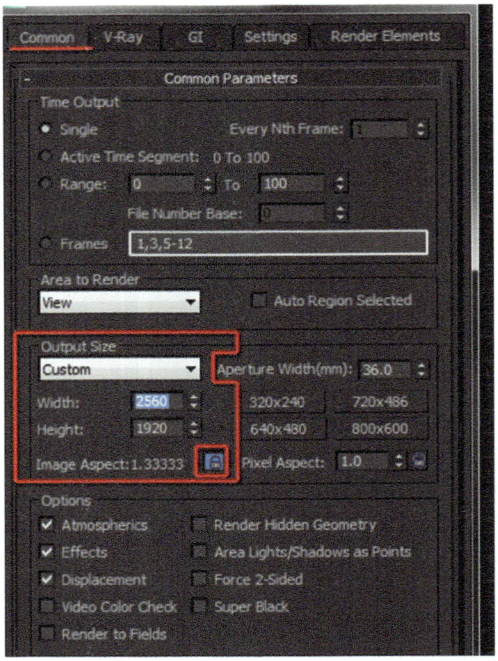

Output Size in 3ds max

Next, load up the background photo in the perspective viewport and use the Shift+F to enable the Show Safe Frames option.

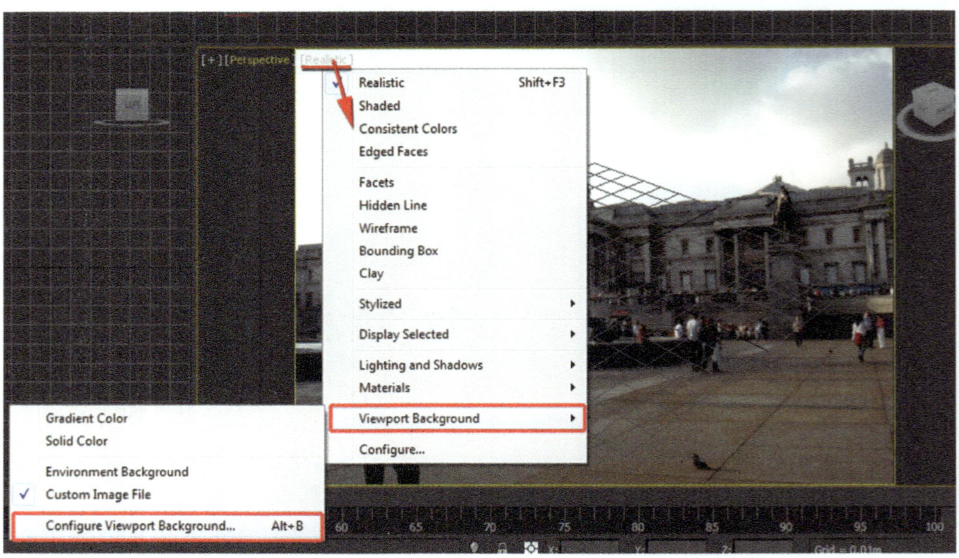

Load up the background photo in the perspective viewport

While the perspective viewport is still selected, click on the Tools from the main toolbar, followed by choosing the Perspective Match option.

The Perspective Match from the Utilities command panel should be prompted automatically. Click on the Hide Vanishing Lines button to make it visible in the viewport.

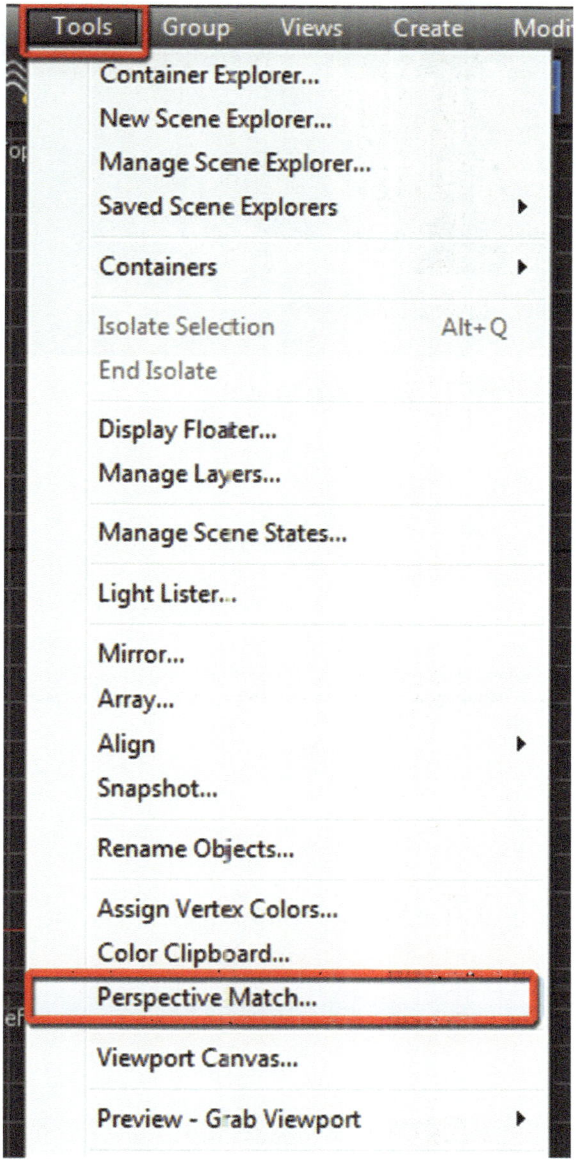

Select the Perspective Match tool

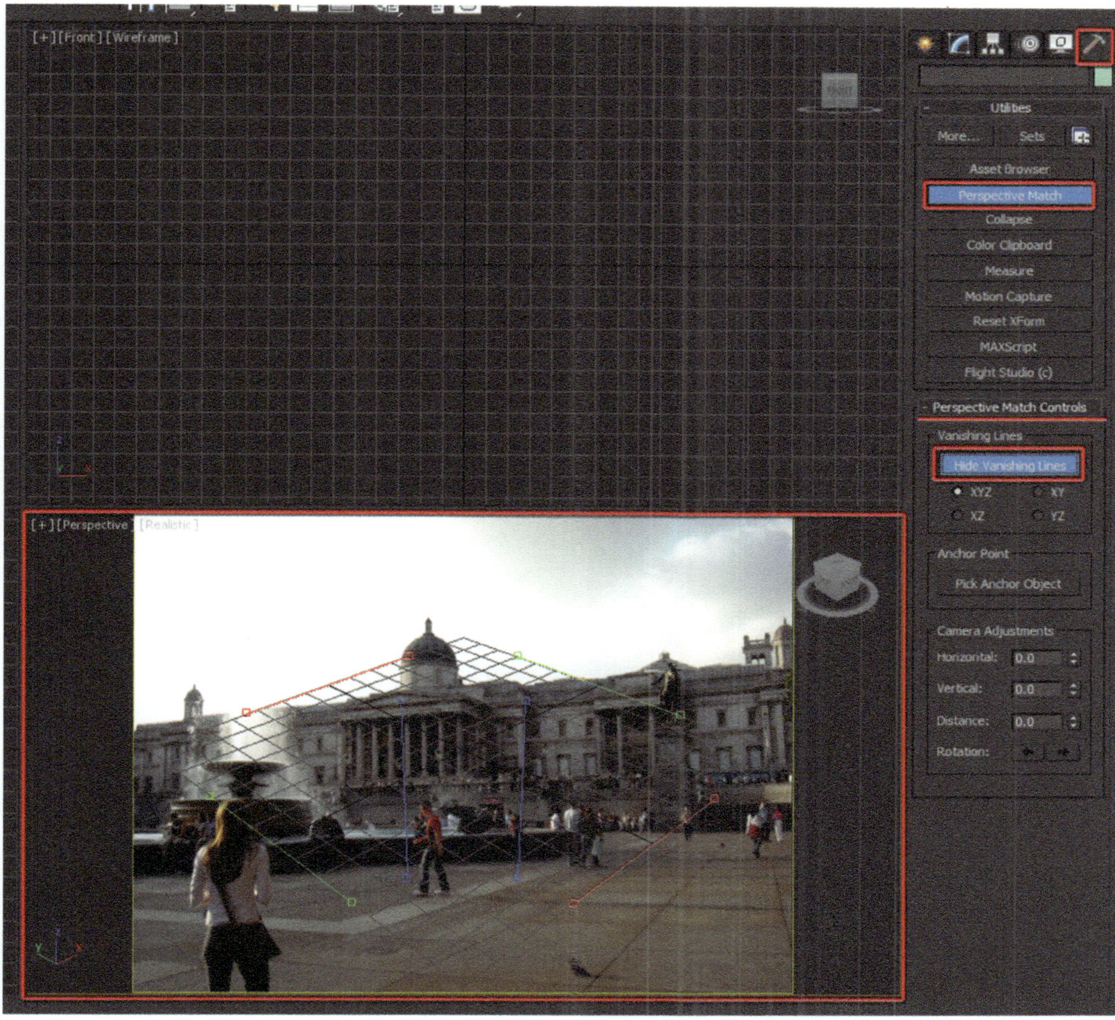

Click on Hide Vanishing Lines button to make it visible

The two Blue Vanishing lines are usually moved to line up closely to two key horizontal lines of the photo.

The two Green vanishing lines are often moved to line up closely to two key perspective lines of the photo (e.g., bottom/foreground and a top perspective line).

The two Red vanishing lines are often moved to line up closely to two key horizontal lines of the photo.

To move a vanishing line as a whole, simply left click on its middle point, followed by moving it.

To move parts of the vanishing line, simply click on one of its handles and move it accordingly.

The rule of thumb is to keep the top vanishing lines (e.g., red and green) on upper areas of the photo, and the lower vanishing lines (e.g., red and green) on the lower areas of the photo.

After much pulling and moving the vanishing lines around, the result should look similar to the figure depicted below.

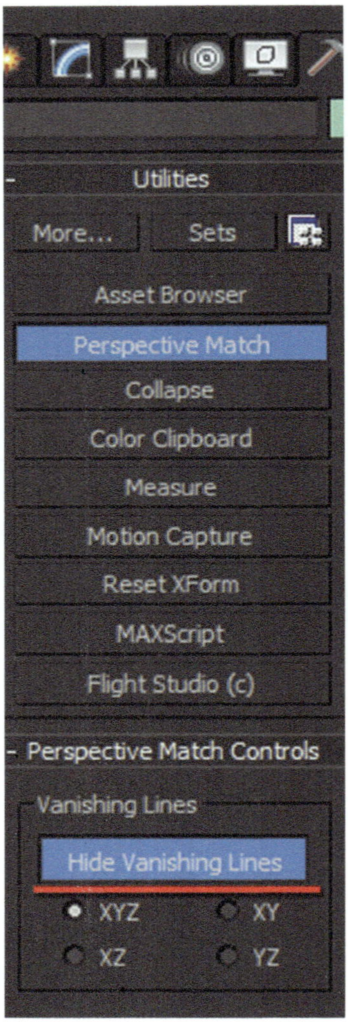

Vanishing lines lined up

Once satisfied with the position of the vanishing lines, simply Create Camera from View (Ctrl+C)

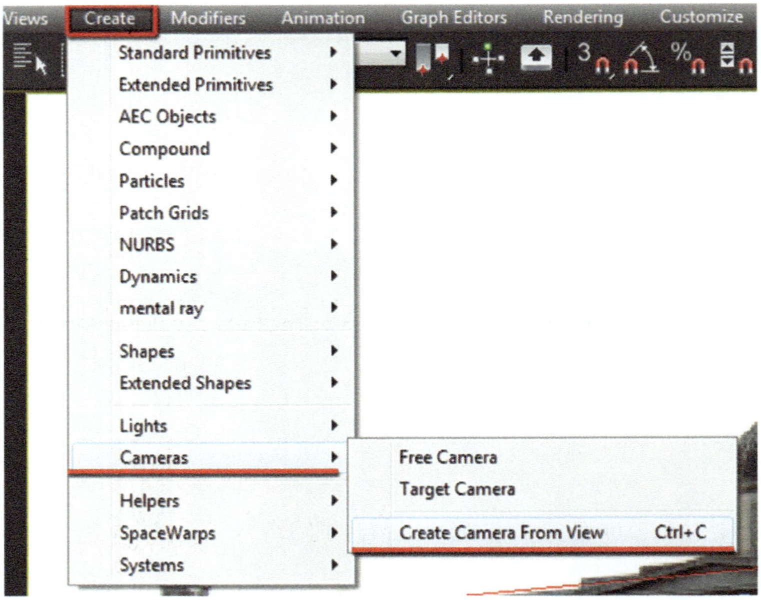
Views
Create
Modifiers
Animation
Graph Editors
Rendering
Customize
Standard Primitives
Extended Primitives
AEC Objects
Compound
Particles
Patch Grids
NURBS
Dynamics
mental ray
Shapes
Extended Shapes
Lights
Cameras
Helpers
SpaceWarps
Systems
Free Camera
Target Camera
Create Camera From View Ctrl+C

Create Camera from View

As mentioned earlier, since cameras are often at eye level (e.g., 1.65 m), one can create a surface (e.g., Box-geometry standard primitive) 1.65 meters below the camera, and increase its width and length to fit the dimensions of the photo reference.

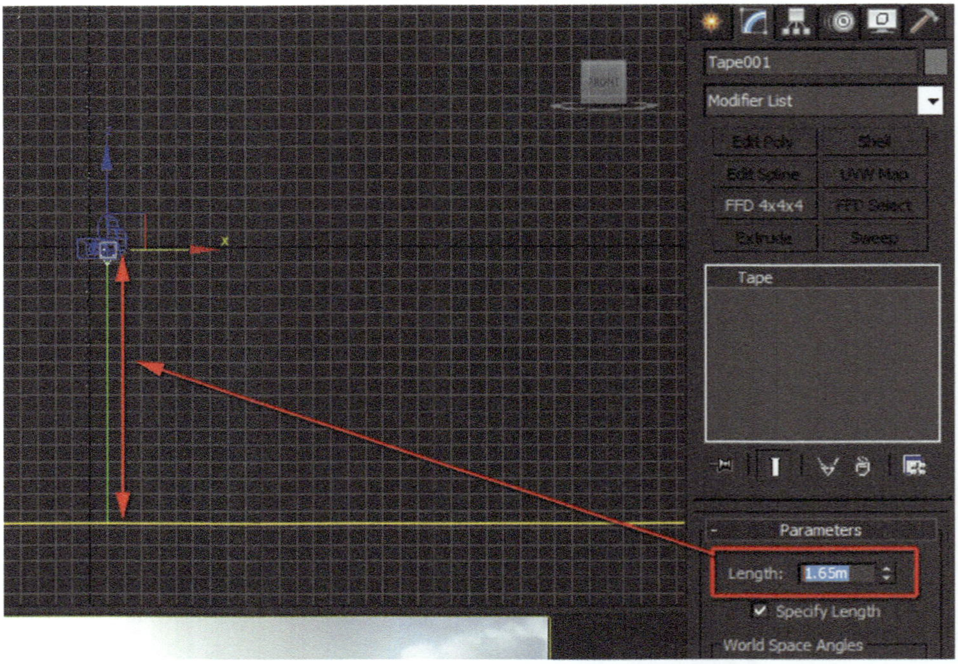

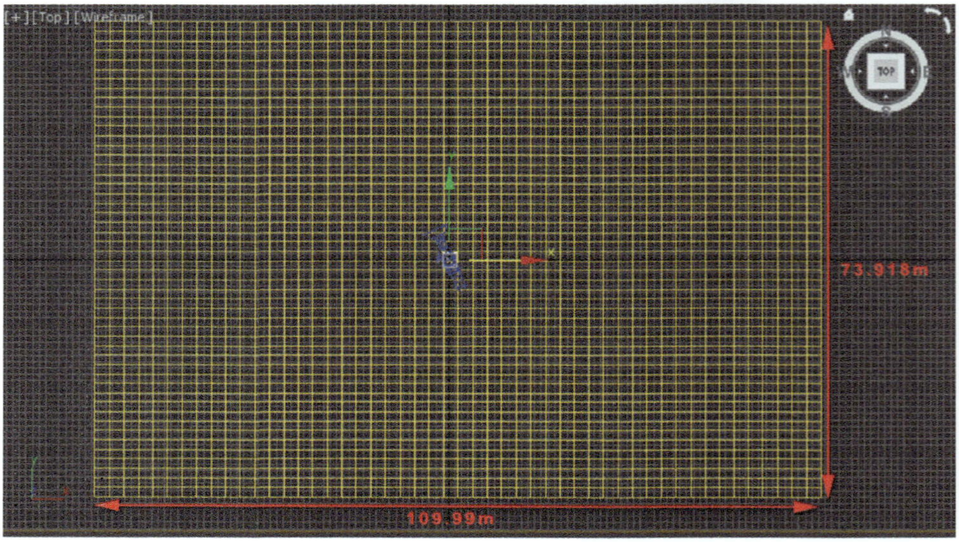

Create a surface 1.65 meters below the camera

From this point onward, one can create other reference points such as people and other objects in the scene.

Since a standard 3ds max camera is currently being used in the scene, one can recreate a similar VRayPhysicalcamera manually or via a script camera converter.

Alternatively, simply keep the current standard 3ds max camera, and open the Environment and Effects dialog (8).

In the Exposure Control rollout parameters, load the VRay Exposure Control option from its dropdown list.

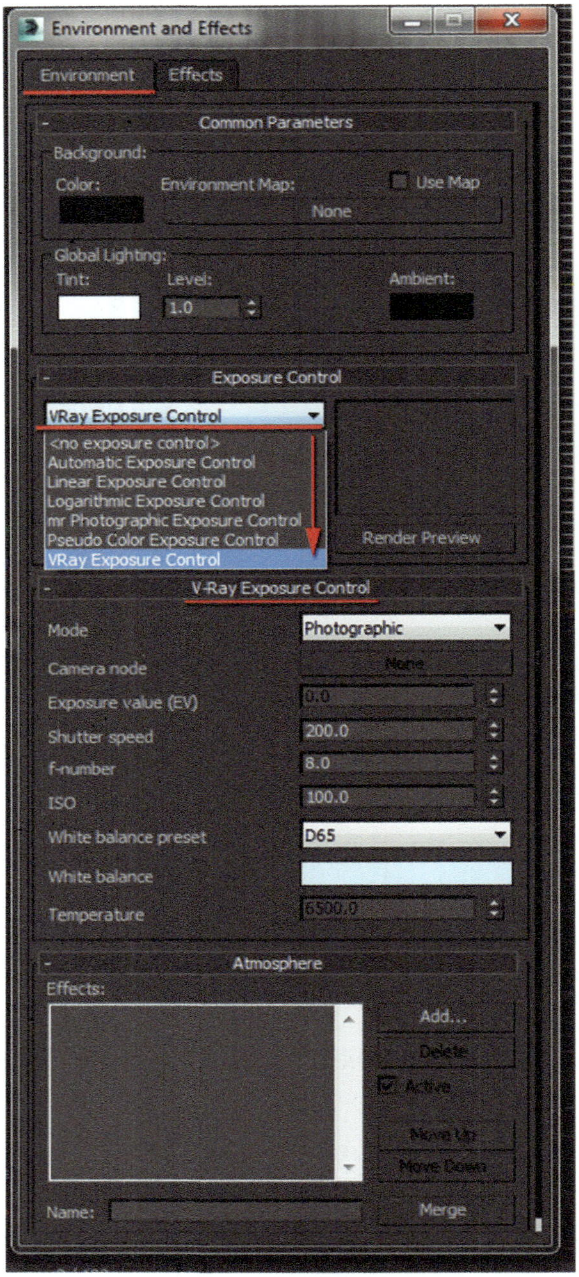
Environment and Effects
Environment
Effects
Common Parameters
Background:
Color:
Environment Map:
Use Map
None
Global Lighting:
Tint:
Level:
1.0
Ambient:
Exposure Control
VRay Exposure Control
<no exposure control>
Automatic Exposure Control
Linear Exposure Control
Logarithmic Exposure Control
mr Photographic Exposure Control
Pseudo Color Exposure Control
VRay Exposure Control
Render Preview
V-Ray Exposure Control
Mode
Photographic
Camera node
Exposure value (EV)
0.0
Shutter speed
200.0
f-number
8.0
ISO
100.0
White balance preset
D65
White balance
Temperature
6500.0
Atmosphere
Effects:
Add...
Delete
Active
Name:
Merge

Load the VRay Exposure Control

Use the background photo Properties Details to enter more accurate camera detail parameters such as Focal Length, F-stop, and ISO speed.

The Origin info from the Properties Details can be used in the Daylight System parameters (Chapter 3) to enter the time, day, and location of the photo taken.

Also, refer to Chapters 9, 12, 16, and 19 to match in post, the overall color, and feel of the render with the background photo.

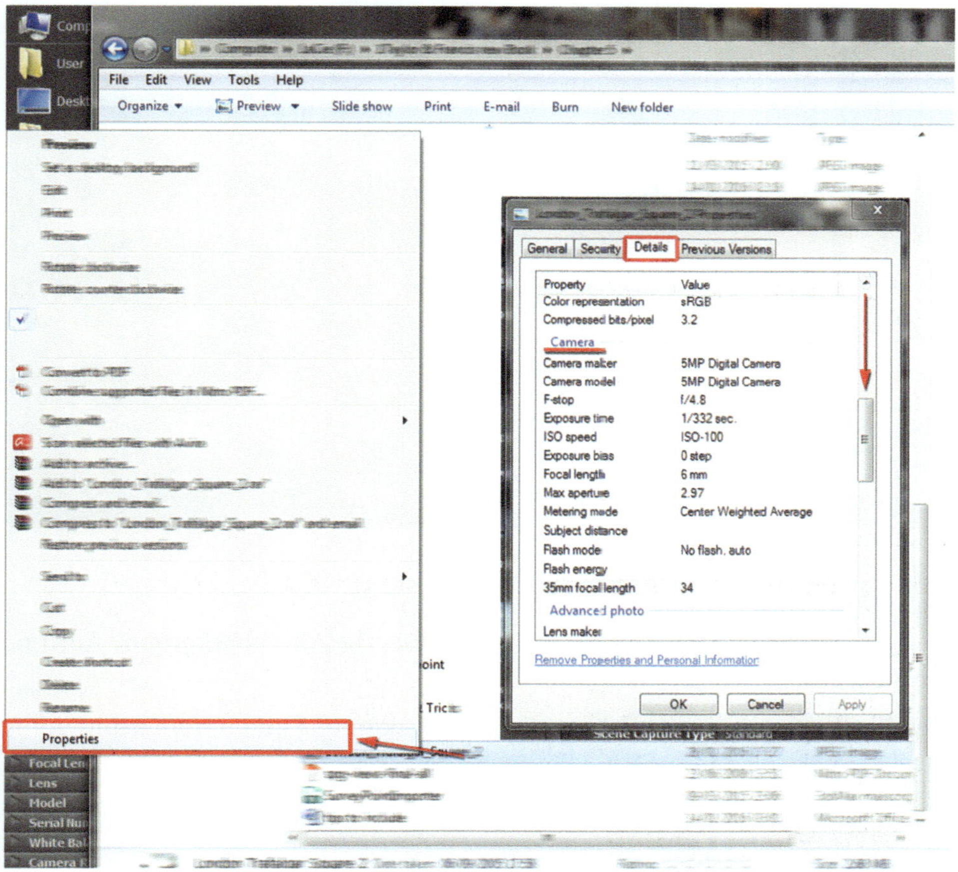

Background photo Properties Details

For aerial shots looking down, the previously described methodology might not work. Instead, users might have to eyeball the correct camera perspective, by constantly rotating, moving, and tilting the camera accordingly.

It often takes a bit of practice to camera-match aerial shots accurately.

5 Tips and Tricks

Integrating Shots in 3ds max

Prior to starting, ensure the background photo is plugged into the Environment Map toggle, and that its Mapping coordinates are set to Screen type.

Background photo plugged in the Environment Map toggle

In the Color mapping rollout parameters, ensure the Affect background function is disabled.

This function will prevent the environment background photo from being affected by the GI and the VRayPhysicalcamera settings (e.g., prevent it from being washed out and overexposed).

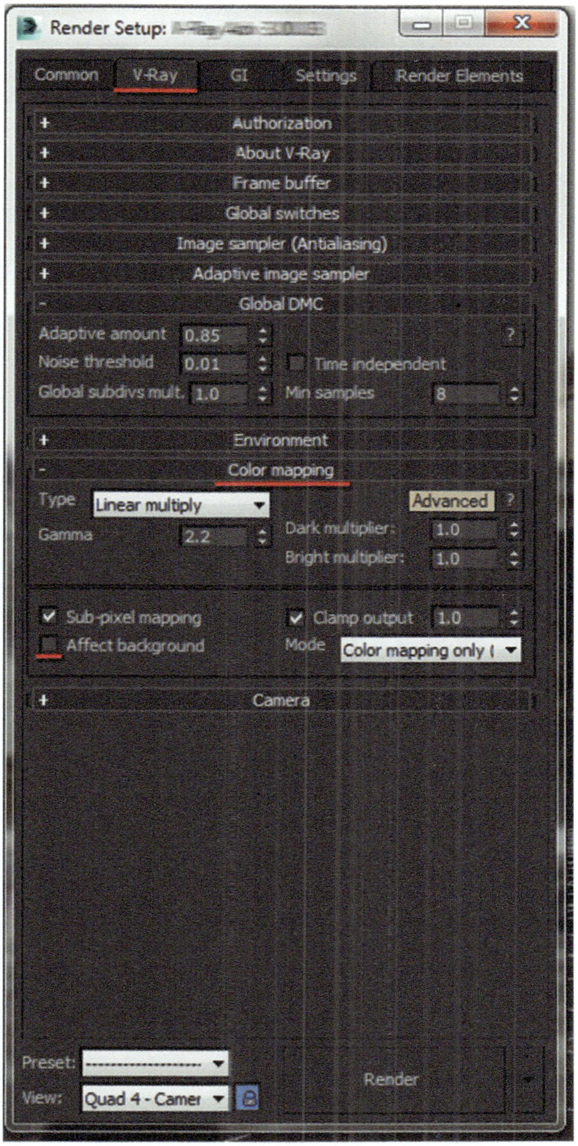

Affect background disabled

Next, ensure the Enable GI option is turned on.

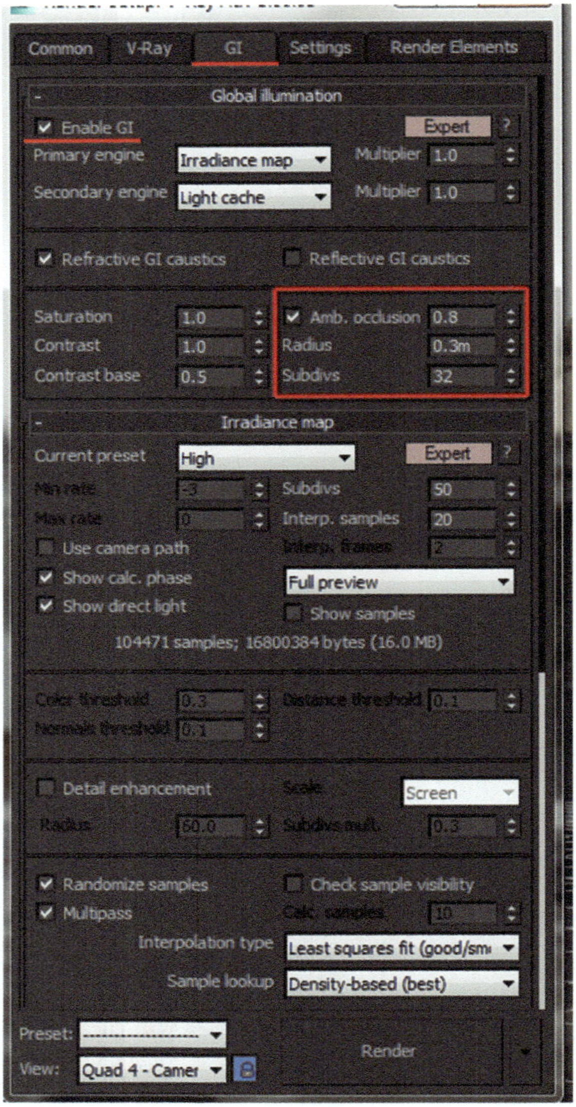

Enable GI option is turned on

If the 3d surface/ground in the scene is to be used as a Matte object to cast shadows, simply do the following:

Select the surface in the scene and right click on it to bring up its quad menu. Select the VRay properties option to open its dialog.

In the Matte properties group, enable the Matte object option and set the Alpha contribution to –1.0.

The value of –1.0 will ensure the 3d surface is not included in the Alpha channel.

To have shadows cast onto its matte surface, simply enable the Shadows option in the Direct light group and Close the dialog.

After closing the dialog, apply a VRay material similar to the ground surface seen in the background photo.

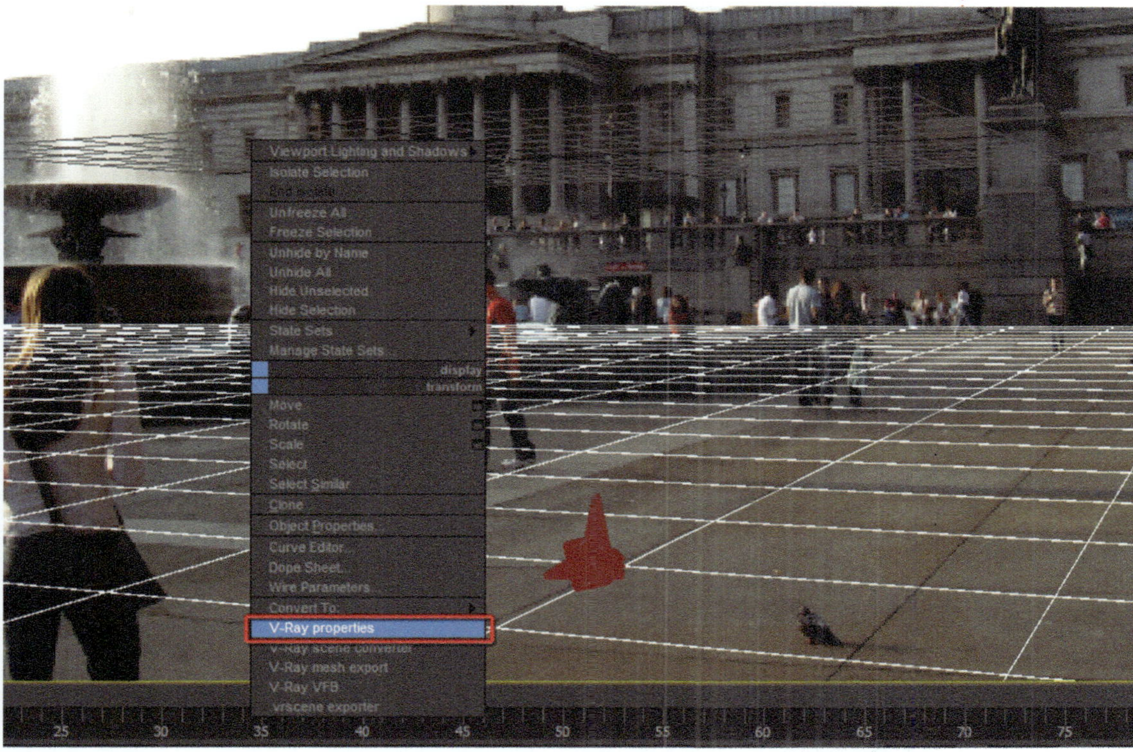

Select the VRay properties option

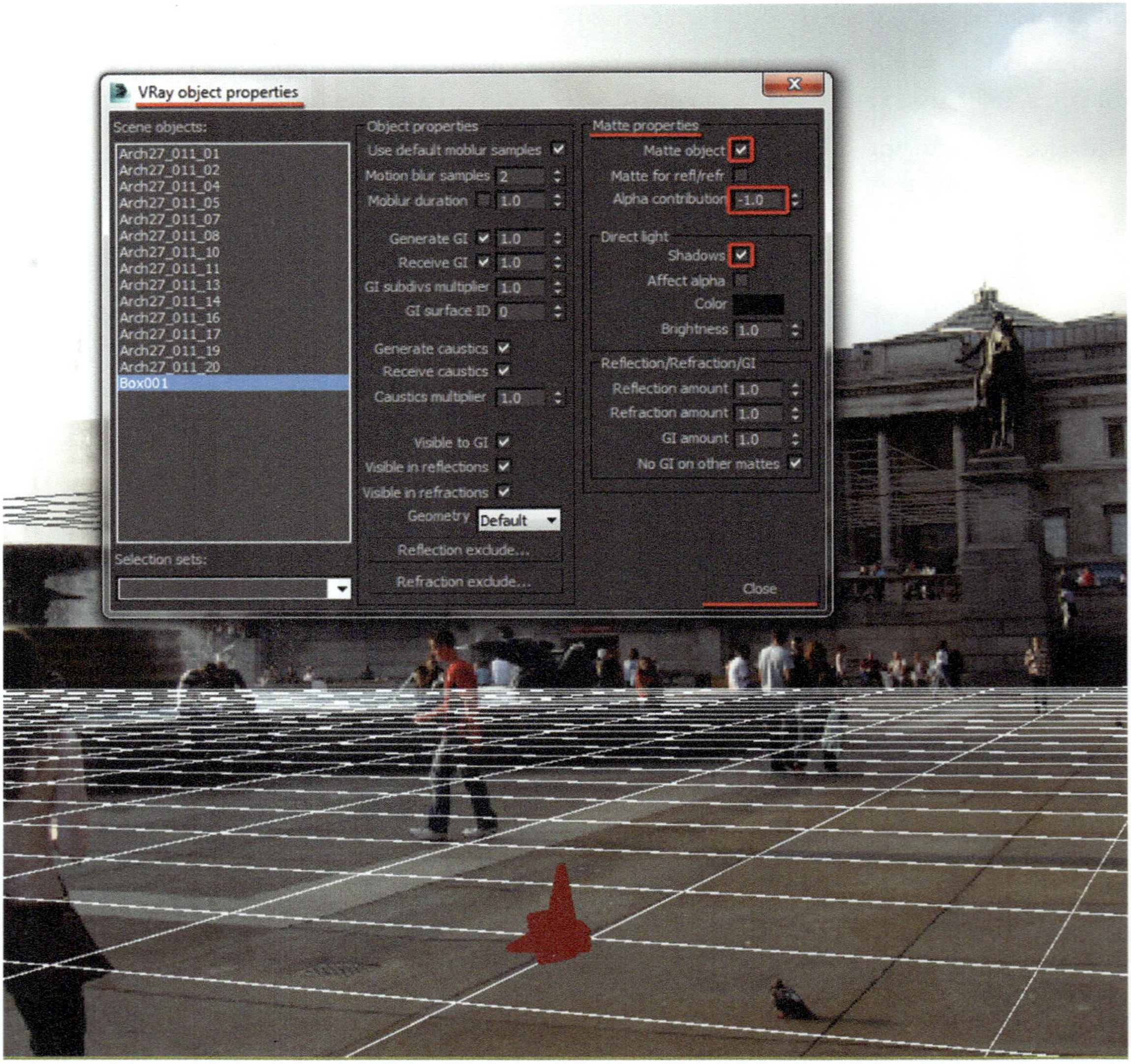

VRay object properties dialog

If it's a daylight shot, ensure a daylight system object is created and the date and time information is accurately entered in its parameters, as previously covered in Chapter 3.

It's utterly imperative to enable the Daylight Saving Time option.

Also, the daylight compass should be placed on the same level as the ground.

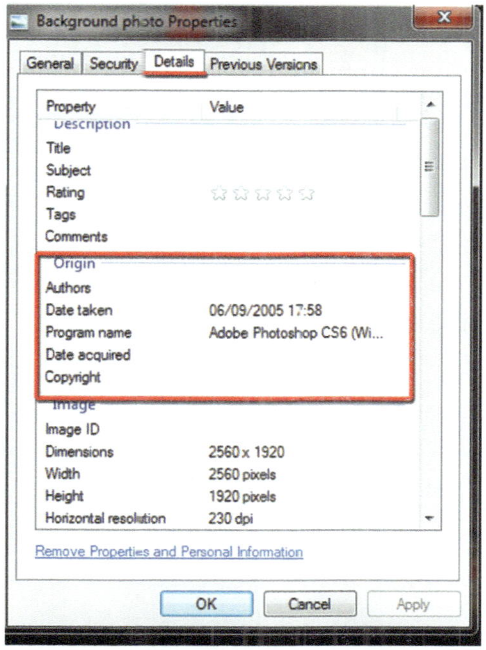

Origin Properties Details

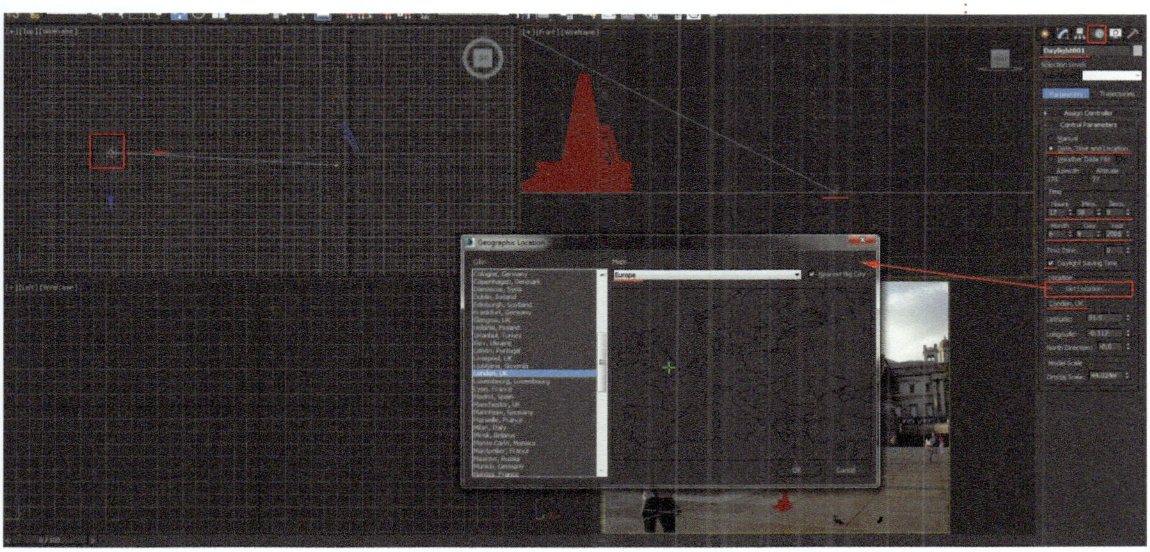

Daylight System position and parameters

To prevent the 3d orange cone in the scene from color bleeding onto the Matte object surface, a VRayOverrideMtl needs to be applied onto the original material.

A VRay black material (or similar) should be plugged into its GI toggle. For more information about this procedural map, refer to Chapter 2.

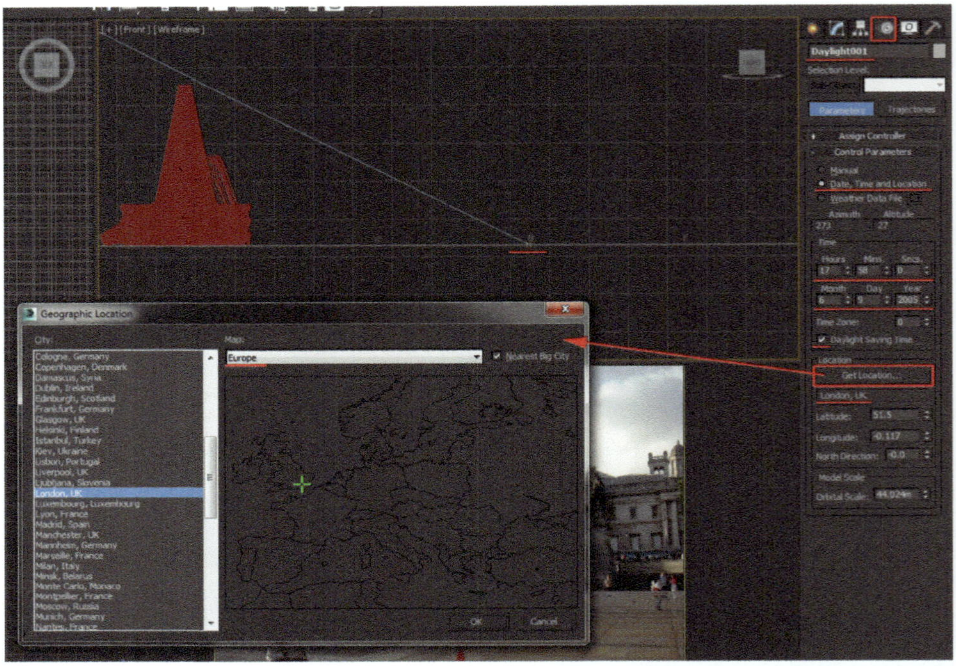

VRayOverrideMtl applied

Also, to make its indirectly lit areas slightly darker, simply open its VRay object properties dialog and set its Receive GI value to about 0.1.

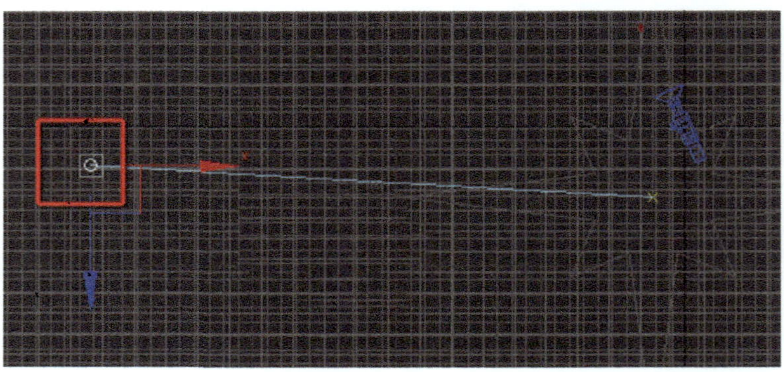

Receive GI value set to 0.1

Next, create a VRay dome light and increase its Intensity value until the shadow color is matched with the background photo.

Tweak with its Color temperature, or simply sample it from the background photo in the viewport.

Alternatively, plug an HDRI to the dome light as depicted in Chapter 3.

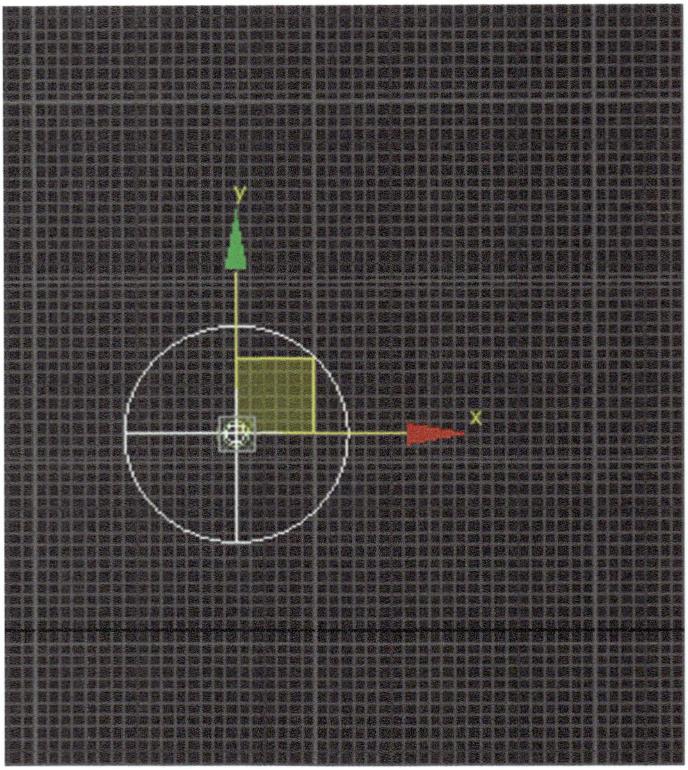

VRay dome light parameters

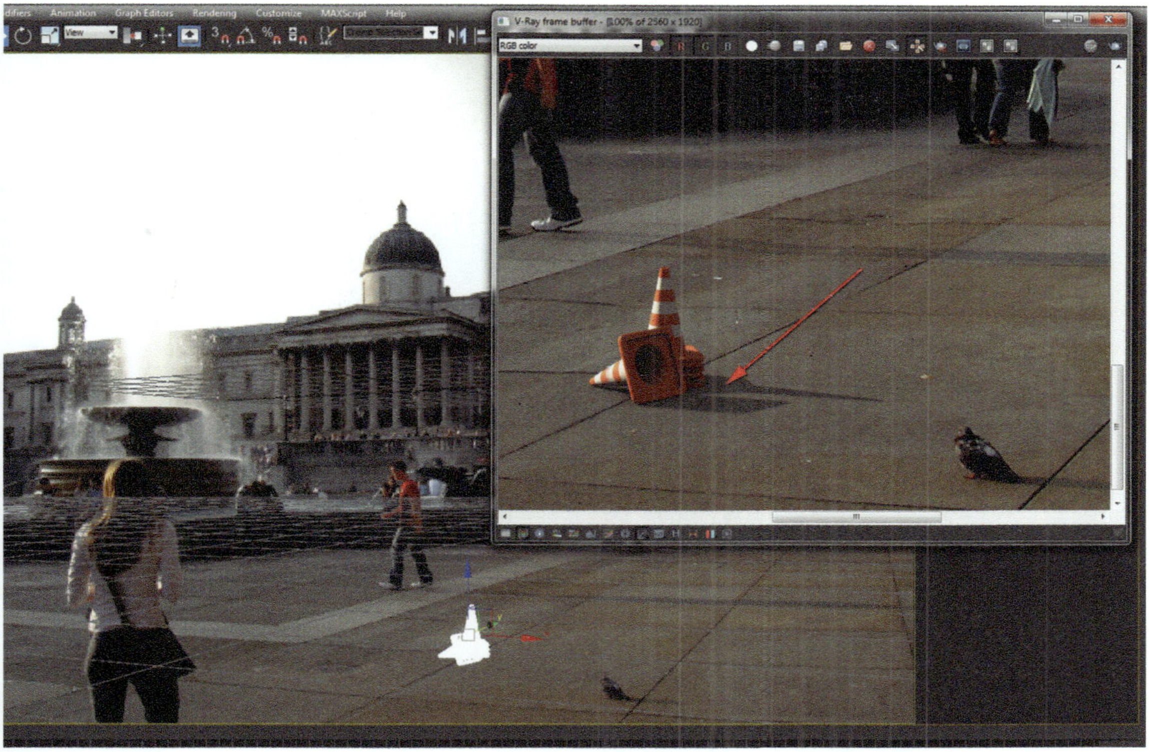

Shadow brightness matched, by increasing the VRay dome light Intensity Multiplier

If it's a Night shot, the daylight system object needs to be deleted or disabled.

By default the 2d reflections/refractions in the scene come from the Environment Map toggle.

To override this, simply open the Environment rollout from the Render Setup dialog and enable the Reflection/refraction environment option.

Following that, simply plug a different bitmap or an HDRI (spherical mapping coordinates type) to its toggle.

To seamlessly match the bright highlights of the render with the background photo, simply go to the Color mapping rollout parameters and increase the Bright multiplier to about 1.8, or higher.

Increase the Bright multiplier value to about 1.8

Final render

Useful Render Elements

In addition to some of the render elements to be covered in later chapters, the following ones are also worth paying attention to:

VRayExtraText: This Render element is often used to add extra details/depth to renders in post, especially in exterior scenes.

To add it, simply open the Render Elements tab and add the VRayExtraText from the Render Elements dialog.

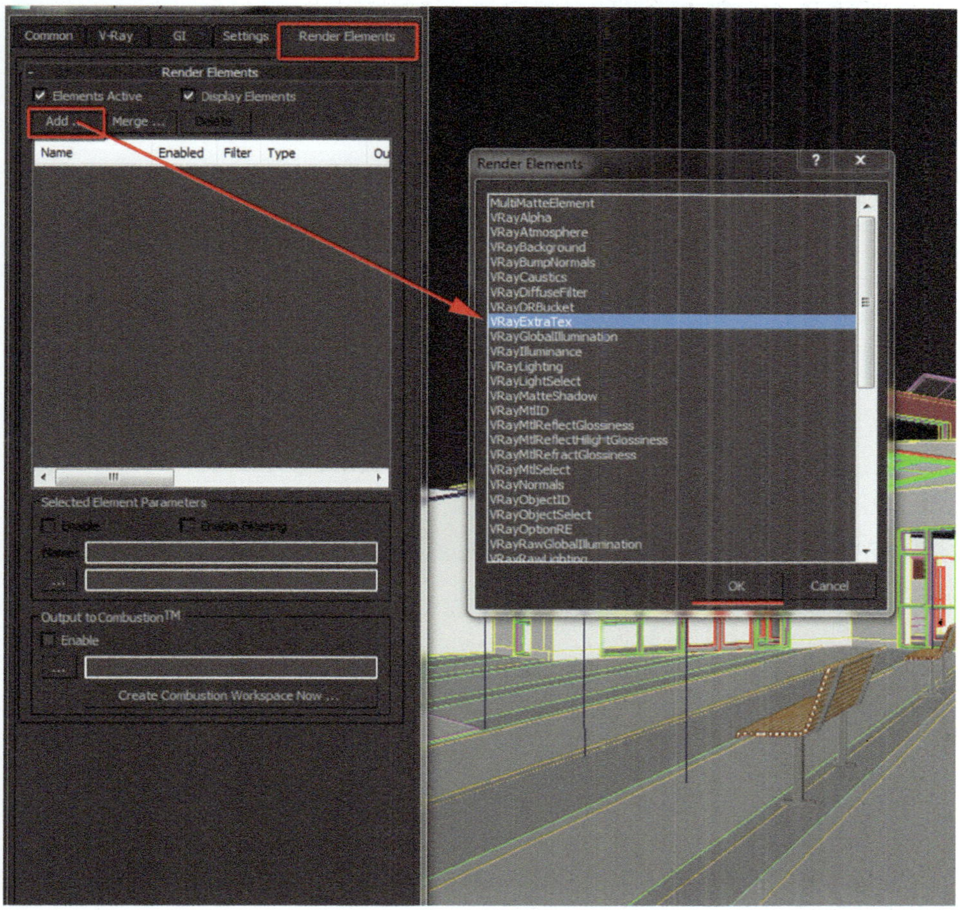

Add the VRayExtraText element

Once loaded, the VRayExtraText element can be renamed in the Name text field (e.g., type in the text+Enter).

The following step is to add the VRayDirt to the texture toggle.

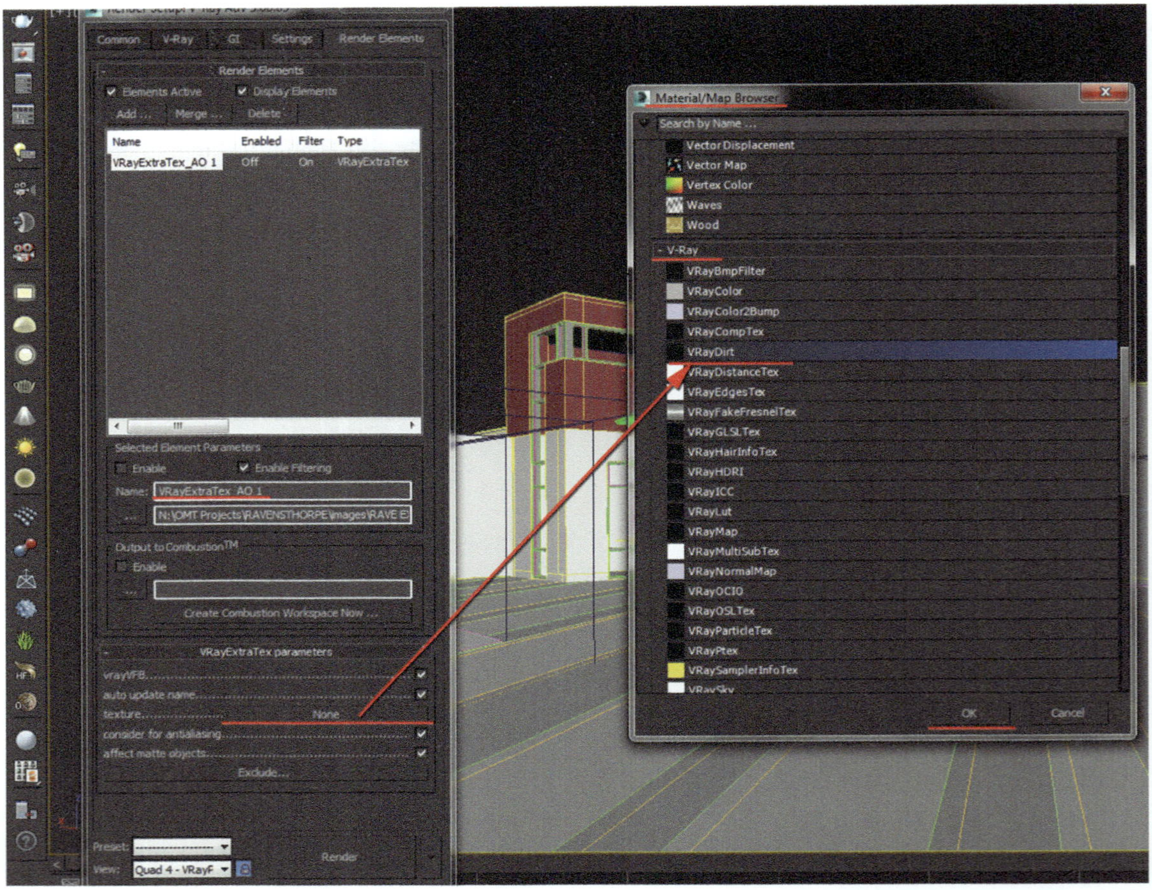
Common
V-Ray
GI
Settings
Render Elements
Elements Active
Display Elements
Add ...
Merge ...
Delete
Name
Enabled
Filter
Type
VRayExtraTex_AO 1
Off
On
VRayExtraTex
Selected Element Parameters
Enable
Enable Filtering
Name:
VRayExtraTex_AO 1
Output to Combustion™
Enable
Create Combustion Workspace Now ...
VRayExtraTex parameters
vrayVFB
auto update name
texture
None
consider for antialiasing
affect matte objects
Exclude...
Preset:
View:
Quad 4 - VRayF
Render
Material/Map Browser
Search by Name ...
Vector Displacement
Vector Map
Vertex Color
Waves
Wood
V-Ray
VRayBmpFilter
VRayColor
VRayColor2Bump
VRayCompTex
VRayDirt
VRayDistanceTex
VRayEdgesTex
VRayFakeFresnelTex
VRayGLSLTex
VRayHairInfoTex
VRayHDRI
VRayICC
VRayLut
VRayMap
VRayMultiSubTex
VRayNormalMap
VRayOCIO
VRayOSLTex
VRayParticleTex
VRayPtex
VRaySamplerInfoTex
OK
Cancel

Add the VRayDirt to the texture toggle

To edit the VRayDirt settings, simply drag it from the texture toggle and drop it onto a material slot as an instanced copy.

Test render its default parameters.

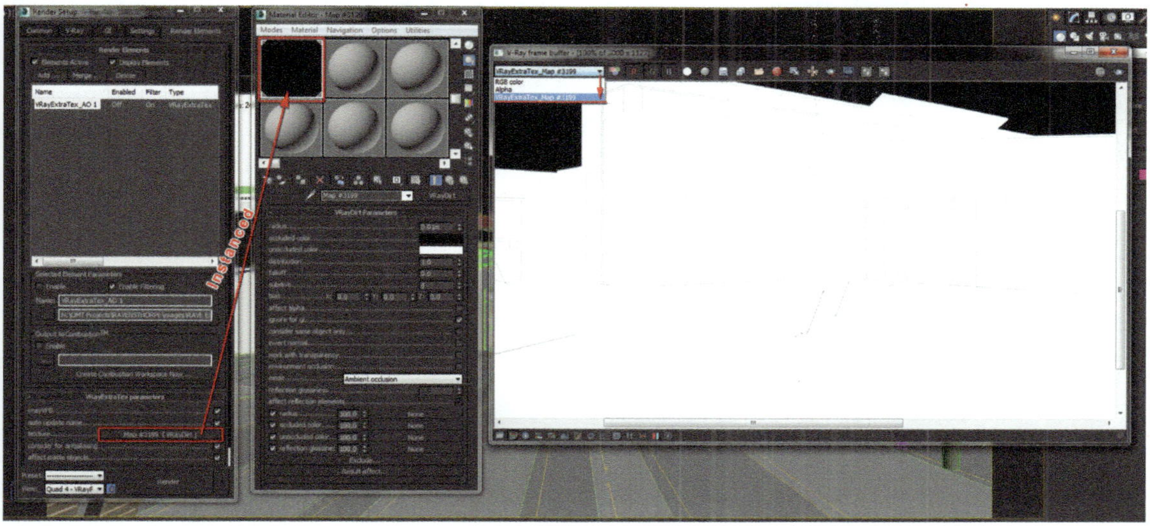

Drag and drop the VRayDirt onto a material slot

Most of VRayDirt parameters are self-explanatory.

The darker areas represent the occluded color; and the white areas represent the unoccluded color.

The radius parameter determines the occluded color radius.

The subdivs parameter controls the smoothness of the occluded color. The default value is 8 (very grainy).

Try different values to see what works best.

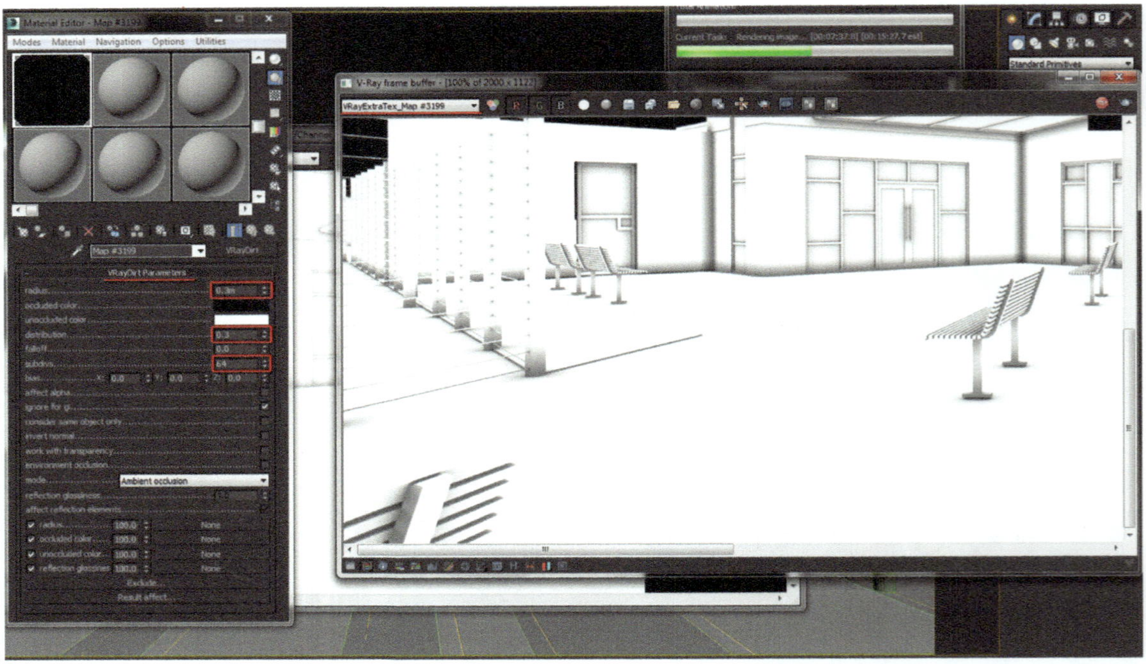
Modes Material Navigation Options Utilities
VRayDirt Parameters
Ambient occlusion
VRayExtraTex_Map #3199

VRayDirt parameters

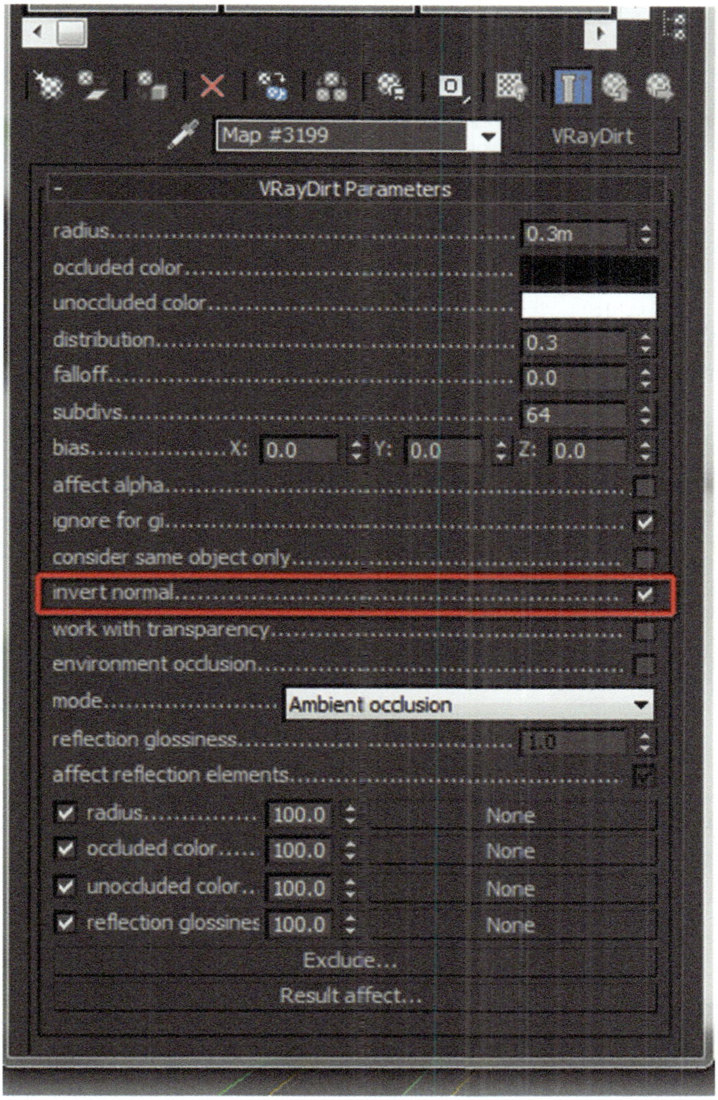

Invert normal enabled

It's widely recommended to use VRayExtraTex element in a separate 3ds max file; as it may contribute to drastic increases of the rendering times.

Blending the VRayDirt in post

For more realistic and complex weathering effects, use a VRay plug-in called Enrichpro.

While film/production companies make discrepancies very prominent in their shots, professional 3d Visualizers tend to make it as subtle as possible, as clients often expect their buildings to appear relatively New (e.g., Architects, Developers).

To make exterior renders more realistic, this unique and utterly useful plug-in can be subtly overlaid in post as multiple render passes.

For more information about it, please visit:

http://www.enrichpro.com/en/richdirt/index.html

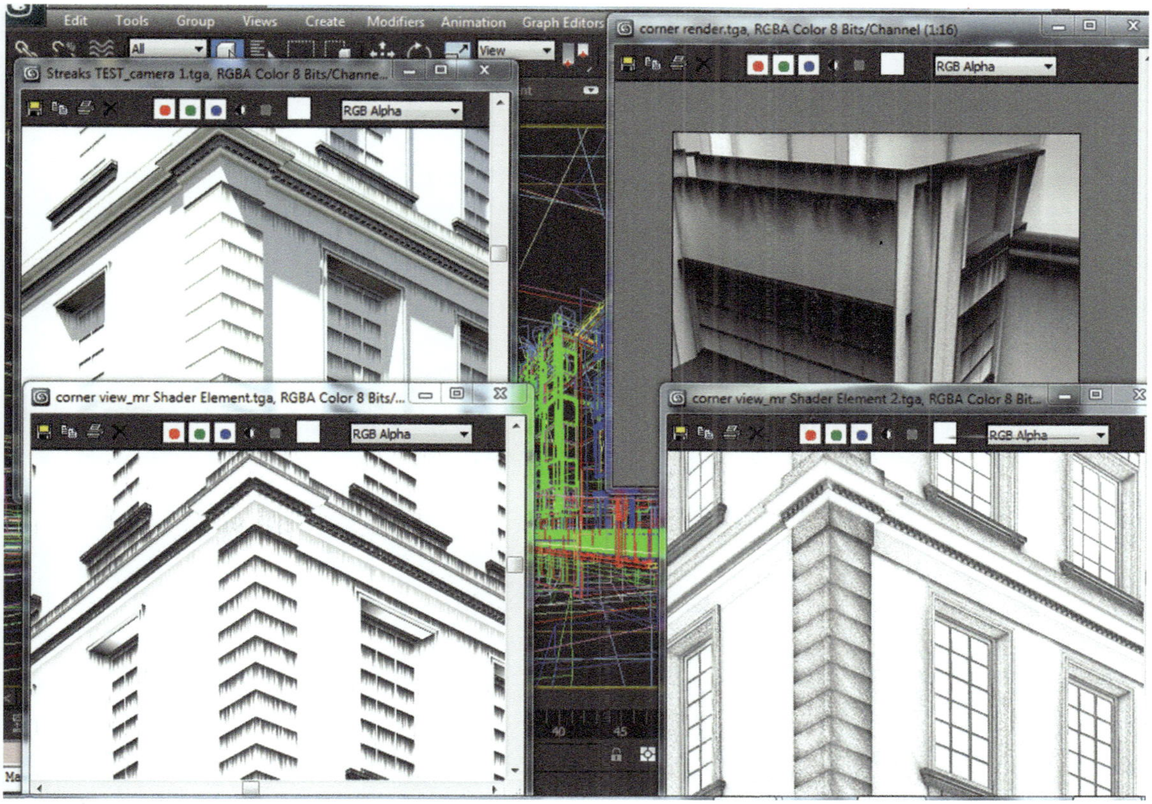

Some of many Enrichpro weathering effects in render elements

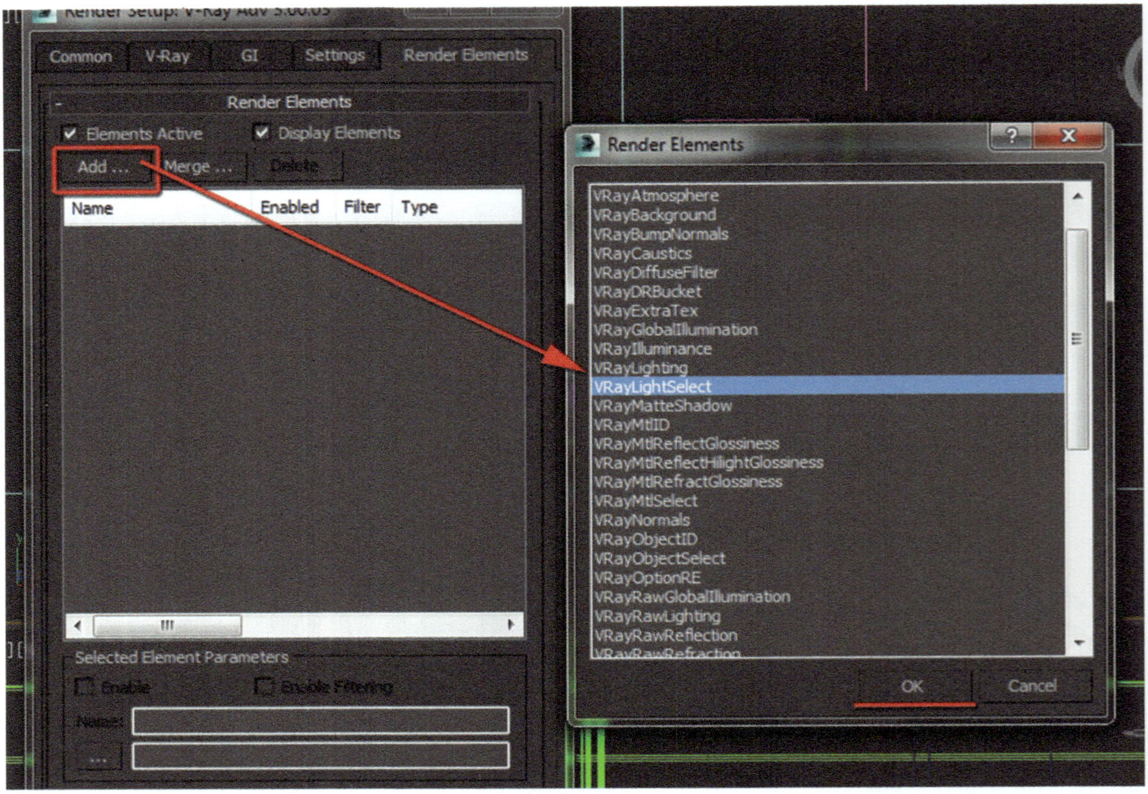

Add the VRayLightSelect to the Render Elements list

Following that, in the Lights group, click on the Add button to select the light/lights in the scene.

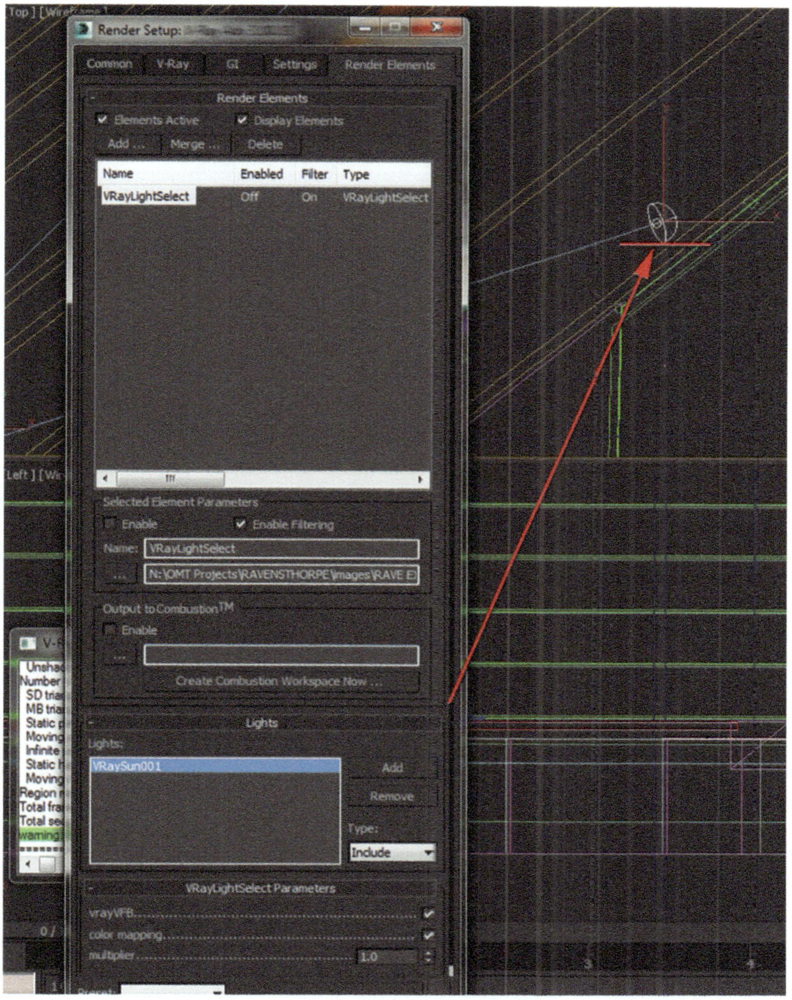

Click on the Ada button to select the light in the scene

If you intend to have different sets of VRayLightSelect elements in the list, simply rename it and press enter.

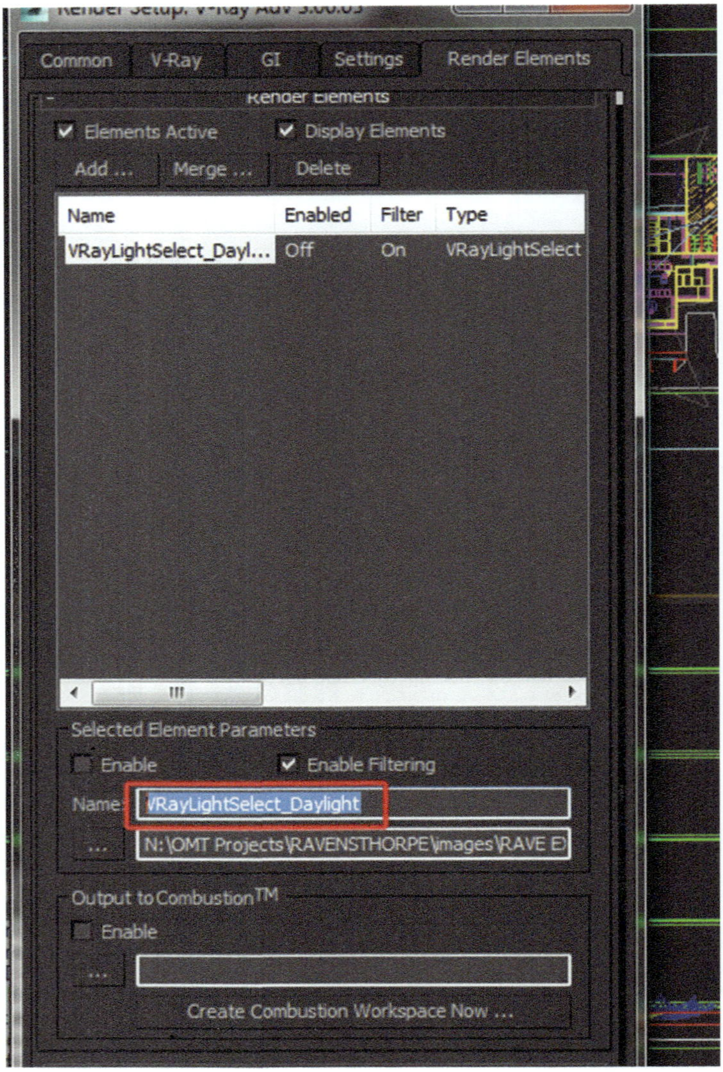

Rename the VRayLightSelect element

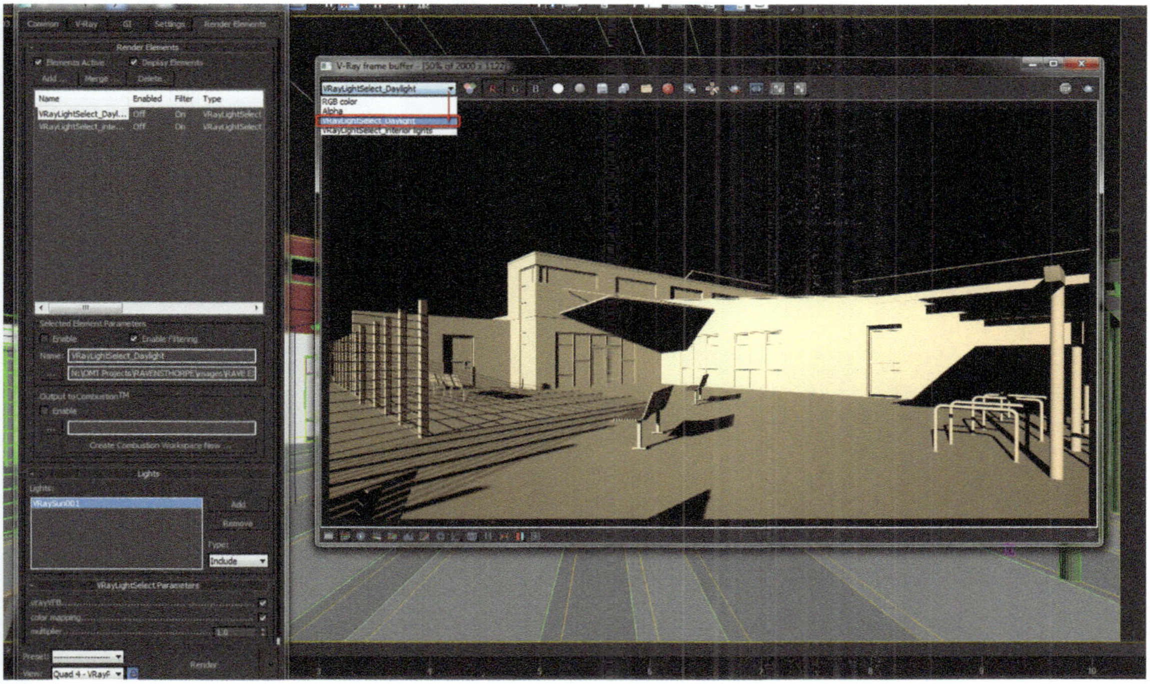

Rendered VRayLightSelect element

To tweak the Rendered VRayLightSelect element in post, simply use some of the techniques covered in Chapters, 9, 12, 16, and 19 to help blend, tweak, and change the color of the VRayLightSelect element.

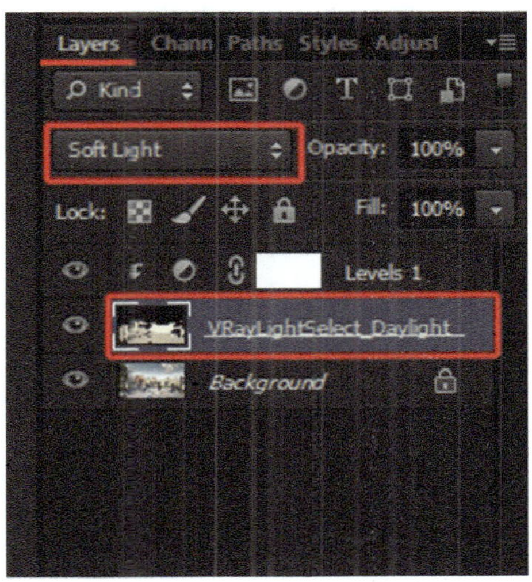

Use Photoshop blending modes to help blend the VRayLightSelect element

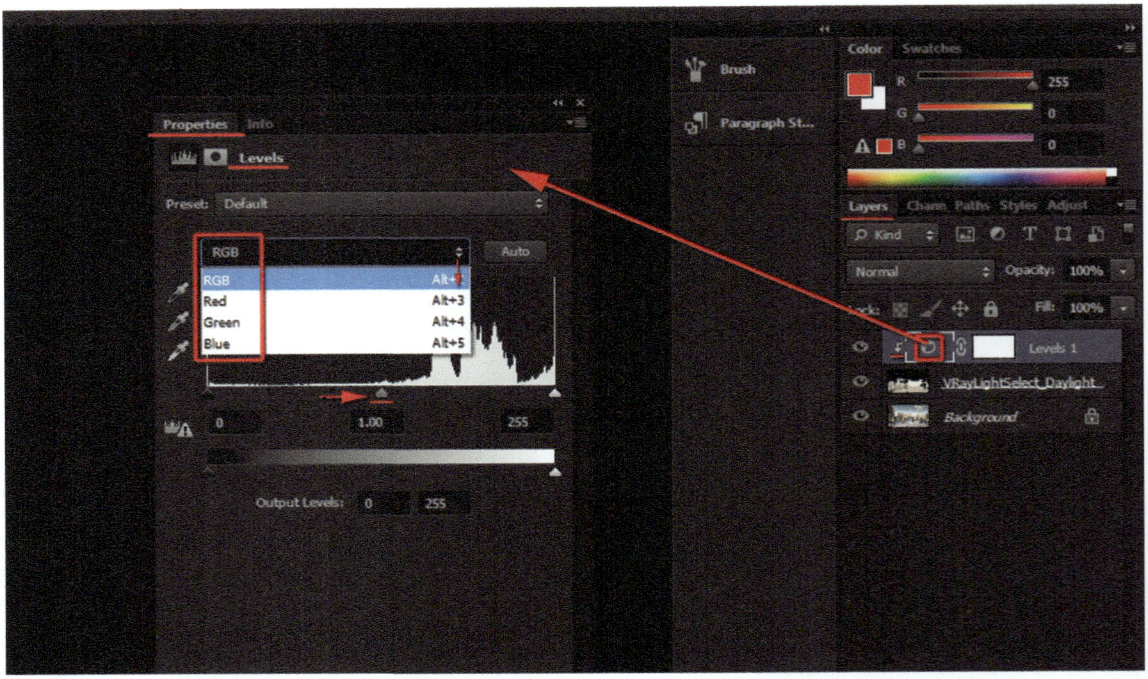

Use clipping layers/masks on adjustment layers to tweak colors and intensity

VRaySampleRate- Users often add this element to closely monitor how VRay is handling the rendering process throughout the scene.

The blue color depicts areas of the scene where little or no render samples are being used.

The Green color highlights areas of the scene where some render samples are being used. These areas often take little or no time to process the render.

The Red color depicts areas of the scene where a substantial/huge number of render samples are being used.

These areas normally take a huge amount of time to process the render. The red areas seen in the frame buffer often contain high-level glossiness/reflectivity, high mesh density, displacement, smooth shadows, etc.

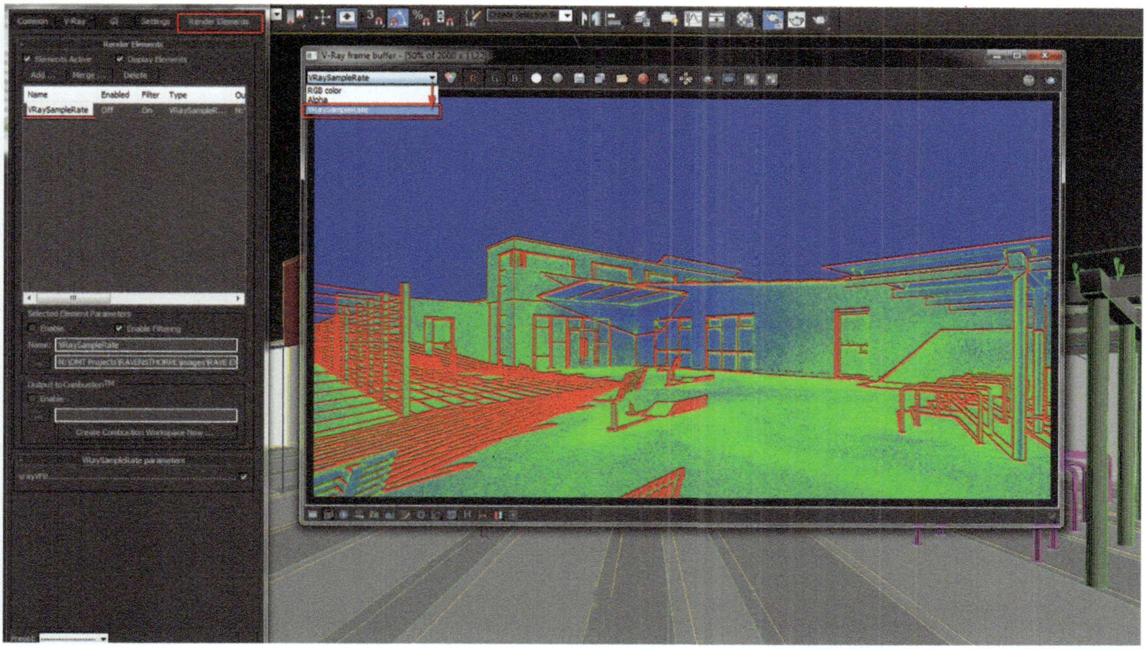

VRaySampleRate in the VRay frame buffer

VRayZDepth: This render element allows users to set the ZDepth of a scene. The render channel can later be used in post to create effects such as depth of field and fog.

The ZDepth min value determines the minimum camera/view value where the ZDepth should start from.

The value of 0.0 is often the default value.

The ZDepth max value determines the maximum camera/view value where the ZDepth should stop (gradient).

The value of 9.0 is often used to cover some of the foreground areas of the view/camera.

The ZDepth channel works best when there's a clear gradient between bright and very dark areas.

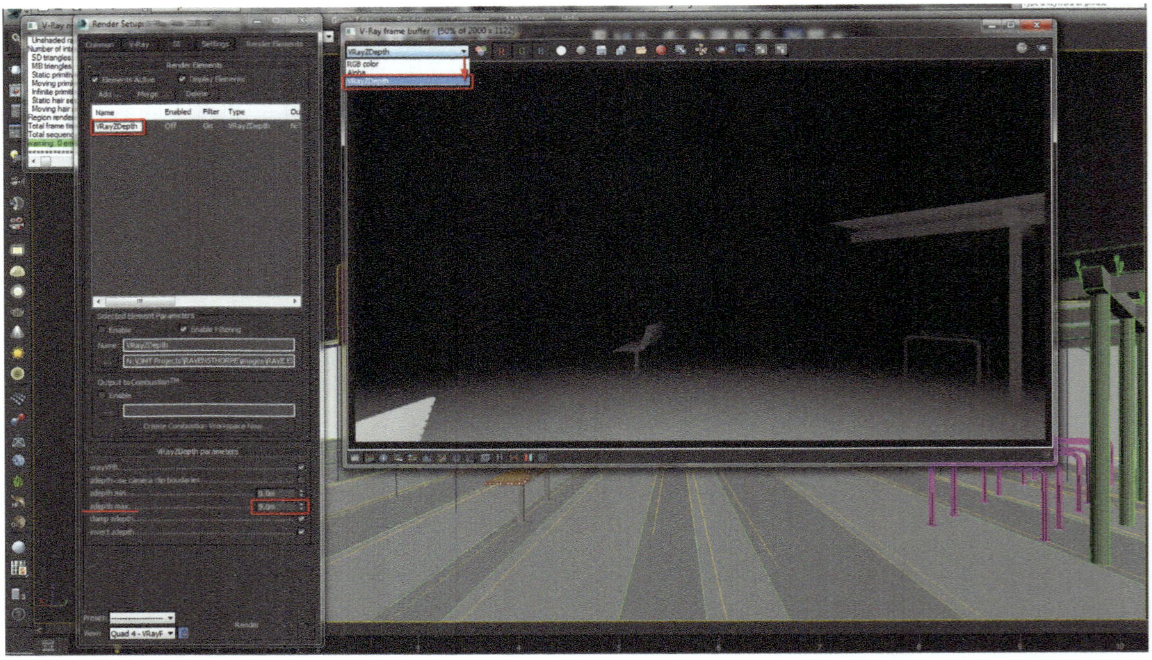

VRayZDepth in the VRay frame buffer

One of the most common ways to use it in Photoshop is to emulate the depth of file (DOF).

To do so, open the VRayZDepth *and* its Channels palette, followed by holding down the Ctrl key and clicking on its RGB Channel to enable the gradient selection.

Enable the VRayZDepth Channels selection in post

While the selection is still on, save it by selecting on the Select main toolbar and choosing the Save Selection option from its dropdown list.

The Save Selection dialog should be prompted. Choose Document Destination to save it, followed by renaming it and clicking OK to close the dialog.

This new saved selection should be added to the Channels palette of the document destination chosen.

It's worth mentioning that, selections can only be saved to a different document when both documents share the same pixels' size (same proportions).

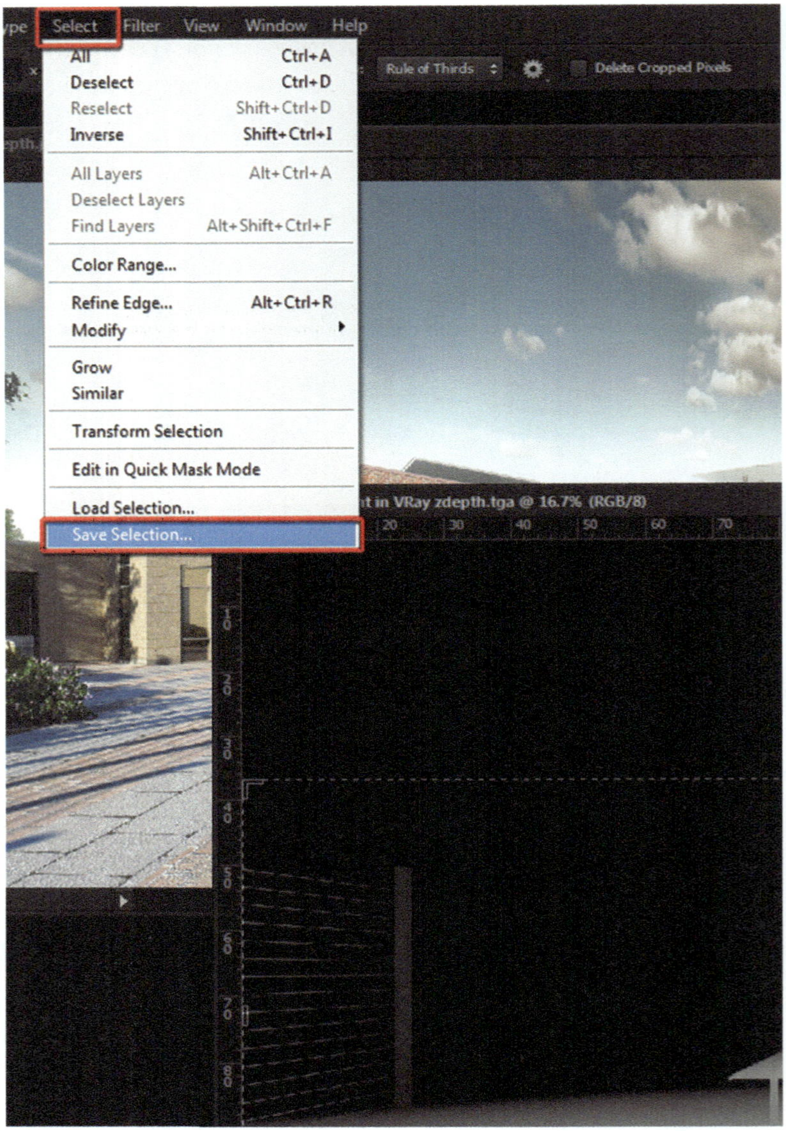
Select
Filter
View
Window
Help
All Ctrl+A
Deselect Ctrl+D
Reselect Shift+Ctrl+D
Inverse Shift+Ctrl+I
All Layers Alt+Ctrl+A
Deselect Layers
Find Layers Alt+Shift+Ctrl+F
Color Range...
Refine Edge... Alt+Ctrl+R
Modify
Grow
Similar
Transform Selection
Edit in Quick Mask Mode
Load Selection...
Save Selection...
Rule of Thirds
Delete Cropped Pixels
VRay zdepth.tga @ 16.7% (RGB/8)

Choose the Save Selection option

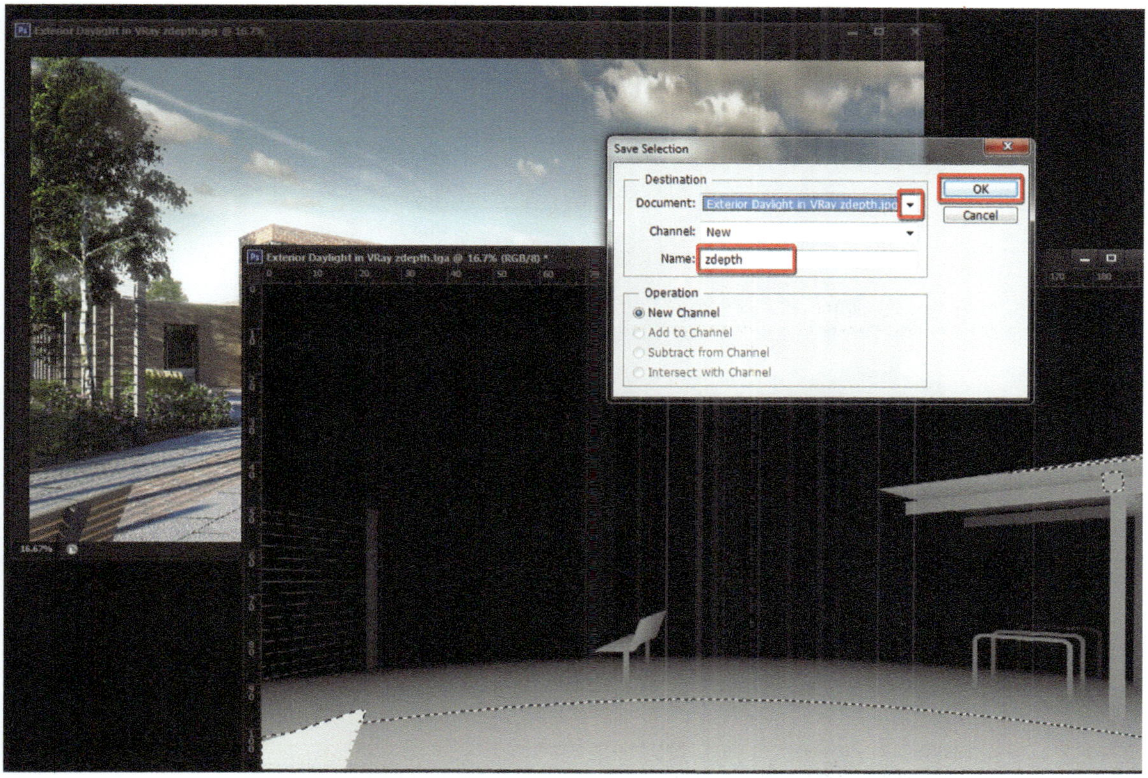

Choose the document destination, rename the selection, and OK to close the Save Selection dialog

Before applying the Lens Blur filter to emulate the DOF effect, duplicate the main layer first, by right clicking on the layer and choosing the duplicate Layer option.

This precautionary measure is to be able to revert back to the original layer, if required.

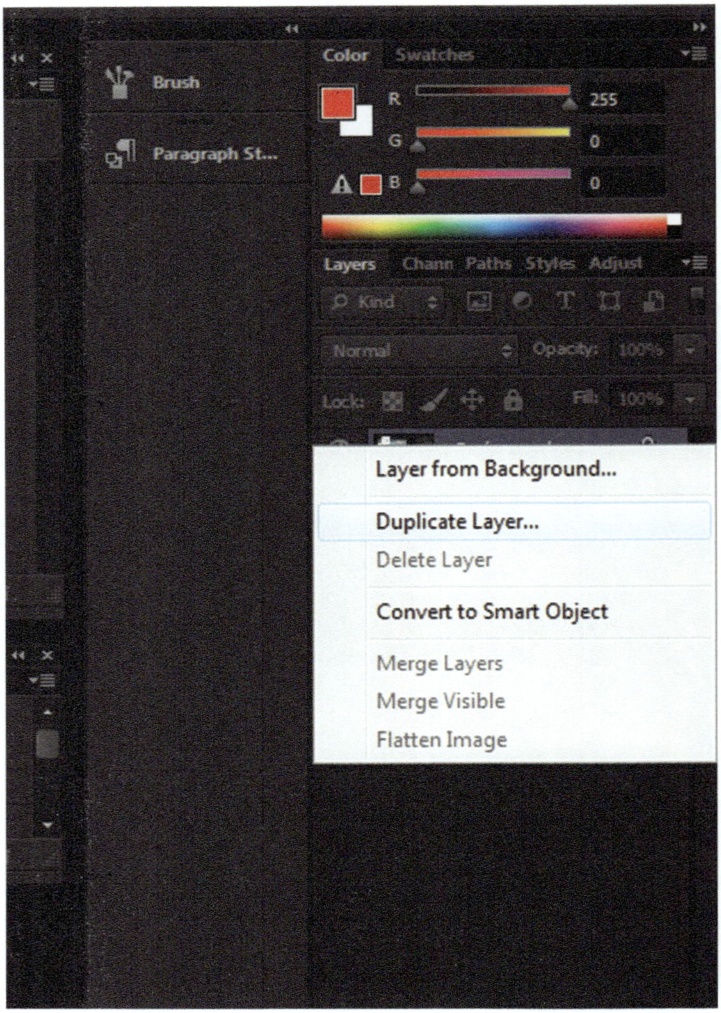

Duplicate Layer

Next, click on the Filter main toolbar and choose the Lens Blur option, from its dropdown list.

Choose the Lens Blur filter

The Lens Blur dialog should appear. To begin using this filter, choose the Depth Map selection, previously saved in this document (e.g., ZDepth).

Enable the Invert function if necessary and begin playing with functions such as Blur Focal Distance, Radius, Shape, and Noise.

Lens Blur dialog

For more professional high-end results Photoshop, use plug-ins such as http://www.dofpro.com/index.htm

VRayDRBucket: This Render element is quite useful to display the machines being used to render each bucket.

In addition, it can also be used to identify render buckets generating artifacts.

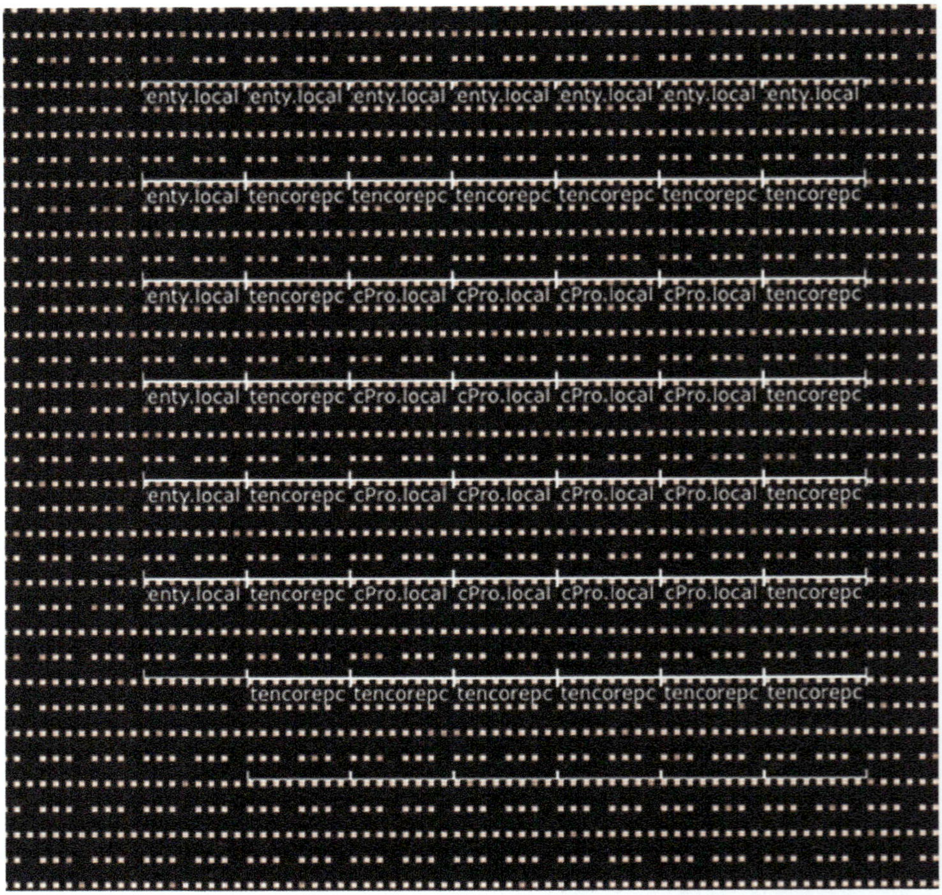

VRayDRBucket

6

Pre-Production

6 Pre-Production

Client Brief

For this project, the main brief was to create a daylight shot, with a camera focused on the main building.

Furthermore, additional requests were made to have a dusk "dramatic shot" to help "sell" the building.

NOTE

This chapter assumes the basic 3d model was supplied by the client or modeled by the studio/ Visualizers, based on 2d drawings. The subsequent steps will be to setup creating the camera, lighting, shading, and rendering.

Photo References and/or Mood Board

To help convey ideas and aspirations, designers and architects often provide users with reference images.

In addition, the studio/artists choose specific photo references to help conceptualize the overall lighting and "mood" of the final render.

It's worth noting that most designers and architects supply the studio/artists with their own design mood boards depicting their furniture, landscape, and material samples.

Some of the chosen furniture can be found at the manufacturer's website, or from websites such as evermotion and 3dsky .

Alternatively, if/when required, users will create bespoke 3d models.

For landscaping, artists often use plug-ins such as Forest Pack and websites such as evermotion to help populate exterior scenes with trees, grass, and flowers, within minutes.

Camera & Lighting ideas

Photo references for camera, lighting, and color

Photo references for material and finishes

Conclusion

The pre-production process is vital to sign off key camera angles and the scene composition as a whole. Also, the studio/artist often use this process to iron out the art direction, furniture, materials, colors, etc., prior to entering the production phase.

7

Scene, Camera, and Lights

7 Scene, Camera, and Lights

Introduction

This chapter will take users through the standard process of setting up the overall scene, camera composition, and lighting.

The initial steps described here are vital in ensuring the subsequent steps are successful.

Setting Up the scene

This chapter assumes the Custom UI and Defaults Switcher are already set to Max.vray, as previously suggested in Chapter 2.

As such, the assigned renderer and materials loaded should be V-Ray 5 by default.

Let's start by opening the file under the name of External daylight scene_Start.max.

If prompted with the Units Mismatch dialog, choose the Adopt the File's Unit Scale.

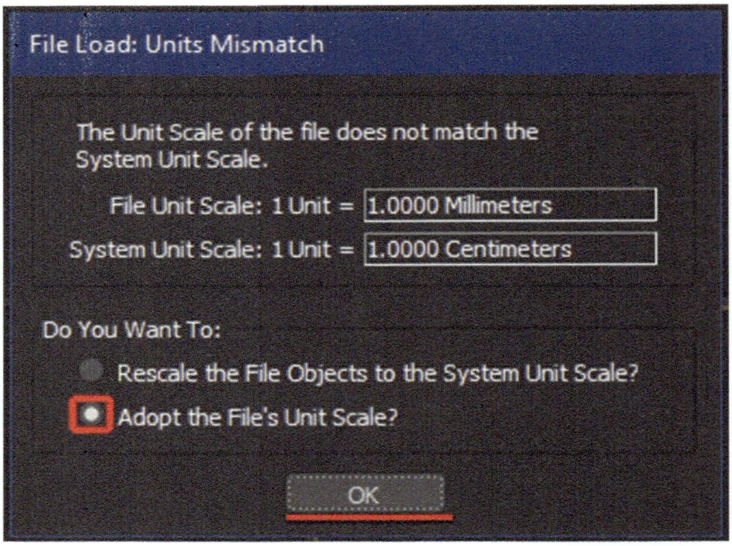

File Load: Units Mismatch

To ensure the framing in the viewport is coherent with what is rendered, click on the Perspective text and choose the option Show Safe Frames (Shift+F).

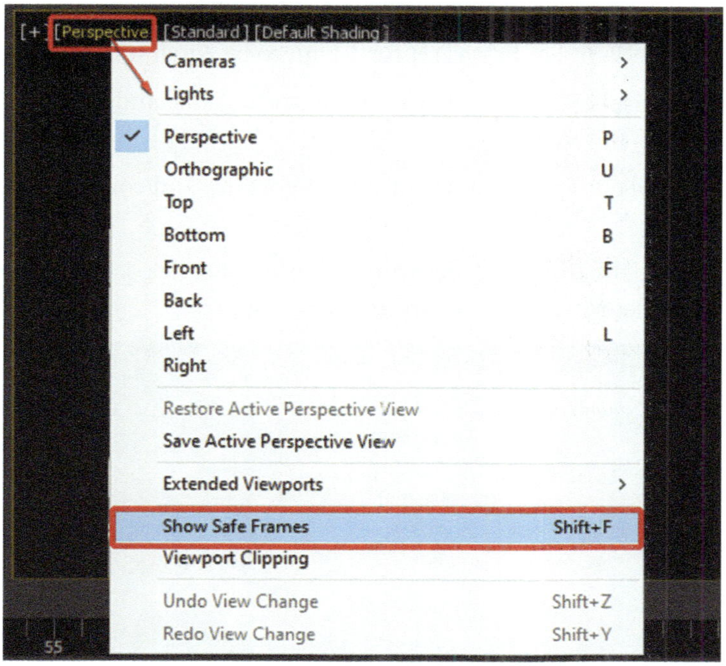

Choose the option Show Safe Frames

Also, to help distinguish different objects in the shaded viewport, simply click on the Default Shading text and choose the Edged Faces option from the list.

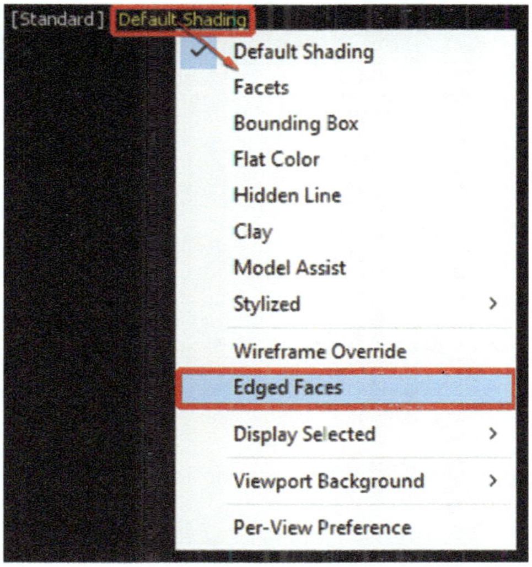

Choose the Edged Faces option

The Display Unit Scale of this scene was set to Metric/millimeters. And the System Unit Setup was set for 1 Unit to be equal to 1 mm.

The Display Unit Scale doesn't affect the scene, and only displays the file's metric system in the viewport.

The System Unit Setup is utterly important, and controls the size of objects in scene.

Before starting to model and/or create lights in a scene, ensure to have these parameters set up properly and accordingly.

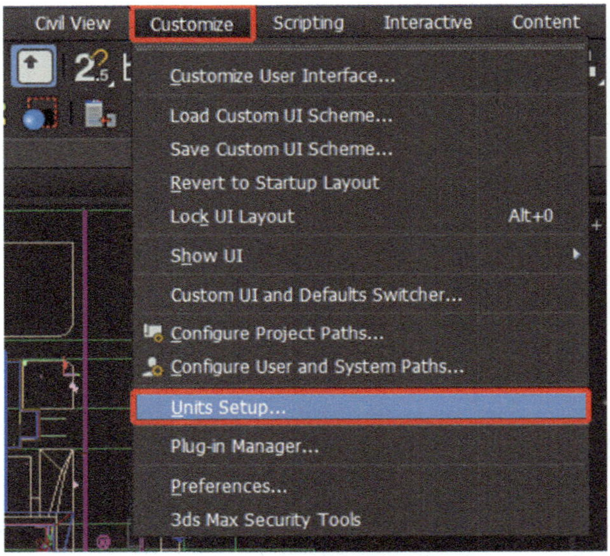

Units Setup toolbar

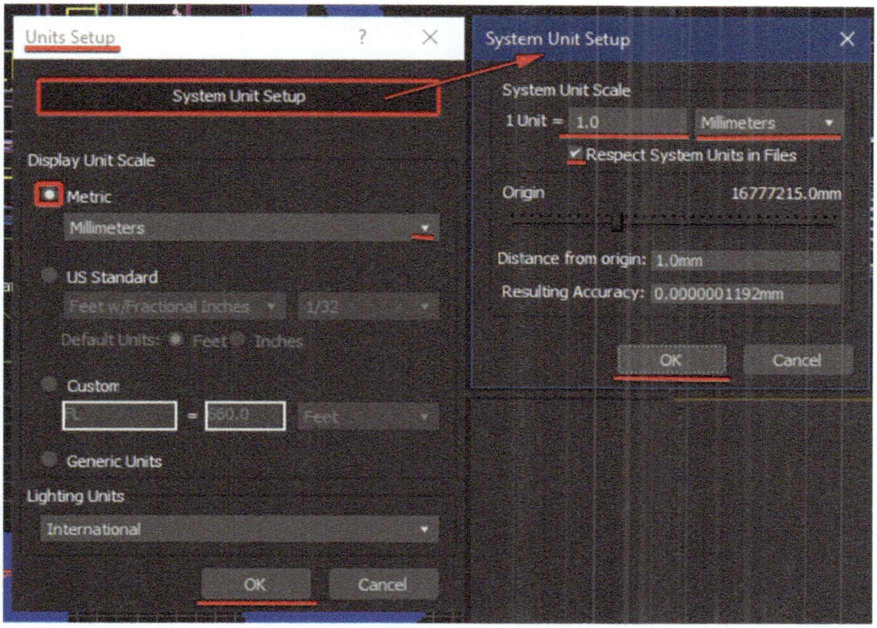

Units and System Unit Setup

Also, go to the Customize toolbar and choose the Preferences option.

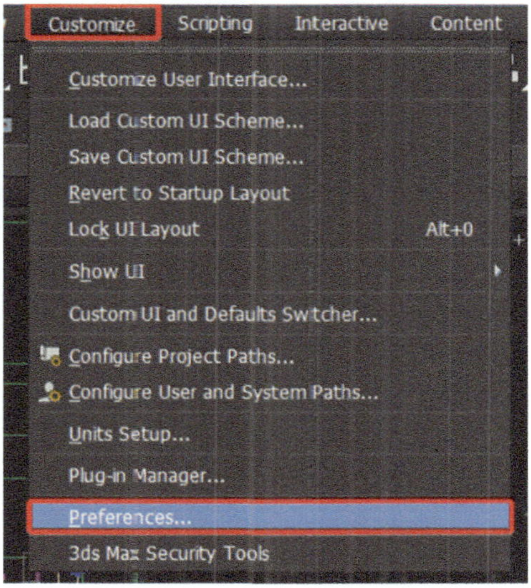

Preferences option

Under Gamma and LUT tab, turn on the Enable Gamma/LUT Correction and set it to 2.2.

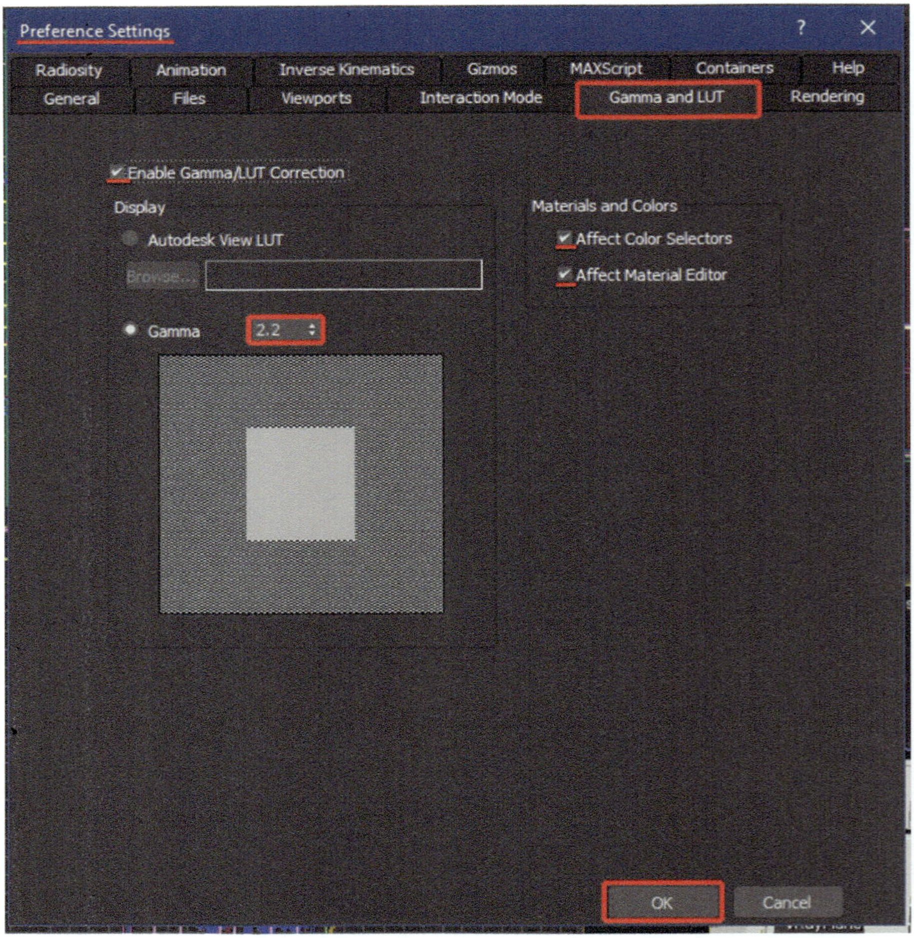

Gamma and LUT tab

Under Files tab, if you happen to be working on a large file that's taking too long to save, you can increase the Backup Interval (minutes) to 30 or higher and choose Compress on Save.

Compressed Max files are automatically reduced to half or less of their original size when saved.

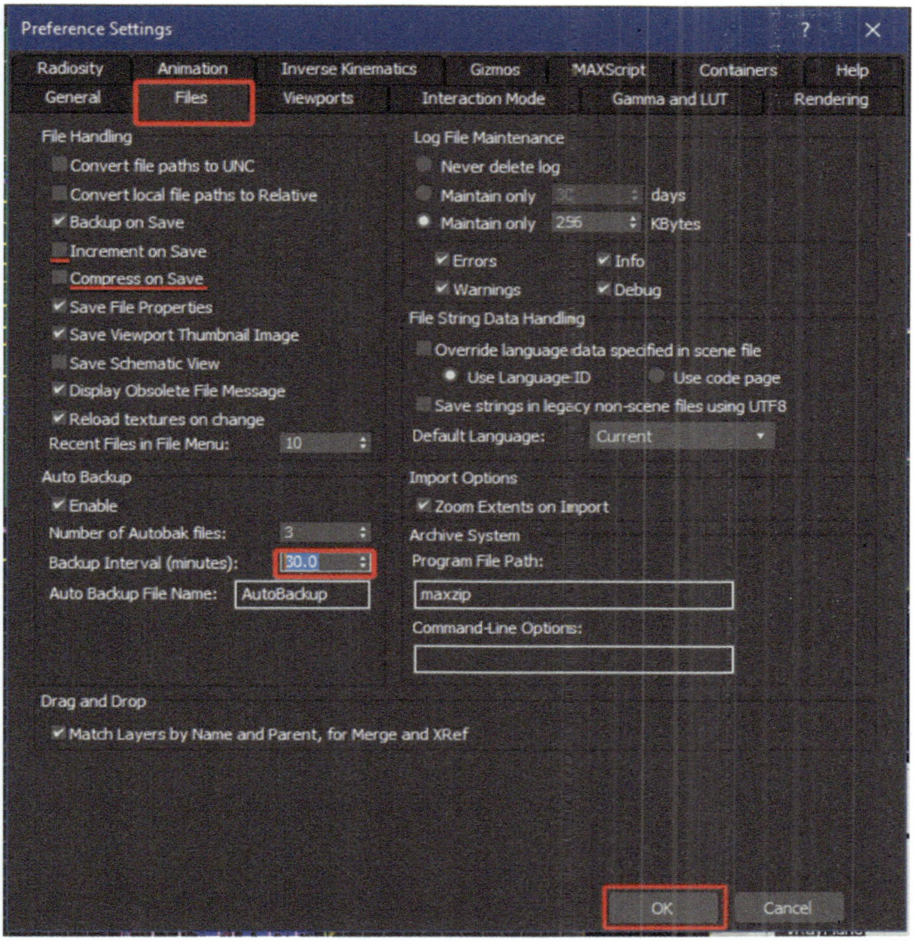

Files Tab

Under General tab, increase the Scene Undo Levels to about 500. This will give you the flexibility to undo (Ctrl+Z) up to 500 levels, if required.

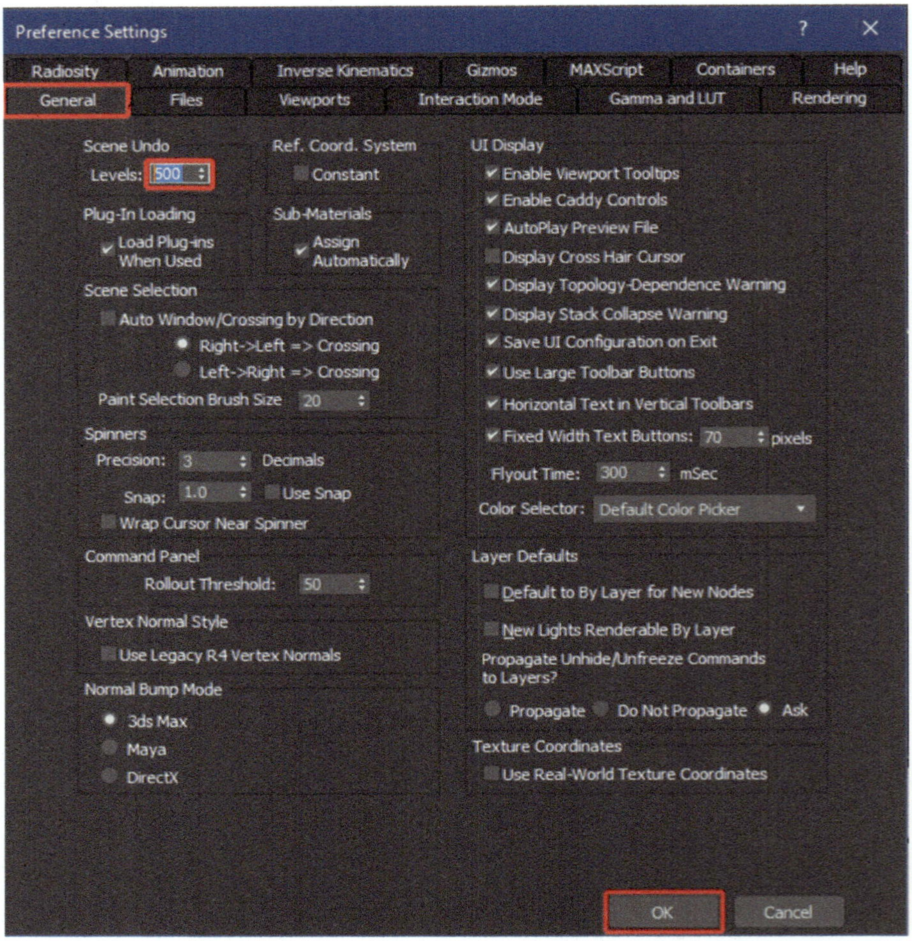

General tab

To configure the viewports, simply click on the + text and choose to Configure Viewports

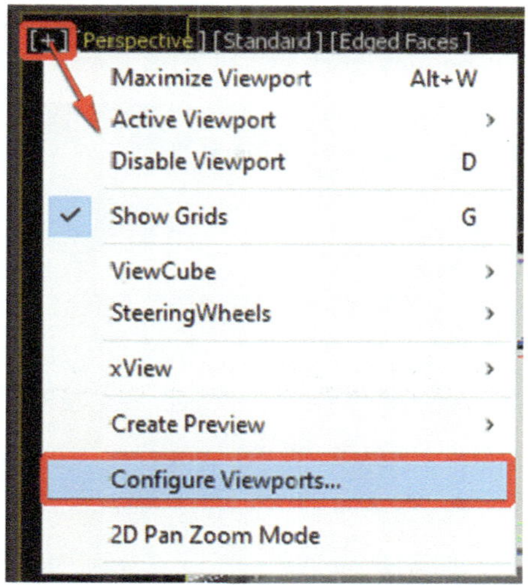

Configure Viewports

Under the Layout tab, select a suitable viewport layout. Users can also right click on a specific layout and choose the viewport.

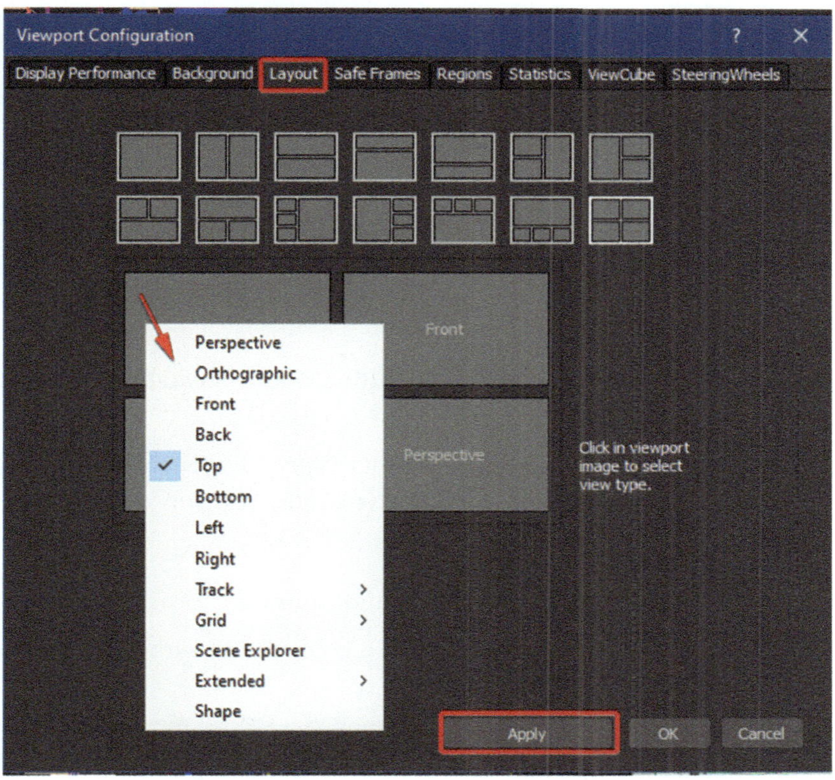

Viewport Layout

NOTE

When creating the sunlight object, it's best to choose a four-viewport layout.

The Display Performance is frequently used to set the display quality of Textures in the viewport, etc.

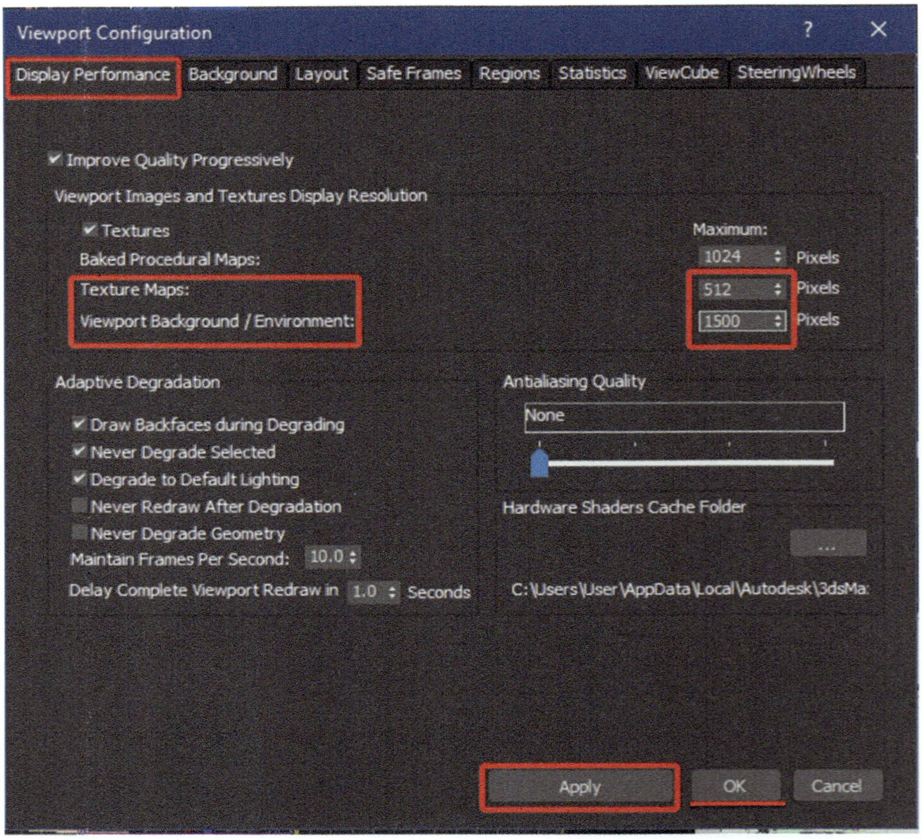

Display Performance tab

NOTE

If you choose another Color Mode type, your saved renders will look either darker or brighter from what is seen in your VFB.

Next, open the Render Setup dialog (F10). Under VRay tab, set the Image filter as VRayLanczosFilter.

Under Color mapping parameters, set its Type to Exponential. This will reduce overly burnt areas in the image, and give a more realistic look to the render.

Set the Gamma value to 2.2.

Under Mode, set it to Color mapping and gamma.

This will ensure what is seen in the VFB is consistent with what is saved into your hard drive.

Scenes saved in earlier versions of 3ds max may require merging in a completely new 3ds max scene with the above Color Mode type in order to override the problem.

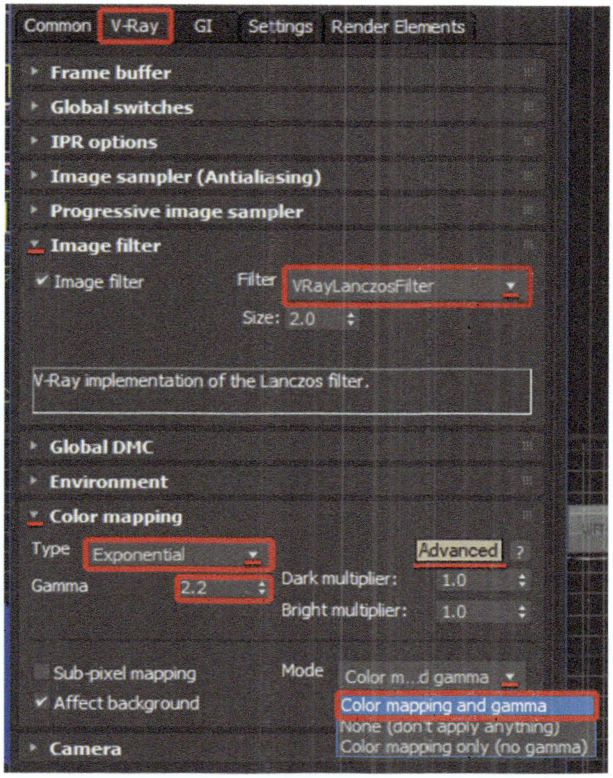

Image filter and Color mapping settings

Camera Composition

Under Create panel, select the Camera button and choose a VRay type from its list.

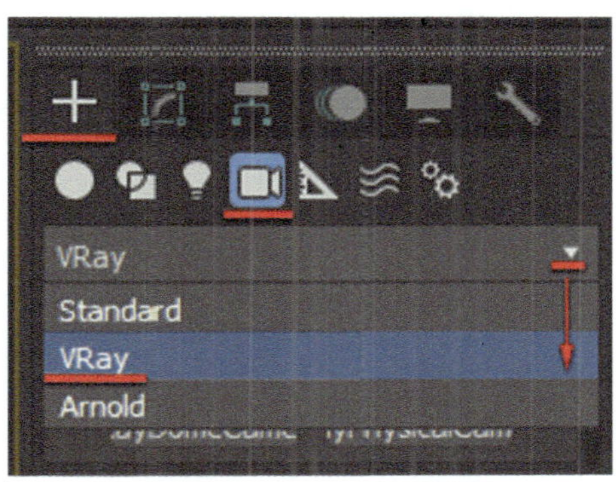

Choose the VRay camera type

Under Object Type group, choose the VRayPhysicalCamera.

In the Top Viewport, click and drag to create the camera and its view direction.

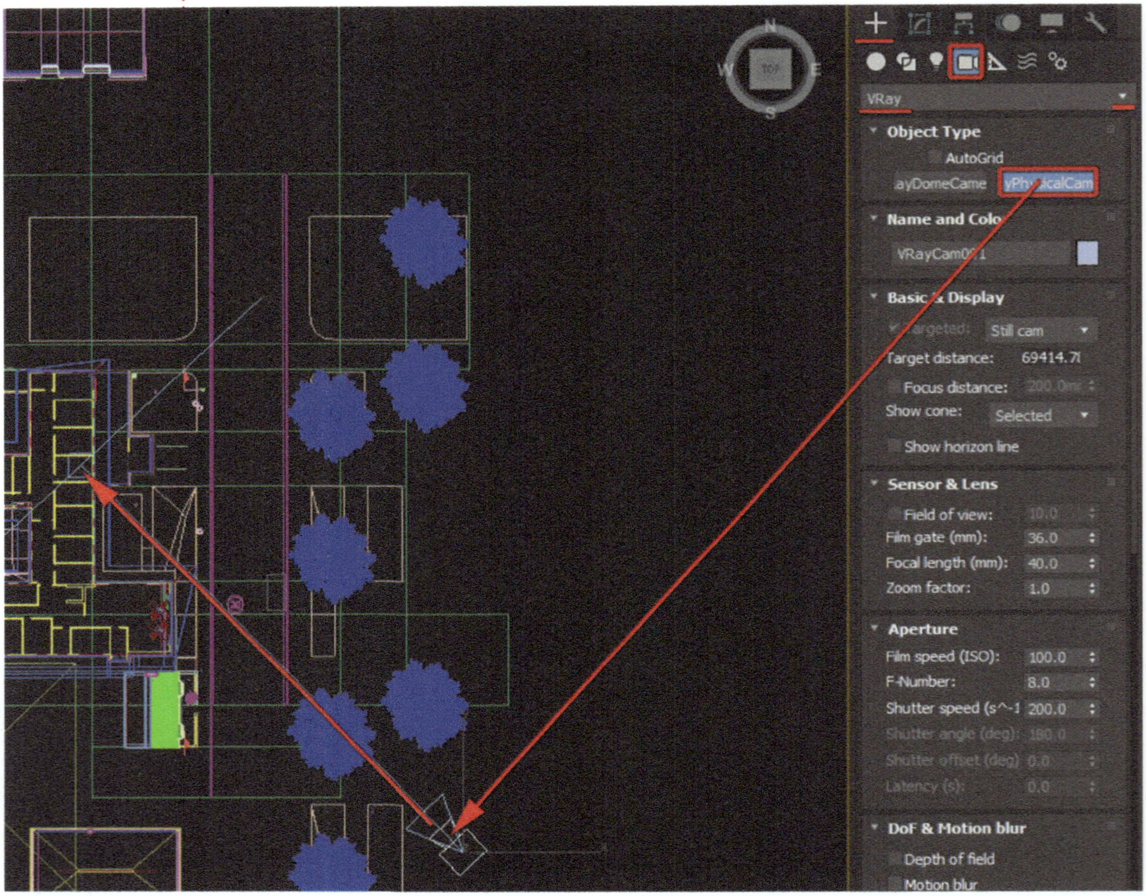

Create the VRayPhysicalCamera in Top viewport

Next, select the Perspective viewport and click on the Perspective text. Choose the Cameras option and select the VRayCam001.

Alternatively, simply select the Perspective viewport and press C on your keyboard.

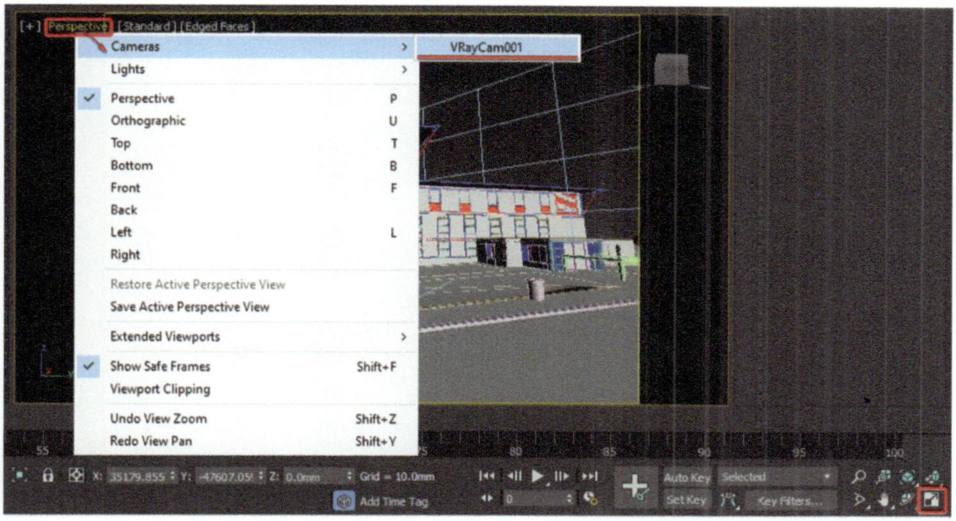

Choose the VRayCam001

For more flexibility to move and rotate the camera, let's open its Modify panel and disable the Targeted option.

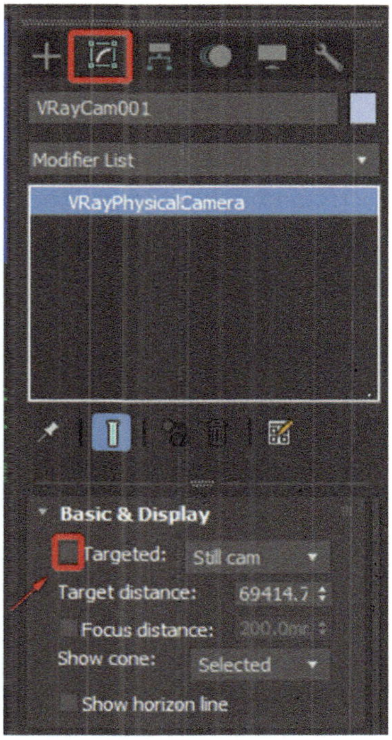

Disable the Targeted option

To ensure you don't accidently select objects while moving and rotating the camera, go to the main toolbar. Under filter options, select the Cameras from it dropdown list.

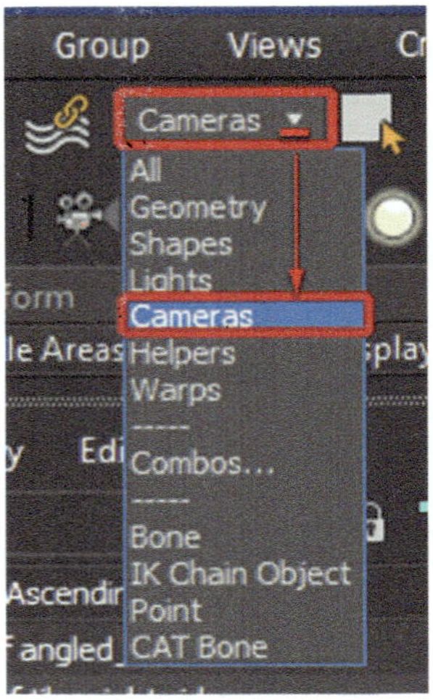

Select Cameras filter options

Begin moving and rotating the camera to capture the main building and a bit of the horizon on the right.

Always use photo references to see how similar buildings are framed.

The final Move values of the camera ended up being X: 9905.408 mm, Y: –24488.455 mm, and Z: 1084.818.

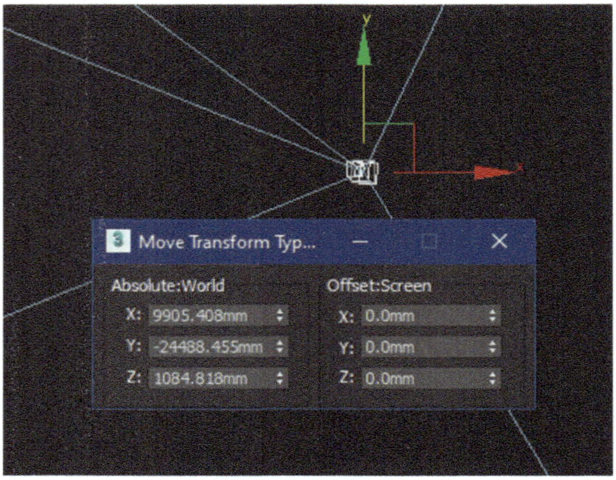

Camera Move values

And the Rotation values were X: 102.865, Y: −0.0, and Z: 56.528.

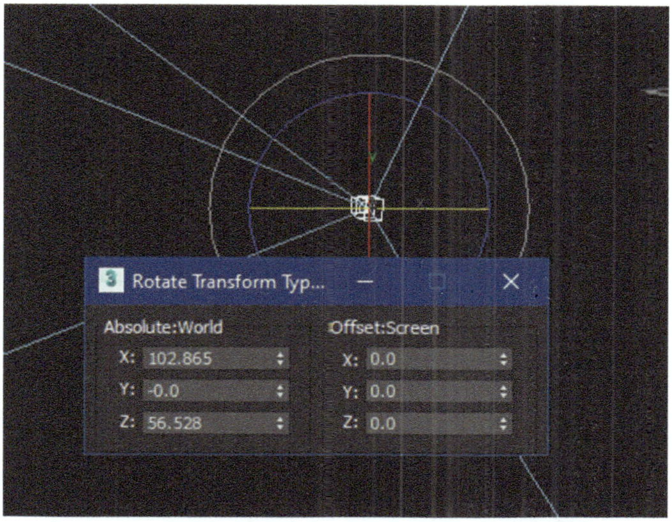

Camera Rotation values

To help frame the building and see a bit of the horizon, go back to the camera's Modify tab. Under Sensor and Lens rollout parameters, change its Film gate (mm) value to about 95.0.

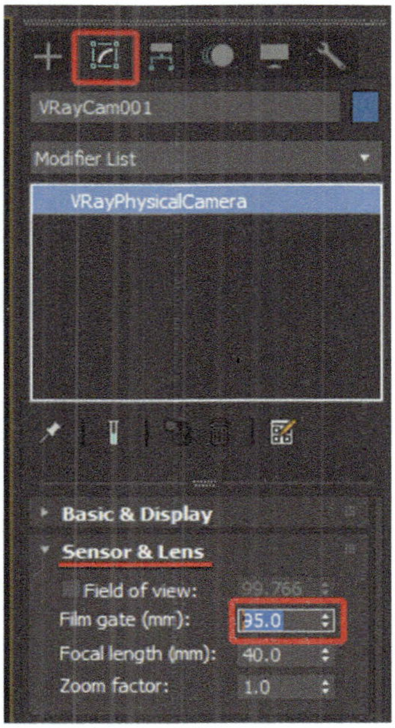

Sensor and lens Film gate set to 95.0

To correct the camera tilt slightly, under Tilt & Shift parameters, set the Vertical Tilt to about 0.1.

A slight tilt was kept to make the camera view more realistic.

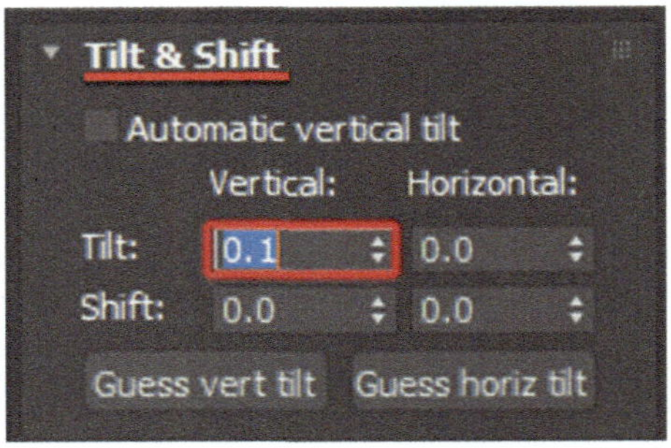

Vertical Tilt set to 0.1

Camera Viewport

To see less of the foreground and frame the camera slightly better, let's go to the Render Setup dialog (F10). Under Common tab, set the Width Output Size to 3500 pixels and the Height to 1750 pixels.

Also, enable the padlock button to lock the Image Aspect ratio.

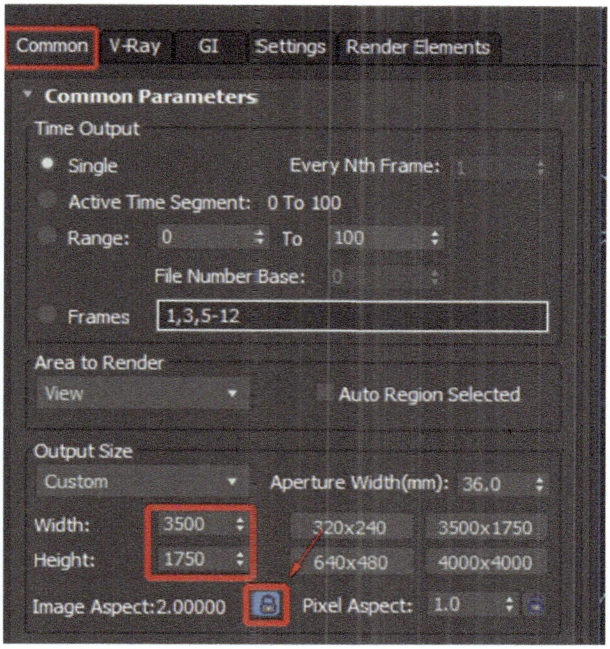

New Output Size locked

Lights

To create the sunlight, ensure to have all four viewports in display (zoomed out).

Go to the Create panel and select the Lights button.

Under Photometric list, choose the VRay type.

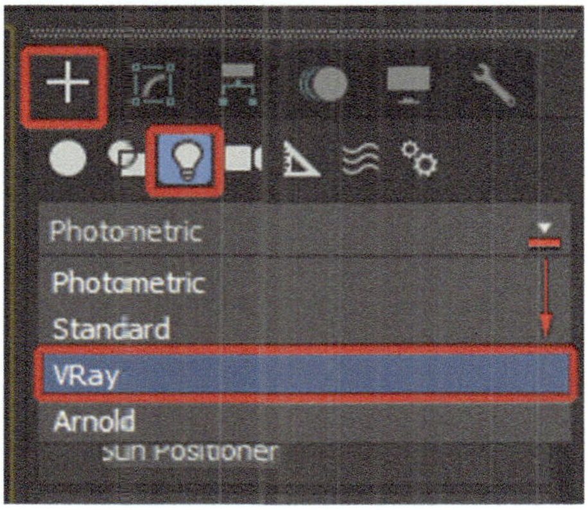

Choose VRay light

Next, select the VRaySun button, followed by clicking and dragging it in the Front viewport to create it.

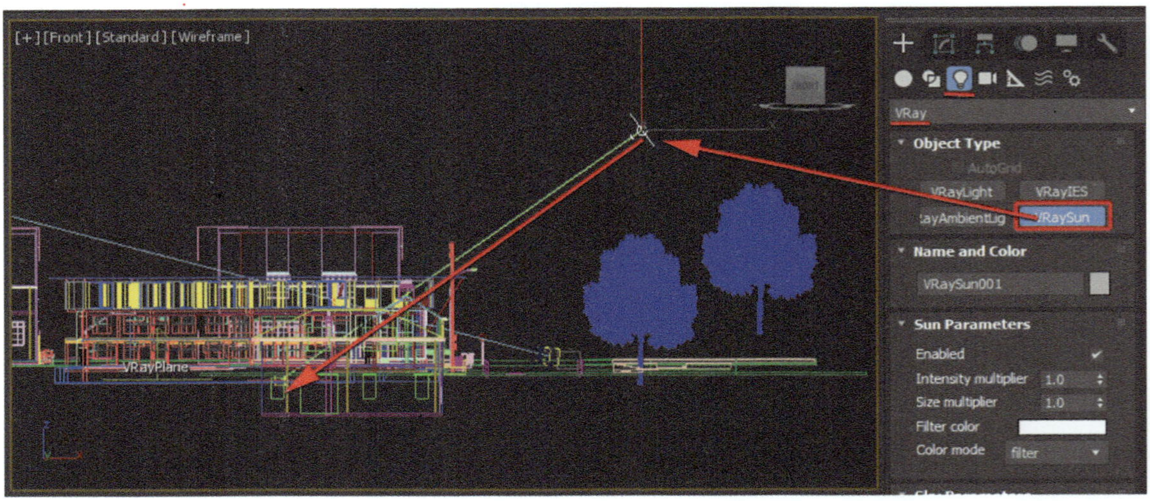

Create VRaySun object

If prompted with the dialog to automatically add a VRaySky environment map, click Yes to accept it.

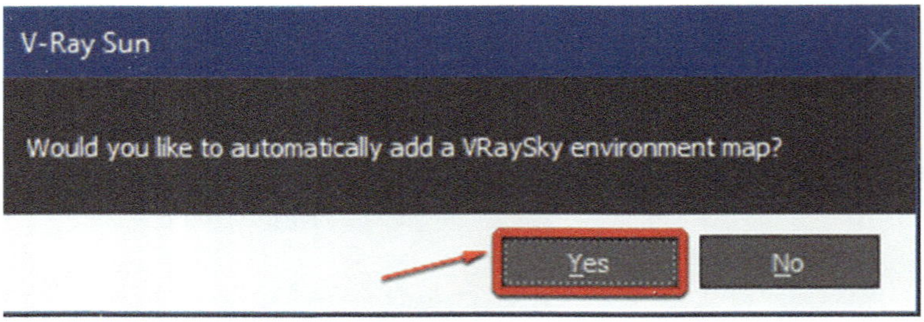

Automatically add a VRaySky environment map dialog

Also, go to the Modify panel and change the default Sky model to Improved.

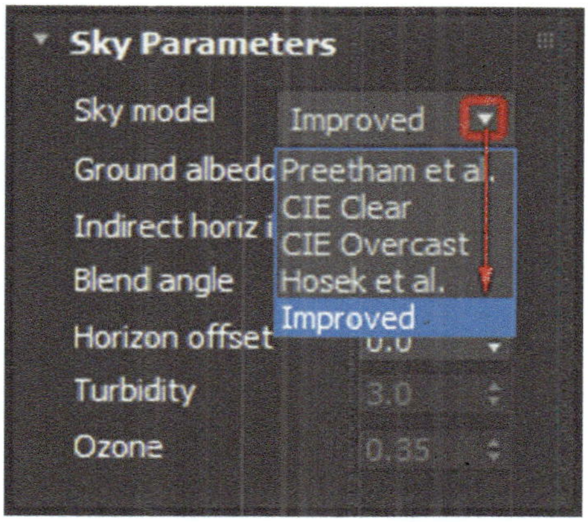

Change the default Sky model to Improved

Next, enable the VRay Viewport IPR option for the camera viewport.

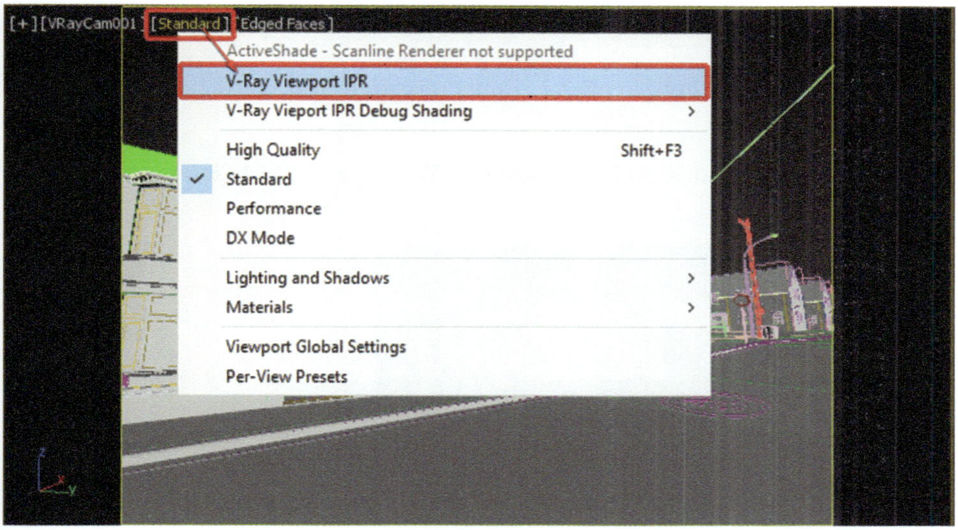

Enable the VRay Viewport IPR option

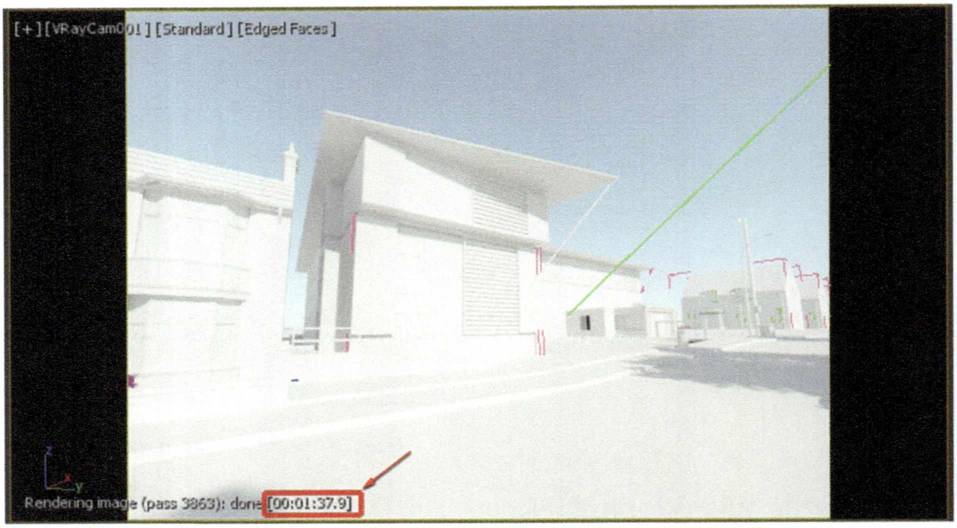

IPR rendered in the viewport in 1:37 minutes

Begin moving the VRaySun object and its target around, until an appealing dusk shot with shadows is achieved.

The final sun head position was X: 26841.133 mm, Y: 108894.687 mm, and Z: 17662.906 mm

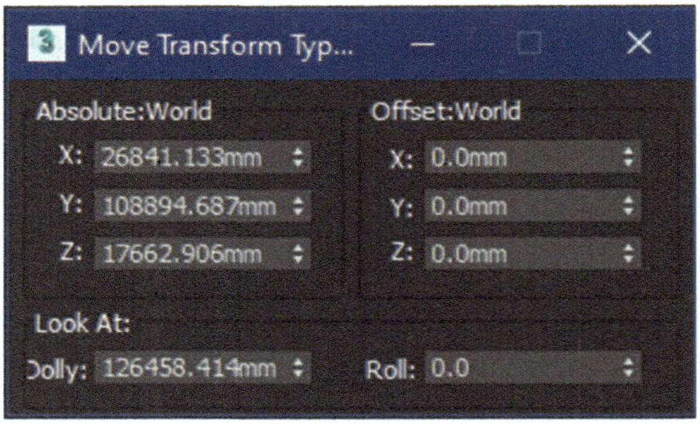

VRay*Sun head position*

Its final target position was X: 7725.571 mm, Y: –14757.275 mm, and Z: –681.522 mm.

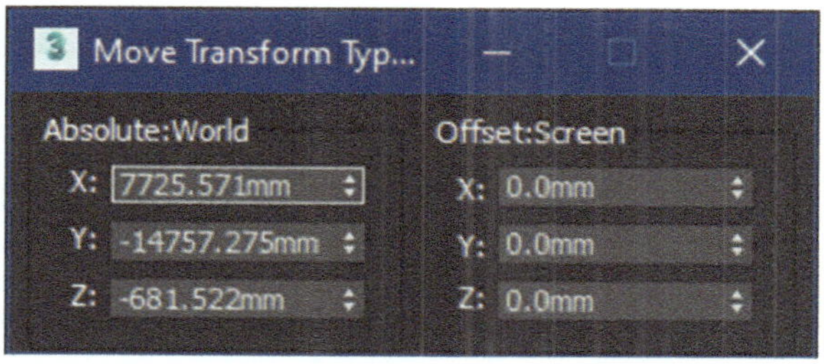

VRaySun target position

Final VRaySun position in the VRay Viewport IPR

Next, go to the Render Setup dialog (F10). Under Render Elements tab, click to Add the VRayLightMix element.

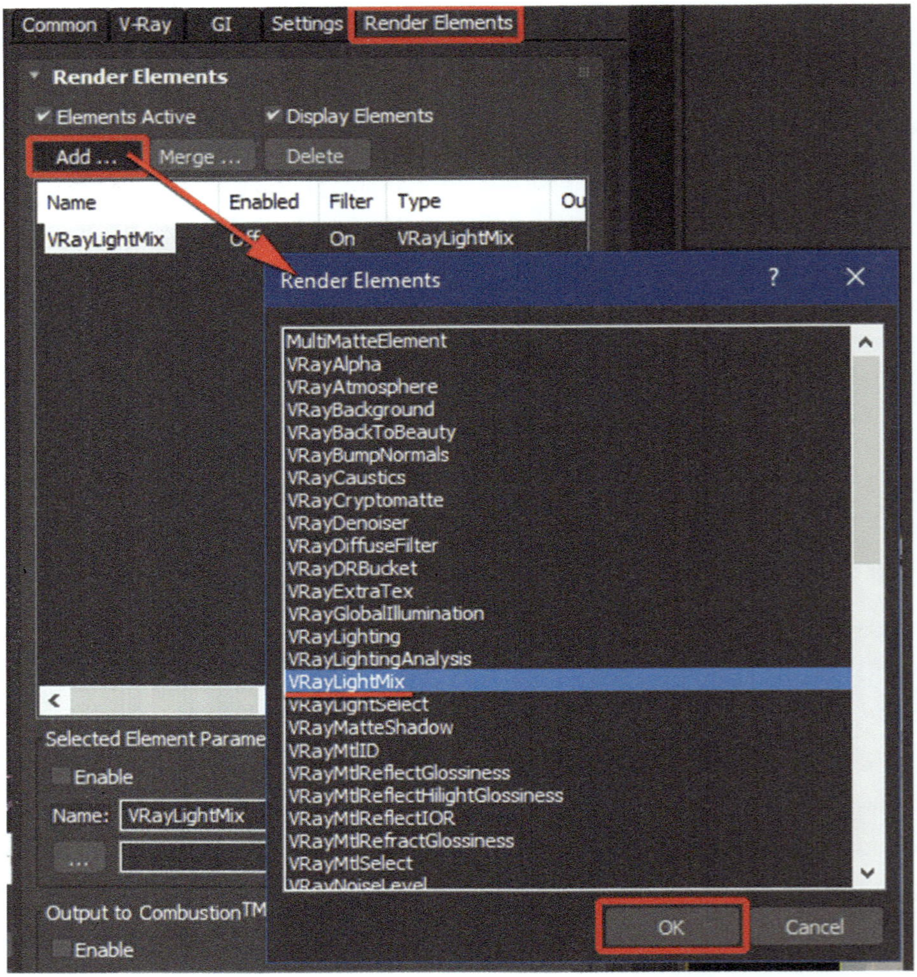

Add the VRayLightMix element

NOTE

By default, it is set to Group by Instanced lights. This option displays all instanced lights in the scene as one Layer in the VFB.

If you want the flexibility to manipulate the instanced lights individually, simply choose the option Group by Individual lights.

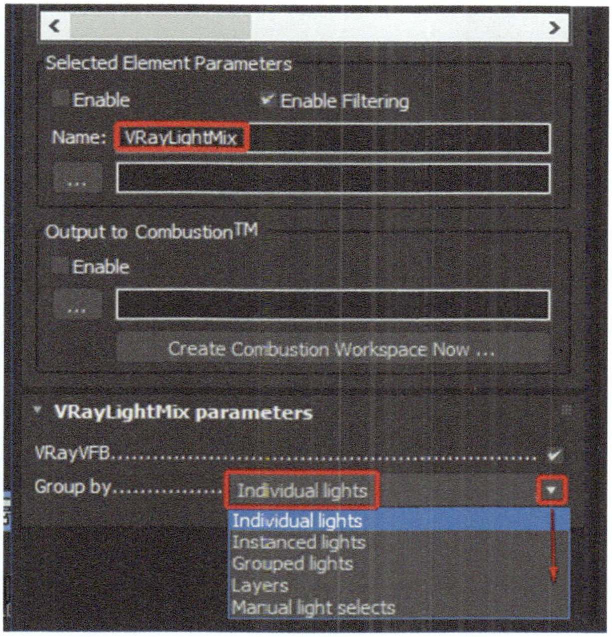

LightMix with instanced lights displayed individually

Open the VRay Frame Buffer dialog and add the Filmic tonemap Layer.

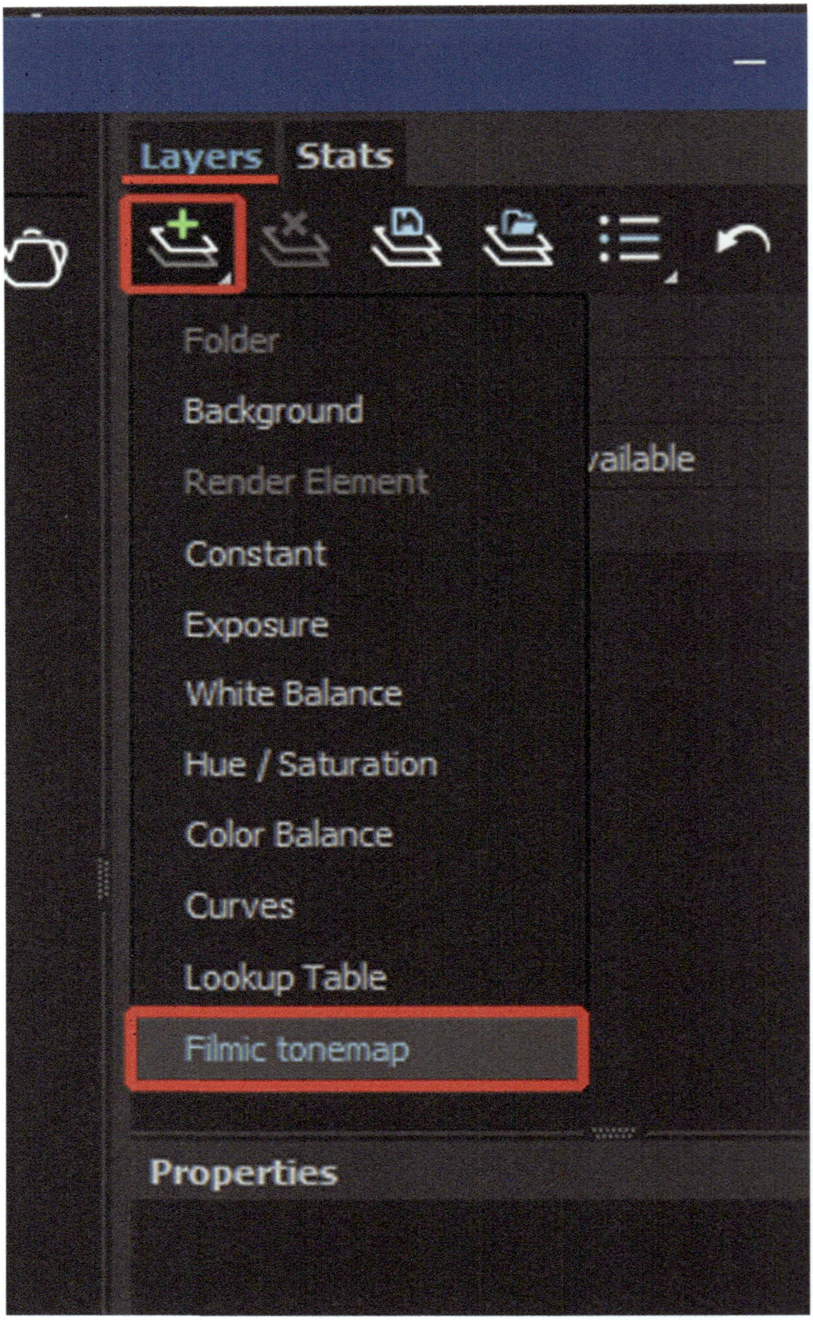
Layers
Stats
Folder
Background
Render Element
Constant
Exposure
White Balance
Hue / Saturation
Color Balance
Curves
Lookup Table
Filmic tonemap
Properties

Add the Filmic tonemap Layer

Under its Properties Type, change it to AMPAS. You should also start seeing changes in the Viewport IPR.

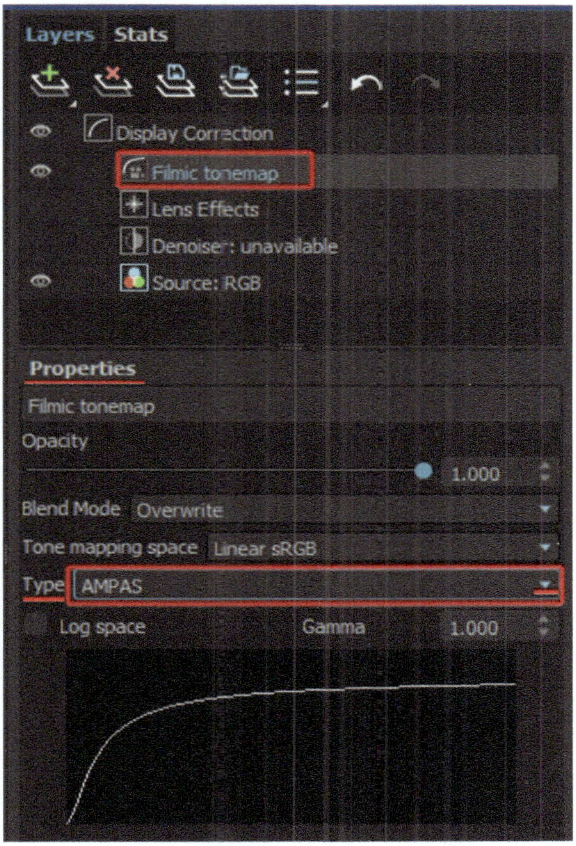

Filmic tonemap: AMPAS Type

Also, add a Lookup Table Layer, and load the LUT file under the name of 3DCollective_sRGB_Agfa_Futura_03Hard.cube.

Disable the function Convert sRGB Space first and enable the Save in image option.

NOTE

You may need to tweak some of its default Properties as materials are added in the scene.

NOTE

This LUT file worked well for this scene. However, feel free to use another LUT file, if desired.

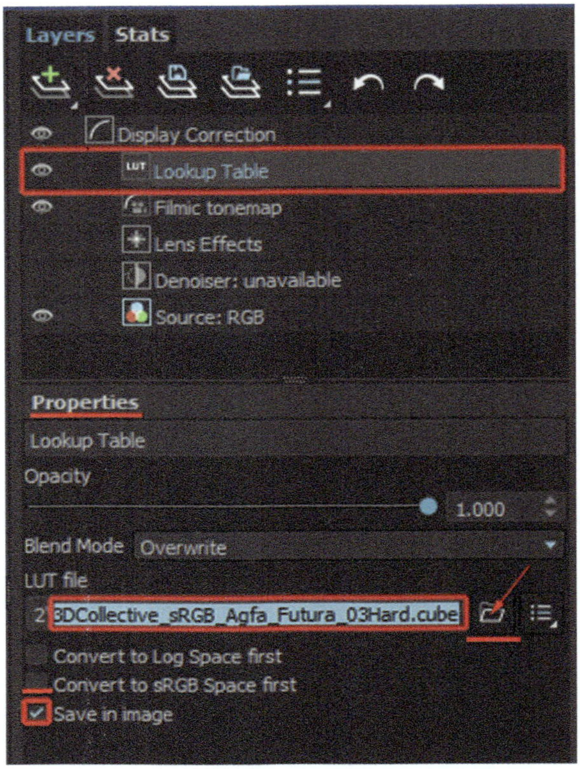

Lookup Table Layer added

To add a bit of contrast to the render, select the camera. In its Modify panel, under Color and Exposure parameters, enable the Vignetting function.

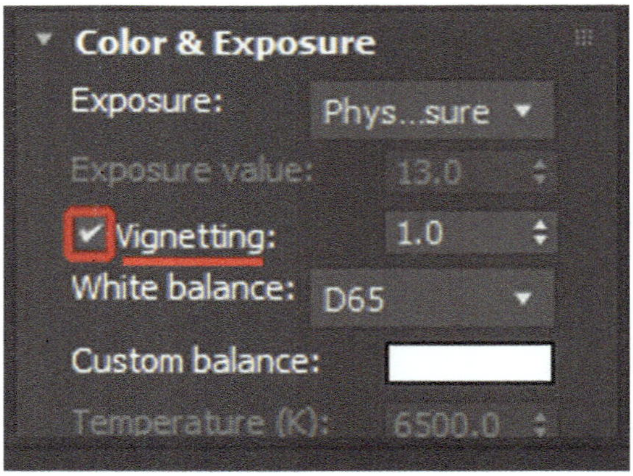

Vignetting enabled in the camera

Final result with VRay Viewport IPR

To add a bit of haze to the sunlight, open the Environment dialog (8). Under the Atmosphere rollout parameters, add the VRayAerialPerspective shader.

Under its General parameters, set the Visibility range (in meters) to about 2000, the Atmosphere height to about 100, and enable the function to Affect environment rays.

These values worked well for this scene. However, feel free to try different values, if desired.

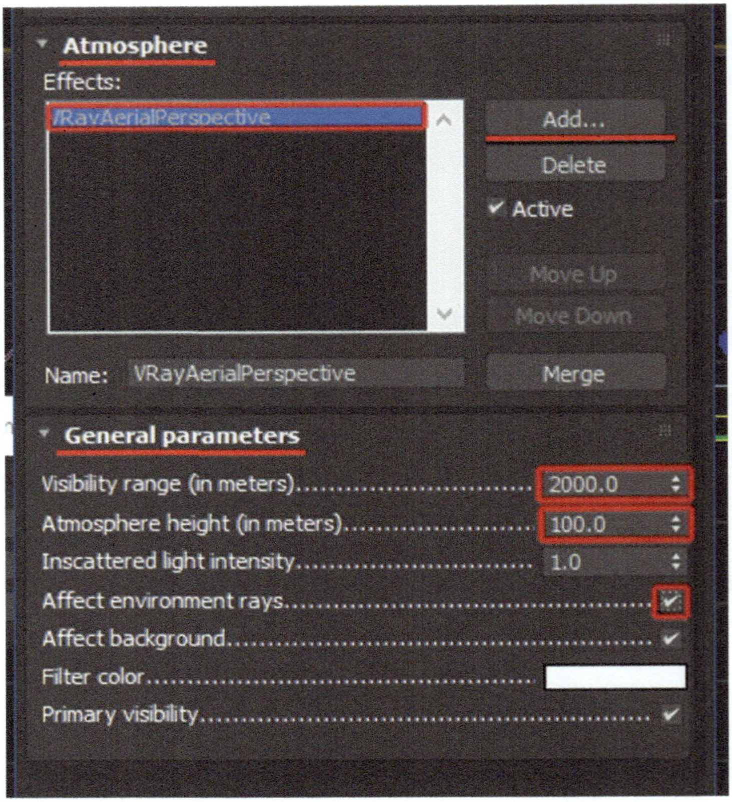

VRayAerialPerspective parameters

NOTE

To check this chapter's final result, simply open the file under the name of External daylight scene _Finished .max.

Conclusion

It's vital to start your 3d scene by setting the System Units Scale accordingly in order for objects and lights to work accurately.

Similarly, the Color mapping and scene Preference Settings will play a crucial role on the input/output render results.

Finally, after lighting a scene, VFB layers will be indispensable to help achieve the final "look and feel" of the final render output.

8

Materials and Final Render

8 Materials and Final Render

Introduction

Creating materials and rendering the final scene are one of the most crucial parts of the entire production process.

As such, the following tutorial will take users through the intricacies of creating materials, setting up the scene for final rendering, and rendering the final image realistically.

Creating Materials

Let's start by opening the file under the name of External daylight scene_ Materials Start.max.

In the scene, select the object under the name of wood and isolate it (Alt+Q).

Also, maximize the camera viewport (Alt+W).

Wood Planks Material

Open the VRay Asset Browser dialog and select the Wood and Laminate Material Library.

Scroll down and pick the Wood_Planks_B01_100cm, followed by right clicking and choosing Apply to selected objects.

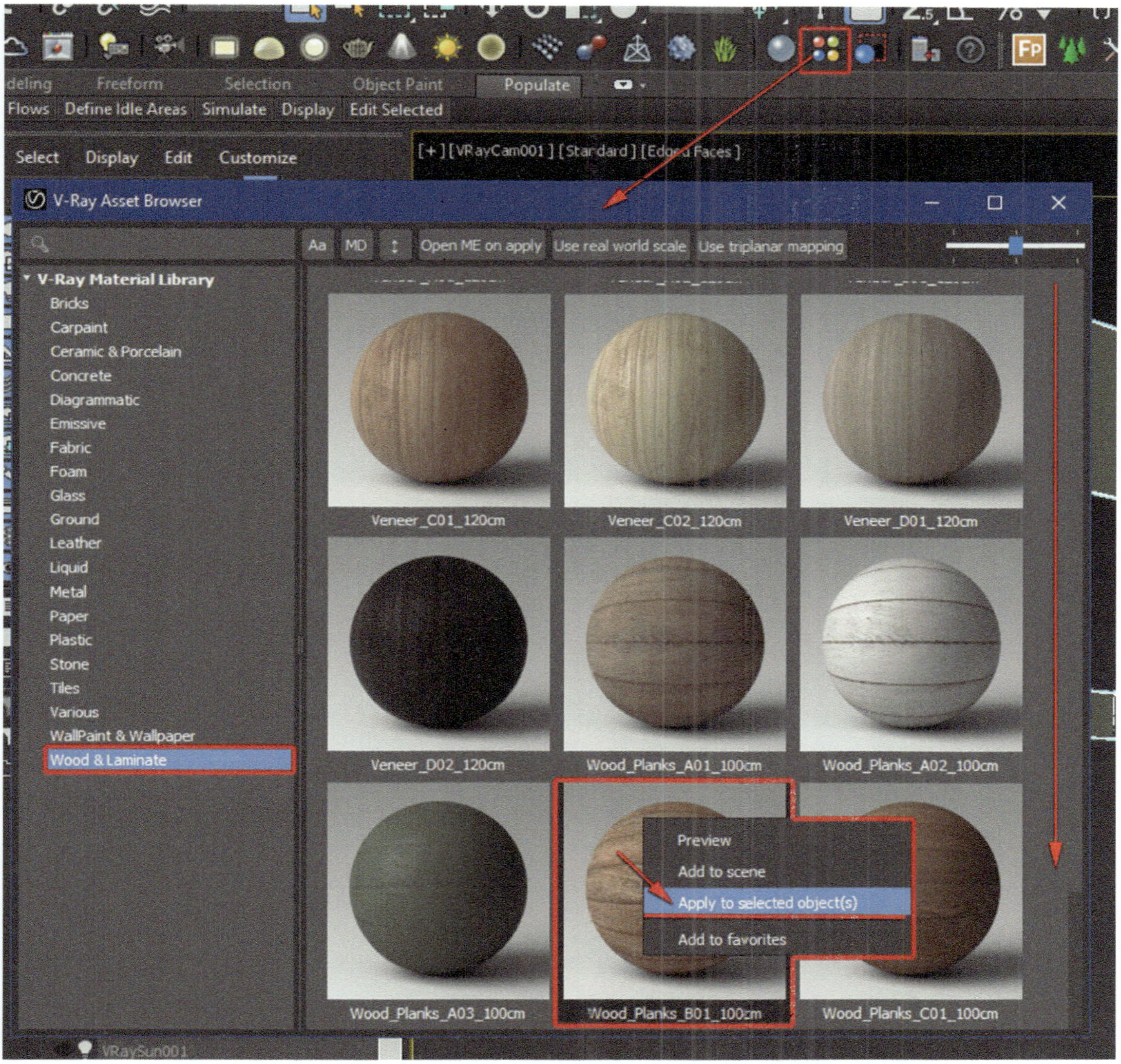

Apply wood material to selected objects

Next, while the wood object is still selected, Open the Modify panel and add the UVW Map modifier to it.

Under Parameters, enable the Box type.

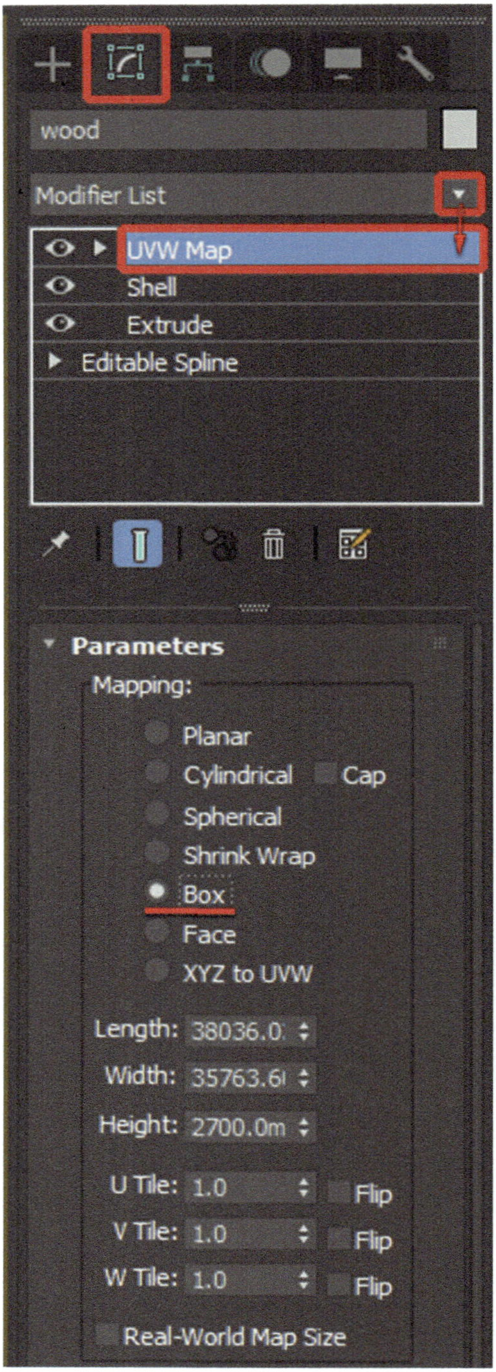
wood
Modifier List
UVW Map
Shell
Extrude
Editable Spline
Parameters
Mapping:
Planar
Cylindrical
Cap
Spherical
Shrink Wrap
Box
Face
XYZ to UVW
Length: 38036.0
Width: 35763.6
Height: 2700.0m
U Tile: 1.0
Flip
V Tile: 1.0
Flip
W Tile: 1.0
Flip
Real-World Map Size

Add the UVW Map modifier

Minimize the VRay Asset Browser dialog and open the Material Editor (M).

Select an empty material slot and enable the button Pick Material from the object, followed by using the sampler to pick material in the scene.

The wood material should appear in the material slot.

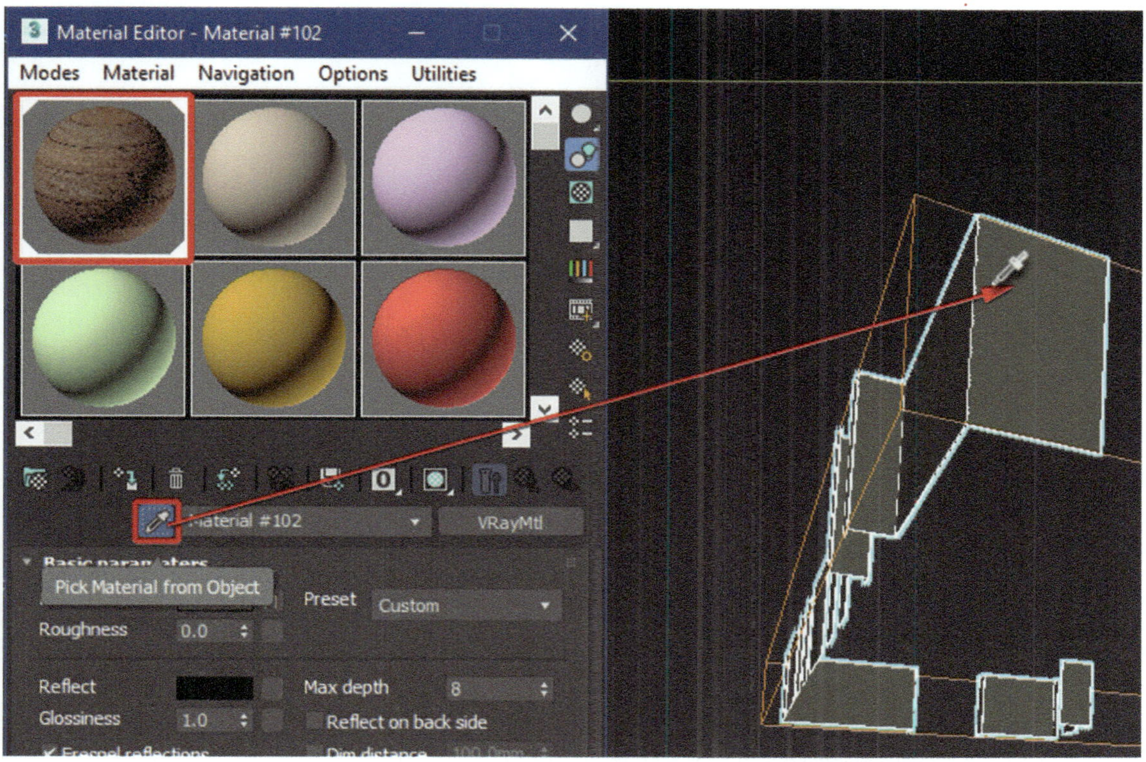

Pick Material from object

To see the texture in the viewport, enable the button named Show Shaded Material in Viewport.

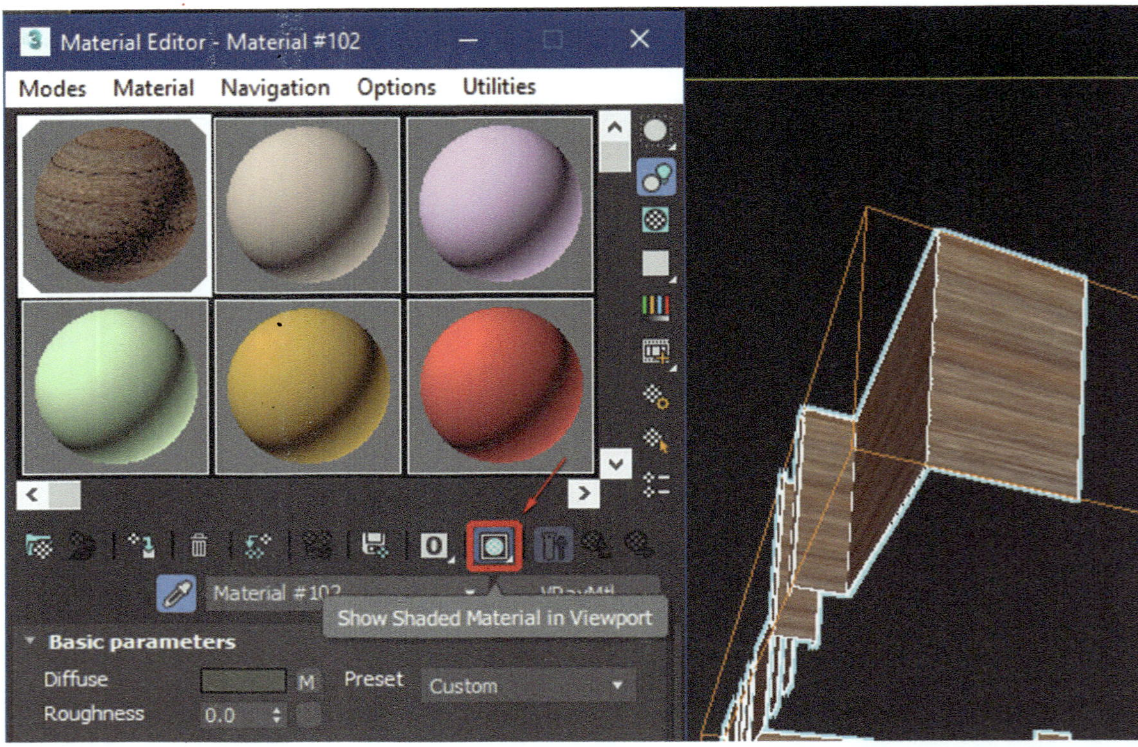

Show Shaded Material in Viewport

To desaturate this material, click on its Diffuse toggle first.

Inside the Diffuse toggle, click on its VRayBitmap toggle to open the Material/Map Browser dialog. Under the General rollout, choose the Color correction procedural map and OK to close the dialog.

Choose the Color correction procedural map

Choose to keep the old map as sub-map and click OK.

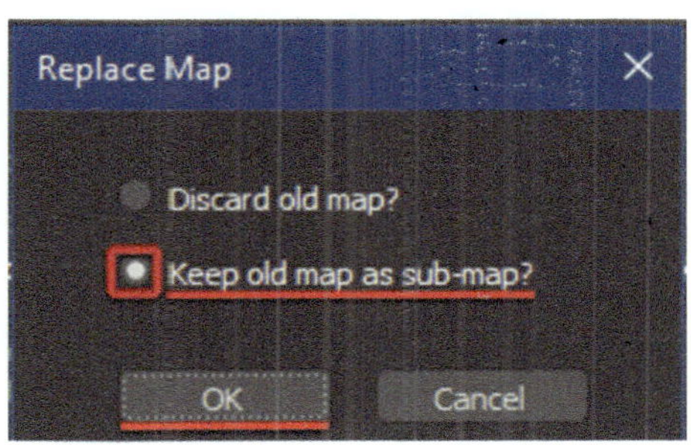

Choose to keep the old map as sub-map

NOTE

This value worked well to desaturate the material. However, feel free to try different values, if desired.

In the Color Correction parameters, decrease the Saturation function to about –32.226.

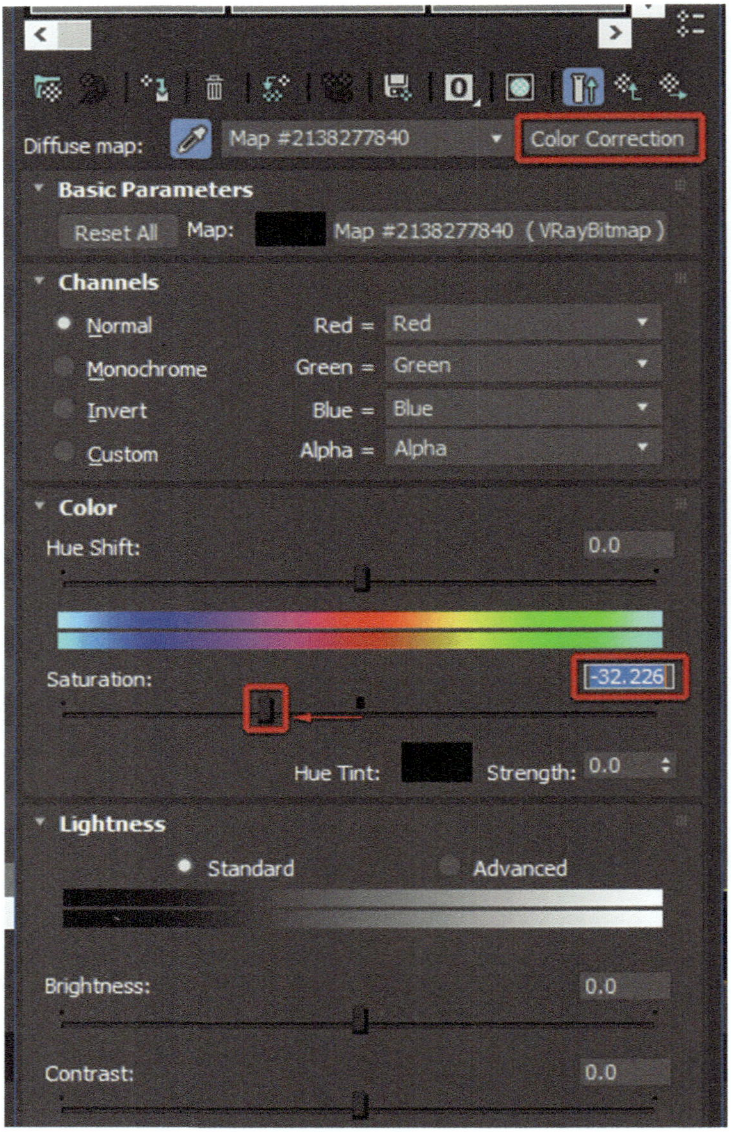

Decrease the Saturation

To add some Dirt streaks on top, let's click on the Color Correction toggle and choose the VRayDirt from the Material/Map Browser dialog.

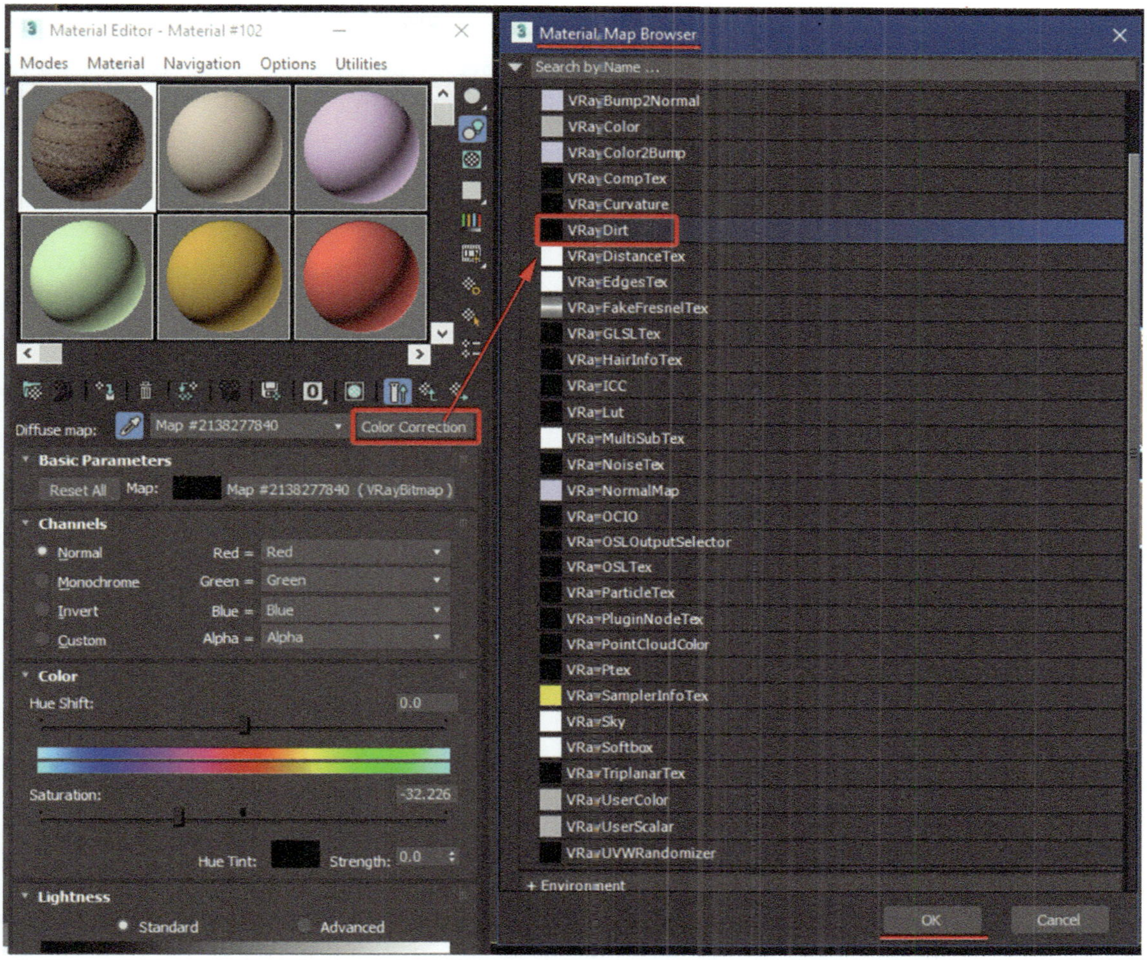

Add VRayDirt

Choose Keep old map as sub-map.

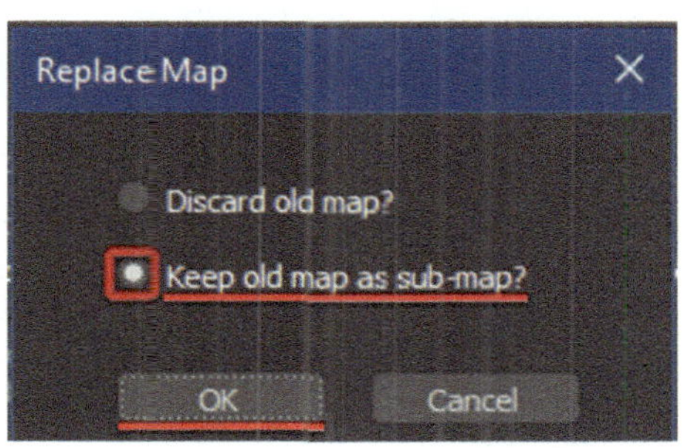

Choose Keep old map as sub-map

NOTE

These values worked well. However, feel free to try different values, if desired.

Under VRayDirt parameters, let's use the same parameters described in Chapter 2.

Increase the Radius to about 700 mm. Set the Bias Z value to about 30.0.

Enable the Streaks ambient and increase the Streaks size to 30.0.

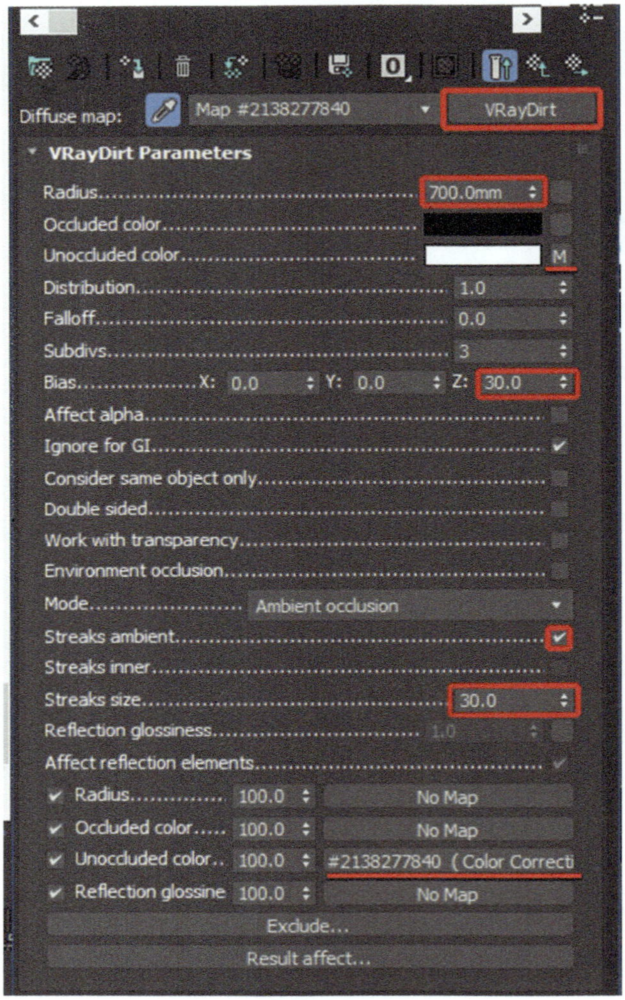

VRayDirt values

Adding the VRayDirt procedural map, subsequently disable the Show Shaded Material in Viewport button (made the texture preview black).

To enable it again, simply go inside the Occluded color toggle and enable the button.

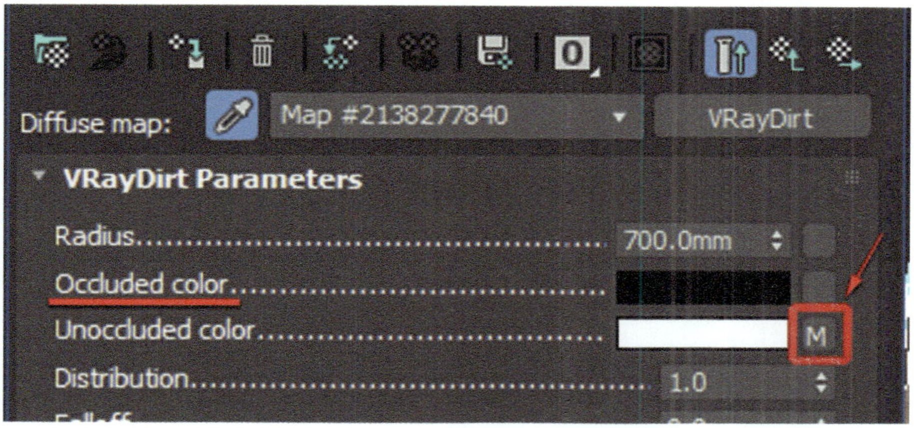

Go inside the Occluded color toggle

Enable the Show Shaded Material in Viewport button

To go back to the main Diffuse parameters, simply click on the Go to Parent button twice.

Go to Parent button

To tile the wood texture evenly, in the UVW Map parameters, set the Length, Width, and Height values to about 3000.0 mm.

Also, set V tile to about 2.0.

NOTE

These values worked well. However, feel free to try different values, if desired.

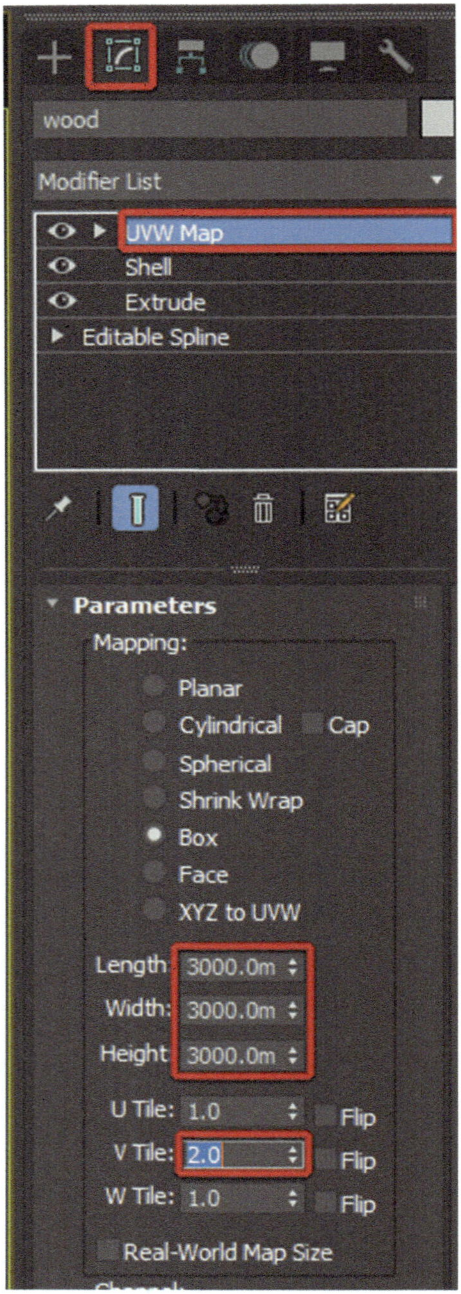

UVW Map tiling

Next, to create more details on the wood material, let's add the VRayDisplacementMod on top. As mentioned earlier, VRayDisplacementMod works best when there's a UVW Map applied previously.

Enable the 2d Mapping option and set it to about 3.0 mm.

Back in the main material parameters, scroll down to the Maps rollout. Drag and drop the Bump toggle into the VRayDisplacementMod Texmap toggle.

Choose the Instance copy Method.

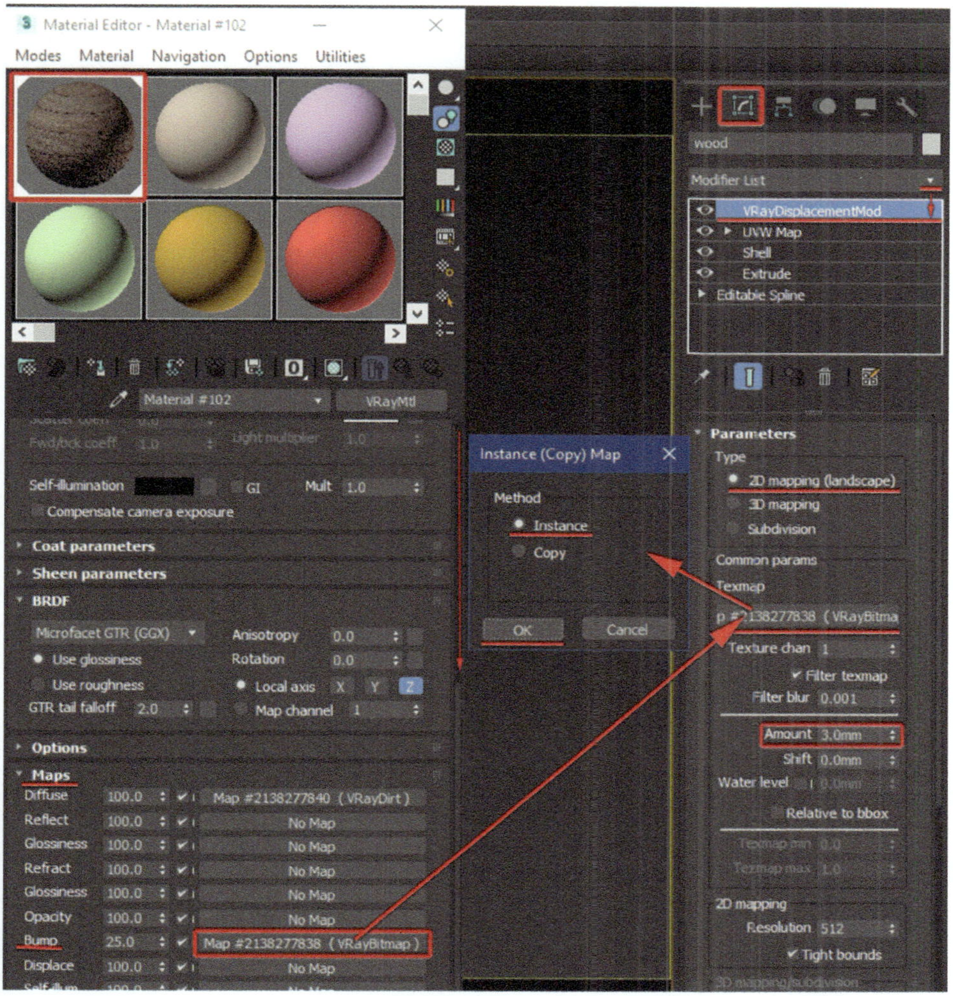

Add the VRayDisplacementMod

Exit the isolation mode (Alt+Q).

NOTE

To make any changes to the UVW Map values, the VRayDisplacementMod needs to be turned off (eye icon) and turned on again after the changes.

Next, in scene, select the object under the name of Box116 and apply the same wood material and modifiers previously used.

Use the right click and copy/paste options to speed up the process. Enable the UVW Map Y Alignment for object, Box116.

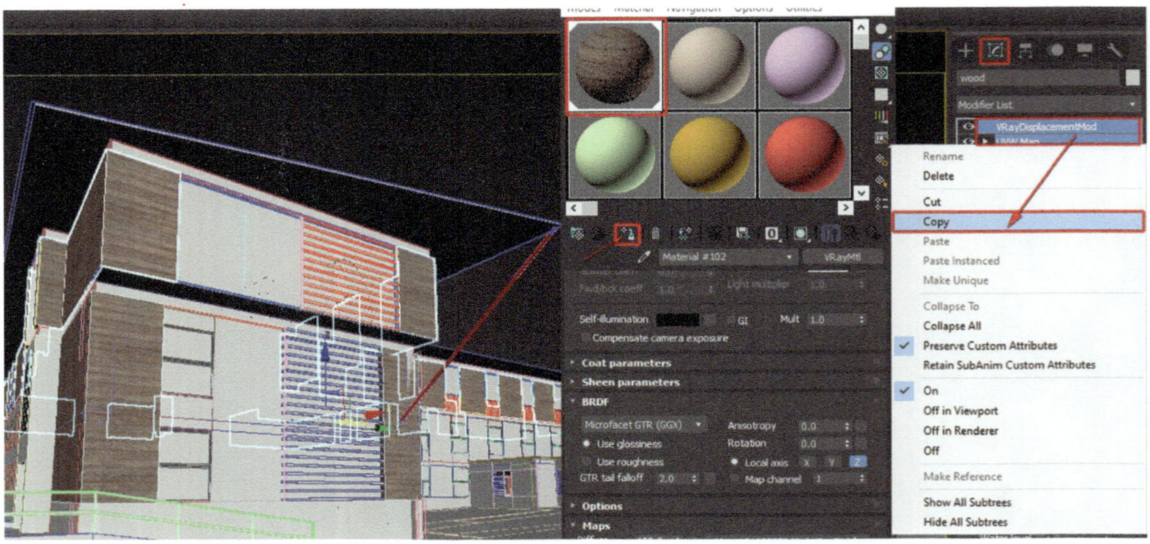

Assign and copy+paste instance modifiers

Rename the wood material as Wood_Planks_B01_100cm, and change its material ID to 1. It's always a good practice to begin changing the material ID numbers from the start.

Rename and change the material ID number

Glass Material

Next, in scene, select objects under the names of Glass, Object034, Rectangle081, and glass. Hold down the Ctrl key+Click to select multiple objects in the scene.

Alternatively, select them one by one and follow the steps.

Isolate the objects (Alt+Q) and open the VRay Asset Browser dialog.

Select the Glass Material Library and select the Glass material slot.

Right click and choose Apply to selected objects.

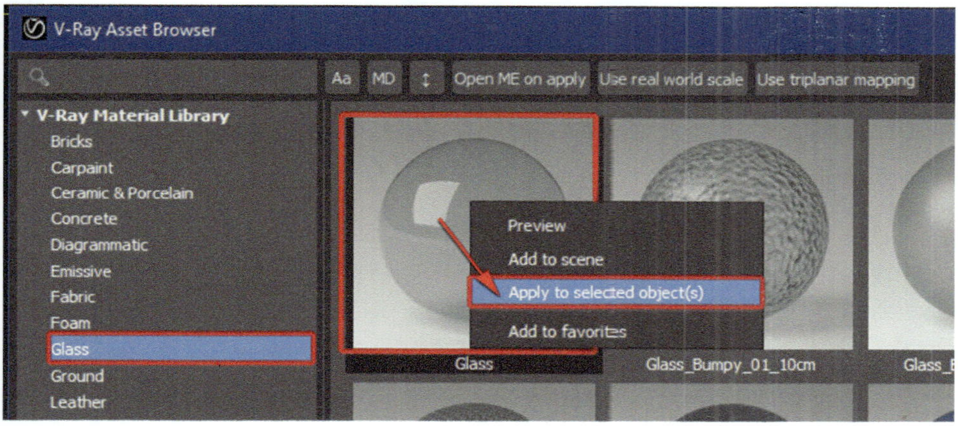

Apply the Glass material>

Minimize the VRay Asset Browser dialog and maximize the Material Editor (M).

Select a new material slot and use the Pick Material from object tool to load the glass material.

The default color of the glass is slightly green. For the purpose of this exercise, let's make it white (218).

It's easier to later change it in post, if required.

To change the glass color, click on its Fog color swatch and change it to white.

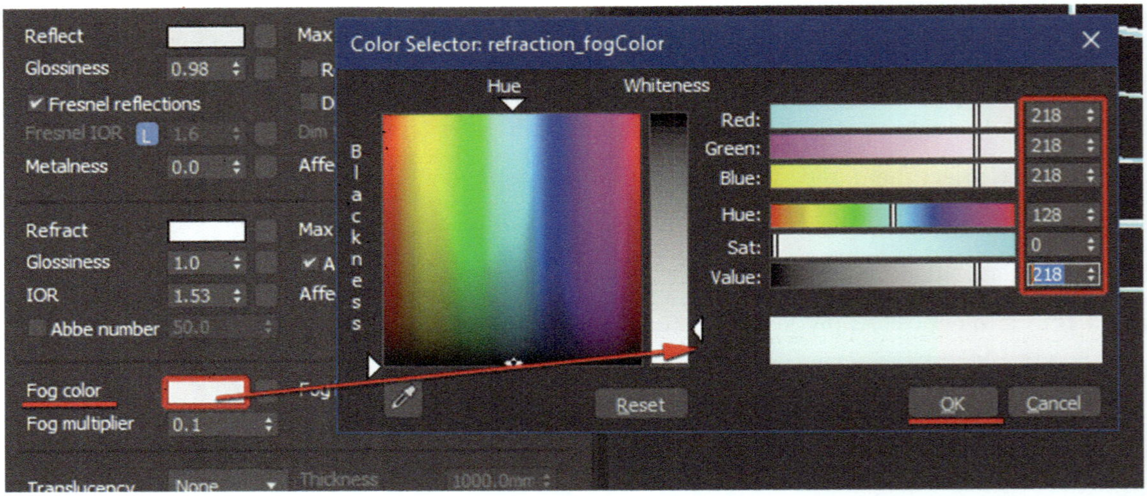

Change Fog color swatch to white (218)

NOTE

These values worked well. However, feel free to try different values, if desired.

Use the viewport IPR to see the material changes happening immediately, while tweaking away parameters.

In the Reflect group, disable the Fresnel reflections to have better control of the reflections and passes.

Decrease the Reflect color swatch to about 15. To add a bit of gloss/specular to the glass, decrease the glossiness value to about 0.88.

To have linear refractions, decrease the Refract IOR value to about 1.1.

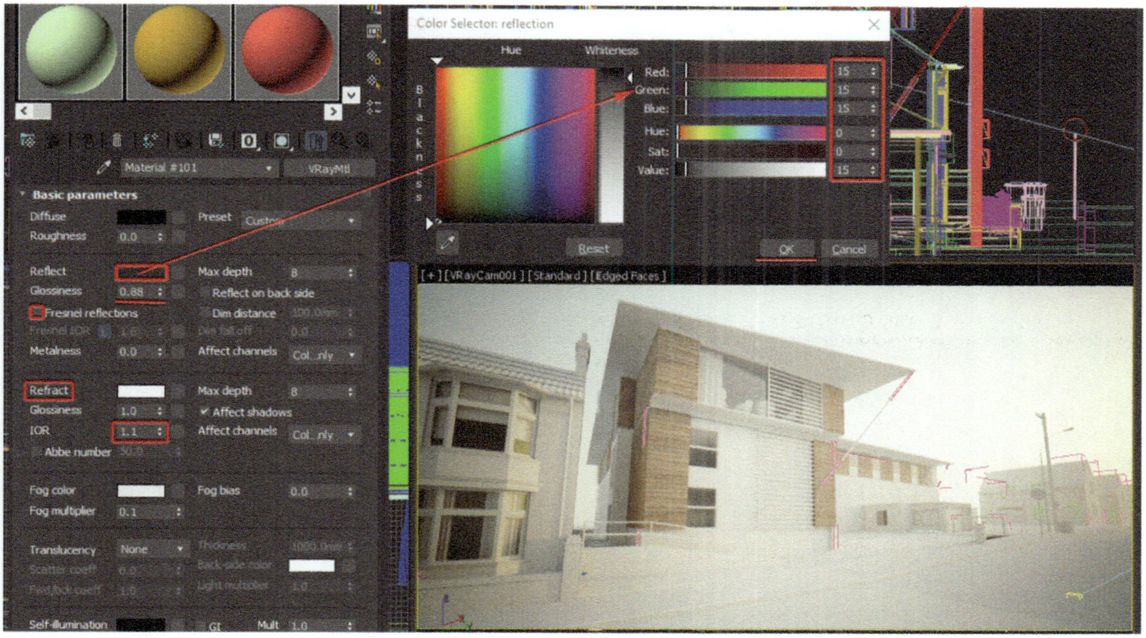

Change Glass material settings

Rename the material as Glass, and change its material ID number to 2.

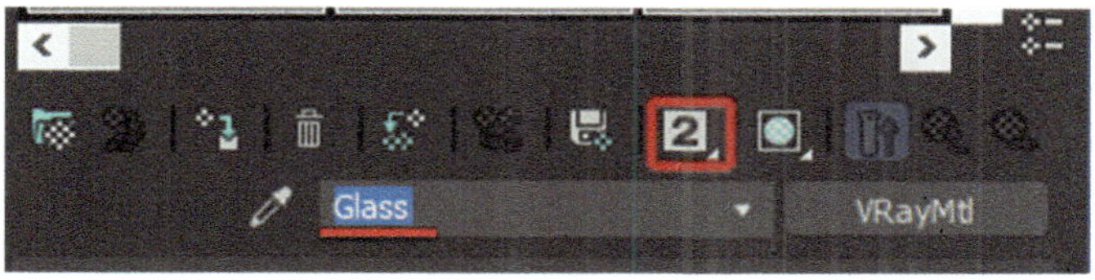

Rename and change material ID

Iron material

In the scene, select objects under the names of roof angled_Base, Rectangle361, Box003, and Rectangle091.

Alternatively, select them one by one and follow the steps.

Isolate the selected objects (Alt+Q).

Select the Metal Material Library and choose the Iron Blurry _5cm slot. Right click and choose Apply to selected objects.

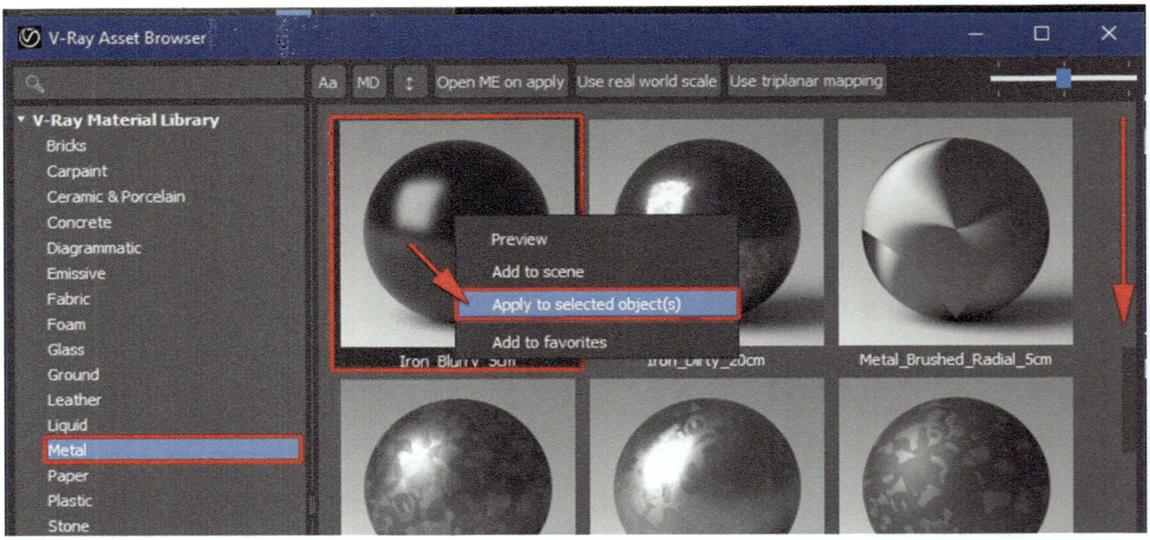

Apply to selected objects

NOTE

These values worked well. However, feel free to try different values, if desired.

Exit the isolation to see the changes in the viewport IPR.

Bring the material into the new material slot with the Pick Material from object tool.

Rename it as Iron Blurry_5cm and change its material ID to 3.

Next, disable the Fresnel reflections function, and decrease the Reflect color swatch to about 20.

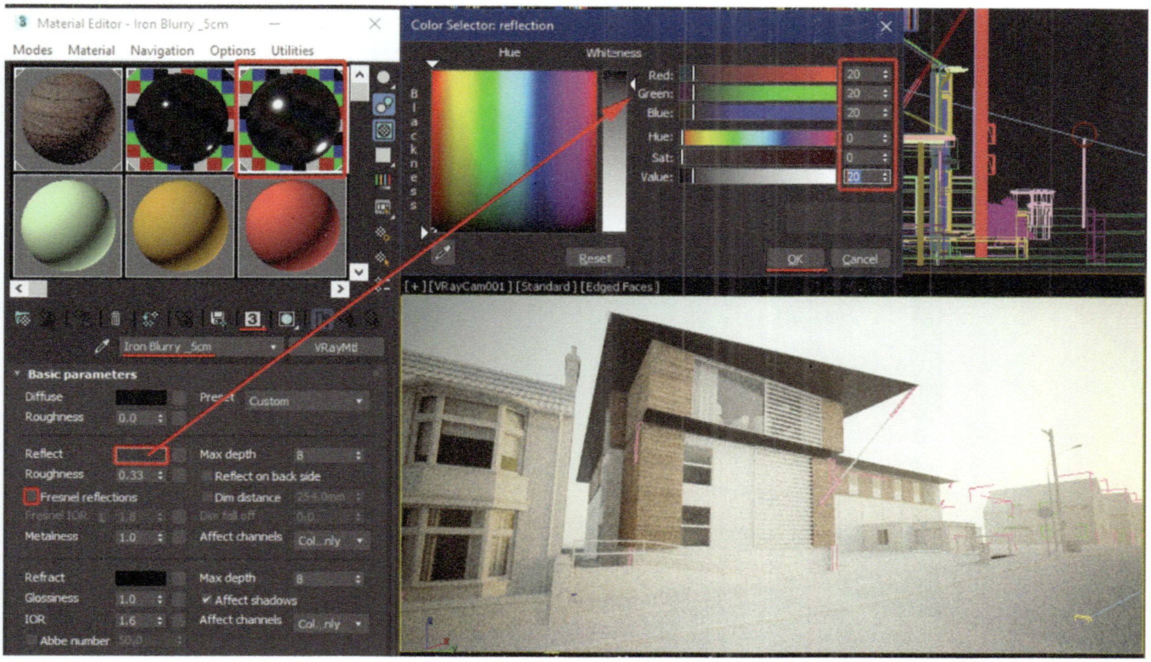

Tweak the material parameters

Wood Laminate Material

In the scene, select the following objects: frames, Line147, Line148, Line151, Line152, Line153, and Line155.

Use the 2d Pan Zoom Mode to zoom into the viewport (using the mouse scroll wheel) and select multiple objects in the scene (Ctrl+click).

Alternatively, select them one by one and follow the steps.

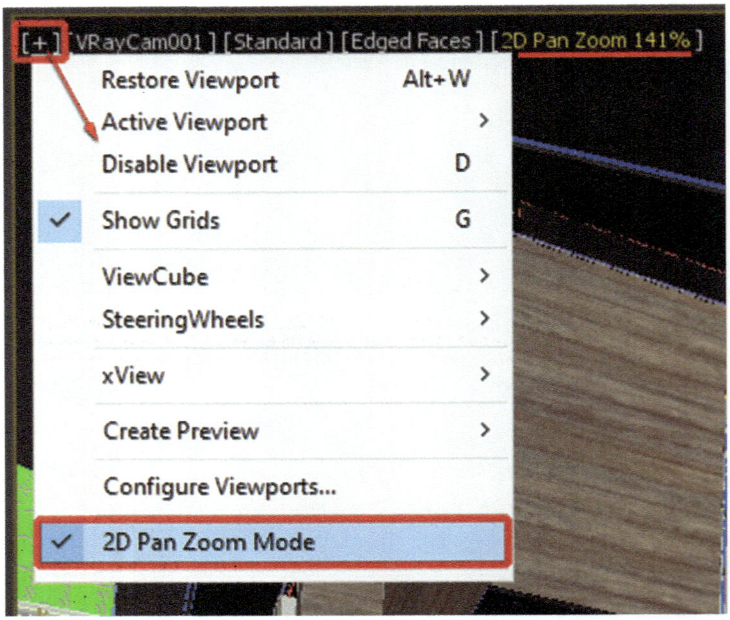

Use the 2d Pan Zoom Mode

Isolate the selected objects (Alt+Q)

In the VRay Asset Browser dialog, select the Wood and Laminate Material Library, followed by choosing the Laminate_B01_120cm slot and right clicking and choosing Apply to selected objects.

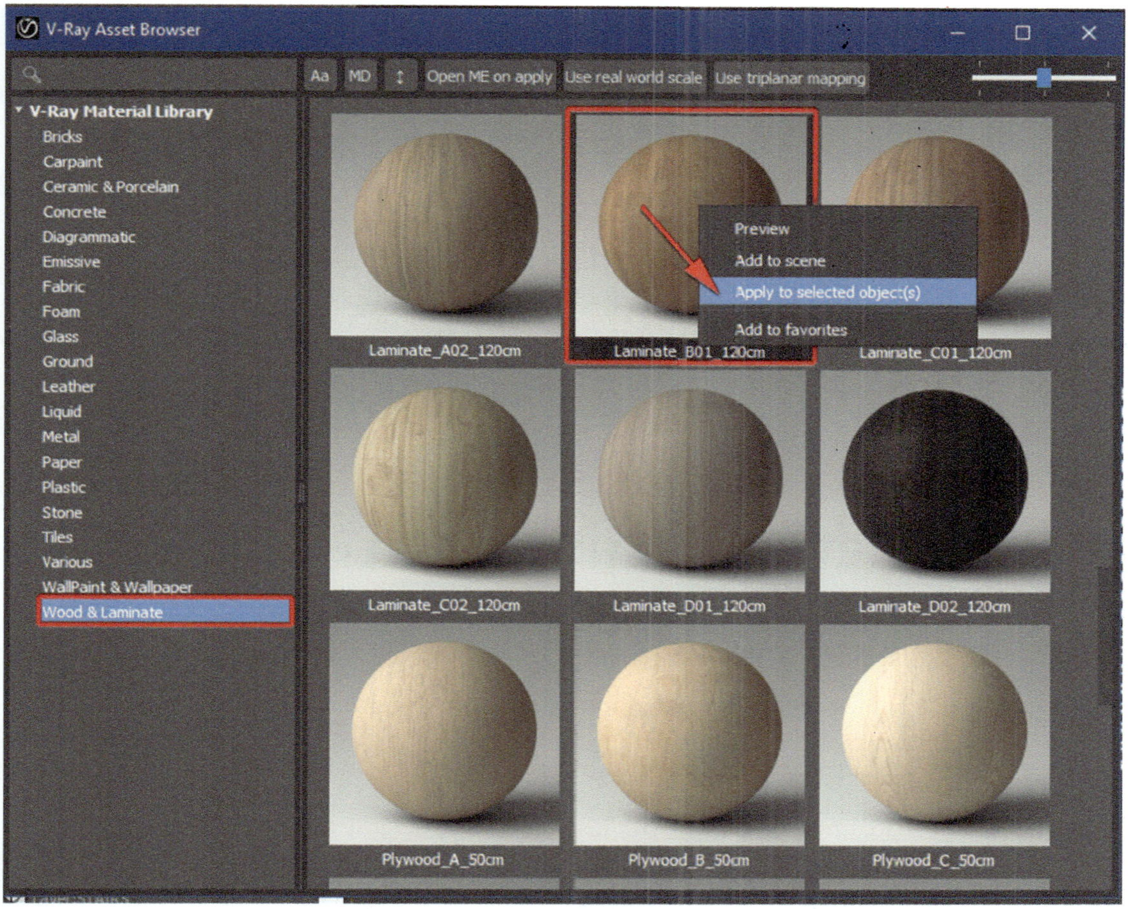

Apply Wood to selected objects

In the Material Editor dialog (M), bring the aminate_B01_120cm material with the Pick Material from object tool.

Rename it as Laminate_B01_120cm and change its material ID to 4. Make the material visible in the viewport with the button Show Shaded material in Viewport.

Also, disable the function of Fresnel reflections.

Next, select its Reflect color swatch and reduce its reflectivity to about 10.

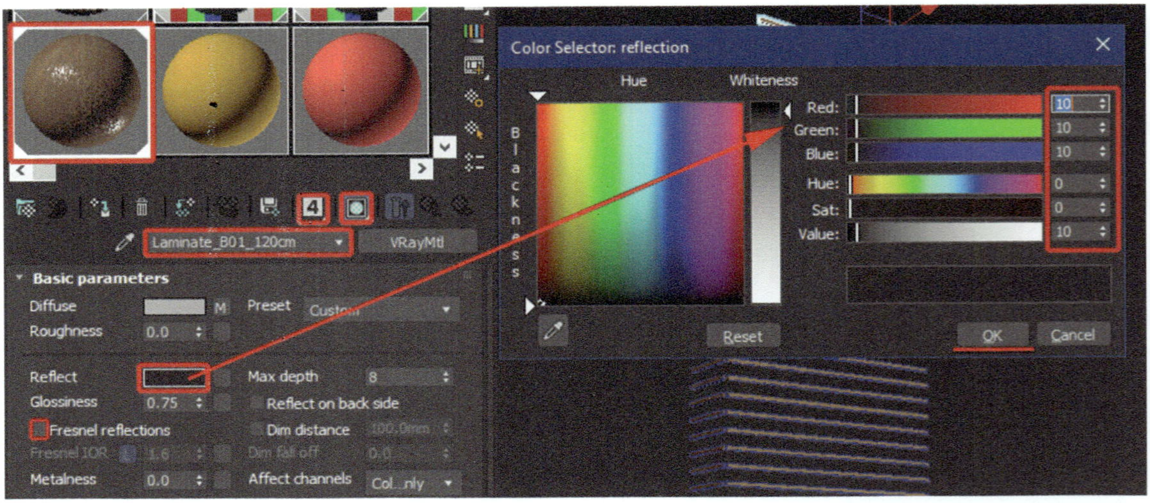

Tweak the Laminate_B01_120cm material parameters

In the scene, select the object under the name of Line148. Open the Modify panel and add the UVW Map modifier from its list.

Enable the Box Mapping type, and set the Length, Width, and Height values to 40 mm. As mentioned earlier, having equal values will ensure the textures are not stretched on any of the sides.

Also, under U, V, and W Tiles, reduce the default values to 0.3.

Under Alignment, enable the X to align the texture horizontally, and click the button Fit material.

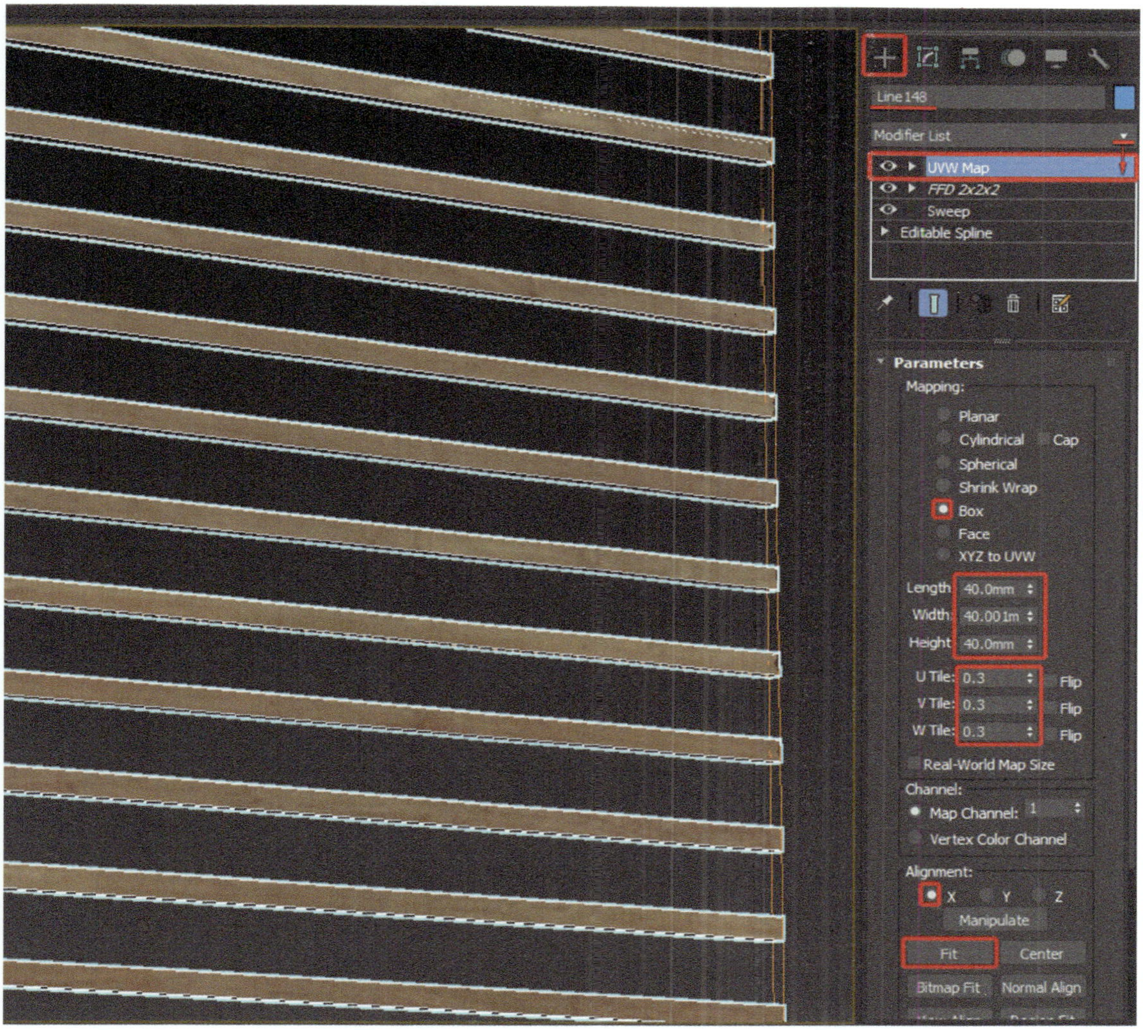

Add the UVW Map modifier and adjust parameters

Select the object, Line155, and add the UVW Map modifier to it. Under Alignment group, click Acquire and select the object, Line148.

Choose Acquire Relative and OK. Object Line155 now has similar UVW Map parameters to object, Line148.

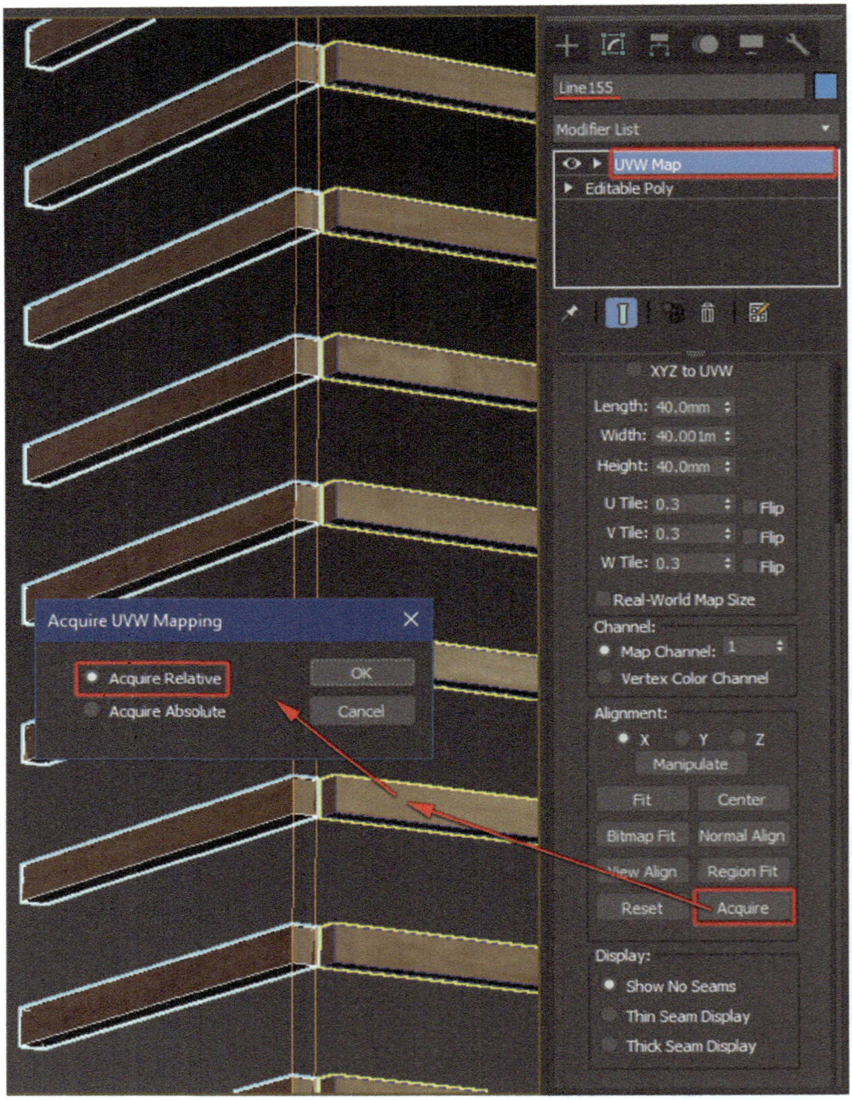

Acquire UVW Mapping

Use the same technique on the remaining objects in the scene with this wood material.

Exit the 2d Pan Zoom Mode and the isolation mode (Alt+Q).

Material progression in the Viewport IPR

Plastic Metallic Material

In the scene, select the following objects: Cylinder009 and Line121.

Next, open the VRay Asset browser dialog. In the Plastic Material Library, select the Plastic_Metallic_Black slot and choose Apply tc selected objects (right click).

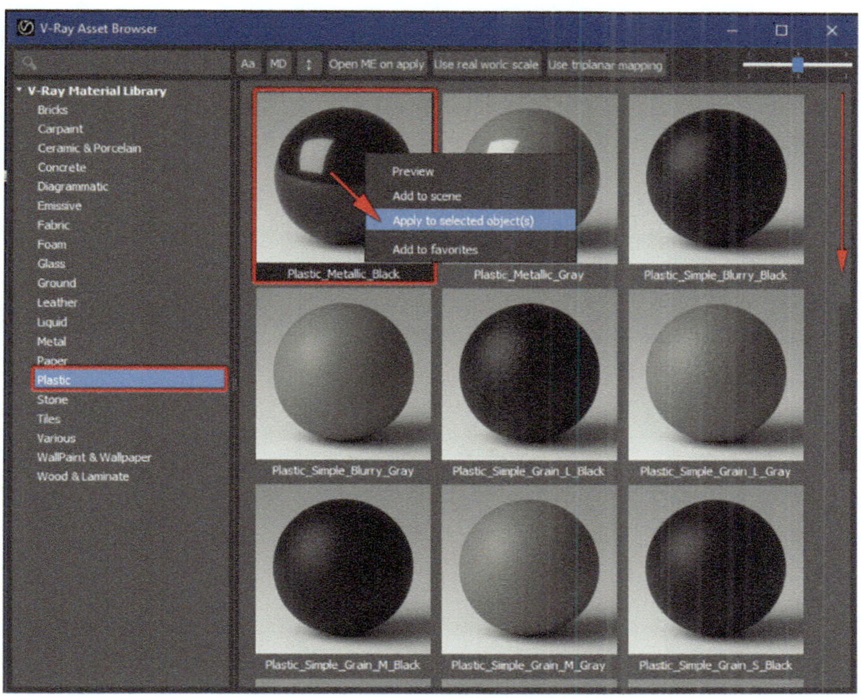

Apply to selected objects

Open the Plastic_Metallic_Black material in the Material Editor (M) and name it as Plastic_Metallic_Black.

Change its ID number to 5 and disable the Fresnel reflections option.

Open the Reflect color swatch and reduce its value to about 5. The glossy highlights are still there but with less reflections.

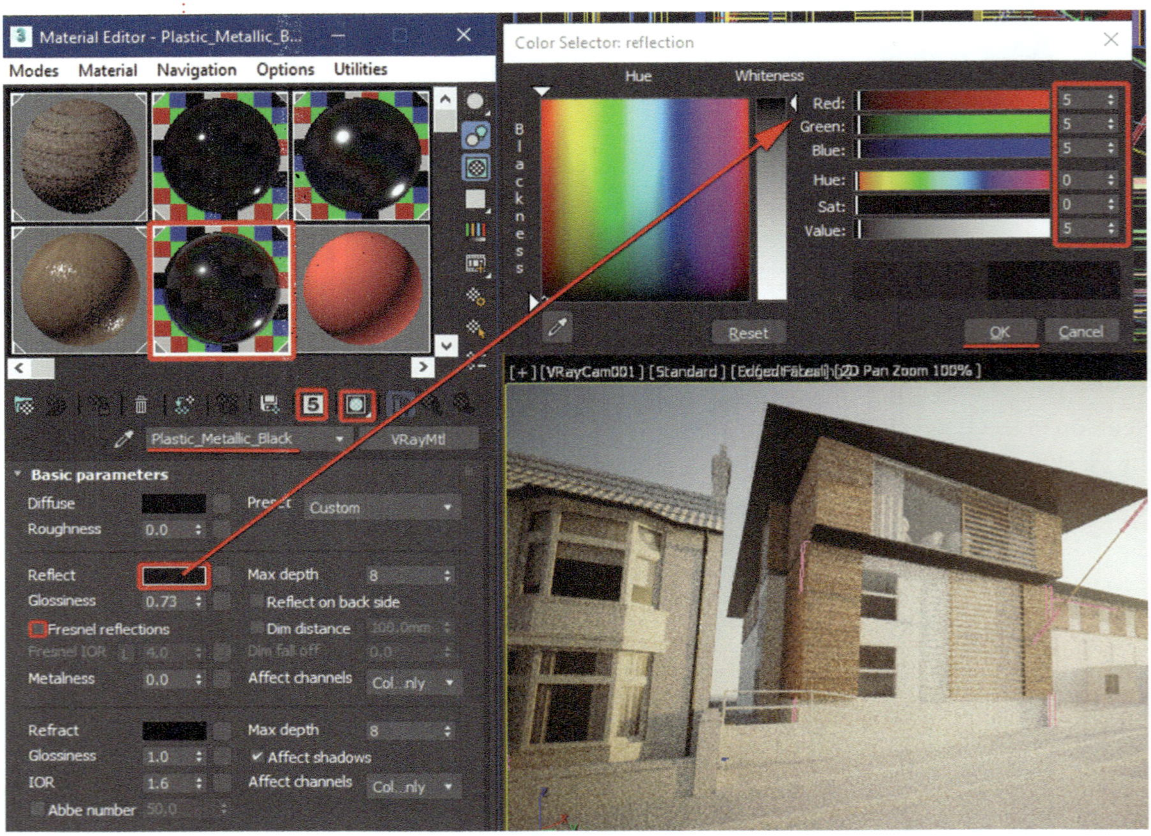

Tweak the Plastic Metallic material

Metallic Paint Copper

In the scene, select the following objects: Rectangle078 and Object035.

Next, open the VRay Asset browser dialog. In the Metal Material Library, select the Metallic_Paint_Copper slot and choose Apply to selected objects (right click).

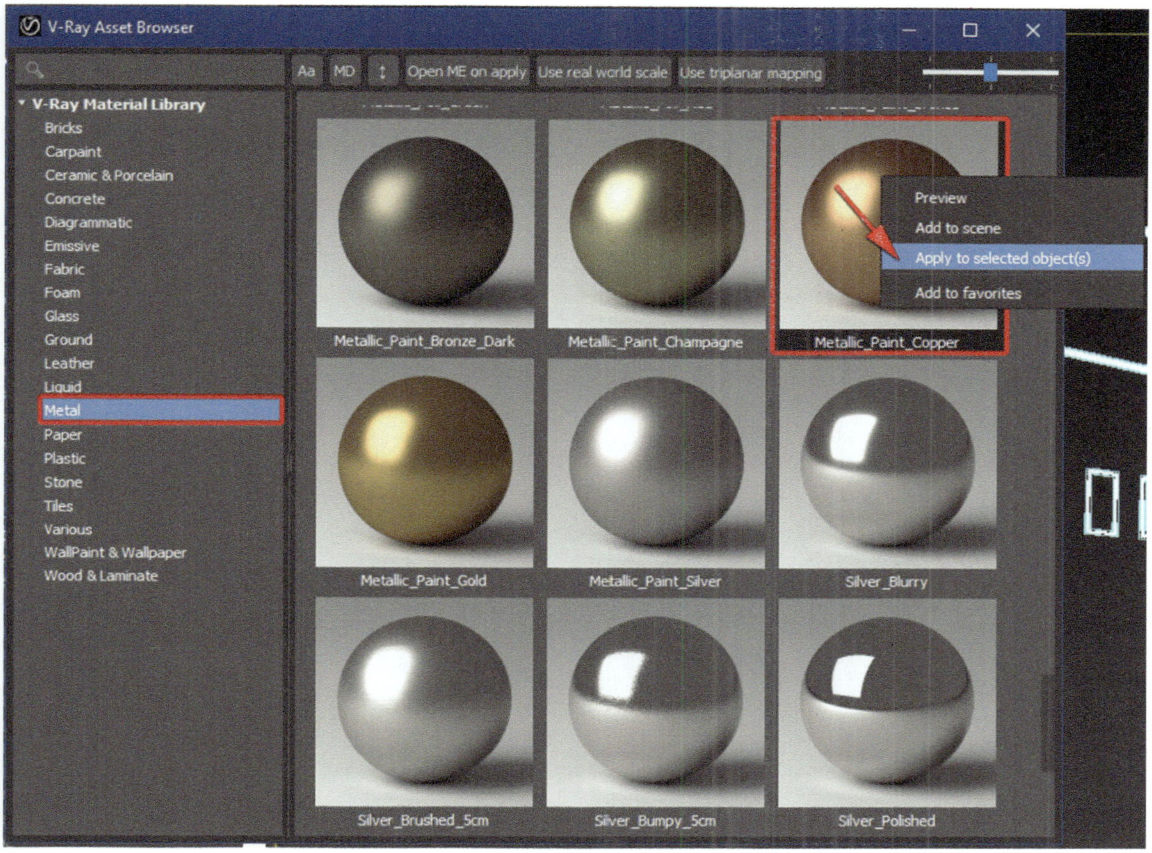

Apply to selected objects

Open the Metallic_Paint_Copper material in the Material Editor (M) and name it as Metallic_Paint_Copper.

Change its ID number to 6 and disable the Fresnel reflections option.

Open the Reflect color swatch and change its color to light brown (19,113,36).

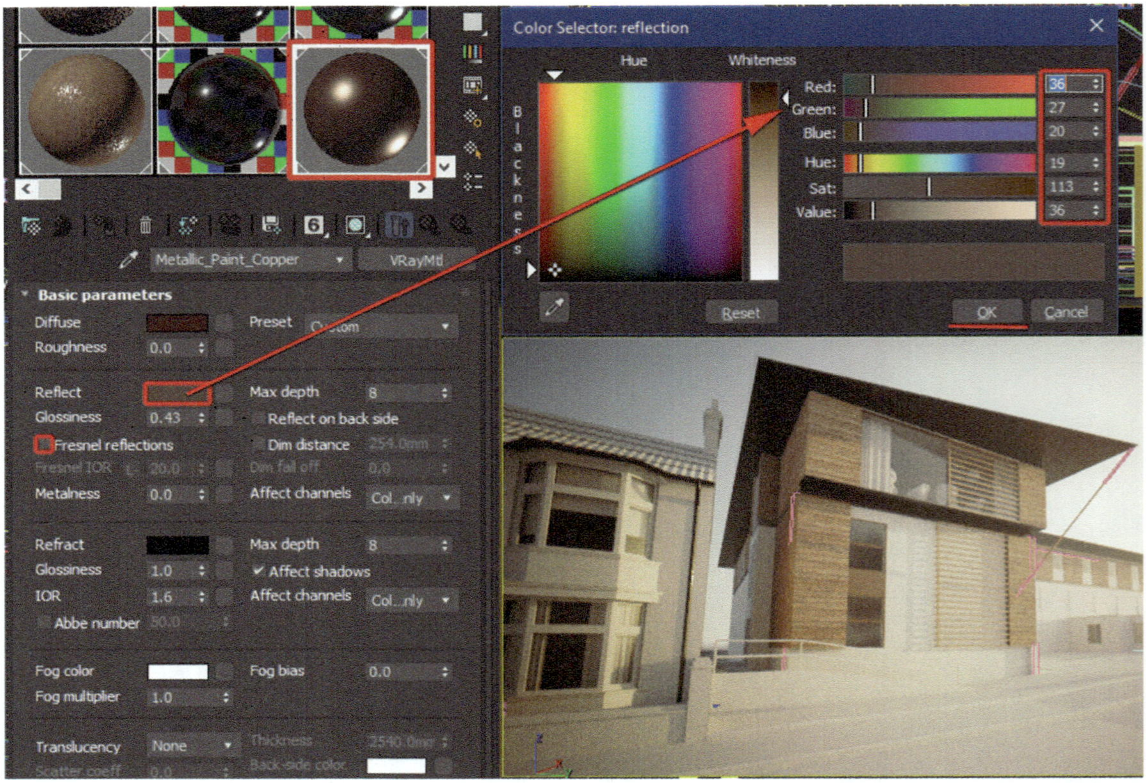

Tweak the Copper material

Also, add VRayDirt on top using the techniques and parameters covered earlier. Copy and paste the Diffuse color into the Unoccluded color (right click).

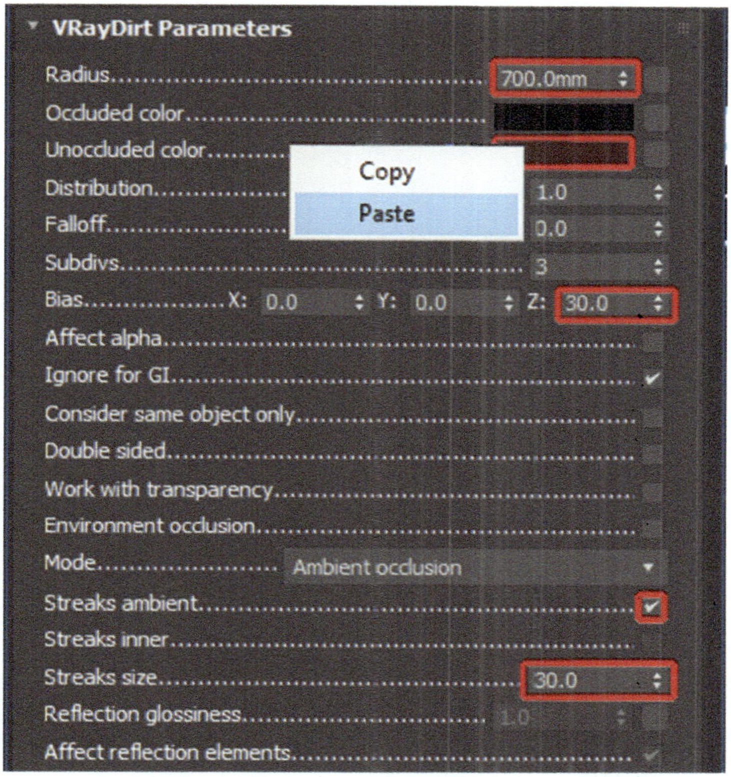

VRayDirt Parameters

Stucco Material

In the scene, select the following objects: Box013 and Box115.

Next, open the VRay Asset browser dialog. In the WallPaint and Wallpaper Material Library, select the Stucco_B01_50cm slot and choose Apply to selected objects (right click).

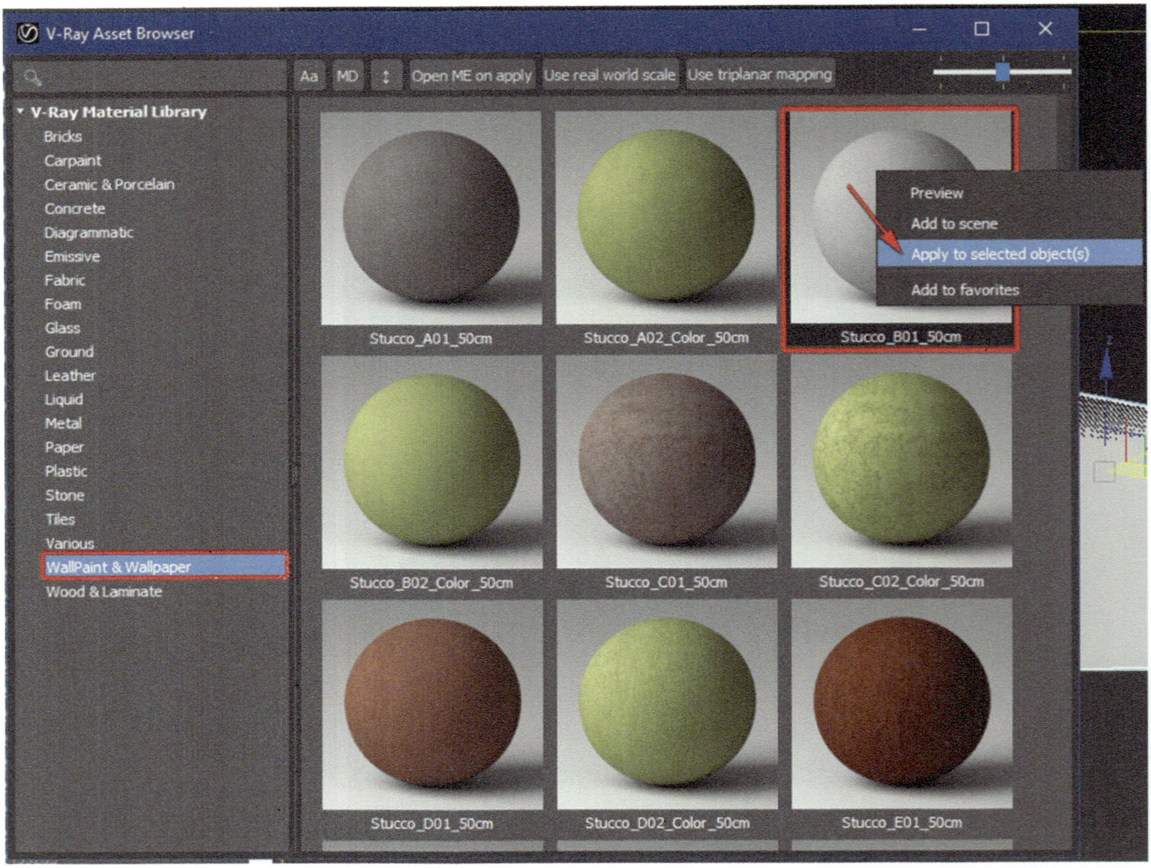

Apply to selected objects

Open the Stucco_B01_50cm material in the Material Editor (M) and name it as Stucco_B01_50cm.

Also, change its ID number to 7.

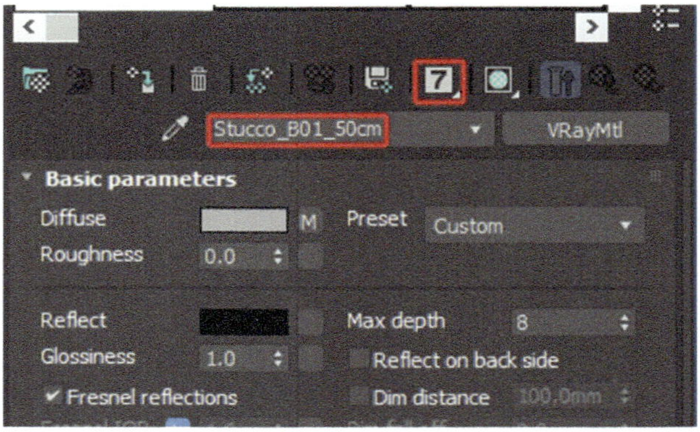

Rename the material and ID number

To change its color, go inside the Diffuse toggle and add a Composite procedural map.

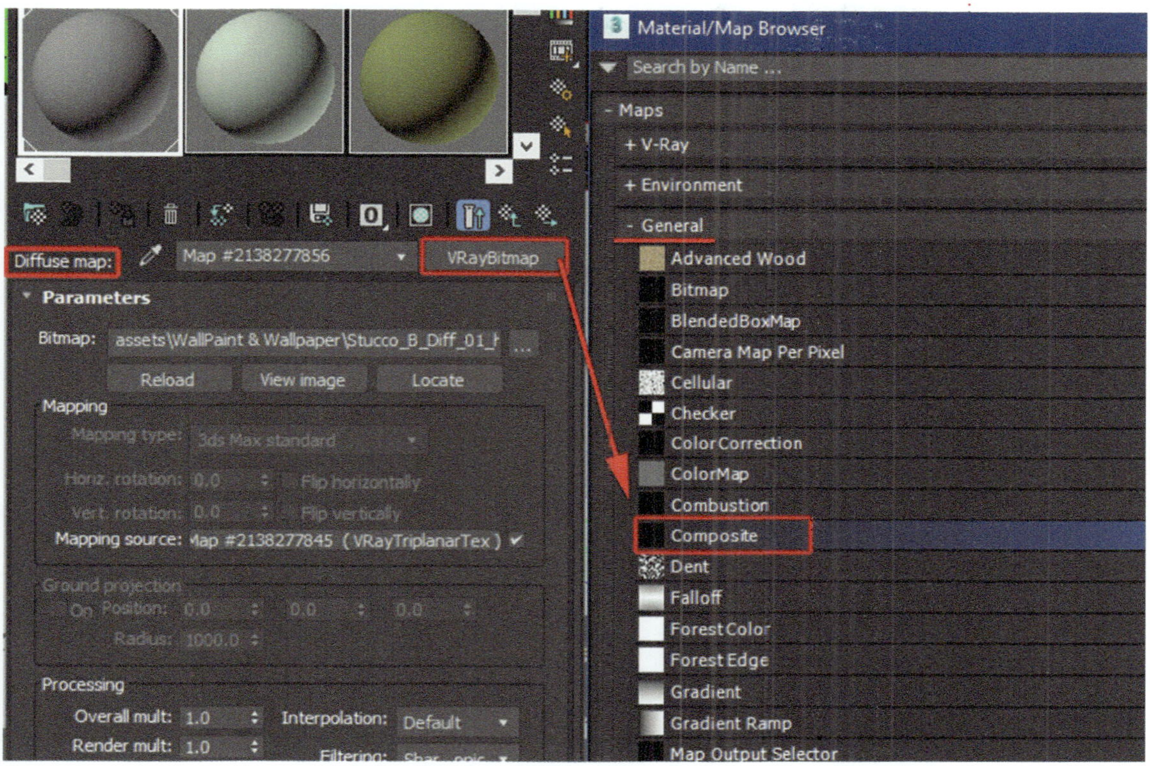

Composite procedural map

Choose Keep old map as sub-map.

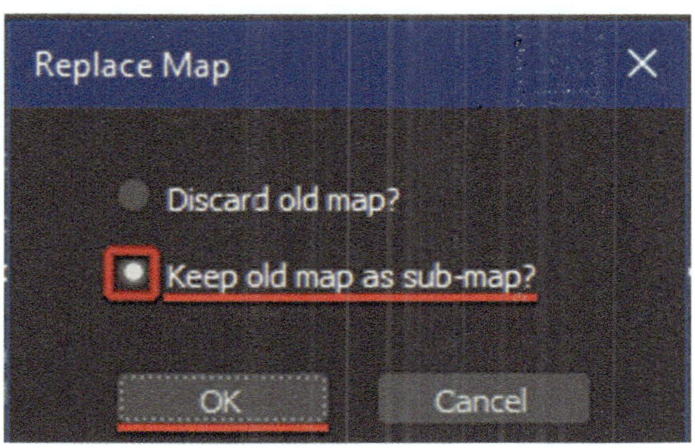

Keep old map as sub-map

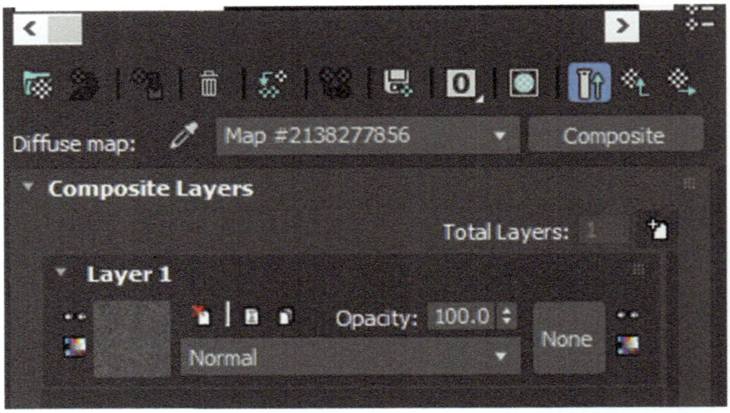

Composite loaded

To add a bit of color, create a new layer by clicking on the Add a New Layer button.

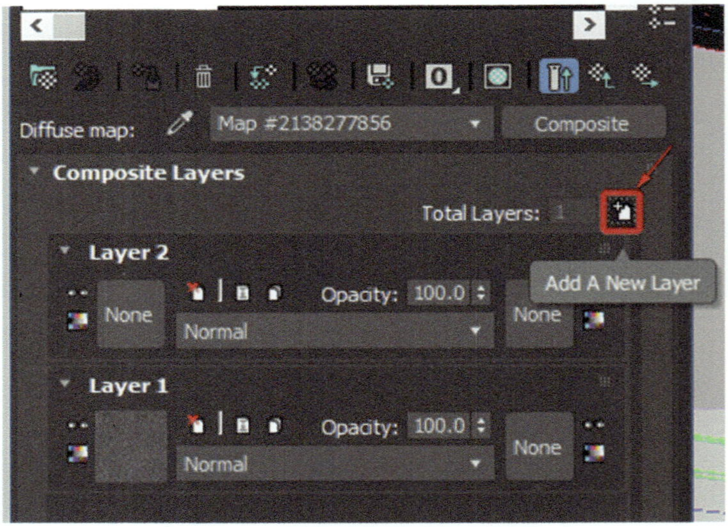

Add a New Layer

Next, move Layer 1 to Layer 2 by clicking and dragging it. Choose the Swap option.

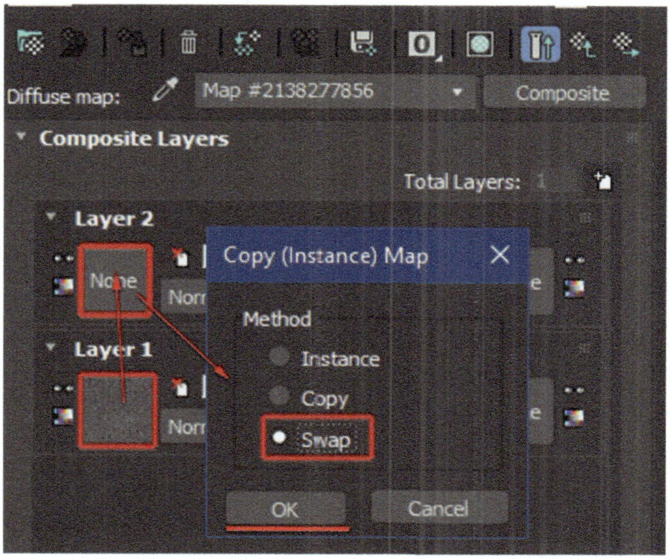

Choose the Swap option

Add a VRayColor procedural map by clicking on the Layer 1 left toggle and choosing it from the Material/Map Browser dialog.

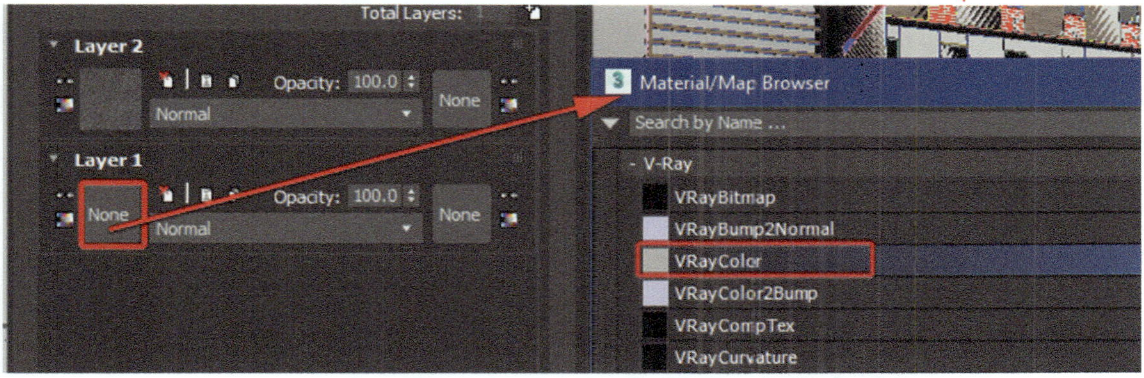

Choose the VRayColor procedural map

In the VRayColor Parameters, change its color to Yellowish (27,203,245).

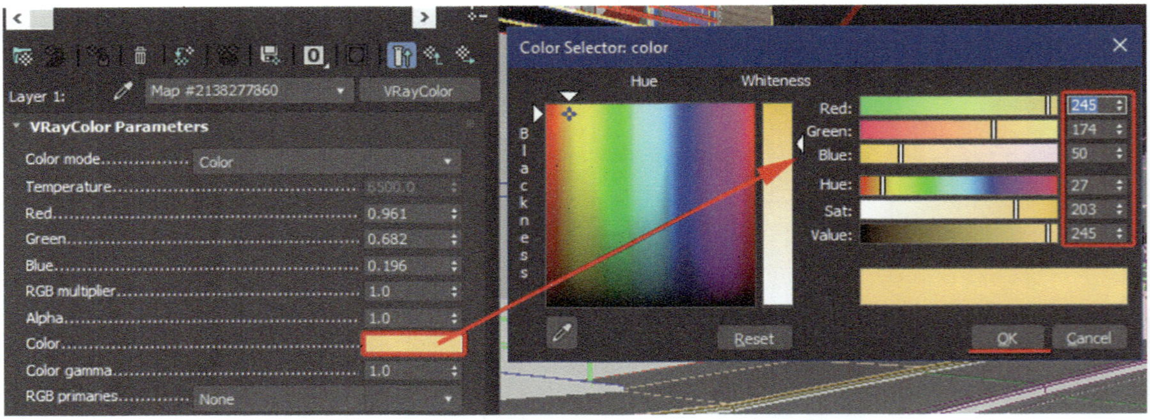

Change the VRayColor

Next, click on the Go to Parent button to go back one level. Change the Layer 2 blending mode from Normal to Screen type. The Stucco material now has a yellow tinge to it.

Change the Layer 2 blending mode to Screen

Add the VRayDirt procedural map on top, and choose Keep old map as sub-map. Use some of the parameters and values previously entered.

Add VRayDirt procedural map

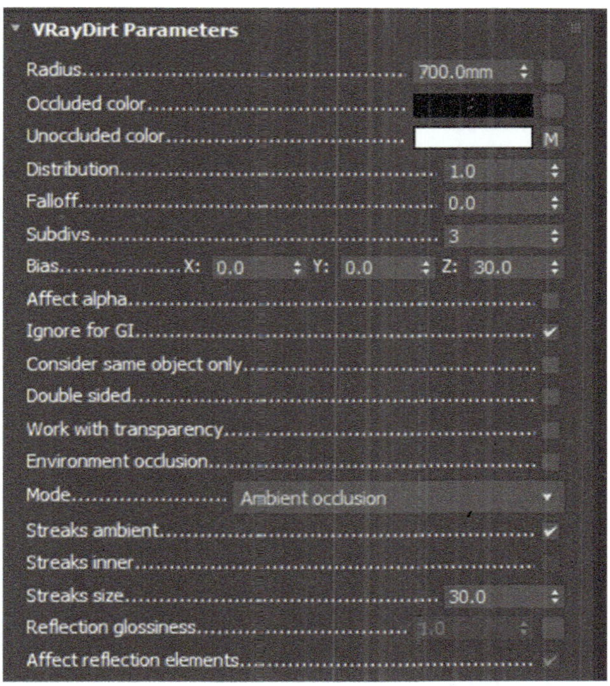

VRayDirt procedural map parameters

8 Materials and Final Render

Viewport IPR progress

Brick Wall Material

In the scene, let's start by selecting the object under the name of Material #2147463750.

Open the VRay Asset Browser dialog and select the Bricks Material Library. Choose the material slot Brick_A01_1m, followed by right clicking and choosing Apply to selected objects (right click).

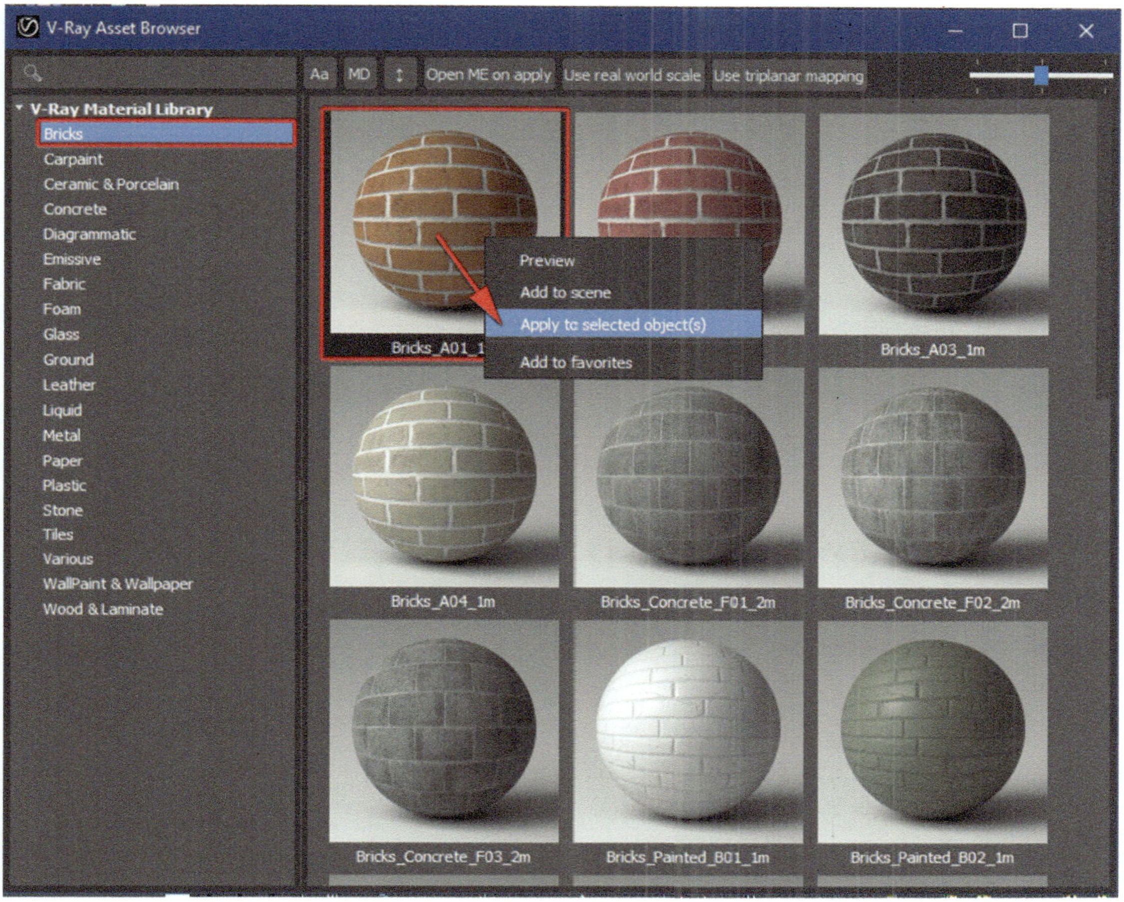

Apply to selected objects

Open the Brick_A01_1m material in the Material Editor (M) and name it as Brick_A01_1m.

Also, enable the Show Shaded Material in Viewport and change its ID number to 8.

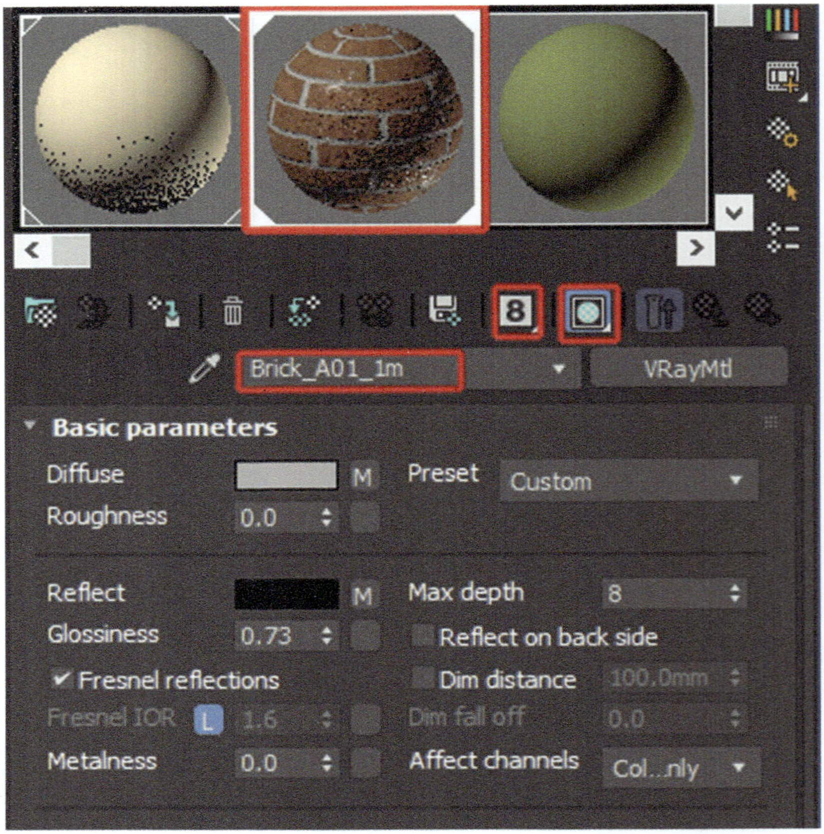

Rename material and change material ID.

NOTE

Use a rectangle shape or the Tape tool to take dimensions.

To tile the material, open the Modify panel and add the UVW Map modifier from the list. Under Mapping, choose the Box type and set the Length, Width, and Height to 750 mm.

Under U Tile, set it to 0.83. These values should result on a standard brick size (250 mm x 65 mm).

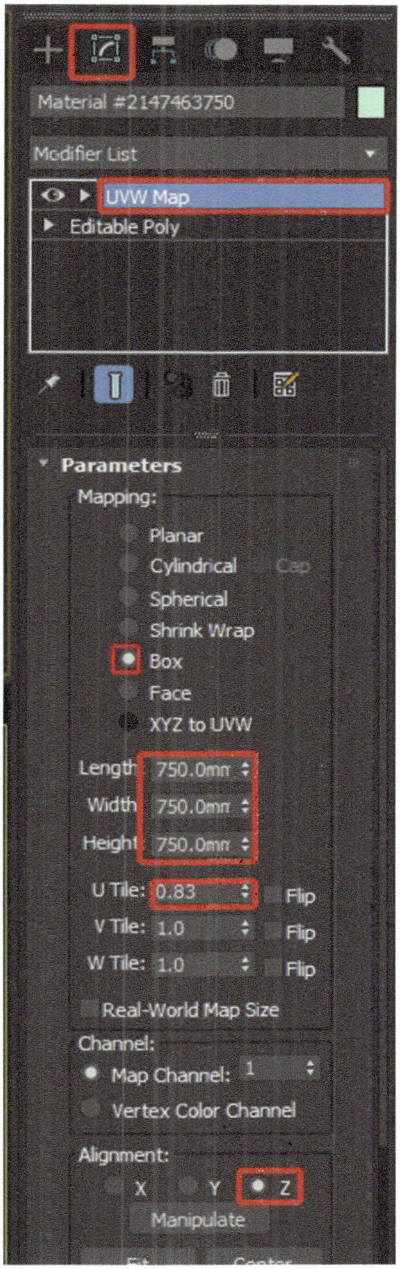

UVW Map parameters

To increase detail on the brick, add the VRayDisplacementMod on top. Enable the 2d mapping type.

Back on the Material Editor (M) main parameters, scroll down to its Maps rollout. Drag and drop its Bump toggle into the Texmap toggle.

Choose the Instance copy type, and set the displacement Amount to about 5.0 mm.

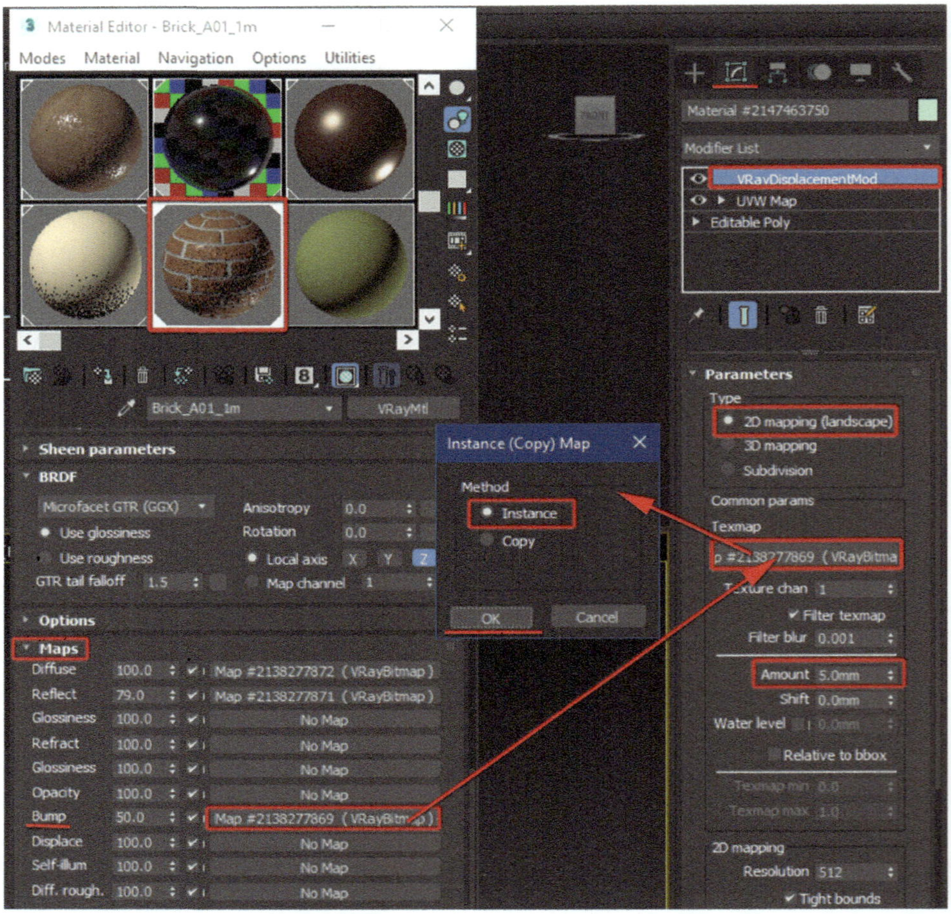

VRayDisplacementMod parameters

In the scene, select objects under the names of Line033 and Box095. Apply this brick material and copy/paste the same modifiers.

Also, select the object under the name of Line167. Apply the same material and copy/paste the same modifiers to it.

To align this texture with the object, Line033, disable the VRayDisplacementMod (eye icon) and select the UVW Map. Under Alignment, choose the Y-axis, followed by clicking the Acquire button.

The Acquire dialog should pop up. Click on the object, Line033, and choose the option Acquire Absolute. Both textures should line up.

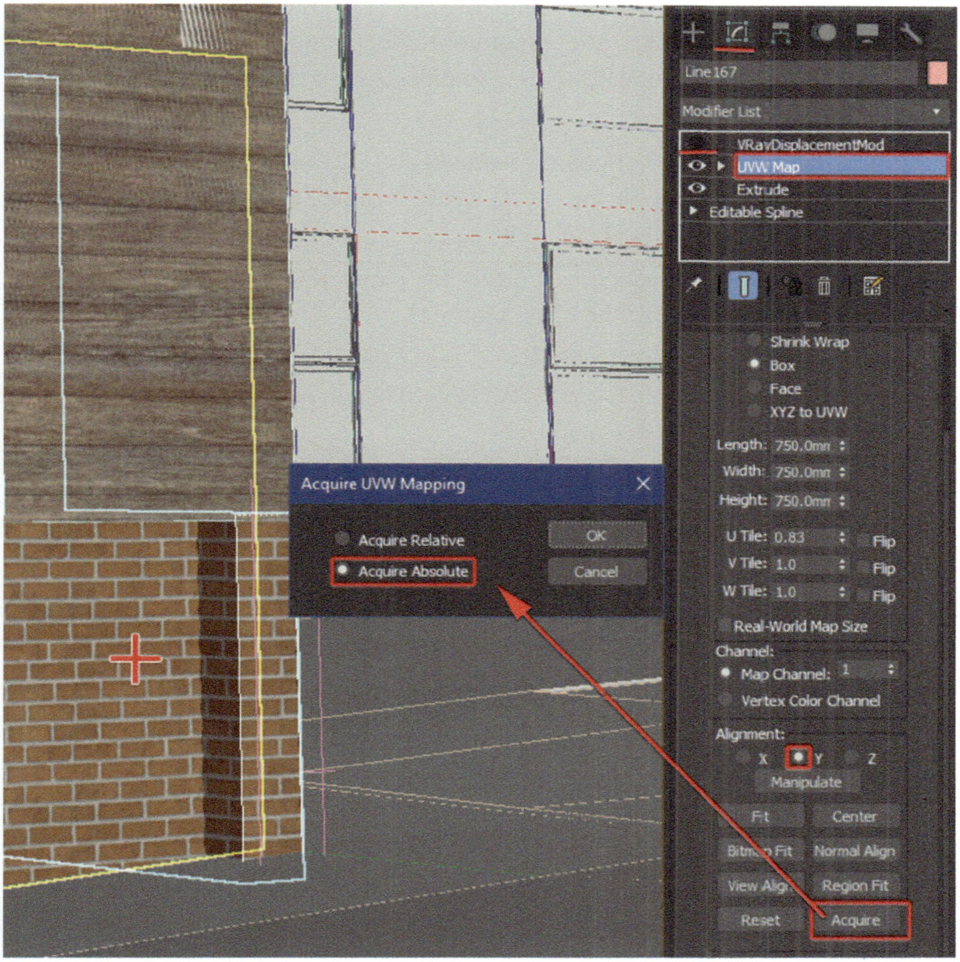

Align brick material

Enable the VRayDisplacementMod back again (eye icon). Apply this brick material and modifiers to objects, Line030 and Line028.

Assigning Previous Materials to More Objects in the Scene

Iron Blurry _5cm: In the scene, select objects, Line056, balcony stripes003, balcony stripes004, balcony stripes005, and balcony stripes006, Line154, and assign the Iron Blurry _5cm material to them.

8 Materials and Final Render

NOTE

The UVW Map Alignment was changed to Y for objects, Box117, Rectangle045.

Wood_Planks_B01_100cm: Next, select the objects under the name of Box117, Rectangle045, Line025, Object077, Line048, Rectangle072, and assign the material, Wood_Planks_B01_100cm to them. Copy and paste the modifiers previously applied to objects with this material.

Stucco_B01_50cm: Select objects named Box112, Box006, Box106, Line026, Rectangle070 Rectangle066, Rectangle077, Line032, and assign them the material, Stucco_B01_50cm, to it.

Glass: In the scene, select objects under the name of Object033, Box2433164, Glass and assign them the Glass material.

Metallic_Paint_Copper: In the scene, select the objects, Object032, Object039, Object060, Object059, Object056, Shape003, and assign them the Metallic_Paint_Copper material.

Asphalt Material

In the scene, select the object under the name of Object068.

Open the VRay Asset Browser dialog and select the Ground Material Library. Choose the material Asphalt_Cracked_D01_200cm, followed by right clicking and choosing Apply to selected objects.

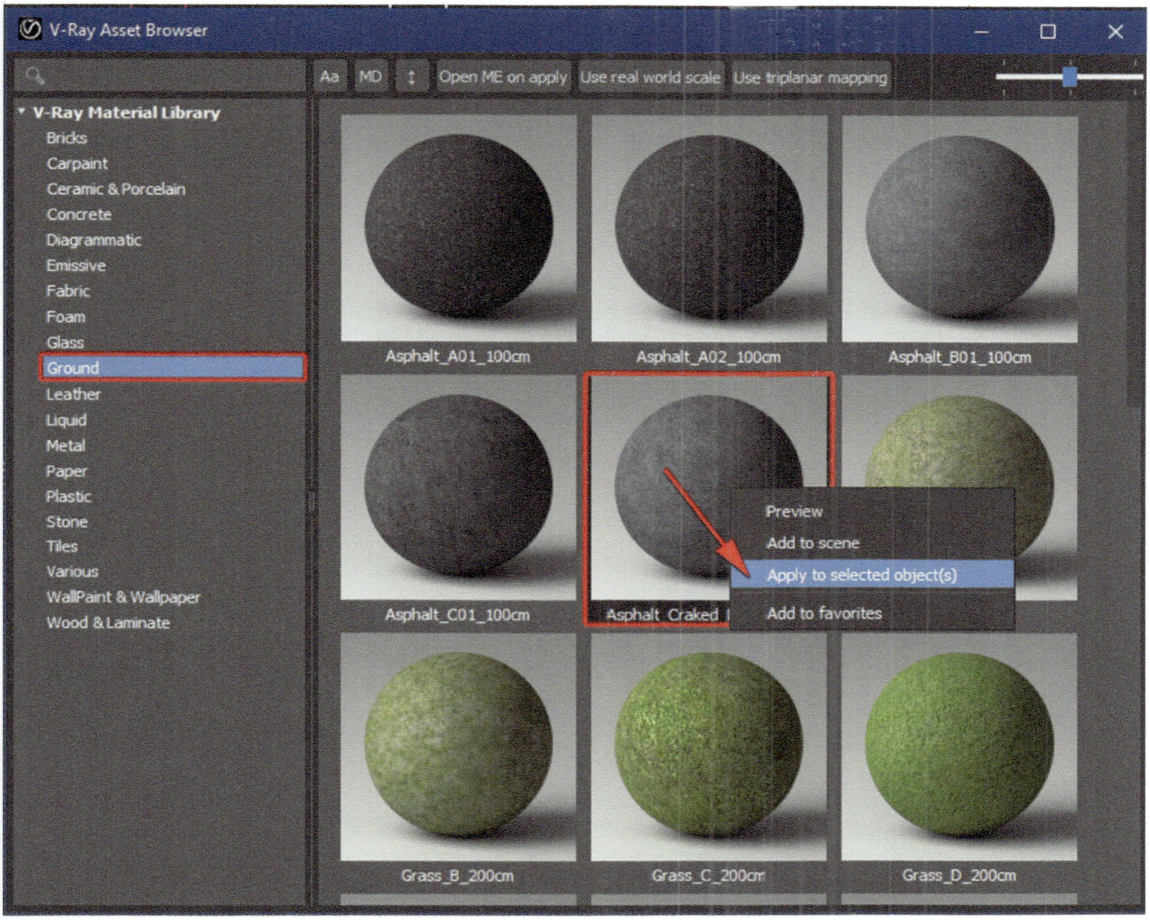

Apply to selected objects

Open the Asphalt in the Material Editor (M) and name it as Asphalt_Cracked_D01_200cm.

Also, enable the Show Shaded Material in Viewport and change its ID number to 9.

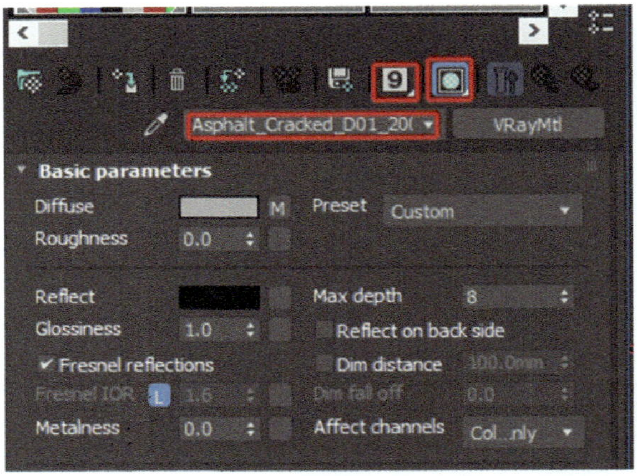

Rename material and change material ID.

NOTE

These values worked well. However, feel free to try different values, if desired.

To tile the material, open the Modify panel and add the UVW Map modifier from the list. Under Mapping, choose the Box type and set the Length, Width, and Height to 9000.0 mm.

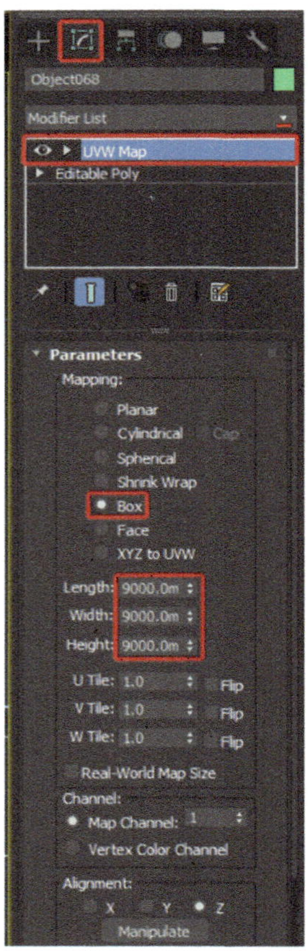

Add the UVW Map modifier from the list

Next, add a VRayDisplacementMod on top, and enable the 2d mapping type. Back on the main parameters of the Material Editor dialog (M), scroll down to the Maps rollout.

Drag and drop its Bump toggle into the Texmap of the VRayDisplacementMod.

Choose the Instance copy method, and set its Amount to 4.0 mm.

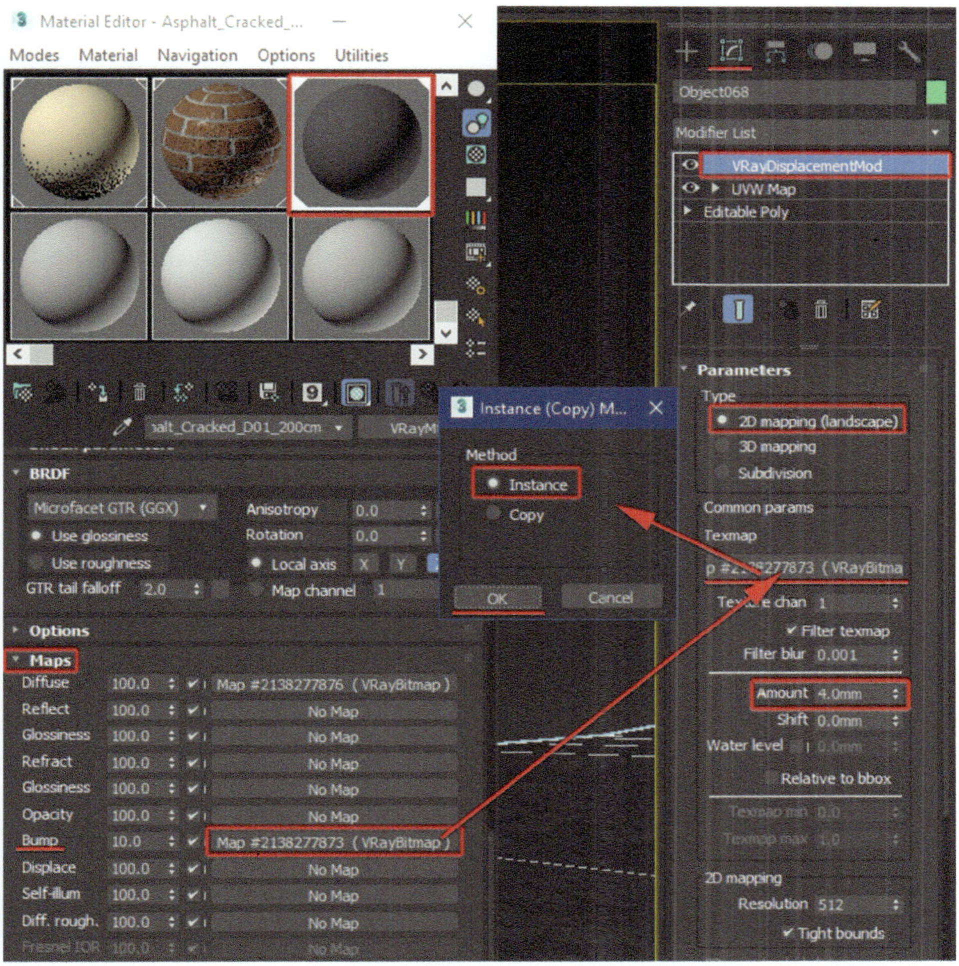

Set the VRayDisplacementMod parameters

Select and apply the material and modifiers to the object named Box096.

NOTE

These values worked well. However, feel free to try different values, if desired.

Viewport IPR progress

Next, go back to the Material Editor (M) and click on its Diffuse toggle. Inside the Diffuse map, replace the current Mapping source (right click and choose Clear VRayTriplanar) with VRayUVWRandomizer.

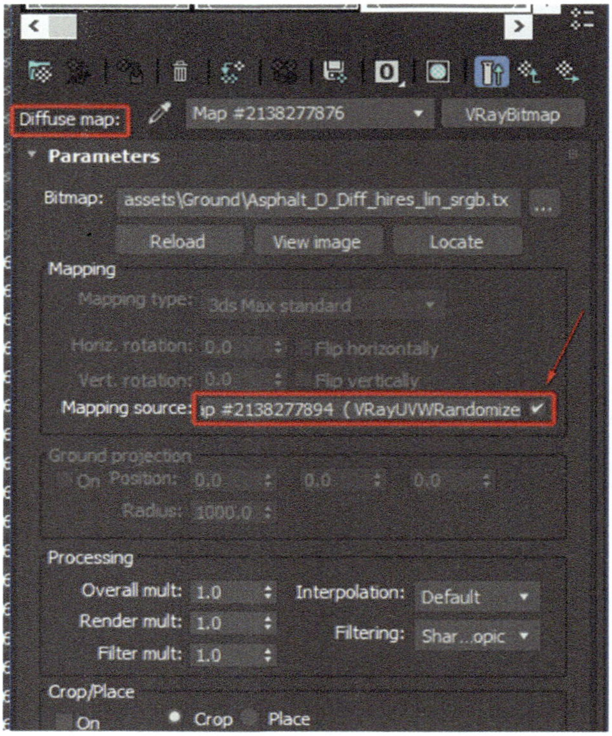

VRayUVWRandomizer

Inside VRayUVWRandomizer Basic parameters, enable the Stochastic tiling function and reduce UV rotation Variance to 0.0.

Repeat the same steps to the Bump toggle.

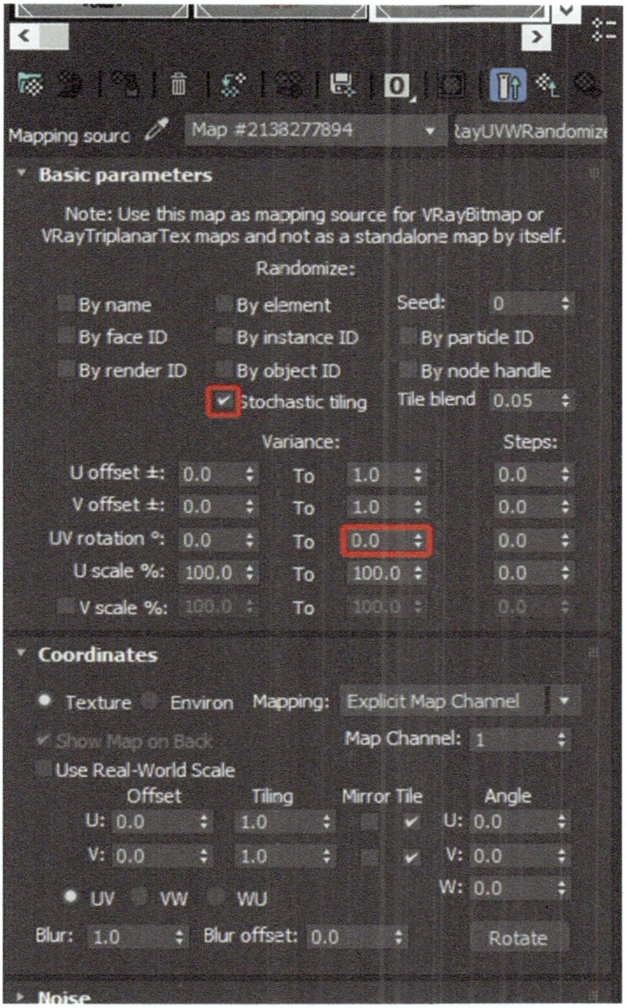

VRayUVWRandomizer Basic parameters

Final Tweaks to the Wood Planks Material

To make the wood planks reflect light in different directions and capture the specular/highlights in the render elements, copy its Bump toggle (right click and choose Copy) and paste it into the Reflect toggle.

Also, disable the Fresnel reflections and reduce the Glossiness to about 0.7.

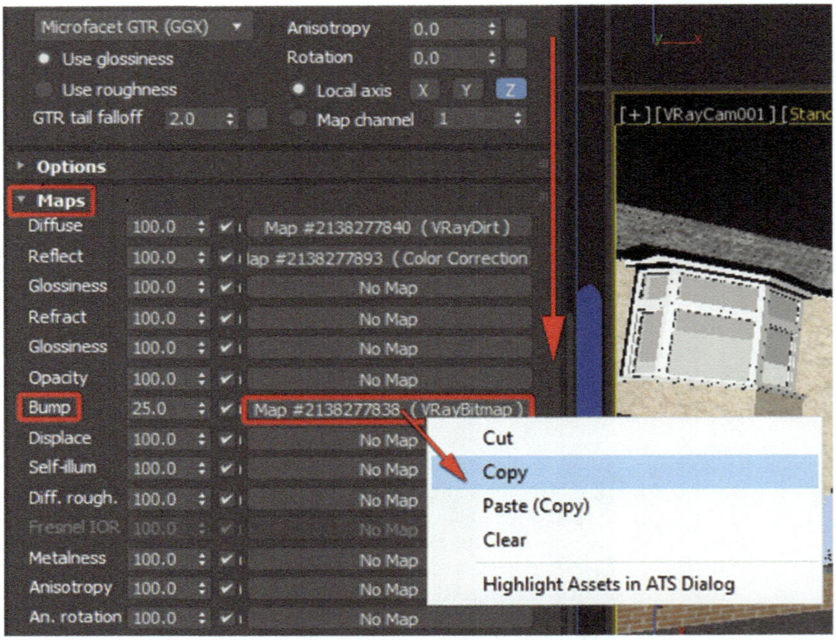

Copy Bump toggle

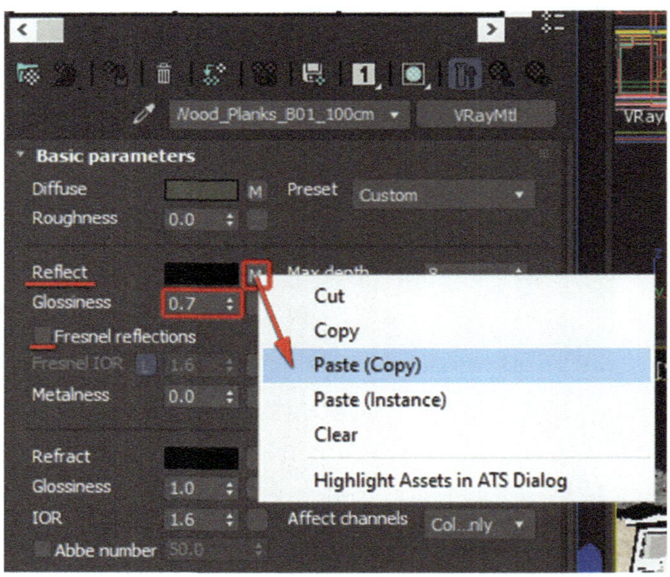

Paste Bump toggle

Next, go inside the Reflect toggle.

Reduce its Color Correction Saturation value to about –100.

Following that, decrease the Brightness value to about –53.488, and the Contrast to about 26.91.

The Reflect map now has enough contrast to reflect light in different directions.

NOTE

By default, when the Wood_Planks_B01_100cm is loaded, its diffuse and Bump toggles are instanced. When the Color Correction was previously applied to the Diffuse toggle, it was also automatically applied to the Bump toggle (hence the Color correction appearing in the copied Reflect map).

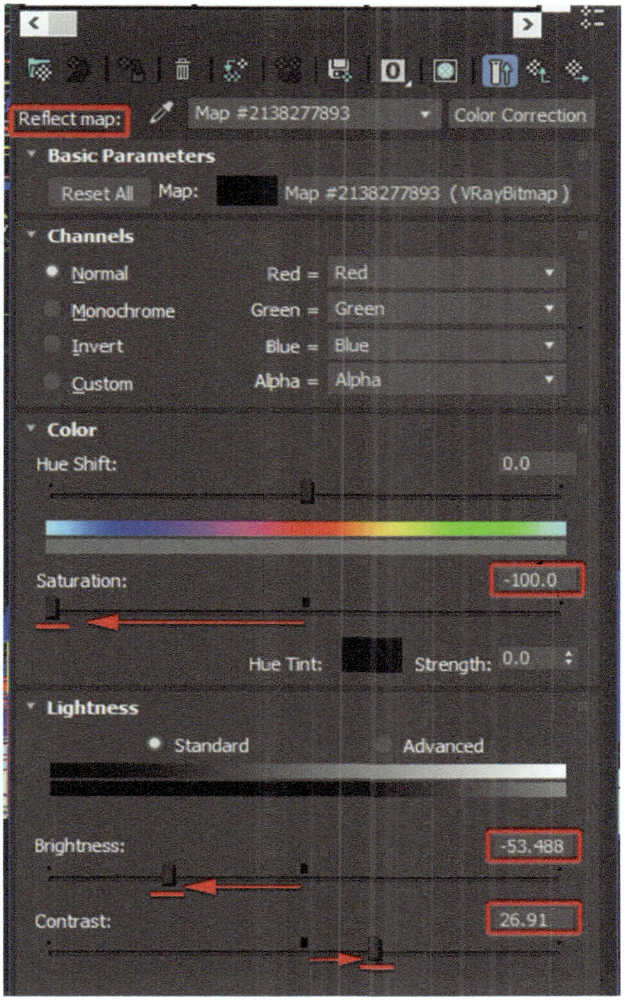

Tweak Color Correction Basic parameters

Next, go inside the Diffuse toggle and open the Unoccluded toggle.

To change the wood color slightly, increase the Hue Shift value to about 13.754.

Also, increase its Saturation to about 14.286.

Change the Hue Tint color to an orange tone (0.061,0.888,0.82) and increase the strength value to about 33.0.

Finally, increase the Brightness value to 11.628.

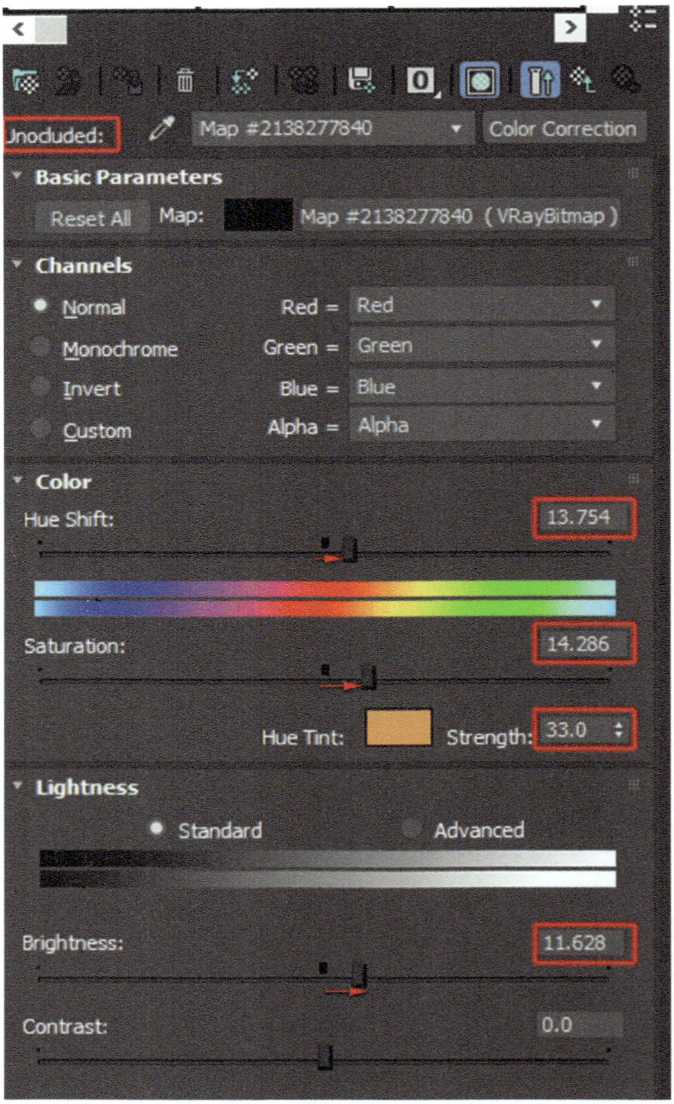

Unoccluded Color Correction Basic parameters

Wood plank final result in the material editor

The remaining materials in the scene were created and applied using some of the techniques described here and in Chapter 2.

Finally, open the 3d scene under the name of External daylight scene_Materials Finished.max to see the final textured file.

NOTE

These values worked well. However, feel free to try different values, if desired.

Merging 3d Assets from Websites such as Evermotion and 3dsky

To make the overall shot more appealing and realistic, the foreground and background need to be populated with 3d assets such as trees and cars.

Evermotion and 3dsky are currently two of the best websites to download such 3d assets from.

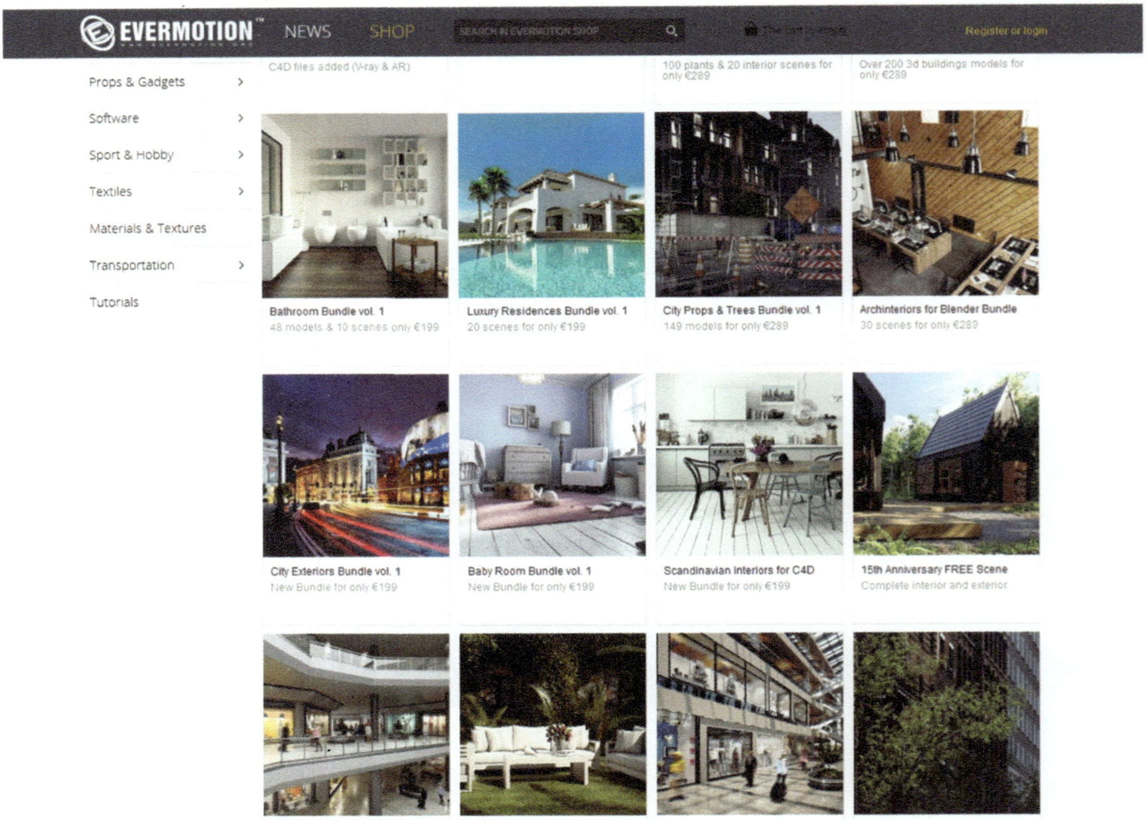
EVERMOTION
NEWS
SHOP
Register or login
Props & Gadgets
Software
Sport & Hobby
Textiles
Materials & Textures
Transportation
Tutorials
C4D files added (V-ray & AR)
100 plants & 20 interior scenes for only €289
Over 200 3d buildings models for only €289
Bathroom Bundle vol. 1
48 models & 10 scenes only €199
Luxury Residences Bundle vol. 1
20 scenes for only €199
City Props & Trees Bundle vol. 1
149 models for only €289
Archinteriors for Blender Bundle
30 scenes for only €289
City Exteriors Bundle vol. 1
New Bundle for only €199
Baby Room Bundle vol. 1
New Bundle for only €199
Scandinavian Interiors for C4D
New Bundle for only €199
15th Anniversary FREE Scene
Complete interior and exterior

Evermotion website

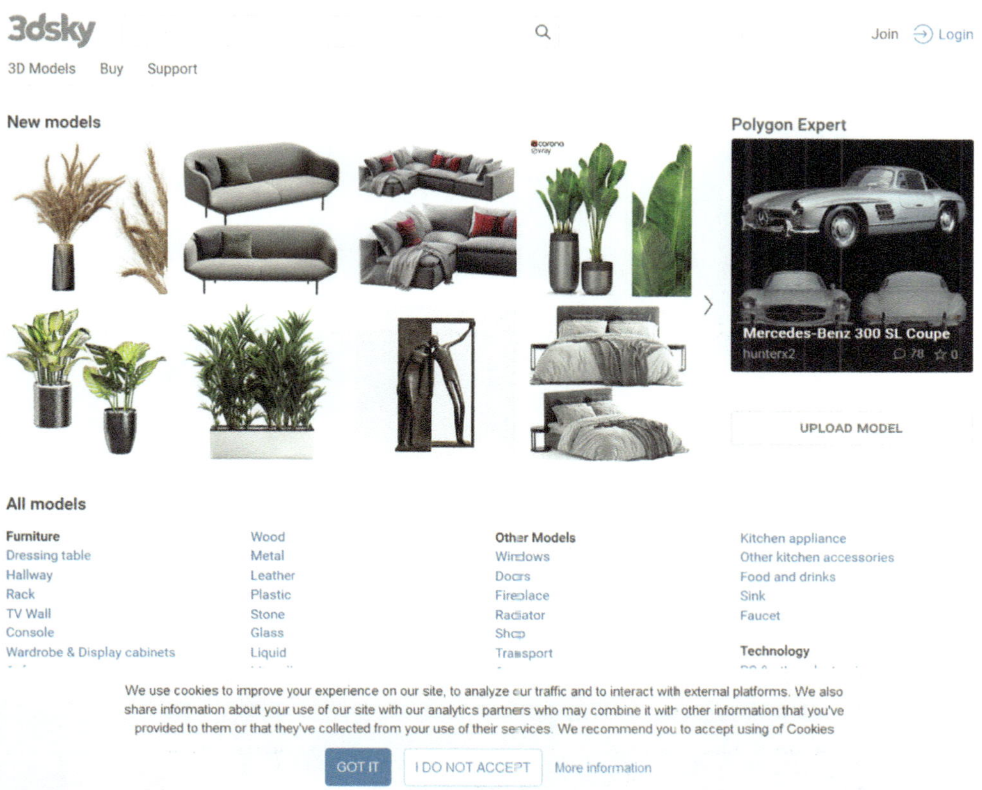

3dsky website

Once the 3d assets are downloaded, to make them lighter in size, they need to be attached as one mesh and converted into separate proxies.

Attaching Mesh Components Before Creating VRayProxies

The following is an example of two objects with separate components. The techniques covered here can be used for trees, cars, and objects with high poly count.

Use the Rectangle Region selection to select the objects you want to collapse in the scene.

NOTE

Ensure to have copies of the original mesh in a separate file to refer back to.

Rectangle Region selection

Objects selected

Next, collapse any potential modifiers used on objects by right clicking and choosing Convert to Editable Poly.

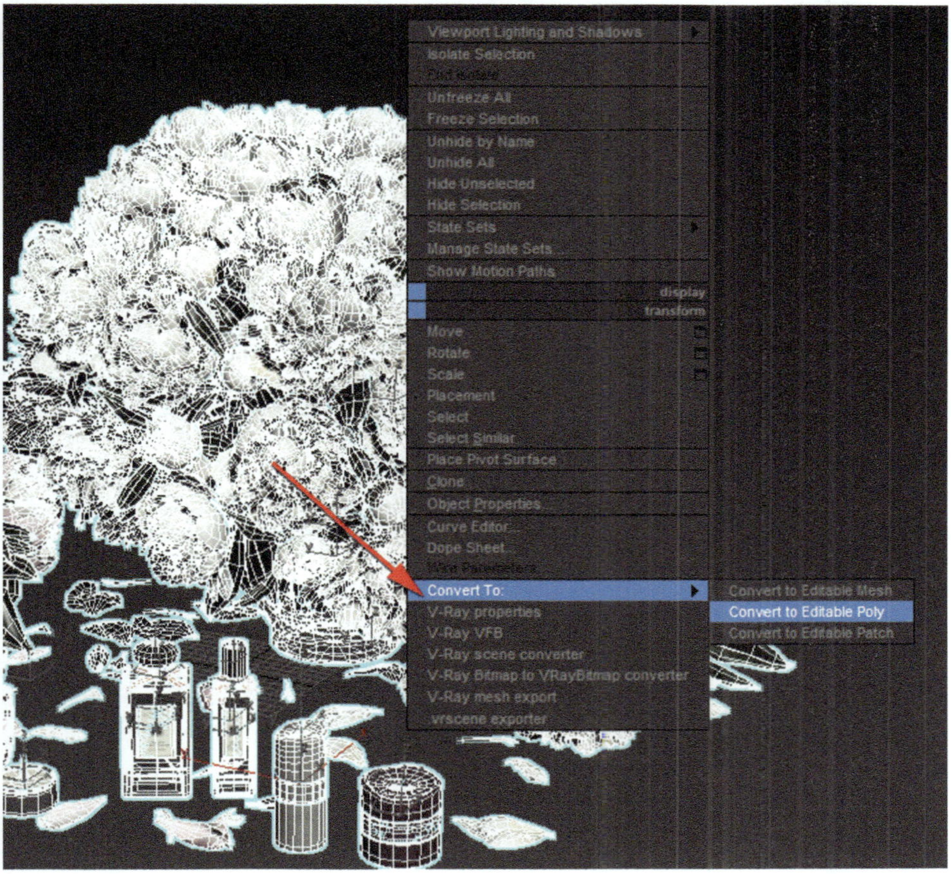

Convert to Editable Poly

Once the objects are collapsed, open the Modify panel. Highlight the Editable Poly and enable the Element selection.

Under Edit Geometry rollout parameters, click on the Attach button and select an object in the scene to attach the object to.

If it has a different material, you should be prompted with the Attach Options dialog.

Choose Match Material IDs to Material and to Condense Material and IDs.

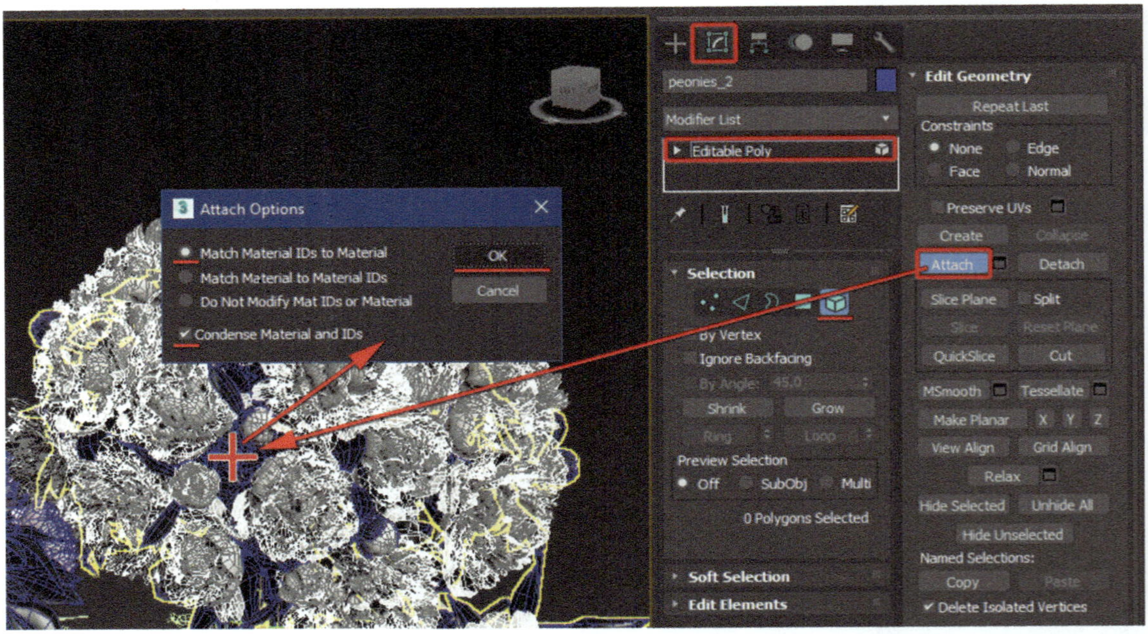

Attach Options

Repeat the same action to other objects you want to attach to this element.

Open the Material Editor (M) and select an empty slot. Use the Pick Material from Object tool to pick and load the object material in the Material Editor slot.

As you can see, different materials from the attached objects have been automatically condensed into a new Multi/Sub-Object material.

Each separate material was automatically assigned to a mesh element with an object ID number. Please refer to Chapter 2 for more information on how to create object ID numbers.

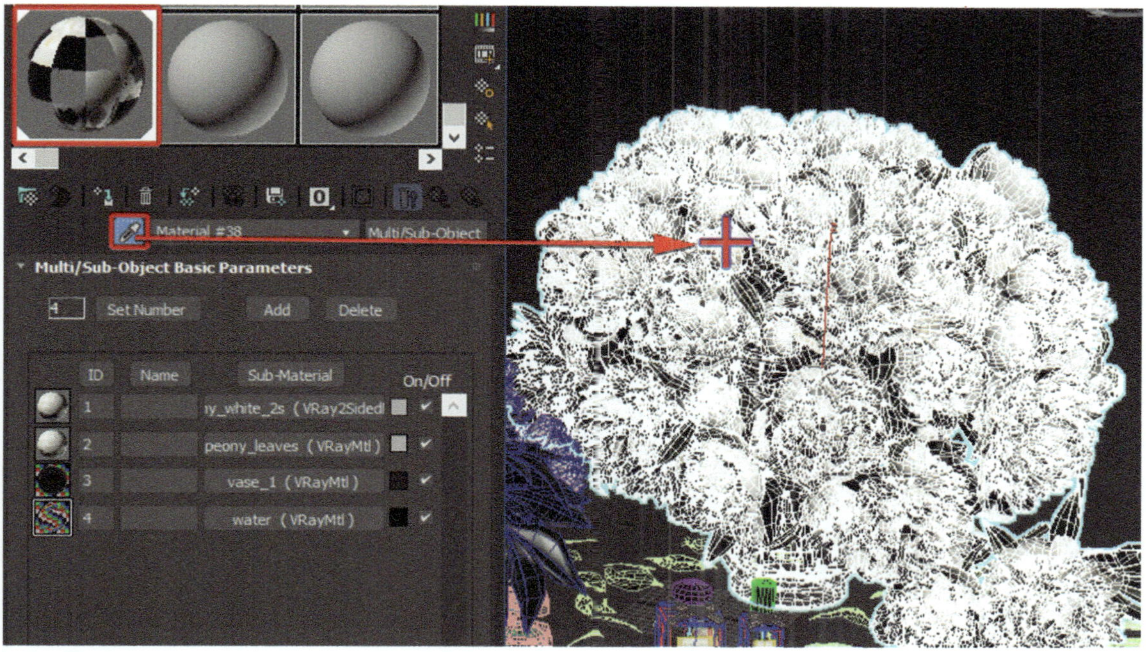

Material loaded as multi/sub-object

Creating VRayProxies

VRayProxies reduce the file size considerably while also speeding up the rendering times.

Whenever you have heavy objects in the scene, or objects you intend to copy multiple times in a scene, it is always best to proxy them first.

Once a VRay proxy is generated, the mesh will be referencing a specific file format under the name of vrmesh.

To convert a previously attached object into a VRayProxy, simply right click and choose VRay mesh export.

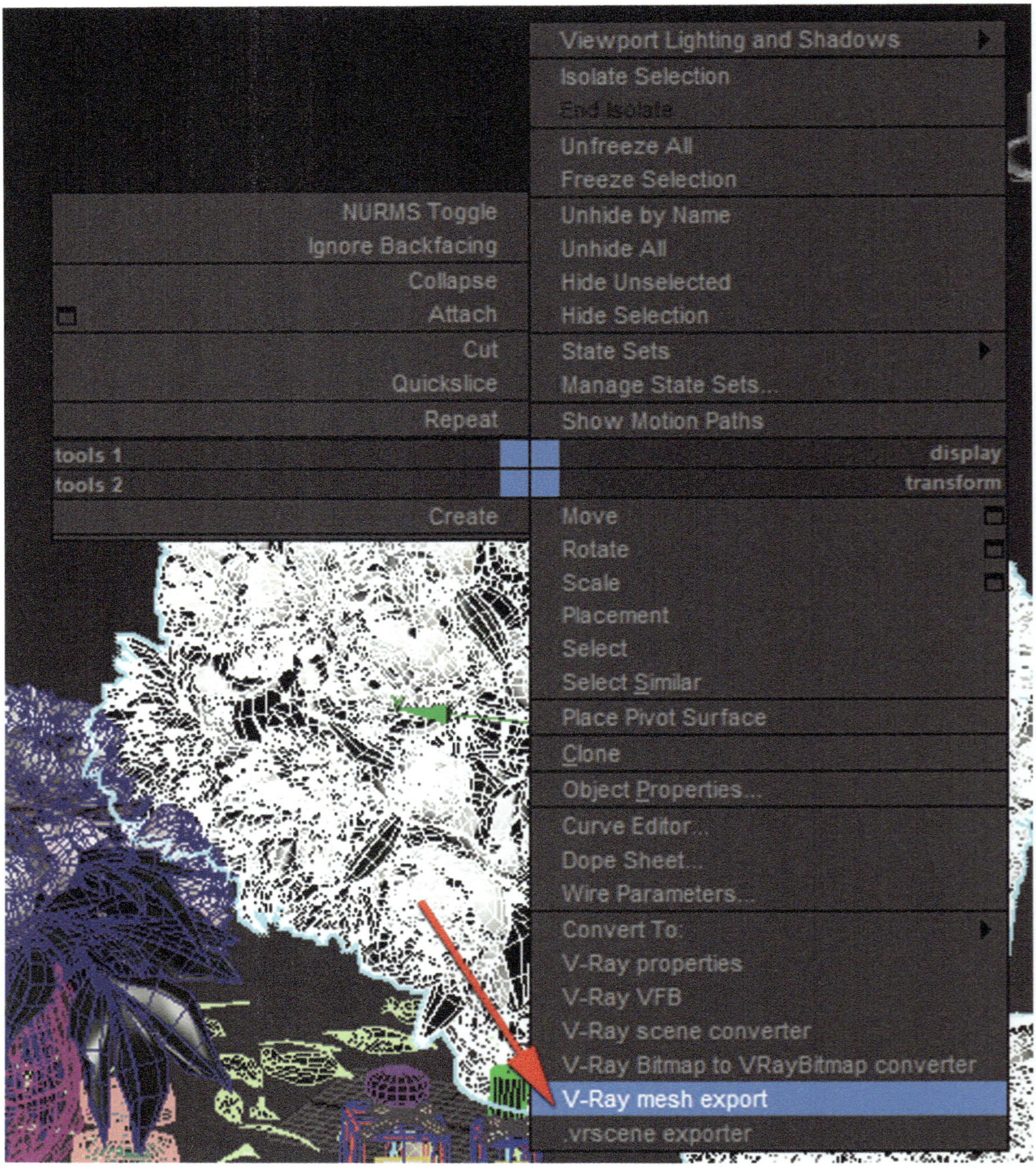

Choose VRay mesh export

The VRay mesh export dialog should be prompted.

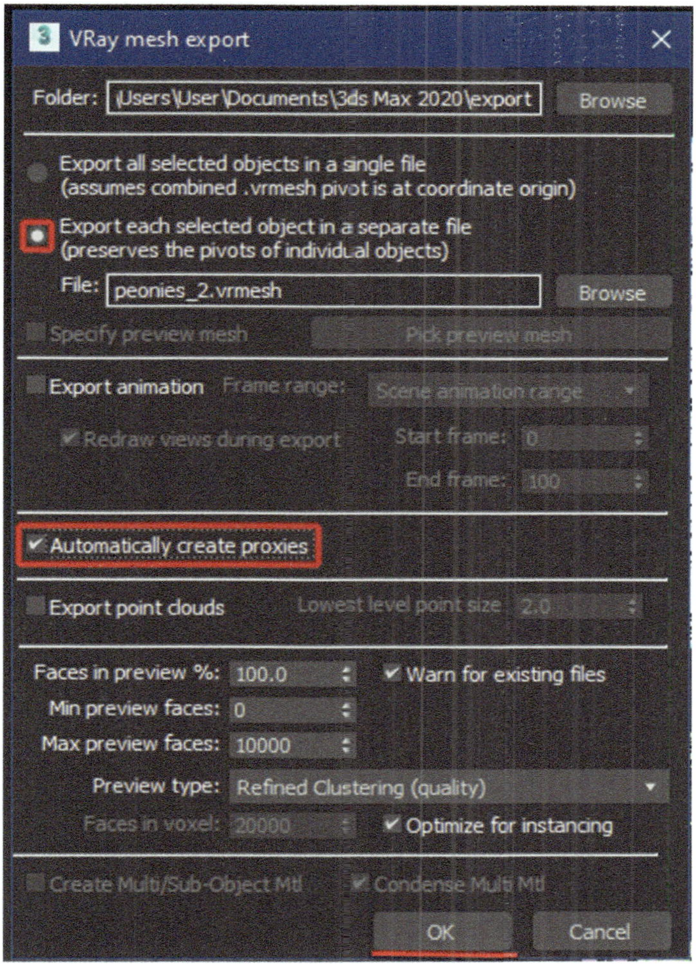

VRay mesh export dialog

Folder: This section specifies the location where the vrmesh will be saved to. The adjacent Browse toggle allows users to change the default file location.

Export all selected objects in a single file: This function allows users to select multiple objects in the scene and automatically convert them to VRayProxies.

Export each selected object in a separate file: This option allows users to select and convert individual objects to VRay proxies.

NOTE

This option sometimes generates proxies with errors.

NOTE

The file extension .vrmesh cannot be changed.

File: This option enables users to rename the default name of the vrmesh. The Adjacent Browse toggle allows users to change the location of the vrmesh.

Export animation: If your object is animated, click on this option to enable other functions such as Frame range, Start frame, End frame, etc.

Automatically create proxies: This function automatically creates a proxy once the OK button is clicked.

Disabled by default.

Export point clouds: When enabled, this function exports the proxy as point clouds.

Faces in preview %: This function controls the percentage faces previewed once the proxy is created. Always keep it at 100%.

Min preview faces: This function controls the minimum number of faces to be previewed in the viewport once the proxy is created.

Always keep it at 0.

Max preview faces: This function controls the maximum number of faces to be previewed once the proxy is created.

Keep it at 10.000 or higher.

Preview type: This option controls the type of proxy preview.

Refined Clustering (quality) is set by default.

Once a proxy is created, the text VRayProxy is automatically added to the original objet name. This is quite useful to differentiate between normal meshes and proxies.

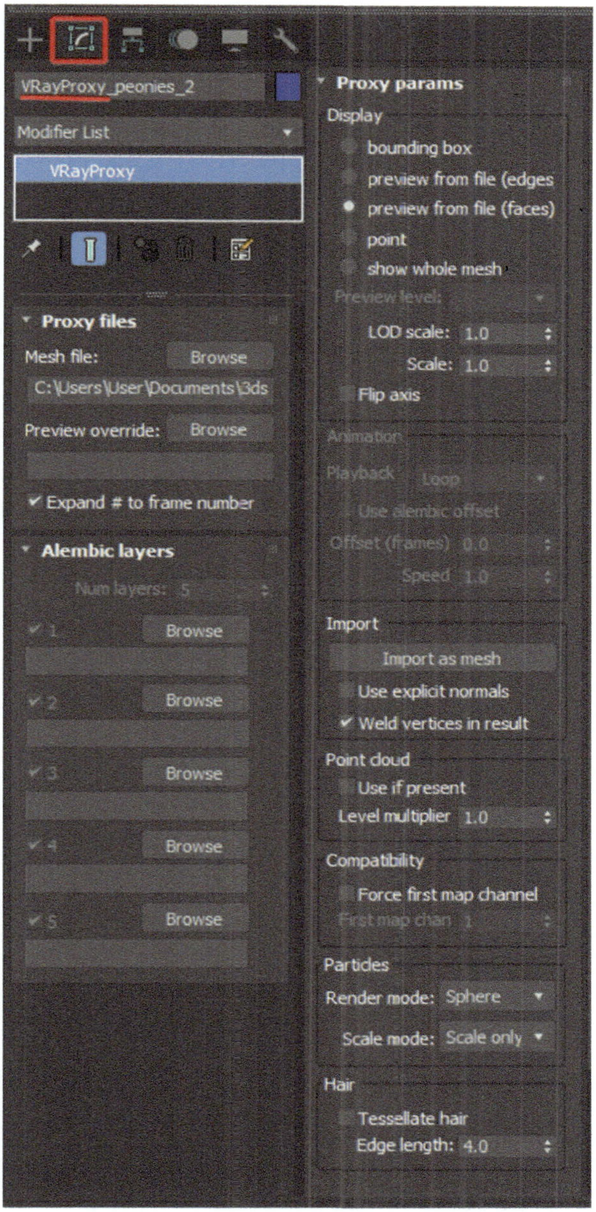

VRayProxy Modify parameters

Mesh file: This function specifies the location of the vrmesh file. It can also be used to replace vrmesh files by clicking the Browse toggle.

Preview override: This function is useful to replace the proxy mesh previewed in the viewport with a different vrmesh or a .abc file format, using the Browse toggle.

Expand # to frame number: This function automatically adds a hashtag symbol to the name of a frame using this proxy file.

Enabled by default.

Alembic layers: This option only becomes available if the proxy file format is a .abc type.

Greyed out with .vrmesh.

Display: This group controls how the VRayProxy file is previewed in the viewport.

Preview from file (faces) is displayed by default.

bounding box: This option displays the proxy as a simple box. This option is quite useful to reduce computer resources when displaying complex objects in the viewport.

Preview from file (edges): This option displays the proxy object with edges.

Preview from file (faces): This option displays the proxy object with edges. Default preview method.

Point: This option displays the proxy object as a single point. This is useful when you have an extremely dense scene.

However, it could be misleading/difficult to evaluate when the file is taken over by a user unfamiliar with the scene.

Show whole mesh: This option displays the proxy with all its original mesh details.

LOD scale: This function controls the maximum number of pixels an edge can span over prior to being subdivided.

Scale: This option allows users to scale a proxy up and down. Default value is 1.0.

Flip axis: This option allows users to flip the axis of proxies. Disabled by default.

Import as mesh: This function allows users to Import the original mesh into the scene (without materials applied).

Use explicit normals: This option is useful when the vertex normals information is explicit prior to converting the original object to a vrmesh.

Weld vertices in result: This option welds vertices when the vrmesh is created.

Point cloud/use if present: This option allows users to use the point cloud data, if available.

Level multiplier: This function controls the waypoint cloud levels loaded.

Compatibility/Force first map channel: When enabled, it forces the map channel specified. Disabled by default.

Prior to moving, scaling, and/or copying proxies, ensure to place the Pivot point on the base of the object.

Before adjusting the pivot, go to the main toolbar and set the Snaps Toggle to 2.5. This will ensure the moving pivot stays on X- and Y-axes only.

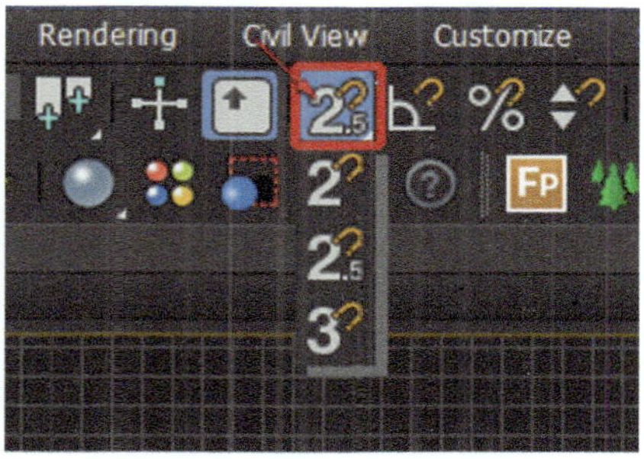

Set the Snaps Toggle to 2.5

Next, right click on the Snaps Toggle toolbar to bring the Grid and Snap Settings dialog.

Under the Snaps tab, enable the functions for Grid Points, Pivot, and Endpoint.

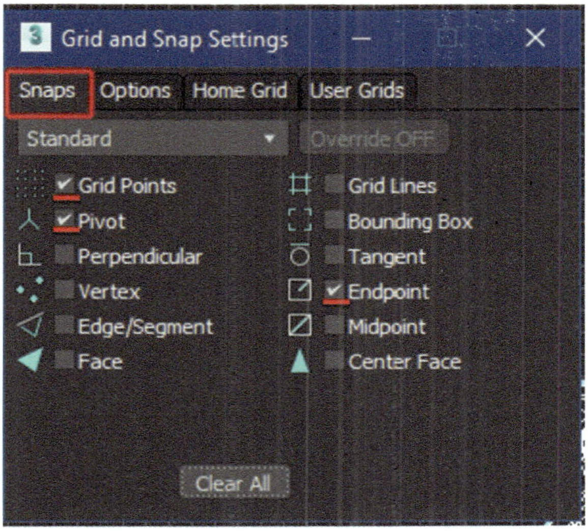

Snaps tab options

Under the Options tab, Enable the functions to Snap to frozen objects, Enable Axis Constraints, and Display rubber band.

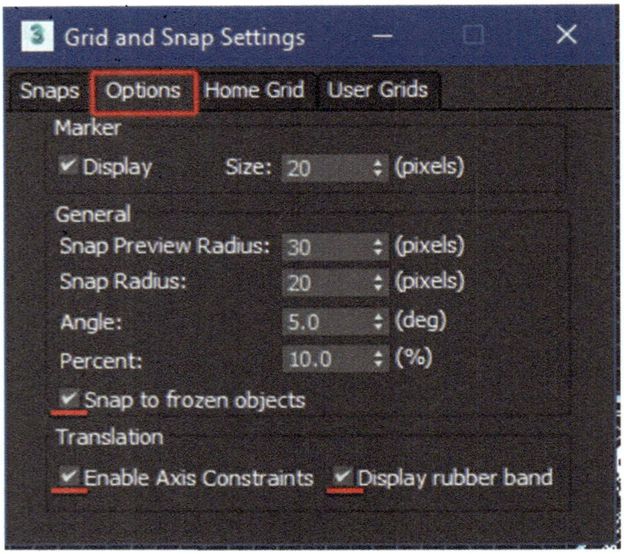

Next, under Hierarchy, click on the Pivot button. Under Adjust Pivot group, click on the Affect Pivot Only, and place the Pivot point on the base of the proxy (using the Move toolbar).

This will ensure the object will always scale from the bottom-up, not from the center of the object.

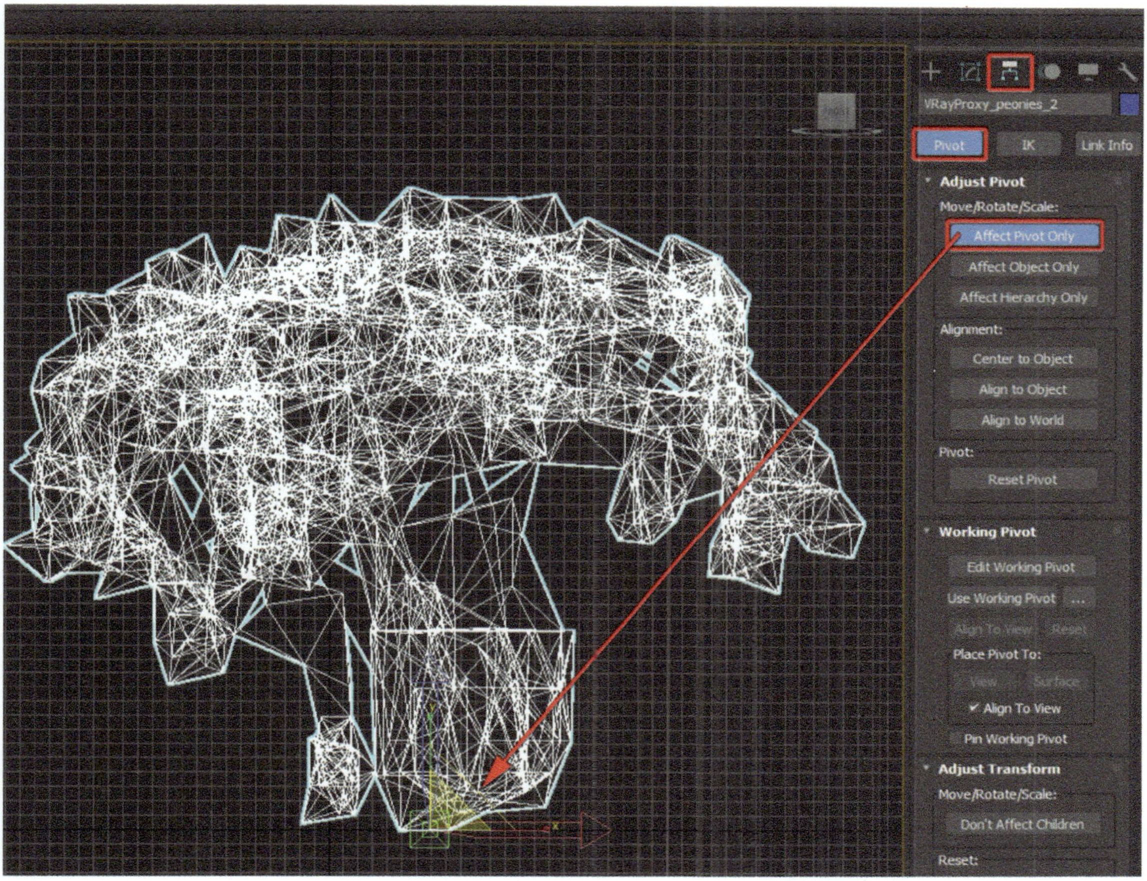

Adjust Pivot

While adjusting the pivot point, click on the Move toolbar, Rotate and Scale toolbar. If the pivot point moves while selecting any of the toolbars, simply adjust it to the base of the object accordingly.

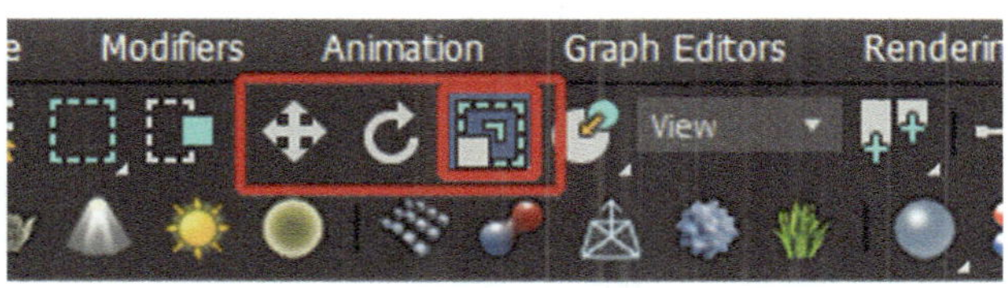

Click the Move, Rotate, and Scale toolbars

To randomize the scene with same proxies, simply copy (Ctrl+V) and choose the Instance option. Move, scale, and rotate each instanced copy randomly with the Scale, Rotate, and Move toolbar.

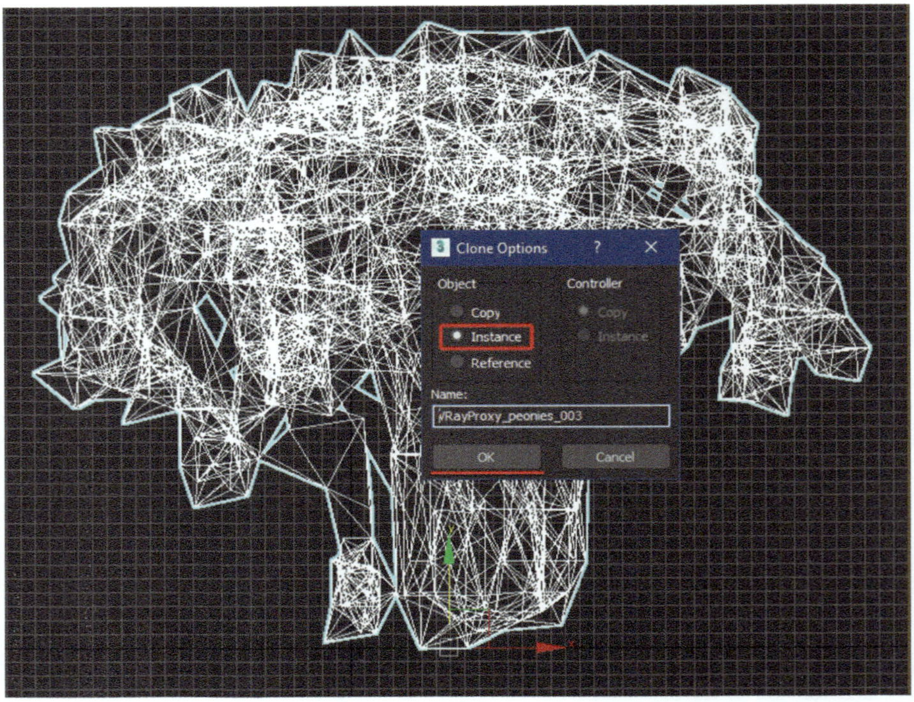

Clone options

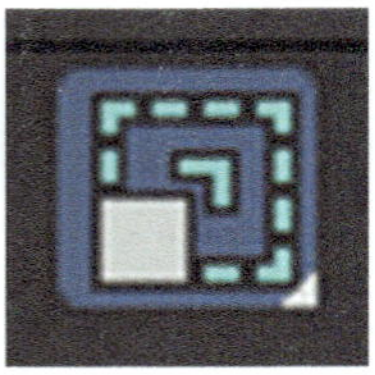

Scale toolbar

NOTE

Always copy/instance VRayProxies as these will be quicker to compute and render.

Merging Proxies and Setting Up for Final Render

Assuming you are currently using the file named External daylight scene_ Materials Finished.max, merge a 3ds max file under the name of Proxies to be merged.max.

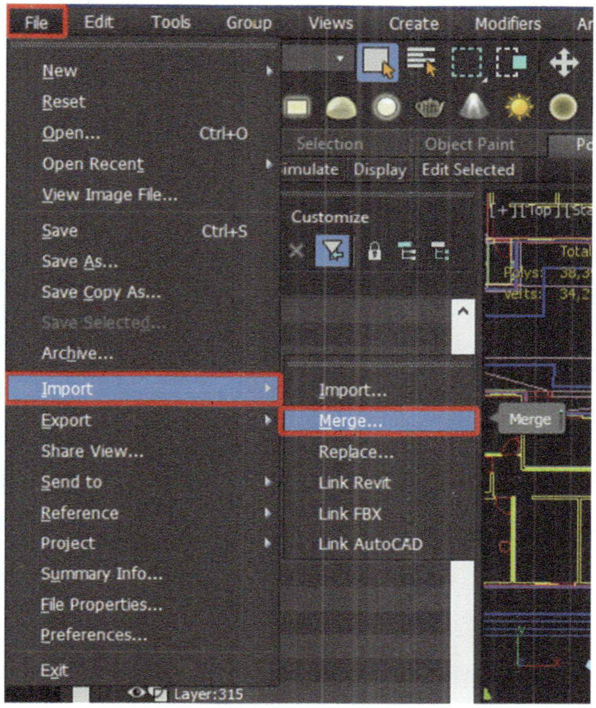
File
Edit
Tools
Group
Views
Create
Modifiers
New
Reset
Open... Ctrl+O
Open Recent
View Image File...
Save Ctrl+S
Save As...
Save Copy As...
Save Selected...
Archive...
Import
Export
Share View...
Send to
Reference
Project
Summary Info...
File Properties...
Preferences...
Exit
Selection
Object Paint
Display
Edit Selected
Customize
Import...
Merge...
Replace...
Link Revit
Link FBX
Link AutoCAD
Merge
Layer:315

Import Merge

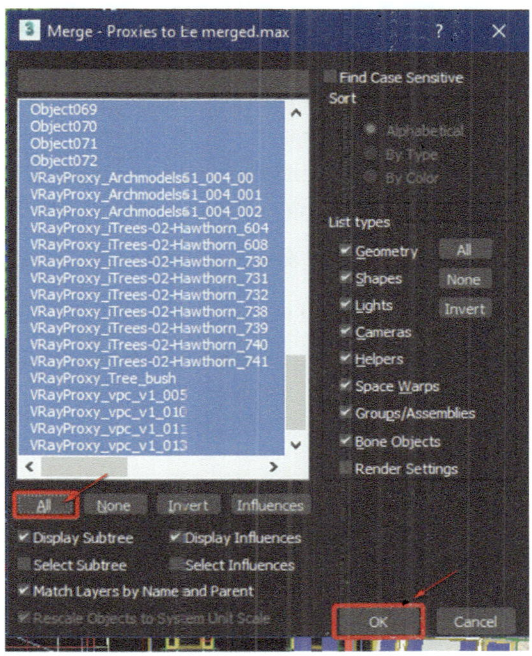
Merge - Proxies to be merged.max
Find Case Sensitive
Sort
Alphabetical
By Type
By Color
Object069
Object070
Object071
Object072
VRayProxy_Archmodels61_004_00
VRayProxy_Archmodels61_004_001
VRayProxy_Archmodels61_004_002
VRayProxy_iTrees-02-Hawthorn_604
VRayProxy_iTrees-02-Hawthorn_608
VRayProxy_iTrees-02-Hawthorn_730
VRayProxy_iTrees-02-Hawthorn_731
VRayProxy_iTrees-02-Hawthorn_732
VRayProxy_iTrees-02-Hawthorn_738
VRayProxy_iTrees-02-Hawthorn_739
VRayProxy_iTrees-02-Hawthorn_740
VRayProxy_iTrees-02-Hawthorn_741
VRayProxy_Tree_bush
VRayProxy_vpc_v1_005
List types
Geometry
All
Shapes
None
Lights
Invert
Cameras
Helpers
Space Warps
Groups/Assemblies
Bone Objects
Render Settings
All
None
Invert
Influences
Display Subtree
Display Influences
Select Subtree
Select Influences
Match Layers by Name and Parent
Rescale Objects to System Unit Scale
OK
Cancel

Merge dialog

The merged 3ds max file contains cars trees and other assets previously attached and converted to proxies.

There are trees behind the camera placed strategically to cast shadows and be used for reflections without being visible to the camera (right click and choose properties).

Merge objects

Prior to sending out the final high-resolution render, let's start by opening the Render setup dialog (F10) and going to the VRay tab.

Change the Image sampler type from Progressive to Bucket.

Furthermore, increase the Min shading rate to 64.

Under Bucket image sampler, increase the Max subdivs to 100 and the noise threshold to 0.008.

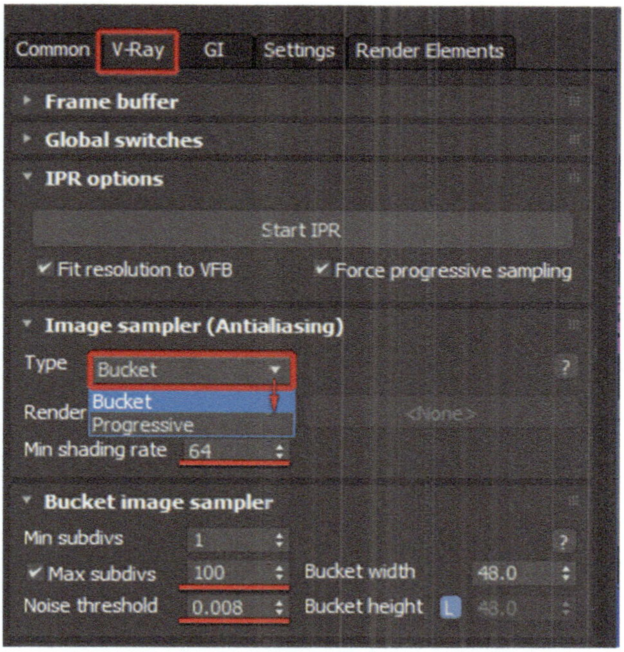

Change Image and Bucket Image sampler parameters

Next, go to the Render Elements tab and add the render elements discussed in Chapter 4.

In addition to VRayLightMix (previously added), ensure you add enough MultiMatteElement to cover most important materials in the shot.

Again, use techniques covered in Chapter 4 to set them up properly.

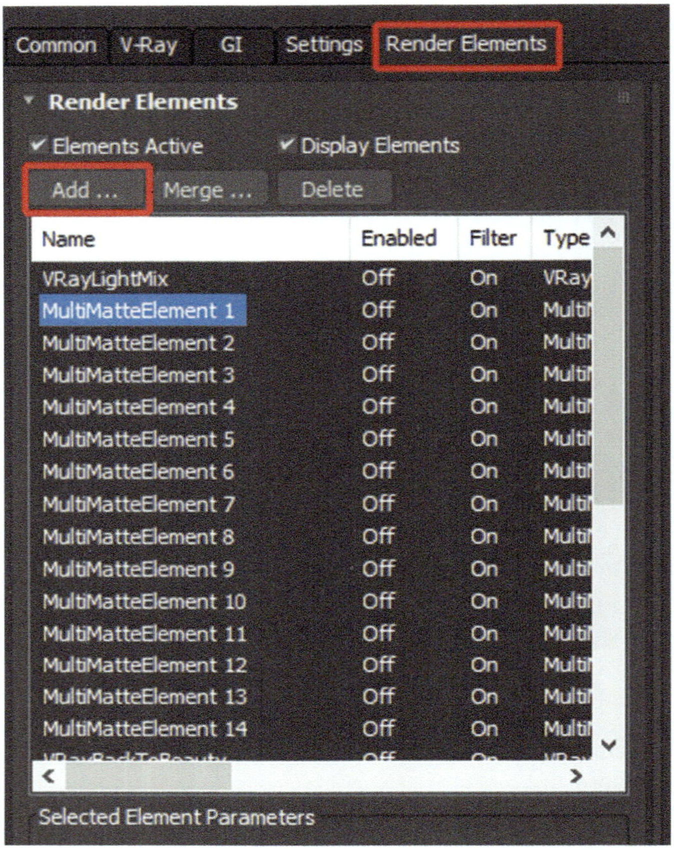

Add render elements

Also, add render elements such as

VRayBackToBeauty
VRayBumpNormals
VRayDiffuseFilter
VRayNormals
VRayRawReflection
VRayRawRefraction
VRayReflection
VRayRefraction

VRaySampleRate: This render element is quite useful to see areas of the scene that are problematic to render (green and red).

VRaySpecular

VRayWireColor

VRayZDepth: For this scene, the *z*-depth max value was set to 7000.0 mm.

VRayLighting

Open the VFB and load a layer tree preset named External daylight scene_Final .vfbl.

Enable the Region render tool and test the quality of lighting and materials.

Region render

Once satisfied with the test renders, disable the Region render tool and go to the VRay tab. Under Frame buffer rollout, name and set the location of your VRay image file (*.vrimg).

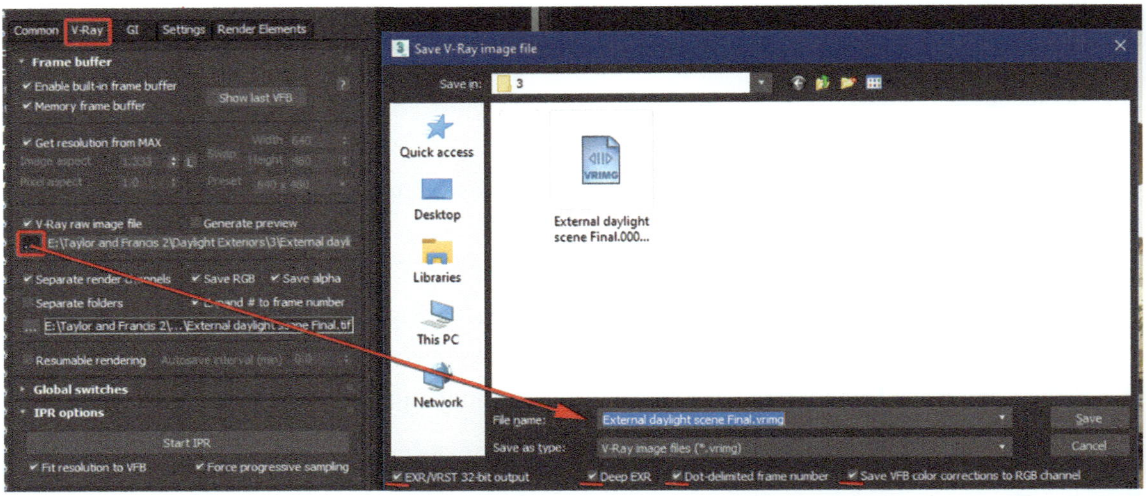

VRay image file (.vrimg)*

Also, enable the Separate render channels option. Name the file, set its format as TIF, and set its location.

For best results, set the TIF image as a 16-bit Color, No Compression, and 300 Dots per Inch (DPI).

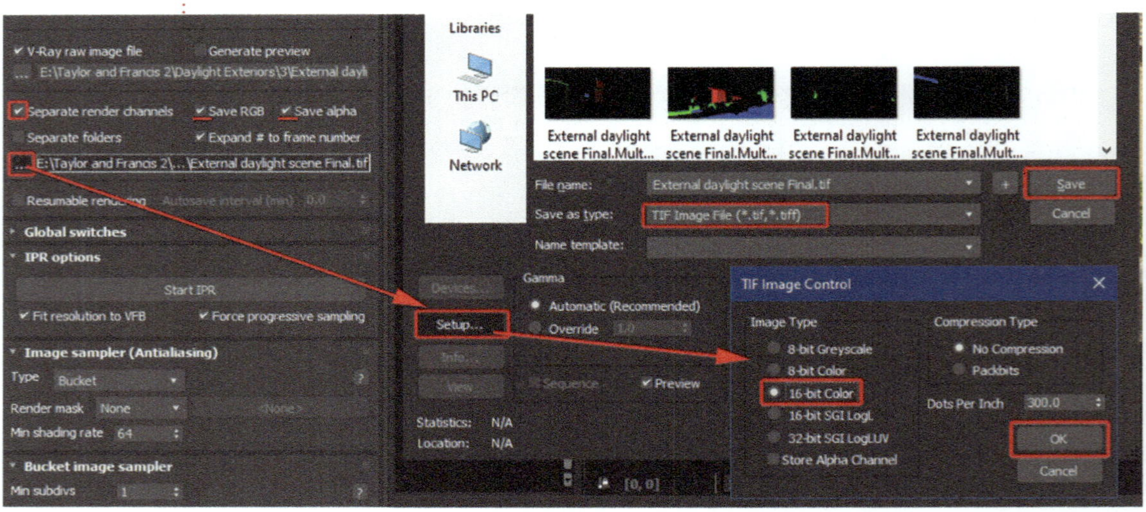

Set up the render channels

While rendering, you may notice some Texture map and other warnings in the VRay messages dialog. They're mostly related to the proxied 3d assets merged in from other websites.

V-Ray 5 removed a number of functions previously available and no longer supported in V-Ray 5.

The messages will not affect the render quality or cause render errors.

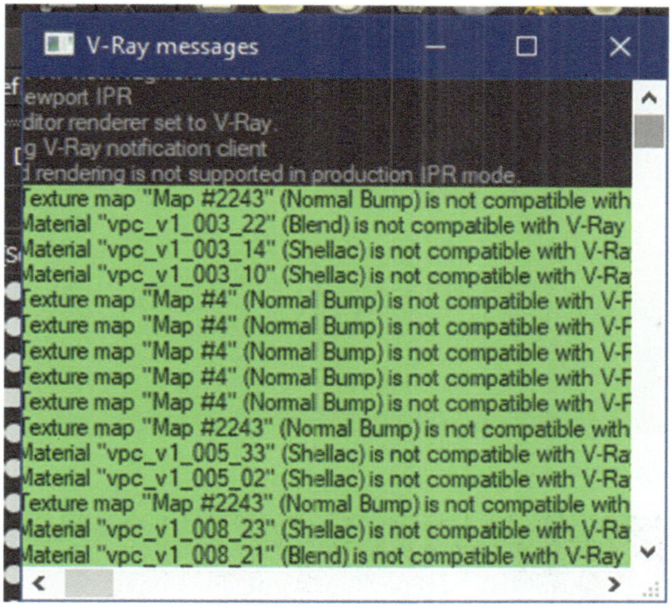

VRay messages dialog

Once the final render is finished, you can always use VFB Layers to tweak the light colors, intensity, LensEffects, etc.

Once happy with the tweaks, simply use the Save current channel tool to save it as a new TIF file.

Alternatively, if you had used an external render farm, simply load the VRay image file (*.vrimg) in the VFB as previously shown in Chapter 4, and tweak with Layers.

Tweak with the VFB Layers and save

Also, you can save and/or load a new vfbl. This final scene can be found under the name of External daylight scene_Final.max

Alternatively, if you would like to try a different sun position, simply open a new 3ds max named External daylight_different time_Final, max.

Conclusion

This chapter guided users through the process of creating VRay materials realistically and setting up the scene for final rendering.

Throughout the process, users were shown how to load and tweak VRay Asset Browser default materials realistically.

Following that, users were guided through the detailed step-by-step methodology of creating proxies, setting up the final scene, carrying out final adjustments, and finalizing the renders in 3ds max.

Finally, the next chapter will take users through the fascinating process of using seasoned post-production techniques to take the render to the next level.

9

Post-Production

9 Post-Production

Introduction

Being the final phase of the entire process, post-production is the most important of all phases.

This final execution often determines the success of an entire project.

Furthermore, this is the phase where the artist can rectify and/or enhance materials, colors, skies, lights, etc., with great ease, without having to rerender the entire scene.

Finally, clients usually capitalize on this final opportunity to address new tweaks and incorporate last-minute changes.

Post-Production

NOTE

This chapter uses Adobe Photoshop CC 2018.

To bring in the prerendered elements, let's start by clicking on the File toolbar, scroll down to Scripts, and choose the Load Files into Stack option.

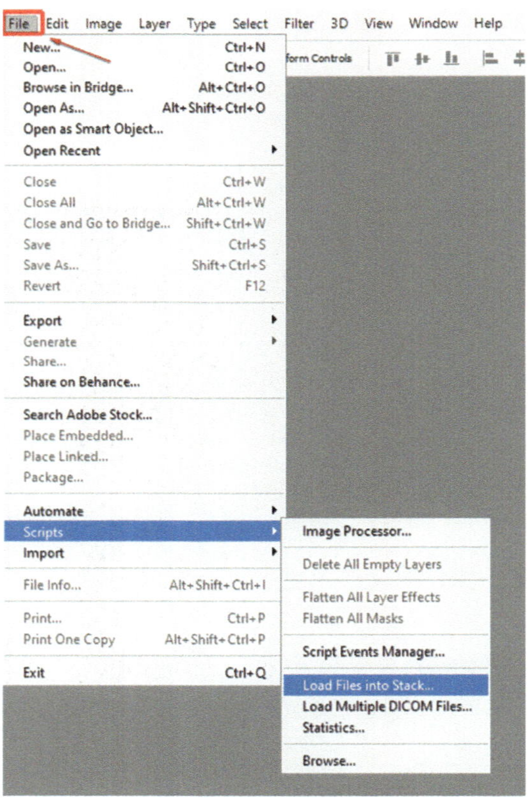

Load Files into Stack script

The Load Layers dialog should be prompted. Click on the Browse toggle to locate the files inside the Render Elements folder.

Select all the prerendered TIF files by selecting the first one, holding down the Shift key, and selecting the last one on the list. All files should be selected.

Click Open to load the files/layers.

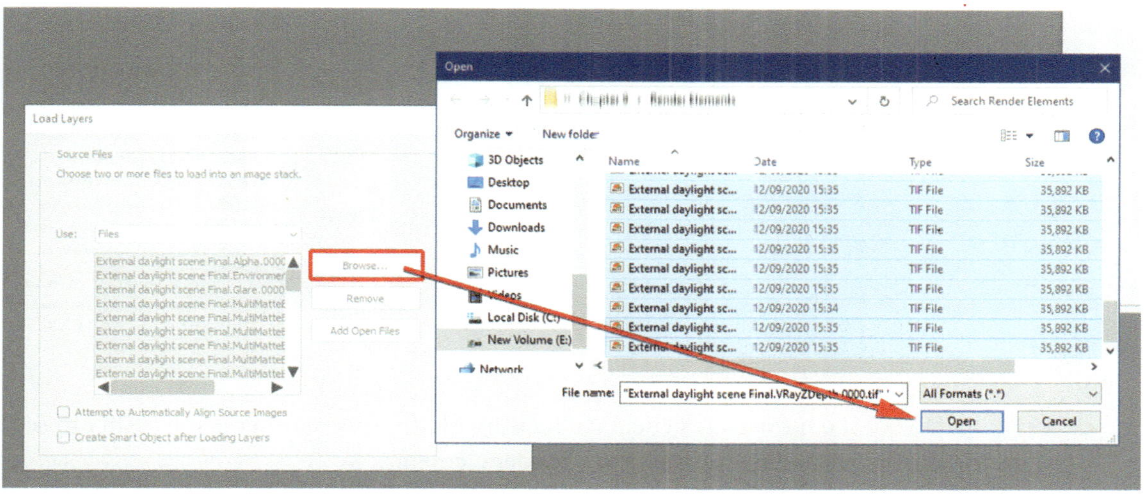

Open Layers

Once the files are loaded in the Loaded Layers dialog, click OK to load them in a stack.

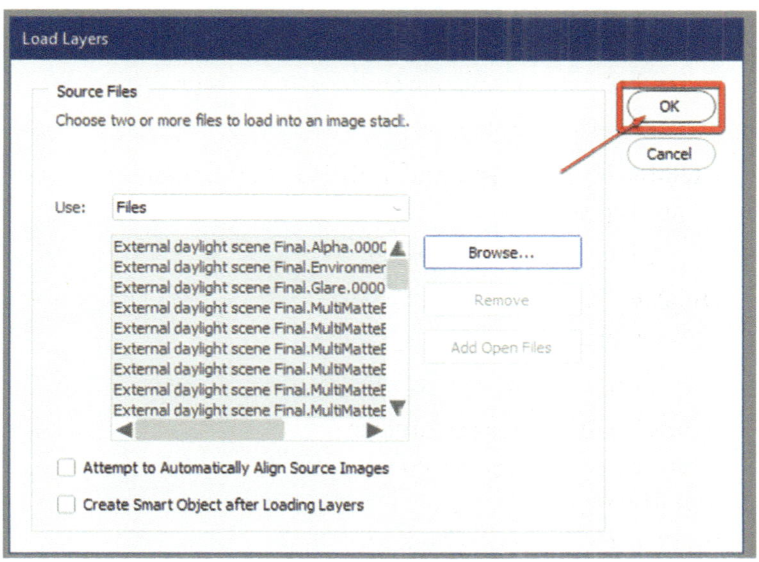

Click OK to load files

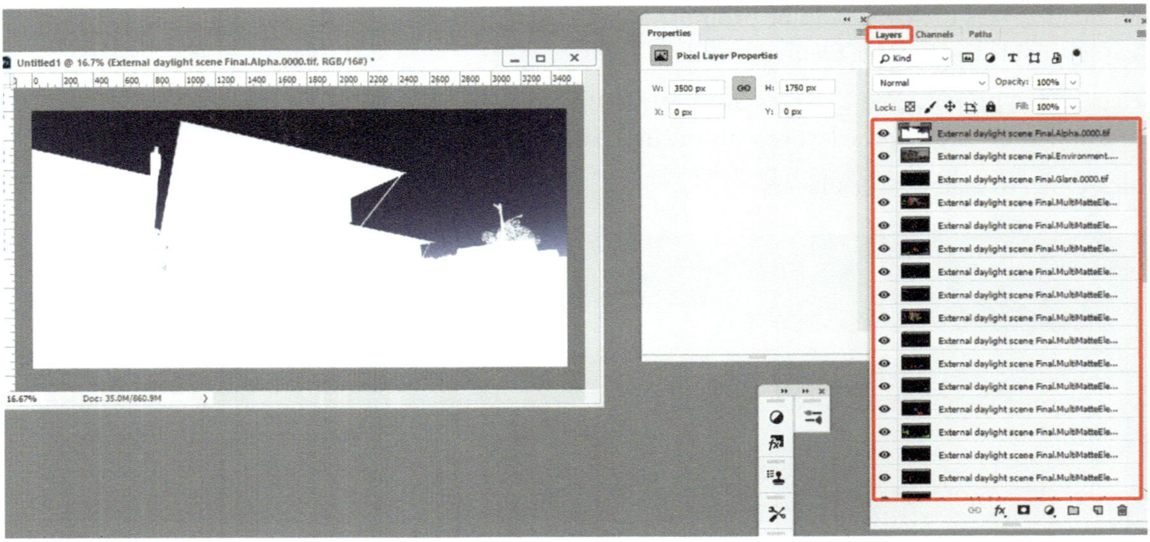

Files loaded

One of the numerous benefits of loading files in this manner is the ability to see the names associated with each render element.

To begin organizing the long list of files, scroll down the Layers' list. Hold down the Alt key and click on the eye icon of the layer named External daylight scene Final.RGB_color.0000.tif.

All but this layer visibility should be turned off. This is the pass with the VFB layers applied to.

Turn off layer visibility of all but one layer

Next, select and move the layer to the bottom of the list. It's good practice to always keep the main layer at the base of the list.

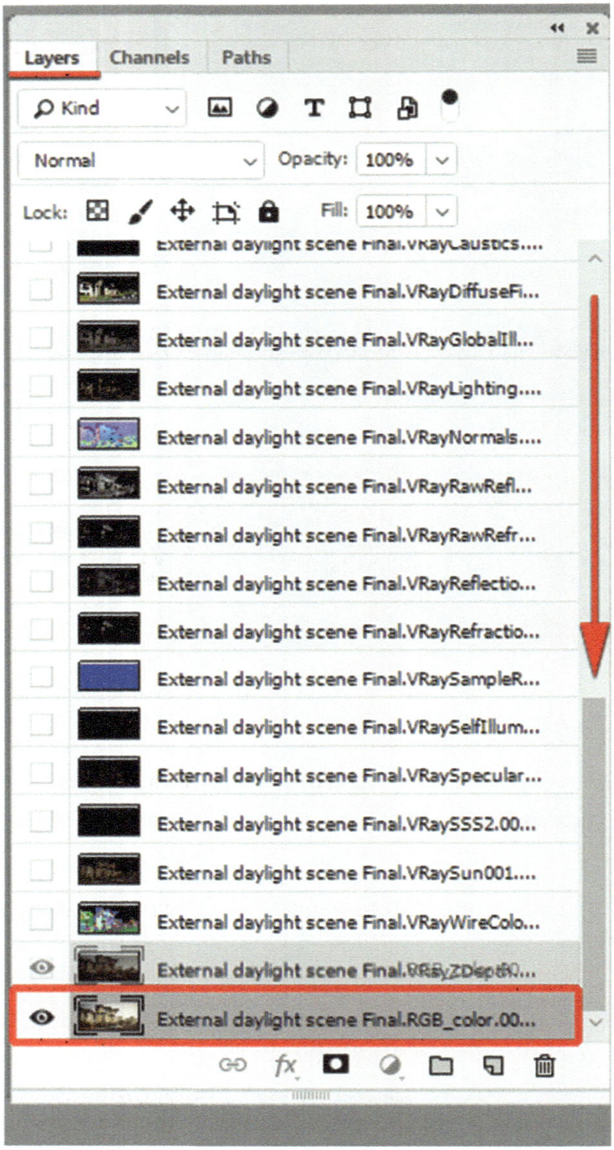

Select and move the layer to the bottom of the list

Following that, select the first invisible layer (at the bottom) and hold down the Shift key. Scroll up and select the top layer.

The entire list of layers should be selected now.

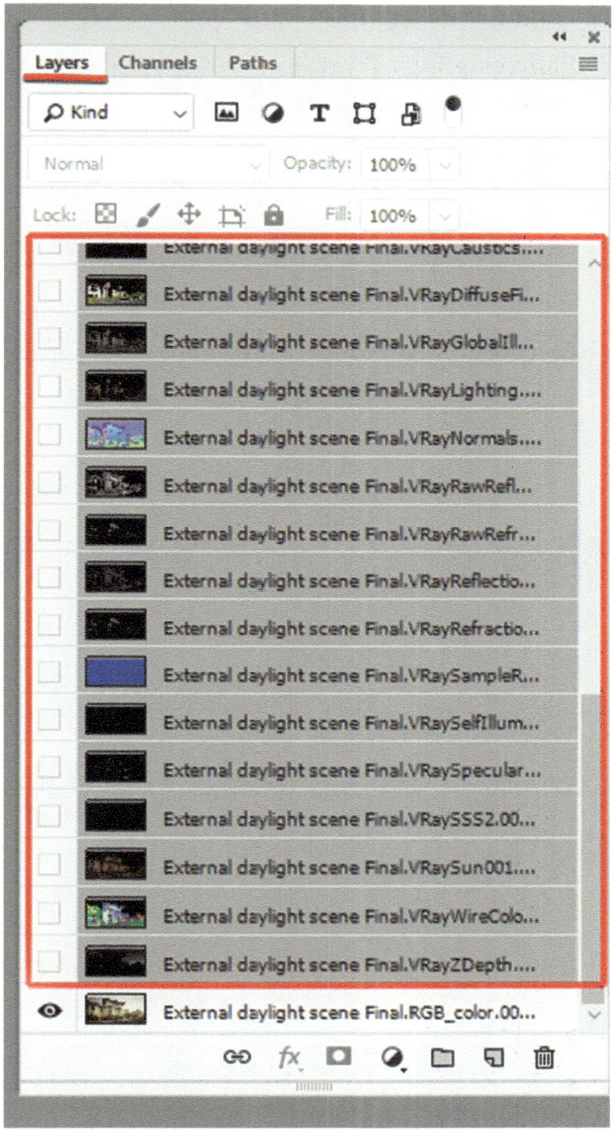

Layers selected

While the layers are still selected, click on the Group layer button to automatically move them to a group.

Alternatively, simply select layers individually, and move them inside a group.

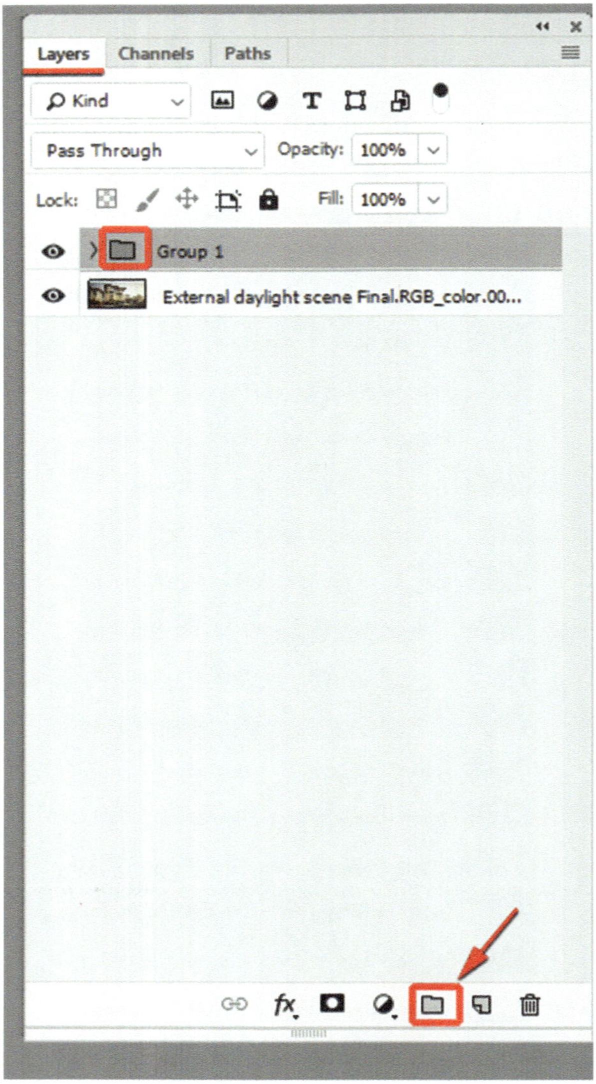

Create a Group with layers inside

Double click on the group name and rename it as =Render Elements=.

Renaming the group and adding will make it easier to select layers inside this group, by right clicking in the document.

Renaming the group

Create a new group and name it as =Adjustments=. This group will be used to add the overall adjustments.

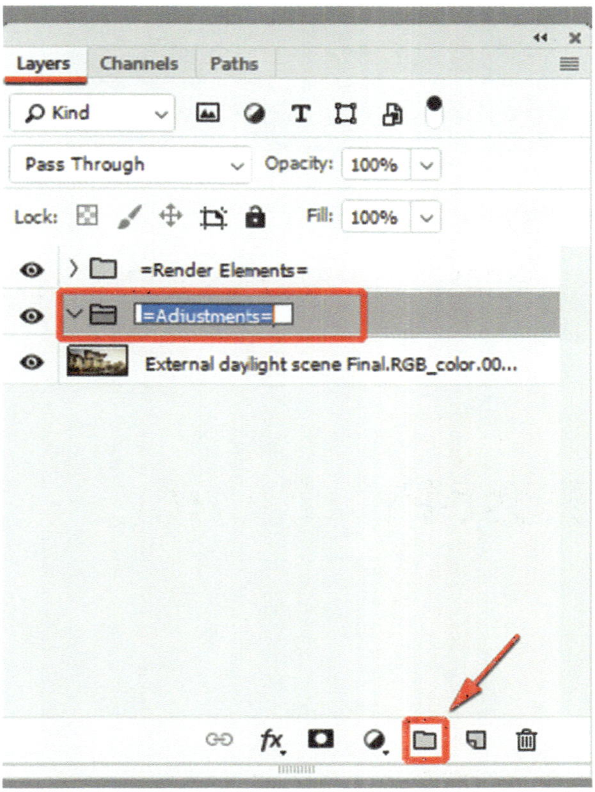

Create a new group

To increase the sunlight effect and the shadows in the render, go inside the =Render Elements= group and select the layer named External daylight scene Final.VRayLighting.0000.tif

To copy and move it, hold down the Alt key and move it inside the =Adjustments= group. Also, enable its visibility eye icon (click on it) and change the blending mode from Normal to Screen type.

The Screen blending mode works best for most render elements.

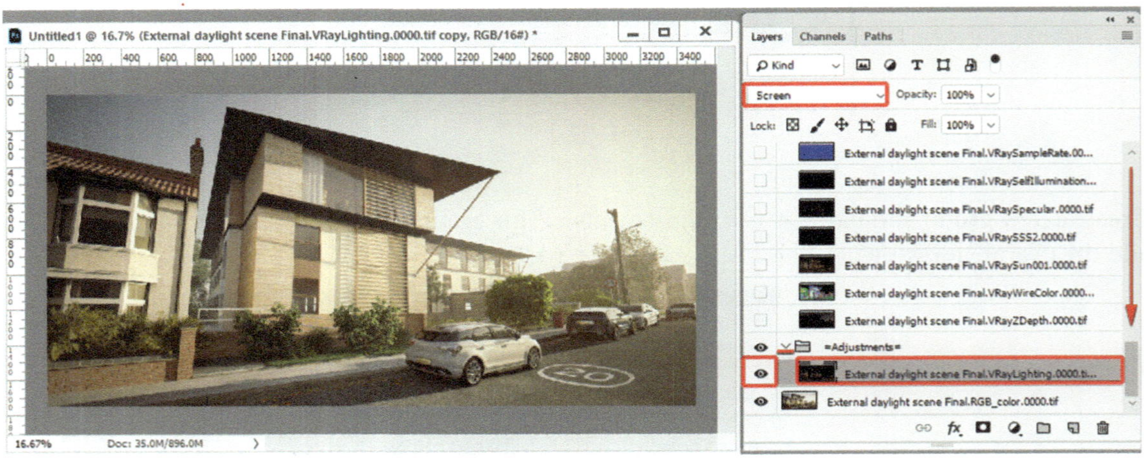

Copy and move VRayLighting pass

To increase this effect, right click on the VRayLighting pass and choose the Duplicate Layer.

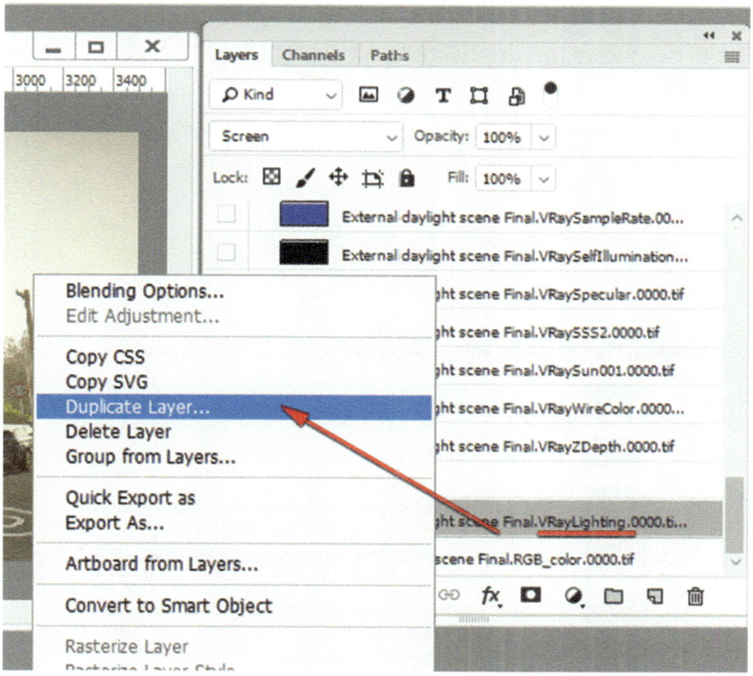

Choose Duplicate Layer

Once the layer is duplicated, decrease its layer Opacity to about 50%. The overall sun intensity should look more appealing.

Decrease layer Opacity

Some of the areas of the left building have become a bit overblown. To correct the problem, while the duplicated layer is still selected, click on the Mask button to create a mask that is attached to the layer.

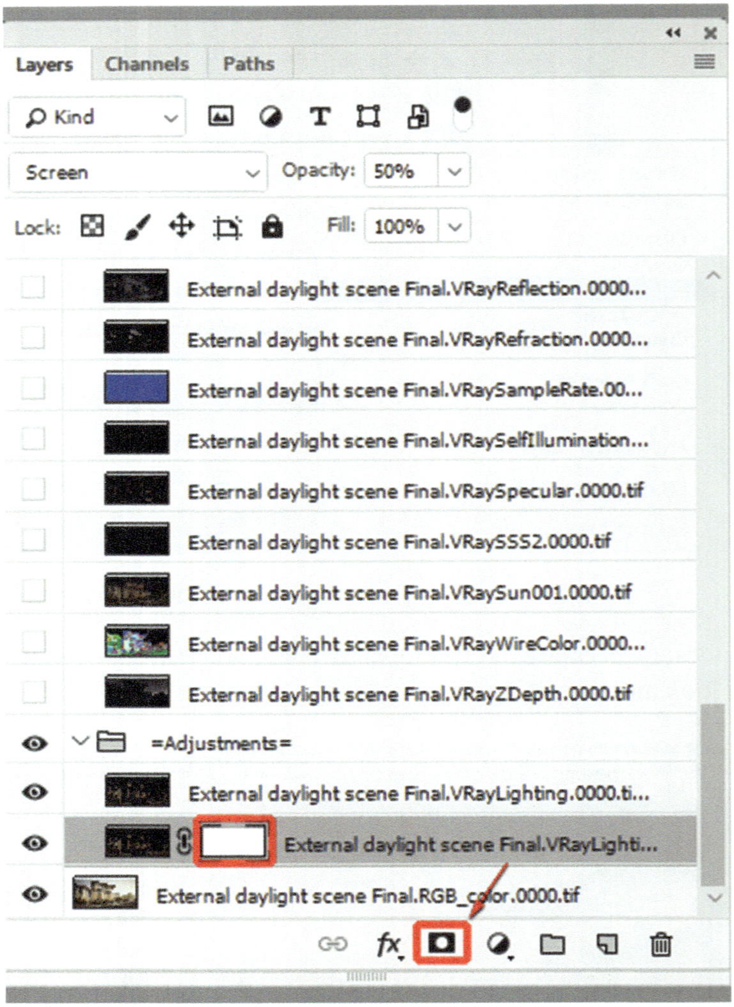

Create a layer mask

Next, enable the brush tool (B) and decrease the Opacity value to about 8%. This value will ensure pixels will be removed or added gradually (as opposed to abruptly at 100%).

When using a layer mask with a brush tool, white/bright colors add pixels, while black/dark colors take away pixels. Use the X key to switch between background colors (black or white).

Also, ensure the layer mask is selected, not the layer itself. Otherwise, the layer will be painted instead.

Enable the Brush tool and Opacity

While the layer mask is selected, begin brushing away the overblown areas of the image. Note the dark areas appearing on the layer mask while brushing away.

Also, use the main toolbar to set brush sizes and smooth the brush pressure.

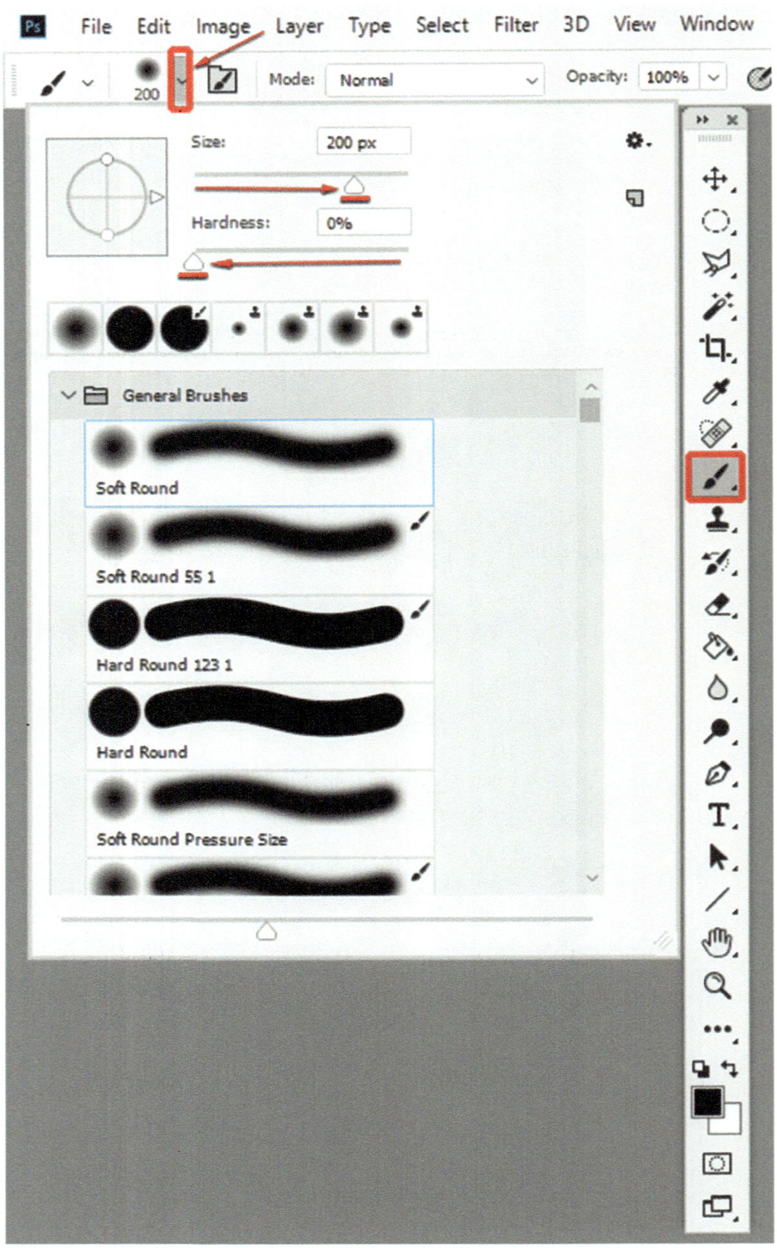
Ps
File
Edit
Image
Layer
Type
Select
Filter
3D
View
Window
200
Mode:
Normal
Opacity:
100%
Size:
200 px
Hardness:
0%
General Brushes
Soft Round
Soft Round 55 1
Hard Round 123 1
Hard Round
Soft Round Pressure Size

Brush options

Brushing away pixels with the layer mask

To add a bit of contrast to the overall image, select the VRayLighting pass (top layer) and click on the Adjustment layer button. Choose the Levels adjustment layer from the list.

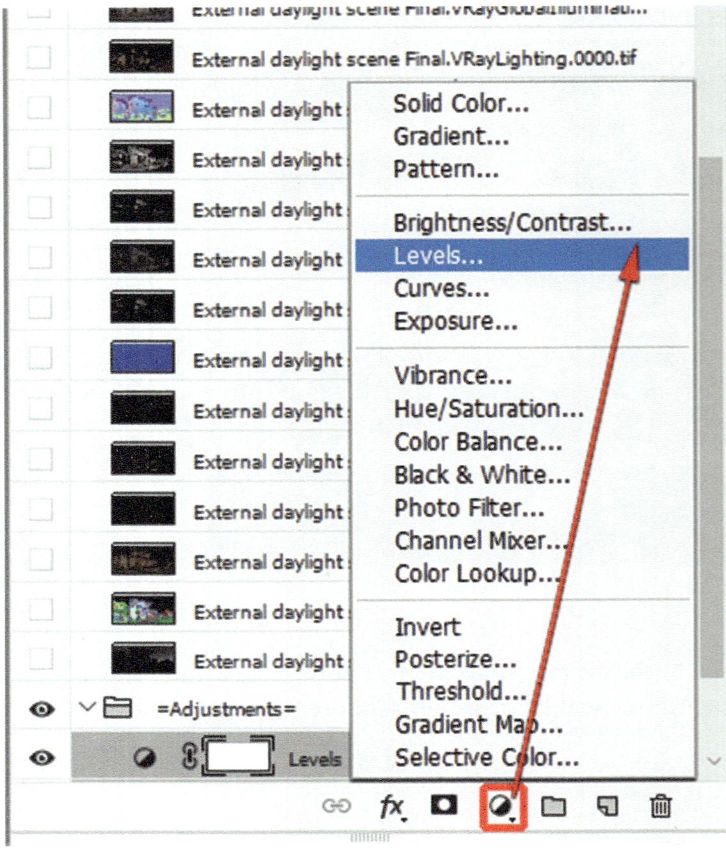

Choose the Levels adjustment layer

Next, move the Levels mid-RGB point slightly to the right (0.67), followed by moving the right point slightly to the left (237).

The overall image should have a nice and appealing contrast.

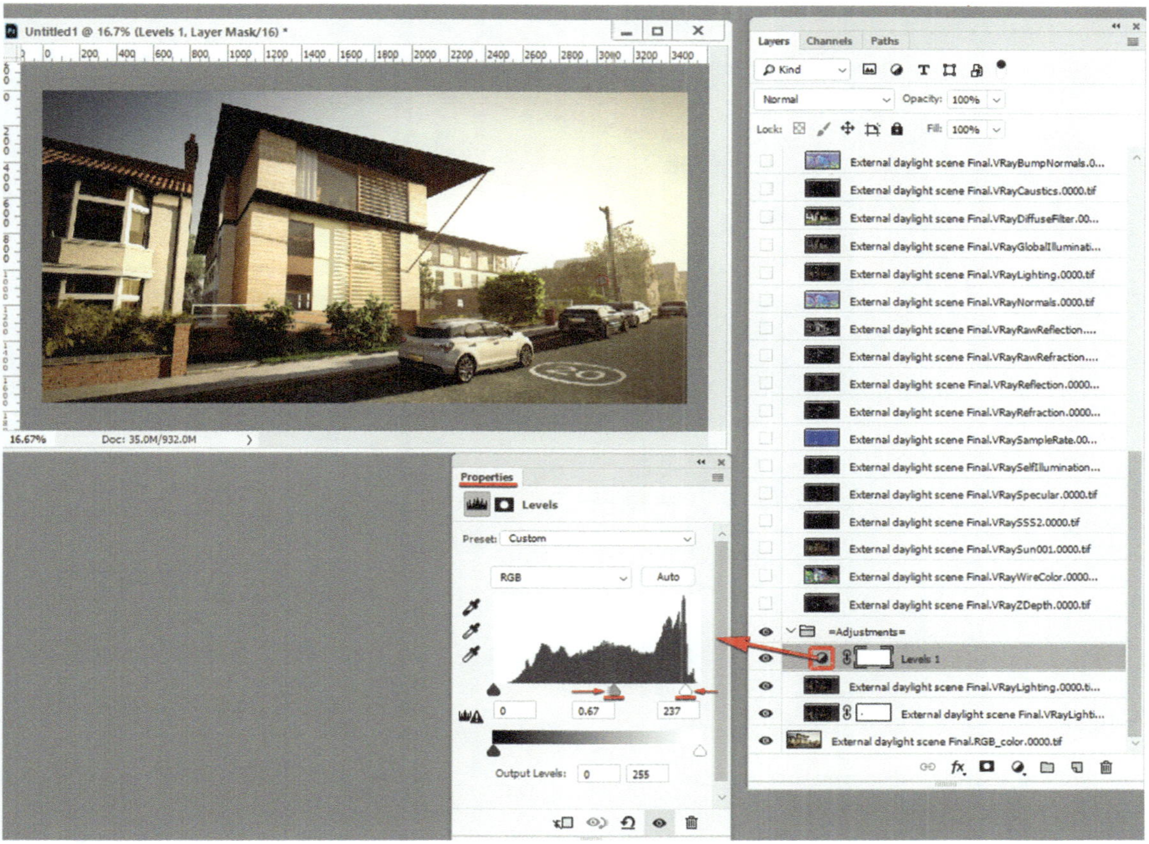

Tweak the Levels adjustment layer

Use the Levels layer mask to brush (B) away pixels on overly bright areas of the image.

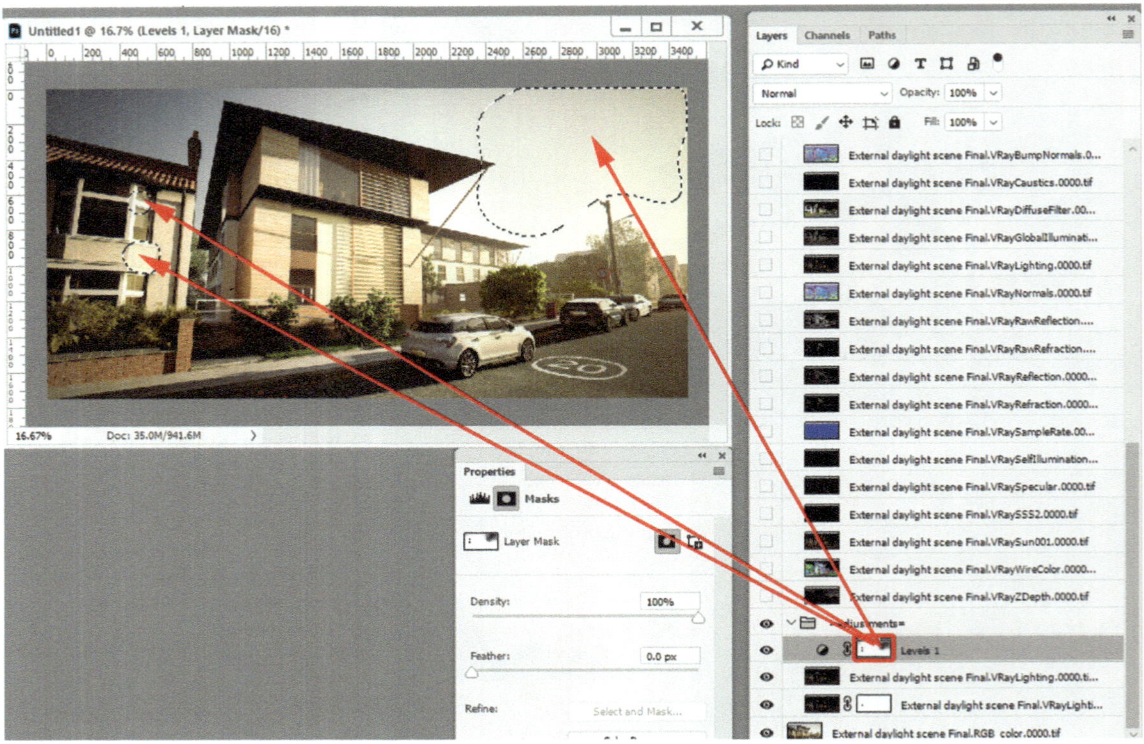

Use the Brush tool to remove overly bright areas

To see the before and after layer mask effects, simply right click and choose Disable Layer Mask.

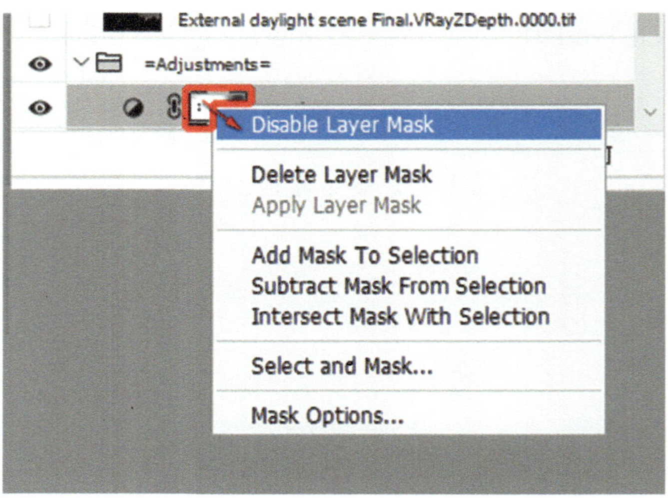

Disable Layer Mask

Also, use the Backslash key (\) to see the masked out areas on the image (in red).

So far, all adjustment layers and passes have been applied to the overall image inside the =Adjustments= group.

The following steps will focus mainly on selecting and adjusting specific objects using groups with masks, render passes, and adjustment layers.

Let's start with the Glass material. In the =Render Elements= group, select and enable the eye icon of the render element named External daylight scene Final .MultiMatteElement_1.0000.tif

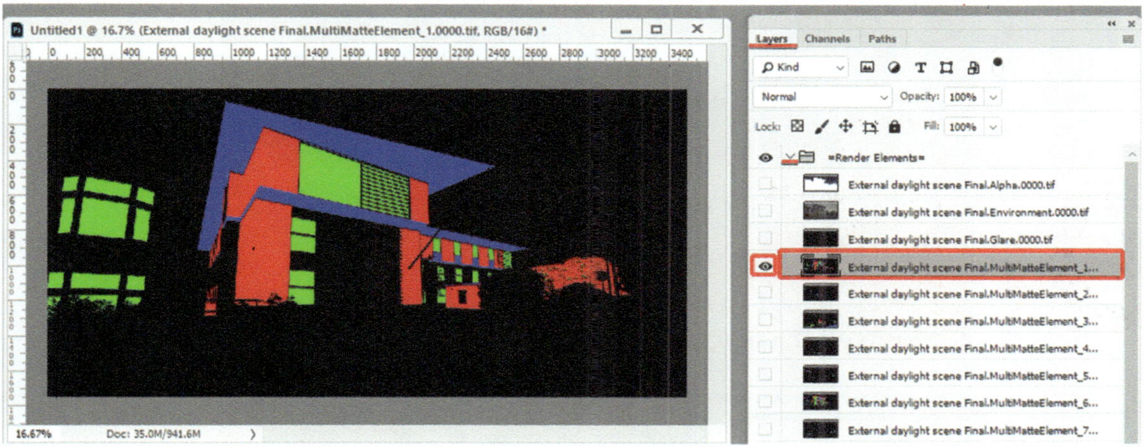

Select and enable layer visibility

Next, go to the Channels tab. Hold down the Ctrl key and click on the Green Channel. The glass areas should be selected.

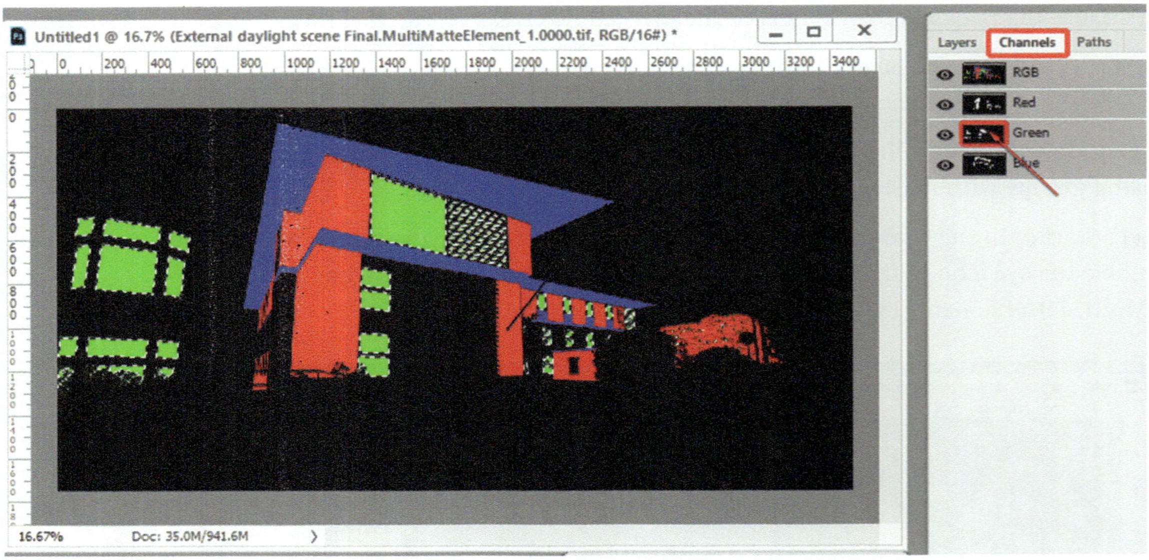

Green Channel selected

Go back to the Layers tab and disable the eye icon of the MultiMatteElement layer to see the selection on the image.

Selection on the image

While the selection is still on, scroll down to the bottom of the layer stack and click to create a new Group.

Following that, click on the Mask button to create a mask based on the selection. Any adjustments created inside this group will be confined within the mask boundaries.

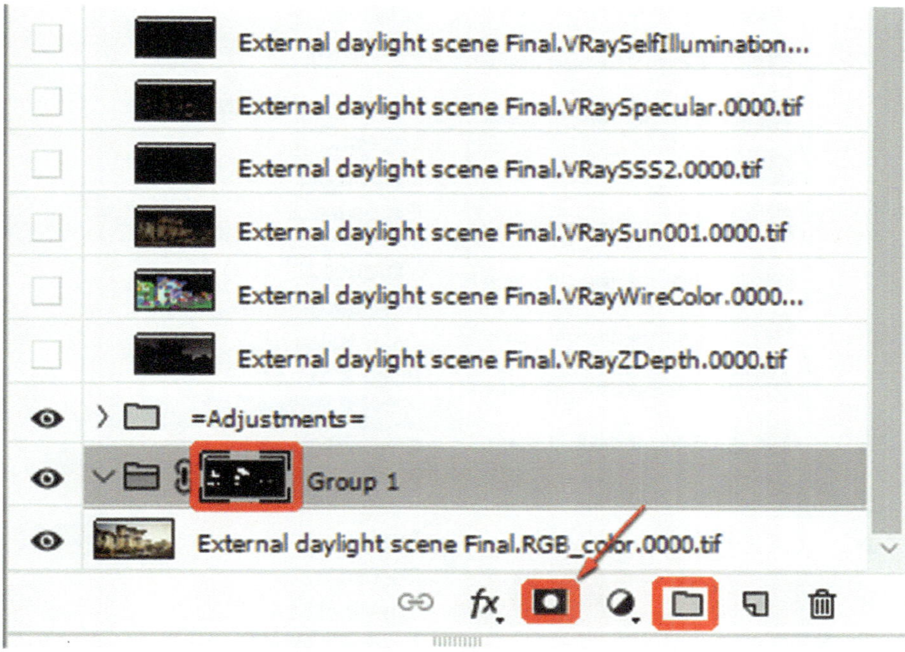

Create a new Group with a Mask

Rename the new group as =Glass=.

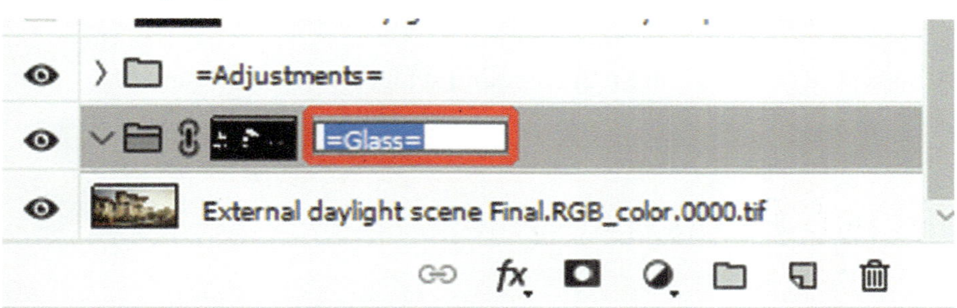

Group renamed

To add a bit of tint to the =Glass= group, create a Photo Filter Adjustment Layer inside it.

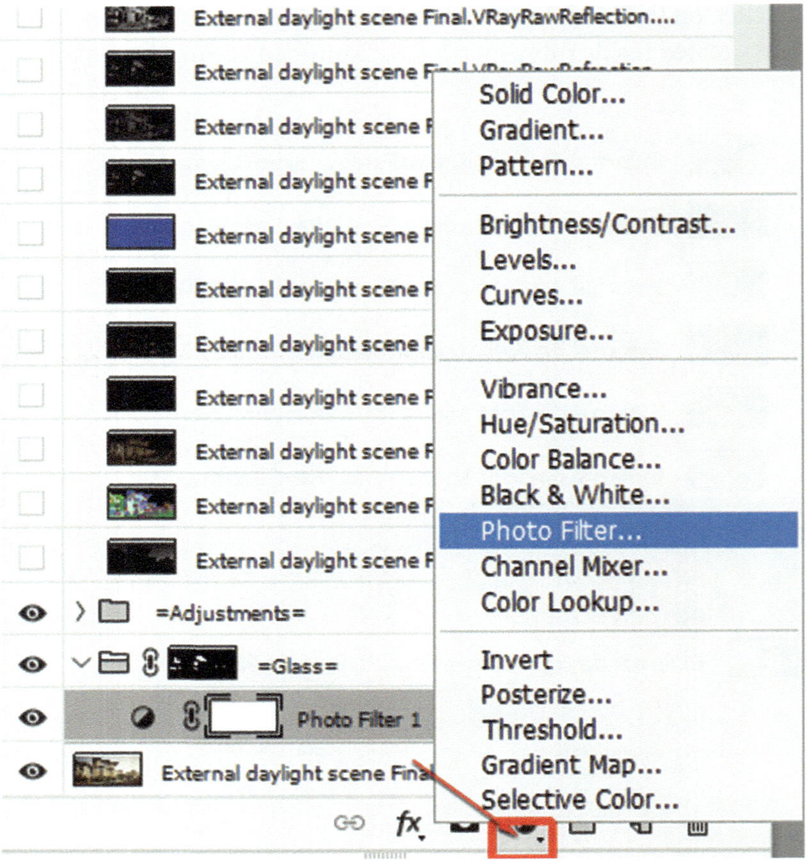

Photo Filter added

Choose the Cooling Filter (82) color and set its Density to about 25%.

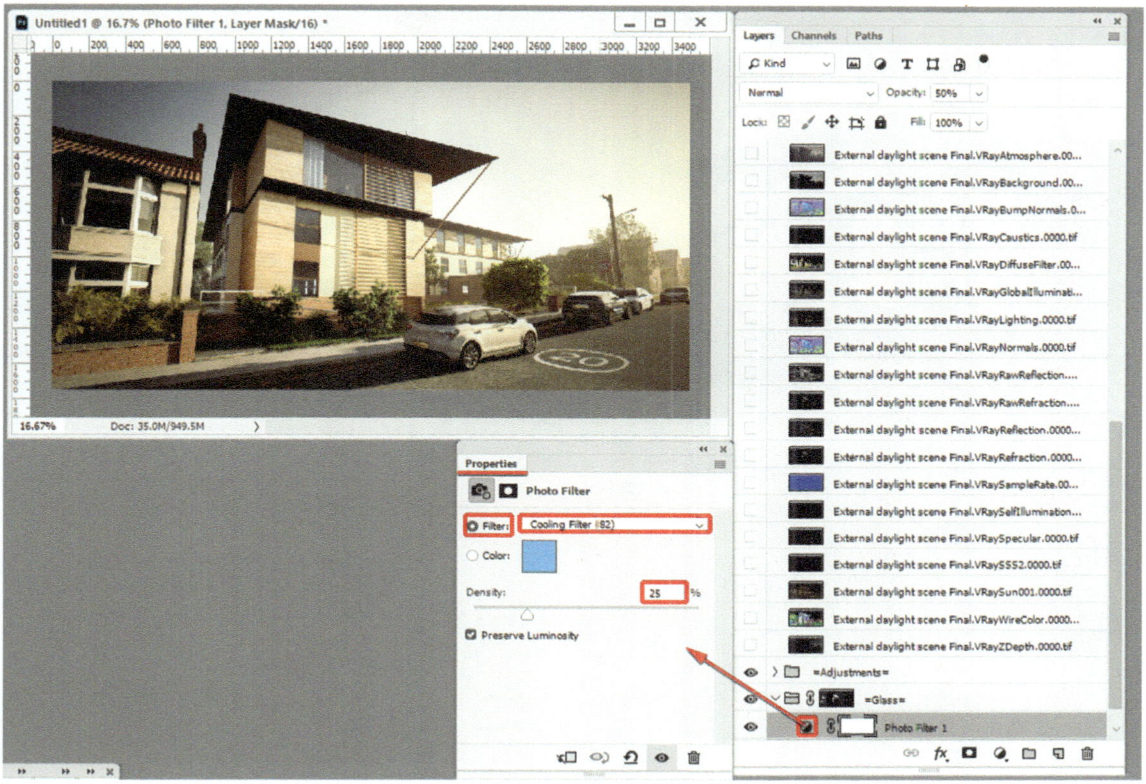

Cooling Filter (82)

Use the Brush tool (B) to brush away pixels of the Photo filer using some of the techniques covered earlier.

Also, use the left and right bracket keys ([ ]) to increase or decrease the brush sizes.

Alternatively, simply use its main toolbar to set brush sizes and smoothen the brush.

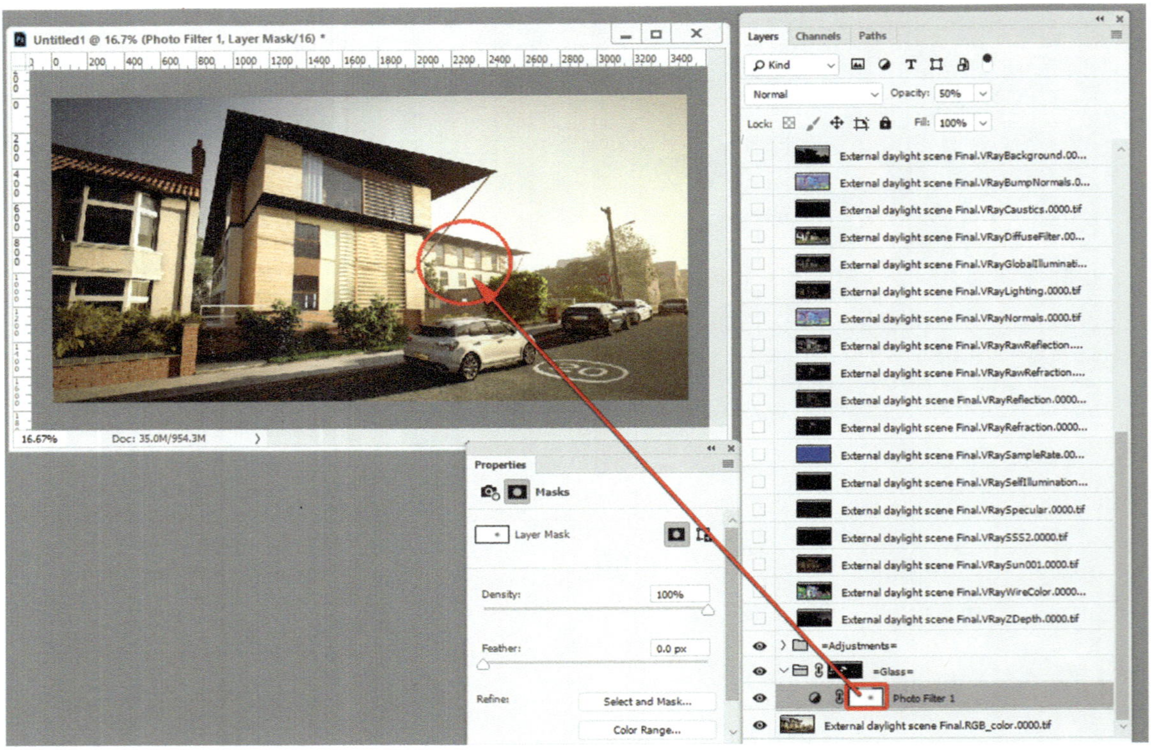

Use the Brush tool to reduce the blue tint

To adjust the Iron material, let's enable again the layer named External daylight scene Final.MultiMatteElement_1.0000.tif.

In the Channels tab, hold down the Ctrl key and click the Blue channel to enable it.

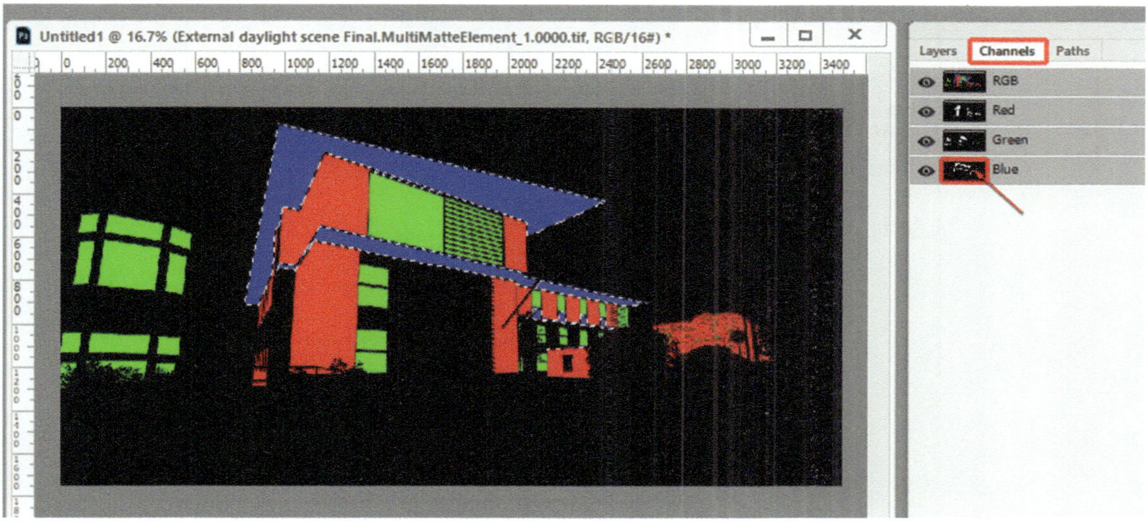

Blue Channel selection

Back to the Layers tab, disable the MultiMatteElement layer. Create a new Group and rename it as =Roof=.

While the selection is still on, click on the Mask button to create a group mask based on the selection.

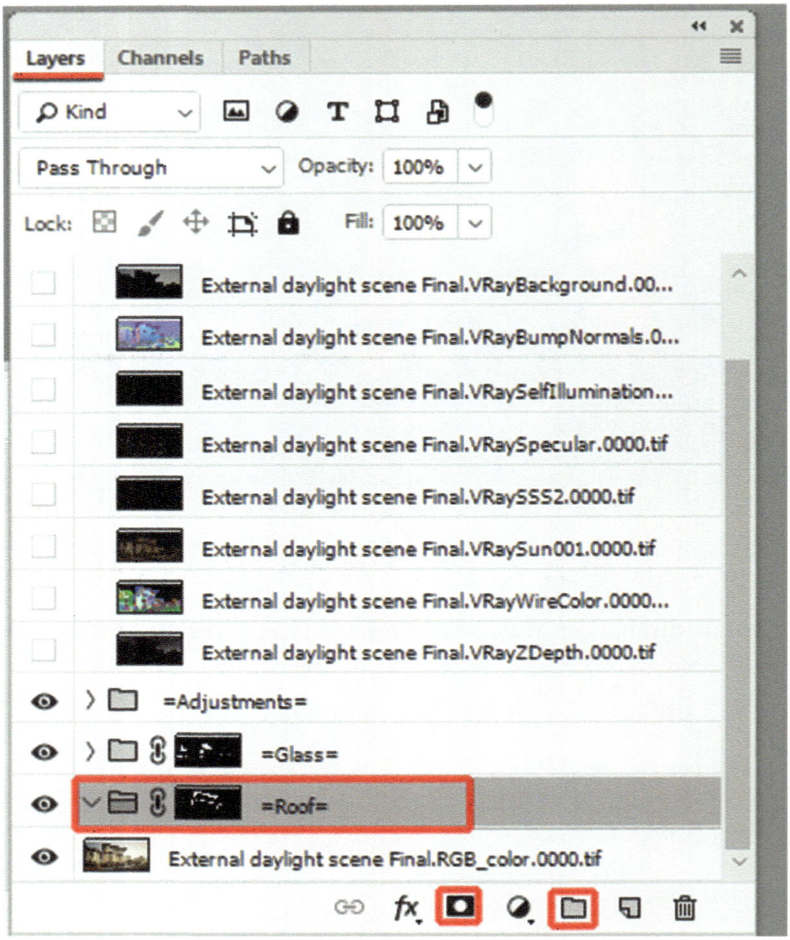

New Group created with a mask

To add a bit of reflectivity to the Iron material, select the layer named External daylight scene Final.VRayRawReflection.0000.tif.

To copy/duplicate the layer, hold down the Alt key and move it inside the =Roof= group. Also, enable its layer visibility eye icon.

Keep the blending mode as Normal and reduce its Opacity value to about 25%. This should increase the Iron material reflectivity.

Raw Reflection added to the Iron material

To adjust the Gutter material, let's start by enabling the layer named External daylight scene Final.MultiMatteElement_2.0000.tif

Next, go to the Channels tab. Hold down the Ctrl key and click on the Green Channel.

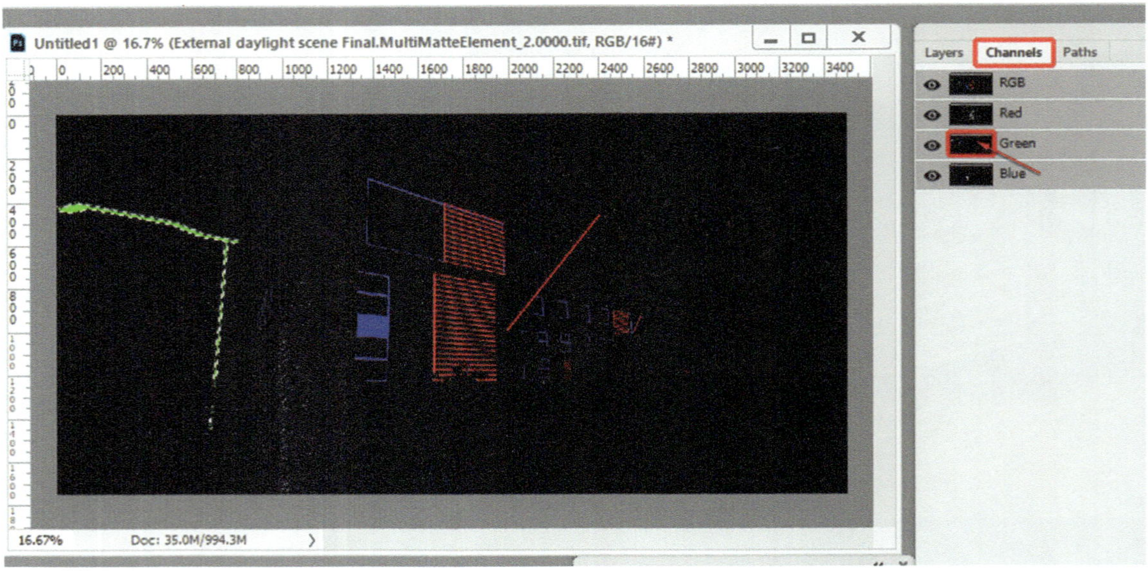

Select the Green Channel

Back to the Layers tab, scroll down and create a new Group. Rename it as =Gutter=.

While the selection is still on, click on the Mask button to create a mask based on the selection.

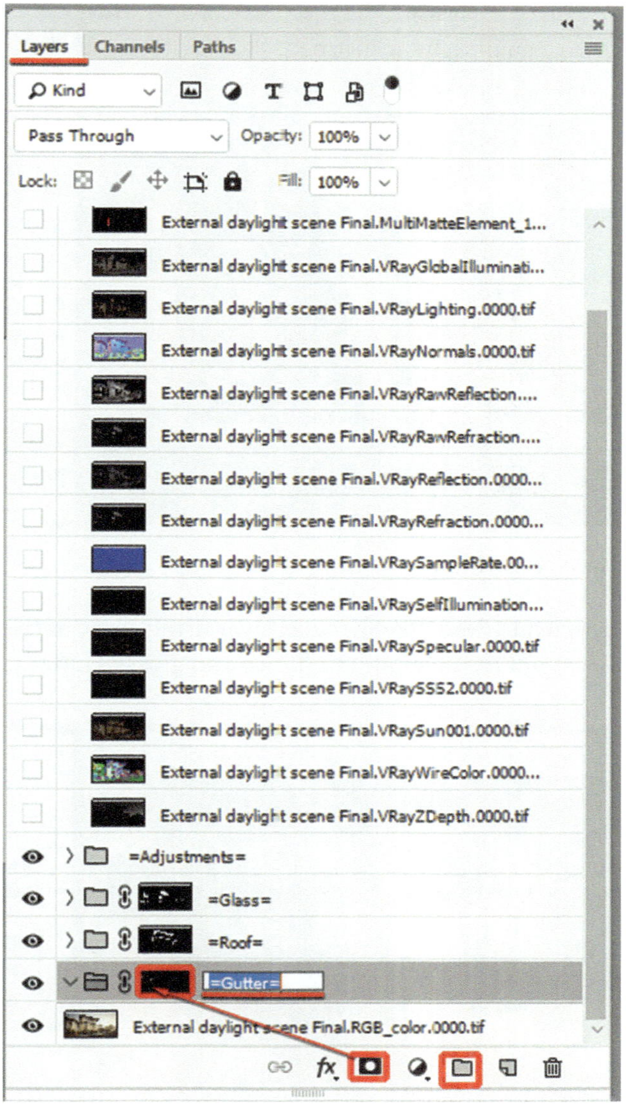

New Group created with a mask

To add a bit of specular/glossiness to the Gutter material, select the layer named External daylight scene Final.VRaySpecular.0000.tif

To copy/duplicate the layer, hold down the Alt key and move it inside the =Gutter= group. Also, enable its layer visibility eye icon.

Change its layer blending mode to Screen type. VRaySpecular works best with Screen type layer blending mode.

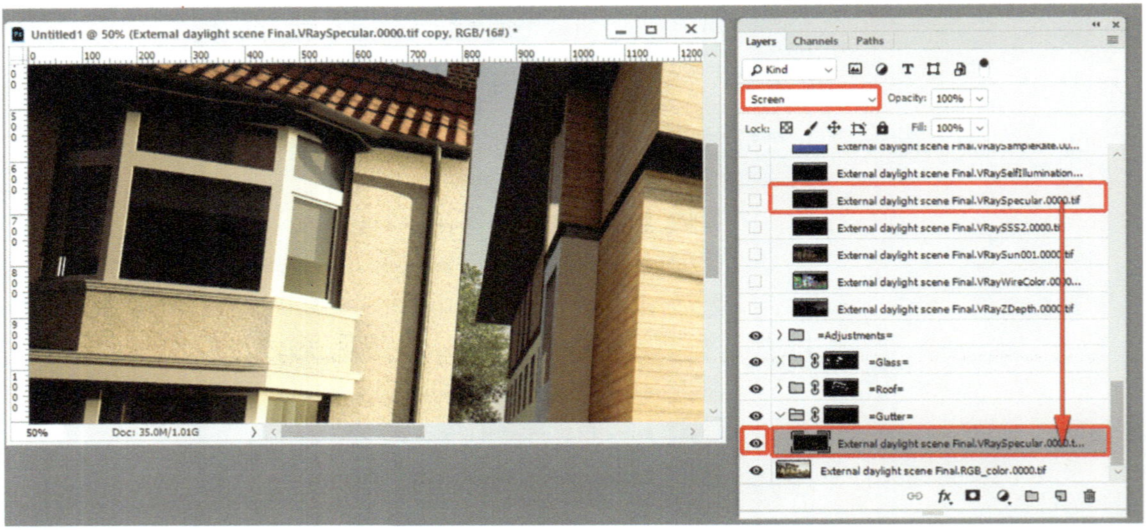

VRaySpecular added to the Gutter group

Duplicate the VRaySpecular layer using some of the techniques described earlier. The final result should be a nice and glossy Gutter material.

Duplicated VRaySpecular passes

The same technique (duplicated VRaySpecular passes) was used to adjust the grass material, plants, and trees.

To add a red color to the back light of the car (right side), zoom in(Z) close to the area first.

Enable the Polygonal Lasso Tool and begin clicking and drawing around it to create a selection shape. Once the drawn shape is closed, a selection should appear.

Drawn selection around the back light

While the selection is still on with Polygonal Tool enabled, hold down the Alt key to see the minus sign, and draw inside the selection to subtract parts of the selection.

Subtract parts of the selection with Alt key

Next, click on the button to create a new Group. Rename it as =BackLight=.

While the selection is still on, click on the button to create a Mask based on the selection.

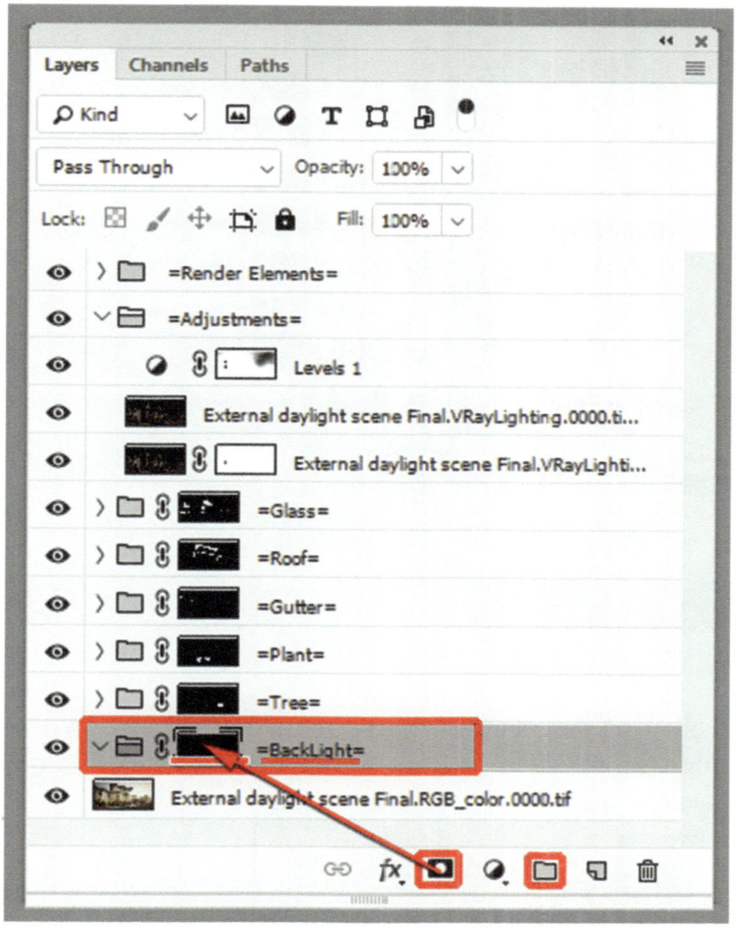

Create a new Group with a Mask

To start adding colors, create a Levels adjustment layer by clicking on its button. Under RGB, move its middle point to the right (0.50) to add a bit of contrast.

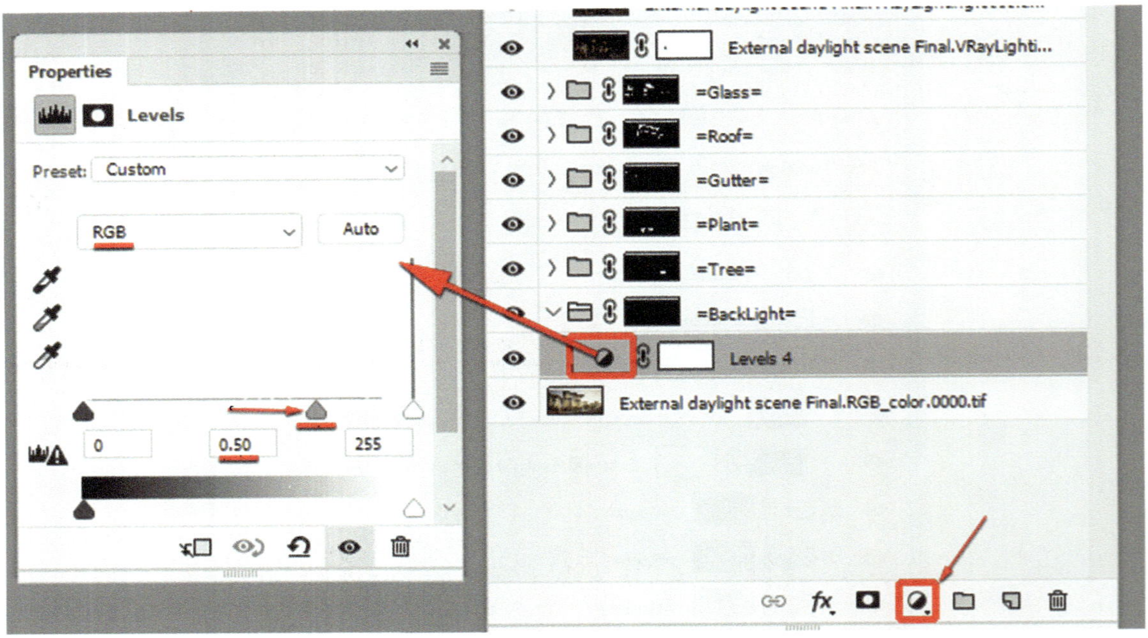

Create a Levels adjustment layer and tweak it

Following that, choose the Red color from the list and move its middle point to the left (1.80). This should add a slight red tint.

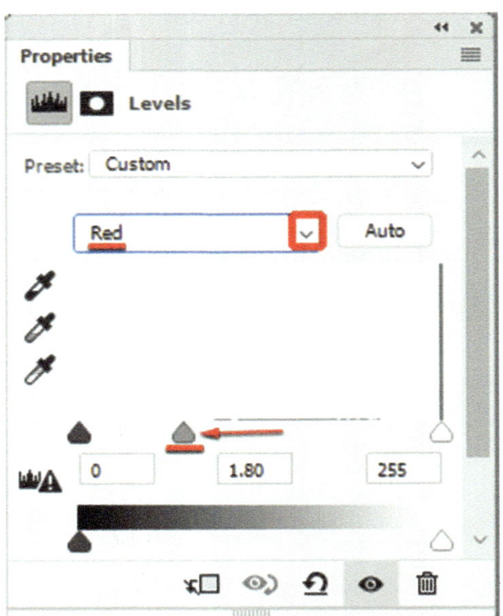

Adjust the Red color

To reinvigorate the color, choose the Blue color from the list and move its midpoint to the right (0.43).

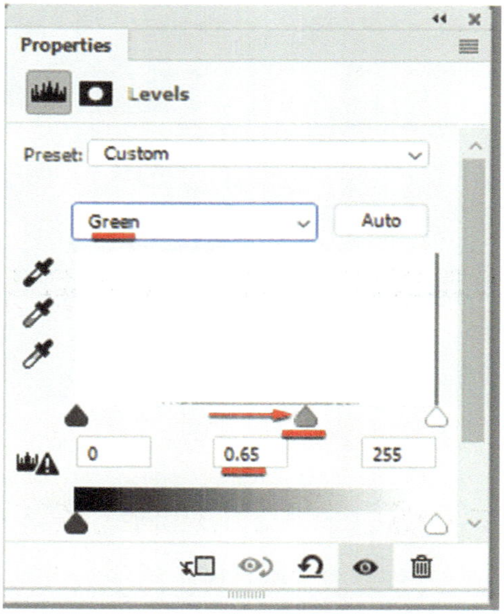

Adjust the Blue color

Finally, choose the Green color from the list and move its midpoint to the right (0.65). The final result should be a matching red tint.

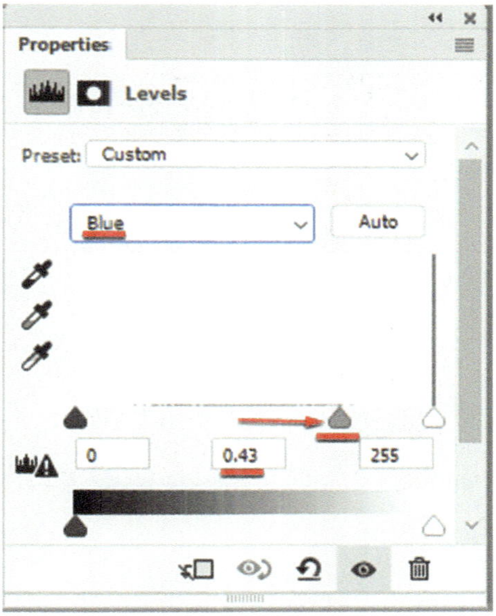

Adjust the Green color

Final result

Save the file as a PSD (Ctrl+S) by going to File and choosing to save as a PSD file format. This Photoshop file format should retain all the layers and masks.

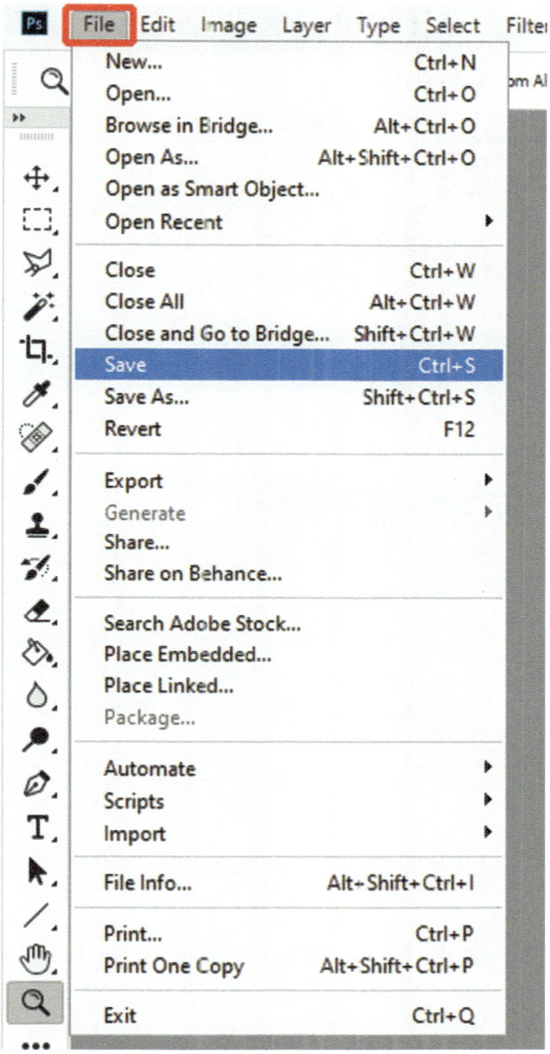

File and Save

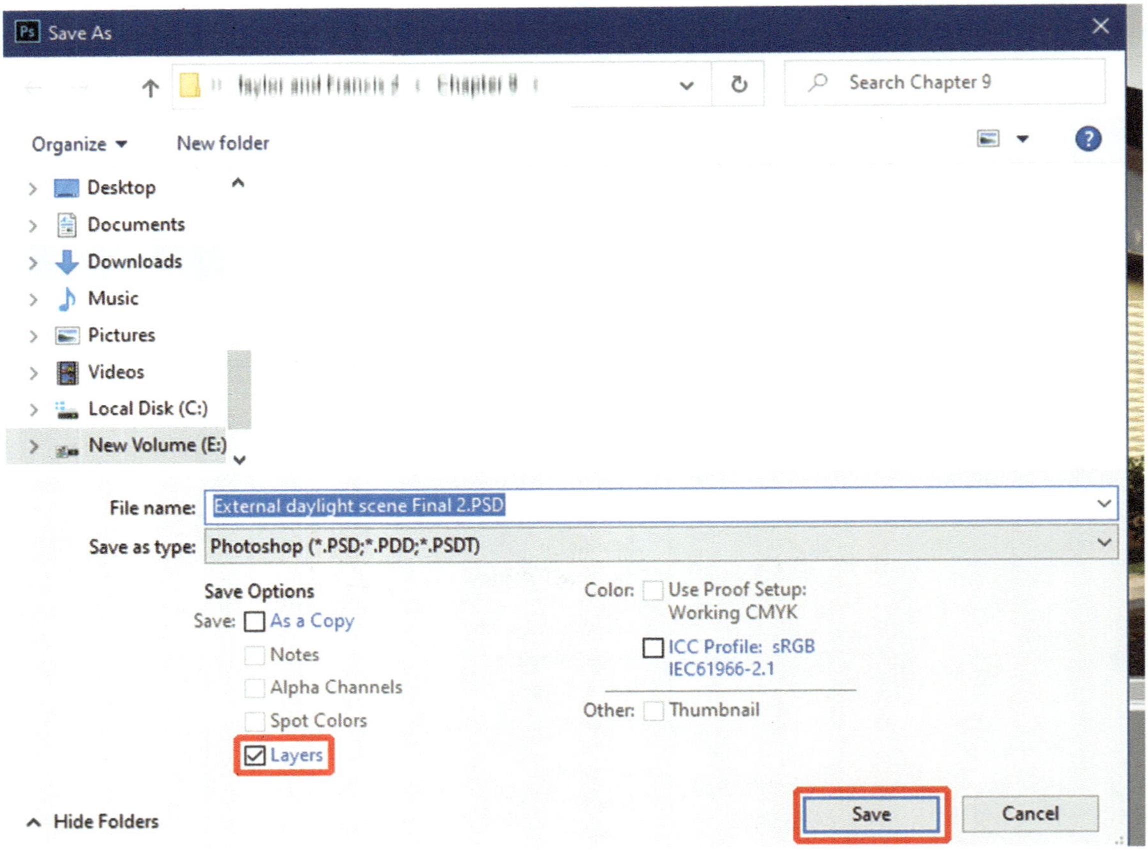

Save as PSD file format

To see the final result, please open the Photoshop file named External daylight scene Final.PSD.

The following step is to add the Camera Raw Filter to create a more appealing image. The Camera Raw Filter can only be applied to a flattened image.

To ensure we work on a separate document, right click on the top edge of the document External daylight scene Final.PSD and choose the option Duplicate.

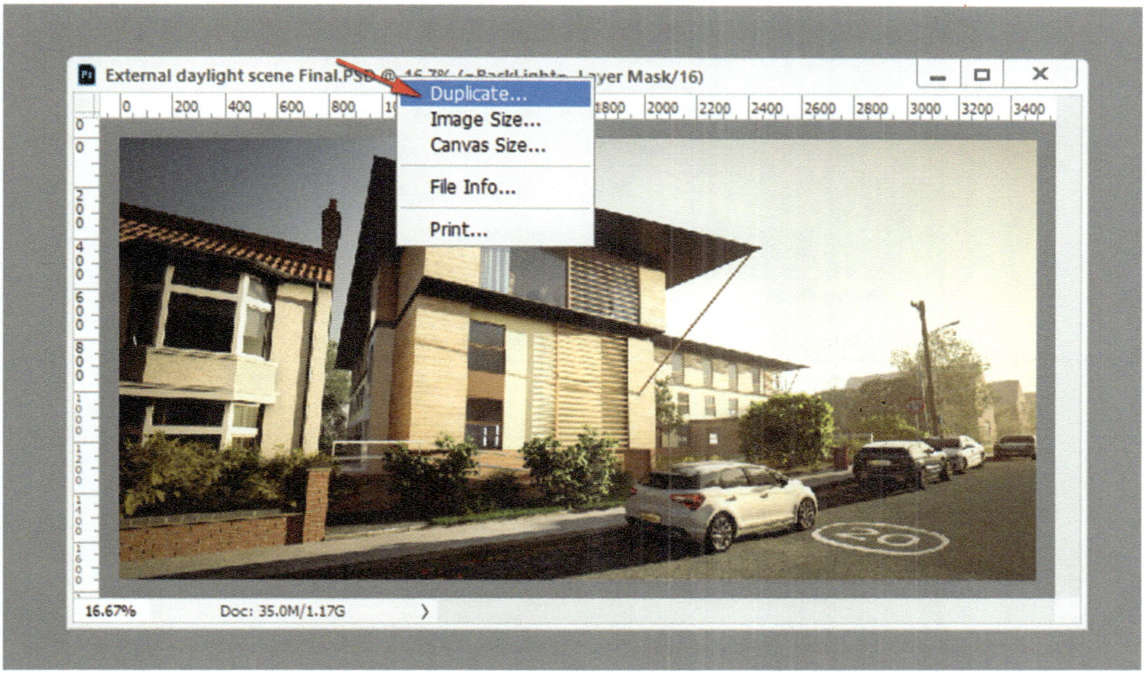

Choose Duplicate

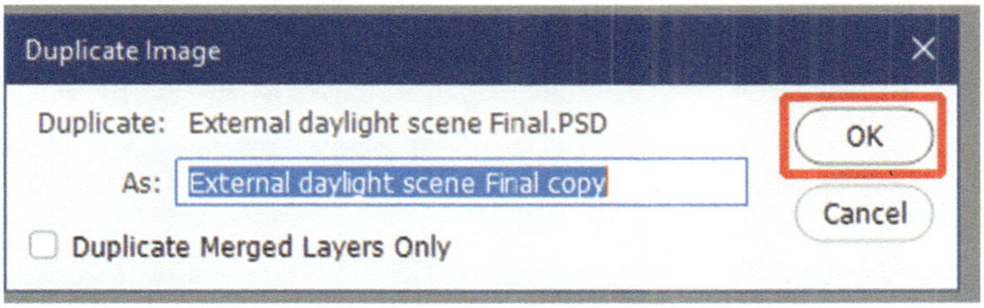

Duplicate image dialog

To flatten the document, select a layer (Not a group), right click, and choose the option Flatten Image.

Click OK to Discard hidden layers, if any.

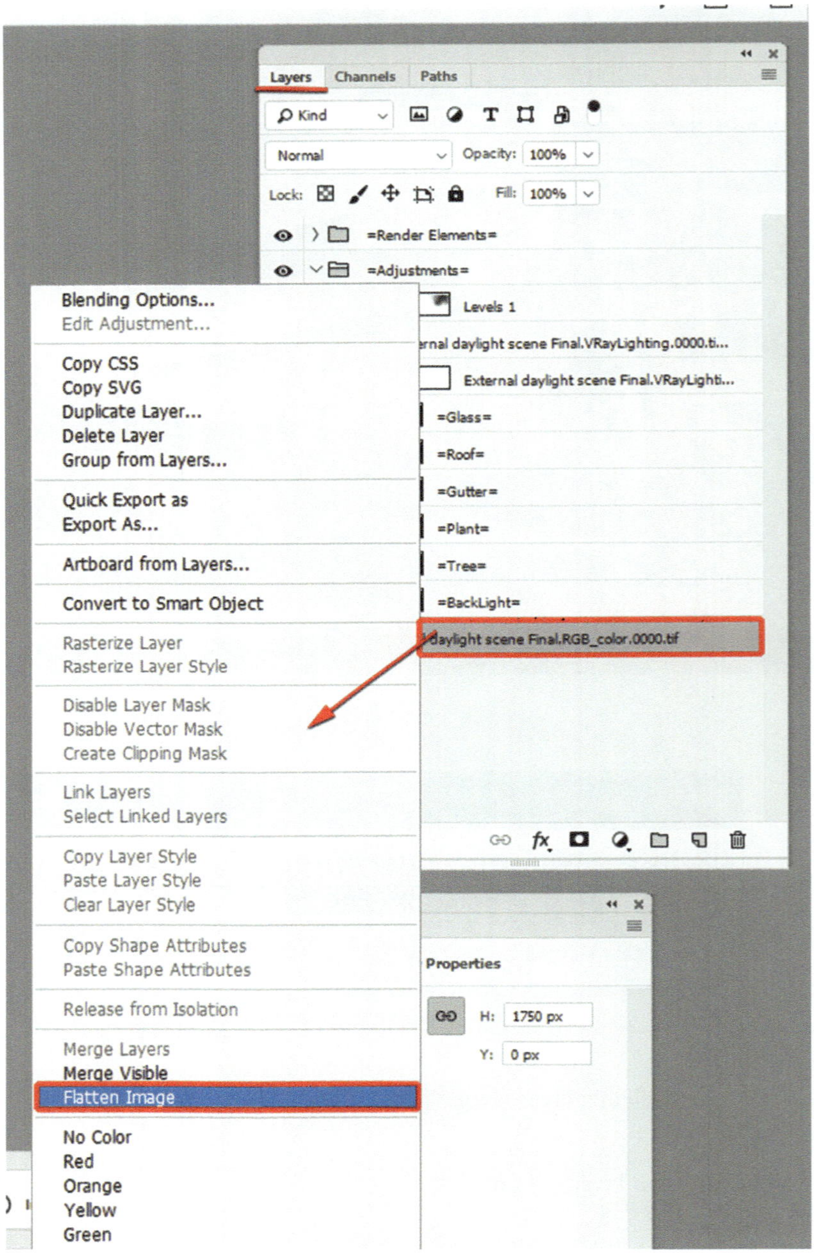
Layers
Channels
Paths
Kind
Normal
Opacity: 100%
Lock:
Fill: 100%
=Render Elements=
=Adjustments=
Levels 1
rnal daylight scene Final.VRayLighting.0000.ti...
External daylight scene Final.VRayLighti...
=Glass=
=Roof=
=Gutter=
=Plant=
=Tree=
=BackLight=
daylight scene Final.RGB_color.0000.tif
Blending Options...
Edit Adjustment...
Copy CSS
Copy SVG
Duplicate Layer...
Delete Layer
Group from Layers...
Quick Export as
Export As...
Artboard from Layers...
Convert to Smart Object
Rasterize Layer
Rasterize Layer Style
Disable Layer Mask
Disable Vector Mask
Create Clipping Mask
Link Layers
Select Linked Layers
Copy Layer Style
Paste Layer Style
Clear Layer Style
Copy Shape Attributes
Paste Shape Attributes
Release from Isolation
Merge Layers
Merge Visible
Flatten Image
No Color
Red
Orange
Yellow
Green
Properties
H: 1750 px
Y: 0 px

Choose Flatten Image

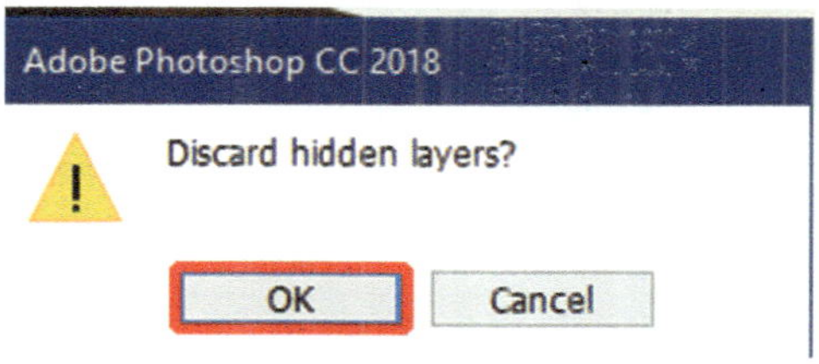

Discard hidden layers dialog

To ensure you don't work on the original layer, Duplicate it and rename the new layer as Raw Camera filter.

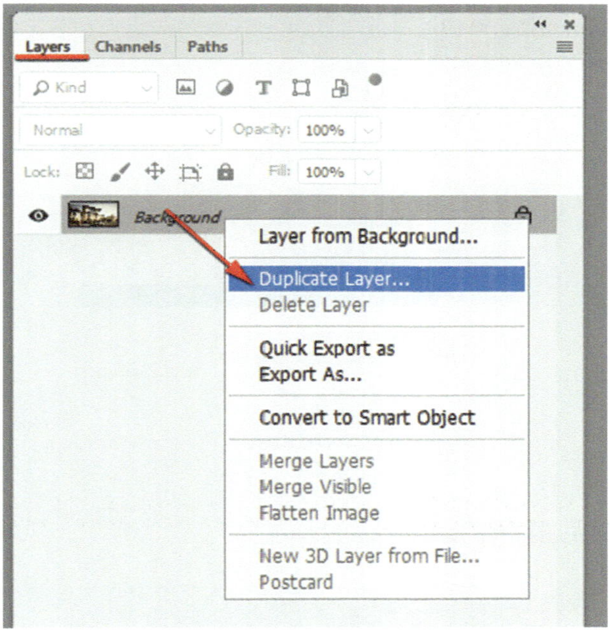

Duplicate Layer option

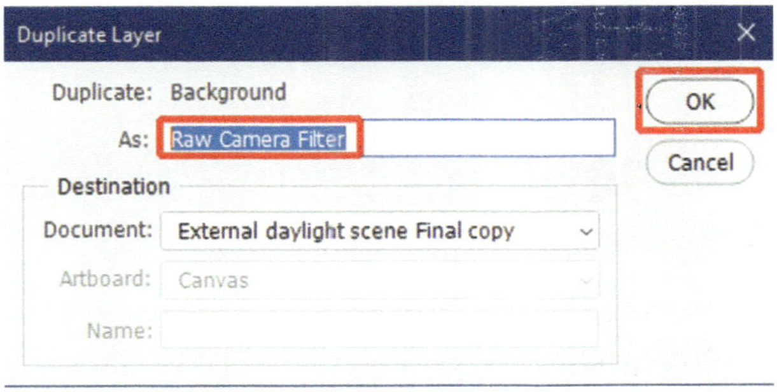

Rename duplicated layer

To retain the parameters of filters applied to an image, the layer needs to become a Smart object first.

To do so, right click on the Raw camera Filter layer and choose to Convert to Smart Object.

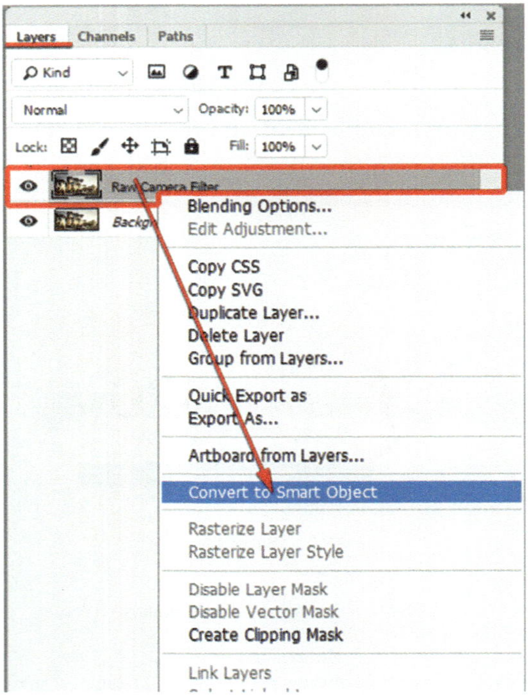

Choose to Convert to Smart Object

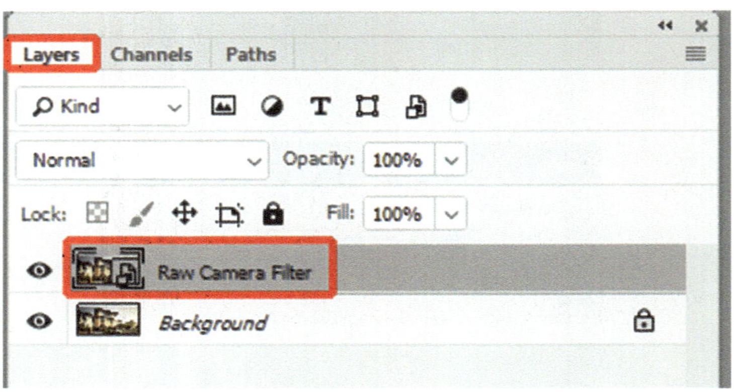

Layer converted to a Smart Object

To add a filter, click on the File toolbar and choose the Camera Raw Filter from the list.

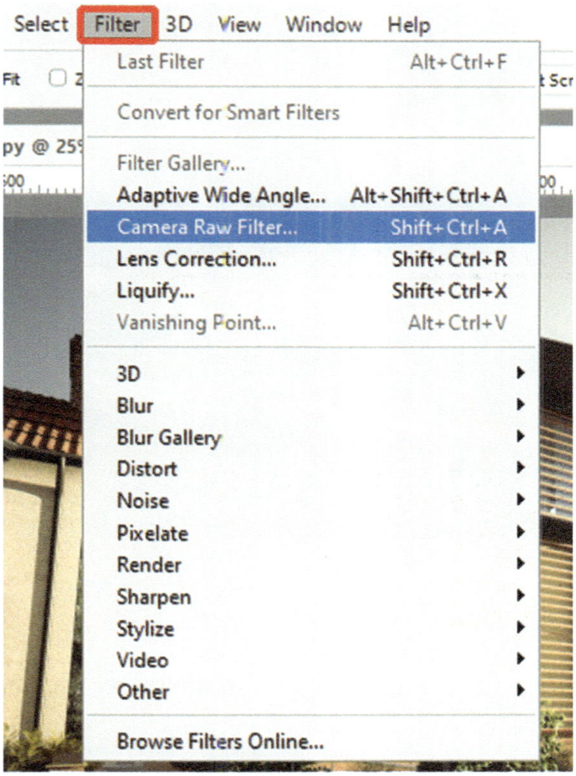

Choose the Camera Raw Filter

In the Camera Raw Filter dialog, let's start by increasing the Highlights to about +18.

Decrease the Shadows to about –13 and the Whites to –58.

Also, increase the Blacks to about +34, along with Clarity to +92.

In addition, increase the Dehaze to +30, and decrease the Vibrance to –10.

Finally, decrease the Saturation to –9.

NOTE

These values worked well. However, feel free to try different values, if desired.

Camera Raw Filter adjusted

Once the dialog is closed, you should see the Camera Raw Filter under the main layer.

If you wish to re-edit the parameters, simply double click on the Camera Raw Filter text to open its dialog.

The eye icon allows users to turn the filter on and off.

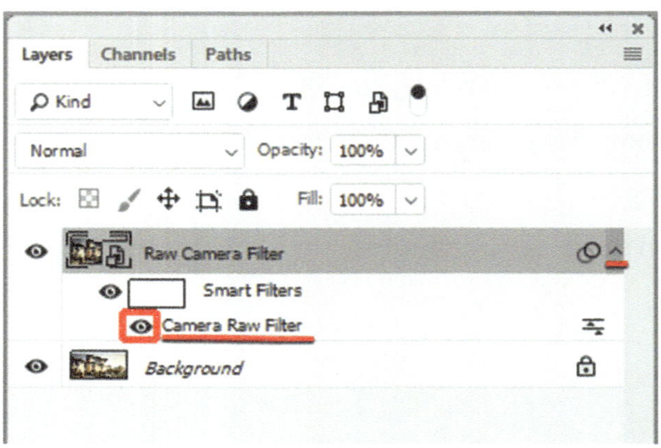

Camera Raw Filter under the main layer

Create a layer mask and mask out (with a brush tool) darker areas of the top-right corner.

Mask out darker areas

Next, let's add a Photoshop LUT by clicking on the Adjustment layer button and choosing the Color Lookup from the list.

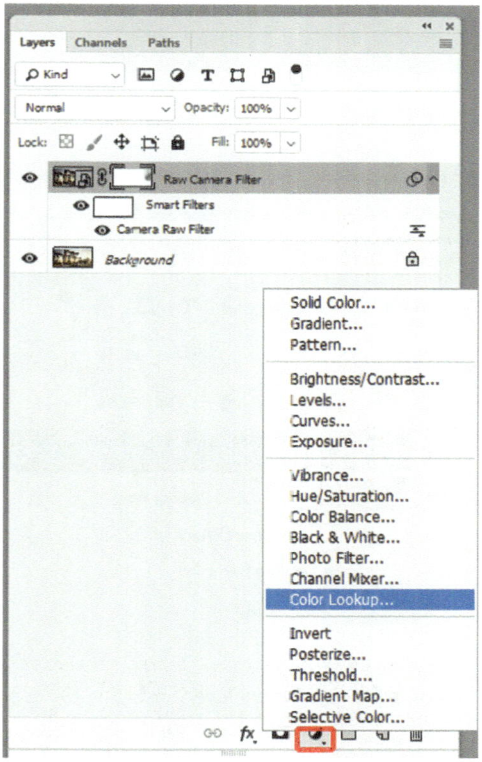

Choose the Color Lookup option

> **NOTE**
>
> This LUT file is specific to Photoshop, and shouldn't be used in 3ds max.

Once the Color Lookup is added, go to its Properties dialog and add the 3DLUT File named C-7050-STD.cube.

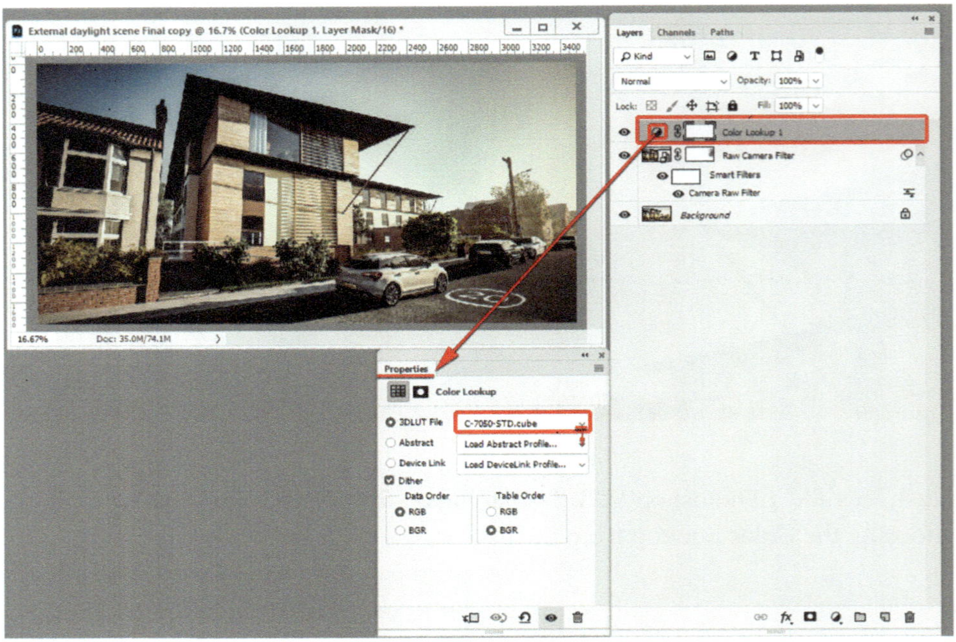

Add the Color Lookup file C-7050-STD.cube

Also, rename the adjustment layer as Color Lookup C-7050-STD.cube.

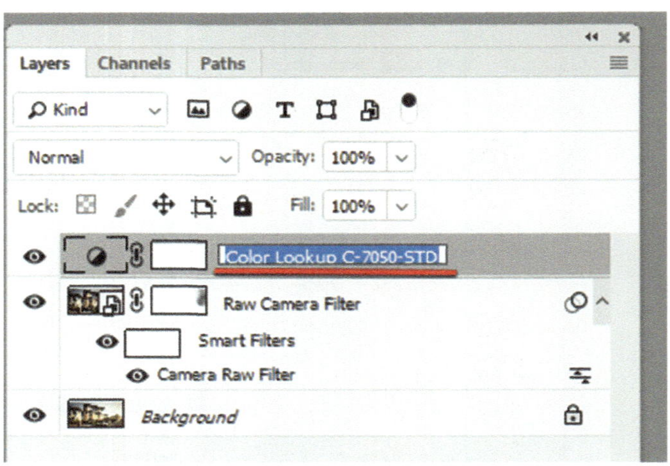

Rename the Adjustment layer

Save this file as a PSD.

To see the final result of adding the Camera Raw Filter and the LUT file, simply open the document named External daylight scene Final_Camera Raw Filters & LUT.PSD

Most real photos have a slight chromatic aberration on pixels. When added in 3d, renders often look more realistic as result.

This effect can only be applied on a flattened document (without any layers).

To add the chromatic aberration effect on this render, simply Duplicate the document first and flatten it, as previously done.

Duplicate document

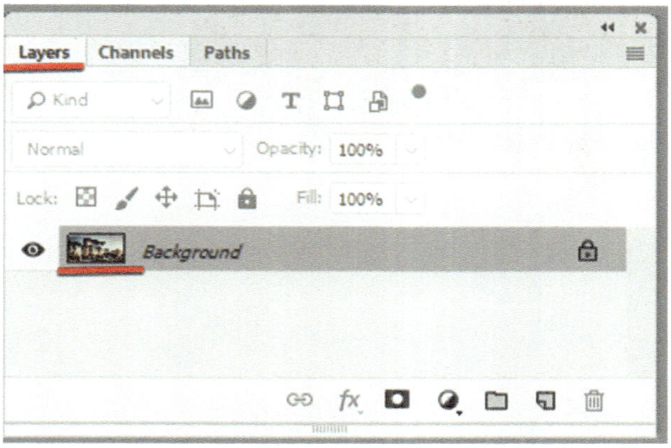

Flatten document

Next, zoom into the document 100%. Alternatively, simply type in 100 on the bottom-left part of the document.

It's utterly important to zoom in 100% to prevent massive color shifts when nudging the channels.

Zoom in 100%

Next, go to the Channels tab and select the Red channel. The image should turn black and white.

Nudge the image up once. To nudge, enable the Move tool (V) and use the arrow on your keyboard (once).

Select the Red channel and nudge it up

Select the Green Channel and nudge it down once (using the arrow). Following that, select the Blue channel and nudge it to the right. Finally, select the RGB channel to see the final result in color.

Select the RGB channel to see the final result

The color shifts are now apparent. Next, we are going to blend this layer with the document External daylight scene Final_Camera Raw Filters & LUT.PSD.

To do so, go to the Layers tab. Right click and choose Duplicate layer.

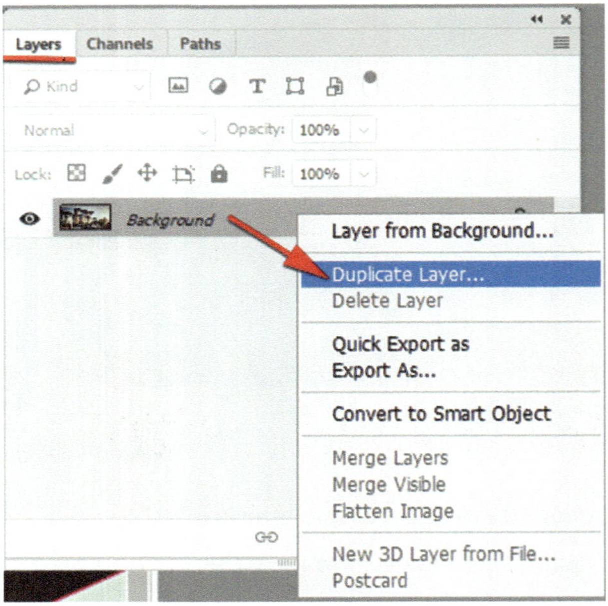

Right click and Duplicate Layer

In the Duplicate Layer dialog, under Destination, choose the document External daylight scene Final_Camera Raw Filters & LUT.PSD.

This duplicated layer with chromatic aberration should appear in the document External daylight scene Final_Camera Raw Filters & LUT.PSD.

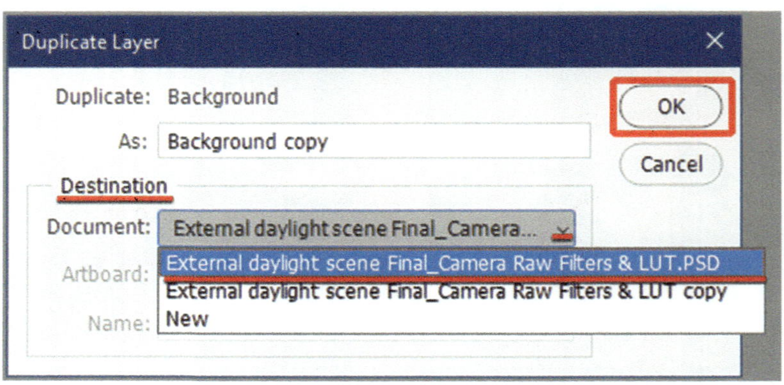

Choose the Destination Document

Back in the document External daylight scene Final_Camera Raw Filters & LUT.PSD, select the duplicated later with chromatic aberration and reduce its layer Opacity to 50%.

This value should make the chromatic aberration less prominent and more appealing.

Reduce the chromatic aberration Opacity

Rename the layer as Chromatic Aberration.

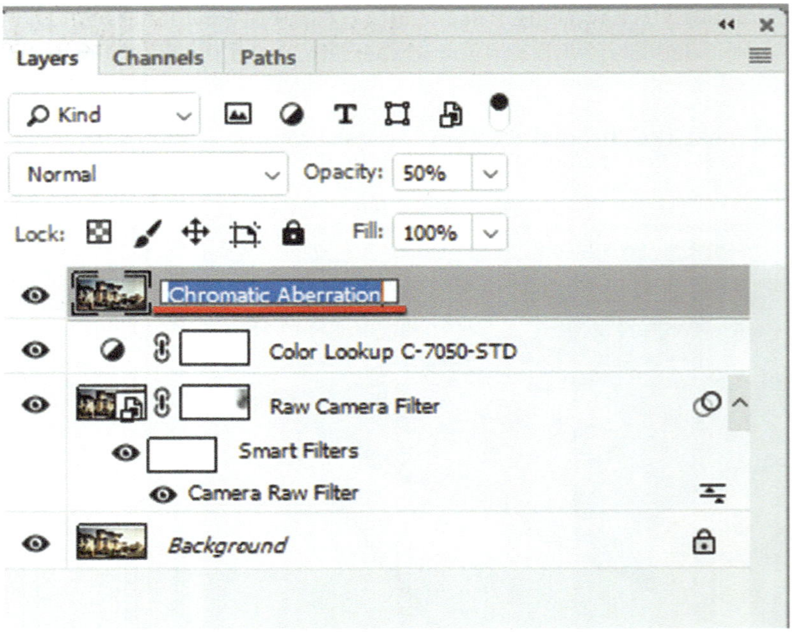

Rename the chromatic aberration layer

Save the PSD file under a different name.

To see the final PSD document with all effects applied, simply open the document named External daylight scene Final_Camera Raw Filters & LUT Chromatic.PSD

Once happy with the final results, click to save the file in TIF format (Shift+Ctrl+S). Ensure to disable the Layers option to flatten the image.

Unlike JPEGs, TIF file formats preserve the quality of renders for high-resolution prints. However, they are often huge in size.

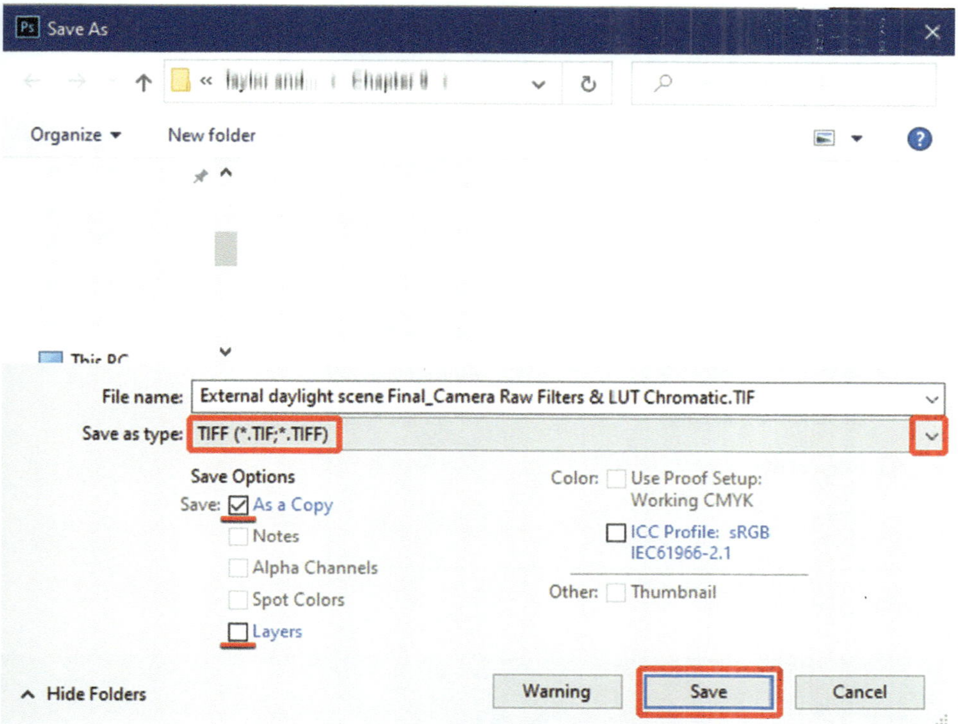

TIF Save options

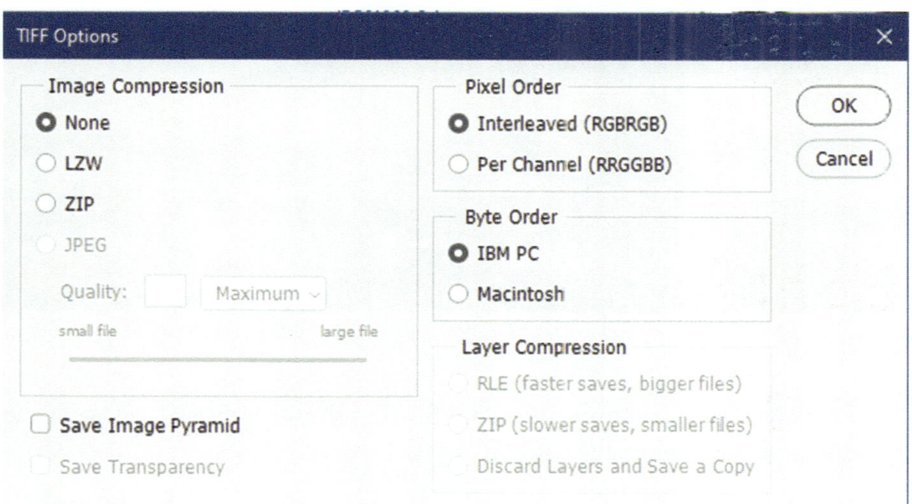

TIF Options dialog

Also, save another version in JPEG file format, for emails, etc.

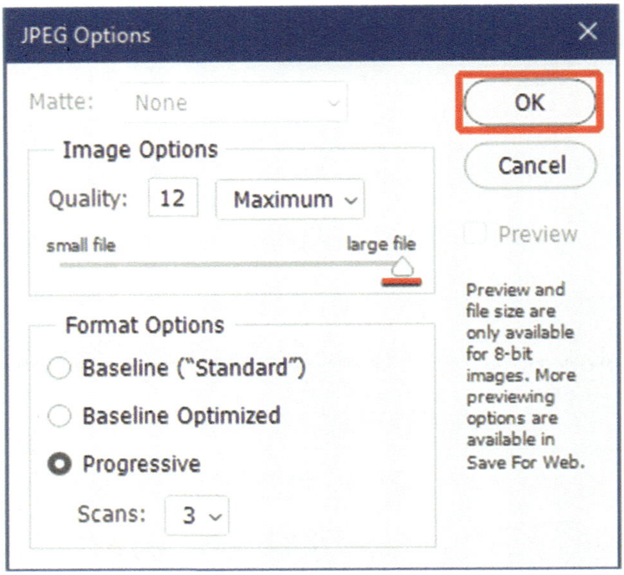

JPEG Options dialog

Final image

In the folder, there are three different PSD files showcasing each phase of the process and the final image (JPEG).

Below is the final result.

NOTE

There's also another version of this image in the folder named Another Version. A different Photoshop LUT file was used (C-8100-STD) with different Camera Raw Filter parameters.

Second version

Conclusion

This chapter has taken users through the unique journey of turning a basic render into a full marketing visual.

The process began by using render elements and Photoshop adjustment layers to control the overall image.

It followed by using render elements such as VRaySpecular, RawReflection, and others, to help bring to life specific objects and elements in the scene.

Finally, users were introduced to key Photoshop filters such as Camera Raw and chromatic aberration techniques to make the overall image more appealing and photorealistic.

10

Pre-Production

10 Pre-Production

Client Brief

For this night shot, the main brief was to highlight the effects of the artificial lights around the grass areas, foreground, inside the main building, and around it.

In addition, a lot of emphasis was put on the overall image to be inviting, atmospheric, and with a lot of spark.

Photo References and/or Mood Board

The images below depict two of many photo references presented to the client.

Lighting/Color Suggestions

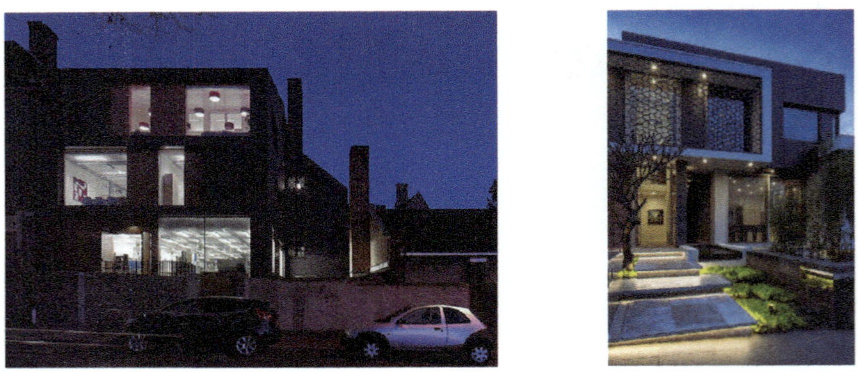

Photo references for lighting and color

Conclusion

While this pre-production stage was notably more straightforward than the previous one, it was equally important to go through the process of selecting the best possible photo references related to the camera shot and the scene composition.

Furthermore, the photo references had to reflect the time of the day requested by the client (night).

11

Lighting and Rendering

11 Lighting and Rendering

Introduction

Lighting an exterior night scene can be challenging at times, especially when dealing with multiple light sources and colors to achieve a nice and balanced scene.

The following tutorial will help users to quickly set up and light an exterior night scene, while using industry-standard techniques and some new ones with V-Ray 5 and LightMix.

Getting Started

Let's start by opening the 3ds max scene under the name of External Night scene_Start.max.

As you can see, the scene still has the sunlight from the daylight scene.

Also, as you open the Render Setup dialog (F10), under VRay tab, the Frame Buffer rollout file outputs are disabled and the Noise threshold is set to 0.01.

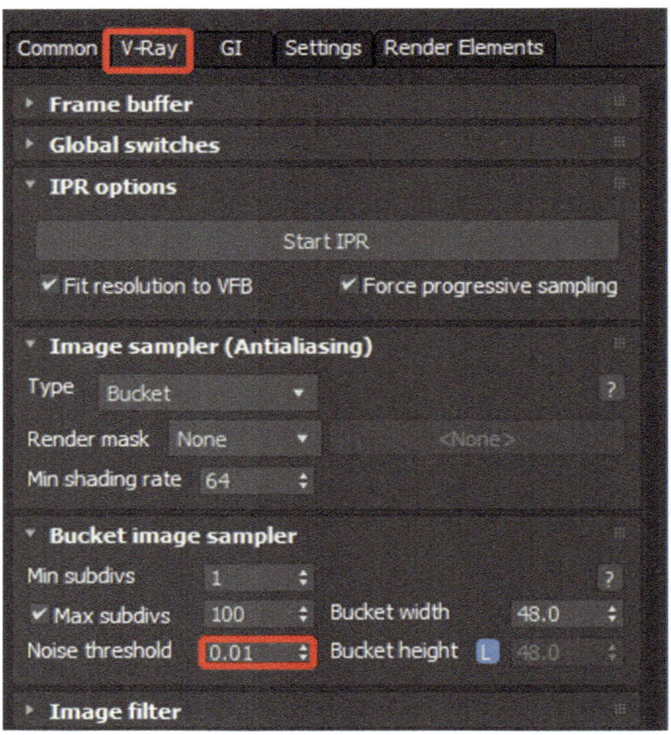

Default scene settings

Finally, the VFB dialog has a Layer tree preset loaded under the name of External Night scene Start.vfbl, and the render elements are the same as previously added in Chapter 8.

Lighting

To set the mood of the scene, in the Front viewport, select the VRaySun001 head and move it down to the ground level. Set its position to X = .133 mm, Y = 108894.687 mm, and Z = 233.769 mm.

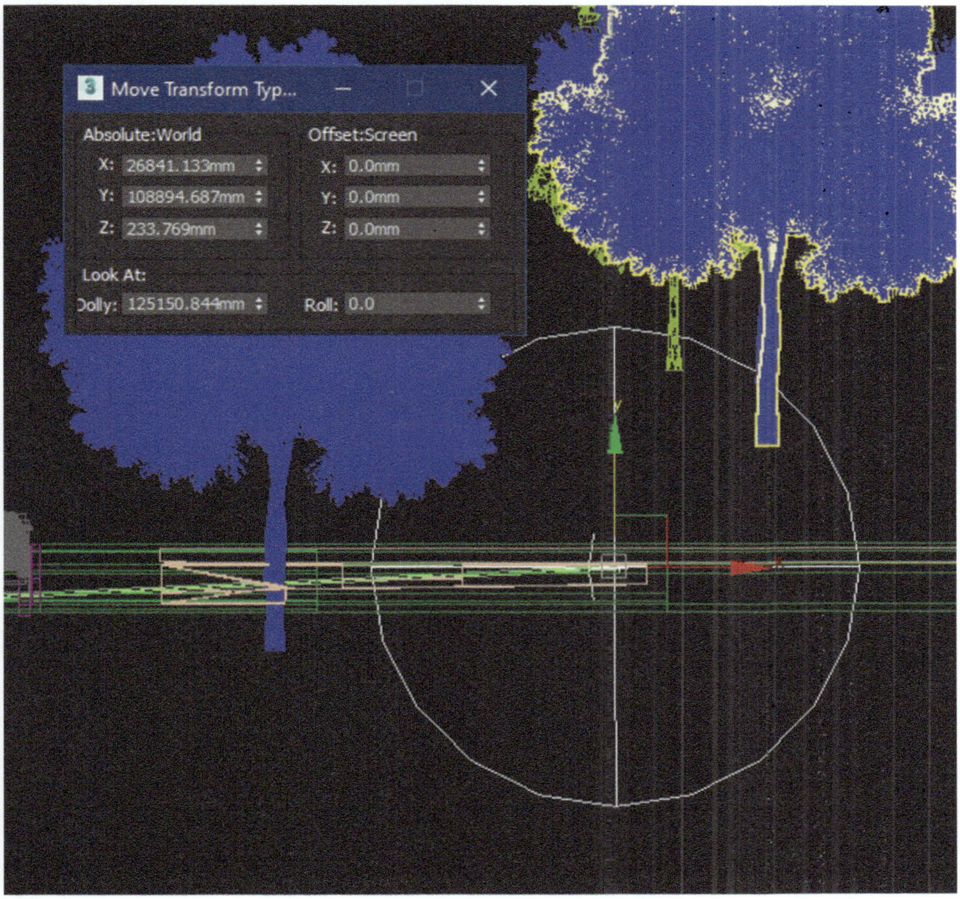

Sun position

Click the Start IPR button for a quick progressive test render.

NOTE

Even though the Image sampler type is set to Bucket, the Start IPR button forces the VFB dialog to automatically render Progressively, without visibly changing the Image sampler rollout.

With the Sky model previously set to Improved, the sky and shadows should look quite appealing.

Start IPR button

To create the first artificial light, open the light panel. Under VRay, choose the VRayLight object.

In the Top viewport, click and drag to create the VRayLight.

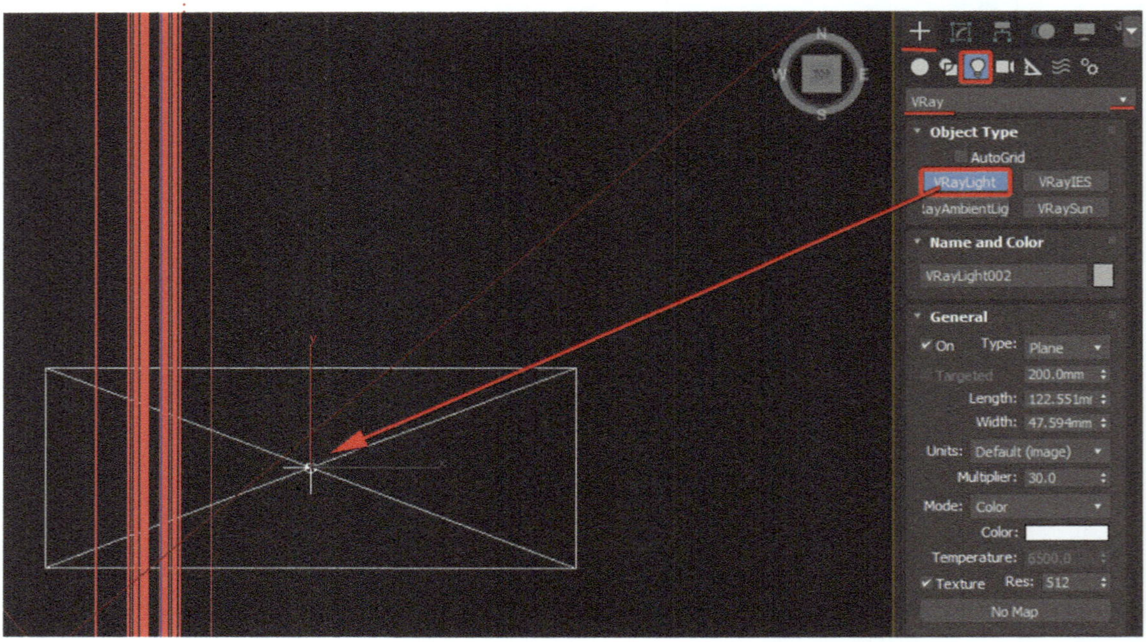

Click and drag to create the VRayLight

While the light is selected, open the Modify panel. Under General parameters, change the light Type to Disc.

Under Radius, set it to about 132.431 mm.

Next, change its default color to yellow (31,183,248).

Also, ensure the light is visible to the camera.

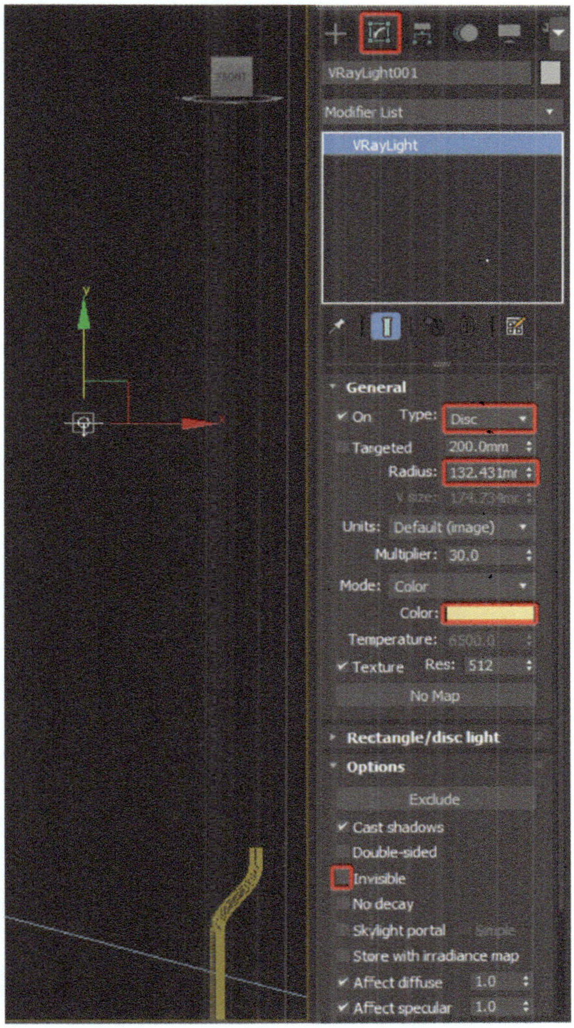

Change light Type to Disc

Following that, move the light inside the first-floor window, next to the sofas.

It's position should be X = –1574.503 mm, Y = –18360.58 mm, and Z = 7905.435 mm.

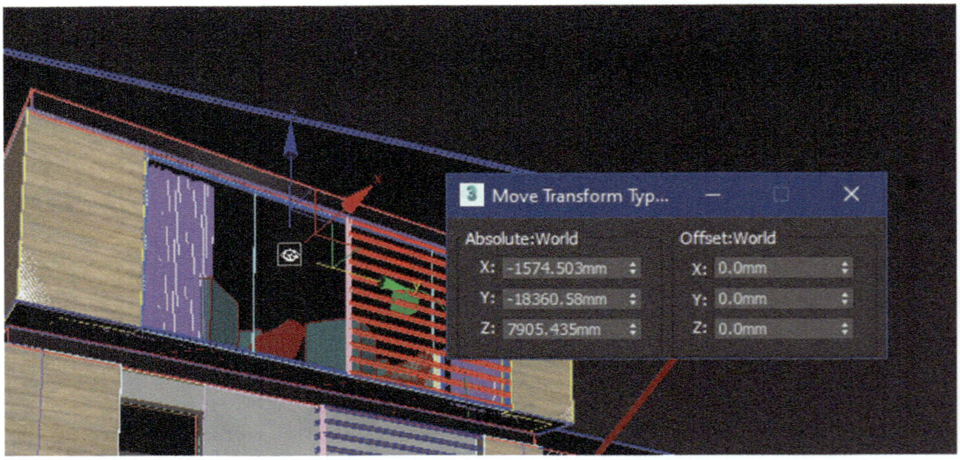

Move the light inside the first floor

Copy instance light (Ctrl+V) and move it further in. It's position should be X = −3104.369 mm,

Y = −18742.895 mm, and Z = 7905.435 mm.

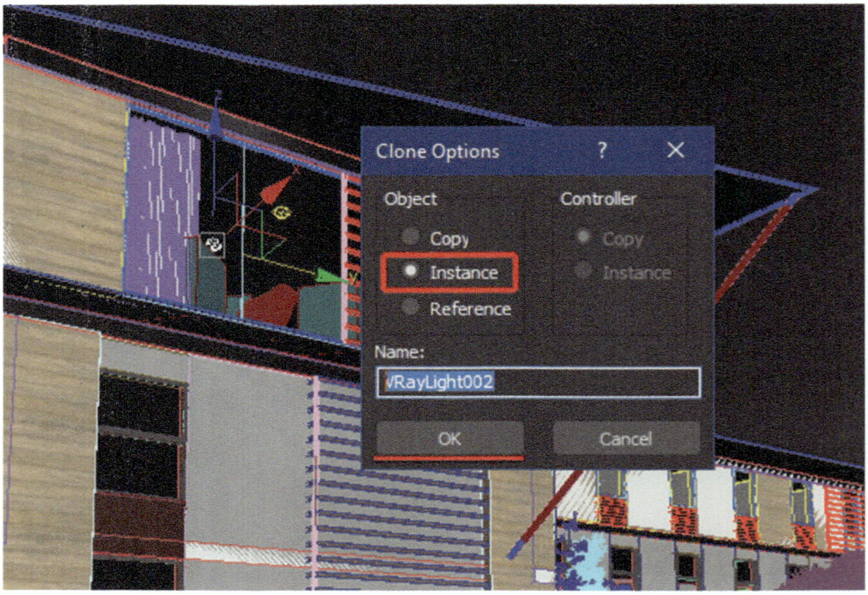

Copy instance light

Copy another instance light and place it below the top window. As mentioned earlier, instanced lights are much faster to compute and render than otherwise.

Copy another instance light

Copy few more instanced disc lights across the windows facing the camera directly.

If you decide to merge the disc lights in the scene, before you do so, ensure to delete all disc lights created thus far (to prevent doubling the number of disc lights in the scene).

Use the IPR to check the progress.

NOTE

To check the final position of all disc lights in the scene, merge or open the 3ds max scene named Disc lights only .max.

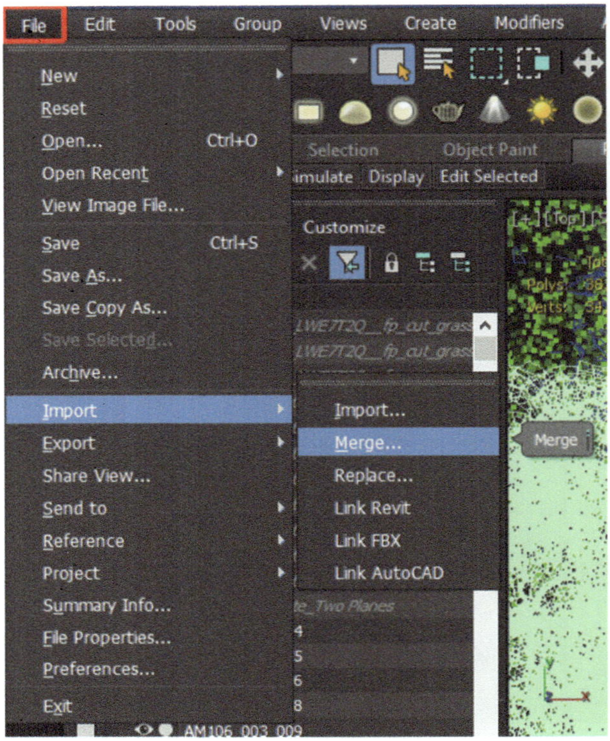

File Merge

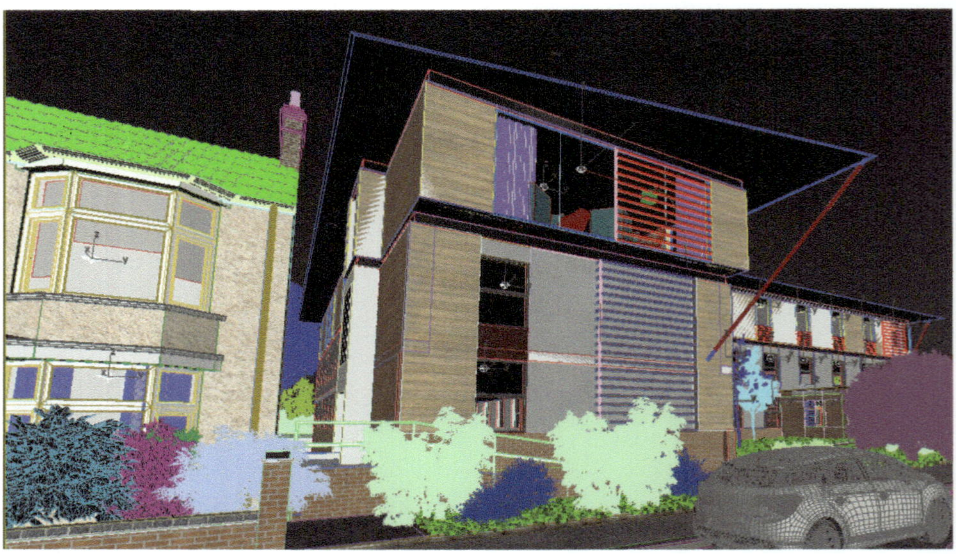

19 Instanced disc lights in the scene

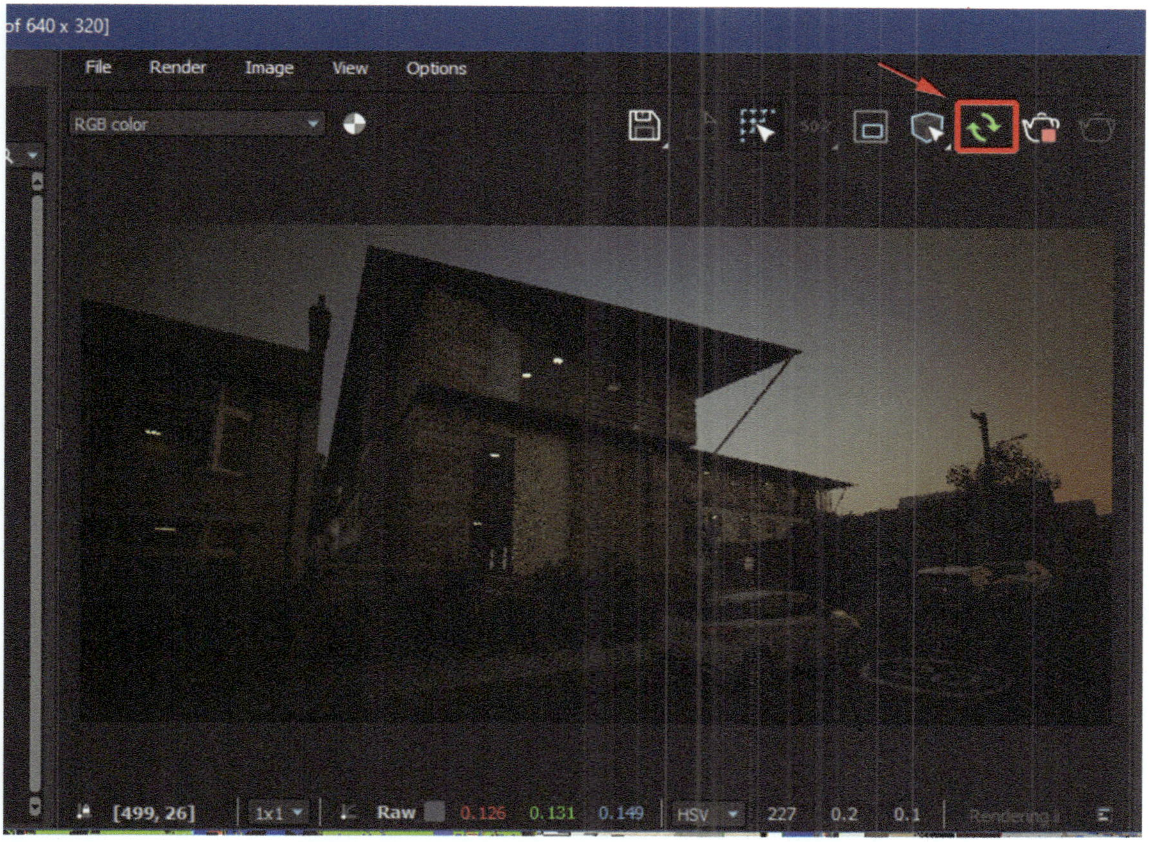

IPR in the VFB

The next step is to create VRay Plane lights along the grass, the main building, and foreground.

As previously done, go to the Lights panel and select the VRayLight button. Set its Length to 304.969 mm, the Width to 1001.018 mm.

Also, change its color to yellow (31,183,248) and make it invisible to the camera.

Next, click and drag to create it in the top viewport.

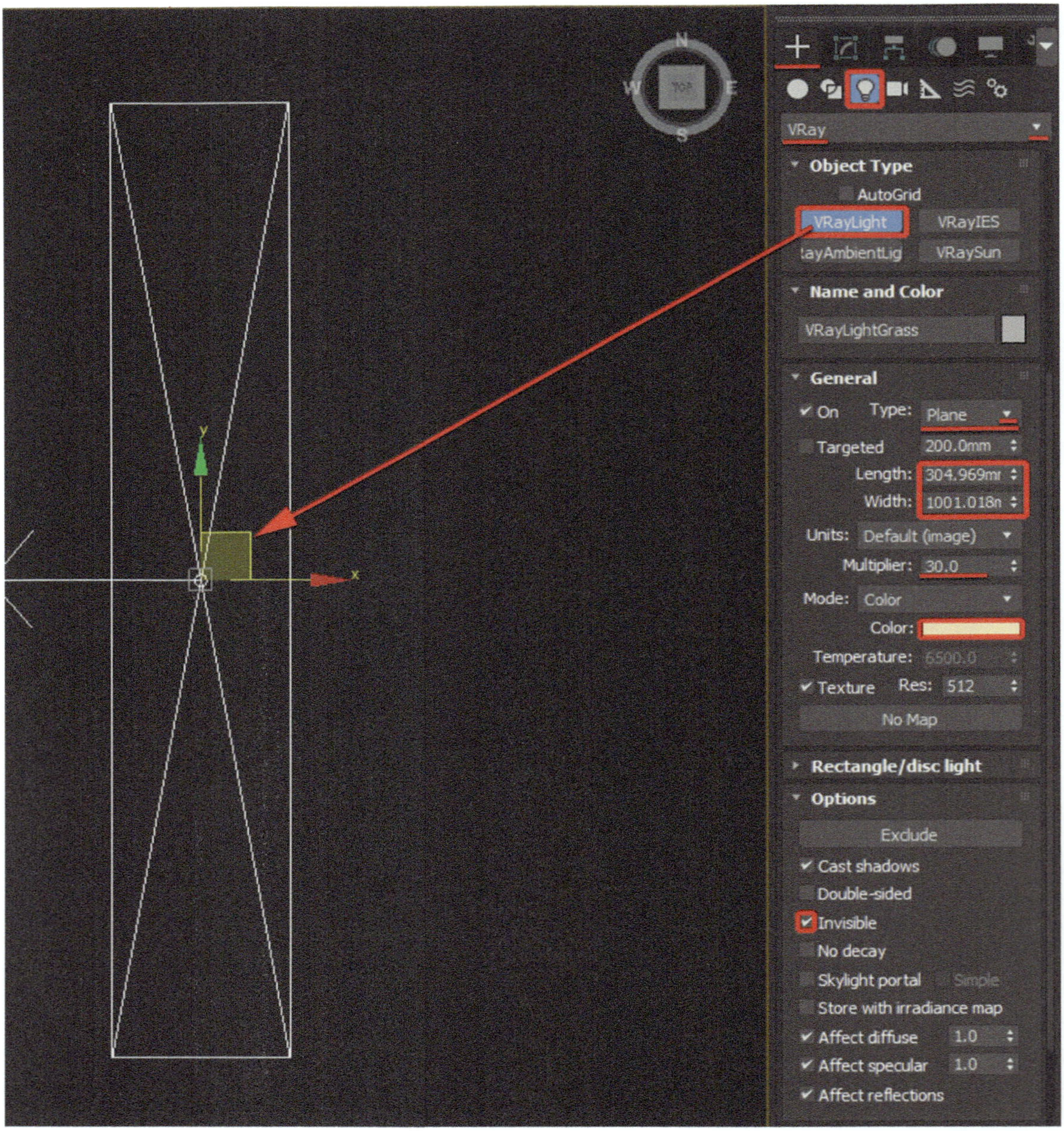

Create a VRay Plane light

The following step is to move the plane light down near the grass edge (X = 1813.959 mm, Y = –21744.816mm, and Z = –450.984 mm).

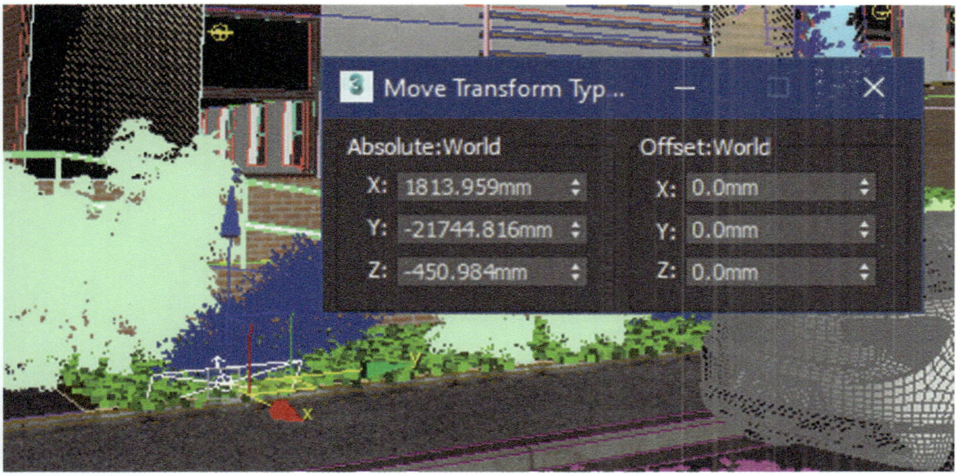

Move the light down

Also, rotate it in Y-axis (Y = 125.942).

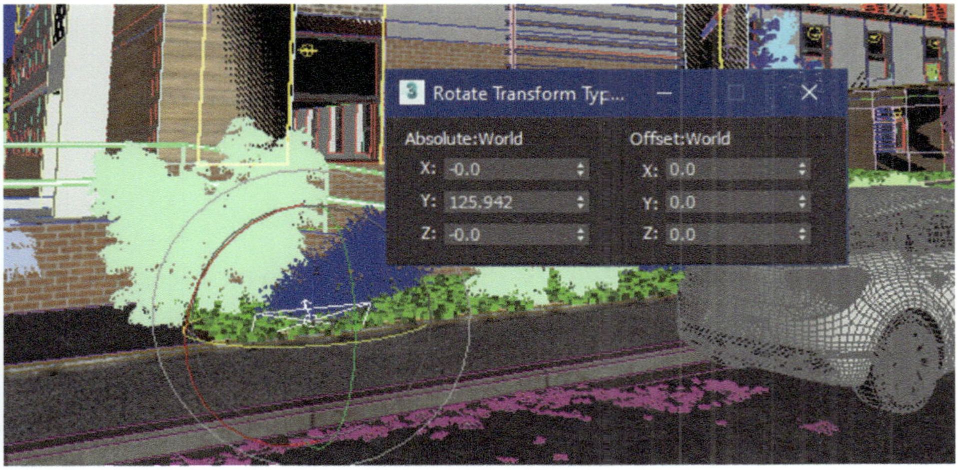

Rotate the Plane light

The next step is to copy few instance lights along the grass area. Also, copy instance lights along the ground of the main building and behind the plants of the left adjacent building.

Finally, copy instance lights and move few more plane lights to the foreground.

You may need to rotate and scale some of them with the scale toolbar.

Instanced plane lights

Select and Uniform Scale

NOTE

To check the final position of all instanced Plane lights in the scene, merge or open the 3ds max scene named Plane lights only.max.

If you decide to merge plane lights in the scene, before you do so, ensure to delete all plane lights created thus far (to prevent doubling the number of plane lights in the scene).

Use the IPR to check the final result in the VRay Frame Buffer dialog.

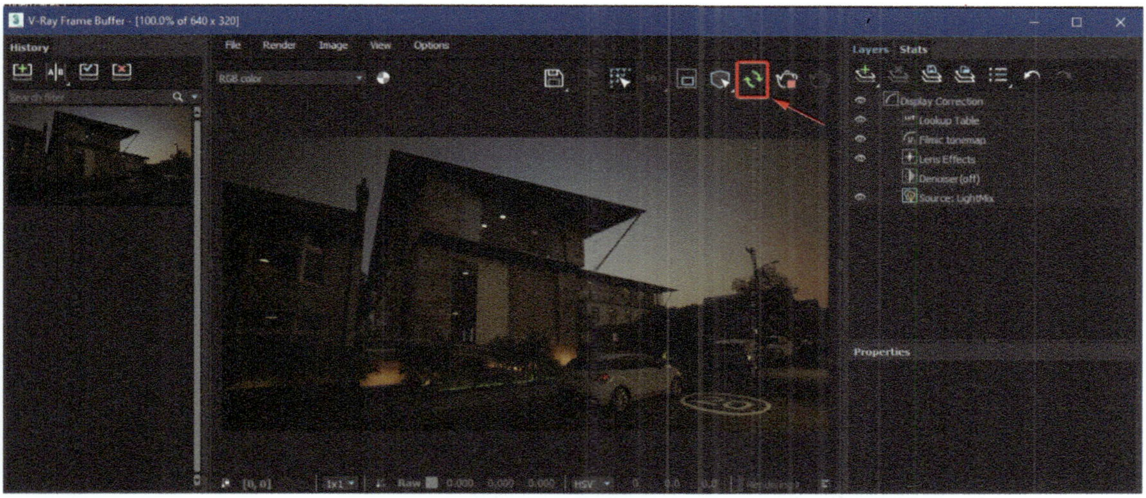

IPR in the VFB

To preview how the Lens Effects Layer will be affecting the overall render, let's tweak some of the LightMix values.

In the VFB Layers list, click on the LightMix layer to display the Properties.

Begin playing/tweaking with some of the light values listed under Properties.

As mentioned earlier, even though most of the lights in the scene are instances, LightMix enables users to tweak their color and values individually when the VRayLightMix render element is set as Individual lights.

After few tweaks with the LightMix, the following values and colors were changed:

VRayLight001: 3.000

VRayLight002: 2.000

VRayLight003: 5.000

VRayLight004: 4.000

VRayLight005: 2.000

VRayLight006: 0.500

VRayLight011: 2.780

VRayLight016: 8.000

VRayLight017: 4.435

VRayLight019: 5.890

VRayLightGrass: 0.500

VRayLightGrass007: 3.000

VRayLightGrass008: 0.500

VRayLightGrass009: 1.475

VRayLightGrass010: 1.275

Etc.

To check the final LightMix result with all values tweaked, simply go to the Load layer tree preset and open the vfbl file named External Night scene Finished.vfbl.

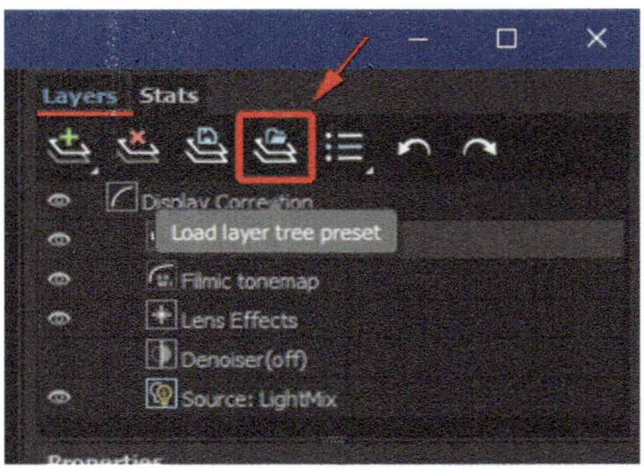

Load layer tree preset button

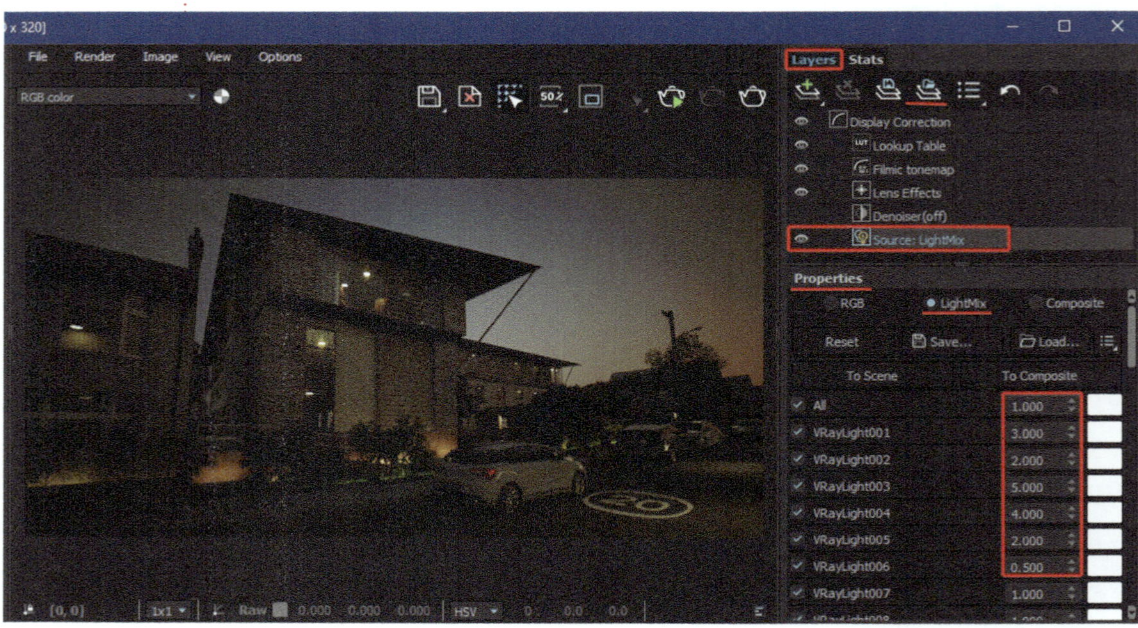

LightMix values tweaked

As you will notice, increasing the LightMix values of the visible light sources behind the glass will generate few speckles in the render.

This is mostly to do with the current render settings being progressive/draft and some of the lights being behind a glass.

Setting Up for Final Render

Open the Render Setup dialog (F10). In the VRay tab, under Frame buffer rollout, enable the VRay raw image file and set its location and name as previously done.

Choose a new folder location and name the files differently (External Night scene Final).

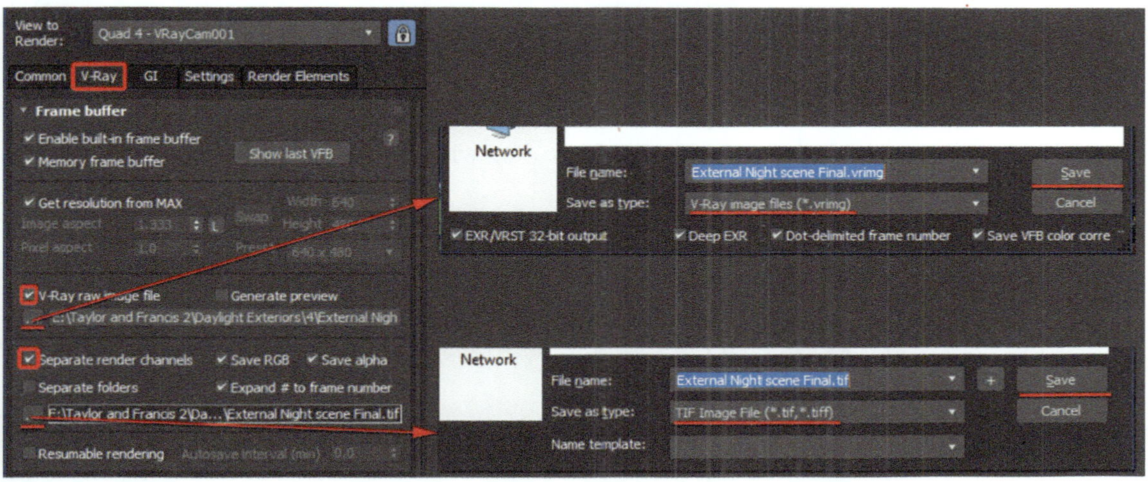

Enable VRay raw image file and separate render channels

Under Bucket image sampler, increase the Min subdivs values to 4 to reduce the light speckles.

Also, to improve the overall quality of the render, decrease the noise threshold to about 0.008.

Finally, click to Render (Shift+Q).

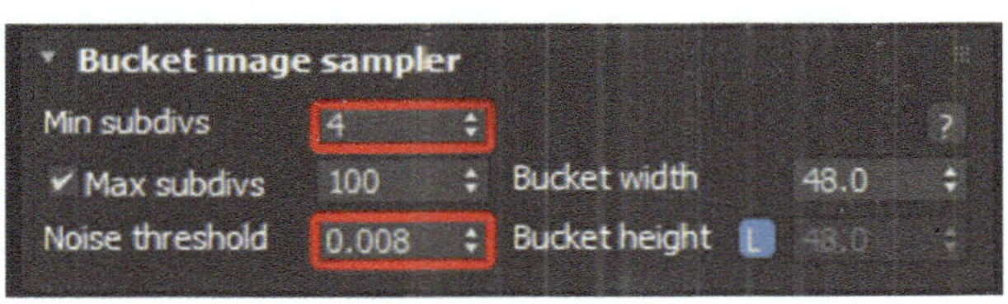

Change Bucket image sampler values

NOTE

Increasing the Min subdivs values will increase the render times slightly.

The final result of this 3ds max file is under the name External Night scene_Final .max.

To see the final render result in the VFB dialog, load the vrimg file named External Night scene Final.0000.vrimg.

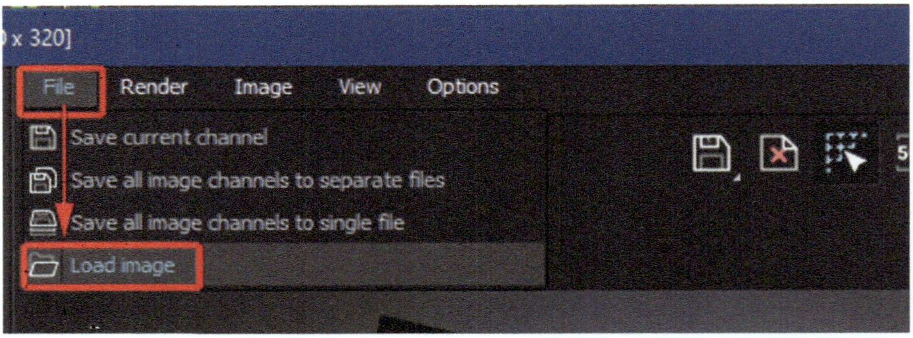

Load image in VFB dialog

The high-resolution file should load up with all its render elements previously saved.

VRay Image file loaded in the VFB

Final Render with LightMix Filter

The following step is to open a photo reference image in the scene and use it as guide to transform the final render with the LightMix Layer Properties.

First, go to file and choose to View Image File. Open the image under the name of Photo Reference.jpg.

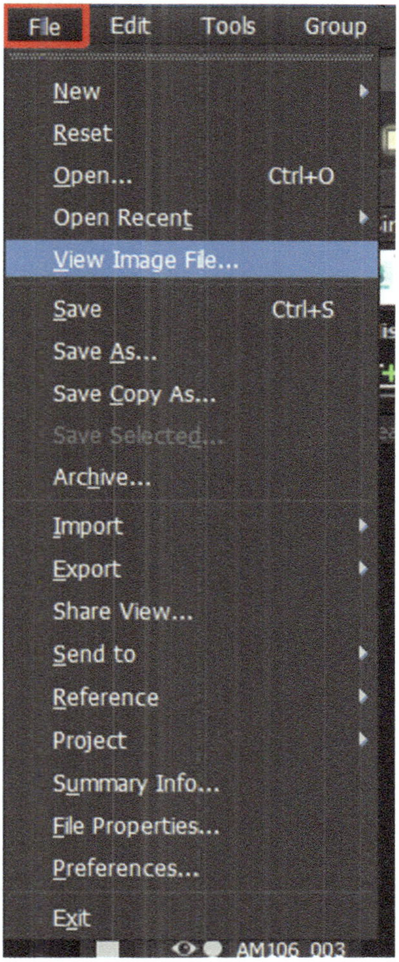

View Image File

Photo Reference.jpg

To start, select the LightMix Layer and scroll down to the Properties list. In the Environment light, increase it to about 3.000.

Also, reduce the size of the photo reference image, by hovering over its corner angles and clicking/pulling to reduce the size.

To match the Environment light to the blue tones of the photo reference, click on its color swatch to open the Select Color dialog.

To sample the color, click on the Pick Screen Color button and select the top part of the photo.

If perchance the color isn't looking exactly as expected, type in the color values (240, 255, 255), and OK to close the dialog.

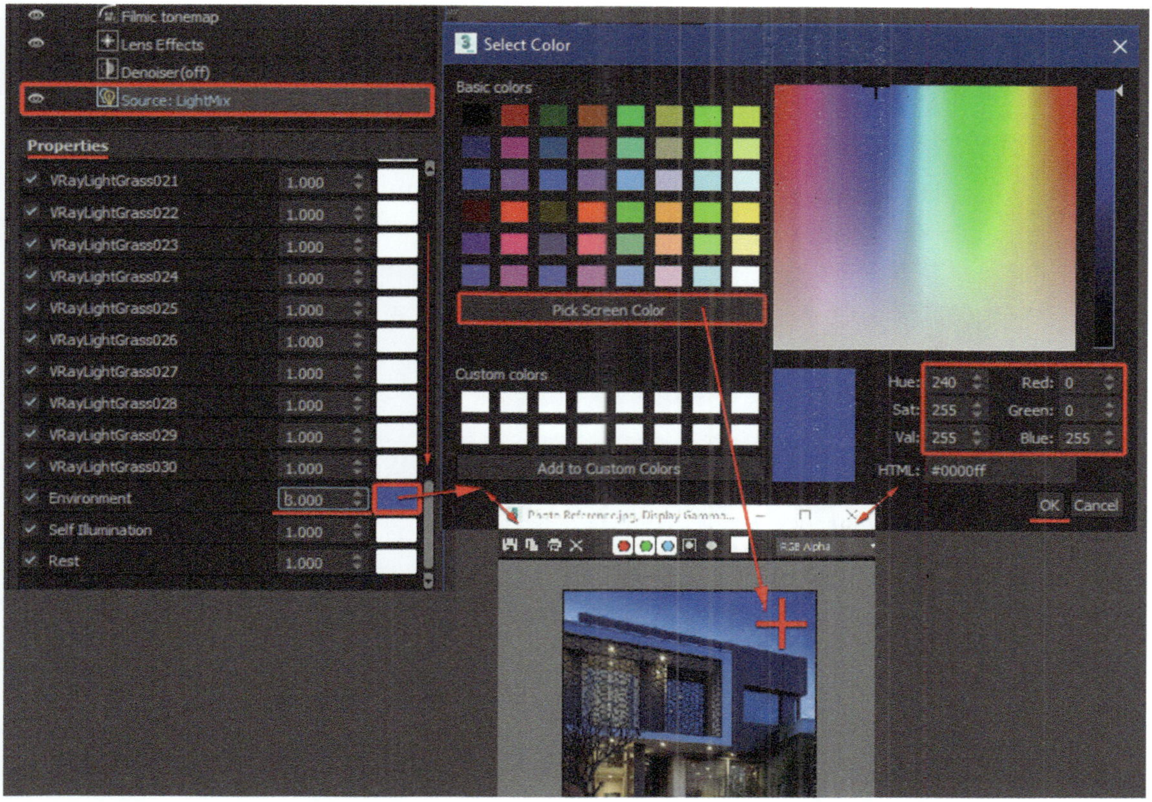

LightMix and Color values

Result in the VFB dialog

Next, decrease the Rest light value to about 0.700 and increase the Self-Illumination value to about 1.450.

Also, increase the VRayLightGrass030 to 1.995 and the VRayLightGrass029 to 1.675.

Furthermore, select the VRayLightGrass028 and increase it to 1.300. Change its color swatch to yellow (60,128,255) to match with the photo reference.

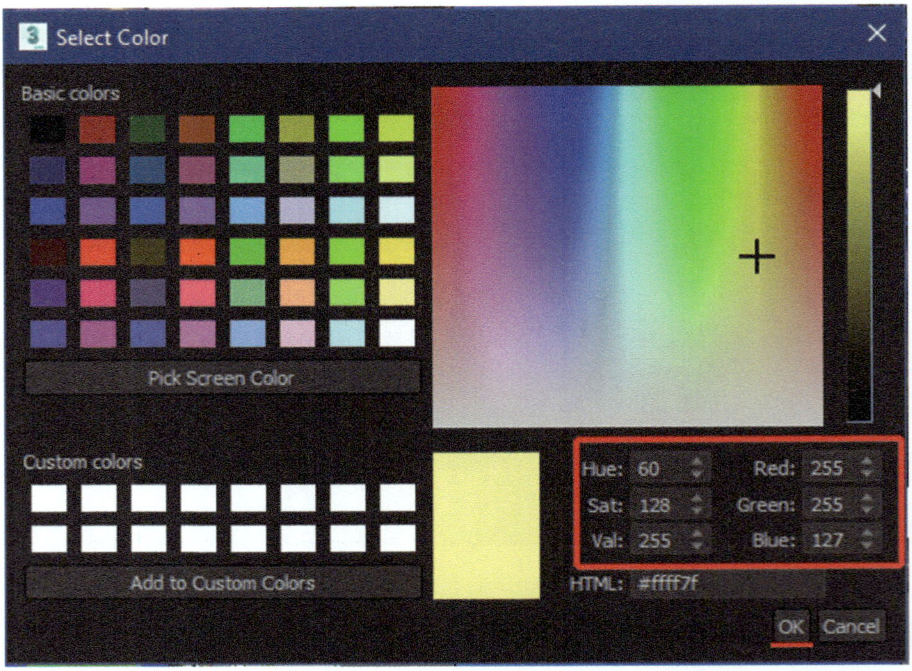

Yellow color values

The overall render should begin to look closer to the photo reference.

After few more tweaks, the following changes were made:

VRayLightGrass027: Increased to 1.280

VRayLightGrass026: Increased to 1.755

VRayLightGrass025: Increased to 2.000

VRayLightGrass024: Increased it 3.000

VRayLightGrass023: Increased 3.430

VRayLightGrass022: Increased to 1.500 and color changed to yellow

VRayLightGrass021: Decreased to 0.700

Etc.

To see the final result with LightMix values and colors tweaked, go to the Load layer tree preset and open the vfbl file under the name of External Night scene Final.vfbl.

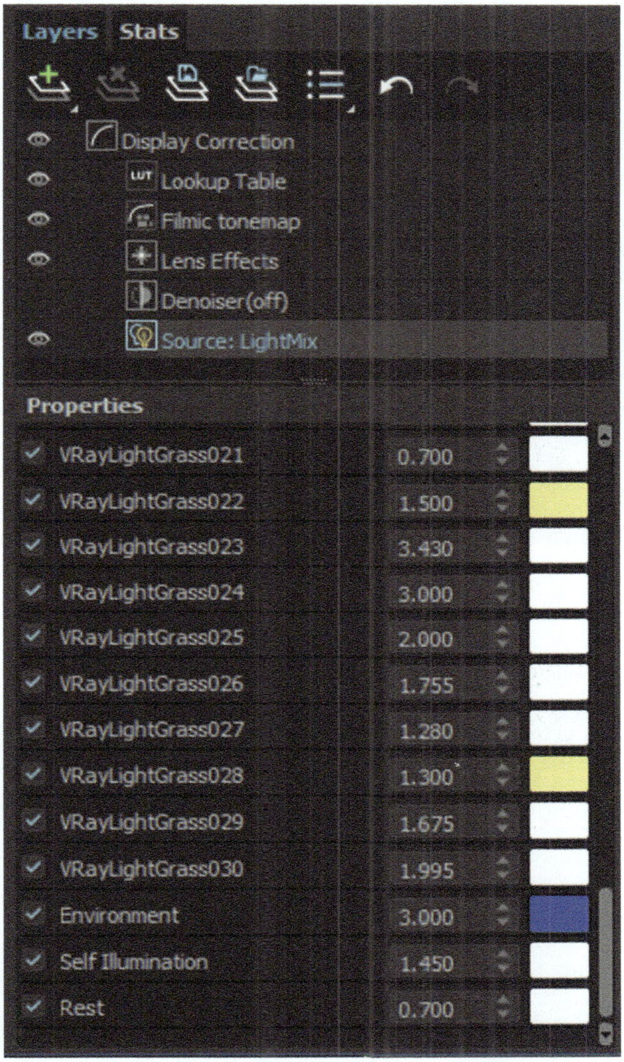

LightMix colors and values

NOTE

The LightMix values and colors used here worked well for this render. However, feel free to try different values and colors, if desired.

Final result

Finally, to save this bluer version of the render separately, in the VFB dialog, go to File and choose Save all image channels to separate files.

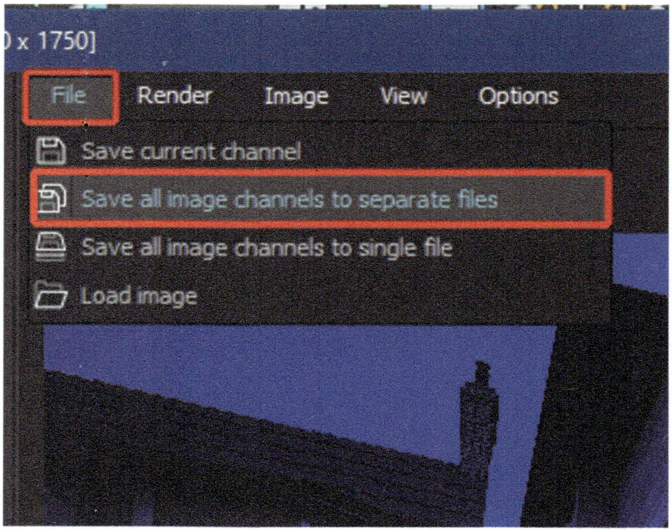

Save all image channels to separate files

Create a new folder.

Create a New Folder

Setup the TIF options and file name.

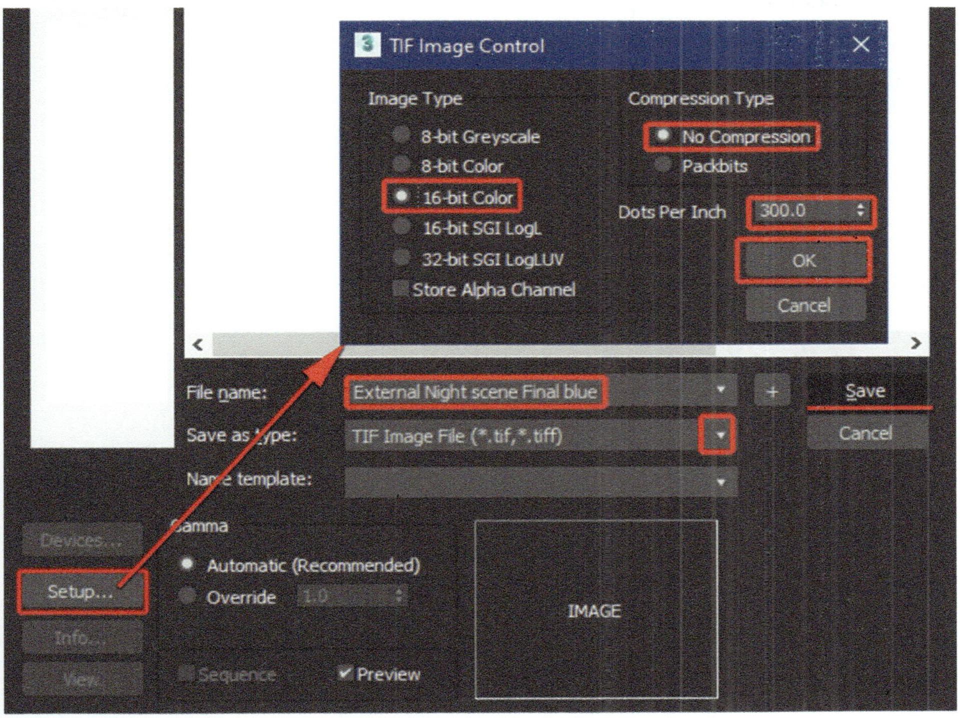

Set up and Save the File as TIF

All channels should be automatically saved in a list.

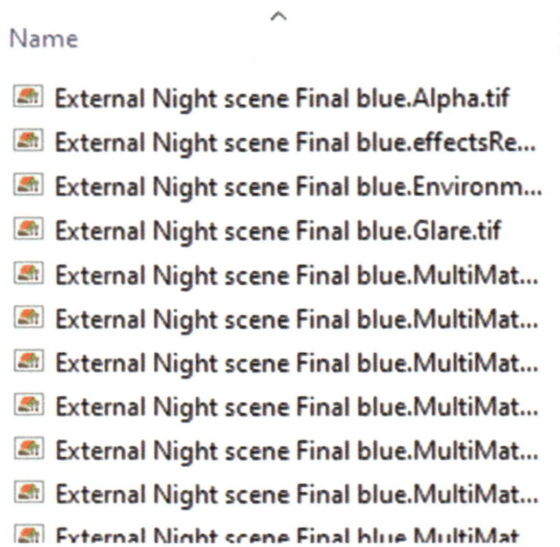

Channels automatically saved in the folder

Conclusion

This chapter has depicted the importance of using the Improved sky model type to display appealing skies.

A lot of emphasis was put on the process of creating specific light types such as Discs and Planes.

Also, using a photo reference as guide has helped to finalize the light colors, positions, and values throughout the scene.

Furthermore, users learnt to use the Start IPR button and the VFB to kick start successive progressive test renders automatically, even when the Image sampler is set to Bucket.

Finally, users were taken through the fascinating process of using the LightMix properties to make key fundamental changes to light values and colors in order to transform the render in the VRay Frame Buffer dialog.

12

Post-Production

12 Post-Production

Introduction

This last step of the production will take users through the process of putting together all the elements previously rendered to enhance the overall image and material details.

During this process, users will also deploy some of the techniques previously covered in Chapter 9 to achieve the final result.

Post-Production

Let's start by using the Load Files into Stack script to select and load the rendered elements on a stack.

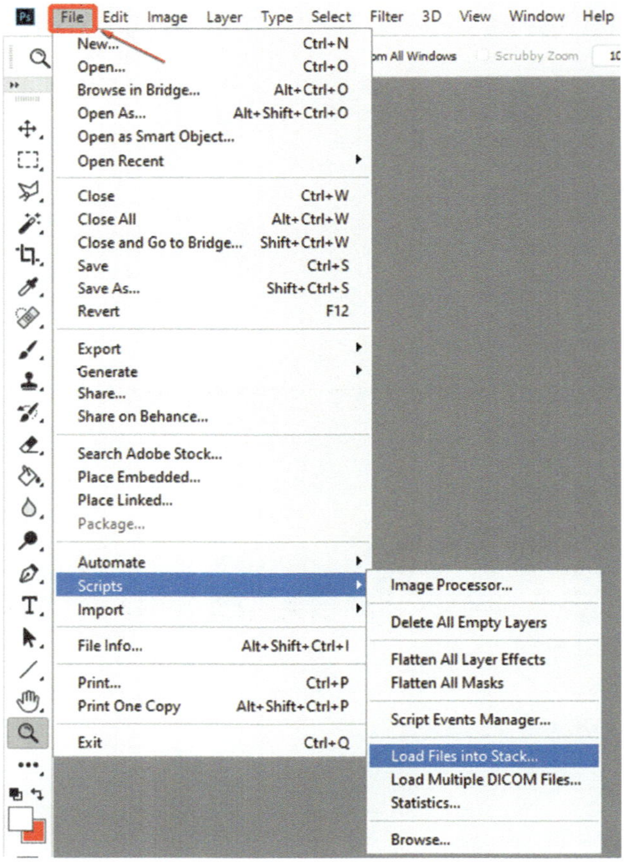

Choose the Load Files into Stack

In the Load Layers dialog, click on the Browse toggle to locate the files inside the folder named Render Elements Blue.

Select all the prerendered elements by selecting the first file, scrolling down, holding down the Shift key, and selecting the last one on the list. All files should be selected.

Click Open to load the files/layers.

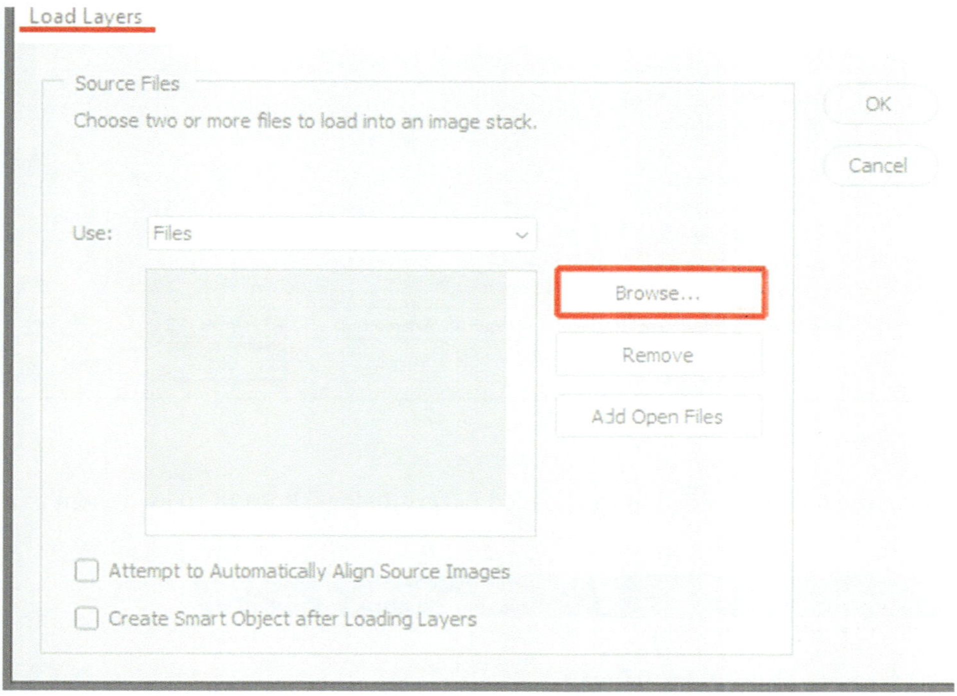

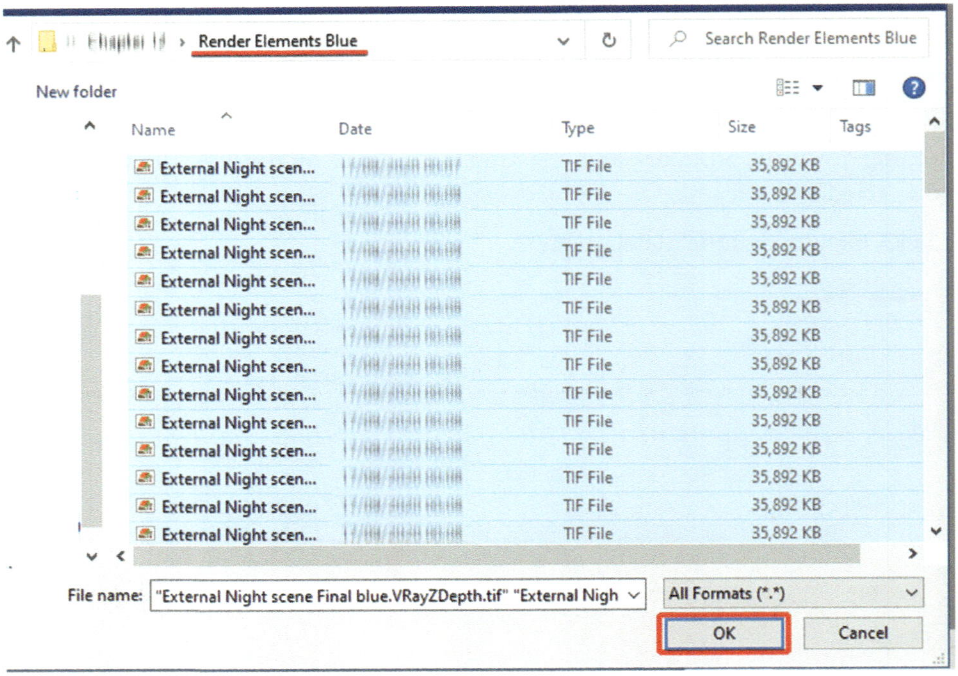

Select Layers

Once the files are loaded in the Loaded Layers dialog, click OK to load them in a stack.

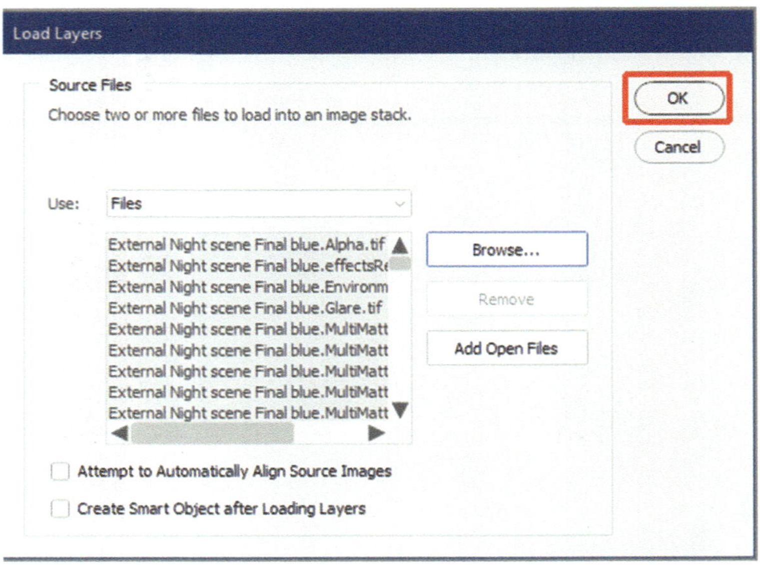

Click OK to load files

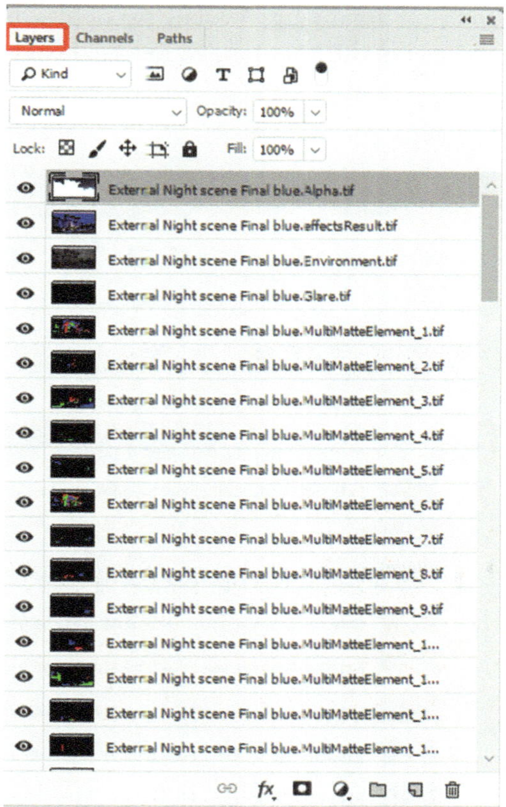

Layers loaded

To begin organizing the long list of files, hold down the Alt key and click on the eye icon of the layer named External Night scene Final blue.effectsResult.tif.

All but this layer visibility should be turned off. This is the pass with the LightMix effects applied.

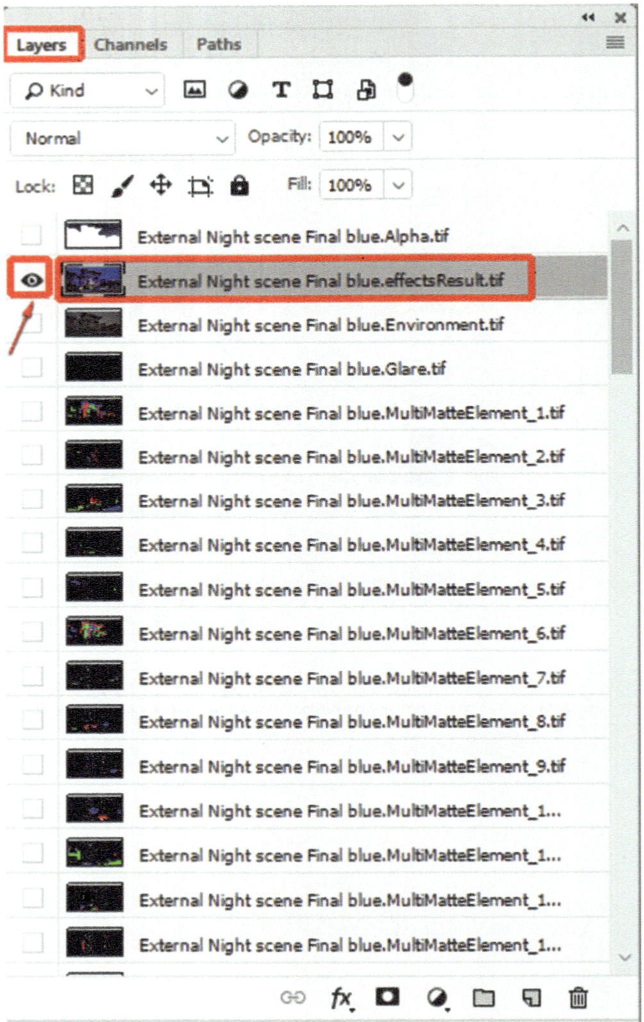

Turn off layer visibility of all but one layer

Next, select and move the layer to the bottom of the list. As mentioned earlier, it's good practice to always keep the main layer at the base of the list.

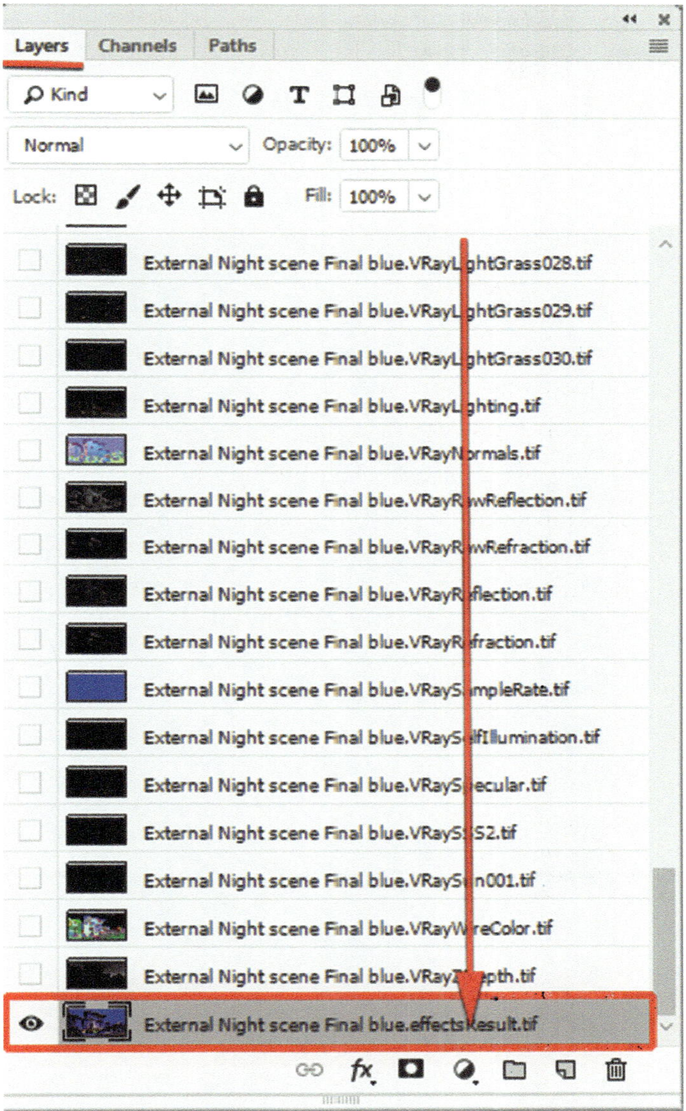

Select and move the layer to the bottom of the list

Following that, select the first invisible layer (at the bottom) and scroll up. Hold down the Shift key and select the top layer.

The entire list of layers should be selected now.

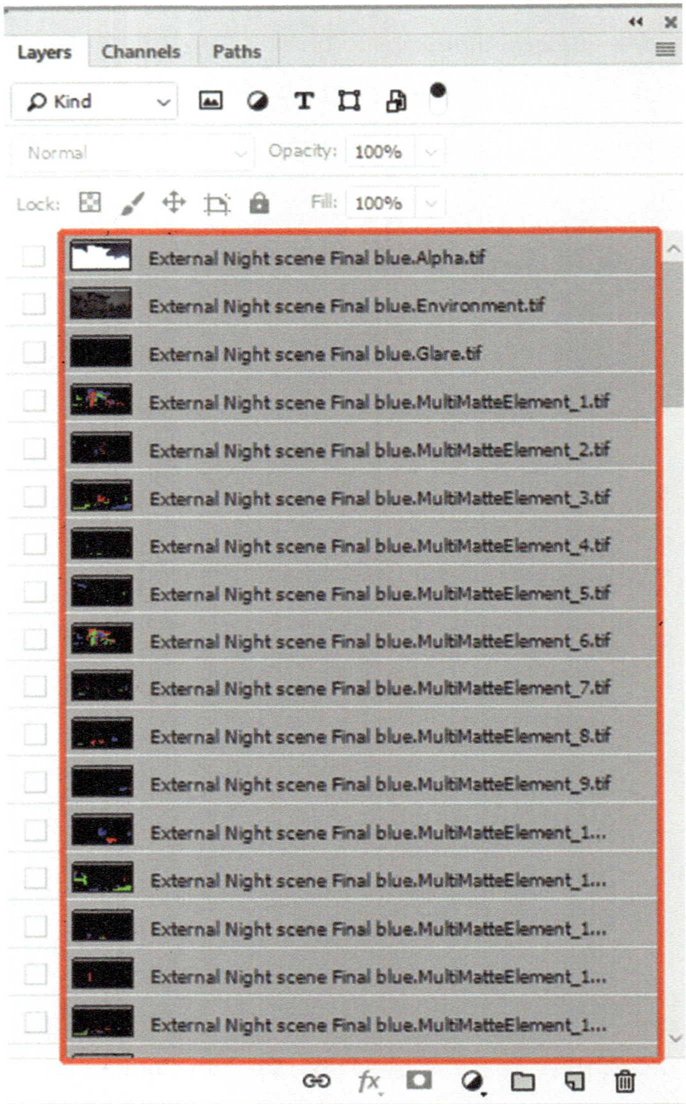

Layers selected

While the layers are still selected, click on the Group layer button to automatically move them to a group.

Alternatively, simply select layers individually and move them inside a group.

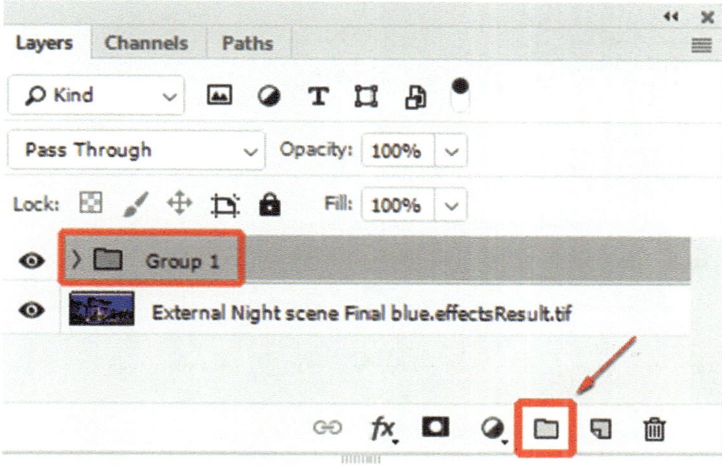

Create a Group with layers inside

Double click on the group name and rename it as =Render Elements=.

Renaming the group and adding = will make it easier to select layers inside this group, by right clicking in the document.

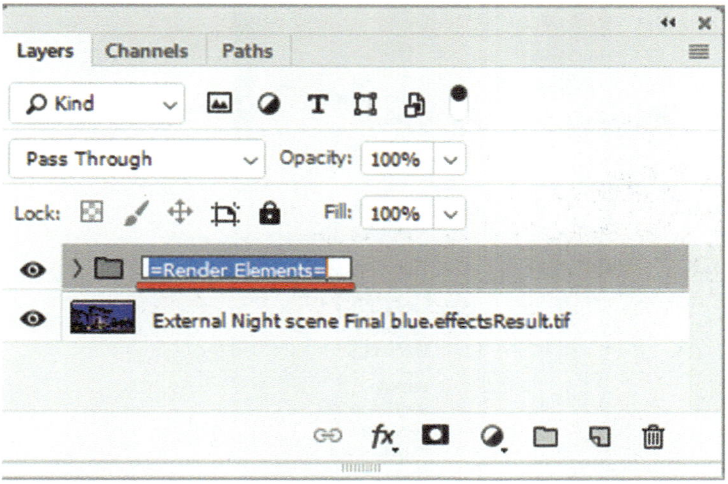

Renaming the group

Select the base layer, External Night scene Final blue.effectsResult.tif, and click to create a new Group. Name it as =Adjustments=.

This group will be used to add the overall adjustments.

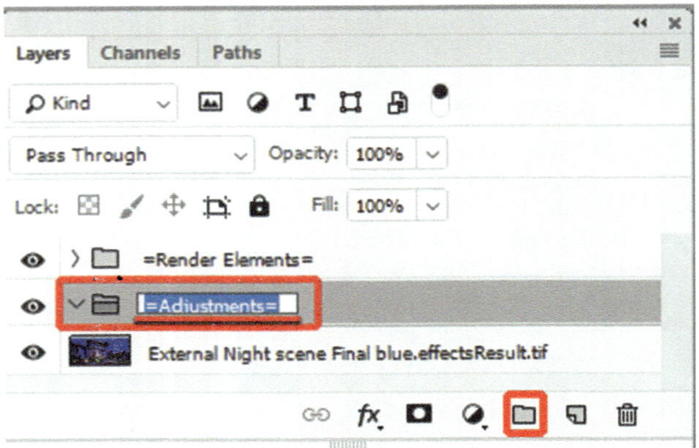

Create a new group and rename it

The following step is to click on the adjustment layer button and choosing the Color Lookup option.

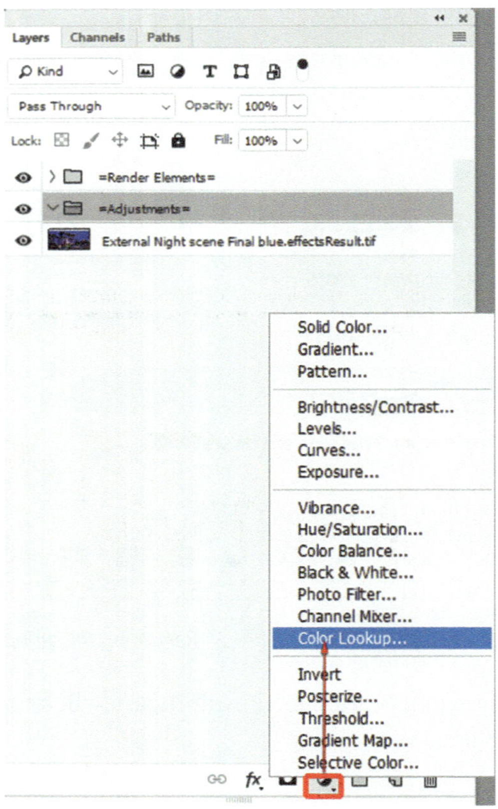

Choose the Color Lookup Adjustment layer

In the Color Lookup adjustment layer Properties, choose the 3DLUT File named, F-8870-STD.cube

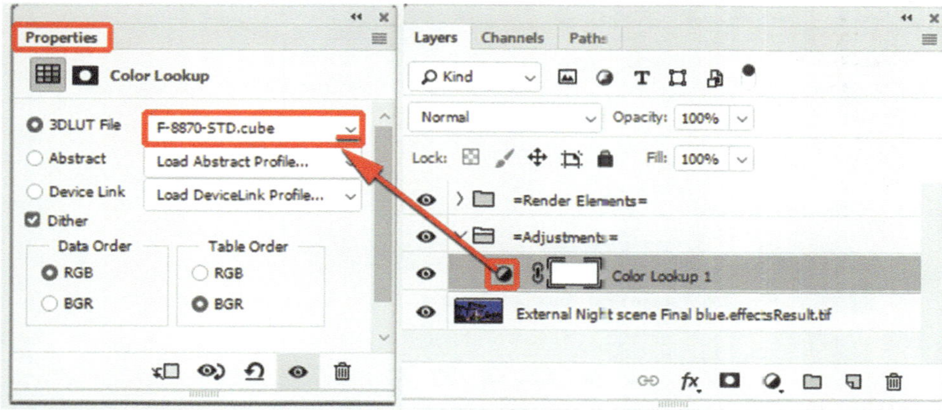

Choose the LUT F-8870-STD.cube

LUT result

Rename the LUT adjustment layer as F-8870-STD.cube. It's standard practice to always name layers accordingly.

NOTE

This LUT file is specific to Photoshop, and shouldn't be used in 3ds max.

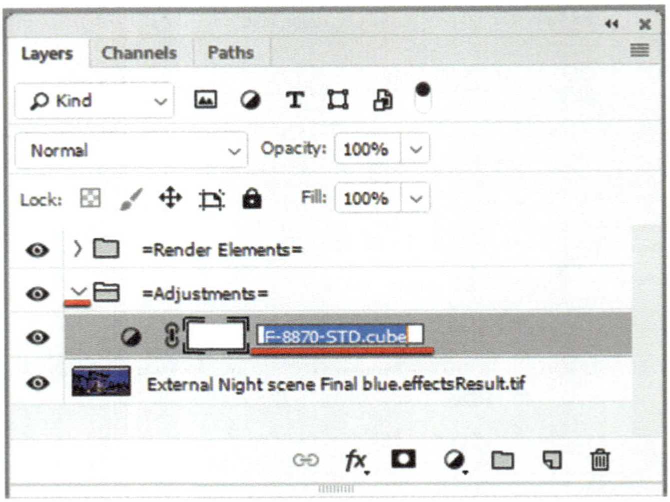

LUT adjustment layer renamed

Next, create a new group and name it =Lights=.

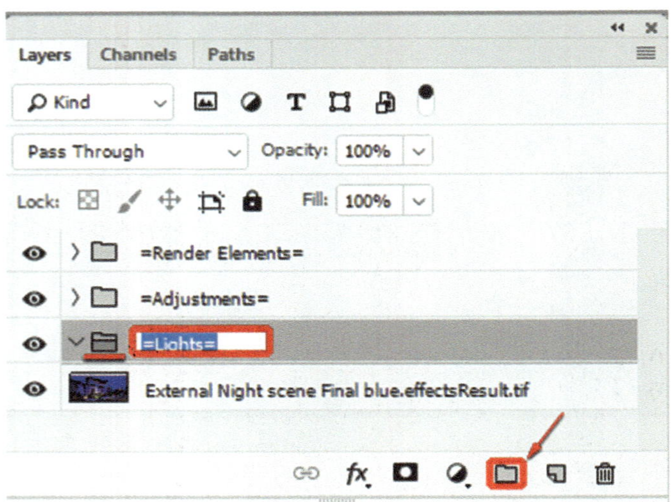

Create and rename a new Group

To enhance the light inside the window of the first floor, open the =Render Elements= group and select the layer named External Night scene Final blue. VRayLight001.tif.

Enable the visibility eye icon.

Also, change its blending mode to a Screen type. VRayLight passes work best with the Screen blending mode.

NOTE

In 3ds max, when renders are set to be saved in a location, VRayLight passes are automatically saved when the LightMix is added in the Render Element tab.

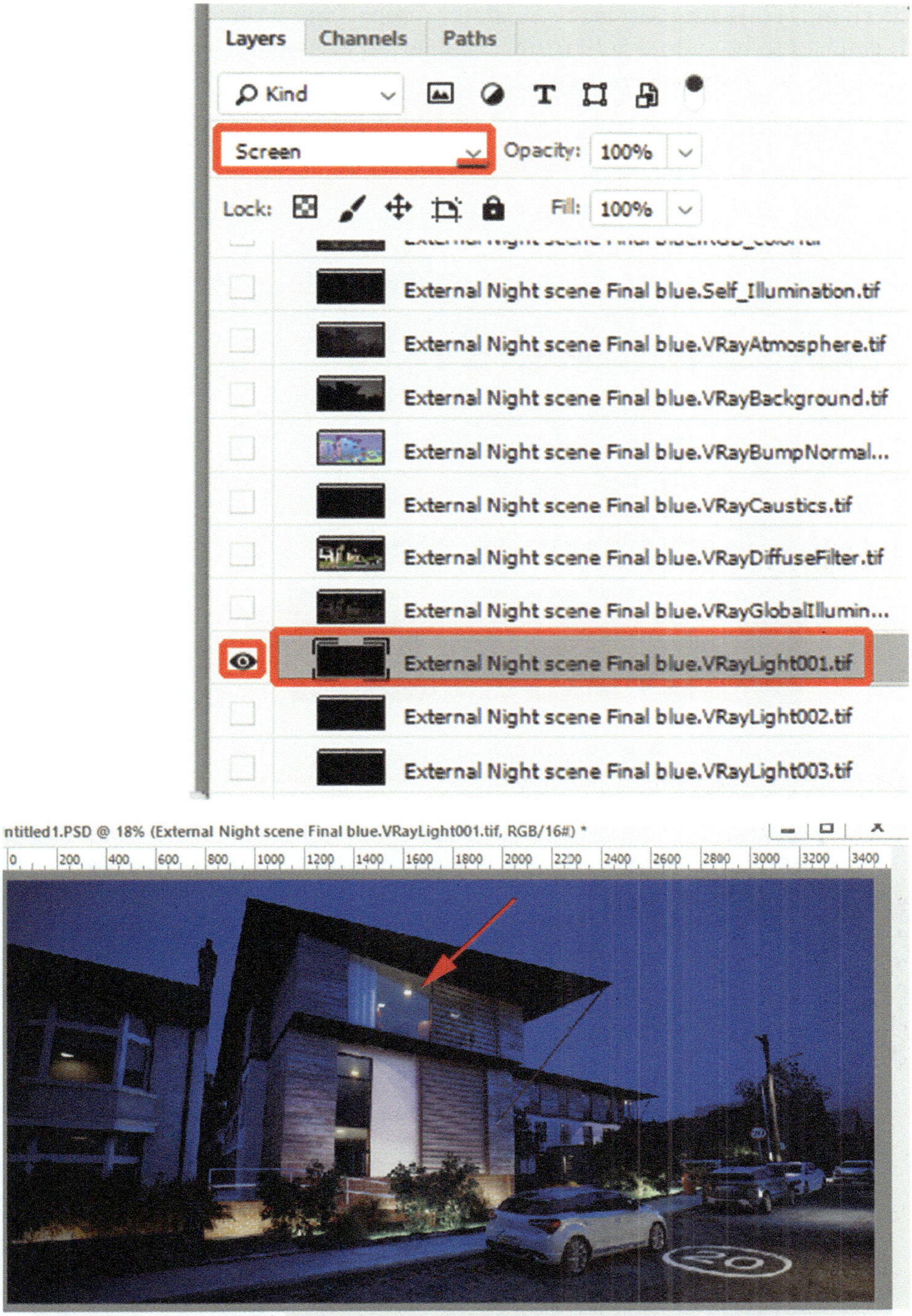
Layers
Channels
Paths
Kind
Screen
Opacity: 100%
Lock:
Fill: 100%
External Night scene Final blue.Self_Illumination.tif
External Night scene Final blue.VRayAtmosphere.tif
External Night scene Final blue.VRayBackground.tif
External Night scene Final blue.VRayBumpNormal...
External Night scene Final blue.VRayCaustics.tif
External Night scene Final blue.VRayDiffuseFilter.tif
External Night scene Final blue.VRayGlobalIllumin...
External Night scene Final blue.VRayLight001.tif
External Night scene Final blue.VRayLight002.tif
External Night scene Final blue.VRayLight003.tif
ntitled1.PSD @ 18% (External Night scene Final blue.VRayLight001.tif, RGB/16#) *

Enable the VRayLight layer

Next, move this layer inside the =Lights= group. If you wish to increase the lighting of the first floor even further, simply duplicate the layer and reduce the layer Opacity slightly.

The following step is to select the layer named External Night scene Final blue .VRayLight008.tif, and repeat the previous actions.

This VRayLight layer should illuminate some of the far-right windows of the main building.

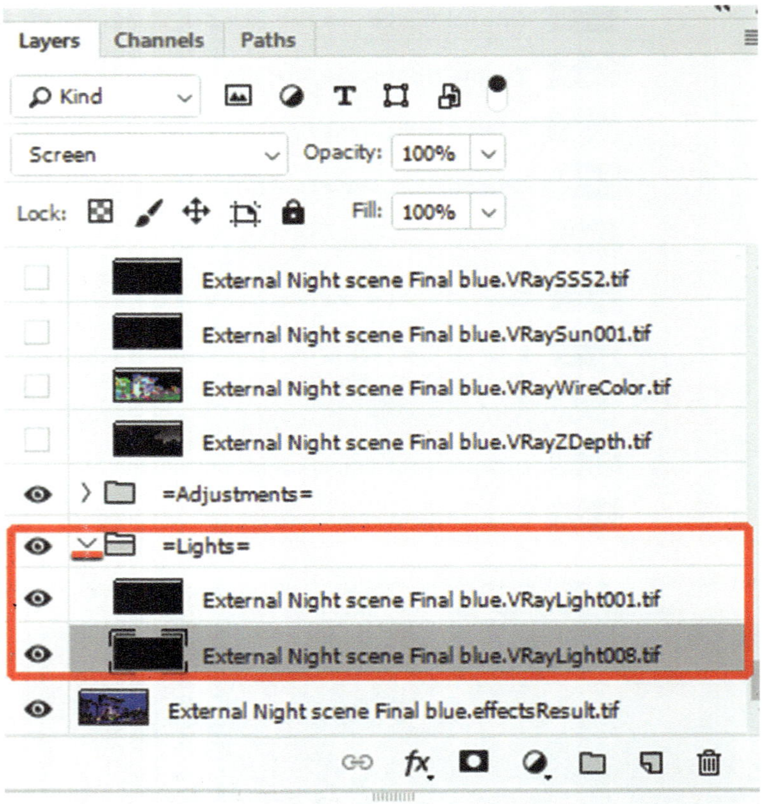

Far-right windows illuminated

The following step is to begin enhancing specific objects such as the roof, plants, and gutters.

As previously done, select and enable the visibility of the layer named External Night scene Final blue.MultiMatteElement_1.tif.

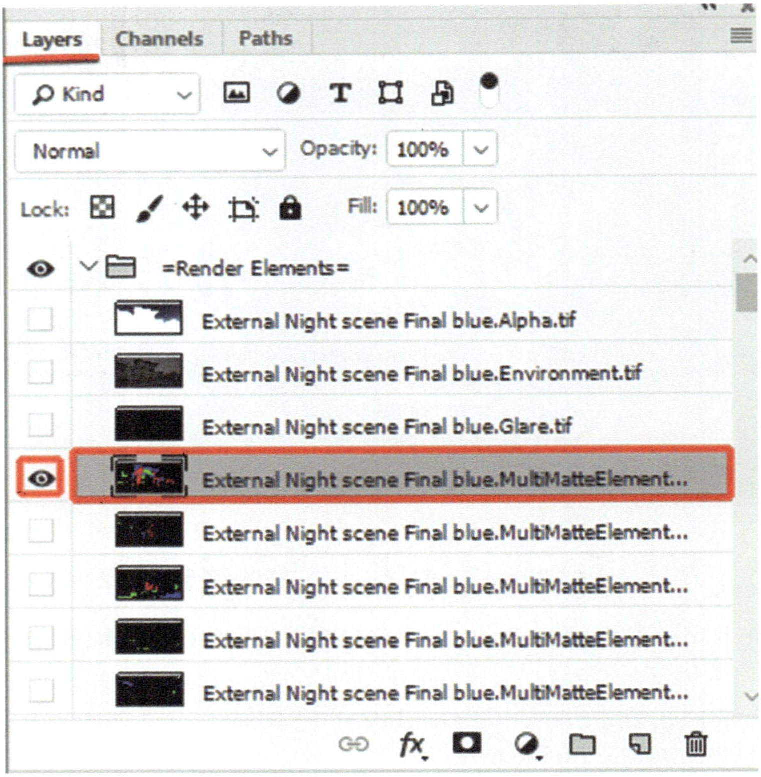

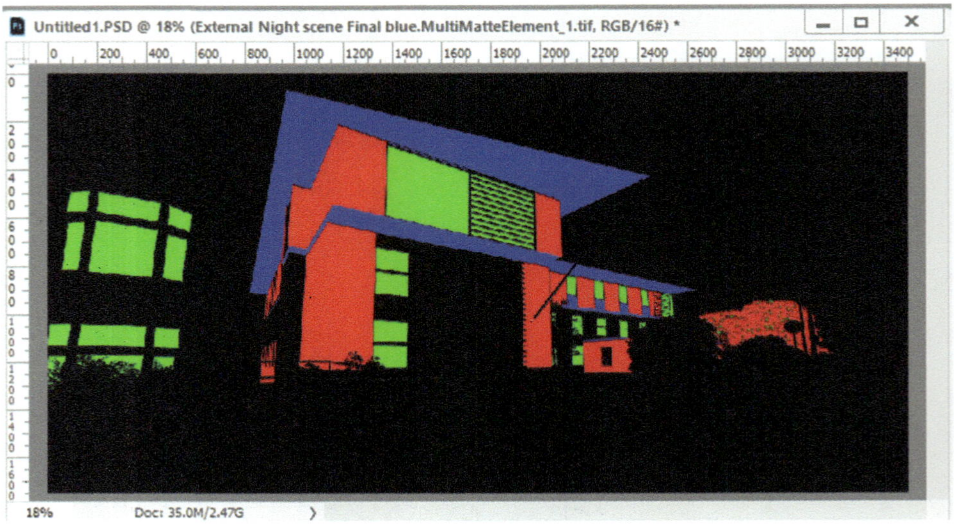

MultiMatteElement enabled

Next, go to the Channels tab. Hold down the Ctrl key and click on the Blue channel to select the Roof color.

The Roof color should be selected.

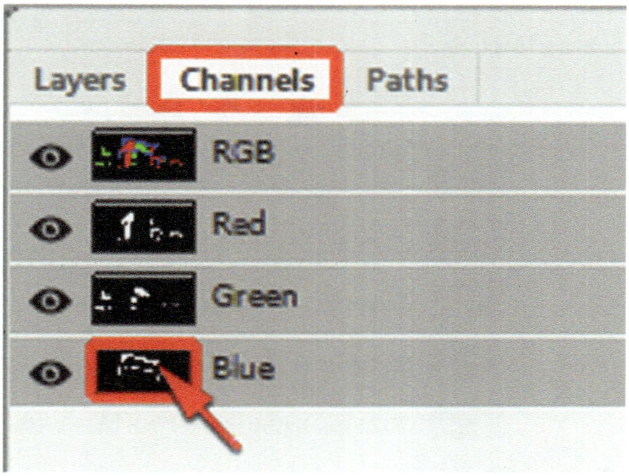

Roof color selected

Go back to the Layers tab and disable the visibility of the MultiMatteElement.

Scroll down and click to create a new Group. Name it as =Roof=.

While the selection is still on, create a mask by clicking on its button.

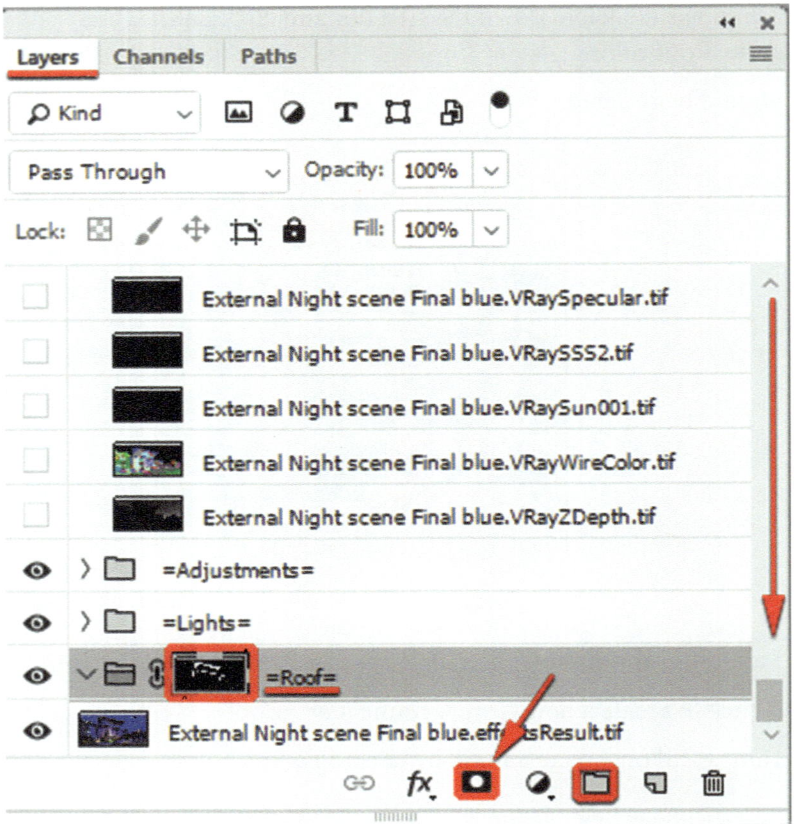

Group and Mask created

To add a bit of reflectivity to the =Roof= group, select the layer named External Night scene Final blue.VRayRawReflection.tif.

Hold down the Alt key and move it inside the =Roof= group. A copy of the VRayRawReflection layer has been created and moved.

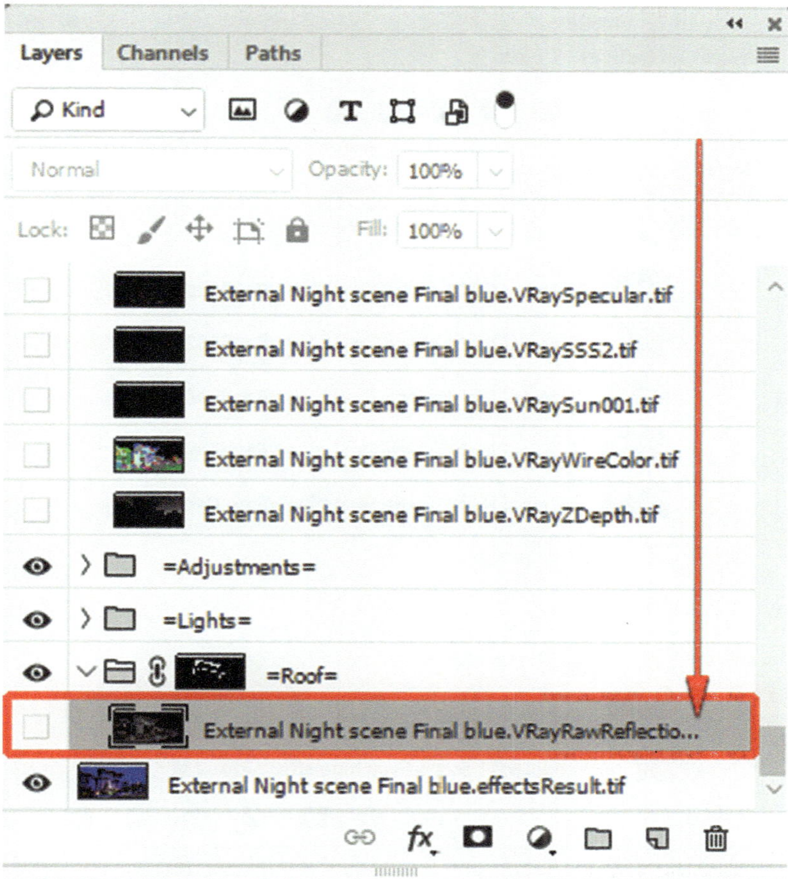

VRayRawReflection layer copied

Turn on the layer visibility eye icon and decrease the layer Opacity to 16%. As mentioned earlier, the VRayRawReflection layer works best with the Normal blending mode.

NOTE

The value of 16% worked well. However, try different values, if desired.

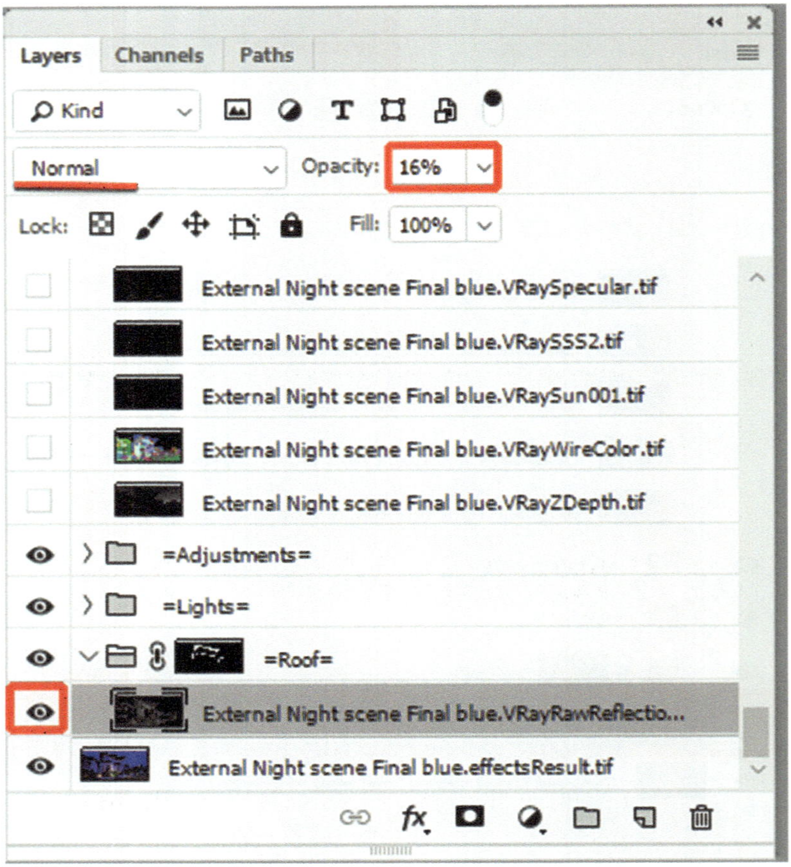

Decrease the Layer Opacity

The following step is to increase the specular/glossiness levels of the plants in the foreground.

Enable the visibility of the layer, External Night scene Final blue .MultiMatteElement_8.tif.

Go to the Channels tab and enable the Red channel selection (Ctrl+Click).

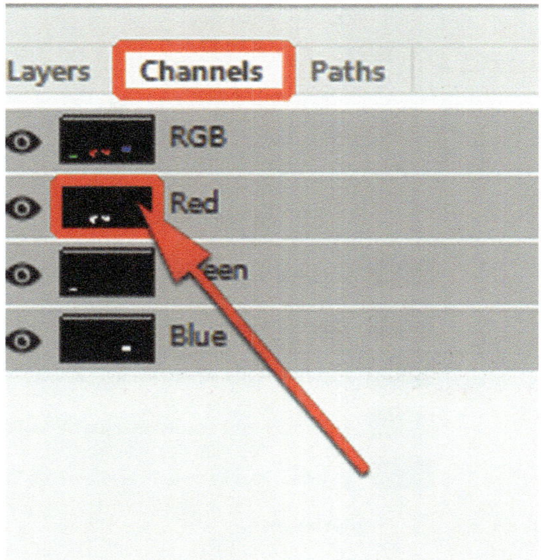

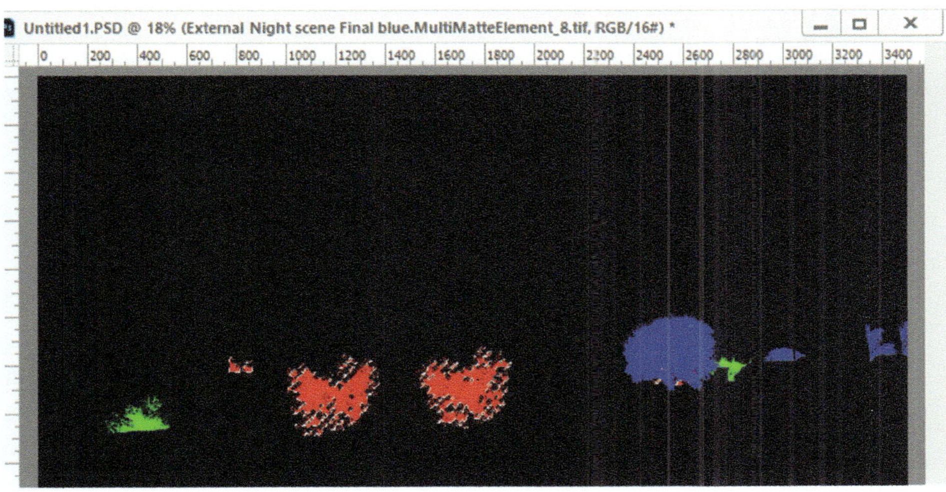

Enable the Red channel selection

Go back to the Layers tab and disable the MultiMatteElement visibility eye icon.

Scroll down and click to create a new Group. Name it as =Plants= and click to create a mask while the selection is on.

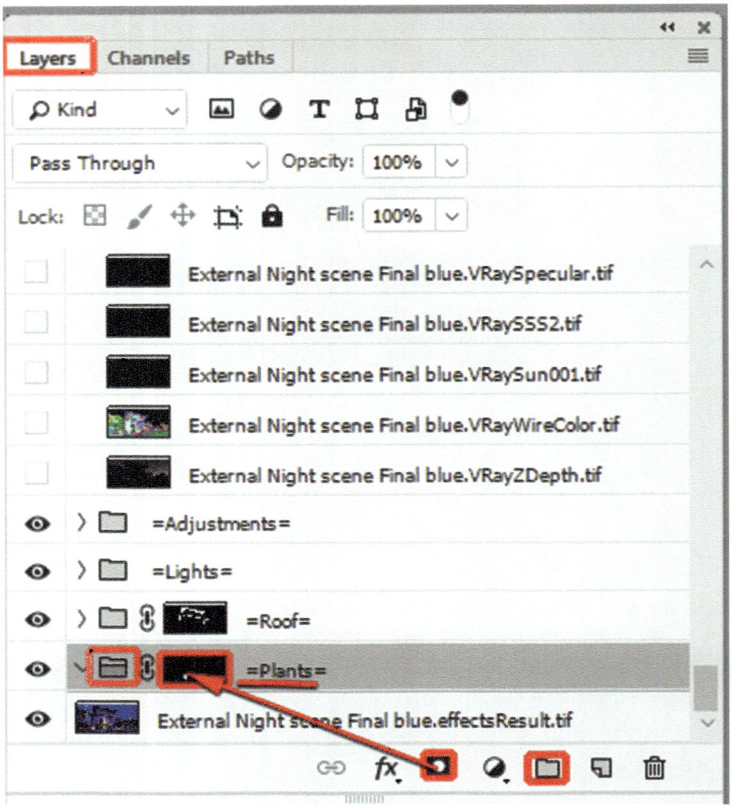

Group and Mask created

Next, select the layer, External Night scene Final blue.VRaySpecular.tif.

Copy and move it inside the =Plants= group, as previously done. Enable the layer visibility and change its blending mode to a Screen type.

As mentioned earlier, VRaySpecular layer works best with a Screen blending mode type.

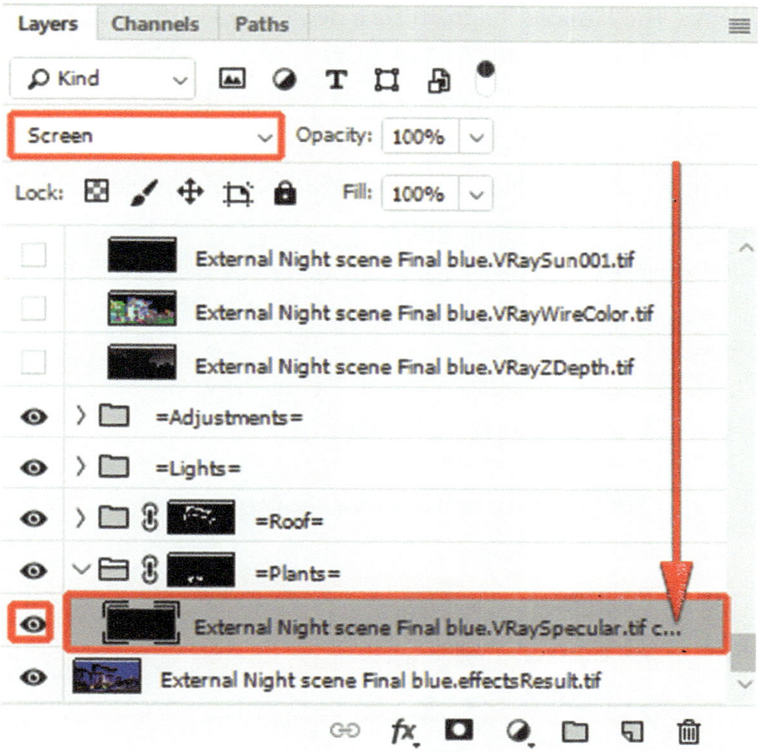

Copy and move the VRaySpecular layer

Repeat the same action to create a new Group with mask for the Gutter object, as previously done. Name it as =Gutter=.

Copy and move the VRaySpecular layer into the =Gutter= group. Duplicate the VRaySpecular layer.

Change their layer blending modes to a Screen type, as previously done.

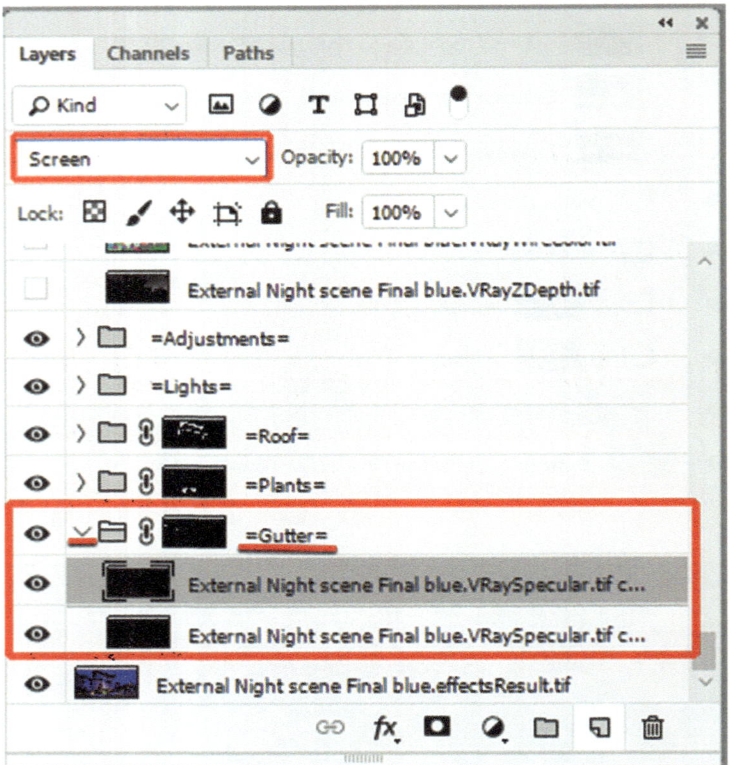

New Group with duplicated Specular layer

Save the PSD file.

To see the final result of this exercise, simply open the Photoshop file (PSD) under the name of External Night scene Final.PSD.

The next step is to add the Camera Raw Filter and apply the final chromatic aberration effect, as previously done.

As mentioned earlier, the Camera Raw Filter can only be applied to a flatten image. To ensure we work on a separate document, right click on the top edge of the document External Night scene Final.PSD and choose the option Duplicate.

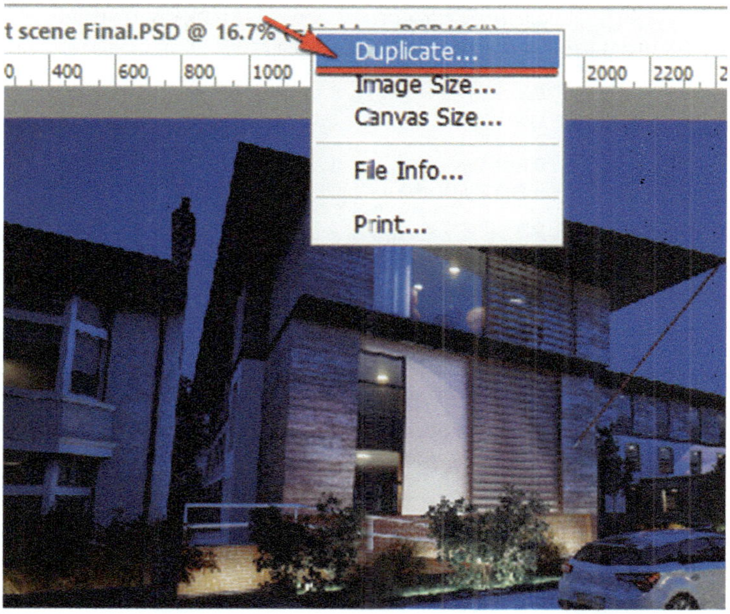

Choose Duplicate document

Accept the Duplicate Image dialog option.

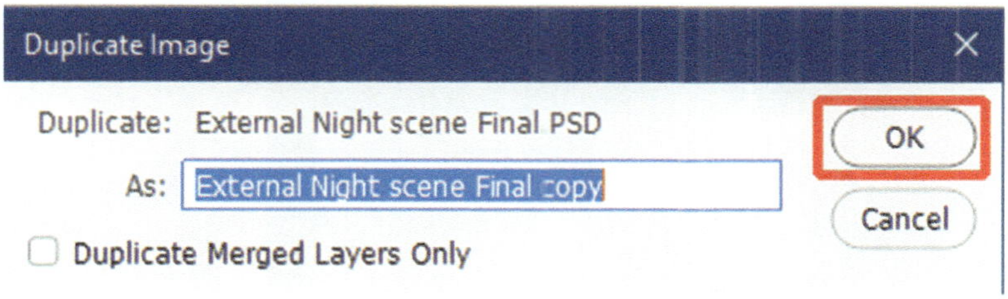

Duplicate Image dialog

Next, select the bottom layer (not groups); right click and choose the Flatten Image.

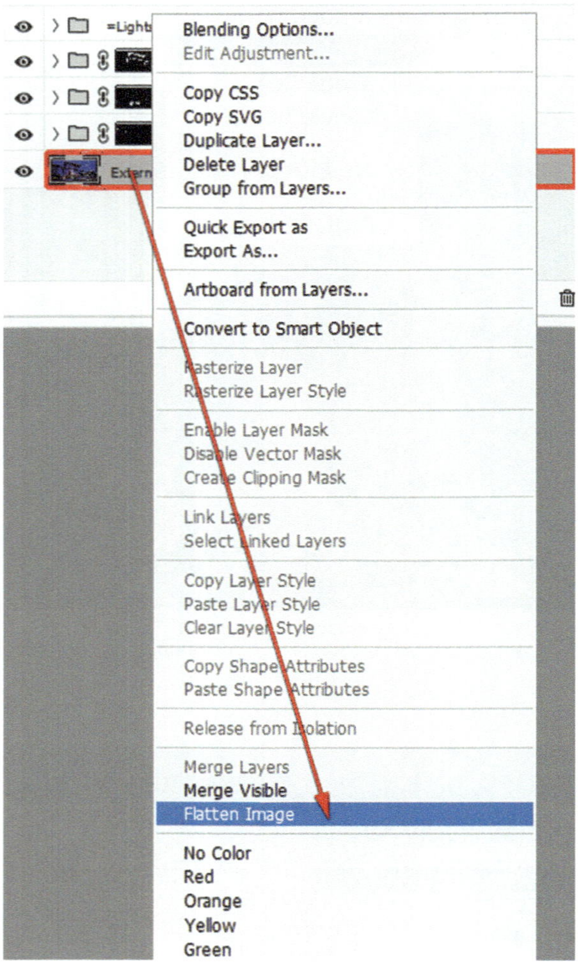

Flatten Image option

Accept to Discard hidden layers.

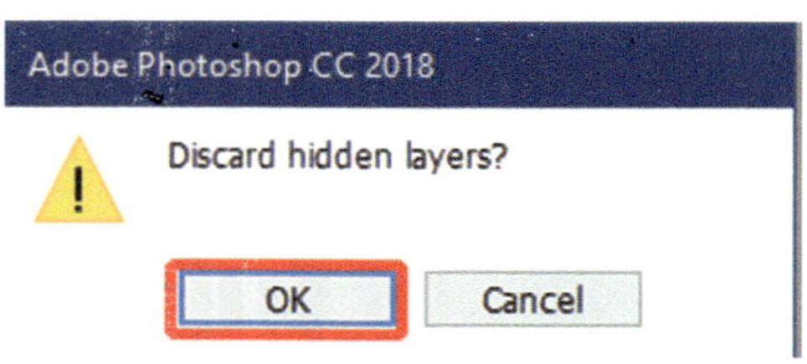

Discard hidden layers dialog

To avoid working on the original layer, in the flatten document, right click and choose Duplicate Layer.

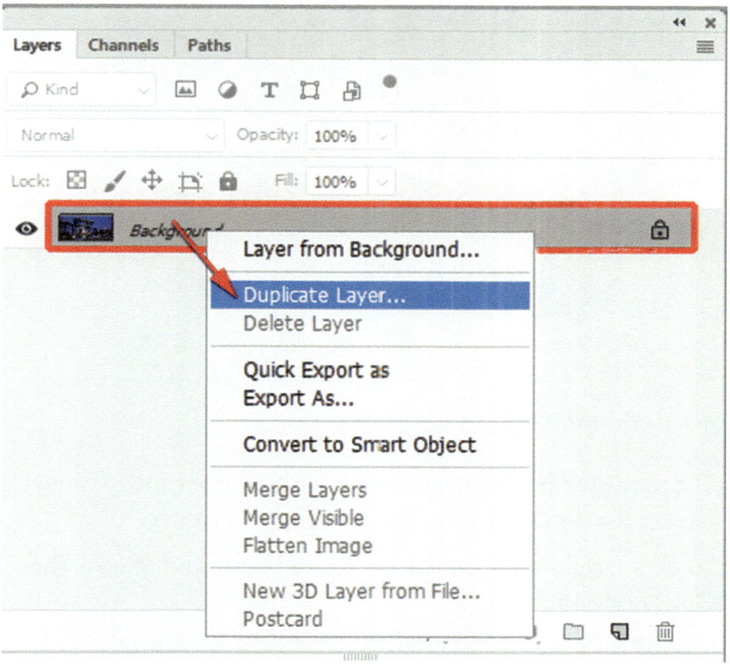

Duplicate Layer option

In the Duplicate Layer dialog, rename the new layer as Camera Raw filter.

Duplicate Layer option

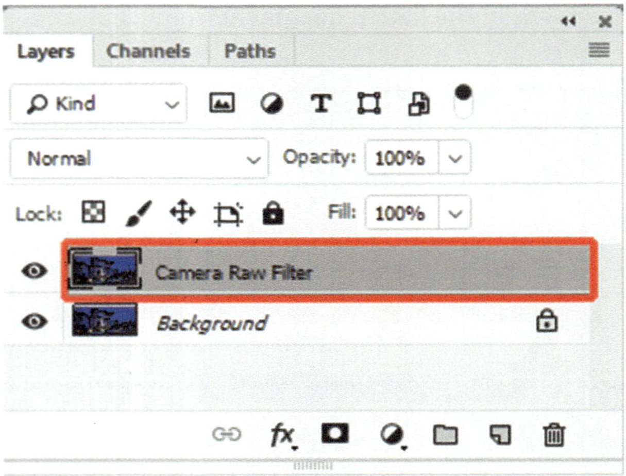

New duplicated layer renamed

The next step is to convert the duplicated layer into a Smart Object. This will ensure users can edit any applied filters in future.

To do so, right click on the duplicated layer and choose the Convert to Smart Object option.

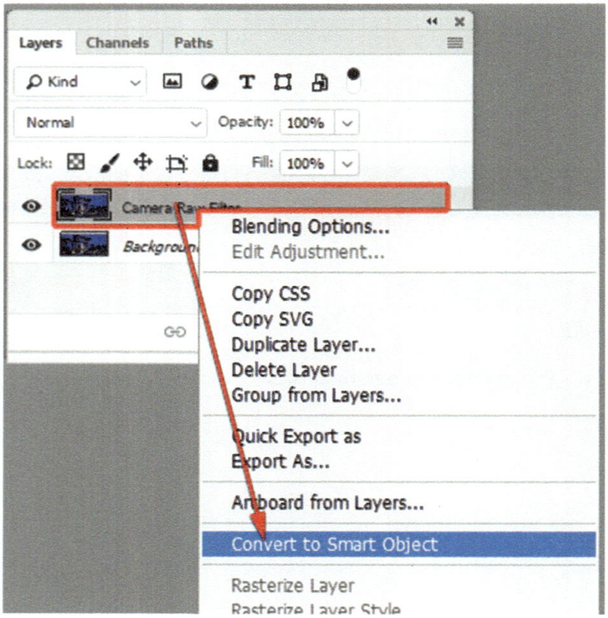

Choose Convert to Smart Object

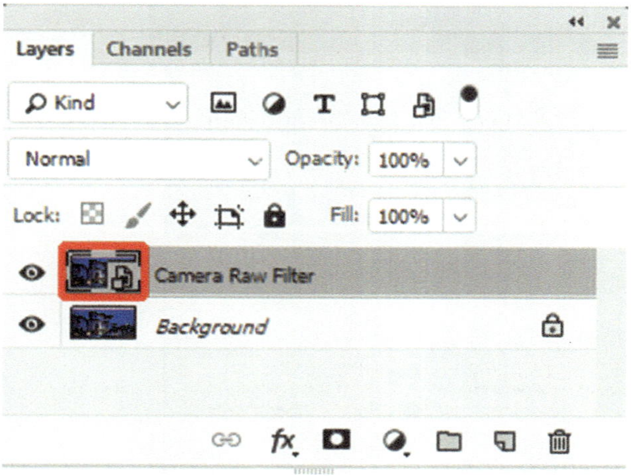

Smart layer

To apply the Camera Raw Filter, click on the Filter main toolbar and choose the Camera Raw Filter from the list (Shift+Ctrl+A).

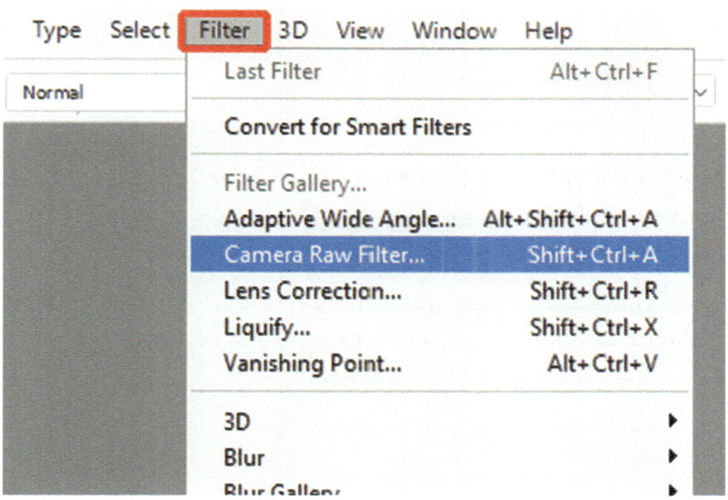

Choose the Camera Raw Filter

In the Camera Raw Filter parameters, begin by increasing the Shadows to about +72.

Next, increase the Whites to about +14, and decrease the Blacks to −6.

Finally, increase the Clarity to about +38 and OK to close the dialog. Note the amazing changes it's making to the image.

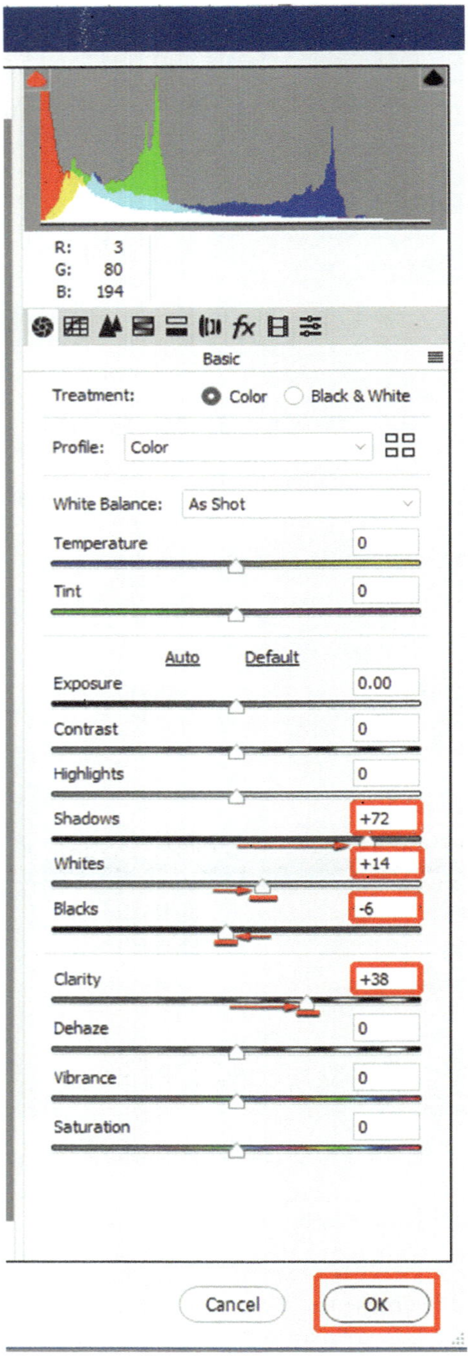
R: 3
G: 80
B: 194
Basic
Treatment:
Color
Black & White
Profile:
Color
White Balance:
As Shot
Temperature
0
Tint
0
Auto
Default
Exposure
0.00
Contrast
0
Highlights
0
Shadows
+72
Whites
+14
Blacks
-6
Clarity
+38
Dehaze
0
Vibrance
0
Saturation
0
Cancel
OK

Camera Raw Filter parameters

If at any point you decide to edit the parameters, simply double click on the Camera Raw Filter text.

Its eye icon allows users to turn the filter on and off.

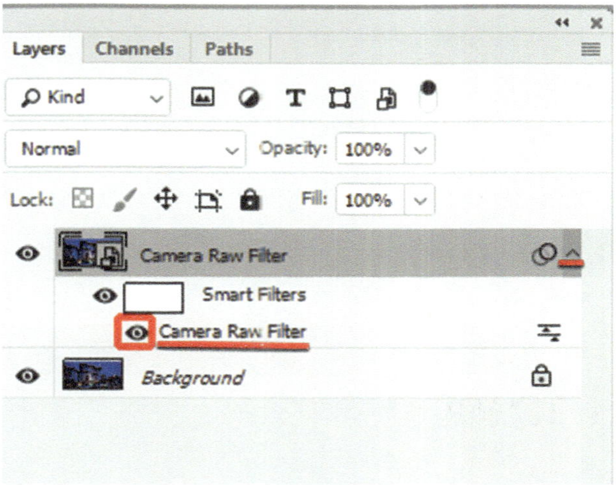

Camera Raw Filter applied

NOTE

These values used here worked well. However, try different values, if desired.

Save the PSD file document (Ctrl+S).

To see the final result of this exercise, simply open the document named External Night scene Final_Camera Raw Filter.PSD.

As mentioned earlier, most real photos have a slight chromatic aberration on pixels. When added in 3d, renders often look more realistic as a result.

This effect can only be applied on a flattened document (without any layers).

To add the chromatic aberration effect on this render, simply Duplicate the document first and flatten it, as previously done.

Choose to Duplicate document

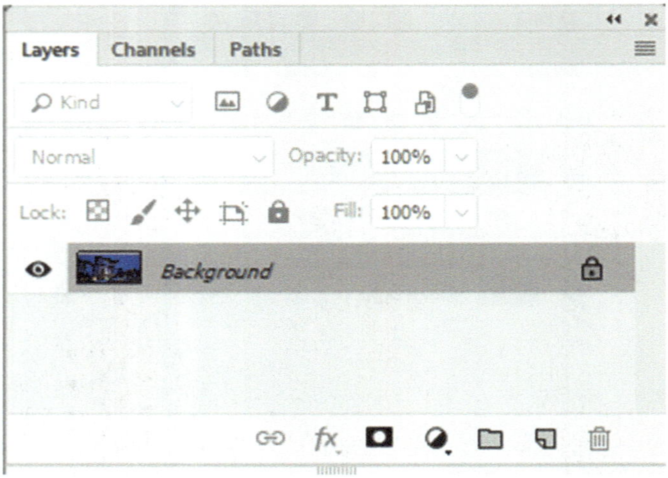

Flattened Document

Next, zoom in 100% into the document. Type in 100% on the bottom left part of the document.

Zoom in 100%

NOTE

It's utterly important to zoom in 100% to prevent massive color shifts when nudging the channels.

Next, go to the Channels tab and select Red channel. Enable the Move tool (V) and use the arrow on your keyboard to nudge the document up once.

Select the Red channel and nudge it up once

Select the Green Channel and nudge it down once (using the arrow).

Select the Green channel and nudge it down once

Following that, select the Blue channel and nudge it to the right (once).

Finally, select the RGB channel to see the final result in color.

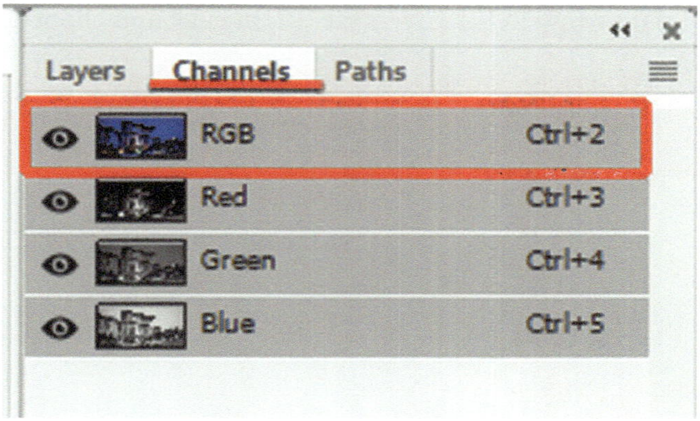

Select the RGB channel to see the final result

The color shifts are now apparent. Next, we are going to blend this layer with the document External Night scene Final_Camera Raw Filter.PSD.

To do so, go to the Layers tab. Right click and choose Duplicate Layer.

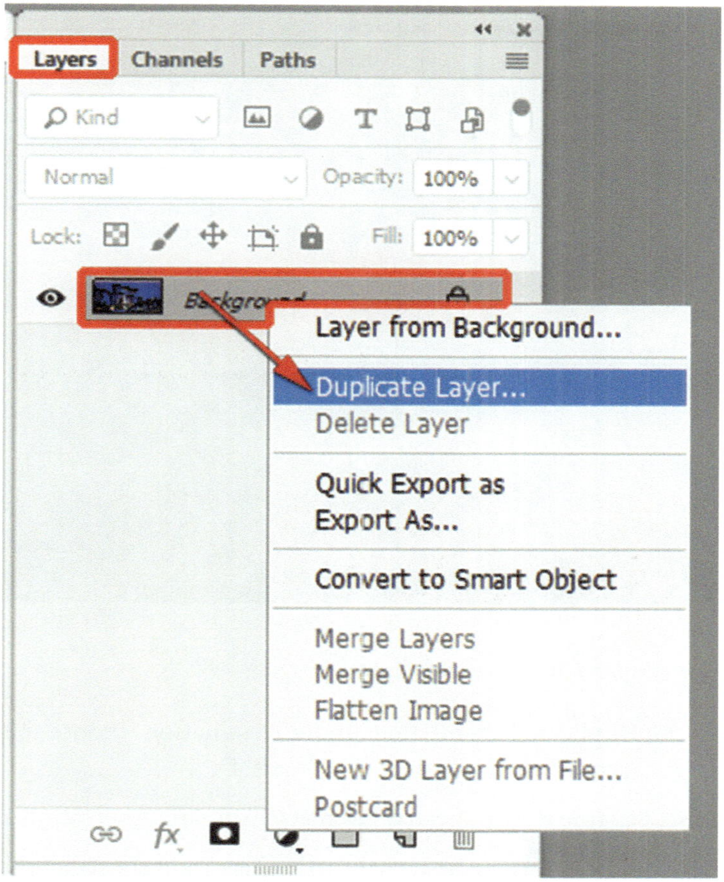
Layers
Channels
Paths
Kind
Normal
Opacity: 100%
Lock:
Fill: 100%
Layer from Background...
Duplicate Layer...
Delete Layer
Quick Export as
Export As...
Convert to Smart Object
Merge Layers
Merge Visible
Flatten Image
New 3D Layer from File...
Postcard

Right click and choose Duplicate Layer

In the Duplicate Layer dialog, under Destination, choose the document External Night scene Final_Camera Raw Filter.PSD.

Also, rename the duplicated layer as Chromatic Aberration.

This duplicated layer with chromatic aberration should appear in the document External Night scene Final_Camera Raw Filter.PSD.

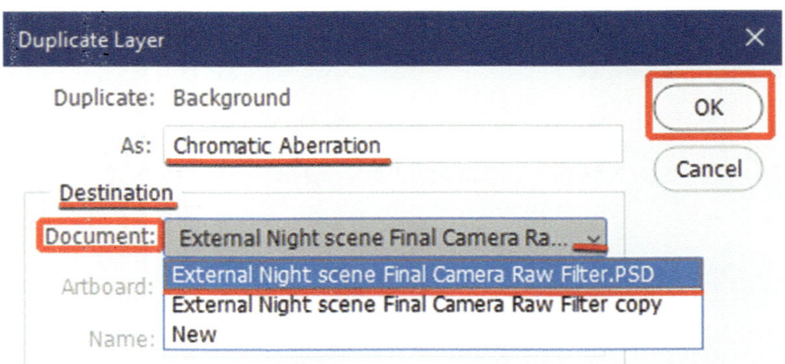

Choose the Destination document

Back in the document External Night scene Final_Camera Raw Filter.PSD, select the Chromatic Aberration layer and reduce its layer Opacity to about 75%.

This value should make the chromatic aberration less prominent and more appealing.

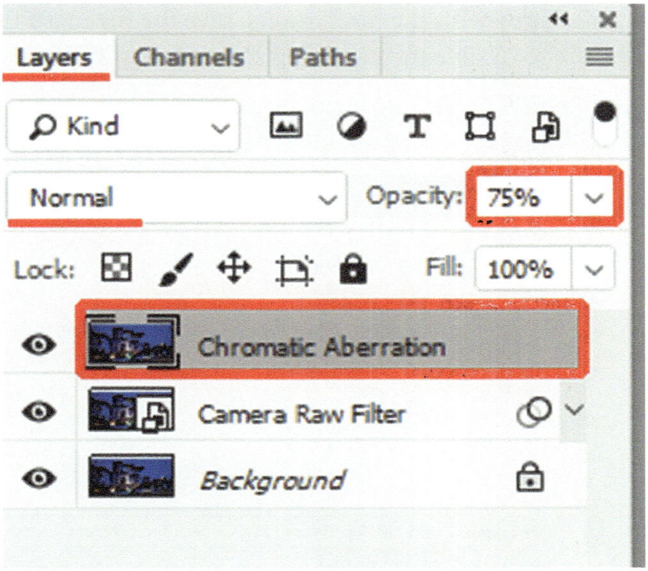

Reduce the chromatic aberration Opacity

NOTE

The value of this layer Opacity worked well for this night scene. However, try different values, if desired.

Save the PSD file under a different name.

To see the final PSD document with all effects applied, simply open the document named External Night scene Final_Camera Raw Filter & Chromatic Aberration. PSD.

Once happy with the final results, save the file in a TIF format (Shift+Ctrl+S). Ensure to disable the Layers option to flatten the image.

Unlike JPEGs, TIF file formats preserve the quality of renders for high-resolution prints. However, they are often big in size.

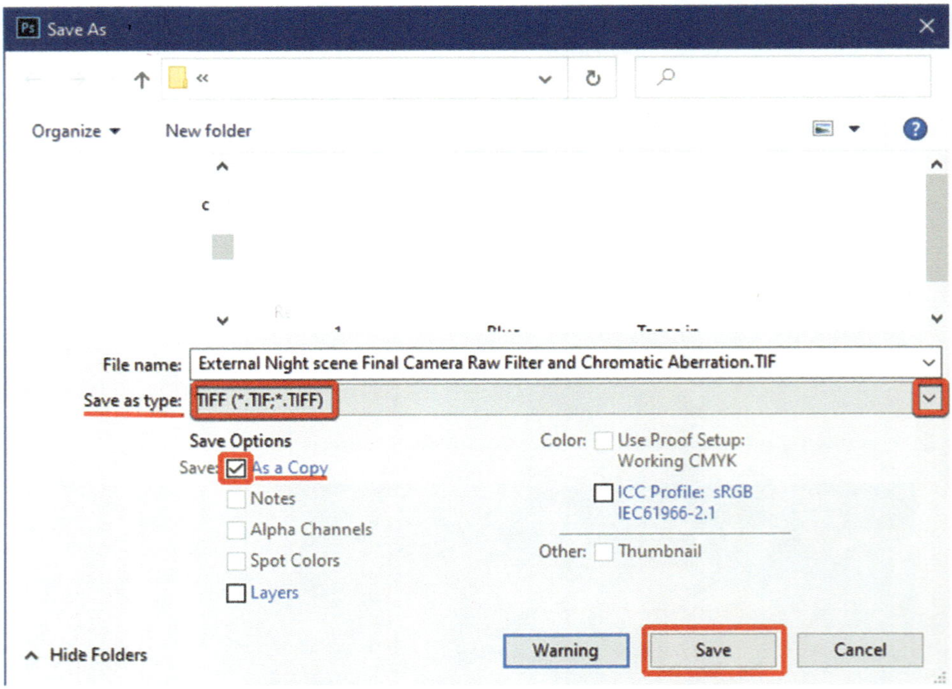

TIF Save options

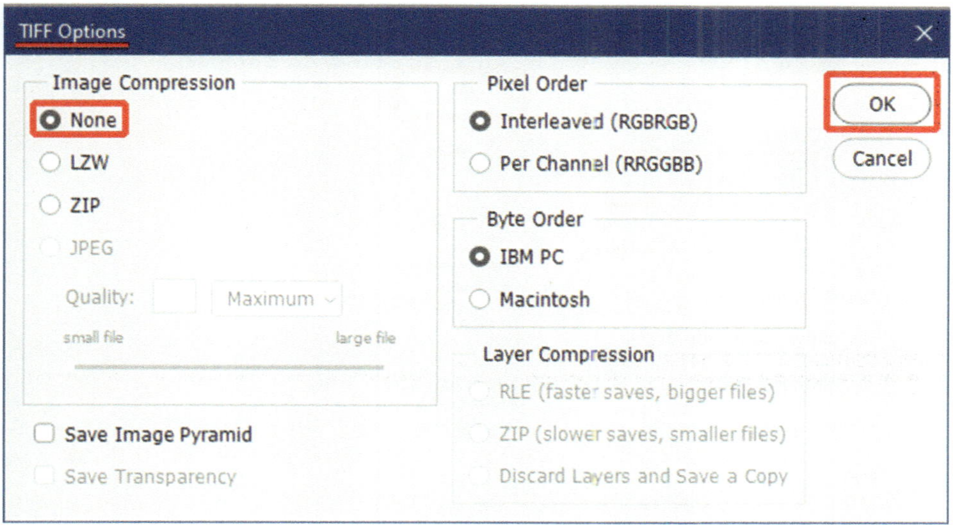

TIF Options dialog

Also, save another version as a JPEG, for emails, etc.

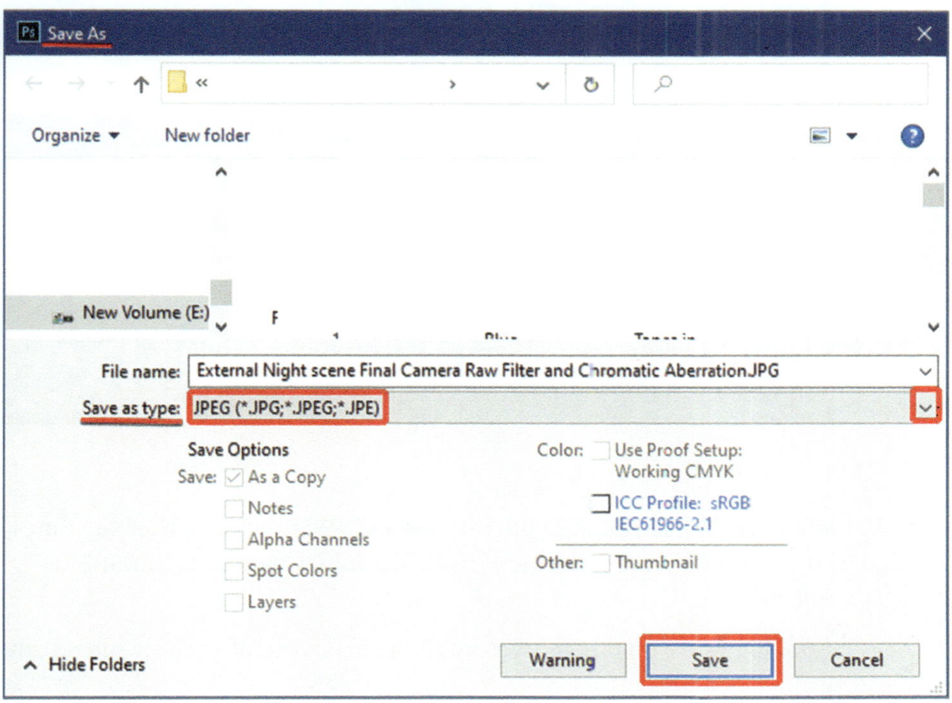

Save as JPEG

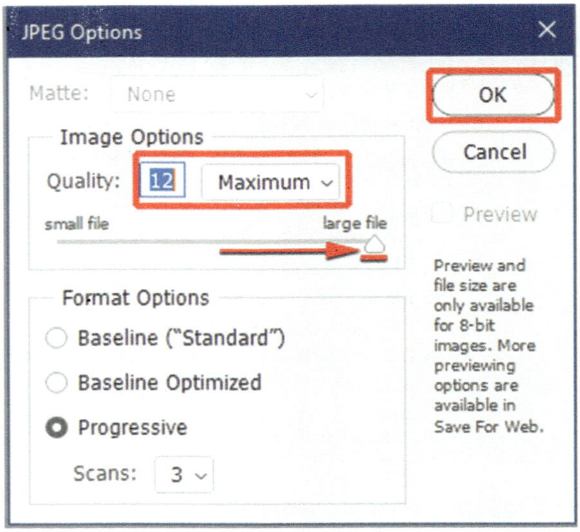

JPEG Options dialog

Final image

Finally, there are other sets of PSD documents and JPGs, without the blue tones applied in the LightMix layer. They are inside the folder named Without Blue Tones in LightMix.

Same methodologies covered here were implemented to achieve the same results.

Final image without blue tones

Conclusion

This chapter has guided users through the fascinating process of transforming a basic render into a full marketing visual.

We've started by using a LUT file and VRayLight passes to set the overall mood of the render, followed by using render elements and Adjustment Layers to enhance physical properties such as reflections and the specular.

The subsequent step was to apply the Camera Raw Filter to help lift the overall image.

Finally, a chromatic aberration effect was used to help create a more photographic image.

Index

Index

Index

Index

Index

Index

Index

Index

Index

Index

For Product Safety Concerns and Information please contact our EU representative GPSR@taylorandfrancis.com Taylor & Francis Verlag GmbH, Kaufingerstraße 24, 80331 München, Germany

Batch number: 10732790

Printed by Printforce, the Netherlands